P9-DNM-522

This book belongs to:

_____

WEBSTER'S
Dictionary
for Students
≡ THIRD EDITION ≡

Created in Cooperation with the Editors of
MERRIAM-WEBSTER

FEDERAL
STREET
PRESS

A Division of Merriam-Webster, Incorporated
Springfield, Massachusetts

This edition published by
Federal Street Press
A Division of Merriam-Webster, Incorporated
P.O. Box 281
Springfield, MA 01102

ISBN 978-1-59695-093-1

3rd Printing   Craftline, Ft. Wayne, IN   7/2010

Printed in the United States of America

Contents

Preface

This newly updated volume defines more than 37,000 words and phrases that reflect the vocabulary level, curriculum requirements, and personal interests of students. In addition to the dictionary, a section including ten general spelling rules and ten rules for forming plurals can be found at the back of the book.

The features of this dictionary are similar to those of larger dictionaries. It is important to understand them to make best use of this valuable language tool.

The **bold** word that begins an entry is known as the main entry word. All of the material in the entry is related to the main entry word or to derived words or phrases that also appear in the entry.

> **as·pen** *n* : a poplar tree whose leaves move easily
> in the breeze

Centered dots in the bold forms show where the words may be hyphenated at the end of a line on a page and they serve as an aid in sounding out the words.

Other bold forms may appear in this entry, such as **variant spellings** and **inflected forms** of the main entry word. Inflected forms are the plurals of nouns, the principal parts of verbs, or the comparative and superlative forms of adjectives.

> ¹**cad·die** or **cad·dy** *n, pl* **cad·dies** : a person who
> carries a golfer's clubs
> ¹**free** *adj* **fre·er; fre·est 1** : given without charge
> **pul·sate** *vb* **pul·sat·ed; pul·sat·ing** : to have or
> show a pulse or beats

Other bold items in the entry may be defined **run-on phrases** that have the main entry word in the phrase, and **run-in entries** that are being explained in the definition itself.

> ¹**stand** *vb* . . . — **stand by** : to be or remain loyal
> or true to — **stand for 1** : to be a symbol for . . .
> **2** : to put up with . . .
> **co·co·nut** *n* : a large nutlike fruit that has a thick
> husk with white flesh . . . and that grows on a tall
> tropical palm (**coconut palm**)

One of the more common bold forms appearing at an entry is the **undefined run-on entry**. This is a word at the end of an entry that is derived from the main entry by the addition of a common word ending (suffix).

> **har·mo·ni·ous** . . . — **har·mo·ni·ous·ly** *adv*

Since you know the meaning of the main entry word and the meaning of the suffix, the meaning of the run-on entry is self-explanatory.

The way a word is used in a sentence, its *function*, sometimes called its *part of speech*, is indicated by any of several *italic* abbreviations: *n* for *noun* (**cat, dog, mother**), *vb* for *verb* (**run, jump, cry**), *adj* for *adjective* (**blue, tall, happy**), *adv* for *adverb* (**easily, fast, nearby**), *pron* for *pronoun* (**who, them, none**), *conj* for *conjunction* (**and, but, if**), *prep* for *preposition* (**about, for, to**), and *interj* for *interjection* (**hello, ahoy**). Others include *helping verb* (**may, can**), *prefix* (**anti-, bio-**), and *suffix* (**-age, -er, -graph**).

When there are two or more words that have the same spelling but are different in their meanings or how they function in a sentence, these are distinguished by a small superscript numeral in front of the spelling. The numeral is not part of the spelling; it is there in this dictionary to distinguish these identically spelled words (called **homographs**).

> [1]**seal** *n* **1** : a sea mammal . . .
> [2]**seal** *n* **1** : something that closes tightly
> [3]**seal** *vb* **1** : to close tightly or completely . . .

One very important way a dictionary saves space when two or more words have the same meaning is by putting the definition at the more common word and linking to that entry by means of a cross-reference in SMALL CAPITALS. Look at the following.

> **abash** *vb* : EMBARRASS

The treatment here tells you to look at the entry **embarrass** for a definition of both *abash* and *embarrass*. And this treatment tells you also that *abash* and *embarrass* are **synonyms**.
Sometimes the synonym cross-reference is used in place of a definition and sometimes following a definition.

> **hare‑brained** *adj* : FOOLISH
> **staunch** *adj* **1** : strongly built : SUBSTANTIAL

When the synonym cross-reference has a following sense number or has a superscript homograph number attached, it tells you which specific sense number and which homograph to look to for the shared meaning.

> **be‑nev‑o‑lence** *n* : KINDNESS 1
> **mom** *n* : [1]MOTHER 1

Your dictionary also guides you in the way a particular word is used. **Usage notes** may follow a definition or be used in place of a definition.

> **air‑wave** *n* : the radio waves used to broadcast
> radio and television programs — usually used in
> *pl.*
> **rev‑er‑end** *adj* . . . **2** — used as a title for a member
> of the clergy

Guidance on capitalization for entries where the main entry word is not shown capitalized is usually shown by an italic note at the beginning of the definition.

> **brus‑sels sprouts** *n pl*, *often cap B* : small leafy
> heads resembling tiny cabbages and eaten as a
> vegetable

WEBSTER'S
Dictionary
for Students

THIRD EDITION

A

¹a *n, pl* **a's** *or* **as** *often cap* **1** : the first letter of the English alphabet **2** : a grade that shows a student's work is excellent **3** : a musical note referred to by the letter A

²a *indefinite article* **1** : someone or something being mentioned for the first time **2** : the same **3** : ¹ANY 1 **4** : for or from each **5** : ²ONE 3 — used before words that do not begin with a vowel sound

a- *prefix* **1** : on : in : at **2** : in (such) a state, condition, or manner **3** : in the act or process of

aard·vark *n* : an African animal with a long snout and a long sticky tongue that feeds mostly on ants and termites and is active at night

AB *abbr* Alberta

ab- *prefix* : from : differing from

aback *adv* : by surprise

aba·cus *n, pl* **aba·ci** *or* **aba·cus·es** : an instrument for doing arithmetic by sliding counters along rods or in grooves

ab·a·lo·ne *n* : a shellfish that is a mollusk which has a flattened shell with a pearly lining

¹aban·don *vb* **aban·doned; aban·don·ing 1** : to leave and never return to : give up completely **2** : to stop having or doing — **aban·don·ment** *n*

²abandon *n* : a feeling of complete freedom

aban·doned *adj* : given up : left empty or unused

abash *vb* **abashed; abash·ing** : EMBARRASS

abate *vb* **abat·ed; abat·ing** : to make or become less — **abate·ment** *n*

ab·bess *n* : the head of an abbey for women

ab·bey *n, pl* **abbeys 1** : MONASTERY, CONVENT **2** : a church that is connected to buildings where nuns or monks live

ab·bot *n* : the head of an abbey for men

abbr *abbr* abbreviation

ab·bre·vi·ate *vb* **ab·bre·vi·at·ed; ab·bre·vi·at·ing** : to make briefer : SHORTEN

ab·bre·vi·a·tion *n* : a shortened form of a word or phrase

ab·di·cate *vb* **ab·di·cat·ed; ab·di·cat·ing** : to give up a position of power or authority — **ab·di·ca·tion** *n*

ab·do·men *n* **1** : the part of the body between the chest and the hips including the cavity containing the stomach and other digestive organs **2** : the hind part of the body of an arthropod (as an insect)

ab·dom·i·nal *adj* : relating to or located in the abdomen

ab·duct *vb* **ab·duct·ed; ab·duct·ing** : to take a person away by force : KIDNAP — **ab·duc·tion** *n*

abed *adv or adj* : in bed

ab·er·ra·tion *n* : an instance of being different from what is normal or usual

ab·hor *vb* **ab·horred; ab·hor·ring** : to dislike very much : LOATHE

ab·hor·rent *adj* : causing or deserving strong dislike

abide *vb* **abode** *or* **abid·ed; abid·ing 1** : to put up with patiently : TOLERATE **2** : ¹LAST 1, ENDURE **3** : to stay or live in a place — **abide by** : to accept the terms of : OBEY

abil·i·ty *n, pl* **abil·i·ties 1** : power to do something **2** : natural talent or acquired skill

-abil·i·ty *also* **-ibil·i·ty** *n suffix, pl* **-abil·i·ties** *also* **-ibil·i·ties** : ability, fitness, or tendency to act or be acted upon in (such) a way

ab·ject *adj* **1** : very bad or severe **2** : low in spirit, strength, or hope — **ab·ject·ly** *adv*

ablaze *adj* **1** : on fire **2** : glowing with light, color, or emotion

able *adj* **abler; ablest 1** : having enough power, resources, or skill to do something **2** : having the freedom or opportunity to do something **3** : having or showing much skill

-able *also* **-ible** *adj suffix* **1** : capable of, fit for, or worthy of being **2** : tending or likely to — **-ably** *also* **-ibly** *adv suffix*

able-bod·ied *adj* : physically fit

ably *adv* : in a skillful way

ab·nor·mal *adj* : differing from the normal usually in a noticeable way — **ab·nor·mal·ly** *adv*

ab·nor·mal·i·ty *n, pl* **ab·nor·mal·i·ties** : something that is not usual, expected, or normal

¹aboard *adv* : on, onto, or within a ship, train, bus, or airplane

²aboard *prep* : on or into especially for passage

¹abode *past of* ABIDE

²abode *n* : the place where someone stays or lives

abol·ish *vb* **abol·ished; abol·ish·ing** : to do away with : put an end to

ab·o·li·tion *n* : a complete elimination of

ab·o·li·tion·ist *n* : a person favoring the abolition of slavery

A–bomb *n* : ATOMIC BOMB

abom·i·na·ble *adj* **1** : deserving or causing disgust **2** : very disagreeable or unpleasant — **abom·i·na·bly** *adv*

abom·i·na·tion *n* : something that causes disgust

ab·orig·i·nal *adj* **1** : being the first of its kind in a region **2** : of or relating to the original people living in a region

ab·orig·i·ne *n, pl* **ab·orig·i·nes** : a member of the original people living in a region : NA-TIVE

abound *vb* **abound·ed; abound·ing 1** : to be plentiful : TEEM **2** : to be fully supplied

¹**about** *adv* **1** : ALMOST, NEARLY **2** : on all sides : AROUND **3** : in the opposite direction **4** : on the verge of

²**about** *prep* **1** : having to do with **2** : on every side of : AROUND **3** : over or in different parts of **4** : near or not far from in time

¹**above** *adv* : in or to a higher place

²**above** *prep* **1** : higher than : OVER **2** : too good for **3** : more than **4** : to a greater degree than **5** : having more power or importance than

³**above** *adj* : said or written earlier

¹**above·board** *adv* : in an honest open way

²**aboveboard** *adj* : free from tricks and secrecy

ab·ra·ca·dab·ra *n* : a magical charm or word

abrade *vb* **abrad·ed; abrad·ing** : to wear away or irritate by rubbing

¹**abra·sive** *n* : a substance for grinding, smoothing, or polishing

²**abrasive** *adj* **1** : causing damage or wear by rubbing **2** : very unpleasant or irritating

abreast *adv or adj* **1** : right beside one another **2** : up to a certain level of knowledge

abridge *vb* **abridged; abridg·ing** : to shorten by leaving out some parts

abridg·ment *or* **abridge·ment** *n* : a shortened form of a written work

abroad *adv or adj* **1** : over a wide area **2** : in the open : OUTDOORS **3** : in or to a foreign country **4** : known to many people

abrupt *adj* **1** : happening without warning : SUDDEN **2** : ¹STEEP 1 **3** : rudely brief — **abrupt·ly** *adv* — **abrupt·ness** *n*

ab·scess *n* : a collection of pus with swollen and red tissue around it — **ab·scessed** *adj*

ab·sence *n* **1** : a failure to be present at a usual or expected place **2** : ²LACK, WANT

ab·sent *adj* **1** : not present **2** : not existing **3** : showing a lack of attention

ab·sen·tee *n* : a person who is not present

ab·sent·mind·ed *adj* : tending to forget or not pay attention — **ab·sent·mind·ed·ly** *adv* — **ab·sent·mind·ed·ness** *n*

ab·so·lute *adj* **1** : ¹TOTAL 1, COMPLETE **2** : not limited in any way **3** : free from doubt : CERTAIN — **ab·so·lute·ly** *adv*

ab·solve *vb* **ab·solved; ab·solv·ing** : to make free from guilt or responsibility

ab·sorb *vb* **ab·sorbed; ab·sorb·ing 1** : to take in or swallow up **2** : to hold the com-

plete attention of **3** : to receive without giving back

ab·sor·ben·cy *n* : the quality or state of being able to draw in or soak up

ab·sor·bent *adj* : able to draw in or soak up

ab·sorp·tion *n* **1** : the process of drawing in or soaking up : absorbing or being absorbed **2** : complete attention

ab·stain *vb* **ab·stained; ab·stain·ing** : to choose not to do or have something — **ab·stain·er** *n*

ab·sti·nence *n* : an avoidance by choice especially of certain foods or of liquor

¹**ab·stract** *adj* **1** : hard to understand **2** : relating to general ideas or qualities rather than specific people, things, or actions — **ab·stract·ly** *adv*

²**ab·stract** *n* : ²SUMMARY

³**ab·stract** *vb* **ab·stract·ed; ab·stract·ing 1** : to take away : SEPARATE **2** : SUMMARIZE

ab·strac·tion *n* **1** : the act of summarizing : the state of being summarized **2** : a thought or thoughts about general qualities or ideas rather than people or things

ab·surd *adj* : completely foolish, unreasonable, or untrue : RIDICULOUS — **ab·surd·ly** *adv*

ab·sur·di·ty *n, pl* **ab·sur·di·ties 1** : the fact of being ridiculous **2** : something that is ridiculous

abun·dance *n* : a large quantity : PLENTY

abun·dant *adj* : more than enough : PLENTI-FUL — **abun·dant·ly** *adv*

¹**abuse** *n* **1** : wrong or unfair treatment or use **2** : the act or practice of improperly using or of using in harmful amounts **3** : harmful treatment of a person or an animal **4** : harsh insulting language **5** : a dishonest practice

²**abuse** *vb* **abused; abus·ing 1** : to treat in a cruel or harmful way **2** : to use wrongly : MISUSE **3** : to use improperly or in harmful amounts **4** : to blame or scold rudely

abu·sive *adj* **1** : using or involving harmful treatment **2** : using harsh insulting language

abut *vb* **abut·ted; abut·ting** : to touch along an edge

abys·mal *adj* : extremely bad

abyss *n* : a gulf so deep or space so great that it cannot be measured

AC *abbr* **1** air-conditioning **2** alternating current **3** area code

ac·a·dem·ic *adj* **1** : of or relating to schools and education **2** : having no practical importance — **ac·a·dem·i·cal·ly** *adv*

acad·e·my *n, pl* **acad·e·mies 1** : a private high school **2** : a high school or college where special subjects are taught **3** : an organization which supports art, science, or literature

ac·cede *vb* **ac·ced·ed; ac·ced·ing** : to agree to

ac·cel·er·ate *vb* **ac·cel·er·at·ed; ac·cel·er·at·ing 1** : to move or cause to move faster **2** : to cause to happen more quickly

ac·cel·er·a·tion *n* : the act or process of speeding up

ac·cel·er·a·tor *n* : a pedal in an automobile for controlling the speed of the motor

¹ac·cent *vb* **ac·cent·ed; ac·cent·ing 1** : to give a greater force or stress **2** : to mark with a written or printed accent

²ac·cent *n* **1** : a way of pronouncing words shared by the people of a particular country or region **2** : greater stress or force given to a syllable of a word in speaking or to a beat in music **3** : a mark (as ' or ˌ) used in writing or printing to show the place of greater stress on a syllable

ac·cen·tu·ate *vb* **ac·cen·tu·at·ed; ac·cen·tu·at·ing** : to make more noticeable

ac·cept *vb* **ac·cept·ed; ac·cept·ing 1** : to receive or take willingly **2** : to agree to **3** : to stop resisting **4** : to admit deserving

ac·cept·able *adj* **1** : worthy of being accepted **2** : ADEQUATE **2** — **ac·cept·ably** *adv*

ac·cep·tance *n* **1** : the act of accepting **2** : the quality or state of being accepted or acceptable

¹ac·cess *n* **1** : the right or ability to approach, enter, or use **2** : a way or means of approaching

²access *vb* **ac·cessed; ac·cess·ing** : to get at : get access to

ac·ces·si·ble *adj* **1** : able to be reached **2** : able to be used or obtained

ac·ces·sion *n* : the rise to a position of power

ac·ces·so·ry *n, pl* **ac·ces·so·ries 1** : a person who helps another in doing wrong **2** : an object or device not necessary in itself but adding to the beauty or usefulness of something else

ac·ci·dent *n* **1** : something that happens by chance or from unknown causes and that often causes injury or damage : MISHAP **2** : ¹CHANCE **1**

ac·ci·den·tal *adj* **1** : happening by chance or unexpectedly **2** : not happening or done on purpose — **ac·ci·den·tal·ly** *adv*

¹ac·claim *vb* **ac·claimed; ac·claim·ing** : ¹PRAISE **1**

²acclaim *n* : ²PRAISE **1**

ac·cli·mate *vb* **ac·cli·mat·ed; ac·cli·mat·ing** : to adjust or change to fit a new climate or new surroundings

ac·cli·ma·tize *vb* **ac·cli·ma·tized; ac·cli·ma·tiz·ing** : ACCLIMATE

ac·com·mo·date *vb* **ac·com·mo·dat·ed; ac·com·mo·dat·ing 1** : to provide with a place to stay or sleep **2** : to provide with something needed : help out **3** : to have room for

ac·com·mo·dat·ing *adj* : ready to help

ac·com·mo·da·tion *n* **1 accommodations** *pl* : a place where travelers can sleep and find other services **2** : something supplied that is useful or handy

ac·com·pa·ni·ment *n* : music played in support of someone singing or playing an instrument

ac·com·pa·nist *n* : a musician who plays in support of someone else who is singing or playing an instrument

ac·com·pa·ny *vb* **ac·com·pa·nied; ac·com·pa·ny·ing 1** : to go with as a companion **2** : to play a musical accompaniment for **3** : to go or occur with

ac·com·plice *n* : a partner in wrongdoing

ac·com·plish *vb* **ac·com·plished; ac·com·plish·ing** : to succeed in doing or reaching

ac·com·plished *adj* : skilled through practice or training : EXPERT

ac·com·plish·ment *n* **1** : the act of successfully doing or reaching **2** : something successfully done or reached especially through effort **3** : an ability or skill gained by practice or training

¹ac·cord *vb* **ac·cord·ed; ac·cord·ing 1** : ¹GIVE **3 2** : to be in harmony : AGREE

²accord *n* **1** : AGREEMENT **1**, HARMONY **2** : willingness to act or to do something

ac·cor·dance *n* : AGREEMENT **1**

ac·cord·ing·ly *adv* **1** : in the necessary way : in the way called for **2** : as a result : CONSEQUENTLY, SO

ac·cord·ing to *prep* **1** : in agreement with **2** : as stated by

ac·cor·di·on *n* : a portable keyboard musical instrument played by forcing air from a bellows past metal reeds

ac·cost *vb* **ac·cost·ed; ac·cost·ing** : to approach and speak to in a demanding or aggressive way

¹ac·count *n* **1** : a record of money received and money paid out **2** : an arrangement with a bank to hold money and keep records of transactions **3** : an arrangement for regular dealings with a business **4** : a statement of explanation or of reasons or causes **5** : a statement of facts or events : REPORT **6** : ²WORTH **1**, IMPORTANCE — **on account of** : for the sake of : because of — **on someone's account** : because of someone

²account *vb* **ac·count·ed; ac·count·ing 1** : to think of as : CONSIDER **2** : to take into consideration **3** : to give an explanation **4** : to be the only or chief reason

ac·coun·tant *n* : someone whose job is keeping the financial records of a person or a business

ac·count·ing *n* : the work of keeping the financial records of a person or a business

ac·cu·mu·late *vb* **ac·cu·mu·lat·ed; ac·cu·mu·lat·ing** **1** : COLLECT 3, GATHER **2** : to increase in quantity or number

ac·cu·mu·la·tion *n* **1** : an act of collecting or gathering **2** : COLLECTION 2

ac·cu·ra·cy *n* : freedom from mistakes

ac·cu·rate *adj* : free from mistakes : RIGHT — **ac·cu·rate·ly** *adv*

ac·cursed *or* **ac·curst** *adj* **1** : being under a curse **2** : greatly or strongly disliked

ac·cu·sa·tion *n* : a claim that someone has done something bad or illegal

ac·cuse *vb* **ac·cused; ac·cus·ing** : to blame for something wrong or illegal — **ac·cus·er** *n*

ac·cus·tom *vb* **ac·cus·tomed; ac·cus·tom·ing** : to cause (someone) to get used to something

ac·cus·tomed *adj* **1** : CUSTOMARY 2, USUAL **2** : familiar with

¹ace *n* **1** : a playing card with one figure in its center **2** : a person who is expert at something

²ace *adj* : of the very best kind

¹ache *vb* **ached; ach·ing** **1** : to suffer a dull continuous pain **2** : to desire very much : YEARN

²ache *n* : a dull continuous pain

achieve *vb* **achieved; achiev·ing** **1** : to get by means of hard work **2** : to become successful

achieve·ment *n* **1** : the state of having gotten through great effort **2** : something gotten especially by great effort

¹ac·id *adj* **1** : having a taste that is sour, bitter, or stinging **2** : harsh or critical in tone **3** : of, relating to, or like an acid — **ac·id·ly** *adv*

²acid *n* : a chemical compound that tastes sour and forms a water solution which turns blue litmus paper red

acid·i·ty *n, pl* **acid·i·ties** : the quality, state, or degree of being acid

ac·knowl·edge *vb* **ac·knowl·edged; ac·knowl·edg·ing** **1** : to admit the truth or existence of **2** : to make known that something has been received or noticed **3** : to recognize the rights or authority of **4** : to express thanks or appreciation for

ac·knowl·edged *adj* : generally accepted

ac·knowl·edg·ment *or* **ac·knowl·edge·ment** *n* **1** : an act of admitting the truth or existence of **2** : an act of praising or thanking for some deed or achievement **3** : a usually written statement saying that a letter or message was received

ac·ne *n* : a skin condition in which pimples and blackheads are present

acorn *n* : the nut of the oak tree

acous·tic *or* **acous·ti·cal** *adj* **1** : of or relating to hearing or sound **2** : not having the sound changed by electrical devices

acous·tics *n pl* : the qualities in a room that affect how well a person in it can hear

ac·quaint *vb* **ac·quaint·ed; ac·quaint·ing** **1** : to cause to know personally **2** : to make familiar

ac·quain·tance *n* **1** : a person someone knows slightly **2** : personal knowledge

ac·qui·esce *vb* **ac·qui·esced; ac·qui·esc·ing** : to accept, agree, or give consent by keeping silent or by not making objections

ac·qui·es·cence *n* : the act of agreeing, accepting, or giving consent

ac·quire *vb* **ac·quired; ac·quir·ing** : to get especially through effort : GAIN

ac·qui·si·tion *n* **1** : the act of gaining especially through effort **2** : something gained especially through effort

ac·quit *vb* **ac·quit·ted; ac·quit·ting** **1** : to declare innocent of a crime or of wrongdoing **2** : to behave in a certain way

ac·quit·tal *n* : the act of declaring someone innocent of a crime or wrongdoing

acre *n* : a measure of land area equal to 43,560 square feet (about 4047 square meters)

acre·age *n* : area in acres

ac·rid *adj* **1** : sharp or bitter in taste or odor **2** : very harsh or unpleasant

ac·ro·bat *n* : a person skillful at performing stunts like jumping, balancing, tumbling, and swinging from a bar

ac·ro·bat·ic *adj* : relating to acrobats or acrobatics

ac·ro·bat·ics *n pl* **1** : the art or performance of an acrobat **2** : difficult or dangerous stunts — used either as a singular or a plural

ac·ro·nym *n* : a word formed from the first letter or letters of the words of a compound term

¹across *adv* **1** : from one side to the other **2** : a measurement from one side to another **3** : on the opposite side

²across *prep* **1** : to or on the opposite side of **2** : so as to pass, go over, or intersect at an angle **3** : in every part of

¹act *n* **1** : something that is done : DEED **2** : a law made by a governing body **3** : a main division of a play **4** : one of the performances in a show **5** : an insincere way of behaving

²act *vb* **act·ed; act·ing** **1** : to do something : MOVE **2** : to behave oneself in a certain way **3** : to perform as a character in a play **4** : to perform a certain function **5** : to have a result : make something happen : WORK — **act up** : to behave badly

act·ing *adj* : serving for a short time only or in place of another

ac·tion *n* **1** : the process by which something produces a change in another thing **2** : the doing of something **3** : something done **4** : the way something runs or works **5** : combat in war

action figure *n* : a model often of a superhero used as a toy

ac·ti·vate *vb* **ac·ti·vat·ed; ac·ti·vat·ing** : to start working or cause to start working

ac·tive *adj* **1** : producing or involving action or movement **2** : showing that the subject of a sentence is the doer of the action represented by the verb **3** : quick in physical movement : LIVELY **4** : taking part in an action or activity — **ac·tive·ly** *adv*

ac·tiv·ist *n* : a person who believes in forceful action for political purposes

ac·tiv·i·ty *n, pl* **ac·tiv·i·ties 1** : energetic action **2** : something done especially for relaxation or fun

ac·tor *n* : a person who acts especially in a play or movie

ac·tress *n* : a woman or girl who acts especially in a play or movie

ac·tu·al *adj* : really existing or happening : not false

ac·tu·al·ly *adv* : in fact : REALLY

acute *adj* **acut·er; acut·est 1** : measuring less than 90 degrees **2** : marked by or showing an ability to understand things that are not obvious **3** : SEVERE 2, SHARP **4** : developing quickly and lasting only a short time **5** : CRITICAL 4, URGENT **6** : very strong and sensitive — **acute·ly** *adv* — **acute·ness** *n*

ad *n* : ADVERTISEMENT

A.D. *abbr* in the year of our Lord — abbreviation for Latin *anno Domini*, which means "in the year of our Lord"

ad·age *n* : an old familiar saying : PROVERB

ad·a·mant *adj* : not giving in

Ad·am's apple *n* : the lump formed in the front of a person's neck by cartilage in the throat

adapt *vb* **adapt·ed; adapt·ing 1** : to change behavior so that it is easier to function in a particular place or situation **2** : to make or become suitable or able to function

adapt·able *adj* : capable of changing or being changed to better suit a situation

ad·ap·ta·tion *n* **1** : the act or process of changing to better suit a situation **2** : a body part or feature or a behavior that helps a living thing survive and function better in its environment

add *vb* **add·ed; add·ing 1** : to combine numbers into a single sum **2** : to join or unite to something **3** : to cause to have **4** : to say something more — **add up 1** : to be added together to equal the expected amount **2** : to make sense

ad·dend *n* : a number that is to be added to another number

ad·den·dum *n, pl* **ad·den·da** : something added (as to a book)

ad·der *n* **1** : a poisonous snake of Europe or Africa **2** : a harmless North American snake

ad·dict *n* **1** : a person who is not able to stop taking drugs **2** : a person who likes or enjoys something excessively

ad·dict·ed *adj* **1** : unable to stop using a drug **2** : having an unusually great need to do or have something — **ad·dic·tion** *n*

ad·di·tion *n* **1** : the act or process of adding numbers to obtain their sum **2** : something added — **in addition** : as something more — **in addition to** : along with or together with

ad·di·tion·al *adj* : ¹EXTRA — **ad·di·tion·al·ly** *adv*

ad·di·tive *n* : a substance added to another in small amounts

ad·dle *vb* **ad·dled; ad·dling** : to make or become confused

¹ad·dress *vb* **ad·dressed; ad·dress·ing 1** : to put directions for delivery on **2** : to speak or write to **3** : to use a specified name or title when speaking or writing to (someone) **4** : to deal with : give attention to

²ad·dress *n* **1** : the place where a person can usually be reached **2** : the directions for delivery placed on mail **3** : the symbols (as numerals or letters) that identify the location where particular information (as a home page) is stored on a computer especially on the Internet **4** : a formal speech **5** : the name of a computer account from which e-mail can be sent or received

ad·dress·ee *n* : the person to whom something is addressed

ad·e·noids *n pl* : fleshy growths near the opening of the nose into the throat

ad·ept *adj* : very good at something — **adept·ly** *adv* — **adept·ness** *n*

ad·e·quate *adj* **1** : ¹ENOUGH **2** : good enough — **ad·e·quate·ly** *adv*

ad·here *vb* **ad·hered; ad·her·ing 1** : to stick tight : CLING **2** : to act in the way that is required by

ad·her·ence *n* : the act of doing what is required by

ad·her·ent *n* : a person who is loyal to a belief, an organization, or a leader

ad·he·sion *n* : the act or state of sticking

¹ad·he·sive *adj* : tending to stick : STICKY

²adhesive *n* : a substance that is used to make things stick together

adj *abbr* adjective

ad·ja·cent *adj* : next to or near something

ad·jec·ti·val *adj* : of, relating to, or function-ing as an adjective — **ad·jec·ti·val·ly** *adv*

ad·jec·tive *n* : a word that says something about a noun or pronoun

ad·join *vb* **ad·joined; ad·join·ing** : to be next to or in contact with

ad·journ *vb* **ad·journed; ad·journ·ing** : to bring or come to a close for a period of time — **ad·journ·ment** *n*

ad·just *vb* **ad·just·ed; ad·just·ing** 1 : to change (something) in a minor way to make it work better 2 : to change the position of (something) 3 : to become used to

ad·just·able *adj* : possible to change to make work or be positioned better

ad·just·ment *n* 1 : a small change that im-proves something or makes it work better 2 : the act or process of changing or adjusting 3 : the decision about and payment of a claim or debt

ad·ju·tant *n* : an officer who assists the officer in command

ad–lib *vb* **ad–libbed; ad–lib·bing** : to make up something and especially music or spo-ken lines during a performance : IMPROVISE

ad·min·is·ter *vb* **ad·min·is·tered; ad·min·is·ter·ing** 1 : to be in charge of : MANAGE 2 : to give out as deserved 3 : to give officially 4 : to give or supply as treatment

ad·min·is·tra·tion *n* 1 : the act or process of administering 2 : the work involved in man-aging something 3 : the people who direct the business of something (as a city or school) 4 : a government department

ad·min·is·tra·tive *adj* : of or assisting in ad-ministration

ad·min·is·tra·tor *n* : a person who administers business, school, or government affairs

ad·mi·ra·ble *adj* : deserving great respect and approval — **ad·mi·ra·bly** *adv*

ad·mi·ral *n* : a high-ranking commissioned officer in the navy or coast guard

ad·mi·ral·ty *adj* : of or relating to conduct on the sea

ad·mi·ra·tion *n* : a feeling of great respect and approval

ad·mire *vb* **ad·mired; ad·mir·ing** : to think very highly of : feel admiration for — **ad·mir·er** *n*

ad·mis·si·ble *adj* : able to be or deserving to be admitted or allowed : ALLOWABLE

ad·mis·sion *n* 1 : acknowledgment by some-one of something about him or her that has not been proved 2 : the right or permission to enter 3 : the price of entrance

ad·mit *vb* **ad·mit·ted; ad·mit·ting** 1 : to make known usually with some unwillingness 2

: to allow to enter : let in 3 : [1]PERMIT 2, ALLOW

ad·mit·tance *n* : permission to enter

ad·mon·ish *vb* **ad·mon·ished; ad·mon·ish·ing** 1 : to criticize or warn gently but seri-ously 2 : to give friendly advice or encour-agement

ad·mo·ni·tion *n* : a gentle or friendly criti-cism or warning

ado *n* : foolish or unnecessary trouble, activ-ity, or excitement

ado·be *n* 1 : brick made of earth or clay dried in the sun 2 : a building made of adobe

ad·o·les·cence *n* : the period of life between childhood and adulthood

ad·o·les·cent *n* : a person who is no longer a child but not yet an adult

adopt *vb* **adopt·ed; adopt·ing** 1 : to legally take a child of other parents to raise 2 : to take up as someone's own 3 : to accept and put into action

adop·tion *n* : the act of adopting : the state of being adopted

ador·able *adj* : CHARMING, LOVELY — **ador·ably** *adv*

ad·o·ra·tion *n* : deep love

adore *vb* **adored; ador·ing** 1 : [2]WORSHIP 1 2 : to be very fond of

adorn *vb* **adorned; adorn·ing** : to make more attractive by adding something

adorn·ment *n* : something added to make a person or thing more attractive

adren·a·line *n* 1 : EPINEPHRINE 2 : excited energy

adrift *adv or adj* : in a drifting state

adroit *adj* : having or showing great skill or cleverness — **adroit·ly** *adv*

ad·u·la·tion *n* : very great admiration

[1]adult *adj* : fully developed and mature

[2]adult *n* : a fully grown person, animal, or plant

adul·ter·ate *vb* **adul·ter·at·ed; adul·ter·at·ing** : to make impure or weaker by adding some-thing different or of poorer quality

adult·hood *n* : the period of being an adult

adv *abbr* adverb

[1]ad·vance *vb* **ad·vanced; ad·vanc·ing** 1 : to move forward 2 : to help the progress of 3 : to raise to a higher rank : PROMOTE 4 : to give ahead of time 5 : PROPOSE 1

[2]advance *n* 1 : a forward movement 2 : progress in development : IMPROVEMENT 3 : a rise in price, value, or amount 4 : a first step or approach 5 : money given ahead of the usual time — **in advance** : before an ex-pected event

ad·vanced *adj* 1 : being far along in years or progress 2 : being beyond the elementary or introductory level

ad·vance·ment *n* **1** : the action of moving forward in position or progress : the state of being moved forward in position or progress **2** : the act of raising to a higher rank or position : the result of being raised to a higher rank or position

ad·van·tage *n* **1** : something that benefits the one it belongs to **2** : the fact of being in a better position or condition **3** : personal benefit or gain

ad·van·ta·geous *adj* : giving a benefit especially that others do not have : giving an advantage — **ad·van·ta·geous·ly** *adv*

ad·vent *n* : the arrival or coming of something

ad·ven·ture *n* **1** : an action that involves unknown dangers and risks **2** : an unusual experience

ad·ven·tur·er *n* : a person who seeks dangerous or exciting experiences

ad·ven·ture·some *adj* : likely to take risks : DARING

ad·ven·tur·ous *adj* **1** : ready to take risks or to deal with new or unexpected problems **2** : DANGEROUS 1, RISKY

ad·verb *n* : a word used to modify a verb, an adjective, or another adverb and often used to show degree, manner, place, or time

ad·ver·bi·al *adj* : of, relating to, or used as an adverb — **ad·ver·bi·al·ly** *adv*

ad·ver·sary *n, pl* **ad·ver·sar·ies** : OPPONENT, ENEMY

ad·verse *adj* **1** : acting against or in an opposite direction **2** : not helping or favoring — **ad·verse·ly** *adv*

ad·ver·si·ty *n, pl* **ad·ver·si·ties** : hard times : MISFORTUNE

ad·ver·tise *vb* **ad·ver·tised; ad·ver·tis·ing** **1** : to call to public attention to persuade to buy **2** : to announce publicly — **ad·ver·tis·er** *n*

ad·ver·tise·ment *n* : a notice or short film advertising something

ad·ver·tis·ing *n* **1** : speech, writing, pictures, or films meant to persuade people to buy something **2** : the business of preparing advertisements

ad·vice *n* : suggestions about a decision or action

ad·vis·able *adj* : reasonable or wise to do

ad·vise *vb* **ad·vised; ad·vis·ing** **1** : to give suggestions about a decision or action : give advice to **2** : to give information about something — **ad·vis·er** *or* **ad·vi·sor** *n*

ad·vi·so·ry *adj* : having the power or right to advise

¹ad·vo·cate *n* **1** : a person who argues for or supports an idea or plan **2** : a person who argues for another especially in court

²ad·vo·cate *vb* **ad·vo·cat·ed; ad·vo·cat·ing** : to speak in favor of : argue for

adze *also* **adz** *n, pl* **adz·es** : a cutting tool that has a thin curved blade at right angles to the handle and is used for shaping wood

ae·on *or* **eon** *n* : a very long period of time

aer- *or* **aero-** *prefix* : air : atmosphere : gas

aer·ate *vb* **aer·at·ed; aer·at·ing** **1** : to supply or cause to be filled with air **2** : to supply (blood) with oxygen by breathing — **aer·a·tor** *n*

aer·a·tion *n* : the process of supplying or filling with air or gas

¹ae·ri·al *adj* **1** : performed or occurring in the air **2** : of aircraft **3** : taken from, used in, or performed using an airplane

²aer·i·al *n* : ANTENNA 2

aero·nau·ti·cal *adj* : of or relating to aeronautics

aero·nau·tics *n* : a science dealing with the building and flying of aircraft

aero·sol *n* **1** : a substance (as an insect repellent or medicine) that is released from a container as a spray of tiny solid or liquid particles in gas **2** : a container (as a can) that dispenses a substance as a spray

¹aero·space *n* **1** : the earth's atmosphere and the space beyond **2** : a science dealing with aerospace

²aerospace *adj* : relating to aerospace, to the vehicles used in aerospace or their manufacture, or to travel in aerospace

aes·thet·ic *adj* : relating to beauty and what is beautiful — **aes·thet·i·cal·ly** *adv*

¹afar *adv* : from, at, or to a great distance

²afar *n* : a long way off

af·fa·ble *adj* : friendly and easy to talk to — **af·fa·bly** *adv*

af·fair *n* **1 affairs** *pl* : work or activities done for a purpose : BUSINESS **2** : something that relates to or involves someone **3** : a social event or activity

¹af·fect *vb* **af·fect·ed; af·fect·ing** : to pretend that a false behavior or feeling is natural or genuine

²affect *vb* **affected; affecting** **1** : to have an effect on **2** : to cause strong emotions in **3** : to cause illness in

af·fect·ed *adj* : not natural or genuine — **af·fect·ed·ly** *adv*

af·fec·tion *n* : a feeling of liking and caring for someone or something

af·fec·tion·ate *adj* : feeling or showing a great liking for a person or thing : LOVING — **af·fec·tion·ate·ly** *adv*

af·fi·da·vit *n* : a written statement signed by a person who swears that the information is true

af·fil·i·ate *vb* **af·fil·i·at·ed; af·fil·i·at·ing** : to associate as a member or partner

af·fin·i·ty *n, pl* **af·fin·i·ties** : a strong liking for or attraction to someone or something

af·firm *vb* **af·firmed; af·firm·ing** : to declare that something is true

af·fir·ma·tion *n* : an act of saying or showing that something is true

¹af·fir·ma·tive *adj* **1** : saying or showing that the answer is "yes" **2** : being positive or helpful

²affirmative *n* **1** : an expression (as the word *yes*) of agreement **2** : the side that supports or votes for something

¹af·fix *vb* **af·fixed; af·fix·ing** **1** : to attach firmly **2** : to add to something else

²af·fix *n* : a letter or group of letters (as a prefix or suffix) that comes at the beginning or end of a word and has a meaning of its own

af·flict *vb* **af·flict·ed; af·flict·ing** : to cause pain or unhappiness to

af·flic·tion *n* **1** : the state of being affected by something that causes pain or unhappiness **2** : something that causes pain or unhappiness

af·flu·ence *n* : the state of having much money and expensive things : WEALTH

af·flu·ent *adj* : having plenty of money and expensive things : WEALTHY

af·ford *vb* **af·ford·ed; af·ford·ing** **1** : to be able to do or bear without serious harm **2** : to be able to pay for **3** : to supply or provide someone with

af·ford·able *adj* : within someone's ability to pay : reasonably priced

¹af·front *vb* **af·front·ed; af·front·ing** : to insult openly : OFFEND

²affront *n* : an act or statement that insults or offends someone

Af·ghan *n* **1** : a person born or living in Afghanistan **2** *not cap* : a blanket or shawl made of wool or cotton knitted or crocheted into patterns

afield *adv* **1** : to, in, or into the countryside **2** : away from home **3** : out of a usual, planned, or proper course

afire *adj* **1** : being on fire **2** : in a state of great excitement or energy

aflame *adj* : burning with flames

afloat *adv or adj* : carried on or as if on water

aflut·ter *adj* **1** : flapping quickly **2** : very excited and nervous

afoot *adv or adj* **1** : on foot **2** : happening now : going on

afore·men·tioned *adj* : mentioned before

afore·said *adj* : named before

afraid *adj* **1** : filled with fear **2** : filled with concern or regret **3** : having a dislike for something

afresh *adv* : again from the beginning

¹Af·ri·can *n* : a person born or living in Africa

²African *adj* : of or relating to Africa or African people

African–American *n* : an American having African and especially black African ancestors — **African–American** *adj*

African violet *n* : a tropical African plant often grown for its showy white, pink, or purple flowers and its velvety leaves

Af·ro–Amer·i·can *n* : AFRICAN-AMERICAN — **Afro–American** *adj*

aft *adv* : toward or at the back part of a ship or the tail of an aircraft

¹af·ter *adv* : following in time or place : at a later time

²after *prep* **1** : behind in time or place **2** : for the reason of catching, seizing, or getting **3** : following in order or in a series **4** : following the actions or departure of **5** : with the name of

³after *conj* : following the time when

af·ter·ef·fect *n* : an effect that follows its cause after some time has passed

af·ter·glow *n* **1** : a glow remaining (as in the sky after sunset) where a light has disappeared **2** : a pleasant feeling that remains after some good experience

af·ter·life *n* : an existence after death

af·ter·math *n* **1** : a result or consequence **2** : the period of time following a bad and usually destructive event

af·ter·noon *n* : the part of the day between noon and evening

af·ter·thought *n* : something done or said that was not thought of originally

af·ter·ward *or* **af·ter·wards** *adv* : at a later time

again *adv* **1** : for another time : once more **2** : on the other hand **3** : in addition

against *prep* **1** : opposed to **2** : not agreeing with or allowed by **3** : as protection from **4** : in or into contact with **5** : in a direction opposite to **6** : before the background of

agape *adj* : having the mouth open in wonder, surprise, or shock

ag·ate *n* : a mineral that is a form of quartz with colors arranged in stripes or patches and that is used especially in jewelry

aga·ve *n* : a plant that has sword-shaped leaves with spiny edges and is sometimes grown for its large stalks of flowers

¹age *n* **1** : the amount of time during which someone or something has lived or existed **2** : the time of life when a person receives some right or capacity **3** : the later part of life **4** : the condition of being old **5** : a period of time associated with a person or thing **6** : a long period of time

²age *vb* **aged** ; **ag·ing** *or* **age·ing** **1** : to become old or older **2** : to cause to become old or to appear to be old **3** : to remain or cause to remain undisturbed until fit for use : MA-TURE

-age *n suffix* **1** : total amount : collection **2** : action : process **3** : result of **4** : rate of **5** : house or place of **6** : state : condition **7** : fee : charge

aged *adj* **1** : very old **2** : having reached a specified age

age·less *adj* **1** : not growing old or showing the effects of age **2** : lasting forever : TIME-LESS

agen·cy *n, pl* **agen·cies** **1** : a person or thing through which power is used or something is achieved **2** : a business that provides a particular service **3** : a part of a government that is responsible for providing a particular service or performing a specific function

agen·da *n* : a list of things to be done or talked about

agent *n* **1** : something that produces an effect **2** : a person who acts or does business for another

ag·gra·vate *vb* **ag·gra·vat·ed; ag·gra·vat·ing** **1** : to make worse or more serious **2** : to make angry usually by bothering again and again

ag·gra·va·tion *n* **1** : an act or the result of making worse or more serious **2** : something that annoys or bothers someone

¹**ag·gre·gate** *vb* **ag·gre·gat·ed; ag·gre·gat·ing** : to collect or gather into a mass or whole

²**ag·gre·gate** *n* **1** : a mass or body of units or parts **2** : the whole sum or amount

ag·gre·ga·tion *n* **1** : the collecting of units or parts into a mass or whole **2** : a group, body, or mass composed of many distinct parts

ag·gres·sion *n* **1** : angry or violent behavior or feelings **2** : hostile action made without reasonable cause

ag·gres·sive *adj* **1** : showing a readiness to fight or argue **2** : engaging in hostile action without reasonable cause **3** : being forceful in getting things done — **ag·gres·sive·ly** *adv* — **ag·gres·sive·ness** *n*

ag·gres·sor *n* : a person or a country that engages in hostile action without reasonable cause

ag·grieved *adj* **1** : having or showing a troubled or unhappy mind **2** : having cause for complaint especially from unfair treatment

aghast *adj* : struck with terror, surprise, or horror

ag·ile *adj* **1** : able to move quickly and easily **2** : having a quick mind — **ag·ile·ly** *adv*

agil·i·ty *n* : the ability to move quickly and easily

aging *present participle of* AGE

ag·i·tate *vb* **ag·i·tat·ed; ag·i·tat·ing** **1** : to move or stir up **2** : to disturb, excite, or an-

ger **3** : to try to stir up public feeling — **ag·i·ta·tor** *n*

ag·i·ta·tion *n* : the act of agitating : the state of being agitated

aglow *adj* **1** : glowing with light or color **2** : feeling or showing excitement and happiness

ago *adv* : before this time

agog *adj* : full of excitement

ag·o·nize *vb* **ag·o·nized; ag·o·niz·ing** : to think or worry very much about something

ag·o·ny *n, pl* **ag·o·nies** : great physical pain or emotional distress

agree *vb* **agreed; agree·ing** **1** : to give approval or permission **2** : to have the same opinion **3** : ADMIT 1 **4** : to be alike **5** : to come to an understanding **6** : to be fitting or healthful

agree·able *adj* **1** : pleasing to the mind or senses **2** : willing to do, allow, or approve something **3** : of a kind that can be accepted — **agree·ably** *adv*

agree·ment *n* **1** : the act or fact of having the same opinion or an understanding **2** : the act or fact of giving approval or permission **3** : an arrangement by which people agree about what is to be done

ag·ri·cul·tur·al *adj* : relating to or used in farming or agriculture

ag·ri·cul·ture *n* : the cultivating of the soil, producing of crops, and raising of livestock

aground *adv or adj* : on or onto the shore or the bottom of a body of water

aha *interj* — used to express discovery or understanding

ahead *adv or adj* **1** : in or toward the front **2** : into or for the future

ahead of *prep* **1** : in front of **2** : earlier than **3** : having a lead over

ahoy *interj* — used in calling out to a passing ship or boat

¹**aid** *vb* **aid·ed; aid·ing** : to provide what is useful or necessary : HELP

²**aid** *n* **1** : the act of helping **2** : help given **3** : someone or something that is of help or assistance

aide *n* : a person who acts as an assistant

AIDS *n* : a serious disease of the human immune system in which large numbers of the cells that help the body fight infection are destroyed by the HIV virus carried in the blood and other fluids of the body

AIDS virus *n* : HIV

ail *vb* **ailed; ail·ing** **1** : to be wrong with **2** : to suffer especially with ill health

ail·ment *n* : a sickness or disease

¹**aim** *vb* **aimed; aim·ing** **1** : to point a weapon toward an object **2** : INTEND **3** : to direct toward an object or goal

²**aim** *n* **1** : the ability to hit a target **2** : the

pointing of a weapon at a target **3** : a goal or purpose

aim·less *adj* : lacking a goal or purpose — **aim·less·ly** *adv*

ain't 1 : am not : are not : is not **2** : have not : has not

¹air *n* **1** : the invisible mixture of odorless tasteless gases that surrounds the earth **2** : the space or sky that is filled with air **3** : air that is compressed **4** : outward appearance : a quality that a person or thing has **5** : AIRCRAFT **6** : AVIATION 1 **7** : a radio or television broadcast **8 airs** *pl* : an artificial way of acting

²air *vb* **aired; air·ing 1** : to place in the air for cooling, freshening, or cleaning **2** : to make known in public

air bag *n* : an automobile safety device consisting of a bag that inflates to cushion a rider in an accident

air base *n* : a base for military aircraft

air·borne *adj* : moving through the air

air–con·di·tion *vb* **air–con·di·tioned; aircon·di·tion·ing** : to equip with a device for cleaning air and controlling its humidity and temperature — **air con·di·tion·er** *n* — **air–con·di·tion·ing** *n*

air·craft *n, pl* **aircraft** : a vehicle (as an airplane or helicopter) that can travel through the air and that is supported either by its own lightness or by the action of the air against its surfaces

air·field *n* : a field or airport where airplanes take off and land

air force *n* : the military organization of a nation for air warfare

air·lift *vb* **air·lift·ed; air·lift·ing** : to move people or cargo by aircraft usually to or from an area that cannot be reached otherwise — **air·lift** *n*

air·line *n* : a company that owns and operates many airplanes which are used for carrying passengers and cargo to different places

air·lin·er *n* : a large airplane used for carrying passengers

¹air·mail *n* **1** : the system of carrying mail by airplanes **2** : mail carried by airplanes

²airmail *vb* **air·mailed; air·mail·ing** : to send by airmail

air·man *n, pl* **air·men 1** : an enlisted person in the air force in one of the ranks below sergeant **2** : ¹PILOT 1, AVIATOR

airman basic *n* : an enlisted person of the lowest rank in the air force

airman first class *n* : an enlisted person in the air force ranking just below that of sergeant

air·plane *n* : an aircraft with wings which do not move, that is heavier than air, is driven by a propeller or jet engine, and is supported by the action of the air against its wings

air·port *n* : a place where aircraft land and take off and where there are usually buildings for passengers to wait in and for aircraft and equipment to be kept

air sac *n* : one of the small pouches in the lungs where oxygen and carbon dioxide are exchanged

air·ship *n* : an aircraft lighter than air that is kept in the air by one or more compartments filled with gas and that has an engine and steering

air·strip *n* : a runway without places (as hangars) for the repair of aircraft or shelter of passengers or cargo

air·tight *adj* : so tightly sealed that no air can get in or out

air·wave *n* : the radio waves used to broadcast radio and television programs — usually used in pl.

air·way *n* **1** : the passage through which air moves from the nose or mouth to the lungs in breathing **2** : a route along which airplanes regularly fly **3** : AIRLINE

airy *adj* **air·i·er; air·i·est 1** : open to the air : BREEZY **2** : high in the air **3** : having a light or careless quality that shows a lack of concern **4** : like air in lightness and delicacy — **air·i·ly** *adv*

aisle *n* **1** : a passage between sections of seats (as in a church or theater) **2** : a passage between shelves (as in a supermarket)

ajar *adv or adj* : slightly open

AK *abbr* Alaska

aka *abbr* also known as

akim·bo *adv or adj* **1** : with the hands on the hips and the elbows turned outward **2** : set in a bent position

akin *adj* **1** : related by blood **2** : SIMILAR

AL *abbr* Alabama

¹-al *adj suffix* : of, relating to, or showing

²-al *n suffix* : action : process

Ala. *abbr* Alabama

al·a·bas·ter *n* : a smooth usually white stone used for carving

à la carte *adv or adj* : with a separate price for each item on the menu

alac·ri·ty *n* : a cheerful readiness to do something

¹alarm *n* **1** : a warning of danger **2** : a device (as a bell) that warns or signals people **3** : ALARM CLOCK **4** : the feeling of fear caused by a sudden sense of danger

²alarm *vb* **alarmed; alarm·ing** : to cause to feel a sense of danger : worry or frighten

alarm clock *n* : a clock that can be set to sound an alarm at a desired time

alas *interj* — used to express unhappiness, pity, disappointment or worry

al·ba·tross *n* : a very large seabird with webbed feet

al·be·it *conj* : even though : ALTHOUGH

al·bi·no *n, pl* **al·bi·nos** **1** : a person or an animal that has little or no coloring matter in skin, hair, and eyes **2** : a plant with little or no coloring matter

al·bum *n* **1** : a book with blank pages in which to put a collection (as of photographs, stamps, or autographs) **2** : one or more recordings (as on tape or disk) produced as a single collection

al·bu·men *n* **1** : the white of an egg **2** : ALBUMIN

al·bu·min *n* : any of various proteins that dissolve in water and occur in blood, the whites of eggs, and in plant and animal tissues

al·che·my *n* : a science that was used in the Middle Ages with the goal of changing ordinary metals into gold

al·co·hol *n* **1** : a colorless flammable liquid that in one form is the substance in liquors (as beer, wine, or whiskey) that can make a person drunk **2** : a drink containing alcohol

¹al·co·hol·ic *adj* **1** : of, relating to, or containing alcohol **2** : affected with alcoholism

²alcoholic *n* : a person affected with alcoholism

al·co·hol·ism *n* : continued, uncontrolled, and greater than normal use of alcoholic drinks accompanied by physical and mental dependence on alcohol

al·cove *n* : a small part of a room set back from the rest of it

al·der *n* : a shrub or small tree that is related to the birch and usually grows in moist soil (as near a river or pond)

al·der·man *n* : a member of a lawmaking body in a city

ale *n* : an alcoholic drink made from malt and flavored with hops that is usually more bitter than beer

¹alert *adj* **1** : watchful and ready especially to meet danger **2** : quick to understand and act — **alert·ly** *adv* — **alert·ness** *n*

²alert *n* **1** : an alarm or signal of danger **2** : the period during which an alert is in effect — **on the alert** : watchful against danger

³alert *vb* **alert·ed; alert·ing** : to make aware of a need to get ready or take action : WARN

al·fal·fa *n* : a plant with purple flowers that is related to the clovers and is grown as a food for horses and cattle

al·ga *n, pl* **al·gae** : any of a large group of simple plants and plant-like organisms (as a seaweed) that usually grow in water and produce chlorophyll like plants but do not produce seeds

al·ge·bra *n* : a branch of mathematics in which symbols (as letters and numbers) are combined according to the rules of arithmetic

Al·gon·qui·an *or* **Al·gon·quin** *n* **1** : a group of American Indian people of southeastern Ontario and southern Quebec or their language — usually *Algonquin* in this sense **2** : a family of American Indian languages spoken by people from Newfoundland and Labrador to North Carolina and westward into the Great Plains **3** : a member of the group of people speaking Algonquian languages

¹ali·as *adv* : otherwise known as

²alias *n* : a false name

al·i·bi *n, pl* **al·i·bis** **1** : the explanation given by a person accused of a crime that he or she was somewhere else when the crime was committed **2** : an excuse intended to avoid blame

¹alien *adj* **1** : different from what is familiar **2** : from another country and not a citizen of the country of residence : FOREIGN **3** : from somewhere other than the planet earth

²alien *n* **1** : a resident who was born elsewhere and is not a citizen of the country in which he or she now lives **2** : a being that comes from somewhere other than the planet earth

alien·ate *vb* **alien·at·ed; alien·at·ing** : to cause (a person who used to be friendly or loyal) to become unfriendly or disloyal

¹alight *vb* **alight·ed; alight·ing** **1** : to get down : DISMOUNT **2** : to come down from the air and settle

²alight *adj* : full of light : lighted up

align *vb* **aligned; align·ing** : to arrange things so that they form a line or are in proper position

align·ment *n* : the state of being arranged in a line or in proper position

¹alike *adv* : in the same way

²alike *adj* : being like each other : similar in appearance, nature, or form

al·i·men·ta·ry canal *n* : DIGESTIVE TRACT

alimentary tract *n* : DIGESTIVE TRACT

al·i·mo·ny *n* : money for living expenses paid regularly by one spouse to another after their legal separation or divorce

alive *adj* **1** : having life : not dead **2** : still in force, existence, or operation **3** : aware of the existence of **4** : filled with life and activity

al·ka·li *n, pl* **al·ka·lies** *or* **al·ka·lis** **1** : a substance that has a bitter taste and reacts with an acid to form a salt : BASE **2** : a salt or a mixture of salts sometimes found in large amounts in the soil of dry regions

al·ka·line *adj* **1** : having the properties of an alkali **2** : containing an alkali

al·ka·lin·i·ty *n* : the quality, state, or degree of being alkaline

¹all *adj* **1** : every one of **2** : the whole of **3** : the whole number of **4** : any whatever **5** : the greatest possible

²all *adv* **1** : COMPLETELY **2** : so much **3** : ²VERY 1 **4** : for each side

³all *pron* **1** : the whole number or amount **2** : EVERYTHING **3** : the only thing

Al·lah *n* : God as named in Islam

all–around *also* **all–round** *adj* **1** : having many good aspects **2** : skillful or useful in many ways

al·lay *vb* **al·layed; al·lay·ing 1** : to make less severe **2** : to put to rest

all but *adv* : very nearly : ALMOST

al·le·ga·tion *n* : a statement that is not supported by proof and that usually accuses someone of wrongdoing

al·lege *vb* **al·leged; al·leg·ing** : to state as fact but without proof

al·le·giance *n* : loyalty and service to a group, country, or idea

al·le·lu·ia *interj* : HALLELUJAH

al·ler·gen *n* : a substance that causes an allergic reaction

al·ler·gic *adj* : of, relating to, causing, or affected by allergy

al·ler·gist *n* : a medical doctor who specializes in treating allergies

al·ler·gy *n, pl* **al·ler·gies** : a condition in which a person is made sick by something that is harmless to most people

al·le·vi·ate *vb* **al·le·vi·at·ed; al·le·vi·at·ing** : to make less painful, difficult, or severe

al·ley *n, pl* **al·leys 1** : a narrow passageway between buildings **2** : a special narrow wooden floor on which balls are rolled in bowling

all fours *n pl* : all four legs of a four-legged animal or both legs and both arms of a person

al·li·ance *n* **1** : a relationship in which people, groups, or countries agree to work together **2** : an association of people, groups, or nations working together for a specific purpose

al·lied *adj* **1** : being connected or related in some way **2** : joined in a relationship in which people, groups, or countries work together

al·li·ga·tor *n* : a large short-legged reptile that has a long body, thick skin, a long broad snout, and sharp teeth and is related to the crocodile and lizards

all·o·sau·rus *n* : a large meat-eating dinosaur related to the tyrannosaur

al·lot *vb* **al·lot·ted; al·lot·ting** : to give out as a share or portion

al·lot·ment *n* **1** : the act of giving out as a share or portion **2** : an amount of something that is given out as a share or portion

all–out *adj* : as great as possible

al·low *vb* **al·lowed; al·low·ing 1** : to give permission to **2** : to fail to prevent **3** : to assign as a share or suitable amount (as of time or money) **4** : to accept as true : CONCEDE **5** : to consider when making a decision or a calculation **6** : to make it possible to have or do something

al·low·able *adj* : not forbidden

al·low·ance *n* **1** : an amount of money given regularly for a specific purpose **2** : a share given out **3** : the act of considering things that could affect a result

al·loy *n* : a substance made of two or more metals melted together

¹all right *adv* **1** : fairly well : well enough **2** — used to show agreement, acceptance, annoyance, reluctance, pleasure, or excitement

²all right *adj* **1** : not ill, hurt, or unhappy : WELL **2** — used to tell someone not to be concerned **3** : within acceptable limits of behavior **4** : suitable or appropriate **5** : fairly good : SATISFACTORY

all–round *variant of* ALL-AROUND

All Saint's Day *n* : November 1 observed as a church holy day in honor of the Christian saints

all–star *adj* : made up mainly or entirely of outstanding participants

al·lude *vb* **al·lud·ed; al·lud·ing** : to talk about or hint at without mentioning directly

¹al·lure *vb* **al·lured; al·lur·ing** : to try to attract or influence by offering what seems to be a benefit or pleasure

²allure *n* : power to attract

al·lu·sion *n* : a statement that refers to something without mentioning it directly

¹al·ly *n, pl* **allies** : a person, group, or nation associated or united with another in a common purpose

²al·ly *vb* **al·lied; al·ly·ing** : to form a connection between : join in an alliance

al·ma·nac *n* : a book containing a calendar of days, weeks, and months and usually facts about weather and astronomy and information of general interest

al·mighty *adj, often cap* : having absolute power over all

al·mond *n* : a nut that is the edible kernel of a small tree related to the peach tree

al·most *adv* : only a little less than : very nearly

alms *n, pl* **alms** : money given to help the poor : CHARITY

aloft *adv* **1** : at or to a great height **2** : in the air : in flight **3** : at, on, or to the top of the mast or the higher rigging of a ship

¹**alone** *adj* **1** : separated from others **2** : not including anyone or anything else

²**alone** *adv* **1** : and nothing or no one else **2** : without company or help

¹**along** *prep* **1** : on or near in a lengthwise direction **2** : at a point on

²**along** *adv* **1** : farther forward or on **2** : as a companion, associate, or useful item **3** : at an advanced point — **all along** : all the time

¹**along·side** *adv* : along or by the side

²**alongside** *prep* : parallel to

¹**aloof** *adv* : at a distance

²**aloof** *adj* : not friendly or outgoing

aloud *adv* : in a voice that can be clearly heard

al·paca *n* : a South American animal related to the camel and llama that is raised for its long woolly hair which is woven into warm strong cloth

al·pha·bet *n* : the letters used in writing a language arranged in their regular order

al·pha·bet·i·cal *or* **al·pha·bet·ic** *adj* : arranged in the order of the letters of the alphabet — **al·pha·bet·i·cal·ly** *adv*

al·pha·bet·ize *vb* **al·pha·bet·ized; al·pha·bet·iz·ing** : to arrange in alphabetical order

al·ready *adv* **1** : before a certain time : by this time **2** : so soon

al·so *adv* : in addition : TOO

alt. *abbr* **1** alternate **2** altitude

Alta *abbr* Alberta

al·tar *n* **1** : a platform or table used as a center of worship **2** : a usually raised place on which sacrifices are offered

al·ter *vb* **al·tered; al·ter·ing** : to change partly but not completely

al·ter·ation *n* **1** : the act or process of changing something **2** : the result of changing : MODIFICATION

¹**al·ter·nate** *adj* **1** : occurring or following by turns **2** : arranged one above, beside, or next to another **3** : every other : every second — **al·ter·nate·ly** *adv*

²**al·ter·nate** *vb* **al·ter·nat·ed; al·ter·nat·ing** : to take place or cause to take place by turns

³**al·ter·nate** *n* : a person named to take the place of another whenever necessary

alternating current *n* : an electric current that reverses its direction of flow regularly many times per second

al·ter·na·tion *n* : the act, process, or result of taking place by turns

¹**al·ter·na·tive** *adj* : offering or expressing a choice — **al·ter·na·tive·ly** *adv*

²**alternative** *n* **1** : a chance to choose between two things **2** : one of the things between which a choice is to be made

al·though *conj* **1** : in spite of the fact that **2** : ¹BUT 1

al·ti·tude *n* **1** : height above a certain level

and especially above sea level **2** : the perpendicular distance from the base of a geometric figure to the vertex or to the side parallel to the base

al·to *n, pl* **altos** **1** : the lowest female singing voice **2** : the second highest part in harmony that has four parts **3** : a singer or an instrument having an alto range or part

al·to·geth·er *adv* **1** : COMPLETELY **2** : with everything taken into consideration **3** : when everything is added together

al·um *n* : either of two aluminum compounds that are used especially in medicine (as to stop bleeding)

alu·mi·num *n* : a silver-white light metallic chemical element that is easily shaped, conducts electricity well, resists weathering, and is the most plentiful metal in the earth's crust

alum·na *n, pl* **alum·nae** : a girl or woman who has attended or has graduated from a school, college, or university

alum·nus *n, pl* **alum·ni** : a person who has attended or has graduated from a school, college, or university

al·ways *adv* **1** : at all times **2** : throughout all time : FOREVER **3** : often, frequently, or repeatedly

am *present first person sing of* BE

Am. *abbr* **1** America **2** American

a.m., A.M. *abbr* before noon — abbreviation for Latin *ante meridiem*, which means "before noon."

amass *vb* **amassed; amass·ing** : to collect or gather together

¹**am·a·teur** *n* **1** : a person who takes part in sports or occupations for pleasure and not for pay **2** : a person who takes part in something without having experience or skill in it — **am·a·teur·ish** *adj*

²**amateur** *adj* : not professional

amaze *vb* **amazed; amaz·ing** : to surprise or puzzle very much

amaze·ment *n* : great surprise

am·bas·sa·dor *n* : a person sent as the chief representative of his or her government in another country — **am·bas·sa·dor·ship** *n*

am·ber *n* **1** : a hard yellowish to brownish clear substance that is a fossil resin from trees long dead and that can be polished and used in making ornamental objects (as beads) **2** : a dark orange yellow : the color of honey

ambi- *prefix* : both

am·bi·dex·trous *adj* : using both hands with equal ease — **am·bi·dex·trous·ly** *adv*

am·bi·gu·i·ty *n, pl* **am·bi·gu·i·ties** : something that can be understood in more than one way

am·big·u·ous *adj* : able to be understood in more than one way — **am·big·u·ous·ly** *adv*

am·bi·tion *n* **1** : a desire for success, honor, or power **2** : something a person hopes to do or achieve **3** : the drive to do things and be active

am·bi·tious *adj* **1** : possessing a desire for success, honor, or power **2** : not easily done or achieved — **am·bi·tious·ly** *adv*

am·ble *vb* **am·bled; am·bling** : to walk at a slow easy pace

am·bu·lance *n* : a vehicle used to carry a sick or injured person

¹am·bush *vb* **am·bushed; am·bush·ing** : to attack by surprise from a hidden place

²ambush *n* **1** : a hidden place from which a surprise attack can be made **2** : a surprise attack made from a hidden place

amen *interj* **1** — used at the end of a prayer **2** — used to express agreement

ame·na·ble *adj* : readily giving in or agreeing

amend *vb* **amend·ed; amend·ing 1** : to change for the better : IMPROVE **2** : to change the wording or meaning of : ALTER

amend·ment *n* : a change in wording or meaning especially in a law, bill, or motion

amends *n pl* : something done or given by a person to make up for a loss or injury he or she has caused — used as singular, but more common as plural

ame·ni·ty *n, pl* **ame·ni·ties 1** : the quality or characteristic of being pleasant or agreeable **2** *amenities pl* : something that makes life easier or more pleasant

Amer. *abbr* **1** America **2** American

¹Amer·i·can *n* **1** : a citizen of the United States **2** : a person born or living in North or South America

²American *adj* **1** : of or relating to the United States or its citizens **2** : of or relating to North or South America or their residents

American Indian *n* : a member of any of the first groups of people to live in North and South America

AmerInd *abbr* American Indian

am·e·thyst *n* : a clear purple or bluish violet quartz used as a gem

ami·a·ble *adj* : having a friendly and pleasant manner — **ami·a·bly** *adv*

am·i·ca·ble *adj* : showing kindness or goodwill — **am·i·ca·bly** *adv*

amid *or* **amidst** *prep* : in or into the middle of

amid·ships *adv* : in or near the middle of a ship

ami·no acid *n* : any of various acids containing carbon and nitrogen that are building blocks of protein and are made by living plant or animal cells or are obtained from the diet

¹amiss *adv* : in the wrong way

²amiss *adj* : not right : WRONG

am·i·ty *n* : a feeling of friendship

am·me·ter *n* : an instrument for measuring electric current in amperes

am·mo·nia *n* **1** : a colorless gas that is a compound of nitrogen and hydrogen, has a sharp smell and taste, can be easily made liquid by cold and pressure, and is used in cleaning products and in making fertilizers and explosives **2** : a solution of ammonia and water

am·mu·ni·tion *n* : objects fired from weapons

am·ne·sia *n* : abnormal and usually complete loss of memory

amoe·ba *n, pl* **amoe·bas** *or* **amoe·bae** : a tiny water animal that is a single cell which flows about and takes in food

amok *or* **amuck** *adv* : in a wild or uncontrolled manner — usually used in the phrase "run amok" or "run amuck"

among *also* **amongst** *prep* **1** : in or through the middle of **2** : in the presence of : WITH **3** : through all or most of **4** : in shares to each of **5** : in the number or group of being considered or compared

¹amount *vb* **amount·ed; amount·ing 1** : to add up **2** : to be the same in meaning or effect

²amount *n* : the total number or quantity

am·pere *n* : a unit for measuring the strength of an electric current

am·per·sand *n* : a character & standing for the word *and*

am·phet·amine *n* : a drug that makes the nervous system more active

am·phib·i·an *n* **1** : any of a group of cold-blooded vertebrate animals (as frogs and toads) that have gills and live in water as larvae but breathe air as adults **2** : an airplane designed to take off from and land on either land or water

am·phib·i·ous *adj* **1** : able to live both on land and in water **2** : meant to be used on both land and water **3** : made by land, sea, and air forces acting together

am·phi·the·ater *n* : an arena with seats rising in curved rows around an open space

am·ple *adj* **am·pler; am·plest** : enough or more than enough of what is needed — **am·ply** *adv*

am·pli·fi·er *n* : a device that increases the strength of electric signals so that sounds played through an electronic system are louder

am·pli·fy *vb* **am·pli·fied; am·pli·fy·ing 1** : to make louder or greater **2** : to give more information about — **am·pli·fi·ca·tion** *n*

am·pu·tate *vb* **am·pu·tat·ed; am·pu·tat·ing** : to cut off

amt. *abbr* amount

amuck *variant of* AMOK

am·u·let *n* : a small object worn as a charm against evil

amuse *vb* **amused; amus·ing** **1** : to entertain with something pleasant **2** : to please the sense of humor of

amuse·ment *n* **1** : something that amuses or entertains **2** : the condition of being amused or entertained

amusement park *n* : a place for entertainment having games and rides

an *indefinite article* : ²A — used before words beginning with a vowel sound

¹**-an** *or* **-ian** *also* **-ean** *n suffix* **1** : one that belongs to **2** : one skilled in or specializing in

²**-an** *or* **-ian** *also* **-ean** *adj suffix* **1** : of or relating to **2** : like : resembling

an·a·bol·ic steroid *n* : a hormone that is used in medicine to help tissue grow and is sometimes abused by athletes to increase muscle size and strength even though it may have unwanted or harmful effects (as stunted growth in teenagers)

an·a·con·da *n* : a large South American snake that coils around and crushes its prey

anal·y·sis *n, pl* **anal·y·ses** **1** : an examination of something to find out how it is made or works or what it is **2** : an explanation of the nature and meaning of something

an·a·lyst *n* : a person who studies or analyzes something

an·a·lyt·ic *or* **an·a·lyt·i·cal** *adj* : of, relating to, or skilled in the careful study of something — **an·a·lyt·i·cal·ly** *adv*

an·a·lyze *vb* **an·a·lyzed; an·a·lyz·ing** **1** : to examine something to find out what it is or what makes it work **2** : to study carefully to understand the nature or meaning of

an·a·tom·i·cal *or* **an·a·tom·ic** *adj* : of or relating to the structural makeup of living things

anat·o·my *n, pl* **anat·o·mies** **1** : a science that has to do with the structure of living things **2** : the structural makeup especially of a person or animal

-ance *n suffix* **1** : action or process **2** : quality or state **3** : amount or degree

an·ces·tor *n* **1** : a person from whom someone is descended **2** : something from which something else develops

an·ces·tral *adj* : of, relating to, or coming from an ancestor

an·ces·try *n, pl* **an·ces·tries** : a person's ancestors

¹**an·chor** *n* **1** : a heavy device attached to a ship by a cable or chain and used to hold the ship in place when thrown overboard **2** : someone or something that provides strength and support

²**anchor** *vb* **an·chored; an·chor·ing** **1** : to hold or become held in place with an anchor **2** : to fasten tightly

an·chor·age *n* : a place where boats can be anchored

¹**an·cient** *adj* **1** : very old **2** : of or relating to a time long past or to those living in such a time

²**ancient** *n* **1** : a very old person **2 ancients** *pl* : the civilized peoples of ancient times and especially of Greece and Rome

-an·cy *n suffix, pl* **-an·cies** : quality or state

and *conj* **1** : added to **2** : AS WELL AS **3** — used to describe an action that is repeated or that occurs for a long time **4** — used to indicate the purpose of an action — **and so forth** : and others or more of the same kind — **and so on** : and so forth

and·iron *n* : one of a pair of metal supports for firewood in a fireplace

an·ec·dote *n* : a short story about something interesting or funny in a person's life

ane·mia *n* : a sickness in which there is too little blood or too few red blood cells or too little hemoglobin in the blood

an·e·mom·e·ter *n* : an instrument for measuring the speed of the wind

anem·o·ne *n* **1** : a plant that blooms in spring and is often grown for its large white or colored flowers **2** : SEA ANEMONE

an·es·the·sia *n* : loss of feeling in all or part of the body with or without loss of consciousness

¹**an·es·thet·ic** *adj* : of, relating to, or capable of producing loss of feeling in all or part of the body

²**anesthetic** *n* : something that produces loss of feeling in all or part of the body

anew *adv* **1** : over again **2** : in a new or different form

an·gel *n* **1** : a spiritual being serving God especially as a messenger **2** : a person who is very good, kind, or beautiful

¹**an·ger** *vb* **an·gered; an·ger·ing** : to make strongly displeased : make angry

²**anger** *n* : a strong feeling of displeasure or annoyance and often of active opposition to an insult, injury, or injustice

¹**an·gle** *n* **1** : the figure formed by two lines meeting at a point **2** : POINT OF VIEW **3** : a sharp corner **4** : the slanting direction in which something is positioned

²**angle** *vb* **an·gled; an·gling** : to turn, move, or point in a direction that is not straight or flat

³**angle** *vb* **an·gled; an·gling** **1** : to fish with hook and line **2** : to try to get something in a sly way

an·gler *n* : a person who fishes with hook and line especially for pleasure

an·gling *n* : fishing with hook and line for pleasure

An·glo- *prefix* **1** : English **2** : English and

¹**An·glo–Sax·on** *n* 1 : a member of the German people who conquered England in the fifth century A.D. 2 : a person whose ancestors were English

²**Anglo–Saxon** *adj* : relating to the Anglo-Saxons

an·go·ra *n* : cloth or yarn made from the long soft silky hair of a special usually white domestic rabbit (**Angora rabbit**) or from the long shiny wool of a goat (**Angora goat**)

an·gry *adj* **an·gri·er; an·gri·est** : feeling or showing great annoyance or displeasure : feeling or showing anger — **an·gri·ly** *adv*

an·guish *n* : great physical or emotional pain

an·guished *adj* : full of physical or emotional pain

an·gu·lar *adj* 1 : having angles or sharp corners 2 : lean and bony

an·i·mal *n* 1 : any member of the kingdom of living things (as earthworms, crabs, birds, and people) that differ from plants typically in being able to move about, in not having cell walls made of cellulose, and in depending on plants and other animals as sources of food 2 : any of the animals lower than humans in the natural order 3 : MAMMAL

animal kingdom *n* : a basic group of natural objects that includes all living and extinct animals

¹**an·i·mate** *adj* : having life

²**an·i·mate** *vb* **an·i·mat·ed; an·i·mat·ing** 1 : to give life or energy to : make alive or lively 2 : to make appear to move

an·i·mat·ed *adj* 1 : full of life and energy : LIVELY 2 : appearing to be alive or moving

an·i·ma·tion *n* 1 : a lively, enthusiastic, or eager state or quality 2 : a way of making a movie that includes moving cartoons

an·i·mos·i·ty *n, pl* **an·i·mos·i·ties** : ¹DISLIKE, HATRED

an·kle *n* 1 : the joint between the foot and the leg 2 : the area containing the ankle joint

an·klet *n* 1 : something (as an ornament) worn around the ankle 2 : a short sock reaching just above the ankle

an·ky·lo·saur *n* : a plant-eating dinosaur with bony plates covering the back

an·nals *n pl* 1 : a record of events arranged in yearly sequence 2 : historical records : HISTORY

an·neal *vb* **an·nealed; an·neal·ing** : to heat (as glass or steel) and then cool so as to toughen and make less brittle

¹**an·nex** *vb* **an·nexed; an·nex·ing** : to add (something) to something else usually so as to become a part of it

²**an·nex** *n* : a building or part of a building attached to or near another building and considered part of it

an·nex·ation *n* : the act of adding new territory

an·ni·hi·late *vb* **an·ni·hi·lat·ed; an·ni·hi·lat·ing** : to destroy entirely : put completely out of existence — **an·ni·hi·la·tion** *n*

an·ni·ver·sa·ry *n, pl* **an·ni·ver·sa·ries** : a date remembered or celebrated every year because of something special that happened on it in an earlier year

an·nounce *vb* **an·nounced; an·nounc·ing** 1 : to make known publicly 2 : to give notice of the arrival, presence, or readiness of

an·nounce·ment *n* 1 : the act of making known publicly 2 : a public notice making something known

an·nounc·er *n* : a person who gives information on television or radio

an·noy *vb* **an·noyed; an·noy·ing** : to cause to feel slightly angry or irritated

an·noy·ance *n* 1 : slight anger or irritation 2 : a source or cause of slight anger or irritation

an·noy·ing *adj* : causing slight anger or irritation — **an·noy·ing·ly** *adv*

¹**an·nu·al** *adj* 1 : coming, happening, done, made, or given once a year 2 : completing the life cycle in one growing season — **an·nu·al·ly** *adv*

²**annual** *n* : an annual plant

annual ring *n* : the layer of wood produced by one year's growth of a woody plant (as in the trunk of a tree)

an·nu·ity *n, pl* **an·nu·ities** : a sum of money paid yearly or at other regular intervals

an·nul *vb* **an·nulled; an·nul·ling** : to cancel by law : take away the legal force of — **an·nul·ment** *n*

an·ode *n* 1 : the positive electrode of an electrolytic cell 2 : the negative end of a battery that is delivering electric current 3 : the electron-collecting electrode of an electron tube

anoint *vb* **anoint·ed; anoint·ing** 1 : to rub or cover with oil or grease 2 : to put oil on as part of a religious ceremony

anom·a·lous *adj* : not regular or usual

anom·a·ly *n, pl* **anom·a·lies** : something different, abnormal, strange, or not easily described

anon. *abbr* anonymous

anon·y·mous *adj* 1 : not named or identified 2 : made or done by someone unknown — **anon·y·mous·ly** *adv*

¹**an·oth·er** *adj* 1 : some other 2 : one more

²**another** *pron* 1 : one more 2 : someone or something different

ans. *abbr* answer

¹**an·swer** *n* 1 : something said or written in reply (as to a question) 2 : a solution of a problem

²**answer** *vb* **an·swered; an·swer·ing 1 :** to speak or write in order to satisfy a question **2 :** to write a response to a letter or e-mail **3 :** to pick up (a ringing telephone) **4 :** to open (a door) when someone knocks on it **5 :** to react to something with an action **6 :** to take responsibility — **answer back :** to reply rudely

an·swer·able *adj* **1 :** RESPONSIBLE 1 **2 :** possible to answer

answering machine *n* **:** a machine that receives telephone calls and records messages from callers

ant *n* **:** a small insect related to the bees and wasps that lives in colonies and forms nests in the ground or in wood in which it stores food and raises its young

ant. *abbr* antonym

ant- *see* ANTI-

¹**-ant** *n suffix* **1 :** one that does or causes a certain thing **2 :** thing that is acted upon in a certain way

²**-ant** *adj suffix* **1 :** doing a certain thing or being a certain way **2 :** causing a certain action

an·tag·o·nism *n* **:** a strong feeling of dislike or disagreement

an·tag·o·nist *n* **:** a person who is against something or someone else **:** OPPONENT

an·tag·o·nis·tic *adj* **:** showing dislike or opposition **:** HOSTILE, UNFRIENDLY

an·tag·o·nize *vb* **an·tag·o·nized; an·tag·o·niz·ing :** to stir up dislike or anger in

ant·arc·tic *adj, often cap* **:** of or relating to the south pole or to the region around it

ante- *prefix* **1 :** before in time **:** earlier **2 :** in front of

ant·eat·er *n* **:** an animal that has a long nose and long sticky tongue and feeds chiefly on ants and termites

an·te·lope *n* **:** an animal chiefly of Africa and southwest Asia that resembles a deer and has horns that extend upward and backward

an·ten·na *n* **1** *pl* **an·ten·nae :** one of two or four threadlike movable feelers on the head of insects and crustaceans (as lobsters) **2** *pl* **an·ten·nas :** a metallic device (as a rod or wire) for sending or receiving radio waves

an·te·room *n* **:** a room used as an entrance to another

an·them *n* **1 :** a sacred song usually sung by a church choir **2 :** a patriotic song

an·ther *n* **:** the enlargement at the tip of a flower's stamen that contains pollen

ant·hill *n* **:** a mound made by ants in digging their nest

an·thol·o·gy *n, pl* **an·thol·o·gies :** a collection of writings (as stories and poems)

an·thra·cite *n* **:** a hard glossy coal that burns without much smoke

an·thrax *n* **:** a serious bacterial disease of warm-blooded animals (as sheep) that can affect humans

an·thro·pol·o·gy *n* **:** a science that studies people and especially their history, development, distribution and culture

anti- *or* **ant-** *prefix* **1 :** opposite in kind, position, or action **2 :** hostile toward

an·ti·bi·ot·ic *n* **:** a substance produced by living things and especially by bacteria and fungi that is used to kill or prevent the growth of harmful germs

an·ti·body *n, pl* **an·ti·bod·ies :** a substance produced by special cells of the body that counteracts the effects of a disease germ or its poisons

an·tic *n* **:** a wildly playful or funny act or action

an·tic·i·pate *vb* **an·tic·i·pat·ed; an·tic·i·pat·ing 1 :** to foresee and deal with or provide for beforehand **2 :** to look forward to

an·tic·i·pa·tion *n* **1 :** excitement about something that's going to happen **2 :** the act of preparing for something

an·ti·cy·clone *n* **:** a system of winds that is like a cyclone but that rotates about a center of high atmospheric pressure instead of low

an·ti·dote *n* **:** something used to reverse or prevent the action of a poison

an·ti·freeze *n* **:** a substance added to the water in an automobile radiator to prevent its freezing

an·ti·mo·ny *n* **:** a silvery white metallic chemical element

an·tip·a·thy *n, pl* **an·tip·a·thies :** a strong feeling of dislike

an·ti·quat·ed *adj* **:** very old and no longer useful or popular **:** OLD-FASHIONED, OBSOLETE

¹**an·tique** *n* **:** an object (as a piece of furniture) made at an earlier time

²**antique** *adj* **:** belonging to or like a former style or fashion

an·tiq·ui·ty *n* **1 :** ancient times **2 :** very great age

¹**an·ti·sep·tic** *adj* **:** killing or preventing the growth or action of germs that cause decay or sickness

²**antiseptic** *n* **:** a substance that helps stop the growth or action of germs

an·ti·so·cial *adj* **1 :** violent or harmful to people **2 :** UNFRIENDLY 1

an·tith·e·sis *n, pl* **an·tith·e·ses :** the exact opposite

an·ti·tox·in *n* **:** a substance that is formed in the blood of one exposed to a disease and that prevents or acts against that disease

ant·ler *n* **:** a bony branching structure that grows from the head of a deer or related animal (as a moose) and that is cast off and grown anew each year — **ant-lered** *adj*

ant lion *n* : an insect having a larva form with long jaws that digs a cone-shaped hole in which it waits for prey (as ants)

an-to-nym *n* : a word of opposite meaning

ant-sy *adj* **ant-si-er; ant-si-est** : impatient and unable to keep still

an-vil *n* : an iron block on which pieces of metal are hammered into shape

anx-i-ety *n, pl* **anx-i-eties** : fear or nervousness about what might happen

anx-ious *adj* **1** : afraid or nervous about what may happen **2** : causing or showing fear or nervousness **3** : wanting very much : EAGER — **anx-ious-ly** *adv*

¹any *adj* **1** : whichever one of **2** : of whatever number or amount

²any *pron* **1** : any one or ones of the people or things in a group **2** : any amount

³any *adv* : to the least amount or degree

any-body *pron* : any person : ANYONE

any-how *adv* **1** : in any way, manner, or order **2** : ANYWAY 1

any-more *adv* : NOWADAYS

any-one *pron* : any person

any-place *adv* : ANYWHERE

any-thing *pron* : a thing of any kind

any-way *adv* **1** : without regard to other considerations **2** : as an additional consideration or thought

any-where *adv* : in, at, or to any place

aor-ta *n* : the main artery that carries blood from the heart for distribution to all parts of the body

Apache *n, pl* **Apache** *or* **Apach-es** **1** : a member of an American Indian people of the southwestern United States **2** : any of the languages of the Apache people

apart *adv* **1** : away from each other **2** : separated by an amount of time **3** : into parts : to pieces **4** : one from another **5** : as something separated : SEPARATELY

apart-ment *n* : a room or set of rooms rented as a home

apartment building *n* : a large building having several apartments

apartment house *n* : APARTMENT BUILDING

ap-a-thy *n* : lack of feeling or of interest : INDIFFERENCE

apato-sau-rus *n* : BRONTOSAURUS

¹ape *n* : any of a group of tailless animals (as gorillas or chimpanzees) that are primates most closely related to humans — **ape-like** *adj*

²ape *vb* **aped; ap-ing** : to imitate (someone) awkwardly

ap-er-ture *n* : an opening or open space : HOLE

apex *n, pl* **apex-es** *or* **api-ces** **1** : the highest point : PEAK **2** : the most successful time

aphid *n* : a small insect that sucks the juices of plants

apiece *adv* : for each one

aplomb *n* : confidence and skill shown especially in a difficult situation

apol-o-get-ic *adj* : sorry for having done or said something wrong — **apol-o-get-i-cal-ly** *adv*

apol-o-gize *vb* **apol-o-gized; apol-o-giz-ing** : to express regret for having done or said something wrong

apol-o-gy *n, pl* **apol-o-gies** : an expression of regret for having done or said something wrong

apos-tle *n* : one of the twelve close followers of Jesus Christ

apos-tro-phe *n* : a mark ' used to show that letters or figures are missing (as in "can't" for "cannot" or "'76" for "1776") or to show the possessive case (as in "Mike's") or the plural of letters or figures (as in "cross your t's")

apoth-e-cary *n, pl* **apoth-e-car-ies** : PHARMACIST

ap-pall *vb* **ap-palled; ap-pall-ing** : to cause to feel shock, horror, or disgust

ap-pall-ing *adj* : being shocking and terrible

ap-pa-ra-tus *n, pl* **ap-pa-ra-tus-es** *or* **apparatus** : the equipment or material for a particular use or job

ap-par-el *n* : things that are worn : CLOTHING

ap-par-ent *adj* **1** : clear to the understanding : EVIDENT **2** : open to view : VISIBLE **3** : appearing to be real or true — **ap-par-ent-ly** *adv*

ap-pa-ri-tion *n* **1** : GHOST **2** : an unusual or unexpected sight

¹ap-peal *n* **1** : the power to cause enjoyment : ATTRACTION **2** : the act of asking for something badly needed or wanted : PLEA **3** : a legal action by which a case is brought to a higher court for review

²appeal *vb* **ap-pealed; ap-peal-ing** **1** : to be pleasing or attractive **2** : to ask for something badly needed or wanted **3** : to take action to have a case or decision reviewed by a higher court

ap-pear *vb* **ap-peared; ap-pear-ing** **1** : to come into sight **2** : to present oneself **3** : SEEM 1 **4** : to come before the public **5** : to come into existence

ap-pear-ance *n* **1** : the way something looks **2** : the act or an instance of appearing

ap-pease *vb* **ap-peased; ap-peas-ing** **1** : to make calm or quiet **2** : to make less severe

ap-pend *vb* **ap-pend-ed; ap-pend-ing** : to add as something extra

ap·pend·age *n* : something (as a leg) attached to a larger or more important thing

ap·pen·di·ci·tis *n* : a condition in which a person's appendix is painful and swollen

ap·pen·dix *n, pl* **ap·pen·dix·es** *or* **ap·pen·di·ces 1** : a part of a book giving added and helpful information (as notes or tables) **2** : a small tubelike part growing out from the large intestine

ap·pe·tite *n* **1** : a natural desire especially for food **2** : a desire or liking for something

ap·pe·tiz·er *n* : a food or drink served before a meal

ap·pe·tiz·ing *adj* : pleasing to the appetite

ap·plaud *vb* **ap·plaud·ed; ap·plaud·ing 1** : to show approval especially by clapping the hands **2** : ¹PRAISE 1

ap·plause *n* : approval shown especially by clapping the hands

ap·ple *n* : a round or oval fruit with red, yellow, or green skin and white flesh that grows on a spreading tree related to the rose

ap·ple·sauce *n* : a sweet sauce made from cooked apples

ap·pli·ance *n* : a piece of household equipment that performs a particular job

ap·pli·ca·ble *adj* : capable of being put to use or put into practice

ap·pli·cant *n* : a person who applies for something (as a job)

ap·pli·ca·tion *n* **1** : the act or an instance of applying **2** : something put or spread on a surface **3** : ¹REQUEST 1 **4** : a document used to make a request for something **5** : ability to be put to practical use **6** : a computer program (as a word processor or browser)

ap·pli·ca·tor *n* : a device for applying a substance (as medicine or polish)

ap·ply *vb* **ap·plied; ap·ply·ing 1** : to request especially in writing **2** : to lay or spread on **3** : to place in contact **4** : to have relation or a connection **5** : to put to use **6** : to give full attention

ap·point *vb* **ap·point·ed; ap·point·ing 1** : to choose for some duty, job, or office **2** : to decide on usually from a position of authority

ap·point·ment *n* **1** : an agreement to meet at a fixed time **2** : the act of choosing for a position or office or of being chosen for a position or office **3** : a position or office to which a person is named **4 appointments** *pl* : FURNISHINGS

ap·po·si·tion *n* : a grammatical construction in which a noun is followed by another that explains it

ap·pos·i·tive *n* : the second of a pair of nouns in apposition

ap·prais·al *n* : an act or instance of setting a value on

ap·praise *vb* **ap·praised; ap·prais·ing** : to set a value on

ap·pre·cia·ble *adj* : large enough to be noticed or measured — **ap·pre·cia·bly** *adv*

ap·pre·ci·ate *vb* **ap·pre·ci·at·ed; ap·pre·ci·at·ing 1** : to be grateful for **2** : to admire greatly and with understanding **3** : to be fully aware of **4** : to increase in number or value

ap·pre·ci·a·tion *n* **1** : a feeling of being grateful **2** : awareness or understanding of worth or value **3** : a rise in value

ap·pre·cia·tive *adj* : having or showing gratitude — **ap·pre·cia·tive·ly** *adv*

ap·pre·hend *vb* **ap·pre·hend·ed; ap·pre·hend·ing 1** : ¹ARREST 1 **2** : to look forward to with fear and uncertainty **3** : UNDERSTAND 1

ap·pre·hen·sion *n* ˙**1** : ²ARREST **2** : fear of or uncertainty about what may be coming **3** : an understanding of something

ap·pre·hen·sive *adj* : fearful of what may be coming — **ap·pre·hen·sive·ly** *adv*

¹ap·pren·tice *n* : a person who is learning a trade or art by experience under a skilled worker

²apprentice *vb* **ap·pren·ticed; ap·pren·tic·ing** : to set at work as an apprentice

ap·pren·tice·ship *n* **1** : service as an apprentice **2** : the period during which a person serves as an apprentice

¹ap·proach *vb* **ap·proached; ap·proach·ing 1** : to come near or nearer : draw close **2** : to begin to deal with **3** : to start talking to for a specific purpose

²approach *n* **1** : an act or instance of drawing near **2** : a way of doing or thinking about something **3** : a way of dealing with something **3** : a path or road to get to a place

ap·proach·able *adj* : easy to meet or deal with

¹ap·pro·pri·ate *adj* : especially fitting or suitable — **ap·pro·pri·ate·ly** *adv* — **ap·pro·pri·ate·ness** *n*

²ap·pro·pri·ate *vb* **ap·pro·pri·at·ed; ap·pro·pri·at·ing 1** : to take possession of especially in an illegal or unfair way **2** : to set apart for a certain purpose or use

ap·pro·pri·a·tion *n* **1** : an act or instance of taking especially illegally or unfairly **2** : the act or an instance of setting apart for a special purpose **3** : a sum of money set apart for a special purpose

ap·prov·al *n* **1** : the belief that something is good or acceptable ˛**2** : permission to do something

ap·prove *vb* **ap·proved; ap·prov·ing 1** : to think of as good **2** : to accept as satisfactory

¹ap·prox·i·mate *adj* : nearly correct or exact
— **ap·prox·i·mate·ly** *adv*

²ap·prox·i·mate *vb* **ap·prox·i·mat·ed; ap-prox·i·mat·ing** : to come near in position, value, or characteristics : APPROACH

ap·prox·i·ma·tion *n* **1** : an estimate or figure that is not intended to be exact **2** : an act or the result of coming near or close

appt. *abbr* appointment

Apr. *abbr* April

apri·cot *n* : a small oval orange-colored fruit that looks like the related peach and plum

April *n* : the fourth month of the year

apron *n* **1** : a piece of cloth worn on the front of the body to keep clothing from getting dirty **2** : a paved area for parking or handling airplanes

apt *adj* **1** : having a tendency : LIKELY **2** : just right : SUITABLE **3** : quick to learn — **apt·ly** *adv* — **apt·ness** *n*

ap·ti·tude *n* **1** : natural ability : TALENT **2** : capacity to learn

aqua *n* : a light greenish blue : the color of water in a swimming pool

aqua·ma·rine *n* : a transparent gem that is blue, blue-green, or green

aquar·i·um *n* **1** : a container (as a tank or bowl) in which fish and other water animals and plants can live **2** : a building in which water animals or water plants are exhibited

Aquar·i·us *n* **1** : a constellation between Capricorn and Pisces imagined as a man pouring water **2** : the eleventh sign of the zodiac or a person born under this sign

aquat·ic *adj* : growing, living, or done in water

aq·ue·duct *n* : an artificial channel used to carry water over a valley

aque·ous *adj* : made of, by, or with water

AR *abbr* Arkansas

-ar *adj suffix* : of or relating to

Ar·ab *n* : a person born or living in the Arabian Peninsula of southwestern Asia — **Arab** *adj*

¹Ara·bi·an *n* : ARAB

²Arabian *adj* : of or relating to Arabs or to the Arabian Peninsula of southwestern Asia

¹Ar·a·bic *n* : a language spoken in the Arabian Peninsula of southwestern Asia, Iraq, Jordan, Lebanon, Syria, Egypt, and parts of northern Africa

²Arabic *adj* : of or relating to the Arabian Peninsula of southwestern Asia, the Arabs, or Arabic

Arabic numeral *n* : one of the number symbols 1, 2, 3, 4, 5, 6, 7, 8, 9, and 0

ar·a·ble *adj* : fit for or cultivated by plowing : suitable for producing crops

Arap·a·ho *or* **Arap·a·hoe** *n, pl* **Arapaho** *or* **Arapahos** *or* **Arapahoe** *or* **Arapahoes 1**

: a member of an American Indian people of the plains region of the United States and Canada **2** : the language of the Arapaho people

ar·bi·trary *adj* **1** : made, chosen, or acting without thought of what is fair or right **2** : seeming to have been made or chosen by chance — **ar·bi·trari·ly** *adv* — **ar·bi·trar·i·ness** *n*

ar·bi·trate *vb* **ar·bi·trat·ed; ar·bi·trat·ing 1** : to settle a disagreement after hearing the arguments of both sides **2** : to refer a dispute to others for settlement

ar·bi·tra·tion *n* : the settling of a disagreement in which both sides present their arguments to a third person or group for decision

ar·bi·tra·tor *n* : a person chosen to settle differences in a disagreement

ar·bor *n* : a shelter shaped like an arch over which vines grow

ar·bo·re·al *adj* **1** : living in or often found in trees **2** : of or relating to a tree

ar·bo·re·tum *n, pl* **ar·bo·re·tums** *or* **ar·bo·re·ta** : a place where trees and plants are grown to be studied

¹arc *n* **1** : a glowing light across a gap in an electric circuit or between electrodes **2** : a part of a curved line between any two points on it

²arc *vb* **arced** ; **arc·ing 1** : to form an electric arc **2** : to follow a curved course

ar·cade *n* **1** : a row of arches supported by columns **2** : an arched or covered passageway between two rows of shops **3** : a place with electronic games that are operated by coins or tokens

¹arch *n* **1** : a usually curved part of a structure that is over an opening and serves as a support (as for the wall above the opening) **2** : something that has a curved shape like an arch — **arched** *adj*

²arch *vb* **arched; arch·ing 1** : to form or shape into an arch : CURVE **2** : to cover with an arch

³arch *adj* **1** : ²CHIEF 2, PRINCIPAL **2** : being clever and mischievous — **arch·ly** *adv*

ar·chae·ol·o·gy *or* **ar·che·ol·o·gy** *n* : a science that deals with past human life and activities as shown by objects (as pottery, tools, and statues) left by ancient peoples

ar·cha·ic *adj* : of, relating to, or existing from an earlier time

arch·an·gel *n* : a chief angel

arch·bish·op *n* : the bishop of highest rank in a group of dioceses

ar·cher *n* : a person who shoots with a bow and arrow

ar·chery *n* : the sport or practice of shooting with bow and arrows

ar·chi·pel·a·go *n, pl* **ar·chi·pel·a·goes** *or* **ar·chi·pel·a·gos** : a group of islands

ar·chi·tect *n* : a person who designs buildings

ar·chi·tec·ture *n* **1** : the art of designing buildings **2** : a style of building — **ar·chi·tec·tur·al** *adj* — **ar·chi·tec·tur·al·ly** *adv*

ar·chive *n* : a place in which public records or historical papers are saved

arch·way *n* **1** : a passage under an arch **2** : an arch over a passage

-archy *n suffix, pl* **-archies** : rule : government

arc·tic *adj* **1** *often cap* : of or relating to the north pole or to the region around it **2** : very cold

ar·dent *adj* : showing or having warmth of feeling : PASSIONATE — **ar·dent·ly** *adv*

ar·dor *n* **1** : warmth of feeling **2** : great eagerness : ZEAL

ar·du·ous *adj* : DIFFICULT 1 — **ar·du·ous·ly** *adv*

are *present second person sing or present pl of* BE

ar·ea *n* **1** : REGION 1 **2** : the amount of surface included within limits **3** : a part of the surface of something **4** : a field of activity or study

area code *n* : a usually three-digit number that represents a telephone service area in a country

are·na *n* **1** : an enclosed area used for public entertainment **2** : a building containing an enclosed area used for public entertainment **3** : a field of activity

aren't : are not

ar·gue *vb* **ar·gued; ar·gu·ing 1** : to discuss some matter usually with different points of view **2** : to give reasons for or against something **3** : to persuade by giving reasons **4** : to disagree or fight using angry words : QUARREL — **ar·gu·er** *n*

ar·gu·ment *n* **1** : an angry disagreement : QUARREL **2** : a reason for or against something **3** : a discussion in which reasons for and against something are given

ar·id *adj* : not having enough rainfall to support agriculture

Ar·ies *n* **1** : a constellation between Pisces and Taurus imagined as a ram **2** : the first sign of the zodiac or a person born under this sign

aright *adv* : in a correct way

arise *vb* **arose** ; **aris·en** ; **aris·ing 1** : to move upward **2** : to get up from sleep or after lying down **3** : to come into existence

ar·is·toc·ra·cy *n, pl* **ar·is·toc·ra·cies 1** : a government that is run by a small class of people **2** : an upper class that is usually based on birth and is richer and more powerful than the rest of a society **3** : people

thought of as being better than the rest of the community

aris·to·crat *n* : a member of an aristocracy

aris·to·crat·ic *adj* : of or relating to the aristocracy or aristocrats — **aris·to·crat·i·cal·ly** *adv*

arith·me·tic *n* **1** : a science that deals with the addition, subtraction, multiplication, and division of numbers **2** : an act or method of adding, subtracting, multiplying, or dividing — **arith·met·ic** *or* **ar·ith·met·i·cal** *adj*

ar·ith·met·ic mean *n* : a quantity formed by adding quantities together and dividing by their number

Ariz. *abbr* Arizona

ark *n, often cap* **1** : the ship in which an ancient Hebrew of the Bible named Noah and his family were saved from a great flood that God sent down on the world because of its wickedness **2** : a cabinet in a synagogue for the scrolls of the Torah

Ark. *abbr* Arkansas

¹arm *n* **1** : a human upper limb especially between the shoulder and wrist **2** : something like an arm in shape or position **3** : SLEEVE 1 **4** : ¹POWER 1 **5** : a foreleg of a four-footed animal

²arm *vb* **armed; arm·ing 1** : to provide with weapons **2** : to provide with a way of fighting, competing, or succeeding

³arm *n* **1** : WEAPON, FIREARM **2** : a branch of an army or of the military forces **3 arms** *pl* : the designs on a shield or flag of a family or government **4 arms** *pl* : actual fighting : WARFARE

ar·ma·da *n* : a large fleet of warships

ar·ma·dil·lo *n, pl* **ar·ma·dil·los** : a small burrowing animal found from Texas to Argentina that has the head and body protected by small bony plates

ar·ma·ment *n* **1** : the military strength and equipment of a nation **2** : the supply of materials for war **3** : the process of preparing for war

ar·ma·ture *n* : the part of an electric motor or generator that turns in a magnetic field

arm·chair *n* : a chair with armrests

¹armed *adj* **1** : carrying weapons **2** : involving the use of weapons

²armed *adj* : having arms of a specified kind or number

armed forces *n pl* : the military, naval, and air forces of a nation

arm·ful *n, pl* **arm·fuls** *or* **arms·ful** : as much as a person's arm can hold

ar·mi·stice *n* : a pause in fighting brought about by agreement between the two sides

ar·mor *n* **1** : a covering (as of metal) to protect the body in battle **2** : a hard covering that provides protection **3** : armored forces and vehicles (as tanks)

ar·mored *adj* : protected by or equipped with armor

ar·mory *n, pl* **ar·mor·ies 1** : a supply of weapons **2** : a place where weapons are kept and where soldiers are often trained **3** : a place where weapons are made

arm·pit *n* : the hollow under a person's arm where the arm joins the shoulder

ar·my *n, pl* **ar·mies 1** : a large body of soldiers trained for land warfare **2** *often cap* : the complete military organization of a nation for land warfare **3** : a great number of people or things

aro·ma *n* : a noticeable and pleasant smell

ar·o·mat·ic *adj* : of, relating to, or having a noticeable and pleasant smell

arose *past of* ARISE

¹around *adv* **1** : in circumference **2** : in or along a curving course **3** : on all sides **4** : NEARBY **5** : in close so as to surround **6** : in many different directions or places **7** : to each in turn **8** : in an opposite direction **9** : almost but not exactly : APPROXIMATELY

²around *prep* **1** : in a curving path along the outside boundary of **2** : on every side of **3** : on or to another side of **4** : here and there in **5** : near in number, time, or amount **6** : in the area near to

arouse *vb* **aroused; arous·ing 1** : to awaken from sleep **2** : to cause to feel **3** : to cause to become active or upset

ar·range *vb* **ar·ranged; ar·rang·ing 1** : to put in order and especially a particular order **2** : to make plans for **3** : to come to an agreement about : SETTLE **4** : to write or change (a piece of music) to suit particular voices or instruments — **ar·rang·er** *n*

ar·range·ment *n* **1** : the act of putting things in order : the order in which things are put **2** : something made by putting things together and organizing them **3** : preparation or planning done in advance **4** : a usually informal agreement **5** : a piece of music written or changed to suit particular voices or instruments

ar·rant *adj* : of the worst kind

¹ar·ray *vb* **ar·rayed; ar·ray·ing 1** : to place in order **2** : to dress especially in fine or beautiful clothing

²array *n* **1** : an impressive group **2** : a group of persons (as soldiers) in a certain order **3** : fine or beautiful clothing **4** : regular order or arrangement **5** : a group of mathematical elements (as numbers or letters) arranged in rows and columns

ar·rears *n pl* **1** : the state of being behind in paying debts **2** : unpaid and overdue debts

¹ar·rest *vb* **ar·rest·ed; ar·rest·ing 1** : to take or keep control over (someone) by authority of law **2** : to stop the progress or movement of : CHECK **3** : to attract and hold the attention of

²arrest *n* : the act of taking or holding a person by authority of law

ar·riv·al *n* **1** : the act of reaching a place **2** : the time when something begins or happens **3** : a person or thing that has come to a place

ar·rive *vb* **ar·rived; ar·riv·ing 1** : to reach the place started out for **2** : COME **4** **3** : to be born — **arrive at** : to reach by effort or thought

ar·ro·gance *n* : a person's sense of his or her own importance that shows itself in a proud and insulting way

ar·ro·gant *adj* : showing the attitude of a person who is overly proud of himself or herself or of his or her own opinions — **ar·ro·gant·ly** *adv*

ar·row *n* **1** : a weapon that is shot from a bow and is usually a stick with a point at one end and feathers at the other **2** : a mark to show direction

ar·row·head *n* : the pointed end of an arrow

ar·row·root *n* : an edible starch obtained from the roots of a tropical plant

ar·se·nal *n* : a place where military equipment is made and stored

ar·se·nic *n* : a solid poisonous chemical element that is usually gray and snaps easily

ar·son *n* : the illegal burning of a building or other property

art *n* **1** : works (as pictures, poems, or songs) made through use of the imagination and creative skills by artists **2** : the methods and skills used for creative visual works (as painting, sculpting, and drawing) **3** : an activity (as painting, music, or writing) whose purpose is making things that are beautiful to look at, listen to, or read **4** : skill that comes through experience or study **5** : an activity that requires skill

ar·tery *n, pl* **ar·ter·ies 1** : one of the branching tubes that carry blood from the heart to all parts of the body **2** : a main road or waterway

art·ful *adj* **1** : done with or showing art or skill **2** : clever at taking advantage — **art·ful·ly** *adv*

ar·thri·tis *n* : a condition in which the joints are painful and swollen

ar·thro·pod *n* : any of a large group of animals (as crabs, insects, and spiders) with jointed limbs and a body made up of segments

ar·ti·choke *n* : the immature flower head of a Mediterranean plant that is cooked and eaten as a vegetable

ar·ti·cle *n* **1** : a piece of writing other than fiction or poetry that forms a separate part of a publication (as a magazine or newspaper) **2** : one of a class of things **3** : a word (as *a*, *an*, or *the*) used with a noun to limit it or make it clearer **4** : a separate part of a document

¹ar·tic·u·late *adj* **1** : clearly understandable **2** : able to express oneself clearly and well — **ar·tic·u·late·ly** *adv*

²ar·tic·u·late *vb* **ar·tic·u·lat·ed; ar·tic·u·lat·ing** : to speak or pronounce clearly

ar·tic·u·la·tion *n* : the making of articulate sounds (as in speaking)

ar·ti·fice *n* : a clever trick or device

ar·ti·fi·cial *adj* **1** : made by humans **2** : not natural in quality **3** : made to seem like something natural — **ar·ti·fi·cial·ly** *adv*

artificial respiration *n* : the forcing of air into and out of the lungs of a person whose breathing has stopped

ar·til·lery *n* **1** : large firearms (as cannon or rockets) **2** : a branch of an army armed with artillery

ar·ti·san *n* : a person who makes things by using skill with the hands

art·ist *n* **1** : a person skilled in one of the arts (as painting, music, or writing) **2** : a person who is very good at something

ar·tis·tic *adj* **1** : relating to art or artists **2** : having or showing skill and imagination — **ar·tis·ti·cal·ly** *adv*

¹-ary *n suffix, pl* **-ar·ies** : thing or person belonging to or connected with

²-ary *adj suffix* : of, relating to, or connected with

¹as *adv* **1** : to the same degree or amount **2** : for example

²as *conj* **1** : in equal amount or degree with **2** : in the way that **3** : at the same time that **4** : for the reason that : BECAUSE

³as *pron* **1** : ¹THAT 1, WHO, WHICH **2** : a fact that

⁴as *prep* **1** : (r)LIKE 1 **2** : in the position or role of

as·bes·tos *n* : a grayish mineral that separates easily into long flexible fibers and has been used especially in the past in making fireproof materials

as·cend *vb* **as·cend·ed; as·cend·ing** **1** : to go or move up **2** : to rise to a higher or more powerful position

as·cen·sion *n* : the act or process of moving or rising up especially to a higher or more powerful position

as·cent *n* **1** : the act of rising or climbing upward **2** : the act of rising to a higher or more powerful position **3** : an upward slope or path

as·cer·tain *vb* **as·cer·tained; as·cer·tain·ing** : to find out with certainty

as·cribe *vb* **as·cribed; as·crib·ing** : to think of as coming from a specified cause, source, or author

asex·u·al *adj* : formed by, characterized by, or being a process of reproduction (as the dividing of one cell into two cells) that does not involve the combining of male and female germ cells — **asex·u·al·ly** *adv*

¹ash *n* : a tree that has seeds with a winglike part, bark with grooves, and hard strong wood

²ash *n* **1** : the solid matter left when something is completely burned **2 ashes** *pl* : the last remains of the dead human body

ashamed *adj* **1** : feeling shame, guilt, or disgrace **2** : kept from doing something by fear of shame or embarrassment

ash·en *adj* **1** : of the color of ashes **2** : very pale

ashore *adv* : on or to the shore

ashy *adj* **ash·i·er; ash·i·est** **1** : of or relating to ashes **2** : very pale

¹Asian *adj* : of or relating to Asia or its people

²Asian *n* : a person born or living in Asia

Asian–Amer·i·can *n* : an American who has Asian ancestors

aside *adv* **1** : to or toward the side **2** : out of the way especially for future use **3** : not included or considered

aside from *prep* : with the exception of

as if *conj* **1** : the way it would be if **2** : as someone would do if **3** : ²THAT 1

ask *vb* **asked; ask·ing** **1** : to seek information by posing a question **2** : to make a request **3** : to set as a price **4** : INVITE 1 **5** : to behave as if seeking a result

askance *adv* **1** : with a side glance **2** : with distrust or disapproval

askew *adv or adj* : not straight : at an angle

aslant *adv or adj* : in a slanting direction

¹asleep *adj* **1** : being in a state of sleep **2** : having no feeling

²asleep *adv* : into a state of sleep

as of *prep* : ¹ON 8, AT

as·par·a·gus *n* : a vegetable that is the young shoots of a garden plant related to the lilies that lives for many years

as·pect *n* **1** : the appearance of something : LOOK **2** : a certain way in which something appears or may be thought of **3** : a position facing a certain direction

as·pen *n* : a poplar tree whose leaves move easily in the breeze

as·phalt *n* **1** : a dark-colored substance obtained from natural deposits in the earth or from petroleum **2** : any of various materials made of asphalt that are used for pavements and as a waterproof cement

as·phyx·i·ate *vb* **as·phyx·i·at·ed; as·phyx·i·at·ing** : to cause (as a person) to become unconscious or die by cutting off the normal taking in of oxygen whether by blocking breathing or by replacing the oxygen of the air with another gas

as·pi·ra·tion *n* **1** : a strong desire to achieve something **2** : something that someone wants very much to achieve

as·pire *vb* **as·pired; as·pir·ing** : to very much want to have or achieve something

as·pi·rin *n* : a white drug used to relieve pain and fever

ass *n* **1** : an animal that looks like but is smaller than the related horse and has shorter hair in the mane and tail and longer ears : DONKEY **2** *sometimes vulgar* : a stupid or stubborn person

as·sail *vb* **as·sailed; as·sail·ing** **1** : to attack violently or angrily with blows or words **2** : to be troubled or bothered by

as·sail·ant *n* : a person who attacks someone violently

as·sas·sin *n* : someone who kills another person usually for pay or from loyalty to a cause

as·sas·si·nate *vb* **as·sas·si·nat·ed; as·sas·si·nat·ing** : to murder a usually important person by a surprise or secret attack

as·sas·si·na·tion *n* : the act of murdering a usually important person by a surprise or secret attack

¹as·sault *n* **1** : a violent or sudden attack **2** : an unlawful attempt or threat to harm someone

²assault *vb* **as·sault·ed; as·sault·ing** : to violently attack

as·sem·blage *n* : a collection of persons or things

as·sem·ble *vb* **as·sem·bled; as·sem·bling** **1** : to collect in one place or group **2** : to fit together the parts of **3** : to meet together in one place — **as·sem·bler** *n*

as·sem·bly *n, pl* **as·sem·blies** **1** : a group of people gathered together **2** *cap* : a group of people who make and change laws for a government or organization **3** : the act of gathering together **4** : the act of connecting together the parts of **5** : a collection of parts that make up a complete unit

assembly line *n* : an arrangement for assembling a product mechanically in which work passes from one operation to the next in a direct line until the product is finished

¹as·sent *vb* **as·sent·ed; as·sent·ing** : to agree to or approve of something

²assent *n* : an act of agreeing to or approving of something

as·sert *vb* **as·sert·ed; as·sert·ing** **1** : to state clearly and strongly **2** : to make others aware of **3** : to speak or act in a way that demands attention or recognition

as·ser·tion *n* **1** : the act of stating clearly and strongly or making others aware **2** : something stated as if certain

as·ser·tive *adj* : having a bold or confident manner

as·sess *vb* **as·sessed; as·sess·ing** **1** : to make a judgment about **2** : to decide on the rate, value, or amount of (as for taxation) **3** : to put a charge or tax on — **as·ses·sor** *n*

as·set *n* **1** : someone or something that provides a benefit **2 assets** *pl* : all the property belonging to a person or an organization

as·sid·u·ous *adj* : showing great care, attention, and effort — **as·sid·u·ous·ly** *adv*

as·sign *vb* **as·signed; as·sign·ing** **1** : to give out as a job or responsibility **2** : to give out to : PROVIDE **3** : to give a particular quality, value, or identity to

as·sign·ment *n* **1** : the act of giving out or assigning **2** : something (as a job or task) that is given out

as·sim·i·late *vb* **as·sim·i·lat·ed; as·sim·i·lat·ing** **1** : to become or cause to become part of a different group or country **2** : to take in and make part of a larger thing **3** : to learn thoroughly

as·sim·i·la·tion *n* : the act or process of assimilating

¹as·sist *vb* **as·sist·ed; as·sist·ing** : to give support or help

²assist *n* : an act of supporting or helping

as·sis·tance *n* **1** : the act of helping **2** : the help given

¹as·sis·tant *adj* : acting as a helper to another

²assistant *n* : a person who assists another

assn. *abbr* association

¹as·so·ci·ate *vb* **as·so·ci·at·ed; as·so·ci·at·ing** **1** : to join or come together as partners, friends, or companions **2** : to connect in thought

²as·so·ci·ate *adj* : having a rank or position that is below the highest level

³as·so·ci·ate *n* **1** : a person who you work with or spend time with

as·so·ci·a·tion *n* **1** : a connection or relationship between things or people **2** : an organization of persons having a common interest **3** : a feeling, memory, or thought connected with a person, place, or thing

as·so·cia·tive *adj* : relating to or being a property of a mathematical operation (as addition or multiplication) in which the result does not depend on how the elements are grouped

as·sort *vb* **as·sort·ed; as·sort·ing** : to sort into groups of like kinds

as·sort·ed *adj* **1** : made up of various kinds **2** : suited to one another : matching or fitting together

as·sort·ment *n* **1** : the act of sorting into groups **2** : a group or collection of various or different things or persons

asst. *abbr* assistant

as·suage *vb* **as·suaged; as·suag·ing** : to make less severe or intense

as·sume *vb* **as·sumed; as·sum·ing 1** : to begin to take on or perform **2** : to take or begin to have **3** : to pretend to have or be **4** : to accept as true

as·sump·tion *n* **1** : the act of taking on **2** : something accepted as true

as·sur·ance *n* **1** : the act of making sure or confident **2** : the state of being sure or confident **3** : SELF-CONFIDENCE

as·sure *vb* **as·sured; as·sur·ing 1** : to give certainty, confidence, or comfort to **2** : to inform positively **3** : to provide a guarantee of

as·sured *adj* **1** : made sure or certain **2** : very confident — **as·sured·ly** *adv*

as·ter *n* : any of various herbs related to the daisies that have leafy stems and white, pink, purple, or yellow flower heads which bloom in the fall

as·ter·isk *n* : a symbol * used in printing or in writing especially to refer a reader to a note usually at the bottom of a page

astern *adv* **1** : in, at, or toward the back of a boat or ship : in, at, or toward the stern **2** : in a reverse direction : BACKWARD

as·ter·oid *n* : one of thousands of rocky objects that move in orbits mostly between those of Mars and Jupiter and have diameters from a fraction of a mile to nearly 500 miles (800 kilometers)

asth·ma *n* : a lung disorder that causes periods of wheezing, coughing, and difficulty with breathing

as to *prep* **1** : with respect to : ABOUT **2** : ACCORDING TO 1

as·ton·ish *vb* **as·ton·ished; as·ton·ish·ing** : to strike with sudden wonder or surprise

as·ton·ish·ment *n* : great surprise or wonder : AMAZEMENT

as·tound *vb* **as·tound·ed; as·tound·ing** : to fill with puzzled wonder

astray *adv or adj* **1** : off the right path or route **2** : in or into error

astride *prep* : with one leg on each side of

as·trin·gent *n* : a substance that is able to shrink or tighten body tissues — **astringent** *adj*

astro- *prefix* : star : heavens : astronomical

as·trol·o·gy *n* : the study of the supposed influences of the stars and planets on people's lives and behavior

as·tro·naut *n* : a person who travels beyond the earth's atmosphere : a traveler in a spacecraft

as·tro·nau·tics *n* : the science of the construction and operation of spacecraft

as·tron·o·mer *n* : a person who is a specialist in astronomy

as·tro·nom·i·cal *or* **as·tro·nom·ic** *adj* **1** : of or relating to astronomy **2** : extremely or unbelievably large — **as·tro·nom·i·cal·ly** *adv*

as·tron·o·my *n* : a science concerned with objects and matter outside the earth's atmosphere and of their motions and makeup

as·tute *adj* : very alert and aware : CLEVER — **as·tute·ly** *adv*

asun·der *adv* : into parts

as well as *conj* : and in addition

asy·lum *n* **1** : a place of protection and shelter **2** : protection given especially to political refugees **3** : a place for the care of the poor or the physically or mentally ill

at *prep* **1** — used to indicate a particular place or time **2** — used to indicate the person or thing toward which an action, motion, or feeling is directed or aimed **3** — used to indicate position or condition **4** — used to tell how or why **5** — used to indicate time, age, or position on a scale

ate *past of* EAT

¹-ate *n suffix* : one acted upon in such a way

²-ate *n suffix* : office : rank : group of persons holding such an office or rank

³-ate *adj suffix* : marked by having

⁴-ate *vb suffix* **1** : cause to be changed or affected by **2** : cause to become **3** : furnish with

athe·ist *n* : a person who believes there is no God

ath·lete *n* : a person who is trained in or good at games and exercises that require physical skill, endurance, and strength

athlete's foot *n* : a fungus infection of the foot marked by blisters, itching, and cracks between and under the toes

ath·let·ic *adj* **1** : of, relating to, or characteristic of athletes or athletics **2** : used by athletes **3** : active in sports or exercises **4** : strong and muscular

ath·let·ics *n pl* : games, sports, and exercises requiring strength, endurance, and skill — used as singular or plural

-ation *n suffix* **1** : action or process **2** : something connected with an action or process

-ative *adj suffix* **1** : of, relating to, or connected with **2** : designed to do something **3** : tending to

at·las *n* : a book of maps

ATM *n* : a computerized machine that performs basic banking functions (as cash withdrawals)

at·mo·sphere *n* **1** : the whole mass of air that surrounds the earth **2** : the gas surrounding a heavenly body (as a planet) **3** : the air in a particular place **4** : a surrounding influence or set of conditions

at·mo·spher·ic *adj* : of or relating to the atmosphere

atoll *n* : a ring-shaped coral island consisting of a coral reef surrounding a lagoon

at·om *n* **1** : the smallest particle of an element that can exist alone or in combination **2** : a tiny particle : BIT

atom·ic *adj* **1** : of or relating to atoms **2** : NUCLEAR 3

atomic bomb *n* : a bomb whose great power is due to the sudden release of the energy in the nuclei of atoms

at·om·iz·er *n* : a device for spraying a liquid (as a perfume or disinfectant)

atone *vb* **atoned; aton·ing** : to do something to make up for a wrong

atone·ment *n* : a making up for an offense or injury

atop *prep* : on top of

atri·um *n* : the part of the heart that receives blood from the veins

atro·cious *adj* **1** : extremely brutal, cruel, or wicked **2** : very bad — **atro·cious·ly** *adv*

atroc·i·ty *n, pl* **atroc·i·ties** : an extremely cruel or terrible act, object, or situation

at sign *n* : the symbol @ used especially as part of an e-mail address

at·tach *vb* **at·tached; at·tach·ing** **1** : to fasten or join one thing to another **2** : to bind by feelings of affection **3** : to think of as belonging to something

at·tach·ment *n* **1** : connection by feelings of affection or regard **2** : an extra part that can be attached to a machine or tool **3** : a connection by which one thing is joined to another

¹at·tack *vb* **at·tacked; at·tack·ing** **1** : to take strong action against : try to hurt, injure, or destroy **2** : to use harsh words against : criticize harshly **3** : to begin to affect or to act upon harmfully **4** : to start to work on in a determined and eager way — **at·tack·er** *n*

²attack *n* **1** : a violent, harmful, or destructive act against someone or something **2** : strong criticism **3** : the setting to work on some undertaking **4** : a sudden short period of suffering from an illness or of being affected by a strong emotion

at·tain *vb* **at·tained; at·tain·ing** **1** : to accomplish or achieve **2** : to come into possession of : OBTAIN **3** : to reach or come to gradually : arrive at — **at·tain·able** *adj*

at·tain·ment *n* **1** : the act of obtaining or doing something difficult : the state of having obtained or done something difficult **2** : ACHIEVEMENT 2

¹at·tempt *vb* **at·tempt·ed; at·tempt·ing** : to try to do, accomplish, or complete

²attempt *n* : the act or an instance of trying to do something

at·tend *vb* **at·tend·ed; at·tend·ing** **1** : to go to or be present at **2** : to look after : take charge of **3** : to direct attention **4** : to pay attention to **5** : to go with especially as a servant or companion **6** : to care for

at·ten·dance *n* **1** : presence at a place **2** : a record of how often a person is present at a place **3** : the number of people present

¹at·ten·dant *n* **1** : a person who goes with or serves another **2** : an employee who waits on or helps customers

²attendant *adj* : coming with or following closely as a result

at·ten·tion *n* **1** : the act or the power of fixing the mind on something : careful listening or watching **2** : notice, interest, or awareness **3** : careful thinking about something so as to be able to take action on it **4** : special care or treatment **5** : an act of kindness or politeness **6** : the way a soldier stands with the body stiff and straight, heels together, and arms at the sides

at·ten·tive *adj* **1** : paying attention **2** : very thoughtful about the needs of others — **at·ten·tive·ly** *adv* — **at·ten·tive·ness** *n*

at·test *vb* **at·test·ed; at·test·ing** : to show or give proof of : say to be true

at·tic *n* : a room or a space just under the roof of a building

¹at·tire *vb* **at·tired; at·tir·ing** : to put clothes and especially special or fine clothes on

²attire *n* : CLOTHING

at·ti·tude *n* **1** : a feeling or way of thinking that affects a person's behavior **2** : a way of positioning the body or its parts

at·tor·ney *n, pl* **at·tor·neys** : a person and usually a lawyer who acts for another in business or legal matters

at·tract *vb* **at·tract·ed; at·tract·ing** **1** : to draw by appealing to interest or feeling **2** : to draw to or toward something else

at·trac·tion *n* **1** : a feeling of interest in something or someone **2** : the act or power of drawing toward something **3** : something that interests or pleases

at·trac·tive *adj* **1** : having the power or quality of drawing interest **2** : having a pleasing appearance — **at·trac·tive·ly** *adv* — **at·trac·tive·ness** *n*

¹at·tri·bute *n* : a quality belonging to a particular person or thing

²at·trib·ute *vb* **at·trib·ut·ed; at·trib·ut·ing** **1**

: to explain as the cause of **2** : to think of as likely to be a quality of a person or thing

atty. *abbr* attorney

atyp·i·cal *adj* : not usual or normal : not typical — **atyp·i·cal·ly** *adv*

au·burn *adj* : of a reddish brown color

¹auc·tion *n* : a public sale at which things are sold to those who offer to pay the most

²auction *vb* **auc·tioned; auc·tion·ing** : to sell at an auction

auc·tion·eer *n* : a person who runs an auction

au·da·cious *adj* **1** : very bold and daring : FEARLESS **2** : disrespectful of authority : INSOLENT — **au·da·cious·ly** *adv*

au·dac·i·ty *n* : a bold and daring quality that is sometimes shocking or rude

au·di·ble *adj* : loud enough to be heard — **au·di·bly** *adv*

au·di·ence *n* **1** : a group that listens or watches (as at a play or concert) **2** : a chance to talk with a person of very high rank **3** : those people who give attention to something said, done, or written

¹au·dio *adj* **1** : of or relating to sound or its reproduction **2** : relating to or used in the transmitting or receiving of sound (as in radio or television)

²audio *n* **1** : the transmitting, receiving, or reproducing of sound **2** : the section of television equipment that deals with sound

au·dio·tape *n* : a magnetic tape recording of sound

au·dio·vi·su·al *adj* : of, relating to, or using both sound and sight

¹au·dit *n* : a thorough check of business accounts

²audit *vb* **au·dit·ed; au·dit·ing** : to thoroughly check the business records of

¹au·di·tion *n* : a short performance to test the talents of someone (as a singer, dancer, or actor)

²audition *vb* **au·di·tioned; au·di·tion·ing** : to test or try out in a short performance

au·di·tor *n* : a person who checks the accuracy of business accounts

au·di·to·ri·um *n* **1** : the part of a building where an audience sits **2** : a large room where people gather as an audience

au·di·to·ry *adj* : of or relating to hearing

Aug. *abbr* August

au·ger *n* : a tool used for boring holes

aught *n* : ZERO 1

aug·ment *vb* **aug·ment·ed; aug·ment·ing** : to increase in size, amount, or degree

au·gust *adj* : being grand and noble : MAJESTIC

Au·gust *n* : the eighth month of the year

auk *n* : a black-and-white diving seabird of cold parts of the northern hemisphere

aunt *n* **1** : a sister of a person's parent **2** : the wife of a person's uncle

au·ra *n* : a feeling that seems to be given off by a person or thing

au·ral *adj* : of or relating to the ear or sense of hearing — **au·ral·ly** *adv*

au·ri·cle *n* : ATRIUM

au·ro·ra bo·re·al·is *n* : broad bands of light that have a magnetic and electrical source and that appear in the sky at night especially in the arctic regions

aus·pic·es *n pl* : support and guidance of a sponsor

aus·pi·cious *adj* : promising success — **aus·pi·cious·ly** *adv*

aus·tere *adj* **1** : seeming or acting serious and unfriendly **2** : ¹PLAIN 1 — **aus·tere·ly** *adv*

aus·ter·i·ty *n* : lack of all luxury

¹Aus·tra·lian *adj* : of or relating to Australia or the Australians

²Australian *n* : a person born or living in Australia

aut- *or* **au·to-** *prefix* **1** : self : same one **2** : automatic

au·then·tic *adj* : being really what it seems to be : GENUINE — **au·then·ti·cal·ly** *adv*

au·then·ti·cate *vb* **au·then·ti·cat·ed; au·then·ti·cat·ing** : to prove or serve as proof that something is authentic

au·thor *n* : a person who writes something (as a novel)

au·thor·i·ta·tive *adj* : having or coming from authority — **au·thor·i·ta·tive·ly** *adv*

au·thor·i·ty *n, pl* **au·thor·i·ties** **1** : power to exercise control **2** : a person looked to as an expert **3** : people having powers to make decisions and enforce rules and laws **4** : a fact or statement used to support a position

au·tho·rize *vb* **au·tho·rized; au·tho·riz·ing** **1** : to give power to : give authority to **2** : to give legal or official approval to

au·thor·ship *n* : the profession of writing

au·to *n, pl* **au·tos** : ¹AUTOMOBILE

auto- — see AUT-

au·to·bi·og·ra·phy *n, pl* **au·to·bi·og·ra·phies** : the biography of a person written by that person

¹au·to·graph *n* : a person's signature written by hand

²autograph *vb* **au·to·graphed; au·to·graph·ing** : to write a person's own signature in or on

au·to·mate *vb* **au·to·mat·ed; au·to·mat·ing** : to run or operate something using machines instead of people

au·to·mat·ic *adj* **1** : INVOLUNTARY 1 **2** : being a machine or device that allows something to work without being directly controlled by a person — **au·to·mat·i·cal·ly** *adv*

au·to·ma·tion *n* **1** : the method of making a machine, a process, or a system work without being directly controlled by a person **2** : automatic working of a machine, process, or system by mechanical or electronic devices that take the place of humans

au·to·mo·bile *n* : a usually four-wheeled vehicle that runs on its own power and is designed to carry passengers

au·to·mo·tive *adj* : of or relating to automobiles

au·tumn *n* : the season between summer and winter

au·tum·nal *adj* : of or relating to autumn

¹aux·il·ia·ry *adj* : available to provide something extra

²auxiliary *n, pl* **aux·il·ia·ries 1** : a group that provides assistance **2** : HELPING VERB

¹avail *vb* **availed; avail·ing 1** : to be of use or help **2** : to make use of

²avail *n* : help toward reaching a goal : USE

avail·able *adj* **1** : SUITABLE, USABLE **2** : possible to get : OBTAINABLE — **avail·abil·i·ty** *n*

av·a·lanche *n* : a large mass of snow and ice or of earth or rock sliding down a mountainside or over a cliff

av·a·rice *n* : strong desire for riches : GREED

av·a·ri·cious *adj* : greedy for riches — **av·a·ri·cious·ly** *adv*

ave. *abbr* avenue

avenge *vb* **avenged; aveng·ing** : to take revenge for — **aveng·er** *n*

av·e·nue *n* **1** : a wide street **2** : a way of reaching a goal

¹av·er·age *n* **1** : a number that is calculated by adding quantities together and dividing the total by the number of quantities : ARITHMETIC MEAN **2** : something usual in a group, class, or series

²average *adj* **1** : equaling or coming close to an average **2** : being ordinary or usual

³average *vb* **av·er·aged; av·er·ag·ing 1** : to amount to usually **2** : to find the average of

averse *adj* : having a feeling of dislike

aver·sion *n* **1** : a strong dislike **2** : something strongly disliked

avert *vb* **avert·ed; avert·ing 1** : to turn away **2** : to keep from happening

avi·ary *n, pl* **avi·ar·ies** : a place (as a large cage or a building) where birds are kept

avi·a·tion *n* **1** : the flying of aircraft **2** : the designing and making of aircraft

avi·a·tor *n* : the pilot of an aircraft

av·id *adj* : very eager — **av·id·ly** *adv*

av·o·ca·do *n, pl* **av·o·ca·dos** : a usually green fruit that is shaped like a pear or an egg,

grows on a tropical American tree, and has a rich oily flesh

av·o·ca·tion *n* : an interest or activity that is not a regular job : HOBBY

avoid *vb* **avoid·ed; avoid·ing 1** : to keep away from **2** : to keep from happening **3** : to keep from doing or being

avoid·ance *n* : the act of avoiding something

avow *vb* **avowed; avow·ing** : to declare openly and frankly

avow·al *n* : an open declaration

await *vb* **await·ed; await·ing 1** : to wait for **2** : to be ready or waiting for

¹awake *vb* **awoke** ; **awo·ken** *or* **awaked** ; **awak·ing 1** : to stop sleeping : wake up **2** : to make or become conscious or aware of something

²awake *adj* : not asleep

awak·en *vb* **awak·ened; awak·en·ing** : ¹AWAKE

¹award *vb* **award·ed; award·ing 1** : to give as deserved or needed **2** : to give by official decision

²award *n* : something (as a prize) that is given in recognition of good work or a good act

aware *adj* : having or showing understanding or knowledge : CONSCIOUS — **aware·ness** *n*

awash *adj* : flooded or covered with water or other liquid

¹away *adv* **1** : from this or that place **2** : in another place or direction **3** : out of existence **4** : from someone's possession **5** : without stopping or slowing down **6** : at or to a great distance in space or time : FAR

²away *adj* **1** : ABSENT 1 **2** : DISTANT 1

¹awe *n* : a feeling of mixed fear, respect, and wonder

²awe *vb* **awed; aw·ing** : to fill with respect, fear, and wonder

awe·some *adj* **1** : causing a feeling of respect, fear, and wonder **2** : extremely good

awe·struck *adj* : filled with awe

¹aw·ful *adj* **1** : very disagreeable or unpleasant **2** : very much **3** : causing fear or terror

²awful *adv* : AWFULLY

aw·ful·ly *adv* **1** : to a very great degree : VERY **2** : in a disagreeable or unpleasant manner

awhile *adv* : for a while : for a short time

awk·ward *adj* **1** : not graceful : CLUMSY **2** : likely to embarrass **3** : difficult to use or handle — **awk·ward·ly** *adv* — **awk·ward·ness** *n*

awl *n* : a pointed tool for making small holes (as in leather or wood)

aw·ning *n* : a cover (as of canvas) that shades or shelters like a roof

awoke *past of* AWAKE

awoken *past participle of* AWAKE

awry *adv or adj* **1** : turned or twisted to one side : ASKEW **2** : out of the right course : AMISS

ax *or* **axe** *n* : a tool that has a heavy head with a sharp edge fixed to a handle and is used for chopping and splitting wood

ax·i·om *n* **1** : MAXIM **2** : a statement thought to be clearly true

ax·is *n, pl* **ax·es** : a straight line about which a body or a geometric figure rotates or may be thought of as rotating

ax·le *n* : a pin or shaft on or with which a wheel or pair of wheels turns

ax·on *n* : a long fiber that carries impulses away from a nerve cell

¹**aye** *adv* : ¹YES 1

²**aye** *n* : a yes vote or voter

AZ *abbr* Arizona

aza·lea *n* : a usually small bush that has flowers of many colors which are shaped like funnels

azure *n* : the blue color of the clear daytime sky

B

b *n, pl* **b's** *or* **bs** *often cap* **1** : the second letter of the English alphabet **2** : a grade that shows a student's work is good **3** : a musical note referred to by the letter B

¹**baa** *n* : the cry of a sheep

²**baa** *vb* **baaed; baa·ing** : to make the cry of a sheep

¹**bab·ble** *vb* **bab·bled; bab·bling** **1** : to make meaningless sounds **2** : to talk foolishly **3** : to make the sound of a brook

²**babble** *n* **1** : talk that is not clear **2** : the sound of a brook

babe *n* : ¹BABY 1

ba·boon *n* : a large monkey of Africa and Asia with a doglike face

¹**ba·by** *n, pl* **babies** **1** : a very young child **2** : a very young animal **3** : the youngest of a group **4** : a childish person — **ba·by·ish** *adj*

²**baby** *adj* **1** : ¹YOUNG 1 **2** : very small

³**baby** *vb* **ba·bied; ba·by·ing** : to treat as a baby : to be overly kind to

ba·by·hood *n* : the time in a person's life when he or she is a baby

ba·by–sit *vb* **ba·by–sat** ; **ba·by–sit·ting** : to care for a child while the child's parents are away

ba·by–sit·ter *n* : a person who cares for a child while the child's parents are away

baby tooth *n* : MILK TOOTH

bach·e·lor : a man who is not married — **bach·e·lor·hood** *n*

¹**back** *n* **1** : the rear part of the human body from the neck to the end of the spine : the upper part of the body of an animal **2** : the part of something that is opposite or away from the front part **3** : a player in a team game who plays behind the forward line of players — **backed** *adj*

²**back** *adv* **1** : to, toward, or at the rear **2** : in or to a former time, state, or place **3** : under control **4** : in return or reply — **back and forth** **1** : toward the back and then toward the front **2** : between two places or people

³**back** *adj* **1** : located at the back **2** : far from a central or main area **3** : not yet paid : OVERDUE **4** : no longer published

⁴**back** *vb* **backed; back·ing** **1** : to give support or help to : UPHOLD **2** : to move back — **back·er** *n* — **back down** : to stop arguing or fighting for something — **back off** : to back down — **back out** : to decide not to do something after agreeing to do it

back·bone *n* **1** : the column of bones in the back enclosing and protecting the spinal cord : SPINAL COLUMN **2** : the strongest part of something **3** : strength of character

¹**back·fire** *vb* **back·fired; back·fir·ing** **1** : to have a result opposite to what was planned **2** : to make a loud engine noise caused by fuel igniting at the wrong time

²**backfire** *n* **1** : a loud engine noise caused by fuel igniting at the wrong time **2** : a fire that is set to stop the spread of a forest fire or a grass fire by burning off a strip of land ahead of it

back·ground *n* **1** : the scenery or ground that is behind a main figure or object **2** : a position that attracts little attention **3** : the total of a person's experience, knowledge, and education

¹**back·hand** *n* **1** : a stroke in sports played with a racket that is made with the back of the hand turned in the direction in which the hand is moving **2** : a catch (as in baseball) made with the arm across the body and the palm turned away from the body

²**backhand** *adv or adj* : with a backhand

back·hand·ed *adj* **1** : using or done with a backhand **2** : not sincere

back·pack *n* : a bag worn on the back for carrying things

back·side *n* **1** : RUMP 1 **2** : the part of the body on which a person sits

back·stage *adv or adj* : in or to the area behind the stage

back·stop n : a fence behind the catcher to keep a baseball from rolling away

back·track vb **back·tracked; back·track·ing** : to go back over a course or a path

back·up n : a person who takes the place of or supports another

¹back·ward or **back·wards** adv **1** : toward the back **2** : with the back first **3** : opposite to the usual way

²backward adj **1** : turned toward the back **2** : done backward **3** : not as advanced in learning and development as others

back·woods n pl **1** : wooded or partly cleared areas away from cities **2** : a place that is backward in culture

back·yard n : an area in the back of a house

ba·con n : salted and smoked meat from the sides and the back of a pig

bac·te·ri·al adj : relating to or caused by bacteria

bac·te·ri·um n, pl **bac·te·ria** : any of a group of single-celled microscopic organisms that are important to humans because of their chemical activities and as causes of disease

bad adj **worse ; worst 1** : not good : POOR **2** : not favorable **3** : not fresh or sound **4** : not good or right : EVIL **5** : not behaving properly **6** : not enough **7** : UNPLEASANT **8** : HARMFUL **9** : SERIOUS 5, SEVERE **10** : not correct **11** : not cheerful or calm **12** : not healthy **13** : SORRY 1 **14** : not skillful — **bad·ness** n

bade past of BID

badge n : something worn to show that a person belongs to a certain group or rank

¹bad·ger n : a furry burrowing animal with short thick legs and long claws on the front feet

²badger vb **bad·gered; bad·ger·ing** : to annoy again and again

bad·ly adv **worse ; worst 1** : in a bad manner **2** : very much

bad·min·ton n : a game in which a shuttlecock is hit back and forth over a net by players using light rackets

baf·fle vb **baf·fled; baf·fling** : to completely confuse — **baffled** adj

¹bag n **1** : a container made of flexible material (as paper or plastic) **2** : ¹PURSE 1, HANDBAG **3** : SUITCASE

²bag vb **bagged; bag·ging 1** : to swell out **2** : to put into a bag **3** : to kill or capture in hunting

ba·gel n : a bread roll shaped like a ring

bag·gage n : the bags, suitcases, and personal belongings of a traveler

bag·gy adj **bag·gi·er; bag·gi·est** : hanging loosely or puffed out like a bag

bag·pipe n : a musical instrument played especially in Scotland that consists of a tube, a

bag for air, and pipes from which the sound comes

¹bail vb **bailed; bail·ing** : to dip and throw out water (as from a boat) — **bail out** : to jump out of an airplane

²bail n : money given to free a prisoner until his or her trial

³bail vb **bailed; bailing** : to get the release of (a prisoner) by giving money as a guarantee of the prisoner's return for trial

¹bait n : something that is used to attract fish or animals so they can be caught

²bait vb **bait·ed; bait·ing 1** : to put something (as food) on or in to attract and catch fish or animals **2** : to torment by mean or unjust attacks

bake vb **baked; bak·ing 1** : to cook or become cooked in a dry heat especially in an oven **2** : to dry or harden by heat

bak·er n : a person who bakes and sells bread, cakes, or pastry

baker's dozen n : THIRTEEN

bak·ery n, pl **bak·er·ies** : a place where bread, cakes, and pastry are made or sold

baking powder n : a powder used to make the dough rise in making baked goods (as cakes)

baking soda n : a white powder used in cooking and medicine

¹bal·ance n **1** : a steady position or condition **2** : something left over : REMAINDER **3** : an instrument for weighing **4** : a state in which things occur in equal or proper amounts **5** : the amount of money in a bank account **6** : an amount of money still owed

²balance vb **bal·anced; bal·anc·ing 1** : to make or keep steady : keep from falling **2** : to make the two sides of (an account) add up to the same total **3** : to be or make equal in weight, number, or amount

bal·co·ny n, pl **bal·co·nies 1** : a platform enclosed by a low wall or a railing built out from the side of a building **2** : a platform inside a theater extending out over part of the main floor

bald adj **bald·er; bald·est 1** : lacking a natural covering (as of hair) **2** : ¹PLAIN 3 — **bald·ness** n

bald eagle n : a North American eagle that when full-grown has white head and neck feathers

¹bale n : a large bundle of goods tightly tied for storing or shipping

²bale vb **baled; bal·ing** : to press together and tightly tie or wrap into a large bundle — **bal·er** n

ba·leen n : a tough material that hangs down from the upper jaw of whales without teeth and is used by the whale to filter small ocean animals out of seawater

balk *vb* **balked; balk·ing** **1 :** to stop short and refuse to go **2 :** to refuse to do something often suddenly

balky *adj* **balk·i·er; balk·i·est :** likely to stop or refuse to go

¹**ball** *n* **1 :** something round or roundish **2 :** a round or roundish object used in a game or sport **3 :** a game or sport (as baseball) played with a ball **4 :** a solid usually round shot for a gun **5 :** the rounded bulge at the base of the thumb or big toe **6 :** a pitched baseball that is not hit and is not a strike

²**ball** *vb* **balled; ball·ing :** to make or come together into a ball

³**ball** *n* **1 :** a large formal party for dancing **2 :** a good time

bal·lad *n* **1 :** a short poem suitable for singing that tells a story in simple language **2 :** a simple song **3 :** a slow usually romantic song

ball–and–socket joint *n* **:** a joint (as in the shoulder) in which a rounded part can move in many directions in a socket

bal·last *n* **1 :** heavy material used to make a ship steady or to control the rising of a balloon **2 :** gravel or broken stone laid in a foundation for a railroad or used in making concrete

ball bearing *n* **1 :** a bearing in which the revolving part turns on metal balls that roll easily in a groove **2 :** one of the balls in a ball bearing

bal·le·ri·na *n* **:** a female ballet dancer

bal·let *n* **1 :** a stage dance that tells a story in movement and pantomime **2 :** a group that performs ballets

¹**bal·loon** *n* **1 :** a bag that rises and floats above the ground when filled with heated air or with a gas that is lighter than air **2 :** a toy or decoration consisting of a rubber bag that can be blown up with air or gas **3 :** an outline containing words spoken or thought by a character (as in a cartoon)

²**balloon** *vb* **bal·looned; bal·loon·ing :** to swell or puff out

bal·lot *n* **1 :** a printed sheet of paper used in voting **2 :** the action or a system of voting **3 :** the right to vote **4 :** the number of votes cast

ball·park *n* **:** a park in which baseball games are played

ball·point *n* **:** a pen whose writing point is a small metal ball that rolls ink on a writing surface

ball·room *n* **:** a large room for dances

balm *n* **:** a greasy substance used for healing or protecting the skin

balmy *adj* **balm·i·er; balm·i·est :** warm, calm, and pleasant

bal·sa *n* **:** the very light but strong wood of a tropical American tree

bal·sam *n* **1 :** a material with a strong pleasant smell that oozes from some plants **2 :** a fir tree that yields balsam

bal·us·ter *n* **:** a short post that supports the upper part of a railing

bal·us·trade *n* **:** a row of balusters topped by a rail to serve as an open fence (as along the side of a bridge or a balcony)

bam·boo *n* **:** a tall treelike tropical grass with a hard hollow jointed stem that is used in making furniture and in building

¹**ban** *vb* **banned; ban·ning :** to forbid especially by law or social pressure

²**ban** *n* **:** an official order forbidding something

ba·nana *n* **:** a fruit that is shaped somewhat like a finger, is usually yellow when ripe, and grows in bunches on a large treelike tropical plant with very large leaves

¹**band** *n* **1 :** a strip of material that holds together or goes around something else **2 :** a strip of something that is different from what it goes around or across **3 :** a range of frequencies (as of radio waves)

²**band** *vb* **band·ed; band·ing** **1 :** to put a strip of material on or around : tie together with a band **2 :** to unite in a group

³**band** *n* **1 :** a group of persons or animals **2 :** a group of musicians performing together

¹**ban·dage** *n* **:** a strip of material used to cover and wrap up wounds

²**bandage** *vb* **ban·daged; ban·dag·ing :** to cover or wrap up (a wound) with a strip of material

ban·dan·na *or* **ban·dana** *n* **:** a large handkerchief usually with a colorful design printed on it

ban·dit *n* **:** a criminal who attacks and steals from travelers and is often a member of a group

band·stand *n* **:** an outdoor platform used for band concerts

band·wag·on *n* **1 :** a wagon carrying musicians in a parade **2 :** a candidate, side, or movement that attracts growing support

¹**bang** *vb* **banged; bang·ing :** to beat, strike, or shut with a loud noise

²**bang** *n* **1 :** a sudden loud noise **2 :** a hard hit or blow **3 :** ²THRILL 1

³**bang** *n* **:** hair cut short across the forehead — usually used in pl.

ban·ish *vb* **ban·ished; ban·ish·ing** **1 :** to force to leave a country **2 :** to cause to go away

ban·ish·ment *n* **:** an act of forcing or of being forced to leave a country

ban·is·ter *n* **1 :** one of the slender posts used to support the handrail of a staircase **2 :** a handrail and its supporting posts **3** : the handrail of a staircase

ban·jo *n, pl* **banjos** : a musical instrument with a round body, long neck, and four or five strings

¹bank *n* **1** : a mound or ridge especially of earth **2** : the side of a hill **3** : the higher ground at the edge of a river, lake, or sea **4** : something shaped like a mound **5** : an undersea elevation : SHOAL

²bank *vb* **banked; bank·ing 1** : to build (a curve) in a road or track with a slope upward from the inside edge **2** : to heap up in a mound or pile **3** : to raise a pile or mound around **4** : to tilt to one side when turning

³bank *n* **1** : a business where people deposit and withdraw their money and borrow money **2** : a small closed container in which money may be saved **3** : a storage place for a reserve supply

⁴bank *vb* **banked; bank·ing 1** : to have an account in a bank **2** : to deposit in a bank

⁵bank *n* : a group or series of objects arranged together in a row

bank·er *n* : a person who is engaged in the business of a bank

bank·ing *n* : the business of a bank or banker

¹bank·rupt *adj* : not having enough money to pay debts

²bankrupt *vb* **bank·rupt·ed; bank·rupt·ing** : to cause to not have enough money to pay debts

³bankrupt *n* : a person or business that does not have enough money to pay debts

bank·rupt·cy *n, pl* **bank·rupt·cies** : the state of not having enough money to pay debts

ban·ner *n* **1** : ¹FLAG **2** : a piece of cloth with a design, a picture, or some writing on it

ban·quet *n* : a formal dinner for many people usually to celebrate a special event

ban·tam *n* : a miniature breed of domestic chicken often raised for exhibiting in shows

¹ban·ter *n* : good-natured teasing and joking

²banter *vb* **ban·tered; ban·ter·ing** : to tease or joke with in a friendly way

bap·tism *n* : the act or ceremony of baptizing

bap·tize *vb* **bap·tized; bap·tiz·ing 1** : to dip in water or sprinkle water on as a part of the ceremony of receiving into the Christian church **2** : to give a name to as in the ceremony of baptism : CHRISTEN

¹bar *n* **1** : a usually slender rigid piece (as of wood or metal) that has a specific use (as for a lever or barrier) **2** : a rectangular solid piece or block of something **3** : a counter on which alcoholic drinks are served **4** : a place of business for the sale of alcoholic drinks **5** : a part of a place of business where a particular food or drink is served **6** : something that blocks the way **7** : a sub-

merged or partly submerged bank along a shore or in a river **8** : a court of law **9** : the profession of law **10** : a straight stripe, band, or line longer than it is wide **11** : a vertical line across a musical staff marking equal measures of time **12** : ¹MEASURE 6

²bar *vb* **barred; bar·ring 1** : to fasten with a bar **2** : to block off **3** : to shut out

³bar *prep* : with the exception of

barb *n* : a sharp point that sticks out and backward (as from the tip of an arrow or fishhook) — **barbed** *adj*

bar·bar·i·an *n* : an uncivilized person

bar·bar·ic *adj* **1** : BARBAROUS **2** : showing a lack of restraint

bar·ba·rous *adj* **1** : not civilized **2** : CRUEL 2, HARSH **3** : very offensive

¹bar·be·cue *vb* **bar·be·cued; bar·be·cu·ing** : to cook over hot coals or on an open fire often in a highly seasoned sauce

²barbecue *n* **1** : an often portable grill **2** : an outdoor meal or party at which food is cooked over hot coals or an open fire

barbed wire *n* : wire that has sharp points and is often used for fences

bar·ber *n* : a person whose business is cutting hair and shaving and trimming beards

bar code *n* : a group of thick and thin lines placed on a product that represents computerized information about the product (as price)

bard *n* **1** : a person in ancient societies skilled at composing and singing songs about heroes **2** : POET

¹bare *adj* **bar·er; bar·est 1** : having no covering : NAKED **2** : ¹EMPTY 1 **3** : having nothing left over or added : MERE **4** : ¹PLAIN 3

²bare *vb* **bared; bar·ing** : UNCOVER

bare·back *adv or adj* : on the bare back of a horse : without a saddle

bare·foot *adv or adj* : with the feet bare

bare·ly *adv* **1** : almost not **2** : with nothing to spare : by a narrow margin

barf *vb* **barfed; barf·ing** : ²VOMIT

¹bar·gain *n* **1** : an agreement settling what each person is to give and receive in a business deal **2** : something bought or offered for sale at a good price

²bargain *vb* **bar·gained; bar·gain·ing** : to talk over the terms of a purchase or agreement

¹barge *n* : a broad boat with a flat bottom used chiefly in harbors and on rivers and canals

²barge *vb* **barged; barg·ing** : to move or push in a fast and often rude way

bar graph *n* : a chart that uses parallel bars whose lengths are in proportion to the numbers represented

bari·tone *n* **1** : a male singing voice between

bass and tenor in range **2** : a singer having a baritone voice

¹bark *vb* **barked; bark·ing 1** : to make the short loud cry of a dog or like a dog's **2** : to shout or speak sharply

²bark *n* : the sound made by a barking dog or a similar sound

³bark *n* : the outside covering of the trunk, branches, and roots of a tree

⁴bark *or* **barque** *n* **1** : a small sailing boat **2** : a three-masted ship with foremast and mainmast square-rigged

⁵bark *vb* **barked; barking** : to rub or scrape the skin off

bark·er *n* : a person who stands at the entrance to a show and tries to attract people to it

bar·ley *n* : a cereal grass grown for its grain which is used mostly to feed farm animals or make malt

bar mitz·vah *n, often cap B&M* **1** : a Jewish boy who at 13 years of age takes on religious responsibilities **2** : the ceremony recognizing a boy as a bar mitzvah

barn *n* : a building used for storing grain and hay and for housing farm animals

bar·na·cle *n* : a small saltwater animal that is a crustacean and becomes permanently attached (as to rocks or the bottoms of boats) as an adult

barn·yard *n* : a usually fenced area next to a barn

ba·rom·e·ter *n* : an instrument that measures air pressure and is used to forecast changes in the weather

bar·on *n* : a man who is a member of the lowest rank of British nobility

bar·on·ess *n* **1** : the wife or widow of a baron **2** : a woman who is a member of the lowest rank of British nobility

bar·on·et *n* : the holder of a rank of honor below a baron but above a knight

ba·ro·ni·al *adj* : of, relating to, or suitable for a baron

barque *variant of* ⁴BARK

bar·rack *n* : a building or group of buildings in which soldiers live — usually used in pl.

bar·rage *n* **1** : continuous artillery or machine-gun fire directed upon a narrow strip of ground **2** : a great amount of something that comes quickly and continuously

¹bar·rel *n* **1** : a round container often with curved sides that is longer than it is wide and has flat ends **2** : the amount contained in a full barrel **3** : something shaped like a cylinder

²barrel *vb* **bar·reled** *or* **bar·relled; bar·rel·ing** *or* **bar·rel·ling** : to move at a high speed

bar·ren *adj* **1** : unable to produce seed, fruit,

or young **2** : growing only poor or few plants

bar·rette *n* : a clasp or bar used to hold hair in place

¹bar·ri·cade *vb* **bar·ri·cad·ed; bar·ri·cad·ing** : to block off with a temporary barrier

²barricade *n* : a temporary barrier for protection against attack or for blocking the way

bar·ri·er *n* **1** : something (as a fence) that blocks the way **2** : something that keeps apart or makes progress difficult

bar·ring *prep* : aside from the possibility of

¹bar·row *n* **1** : WHEELBARROW **2** : PUSHCART

²barrow *n* : a castrated male pig

¹bar·ter *vb* **bar·tered; bar·ter·ing** : to trade by exchanging one thing for another without the use of money — **bar·ter·er** *n*

²barter *n* : the exchange of goods without use of money

¹base *n* **1** : a thing or a part on which something rests : BOTTOM, FOUNDATION **2** : a starting place or goal in various games **3** : any of the four stations a runner in baseball must touch in order to score **4** : the main place or starting place of an action or operation **5** : a place where a military force keeps its supplies or from which it starts its operations **6** : a line or surface of a geometric figure upon which an altitude is or is thought to be constructed **7** : the main substance in a mixture **8** : a number with reference to which a system of numbers is constructed **9** : a chemical substance (as lime or ammonia) that reacts with an acid to form a salt and turns red litmus paper blue

²base *vb* **based; bas·ing 1** : to make or develop from a starting point **2** : to use as a main place of operation or action

³base *adj* **bas·er; bas·est 1** : of low value and not very good in some ways **2** : not honorable

base·ball *n* **1** : a game played with a bat and ball by two teams of nine players on a field with four bases that mark the course a runner must take to score **2** : the ball used in the game of baseball

base·board *n* : a line of boards or molding extending around the walls of a room and touching the floor

base·ment *n* : the part of a building that is partly or entirely below ground level

bash *vb* **bashed; bash·ing** : to hit very hard

bash·ful *adj* **1** : uneasy in the presence of others **2** : showing shyness

¹ba·sic *adj* **1** : relating to or forming the basis or most important part of something **2** : relating to or characteristic of a chemical base — **ba·si·cal·ly** *adv*

²basic *n* : something that is one of the simplest and most important parts of something

ba·sil *n* : a fragrant mint used in cooking

ba·sin *n* **1** : a wide shallow usually round dish or bowl for holding liquids **2** : the amount that a basin holds **3** : the land drained by a river and its branches **4** : a partly enclosed area of water for anchoring ships

ba·sis *n, pl* **ba·ses** : something on which another thing is based or established : FOUNDATION

bask *vb* **basked; bask·ing** **1** : to lie or relax in pleasantly warm surroundings **2** : to take pleasure or derive enjoyment

bas·ket *n* **1** : a container usually made by weaving together materials (as reeds, straw, or strips of wood) **2** : the contents of a basket **3** : a net hanging from a metal ring through which a ball is shot in basketball **4** : a shot that scores in basketball — **bas·ket·like** *adj*

bas·ket·ball *n* **1** : a game in which two teams try to throw a ball through a hanging net **2** : the ball used in basketball

bas·ket·ry *n* **1** : the making of objects (as baskets) by weaving or braiding long slender pieces of material (as reed or wood) **2** : objects made of interwoven material

bas mitzvah *variant of* BAT MITZVAH

¹bass *n, pl* **bass** *or* **bass·es** : any of numerous freshwater or saltwater fishes that are caught for sport and food

²bass *n* **1** : a tone of low pitch **2** : the lowest part in harmony that has four parts **3** : the lower half of the musical pitch range **4** : the lowest male singing voice **5** : a singer or an instrument having a bass range or part

³bass *adj* : having a very low sound or range

bas·soon *n* : a woodwind instrument with two bound reeds and with a usual range two octaves lower than an oboe

¹baste *vb* **bast·ed; bast·ing** : to sew with long loose stitches so as to hold the cloth temporarily in place

²baste *vb* **bast·ed; bast·ing** : to moisten (as with melted fat or juices) while roasting

¹bat *n* **1** : a sharp blow or slap **2** : an implement used for hitting the ball in various games **3** : a turn at batting

²bat *vb* **bat·ted; bat·ting** **1** : to strike with or as if with a bat **2** : to take a turn at bat

³bat *n* : any of a group of mammals that fly by means of long front limbs modified into wings

batch *n* **1** : an amount used or made at one time **2** : a group of persons or things

bate *vb* **bat·ed; bat·ing** : to reduce the force or intensity of

bath *n, pl* **baths** **1** : an act of washing the body usually in a bathtub **2** : water for bathing **3** : a place, room, or building where

people may bathe **4** : BATHROOM **5** : BATHTUB

bathe *vb* **bathed; bath·ing** **1** : to take a bath **2** : to give a bath to **3** : to go swimming **4** : to apply a liquid to for washing or rinsing **5** : to cover with or as if with a liquid — **bath·er** *n*

bathing suit *n* : SWIMSUIT

bath·robe *n* : a robe that is worn especially before or after a bath

bath·room *n* : a room containing a sink and toilet and usually a bathtub or shower

bath·tub *n* : a tub in which to take a bath

bat mitz·vah *also* **bas mitz·vah** *n, often cap B&M* **1** : a Jewish girl who at twelve or more years of age takes on religious responsibilities **2** : the ceremony recognizing a girl as a bat mitzvah

ba·ton *n* **1** : a thin stick with which a leader directs an orchestra or band **2** : a rod with a ball at one or both ends that is carried by a person leading a marching band **3** : a stick that is passed from one runner to the next in a relay race

bat·tal·ion *n* : a part of an army consisting of two or more companies

bat·ten *vb* **bat·tened; bat·ten·ing** **1** : to secure by or as if by fastening — often used with *down* **2** : to prepare for possible trouble or difficulty — often used with *down*

¹bat·ter *vb* **bat·tered; bat·ter·ing** **1** : to beat with repeated violent blows **2** : to damage by blows or hard use

²batter *n* : a mixture made chiefly of flour and a liquid that is cooked and eaten

³batter *n* : the player whose turn it is to bat

bat·tered *adj* : worn down or injured by hard use

bat·ter·ing ram *n* **1** : an ancient military machine that consisted of a heavy beam with an iron tip swung back and forth in order to batter down walls **2** : a heavy metal bar with handles used (as by firefighters) to break down doors or walls

bat·tery *n, pl* **bat·ter·ies** **1** : two or more big military guns that are controlled as a unit **2** : an electric cell or connected electric cells for providing electric current **3** : a number of similar items or devices grouped together **4** : an unlawful touching or use of force on a person against his or her will

bat·ting *n* : sheets of soft material (as cotton or wool) used mostly for stuffing quilts or packaging goods

¹bat·tle *n* **1** : a fight between armies, warships, or airplanes **2** : a fight between two persons or animals **3** : a long or hard struggle or contest **4** : WARFARE 1, COMBAT

²battle *vb* **bat·tled; bat·tling** **1** : to engage in fighting **2** : to try to stop or defeat

bat·tle–ax *or* **bat·tle–axe** *n* : an ax with a broad blade formerly used as a weapon

bat·tle·field *n* : a place where a military battle is fought or was once fought

bat·tle·ground *n* : BATTLEFIELD

bat·tle·ment *n* : a low wall (as at the top of a castle) with openings to shoot through

bat·tle·ship *n* : a large warship with heavy armor and large guns

bat·ty *adj* **bat·ti·er; bat·ti·est** : CRAZY 1

¹bawl *vb* **bawled; bawl·ing 1** : to shout or cry loudly **2** : to weep noisily — **bawl out** : to scold severely

²bawl *n* : a loud cry

¹bay *n* **1** : a reddish-brown horse with black mane, tail, and lower legs **2** : a reddish brown

²bay *vb* **bayed; bay·ing** : to bark or bark at with long deep tones

³bay *n* **1** : a deep bark **2** : the position of an animal or a person forced to face pursuers when it is impossible to escape **3** : the position of someone or something held off or kept back

⁴bay *n* : a part of a large body of water extending into the land

⁵bay *n* : the laurel or a related tree or shrub

bay·ber·ry *n, pl* **bay·ber·ries** : a shrub with leathery leaves and clusters of small berries covered with grayish white wax

¹bay·o·net *n* : a weapon like a dagger made to fit on the end of a rifle

²bayonet *vb* **bay·o·net·ted; bay·o·net·ting** : to stab with a bayonet

bay·ou *n* : a body of water (as a creek) that flows slowly through marshy land

bay window *n* : a large window or a set of windows that sticks out from the wall of a building

ba·zaar *n* **1** : a marketplace (as in southwestern Asia and northern Africa) that has rows of small shops **2** : a place where many kinds of goods are sold **3** : a fair for the sale of goods especially for charity

ba·zoo·ka *n* : a portable gun that rests on a person's shoulder and consists of a tube open at both ends that shoots an explosive rocket

BC *abbr* British Columbia

B.C. *abbr* before Christ

be *vb, past first person & third person sing* **was** ; *second person sing* **were** ; *pl* **were;** *past subjunctive* **were;** *past participle* **been** ; *present participle* **be·ing** ; *present first person sing* **am** ; *second person sing* **are** ; *third person sing* **is** ; *pl* **are;** *present subjunctive* **be 1** : to equal in meaning or identity **2** : to have a specified character, quality, or condition **3** : to belong to the group or class of **4** : to exist or live **5** : to occupy a place, situa-

tion, or position **6** : to take place **7** : ¹COST 1 **8** — used as a helping verb with other verbs

be- *prefix* **1** : on : around : over **2** : provide with or cover with : dress up with **3** : about : to : upon **4** : make : cause to be

¹beach *n* : a sandy or gravelly part of the shore of an ocean or a lake

²beach *vb* **beached; beach·ing** : to run or drive ashore

bea·con *n* **1** : a guiding or warning light or fire on a high place **2** : a radio station that sends out signals to guide aircraft **3** : someone or something that guides or gives hope to others

¹bead *n* **1** : a small piece of solid material with a hole through it by which it can be strung on a thread **2** : a small round drop of liquid

²bead *vb* **bead·ed; bead·ing** : to decorate or cover with beads

beady *adj* **bead·i·er; bead·i·est** : like a bead especially in being small, round, and shiny

bea·gle *n* : a small hound with short legs and a smooth coat

beak *n* **1** : the bill of a bird **2** : a part shaped like or resembling a bird's bill — **beaked** *adj*

bea·ker *n* : a cup or glass with a wide mouth and usually a lip for pouring that is used especially in science laboratories for holding and measuring liquids

¹beam *n* **1** : a long heavy piece of timber or metal used as a main horizontal support of a building or a ship **2** : a ray of light **3** : a radio wave sent out from an airport to guide pilots

²beam *vb* **beamed; beam·ing 1** : to send out beams of light **2** : to smile with joy **3** : to aim a radio broadcast by use of a special antenna

bean *n* **1** : the edible seed or pod of a bushy or climbing garden plant related to the peas and clovers **2** : a seed or fruit like a bean

¹bear *n, pl* **bears 1** *or pl* **bear** : a large heavy mammal with long shaggy hair and a very short tail **2** : a person resembling a bear in size or behavior

²bear *vb* **bore; borne; bear·ing 1** : ¹SUPPORT 4 **2** : to move while holding up and supporting : CARRY **3** : to hold in the mind **4** : to put up with **5** : to assume or accept **6** : to have as a feature or characteristic **7** : to give birth to **8** : ¹PRODUCE 1 **9** : to push down on : ²PRESS **10** : to move or lie in the indicated direction **11** : to have a relation to the matter at hand — **bear in mind** : to think of especially as a warning — **bear up** : to have strength or courage — **bear with** : to be patient with

bear·able *adj* : possible to put up with

beard *n* **1** : the hair that grows on a man's face often not including the mustache **2** : a hairy growth or tuft (as on the chin of a goat) — **beard·ed** *adj*

bear·er *n* **1** : someone or something that bears, supports, or carries **2** : a person who has a check or an order for payment

bear·ing *n* **1** : the manner in which a person carries or conducts himself or herself **2** : a part of a machine in which another part turns **3** : the position or direction of one point with respect to another or to the compass **4** : a determination of position **5 bearings** *pl* : understanding of position or situation **6** : a relation or connection

beast *n* **1** : a mammal with four feet (as a bear or deer) especially as distinguished from human beings **2** : a wild animal that is large, dangerous, or unusual **3** : a farm animal especially when kept for work **4** : a horrid person

beast·ly *adj* : very unpleasant : HORRIBLE

¹beat *vb* **beat; beat·en** *or* **beat; beat·ing 1** : to hit or strike again and again **2** : to hit repeatedly in order to cause pain or injury — often used with *up* **3** : to mix by stirring rapidly **4** : to win against : DEFEAT **5** : to come, arrive, or act before **6** : ¹THROB 2, PULSATE **7** : to flap against **8** : to move with an up and down motion : FLAP **9** : to do or be better than **10** : to find hard to figure out **11** : to make by walking or riding over — **beat·er** *n* — **beat it** : to go away quickly

²beat *n* **1** : a blow or a stroke made again and again **2** : a single pulse (as of the heart) **3** : a sound produced by or as if by beating **4** : a measurement of time in music : an accent or regular pattern of accents in music or poetry **5** : an area or place regularly visited or traveled through as part of a job

³beat *adj* : very tired

beat·en *adj* **1** : worn smooth by passing feet **2** : having lost all hope or spirit

beat–up *adj* : badly worn or damaged by use or neglect

beau·te·ous *adj* : BEAUTIFUL

beau·ti·cian *n* : a person who gives beauty treatments (as to skin and hair)

beau·ti·ful *adj* **1** : having qualities of beauty : giving pleasure to the mind or senses **2** : very good : EXCELLENT — **beau·ti·ful·ly** *adv*

beau·ti·fy *vb* **beau·ti·fied; beau·ti·fy·ing** : to make beautiful

beau·ty *n, pl* **beauties 1** : the qualities of a person or a thing that give pleasure to the senses or to the mind **2** : a beautiful or excellent person or thing

bea·ver *n* : an animal that has thick brown fur, webbed hind feet, and a broad flat tail, that cuts down trees with its teeth, and that builds dams and houses of sticks and mud in water

became *past of* BECOME

be·cause *conj* : for the reason that — **because of** : for the reason of

beck·on *vb* **beck·oned; beck·on·ing 1** : to call or signal by a motion (as a wave or nod) **2** : to appear inviting

be·come *vb* **be·came ; become; be·com·ing 1** : to come or grow to be **2** : to be suitable to especially in a pleasing way — **become of** : to happen to

be·com·ing *adj* : having a flattering effect

¹bed *n* **1** : a piece of furniture on which a person sleeps or rests **2** : a place for sleeping or resting **3** : sleep or a time for sleeping **4** : a piece of ground prepared for growing plants **5** : the bottom of something **6** : ¹LAYER 1

²bed *vb* **bed·ded; bed·ding** : to put or go to bed

bed·bug *n* : a small wingless insect that sucks blood and is sometimes found in houses and especially in beds

bed·clothes *n pl* : coverings (as sheets and blankets) for a bed

bed·ding *n* **1** : BEDCLOTHES **2** : material for a bed

be·deck *vb* **be·decked; be·deck·ing** : to dress up or decorate with showy things

be·dev·il *vb* **be·dev·iled; be·dev·ils** : to trouble or annoy again and again

bed·lam *n* : a place, scene, or state of uproar and confusion

be·drag·gled *adj* : limp, wet, or dirty from or as if from rain or mud

bed·rid·den *adj* : forced to stay in bed by sickness or weakness

bed·rock *n* : the solid rock found under surface materials (as soil)

bed·room *n* : a room used for sleeping

bed·side *n* : the place next to a bed

bed·spread *n* : a decorative top covering for a bed

bed·stead *n* : the framework of a bed

bed·time *n* : time to go to bed

bee *n* **1** : an insect with four wings that is related to the wasps, gathers pollen and nectar from flowers from which it makes beebread and honey for food, and usually lives in large colonies **2** : a gathering of people to do something together or engage in a competition

bee·bread *n* : a bitter yellowish brown food

material prepared by bees from pollen and stored in their honeycomb

beech *n* : a tree with smooth gray bark, deep green leaves, and small edible nuts

¹**beef** *n, pl* **beefs** *or* **beeves** **1** : the meat of a steer, cow, or bull **2** : a steer, cow, or bull especially when fattened for food **3** *pl* **beefs** : COMPLAINT 2

²**beef** *vb* **beefed; beef·ing** : COMPLAIN — **beef up** : to add weight, strength, or power to

bee·hive *n* : HIVE

bee·line *n* : a straight direct course

been *past participle of* BE

¹**beep** *n* : a sound that signals or warns

²**beep** *vb* **beeped; beep·ing** : to make or cause to make a sound that signals or warns

beer *n* : an alcoholic drink made from malt and flavored with hops

bees·wax *n* : wax made by bees and used by them in building honeycomb

beet *n* **1** : a leafy plant with a thick juicy root that is used as a vegetable or as a source of sugar **2** : the root of a beet plant

bee·tle *n* **1** : any of a group of insects with four wings the outer pair of which are stiff cases that cover the others when folded **2** : an insect that looks like a beetle

beeves *pl of* BEEF

be·fall *vb* **be·fell** ; **be·fall·en** ; **be·fall·ing** : to happen to

be·fit *vb* **be·fit·ted; be·fit·ting** : to be suitable to or proper for

¹**be·fore** *adv* **1** : at an earlier time **2** : AHEAD

²**before** *prep* **1** : in front of **2** : earlier than **3** : before in order **4** : in the presence of

³**before** *conj* **1** : ahead of the time when **2** : sooner or quicker than **3** : more willingly than **4** : until the time that

be·fore·hand *adv* : at an earlier or previous time

be·friend *vb* **be·friend·ed; be·friend·ing** : to act as a friend to

be·fud·dle *vb* **be·fud·dled; be·fud·dling** : CONFUSE 1

beg *vb* **begged; beg·ging** **1** : to ask for money, food, or help as charity **2** : to ask as a favor in an earnest or polite way : PLEAD

beg·gar *n* : a person who lives by begging

be·gin *vb* **be·gan** ; **be·gun** ; **be·gin·ning** **1** : to do the first part of an action **2** : to come into existence **3** : to start to have a feeling or thought **4** : to have a starting point **5** : to do or succeed in the least degree

be·gin·ner *n* : a person who is doing something for the first time

be·gin·ning *n* **1** : the point at which something begins **2** : the first part

be·gone *vb* : to go away — used as a command

be·go·nia *n* : a plant with a juicy stem, ornamental leaves, and bright waxy flowers

be·grudge *vb* **be·grudged; be·grudg·ing** : to give or allow reluctantly

be·guile *vb* **be·guiled; be·guil·ing** **1** : ²TRICK, DECEIVE **2** : to cause time to pass pleasantly **3** : to attract or interest by or as if by charm

begun *past of* BEGIN

be·half *n* : a person's interest or support — **on behalf of** *or* **in behalf of** **1** : in the interest of **2** : as a representative of

be·have *vb* **be·haved; be·hav·ing** **1** : to act in a particular manner **2** : to act in a proper or acceptable way **3** : to act or function in a particular way

be·hav·ior *n* **1** : the manner in which a person acts **2** : the whole activity of something and especially a living being

be·head *vb* **be·head·ed; be·head·ing** : to cut off the head of

¹**be·hind** *adv* **1** : in a place that is being or has been left **2** : in, to, or toward the back **3** : not up to the general level **4** : not keeping up to a schedule

²**behind** *prep* **1** : at or to the back of **2** : not up to the level of **3** : out of the thoughts of **4** : responsible for **5** : in support of

be·hold *vb* **be·held** ; **be·hold·ing** : to look upon : SEE — **be·hold·er** *n*

be·hold·en *adj* : owing the return of a gift or favor

be·hoove *vb* **be·hooved; be·hoov·ing** : to be necessary or proper for

beige *n* : a yellowish brown — **beige** *adj*

be·ing *n* **1** : the state of having life or existence **2** : a living thing **3** : an entity believed to be divine

be·la·bor *vb* **be·la·bored; be·la·bor·ing** : to keep explaining or insisting on to excess

be·lat·ed *adj* : happening or coming very late or too late — **be·lat·ed·ly** *adv*

¹**belch** *vb* **belched; belch·ing** **1** : to force out gas suddenly from the stomach through the mouth usually with a sound **2** : to throw out or be thrown out with force

²**belch** *n* : a forcing out of gas from the stomach through the mouth

bel·fry *n, pl* **belfries** : a tower or room in a tower for a bell or set of bells

¹**Bel·gian** *adj* : of or relating to Belgium or the Belgians

²**Belgian** *n* : a person born or living in Belgium

be·lie *vb* **be·lied; be·ly·ing** **1** : to give a false idea of **2** : to show to be false

be·lief *n* 1 : a feeling of being sure that a person or thing exists or is true or trustworthy 2 : religious faith 3 : something believed

be·liev·able *adj* : possible to believe

be·lieve *vb* **be·lieved; be·liev·ing** 1 : to have faith or confidence in the existence or worth of 2 : to accept as true 3 : to accept the word of 4 : to hold an opinion : THINK

be·liev·er *n* : someone who has faith or confidence in the existence or worth of something

be·lit·tle *vb* **be·lit·tled; be·lit·tling** : to make (a person or a thing) seem small or unimportant

bell *n* 1 : a hollow metallic device that is shaped somewhat like a cup and makes a ringing sound when struck 2 : DOORBELL 3 : the stroke or sound of a bell that tells the hour 4 : the time indicated by the stroke of a bell 5 : a half-hour period of watch on shipboard 6 : something shaped like a bell

bell·boy *n* : BELLHOP

belle *n* : an attractive and popular girl or woman

bell·hop *n* : a hotel or club employee who takes guests to rooms, moves luggage, and runs errands

bel·lied *adj* : having a belly of a certain kind

¹bel·lig·er·ent *adj* 1 : carrying on war 2 : feeling or showing readiness to fight

²belligerent *n* 1 : a nation at war 2 : a person taking part in a fight

bell jar *n* : a usually glass vessel shaped like a bell and used to cover objects, hold gases, or keep a vacuum

¹bel·low *vb* **bel·lowed; bel·low·ing** 1 : to shout in a deep voice 2 : to make a deep and loud sound

²bellow *n* : a loud deep sound

bel·lows *n pl* : a device that produces a strong current of air when its sides are pressed together — used as singular or plural

bel·ly *n, pl* **bellies** 1 : the front part of the body between the chest and the hips 2 : the under part of an animal's body 3 : ¹STOMACH 1 4 : a space inside something

belly button *n* : NAVEL

be·long *vb* **be·longed; be·long·ing** 1 : to be in a proper place 2 : to be the property of a person or group of persons 3 : to be a part of : be connected with : go with

be·long·ings *n pl* : the things that belong to a person

be·lov·ed *adj* : greatly loved : very dear

¹be·low *adv* 1 : in or to a lower place 2 : below zero

²below *prep* 1 : in or to a lower place than : BENEATH 2 : at the bottom of : directly underneath 3 : lower in number, size, or amount

¹belt *n* 1 : a strip of flexible material (as leather or cloth) worn around a person's body for holding in or supporting something (as clothing or weapons) or for ornament 2 : a flexible endless band running around wheels or pulleys and used for moving or carrying something 3 : a region suited to or producing something or having some special feature — **belt·ed** *adj*

²belt *vb* **belt·ed; belt·ing** 1 : to put a belt on or around 2 : to hit hard 3 : to sing in a loud and forceful way

belying *present participle of* BELIE

be·moan *vb* **be·moaned; be·moan·ing** : to express sadness, distress, or displeasure over

be·muse *vb* **be·mused; be·mus·ing** : to cause to be confused and often also somewhat amused

bench *n* 1 : a long seat for two or more persons 2 : a long table for holding work and tools 3 : the position or rank of a judge

¹bend *vb* **bent ; bend·ing** 1 : to make, be, or become curved or angular rather than straight or flat 2 : to move out of a straight line or position 3 : to not follow or tell exactly

²bend *n* : something that is bent : a curved part of something

¹be·neath *adv* 1 : in a lower place 2 : directly under

²beneath *prep* 1 : in or to a lower position than : BELOW 2 : directly under (something or someone) 3 : not worthy of

bene·dic·tion *n* 1 : a short blessing said especially at the end of a religious service 2 : an expression of good wishes

ben·e·fac·tor *n* : someone who helps another especially by giving money

ben·e·fi·cial *adj* : producing good results or effects : HELPFUL

ben·e·fi·cia·ry *n, pl* **ben·e·fi·cia·ries** : a person who benefits or will benefit from something

¹ben·e·fit *n* 1 : a good or helpful result or effect 2 : useful assistance : HELP 3 : money paid in time of death, sickness, or unemployment or in old age (as by an insurance company)

²benefit *vb* **ben·e·fit·ed; ben·e·fit·ing** 1 : to be useful or profitable to 2 : to be helped

be·nev·o·lence *n* : KINDNESS 1, GENEROSITY

be·nev·o·lent *adj* 1 : having a desire to do good : KINDLY 2 : marked by or suggestive of a kindly feeling — **be·nev·o·lent·ly** *adv*

be·nign *adj* 1 : marked by gentleness and kindness 2 : not causing death or serious harm — **be·nign·ly** *adv*

¹**bent** *adj* **1** : changed by bending : CROOKED **2** : strongly favorable to : quite determined

²**bent** *n* : a natural talent or interest

be·queath *vb* **be·queathed; be·queath·ing 1** : to give or leave by means of a will **2** : to hand down

be·quest *n* **1** : the act of leaving property by means of a will **2** : something given or left by a will

be·rate *vb* **be·rat·ed; be·rat·ing** : to scold in a loud and angry way

be·reaved *adj* : grieving over the death of a loved one

be·reft *adj* **1** : not having something needed, wanted, or expected **2** : BEREAVED

be·ret *n* : a soft round flat cap without a visor

berg *n* : ICEBERG

beri·beri *n* : a disease marked by weakness, wasting, and damage to nerves and caused by a lack of the vitamin thiamin in the diet

ber·ry *n, pl* **berries 1** : a small juicy and usually edible fruit (as a strawberry) **2** : a fruit (as a grape or tomato) in which the ripened ovary wall is fleshy **3** : a dry seed (as of the coffee plant)

ber·serk *adj* : out of control especially due to extreme anger or excitement

berth *n* **1** : a place in the water where a ship stops and stays when anchored or at a wharf **2** : a bed on a ship or train **3** : an amount of distance kept for the sake of safety

be·seech *vb* **be·sought** *or* **be·seeched; be·seech·ing** : to ask in a serious and emotional way

be·set *vb* **be·set; be·set·ting 1** : to attack violently **2** : SURROUND **3** : to cause problems or difficulties for

be·side *prep* **1** : at or by the side of **2** : compared with **3** : ¹BESIDES **4** : not relating to

¹**be·sides** *prep* **1** : in addition to **2** : other than

²**besides** *adv* : in addition : ALSO

be·siege *vb* **be·sieged; be·sieg·ing 1** : to surround with armed forces for the purpose of capturing **2** : to crowd around **3** : to overwhelm with questions or requests

¹**best** *adj, superlative of* GOOD **1** : better than all others **2** : most appropriate, useful, or helpful — **best part** : ³MOST

²**best** *adv, superlative of* WELL **1** : in a way that is better than all the others **2** : ²MOST 1

³**best** *n* **1** : a person or thing or part of a thing that is better than all the others **2** : someone's greatest effort

⁴**best** *vb* **best·ed; best·ing** : to do better than : defeat or outdo

be·stir *vb* **be·stirred; be·stir·ring** : to stir up : rouse to action

be·stow *vb* **be·stowed; be·stow·ing** : to give as a gift or honor

¹**bet** *n* **1** : an agreement requiring the person who guesses wrong about the result of a contest or the outcome of an event to give something to the person who guesses right **2** : the money or thing risked in a bet **3** : a choice made by considering what might happen

²**bet** *vb* **bet** *or* **bet·ted; bet·ting 1** : to risk in a bet **2** : to make a bet with **3** : to be sure enough to make a bet

bet. *abbr* between

be·tray *vb* **be·trayed; be·tray·ing 1** : to give over to an enemy by treason or treachery **2** : to be unfaithful to **3** : to reveal or show without meaning to **4** : to tell in violation of a trust

be·troth *vb* **be·trothed; be·troth·ing** : to promise to marry or give in marriage

be·troth·al *n* : an engagement to be married

¹**bet·ter** *adj, comparative of* GOOD **1** : more satisfactory or skillful than another **2** : improved in health — **better part** : more than half

²**better** *vb* **bet·tered; bet·ter·ing** : to make or become more satisfactory

³**better** *adv, comparative of* WELL **1** : in a superior or more excellent way **2** : to a higher or greater degree

⁴**better** *n* **1** : something that is more satisfactory **2** : ADVANTAGE 2, VICTORY

bet·ter·ment *n* : the act or result of making something more satisfactory : IMPROVEMENT

bet·tor *or* **bet·ter** *n* : someone that bets

¹**be·tween** *prep* **1** : in the time or space that separates **2** : functioning to separate or tell apart **3** : by the efforts of each of **4** : by comparing **5** : shared by **6** : in shares to each of **7** : to and from

²**between** *adv* : in a position between others

be·twixt *prep* : BETWEEN 1

¹**bev·el** *n* : a slant or slope of one surface or line against another

²**bevel** *vb* **bev·eled** *or* **bev·elled; bev·el·ing** *or* **bev·el·ling** : to cut or shape (an edge or surface) at an angle or slant

bev·er·age *n* : a liquid for drinking

be·ware *vb* : to be cautious or careful — used only in the forms *beware* or *to beware*

be·whis·kered *adj* : having whiskers

be·wil·der *vb* **be·wil·dered; be·wil·der·ing** : CONFUSE 1 — **be·wil·der·ment** *n*

be·witch *vb* **be·witched; be·witch·ing 1** : to gain an influence over by means of magic or witchcraft **2** : to attract or delight as if by magic

¹**be·yond** *adv* : on or to the farther side

²**beyond** *prep* **1** : on the other side of **2** : out of the limits or range of

bi- *prefix* **1** : two **2** : coming or occurring

every two **3** : into two parts **4** : twice : doubly : on both sides

¹bi·as *n* **1** : a seam, cut, or stitching running in a slant across cloth **2** : a favoring of some ideas or people over others : PREJUDICE

²bias *vb* **bi·ased** *or* **bi·assed; bi·as·ing** *or* **bi·as·sing** : to give a prejudiced outlook to

bib *n* **1** : a cloth or plastic shield tied under the chin (as of a young child) to protect the clothes **2** : the upper part of an apron or of overalls

Bi·ble *n* **1** : the book of sacred writings accepted by Christians as coming from God **2** : a book containing the sacred writings of a religion

bib·li·cal *adj* : relating to, taken from, or found in the Bible

bib·li·og·ra·phy *n, pl* **bib·li·og·ra·phies** **1** : a list of materials (as books or magazine articles) used in the preparation of a written work or mentioned in a text **2** : a list of writings about an author or a subject — **bib·lio·graph·ic** *also* **bib·lio·graph·i·cal** *adj*

bi·car·bon·ate of soda *n* : BAKING SODA

bi·ceps *n, pl* **biceps** *also* **bi·ceps·es** : a large muscle of the front of the upper arm

bick·er *vb* **bick·ered; bick·er·ing** : to quarrel in an irritating way especially over unimportant things

bi·cus·pid *n* : either of the two teeth with double points on each side of each jaw of a person

¹bi·cy·cle *n* : a light vehicle having two wheels one behind the other, handlebars, a seat, and pedals by which it is made to move

²bicycle *vb* **bi·cy·cled; bi·cy·cling** : to ride a bicycle

bi·cy·clist *n* : a person who rides a bicycle

¹bid *vb* **bade** *or* **bid; bid·den** *or* **bid; bid·ding** **1** : ¹ORDER 2, COMMAND **2** : to express to **3** : to make an offer for something (as at an auction) — **bid·der** *n*

²bid *n* **1** : an offer to pay a certain sum for something or to do certain work at a stated fee **2** : an attempt to win, achieve, or attract

bide *vb* **bode** *or* **bid·ed** ; **bid·ed; bid·ing** : to wait or wait for

¹bi·en·ni·al *adj* **1** : occurring every two years **2** : growing stalks and leaves one year and flowers and fruit the next before dying — **bi·en·ni·al·ly** *adv*

²biennial *n* : a biennial plant

bier *n* : a stand on which a corpse or coffin is placed

big *adj* **big·ger; big·gest** **1** : large in size **2** : large in number or amount **3** : of great importance **4** : of great strength or force — **big·ness** *n*

Big Dipper *n* : a group of seven stars in the northern sky arranged in a form like a dipper with the two stars that form the side opposite the handle pointing to the North Star

big·horn *n* : a grayish brown wild sheep of mountainous western North America

big·ot *n* : a person who hates or refuses to accept the members of a particular group — **big·ot·ed** *adj*

big·ot·ry *n* : acts or beliefs characteristic of a bigot

big tree *n* : GIANT SEQUOIA

¹bike *n* **1** : ¹BICYCLE **2** : MOTORCYCLE

²bike *vb* **biked; bik·ing** : ²BICYCLE

bik·er *n* : a person who rides a bicycle or motorcycle

bile *n* : a thick bitter yellow or greenish fluid produced by the liver to aid in digestion of fats in the small intestine

bi·lin·gual *adj* **1** : using or expressed in two languages **2** : able to speak two languages

¹bill *n* **1** : the jaws of a bird together with their horny covering **2** : a part of an animal (as a turtle) that resembles the bill of a bird — **billed** *adj*

²bill *n* **1** : a draft of a law presented to a legislature for consideration **2** : a record of goods sold, services performed, or work done with the cost involved **3** : a piece of paper money **4** : a sign or poster advertising something

³bill *vb* **billed; bill·ing** : to send a bill to

bill·board *n* : a flat surface on which outdoor advertisements are displayed

bill·fold *n* : WALLET

bil·liards *n* : a game played by driving solid balls with a cue into each other or into pockets on a large rectangular table

Bill of Rights *n* : the first ten amendments to the United States Constitution

bil·lion *n* **1** : a thousand millions **2** : a very large number

¹bil·lionth *adj* : being last in a series of a billion

²billionth *n* : number 1,000,000,000 in a series

¹bil·low *n* **1** : a large wave **2** : a moving cloud or mass (as of smoke or flame)

²billow *vb* **bil·lowed; bil·low·ing** **1** : to rise or roll in large waves **2** : to move as a large cloud or mass **3** : to bulge or swell out

bil·lowy *adj* **1** : full of large waves **2** : bulging or puffing out

bil·ly club *n* : NIGHTSTICK

billy goat *n* : a male goat

bin *n* : a box or enclosed place used for storage

bi·na·ry *adj* : of, relating to, or being a number system with a base of 2

¹bind *vb* **bound** ; **bind·ing** **1** : to tie or wrap securely (as with string or rope) **2** : to hold or restrict by force or obligation **3** : to wrap or cover with a bandage **4** : to cause to be joined together closely **5** : to fasten together and enclose in a cover

²bind *n* : a difficult situation

bind·er *n* **1** : a person who binds books **2** : a cover for holding together loose sheets of paper **3** : a machine that cuts grain and ties it into bundles

bind·ing *n* **1** : the cover and the fastenings of a book **2** : a narrow strip of fabric used along the edge of an article of clothing **3** : a device that attaches a boot to a ski

bin·go *n* : a game of chance played by covering a numbered space on a card when the number is matched by one drawn at random and won by the first player to cover five spaces in a row

bin·oc·u·lar *adj* : of, using, or suited for the use of both eyes

bin·oc·u·lars *n pl* : a hand-held instrument for seeing at a distance that is made up of two telescopes usually having prisms and a focusing device

bio- *prefix* : life : living organisms

bio·de·grad·able *adj* : possible to break down into very small harmless parts by the action of living things (as bacteria)

bio·di·ver·si·ty *n* : the existence of many different kinds of plants and animals in an environment

bi·og·ra·pher *n* : someone who tells the account of a real person's life

bio·graph·i·cal *adj* : of or relating to an account of a real person's life

bi·og·ra·phy *n, pl* **bi·og·ra·phies** : a usually written account of a real person's life

bi·o·log·i·cal *adj* : of or relating to biology or to life and living things

bi·ol·o·gist *n* : a person specializing in biology

bi·ol·o·gy *n* : a science that deals with living things and their relationships, distribution, and behavior

bi·ome *n* : a major type of community of distinctive plants and animals living together in a particular climate and physical environment

bio·tech·nol·o·gy *n* : the use of techniques from genetics to combine inherited characteristics selected from different kinds of organisms into one organism in order to produce useful products (as drugs)

bi·ped *n* : an animal (as a person) that has only two feet

bi·plane *n* : an airplane with two wings on each side usually placed one above the other

birch *n* : a tree with hard wood and a smooth bark that can be peeled off in thin layers

bird *n* : an animal that lays eggs and has wings and a body covered with feathers

bird·bath *n* : a basin for birds to bathe in

bird·house *n* : an artificial nesting place (as a wooden box) for birds

bird of prey *n, pl* **birds of prey** : a bird (as an eagle or owl) that feeds almost entirely on meat taken by hunting

bird's–eye *adj* : seen from above as if by a flying bird

birth *n* **1** : the coming of a new individual from the body of its parent **2** : the act of bringing into life **3** : LINEAGE 1 **4** : ORIGIN 3

birth·day *n* **1** : the return each year of the date on which a person was born or something began **2** : the day on which a person is born **3** : a day of beginning

birth·mark *n* : an unusual mark or blemish on the skin at birth

birth·place *n* : the place where a person was born or where something began

birth·right *n* : a right belonging to a person because of his or her birth

bis·cuit *n* : a small light bread

bi·sect *vb* **bi·sect·ed; bi·sect·ing** **1** : to divide into two equal parts **2** : INTERSECT

bish·op *n* **1** : a member of the clergy of high rank **2** : a piece in the game of chess

bis·muth *n* : a heavy grayish white metallic chemical element that is used in alloys and in medicines

bi·son *n, pl* **bison** : a large animal with short horns and a shaggy mane that is related to the cows and oxen

¹bit *n* **1** : a small piece or quantity **2** : a short time **3** : ¹SOMEWHAT — **bit by bit** : by small steps or amounts : GRADUALLY

²bit *n* **1** : a part of a bridle that is put in the horse's mouth **2** : the cutting or boring edge or part of a tool

³bit *n* : a unit of computer information that represents the selection of one of two possible choices (as *on* or *off*)

bitch *n* : a female dog

¹bite *vb* **bit; bit·ten; bit·ing** **1** : to seize, grip, or cut into with or as if with teeth **2** : to wound or sting usually with a stinger or fang **3** : to take a bait

²bite *n* **1** : an act of seizing or cutting into with the teeth **2** : a wound made by biting : STING **3** : the amount of food taken at a bite **4** : a sharp or biting sensation

bit·ing *adj* : causing intense discomfort

bit·ter *adj* **bit·ter·er; bit·ter·est** **1** : sharp, biting, and unpleasant to the taste **2** : unhappy and angry because of unfair treatment **3** : hard to put up with **4** : caused by anger, distress, or sorrow **5** : very harsh or sharp : BITING — **bit·ter·ly** *adv* — **bit·ter·ness** *n*

bit·tern *n* : a brownish marsh bird which has a loud booming cry

¹**bit·ter·sweet** *n* **1** : a poisonous vine originally of Europe and Asia with purple flowers and red berries **2** : a poisonous North American woody climbing plant with orange seedcases that open when ripe to reveal red seeds

²**bittersweet** *adj* : being partly bitter or sad and partly sweet or happy

bi·tu·mi·nous coal *n* : a soft coal that gives a lot of smoke when burned

bi·zarre *adj* : very strange or odd

blab *vb* **blabbed; blab·bing 1** : to reveal a secret **2** : to talk too much

¹**black** *adj* **black·er; black·est 1** : of the color of coal : colored black **2** : very dark **3** *often cap* : of or relating to any peoples having dark skin and especially any of the original peoples of Africa south of the Sahara **4** : of or relating to Americans having ancestors from Africa south of the Sahara **5** : WICKED **6** : very sad or gloomy **7** : UNFRIENDLY — **black·ish** *adj* — **black·ness** *n*

²**black** *n* **1** : the color of coal : the opposite of white **2** : black clothing **3** : a person belonging to a race of people having dark skin **4** : an American having black African ancestors : AFRICAN-AMERICAN **5** : total or near total darkness **6** : the condition of making a profit

³**black** *vb* **blacked; black·ing** : BLACKEN 1 — **black out** : to lose consciousness or the ability to see for a short time

black–and–blue *adj* : darkly discolored (as from a bruise)

black·ber·ry *n, pl* **black·ber·ries** : the black or dark purple sweet juicy berry of a prickly plant related to the raspberry

black·bird *n* : any of several birds of which the males are mostly black

black·board *n* : a hard smooth dark surface used for writing or drawing on with chalk

black·en *vb* **black·ened; black·en·ing 1** : to make or become dark or black **2** : ²SPOIL 2

black–eyed Su·san *n* : a daisy with yellow or orange petals and a dark center

black·head *n* : a darkened bit of oily material that blocks the opening of a gland in the skin

¹**black·mail** *n* **1** : the act of forcing someone to pay money by threatening to reveal a secret that might bring disgrace on him or her **2** : money paid under threat of revealing a secret

²**blackmail** *vb* **black·mailed; black·mail·ing** : to threaten with the revealing of a secret unless money is paid — **black·mail·er** *n*

black·out *n* **1** : a period of darkness enforced as a protection against enemy attack by airplanes during a war **2** : a period of darkness caused by power failure **3** : a temporary loss of vision or consciousness

black·smith *n* : a person who makes things out of iron by heating and hammering it

black·snake *n* : either of two harmless snakes of the United States with blackish skins

black·top *n* : a black material used especially to pave roads

black widow *n* : a poisonous spider the female of which is black with a red mark shaped like an hourglass on the underside of the abdomen

blad·der *n* **1** : an organ in the body resembling a pouch into which urine passes from the kidneys and is temporarily stored until discharged from the body **2** : a container that can be filled with air or gas

blade *n* **1** : a leaf of a plant and especially of a grass **2** : the broad flat part of a leaf **3** : something that widens out like the blade of a leaf **4** : the cutting part of a tool, machine, or weapon **5** : SWORD **6** : the runner of an ice skate — **blad·ed** *adj*

¹**blame** *vb* **blamed; blam·ing 1** : to find fault with **2** : to hold responsible **3** : to place responsibility for

²**blame** *n* **1** : responsibility for something that fails or is wrong **2** : expression of disapproval — **blame·less** *adj*

blame·wor·thy *adj* : deserving blame

blanch *vb* **blanched; blanch·ing 1** : ¹BLEACH, WHITEN **2** : to scald so as to remove the skin from **3** : to turn pale

bland *adj* **bland·er; bland·est 1** : not interesting or exiciting **2** : not having much flavor **3** : not showing emotion

¹**blank** *adj* **1** : not having any writing or marks **2** : having empty spaces to be filled in **3** : not showing emotion or understanding

²**blank** *n* **1** : an empty space in a line of writing or printing **2** : a paper with empty spaces to be filled in **3** : a cartridge loaded with powder but no bullet **4** : events or a time that cannot be remembered

¹**blan·ket** *n* **1** : a heavy woven covering used especially for beds **2** : a covering layer

²**blanket** *vb* **blanket·ed; blanket·ing** : to cover with or as if with a blanket

¹**blare** *vb* **blared; blar·ing 1** : to sound loud and harsh **2** : to present in a harsh noisy manner

²**blare** *n* : a harsh loud noise

¹**blast** *n* **1** : the sound made by a wind instrument **2** : EXPLOSION 1 **3** : a strong gust of wind **4** : a stream of air or gas forced through an opening **5** : a very enjoyable experience

²**blast** *vb* **blast·ed; blast·ing 1** : to break to pieces by an explosion : SHATTER **2** : to hit with great force **3** : to make a loud unpleas-

ant sound **4** : to strongly criticize **5** : ²BLIGHT — **blast off** : to take off

blast-off *n* : an instance of taking off (as of a rocket)

bla·tant *adj* : completely obvious in a disagreeable way

¹**blaze** *n* **1** : an intense and dangerous fire **2** : great brightness and heat **3** : a bright display **4** : OUTBURST 1

²**blaze** *vb* **blazed; blaz·ing 1** : to burn brightly **2** : to shine as if on fire

³**blaze** *n* **1** : a white stripe down the center of an animal's face **2** : a mark made on a tree to show a trail

⁴**blaze** *vb* **blazed; blaz·ing** : to show a path by making marks on trees

bldg. *abbr* building

¹**bleach** *vb* **bleached; bleach·ing** : to make white by removing the color or stains from

²**bleach** *n* : a chemical used for bleaching

bleach·er *n* : one of a set of open seats arranged like steps for people to sit on while watching a game or performance — usually used in pl.

bleak *adj* **bleak·er; bleak·est 1** : open to wind or weather **2** : being cold and raw or uncheerful **3** : not hopeful or encouraging — **bleak·ly** *adv* — **bleak·ness** *n*

¹**bleat** *vb* **bleat·ed; bleat·ing** : to make the cry of a sheep, goat, or calf

²**bleat** *n* : the sound made by a sheep, goat, or calf

bleed *vb* **bled** ; **bleed·ing 1** : to lose or shed blood **2** : to feel pain or pity **3** : to draw a liquid or gas from **4** : to spread into something else

¹**blem·ish** *n* : a mark that makes something imperfect : an unwanted mark on a surface

²**blemish** *vb* **blem·ished; blem·ish·ing** : to spoil by or as if by an ugly mark

¹**blend** *vb* **blend·ed; blend·ing 1** : to mix so completely that the separate things mixed cannot be told apart **2** : to exist agreeably with each other — **blend in** : to look like part of something

²**blend** *n* **1** : a thorough mixture : a product made by blending **2** : a word formed by combining parts of two or more other words so that they overlap

blend·er *n* : an appliance used to chop, mix, blend, and liquefy

bless *vb* **blessed** *also* **blest; bless·ing 1** : to make holy by a religious ceremony or words **2** : to ask the favor or protection of God for — used to wish good health especially to someone who has just sneezed **3** : to praise or honor as holy **4** : to give happiness or good fortune to

bless·ed *adj* **1** : HOLY 1 **2** : enjoying happiness — **bless·ed·ness** *n*

bless·ing *n* **1** : the act of one who blesses **2** : APPROVAL **3** : something that makes a person happy or content **4** : a short prayer

blew *past of* BLOW

¹**blight** *n* : a disease that makes parts of plants dry up and die

²**blight** *vb* **blight·ed; blight·ing** : to injure or destroy by or as if by a blight

blimp *n* : an airship filled with gas like a balloon

¹**blind** *adj* **blind·er; blind·est 1** : unable or nearly unable to see **2** : lacking in judgment or understanding **3** : UNQUESTIONING **4** : closed at one end — **blind·ly** *adv* — **blind·ness** *n*

²**blind** *vb* **blind·ed; blind·ing 1** : to cause the permanent loss of sight in **2** : to make it impossible to see well for a short time

³**blind** *n* **1** : a device to reduce sight or keep out light **2** : a place of hiding

⁴**blind** *adv* : with only instruments as guidance

¹**blind·fold** *vb* **blind·fold·ed; blind·fold·ing** : to cover the eyes of with a piece of cloth

²**blindfold** *n* : a covering over the eyes

blind·man's buff *n* : a game in which a blindfolded player tries to catch and identify one of the other players

blink *vb* **blinked; blink·ing 1** : to shut and open the eyes quickly **2** : to shine with a light that goes or seems to go on and off

blink·er *n* : a light that blinks to indicate that a vehicle will be turning

bliss *n* : great happiness : JOY — **bliss·ful** *adj* — **bliss·ful·ly** *adv*

¹**blis·ter** *n* **1** : a small raised area of the skin filled with a watery liquid **2** : a swelling (as in paint) that looks like a blister of the skin

²**blister** *vb* **blis·tered; blis·ter·ing 1** : to develop a blister or blisters **2** : to cause blisters on

blithe *adj* **blith·er; blith·est** : free from worry : MERRY, CHEERFUL — **blithe·ly** *adv*

bliz·zard *n* : a long heavy snowstorm

bloat *vb* **bloat·ed; bloat·ing** : to make swollen with or as if with fluid

blob *n* : a small lump or drop of something thick

¹**block** *n* **1** : a solid piece of some material usually with one or more flat sides **2** : an area of land surrounded by four streets in a city **3** : the length of one side of a city block **4** : a number of things thought of as forming a group or unit **5** : a large building divided into separate houses or shops **6** : an action that stops or slows down an opponent (as in football) **7** : something that prevents a person from thinking about certain things **8** : something that stops or makes passage or

progress difficult : OBSTRUCTION **9** : a case enclosing one or more pulleys

²block *vb* **blocked; block·ing 1** : to stop or make passage through difficult : OBSTRUCT **2** : to stop or make the passage of difficult **3** : to make an opponent's movement (as in football) difficult

¹block·ade *vb* **block·ad·ed; block·ad·ing** : to close off a place to prevent the coming in or going out of people or supplies

²blockade *n* : the closing off of a place (as by warships) to prevent the coming in or going out of people or supplies

block and tackle *n* : an arrangement of pulleys in blocks with rope or cable for lifting or hauling

block·house *n* : a building (as of heavy timbers or of concrete) built with holes in its sides through which people inside may fire out at an enemy

block letter *n* : a capital letter often printed by hand that has all lines of equal thickness

¹blond *or* **blonde** *adj* **blond·er; blond·est 1** : of a golden or pale yellowish brown color **2** : having hair of a light color

²blond *or* **blonde** *n* : someone with golden or pale yellowish brown hair

blood *n* **1** : the red fluid that circulates in the heart, arteries, capillaries, and veins of persons and animals and that brings nourishment and oxygen to and carries away waste products from all parts of the body **2** : relationship through a common ancestor : KINSHIP — **blood·ed** *adj*

blood·cur·dling *adj* : causing great horror or fear

blood·hound *n* : a large hound with long drooping ears, a wrinkled face, and a very good sense of smell

blood pressure *n* : pressure of the blood on the walls of blood vessels and especially arteries

blood·shed *n* : serious injury or death caused by violence

blood·shot *adj* : red and sore

blood·stream *n* : the circulating blood in the living body

blood·suck·er *n* : an animal (as a leech) that sucks blood — **blood·suck·ing** *adj*

blood·thirsty *adj* : eager to kill or hurt

blood vessel *n* : an artery, vein, or capillary of the body

bloody *adj* **blood·i·er; blood·i·est 1** : bleeding or covered with blood **2** : causing or accompanied by bloodshed

¹bloom *n* **1** : ¹FLOWER 1 **2** : the period or state of producing flowers **3** : a condition or time of beauty, freshness, and strength **4** : the rosy color of the cheek

²bloom *vb* **bloomed; bloom·ing 1** : to pro-

duce flowers **2** : to change, grow, or develop fully

¹blos·som *n* **1** : ¹FLOWER 1 **2** : ¹BLOOM 2

²blossom *vb* **blos·somed; blos·som·ing 1** : ²BLOOM 1 **2** : to appear, change, grow, or develop

¹blot *n* **1** : a spot or stain of dirt or ink **2** : a mark of shame or dishonor

²blot *vb* **blot·ted; blot·ting 1** : ²SPOT 1 **2** : to dry by pressing with paper or cloth — **blot out 1** : to make (something) difficult to see **2** : to destroy completely

blotch *n* **1** : a blemish on the skin **2** : a large irregular spot of color or ink — **blotched** *adj*

blotchy *adj* **blotch·i·er; blotch·i·est** : marked with irregular spots

blot·ter *n* : a piece of blotting paper

blot·ting paper *n* : a soft spongy paper used to absorb wet ink

blouse *n* **1** : a loose garment for women covering the body from the neck to the waist **2** : the jacket of a uniform

¹blow *vb* **blew; blown; blow·ing 1** : to move or be moved usually with speed and force **2** : to move in or with the wind **3** : to send forth a strong stream of air from the mouth or from a bellows **4** : to make a sound or cause to sound by blowing **5** : to clear by forcing air through **6** : to shape by forcing air into **7** : to enter or leave very quickly **8** : to fail in performing or keeping — **blow·er** *n* — **blow over** : to pass without effect — **blow up 1** : EXPLODE 1 **2** : to fill with a gas

²blow *n* : a blowing of wind : GALE

³blow *n* **1** : a hard hit with a part of the body or an object **2** : a sudden happening that causes suffering or loss

blow·gun *n* : a tube from which a dart may be shot by the force of the breath

blow·torch *n* : a small portable burner in which the flame is made hotter by a blast of air or oxygen

¹blub·ber *vb* **blub·bered; blub·ber·ing 1** : to weep noisily **2** : to utter while weeping

²blubber *n* : the fat of various sea mammals (as whales and seals) from which oil can be obtained

¹blue *n* **1** : the color of the clear daytime sky **2** : blue clothing or cloth **3** : SKY **4** : SEA — **blu·ish** *adj* — **out of the blue** : suddenly and unexpectedly

²blue *adj* **blu·er; blu·est 1** : of the color of the sky : of the color blue **2** : SAD 1

blue·bell *n* : a plant with blue flowers shaped like bells

blue·ber·ry *n, pl* **blue·ber·ries** : a sweet blue or blackish berry that grows on a bush and has many small soft seeds

blue-bird *n* : a small North American song-bird that is blue above and reddish brown or pale blue below

blue-bot-tle *n* : a large blue hairy fly

blue cheese *n* : cheese ripened by and full of greenish blue mold

blue-fish *n* : a saltwater fish that is bluish above with silvery sides and is often used for food

blue-grass *n* **1** : a grass with bluish green stems **2** : a type of traditional American music that is played on stringed instruments

blue jay *n* : a crested and mostly blue North American bird related to the crows

blue jeans *n pl* : pants made of blue denim

blue-print *n* **1** : a photographic print made with white lines on a blue background and showing how something will be made **2** : a detailed plan of something to be done

blue ribbon *n* : a decorative ribbon colored blue that is given to the winner in a competition

blues *n pl* **1** : low spirits **2** : a style of music that was created by African-Americans and that expresses feelings of sadness

blue whale *n* : a very large whale that is generally considered the largest living animal

¹bluff *adj* **1** : rising steeply with a broad front **2** : frank and outspoken in a rough but good-natured way

²bluff *n* : a high steep bank : CLIFF

³bluff *vb* **bluffed; bluff-ing** : to deceive or frighten by pretending to have more strength or confidence than is really true

⁴bluff *n* : an act or instance of pretending to have more strength, confidence, or ability than is really true

¹blun-der *vb* **blun-dered; blun-der-ing** **1** : to move in a clumsy way **2** : to make a mistake

²blunder *n* : a bad or stupid mistake

blun-der-buss *n* : a short gun that has a barrel which is larger at the end and that was used long ago for shooting at close range without taking exact aim

¹blunt *adj* **blunt-er; blunt-est** **1** : having a thick edge or point : DULL **2** : speaking or spoken in plain language without thought for other people's feelings — **blunt-ly** *adv*

²blunt *vb* **blunt-ed; blunt-ing** : to make or become less sharp

¹blur *n* **1** : something that cannot be seen clearly **2** : something that is difficult to remember

²blur *vb* **blurred; blur-ring** **1** : to make unclear or hard to see or remember **2** : to make or become unclear or confused

blur-ry *adj* **blur-ri-er; blur-ri-est** : not in sharp focus

blurt *vb* **blurt-ed; blurt-ing** : to say or tell suddenly and without thinking

¹blush *vb* **blushed; blush-ing** **1** : to become red in the face from shame, confusion, or embarrassment **2** : to feel ashamed or embarrassed

²blush *n, pl* **blush-es** **1** : a reddening of the face from shame, confusion, or embarrassment **2** : a rosy color

¹blus-ter *vb* **blus-tered; blus-ter-ing** **1** : to talk or act in a noisy boastful way **2** : to blow hard and noisily

²bluster *n* : noisy violent action or speech

blvd. *abbr* boulevard

boa *n* : a large snake (as a python) that coils around and crushes its prey

boar *n* **1** : a male pig **2** : WILD BOAR

¹board *n* **1** : a sawed piece of lumber that is much broader and longer than it is thick **2** : a usually rectangular piece of rigid material used for some special purpose **3** : BLACKBOARD **4** : a number of persons having authority to manage or direct something **5** : meals given at set times for a price **6** **boards** *pl* : the low wooden wall enclosing a hockey rink **7** : a sheet of insulating material carrying electronic parts (as for a computer) — **on board** : ¹ABOARD

²board *vb* **board-ed; board-ing** **1** : to go aboard **2** : to cover with boards **3** : to give or get meals and a place to live for a price

board-er *n* : a person who pays for meals and a place to live at another's house

board-ing-house *n* : a house at which people are given meals and often a place to live

boarding school *n* : a school at which most of the students live during the school year

board-walk *n* : a walk made of planks especially along a beach

¹boast *vb* **boast-ed; boast-ing** **1** : to express too much pride in a person's own qualities, possessions, or achievements **2** : to have and be proud of having

²boast *n* **1** : an act of expressing too much pride in a person's own qualities, possessions, or achievements **2** : a cause for pride — **boast-ful** *adj* — **boast-ful-ly** *adv*

¹boat *n* **1** : a small vessel driven on the water by oars, paddles, sails, or a motor **2** : ¹SHIP 1

²boat *vb* **boat-ed; boat-ing** : to use a boat — **boat-er** *n*

boat-house *n* : a house or shelter for boats

boat-man *n, pl* **boat-men** : a person who works on, handles, or operates boats

boat-swain *n* : a warrant officer on a warship or a petty officer on a commercial ship who has charge of the hull, anchors, boats, and rigging

¹bob *vb* **bobbed; bob-bing** **1** : to move or cause to move with a short jerky up-and-down motion **2** : to try to seize something with the teeth

²bob *n* : a short jerky up-and-down motion

³bob *n* **1** : a float used to buoy up the baited end of a fishing line **2** : a woman's or child's short haircut

⁴bob *vb* **bobbed; bob·bing 1** : to cut (hair) in the style of a bob **2** : to cut shorter

bob·by pin *n* : a flat metal hairpin with the two ends pressed close together

bob·cat *n* : a North American wildcat that is a small rusty brown type of lynx

bob·o·link *n* : a North American songbird related to the blackbirds

bob·sled *n* : a racing sled made with two sets of runners, a hand brake, and often a steering wheel

bob·tail *n* **1** : a short tail : a tail cut short **2** : an animal (as a dog) with a short tail

bob·white *n* : a North American quail with gray, white, and reddish brown coloring

¹bode *vb* **bod·ed; bod·ing** : to be a sign of (a future event)

²bode *past of* BIDE

bod·ice *n* : the upper part of a dress

¹bod·i·ly *adj* : of or relating to the body

²bodily *adv* **1** : by the body **2** : as a whole

body *n, pl* **bod·ies 1** : the physical whole of a live or dead person or animal **2** : the main part of a person, animal, or plant **3** : a human being **4** : the main or central part **5** : the main part of a motor vehicle **6** : a group of persons or things united for some purpose **7** : a mass or portion of something distinct from other masses — **bod·ied** *adj*

body·guard *n* : a person or a group of persons whose duty it is to protect someone

¹bog *n* : wet spongy ground that is usually acid and found next to a body of water (as a pond)

²bog *vb* **bogged; bog·ging** : to sink or stick fast in or as if in a bog

bo·gey *also* **bo·gie** *or* **bo·gy** *n, pl* **bogeys** *or* **bogies 1** : GHOST, GOBLIN **2** : something a person is afraid of without reason

bo·gus *adj* : not genuine

¹boil *n* : a red painful lump in the skin that contains pus and is caused by infection

²boil *vb* **boiled; boil·ing 1** : to heat or become heated to the temperature (**boiling point**) at which bubbles rise and break at the surface **2** : to cook or become cooked in boiling water **3** : to feel angry or upset

³boil *n* : the state of something that is boiling

boil·er *n* **1** : a container in which something is boiled **2** : a tank heating and holding water **3** : a strong metal container used in making steam (as to heat buildings)

bois·ter·ous *adj* : being rough and noisy — **bois·ter·ous·ly** *adv*

bold *adj* **bold·er; bold·est 1** : willing to meet danger or take risks : DARING **2** : not polite and modest : FRESH **3** : showing or calling for courage or daring **4** : standing out prominently — **bold·ly** *adv* — **bold·ness** *n*

bold·face *n* : a heavy black type — **bold·faced** *adj*

boll *n* : the seedpod of a plant (as cotton)

boll weevil *n* : a grayish or brown insect that lays its eggs in cotton bolls

bo·lo·gna *n* : a large smoked sausage usually made of beef, veal, and pork

¹bol·ster *n* : a long pillow or cushion sometimes used to support bed pillows

²bolster *vb* **bol·stered; bol·ster·ing** : to support with or as if with a bolster

¹bolt *n* **1** : a stroke of lightning : THUNDERBOLT **2** : a sliding bar used to fasten a door **3** : the part of a lock worked by a key **4** : a metal pin or rod with a head at one end and a screw thread at the other that is used to hold something in place **5** : a roll of cloth or wallpaper

²bolt *vb* **bolt·ed; bolt·ing 1** : to move suddenly and rapidly **2** : to run away **3** : to fasten with a bolt **4** : to swallow hastily or without chewing

¹bomb *n* **1** : a hollow case or shell filled with explosive material **2** : a container in which something (as an insecticide) is stored under pressure and from which it is released in a fine spray **3** : something that is a complete failure

²bomb *vb* **bombed; bomb·ing 1** : to attack with bombs **2** : to fail completely

bom·bard *vb* **bom·bard·ed; bom·bard·ing 1** : to attack with heavy fire from big guns : SHELL **2** : to attack again and again

bomb·er *n* : an airplane specially made for dropping bombs

bo·na fide *adj* : GENUINE 1

bon·bon *n* : a candy with a soft coating and a creamy center

¹bond *n* **1** : something that binds **2** : the condition of being held together **3** : a force or influence that brings or holds together **4** : a chain or rope used to prevent someone from moving or acting freely **5** : a promise to do something **6** : a legal agreement in which a person agrees to pay a sum of money if he or she fails to do a certain thing **7** : a government or business certificate promising to pay a certain sum by a certain day

²bond *vb* **bond·ed; bond·ing 1** : to stick or cause to stick together **2** : to form a close relationship

bond·age *n* : SLAVERY

¹bone *n* **1** : any of the hard pieces that form

the skeleton of most animals **2** : the hard material of which the skeleton of most animals is formed — **bone·less** *adj*

²bone *vb* **boned; bon·ing** : to remove the bones from

bone marrow *n* : a soft tissue rich in blood vessels that fills the spaces of most bones and includes one type that is red and produces red blood cells and white blood cells and another type that is yellow and contains fat

bon·fire *n* : a large fire built outdoors

bong *n* : a deep sound like that of a large bell

bon·go *n, pl* **bongos** *also* **bongoes** : either of a pair of small drums of different sizes fitted together and played with the fingers

bon·net *n* : a child's or woman's hat usually tied under the chin by ribbons or strings

bon·ny *also* **bon·nie** *adj* **bon·ni·er; bon·ni·est** *chiefly British* : HANDSOME 1, BEAUTIFUL

bo·nus *n* : something given to somebody (as a worker) in addition to what is usual or owed

bony *adj* **bon·i·er; bon·i·est** **1** : of or relating to bone **2** : like bone especially in hardness **3** : having bones and especially large or noticeable bones **4** : very thin

¹boo *interj* — used to express disapproval or to startle or frighten

²boo *n, pl* **boos** : a cry expressing disapproval

³boo *vb* **booed; boo·ing** : to express disapproval of with boos

boo·by trap *n* **1** : a hidden bomb that explodes when the object connected to it is touched **2** : a trap set for an unsuspecting person

boo·by-trap *vb* **boo·by-trapped; boo·by-trap·ping** : to set up as a booby trap

¹book *n* **1** : a set of sheets of paper bound together **2** : a long written work **3** : a large division of a written work **4** : a pack of small items bound together **5** : the records of a business's accounts — often used in pl.

²book *vb* **booked; book·ing** : to reserve for future use

book·case *n* : a set of shelves to hold books

book·end *n* : a support at the end of a row of books to keep them standing up

book·keep·er *n* : a person who keeps financial records for a business

book·keep·ing *n* : the work of keeping business records

book·let *n* : a little book usually having paper covers and few pages

book·mark *n* **1** : something placed in a book to show the page the reader wants to return

to **2** : something on a computer screen that serves as a shortcut (as to a Web site)

book·mo·bile *n* : a truck with shelves of books that is a traveling library

book·worm *n* : a person who reads a lot

¹boom *vb* **boomed; boom·ing** **1** : to make a deep, hollow and loud sound **2** : to increase or develop rapidly

²boom *n* **1** : a deep, hollow, and loud sound **2** : a rapid increase in activity or popularity

³boom *n* **1** : a long pole attached to the bottom of a sail **2** : a long beam sticking out from the mast of a derrick to support or guide something that is being lifted **3** : a long pole for holding a microphone

boom box *n* : a large portable radio and CD or tape player

boo·mer·ang *n* : a curved club that can be thrown so as to return to the thrower

boom·ing *adj* **1** : making a deep sound **2** : forcefully or powerfully done

boon *n* **1** : something asked or granted as a favor **2** : something pleasant or helpful that comes at just the right time

¹boost *vb* **boost·ed; boost·ing** **1** : to raise or push up from below **2** : to make bigger or greater — **boost·er** *n*

²boost *n* : a push up : an act of boosting

¹boot *n* : a covering usually of leather or rubber for the foot and part of the leg

²boot *vb* **boot·ed; boot·ing** : ¹KICK 1

boo·tee *or* **boo·tie** *n* : an infant's knitted sock

booth *n, pl* **booths** **1** : partly enclosed area or small building used for a particular purpose **2** : table in a restaurant between two benches with high backs

boo·ty *n* **1** : goods seized from an enemy in war or by robbery : PLUNDER **2** : a valuable gain or prize

¹bop *vb* **bopped; bop·ping** : ¹HIT 1

²bop *n* : ²HIT 1

¹bor·der *n* **1** : a boundary especially of a country or state **2** : the outer edge of something **3** : a decorative strip on or near the edge of something

²border *vb* **bor·dered; bor·der·ing** **1** : to put a border on **2** : to be close or next to

bor·der·line *adj* : not quite average, standard, or normal

¹bore *vb* **bored; bor·ing** **1** : to make a hole in especially with a drill **2** : to make by piercing or drilling — **bor·er** *n*

²bore *n* **1** : a hole made by boring **2** : a space (as in a gun barrel) shaped like a cylinder **3** : the diameter of a hole or cylinder

³bore *past of* BEAR

⁴bore *n* : an uninteresting person or thing

⁵bore *vb* **bored; bor·ing** : to make tired and restless by being uninteresting

bore·dom *n* : the state of being bored

bo·ric acid *n* : a weak acid containing boron used to kill germs

bor·ing *adj* : dull and uninteresting

born *adj* **1** : brought into life by birth **2** : brought into existence **3** : having a certain characteristic from or as if from birth

borne *past participle of* BEAR

bo·ron *n* : a powdery or hard solid chemical element that is used especially in making glass and detergents

bor·ough *n* **1** : a town, village, or part of a large city that has its own government **2** : one of the five political divisions of New York City

bor·row *vb* **bor·rowed; bor·row·ing 1** : to take and use something with the promise of returning it **2** : to use something begun or thought up by another : ADOPT **3** : to adopt into one language from another — **bor·row·er** *n*

¹bos·om *n* **1** : the front of the human chest **2** : the breasts of a woman

²bosom *adj* : very close

¹boss *n* **1** : the person at a job who tells workers what to do **2** : the head of a group (as a political organization)

²boss *vb* **bossed; boss·ing** : to give orders to

bossy *adj* **boss·i·er; boss·i·est** : liking to order people around

bo·tan·i·cal *adj* : of or relating to the study of plants

bot·a·nist *n* : a person specializing in botany

bot·a·ny *n* : a branch of biology dealing with plants

¹botch *vb* **botched; botch·ing** : to do clumsily and unskillfully : BUNGLE

²botch *n* : a badly done job

¹both *pron* : each one of two things or people : the two

²both *conj* — used before two words or phrases connected with *and* to stress that each is included

³both *adj* : the two

¹both·er *vb* **both·ered; both·er·ing 1** : to trouble (someone) in body or mind : ANNOY **2** : to cause to worry **3** : to take the time or trouble **4** : to intrude upon : INTERRUPT

²bother *n* **1** : someone or something that is annoying **2** : COMMOTION **3** : a state of worry or annoyance

both·er·some *adj* : ANNOYING

¹bot·tle *n* **1** : a container (as of glass or plastic) usually having a narrow neck and mouth and no handle **2** : the quantity held by a bottle

²bottle *vb* **bot·tled; bot·tling 1** : to put into a bottle **2** : to shut up as if in a bottle

bot·tle·neck *n* : a place or condition where improvement or movement is held up

bot·tom *n* **1** : the lowest part of something **2** : the under surface of something **3** : a supporting surface or part : BASE **4** : the lowest or worst level or position **5** : clothing that covers the lower part of the body **6** : the bed of a body of water **7** : low land along a river **8** : the most basic part **9** : the second half of an inning of baseball

bot·tom·less *adj* **1** : having no bottom **2** : very deep

bough *n* : a usually large or main branch of a tree

bought *past and past participle of* BUY

bouil·lon *n* : a clear soup or stock made from meat or vegetables

boul·der *n* : a very large rounded piece of rock

bou·le·vard *n* : a wide usually major street often having strips with trees, grass, or flowers planted along its center or sides

¹bounce *vb* **bounced; bounc·ing 1** : to spring back or up after hitting a surface **2** : to cause to spring back **3** : to jump or move up and down **4** : to leap suddenly

²bounce *n* **1** : the action of springing back after hitting something **2** : a sudden leap — **bouncy** *adj*

¹bound *adj* : going or intending to go

²bound *n* **1** : a boundary line **2** : a point or line beyond which a person or thing cannot go

³bound *past and past participle of* BIND

⁴bound *vb* **bound·ed; bound·ing** : to form the boundary of

⁵bound *adj* **1** : tied or fastened with or as if with bands **2** : required by law or duty **3** : under the control of something **4** : covered with binding **5** : firmly determined **6** : very likely : CERTAIN

⁶bound *n* : a leap or long jump

⁷bound *vb* **bounded; bounding** : to make a long leap or move in leaps

bound·ary *n, pl* **bound·aries** : something that points out or shows a limit or end : a dividing line

bound·less *adj* : having no limits

boun·te·ous *adj* **1** : GENEROUS 1 **2** : given in plenty : ABUNDANT

boun·ti·ful *adj* **1** : giving freely or generously **2** : PLENTIFUL 1

boun·ty *n, pl* **boun·ties 1** : GENEROSITY 1 **2** : things given in generous amounts **3** : money given as a reward

bou·quet *n* : a bunch of flowers

bout *n* **1** : a contest of skill or strength **2** : ²ATTACK 4, OUTBREAK

bou·tique *n* : a small fashionable shop

¹bow *vb* **bowed; bow·ing 1** : to bend the

head or body as an act of politeness or respect **2 :** to stop resisting : YIELD
²**bow** *n* **:** the act of bending the head or body
to express politeness or respect
³**bow** *n* **1 :** a weapon used for shooting arrows and usually made of a strip of wood
bent by a cord connecting the two ends **2**
: something shaped in a curve **3 :** a knot
made with one or more loops **4 :** a rod with
horsehairs stretched from end to end used
for playing a stringed instrument (as a
violin)
⁴**bow** *vb* **bowed; bow·ing :** to bend or cause
to bend into a curve
⁵**bow** *n* **:** the forward part of a ship
bow·el *n* **1 :** INTESTINE — usually used in pl.
2 : a part of the intestine
bow·er *n* **:** a shelter in a garden made of
boughs of trees or vines
¹**bowl** *n* **1 :** a round hollow dish without handles **2 :** the contents of a bowl **3 :** something in the shape of a bowl (as part of a
spoon or pipe)
²**bowl** *vb* **bowled; bowl·ing 1 :** to play a
game of bowling **2 :** to move rapidly and
smoothly — **bowl over 1 :** to hit and push
down while moving quickly **2 :** to surprise
or impress very much
bow·legged *adj* **:** having the legs bowed outward
bow·line *n* **:** a knot used for making a loop
that will not slip
bowl·ing *n* **:** a game in which large heavy
balls are rolled so as to knock down pins
bow·sprit *n* **:** a large spar sticking out forward from the bow of a ship
bow·string *n* **:** the cord connecting the two
ends of a bow
¹**box** *n* **:** an evergreen shrub or small tree used
for hedges
²**box** *n* **1 :** a container usually having four
sides, a bottom, and a cover **2 :** the contents
of a box **3 :** a four-sided shape on a piece of
paper or computer screen **4 :** an enclosed
place for one or more persons
³**box** *vb* **boxed; box·ing :** to enclose in or as
if in a box
⁴**box** *vb* **boxed; boxing :** to fight with the
fists
box·car *n* **:** a roofed freight car usually having sliding doors in the sides
box elder *n* **:** a North American maple with
leaves divided into several leaflets
¹**boxer** *n* **:** a person who engages in the sport
of boxing
²**boxer** *n* **:** a compact dog of German origin
that is of medium size with a square build
and has a short and often tan coat
box·ing *n* **:** the sport of fighting with the fists
box office *n* **:** a place where tickets to public

entertainments (as sports or theatrical
events) are sold
boy *n* **1 :** a male child from birth to young
manhood **2 :** SON **3 :** a male servant
¹**boy·cott** *vb* **boy·cot·ted; boy·cot·ting :** to
join with others in refusing to deal with
someone (as a person, organization, or
country) as a way of protesting or forcing
changes
²**boycott** *n* **:** the process or an instance of
joining with others in refusing to deal with
someone (as a person, organization, or
country) as a way of protesting or forcing
changes
boy·friend *n* **:** a man or boy involved in a romantic relationship
boy·hood *n* **:** the time or condition of being a
boy
boy·ish *adj* **:** relating to or having qualities
often felt to be typical of boys
Boy Scout *n* **:** a member of a scouting program (as the Boy Scouts of America)
bp *abbr* birthplace
Br. *abbr* **1** Britain **2** British
bra *n* **:** a woman's undergarment for breast
support
¹**brace** *vb* **braced; brac·ing 1 :** to make
strong, firm, or steady **2 :** to get ready
²**brace** *n* **1 :** something that adds strength or
support **2 brac·es** *pl* **:** a usually wire device
worn to correct the position of teeth **3 :** one
of a pair of marks { } used to connect words
or items to be considered together **4 :** two of
a kind **5 :** a tool with a U-shaped bend that
is used to turn wood-boring bits
brace·let *n* **:** a decorative band or chain usually worn on the wrist or arm
brack·en *n* **:** a large branching fern
¹**brack·et** *n* **1 :** a support for a weight (as a
shelf) that is usually attached to a wall **2**
: one of a pair of marks [ ] (**square brackets**) used to enclose letters or numbers or in
mathematics to enclose items to be treated
together **3 :** one of a pair of marks ⟨ ⟩
(**angle brackets**) used to enclose letters or
numbers **4 :** ¹GROUP 1, CATEGORY
²**bracket** *vb* **brack·et·ed; brack·et·ing 1 :** to
place within brackets **2 :** to put into the
same class : GROUP
brack·ish *adj* **:** somewhat salty
brad *n* **:** a thin nail with a small usually indented head
brag *vb* **bragged; brag·ging :** to speak in a
way that shows too much pride : BOAST —
brag·ger *n*
brag·gart *n* **:** a person who boasts a lot
¹**braid** *vb* **braid·ed; braid·ing :** to weave
three strands together
²**braid** *n* **:** a length of cord, ribbon, or hair

formed of three or more strands woven together

braille *n, often cap* : a system of printing for the blind in which the letters are represented by raised dots

¹brain *n* **1** : the part of the nervous system that is inside the skull, consists of grayish nerve cells and whitish nerve fibers, and is the organ of thought and the central control point for the nervous system **2** : the ability to think : INTELLIGENCE **3** : someone who is very smart

²brain *vb* **brained; brain·ing** : to hit on the head very hard

brain·storm *n* : a sudden inspiration or idea

brainy *adj* **brain·i·er; brain·i·est** : very smart

¹brake *n* : a device for slowing or stopping motion (as of a wheel) usually by friction

²brake *vb* **braked; brak·ing** : to slow or stop by using a brake

brake·man *n, pl* **brake·men** : a crew member on a train who inspects the train and helps the conductor

bram·ble *n* : a rough prickly bush or vine — usually used in pl.

bran *n* : the broken coat of the seed of cereal grain separated (as by sifting) from the flour or meal

¹branch *n* **1** : a part of a tree that grows out from the trunk or from a main division of the trunk **2** : something extending from a main line or body like a branch **3** : a division or subordinate part of something — **branched** *adj*

²branch *vb* **branched; branch·ing** : to spread or divide into smaller or attached parts : send out a branch

¹brand *n* **1** : a mark made by burning (as on cattle) or by stamping or printing (as on manufactured goods) to show ownership, maker, or quality **2** : a category of goods identified by a name as being made by a certain company **3** : TRADEMARK **4** : a particular type **5** : a mark of disgrace

²brand *vb* **brand·ed; brand·ing** **1** : put a mark on to show ownership **2** : to show or claim (something) to be bad or wrong

bran·dish *vb* **bran·dished; bran·dish·ing** : to wave or shake in a threatening manner

brand–new *adj* : completely new

bran·dy *n, pl* **brandies** : an alcoholic liquor made from wine or fruit juice

brass *n* **1** : an alloy made by combining copper and zinc **2** : the musical instruments of an orchestra or band that are usually made of brass and include the cornets, trumpets, trombones, French horns, and tubas

brat *n* : a naughty annoying child

¹brave *adj* **brav·er; brav·est** : feeling or showing no fear — **brave·ly** *adv*

²brave *vb* **braved; brav·ing** : to face or handle without fear

³brave *n* : an American Indian warrior

brav·ery *n* : COURAGE

¹brawl *vb* **brawled; brawl·ing** : to quarrel or fight noisily

²brawl *n* : a noisy quarrel or fight

brawn *n* : muscular strength

brawny *adj* **brawn·i·er; brawn·i·est** : having large strong muscles

¹bray *vb* **brayed; bray·ing** : to make the loud harsh cry of a donkey

²bray *n* : the loud harsh cry of a donkey

bra·zen *adj* **1** : made of brass **2** : sounding loud and usually harsh **3** : done or acting in a very bold and shocking way without shame

Bra·zil nut *n* : a dark three-sided nut with a white kernel

¹breach *n* **1** : a failure to act in a promised or required way **2** : an opening made by breaking

²breach *vb* **breached; breach·ing** **1** : to fail to do as promised or required by **2** : to make a break in

¹bread *n* **1** : a baked food made from flour or meal **2** : FOOD 1

²bread *vb* **bread·ed; bread·ing** : to cover with bread crumbs

breadth *n* **1** : distance measured from side to side **2** : SCOPE 2

¹break *vb* **broke; bro·ken; break·ing** **1** : to separate into parts especially suddenly or forcibly **2** : to cause (a bone) to separate into two or more pieces **3** : to stop working or cause to stop working because of damage or wear **4** : to fail to keep **5** : to force a way **6** : to cut into and turn over **7** : to go through : PENETRATE **8** : ²TAME 1 **9** : to do better than **10** : to interrupt or put an end to : STOP **11** : to reduce the force of **12** : to develop or burst out suddenly **13** : to make known **14** : SOLVE **15** : ¹CHANGE 4 **16** : to run or flee suddenly — **break down 1** : to stop working properly **2** : to separate or become separated into simpler substances : DECOMPOSE **3** : to be overcome by emotion **4** : to knock down — **break out 1** : to develop a skin rash **2** : to start up suddenly — **break up 1** : to separate into parts **2** : to bring or come to an end **3** : to end a romantic relationship

²break *n* **1** : an act of breaking **2** : something produced by breaking **3** : a period of time when an activity stops **4** : an accidental event

break·down *n* **1** : a failure to function properly **2** : a sudden failure of mental or physical health

brea·ker *n* **1** : a person or thing that breaks something **2** : a wave that breaks on shore

¹**break·fast** *n* : the first meal of the day

²**breakfast** *vb* **break·fast·ed; break·fast·ing** : to eat breakfast

break·neck *adj* : very fast or dangerous

break·through *n* : a sudden advance or successful development

break·wa·ter *n* : an offshore wall to protect a beach or a harbor from the sea

breast *n* **1** : either of the two enlarged soft parts on a woman's chest that contain a gland that produces milk when she has a baby **2** : the front part of the body between the neck and the stomach **3** : the front part of a bird's body below the neck — **breast·ed** *adj*

breast·bone *n* : a flat narrow bone in the middle of the chest to which the ribs are connected

breast-feed *vb* **breast-fed; breast-feed·ing** : to feed (a baby) from a mother's breast

breast·plate *n* : a piece of armor for covering the breast

breast·work *n* : a wall thrown together to serve as a defense in battle

breath *n* **1** : ability to breathe : ease of breathing **2** : air taken in or sent out by the lungs **3** : a slight breeze — **out of breath** : breathing very rapidly as a result of hard exercise — **under someone's breath** : very quietly

breathe *vb* **breathed; breath·ing** **1** : to draw air into and expel it from the lungs **2** : to take in by inhaling **3** : ¹LIVE 1 **4** : ¹SAY 1, UTTER

breath·er *n* : a pause for rest

breath·less *adj* **1** : panting from exertion **2** : filled with excitement or tension — **breath·less·ly** *adv*

breath·tak·ing *adj* : very exciting or beautiful

breech·es *n pl* **1** : short pants fastening below the knee **2** : PANTS

¹**breed** *vb* **bred ; breed·ing** **1** : to produce or increase (animals or plants) by sexual reproduction **2** : to produce offspring by sexual reproduction **3** : to bring up : TRAIN **4** : to bring about : CAUSE — **breed·er** *n*

²**breed** *n* **1** : a kind of animal or plant that is found only under human care and is different from related kinds **2** : ¹CLASS 6, KIND

breed·ing *n* : training especially in manners

breeze *n* **1** : a gentle wind **2** : something that is easy to do

breezy *adj* **breez·i·er; breez·i·est** **1** : somewhat windy **2** : lively and somewhat carefree — **breez·i·ly** *adv*

breth·ren *pl of* BROTHER — used chiefly in formal situations

breve *n* : a mark ˘ placed over a vowel to show that the vowel is short

brev·i·ty *n* : the condition of being short or brief

¹**brew** *vb* **brewed; brew·ing** **1** : to make (beer) from water, malt, and hops **2** : to prepare by soaking in hot water **3** : ²PLAN 2 **4** : to start to form — **brew·er** *n*

²**brew** *n* : something made by brewing

brew·ery *n, pl* **brew·er·ies** : a place where malt liquors are brewed

bri·ar *also* **bri·er** *n* : a plant (as the rose or blackberry) with a thorny or prickly stem

¹**bribe** *n* : something given or promised to a person in order to influence dishonestly a decision or action

²**bribe** *vb* **bribed; brib·ing** : to influence or try to influence dishonestly by giving or promising something

brib·ery *n, pl* **brib·er·ies** : the act of giving or taking a bribe

¹**brick** *n* **1** : a building or paving material made from clay molded into blocks and baked **2** : a block made of brick

²**brick** *vb* **bricked; brick·ing** : to close, face, or pave with bricks

brick·lay·er *n* : a person who builds or paves with bricks

brid·al *adj* : of or relating to a bride or a wedding

bride *n* : a woman just married or about to be married

bride·groom *n* : a man just married or about to be married

brides·maid *n* : a woman who attends a bride at her wedding

¹**bridge** *n* **1** : a structure built over something (as water, a low place, or a railroad) so people can cross **2** : the place on a ship where the ship is steered **3** : something that joins or connects : something like a bridge

²**bridge** *vb* **bridged; bridg·ing** : to make a bridge over or across

³**bridge** *n* : a card game for four players in two teams

¹**bri·dle** *n* : a device for controlling a horse made up of a set of straps enclosing the head, a bit, and a pair of reins

²**bridle** *vb* **bri·dled; bri·dling** **1** : to put a bridle on **2** : RESTRAIN 2 **3** : to hold the head high and draw in the chin as an expression of resentment

¹**brief** *adj* **brief·er; brief·est** : not very long : SHORT — **brief·ly** *adv*

²**brief** *vb* **briefed; brief·ing** : to give information or instructions to

brief·case *n* : a flat case for carrying papers or books

briefs *n pl* : short snug underpants

brier *variant of* BRIAR

brig *n* : a square-rigged sailing ship with two masts

bri·gade *n* **1** : a body of soldiers consisting of two or more regiments **2** : a group of persons organized for acting together

brig·a·dier general *n* : a commissioned officer in the army, air force, or marine corps ranking above a colonel

bright *adj* **1** : giving off or filled with much light **2** : very clear or vivid in color **3** : INTELLIGENT 1, CLEVER **4** : CHEERFUL 1 **5** : likely to be good — **bright·ly** *adv* — **bright·ness** *n*

bright·en *vb* **bright·ened; bright·en·ing 1** : to add more light to **2** : to make or become cheerful

bril·liance *n* : great brightness

bril·liant *adj* **1** : flashing with light : very bright **2** : very impressive **3** : very smart or clever — **bril·liant·ly** *adv*

¹brim *n* **1** : the edge or rim of something hollow **2** : the part of a hat that sticks out around the lower edge

²brim *vb* **brimmed; brim·ming** : to be or become full to overflowing

brin·dled *adj* : having dark streaks or spots on a gray or brownish background

brine *n* **1** : a mixture of salty water used especially to preserve or season food **2** : the salty water of the ocean

bring *vb* **brought ; bring·ing 1** : to cause to come by carrying or leading : take along **2** : to cause to reach a certain state or take a certain action **3** : to cause to arrive or exist **4** : to sell for — **bring·er** *n* — **bring about** : to cause to happen — **bring back** : to cause to return to a person's memory — **bring forth** : to cause to happen or exist : PRODUCE — **bring on** : to cause to happen to — **bring out 1** : to produce and make available **2** : to cause to appear — **bring to** : to bring back from unconsciousness : REVIVE — **bring up 1** : to bring to maturity through care and education **2** : to mention when talking

brink *n* **1** : the edge at the top of a steep place **2** : a point of beginning

briny *adj* **brin·i·er; brin·i·est** : SALTY

brisk *adj* **1** : done or spoken with quickness and energy **2** : quick and efficient **3** : very refreshing — **brisk·ly** *adv*

¹bris·tle *n* **1** : a short stiff hair **2** : a stiff hair or something like a hair fastened in a brush

²bristle *vb* **bris·tled; bris·tling 1** : to rise up and stiffen like bristles **2** : to show signs of anger **3** : to be covered with

bris·tly *adj* **bris·tli·er; bris·tli·est** : of, like, or having many bristles

Brit. *abbr* **1** Britain **2** British

britch·es *n pl* **1** : BREECHES 1 **2** : PANTS

¹Brit·ish *adj* : of or relating to Great Britain (England, Scotland, and Wales) or the British

²British *n pl* : the people of Great Britain

brit·tle *adj* **brit·tler; brit·tlest** : hard but easily broken — **brit·tle·ness** *n*

bro *abbr* brother

broach *vb* **broached; broach·ing** : to bring up as a subject for discussion

broad *adj* **broad·er; broad·est 1** : not narrow : WIDE **2** : extending far and wide : SPACIOUS **3** : ¹COMPLETE 1, FULL **4** : not limited **5** : covering only the main points : GENERAL — **broad·ly** *adv*

¹broad·cast *vb* **broadcast; broad·cast·ing 1** : to send out by radio or television from a transmitting station **2** : to make widely known **3** : to scatter far and wide — **broad·cast·er** *n*

²broadcast *n* **1** : an act of broadcasting **2** : a radio or television program

broad·cloth *n* : a fine cloth with a firm smooth surface

broad·en *vb* **broad·ened; broad·en·ing** : to make or become wide or wider

broad–mind·ed *adj* : willing to consider unusual or different opinions, beliefs, and practices

¹broad·side *n* **1** : the part of a ship's side above the waterline **2** : a firing of all of the guns that are on the same side of a ship

²broadside *adv* **1** : with one side forward **2** : from the side

broad·sword *n* : a sword having a broad blade

bro·cade *n* : a cloth with a raised design woven into it — **bro·cad·ed** *adj*

broc·co·li *n* : a vegetable that has green stalks and green or purplish clustered flower buds

brogue *n* : an Irish or Scottish accent

broil *vb* **broiled; broil·ing 1** : to cook or be cooked directly over or under a heat source **2** : to make or feel extremely hot

broil·er *n* : a young chicken suitable for broiling

¹broke *past of* BREAK

²broke *adj* : having no money

¹broken *past participle of* BREAK

²bro·ken *adj* **1** : separated into parts or pieces **2** : not working properly **3** : having gaps or breaks **4** : not kept or followed **5** : imperfectly spoken

bro·ken·heart·ed *adj* : very sad

bro·ker *n* : a person who acts as an agent for others in the buying or selling of property

bro·mine *n* : a chemical element that is a deep red liquid giving off an irritating smelly vapor

bron·chi·al *adj* : of or relating to either of the

two branches (**bronchial tubes**) of the trachea that carry air into the lungs

bron·chi·tis *n* : a sore raw state of the bronchial tubes

bron·co *n, pl* **bron·cos** : MUSTANG

bron·to·sau·rus *n* : a huge plant-eating dinosaur with a long neck and tail and four thick legs

¹bronze *n* **1** : an alloy of copper and tin and sometimes other elements **2** : a yellowish brown color **3** : a medal made of bronze given to the third place winner in a competition

²bronze *adj* **1** : made of bronze **2** : having a yellowish brown color

brooch *n* : a piece of jewelry fastened to clothing with a pin

¹brood *vb* **brood·ed; brood·ing** **1** : to sit on eggs to hatch them **2** : to cover (young) with the wings for warmth and protection **3** : to think long and anxiously about something

²brood *n* **1** : the young of birds hatched at the same time **2** : a group of young children or animals having the same mother

brood·er *n* : a building or a compartment that can be heated and is used for raising young fowl

brook *n* : a small stream

broom *n* **1** : a brush with a long handle used for sweeping **2** : a plant with long slender branches along which grow many yellow flowers

broom·stick *n* : the handle of a broom

bros *abbr* brothers

broth *n* : the liquid in which a meat, fish, or vegetable has been cooked

broth·er *n, pl* **brothers** *also* **breth·ren** **1** : a male person or animal related to another person or animal by having one or both parents in common **2** : a fellow member of an organization

broth·er·hood *n* **1** : the state of being a brother **2** : a group of people who are engaged in the same business or have a similar interest **3** : feelings of friendship, support, and understanding between people

broth·er–in–law *n, pl* **broth·ers–in–law** **1** : the brother of a person's husband or wife **2** : the husband of a person's sister

broth·er·ly *adj* **1** : of or relating to brothers **2** : ¹KINDLY 1, AFFECTIONATE

brought *past and past participle of* BRING

brow *n* **1** : EYEBROW **2** : FOREHEAD **3** : the upper edge of a steep slope

¹brown *adj* **1** : of the color of coffee : colored brown **2** : having a dark or tanned complexion

²brown *n* : a color like that of coffee or chocolate — **brown·ish** *adj*

³brown *vb* **browned; brown·ing** : to make or become brown

brown·ie *n* **1** : a small square piece of chewy chocolate cake **2** *cap* : a member of a program of the Girl Scouts for girls in the first through third grades in school **3** : a cheerful elf believed to perform helpful services at night

brown sugar *n* : sugar that contains molasses

browse *vb* **browsed; brows·ing** **1** : to read or look in a casual way **2** : to nibble young shoots and foliage

brows·er *n* **1** : a person or animal that browses **2** : a computer program providing access to sites on the World Wide Web

bru·in *n* : ¹BEAR 1

¹bruise *vb* **bruised; bruis·ing** : to injure the flesh (as by a blow) without breaking the skin

²bruise *n* : a black-and-blue spot on the body or a dark spot on fruit caused by an injury or damage

brunch *n* : a meal that combines breakfast and lunch and is usually eaten in late morning

bru·net *or* **bru·nette** *adj* : having dark brown or black hair and dark eyes — spelled *brunet* when used of a boy or man and usually *brunette* when used of a girl or woman — **brunet** *or* **brunette** *n*

brunt *n* : the main force or stress (as of an attack)

¹brush *n* **1** : a tool made of bristles set in a handle and used for cleaning, smoothing, or painting **2** : an act of smoothing or scrubbing with a brush **3** : a light stroke **4** : a bushy tail

²brush *vb* **brushed; brush·ing** **1** : to scrub or smooth with a brush **2** : to remove with or as if with a brush **3** : to pass lightly across

³brush *n* **1** : branches and twigs cut from trees **2** : a heavy growth of small trees and bushes

⁴brush *n* : a brief fight or quarrel

brush·wood *n* : ³BRUSH

brusque *adj* : so abrupt and frank in manner or speech as to be impolite — **brusque·ly** *adj* — **brusque·ness** *n*

brus·sels sprouts *n pl, often cap B* : small leafy heads resembling tiny cabbages and eaten as a vegetable

bru·tal *adj* : cruel and harsh — **bru·tal·ly** *adv*

bru·tal·i·ty *n, pl* **bru·tal·i·ties** **1** : the quality of being cruel and harsh **2** : a cruel and harsh act or course of action

¹brute *adj* : typical of beasts : like that of a beast

²brute *n* **1** : a four-footed animal especially when wild **2** : a cruel or rough person

brut·ish *adj* : being unfeeling and stupid

BSA *abbr* Boy Scouts of America

BTW *abbr* by the way

bu. *abbr* bushel

¹**bub·ble** *n* 1 : a tiny round body of air or gas in a liquid 2 : a round body of air within a solid 3 : a thin film of liquid filled with air or gas — **bub·bly** *adj*

²**bubble** *vb* **bub·bled; bub·bling** 1 : to form or produce bubbles 2 : to flow with a gurgle

bu·bon·ic plague *n* : a dangerous disease which is spread by rats and in which fever, weakness, and swollen lymph nodes are present

buc·ca·neer *n* : PIRATE

¹**buck** *n* 1 : the male of an animal (as a deer or rabbit) the female of which is called *doe* 2 : DOLLAR 3 : ¹MAN 1, FELLOW

²**buck** *vb* **bucked; buck·ing** 1 : to spring or jump upward with head down and back arched 2 : to charge or push against 3 : to go against : OPPOSE — **buck up** : to become more confident

buck·board *n* : a lightweight carriage with four wheels that has a seat supported by a springy platform

buck·et *n* 1 : a usually round container with a handle for holding or carrying liquids or solids 2 : a large container that is part of a machine and is used for collecting, scooping, or carrying 3 : BUCKETFUL

buck·et·ful *n, pl* **buck·et·fuls** *or* **buck·ets·ful** 1 : as much as a bucket will hold 2 : a large quantity

buck·eye *n* : a tree with showy clusters of flowers and large brown inedible nutlike seeds

¹**buck·le** *n* : a fastening device which is attached to one end of a belt or strap and through which the other end is passed and held

²**buckle** *vb* **buck·led; buck·ling** 1 : to fasten with a buckle 2 : to start to work hard — usually used with *down* 3 : to bend, crumple, or give way

buck·skin *n* : a soft flexible leather usually having a suede finish

buck·wheat *n* : a plant with pinkish white flowers that is grown for its dark triangular seeds which are used as a cereal grain

¹**bud** *n* 1 : a small growth at the tip or on the side of a stem that later develops into a flower, leaf, or branch 2 : a flower that has not fully opened 3 : an early stage of development

²**bud** *vb* **bud·ded; bud·ding** 1 : to form or put forth a small growth that develops into a flower, leaf, or branch 2 : to reproduce by asexual means by forming a small growth that pinches off and develops into a new organism

Bud·dha *n* 1 : the founder of Buddhism originally known as Siddhartha Gautama 2 : a statue that represents Buddha

Bud·dhism *n* : a religion of eastern and central Asia based on the teachings of Gautama Buddha — **Bud·dhist** *n*

bud·dy *n, pl* **buddies** : a close friend

budge *vb* **budged; budg·ing** 1 : to move or cause to move especially slightly 2 : to give in

¹**bud·get** *n* 1 : a statement of estimated income and expenses for a period of time 2 : a plan for using money

²**budget** *vb* **bud·get·ed; bud·get·ing** 1 : to include in a plan for using money 2 : to plan for efficient use

¹**buff** *n* 1 : a pale orange yellow 2 : a stick or wheel with a soft surface for applying polish 3 : ³FAN

²**buff** *vb* **buffed; buff·ing** : to polish with or as if with a buff

buf·fa·lo *n, pl* **buffalo** *or* **buf·fa·loes** : any of several wild oxen and especially the American bison

buffalo wing *n* : a deep-fried chicken wing coated with a spicy sauce and usually served with blue cheese dressing

¹**buf·fet** *vb* **buf·fet·ed; buf·fet·ing** : to pound repeatedly : BATTER

²**buf·fet** *n* 1 : a cabinet or set of shelves for the display of dishes and silver : SIDEBOARD 2 : a meal set out on a buffet or table from which people may serve themselves

buf·foon *n* : a foolish or stupid person

¹**bug** *n* 1 : any of a large group of insects that have four wings, suck liquid food (as plant juices or blood), and have young which resemble the adults but lack wings 2 : an insect or other small creeping or crawling animal 3 : FLAW

²**bug** *vb* **bugged; bug·ging** 1 : ¹BOTHER 1, ANNOY 2 : to stick out — often used with *out*

bug·gy *n, pl* **buggies** : a light carriage with a single seat that is usually drawn by one horse

bu·gle *n* : an instrument like a simple trumpet used chiefly for giving military signals

¹**build** *vb* **built** ; **build·ing** 1 : to make by putting together parts or materials 2 : to produce or create gradually by effort 3 : to grow or increase to a high point or level

²**build** *n* : the shape and size of a person's or animal's body

build·er *n* : a person whose business is the construction of buildings

build·ing *n* 1 : a permanent structure built as a dwelling, shelter, or place for human activities or for storage **2** : the art, work, or business of assembling materials into a structure

built–in *adj* : forming a permanent part of a structure

bulb *n* **1** : LIGHT BULB **2** : a resting stage of a plant that is formed underground and consists of a very short stem with one or more flower buds surrounded by special thick leaves **3** : a plant structure (as a tuber) that is somewhat like a bulb **4** : a rounded object or part

bul·bous *adj* : round or swollen

¹**bulge** *vb* **bulged; bulg·ing** : to swell or curve outward

²**bulge** *n* : a swelling part : a part that sticks out

bulk *n* **1** : greatness of size or volume **2** : the largest or chief part — **in bulk** : in large amounts

bulk·head *n* : a wall separating sections in a ship

bulky *adj* **bulk·i·er; bulk·i·est 1** : great in size or volume **2** : being large and awkward to handle

bull *n* : an adult male ox or an adult male of certain other large animals (as the elephant and the whale)

bull·dog *n* : a dog of English origin with short hair and a stocky powerful build

bull·doz·er *n* : a motor vehicle with tracks instead of tires and a large wide blade for pushing (as in clearing land of trees)

bul·let *n* : a small piece of metal made to be shot from a firearm

bul·le·tin *n* : a short public notice usually coming from an informed or official source

bulletin board *n* : a board for posting bulletins and announcements

bul·let·proof *adj* : made to stop bullets from going through

bull·fight *n* : a public entertainment popular especially in Spain in which a person (**bullfight·er**) displays skill in escaping the charges of a bull and usually finally kills it with a sword

bull·finch *n* : a European songbird that has a thick bill and a red breast

bull·frog *n* : a large heavy frog that makes a booming or bellowing sound

bull·head *n* : any of various fishes with large heads

bul·lion *n* : gold or silver metal in bars or blocks

bull·ock *n* **1** : a young bull **2** : ¹STEER

bull's–eye *n* **1** : the center of a target **2** : a shot that hits the center of a target

¹**bul·ly** *n, pl* **bul·lies** : a person who teases, hurts, or threatens smaller or weaker persons

²**bully** *vb* **bul·lied; bul·ly·ing** : to tease, hurt,

or threaten a smaller or weaker person : to act like a bully toward

bul·rush *n* : any of several large rushes or sedges that grow in wet places

bul·wark *n* **1** : a solid structure like a wall built for defense against an enemy **2** : something that defends or protects

¹**bum** *n* **1** : a person who avoids work **2** : ²TRAMP 1, HOBO

²**bum** *vb* **bummed; bum·ming** : to obtain by asking or begging

bum·ble *vb* **bum·bled; bum·bling** : to act, move, or speak in a clumsy way

bum·ble·bee *n* : a large hairy bee that makes a loud humming sound

¹**bump** *n* **1** : a rounded swelling of flesh as from an injury **2** : a small raised area on a surface **3** : a sudden heavy impact or jolt

²**bump** *vb* **bumped; bump·ing 1** : to strike or knock against something **2** : to move along unevenly : JOLT

¹**bump·er** *n* : a bar across the front or back of a motor vehicle intended to lessen shock or damage from collision

²**bum·per** *adj* : larger or finer than usual

bumpy *adj* **bump·i·er; bump·i·est 1** : having or covered with bumps **2** : having sudden up-and-down movements

bun *n* : a sweet or plain round roll

¹**bunch** *n* **1** : a number of things of the same kind growing together **2** : ¹GROUP 1

²**bunch** *vb* **bunched; bunch·ing** : to gather in a bunch

¹**bun·dle** *n* : a number of things fastened or wrapped together : PACKAGE

²**bundle** *vb* **bun·dled; bun·dling 1** to fasten, tie, or wrap a group of things together **2** : to move or push into or out of a place quickly — **bundle up** : to dress warmly

bung *n* : a stopper that closes or covers a hole in a barrel

bun·ga·low *n* : a house with a main level and a smaller second level above

bun·gle *vb* **bun·gled; bun·gling** : to act, do, make, or work badly — **bun·gler** *n*

bun·ion *n* : a sore reddened swelling of the first joint of a big toe

¹**bunk** *n* **1** : BUNK BED **2** : a built-in bed (as on a ship or train) **3** : a sleeping place

²**bunk** *vb* **bunked; bunk·ing** : to stay overnight

bunk bed *n* : one of two single beds usually placed one above the other

bun·ny *n, pl* **bunnies** : RABBIT

bunt *vb* **bunt·ed; bunt·ing** : to hit a baseball lightly so that the ball rolls for a short distance — **bunt** *n*

¹**bun·ting** *n* : a bird similar to a sparrow in size and habits but having a stout bill

²bunting *n* : flags or decorations made of a thin cloth

¹buoy *n* **1** : a floating object anchored in a body of water to mark a channel or to warn of danger **2** : LIFE BUOY

²buoy *vb* **buoyed; buoy·ing 1** : to keep from sinking : keep afloat **2** : to brighten the mood of

buoy·an·cy *n* **1** : the power of rising and floating (as on water or in air) **2** : the power of a liquid to hold up a floating body

buoy·ant *adj* **1** : able to rise and float in the air or on the top of a liquid **2** : able to keep a body afloat **3** : LIGHTHEARTED, CHEERFUL

bur *or* **burr** *n* : a rough or prickly covering or shell of a seed or fruit

¹bur·den *n* **1** : something carried : LOAD **2** : something that is hard to take **3** : the capacity of a ship for carrying cargo

²burden *vb* **bur·dened; bur·den·ing 1** : to have a heavy load or put a heavy load on **2** : to cause to have or deal with

bur·den·some *adj* : so heavy or hard to take as to be a burden

bur·dock *n* : a tall weed related to the thistles that has prickly purplish heads of flowers

bu·reau *n* **1** : a low chest of drawers for use in a bedroom **2** : a division of a government department **3** : a business office that provides services

bur·ger *n* **1** : HAMBURGER 1 **2** : a sandwich like a hamburger

bur·glar *n* : a person who commits burglary

bur·glary *n, pl* **bur·glar·ies** : the act of breaking into a building especially at night with the intent to commit a crime (as theft)

buri·al *n* : the act of placing a dead body in a grave or tomb

bur·lap *n* : a rough cloth made usually from jute or hemp and used mostly for bags

bur·ly *adj* **bur·li·er; bur·li·est** : strongly and heavily built

¹burn *vb* **burned** *or* **burnt** ; **burn·ing 1** : to be on fire or to set on fire **2** : to destroy or be destroyed by fire or heat **3** : to make or produce by fire or heat **4** : to give light **5** : to injure or affect by or as if by fire or heat **6** : to ruin by cooking too long or with too much heat **7** : to feel or cause to feel as if on fire **8** : to feel a strong emotion **9** : to record music or data on a computer disk **10** : to get a sunburn

²burn *n* : an injury produced by burning or by something rubbing away the skin

burn·er *n* : the part of a stove or furnace where the flame or heat is produced

bur·nish *vb* **bur·nished; bur·nish·ing** : to make shiny

¹burp *vb* **burped; burp·ing 1** : ¹BELCH 1 **2** : to help (a baby) let out gas from the stomach especially by patting or rubbing the baby's back

²burp *n* : ²BELCH

burr *variant of* BUR

bur·ro *n, pl* **burros** : a small donkey often used to carry loads

¹bur·row *n* : a hole in the ground made by an animal (as a rabbit or fox) for shelter or protection

²burrow *vb* **bur·rowed; bur·row·ing 1** : to hide in or as if in a burrow **2** : to make a burrow **3** : to proceed by or as if by digging

¹burst *vb* **burst; burst·ing 1** : to break open or in pieces (as by an explosion from within) **2** : to suddenly show one's feelings **3** : to come or go suddenly **4** : to be filled to the maximum

²burst *n* : a sudden release or effort

bury *vb* **bur·ied; bury·ing 1** : to place in the ground and cover over for concealment **2** : to put (a dead body) in a grave or tomb **3** : to cover with something **4** : to cover up : HIDE

bus *n, pl* **bus·es** *or* **bus·ses** : a large motor vehicle for carrying passengers

bus·boy *n* : a person hired by a restaurant to clear and set tables

bush *n* **1** : a usually low shrub with many branches **2** : a stretch of uncleared or lightly settled country

bush·el *n* : a unit of measure (as of grain, produce, or seafood) equal to four pecks or 32 quarts (about 35 liters)

bushy *adj* **bush·i·er; bush·i·est 1** : being thick and spreading **2** : overgrown with bushes

busi·ness *n* **1** : the activity of making, buying, and selling goods or services **2** : a commercial enterprise **3** : the normal activity of a person or group **4** : personal concerns **5** : ¹MATTER 1

busi·ness·man *n, pl* **busi·ness·men** : a man in business especially as an owner or a manager

busi·ness·wom·an *n, pl* **busi·ness·wom·en** : a woman in business especially as an owner or a manager

¹bust *n* **1** : a piece of sculpture representing the upper part of the human figure including the head and neck **2** : a woman's bosom

²bust *vb* **bust·ed; bust·ing 1** : to hit with the fist **2** : ¹BREAK 1

¹bus·tle *vb* **bus·tled; bus·tling** : to move about in a busy or noisy way

²bustle *n* : busy or noisy activity

¹busy *adj* **busi·er; busi·est 1** : actively at work **2** : being used **3** : full of activity — **busi·ly** *adv*

²busy *vb* **bus·ied; busy·ing** : to make busy

busy·body *n, pl* **busy·bod·ies** : a person who is too interested in the affairs of other people

¹but *conj* **1** : yet nevertheless **2** : while just the opposite **3** : except that : UNLESS

²but *prep* : other than : EXCEPT

³but *adv* : ²ONLY 1

¹**butch·er** *n* **1** : a person whose business is killing animals for sale as food **2** : a dealer in meat **3** : a person who kills in large numbers or in a brutal manner

²**butcher** *vb* **butch·ered; butch·er·ing 1** : to kill and prepare (an animal) for food **2** : ²MASSACRE **3** : to make a mess of : BOTCH

but·ler *n* : the chief male servant of a household

¹**butt** *n* : a target of ridicule or hurtful humor

²**butt** *n* **1** : the part of the body on which a person sits **2** : the thicker or bottom end of something **3** : an unused remainder

³**butt** *vb* **butt·ed; butt·ing** : to strike or thrust with the head or horns — **butt in** : to intrude on someone else's activity or conversation

⁴**butt** *n* : a blow or thrust with the head or horns

butte *n* : an isolated hill with steep sides

¹**but·ter** *n* **1** : a solid yellowish fatty food obtained from cream or milk by churning **2** : a spreadable food made of cooked and crushed nuts or fruit

²**butter** *vb* **but·tered; but·ter·ing** : to spread with or as if with butter

but·ter·cup *n* : a common wildflower with bright yellow blossoms

but·ter·fat *n* : the natural fat of milk that is the chief ingredient of butter

but·ter·fly *n, pl* **but·ter·flies** : an insect that has a slender body and large colored wings covered with tiny overlapping scales and that flies mostly in the daytime

but·ter·milk *n* : the liquid left after churning butter from milk or cream

but·ter·nut *n* : an eastern North American tree that has sweet egg-shaped nuts and is related to the walnuts

but·ter·scotch *n* : a candy made from sugar, corn syrup, and water

but·tock *n* **1** : the back of the hip which forms one of the rounded parts on which a person sits **2 buttocks** *pl* : RUMP 1

¹**but·ton** *n* **1** : a small ball or disk used for holding parts of a garment together or as an ornament **2** : a small often round part of a machine that makes the machine do something when pushed

²**button** *vb* **but·toned; but·ton·ing** : to close or fasten with buttons

but·ton·hole *n* : a slit or loop for fastening a button

but·ton·wood *n* : SYCAMORE 2

¹**but·tress** *n* **1** : a structure built against a wall or building to give support and strength **2** : something that supports, props, or strengthens

²**buttress** *vb* **but·tressed; but·tress·ing** : to support or strengthen : to support with or as if with a buttress

bux·om *adj* : having a healthy plump form

¹**buy** *vb* **bought** ; **buy·ing** : to get by paying for : PURCHASE — **buy·er** *n*

²**buy** *n* : ¹BARGAIN 2

¹**buzz** *vb* **buzzed; buzz·ing 1** : to make a low humming sound like that of bees **2** : to be filled with a low hum or murmur **3** : to fly an airplane low over

²**buzz** *n* : a low humming sound

buz·zard *n* : a usually large bird of prey that flies slowly

buzz·er *n* : an electric signaling device that makes a buzzing sound

¹**by** *prep* **1** : close to : NEAR **2** : so as to go on **3** : so as to go through **4** : so as to pass **5** : AT 1, DURING **6** : no later than **7** : with the use or help of **8** : through the action of **9** : ACCORDING TO 1 **10** : with respect to **11** : to the amount of **12** — used to join two or more measurements or to join the numbers in a statement of multiplication or division

²**by** *adv* **1** : near at hand **2** : ⁴PAST — **by and by** : after a while

¹**by·gone** *adj* : gone by : PAST

²**by·gone** *n* : an event that is over and done with

¹**by·pass** *n* : a road serving as a substitute route around a blocked or crowded area

²**bypass** *vb* **by·passed; by·pass·ing 1** : to make a detour around **2** : AVOID 1, FORGO

by–prod·uct *n* : something produced (as in manufacturing) in addition to the main product

by·stand·er *n* : a person present or standing near but taking no part in what is going on

byte *n* : a group of eight bits that a computer handles as a unit

by·way *n* : a road that is not used very much

C

c *n, pl* **c's** *or* **cs** *often cap* **1** : the third letter of the English alphabet **2** : the number 100 in Roman numerals **3** : a musical note referred to by the letter C **4** : a grade that shows a student's work is fair or average

c. *abbr* **1** carat **2** cent **3** centimeter **4** century **5** chapter **6** cup

C *abbr* **1** Celsius **2** centigrade

CA *abbr* California

cab *n* **1** : a light closed carriage pulled by a

horse **2** : TAXICAB **3** : the covered compartment for the engineer and the controls of a locomotive or for the operator of a truck, tractor, or crane

ca·bana *n* : a shelter usually with an open side used by people at a beach or swimming pool

cab·bage *n* : a garden plant related to the turnips that has a round firm head of leaves used as a vegetable

cab·in *n* **1** : a small simple dwelling usually having only one story **2** : a private room on a ship **3** : a place below deck on a small boat for passengers or crew **4** : a part of an airplane for cargo, crew, or passengers

cab·i·net *n* **1** : a case or cupboard with shelves or drawers for storing or displaying things **2** : a group of people who act as advisers (as to the head of a country)

¹ca·ble *n* **1** : a very strong rope, wire, or chain **2** : a bundle of wires to carry electric current **3** : TELEGRAM **4** : CABLE TELEVISION

²cable *vb* **ca·bled; ca·bling** : to send a message by telegraph

cable television *n* : a television system in which paying customers receive the television signals over electrical wires

ca·boose *n* : a car usually at the rear of a freight train for the use of the train crew

ca·cao *n, pl* **cacaos** : a South American tree with fleshy yellow pods that contain fatty seeds from which chocolate is made

¹cache *n* **1** : a place for hiding, storing, or preserving treasure or supplies **2** : something hidden or stored in a cache

²cache *vb* **cached; cach·ing** : to put or store so as to be safe or hidden : place in a cache

¹cack·le *vb* **cack·led; cack·ling** **1** : to make the noise or cry a hen makes especially after laying an egg **2** : to laugh or chatter noisily

²cackle *n* : a sound made by a hen or like that made by a hen

cac·tus *n, pl* **cac·ti** *or* **cac·tus·es** : any of a large group of flowering plants of dry regions that have thick juicy stems and branches with scales or spines

ca·dav·er *n* : CORPSE

¹cad·die *or* **cad·dy** *n, pl* **cad·dies** : a person who carries a golfer's clubs

²caddie *or* **caddy** *vb* **cad·died; cad·dy·ing** : to carry a golfer's clubs

cad·dis fly *n* : an insect that has four wings and a larva which lives in water in a silk case covered especially with bits of wood, gravel, sand, or plant matter

ca·dence *n* : a regular beat or rhythm

ca·det *n* : a student in a military school or college

ca·fé *also* **ca·fe** *n* : a small restaurant serving usually simple meals

caf·e·te·ria *n* : a place where people get food at a counter and carry it to a table for eating

caf·feine *n* : a substance found especially in coffee and tea that makes a person feel more awake

¹cage *n* **1** : a box or enclosure that has large openings covered usually with wire net or bars and is used for keeping birds or animals **2** : an enclosure like a cage in shape or purpose

²cage *vb* **caged; cag·ing** : to put or keep in or as if in a cage

ca·gey *adj* **ca·gi·er; ca·gi·est** **1** : unwilling to act or speak in a direct or open way **2** : clever in a tricky way

ca·hoot *n* : a secret partnership — usually used in pl.

ca·jole *vb* **ca·joled; ca·jol·ing** : to coax or persuade especially by flattery or false promises

¹cake *n* **1** : a baked food made from a sweet batter or dough **2** : a usually flat round piece of food that is baked or fried **3** : a substance hardened or molded into a solid piece

²cake *vb* **caked; cak·ing** **1** : ENCRUST **2** : to become dry and hard

Cal. *abbr* California

cal·a·mine *n* : a skin lotion used especially to reduce itching (as from an insect bite or poison ivy)

ca·lam·i·ty *n, pl* **ca·lam·i·ties** **1** : great distress or misfortune **2** : an event that causes great harm and suffering : DISASTER — **ca·lam·i·tous** *adj*

cal·ci·um *n* : a silvery soft metallic chemical element that is essential for strong healthy bones

calcium carbonate *n* : a solid substance that is found as limestone and marble and in plant ashes, bones, and shells

cal·cu·late *vb* **cal·cu·lat·ed; cal·cu·lat·ing** **1** : to find by adding, subtracting, multiplying, or dividing : COMPUTE **2** : ¹ESTIMATE **3** : to plan by careful thought : INTEND

cal·cu·lat·ing *adj* : carefully thinking about and planning actions for selfish or improper reasons

cal·cu·la·tion *n* : the process or result of adding, subtracting, multiplying, or dividing

cal·cu·la·tor *n* **1** : a person who calculates **2** : a usually small electronic device for solving mathematical problems

cal·cu·lus *n* : an advanced branch of mathematics that deals mostly with rates of change and with finding lengths, areas, and volumes

caldron *variant of* CAULDRON

cal·en·dar *n* **1** : a chart showing the days,

weeks, and months of the year **2** : a schedule of planned events or activities

¹calf *n, pl* **calves 1** : a young cow **2** : the young of various large animals (as the elephant, moose, or whale)

²calf *n, pl* **calves** : the muscular back part of the leg below the knee

calf·skin *n* : leather made from the skin of a calf

cal·i·ber *or* **cal·i·bre** *n* **1** : level of excellence, skill, or importance **2** : the diameter of a bullet or of the hole in the barrel of a gun

¹cal·i·co *n, pl* **cal·i·coes** *or* **cal·i·cos** : cotton cloth especially with a colored pattern printed on one side

²calico *adj* : marked with blotches of color

Calif. *abbr* California

cal·i·per *n* : an instrument with two adjustable legs used to measure the thickness of objects or the distance between surfaces — usually used in pl.

ca·liph *or* **ca·lif** *n* : an important Muslim political and religious leader

cal·is·then·ics *n pl* : exercises (as push-ups and jumping jacks) to develop strength and flexibility that are done without special equipment — used as singular or plural

¹call *vb* **called; call·ing 1** : to speak in a loud clear voice so as to be heard at a distance : SHOUT **2** : to say loudly or with authority **3** : to tell, order, or ask to come **4** : to give the order for **5** : to utter a cry **6** : to make a request or demand **7** : to get in touch with by telephone **8** : to make a short visit **9** : ²NAME 1 **10** : to address someone or something as **11** : to regard as being of a certain kind **12** : to say or guess what the result will be **13** : to estimate as being **14** : SUSPEND 3, END — **call for** : to require as necessary or suitable — **call off 1** : CANCEL 2 **2** : to cause or tell to stop attacking or chasing — **call on** : to choose to answer

²call *n* **1** : a loud shout or cry **2** : a cry of an animal **3** : a loud sound or signal **4** : a public request or command **5** : ¹REQUEST 1 **6** : a short visit **7** : somehing called or announced **8** : the act of calling on the telephone **9** : DECISION 1 **10** : the attraction or appeal of a particular place or condition

call·er *n* : someone who calls

cal·li·gra·phy *n* **1** : beautiful artistic handwriting **2** : the art of producing beautiful handwriting

call·ing *n* : a profession especially that a person feels strongly about

cal·lous *adj* : feeling or showing no sympathy for others

cal·lus *n, pl* **cal·lus·es** : a hard thickened area on the skin and especially on the hands and feet

¹calm *n* **1** : a period or condition of freedom from storm, wind, or rough water **2** : a quiet and peaceful state

²calm *vb* **calmed; calm·ing** : to make or become less active or disturbed — often used with *down*

³calm *adj* **calm·er; calm·est 1** : not stormy or windy **2** : not excited or upset — **calm·ly** *adv* — **calm·ness** *n*

cal·o·rie *n* **1** : a unit for measuring heat equal to the amount of heat required to raise the temperature of one gram of water one degree Celsius **2** : a unit of heat used to indicate the amount of energy foods produce in the human body that is equal to 1000 calories

calve *vb* **calved; calv·ing** : to give birth to a calf

calves *pl of* CALF

ca·lyp·so *n, pl* **calypsos** : a lively folk song or style of singing of the West Indies

ca·lyx *n, pl* **ca·lyx·es** *or* **ca·ly·ces** : the usually green outer part of a flower consisting of sepals

cam·bi·um *n, pl* **cam·bi·ums** *or* **cam·bia** : soft tissue in woody plants from which new wood and bark grow

cam·cord·er *n* : a small video camera

came *past of* COME

cam·el *n* : a large hoofed animal that has one or two large humps on its back and is used in the deserts of Asia and Africa for carrying passengers and loads

cam·era *n* **1** : a device that has a lens on one side to let light in and is used for taking pictures **2** : the part of a television sending device in which the image to be sent out is formed

¹cam·ou·flage *n* **1** : the hiding or disguising of something by covering it up or changing the way it looks **2** : something (as color or shape) that protects an animal from attack by making it difficult to see in the area around it

²camouflage *vb* **cam·ou·flaged; cam·ou·flag·ing** : to hide or disguise by covering or making harder to see

¹camp *n* **1** : a place where temporary shelters are erected **2** : a place or program for recreation or instruction usually during the summer

²camp *vb* **camped; camp·ing 1** : to make or occupy a camp **2** : to sleep outdoors usually in a tent

¹cam·paign *n* **1** : a series of activities meant to produce a particular result **2** : a series of military operations in a certain area or for a certain purpose

²campaign *vb* **cam·paigned; cam·paign·ing** : to take part in a series of activities meant to produce a particular result — **campaign·er** *n*

camp·er *n* **1** : a person who sleeps outdoors (as in a tent) **2** : a type of vehicle or special trailer that people can live and sleep in when they are traveling or camping **3** : a young person who goes to a camp during the summer

Camp Fire Girl *n* : a member of a national organization for girls from ages 5 to 18

camp·ground *n* : an area used for a camp or for camping

cam·phor *n* : a white fragrant solid that comes from the wood and bark of a tall Asian tree (**camphor tree**) and is used mostly in medicine, in making plastics, and to repel moths

camp·site *n* : a place used for camping

cam·pus *n* : the grounds and buildings of a college or school

¹can *helping verb, past* **could** ; *present sing & pl* **can 1** : know how to **2** : be able to **3** : be permitted by conscience or feeling to **4** : have permission to **5** : to be possible

²can *n* **1** : a metal container usually shaped like a cylinder **2** : the contents of a can

³can *vb* **canned; can·ning** : to prepare for later use by sealing in an airtight can or jar

Can., Canad. *abbr* **1** Canada **2** Canadian

¹Ca·na·di·an *adj* : of or relating to Canada or its people

²Canadian *n* : a person born or living in Canada

ca·nal *n* **1** : an artificial waterway for boats or for irrigation of land **2** : a tubelike passage in the body

ca·nary *n, pl* **ca·nar·ies** : a small usually yellow songbird often kept in a cage

can·cel *vb* **can·celed** *or* **can·celled; can·cel·ing** *or* **can·cel·ling 1** : to take back : stop from being in effect **2** : to cause to not happen **3** : to be equal in force or importance but have opposite effect **4** : to remove (a common divisor) from numerator and denominator : remove (equivalents) on opposite sides of an equation **5** : to cross out or strike out with a line **6** : to mark (as a postage stamp) so as to make impossible to use again

can·cel·la·tion *n* **1** : an act of causing something to end or no longer be in effect **2** : a mark that makes something impossible to use again

can·cer *n* : a serious sometimes deadly disease characterized by the growth of abnormal cells that form tumors which may damage or destroy normal body tissue

can·de·la·bra *n* : a candlestick or lamp that has several branches for lights

can·de·la·brum *n, pl* **can·de·la·bra** *also* **can·de·la·brums** : CANDELABRA

can·did *adj* **1** : marked by or showing honesty : FRANK **2** : relating to photography of people acting naturally without being posed — **can·did·ly** *adv*

can·di·da·cy *n, pl* **can·di·da·cies** : the position of a person who is trying to be elected : the state of being a candidate

can·di·date *n* **1** : a person who is trying to be elected **2** : a person who is being considered for a position or honor

can·died *adj* : cooked in or coated with sugar

¹can·dle *n* : a stick of tallow or wax containing a wick and burned to give light

²candle *vb* **can·dled; can·dling** : to examine (an egg) by holding between the eye and a light — **can·dler** *n*

can·dle·light *n* : the light of a candle — **can·dle·lit** *adj*

can·dle·stick *n* : a holder for a candle

can·dor *n* : sincere and honest expression

¹can·dy *n, pl* **can·dies** : a sweet made of sugar often with flavoring and filling

²candy *vb* **can·died; can·dy·ing** : to coat or become coated with sugar often by cooking

cane *n* **1** : an often hollow, slender, and somewhat flexible plant stem **2** : a tall woody grass or reed (as sugarcane) **3** : a rod made especially of wood or metal that often has a curved handle and is used to help someone walk **4** : a rod for beating

¹ca·nine *n* **1** : a pointed tooth next to the incisors **2** : a domestic dog or a related animal (as a wolf or fox)

²canine *adj* **1** : of or relating to the domestic dog or a related animal **2** : like or typical of a dog

can·is·ter *n* : a small box or can for holding a dry product

can·ker sore *n* : a small painful sore of the mouth

can·nery *n, pl* **can·ner·ies** : a factory where foods are canned

can·ni·bal *n* **1** : a human being who eats human flesh **2** : an animal that eats other animals of its own kind

can·non *n, pl* **cannons** *or* **cannon** : a large heavy weapon consisting mostly of a metal tube that is mounted on wheels and is used for firing cannonballs

can·non·ball *n* **1** : a usually round solid missile (as of stone or metal) for firing from a cannon **2** : a jump into water made with the arms holding the knees tight against the chest

can·not : can not

can·ny *adj* **can·ni·er; can·ni·est** : clever especially in taking advantage of opportunities : SHREWD — **can·ni·ly** *adv*

capitalize

¹**ca·noe** *n* : a long light narrow boat with pointed ends and curved sides that is usually moved by a paddle

²**canoe** *vb* **ca·noed; ca·noe·ing** : to travel or carry in a canoe — **ca·noe·ist** *n*

can·on *n* **1** : a rule or law of a church **2** : an accepted rule

can·o·py *n, pl* **can·o·pies 1** : a covering fixed over a bed or throne or carried on poles (as over a person of high rank) **2** : something that hangs over and shades or shelters something else **3** : the uppermost spreading layer of a forest

can't : can not

can·ta·loupe *n* : a melon usually with a hard rough skin and reddish orange flesh

can·tan·ker·ous *adj* : CRABBY, QUARRELSOME

can·ta·ta *n* : a piece of music that features solos, duets, and choruses with instrumental accompaniment and is sometimes based on a poem, play, or story

can·teen *n* **1** : a store (as in a camp or factory) in which food, drinks, and small supplies are sold **2** : a place of recreation and entertainment for people in military service **3** : a small container for carrying water or another liquid

¹**can·ter** *n* : a horse's gait resembling but slower than a gallop

²**canter** *vb* **can·tered; can·ter·ing** : to run with a movement that resembles but is slower than a gallop

can·ti·le·ver *n* **1** : a beam or similar support fastened (as by being built into a wall) only at one end **2** : either of two structures that stick out from piers toward each other and when joined form a span in a bridge (**cantilever bridge**)

can·to *n, pl* **can·tos** : one of the major divisions of a long poem

can·ton *n* : a division of a country (as Switzerland)

can·tor *n* : a synagogue official who sings religious music and leads the congregation in prayer

can·vas *n* **1** : a strong cloth of hemp, flax, or cotton **2** : a specially prepared piece of cloth used as a surface for painting

can·vas·back *n* : a North American wild duck with reddish brown head and grayish back

can·vass *vb* **can·vassed; can·vass·ing** : to go to (people) to ask for votes, contributions, or orders for goods or to determine public opinion — **can·vass·er** *n*

can·yon *n* : a deep valley with steep sides and often a stream flowing through it

cap. *abbr* **1** capital **2** capitalize **3** capitalized

¹**cap** *n* **1** : a head covering and especially one having a visor and no brim **2** : something that serves as a cover or protection for something **3** : a part that forms the top of something **4** : an upper limit **5** : a paper or metal container holding a small explosive charge

²**cap** *vb* **capped; cap·ping 1** : to cover or provide with a top or cover **2** : to bring to a high point or end **3** : to match or follow with something equal or better **4** : to put an upper limit on

ca·pa·bil·i·ty *n, pl* **ca·pa·bil·i·ties** : ABILITY 1

ca·pa·ble *adj* **1** : having the qualities or abilities that are needed to do or accomplish something **2** : able to do something well — **ca·pa·bly** *adv*

ca·pa·cious *adj* : able to hold a great deal

ca·pac·i·ty *n, pl* **ca·pac·i·ties 1** : ability to contain or deal with something **2** : mental or physical power **3** : VOLUME 3 **4** : ROLE 1, STATUS

¹**cape** *n* : a point of land that juts out into the sea or into a lake

²**cape** *n* : a sleeveless garment worn so as to hang over the shoulders, arms, and back

¹**ca·per** *vb* **ca·pered; ca·per·ing** : to leap about in a lively way

²**caper** *n* **1** : a playful or mischievous trick **2** : a lively leap or spring **3** : an illegal or questionable act

¹**cap·il·lary** *adj* **1** : having a long slender form and a small inner diameter **2** : of or relating to capillary action or a capillary

²**capillary** *n, pl* **cap·il·lar·ies** : one of the slender hairlike tubes that are the smallest blood vessels and connect arteries with veins

capillary action *n* : the action by which the surface of a liquid where it is in contact with a solid (as in a capillary tube) is raised or lowered

¹**cap·i·tal** *adj* **1** : being like the letters A, B, C, etc. rather than a, b, c, etc. **2** : being the location of a government **3** : punishable by or resulting in death **4** : of or relating to accumulated wealth **5** : EXCELLENT

²**capital** *n* : **1** : a capital letter **2** : a capital city **3** : the money and property that a person owns **4** : profitable use

³**capital** *n* : the top part of an architectural column

cap·i·tal·ism *n* : a system under which the ownership of land and wealth is for the most part in the hands of private individuals

cap·i·tal·ist *n* **1** : a person who has usually a lot of money which is used to make more money **2** : a person who supports capitalism

cap·i·tal·ize *vb* **cap·i·tal·ized; cap·i·tal·iz·ing 1** : to write with a beginning capital letter or in all capital letters **2** : to provide money needed to start or develop (a business) **3** : to

gain by turning something to advantage —
cap·i·tal·i·za·tion n

cap·i·tol n 1 : the building in which a state
legislature meets 2 cap : the building in
Washington, D.C., in which the United
States Congress meets

ca·pon n : a castrated male chicken

ca·price n : a sudden change in feeling, opinion, or action : WHIM

ca·pri·cious adj 1 : moved or controlled by a
sudden desire 2 : likely to change suddenly
— **ca·pri·cious·ly** adv

cap·size vb **cap·sized; cap·siz·ing** : to turn
over : UPSET

cap·stan n : a device that consists of a drum
to which a rope is fastened and that is used
especially on ships for raising the anchor

cap·sule n 1 : a case enclosing the seeds or
spores of a plant 2 : a small case of material
that contains medicine to be swallowed 3 : a
closed compartment for travel in space

Capt. abbr captain

¹**cap·tain** n 1 : the commanding officer of a
ship 2 : a leader of a group : one in command 3 : an officer of high rank in a police
or fire department 4 : a commissioned officer in the navy or coast guard ranking above
a commander 5 : a commissioned officer in
the army, air force, or marine corps ranking
below a major

²**captain** vb **cap·tained; cap·tain·ing** : to be
captain of

cap·tion n : a comment or title that goes with
a picture

cap·ti·vate vb **cap·ti·vat·ed; cap·ti·vat·ing** : to
fascinate by some special charm

¹**cap·tive** adj 1 : taken and held prisoner 2
: kept within bounds or under control 3 : as
a prisoner 4 : unable to avoid watching or
listening to something

²**captive** n : someone who is held prisoner

cap·tiv·i·ty n : the state of being held prisoner
: the state of being captive

cap·tor n : someone who has captured a person or thing

¹**cap·ture** vb **cap·tured; cap·tur·ing** 1 : to
take and hold especially by force 2 : to get
and hold 3 : to put into a lasting form

²**capture** n : the act of taking and holding especially by force

car n 1 : a vehicle that moves on wheels 2
: a separate section of a train 3 : the part of
an elevator that holds passengers

ca·rafe n : a bottle that has a wide mouth and
is used to hold water or beverages

car·a·mel n 1 : a firm chewy candy 2 : burnt
sugar used for coloring and flavoring

car·at n : a unit of weight for gemstones (as
diamonds) equal to 200 milligrams

car·a·van n 1 : a group (of people or animals) traveling together on a long journey 2
: a group of vehicles traveling together one
behind the other

car·a·vel n : a small sailing ship of the 15th
and 16th centuries with a broad bow and
high stern and three or four masts

car·a·way n : the dried seeds of a white-flowered plant that are used especially in seasoning foods

car·bine n : a short light rifle

car·bo·hy·drate n : a substance (as a starch or
sugar) that is rich in energy and is made up
of carbon, hydrogen, and oxygen

car·bon n : a chemical element occurring as
diamond and graphite, in coal and petroleum, and in plant and animal bodies

car·bon·ate vb **car·bon·at·ed; car·bon·at·ing**
: to fill with carbon dioxide which escapes in
the form of bubbles

carbon di·ox·ide n : a heavy colorless gas
that is formed by burning fuels, by the
breakdown or burning of animal and plant
matter, and by the act of breathing and that
is absorbed from the air by plants in photosynthesis

carbon mon·ox·ide n : a colorless odorless
very poisonous gas formed by incomplete
burning of carbon

car·bu·re·tor n : the part of an engine in
which liquid fuel (as gasoline) is mixed with
air to make it burn easily

car·cass n : the body of an animal prepared
for use as meat

card n 1 : a decorated piece of thick paper
that contains a greeting or is used to write a
message 2 : a thick stiff piece of paper or
plastic that contains information about a
person or business 3 : PLAYING CARD 4
cards pl : a game played with playing cards
5 : a thick stiff piece of paper that has a picture on one side and is traded or collected 6
: CREDIT CARD

card·board n : a stiff material made of wood
pulp that has been pressed and dried

car·di·ac adj : of, relating to, or affecting the
heart

¹**car·di·nal** n 1 : a high official of the Roman
Catholic Church ranking next below the
pope 2 : a bright red songbird with a crest
and a whistling call

²**cardinal** adj : of first importance : MAIN,
PRINCIPAL

cardinal number n : a number (as 1, 5, 22)
that is used in simple counting and answers
the question "how many?"

cardinal point n : one of the four chief points
of the compass which are north, south, east,
west

car·dio·pul·mo·nary re·sus·ci·ta·tion n : a
method used in an emergency to save the life

of a person whose heart has stopped beating that involves breathing into the victim's mouth to force air into the lungs and pressing on the victim's chest to cause blood to flow through the body

¹care *n* **1** : serious attention **2** : PROTECTION 1, SUPERVISION **3** : proper maintenance of property or equipment **4** : a feeling of concern or worry

²care *vb* **cared; car·ing 1** : to feel interest or concern **2** : to provide help, protection, or supervision to : look after **3** : to have a liking or desire

ca·reen *vb* **ca·reened; ca·reen·ing** : to go at high speed without control

ca·reer *n* **1** : a period of time spent in a job or profession **2** : a job followed as a life's work

care-free *adj* : free from care or worry

care-ful *adj* **1** : using care **2** : made, done, or said with care — **care·ful·ly** *adv*

care-less *adj* **1** : not taking proper care **2** : done, made, or said without being careful **3** : CAREFREE — **care·less·ly** *adv* — **care·less·ness** *n*

¹ca·ress *n* : a tender or loving touch or hug

²caress *vb* **ca·ressed; ca·ress·ing** : to touch in a tender or loving way

care-tak·er *n* : a person who takes care of property for someone else

car·go *n, pl* **cargoes** *or* **cargos** : the goods carried by a ship, airplane, or vehicle

car·i·bou *n* : a large deer of northern and arctic regions that has antlers in both the male and female — used especially for one in the New World

car·ies *n, pl* **caries** : a decayed condition of a tooth or teeth

car·il·lon *n* : a set of bells sounded by hammers controlled by a keyboard

car·nage *n* : ¹SLAUGHTER 3

car·na·tion *n* : a fragrant usually white, pink, or red garden or greenhouse flower

car·ne·lian *n* : a hard reddish quartz used as a gem

car·ni·val *n* **1** : a form of entertainment that travels from town to town and includes rides and games **2** : an organized program of entertainment or exhibition : FESTIVAL

car·ni·vore *n* : an animal that feeds on meat

car·niv·o·rous *adj* : feeding on animal flesh or tissue

¹car·ol *n* : a usually religious song of joy

²carol *vb* **car·oled** *or* **car·olled; car·ol·ing** *or* **car·ol·ling 1** : to sing in a joyful manner **2** : to sing carols and especially Christmas carols — **car·ol·er** *or* **car·ol·ler** *n*

¹car·om *n* : the act of bouncing back at an angle

²carom *vb* **car·omed; car·om·ing** : to hit and bounce back at an angle

car·ou·sel : MERRY-GO-ROUND

¹carp *vb* **carped; carp·ing** : to complain in an annoying way

²carp *n* : a freshwater fish that lives a long time and is often used for food

car·pel *n* : the female reproductive structure of a flower that encloses the ovules

car·pen·ter *n* : a worker who builds or repairs wooden things

car·pen·try *n* : the skill or work of building or repairing wooden things

¹car·pet *n* **1** : a heavy woven fabric used especially as a floor covering **2** : a covering like a carpet

²carpet *vb* **car·pet·ed; car·pet·ing** : to cover with or as if with a carpet

car pool *n* : an arrangement by a group of automobile owners in which each takes turns driving his or her own car and giving the others a ride

car·riage *n* **1** : a vehicle with wheels used for carrying people **2** : a support with wheels used for carrying a load **3** : a movable part of a machine that carries or supports some other moving part **4** : the manner of holding the body : POSTURE

car·ri·er *n* **1** : a person or thing that carries **2** : a person or business that transports passengers or goods or provides a certain service **3** : a person, animal, or plant that carries disease germs without showing symptoms and passes them on to others

car·ri·on *n* : dead and decaying flesh

car·rot *n* : a long orange root of a garden plant that is eaten as a vegetable

car·ry *vb* **car·ried; car·ry·ing 1** : to take or transfer from one place to another **2** : to contain and direct the course of **3** : to wear or have on or within the body **4** : to have as an element, quality, or part **5** : to have for sale **6** : to go over or travel a distance **7** : ¹SUPPORT 4, BEAR **8** : WIN 4 **9** : to hold or bear the body or some part of it **10** : to sing in correct pitch **11** : to present to the public — **carry away** : to cause strong feeling in — **carry on 1** : to behave in an improper or excited manner **2** : MANAGE 1 **3** : to continue in spite of difficulties — **carry out** : to put into action or effect

car seat *n* : a seat for a small child that attaches to an automobile seat and holds the child safely

¹cart *n* **1** : a heavy vehicle with two wheels usually drawn by horses and used for hauling **2** : a light vehicle pushed or pulled by hand

²cart *vb* **cart·ed; cart·ing 1 :** to carry in a cart **2 :** CARRY 1 — **cart·er** *n*

car·ti·lage *n* : tough flexible tissue that makes up most of the skeleton of vertebrates during early development and except for in a few places in the body (as the nose or outer ear) is replaced by bone

car·ti·lag·i·nous *adj* : relating to or made of cartilage

car·ton *n* : a cardboard container

car·toon *n* **1 :** a movie or television program made by photographing a series of drawings **2 :** a drawing (as in a newspaper) making people or objects look funny or foolish **3 :** COMIC STRIP

car·toon·ist *n* : a person who draws cartoons

car·tridge *n* **1 :** a case or shell containing gunpowder and shot or a bullet for use in a firearm **2 :** a container that is inserted into a machine to make it work

cart·wheel *n* : a handspring made to the side with arms and legs sticking out

carve *vb* **carved; carv·ing 1 :** to cut with care **2 :** to make or get by cutting **3 :** to slice and serve (meat) — **carv·er** *n*

carv·ing *n* **1 :** the art or act of a person who carves **2 :** an object or design that has been carved

¹cas·cade *n* : a steep usually small waterfall

²cascade *vb* **cas·cad·ed; cas·cad·ing :** to flow or fall rapidly and in large quantity

¹case *n* **1 :** a particular instance, situation, or example **2 :** a situation or an object that calls for investigation or action (as by the police) **3 :** a question to be settled in a court of law **4 :** a form of a noun, pronoun, or adjective showing its grammatical relation to other words **5 :** the actual situation **6 :** a convincing argument **7 :** an instance of disease, injury, or discomfort — **in any case** : no matter what has happened or been said — **in case** : for the purpose of being ready for something that might happen

²case *n* **1 :** a container (as a box) for holding something **2 :** a box and its contents **3 :** an outer covering

ca·sein *n* : a whitish to yellowish protein that is found in milk and cheese and is used in making paints, plastics, and adhesives

case·ment *n* **1 :** a window sash opening on hinges **2 :** a window with a casement

¹cash *n* **1 :** money in the form of coins or bills **2 :** money or its equivalent (as a check) paid for goods at the time of purchase or delivery

²cash *vb* **cashed; cash·ing :** to give or get cash for

cash·ew *n* : a curved edible nut that comes from a tropical American tree

cash·ier *n* : a person who is responsible for giving out or taking in money (as in a bank or store)

cash·mere *n* : a soft yarn or fabric once made from the fine wool of an Indian goat but now often from sheep's wool

cash register *n* : a machine used in a business to calculate the amount of cash due for a sale and having a drawer to hold money

cas·ing *n* : something that covers or encloses

cask *n* **1 :** a container that is shaped like a barrel and is usually used for liquids **2 :** the amount contained in a cask

cas·ket *n* **1 :** COFFIN **2 :** a small box for storage or safekeeping (as for jewels)

cas·se·role *n* **1 :** a mix of food baked and served in a deep dish **2 :** a deep dish in which food can be baked and served

cas·sette *n* **1 :** a container that holds audiotape or videotape and in which the tape passes from one reel to another when being played **2 :** a container holding photographic film or plates that can be easily loaded into a camera

¹cast *vb* **cast; cast·ing 1 :** ¹THROW 1 **2 :** to direct to or toward something or someone **3 :** to send out or forward **4 :** to put under the influence of **5 :** to throw out, off, or away : SHED **6 :** to make (a vote) formally **7 :** to assign a part or role to **8 :** to give shape to liquid material by pouring it into a mold and letting it harden

²cast *n* **1 :** an act of throwing **2 :** the characters or the people acting in a play or story **3 :** a stiff dressing (as of plaster) hardened around a part of the body to allow a broken bone to heal **4 :** a hint of color **5 :** the container used to give a shape to the thing made in it **6 :** something formed by casting in a mold or form **7 :** the distance to which a thing can be thrown **8 :** ²SHAPE 1 **9 :** something (as the skin of an insect or the waste of an earthworm) that is shed or thrown out or off

cas·ta·net *n* : a rhythm instrument that consists of two small flat round parts fastened to the thumb and clicked by the fingers — usually used in pl.

¹cast·away *adj* **1 :** thrown away **2 :** cast adrift or ashore

²castaway *n* : a person who is stranded in a place where there are no other people (as because of a shipwreck)

caste *n* **1 :** one of the classes into which the Hindu people of India were formerly divided **2 :** a division or class of society based on wealth, rank, or occupation **3 :** social rank : PRESTIGE

cast·er *n* : one of a set of small wheels on a piece of furniture that makes it easier to move

cas·ti·gate *vb* **cas·ti·gat·ed; cas·ti·gat·ing**
: to punish or criticize harshly

cast·ing *n* **1** : the act or action of one that
casts **2** : something that is cast in a mold **3**
: ²CAST 9

cast iron *n* : a hard and brittle alloy of iron,
carbon, and silicon shaped by being poured
into a mold while melted

cas·tle *n* **1** : a large building or group of
buildings usually having high walls with
towers that was built in the past to protect
against attack **2** : a large or impressive
house

cast-off *n* : a person or thing that has been
thrown aside or rejected

cast–off *adj* : thrown away or aside

cas·tor oil *n* : a thick yellowish liquid that
comes from the seeds (**castor beans**) of a
tropical herb and is used as a lubricant and
as a strong laxative

cas·trate *vb* **cas·trat·ed; cas·trat·ing** : to remove the sex glands of

ca·su·al *adj* **1** : happening unexpectedly or
by chance : not planned or foreseen **2** : occurring without regularity : OCCASIONAL **3**
: showing or feeling little concern : NON-
CHALANT **4** : meant for informal use — **ca-
su·al·ly** *adv*

ca·su·al·ty *n, pl* **ca·su·al·ties 1** : a person
who is hurt or killed in a war, disaster, or accident **2** : a person or thing injured, lost, or
destroyed

cat *n* **1** : a common furry meat-eating animal
kept as a pet or for catching mice and rats **2**
: any of a family of mammals (as the lion,
tiger, and leopard) to which the domestic cat
belongs

¹**cat·a·log** *or* **cat·a·logue** *n* **1** : a book containing brief descriptions of things that can
be purchased or signed up for **2** : a list of
names, titles, or articles arranged by some
system

²**catalog** *or* **catalogue** *vb* **cat·a·loged** *or*
cat·a·logued; cat·a·log·ing *or* **cat·a·logu·
ing 1** : to make a catalog of **2** : to enter
in a catalog — **cat·a·log·er** *or* **cat·a·logu-
er** *n*

ca·tal·pa *n* : a tree of North America and Asia
with broad leaves, showy flowers, and long
pods

¹**cat·a·pult** *n* **1** : an ancient military machine
for hurling stones and arrows **2** : a device
for launching an airplane from the deck of
a ship

²**catapult** *vb* **cat·a·pult·ed; cat·a·pult·ing 1**
: to throw by or as if by a catapult **2** : to
quickly advance

cat·a·ract *n* **1** : a clouding of the lens of the
eye or of the cover around the lens that

blocks the passage of light **2** : a large waterfall **3** : a sudden rush or flow like a waterfall

ca·tas·tro·phe *n* **1** : a sudden disaster **2**
: complete failure : FIASCO

cat·bird *n* : a dark gray songbird that has a
call like a cat's meow

cat·boat *n* : a sailboat with a single mast set
far forward and a single large sail with a
long boom

cat·call *n* : a sound like the cry of a cat or a
noise expressing disapproval (as at a sports
event)

¹**catch** *vb* **caught ; catch·ing 1** : to capture
and hold **2** : to discover unexpectedly **3**
: to stop suddenly before doing something
4 : to take hold of **5** : to become affected
by **6** : to take or get briefly or quickly **7**
: to be in time for **8** : to grasp by the
senses or the mind **9** : to play catcher on a
baseball team **10** : to get tangled **11** : to
hold firmly : FASTEN **12** to recover by
resting — **catch on 1** : to realize something **2** : to become popular — **catch up**
: to move or progress fast enough to join another

²**catch** *n* **1** : something caught : the amount
caught at one time **2** : the act of catching **3**
: a pastime in which a ball is thrown and
caught **4** : something that checks, fastens,
or holds immovable **5** : a hidden difficulty

catch·er *n* **1** : someone or something that
catches **2** : a baseball player who plays behind home plate

catch·ing *adj* **1** : INFECTIOUS 1, CONTAGIOUS
2 : likely to spread as if infectious

catchy *adj* **catch·i·er; catch·i·est** : likely to
attract and be remembered

cat·e·chism *n* **1** : a series of questions and
answers used in giving religious instruction
2 : a set of formal questions

cat·e·go·ry *n, pl* **cat·e·go·ries** : a basic division or grouping of things

ca·ter *vb* **ca·tered; ca·ter·ing 1** : to provide a
supply of food **2** : to supply what is needed
or wanted — **ca·ter·er** *n*

cat·er·pil·lar *n* : a wormlike often hairy larva
of an insect and usually a butterfly or moth

cat·fish *n* : a fish with a large head and feelers about the mouth

cat·gut *n* : a tough cord made from intestines
of animals (as sheep) and used for strings of
musical instruments and rackets and for
sewing in surgery

ca·the·dral *n* : the principal church of a district headed by a bishop

cath·o·lic *adj* **1** : including many different
things or types **2** *cap* : of or relating to the
Roman Catholic church

Catholic *n* : a member of the Roman Catholic church

cat·kin *n* : a flower cluster (as of the willow and birch) in which the flowers grow in close circular rows along a slender stalk

cat·nap *n* : a very short light nap

cat·nip *n* : a plant that is a mint with a smell especially attractive to cats

catsup *variant of* KETCHUP

cat·tail *n* : a tall plant with long flat leaves and tall furry stalks that grows in marshy areas

cat·tle *n, pl* **cattle** : domestic animals with four feet and especially cows, bulls, and calves

cat·walk *n* : a narrow walk or way (as along a bridge)

caught *past and past participle of* CATCH

caul·dron *also* **cal·dron** *n* : a large kettle

cau·li·flow·er *n* : a vegetable that is a white head of undeveloped flowers and is related to the cabbage

¹caulk *vb* **caulked; caulk·ing** : to fill up a crack, seam, or joint so as to make it watertight

²caulk *also* **caulk·ing** *n* : material used to fill up a crack, seam, or joint so as to make it watertight

¹cause *n* **1** : a person or thing that brings about a result **2** : a good or good enough reason for something **3** : something supported or deserving support

²cause *vb* **caused; caus·ing** : to make happen or exist

³cause *conj* : BECAUSE

cause·way *n* : a raised road or way across wet ground or water

caus·tic *adj* **1** : capable of eating away by chemical action : CORROSIVE **2** : very harsh and critical

¹cau·tion *n* **1** : care taken to avoid trouble or danger : PRECAUTION **2** : WARNING

²caution *vb* **cau·tioned; cau·tion·ing** : to warn about danger

cau·tious *adj* : showing or using care to avoid trouble or danger — **cau·tious·ly** *adv*

cav·al·cade *n* **1** : a procession especially of riders or carriages **2** : a dramatic series (as of related events)

¹cav·a·lier *n* **1** : a mounted soldier **2** : a brave and courteous gentleman

²cavalier *adj* **1** : easy and lighthearted in manner **2** : having or showing no concern for a serious or important matter

cav·al·ry *n, pl* **cav·al·ries** : a unit of troops mounted on horseback or moving in motor vehicles

¹cave *n* : a hollow underground place with an opening on the surface

²cave *vb* **caved; cav·ing** : to fall or cause to fall in or down : COLLAPSE

cave·man *n, pl* **cave·men** : a person living in a cave especially during the Stone Age

cav·ern *n* : a cave often of large or unknown size

cav·ern·ous *adj* **1** : having caverns or hollow places **2** : like a cavern in being large and hollow

cav·i·ty *n, pl* **cav·i·ties** **1** : a small hole formed in a tooth by decay **2** : a hollow place

ca·vort *vb* **ca·vort·ed; ca·vort·ing** : to move or hop about in a lively way

¹caw *n* : the cry of a crow or a raven

²caw *vb* **cawed; caw·ing** : to make the sound of a crow or raven

cay *n* : ⁴KEY

cay·enne pepper *n* : dried ripe hot peppers ground and used to add flavor to food

CD *n* : a small plastic disk on which information (as music or computer data) is recorded

CD–ROM *n* : a CD that contains computer data that cannot be changed

cease *vb* **ceased; ceas·ing** : to come or bring to an end : STOP

cease·less *adj* : occurring without stop or over and over again

ce·cro·pia moth *n* : a colorful moth that is the largest moth of North America

ce·dar *n* : a tree having cones and a strong wood with a pleasant smell

cede *vb* **ced·ed; ced·ing** : to give up especially by treaty

ceil·ing *n* **1** : the overhead inside surface of a room **2** : the greatest height at which an airplane can fly properly **3** : the height above the ground of the bottom of the lowest layer of clouds **4** : an upper limit

cel·e·brate *vb* **cel·e·brat·ed; cel·e·brat·ing** **1** : to observe (a holiday or important occasion) in some special way **2** : to perform (a religious ceremony) **3** : ¹PRAISE 1

cel·e·brat·ed *adj* : widely known and praised

cel·e·bra·tion *n* **1** : the act of doing something to observe a special occasion **2** : the activities or ceremonies for observing a special occasion

ce·leb·ri·ty *n, pl* **ce·leb·ri·ties** **1** : FAME **2** : a famous person

cel·ery *n* : a vegetable that has crisp light green leafstalks that are eaten raw or cooked

ce·les·tial *adj* **1** : of, relating to, or suggesting heaven **2** : of or relating to the sky

cell *n* **1** : a very small room (as in a prison or a monastery) **2** : the basic structural unit of living things that is made up of cytoplasm enclosed by a membrane and that typically includes a nucleus and other smaller parts (as mitochondria or chloroplasts) which perform specific functions necessary for life **3** : a small enclosed part or division (as in a honeycomb) **4** : a container with substances which can produce an electric current by chemical action **5** : a device that converts light (as sunlight) that falls on it into electrical energy that is used as a power source **6** : CELL PHONE — **celled** *adj*

cel·lar *n* : a room or set of rooms below the surface of the ground : BASEMENT

cell membrane *n* : the thin outside layer that surrounds the cytoplasm of a cell and controls the movement of materials into and out of the cell

cel·lo *n, pl* **cel·los** : a large stringed instrument of the violin family that plays the bass part

cel·lo·phane *n* : a thin clear material made from cellulose and used as a wrapping

cell phone *n* : a portable telephone that connects to other telephones by radio through a system of transmitters each of which covers a limited geographical area

cel·lu·lar *adj* **1** : of, relating to, or made up of cells **2** : of, relating to, or being a cell phone

cel·lu·lose *n* : a substance that is the chief part of the cell walls of plants and is used in making various products (as paper and rayon)

cell wall *n* : the firm outer nonliving layer that surrounds the cell membrane and encloses and supports the cells of most plants, bacteria, and fungi

Cel·si·us *adj* : relating to or having a thermometer scale on which the interval between the freezing point and the boiling point of water is divided into 100 degrees with 0 representing the freezing point and 100 the boiling point

¹**ce·ment** *n* **1** : a powder that is made mainly from compounds of aluminum, calcium, silicon, and iron heated together and then ground and mixed with water to make mortar and concrete **2** : ²CONCRETE, MORTAR **3** : a substance used to make things stick together firmly

²**cement** *vb* **ce·ment·ed; ce·ment·ing 1** : to join together with or as if with cement **2** : to make stronger

ce·men·tum *n* : a thin bony layer covering the part of a tooth inside the gum

cem·e·tery *n, pl* **cem·e·ter·ies** : a place where dead people are buried : GRAVEYARD

Ce·no·zo·ic *n* : an era of geological history lasting from 70 million years ago to the present time in which there has been a rapid evolution of mammals and birds and of flowering plants

¹**cen·sor** *n* : an official who checks writings or movies to take out things considered offensive or immoral

²**censor** *vb* **cen·sored; cen·sor·ing** : to examine (as a book) to take out things considered offensive or immoral

cen·sor·ship *n* : the system or practice of examining writings or movies and taking out things considered offensive or immoral

¹**cen·sure** *n* **1** : the act of finding fault with or blaming **2** : an official criticism

²**censure** *vb* **cen·sured; cen·sur·ing** : to find fault with especially publicly

cen·sus *n* : a count of the number of people in a country, city, or town

cent *n* **1** : a hundredth part of the unit of the money system in a number of different countries **2** : a coin, token, or note representing one cent

cent. *abbr* **1** centigrade **2** century

cen·taur *n* : a creature in Greek mythology that is part man and part horse

cen·ten·ni·al *n* : a 100th anniversary or a celebration of it — **centennial** *adj*

¹**cen·ter** *n* **1** : the middle part of something **2** : a person or thing characterized by a particular concentration or activity **3** : a place used for a particular purpose **4** : the middle point of a circle or a sphere equally distant from every point on the circumference or surface **5** : a player occupying a middle position on a basketball, football, hockey, lacrosse, or soccer team

²**center** *vb* **cen·tered; cen·ter·ing 1** : to place or fix at or around a center or central area **2** : to collect or concentrate at or around one point, group, or person

center of gravity *n, pl* **centers of gravity** : the point at which the entire weight of a body may be thought of as centered so that if supported at this point the body would balance perfectly

cen·ter·piece *n* : a piece put in the center of something and especially a decoration (as flowers) for a table

centi- *prefix* : hundredth part — used in terms of the metric system

cen·ti·grade *adj* : CELSIUS

cen·ti·gram *n* : a unit of weight equal to $\frac{1}{100}$ gram

cen·ti·li·ter *n* : a unit of liquid capacity equal to $\frac{1}{100}$ liter

cen·ti·me·ter *n* : a unit of length equal to $\frac{1}{100}$ meter

cen·ti·pede *n* : an animal that is an arthropod with a long somewhat flattened body with one pair of legs on most of its many body sections

cen·tral *adj* : **1** : located or placed at, in, or near the center **2** : most important : CHIEF — **cen·tral·ly** *adv*

¹**Central American** *adj* : of or relating to Central America or the Central Americans

²Central American *n* : a person born or living in Central America

central angle *n* : an angle with its vertex at the center of a circle and with sides that are radii of the circle

cen·tral·ize *vb* **cen·tral·ized; cen·tral·iz·ing** : to bring to a central point or under a single control

central processing unit *n* : PROCESSOR 3

cen·tre *chiefly British variant of* CENTER

cen·trif·u·gal force *n* : the force that tends to cause a thing or parts of a thing to go outward from a center of rotation

cen·tu·ry *n, pl* **cen·tu·ries** : a period of 100 years

ce·ram·ic *n* **1** ceramics *pl* : the art of making things (as pottery or tiles) of baked clay **2** : a product made by baking clay

cereal *n* **1** : a plant (as a grass) that produces grain for food **2** : a food prepared from grain

cer·e·bel·lum *n, pl* **cer·e·bel·lums** *or* **cer·e·bel·la** : the lower back part of the brain whose chief functions are controlling the coordination of muscles and keeping the body in proper balance

ce·re·bral *adj* **1** : of or relating to the brain or mind **2** : of, relating to, or affecting the cerebrum

ce·re·brum *n, pl* **ce·re·brums** *or* **ce·re·bra** : the enlarged front and upper part of the brain that is the center of thinking

¹cer·e·mo·ni·al *adj* : of, used in, or being a ceremony — **cer·e·mo·ni·al·ly** *adv*

²ceremonial *n* : a special ceremony

cer·e·mo·ni·ous *adj* **1** : ¹CEREMONIAL **2** : ¹FORMAL 1 — **cer·e·mo·ni·ous·ly** *adv*

cer·e·mo·ny *n, pl* **cer·e·mo·nies** **1** : an act or series of acts performed in some regular way according to fixed rules especially as part of a social or religious event **2** : very polite behavior : FORMALITY

¹cer·tain *adj* **1** : without any doubt : SURE **2** : known to be true **3** : known but not named **4** : being fixed or settled **5** : bound by the way things are **6** : sure to have an effect

²certain *pron* : known ones that are not named

cer·tain·ly *adv* **1** : without fail **2** : without doubt

cer·tain·ty *n, pl* **cer·tain·ties** **1** : something that is sure **2** : the quality or state of being sure

cer·tif·i·cate *n* **1** : a written or printed statement that is proof of some fact **2** : a paper showing that a person has met certain requirements **3** : a paper showing ownership

cer·ti·fy *vb* **cer·ti·fied; cer·ti·fy·ing** **1** : to show to be true or as claimed by a formal or official statement **2** : to guarantee the qual-

ity, fitness, or value of officially **3** : to show to have met certain requirements

ces·sa·tion *n* : a coming to a stop

ch. *abbr* **1** chapter **2** church

chafe *vb* **chafed; chaf·ing** **1** : to become irritated or impatient **2** : to rub so as to wear away or make sore

¹chaff *n* **1** : the husks of grains and grasses separated from the seed in threshing **2** : something worthless

²chaff *vb* **chaffed; chaff·ing** : to tease in a friendly way

cha·grin *n* : a feeling of being annoyed by failure or disappointment

¹chain *n* **1** : a series of connected links or rings usually of metal **2** : a series of things joined together as if by links **3** : a group of businesses that have the same name and sell the same products or services

²chain *vb* **chained; chain·ing** : to fasten, bind, or connect with or as if with a chain

chain reaction *n* : a series of events in which each event causes the next one

chain saw *n* : a portable saw that cuts using teeth that are linked together to form a continuous chain

chair *n* **1** : a seat for one person usually having a back and four legs **2** : a person who leads a meeting, group, or event

chair·man *n, pl* **chair·men** **1** : CHAIR 2 **2** : a person who is in charge of a company — **chair·man·ship** *n*

chair·per·son *n* : CHAIR 2

chair·wom·an *n, pl* **chair·wom·en** **1** : a woman who leads a meeting, group, or event : CHAIR **2** : a woman who is in charge of a company

cha·let *n* **1** : a Swiss dwelling with a steep roof that sticks far out past the walls **2** : a cottage or house built to look like a Swiss chalet

chal·ice *n* : GOBLET

¹chalk *n* **1** : a soft white, gray, or buff limestone made up mainly of the shells of tiny saltwater animals **2** : a material like chalk especially when used for writing or drawing

²chalk *vb* **chalked; chalk·ing** : to rub, mark, write, or draw with chalk — **chalk up 1** : to attribute to a supposed cause or source **2** : to earn or achieve

chalk·board *n* : BLACKBOARD

chalky *adj* **chalk·i·er; chalk·i·est** **1** : made of or like chalk **2** : very pale

¹chal·lenge *vb* **chal·lenged; chal·leng·ing** **1** : to object to as bad or incorrect : DISPUTE **2** : to confront or defy boldly **3** : to invite or dare to take part in a contest **4** : to be difficult enough to be interesting to : test the skill or ability of **5** : to halt and demand identification from — **chal·leng·er** *n*

²challenge *n* **1 :** an objection to something as not being true, genuine, correct, or proper or to a person (as a juror) as not being correct, qualified, or approved **2 :** a call or dare for someone to compete in a contest or sport **3 :** a difficult task or problem **4 :** an order to stop and provide identification

challenged *adj* **:** having a disability or deficiency

cham·ber *n* **1 :** an enclosed space, cavity, or compartment **2 :** a room in a house and especially a bedroom **3 :** a room used for a special purpose **4 :** a meeting hall of a government body **5 :** a room where a judge conducts business outside of the courtroom **6 :** a group of people organized into a lawmaking body **7 :** a board or council of volunteers (as businessmen) — **cham·bered** *adj*

cham·ber·lain *n* **1 :** a chief officer in the household of a ruler or noble **2 :** TREASURER

cham·ber·maid *n* **:** a maid who takes care of bedrooms (as in a hotel)

chamber music *n* **:** instrumental music to be performed in a room or small hall

cha·me·leon *n* **:** a lizard that has the ability to change the color of its skin

cham·ois *n, pl* **cham·ois 1 :** a goatlike animal of the mountains of Europe and Asia **2 :** a soft yellowish leather made from the skin of the chamois or from sheepskin

¹champ *vb* **champed; champ·ing :** to bite and chew noisily — **champing at the bit :** waiting in an impatient way

²champ *n* **1 :** ¹CHAMPION 2 **2 :** ¹CHAMPION 3

¹cham·pi·on *n* **1 :** a person who fights or speaks for another person or in favor of a cause **2 :** a person accepted as better than all others in a sport or in a game of skill **3 :** the winner of first place in a competition

²champion *vb* **cham·pi·oned; cham·pi·on·ing :** to fight or speak publicly in support of

cham·pi·on·ship *n* **:** the position or title of best or winning player or team in a sport or game of skill **2 :** a contest held to determine the best or winning player or team in a sport or game

¹chance *n* **1 :** the unplanned or uncontrolled happening of events **2 :** OPPORTUNITY 1 **3 :** ¹RISK 1, GAMBLE **4 :** the possibility that something will happen **5 :** a ticket in a raffle

²chance *vb* **chanced; chanc·ing 1 :** to take place without planning **:** to happen by luck **2 :** to find or meet unexpectedly **3 :** to accept the danger of **:** RISK

³chance *adj* **:** happening without being planned

chan·cel·lor *n* **1 :** a high government official (as in Germany) **2 :** the head of a university

chan·de·lier *n* **:** a lighting fixture with several branches that usually hangs from the ceiling

¹change *vb* **changed; chang·ing 1 :** to make or become different **2 :** to give a different position, course, or direction to **3 :** to put one thing in the place of another **:** SWITCH **4 :** to give or receive an equal amount of money in usually smaller units of value or in the money of another country **5 :** to put fresh clothes or covering on **6 :** to put on different clothes — **change hands :** to pass from one person's possession or ownership to another's

²change *n* **1 :** the act, process, or result of making or becoming different **2 :** something that is different from what is usual or expected **3 :** a fresh set of clothes **4 :** money in small units of value received in exchange for an equal amount in larger units **5 :** money returned when a payment is more than the amount due **6 :** money in coins

change·able *adj* **:** able or likely to become different

¹chan·nel *n* **1 :** the bed of a stream **2 :** the deeper part of a waterway (as a river or harbor) **3 :** a strait or a narrow sea **4 :** a passage (as a tube) through which something flows **5 :** a long groove **6 :** a means by which something is passed or carried from one place or person to another **7 :** a band of frequencies used by a single radio or television station in broadcasting

²channel *vb* **chan·neled** *or* **chan·nelled; chan·nel·ing** *or* **chan·nel·ling :** to direct into or through a passage or channel

¹chant *vb* **chant·ed; chant·ing 1 :** to sing using a small number of musical tones **2 :** to recite or speak in a rhythmic usually loud way

²chant *n* **1 :** a melody in which several words or syllables are sung on one tone **2 :** something spoken in a rhythmic usually loud way

Chanukah *variant of* HANUKKAH

cha·os *n* **:** complete confusion and disorder

cha·ot·ic *adj* **:** in a state of or characterized by complete confusion and disorder

¹chap *vb* **chapped; chap·ping :** to open in slits **:** CRACK

²chap *n* **:** ¹FELLOW 1

chap·el *n* **1 :** a building or a room or place for prayer or special religious services **2 :** a religious service or assembly held in a school or college

¹chap·er·one *or* **chap·er·on** *n* **:** a person who goes with and is responsible for a group of young people

²chaperone *or* **chaperon** *vb* **chap·er·oned; chap·er·on·ing :** to go with and supervise

a group of young people : act as a chap-
erone

chap·lain *n* : a member of the clergy who
performs religious services for a special
group (as the army)

chaps *n pl* : leather coverings for the legs
worn over pants

chap·ter *n* **1** : a main division of a book or
story **2** : a local branch of a club or organization

char *vb* **charred; char·ring** : to burn slightly

char·ac·ter *n* **1** : a mark, sign, or symbol (as
a letter or figure) used in writing or printing
2 : the group of qualities that make a person, group, or thing different from others **3**
: a distinguishing feature : CHARACTERISTIC
4 : a person who says or does funny or unusual things **5** : a person in a story or play **6**
: the usually good opinions that most people
have about a particular person : REPUTATION
7 : moral excellence

¹char·ac·ter·is·tic *n* : a special quality or appearance that makes an individual or a group
different from others

²characteristic *adj* : serving to distinguish
an individual or a group : typical of a person,
thing, or group — **char·ac·ter·is·ti·cal·ly**
adv

char·ac·ter·ize *vb* **char·ac·ter·ized; char·ac·
ter·iz·ing 1** : to describe the special qualities
of **2** : to be a typical or distinguishing quality of

char·coal *n* : a black or dark absorbent fuel
made by heating wood in the absence of air

¹charge *n* **1** : the responsibility of managing,
controlling, or caring for **2** : a task or duty
given to a person : OBLIGATION **3** : a person
or thing given to someone to look after **4**
: the price asked especially for a service **5**
: an amount listed as a debt on an account **6**
: ACCUSATION **7** : an instruction or command based on authority **8** : the amount of
an explosive material (as dynamite) used in
a single blast **9** : an amount of electricity
10 : a rushing attack **11** : the signal for attack

²charge *vb* **charged; charg·ing 1** : to give
an electric charge to **2** : to refill (as an exhausted battery) with available energy **3** : to
give a task, duty, or responsibility to **4** : to
instruct or command with authority **5** : to
accuse especially formally **6** : to rush toward or against **7** : to ask for payment from
8 : to ask or set as a price or fee **9** : to enter
as a debt or responsibility on a record

charg·er *n* **1** : a device that restores energy to
an exhausted battery **2** : a cavalry horse

char·i·ot *n* : a vehicle of ancient times that
had two wheels, was pulled by horses, and
was used in battle and in races and parades

char·i·ta·ble *adj* **1** : freely giving money or
help to needy persons : GENEROUS **2** : given
for the needy : of service to the needy **3**
: kindly especially in judging other people

char·i·ty *n, pl* **char·i·ties 1** : love for others **2**
: kindliness especially in judging others **3**
: the giving of aid to the needy **4** : aid (as
food or money) given to those in need **5** : an
organization or fund for helping the needy

char·la·tan *n* : a person who falsely pretends
to know or be something

char·ley horse *n* : a painful cramp in a muscle (as of the leg)

¹charm *n* **1** : an action, word, or phrase believed to have magic powers **2** : something
believed to keep away evil and bring good
luck **3** : a small decorative object worn on a
chain or bracelet **4** : a quality that attracts
and pleases

²charm *vb* **charmed; charm·ing 1** : to affect
or influence by or as if by a magic spell **2**
: FASCINATE **2, DELIGHT 3** : to attract by
being graceful, beautiful, or welcoming **4**
: to protect by or as if by a charm

charm·ing *adj* : very pleasing

¹chart *n* **1** : a sheet giving information in a
table or lists or by means of diagrams **2** : a
map showing features (as coasts, currents,
and depths of water) of importance to sailors
3 : a diagram of an area showing information other than natural features

²chart *vb* **chart·ed; chart·ing 1** : to make a
map or chart of **2** : to make a plan for

¹char·ter *n* **1** : an official document setting
out the rights and duties of a group **2** : a
document which declares that a city, town,
school, or corporation has been established
3 : a document that describes the basic laws
or principles of a group

²charter *vb* **char·tered; char·ter·ing 1** : to
grant a charter to **2** : to hire (as a bus or an
aircraft) for temporary use

charter school *n* : a public school that is established by a charter describing its programs and goals and is supported by taxes
but does not have to be run according to
many of the rules of a city or state

¹chase *n* : the act of following quickly in
order to capture or catch up with : PURSUIT

²chase *vb* **chased; chas·ing 1** : to follow
quickly in order to catch up with or capture
2 : to drive away or out

chasm *n* : a deep split or gap in the earth

chas·sis *n, pl* **chas·sis** : the supporting
frame of a structure (as an automobile or television)

chaste *adj* **chast·er; chast·est 1** : pure in
thought and act : MODEST **2** : simple or plain
in design

chas·ten *vb* **chas·tened; chas·ten·ing** : to correct by punishment : DISCIPLINE

chas·tise *vb* **chas·tised; chas·tis·ing 1** : to punish severely (as by whipping) **2** : to criticize harshly — **chas·tise·ment** *n*

chas·ti·ty *n* : the quality or state of being pure in thought and act

¹**chat** *vb* **chat·ted; chat·ting** : to talk in a friendly way about things that are not serious

²**chat** *n* : a light friendly conversation

châ·teau *n, pl* **châ·teaus** *or* **châ·teaux** : a castle or a large house especially in France

¹**chat·ter** *vb* **chat·tered; chat·ter·ing 1** : to talk fast without thinking or without stopping **2** : to make quick sounds that suggest speech but lack meaning **3** : to make clicking sounds by hitting together again and again

²**chatter** *n* **1** : the act or sound of chattering **2** : quick or unimportant talk

chat·ter·box *n* : a person who talks a lot

chat·ty *adj* **chat·ti·er; chat·ti·est 1** : tending to talk a lot : TALKATIVE **2** : having the style and manner of friendly conversation

chauf·feur *n* : a person hired to drive people around in a car

¹**cheap** *adj* **cheap·er; cheap·est 1** : not costing much **2** : charging low prices **3** : worth little : of low quality **4** : gained without much effort **5** : having little self-respect **6** : not willing to share or spend money : STINGY — **cheap·ly** *adv*

²**cheap** *adv* : at low cost

cheap·en *vb* **cheap·ened; cheap·en·ing** : to cause to be of lower quality, value, or importance

cheap·skate *n* : a stingy person

¹**cheat** *vb* **cheat·ed; cheat·ing 1** : to use unfair or dishonest methods to gain an advantage **2** : to take something away from or keep from having something by dishonest tricks — **cheat·er** *n*

²**cheat** *n* : a dishonest person

¹**check** *n* **1** : a sudden stopping of progress : PAUSE **2** : something that delays, stops, or holds back **3** : EXAMINATION 1, INVESTIGATION **4** : a written order telling a bank to pay out money from a person's account to the one named on the order **5** : a ticket or token showing a person's ownership, identity, or claim to something **6** : a slip of paper showing the amount due **7** : a pattern in squares **8** : a mark ✓ typically placed beside a written or printed item to show that something has been specially noted **9** : an act of hitting or stopping a player in hockey **10** : a situation in chess in which a player's king can be captured on the opponent's next turn — **in check** : under control

²**check** *vb* **checked; check·ing 1** : to slow or bring to a stop **2** : to hold back or under control **3** : to make sure that something is correct or satisfactory **4** : to get information by examining **5** : to mark with a check **6** : to leave or accept for safekeeping or for shipment **7** : to stop or hit (a player) in hockey — **check out 1** : to look at **2** : to borrow from a library **3** : to pay for purchases

checked *adj* : CHECKERED

check·er·board *n* : a board marked with 64 squares in two colors and used for games (as checkers)

check·ered *adj* : having a pattern made up of squares of different colors

check·ers *n* : a game played on a checkerboard by two players each having twelve pieces

checking account *n* : an account in a bank from which the depositor can draw money by writing checks

check·mate *n* : a situation in chess in which a player loses because the player's king is in a position from which it cannot escape capture

check·up *n* **1** : INSPECTION, EXAMINATION **2** : a general physical examination made by a doctor or veterinarian

cheek *n* **1** : the side of the face below the eye and above and to the side of the mouth **2** : disrespectful speech or behavior

cheeky *adj* **cheek·i·er; cheek·i·est** : showing disrespect : RUDE

¹**cheep** *vb* : ³PEEP, CHIRP

²**cheep** *n* : ¹CHIRP

¹**cheer** *n* **1** : a happy feeling : good spirits **2** : something that gladdens **3** : a shout of praise or encouragement

²**cheer** *vb* **cheered; cheer·ing 1** : to give hope to or make happier : COMFORT **2** : to grow or be cheerful — usually used with *up* **3** : to urge on especially with shouts or cheers **4** : to shout with joy, approval, or enthusiasm

cheer·ful *adj* **1** : feeling or showing happiness **2** : causing good feelings or happiness **3** : pleasantly bright — **cheer·ful·ly** *adv* — **cheer·ful·ness** *n*

cheer·less *adj* : offering no happiness or cheer : GLOOMY

cheery *adj* **cheer·i·er; cheer·i·est** : merry and bright in manner or effect : CHEERFUL — **cheer·i·ly** *adv* — **cheer·i·ness** *n*

cheese *n* : the curd of milk pressed for use as food

cheese·cloth *n* : a thin loosely woven cotton cloth

cheesy *adj* **chees·i·er; chees·i·est 1** : resembling cheese especially in appearance or smell **2** : containing cheese **3** : of poor quality : lacking style or good taste

chee·tah *n* : a long-legged spotted African and formerly Asian animal of the cat family that is the fastest animal on land

chef *n* **1** : a professional cook who is usually in charge of a kitchen in a restaurant **2** : ¹COOK

¹chem·i·cal *adj* : of or relating to chemistry or chemicals — **chem·i·cal·ly** *adv*

²chemical *n* : any substance (as an acid) that is formed when two or more other substances act upon one another or that is used to produce a change in another substance

chem·ist *n* : a person trained or engaged in chemistry

chem·is·try *n* **1** : a science that deals with the composition and properties of substances and of the changes they undergo **2** : chemical composition and properties

cher·ish *vb* **cher·ished; cher·ish·ing 1** : to hold dear : feel or show affection for **2** : remember or hold in a deeply felt way

Cher·o·kee *n, pl* **Cherokee** *or* **Cherokees 1** : a member of an American Indian people originally of Tennessee and North Carolina **2** : the language of the Cherokee people

cher·ry *n, pl* **cherries 1** : the small round yellow to deep red smooth-skinned fruit of a tree that is related to the plum tree **2** : a medium red

cher·ub *n* **1** : a beautiful child usually with wings in paintings and drawings **2** : a cute chubby child

chess *n* : a game for two players in which each player moves 16 pieces according to fixed rules across a checkerboard and tries to place the opponent's king in a position from which it cannot escape

chest *n* **1** : a container (as a box or case) for storing, safekeeping, or shipping **2** : the front part of the body enclosed by the ribs and breastbone **3** : a fund of public money — **chest·ed** *adj*

chest·nut *n* **1** : a sweet edible nut that grows in burs on a tree related to the beech **2** : a reddish brown

chev·ron *n* : a sleeve badge of one or more bars or stripes usually in the shape of an upside-down V indicating the wearer's rank (as in the armed forces)

¹chew *vb* **chewed; chew·ing** : to crush or grind with the teeth

²chew *n* **1** : the act of crushing or grinding with the teeth **2** : something that a person or animal chews

chew·ing gum *n* : a sweetened and flavored soft material (as of chicle) that is chewed but not swallowed

chewy *adj* **chew·i·er; chew·i·est** : requiring a lot of chewing

Chey·enne *n, pl* **Cheyenne** *or* **Chey·ennes** : a member of an American Indian people of the western plains ranging between the Arkansas and Missouri rivers **2** : the language of the Cheyenne people

¹chic *n* : fashionable style

²chic *adj* **chic·er; chic·est** : STYLISH, FASHIONABLE

Chi·ca·na *n* : an American woman or girl of Mexican ancestry

¹Chi·ca·no *n, pl* **Chicanos** : an American of Mexican ancestry

²Chicano *adj* : of or relating to Chicanos

chick *n* : a baby bird and especially a baby chicken

chick·a·dee *n* : a small mostly grayish bird with the top of the head black

¹chick·en *n* **1** : a bird that is commonly raised by people for its eggs and meat : a hen or rooster **2** : the meat of a chicken used as food **3** : COWARD

²chicken *adj* : COWARDLY 1

chicken out *vb* **chickened out; chickening out** : to become too scared to do something

chicken pox *n* : a contagious illness especially of children in which there is fever and the skin breaks out in watery blisters

chick·pea *n* : an edible roundish pale yellow seed from the pod of an Asian plant that is cooked and eaten as a vegetable

chi·cle *n* : a gum obtained from the sap of a tropical American tree and used in making chewing gum

chide *vb* **chid·ed; chid·ing** : to scold gently

¹chief *n* : the head of a group : LEADER — **in chief** : in the highest ranking position or place

²chief *adj* **1** : highest in rank or authority **2** : most important : MAIN

chief·ly *adv* **1** : above all : most importantly **2** : for the most part

chief master sergeant *n* : a noncommissioned officer in the air force ranking above a senior master sergeant

chief petty officer *n* : a petty officer in the navy or coast guard ranking above a petty officer first class

chief·tain *n* : a chief especially of a band, tribe, or clan

chief warrant officer *n* : a warrant officer in any of the three top grades

chig·ger *n* : the six-legged larva of a mite that clings to the skin and causes itching

chil·blain *n* : a red swollen itchy condition caused by cold that occurs especially on the hands or feet

child *n, pl* **chil·dren 1** : an unborn or recently born person **2** : a young person of ei-

ther sex between infancy and youth **3** : a
son or daughter of any age

child·birth *n* : the act or process of giving
birth to a child

child·hood *n* : the period of life between infancy and youth

child·ish *adj* **1** : of, like, or thought to be
suitable to children **2** : showing the less
pleasing qualities (as silliness) often thought
to be those of children

child·like *adj* **1** : like that of a child **2**
: showing the more pleasing qualities (as innocence and trustfulness) often thought to
be those of children

child·proof *adj* **1** : made to prevent opening
by children **2** : made safe for children

chili *also* **chile** *or* **chil·li** *n, pl* **chil·ies** *also*
chil·es *or* **chil·is** *or* **chil·lies** **1** : a small pepper with a very hot flavor **2** : a spicy stew of
ground beef and chilies usually with beans

¹chill *n* **1** : coldness that is unpleasant but not
extreme **2** : a feeling of coldness accompanied by shivering **3** : a feeling of coldness
caused by fear

²chill *adj* **1** : unpleasantly cold : RAW **2** : not
friendly

³chill *vb* **chilled; chill·ing** **1** : to make or become cold or chilly **2** : to make cool especially without freezing **3** : to cause to feel
cold from fear

chill·ing *adj* : very upsetting or frightening

chilly *adj* **chill·i·er; chill·i·est** : noticeably
cold

¹chime *vb* **chimed; chim·ing** **1** : to make
sounds like a bell **2** : to call or indicate by
chiming — **chime in** : to interrupt or join in
a conversation

²chime *n* **1** : a set of bells tuned to play
music **2** : the sound from a set of bells —
usually used in pl.

chim·ney *n, pl* **chimneys** : a structure that allows smoke to escape (as from a fireplace)
and that is often made of brick

chimney sweep *n* : a person who cleans soot
from chimneys

chimney swift *n* : a small dark gray bird with
long narrow wings that often builds its nest
inside chimneys

chimp *n* : CHIMPANZEE

chim·pan·zee *n* : an African ape that lives
mostly in trees and is smaller than the related gorilla

chin *n* : the part of the face below the mouth
and including the point of the lower jaw

chi·na *n* **1** : PORCELAIN **2** : dishes of pottery
or porcelain for use as tableware

chin·chil·la *n* : a South American animal that
is somewhat like a squirrel and is often
raised for its soft silvery gray fur

¹Chi·nese *adj* : of or relating to China, the
Chinese people, or the languages of China

²Chinese *n, pl* **Chinese** **1** : a person born or
living in China **2** : a group of related languages used in China

chink *n* : a narrow slit or crack (as in a wall)

¹chip *n* **1** : a small piece cut or broken off **2**
: a thin crisp piece of food and especially potato **3** : a small bit of candy used in baking
4 : a flaw left after a small piece has been
broken off **5** : INTEGRATED CIRCUIT **6** : a
small slice of silicon containing a number of
electronic circuits (as for a computer)

²chip *vb* **chipped; chip·ping** **1** : to cut or
break a small piece from **2** : to break off in
small pieces

chip·munk *n* : a small striped animal related
to the squirrels

¹chirp *n* : the short high-pitched sound made
by crickets and some small birds

²chirp *vb* **chirped; chirp·ing** : to make a
short high-pitched sound

¹chis·el *n* : a metal tool with a sharp edge at
the end of a usually flat piece used to chip
away stone, wood, or metal

²chisel *vb* **chis·eled** *or* **chis·elled; chis·el·**
ing *or* **chis·el·ling** : to cut, shape, or carve
with a chisel

chit·chat *n* : friendly conversation

chiv·al·rous *adj* **1** : of or relating to a knight
or knighthood **2** : having or showing honor,
generosity, and courtesy **3** : showing special courtesy and regard to women

chiv·al·ry *n* **1** : the system, spirit, ways, or
customs of knighthood **2** : very honorable
and courteous behavior

chlo·rine *n* : a chemical element that is a
greenish yellow irritating gas of strong odor
used as a bleach and as a disinfectant to pu-
rify water

chlo·ro·form *n* : a colorless heavy liquid used
especially to dissolve fatty substances

chlo·ro·phyll *n* : the green coloring matter
found mainly in the chloroplasts of plants
that absorbs energy from sunlight to produce carbohydrates from carbon dioxide
and water during photosynthesis

chlo·ro·plast *n* : one of the tiny parts in a
plant cell that contains chlorophyll and is
the place where photosynthesis occurs

chock–full *adj* : very full

choc·o·late *n* **1** : a food prepared from
ground roasted cacao beans **2** : a candy
made or coated with chocolate **3** : a beverage of chocolate in water or milk — **choco-**
late *adj*

Choc·taw *n, pl* **Choctaw** *or* **Choc·taws** **1** : a
member of an American Indian people of
Mississippi, Alabama, and Louisiana **2** : the
language of the Choctaw people

¹**choice** *n* **1** : the act of picking between two or more possibilities **2** : the power of choosing : OPTION **3** : a person or thing chosen **4** : a range of possibilities to choose from

²**choice** *adj* **choic·er; choic·est** : of very good quality

choir *n* **1** : an organized group of singers especially in a church **2** : the part of a church set aside for the singers

choke *vb* **choked; chok·ing** **1** : to keep from breathing in a normal way by cutting off the supply of air **2** : to have the trachea blocked entirely or partly **3** : to slow or prevent the growth or action of **4** : to block by clogging — **choke down** : to eat with difficulty — **choke up** : to become too emotional to speak

choke·cher·ry *n, pl* **choke·cher·ries** : a wild cherry tree with clusters of bitter reddish black fruits

chol·era *n* : a serious disease that causes severe vomiting and diarrhea

choose *vb* **chose; cho·sen; choos·ing** **1** : to select freely and after careful thought **2** : to decide what to do **3** : to see fit

choosy *adj* **choos·i·er; choos·i·est** : careful in making choices

¹**chop** *vb* **chopped; chop·ping** **1** : to cut by striking especially over and over with something sharp **2** : to cut into small pieces : MINCE

²**chop** *n* **1** : a sharp downward blow or stroke (as with an ax) **2** : a small cut of meat often including a part of a rib

chop·per *n* **1** : someone or something that chops **2** : HELICOPTER

choppy *adj* **chop·pi·er; chop·pi·est** **1** : rough with small waves **2** : marked by sudden stops and starts : not smooth

chops *n pl* : the fleshy covering of the jaws

chop·stick *n* : one of two thin sticks used chiefly in Asian countries to pick up and eat food

cho·ral *adj* : of or relating to a choir or chorus

cho·rale *n* **1** : a hymn sung by the choir or congregation at a church service **2** : CHORUS 1

¹**chord** *n* : a group of tones sounded together to form harmony

²**chord** *n* : a straight line joining two points on a curve

chore *n* **1** : a small job that is done regularly **2** : a dull, unpleasant, or difficult task

cho·re·og·ra·phy *n* **1** : the art of arranging the movements of dancers for a performance and especially a ballet **2** : the arrangement of a dance — **cho·re·og·ra·pher** *n*

chor·tle *vb* **chor·tled; chor·tling** : to chuckle in amusement or joy

¹**cho·rus** *n* **1** : a group of singers : CHOIR **2** : a group of dancers and singers (as in a musical comedy) **3** : a part of a song or hymn that is repeated every so often : REFRAIN **4** : a song meant to be sung by a group : group singing **5** : sounds uttered by a group of persons or animals together

²**chorus** *vb* **cho·rused; cho·rus·ing** : to speak, sing, or sound at the same time or together

chose *past of* CHOOSE

¹**chosen** *past participle of* CHOOSE

²**cho·sen** *adj* **1** : carefully selected **2** : picked to be shown favor or given special privilege

chow·der *n* : a soup or stew made of fish, clams, or a vegetable usually simmered in milk

Christ *n* : JESUS CHRIST

chris·ten *vb* **chris·tened; chris·ten·ing** **1** : BAPTIZE 1 **2** : to name at baptism **3** : ²NAME 1 **4** : to name or dedicate (as a ship) in a ceremony

chris·ten·ing *n* : BAPTISM

¹**Chris·tian** *n* **1** : a person who believes in Jesus Christ and follows his teachings **2** : a member of a Christian church

²**Christian** *adj* **1** : of or relating to Jesus Christ or the religion based on his teachings **2** : of or relating to people who follow the teachings of Jesus Christ **3** : being what a person who practices Christianity should be or do

Chris·tian·i·ty *n* : the religion based on the teachings of Jesus Christ

Christian name *n* : the personal name given to a person at birth or christening

Christ·mas *n* : December 25 celebrated in honor of the birth of Jesus Christ

Christ·mas·tide *n* : the season of Christmas

Christmas tree *n* : a usually evergreen tree decorated at Christmas

chro·mat·ic scale *n* : a musical scale that has all half steps

chrome *n* **1** : CHROMIUM **2** : something plated with an alloy of chromium

chro·mi·um *n* : a bluish white metallic chemical element used especially in alloys

chro·mo·some *n* : one of the rod-shaped or threadlike structures of a cell nucleus that contain genes and divide when the cell divides

chron·ic *adj* **1** : continuing for a long time or returning often **2** : happening or done frequently or by habit — **chron·i·cal·ly** *adv*

¹**chron·i·cle** *n* : an account of events in the order that they happened : HISTORY

²**chronicle** *vb* **chron·i·cled; chron·i·cling** : to record in the order of occurrence

chron·o·log·i·cal *adj* : arranged in or according to the order of time — **chron·o·log·i·cal·ly** *adv*

chrys·a·lis *n* **1** : a moth or butterfly pupa that is enclosed in a hardened protective case **2** : the hardened protective case made by and enclosing a moth or butterfly pupa

chry·san·the·mum *n* : a plant related to the daisies that has brightly colored flower heads

chub·by *adj* **chub·bi·er; chub·bi·est** : somewhat fat

chuck *vb* **chucked; chuck·ing** **1** : to give a pat or tap to **2** : ¹TOSS 2

¹**chuck·le** *vb* **chuck·led; chuck·ling** : to laugh in a quiet way

²**chuckle** *n* : a low quiet laugh

chuck wagon *n* : a wagon carrying a stove and food for cooking

chug *vb* **chugged; chug·ging** : to move with repeated low sounds like that of a steam engine

¹**chum** *n* : a close friend : PAL

²**chum** *vb* **chummed; chum·ming** : to spend time with as a friend

chum·my *adj* **chum·mi·er; chum·mi·est** : very friendly

chunk *n* : a short thick piece

chunky *adj* **chunk·i·er; chunk·i·est** **1** : heavy, thick, and solid **2** : having a short and thick body **3** : containing many solid pieces

church *n* **1** : a building for public worship and especially Christian worship **2** *often cap* : an organized body of religious believers **3** : public worship

church·yard *n* : an area of land that belongs to and usually surrounds a church and that is often used as a burial ground

¹**churn** *n* : a container in which milk or cream is stirred or shaken in making butter

²**churn** *vb* **churned; churn·ing** **1** : to stir or shake in a churn (as in making butter) **2** : to stir or shake forcefully **3** : to feel the effects of an emotion (as fear) **4** : to move by or as if by forceful stirring action

chute *n* **1** : a tube or passage down or through which people slide or things are slid or dropped **2** : ¹PARACHUTE

ci·ca·da *n* : an insect that has transparent wings and a stout body and the males of which make a loud buzzing noise

-cide *n suffix* **1** : killer **2** : killing

ci·der *n* : the juice pressed out of fruit (as apples) and used especially as a drink and in making vinegar

ci·gar *n* : a small roll of tobacco leaf for smoking

cig·a·rette *n* : a small roll of cut tobacco wrapped in paper for smoking

cil·i·um *n, pl* **cil·ia** : a tiny hairlike structure on the surface of some cells

¹**cinch** *n* **1** : a sure or an easy thing **2** : GIRTH 2

²**cinch** *vb* **cinched; cinch·ing** : to fasten (as a belt or strap) tightly

cin·cho·na *n* : a South American tree whose bark yields quinine

cin·der *n* **1** : a piece of partly burned coal or wood that is not burning **2** : EMBER **3 cinders** *pl* : ²ASH 1

cin·e·ma *n* **1** : a movie theater **2** : the movie industry

cin·na·mon *n* : a spice that is made from the fragrant bark of a tropical Asian tree and is used especially in cooking and baking

¹**ci·pher** *n* **1** : ZERO 1 **2** : a method of secret writing or the alphabet or letters and symbols used in such writing **3** : a message in code

²**cipher** *vb* **ci·phered; ci·pher·ing** : to use figures in doing a problem in arithmetic : CALCULATE

¹**cir·cle** *n* **1** : a line that is curved so that its ends meet and every point on the line is the same distance from the center **2** : something in the form of a circle or part of a circle **3** : ¹CYCLE 2, ROUND **4** : a group of people sharing a common interest

²**circle** *vb* **cir·cled; cir·cling** **1** : to form or draw a circle around **2** : to move or revolve around **3** : to move in or as if in a circle

cir·cuit *n* **1** : a boundary line around an area **2** : an enclosed space **3** : movement around something **4** : a regular tour of service (as by a judge) around an assigned territory : a course so traveled **5** : a series of performances, competitions, or appearances held at many different places **6** : the complete path of an electric current **7** : a group of electronic parts

circuit breaker *n* : a switch that automatically stops the flow of electric current if a circuit becomes overloaded

¹**cir·cu·lar** *adj* **1** : shaped like a circle or part of a circle : ROUND **2** : passing or going around in a circle **3** : not said in simple or sincere language

²**circular** *n* : a printed notice or advertisement given or sent to many people

cir·cu·late *vb* **cir·cu·lat·ed; cir·cu·lat·ing** **1** : to move around in a course **2** : to pass or be passed from place to place or from person to person

cir·cu·la·tion *n* **1** : movement through something **2** : passage from place to place or person to person **3** : the average number of copies (as of a newspaper) sold in a given period

cir·cu·la·to·ry *adj* : of or relating to circulation and especially the circulation of blood in the body

circulatory system *n* : the system of the body that circulates blood and lymph and includes the heart and blood vessels

circum- *prefix* : around : about

cir·cum·fer·ence *n* **1** : the line that goes around a circle **2** : a boundary line enclosing an area **3** : the distance around something

cir·cum·nav·i·gate *vb* **cir·cum·nav·i·gat·ed; cir·cum·nav·i·gat·ing** : to go completely around (as the earth) especially by water

cir·cum·po·lar *adj* **1** : continually visible above the horizon **2** : surrounding or found near a pole of the earth

cir·cum·stance *n* **1** : a fact or event that affects a situation **2 circumstances** *pl* : conditions at a certain time or place **3 circumstances** *pl* : the way something happens **4 circumstances** *pl* : the conditions in which someone lives **5** : an uncontrollable event or situation

cir·cum·vent *vb* **cir·cum·vent·ed; cir·cum·vent·ing** : to avoid the force or effect of by cleverness

cir·cus *n* : a traveling show that often takes place under a tent and that usually includes acts performed by acrobats, clowns, and trained animals

cir·rus *n, pl* **cir·ri** : a thin white cloud of tiny ice crystals that forms at a very high altitude

cis·tern *n* : an artificial reservoir or tank for storing water usually underground

cit·a·del *n* : a fortress that sits high above a city

ci·ta·tion *n* **1** : an official order to appear in court **2** : an act or instance of quoting **3** : QUOTATION **4** : a formal public statement praising a person for doing something good

cite *vb* **cit·ed; cit·ing** **1** : to order to appear in court **2** : to quote as an example, authority, or proof **3** : to refer to especially in praise

cit·i·zen *n* **1** : a person who lives in a particular place **2** : a person who legally belongs to, gives allegiance to, and has the rights and protections of a country

cit·i·zen·ry *n* : all the citizens of a place

cit·i·zen·ship *n* **1** : the state of being a citizen **2** : the behavior expected of a person as a member of a community

cit·ron *n* **1** : a citrus fruit like the smaller lemon and having a thick rind that is preserved for use in cakes and puddings **2** : a small hard watermelon used especially in pickles and preserves

cit·rus *n, pl* **citrus** *or* **cit·rus·es** : a juicy fruit (as a lemon, orange, or grapefruit) with a thick rind that comes from a tree or shrub that grows in warm regions

city *n, pl* **cit·ies** **1** : a place in which people live and work that is larger than a town **2** : the people of a city

city hall *n* : the main administrative building of a city

civ·ic *adj* : of or relating to a citizen, a city, or citizenship

civ·ics *n* : the study of the rights and duties of citizens and of how government works

civ·il *adj* **1** : of or relating to citizens **2** : of or relating to matters within a country **3** : of or relating to the regular business of citizens or government that is not connected to the military or a religion **4** : polite without being friendly **5** : relating to laws about private rights — **civ·il·ly** *adv*

¹ci·vil·ian *n* : a person who is not a member of a military, police, or firefighting force

²civilian *adj* : of or relating to people who are not members of a military, police, or firefighting force

ci·vil·i·ty *n, pl* **ci·vil·i·ties** **1** : polite behavior **2** : a polite act or thing to say

civ·i·li·za·tion *n* **1** : an advanced stage (as in art, science, and government) in the development of society **2** : the way of life of a people **3** : all the societies of the world

civ·i·lize *vb* **civ·i·lized; civ·i·liz·ing** : to cause to have a more advanced or modern way of living

civil rights *n* : the nonpolitical rights of a citizen guaranteed by the Constitution and acts of Congress

civil service *n* : the branch of a government that takes care of the business of running the government and its programs but that does not include the legislature, the military, or the courts

civil war *n* : a war between opposing groups of citizens of the same country

¹clack *vb* **clacked; clack·ing** **1** : to talk rapidly and without stopping **2** : to make or cause to make a short sharp sound

²clack *n* **1** : rapid continuous talk **2** : a sound of clacking

¹clad *past and past participle of* CLOTHE

²clad *adj* **1** : being covered **2** : being dressed

¹claim *vb* **claimed; claim·ing** **1** : to ask for as something that is a right or is deserved **2** : to take as the rightful owner **3** : to state as a fact **4** : to cause the end or death of

²claim *n* **1** : a demand for something believed to be owed **2** : a right to something **3** : something (as an area of land) claimed as one's own **4** : a statement that others may dispute

clam *n* : a shellfish that lives in sand or mud and has a soft body surrounded by a hinged shell with two parts and that is often eaten as food

clam·bake *n* : an outdoor party where clams

and other foods are cooked usually on heated rocks covered by seaweed

clam·ber *vb* **clam·bered; clam·ber·ing** : to climb in an awkward way (as by scrambling)

clam·my *adj* **clam·mi·er; clam·mi·est** : unpleasantly damp, sticky, and cool

¹clam·or *n* **1** : a noisy shouting **2** : a loud continuous noise **3** : strong and loud demand

²clamor *vb* **clam·ored; clam·or·ing** : to make a loud noise or demand

¹clamp *n* : a device that holds or presses parts together firmly

²clamp *vb* **clamped; clamp·ing** : to fasten or to hold tightly with or as if with a clamp

clan *n* **1** : a group (as in the Scottish Highlands) made up of households whose heads claim to have a common ancestor **2** : a large family

¹clang *vb* **clanged; clang·ing** : to make or cause to make the loud ringing sound of metal hitting something

²clang *n* : a loud ringing sound like that made by pieces of metal striking together

¹clank *vb* **clanked; clank·ing 1** : to make or cause to make a clank or series of clanks **2** : to move with a clank

²clank *n* : a sharp short ringing sound

¹clap *vb* **clapped; clap·ping 1** : to hit (the palms of the hands) together usually more than once **2** : to hit or touch with the open hand **3** : to hit together noisily **4** : to put or place quickly or with force

²clap *n* **1** : a loud sharp sound **2** : a hard or a friendly slap

clap·board *n* : a narrow board thicker at one edge than at the other used as siding for a building

clap·per *n* : the part hanging inside a bell that hits the sides to make the bell ring

clar·i·fy *vb* **clar·i·fied; clar·i·fy·ing 1** : to make or to become pure or clear **2** : to make or become more easily understood

clar·i·net *n* : a woodwind instrument with a single reed, a straight body formed like a tube, and keys

clar·i·ty *n* : clear quality or state

¹clash *vb* **clashed; clash·ing 1** : to make or cause to make the loud sound of metal objects hitting **2** : to come into conflict **3** : to not go together well

²clash *n* **1** : a loud sharp sound usually of metal striking metal **2** : a struggle or strong disagreement

¹clasp *n* **1** : a device for holding together objects or parts of something **2** : a firm hold with the hands or arms

²clasp *vb* **clasped; clasp·ing 1** : to fasten

with or as if with a clasp **2** : to hold firmly with the hands or arms

¹class *n* **1** : a group of students who are taught together regularly **2** : one of the meetings of students being taught **3** : a course of instruction **4** : a group of students who graduate together **5** : a group of people in a society who are at the same level of wealth or social status **6** : a group of related living things (as plants or animals) that ranks above the order and below the phylum or division in scientific classification **7** : a category (as of goods or services) based on quality

²class *vb* **classed; class·ing** : CLASSIFY

¹clas·sic *adj* **1** : serving as a model of the best of its kind **2** : fashionable year after year **3** : of or relating to the ancient Greeks and Romans or their culture **4** : being typical of its kind

²classic *n* **1** : a written work or author of ancient Greece or Rome **2** : a great work of art **3** : something long regarded as outstanding of its kind

clas·si·cal *adj* **1** : of a kind that has long been considered great **2** : of or relating to the ancient Greek and Roman world and especially to its language and arts **3** : relating to music in a European tradition that includes opera and symphony and that is generally considered more serious than other kinds of music **4** : concerned with a general study of the arts and sciences

clas·si·fi·ca·tion *n* **1** : the act of arranging into groups of similar things **2** : an arrangement into groups of similar things

clas·si·fied *adj* **1** : arranged in groups with other similar things **2** : kept secret from all but a few people in government

clas·si·fy *vb* **clas·si·fied; clas·si·fy·ing** : to arrange in groups based on similarities

class·mate *n* : a member of the same class in a school or college

class·room *n* : a room where classes are held in a school

¹clat·ter *vb* **clat·tered; clat·ter·ing 1** : to make or cause to make a rattling sound **2** : to move or go with a rattling sound

²clatter *n* **1** : a rattling sound (as of hard objects striking together) **2** : COMMOTION

clause *n* **1** : a separate part of a document (as a will) **2** : a group of words having its own subject and predicate

clav·i·cle *n* : COLLARBONE

¹claw *n* **1** : a sharp usually thin and curved nail on the finger or toe of an animal (as a cat or bird) **2** : the end of a limb of some animals (as an insect, scorpion, or lobster) that is pointed or used for grasping

²claw *vb* **clawed; claw·ing :** to scratch, seize, or dig with claws or fingers

clay *n* **1 :** an earthy material that is sticky and easily molded when wet and hard when baked **2 :** a substance like clay that is used for modeling

¹clean *adj* **clean·er; clean·est 1 :** free of dirt or pollution **2 :** not yet used **3 :** not involving or showing involvement with anything wrong or illegal **4 :** not offensive **5 :** THOROUGH 1 **6 :** having a simple graceful form **:** TRIM **7 :** ¹SMOOTH 1 **— clean·ly** *adv*

²clean *adv* **:** all the way **:** COMPLETELY

³clean *vb* **cleaned; clean·ing :** to make or become free of dirt or disorder **— clean·er** *n*

clean·li·ness *n* **:** the condition of being clean **:** the habit of keeping clean

cleanse *vb* **cleansed; cleans·ing :** to make clean

cleans·er *n* **:** a substance (as a scouring powder) used for cleaning

¹clear *adj* **clear·er; clear·est 1 :** easily heard, seen, noticed, or understood **2 :** free of clouds, haze, or mist **3 :** free from feelings of guilt **4 :** easily seen through **5 :** free from doubt or confusion **:** SURE **6 :** free of blemishes **7 :** not blocked **8 :** BRIGHT 1, LUMINOUS **— clear·ly** *adv* **— clear·ness** *n*

²clear *vb* **cleared; clear·ing 1 :** to free of things blocking **2 :** to make or become free of clouds, haze, or mist **3 :** to get rid of **:** REMOVE **4 :** to go over or by without touching **5 :** to go away **:** DISPERSE **6 :** EXPLAIN 1 **7 :** to free from blame **8 :** to approve or be approved by **9 :** to make as profit

³clear *adv* **1 :** in a way that is easy to hear **2 :** all the way

clear·ance *n* **1 :** the act or process of removing something **2 :** the distance by which one object avoids hitting or touching another **3 :** official permission

clear·ing *n* **:** an open area of land in which there are no trees

cleat *n* **1 :** a wooden or metal device used to fasten a line or a rope **2 :** a strip or projection fastened to the bottom of a shoe to prevent slipping **3** *pl* **:** shoes equipped with cleats

cleav·age *n* **1 :** the tendency of a rock or mineral to split readily in one or more directions **2 :** the action of splitting **3 :** the state of being split

¹cleave *vb* **cleaved** *or* **clove ; cleav·ing :** to cling to a person or thing closely

²cleave *vb* **cleaved** *also* **cleft** *or* **clove; cleaved** *also* **cleft** *or* **clo·ven; cleav·ing :** to divide by or as if by a cutting blow **:** SPLIT

cleav·er *n* **:** a heavy knife used for cutting up meat

clef *n* **:** a sign placed on the staff in writing music to show what pitch is represented by each line and space

¹cleft *n* **1 :** a space or opening made by splitting or cracking **:** CREVICE **2 :** ¹NOTCH 1

²cleft *adj* **:** partly split or divided

clem·en·cy *n, pl* **clemencies 1 :** MERCY 1 **2 :** an act of mercy

clench *vb* **clenched; clench·ing 1 :** to hold tightly **:** CLUTCH **2 :** to set or close tightly

cler·gy *n, pl* **clergies :** the group of religious officials (as priests, ministers, and rabbis) specially prepared and authorized to lead religious services

cler·gy·man *n, pl* **cler·gy·men :** a member of the clergy

cler·i·cal *adj* **1 :** relating to the clergy **2 :** relating to a clerk or office worker

¹clerk *n* **1 :** a person whose job is to keep records or accounts **2 :** a salesperson in a store

²clerk *vb* **clerked; clerk·ing :** to act or work as a clerk

clev·er *adj* **clev·er·er; clev·er·est 1 :** having a quick inventive mind **2 :** showing intelligence, wit, or imagination **3 :** showing skill in using the hands **— clev·er·ly** *adv* **— clev·er·ness** *n*

¹click *vb* **clicked; click·ing 1 :** to make or cause to make a slight sharp noise **2 :** to fit in or work together smoothly **3 :** to select or make a selection especially on a computer by pressing a button on a control device (as a mouse)

²click *n* **:** a slight sharp noise

click·er *n* **:** REMOTE CONTROL 1

cli·ent *n* **:** a person who uses the professional advice or services of another

cli·en·tele *n* **:** a group of clients

cliff *n* **:** a high steep surface of rock

cli·mate *n* **:** the average weather conditions of a place over a period of years

cli·max *n* **:** the most interesting, exciting, or important time or part of something

¹climb *vb* **climbed; climb·ing 1 :** to move in a way that involves going up or down **2 :** to go up or down on often with the help of the hands **3 :** to rise little by little to a higher point **4 :** to go upward in growing (as by winding around something) **5 :** to increase in amount, value, or level **— climb·er** *n*

²climb *n* **1 :** a place where climbing is necessary **2 :** the act of climbing

clime *n* **:** CLIMATE

clinch *vb* **clinched; clinch·ing :** to show to be certain or true

cling *vb* **clung ; cling·ing 1 :** to hold fast by grasping or winding around **2 :** to remain close **3 :** to hold fast or stick closely to a surface **4 :** to continue to believe in

clin·ic *n* **1** : a place where people can receive medical treatment usually for minor ailments **2** : a group meeting for teaching a certain skill and working on individual problems

¹clink *vb* **clinked; clink·ing** : to make or cause to make a slight short sound like that of metal being struck

²clink *n* : a slight sharp ringing sound

¹clip *n* : a device that holds or hooks

²clip *vb* **clipped; clip·ping** : to fasten with a clip

³clip *vb* **clipped; clip·ping** **1** : to shorten or remove by cutting **2** : to cut off or trim the hair or wool of **3** : to cut out or off

⁴clip *n* **1** : a sharp blow **2** : a rapid pace **3** : a short section of a recording

clip·board *n* **1** : a small board with a clip at the top for holding papers **2** : a part of computer memory that is used to store data (as items to be copied to another file) temporarily

clip·per *n* **1 clippers** *pl* : a device used for clipping **2** : a fast sailing ship with three tall masts and large square sails **3** : a person who clips

clip·ping *n* : something cut out or off

clique *n* : a small group of friends who are not friendly to others

¹cloak *n* **1** : a long loose outer garment **2** : something that hides or covers

²cloak *vb* **cloaked; cloak·ing** : to cover or hide completely

cloak·room *n* : a room (as in a school) in which coats and hats may be kept

clob·ber *vb* **clob·bered; clob·ber·ing** **1** : to hit with force **2** : to defeat very easily

¹clock *n* : a device for measuring or telling the time and especially one not meant to be worn or carried by a person — **around the clock** : at every hour of the day

²clock *vb* **clocked; clock·ing** **1** : to measure the amount of time it takes to do something **2** : to show (as time or speed) on a recording device

clock·wise *adv or adj* : in the direction in which the hands of a clock turn

clock·work *n* : machinery that makes the parts of a device move — **like clockwork** : in a very regular or exact way

clod *n* **1** : a lump or mass especially of earth or clay **2** : a clumsy or stupid person

¹clog *vb* **clogged; clog·ging** : to make passage through difficult or impossible : PLUG

²clog *n* **1** : something that hinders or holds back **2** : a shoe having a thick usually wooden sole

clois·ter *n* **1** : MONASTERY, CONVENT **2** : a covered passage with arches along or around the walls of a courtyard

clomp *vb* **clomped; clomp·ing** : to walk with loud heavy steps

clop *n* : a sound like that of a hoof against pavement

¹close *vb* **closed; clos·ing** **1** : to cover the opening of **2** : to change the position of so as to prevent passage through an opening : SHUT **3** : to bring or come to an end **4** : to end the operation of for a period of time or permanently **5** : to bring the parts or edges of together **6** : ¹APPROACH 1 **7** : ¹DECREASE — **close in** : to come or move nearer or closer

²close *n* : the point at which something ends

³close *adj* **clos·er; clos·est** **1** : not far apart in space, time, degree, or effect **2** : very similar **3** : almost reaching a particular condition **4** : having a strong liking each one for the other **5** : strict and careful in attention to details **6** : decided by a narrow margin **7** : ¹SHORT 1 **8** : having little extra space **9** : kept secret or tending to keep secrets **10** : lacking fresh or moving air — **close·ly** *adv* — **close·ness** *n*

⁴close *adv* **clos·er; clos·est** : a short distance or time away

close call *n* : a barely successful escape from a difficult or dangerous situation

closed *adj* : not open

clos·et *n* : a small room for clothing or for supplies for the house

close–up *n* : a photograph taken at close range

clo·sure *n* **1** : an act of closing **2** : the condition of being closed

¹clot *n* : a lump made by some substance getting thicker and sticking together

²clot *vb* **clot·ted; clot·ting** : to become thick and partly solid

cloth *n, pl* **cloths 1** : a woven or knitted material (as of cotton or nylon) **2** : a piece of cloth for a certain use **3** : TABLECLOTH

clothe *vb* **clothed** *or* **clad; cloth·ing** **1** : to cover with or as if with clothing : DRESS **2** : to provide with clothes

clothes *n pl* : CLOTHING

clothes·pin *n* : a small object used for holding clothes in place on a line

cloth·ing *n* : the things people wear to cover their bodies

¹cloud *n* **1** : a visible mass of tiny bits of water or ice hanging in the air usually high above the earth **2** : a visible mass of small particles in the air **3** : a large number of things that move together in a group **4** : an overwhelming feeling — **cloud·less** *adj*

²cloud *vb* **cloud·ed; cloud·ing** **1** : to make or become cloudy **2** : to have a bad effect on **3** : to make confused

cloud·burst *n* : a sudden heavy rainfall

cloudy *adj* **cloud·i·er; cloud·i·est** **1** : overspread with clouds **2** : not clear — **cloud·i·ness** *n*

¹clout *n* **1** : a blow especially with the hand **2** : the power to influence or control situations

²clout *vb* **clout·ed; clout·ing** : to hit hard

¹clove *n* : the dried flower bud of a tropical tree used in cooking as a spice

²clove *past of* CLEAVE

cloven *past participle of* ²CLEAVE

cloven hoof *n* : a hoof (as of a sheep or cow) with the front part divided into two sections

clo·ver *n* : a small plant that has leaves with three leaflets and usually roundish red, white, yellow, or purple flower heads and is sometimes grown for hay or pasture

¹clown *n* **1** : a performer (as in a circus) who entertains by playing tricks and who usually wears comical clothes and makeup **2** : someone who does things to make people laugh

²clown *vb* **clowned; clown·ing** : to act in a funny or silly way : act like a clown

¹club *n* **1** : a heavy usually wooden stick used as a weapon **2** : a stick or bat used to hit a ball in various games **3** : a group of people associated because of a shared interest **4** : the meeting place of a club

²club *vb* **clubbed; club·bing** : to beat or strike with or as if with a club

club·house *n* **1** : a building used by a club **2** : locker rooms used by an athletic team

¹cluck *vb* **clucked; cluck·ing** : to make the low sound of or like a hen

²cluck *n* : the sound made by a hen

clue *n* : something that helps a person to find something or to solve a mystery

¹clump *n* **1** : a group of things clustered together **2** : a cluster or lump of something **3** : a heavy tramping sound

²clump *vb* **clumped; clump·ing** **1** : to form or cause to form a clump or clumps **2** : to walk with loud heavy steps : CLOMP

clum·sy *adj* **clum·si·er; clum·si·est** **1** : lacking skill or grace in movement **2** : awkwardly or carelessly made or done **3** : awkward to handle — **clum·si·ly** *adv* — **clum·si·ness** *n*

clung *past and past participle of* CLING

clunk *n* : a loud dull sound

¹clus·ter *n* : a number of similar things growing or grouped closely together : BUNCH

²cluster *vb* **clus·tered; clus·ter·ing** : to grow, collect, or assemble in a bunch

¹clutch *vb* **clutched; clutch·ing** **1** : to grasp or hold tightly with or as if with the hands or claws **2** : to make a grab

²clutch *n* **1** : control or power someone has over someone else — usually used in pl. **2** : a coupling for connecting and disconnecting a driving and a driven part in machinery **3** : a lever or pedal operating a clutch

³clutch *n* **1** : a group of eggs that is laid by a bird at one time **2** : a small group of things or people

¹clut·ter *vb* **clut·tered; clut·ter·ing** : to fill or cover with scattered things

²clutter *n* : a collection of scattered things

cm *abbr* centimeter

co. *abbr* **1** company **2** county

CO *abbr* Colorado

co- *prefix* **1** : with : together : joint : jointly **2** : in or to the same degree **3** : fellow : partner

¹coach *n* **1** : a large carriage that has four wheels and a raised seat outside in front for the driver and is drawn by horses **2** : a person who instructs or trains a performer or team **3** : a person who teaches students individually **4** : a railroad passenger car without berths **5** : the least expensive seats on an airplane or a train

²coach *vb* **coached; coach·ing** : to teach and train

coach·man *n, pl* **coach·men** : a person whose business is driving a coach or carriage

co·ag·u·late *vb* **co·ag·u·lat·ed; co·ag·u·lat·ing** : to gather into a thick compact mass : CLOT

coal *n* **1** : a piece of glowing or charred wood : EMBER **2** : a black solid mineral substance that is formed by the partial decay of plant matter under the influence of moisture and often increased pressure and temperature within the earth and is mined for use as a fuel

coarse *adj* **coars·er; coars·est** **1** : having a harsh or rough quality **2** : made up of large particles **3** : crude in taste, manners, or language **4** : of poor or ordinary quality — **coarse·ly** *adv* — **coarse·ness** *n*

coars·en *vb* **coars·ened; coars·en·ing** : to make or become rough or rougher

¹coast *n* : the land near a shore

²coast *vb* **coast·ed; coast·ing** **1** : to move downhill by the force of gravity **2** : to sail close to shore along a coast

coast·al *adj* : of, relating to, or located on, near, or along a coast

coast·er *n* **1** : a ship that sails or trades along a coast **2** : a small mat on which a glass is placed to protect the surface of a table

coast guard *n* : a military force that guards a coast and helps people on boats and ships that are in trouble

¹coat *n* **1** : an outer garment worn especially for warmth **2** : the outer covering (as fur or feathers) of an animal **3** : a layer of material covering a surface — **coat·ed** *adj*

²**coat** *vb* **coat·ed; coat·ing** : to cover with a coat or covering

coat·ing *n* : ¹COAT 3, COVERING

coat of arms *n, pl* **coats of arms** : a special group of pictures or symbols belonging to a person, family, or group and shown on a shield

coat of mail *n, pl* **coats of mail** : a garment of metal scales or rings worn long ago as armor

co·au·thor *n* : an author who works with another author

coax *vb* **coaxed; coax·ing 1** : to influence by gentle urging, special attention, or flattering **2** : to get or win by means of gentle urging or flattery

cob *n* **1** : a male swan **2** : CORNCOB

co·balt *n* : a tough shiny silvery white metallic chemical element found with iron and nickel

cob·bled *adj* : paved or covered with cobblestones

cob·bler *n* **1** : a person who mends or makes shoes **2** : a fruit pie with a thick upper crust and no bottom crust that is baked in a deep dish

cob·ble·stone *n* : a rounded stone used especially in the past to pave streets

co·bra *n* : a very poisonous snake of Asia and Africa that puffs out the skin around its neck into a hood when threatened

cob·web *n* **1** : SPIDERWEB **2** : tangles of threads of old spiderwebs usually covered with dirt and dust

co·caine *n* : a habit-forming drug obtained from the leaves of a South American shrub and sometimes used as a medicine to deaden pain

coc·cus *n, pl* **coc·ci** : a bacterium shaped like a ball

co·chlea *n, pl* **co·chle·as** *or* **co·chle·ae** : a coiled tube in the inner part of the ear that contains the endings of the nerve which carries information about sound to the brain

¹**cock** *n* **1** : a male bird : ROOSTER **2** : a faucet or valve for controlling the flow of a liquid or a gas

²**cock** *vb* **cocked; cock·ing 1** : to turn or tip upward or to one side **2** : to set or draw back in readiness for some action **3** : to draw back the hammer of (a gun) in readiness for firing

³**cock** *n* : the act of tipping or turning at an angle : TILT

cock·a·too *n, pl* **cock·a·toos** : a large, noisy,

and usually brightly colored crested parrot mostly of Australia

cock-eyed *adj* **1** : tilted to one side **2** : FOOLISH

cock·le *n* : an edible shellfish with a shell that has two parts and is shaped like a heart

cock·le·bur *n* : a plant with prickly fruit that is related to the thistles

cock·le·shell *n* : a shell of a cockle

cock·pit *n* **1** : an open space in the deck from which a small boat (as a yacht) is steered **2** : a space in an airplane for the pilot

cock·roach *n* : a black or brown insect that is active chiefly at night and can be a troublesome pest in homes

cocky *adj* **cock·i·er; cock·i·est** : very sure of oneself : boldly self-confident

co·coa *n* **1** : a brown powder that is made from the roasted seeds (**cocoa beans**) of the cacao tree after some of its fat is removed and that is used to make chocolate **2** : a hot drink made from cocoa powder mixed with water or milk

co·co·nut *n* : a large nutlike fruit that has a thick husk with white flesh and a watery liquid inside it and that grows on a tall tropical palm (**coconut palm**)

co·coon *n* : the silky covering which moth caterpillars make around themselves and in which they are protected while changing into a moth

cod *n, pl* **cod** : a large fish found in the deep colder parts of the northern Atlantic Ocean and often used for food

COD *abbr* **1** cash on delivery **2** collect on delivery

cod·dle *vb* **cod·dled; cod·dling** : to treat with too much care : PAMPER

¹**code** *n* **1** : a system of rules or principles **2** : a system of signals or letters and symbols with special meanings used for sending messages **3** : a collection of laws **4** : GENETIC CODE **5** : a set of instructions for a computer

²**code** *vb* **cod·ed; cod·ing** : to put in the form of a code

cod·fish *n, pl* **codfish** *or* **cod·fish·es** : COD

cod·ger *n* : an odd or cranky man

co·erce *vb* **co·erced; co·erc·ing** : ²FORCE 1, COMPEL

cof·fee *n* **1** : a drink made from the roasted and ground seeds (**coffee beans**) of a tropical plant **2** : the roasted seeds of the coffee plant when whole or ground

coffee table *n* : a low table usually placed in front of a sofa

cof·fer *n* : a box used especially for holding money and valuables

cof·fin *n* : a box or case to hold a dead body for burial

cog *n* : a tooth on the rim of a wheel or gear

cog·i·tate *vb* **cog·i·tat·ed; cog·i·tat·ing** : to think over : PONDER

cog·i·ta·tion *n* : careful consideration

cog·wheel *n* : a wheel with cogs on the rim

co·her·ent *adj* **1** : logical and well-organized **2** : to be able to speak well

co·he·sion *n* **1** : the action of sticking together **2** : the force of attraction between the molecules in a mass

¹coil *n* **1** : a circle, a series of circles, or a spiral made by coiling **2** : a long thin piece of material that is wound into circles

²coil *vb* **coiled; coil·ing 1** : to wind into rings or a spiral **2** : to form or lie in a coil

¹coin *n* **1** : a piece of metal put out by government authority as money **2** : metal money

²coin *vb* **coined; coin·ing 1** : to make coins especially by stamping pieces of metal : MINT **2** : to make metal (as gold or silver) into coins **3** : to make up (a new word or phrase)

coin·age *n* **1** : the act or process of making coins **2** : money in the form of coins **3** : a word or phrase that has recently been invented

co·in·cide *vb* **co·in·cid·ed; co·in·cid·ing 1** : to happen at the same time **2** : to agree exactly **3** : to occupy the same space

co·in·ci·dence *n* **1** : a situation in which things happen at the same time without planning **2** : a condition of coming together in space or time

coke *n* : gray lumps of fuel made by heating soft coal in a closed chamber until some of its gases have passed off

col. *abbr* column

Col. *abbr* **1** colonel **2** Colorado

col- — see COM-

co·la *n, pl* **co·las** : a sweet brown carbonated soft drink that contains flavoring from the nut of a tropical tree

col·an·der *n* : a bowl-shaped utensil with small holes for draining foods

¹cold *adj* **cold·er; cold·est 1** : having a low temperature or one much below normal **2** : suffering from lack of warmth **3** : cooled after being cooked **4** : served at a low temperature or with ice **5** : lacking warmth of feeling : UNFRIENDLY — **cold·ly** *adv* — **cold·ness** *n* — **in cold blood** : with planning beforehand

²cold *n* **1** : a condition of low temperature : cold weather **2** : the bodily feeling produced by lack of warmth : CHILL **3** : COMMON COLD

cold–blood·ed *adj* **1** : having a body temperature that varies with the temperature of the environment **2** : lacking or showing a lack of normal human feelings

cold cuts *n pl* : slices of cold cooked meats

cole·slaw *n* : a salad made with chopped raw cabbage

co·le·us *n* : a plant grown as a houseplant or a garden plant for its many-colored leaves

col·ic *n* **1** : sharp pain in the intestines **2** : a condition in which a healthy baby is uncomfortable and cries for long periods of time — **col·icky** *adj*

col·i·se·um *n* : a large structure (as a stadium) for athletic contests or public entertainment

col·lab·o·rate *vb* **col·lab·o·rat·ed; col·lab·o·rat·ing 1** : to work with others (as in writing a book) **2** : to cooperate with an enemy force that has taken over a person's country

col·lage *n* : a work of art made by gluing pieces of different materials to a flat surface

¹col·lapse *vb* **col·lapsed; col·laps·ing 1** : to break down completely : fall in **2** : to completely relax **3** : to suffer a physical or mental breakdown **4** : to fail or stop working suddenly **5** : to fold together

²collapse *n* : the act or an instance of breaking down

col·laps·ible *adj* : capable of collapsing or possible to collapse

¹col·lar *n* **1** : the part of a piece of clothing that fits around a person's neck **2** : a band of material worn around an animal's neck **3** : a ring used to hold something (as a pipe) in place — **col·lar·less** *adj*

²collar *vb* **col·lared; col·lar·ing** : to seize by or as if by the collar : CAPTURE, GRAB

col·lar·bone *n* : a bone of the shoulder joined to the breastbone and the shoulder blade

col·league *n* : an associate in a profession : a fellow worker

col·lect *vb* **col·lect·ed; col·lect·ing 1** : to gather from a number of sources **2** : to receive payment for **3** : to bring or come together into one body or place **4** : to gain or regain control of **5** : to increase in amount **6** : to get and bring

col·lect·ed *adj* : ³CALM 2

col·lect·ible *adj* : considered valuable by collectors — **collectible** *n*

col·lec·tion *n* **1** : the act or process of gathering together **2** : a group of things that have been gathered **3** : a group of objects gathered for study or exhibition or as a hobby **4** : the act of gathering money (as for charitable purposes) **5** : money gathered for a charitable purpose

col·lec·tive *adj* **1** : having to do with a number of persons or things thought of as a whole **2** : done or shared by a number of persons as a group — **col·lec·tive·ly** *adv*

col·lec·tor *n* **1** : a person or thing that collects **2** : a person whose business it is to collect money

col·lege *n* : a school that offers more advanced classes than a high school

col·le·giate *adj* **1** : having to do with a college **2** : of, relating to, or characteristic of college students

col·lide *vb* **col·lid·ed; col·lid·ing 1** : to strike against each other with strong force **2** : ¹CLASH 2

col·lie *n* : a large usually long-haired dog of Scottish origin that has been used to herd sheep

col·li·sion *n* : an act or instance of colliding

col·lo·qui·al *adj* : used in or suited to familiar and informal conversation

col·lo·qui·al·ism *n* : a word or expression used in or suited to familiar and informal conversation

co·logne *n* : a perfumed liquid made up of alcohol and fragrant oils

¹co·lon *n* : the main part of the large intestine

²colon *n* : a punctuation mark : used mostly to call attention to what follows (as a list, explanation, or quotation)

col·o·nel *n* : a commissioned officer in the army, air force, or marine corps ranking above a major and below a general

¹co·lo·nial *adj* **1** : of, relating to, or characteristic of a colony **2** *often cap* : of or relating to the original 13 colonies that formed the United States

²colonial *n* : a member of or a person living in a colony

col·o·nist *n* **1** : a person living in a colony **2** : a person who helps to found a colony

col·o·nize *vb* **col·o·nized; col·o·niz·ing 1** : to establish a colony in or on **2** : to settle in a colony

col·on·nade *n* : a row of columns usually supporting a roof

col·o·ny *n, pl* **col·o·nies 1** : a distant territory belonging to or under the control of a nation **2** : a group of people sent out by a government to a new territory **3** : a group of living things of one kind living together **4** : a group of people with common qualities or interests located in close association

¹col·or *n* **1** : the appearance of a thing apart from size and shape when light strikes it **2** : skin tone as a mark of race **3** : the rosy tint of a light-skinned person's face **4** : ²BLUSH 1 **5 colors** *pl* : an identifying flag **6** : ¹INTEREST 2

²color *vb* **col·ored; col·or·ing 1** : to give color to **2** : to change the color of **3** : to fill in the outlines of a shape or picture with color **4** : to take on or change color : BLUSH **5** : ²INFLUENCE

col·or·ation *n* : use or arrangement of colors or shades : COLORING

color–blind *adj* : unable to see the difference between certain colors

col·ored *adj* : having color

col·or·ful *adj* **1** : having bright colors **2** : full of variety or interest

col·or·ing *n* **1** : the act of applying colors **2** : something that produces color **3** : the effect produced by the use of color **4** : natural color **5** : COMPLEXION

coloring book *n* : a book of drawings made in solid lines for coloring

col·or·less *adj* **1** : having no color **2** : WAN, PALE **3** : ¹DULL 3

co·los·sal *adj* : very large : HUGE

col·our *chiefly British variant of* COLOR

colt *n* : a young male horse

col·um·bine *n* : a plant that has leaves with three parts and showy flowers usually with five petals that are thin and pointed

col·umn *n* **1** : one of two or more vertical sections of a printed page **2** : a group of items shown one under the other down a page **3** : a regular feature in a newspaper or magazine **4** : a pillar used to support a building **5** : something that is tall or thin in shape or arrangement **6** : a long straight row

col·um·nist *n* : a writer of a column in a newspaper or magazine

com *abbr* commercial organization

com- *or* **col-** *or* **con-** *prefix* : with : together : jointly — usually *com-* before *b, p,* or *m, col-* before *l* and *con-* before other sounds

co·ma *n* : a deep sleeplike state caused by sickness or injury

Co·man·che *n, pl* **Comanche** *or* **Co·man·ches 1** : a member of an American Indian people ranging from Wyoming and Nebraska into New Mexico and northwestern Texas **2** : the language of the Comanche people

¹comb *n* **1** : a toothed implement used to smooth and arrange the hair or worn in the hair to hold it in place **2** : a soft fleshy part on top of the head of a chicken or some related birds **3** : HONEYCOMB

²comb *vb* **combed; comb·ing 1** : to smooth, arrange, or untangle with a comb **2** : to search over or through carefully

¹com·bat *n* **1** : a fight or contest between individuals or groups **2** : active military fighting

²com·bat *vb* **com·bat·ed** *or* **com·bat·ted; com·bat·ing** *or* **com·bat·ting** : to fight with : fight against : OPPOSE

com·bat·ant *n* : a person who takes part in a combat

com·bi·na·tion *n* **1** : a result or product of

combining or being combined **2** : a series of numbers or letters that is used to open a lock

combination lock *n* : a lock with one or more dials or rings marked usually with numbers which are used to open the lock by moving them in a certain order to certain positions

¹**com·bine** *vb* **com·bined; com·bin·ing 1** : to mix together so as to make or to seem one thing **2** : to be or cause to be together for a purpose

²**com·bine** *n* **1** : a union of persons or groups that work together to achieve a common goal **2** : a machine that harvests and threshes grain

com·bus·ti·ble *adj* : catching fire or burning easily

com·bus·tion *n* : the process of burning

come *vb* **came** ; **come; com·ing 1** : to move toward : APPROACH **2** : to go or travel to a place **3** : ORIGINATE 2, ARISE **4** : to reach the point of being or becoming **5** : to add up : AMOUNT **6** : to happen or occur **7** : to be available **8** : ¹REACH 3 — **come about** : HAPPEN 1 — **come across** : to meet or find by chance — **come along 1** : to go somewhere with someone **2** : to make progress **3** : to appear or occur as a possibility — **come by 1** : to make a visit to **2** : ACQUIRE — **come down** : to fall sick — **come over** : to affect suddenly and strangely — **come to** : to become conscious again — **come upon** : to meet or find by chance

co·me·di·an *n* **1** : a performer who makes people laugh **2** : an amusing person

com·e·dy *n, pl* **com·e·dies 1** : an amusing play that has a happy ending **2** : an amusing and often ridiculous event

come·ly *adj* **come·li·er; come·li·est** : physically attractive

com·et *n* : a small bright heavenly body that develops a cloudy tail as it moves in an orbit around the sun

¹**com·fort** *vb* **com·fort·ed; com·fort·ing** : to ease the grief or trouble of

²**comfort** *n* **1** : acts or words that bring relief from grief or trouble **2** : the feeling of being cheered **3** : something that makes a person comfortable

com·fort·able *adj* **1** : giving physical ease **2** : more than what is needed **3** : physically at ease — **com·fort·ably** *adj*

com·fort·er *n* **1** : a person or thing that gives relief to someone suffering grief or trouble **2** : ¹QUILT

com·ic *adj* **1** : of, relating to, or characteristic of comedy **2** : ¹FUNNY 1

com·i·cal *adj* : ¹FUNNY 1, RIDICULOUS — **com·i·cal·ly** *adv*

comic book *n* : a magazine made up of a series of comic strips

comic strip *n* : a series of cartoons that tell a story or part of a story

com·ma *n* : a punctuation mark , used chiefly to show separation of words or word groups within a sentence

¹**com·mand** *vb* **com·mand·ed; com·mand·ing 1** : to order with authority **2** : to have power or control over : be commander of **3** : to demand as right or due : EXACT **4** : to survey from a good position

²**command** *n* **1** : an order given **2** : the authority, right, or power to command : CONTROL **3** : the ability to control and use : MASTERY **4** : the people, area, or unit (as of soldiers and weapons) under a commander **5** : a position from which military operations are directed

com·man·dant *n* : an officer who is in charge of a group of soldiers

com·mand·er *n* : a commissioned officer in the navy or coast guard ranking above a lieutenant and below a captain

commander in chief *n, pl* **commanders in chief** : a person who holds supreme command of the armed forces of a nation

com·mand·ment *n* **1** : something given as a command **2** : one of ten rules given by God that are mentioned in the Bible

com·man·do *n, pl* **com·man·dos** *or* **com·man·does 1** : a unit of troops trained for making surprise raids into enemy territory **2** : a member of a commando

command sergeant major *n* : a noncommissioned officer in the army ranking above a first sergeant

com·mem·o·rate *vb* **com·mem·o·rat·ed; com·mem·o·rat·ing 1** : to observe with a ceremony **2** : to serve as a memorial of

com·mem·o·ra·tion *n* **1** : the act of commemorating **2** : something (as a ceremony) that commemorates

com·mence *vb* **com·menced; com·menc·ing** : BEGIN 1, START

com·mence·ment *n* **1** : graduation exercises **2** : the act or the time of beginning

com·mend *vb* **com·mend·ed; com·mend·ing 1** : to give into another's care : ENTRUST **2** : to speak or write of with approval : PRAISE

com·mend·able *adj* : deserving praise or approval

com·men·da·tion *n* **1** : ²PRAISE 1, APPROVAL **2** : an expression of approval

¹**com·ment** *n* **1** : an expression of opinion either in speech or writing **2** : mention of something that deserves notice

²**comment** *vb* **com·ment·ed; com·ment·ing**

: to make a statement about someone or something : make a comment

com·men·ta·tor *n* : a person who describes or analyzes a news, sports, or entertainment event (as over radio or on television)

com·merce *n* : the buying and selling of goods especially on a large scale and between different places : TRADE

¹com·mer·cial *n* : an advertisement broadcast on radio or television

²commercial *adj* **1** : having to do with the buying and selling of goods and services **2** : used to earn a profit — **com·mer·cial·ly** *adv*

com·mer·cial·ize *vb* **com·mer·cial·ized; com·mer·cial·iz·ing** : to handle with the idea of making a profit

¹com·mis·sion *n* **1** : an order granting the power to perform various acts or duties : the right or duty to be performed **2** : a certificate that gives military or naval rank and authority : the rank and authority given **3** : authority to act as agent for another : a task or piece of business entrusted to an agent **4** : a group of persons given orders and authority to perform specified duties **5** : an act of doing something wrong **6** : a fee paid to an agent for taking care of a piece of business

²commission *vb* **com·mis·sioned; com·mis·sion·ing 1** : to give a commission to **2** : to put (a ship) into service

commissioned officer *n* : an officer in the armed forces who ranks above the enlisted persons or warrant officers and who is appointed by the President

com·mis·sion·er *n* **1** : a member of a commission **2** : an official who is the head of a government department

com·mit *vb* **com·mit·ted; com·mit·ting 1** : to bring about : PERFORM **2** : to make secure or put in safekeeping : ENTRUST **3** : to place in or send to a prison or mental hospital **4** : to pledge to do some particular thing — **com·mit·ment** *n*

com·mit·tee *n* : a group of persons appointed or elected to study a problem, plan an event, or perform a specific duty

com·mod·i·ty *n, pl* **com·mod·i·ties** : something produced by agriculture, mining, or manufacture

com·mo·dore *n* : an officer of high rank in the navy

¹com·mon *adj* **1** : affecting, belonging to, needed by, or used by everybody **2** : shared by two or more individuals or by the members of a family or group **3** : ¹GENERAL 1 **4** : occurring, appearing, or used frequently **5** : not above the average in rank or status **6** : not privileged or elite **7** : expected from

polite and decent people — **in common** : shared together

²common *n* : land (as a park) owned and used by a community

common cold *n* : a contagious illness which causes the lining of the nose and throat to be sore, swollen, and red and in which there is usually much mucus and coughing and sneezing

common denominator *n* : a common multiple of the denominators of a number of fractions

common·er *n* : a person who is not privileged or high in social status

common multiple *n* : a multiple of each of two or more numbers

common noun *n* : a noun that names a class of persons or things or any individual of a class and that may occur with a limiting modifier (as *a*, *the*, *some*, or *every*)

¹com·mon·place *adj* : often seen or met with : ORDINARY

²commonplace *n* : something that is often seen or met with

common sense *n* : ordinary good sense and judgment — **com·mon·sense** *adj*

com·mon·wealth *n* **1** : a political unit (as a nation or state) **2** : one of four states of the United States—Kentucky, Massachusetts, Pennsylvania, or Virginia

com·mo·tion *n* : noisy excitement and confusion : TURMOIL

com·mune *vb* **com·muned; com·mun·ing** : to be in close accord or communication with someone or something

com·mu·ni·ca·ble *adj* : able to be passed to another person

com·mu·ni·cate *vb* **com·mu·ni·cat·ed; com·mu·ni·cat·ing 1** : to get in touch **2** : to make known **3** : to pass (as a disease) from one to another : SPREAD

com·mu·ni·ca·tion *n* **1** : the exchange (as by speech or letter) of information between persons **2** : information exchanged **3 communications** *pl* : a system of sending information **4 communications** *pl* : a system of routes for transportation

com·mu·nion *n* **1** : a close relationship **2** *cap* : a Christian ceremony commemorating with bread and wine the last supper of Jesus Christ **3** : a body of Christians having similar beliefs

com·mu·nism *n* : a social system or theory in which property and goods are held in common

com·mu·nist *n* : a person who supports communism

com·mu·ni·ty *n, pl* **com·mu·ni·ties 1** : the people living in a certain place (as a village or city) : the area itself **2** : a natural group (as of kinds of plants and animals) living together and depending on one another for various necessities of life (as food or shelter) **3** : a group of people with common interests **4** : a feeling of caring about others in a group

com·mu·ta·tive *adj* : being a property of a mathematical operation (as addition or multiplication) in which the result does not depend on the order of the elements

com·mute *vb* **com·mut·ed; com·mut·ing 1** : to travel back and forth regularly **2** : to change (as a penalty) to something less severe — **com·mut·er** *n*

¹com·pact *adj* **1** : closely united or packed **2** : arranged so as to save space — **com·pact·ly** *adv* — **com·pact·ness** *n*

²compact *vb* **com·pact·ed; com·pact·ing 1** : to draw together : COMBINE **2** : to press together tightly

³com·pact *n* **1** : a small case for cosmetics **2** : a somewhat small automobile

⁴com·pact *n* : AGREEMENT 3

compact disc *n* : CD

com·pan·ion *n* **1** : a person or thing that accompanies another **2** : one of a pair of things that go together **3** : a person employed to live with and assist another

com·pan·ion·ship *n* : FELLOWSHIP 1, COMPANY

com·pa·ny *n, pl* **com·pa·nies 1** : an association of persons operating a business **2** : the presence of someone who brings comfort **3** : a person or thing someone enjoys being with **4** : a person's companions or associates **5** : guests or visitors especially at a person's home **6** : a group of persons or things **7** : a body of soldiers **8** : a band of musical or dramatic performers

com·pa·ra·ble *adj* : being similar or about the same

¹com·par·a·tive *adj* **1** : not entirely but more so than others : RELATIVE **2** : of or relating to the form of an adjective or adverb that shows an increase in the quality that the adjective or adverb expresses — **com·par·a·tive·ly** *adv*

²comparative *n* : the degree or form in a language that indicates an increase in the quality expressed by an adjective or adverb

com·pare *vb* **com·pared; com·par·ing 1** : to point out as similar : LIKEN **2** : to examine for similarity or differences **3** : to appear in relation to others **4** : to state the positive, comparative, and superlative forms of an adjective or adverb

com·par·i·son *n* **1** : the act of examining things to see if they are similar or different : the condition of being examined to find similarity or difference **2** : SIMILARITY **3**

: change in the form and meaning of an adjective or an adverb (as by adding *-er* or *-est* to the word or by adding *more* or *most* before the word) to show different levels of quality, quantity, or relation

com·part·ment *n* **1** : a small chamber, receptacle, or container **2** : one of the separate areas of a train, airplane, or automobile

com·pass *n* **1** : a device having a magnetic needle that indicates direction on the earth's surface by pointing toward the north **2** : an instrument for drawing circles or marking measurements consisting of two pointed legs joined at the top by a pivot — usually used in pl. **3** : ¹RANGE 2, SCOPE

com·pas·sion *n* : pity for and a desire to help someone

com·pas·sion·ate *adj* : having or showing pity for and desire to help someone

com·pat·i·ble *adj* : capable of existing together in harmony

com·pa·tri·ot *n* : a person from the same country as someone else

com·pel *vb* **com·pelled; com·pel·ling 1** : to make (as a person) do something by the use of physical, moral, or mental pressure : FORCE **2** : to make happen by force

com·pen·sate *vb* **com·pen·sat·ed; com·pen·sat·ing 1** : to make up for **2** : to give money to make up for something

com·pen·sa·tion *n* **1** : something that makes up for or is given to make up for something else **2** : money paid regularly

com·pete *vb* **com·pet·ed; com·pet·ing** : to strive for something (as a prize or a reward) for which another is also striving

com·pe·tence *n* : the quality or state of being capable

com·pe·tent *adj* : CAPABLE 2, EFFICIENT — **com·pe·tent·ly** *adv*

com·pe·ti·tion *n* **1** : the act or process of trying to get or win something others are also trying to get or win **2** : a contest in which all who take part strive for the same thing **3** : all of a person's competitors

com·pet·i·tive *adj* : characterized by or based on a situation in which more than one person is striving for the same thing

com·pet·i·tor *n* : someone or something that is trying to beat or do better than others in a contest or in the selling of goods or services : RIVAL

com·pile *vb* **com·piled; com·pil·ing 1** : to create by gathering things together **2** : to put things together in a publication or collection

com·pla·cen·cy *n* : a feeling of being satisfied with the way things are and not wanting to make them better

com·pla·cent *adj* : feeling or showing satisfaction and lack of worry or caution

com·plain *vb* **com·plained; com·plain·ing** : to express grief, pain, or discontent : find fault — **com·plain·er** *n*

com·plaint *n* **1** : expression of grief, pain, or discontent **2** : a cause or reason for expressing grief, pain, or discontent **3** : a sickness or disease of the body **4** : a charge of wrongdoing against a person

¹**com·ple·ment** *n* **1** : something that makes whole or better **2** : the number or quantity of something that is needed or used

²**com·ple·ment** *vb* **com·ple·ment·ed; com·ple·ment·ing** : to serve as something necessary to make whole or better

com·ple·men·ta·ry *adj* : serving to make whole or improve something

¹**com·plete** *adj* **1** : having all necessary parts : not lacking anything **2** : entirely done **3** : THOROUGH 1 — **com·plete·ness** *n*

²**complete** *vb* **com·plet·ed; com·plet·ing 1** : to bring to an end : FINISH **2** : to make whole or perfect

com·plete·ly *adv* : as much as possible : in every way or detail

com·ple·tion *n* : the act or process of making whole or finishing : the condition of being whole or finished

com·plex *adj* **1** : not easy to understand or explain : not simple **2** : having parts that go together in complicated ways

complex fraction *n* : a fraction with a fraction or mixed number in the numerator or denominator or both

com·plex·ion *n* : the color or appearance of the skin and especially of the face

com·plex·i·ty *n, pl* **com·plex·i·ties 1** : the quality or condition of being difficult to understand or of lacking simplicity **2** : something difficult to understand or lacking simplicity

com·pli·cate *vb* **com·pli·cat·ed; com·pli·cat·ing** : to make or become difficult or lacking in simplicity

com·pli·cat·ed *adj* : difficult to understand or explain

com·pli·ca·tion *n* : something that makes a situation more difficult

¹**com·pli·ment** *n* **1** : an act or expression of praise, approval, respect, or admiration **2** **compliments** *pl* : best wishes

²**com·pli·ment** *vb* **com·pli·ment·ed; com·pli·ment·ing** : to express praise, approval, respect, or admiration to

com·pli·men·ta·ry *adj* **1** : expressing or containing praise, approval, respect, or admiration **2** : given free as a courtesy or favor

com·ply *vb* **com·plied; com·ply·ing** : to act in agreement with another's wishes or in obedience to a rule

com·po·nent *n* : one of the parts or units of a combination, mixture, or system

com·pose *vb* **com·posed; com·pos·ing 1** : to form by putting together **2** : to be the parts or materials of **3** : to create and write **4** : to make calm : get under control

com·posed *adj* : being calm and in control emotionally

com·pos·er *n* : a writer of music

com·pos·ite *adj* : made up of different parts or elements

composite number *n* : an integer that is a product of two or more whole numbers each greater than 1

com·po·si·tion *n* **1** : a short piece of writing done as a school exercise **2** : the act of writing words or music **3** : the manner in which the parts of a thing are put together : MAKEUP, CONSTITUTION **4** : a literary, musical, or artistic production

com·post *n* : decayed organic material (as of leaves and grass) used to improve soil especially for growing crops

com·po·sure *n* : calmness especially of mind, manner, or appearance

¹**com·pound** *vb* **com·pound·ed; com·pound·ing 1** : to form by combining separate things **2** : to make worse **3** : to pay (interest) on both an original amount of money and on the interest it has already earned

²**com·pound** *adj* : made of or by the union of two or more parts

³**com·pound** *n* **1** : a word made up of parts that are themselves words **2** : something (as a chemical) that is formed by combining two or more parts or elements

⁴**com·pound** *n* : an enclosed area containing a group of buildings

com·pre·hend *vb* **com·pre·hend·ed; com·pre·hend·ing 1** : to understand fully **2** : to take in : INCLUDE

com·pre·hen·sion *n* : ability to understand

com·pre·hen·sive *adj* : including much : INCLUSIVE

¹**com·press** *vb* **com·pressed; com·press·ing 1** : to press or squeeze together **2** : to reduce in size, quantity, or volume by or as if by pressure

²**com·press** *n* : a pad (as of folded cloth) applied firmly to a part of the body (as to stop bleeding)

com·pres·sion *n* : the act, process, or result of pressing something together

com·pres·sor *n* : a machine for reducing the volume of something (as air) by pressure

com·prise *vb* **com·prised; com·pris·ing 1** : to be made up of : consist of **2** : ²FORM 3

¹**com·pro·mise** *n* **1** : an agreement over a

dispute reached by each side changing or giving up some demands **2** : something agreed upon as a result of each side changing or giving up some demands

²com·pro·mise *vb* **com·pro·mised; com·pro·mis·ing 1** : to settle by agreeing that each side will change or give up some demands **2** : to expose to risk, suspicion, or disgrace

com·pul·sion *n* **1** : a very strong urge to do something **2** : a force that makes someone do something **3** : an act or the state of forcing an action

com·pul·so·ry *adj* **1** : required by or as if by law **2** : having the power of forcing someone to do something

com·pu·ta·tion *n* **1** : the act or action of determining by use of mathematics **2** : a result obtained by using mathematics

com·pute *vb* **com·put·ed; com·put·ing** : to find out by using mathematics

com·put·er *n* : an automatic electronic machine that can store and process data

com·put·er·ize *vb* **com·put·er·ized; com·put·er·iz·ing 1** : to carry out, control, or produce on a computer **2** : to equip with computers **3** : to put in a form that a computer can use

com·rade *n* : COMPANION 1

¹con *adv* : on the negative side

²con *n* : an opposing argument, person, or position

con- — see COM-

con·cave *adj* : hollow or rounded inward like the inside of a bowl

con·ceal *vb* **con·cealed; con·ceal·ing 1** : to hide from sight **2** : to keep secret

con·ceal·ment *n* **1** : the act of hiding : the state of being hidden **2** : a hiding place

con·cede *vb* **con·ced·ed; con·ced·ing 1** : to admit to be true **2** : to grant or yield usually unwillingly

con·ceit *n* : too much pride in a person's own abilities or qualities : excessive self-esteem

con·ceit·ed *adj* : VAIN 2

con·ceiv·able *adj* : possible to imagine or understand

con·ceive *vb* **con·ceived; con·ceiv·ing 1** : to form an idea of : IMAGINE **2** : THINK 2

con·cen·trate *vb* **con·cen·trat·ed; con·cen·trat·ing 1** : to focus thought or attention on something **2** : to bring or come to or direct toward a common center **3** : to make stronger or thicker by removing something (as water)

con·cen·tra·tion *n* **1** : close attention to or thought about a subject **2** : the ability to pay close attention **3** : a large amount of something or a large number of people in one place

con·cept *n* : something thought of : a general idea

¹con·cern *vb* **con·cerned; con·cern·ing 1** : to relate to : be about **2** : to be of interest or importance to : AFFECT **3** : to make worried **4** : ENGAGE 2, OCCUPY

²concern *n* **1** : a feeling of worry or care about a person or thing **2** : something that causes worry or is regarded as important **3** : something that relates to or involves a person : AFFAIR **4** : a business organization

con·cerned *adj* : feeling interest and worry

con·cern·ing *prep* : relating to : ABOUT

con·cert *n* : a musical performance by several voices or instruments or by both — **in concert** : TOGETHER 5

con·cer·ti·na *n* : a small musical instrument like an accordion

con·cer·to *n, pl* **con·cer·tos** : a musical composition usually in three parts for orchestra with one or more principal instruments

con·ces·sion *n* **1** : the act or an instance of giving up or admitting something **2** : something given up **3** : a right to engage in business given by an authority **4** : a small business where things are sold (as at a sports facility or public place)

conch *n, pl* **conchs** *or* **conch·es** : a very large sea snail with a tall thick spiral shell

con·cil·i·ate *vb* **con·cil·i·at·ed; con·cil·i·at·ing 1** : to bring into agreement : RECONCILE **2** : to gain or regain the goodwill or favor of — **con·cil·i·a·to·ry** *adj*

con·cise *adj* : expressing much in few words

con·clude *vb* **con·clud·ed; con·clud·ing 1** : to bring or come to an end : FINISH **2** : to decide after a period of thought or research **3** : to bring about as a result

con·clu·sion *n* **1** : final decision reached by reasoning **2** : the last part of something **3** : a final settlement

con·clu·sive *adj* : DECISIVE 1 — **con·clu·sive·ly** *adv*

con·coct *vb* **con·coct·ed; con·coct·ing 1** : to prepare (as food) by putting several different things together **2** : to make up : DEVISE

con·cord *n* : a state of agreement

con·course *n* **1** : a flocking, moving, or flowing together (as of persons or streams) : GATHERING **2** : an open space or hall (as in a mall or airport)

¹con·crete *adj* **1** : made of or relating to concrete **2** : being specific and useful **3** : being real and useful

²con·crete *n* : a hardened mixture of cement, sand, and water with gravel or broken stone used in construction

con·cur *vb* **con·curred; con·cur·ring 1** : to act or happen together **2** : to be in agreement (as in action or opinion) : ACCORD

con·cus·sion *n* : injury to the brain caused by a hard hit on the head

con·demn *vb* **con·demned; con·demn·ing 1** : to cause to suffer or live in difficult or unpleasant conditions **2** : to sentence to a usually severe punishment **3** : to declare to be wrong **4** : to declare to be unfit for use

con·dem·na·tion *n* **1** : CRITICISM 1, DISAP-PROVAL **2** : the act of condemning or state of being condemned

con·den·sa·tion *n* **1** : the act or process of making more compact or concise **2** : something that has been made more compact or concise **3** : the conversion of a vapor to a liquid (as by cooling)

con·dense *vb* **con·densed; con·dens·ing 1** : to make or become more compact or concise **2** : to change or cause to change from a vapor to a liquid (as by cooling)

con·de·scend *vb* **con·de·scend·ed; con·de·scend·ing 1** : to stoop to the level of someone considered less important **2** : to grant favors with a show of being better than others

con·di·ment *n* : something added to food to make it taste better

¹con·di·tion *n* **1** : state of physical fitness or readiness for use **2** : something agreed upon or necessary if some other thing is to take place **3 conditions** *pl* : the way things are at a certain time or in a certain place **4** : state of being **5** : situation in life

²condition *vb* **con·di·tioned; con·di·tion·ing 1** : to put into the proper or desired state **2** : to change the habits of usually by training

con·di·tion·al *adj* : of or relating to something that will happen only if something else happens

con·do *n, pl* **con·dos** : CONDOMINIUM

con·do·min·i·um *n* : an individually owned unit in a building with many units

con·dor *n* : a very large American vulture having a bare head and neck and a frill of feathers on the neck

¹con·duct *vb* **con·duct·ed; con·duct·ing 1** : to plan and put into operation from a position of command : LEAD **2** : ²GUIDE 1 **3** : BEHAVE 1 **4** : to direct the performance of (musicians or singers) **5** : to have the quality of transmitting light, heat, sound, or electricity

²con·duct *n* **1** : personal behavior **2** : the act or way of managing something

con·duc·tion *n* **1** : the act of transporting something **2** : transmission through a conductor

con·duc·tor *n* **1** : a person in charge of a public means of transportation (as a train) **2** : a person or thing that directs or leads **3** : a

substance or body capable of transmitting light, electricity, heat, or sound

cone *n* **1** : a thin crisp cookie shaped to hold ice cream **2** : a scaly structure of certain trees (as the pine or fir) that produces pollen or egg cells and seeds **3** : a shape with a circular base and sides that taper evenly to a point **4** : a cell of the retina of the eye that is sensitive to colored light

con·fec·tion *n* : a very fancy and usually sweet food

con·fec·tion·er *n* : a maker of or dealer in sweet foods (as candies)

con·fed·er·a·cy *n, pl* **con·fed·er·a·cies 1** : a league of persons, parties, or states **2** *cap* : the eleven southern states that seceded from the United States in 1860 and 1861 to form their own government

¹con·fed·er·ate *adj* **1** : united in a league **2** *cap* : of or relating to the southern Confederacy

²confederate *n* **1** : a member of a league of persons, parties, or states **2** : ACCOMPLICE **3** *cap* : a soldier of or a person who sided with the southern Confederacy

con·fer *vb* **con·ferred; con·fer·ring 1** : BE-STOW, PRESENT **2** : to compare views especially in studying a problem

con·fer·ence *n* : a meeting for discussion or exchange of opinions

con·fess *vb* **con·fessed; con·fess·ing 1** : to tell of doing something wrong or illegal or of something embarrassing : ADMIT **2** : to admit committing sins to God or to a priest

con·fes·sion *n* **1** : an act of telling of sins or wrong, illegal, or embarrassing acts **2** : a written or spoken admission of guilt of a crime

con·fet·ti *n* : small bits of brightly colored paper made for throwing at celebrations

con·fide *vb* **con·fid·ed; con·fid·ing 1** : to have or show faith **2** : to display trust by telling secrets **3** : to tell without anyone else knowing **4** : ENTRUST 2

con·fi·dence *n* **1** : a feeling of trust or belief **2** : SELF-CONFIDENCE **3** : reliance on another's secrecy or loyalty **4** : ²SECRET

con·fi·dent *adj* : having or showing sureness and optimism — **con·fi·dent·ly** *adv*

con·fi·den·tial *adj* **1** : ¹SECRET 1 **2** : indicating a need for secrecy **3** : trusted with secret matters — **con·fi·den·tial·ly** *adv*

con·fine *vb* **con·fined; con·fin·ing 1** : to keep within limits **2** : to shut up : IMPRISON **3** : to keep indoors — **con·fine·ment** *n*

con·fines *n pl* : the boundary or limits of something

con·firm *vb* **con·firmed; con·firm·ing 1** : to make sure of the truth of **2** : to make firm or firmer (as in a habit, in faith, or in intention)

: STRENGTHEN **3** : APPROVE 2, ACCEPT **4** : to perform a ceremony admitting a person into a church or synagogue

con·fir·ma·tion *n* **1** : an act of ensuring the truth of, strengthening, or approving **2** : a religious ceremony admitting a person to full privileges in a church or synagogue **3** : something that ensures the truth of, strengthens, or approves

con·firmed *adj* : unlikely to change

con·fis·cate *vb* **con·fis·cat·ed; con·fis·cat·ing** : to seize by or as if by public authority — **con·fis·ca·tion** *n*

con·fla·gra·tion *n* : a large destructive fire

¹con·flict *n* **1** : an extended struggle : BATTLE **2** : a clashing disagreement (as between ideas or interests)

²con·flict *vb* **con·flict·ed; con·flict·ing** : to be in opposition

con·form *vb* **con·formed; con·form·ing** **1** : to make or be like : AGREE, ACCORD **2** : COMPLY

con·for·mi·ty *n, pl* **con·for·mi·ties** **1** : agreement in form, manner, or character **2** : action in accordance with some standard or authority

con·found *vb* **con·found·ed; con·found·ing** : CONFUSE 1

con·front *vb* **con·front·ed; con·front·ing** **1** : to face especially in challenge : OPPOSE **2** : to cause to face or meet — **con·fron·ta·tion** *n*

con·fuse *vb* **con·fused; con·fus·ing** **1** : to make uncertain or unable to understand : PERPLEX **2** : to fail to tell apart

con·fu·sion *n* **1** : difficulty in understanding or in being able to tell one thing from a similar thing **2** : a feeling or state of uncertainty

con·geal *vb* **con·gealed; con·geal·ing** **1** : to change from a fluid to a solid state by or as if by cold : FREEZE **2** : to make or become hard, stiff, or thick

con·ge·nial *adj* **1** : alike or sympathetic in nature, disposition, or tastes **2** : existing together in harmony **3** : tending to please or satisfy **4** : FRIENDLY 1

con·gest *vb* **con·gest·ed; con·gest·ing** : to make too crowded or full : CLOG

con·gest·ed *adj* : blocked or clogged with fluid and especially mucus

con·glom·er·ate *n* **1** : a mass (as a rock) formed of fragments from various sources **2** : a corporation engaging in many different kinds of business

con·grat·u·late *vb* **con·grat·u·lat·ed; con·grat·u·lat·ing** : to express pleasure on account of success or good fortune — **con·grat·u·la·to·ry** *adj*

con·grat·u·la·tion *n* **1** : the act of expressing pleasure at another person's success or good fortune **2** : an expression of pleasure at another person's success or good fortune — usually used in pl.

con·gre·gate *vb* **con·gre·gat·ed; con·gre·gat·ing** : to collect or gather into a crowd or group : ASSEMBLE

con·gre·ga·tion *n* **1** : an assembly of persons gathered for religious worship **2** : a gathering or collection of people or things **3** : the membership of a church or synagogue

con·gress *n* **1** : the chief lawmaking body of a republic that in the United States is made up of the Senate and the House of Representatives **2** : a formal meeting of delegates for discussion and action : CONFERENCE — **con·gres·sio·nal** *adj*

con·gress·man *n, pl* **con·gress·men** : a member of a congress and especially of the United States House of Representatives

con·gress·wom·an *n, pl* **con·gress·wom·en** : a woman member of a congress and especially of the United States House of Representatives

con·gru·ent *adj* : having the same size and shape

con·i·cal *adj* : shaped like a cone

co·ni·fer *n* : any of a group of mostly evergreen trees and shrubs (as pines) that typically produce cones and have leaves resembling needles or scales in shape — **co·nif·er·ous** *adj*

conj *abbr* conjunction

¹con·jec·ture *n* : ²GUESS

²conjecture *vb* **con·jec·tured; con·jec·tur·ing** : ¹GUESS 1, SURMISE

con·ju·gate *vb* **con·ju·gat·ed; con·ju·gat·ing** : to give the various forms of a verb in order — **con·ju·ga·tion** *n*

con·junc·tion *n* **1** : a joining together : UNION **2** : a word or expression that joins together sentences, clauses, phrases, or words

con·jure *vb* **con·jured; con·jur·ing** **1** : to practice magical arts **2** : IMAGINE 1 **3** : to produce by or as if by magic

Conn. *abbr* Connecticut

con·nect *vb* **con·nect·ed; con·nect·ing** **1** : to join or link together **2** : to have something to do with **3** : to bring together in thought — **con·nec·tor** *n*

con·nec·tion *n* **1** : the act of linking together **2** : the fact or condition of having a link : RELATIONSHIP **3** : a thing that links **4** : a person having a relationship with another by kinship, friendship, or common interest **5** : a social, professional, or commercial relationship **6** : the act or the means of continuing a journey by transferring (as to another train)

con·nois·seur *n* : a person qualified to act as

a judge in matters involving taste and appreciation

con·quer *vb* **con·quered; con·quer·ing 1** : to get or gain by force : win by fighting **2** : OVERCOME 1

con·quer·or *n* : a person who gains something by force

con·quest *n* **1** : the act or process of getting or gaining especially by force **2** : something that is gotten or gained especially by force

con·quis·ta·dor *n, pl* **con·quis·ta·do·res** *or* **con·quis·ta·dors** : a leader in the Spanish conquest especially of Mexico and Peru in the 16th century

con·science *n* : a sense of right and wrong and a feeling that what is right should be done

con·sci·en·tious *adj* **1** : guided by or agreeing with a sense of doing what is right **2** : using or done with care

con·scious *adj* **1** : aware of facts, feelings, or some particular condition or situation **2** : known or felt by a person's inner self **3** : mentally awake or active **4** : INTENTIONAL — **con·scious·ly** *adv*

con·scious·ness *n* **1** : the condition of being mentally awake and active **2** : the part of the mind involving thought and awareness **3** : knowledge of something specified

con·se·crate *vb* **con·se·crat·ed; con·se·crat·ing** : to declare to be sacred or holy : set apart for a sacred purpose

con·sec·u·tive *adj* : following one another in order without gaps

¹con·sent *vb* **con·sent·ed; con·sent·ing** : to express willingness or approval : AGREE

²consent *n* : approval of or agreement with what is done or suggested by another person

con·se·quence *n* **1** : something produced by a cause or following from a condition **2** : real importance

con·se·quent *adj* : following as a result or effect

con·se·quent·ly *adv* : as a result

con·ser·va·tion *n* : planned management of something (as natural resources or historic places) to prevent waste, destruction, damage, or neglect

¹con·ser·va·tive *adj* **1** : favoring a policy of keeping things as they are : opposed to change **2** : favoring established styles and standards **3** : likely to be lower than what the real amount or number is — **con·ser·va·tive·ly** *adv*

²conservative *n* : a person who is opposed to change : a cautious person

con·ser·va·to·ry *n, pl* **con·ser·va·to·ries 1** : a

place of instruction in some special study (as music) **2** : GREENHOUSE

¹con·serve *vb* **con·served; con·serv·ing 1** : to prevent the waste of **2** : to keep in a safe condition : SAVE

²con·serve *n* : a rich fruit preserve

con·sid·er *vb* **con·sid·ered; con·sid·er·ing 1** : to think over carefully : PONDER, REFLECT **2** : to treat in a kind or thoughtful way **3** : to think of in a certain way : BELIEVE

con·sid·er·able *adj* : rather large in extent, amount, or size — **con·sid·er·ably** *adv*

con·sid·er·ate *adj* : thoughtful of the rights and feelings of others

con·sid·er·ation *n* **1** : careful thought : DELIBERATION **2** : thoughtfulness for other people **3** : something that needs to be thought over carefully before deciding or acting **4** : a payment made in return for something

con·sid·er·ing *prep* : taking into account

con·sign *vb* **con·signed; con·sign·ing 1** : to send (as goods) to an agent to be sold or cared for **2** : to put (something) in a place to store it or get rid of it — **con·sign·ment** *n*

con·sist *vb* **con·sist·ed; con·sist·ing** : to be made up or composed

con·sis·ten·cy *n, pl* **con·sis·ten·cies 1** : degree of compactness, firmness, or stickiness **2** : agreement or harmony between parts or elements **3** : a pattern of sticking with one way of thinking or acting

con·sis·tent *adj* **1** : always the same **2** : being in harmony — **con·sis·tent·ly** *adv*

con·so·la·tion *n* **1** : something that lessens disappointment, misery, or grief **2** : the act of comforting or the state of being comforted

¹con·sole *vb* **con·soled; con·sol·ing** : to comfort in a time of grief or distress

²con·sole *n* **1** : a panel on which are dials and switches for controlling an electronic or mechanical device **2** : a cabinet (as for a television) that stands on the floor **3** : the part of an organ at which the organist sits and which contains the keyboard and controls

con·sol·i·date *vb* **con·sol·i·dat·ed; con·sol·i·dat·ing 1** : to join together into one whole : UNITE **2** : STRENGTHEN

con·so·nant *n* **1** : a letter in the English alphabet other than *a, e, i, o,* or *u* **2** : a speech sound (as \p\, \n\, or \s\) produced by partly or completely stopping the flow of air breathed out of the mouth

¹con·sort *n* : a wife or husband especially of a king or queen

²con·sort *vb* **con·sort·ed; con·sort·ing** : to spend time with as a companion : ASSOCIATE

con·spic·u·ous *adj* **1** : easily seen **2** : attracting attention : PROMINENT — **con·spic·u·ous·ly** *adv*

con·spir·a·cy *n, pl* **con·spir·a·cies** **1** : a secret agreement to do something harmful or unlawful **2** : the act of plotting with others to do something harmful or unlawful **3** : a group of people plotting to do something unlawful

con·spir·a·tor *n* : a person who plots with others to do something harmful or unlawful

con·spire *vb* **con·spired; con·spir·ing** **1** : to make an agreement with others especially in secret to do an unlawful act **2** : to act together

con·sta·ble *n* : a police officer usually of a village or small town

con·stan·cy *n* : firmness and loyalty in beliefs or personal relationships

con·stant *adj* **1** : remaining steady and unchanged **2** : occurring continuously or following one after another **3** : always faithful and true — **con·stant·ly** *adv*

con·stel·la·tion *n* : any of 88 named groups of stars forming patterns

con·ster·na·tion *n* : amazement, alarm, or disappointment that results in a feeling of helplessness or confusion

con·sti·pa·tion *n* : difficult or infrequent passage of dry hard material from the bowels

¹con·stit·u·ent *n* **1** : one of the parts or materials of which something is made : ELEMENT, INGREDIENT **2** : any of the voters who elect a person to represent them

²constituent *adj* : forming part of a whole

con·sti·tute *vb* **con·sti·tut·ed; con·sti·tut·ing** **1** : to form the whole of **2** : to establish or create

con·sti·tu·tion *n* **1** : the physical makeup of an individual **2** : the basic structure of something **3** : the basic beliefs and laws of a nation, state, or social group by which the powers and duties of the government are established and certain rights are guaranteed to the people or a document that sets forth these beliefs and laws

¹con·sti·tu·tion·al *adj* **1** : having to do with a person's physical or mental makeup **2** : relating to or in agreement with a constitution (as of a nation)

²constitutional *n* : a walk taken to maintain health

con·strain *vb* **con·strained; con·strain·ing** **1** : COMPEL 1, FORCE **2** : to restrict or limit

con·straint *n* **1** : control that limits or restricts **2** : something that limits or restricts

con·strict *vb* **con·strict·ed; con·strict·ing** : to make narrower, smaller, or tighter by drawing together : SQUEEZE

con·stric·tion *n* : an act or instance of drawing together

con·stric·tor *n* : a snake (as a boa) that kills its prey by coiling around and crushing it

con·struct *vb* **con·struct·ed; con·struct·ing** : to make or form by combining parts

con·struc·tion *n* **1** : the process, art, or manner of building something **2** : something built or put together : STRUCTURE **3** : the arrangement of words and the relationship between words in a sentence

construction paper *n* : a thick paper available in many colors for school art work

con·struc·tive *adj* : helping to develop or improve something — **con·struc·tive·ly** *adv*

con·strue *vb* **con·strued; con·stru·ing** : to understand or explain the sense or intention of

con·sul *n* : an official appointed by a government to live in a foreign country in order to look after the commercial interests of citizens of the appointing country

con·sult *vb* **con·sult·ed; con·sult·ing** **1** : to seek the opinion or advice of **2** : to seek information from **3** : to talk something over

con·sul·tant *n* : a person who gives professional advice or services

con·sul·ta·tion *n* **1** : a meeting held to talk things over **2** : the act of talking things over

con·sume *vb* **con·sumed; con·sum·ing** **1** : to destroy by or as if by fire **2** : to eat or drink up **3** : to use up **4** : to take up the interest or attention of

con·sum·er *n* : a person who buys and uses up goods

con·sump·tion *n* **1** : the act or process of using up something (as food or coal) **2** : a wasting away of the body especially from tuberculosis of the lungs

cont. *abbr* continued

¹con·tact *n* **1** : a meeting or touching of persons or things **2** : communication with other people **3** : a person someone knows who serves as a connection especially in the business or political world **4** : CONTACT LENS

²contact *vb* **con·tact·ed; con·tact·ing** **1** : to touch or make touch physically **2** : to get in touch or communication with

³contact *adj* : involving or activated by physical interaction

contact lens *n* : a thin lens used to correct bad eyesight and worn over the cornea of the eye

con·ta·gion *n* **1** : the passing of a disease from one individual to another as a result of some contact between them **2** : a contagious disease

con·ta·gious *adj* **1** : able to be passed from one individual to another through contact **2** : having a sickness that can be passed to someone else **3** : causing other people to feel or act a similar way

con·tain *vb* **con·tained; con·tain·ing 1** : to have within : HOLD **2** : to consist of or include **3** : to keep within limits : RESTRAIN, CHECK

con·tain·er *n* : something into which other things can be put (as for storage)

con·tam·i·nate *vb* **con·tam·i·nat·ed; con·tam·i·nat·ing 1** : to soil, stain, or infect by contact or association **2** : to make unfit for use by adding something harmful or unpleasant

con·tem·plate *vb* **con·tem·plat·ed; con·tem·plat·ing 1** : to look at with careful and thoughtful attention **2** : to think about deeply and carefully **3** : to have in mind : plan on

con·tem·pla·tion *n* **1** : the act of thinking about spiritual things : MEDITATION **2** : the act of looking at or thinking about something for some time

¹con·tem·po·rary *adj* **1** : living or occurring at the same period of time **2** : MODERN 1

²contemporary *n, pl* **con·tem·po·rar·ies** : a person who lives at the same time or is about the same age as another

con·tempt *n* **1** : a feeling of disrespect or disapproval of something or someone **2** : the state of being despised **3** : lack of proper respect for a judge or court

con·tempt·ible *adj* : deserving or causing a person to be despised

con·temp·tu·ous *adj* : SCORNFUL

con·tend *vb* **con·tend·ed; con·tend·ing 1** : COMPETE **2** : to try hard to deal with **3** : to argue or state earnestly

con·tend·er *n* : a person who is in competition with others

¹con·tent *n* **1** : the things that are within — usually used in pl. **2** : the subject or topic treated (as in a book) — usually used in pl. **3** : the important part or meaning (as of a book) **4** : a certain amount

²con·tent *adj* : pleased and satisfied

³content *vb* **con·tent·ed; con·tent·ing** : to make pleased : SATISFY

⁴content *n* : freedom from care or discomfort

con·tent·ed *adj* : satisfied or showing satisfaction — **con·tent·ed·ly** *adv*

con·ten·tion *n* **1** : something that is argued **2** : anger and disagreement **3** : a state or situation of having a chance to win

con·tent·ment *n* : freedom from worry or restlessness : peaceful satisfaction

¹con·test *n* : a struggle for victory : COMPETITION

²con·test *vb* **con·test·ed; con·test·ing** : to make (something) a cause of dispute or fighting

con·tes·tant *n* : a person who takes part in a competition

con·text *n* **1** : the words that are used with a certain word in writing or speaking **2** : the situation in which something happens

con·ti·nent *n* : one of the great divisions of land on the globe—Africa, Antarctica, Asia, Australia, Europe, North America, or South America

con·ti·nen·tal *adj* **1** : being the mainland part and not including islands **2** *often cap* : of the colonies later forming the United States

con·tin·gent *adj* : depending on something else that may or may not exist or occur

con·tin·u·al *adj* **1** : going on or lasting without stop **2** : occurring again and again within short periods of time — **con·tin·u·al·ly** *adv*

con·tin·u·ance *n* : the act of going on or lasting for a long time

con·tin·u·a·tion *n* **1** : something that begins where something else ends and follows a similar pattern **2** : the act of beginning again after an interruption

con·tin·ue *vb* **con·tin·ued; con·tinu·ing 1** : to do or cause to do the same thing without changing or stopping **2** : to begin again after stopping

con·ti·nu·i·ty *n, pl* **con·ti·nu·i·ties** : the quality or state of going on without stop

con·tin·u·ous *adj* : going on without stop — **con·tin·u·ous·ly** *adv*

con·tort *vb* **con·tort·ed; con·tort·ing** : to give an unusual appearance or unnatural shape to by twisting

con·tor·tion *n* : the act or result of twisting out of shape

con·tour *n* : the outline of a figure, body, or surface

contra- *prefix* **1** : against : contrary : contrasting **2** : pitched below normal bass

con·tra·band *n* : goods forbidden by law to be owned or to be brought into or out of a country

¹con·tract *n* **1** : a legal agreement **2** : a written document that shows the terms and conditions of a legal agreement

²con·tract *vb* **con·tract·ed; con·tract·ing 1** : to agree by contract **2** : to become sick with : CATCH **3** : to draw together and make shorter and broader **4** : to make or become smaller : SHRINK **5** : to make (as a word) shorter by dropping sounds or letters

con·trac·tion *n* **1** : the act, process, or result of making or becoming smaller or shorter and broader **2** : a short form of a word or word group (as *don't* or *they've*) produced by leaving out a letter or letters

con·tra·dict *vb* **con·tra·dict·ed; con·tra·dict·ing 1** : to deny the truth of a statement : say the opposite of what someone else has said **2** : to be opposed to

con·tra·dic·tion *n* : something (as a statement) that is the opposite of or is much different from something else

con·tra·dic·to·ry *adj* : involving, causing, or being the opposite of or much different from something else

con·tral·to *n, pl* **con·tral·tos** **1** : the lowest female singing voice : ALTO **2** : a singer with a low female singing voice

con·trap·tion *n* : GADGET

¹con·trary *n, pl* **con·trar·ies** : something opposite — **on the contrary** : just the opposite : NO

²con·trary *adj* **1** : exactly opposite **2** : being against what is usual or expected **3** : not favorable **4** : unwilling to accept control or advice

¹con·trast *vb* **con·trast·ed; con·trast·ing** **1** : to show noticeable differences **2** : to compare two persons or things so as to show the differences between them

²con·trast *n* **1** : something that is different from another **2** : difference or the amount of difference (as in color or brightness) between parts **3** : difference or amount of difference between related or similar things

con·trib·ute *vb* **con·trib·ut·ed; con·trib·ut·ing** **1** : to give along with others **2** : to have a share in something **3** : to supply (as an article) for publication especially in a magazine — **con·trib·u·tor** *n*

con·tri·bu·tion *n* : the act of giving something or something given : DONATION

con·trite *adj* : feeling or showing sorrow for some wrong that one has done : REPENTANT

con·triv·ance *n* : something (as a scheme or a mechanical device) produced with skill and cleverness

con·trive *vb* **con·trived; con·triv·ing** **1** : ²PLAN 1, PLOT **2** : to form or make in some skillful or clever way **3** : to manage to bring about or do

¹con·trol *vb* **con·trolled; con·trol·ling** **1** : to have power over **2** : to direct the actions or behavior of **3** : to keep within bounds : RESTRAIN **4** : to direct the function of

²control *n* **1** : the power or authority to manage **2** : ability to keep within bounds or direct the operation of **3** : SELF-RESTRAINT **4** : REGULATION 1 **5** : a device used to start, stop, or change the operation of a machine or system **6** : something that is not treated or exposed to testing in an experiment in order to serve as a comparison to others that have undergone treatment or exposure

con·tro·ver·sial *adj* : relating to or causing disagreement or argument

con·tro·ver·sy *n, pl* **con·tro·ver·sies** **1** : an

often long or heated discussion of something about which there is great difference of opinion **2** : ¹QUARREL 1

co·nun·drum *n* : ¹RIDDLE 1

con·va·lesce *vb* **con·va·lesced; con·va·lesc·ing** : to regain health and strength gradually after sickness or injury

con·va·les·cence *n* : the period or process of becoming well again after a sickness or injury

¹con·va·les·cent *adj* : going through or used for the process of becoming well again after a sickness or injury

²convalescent *n* : a person who is in the process of becoming well again after a sickness or injury

con·vec·tion *n* : motion in a gas (as air) or a liquid in which the warmer portions rise and the colder portions sink

con·vene *vb* **con·vened; con·ven·ing** : to come or bring together as an assembly

con·ve·nience *n* **1** : the quality or state of being available, easy to use, useful, or helpful **2** : personal comfort **3** : OPPORTUNITY 1 **4** : something that gives comfort or advantage

con·ve·nient *adj* **1** : suited to a person's comfort or ease **2** : suited to a certain use **3** : easy to get to — **con·ve·nient·ly** *adv*

con·vent *n* **1** : a group of nuns living together **2** : a house or a set of buildings occupied by a community of nuns

con·ven·tion *n* **1** : a meeting of people for a common purpose **2** : a custom or a way of acting and doing things that is widely accepted and followed **3** : AGREEMENT 3

con·ven·tion·al *adj* **1** : following the usual or widely accepted way of doing things **2** : used or accepted through general agreement

con·ver·sa·tion *n* : a talk between two or more people : the act of talking — **con·ver·sa·tion·al** *adj*

con·verse *vb* **con·versed; con·vers·ing** : to talk to another person or to other people

con·ver·sion *n* **1** : the act of changing : the process of being changed **2** : a change of religion

¹con·vert *vb* **con·vert·ed; con·vert·ing** **1** : to change from one form to another **2** : to change from one belief, religion, view, or party to another **3** : to exchange for an equivalent

²con·vert *n* : a person who has been convinced to change to a different belief, religion, view, or party

¹con·vert·ible *adj* : possible to change in form or use

²convertible *n* **1** : an automobile with a top that can be raised, lowered, or removed **2**

: something that can be changed into a different form

con·vex *adj* : rounded like the outside of a ball or circle

con·vey *vb* **con·veyed; con·vey·ing 1** : to carry from one place to another : TRANSPORT **2** : to make known : COMMUNICATE

con·vey·ance *n* **1** : the act of carrying from one place to another **2** : something used to carry goods or passengers

¹con·vict *vb* **con·vict·ed; con·vict·ing** : to prove or find guilty

²con·vict *n* : a person serving a prison sentence

con·vic·tion *n* **1** : a strong belief or opinion **2** : the state of mind of a person who is sure that what he or she believes or says is true **3** : the act of proving or finding guilty : the state of being proven guilty

con·vince *vb* **con·vinced; con·vinc·ing** : to argue so as to make a person agree or believe

con·vinc·ing *adj* : causing someone to believe or agree : PERSUASIVE — **con·vinc·ing·ly** *adv*

¹con·voy *n, pl* **con·voys** : a group traveling together for protection

²con·voy *vb* **con·voyed; con·voy·ing** : to travel with and protect

con·vulse *vb* **con·vulsed; con·vuls·ing** : to shake violently or with jerky motions

con·vul·sion *n* : an attack of powerful involuntary muscular contractions

con·vul·sive *adj* : causing or marked by violent, frantic, or jerky movement — **con·vul·sive·ly** *adv*

¹coo *vb* **cooed; coo·ing 1** : to make the soft sound made by doves and pigeons or a similar sound **2** : to talk or say fondly or lovingly

²coo *n, pl* **coos** : a sound of or similar to that made by doves and pigeons

¹cook *n* : a person who prepares food for eating

²cook *vb* **cooked; cook·ing 1** : to prepare food for eating by the use of heat **2** : to go through the process of being heated in preparation for being eaten **3** : to create through thought and imagination — usually used with *up*

cook·book *n* : a book of recipes and directions for the preparation of food

cook·ie *n, pl* **cook·ies** : a small sweet cake

cook·out *n* : an outing at which a meal is cooked and served outdoors

¹cool *adj* **cool·er; cool·est 1** : somewhat cold : not warm **2** : not letting or keeping in heat **3** : ³CALM 2 **4** : not friendly or interested : INDIFFERENT **5** : fashionable, stylish,

or attractive in a way that is widely approved of — **cool·ly** *adv* — **cool·ness** *n*

²cool *vb* **cooled; cool·ing** : to make or become less warm

³cool *n* **1** : a time or place that is not warm **2** : a calm state of mind

cool·er *n* : a container for keeping food or drink somewhat cold

coon *n* : RACCOON

¹coop *n* : a cage or small building for keeping poultry

²coop *vb* **cooped; coop·ing** : to restrict to a small space

coo·per *n* : a worker who makes or repairs wooden casks, tubs, or barrels

co·op·er·ate *vb* **co·op·er·at·ed; co·op·er·at·ing** : to act or work together so as to get something done

co·op·er·a·tion *n* : the act or process of working together to get something done

¹co·op·er·a·tive *adj* **1** : willing to work with others **2** : relating to an organization owned by and operated for the benefit of the people who use its services

²cooperative *n* : an organization owned by and operated for the benefit of the people who use its services

¹co·or·di·nate *n* : any of a set of numbers used to locate a point on a line or surface or in space

²co·or·di·nate *vb* **co·or·di·nat·ed; co·or·di·nat·ing** : to work or cause to work together smoothly

co·or·di·na·tion *n* : smooth working together (as of parts)

cop *n* : POLICE OFFICER

cope *vb* **coped; cop·ing** : to struggle or try to manage especially with some success

copi·er *n* : a machine for making duplicates

co·pi·lot *n* : a person who assists in flying an airplane

co·pi·ous *adj* : very plentiful : ABUNDANT — **co·pi·ous·ly** *adv*

cop·per *n* **1** : a tough reddish metallic chemical element that is one of the best conductors of heat and electricity **2** : a coin having little value

cop·per·head *n* : a poisonous snake of the eastern and central United States with a reddish brown head

cop·pice *n* : a thicket, grove, or growth of small trees

copse *n* : COPPICE

¹copy *n, pl* **cop·ies 1** : something that is made to look exactly like something else : DUPLICATE **2** : one of the total number of books, magazines, or papers printed at one time **3** : written material to be published

²**copy** *vb* **cop·ied; copy·ing** **1** : to make a duplicate of **2** : IMITATE 1

copy·cat *n* : a person who imitates another person

¹**copy·right** *n* : the legal right to be the only one to reproduce, publish, and sell the contents and form of a literary or artistic work — **copyright** *vb*

²**copyright** *vb* **copy·right·ed; copy·right·ing** : to get a copyright on

¹**cor·al** *n* **1** : a stony material consisting of the skeletons of tiny sea animals that live in colonies and that are related to the jellyfish **2** : one or a colony of the animals that form coral **3** : a dark pink

²**coral** *adj* **1** : made of coral **2** : of a dark pink color

coral snake *n* : a small poisonous tropical American snake brightly ringed with red, black, and yellow or white

cord *n* **1** : a covered electrical wire used to connect an electrical appliance with an outlet **2** : material like a small thin rope that is used mostly for tying things **3** : an amount of firewood equal to a pile of wood eight feet long, four feet high, and four feet wide or 128 cubic feet (about 3.6 cubic meters) **4** : a rib or ridge woven into cloth **5** : a ribbed fabric

cor·dial *adj* : warm and friendly — **cor·dial·ly** *adv*

cor·du·roy *n* **1** : a heavy ribbed usually cotton cloth **2** **corduroys** *pl* : trousers made of a heavy ribbed cloth

¹**core** *n* **1** : the usually inedible central part of some fruits (as a pineapple or pear) **2** : the central part of a heavenly body (as the earth or sun) **3** : the central or most important part of something

²**core** *vb* **cored; cor·ing** : to remove the core from

¹**cork** *n* **1** : the light but tough material that is the outer layer of bark of a tree (**cork oak**) and is used especially for stoppers and insulation **2** : a stopper for a bottle or jug

²**cork** *vb* **corked; cork·ing** : to stop with a stopper

¹**cork·screw** *n* : a pointed spiral piece of metal with a handle that is screwed into corks to pull them from bottles

²**corkscrew** *adj* : having a spiral shape

cor·mo·rant *n* : a black seabird with webbed feet, a long neck, and a slender hooked beak

¹**corn** *n* **1** : a tall American cereal grass plant widely grown for its large ears of starchy grain which come in many varieties **2** : the seeds of a corn plant that are used especially as food for humans and animals and are typically yellow or whitish **3** : an ear of corn with or without its leafy outer covering

²**corn** *n* : a hardening and thickening of the skin (as on a person's toe)

corn bread *n* : bread made with cornmeal

corn·cob *n* : the woody core on which grains of corn grow

cor·nea *n* : the transparent outer layer of the front of the eye covering the pupil and iris

corned beef *n* : beef that has been preserved in salt water

¹**cor·ner** *n* **1** : the point or place where edges or sides meet **2** : the place where two streets or passageways meet **3** : a position from which escape or retreat is difficult or impossible **4** : a place away from ordinary life or business — **cor·nered** *adj*

²**corner** *adj* **1** : located at a corner **2** : used or usable in or on a corner

³**corner** *vb* **cor·nered; cor·ner·ing** : to force into a place from which escape is difficult or into a difficult position

cor·net *n* : a brass musical instrument similar to but shorter than a trumpet

corn·flow·er *n* : a European plant related to the daisies that is often grown for its bright heads of blue, pink, or white flowers

cor·nice *n* **1** : an ornamental piece that forms the top edge of the front of a building or pillar **2** : an ornamental molding placed where the walls meet the ceiling of a room

corn·meal *n* : coarse flour made from ground corn

corn·stalk *n* : a stalk of corn

corn·starch *n* : a fine powder made from corn and used to thicken foods when cooking

corn syrup *n* : a syrup made from cornstarch

cor·nu·co·pia *n* : a container in the shape of a horn overflowing with fruits and flowers used as a symbol of plenty

corny *adj* **corn·i·er; corn·i·est** : so simple, sentimental, or old-fashioned as to be annoying

co·rol·la *n* : the part of a flower that is formed by the petals

cor·o·nary *adj* : of or relating to the heart or its blood vessels

cor·o·na·tion *n* : the act or ceremony of crowning a king or queen

cor·o·ner *n* : a public official responsible for determining the causes of deaths which are not due to natural causes

cor·o·net *n* **1** : a small crown worn by a person of noble but less than royal rank **2** : an ornamental wreath or band worn around the head

¹**cor·po·ral** *adj* : of or relating to the body

²**corporal** *n* : a noncommissioned officer ranking above a private in the army or above a lance corporal in the marine corps

cor·po·ra·tion *n* : a business or organization

authorized by law to carry on an activity with the rights and duties of a single person

cor·po·re·al *adj* : having, consisting of, or relating to a physical body

corps *n, pl* **corps** **1** : an organized branch of a country's military forces **2** : a group of persons acting under one authority

corpse *n* : a dead body

cor·pu·lent *adj* : very fat

cor·pus·cle *n* : a very small cell (as a red blood cell) that floats freely in the blood

¹cor·ral *n* : an enclosure for keeping or capturing animals

²corral *vb* **cor·ralled; cor·ral·ling** **1** : to confine in or as if in an enclosure **2** : to gather or get control over

¹cor·rect *vb* **cor·rect·ed; cor·rect·ing** **1** : to make or set right **2** : to change or adjust so as to bring to some standard or to a required condition **3** : to punish in order to improve **4** : to show how a thing can be improved or made right

²correct *adj* **1** : free from mistakes : ACCURATE **2** : meeting or agreeing with some standard : APPROPRIATE — **cor·rect·ly** *adv* — **cor·rect·ness** *n*

cor·rec·tion *n* **1** : the act of making something agree with what is right or standard **2** : a change that makes something right **3** : PUNISHMENT 1 — **cor·rec·tion·al** *adj*

cor·re·spond *vb* **cor·re·spond·ed; cor·re·spond·ing** **1** : to be alike : AGREE **2** : to compare closely **3** : to communicate with a person by exchanging letters

cor·re·spon·dence *n* **1** : communication by means of letters or e-mail : the letters or e-mail exchanged **2** : agreement between certain things

cor·re·spon·dent *n* **1** : a person with whom another person communicates by letter or e-mail **2** : a person who sends news stories or comment to a newspaper, magazine, or broadcasting company especially from a distant place

cor·ri·dor *n* : a passage into which rooms open

cor·rob·o·rate *vb* **cor·rob·o·rat·ed; cor·rob·o·rat·ing** : to support with evidence or authority

cor·rode *vb* **cor·rod·ed; cor·rod·ing** **1** : to wear away little by little (as by rust or acid) **2** : to gradually destroy or weaken

cor·ro·sion *n* : the process or effect of destroying, weakening, or wearing away little by little

cor·ro·sive *adj* : tending or able to destroy, weaken, or wear away little by little

cor·ru·gat·ed *adj* : having a wavy surface

¹cor·rupt *vb* **cor·rupt·ed; cor·rupt·ing** **1** : to change (as in morals, manners, or actions) from good to bad **2** : to influence a public official in an improper way (as by a bribe)

²corrupt *adj* **1** : behaving in a bad or improper way : doing wrong **2** : morally bad : EVIL

cor·rup·tion *n* **1** : dishonest or illegal behavior **2** : the process of causing someone else to do something wrong **3** : the act of changing or damaging something

cor·sage *n* : a small bouquet of flowers usually worn on the shoulder

corse·let *or* **cors·let** *n* : the body armor worn by a knight especially on the upper part of the body

cor·set *n* : a tight undergarment worn to support or give shape to waist and hips

cos·met·ic *n* : a material (as a cream, lotion, or powder) used to improve a person's appearance

cos·mic *adj* : of or relating to the whole universe

cosmic ray *n* : a stream of very penetrating particles that enter the earth's atmosphere from outer space at high speed

cos·mo·naut *n* : a Russian or Soviet astronaut

cos·mos *n* **1** : the universe especially as thought of as an orderly system **2** : a tall garden plant related to the daisies that has showy white, pink, or rose-colored flower heads

¹cost *vb* **cost; cost·ing** **1** : to have a price of **2** : to cause the payment, spending, or loss of

²cost *n* **1** : the amount paid or charged for something : PRICE **2** : loss or penalty involved in gaining something

cost·ly *adj* **cost·li·er; cost·li·est** **1** : having a high price or value : EXPENSIVE **2** : causing loss or suffering

¹cos·tume *n* **1** : special or fancy dress (as for wear on the stage or at a masquerade) **2** : style of clothing, ornaments, and hair used during a certain period, in a certain region, or by a certain class or group

²costume *vb* **cos·tumed; cos·tum·ing** : to provide with a special or fancy outfit

cot *n* : a narrow bed often made to fold up

cot·tage *n* : a small house usually in the country or for vacation use

cottage cheese *n* : a very soft white cheese made from soured skim milk

cot·ton *n* **1** : a soft fluffy usually white material made up of twisted hairs that surrounds the seeds of a tall plant of warm regions and is spun into thread or yarn **2** : thread, yarn, or cloth made from cotton — **cotton** *adj*

cotton gin *n* : a machine for removing seeds from cotton

cot·ton·mouth *n* : WATER MOCCASIN

cot·ton·seed *n* : the seed of the cotton plant from which comes an oil used especially in cooking and a protein-rich meal used in livestock feed

cot·ton·tail *n* : a small rabbit with a white tail

cot·ton·wood *n* : a poplar tree that has seeds with bunches of hairs resembling cotton

couch *n* : a long piece of furniture that a person can sit or lie on

cou·gar *n* : a large yellowish brown wild animal of North and South America related to the domestic cat

¹cough *vb* **coughed; cough·ing** **1** : to force air from the lungs suddenly with a sharp short noise or series of noises **2** : to get rid of by coughing

²cough *n* **1** : a condition in which there is severe or frequent coughing **2** : an act or sound of coughing

could *past of* CAN **1** — used as a helping verb in the past **2** — used as a polite form instead of *can* **3** — used to say something is possible

couldn't : could not

coun·cil *n* : a group of people appointed or elected to make laws or give advice

coun·cil·lor *or* **coun·cil·or** *n* : a member of a group of people appointed or elected to make laws or give advice : a member of a council

¹coun·sel *n* **1** : advice given **2** *pl* **counsel** : a lawyer representing someone in court

²counsel *vb* **coun·seled** *or* **coun·selled; coun·sel·ing** *or* **coun·sel·ling** **1** : to give advice to : ADVISE **2** : to suggest or recommend

coun·sel·or *or* **coun·sel·lor** *n* **1** : a person who gives advice **2** : a supervisor of campers or activities at a summer camp **3** : LAWYER

¹count *vb* **count·ed; count·ing** **1** : to add one by one in order to find the total number **2** : to name the numbers one by one, by groups, or in order up to a particular point **3** : to include in thinking about **4** : to rely or depend on **5** : ²PLAN 1 **6** : to have value, force, or importance **7** : to consider or judge to be

²count *n* **1** : the act or process of naming numbers or adding one by one **2** : a total arrived at by adding **3** : any one crime that a person is charged with

³count *n* : a European nobleman whose rank is like that of a British earl

count·down *n* : the process of subtracting the time remaining before an event (as the launching of a rocket)

¹coun·te·nance *n* : the human face or its expression

²countenance *vb* **coun·te·nanced; coun·te·nanc·ing** : to give approval or tolerance to

¹count·er *n* **1** : a level surface usually higher than a table that is used especially for selling, serving food, displaying things, or working on **2** : a piece used in games or to find a total in adding

²count·er *n* **1** : a person whose job is to determine a total **2** : a device for showing a number or amount

³coun·ter *vb* **coun·tered; coun·ter·ing** **1** : to say in response to something said **2** : to act in opposition to : OPPOSE

⁴coun·ter *adv* : in another or opposite direction

⁵coun·ter *n* : an answering or opposing force or blow

coun·ter- *prefix* **1** : opposite **2** : opposing **3** : like : matching **4** : duplicate : substitute

coun·ter·act *vb* **coun·ter·act·ed; coun·ter·act·ing** : to make (something) have less of an effect or no effect at all

coun·ter·clock·wise *adv or adj* : in a direction opposite to that in which the hands of a clock move

¹coun·ter·feit *adj* **1** : made in exact imitation of something genuine and meant to be taken as genuine **2** : not sincere

²counterfeit *vb* **coun·ter·feit·ed; coun·ter·feit·ing** **1** : to imitate or copy especially in order to deceive **2** : ¹PRETEND 2 — **coun·ter·feit·er** *n*

³counterfeit *n* : something made to imitate another thing with the desire to deceive

coun·ter·part *n* : a person or thing that is very like or equivalent to another person or thing

coun·ter·sign *n* : a secret signal that must be given by a person wishing to pass a guard : PASSWORD

count·ess *n* **1** : the wife or widow of a count or an earl **2** : a woman who holds the rank of a count or an earl in her own right

counting number *n* : NATURAL NUMBER

count·less *adj* : too many to be counted

coun·try *n, pl* **coun·tries** **1** : a land lived in by a people with a common government **2** : REGION 1, DISTRICT **3** : open rural land away from big towns and cities **4** : the people of a nation

country and western *n* : COUNTRY MUSIC

coun·try·man *n, pl* **coun·try·men** **1** : a person born in the same country as another : a fellow citizen **2** : a person living or raised in a place away from big towns and cities

country music *n* : a style of music that developed in the southern and western United States, that is similar to folk music, and that often has lyrics about people who live in the country

coun·try·side *n* : a rural area or its people

coun·ty *n, pl* **coun·ties** : a division of a state or country for local government

cou·pé *or* **coupe** *n* **1** : a carriage with four wheels and an enclosed body seating two persons and with an outside seat for the driver in front **2** : an enclosed two-door automobile for two persons

¹cou·ple *n* **1** : two people who are married or in a romantic relationship **2** : two people or things paired together **3** : two things that are of the same kind or that are thought of together

²couple *vb* **cou·pled; cou·pling 1** : to join or link together : CONNECT **2** : to join in pairs

cou·plet *n* : two rhyming lines of verse one after another

cou·pling *n* **1** : the act of bringing or coming together **2** : something that connects two parts or things

cou·pon *n* **1** : a ticket or form that allows the holder to receive some service, payment, or discount **2** : a part of an advertisement meant to be cut out for use as an order blank

cour·age *n* : the ability to meet danger and difficulties with firmness

cou·ra·geous *adj* : having or showing the ability to meet danger and difficulties with firmness — **cou·ra·geous·ly** *adv*

cou·ri·er *n* : MESSENGER

¹course *n* **1** : motion from one point to another : progress in space or time **2** : the path over which something moves **3** : a natural channel for water **4** : a way of doing something **5** : the ordinary way something happens over time **6** : a series of acts or proceedings arranged in regular order **7** : a series of classes in a subject **8** : a part of a meal served separately — **of course** : as might be expected

²course *vb* **coursed; cours·ing 1** : to run through or over **2** : to move rapidly : RACE

¹court *n* **1** : a space arranged for playing a certain game **2** : an official meeting led by a judge for settling legal questions or the place where it is held **3** : a judge or the judges presiding in a courtroom **4** : the home of a ruler (as a king) **5** : a ruler's assembly of advisers and officers as a governing power **6** : the family and people who follow a ruler **7** : an open space completely or partly surrounded by buildings **8** : a short street **9** : respect meant to win favor

²court *vb* **court·ed; court·ing 1** : to seek the love or companionship of **2** : to try to gain or get the support of : SEEK **3** : to seem to be asking for : TEMPT

cour·te·ous *adj* : showing respect and consideration for others : POLITE — **cour·te·ous·ly** *adv*

cour·te·sy *n, pl* **cour·te·sies 1** : the quality or state of being respectful and considerate of others **2** : a polite or generous act or expression **3** : something that is a favor and not a right

court·house *n* **1** : a building in which courts of law are held **2** : a building in which county offices are housed

court·i·er *n* : a member of a royal court

court·ly *adj* **court·li·er; court·li·est** : polite and graceful in a formal way

court·room *n* : a room in which formal legal meetings and trials take place

court·ship *n* : the act of seeking the love or companionship of someone

court·yard *n* : ¹COURT 7

cous·in *n* : a child of a person's uncle or aunt

cove *n* : a small sheltered inlet or bay

cov·e·nant *n* : a formal or serious agreement or promise

¹cov·er *vb* **cov·ered; cov·er·ing 1** : to place or spread something over **2** : to be spread with or extend over much or all of the surface of **3** : to form a covering over **4** : to pass over or through **5** : to provide protection to or against **6** : to maintain a check on by patrolling **7** : to hide from sight or knowledge **8** : to deal with as a subject **9** : to have as a field of activity or interest **10** : to provide insurance for

²cover *n* **1** : something that protects, shelters, or hides **2** : a covering (as a blanket) used on a bed **3** : a binding or a protecting case **4** : something that is placed over or about another thing : LID, TOP

cov·er·age *n* **1** : insurance against something **2** : the value or amount of insurance **3** : treatment of an event or subject

cov·er·all *n* : an outer garment that combines shirt and pants and is worn to protect a person's regular clothes — usually used in pl.

covered wagon *n* : a large long wagon with a curving canvas top

cov·er·ing *n* : something that shelters, protects, or conceals

cov·er·let *n* : BEDSPREAD

¹co·vert *adj* : made or done secretly — **co·vert·ly** *adv*

²covert *n* **1** : a hiding place (as a thicket that gives shelter to game animals) **2** : one of the small feathers around the bottom of the quills on the wings and tail of a bird

cov·et *vb* **cov·et·ed; cov·et·ing** : to wish for greatly or with envy

cov·et·ous *adj* : having or showing too much desire for wealth or possessions or for something belonging to another person

cov·ey *n, pl* **coveys 1 :** a small flock of birds **2 :** ¹GROUP 1

¹cow *n* **:** the adult female of cattle or of any of various other large animals (as moose or seals)

²cow *vb* **cowed; cow·ing :** to make afraid

cow·ard *n* **:** a person who shows shameful fear

cow·ard·ice *n* **:** shameful fear

cow·ard·ly *adj* **1 :** shamefully fearful **2 :** showing shameful fear — **cow·ard·li·ness** *n*

cow·bell *n* **:** a bell hung around the neck of a cow to tell where it is

cow·bird *n* **:** a small North American blackbird that lays its eggs in the nests of other birds

cow·boy *n* **:** a man or boy who works on a ranch or performs at a rodeo

cow·catch·er *n* **:** a strong frame on the front of a railroad engine for moving things blocking the track

cow·er *vb* **cow·ered; cow·er·ing :** to shrink away or crouch down shivering (as from fear)

cow·girl *n* **:** a girl or woman who works on a ranch or performs at a rodeo

cow·hand *n* **:** a person who works on a cattle ranch

cow·herd *n* **:** a person who tends cows

cow·hide *n* **1 :** the hide of cattle or leather made from it **2 :** a whip of rawhide or braided leather

cowl *n* **:** a hood or long hooded cloak especially of a monk

cow·lick *n* **:** a small bunch of hair that sticks out and will not lie flat

cox·swain *n* **:** the person who steers or directs the rowers of a boat

coy *adj* **:** falsely shy or modest

coy·ote *n* **:** a yellowish to reddish gray doglike animal chiefly of western North America that is closely related to but smaller than the wolf

¹co·zy *adj* **co·zi·er; co·zi·est :** enjoying or providing warmth and comfort — **co·zi·ly** *adv* — **co·zi·ness** *n*

²cozy *n, pl* **co·zies :** a padded covering for a container (as a teapot) to keep the contents hot

CPR *abbr* cardiopulmonary resuscitation

cpu *n, often cap C&P&U* **:** the part of a computer that does most of the processing of data

¹crab *n* **:** a sea animal that is a crustacean related to the lobsters and has a short broad flat shell and a front pair of legs with small claws

²crab *n* **:** a person who is usually grouchy

³crab *vb* **crabbed; crab·bing :** COMPLAIN

crab apple *n* **1 :** an apple tree grown for its white, pink, or red flowers or its small usually brightly colored sour fruit **2 :** the small sour fruit of a crab apple tree

crab·bed *adj* **:** CRABBY

crab·by *adj* **crab·bi·er; crab·bi·est :** GROUCHY

crab·grass *n* **:** a weedy grass with coarse stems that root at the joints

¹crack *vb* **cracked; crack·ing 1 :** to break or cause to break with a sudden sharp sound **2 :** to break often without completely separating into parts **3 :** to make or cause to make a sound as if breaking **4 :** to open a small amount **5 :** to tell (a joke) especially in a clever way **6 :** to lose self-control **7 :** to change in tone quality **8 :** to strike or receive a sharp blow **9 :** SOLVE — **crack up 1 :** to have a reputation as a result of praise **2 :** to damage or destroy (a vehicle) by crashing **3 :** to laugh or cause to laugh

²crack *n* **1 :** a narrow break or opening **2 :** a sudden sharp noise **3 :** a sharp clever remark **4 :** a broken tone of the voice **5 :** the beginning moment **6 :** a sharp blow **7 :** ²ATTEMPT

³crack *adj* **:** of high quality or ability

crack·er *n* **:** a dry thin baked food made of flour and water

¹crack·le *vb* **crack·led; crack·ling 1 :** to make many small sharp noises **2 :** to form little cracks in a surface

²crackle *n* **:** the noise of repeated small cracks (as of burning wood)

crack–up *n* **1 :** BREAKDOWN 2 **2 :** ²CRASH 3, WRECK

¹cra·dle *n* **1 :** a baby's bed usually on rockers **2 :** place of beginning **3 :** the earliest period of life **4 :** a framework or support resembling a baby's bed in appearance or use

²cradle *vb* **cra·dled; cra·dling :** to hold or support in or as if in a cradle

¹craft *n* **1 :** skill in making things especially with the hands **2 :** an occupation or trade requiring skill with the hands or as an artist **3** *pl usually* **craft :** a boat especially when of small size **4** *pl usually* **craft :** AIRCRAFT **5 :** skill and cleverness often used to trick people

²craft *vb* **craft·ed; craft·ing :** to make or produce with care or skill

crafts·man *n, pl* **crafts·men 1 :** a person who works at a trade or handicraft **2 :** a highly skilled worker

crafty *adj* **craft·i·er; craft·i·est :** skillful at tricking others : CUNNING — **craft·i·ly** *adv* — **craft·i·ness** *n*

crag *n* **:** a steep rock or cliff

crag·gy *adj* **crag·gi·er; crag·gi·est :** having many steep rocks or cliffs

cram *vb* **crammed; cram·ming** **1 :** to stuff or pack tightly **2 :** to fill full **3 :** to study hard just before a test

¹cramp *n* **1 :** a sudden painful tightening of a muscle **2 :** sharp pain in the abdomen — usually used in pl.

²cramp *vb* **cramped; cramp·ing 1 :** to cause or experience a sudden painful muscular tightening in **2 :** to hold back from free action or expression : HAMPER

cramped *adj* **1 :** having too little space **2 :** unable to move freely because of lack of space

cran·ber·ry *n, pl* **cran·ber·ries :** a sour bright red berry that is eaten in sauces and jelly and is the fruit of an evergreen swamp plant related to the blueberries

¹crane *n* **1 :** a large tall wading bird with a long neck, bill, and legs **2 :** a machine with a swinging arm for lifting and carrying heavy weights

²crane *vb* **craned; cran·ing :** to stretch the neck to see better

cra·ni·al *adj* **:** of or relating to the skull and especially the part enclosing the brain

cra·ni·um *n, pl* **cra·ni·ums** *or* **cra·nia 1 :** SKULL **2 :** the part of the skull enclosing the brain

¹crank *n* **1 :** a bent part with a handle that is turned to start or run machinery **2 :** a person with strange ideas **3 :** a cross or irritable person

²crank *vb* **cranked; crank·ing 1 :** to start or run by or as if by turning a part with a handle **2 :** to make or become greater in speed or intensity — **crank out :** to produce quickly and often carelessly

cranky *adj* **crank·i·er; crank·i·est :** easily angered or irritated — **crank·i·ness** *n*

cran·ny *n, pl* **cran·nies 1 :** a small break or slit (as in a cliff) **2 :** a place that is not generally known or noticed

crap·pie *n* **:** either of two silvery sunfish that are caught for sport or for food

¹crash *vb* **crashed; crash·ing 1 :** to break or go to pieces with or as if with violence and noise : SMASH **2 :** to fall or strike something with noise and damage **3 :** to hit or cause to hit something with force and noise **4 :** to make or cause to make a loud noise **5 :** to move roughly and noisily **6 :** to stay for a short time where someone else lives

²crash *n* **1 :** a loud sound (as of things smashing) **2 :** an instance of hitting something with force **3 :** a collision involving a vehicle **4 :** a sudden weakening or failure (as of a business or prices)

¹crate *n* **:** a box or frame of wooden slats or boards for holding and protecting something in shipment

²crate *vb* **crat·ed; crat·ing :** to pack in a wooden box or frame

cra·ter *n* **1 :** the area around the opening of a volcano or geyser that is shaped like a bowl **2 :** a hole (as in the surface of the earth or moon) formed by an impact (as of a meteorite)

cra·vat *n* **:** NECKTIE

crave *vb* **craved; crav·ing 1 :** to want greatly : long for **2 :** to ask for earnestly

cra·ven *adj* **:** COWARDLY

crav·ing *n* **:** a great desire or longing

craw *n* **1 :** ¹CROP 3 **2 :** the stomach of an animal

craw·fish *n, pl* **crawfish 1 :** CRAYFISH **2 :** SPINY LOBSTER

¹crawl *vb* **crawled; crawl·ing 1 :** to move slowly with the body close to the ground : move on hands and knees **2 :** to go very slowly or carefully **3 :** to be covered with or have the feeling of being covered with creeping things

²crawl *n* **1 :** the act or motion of going very slowly **2 :** a swimming stroke performed by moving first one arm over the head and then the other while kicking the legs

cray·fish *n, pl* **crayfish 1 :** a freshwater shellfish that looks like the related lobster but is much smaller **2 :** SPINY LOBSTER

¹cray·on *n* **:** a stick of colored wax or sometimes chalk used for writing or drawing

²crayon *vb* **cray·oned; cray·on·ing :** to draw or color with a crayon

craze *n* **:** something that is very popular for a short while

cra·zy *adj* **cra·zi·er; cra·zi·est 1 :** having a severe mental illness : INSANE **2 :** not sensible or logical **3 :** very excited or pleased **4 :** very annoyed — **cra·zi·ly** *adv* — **cra·zi·ness** *n*

¹creak *vb* **creaked; creak·ing :** to make a long scraping or squeaking sound

²creak *n* **:** a long squeaking or scraping noise

creaky *adj* **creak·i·er; creak·i·est :** making or likely to make a long squeaking or scraping sound

¹cream *n* **1 :** the thick yellowish part of milk that contains butterfat **2 :** a food prepared with cream **3 :** a very thick liquid used to soften, protect, or heal the skin **4 :** the best part **5 :** a pale yellow

²cream *vb* **creamed; cream·ing 1 :** to stir (as butter) until smooth and soft **2 :** to defeat easily and completely

cream cheese *n* **:** a soft white cheese made from whole milk enriched with cream

cream·ery *n, pl* **cream·er·ies :** a place where milk is made into other products (as cream and cheese)

creamy *adj* **cream·i·er; cream·i·est 1 :** full of or containing cream **2 :** smooth and soft — **cream·i·ness** *n*

¹crease *n* **:** a line or mark made by folding, pressing, or wrinkling

²crease *vb* **creased; creas·ing :** to make a line or lines in or on

cre·ate *vb* **cre·at·ed; cre·at·ing :** to cause to exist : bring into existence : PRODUCE

cre·a·tion *n* **1 :** the act of bringing the world into existence out of nothing **2 :** the act of making, inventing, or producing something **3 :** something produced by human intelligence or imagination **4 :** a wide range of places **5 :** a living thing or living things

cre·a·tive *adj* **:** able to invent or produce new and original things — **cre·a·tive·ly** *adv* — **cre·a·tive·ness** *n*

cre·a·tor *n* **1 :** someone that invents or produces **2** *cap* **:** GOD 1

crea·ture *n* **1 :** a lower animal **2 :** PERSON 1 **3 :** an imaginary or strange being

cred·i·ble *adj* **:** possible to believe : deserving belief — **cred·i·bly** *adv*

¹cred·it *n* **1 :** recognition or honor received for some quality or work **2 :** the balance in an account in a person's favor **3 :** money or goods or services allowed to a person by a bank or business with the expectation of payment later **4 :** good reputation especially for honesty : high standing **5 :** a source of honor or pride **6 :** a unit of schoolwork **7 :** belief or trust in the truth of something

²credit *vb* **cred·it·ed; cred·it·ing 1 :** to give recognition or honor to for something **2 :** to place something in a person's favor on (a business account) **3 :** BELIEVE 2

cred·it·able *adj* **:** good enough to deserve praise

credit card *n* **:** a card with which a person can buy things and pay for them later

cred·i·tor *n* **:** a person to whom a debt is owed

creed *n* **1 :** a statement of the basic beliefs of a religious faith **2 :** a set of guiding rules or beliefs

creek *n* **:** a stream of water usually larger than a brook and smaller than a river

Creek *n* **1 :** a confederacy of American Indian people once occupying most of Alabama and Georgia **2 :** the language of the Creek people

creel *n* **:** a basket for holding caught fish

¹creep *vb* **crept ; creep·ing 1 :** to move along with the body close to the ground or floor : move slowly on hands and knees : CRAWL **2 :** to move or advance slowly, timidly, or quietly **3 :** to grow or spread along the ground or along a surface

²creep *n* **1 :** a strange or unlikable person **2 :** a slow, timid, or quiet movement **3 :** a feeling of nervousness or fear — usually used in pl.

creep·er *n* **1 :** a person or animal that moves slowly, timidly, or quietly **2 :** a small bird that creeps about trees and bushes in search of insects **3 :** a plant (as ivy) that grows by spreading over a surface

creepy *adj* **creep·i·er; creep·i·est 1 :** EERIE **2 :** annoyingly unpleasant — **creep·i·ness** *n*

cre·mate *vb* **cre·mat·ed; cre·mat·ing :** to burn (as a dead body) to ashes — **cre·ma·tion** *n*

crepe *n* **1 :** a thin crinkled fabric (as of silk or wool) **2 :** a very thin pancake

crepe paper *n* **:** paper with a crinkled or puckered look and feel

crept *past and past participle of* CREEP

cre·scen·do *n, pl* **cre·scen·dos :** a gradual increase in the loudness of music

¹cres·cent *n* **1 :** the shape of the visible part of the moon when it is less than half full **2 :** something shaped like a crescent moon

²crescent *adj* **:** shaped like the crescent moon

cress *n* **:** a small plant having leaves with a sharp taste that are eaten in salads

crest *n* **1 :** a showy growth (as of flesh or feathers) on the head of an animal **2 :** the highest part or point of something **3 :** an emblem or design used to represent a family, group, or organization — **crest·ed** *adj*

crest·fall·en *adj* **:** feeling disappointment and loss of pride

crev·ice *n* **:** a narrow opening (as in the earth) caused by cracking or splitting : FISSURE

crew *n* **1 :** the group of people who operate a ship, train, or airplane **2 :** a group of people working together **3 :** a gathering of people

crib *n* **1 :** a small bed frame with high sides for a child **2 :** a building or bin for storage **3 :** a long open box for feeding animals

¹crick·et *n* **:** a small leaping insect noted for the chirping sound made by the males rubbing part of the wings together

²cricket *n* **:** a game played on a large field with bats, ball, and wickets by two teams of eleven players

cri·er *n* **:** a person whose job is to call out orders or announcements

crime *n* **1 :** the act of doing something forbidden by law or the failure to do an act required by law **2 :** an act that is foolish or wrong

¹crim·i·nal *adj* **1 :** being or guilty of an act that is unlawful, foolish, or wrong **2 :** relating to unlawful acts or their punishment — **crim·i·nal·ly** *adv*

²crim·i·nal *n* : a person who has committed an unlawful act

crimp *vb* **crimped; crimp·ing** : to make wavy or bent

crim·son *n* : a deep purplish red

cringe *vb* **cringed; cring·ing 1** : to shrink in fear : COWER **2** : to show disgust or embarrassment at something

crin·kle *vb* **crin·kled; crin·kling 1** : to form or cause little waves or wrinkles on the surface : WRINKLE **2** : ¹RUSTLE 1

crin·kly *adj* **crin·kli·er; crin·kli·est** : full of small wrinkles

¹crip·ple *n, sometimes offensive* : a disabled person who is unable to fully use one or both of his or her arms or legs

²cripple *vb* **crip·pled; crip·pling 1** : to cause to lose the use of one or more arms or legs **2** : to make useless or powerless

cri·sis *n, pl* **cri·ses** : a difficult or dangerous situation that needs serious attention

¹crisp *adj* **crisp·er; crisp·est 1** : being thin, hard, and easily crumbled **2** : pleasantly firm and fresh **3** : being clear and brief **4** : pleasantly cool and invigorating : BRISK **5** : having clear details — **crisp·ly** *adv* — **crisp·ness** *n*

²crisp *vb* **crisped; crisp·ing** : to make or keep something crispy or fresh

crispy *adj* : pleasantly thin, dry, and crunchy

criss·cross *vb* **criss·crossed; criss·cross·ing 1** : to go, pass, or extend back and forth or cover with something that extends back and forth **2** : to mark with or make lines that go across one another

crit·ic *n* **1** : a person who makes or gives a judgment of the value, worth, beauty, or quality of something **2** : a person who finds fault or complains

crit·i·cal *adj* **1** : likely or eager to find fault **2** : consisting of or involving judgment of value, worth, beauty, or quality **3** : using or involving careful judgment **4** : extremely important — **crit·i·cal·ly** *adv*

crit·i·cism *n* **1** : the act of finding fault **2** : a remark that expresses disapproval **3** : a careful judgment or review especially by a person whose job is to judge the value, worth, beauty, or quality of something

crit·i·cize *vb* **crit·i·cized; crit·i·ciz·ing 1** : to examine and judge **2** : to find fault with

crit·ter *n* : a small animal

¹croak *vb* **croaked; croak·ing 1** : to utter with a rough low voice **2** : to make a deep harsh sound

²croak *n* : a hoarse harsh sound or cry

¹cro·chet *vb* **cro·cheted; cro·chet·ing** : to make (something) or create a fabric with a hooked needle by forming and weaving loops in a thread

²crochet *n* : work done or a fabric formed by weaving loops in a thread using a hooked needle

crock *n* : a thick pot or jar of baked clay

crock·ery *n* : EARTHENWARE

croc·o·dile *n* : a reptile that resembles the related alligator but that has a long narrow snout

cro·cus *n* : a small plant having grasslike leaves and colorful flowers that bloom in the spring

cro·ny *n, pl* **cro·nies** : a close companion : CHUM

¹crook *vb* **crooked ; crook·ing** : ¹BEND 1, CURVE

²crook *n* **1** : a dishonest person (as a thief) **2** : a shepherd's staff with one end curved into a hook **3** : a curved or hooked part of a thing : BEND

crook·ed *adj* **1** : having bends and curves **2** : not set or placed straight **3** : DISHONEST — **crook·ed·ly** *adv* — **crook·ed·ness** *n*

croon *vb* **crooned; croon·ing** : to hum or sing in a low soft voice

¹crop *n* **1** : the amount gathered or harvested : HARVEST **2** : a short riding whip **3** : an enlargement just above the stomach of a bird or insect in which food is temporarily stored **4** : BATCH 2, LOT **5** : a close cut of the hair

²crop *vb* **cropped; crop·ping 1** : to remove (as by cutting or biting) the upper or outer parts of : TRIM **2** : to grow or yield a crop (as of grain) : cause (land) to bear a crop **3** : to come or appear when not expected

cro·quet *n* : a game in which players hit wooden balls with mallets through a series of wickets set out on a lawn

cro·quette *n* : a roll or ball of hashed meat, fish, or vegetables fried in deep fat

¹cross *n* **1** : a structure, object, or mark consisting of one line or bar extending across another at right angles **2** *often cap* : the structure on which Jesus Christ was crucified used as a symbol of Christianity **3** : sorrow or suffering as a test of patience or virtue **4** : mixture of two different things, types, or qualities

²cross *vb* **crossed; cross·ing 1** : to move, pass, or extend across or past **2** : to place one over the other **3** : to lie or be situated across **4** : to go across : INTERSECT **5** : to turn (the eyes) toward the nose **6** : to occur to **7** : to make a gesture by touching the hand to the forehead, breast, and shoulders (as in prayer) **8** : to draw a line across **9** : to cancel by drawing a line through **10** : to act against : OPPOSE **11** : to cause (an animal or plant) to breed with one of another kind : produce hybrids **12** : to pass going in opposite directions

cross

³**cross** *adj* **cross·er; cross·est 1** : hard to get along with : IRRITABLE **2** : lying, falling, or passing across — **cross·ly** *adv*

cross·bar *n* : a piece or stripe placed crosswise or across something

cross·bones *n pl* : two leg or arm bones placed or pictured as lying across each other

cross·bow *n* : a short strip mounted crosswise near the end of a wooden stock that shoots short arrows

cross–ex·am·ine *vb* **cross–ex·am·ined; cross–ex·am·in·ing** : to question (a witness) in an effort to show that statements or answers given earlier in the legal hearing were false

cross–eyed *adj* : having one or both eyes turned toward the nose

cross·ing *n* **1** : a point where a line, track, or street intersects another line, track, or street **2** : a place provided for going across a street, railroad tracks, or a stream **3** : a voyage across a body of water

cross·piece *n* : something placed so as to lie across something else

cross–ref·er·ence *n* : a note (as in a dictionary) that directs a user to information at another place

cross·road *n* : a place where roads run across each other — usually used in pl.

cross section *n* **1** : a cutting made across something (as a log or an apple) **2** : a view showing what the inside of something looks like after a cut has been made through it **3** : a small group that includes examples of the different types of people or things in a larger group

cross·walk *n* : a specially marked path for people to walk across a street

cross·wise *adv* : so as to cross something

cross·word puzzle *n* : a puzzle in which words are filled into a pattern of numbered squares in answer to clues so that they read across and down

crotch *n* **1** : the part of the body where the legs join together **2** : an angle formed by the spreading apart of two legs or branches or of a limb from its trunk

crotch·ety *adj* : very grumpy or unpleasant

¹**crouch** *vb* **crouched; crouch·ing** : to stoop or bend low with the arms and legs close to the body

²**crouch** *n* : the position of stooping with the arms and legs close to the body

croup *n* : an illness that usually affects young children and causes a hoarse cough and difficult breathing

¹**crow** *n* **1** : a glossy black bird that has a harsh cry **2** *cap* : a member of an American Indian people of Montana **3** : the language of the Crow people

²**crow** *vb* **crowed; crow·ing 1** : to make the loud cry of a rooster **2** : to make sounds of delight **3** : ¹BOAST 1 **4** : to say with delight

³**crow** *n* **1** : the cry of a rooster **2** : a cry of triumph

crow·bar *n* : a metal bar used as a lever (as for prying things apart)

¹**crowd** *vb* **crowded; crowd·ing 1** : to push into a small space **2** : to form a tight group **3** : to collect in numbers **4** : to fill or pack by pressing together

²**crowd** *n* **1** : a large number of people in one place **2** : the population as a whole : ordinary people **3** : a group of people who spend time together or have a common interest

¹**crown** *n* **1** : a royal headdress **2** : a wreath or band worn especially as a symbol of victory or honor **3** : the top of the head **4** : the highest part (as of a tree or mountain) **5** *often cap* : royal power or authority, a person having such power, or the government of a country ruled by a king or queen **6** : any of various coins (as a British coin worth five shillings) **7** : the top part of a hat **8** : the part of a tooth outside of the gum or an artificial substitute for it — **crowned** *adj*

²**crown** *vb* **crowned; crown·ing 1** : to place a royal headdress on : give the title of king or queen to **2** : to declare officially to be **3** : to cover or be situated on the top of **4** : to bring to a conclusion **5** : to put an artificial crown on a damaged tooth **6** : to hit on the head

crow's nest *n* : a partly enclosed place to stand high on the mast of a ship for use as a lookout

cru·cial *adj* **1** : being a final or very important test or decision : DECISIVE **2** : very important : SIGNIFICANT

cru·ci·ble *n* : a pot in which metals or other substances are heated to a very high temperature or melted

cru·ci·fix *n* : a cross with a figure representing Jesus crucified on it

cru·ci·fix·ion *n* **1** : the act of killing someone by nailing his or her feet and hands to a cross **2** *cap* : the crucifying of Jesus on a cross

cru·ci·fy *vb* **cru·ci·fied; cru·ci·fy·ing 1** : to put to death by nailing or binding the hands and feet to a cross **2** : to treat cruelly or harshly

crude *adj* **crud·er; crud·est 1** : in a natural state and not changed by special treatment : RAW **2** : planned or done in a rough or unskilled way **3** : not having or showing good manners : VULGAR — **crude·ly** *adv* — **crude·ness** *n*

cru·el *adj* **cru·el·er** *or* **cru·el·ler; cru·el·est** *or* **cru·el·lest** **1** : wanting to cause others to suffer **2** : causing or helping to cause suffering — **cru·el·ly** *adv*

cru·el·ty *n, pl* **cru·el·ties** **1** : the quality or state of causing or wanting to cause suffering **2** : treatment that causes suffering

¹cruise *vb* **cruised; cruis·ing** **1** : to travel by ship often stopping at a series of ports **2** : to travel at a steady pace

²cruise *n* : a trip on a ship

cruis·er *n* **1** : a police car used for patrolling streets and equipped with radio for communicating with headquarters **2** : a warship that is smaller than a battleship **3** : a motorboat equipped for living aboard

crumb *n* **1** : a very small piece of food **2** : a little bit

crum·ble *vb* **crum·bled; crum·bling** **1** : to break into small pieces **2** : to fall to pieces : fall into ruin

crum·bly *adj* **crum·bli·er; crum·bli·est** : easily broken into small pieces

crum·my *adj* **crum·mi·er; crum·mi·est** : very poor

crum·ple *vb* **crum·pled; crum·pling** **1** : to press or crush out of shape **2** : to become full of wrinkles **3** : ¹COLLAPSE 1

¹crunch *vb* **crunched; crunch·ing** **1** : to chew or grind with a crushing noise **2** : to make the sound of being crushed or squeezed

²crunch *n* : an act or sound of crushing

crunchy *adj* **crunch·i·er; crunch·i·est** : being firm and making a sharp sound when chewed or crushed

¹cru·sade *n* **1** *cap* : one of the military expeditions made by Christian countries in the eleventh, twelfth, and thirteenth centuries to recover the Holy Land from the Muslims **2** : a campaign to get things changed for the better

²crusade *vb* **cru·sad·ed; cru·sad·ing** **1** : to take part in a medieval military expedition to recover the Holy Land **2** : to take part in a campaign to make things better — **cru·sad·er** *n*

¹crush *vb* **crushed; crush·ing** **1** : to squeeze together so as to change or destroy the natural shape or condition **2** : to break into fine pieces by pressure **3** : OVERWHELM 1 **4** : to defeat in spirit

²crush *n* **1** : a tightly packed crowd **2** : a foolish or very strong liking : INFATUATION

crust *n* **1** : the hardened outside surface of bread **2** : a hard dry piece of bread **3** : the pastry cover of a pie **4** : a hard outer covering or surface layer **5** : the outer part of the earth

crus·ta·cean *n* : any of a large group of

mostly water animals (as crabs, lobsters, and shrimps) with a body made of segments, a tough outer shell, two pairs of antennae, and limbs that are jointed

crusty *adj* **crust·i·er; crust·i·est** **1** : having a thick or crispy crust **2** : ³CROSS 1

crutch *n* **1** : a long stick usually made with a piece at the top to fit under the armpit that is used as an aid in walking **2** : something that a person depends on to help deal with problems

¹cry *vb* **cried; cry·ing** **1** : to shed tears : WEEP **2** : to make a loud call : SHOUT, EXCLAIM **3** : to utter a special sound or call

²cry *n, pl* **cries** **1** : a loud call or shout (as of pain, fear, or joy) **2** : ¹APPEAL 2 **3** : an act or period of weeping **4** : the special sound made by an animal

cry·ba·by *n, pl* **cry·ba·bies** : a person who cries easily or who complains often

cryp·tic *adj* : difficult to understand or make sense of

¹crys·tal *n* **1** : quartz that is colorless and clear or nearly so **2** : a body formed by a substance hardening so that it has flat surfaces in an even arrangement **3** : a clear colorless glass of very good quality **4** : something clear like colorless quartz **5** : the clear cover over a clock or watch dial

²crystal *adj* **1** : made of or being like a clear colorless glass of very good quality **2** : ¹CLEAR 4

crys·tal·line *adj* **1** : made of crystal or composed of crystals **2** : ¹CLEAR 4

crys·tal·lize *vb* **crys·tal·lized; crys·tal·liz·ing** **1** : to form or cause to form crystals or grains **2** : to take or cause to take definite form

ct. *abbr* **1** cent **2** court

CT *abbr* Connecticut

cu. *abbr* cubic

cub *n* **1** : the young of various animals (as the bear, fox, or lion) **2** : CUB SCOUT

cub·by·hole *n* : a snug place (as for storing things)

¹cube *n* **1** : a solid body having six equal square sides **2** : the product obtained by multiplying the square of a number by the number itself

²cube *vb* **cubed; cub·ing** **1** : to take (a number) as a factor three times **2** : to cut food into solid squares

cu·bic *adj* **1** : having the shape of a cube **2** : being the volume of a cube whose edge has a specified length

cu·bit *n* : a unit of length usually equal to about 18 inches (46 centimeters)

Cub Scout *n* : a member of a program of the Boy Scouts for boys in the first through fifth grades in school

cuck·oo *n, pl* **cuckoos** **1** : a grayish brown European bird that lays eggs in the nests of other birds which hatch and raise them **2** : the call of the cuckoo

cu·cum·ber *n* : a long usually green-skinned vegetable that is used in salads and for making pickles and is the fruit of a vine related to the melons and gourds

cud *n* : a portion of food brought up from the first stomach compartment of some animals (as the cow and sheep) to be chewed again

cud·dle *vb* **cud·dled; cud·dling** **1** : to hold close for warmth or comfort or in affection **2** : to lie close : NESTLE, SNUGGLE

¹cud·gel *n* : a short heavy club

²cudgel *vb* **cud·geled** *or* **cud·gelled; cud·gel·ing** *or* **cud·gel·ling** : to beat with or as if with a short heavy club

¹cue *n* **1** : something serving as a signal or suggestion : HINT **2** : a word, phrase, or action in a play serving as a signal for the next actor to speak or to do something

²cue *n* : a straight tapering stick used in playing billiards and pool

¹cuff *n* **1** : a band or turned-over piece at the end of a sleeve **2** : the turned-back hem of a pant leg

²cuff *vb* **cuffed; cuff·ing** : to strike especially with or as if with the palm of the hand : SLAP

³cuff *n* : ²SLAP 1

cu·li·nary *adj* : of or relating to the kitchen or cooking

¹cull *vb* **culled; cull·ing** **1** : to select from a group **2** : to identify and remove less desirable members from

²cull *n* : something rejected from a group because it is not as good as the rest

cul·mi·nate *vb* **cul·mi·nat·ed; cul·mi·nat·ing** : to reach the end or the final result of

cul·prit *n* : a person accused of, charged with, or guilty of a crime or fault

cul·ti·vate *vb* **cul·ti·vat·ed; cul·ti·vat·ing** **1** : to prepare land for the raising of crops **2** : to raise or assist the growth of crops by tilling or by labor and care **3** : to improve or develop by careful attention, training, or study : devote time and thought to **4** : to seek the company and friendship of

cul·ti·vat·ed *adj* **1** : raised or grown on a farm or under other controlled conditions **2** : having or showing good education and proper manners

cul·ti·va·tion *n* **1** : the act or process of preparing the soil for the raising of crops **2** : REFINEMENT 2

cul·ti·va·tor *n* : a tool or machine for loosening the soil between rows of a crop

cul·tur·al *adj* **1** : relating to the habits, beliefs, and traditions of a certain people **2** : relating to the arts (as music, dance, or painting) — **cul·tur·al·ly** *adv*

cul·ture *n* **1** : CULTIVATION 1 **2** : the raising or development (as of a crop or product) by careful attention **3** : the appreciation and knowledge of the arts (as music, dance, and painting) **4** : the habits, beliefs, and traditions of a particular people, place, or time

cul·tured *adj* **1** : having or showing refinement in taste, speech, or manners **2** : produced under artificial conditions

cul·vert *n* : a drain or waterway crossing under a road or railroad

cum·ber·some *adj* : hard to handle or manage because of size or weight

cu·mu·la·tive *adj* : increasing (as in force, strength, amount, or importance) over time

cu·mu·lus *n, pl* **cu·mu·li** : a massive cloud form having a flat base and rounded outlines often piled up like a mountain

cu·ne·i·form *adj* : made up of or written with marks or letters shaped like wedges — **cuneiform** *n*

¹cun·ning *adj* **1** : skillful and clever at using special knowledge or at getting something done **2** : showing craftiness and trickery

²cunning *n* **1** : SKILL 1, DEXTERITY **2** : cleverness in getting what one wants often by tricks or deception

¹cup *n* **1** : a container to drink out of in the shape of a small bowl usually with a handle **2** : the contents of a small drinking container : CUPFUL **3** : a unit of measure that equals half a pint or eight fluid ounces **4** : a trophy in the shape of a cup with two handles **5** : something like a small bowl in shape or use

²cup *vb* **cupped; cup·ping** **1** : to curve the hand or hands into the shape of a small bowl **2** : to put the hands in a curved shape around

cup·board *n* : a closet usually with shelves for dishes or food

cup·cake *n* : a small cake baked in a mold shaped like a cup

cup·ful *n, pl* **cup·fuls** *also* **cups·ful** **1** : the amount held by a cup **2** : a half pint : eight ounces (about 236 milliliters)

cu·pid *n* **1** *cap* : the god of love in ancient Roman mythology **2** : a picture or statue of a naked child with wings holding a bow and arrow and symbolizing love

cu·po·la *n* **1** : a small structure built on top of a roof **2** : a rounded roof or ceiling : DOME

cur *n* : a worthless or mongrel dog

cur·able *adj* : possible to bring about recovery from : possible to cure

cu·rate *n* : a member of the clergy who assists the rector or vicar of a church

cu·ra·tor *n* : a person in charge of a museum or zoo

¹curb *n* **1** : an enclosing border (as of stone or concrete) often along the edge of a street **2** : ¹CHECK 2

²curb *vb* **curbed; curb·ing** : to control or limit

curb·ing *n* **1** : material for making an enclosing border along the edge of a street **2** : ¹CURB 1

curd *n* : the thickened or solid part of milk that separates from the whey after milk sours and is used to make cheese

cur·dle *vb* **cur·dled; cur·dling** : to thicken or cause to become thickened with or as if with curds

¹cure *n* **1** : something (as a drug or medical treatment) that brings about recovery from a disease or illness : REMEDY **2** : recovery or relief from a disease **3** : something that solves a problem or improves a bad situation

²cure *vb* **cured; cur·ing 1** : to make or become healthy or sound again **2** : to bring about recovery from **3** : to prepare by or undergo a chemical or physical process for use or storage **4** : to provide a solution for

cur·few *n* : a rule requiring certain or all people to be off the streets or at home at a stated time

cu·rio *n, pl* **cu·ri·os** : a rare or unusual article : CURIOSITY

cu·ri·os·i·ty *n, pl* **cu·ri·os·i·ties 1** : an eager desire to learn and often to learn things that are another's concern **2** : something strange or unusual **3** : an object or article valued because it is strange or rare

cu·ri·ous *adj* **1** : eager to learn : INQUISITIVE **2** : showing an eagerness to learn **3** : attracting attention by being strange or unusual : ODD — **cu·ri·ous·ly** *adv*

¹curl *vb* **curled; curl·ing 1** : to twist or form into ringlets **2** : to take or move in a curved form — **curl up** : to arrange the body into a ball

²curl *n* **1** : a lock of hair that curls : RINGLET **2** : something having a spiral or winding form : COIL

cur·li·cue *n* : a fancy shape having curves in it

curly *adj* **curl·i·er; curl·i·est 1** : having coils **2** : having a curved shape

cur·rant *n* **1** : a small seedless raisin used in baking and cooking **2** : a sour red, white, or black edible berry that is often used in making jams and jellies

cur·ren·cy *n, pl* **cur·ren·cies 1** : common use or acceptance **2** : money in circulation

¹cur·rent *adj* **1** : now passing **2** : occurring in or belonging to the present time **3** : generally and widely accepted, used, or practiced

²current *n* **1** : a body of fluid (as air or water) moving in a specified direction **2** : the swiftest part of a stream **3** : the general course : TREND **4** : a flow of electricity

cur·ric·u·lum *n, pl* **cur·ric·u·la** *also* **cur·ric·u·lums** : all the courses of study offered by a school

cur·ry favor *vb* **cur·ried favor; cur·ry·ing favor** : to try to win approval by saying or doing nice things

¹curse *n* **1** : a series of words calling for harm to come to someone **2** : a word or an expression used in swearing or in calling for harm to come to someone **3** : evil or misfortune that comes as if in answer to someone's request **4** : a cause of great harm or evil

²curse *vb* **cursed; curs·ing 1** : to call upon divine power to send harm or evil upon **2** : SWEAR 5 **3** : to bring unhappiness or evil upon : AFFLICT **4** : to say or think bad things about (someone or something)

cur·sive *n* : a type of handwriting in which all the letters of a word are connected to each other — **cursive** *adj*

cur·sor *n* : a symbol (as an arrow or blinking line) on a computer screen that shows where the user is working

cur·so·ry *adj* : done or made quickly

curt *adj* **curt·er; curt·est** : rudely brief in language — **curt·ly** *adv*

cur·tail *vb* **cur·tailed; cur·tail·ing** : to shorten or reduce by cutting off the end or a part of

¹cur·tain *n* **1** : a piece of material (as cloth) hung up to darken, hide, divide, or decorate **2** : something that covers, hides, or separates like a curtain

²curtain *vb* **cur·tained; cur·tain·ing 1** : to furnish with cloth that darkens, hides, divides, or decorates **2** : to hide or shut off

¹curt·sy *also* **curt·sey** *vb* **curt·sied** *also* **curt·seyed; curt·sy·ing** *also* **curt·sey·ing** : to lower the body slightly by bending the knees as an act of politeness or respect

²curtsy *also* **curtsey** *n, pl* **curtsies** *also* **curtseys** : an act of politeness or respect made by women and consisting of a slight lowering of the body by bending the knees

cur·va·ture *n* : a part having a somewhat round shape

¹curve *vb* **curved; curv·ing** : to turn or cause to turn from a straight line or course

²curve *n* **1** : a smooth rounded line or surface **2** : something having a somewhat round shape **3** : a ball thrown so that it moves away from a straight course

¹cush·ion *n* **1** : a soft pillow or pad to rest on or against **2** : something soft like a pad **3**

: something that serves to soften or lessen the effects of something bad or unpleasant

²cushion *vb* **cush·ioned; cush·ion·ing 1** : to place on or as if on a soft pillow or pad **2** : to furnish with a soft pillow or pad **3** : to soften or lessen the force or shock of

cusp *n* : a point or pointed end

cus·pid *n* : ¹CANINE 1

cuss *vb* **cussed; cuss·ing** : SWEAR 5

cus·tard *n* : a sweetened mixture of milk and eggs baked, boiled, or frozen

cus·to·di·an *n* : a person who guards and protects or takes care of

cus·to·dy *n* **1** : direct responsibility for care and control **2** : the state of being arrested or held by police

¹cus·tom *n* **1** : the usual way of doing things : the usual practice **2 customs** *pl* : duties or taxes paid on imports or exports **3** : support given to a business by its customers

²custom *adj* **1** : made or done to personal order **2** : specializing in work done to personal order

cus·tom·ary *adj* **1** : usual in a particular situation or at a particular place or time **2** : typical of a particular person

cus·tom·er *n* : a person who buys from or uses the services of a company especially regularly

¹cut *vb* **cut; cut·ting 1** : to penetrate or divide with or as if with an edged tool : CLEAVE **2** : to undergo shaping or penetrating with an edged tool **3** : to divide into two or more parts **4** : to shorten or remove with scissors, a knife, or clippers **5** : to go by a short or direct path or course **6** : to destroy the connection of **7** : to intentionally not attend **8** : to move quickly or suddenly **9** : to make less **10** : to experience the growth of through the gum **11** : to stop or cause to stop **12** : to cause painful feelings **13** : to shape by carving or grinding — **cut down 1** : to knock down and wound or kill **2** : to reduce the size or amount of — **cut off 1** : ISOLATE **2** : DISCONTINUE **3** : to stop or interrupt while speaking — **cut out 1** : to form by removing with scissors, a knife, or a saw **2** : to assign through necessity **3** : to put an end to

²cut *n* **1** : something (as a gash or wound) produced by a sharp object **2** : REDUCTION 1 **3** : something resulting from shortening, division, or removal **4** : ¹SHARE 1 **5** : a sharp stroke or blow **6** : the way in which a thing is styled, formed, or made **7** : something done or said that hurts someone's feelings

cute *adj* **cut·er; cut·est 1** : attractive in looks or actions **2** : CLEVER 2 **3** : clever in a way that annoys

cu·ti·cle *n* **1** : an outer layer (as of skin or a leaf) often produced by the cells beneath **2** : a dead or hard layer of skin especially around a fingernail

cut·lass *n* : a short heavy curved sword

cut·lery *n* **1** : cutting tools (as knives and scissors) **2** : utensils used in cutting, serving, and eating food

cut·let *n* **1** : a small thin slice of meat **2** : meat, fish, or vegetables pressed into a flat piece, covered with bread crumbs, and fried in oil

cut·out *n* : a shape or picture that has been formed or removed with scissors, a knife, or a saw

cut·ter *n* **1** : someone or something that cuts **2** : a boat used by warships for carrying passengers and stores to and from the shore **3** : a small sailing boat with one mast **4** : a small military ship

cut·ting *n* : a part (as a shoot) of a plant able to grow into a whole new plant

cut·tle·fish *n* : a sea animal with ten arms that is related to the squid and octopus

cut·up *n* : a person who behaves in a silly way and tries to make other people laugh

cut·worm *n* : a moth caterpillar that has a smooth body and feeds on the stems of plants at night

-cy *n suffix, pl* **-cies 1** : action : practice **2** : rank : office **3** : body : class **4** : state : quality

cy·a·nide *n* : any of several compounds containing carbon and nitrogen and including two very poisonous substances

cyber- *prefix* : relating to computers or computer networks

cy·ber·space *n* : the online world of computer networks and especially the Internet

cy·cad *n* : a tropical plant like a palm but related to the conifers

¹cy·cle *n* **1** : a period of time taken up by a series of events or actions that repeat themselves again and again in the same order **2** : a complete round or series **3** : ¹BICYCLE **4** : MOTORCYCLE

²cycle *vb* **cy·cled; cy·cling** : to ride a bicycle or motorcycle

cy·clist *n* : a person who rides a bicycle

cy·clone *n* **1** : a storm or system of winds that rotates about a center of low atmospheric pressure and that moves forward at a speed of 20 to 30 miles (30 to 50 kilometers) an hour and often brings heavy rain **2** : TORNADO

cyl·in·der *n* : a long round body whether hollow or solid

cy·lin·dri·cal *adj* : having a long round shape

cym·bal *n* : a musical instrument in the form of a brass plate that is struck with a drumstick or is used in pairs struck together

cyn·i·cal *adj* : believing that people are selfish and dishonest

cy·press *n* : an evergreen tree or shrub with small overlapping leaves resembling scales

cyst *n* **1** : an abnormal lump or sac that forms in or on the body **2** : a saclike structure with a protective covering or a body (as a spore) with such a covering

cy·to·plasm *n* : the jellylike material that fills most of the space in a cell and surrounds the nucleus

CZ *abbr* Canal Zone

czar *n* : the ruler of Russia before 1917

cza·ri·na *n* : the wife of a czar

D

d *n, pl* **d's** *or* **ds** *often cap* **1** : the fourth letter of the English alphabet **2** : 500 in Roman numerals **3** : a grade that shows a student's work is poor **4** : a musical note referred to by the letter D

d. *abbr* **1** day **2** dead **3** deceased **4** penny

¹dab *n* **1** : a small amount **2** : a light quick touch

²dab *vb* **dabbed; dab·bing 1** : to strike or touch lightly **2** : to apply with light or uneven strokes

dab·ble *vb* **dab·bled; dab·bling 1** : to wet by splashing : SPATTER **2** : to paddle or play in or as if in water **3** : to work without any deep involvement — **dab·bler** *n*

dace *n, pl* **dace** : a small freshwater fish related to the carp

dachs·hund *n* : a small dog of German origin with a long body, short legs, and long drooping ears

dad *n* : ¹FATHER 1

dad·dy *n, pl* **daddies** : ¹FATHER 1

dad·dy long·legs *n, pl* **daddy longlegs 1** : a small animal like the related spider but with longer more slender legs **2** : a two-winged fly with long legs that resembles a large mosquito but does not bite

daf·fo·dil *n* : a plant that grows from a bulb and has long slender leaves and usually yellow or white flowers with petals whose inner parts are arranged to form a trumpet-shaped tube

daf·fy *adj* **daf·fi·er; daf·fi·est** : silly or oddly funny

daft *adj* **daft·er; daft·est** : FOOLISH, CRAZY

dag·ger *n* : a short knife used for stabbing

dahl·ia *n* : a plant related to the daisies and grown for its brightly colored flowers

¹dai·ly *adj* **1** : occurring, done, produced, appearing, or used every day or every weekday **2** : figured by the day

²daily *adv* : every day

³daily *n, pl* **dai·lies** : a newspaper published every weekday

¹dain·ty *n, pl* **dain·ties** : a delicious food : DELICACY

²dainty *adj* **dain·ti·er; dain·ti·est 1** : tasting good **2** : pretty in a delicate way **3** : having or showing delicate or finicky taste — **dain·ti·ly** *adv*

dairy *n, pl* **dair·ies 1** : a place where milk is stored or is made into butter and cheese **2** : a farm that produces milk **3** : a company or a store that sells milk products

da·is *n* : a raised platform (as in a hall or large room)

dai·sy *n, pl* **daisies** : a plant with flower heads consisting of one or more rows of white or colored flowers like petals around a central disk of tiny often yellow flowers closely packed together

Da·ko·ta *n, pl* **Da·ko·tas** *also* **Dakota 1** : a member of an American Indian people of the area that is now Minnesota, North Dakota, and South Dakota **2** : the language of the Dakota people

dale *n* : VALLEY

dal·ly *vb* **dal·lied; dal·ly·ing 1** : to act playfully **2** : to waste time **3** : LINGER 1, DAWDLE

dal·ma·tian *n, often cap* : a large dog having a short white coat with black or brown spots

¹dam *n* : the female parent of a domestic animal (as a dog or horse)

²dam *n* : a barrier (as across a stream) to hold back a flow of water

³dam *vb* **dammed; dam·ming** : to hold back or block with or as if with a dam

¹dam·age *n* **1** : loss or harm caused by injury to a person's body or property **2 damages** *pl* : money demanded or paid according to law for injury or damage

²damage *vb* **dam·aged; dam·ag·ing** : to cause harm or loss to

dame *n* : a woman of high rank or social position

¹damn *vb* **damned; damn·ing 1** : to condemn to everlasting punishment especially in hell **2** : to declare to be bad or a failure **3** : to swear at : CURSE

²damn *or* **damned** *adj* **1** : very bad **2** — used to make a statement more forceful

¹damp *n* **1** : MOISTURE **2** : a harmful gas found especially in coal mines

²damp vb **damped; damp·ing** : DAMPEN

³damp adj **damp·er; damp·est** : slightly wet : MOIST — **damp·ness** n

damp·en vb **damp·ened; damp·en·ing 1** : to make or become slighty wet **2** : to make dull or less active

damp·er n **1** : something that discourages or deadens **2** : a valve or movable plate for controlling a flow of air

dam·sel n : GIRL 1, MAIDEN

¹dance vb **danced; danc·ing 1** : to step or move through a series of movements usually in time to music **2** : to move about or up and down quickly and lightly — **danc·er** n

²dance n **1** : an act of stepping or moving through a series of movements usually in time to music **2** : a social gathering for dancing **3** : a set of movements or steps for dancing usually in time to special music **4** : the art of dancing

dan·de·li·on n : a weedy plant that has bright yellow flowers with hollow stems and long deeply toothed leaves that are often eaten

dan·der n **1** : tiny scales from hair, feathers, or skin that may cause allergic reactions **2** : ²ANGER

dan·druff n : thin dry whitish flakes of dead skin that form on the scalp and come off freely

¹dan·dy n, pl **dandies 1** : a man who is extremely interested in his clothes and appearance **2** : something excellent or unusual

²dandy adj **dan·di·er; dan·di·est** : very good

Dane n : a person born or living in Denmark

dan·ger n **1** : the state of not being protected from harm or evil : PERIL **2** : something that may cause injury or harm

dan·ger·ous adj **1** : involving possible harm or death : full of danger **2** : able or likely to injure — **dan·ger·ous·ly** adv

dan·gle vb **dan·gled; dan·gling 1** : to hang loosely especially with a swinging motion **2** : to cause to hang loosely

¹Dan·ish adj : belonging to or relating to Denmark, the Danes, or the Danish language

²Danish n **1** : the language of the Danes **2** : a piece of Danish pastry

Danish pastry n : a pastry made of rich raised dough

dank adj **dank·er; dank·est** : unpleasantly wet or moist

dap·per adj : neat and trim in dress or appearance

dap·ple vb **dap·pled; dap·pling** : to mark or become marked with rounded spots of color

¹dare vb **dared; dar·ing 1** : to have courage enough for some purpose : be bold enough — sometimes used as a helping verb **2** : to

challenge to do something especially as a proof of courage **3** : to face with courage

²dare n : a challenge to do something as proof of courage

dare·dev·il n : a person who does dangerous things especially for attention

¹dar·ing adj : ready to take risks : BOLD, VENTURESOME

²daring n : bold fearlessness : readiness to take chances

¹dark adj **dark·er; dark·est 1** : without light or without much light **2** : not light in color **3** : not bright and cheerful : GLOOMY **4** : arising from or characterized by evil

²dark n **1** : absence of light : DARKNESS **2** : a place or time of little or no light

Dark Ages n pl : the period of history from about A.D. 476 to about 1000

dark·en vb **dark·ened; dark·en·ing 1** : to make or grow dark or darker **2** : to make or become gloomy

dark·ly adv **1** : with a dark or blackish color **2** : with a gloomy or threatening manner or quality

dark·ness n **1** : absence of light **2** : NIGHT 1 **3** : ²EVIL 1, WICKEDNESS

dark·room n : a usually small dark room used in developing photographic plates and film

¹dar·ling n **1** : a dearly loved person **2** : ¹FAVORITE

²darling adj **1** : dearly loved **2** : very pleasing : CHARMING

¹darn vb **darned; darn·ing** : to mend by sewing

²darn interj — used to express anger or annoyance

³darn or **darned** adj **1** : very bad **2** — used to make a statement more forceful

darning needle n : DRAGONFLY

¹dart n **1** : a small pointed object that is meant to be thrown **2** **darts** pl : a game in which darts are thrown at a target **3** : a quick sudden movement **4** : a fold sewed into a piece of clothing

²dart vb **dart·ed; dart·ing** : to move or shoot out suddenly and quickly

¹dash vb **dashed; dash·ing 1** : to knock, hurl, or shove violently **2** : ²SMASH 1 **3** : ¹SPLASH 2 **4** : ¹RUIN 2 **5** : to complete or do hastily **6** : to move with sudden speed

²dash n **1** : a sudden burst or splash **2** : a punctuation mark — that is used most often to show a break in the thought or structure of a sentence **3** : a small amount : TOUCH **4** : liveliness in style and action **5** : a sudden rush or attempt **6** : a short fast race **7** : a long click or buzz forming a letter or part of a letter (as in Morse code) **8** : DASHBOARD

dash·board n : a panel across an automobile

or aircraft below the windshield usually containing dials and controls

dash·ing *adj* : very attractive

das·tard·ly *adj* : very mean and tricky

da·ta *n pl* **1** : facts about something that can be used in calculating, reasoning, or planning **2** : information expressed as numbers for use especially in a computer — used as singular or plural

da·ta·base *n* : a collection of data that is organized especially to be used by a computer

¹date *n* : the sweet brownish fruit of an Old World palm (**date palm**)

²date *n* **1** : the day, month, or year on which an event happens or happened **2** : a statement of time on something (as a coin, letter, book, or building) **3** : APPOINTMENT 1 **4** : an arrangement to meet between two people usually with romantic feelings for each other **5** : either of two people who meet for a usually romantic social engagement

³date *vb* **dat·ed; dat·ing 1** : to write the date on **2** : to find or show the date or age of **3** : to belong to or have survived from a time **4** : to make or have a date with **5** : to go together regularly on romantic social engagements

da·tum *n, pl* **da·ta** *or* **da·tums** : a single piece of information : FACT

¹daub *vb* **daubed; daub·ing** : to cover with something soft and sticky

²daub *n* : a small amount of something

daugh·ter *n* **1** : a female child or offspring **2** : a woman or girl associated with or thought of as a child of something (as a country, race, or religion)

daugh·ter–in–law *n, pl* **daugh·ters–in–law** : the wife of a person's son

daunt *vb* **daunt·ed; daunt·ing** : DISCOURAGE 1, FRIGHTEN

daunt·ing *adj* : likely to discourage or frighten

daunt·less *adj* : bravely determined

daw·dle *vb* **daw·dled; daw·dling 1** : to spend time wastefully : DALLY **2** : to move slowly and without purpose

¹dawn *vb* **dawned; dawn·ing 1** : to begin to grow light as the sun rises **2** : to start becoming plain or clear

²dawn *n* **1** : the time when the sun comes up in the morning **2** : a first appearance : BEGINNING

day *n* **1** : the time between sunrise and sunset : DAYLIGHT **2** : the time a planet or moon takes to make one turn on its axis **3** : a period of 24 hours beginning at midnight **4** : a specified day or date **5** : a particular time : AGE **6** : the time set apart by custom or law for work

day·break *n* : ²DAWN 1

day care *n* : a program in which or a place where care is provided during the day for young children

¹day·dream *n* : a person's pleasant and usually wishful thoughts about life

²daydream *vb* **day·dreamed; day·dream·ing** : to think pleasant and usually wishful thoughts while awake

day·light *n* **1** : the light of day **2** : DAYTIME **3** : ²DAWN 1

daylight saving time *n* : time usually one hour ahead of standard time

day·time *n* : the period of daylight

¹daze *vb* **dazed; daz·ing 1** : to stun by or as if by a blow **2** : to dazzle with light

²daze *n* : a state of not being able to think or act as quickly as normal

daz·zle *vb* **daz·zled; daz·zling 1** : to overpower with too much light **2** : to confuse, surprise, or delight by being or doing something special and unusual — **daz·zling·ly** *adv*

DC *abbr* **1** District of Columbia **2** direct current

DDS *abbr* doctor of dental surgery

DDT *n* : a chemical that was used as an insecticide until it was found to damage the environment

DE *abbr* Delaware

de- *prefix* **1** : do the opposite of **2** : reverse of **3** : remove or remove from something **4** : reduce **5** : get off of

dea·con *n* **1** : an official in some Christian churches ranking just below a priest **2** : a church member in some Christian churches who has special duties

¹dead *adj* **1** : no longer living **2** : having the look of death **3** : ¹NUMB 1 **4** : very tired **5** : lacking motion, activity, energy, or power to function **6** : no longer in use : **7** : no longer active **8** : lacking warmth or vigor **9** : not lively **10** : ACCURATE, PRECISE **11** : being sudden and complete **12** : ¹COMPLETE 1, TOTAL **13** : facing certain punishment

²dead *n, pl* **dead 1** : a person who is no longer alive — usually used for all people who are no longer alive **2** : the time of greatest quiet or least activity

³dead *adv* **1** : in a whole or complete manner **2** : suddenly and completely **3** : ²STRAIGHT

dead·en *vb* **dead·ened; dead·en·ing** : to take away some of the force of : make less

dead end *n* : an end (as of a street) with no way out

dead·line *n* : a date or time by which something must be done

¹dead·lock *n* : a situation in which a disagreement cannot be ended because neither side will give in

²**dead·lock** *vb* **dead·locked; dead·lock·ing** : to be unable to end a disagreement because neither side will give in

¹**dead·ly** *adj* **dead·li·er; dead·li·est** 1 : causing or capable of causing death 2 : meaning or hoping to kill or destroy 3 : very accurate 4 : ¹EXTREME 1

²**deadly** *adv* 1 : in a way suggestive of death 2 : to an extreme degree

deaf *adj* 1 : wholly or partly unable to hear 2 : unwilling to hear or listen — **deaf·ness** *n*

deaf·en *vb* **deaf·ened; deaf·en·ing** : to make unable to hear

¹**deal** *n* 1 : an indefinite amount 2 : a person's turn to pass out the cards in a card game

²**deal** *vb* **dealt** ; **deal·ing** 1 : to give out as a person's share 2 : ¹GIVE 8, ADMINISTER 3 : to have to do 4 : to take action 5 : to buy and sell regularly : TRADE — **deal·er** *n*

³**deal** *n* 1 : an agreement to do business 2 : treatment received 3 : an arrangement that is good for everyone involved

deal·ing *n* 1 **deal·ings** *pl* : friendly or business relations 2 : a way of acting or doing business

dean *n* 1 : a church official in charge of a cathedral 2 : the head of a section (as a college) of a university 3 : an official in charge of students or studies in a school or college

¹**dear** *adj* 1 : greatly loved or cared about 2 — used as a form of address especially in letters 3 : having a high price 4 : deeply felt : EARNEST — **dear·ly** *adv*

²**dear** *adv* : with love

³**dear** *n* : a loved one : DARLING

dearth *n* : SCARCITY, LACK

death *n* 1 : the end or ending of life 2 : the cause of loss of life 3 : the state of being dead 4 : ²RUIN 1, EXTINCTION — **death-like** *adj* — **to death** : VERY, EXTREMELY

death·bed *n* : the bed a person dies in — **on someone's deathbed** : very close to death

¹**death·ly** *adj* : relating to or suggesting death

²**deathly** *adv* : in a way suggesting death

de·bat·able *adj* : possible to question or argue about

¹**de·bate** *n* 1 : a discussion or argument carried on between two teams or sides 2 : a discussion of issues

²**debate** *vb* **de·bat·ed; de·bat·ing** 1 : to discuss a question by giving arguments on both sides : take part in a debate 2 : to consider reasons for and against : give serious and careful thought to — **de·bat·er** *n*

de·bil·i·tate *vb* **de·bil·i·tat·ed; de·bil·i·tat·ing** : to make feeble : WEAKEN

de·bil·i·ty *n, pl* **de·bil·i·ties** : a weakened state especially of health

¹**deb·it** *vb* **deb·it·ed; deb·it·ing** : to record as money paid out or as a debt

²**debit** *n* : an entry in a business record showing money paid out or owed

deb·o·nair *adj* : gracefully charming

de·bris *n, pl* **de·bris** : the junk or pieces left from something broken down or destroyed

debt *n* 1 : ¹SIN 1 2 : something owed to another 3 : the condition of owing something

debt·or *n* : a person who owes a debt

¹**de·but** *n* 1 : a first public appearance 2 : the formal entrance of a young woman into society

²**debut** *vb* **de·but·ing; de·but·ed** 1 : to make a first public appearance 2 : to present to the public for the first time

deb·u·tante *n* : a young woman making her debut

Dec. *abbr* December

deca- *or* **dec-** *or* **deka-** *or* **dek-** *prefix* : ten

de·cade *n* : a period of ten years

deca·gon *n* : a closed figure having ten angles and ten sides

de·cal *n* : a design made to be transferred (as to glass) from specially prepared paper

de·camp *vb* **de·camped; de·camp·ing** 1 : to pack up gear and leave a camp 2 : to go away suddenly

de·cant·er *n* : an ornamental glass bottle used especially for serving wine

de·cap·i·tate *vb* **de·cap·i·tat·ed; de·cap·i·tat·ing** : to cut off the head of : BEHEAD

¹**de·cay** *vb* **de·cayed; de·cay·ing** 1 : to break down or cause to break down slowly by natural processes 2 : to slowly worsen in condition

²**decay** *n* 1 : the process or result of slowly breaking down by natural processes 2 : a gradual worsening in condition 3 : a natural change of a radioactive element into another form of the same element or into a different element

de·ceased *n, pl* **deceased** : a dead person

de·ce·dent *n* : a dead person

de·ceit *n* 1 : the act or practice of making someone believe something that is not true : DECEPTION 2 : a statement or act that misleads a person or causes him or her to believe something that is not true : TRICK 3 : the quality of being dishonest

de·ceit·ful *adj* : not honest : full of deceit

de·ceive *vb* **de·ceived; de·ceiv·ing** 1 : to cause to believe what is not true : MISLEAD 2 : to be dishonest and misleading

de·cel·er·ate *vb* **de·cel·er·at·ed; de·cel·er·at·ing** : to slow down

De·cem·ber *n* : the twelfth month of the year

de·cen·cy *n, pl* **de·cen·cies** : a way or habit

of behaving with good manners or good morals

de·cent *adj* **1** : meeting an accepted standard of good taste (as in speech, dress, or behavior) **2** : being moral and good **3** : not offensive **4** : fairly good — **de·cent·ly** *adv*

de·cep·tion *n* **1** : the act of making someone believe something that is not true **2** : ¹TRICK 1

de·cep·tive *adj* : tending or able to deceive — **de·cep·tive·ly** *adv*

deci- *prefix* : tenth part

deci·bel *n* : a unit for measuring the loudness of sounds

de·cide *vb* **de·cid·ed; de·cid·ing** **1** : to make a judgment on **2** : to bring to an end in a particular way **3** : to make a choice especially after careful thought

de·cid·ed *adj* **1** : UNMISTAKABLE **2** : free from doubt — **de·cid·ed·ly** *adv*

de·cid·u·ous *adj* : made up of or having a part that falls off at the end of a period of growth and use

¹dec·i·mal *adj* **1** : based on the number 10 : numbered or counting by tens **2** : expressed in or including a decimal

²decimal *n* : a proper fraction in which the denominator is 10 or 10 multiplied one or more times by itself and is indicated by a point placed at the left of the numerator

decimal point *n* : the dot at the left of a decimal (as .05) or between the decimal and whole parts of a mixed number (as 3.125)

deci·me·ter *n* : a unit of length equal to one tenth of a meter

de·ci·pher *vb* **de·ci·phered; de·ci·pher·ing** **1** : to translate from secret or mysterious writing : DECODE **2** : to make out the meaning of something not clear

de·ci·sion *n* **1** : the act or result of making a choice especially after careful thought **2** : the ability to make choices quickly and confidently

de·ci·sive *adj* **1** : causing something to end in a certain way **2** : UNMISTAKABLE, UNQUESTIONABLE **3** : firmly determined — **de·ci·sive·ly** *adv*

¹deck *n* **1** : a floor that goes from one side of a ship to the other **2** : something like the deck of a ship **3** : a pack of playing cards

²deck *vb* **decked; deck·ing** : to dress or decorate especially in a fancy way

dec·la·ra·tion *n* **1** : an act of formally or confidently stating something **2** : something formally or confidently stated or a document containing such a statement

de·clar·a·tive *adj* : making a statement

de·clare *vb* **de·clared; de·clar·ing** **1** : to make known in a clear or formal way **2** : to state as if certain

¹de·cline *vb* **de·clined; de·clin·ing** **1** : to bend or slope downward **2** : to pass toward a lower, worse, or weaker level **3** : to refuse to accept, do, or agree

²decline *n* **1** : a process of becoming worse or weaker in condition **2** : a change to a lower state or level **3** : the time when something is nearing its end

de·code *vb* **de·cod·ed; de·cod·ing** : to change a message in code into ordinary language

de·com·pose *vb* **de·com·posed; de·com·pos·ing** **1** : to break down or be broken down into simpler parts or substances especially by the action of living things (as bacteria and fungi) **2** : to separate a substance into simpler compounds

de·com·pos·er *n* : a living thing (as a bacterium, fungus, or insect) that feeds on and breaks down plant and animal matter into simpler parts or substances

de·com·po·si·tion *n* : the process of breaking down or being broken down into simpler parts or substances especially by the action of living things

dec·o·rate *vb* **dec·o·rat·ed; dec·o·rat·ing** **1** : to make more attractive by adding beautiful or festive things **2** : to award a badge of honor to

dec·o·ra·tion *n* **1** : the act of adding things to improve the appearance of something **2** : something that adds beauty **3** : a badge of honor

dec·o·ra·tive *adj* : serving to improve appearance : ORNAMENTAL

dec·o·ra·tor *n* : a person who decorates especially the rooms of houses

de·co·rum *n* : proper behavior

¹de·coy *n* : a person or thing (as an artificial bird) used to lead or lure into a trap or snare

²decoy *vb* **de·coy·ed; de·coy·ing** : to lure by or as if by a decoy

¹de·crease *vb* **de·creased; de·creas·ing** : to grow less or cause to grow less

²de·crease *n* **1** : the process of growing less **2** : the amount by which something grows less

¹de·cree *n* : an order or decision given by a person or group in authority

²decree *vb* **de·creed; de·cree·ing** : to give an order as an authority

de·crep·it *adj* : broken down with age : WORN-OUT

de·cre·scen·do *n* : a gradual decrease in the loudness of music

ded·i·cate *vb* **ded·i·cat·ed; ded·i·cat·ing** **1** : to set apart for some purpose : DEVOTE **2** : to commit to a goal or way of life **3** : to say or write that something (as a book or song) is written or performed as a compliment to someone

ded·i·ca·tion *n* **1** : an act of setting apart for a special purpose **2** : a message at the beginning of a work of art (as a book or a song) saying that it is written or performed to honor someone **3** : extreme devotion

de·duce *vb* **de·duced; de·duc·ing** : to figure out by using reason or logic

de·duct *vb* **de·duct·ed; de·duct·ing** : to take away an amount of something : SUBTRACT

de·duc·tion *n* **1** : SUBTRACTION **2** : an amount deducted **3** : a conclusion reached by reasoning

¹deed *n* **1** : something that is done : ACT **2** : a legal document by which a person transfers land or buildings to another

²deed *vb* **deed·ed; deed·ing** : to transfer by a deed

deem *vb* **deemed; deem·ing** : to have as an opinion

¹deep *adj* **deep·er; deep·est 1** : reaching far down below the surface **2** : reaching far inward or back from the front or outer part **3** : located well below the surface or well within the boundaries of **4** : coming from well within **5** : completely absorbed **6** : hard to understand **7** : MYSTERIOUS **8** : extreme in degree : HEAVY **9** : dark and rich in color **10** : low in tone — **deep·ly** *adv*

²deep *adv* **deep·er; deep·est 1** : to a great depth : DEEPLY **2** : ²LATE 1

³deep *n* **1** : a very deep place or part **2** : OCEAN 1 **3** : the middle or most intense part

deep·en *vb* **deep·ened; deep·en·ing** : to make or become deep or deeper

deep fat *n* : hot fat or oil deep enough in a cooking utensil to cover the food to be fried

deep–fry *vb* **deep–fry·ing; deep–fried** : to cook in deep fat

deep·ly *adv* **1** : at or to a great depth : far below the surface **2** : in a high degree : THOROUGHLY **3** : with intensity of color

deer *n, pl* **deer** : a mammal that has cloven hoofs and in the male antlers which are often branched

deer·skin *n* : leather made from the skin of a deer or a garment made of such leather

de·face *vb* **de·faced; de·fac·ing** : to damage the face or surface of

¹de·fault *n* : failure to do something especially that is required by law or duty

²default *vb* **de·fault·ed; de·fault·ing** : to fail to do something required

¹de·feat *vb* **de·feat·ed; de·feat·ing 1** : to win victory over **2** : to cause to fail or be destroyed

²defeat *n* : loss of a contest or battle

de·fect *n* **1** : something that makes a thing imperfect : FLAW **2** : a lack of something needed for perfection

de·fec·tive *adj* : FAULTY

de·fence *chiefly British variant of* DEFENSE

de·fend *vb* **de·fend·ed; de·fend·ing 1** : to protect from danger or attack **2** : to act or speak in favor of when others are opposed

de·fend·er *n* **1** : a person or thing that protects from danger or attack **2** : a player in a sport who tries to keep the other team from scoring

de·fense *n* **1** : the act of protecting or defending **2** : something that defends or protects **3** : the players on a team who try to stop the other team from scoring — **de·fense·less** *adj*

¹de·fen·sive *adj* **1** : serving or meant to defend or protect **2** : relating to the attempt to keep an opponent from scoring **3** : showing a dislike for criticism — **de·fen·sive·ly** *adv*

²defensive *n* : a position or attitude that is meant to defend

¹de·fer *vb* **de·ferred; de·fer·ring** : to put off to a future time : POSTPONE

²defer *vb* **de·ferred; de·fer·ring** : to give in or yield to the opinion or wishes of another

def·er·ence *n* : respect and consideration for the wishes of another

de·fer·ment *n* : the act of postponing

de·fi·ance *n* **1** : a refusal to obey **2** : a willingness to resist

de·fi·ant *adj* : showing a willingness to resist — **de·fi·ant·ly** *adv*

de·fi·cien·cy *n, pl* **de·fi·cien·cies** : the condition of being without something necessary and especially something required for health

de·fi·cient *adj* : lacking something necessary for completeness or health

def·i·cit *n* : a shortage especially in money

de·fine *vb* **de·fined; de·fin·ing 1** : to explain the meaning of **2** : to make clear especially in outline

def·i·nite *adj* **1** : having certain or distinct limits **2** : clear in meaning **3** : UNQUESTIONABLE — **def·i·nite·ly** *adv*

definite article *n* : the article *the* used to show that the following noun refers to one or more specific persons or things

def·i·ni·tion *n* **1** : a statement of the meaning of a word or a word group **2** : clearness of outline or detail

de·flate *vb* **de·flat·ed; de·flat·ing 1** : to let the air or gas out of something that has been blown up **2** : to reduce in size or importance

de·flect *vb* **de·flect·ed; de·flect·ing** : to change or cause to change direction

de·for·est *vb* **de·for·est·ed; de·for·est·ing** : to clear of forests — **de·for·es·ta·tion** *n*

de·form *vb* **de·formed; de·form·ing** : to spoil the form or the natural appearance of

de·for·mi·ty *n, pl* **de·for·mi·ties 1 :** the condition of having a physical flaw **2 :** a flaw in something and especially in the body of a person or animal

de·fraud *vb* **de·fraud·ed; de·fraud·ing :** to get something from by trickery : CHEAT

de·frost *vb* **de·frost·ed; de·frost·ing 1 :** to thaw out **2 :** to remove ice from — **de·frost·er** *n*

deft *adj* **deft·er; deft·est :** quick and skillful in action — **deft·ly** *adv*

de·fy *vb* **de·fied; de·fy·ing 1 :** to refuse boldly to obey or yield to **2 :** to challenge to do something thought to be impossible : DARE **3 :** to resist attempts at : WITHSTAND

de·grade *vb* **de·grad·ed; de·grad·ing 1 :** to lower in character or dignity **2 :** to break down or separate into simpler parts or substances **3 :** to reduce from a higher to a lower rank or degree

de·gree *n* **1 :** a step in a series **2 :** amount of something as measured by a series of steps **3 :** one of the three forms an adjective or adverb may have when it is compared **4 :** a title given (as to students) by a college or university **5 :** one of the divisions marked on a measuring instrument (as a thermometer) **6 :** a 360th part of the circumference of a circle **7 :** a line or space of the staff in music or the difference in pitch between two notes

de·hu·mid·i·fy *vb* **de·hu·mid·i·fied; de·hu·mid·i·fy·ing :** to take moisture from (as the air) — **de·hu·mid·i·fi·er** *n*

de·hy·drate *vb* **de·hy·drat·ed; de·hy·drat·ing 1 :** to take water from (as foods) **2 :** to lose water or body fluids — **de·hy·dra·tion** *n*

deign *vb* **deigned; deign·ing :** to do something a person considers below his or her dignity

de·i·ty *n, pl* **de·i·ties 1** *cap* **:** GOD 1 **2 :** GOD 2, GODDESS

de·ject·ed *adj* **:** SAD 1 — **de·ject·ed·ly** *adv*

de·jec·tion *n* **:** a feeling of sadness

deka- *or* **dek-** — see DECA-

Del. *abbr* Delaware

Del·a·ware *n, pl* **Delaware** *or* **Del·a·wares 1 :** a member of an American Indian people originally of the region from southeastern New York to northern Delaware **2 :** the language of the Delaware people

¹de·lay *n* **1 :** a putting off of something **2 :** the time during which something is delayed

²delay *vb* **de·layed; de·lay·ing 1 :** to put off **2 :** to stop or prevent for a time **3 :** to move or act slowly

de·lec·ta·ble *adj* **1 :** very pleasing : DELIGHTFUL **2 :** DELICIOUS

¹del·e·gate *n* **:** a person sent with power to act for another or others

²del·e·gate *vb* **del·e·gat·ed; del·e·gat·ing 1 :** to entrust to another **2 :** to make responsible for getting something done

del·e·ga·tion *n* **1 :** the act of giving someone authority or responsibility for **2 :** one or more persons chosen to represent others

de·lete *vb* **de·let·ed; de·let·ing :** to take out especially by erasing, crossing out, or cutting

de·le·tion *n* **1 :** an act of taking out **2 :** something taken out

deli *n, pl* **del·is :** DELICATESSEN

¹de·lib·er·ate *vb* **de·lib·er·at·ed; de·lib·er·at·ing :** to think about carefully

²de·lib·er·ate *adj* **1 :** showing careful thought **2 :** done or said on purpose **3 :** slow in action : not hurried — **de·lib·er·ate·ly** *adv*

de·lib·er·a·tion *n* **1 :** careful thought : CONSIDERATION **2 :** the quality of being deliberate

del·i·ca·cy *n, pl* **del·i·ca·cies 1 :** something pleasing to eat that is rare or a luxury **2 :** fineness of structure **3 :** weakness of body : FRAILTY **4 :** a need for careful treatment **5 :** consideration for the feelings of others

del·i·cate *adj* **1 :** pleasing because of fineness or mildness **2 :** able to sense very small differences **3 :** calling for skill and careful treatment **4 :** easily damaged **5 :** SICKLY 1 **6 :** requiring tact — **del·i·cate·ly** *adv*

del·i·ca·tes·sen *n* **:** a store where prepared foods (as salads and meats) are sold

de·li·cious *adj* **:** giving great pleasure especially to the taste or smell — **de·li·cious·ly** *adv*

¹de·light *n* **1 :** great pleasure or satisfaction : JOY **2 :** something that gives great pleasure

²delight *vb* **de·light·ed; de·light·ing 1 :** to take great pleasure **2 :** to give joy or satisfaction to

de·light·ed *adj* **:** very pleased

de·light·ful *adj* **:** giving delight : very pleasing — **de·light·ful·ly** *adv*

de·lin·quent *n* **:** a usually young person who is guilty of improper or illegal behavior

de·lir·i·ous *adj* **1 :** not able to think or speak clearly usually because of a high fever or other illness **2 :** wildly excited — **de·lir·i·ous·ly** *adv*

de·lir·i·um *n* **1 :** a condition of mind in which thought and speech are confused usually because of a high fever or other illness **2 :** wild excitement

de·liv·er *vb* **de·liv·ered; de·liv·er·ing 1 :** to take and give to or leave for another **2 :** to set free : RESCUE **3 :** to give birth to or help in giving birth to **4 :** ¹SAY 1 **5 :** to send to an intended target **6** : to do what is expected — **de·liv·er·er** *n*

de·liv·er·ance *n* : a setting free

de·liv·ery *n, pl* **de·liv·er·ies 1** : the transfer of something from one place or person to another **2** : a setting free from something that restricts or burdens **3** : the act of giving birth **4** : speaking or manner of speaking (as of a formal speech) **5** : the act or way of throwing

dell *n* : a small valley usually covered with trees

del·ta *n* : a piece of land in the shape of a triangle or fan made by deposits of mud and sand at the mouth of a river

de·lude *vb* **de·lud·ed; de·lud·ing** : DECEIVE 1, MISLEAD

¹del·uge *n* **1** : a flooding of land by water : FLOOD **2** : a drenching rain **3** : a sudden huge stream of something

²deluge *vb* **del·uged; del·ug·ing 1** : ²FLOOD 1 **2** : to overwhelm as if with a flood

de·lu·sion *n* : a false belief that continues in spite of the facts

de·luxe *adj* : very fine or luxurious

delve *vb* **delved; delv·ing 1** : to dig or work hard with or as if with a shovel **2** : to work hard looking for information

¹de·mand *n* **1** : a forceful expression of what is desired **2** : something claimed as owed **3** : an expressed desire to own or use something **4** : a seeking or being sought after

²demand *vb* **de·mand·ed; de·mand·ing 1** : to claim as a right **2** : to ask earnestly or in the manner of a command **3** : to call for : REQUIRE — **on demand** : when requested or needed

de·mand·ing *adj* : requiring or expecting much effort

¹de·mean *vb* **de·meaned; de·mean·ing** : BEHAVE 2

²demean *vb* **de·meaned; de·mean·ing** : to lower in character or dignity

de·mean·or *n* : outward manner or behavior

de·ment·ed *adj* : INSANE 1, MAD

de·mer·it *n* : a mark placed against a person's record for doing something wrong

demi- *prefix* : half or partly

de·mise *n* **1** : DEATH 1 **2** : an ending of existence or activity

de·mo·bi·lize *vb* **de·mo·bi·lized; de·mo·bi·liz·ing 1** : to let go from military service **2** : to change from a state of war to a state of peace

de·moc·ra·cy *n, pl* **de·moc·ra·cies 1** : government by the people : majority rule **2** : government in which the highest power is held by the people and is usually used through representatives **3** : a political unit (as a nation) governed by the people **4** : be-lief in or practice of the idea that all people are socially equal

dem·o·crat *n* **1** : a person who believes in or practices democracy **2** *cap* : a member of the Democratic party of the United States

dem·o·crat·ic *adj* **1** : relating to or favoring political democracy **2** : relating to a major political party in the United States that is associated with helping common people **3** : believing in or practicing the idea that people are socially equal — **dem·o·crat·i·cal·ly** *adv*

de·mol·ish *vb* **de·mol·ished; de·mol·ish·ing 1** : to destroy by breaking apart **2** : to ruin completely : SHATTER

de·mo·li·tion *n* : the act of destroying by breaking apart especially using explosives

de·mon *n* **1** : an evil spirit : DEVIL **2** : a person of great energy or enthusiasm

dem·on·strate *vb* **dem·on·strat·ed; dem·on·strat·ing 1** : to show clearly **2** : to prove or make clear by reasoning **3** : to explain (as in teaching) by use of examples or experiments **4** : to show to people the good qualities of an article or a product **5** : to make a public display (as of feelings or military force)

dem·on·stra·tion *n* **1** : an outward expression (as a show of feelings) **2** : an act or a means of showing **3** : a showing or using of an article for sale to display its good points **4** : a parade or a gathering to show public feeling

de·mon·stra·tive *adj* **1** : pointing out the one referred to and showing that it differs from others **2** : showing feeling freely

dem·on·stra·tor *n* **1** : a person who makes or takes part in a demonstration **2** : a manufactured article (as a automobile) used for demonstration

de·mor·al·ize *vb* **de·mor·al·ized; de·mor·al·iz·ing** : to weaken the spirit or confidence of

de·mote *vb* **de·mot·ed; de·mot·ing** : to reduce to a lower grade or rank

de·mure *adj* **1** : proper and reserved in behavior and speech **2** : pretending to be proper and reserved : COY — **de·mure·ly** *adv*

den *n* **1** : the shelter or resting place of a wild animal **2** : a quiet or private room in a home **3** : a hiding place (as for thieves)

den·drite *n* : any of the usually branched fibers that carry nerve impulses toward a nerve cell body

de·ni·al *n* **1** : a refusal to give or agree to something asked for **2** : a refusal to admit the truth of a statement **3** : a refusal to accept or believe in someone or something **4** : a cutting down or limiting

den·im *n* **1** : a firm often coarse cotton cloth

2 denims *pl* : overalls or pants of usually blue denim

de·nom·i·na·tion *n* **1** : a value in a series of values (as of money) ∼ **2** : a name especially for a class of things **3** : a religious body made up of a number of congregations having the same beliefs

de·nom·i·na·tor *n* : the part of a fraction that is below the line

de·note *vb* **de·not·ed; de·not·ing 1** : to serve as a mark or indication of **2** : to have the meaning of : MEAN

de·nounce *vb* **de·nounced; de·nounc·ing 1** : to point out as wrong or evil : CONDEMN **2** : to inform against : ACCUSE

dense *adj* **dens·er; dens·est 1** : having its parts crowded together : THICK **2** : STUPID 1 — **dense·ly** *adv*

den·si·ty *n, pl* **den·si·ties 1** : the condition of having parts that are close together **2** : the amount of something in a specified volume or area

1dent *vb* **dent·ed; dent·ing 1** : to make a hollow mark in or on **2** : to become damaged by a hollow mark

2dent *n* : a notch or hollow mark made in a surface by a blow or by pressure

den·tal *adj* : relating to the teeth or dentistry

dental floss *n* : a special thread used for cleaning between teeth

den·tin *or* **den·tine** *n* : a calcium-containing material that is similar to bone but harder and that makes up the main part of a tooth

den·tist *n* : a person whose profession is the care, treatment, and repair of the teeth

den·tist·ry *n* : the profession or practice of a dentist

de·nude *vb* **de·nud·ed; de·nud·ing** : to make bare

de·ny *vb* **de·nied; de·ny·ing 1** : to declare not to be true **2** : to refuse to grant **3** : to refuse to admit

de·odor·ant *n* : something used to remove or hide unpleasant odors

de·odor·ize *vb* **de·odor·ized; de·odor·iz·ing** : to remove odor and especially a bad smell from

de·part *vb* **de·part·ed; de·part·ing 1** : to go away or go away from : LEAVE **2** : 1DIE 1 **3** : to turn away from

de·part·ment *n* : a special part or division of an organization (as a government or college)

department store *n* : a store having individual departments for different kinds of goods

de·par·ture *n* **1** : an act of leaving or setting out **2** : an act of turning away or aside (as from a way of doing things)

de·pend *vb* **de·pend·ed; de·pend·ing 1** : to rely for support **2** : to be determined by or based on a person, action, or condition **3** : 2TRUST 1, RELY

de·pend·able *adj* : TRUSTWORTHY, RELIABLE

de·pen·dence *n* **1** : a condition of being influenced and caused by something else **2** : a state of having to rely on someone or something **3** : 1TRUST 1, RELIANCE **4** : the reliance on or addiction to a drug or alcohol

1de·pen·dent *adj* **1** : determined by something or someone else **2** : relying on someone else for support **3** : requiring or addicted to a drug or alcohol

2dependent *n* : a person who depends upon another for support

de·pict *vb* **de·pict·ed; de·pict·ing 1** : to represent by a picture **2** : to describe in words

de·pic·tion *n* **1** : a representation of something using a picture **2** : DESCRIPTION 1

de·plete *vb* **de·plet·ed; de·plet·ing** : to reduce in amount by using up

de·plor·able *adj* **1** : deserving to be deplored : REGRETTABLE **2** : very bad : WRETCHED

de·plore *vb* **de·plored; de·plor·ing 1** : to regret strongly **2** : to disapprove of

de·port *vb* **de·port·ed; de·port·ing 1** : BEHAVE 1, CONDUCT **2** : to force (a person who is not a citizen) to leave a country

de·por·ta·tion *n* : the removal from a country of a person who is not a citizen

de·pose *vb* **de·posed; de·pos·ing** : to remove from a high office

1de·pos·it *vb* **de·pos·it·ed; de·pos·it·ing 1** : to place for or as if for safekeeping **2** : to give as a pledge that a purchase will be made or a service used **3** : to lay down : PUT **4** : to let fall or sink

2deposit *n* **1** : the state of being deposited **2** : money that is deposited **3** : something given as a pledge or as part payment **4** : something laid or thrown down **5** : mineral matter built up in nature

de·pos·i·tor *n* : a person who makes a deposit especially of money in a bank

de·pot *n* **1** : a place where military supplies are kept **2** : STOREHOUSE 1 **3** : a railroad or bus station

de·pre·ci·ate *vb* **de·pre·ci·at·ed; de·pre·ci·at·ing 1** : BELITTLE **2** : to lower the price or value of **3** : to lose value

de·press *vb* **de·pressed; de·press·ing 1** : to press down **2** : to make sad or discouraged **3** : to lessen the activity or strength of

de·pres·sant *n* : a drug that slows the activity of the nervous system

de·pressed *adj* **1** : SAD 1 **2** : suffering from bad economic times

de·pres·sion *n* **1** : an act of pressing down **2** : a hollow place or part **3** : a feeling of sadness **4** : a period of low activity in business with much unemployment

de·pri·va·tion *n* **1** : a taking or keeping away **2** : the state of having something taken away

de·prive *vb* **de·prived; de·priv·ing** : to take something away from or keep from having something

de·prived *adj* : not having the things that are needed for a good or healthful life

dept. *abbr* department

depth *n* **1** : measurement from top to bottom or from front to back **2** : a place far below a surface or far inside something (as a sea or a forest) **3** : the middle of time **4** : INTENSITY 2 **5** : ABUNDANCE, COMPLETENESS

dep·u·tize *vb* **dep·u·tized; dep·u·tiz·ing** : to appoint as deputy

dep·u·ty *n, pl* **dep·u·ties** : a person who officially acts for or in place of another

de·rail *vb* **de·railed; de·rail·ing** **1** : to leave or cause to leave the rails **2** : to make progress or success difficult for

der·by *n, pl* **der·bies** **1** : a race for three-year-old horses usually held every year **2** : a race or contest open to anyone **3** : a stiff felt hat with a narrow brim and a rounded top

¹**der·e·lict** *adj* **1** : abandoned by the owner or occupant **2** : in poor condition : RUN-DOWN **3** : failing to do what should be done

²**derelict** *n* **1** : something abandoned (as a boat) **2** : ¹BUM 1, VAGRANT

de·ride *vb* **de·rid·ed; de·rid·ing** : to laugh at in scorn : make fun of : RIDICULE

de·ri·sion *n* : a feeling of dislike or disrespect often shown by the use of insults

der·i·va·tion *n* **1** : the formation of a word from an earlier word or root **2** : ETYMOLOGY **3** : ORIGIN 1, SOURCE **4** : an act or process by which one thing is formed from another

¹**de·riv·a·tive** *n* **1** : a word formed from an earlier word or root **2** : something that is formed from something else

²**derivative** *adj* : formed from something else — **de·riv·a·tive·ly** *adv*

de·rive *vb* **de·rived; de·riv·ing** **1** : to take or get from a source **2** : to come from a certain source **3** : to trace the origin or source of

der·mal *adj* : of or relating to skin

der·mis *n* : the inner sensitive layer of the skin

de·rog·a·to·ry *adj* : expressing a low opinion of a person or thing

der·rick *n* **1** : a machine for moving or lifting heavy weights by means of a long arm fitted with ropes and pulleys **2** : a framework or tower over an oil well used to support machinery

de·scend *vb* **de·scend·ed; de·scend·ing** **1** : to come or go down from a higher place or level to a lower one **2** : to move down or

down along **3** : to slope or lead downward **4** : to come down from an earlier time **5** : to come down from a source or ancestor : DERIVE **6** : to be handed down to an heir **7** : to arrive from or as if from the sky **8** : to sink in dignity or respectability : STOOP **9** : to sink to a worse condition

de·scen·dant *n* **1** : someone related to a person or group of people who lived at an earlier time **2** : a thing that comes from something that existed at an earlier time

de·scent *n* **1** : an act of coming or going down in location or condition **2** : a downward slope **3** : a person's ancestors

de·scribe *vb* **de·scribed; de·scrib·ing** **1** : to write or tell about **2** : to draw the outline of

de·scrip·tion *n* **1** : a written or spoken statement about something that enables a reader or listener to picture it **2** : ¹SORT 1, KIND

de·scrip·tive *adj* : giving information about what something is like

des·e·crate *vb* **des·e·crat·ed; des·e·crat·ing** : to treat a sacred place or sacred object shamefully or with great disrespect

de·seg·re·gate *vb* **de·seg·re·gat·ed; de·seg·re·gat·ing** : to end by law the separation of members of different races

de·seg·re·ga·tion *n* : the act or process or an instance of ending a law or practice that separates people of different races

¹**des·ert** *n* : a dry land with few plants and little rainfall

²**de·sert** *n* : a reward or punishment that a person deserves

³**de·sert** *vb* **de·sert·ed; de·sert·ing** **1** : to leave usually without intending to return **2** : to leave a person or a thing that one should stay with **3** : to fail in time of need — **de·sert·er** *n*

de·serve *vb* **de·served; de·serv·ing** : to have earned because of some act or quality

de·served·ly *adv* : as earned by acts or qualities

de·serv·ing *adj* : WORTHY

¹**de·sign** *vb* **de·signed; de·sign·ing** **1** : to think up and plan out in the mind **2** : to set apart for or have as a special purpose : INTEND **3** : to make a pattern or sketch of

²**design** *n* **1** : an arrangement of parts in a structure or a work of art **2** : the art or process of planning and creating something **3** : a sketch, model, or plan of something made or to be made **4** : a decorative pattern **5** : ¹PLAN 1, SCHEME **6** : a planned intention **7** : a secret purpose : PLOT

des·ig·nate *vb* **des·ig·nat·ed; des·ig·nat·ing** **1** : to appoint or choose for a special purpose **2** : to call by a name or title **3** : to mark or point out : INDICATE

des·ig·na·tion *n* **1** : an act of choosing to be

or do something **2** : a name, sign, or title that identifies something

de·sign·er *n* : a person who plans how to make or change something

de·sir·able *adj* **1** : having pleasing qualities : ATTRACTIVE **2** : worth having or seeking

¹de·sire *vb* **de·sired; de·sir·ing 1** : to long for : wish for in earnest **2** : to express a wish for : REQUEST

²desire *n* **1** : a strong wish : LONGING **2** : something longed for

de·sist *vb* **de·sist·ed; de·sist·ing** : to stop doing something

desk *n* **1** : a piece of furniture with a flat or sloping surface for use in writing or reading **2** : a counter at which a person works especially to help customers

desk·top *n* **1** : the top of a desk **2** : a computer that is used on a desk or table and is too big to be moved easily **3** : an area on a computer screen in which items are arranged as if they were objects on top of a desk

¹des·o·late *adj* **1** : having no comfort or companionship : LONELY **2** : left neglected or in ruins **3** : without signs of life : BARREN **4** : CHEERLESS, GLOOMY — **des·o·late·ly** *adv*

²des·o·late *vb* **des·o·lat·ed; des·o·lat·ing** : to ruin or leave without comfort or companionship

des·o·la·tion *n* **1** : the state of being deserted or ruined **2** : sadness resulting from grief or loneliness

¹de·spair *vb* **de·spaired; de·spair·ing** : to give up or lose all hope or confidence

²despair *n* **1** : loss of hope : a feeling of complete hopelessness **2** : a cause of hopelessness

de·spair·ing *adj* : having or showing no hope — **de·spair·ing·ly** *adv*

des·per·ate *adj* **1** : very sad and worried and with little or no hope **2** : showing great worry and loss of hope **3** : giving little reason to hope : causing despair **4** : reckless because of despair : RASH **5** : very severe

des·per·ate·ly *adv* **1** : in a way showing great worry and weakening hope **2** : in such a way as to leave little hope **3** : with great intensity

des·per·a·tion *n* : a condition of hopelessness often leading to recklessness

de·spi·ca·ble *adj* : very bad : deserving to be despised

de·spise *vb* **de·spised; de·spis·ing** : to feel scorn and dislike for

de·spite *prep* : in spite of

de·spon·den·cy *n* : DEJECTION, SADNESS

de·spon·dent *adj* : very sad — **de·spon·dent·ly** *adv*

des·pot *n* : a ruler having absolute power and authority and especially one who rules cruelly

des·sert *n* : a sweet food eaten at the end of a meal

des·ti·na·tion *n* : a place that a person starts out for or that something is sent to

des·tine *vb* **des·tined; des·tin·ing 1** : to decide in advance on the future condition, use, or action of **2** : to be bound or directed

des·ti·ny *n, pl* **des·ti·nies 1** : what happens to someone or something in the future **2** : the course of events believed to be controlled by a superhuman power **3** : a power that is believed to control the future

des·ti·tute *adj* **1** : lacking something needed or desirable **2** : very poor

des·ti·tu·tion *n* : the condition of being very poor

de·stroy *vb* **de·stroyed; de·stroy·ing 1** : to put an end to : do away with **2** : ¹KILL 1

de·stroy·er *n* **1** : someone or something that ruins or ends something **2** : a small fast warship armed with guns, torpedoes, and sometimes missiles

de·struc·tion *n* **1** : the act or process of killing, ruining, or putting an end to something **2** : the state or fact of being killed, ruined, or brought to an end

de·struc·tive *adj* **1** : causing great damage or ruin **2** : not positive or helpful

de·tach *vb* **de·tached; de·tach·ing** : to separate from something else or from others especially for a certain purpose — **de·tach·able** *adj*

de·tached *adj* **1** : not joined or connected : SEPARATE **2** : not taking sides or being influenced by others

de·tach·ment *n* **1** : SEPARATION 1 **2** : the sending out of a body of troops or ships on a special duty **3** : a small unit of troops or ships sent out for a special duty **4** : lack of interest in worldly concerns **5** : freedom from the favoring of one side over another

¹de·tail *n* **1** : a dealing with something with attention to each item **2** : a small part of something larger : ITEM **3** : a soldier or group of soldiers picked for special duty

²detail *vb* **de·tailed; de·tail·ing 1** : to report with attention to each item **2** : to select for some special duty

de·tailed *adj* : including many small items or parts

de·tain *vb* **de·tained; de·tain·ing 1** : to hold or keep in or as if in prison **2** : to stop especially from going on : DELAY

de·tect *vb* **de·tect·ed; de·tect·ing** : to learn that something or someone is or was there — **de·tec·tor** *n*

de·tec·tion *n* : the act of learning that something or someone is or was there : DISCOVERY

de·tec·tive *n* : a person (as a police officer) whose business is solving crimes and catching criminals or gathering information that is not easy to get

de·ten·tion *n* **1** : the act of holding back or delaying : the condition of being held or delayed **2** : the punishment of being kept after school

de·ter *vb* **de·terred; de·ter·ring** : to discourage or prevent from doing something

de·ter·gent *n* : a substance that cleans

de·te·ri·o·rate *vb* **de·te·ri·o·rat·ed; de·te·ri·o·rat·ing** : to make or become worse or of less value

de·ter·mi·na·tion *n* **1** : firm or fixed intention **2** : an act of deciding or the decision reached **3** : an act of making sure of the position, size, or nature of something

de·ter·mine *vb* **de·ter·mined; de·ter·min·ing 1** : to come to a decision **2** : to learn or find out exactly **3** : to be the cause of or reason for **4** : to fix exactly and with certainty

de·ter·mined *adj* **1** : free from doubt about doing something **2** : not weak or uncertain : FIRM

de·ter·min·er *n* : a word belonging to a group of noun modifiers that can occur before descriptive adjectives modifying the same noun

de·test *vb* **de·test·ed; de·test·ing** : to dislike very much

de·throne *vb* **de·throned; de·thron·ing** : to drive from a throne : DEPOSE

¹de·tour *n* : a roundabout way that temporarily replaces part of a regular route

²detour *vb* **de·toured; de·tour·ing** : to go or make go on a different route than usual

de·tract *vb* **de·tract·ed; de·tract·ing** : to take away (as from value or importance)

det·ri·ment *n* : injury or damage or its cause : HARM

dev·as·tate *vb* **dev·as·tat·ed; dev·as·tat·ing 1** : to destroy entirely or nearly entirely **2** : to cause to suffer emotionally

dev·as·ta·tion *n* : the action of destroying or damaging greatly : the state of being greatly damaged or destroyed

de·vel·op *vb* **de·vel·oped; de·vel·op·ing 1** : to make or become plain little by little : UNFOLD **2** : to apply chemicals to exposed photographic material (as a film) in order to bring out the picture **3** : to bring out the possibilities of : IMPROVE **4** : to make more available or usable **5** : to begin to have grad-

ually **6** : to begin to exist or be present gradually **7** : to create over time **8** : to grow or cause to grow bigger or more advanced — **de·vel·op·er** *n*

de·vel·oped *adj* **1** : having many large industries and a complex economic system **2** : bigger or more advanced

de·vel·op·ment *n* **1** : the act, process, or result of developing **2** : the state of being developed

de·vi·ate *vb* **de·vi·at·ed; de·vi·at·ing** : to follow a course, principle, standard, or topic that is different from usual

de·vice *n* **1** : a piece of equipment made for a special purpose **2** : choice of what to do **3** : a thing or act used to deceive : TRICK

dev·il *n* **1** *often cap* : the most powerful spirit of evil **2** : an evil spirit : DEMON, FIEND **3** : a wicked or cruel person **4** : an attractive, mischievous, or unfortunate person

dev·iled *adj* : spicy or highly seasoned

dev·il·ish *adj* **1** : evil and cruel **2** : MISCHIEVOUS 2

dev·il·ment *n* : MISCHIEF 2

de·vi·ous *adj* **1** : SNEAKY, DISHONEST **2** : not straight : having many twists and turns

de·vise *vb* **de·vised; de·vis·ing** : to think up : PLAN, INVENT

de·void *adj* : completely without

de·vote *vb* **de·vot·ed; de·vot·ing 1** : to set apart for a special purpose **2** : to give up to entirely or in part

de·vot·ed *adj* **1** : completely loyal **2** : AFFECTIONATE, LOVING — **de·vot·ed·ly** *adv*

de·vo·tion *n* **1** : deep love or loyalty **2** : an act of giving (as effort or time) to something **3** : a religious exercise or practice (as prayers) especially that is private

de·vour *vb* **de·voured; de·vour·ing 1** : to eat up hungrily **2** : to take in eagerly by the senses or mind **3** : to destroy as if by eating

de·vout *adj* **1** : deeply religious **2** : strongly loyal or devoted **3** : warmly sincere and earnest — **de·vout·ly** *adv*

dew *n* : moisture that collects on cool surfaces at night

dew·lap *n* : loose skin hanging under the neck of some animals (as cows)

dew point *n* : the temperature at which the moisture in the air begins to turn to dew

dewy *adj* **dew·i·er; dew·i·est** : moist with or as if with dew

dex·ter·i·ty *n, pl* **dex·ter·i·ties 1** : skill and ease in the use of the hands or body **2** : the ability to think and act quickly and cleverly

dex·ter·ous *adj* **1** : skillful with the hands **2** : CLEVER 2 **3** : done with skill — **dex·ter·ous·ly** *adv*

di·a·be·tes *n* : a disease in which too little or no insulin is produced or insulin is produced but cannot be used normally resulting in high levels of sugar in the blood

di·a·bet·ic *n* : a person with diabetes

di·a·crit·i·cal mark *n* : a mark that is placed over, under, or through a letter in some languages to show that the letter should be pronounced in a particular way

di·ag·nose *vb* **di·ag·nosed; di·ag·nos·ing** : to recognize (as a disease) by signs and symptoms

di·ag·no·sis *n, pl* **di·ag·no·ses** 1 : the act of recognizing a disease from its signs and symptoms 2 : the conclusion that is reached following examination and testing

¹di·ag·o·nal *adj* 1 : running from one corner to the opposite corner of a four-sided shape (as a square) 2 : running in a slanting direction — **di·ag·o·nal·ly** *adv*

²diagonal *n* : a line, direction, or pattern that runs in a slanting direction

¹di·a·gram *n* : a drawing, plan, or chart that makes something clearer or easier to understand

²diagram *vb* **di·a·grammed** *or* **di·a·gramed** ; **di·a·gram·ming** *or* **di·a·gram·ing** : to put in the form of a drawing, plan, or chart

¹di·al *n* 1 : the face of a watch or clock 2 : SUNDIAL 3 : a usually flat round part of a piece of equipment with numbers or marks to show some measurement usually by means of a pointer 4 : a part of a machine or device (as a radio) that may be turned to operate or adjust it

²dial *vb* **di·aled** *or* **di·alled; di·al·ing** *or* **di·al·ling** : to use a knob, button, or other control to operate or select

di·a·lect *n* : a form of a language that is spoken in a certain region or by a certain group

di·a·logue *also* **di·a·log** *n* 1 : conversation given in a written story or a play 2 : a conversation between two or more people or groups

di·am·e·ter *n* 1 : a straight line that runs from one side of a figure and passes through the center 2 : the distance through the center of an object from one side to the other : THICKNESS

di·a·mond *n* 1 : a very hard mineral that is a form of carbon, is usually nearly colorless, and is used especially in jewelry 2 : a flat figure ♦ like one of the surfaces of certain cut diamonds 3 : INFIELD 1

di·a·per *n* : a piece of absorbent material for a baby worn pulled up between the legs and fastened around the waist

di·a·phragm *n* 1 : a muscular wall that separates the lungs from the stomach area and assists in breathing in 2 : a thin disk (as in a microphone) that vibrates when sound strikes it

di·ar·rhea *n* : abnormally frequent and watery bowel movements

di·a·ry *n, pl* **di·a·ries** 1 : a daily written record especially of personal experiences and thoughts 2 : a book for keeping a record of experiences and thoughts

¹dice *n, pl* **dice** : ²DIE 1

²dice *vb* **diced; dic·ing** : to cut into small cubes

¹dic·tate *vb* **dic·tat·ed; dic·tat·ing** 1 : to speak or read for someone else to write down or for a machine to record 2 : to say or state with authority : ORDER 3 : to make necessary

²dictate *n* 1 : a statement made or direction given with authority : COMMAND 2 : a guiding rule or principle

dic·ta·tion *n* : the act of speaking words for someone else to write down or for a machine to record the words spoken

dic·ta·tor *n* : a person who rules with total power and often in a cruel manner — **dic·ta·tor·ship** *n*

dic·tion *n* 1 : choice of words especially with regard to correctness, clearness, and effectiveness 2 : the ability to say words

dic·tio·nary *n, pl* **dic·tio·nar·ies** 1 : a book giving the meaning and usually the pronunciation of words listed in alphabetical order 2 : a reference book explaining words of a particular subject listed in alphabetical order 3 : a book listing words of one language in alphabetical order with definitions in another language

did *past of* DO

didn't : did not

¹die *vb* **died; dy·ing** 1 : to stop living 2 : to come to an end 3 : to disappear little by little 4 : to want badly 5 : to stop working or running — **die out** : to disappear gradually

²die *n* 1 *pl* **dice** : a small cube marked on each side with one to six spots and used in games 2 *pl* **dies** : a device for forming or cutting material by pressure

die·sel *n* 1 : DIESEL ENGINE 2 : a vehicle that has a diesel engine 3 : DIESEL FUEL

diesel engine *n* : an engine in which the mixture of air and fuel is compressed until enough heat is created to ignite the mixture that uses diesel fuel instead of gasoline

diesel fuel *n* : a heavy oil used as fuel in diesel engines

¹di·et *n* 1 : the food and drink that a person or animal usually takes 2 : the kind and amount of food selected or allowed in certain circumstances (as poor health)

²diet *vb* **di·et·ed; di·et·ing** : to eat less or according to certain rules in order to lose weight — **di·et·er** *n*

³**diet** *adj* : reduced in calories

di·e·tary *adj* : relating to a diet

di·e·ti·tian *or* **di·e·ti·cian** *n* : a person trained to give advice about diet and nutrition

dif·fer *vb* **dif·fered; dif·fer·ing** **1** : to be unlike : be different **2** : DISAGREE 1

dif·fer·ence *n* **1** : what makes two or more persons or things not the same **2** : a disagreement about something **3** : the number that is left after subtracting one number from another **4** : an important change

dif·fer·ent *adj* **1** : not of the same kind **2** : not the same **3** : not ordinary — **dif·fer·ent·ly** *adv*

dif·fer·en·ti·ate *vb* **dif·fer·en·ti·at·ed; dif·fer·en·ti·at·ing** **1** : to make or become different **2** : to recognize or state the difference between

dif·fer·en·ti·a·tion *n* : the process of change by which immature living structures develop to maturity

dif·fi·cult *adj* **1** : not easy : hard to do or make **2** : hard to deal with **3** : hard to understand

dif·fi·cul·ty *n, pl* **dif·fi·cul·ties** **1** : the state of being hard to do **2** : great effort **3** : something that makes something hard to do : OBSTACLE **4** : a troublesome situation

dif·fi·dent *adj* **1** : lacking confidence **2** : cautious about acting or speaking

dif·fuse *vb* **dif·fused; dif·fus·ing** : to spread or allow to spread freely

dif·fu·sion *n* **1** : the act of spreading or allowing to spread freely **2** : the mixing of particles of liquids or gases so that they move from a region of high concentration to one of lower concentration

¹**dig** *vb* **dug** ; **dig·ging** **1** : to turn up, loosen, or remove the soil **2** : to turn up or remove with a shovel or by similar means **3** : to form by removing earth **4** : to uncover or search by or as if by turning up earth **5** : ¹PROD 1, POKE — **dig in** : to begin eating — **dig into** **1** : to begin eating **2** : to try to discover information — **dig up** **1** : to uncover or remove (as from soil) **2** : DISCOVER

²**dig** *n* **1** : ²POKE **2** : a place where buried objects are being uncovered **3** : a project to uncover buried objects **4** : a nasty remark

¹**di·gest** *n* : information in shortened form

²**di·gest** *vb* **di·gest·ed; di·gest·ing** **1** : to change or become changed into simpler forms that can be used by the body **2** : to think over and try to understand

di·gest·ible *adj* : possible to digest

di·ges·tion *n* : the body's process or power of changing food into simpler forms that can be taken up and used

di·ges·tive *adj* : relating to or functioning in the body's process of changing food into simpler forms that can be taken up and used

digestive system *n* : the system of the body that takes in, breaks down, and absorbs food and discharges solid waste and consists of the digestive tract and related glands (as the salivary glands and pancreas)

digestive tract *n* : the tube-shaped passage including the mouth, pharynx, esophagus, stomach, and intestines that is concerned with taking in, breaking down, and absorbing food and discharging solid waste

dig·it *n* **1** : any of the numerals 1 to 9 and the symbol 0 **2** : a finger or toe

dig·i·tal *adj* **1** : relating to or using calculation directly with digits rather than through measurable physical quantities **2** : of or relating to data in the form of numerical digits **3** : providing displayed or recorded information in numerical digits from an automatic device — **dig·i·tal·ly** *adv*

digital camera *n* : a camera that takes pictures without using film by recording the images as electronic data

dig·ni·fied *adj* : having or showing dignity

dig·ni·fy *vb* **dig·ni·fied; dig·ni·fy·ing** **1** : to give dignity or importance to **2** : to treat with respect or seriousness that is not deserved

dig·ni·tary *n, pl* **dig·ni·tar·ies** : a person of high position or honor

dig·ni·ty *n, pl* **dig·ni·ties** **1** : the quality or state of being worthy of honor and respect **2** : a serious and admirable look or way of behaving

dike *n* **1** : a long trench dug in the earth to carry water **2** : a mound of earth built to control water

di·lap·i·dat·ed *adj* : falling apart or ruined from age or from lack of care

di·late *vb* **di·lat·ed; di·lat·ing** : to make or grow larger or wider

di·lem·ma *n* : a situation in which a person has to choose between things that are all bad or unsatisfactory

dil·i·gence *n* : careful and continued hard work

dil·i·gent *adj* : showing steady and earnest care and hard work — **dil·i·gent·ly** *adv*

dill *n* : an herb that is related to the carrot plant and has fragrant leaves and seeds used in flavoring foods and especially pickles

dil·ly·dal·ly *vb* **dil·ly·dal·lied; dil·ly·dal·ly·ing** : to waste time : DAWDLE

di·lute *vb* **di·lut·ed; di·lut·ing** : to make thinner or more liquid by adding something

di·lu·tion *n* **1** : the act of making thinner or more liquid : the state of being made thinner or more liquid **2** : something (as a solution) that has had something added to it to make it thinner or more liquid

¹dim *adj* **dim·mer; dim·mest** **1** : not bright or distinct : FAINT **2** : not seeing or understanding clearly — **dim·ly** *adv* — **dim·ness** *n*

²dim *vb* **dimmed; dim·ming** : to make or become less bright or clear

dime *n* : a United States coin worth ten cents

di·men·sion *n* : the length, width, or height of something

di·men·sion·al *adj* : relating to the length, width, or height of something

di·min·ish *vb* **di·min·ished; di·min·ish·ing** **1** : to make less or cause to seem less **2** : BELITTLE **3** : to become gradually less or smaller : DWINDLE — **di·min·ish·ment** *n*

di·min·u·en·do *n, pl* **di·min·u·en·dos** *or* **di·min·u·en·does** : DECRESCENDO

di·min·u·tive *adj* : very small : TINY

dim·ple *n* : a slight hollow spot especially in the cheek or chin

din *n* : loud confused noise

dine *vb* **dined; din·ing** : to eat dinner — **dine out** : to eat at a restaurant

din·er *n* **1** : a person eating dinner **2** : a railroad dining car or a restaurant that looks like one

di·nette *n* : a small room or separate area near a kitchen that is used for dining

ding-dong *n* : the sound of a bell ringing

din·ghy *n, pl* **dinghies** **1** : a small light rowboat **2** : a rubber life raft

din·gy *adj* **din·gi·er; din·gi·est** : rather dark and dirty

din·ner *n* **1** : the main meal of the day **2** : a usually large formal event at which a meal is served

di·no·saur *n* : any of a group of extinct often very large mostly land-dwelling reptiles that lived millions of years ago

dint *n* : the force or power of something — used in the phrase *by dint of.*

di·o·cese *n* : the area that is under the authority of a bishop

¹dip *vb* **dipped; dip·ping** **1** : to lower or push briefly into a liquid to wet or coat **2** : to take out or serve with or as if with a ladle **3** : to lower and quickly raise again : drop or sink and quickly rise again **4** : to sink out of sight **5** : to slope downward

²dip *n* **1** : a short swim **2** : something obtained by or as if by a ladle **3** : a sauce into which solid food may be dipped **4** : a downward slope

diph·the·ria *n* : a contagious disease that often makes breathing and swallowing difficult

diph·thong *n* : two vowel sounds joined in one syllable to form one speech sound

di·plo·ma *n* : a certificate that shows a person has finished a course or graduated from a school

di·plo·ma·cy *n* **1** : the work of keeping good relations between the governments of different countries **2** : skill in dealing with people

dip·lo·mat *n* **1** : a person whose work is keeping good relations between the governments of different countries **2** : a person who is good at dealing with people in a way that avoids bad feelings

dip·lo·mat·ic *adj* **1** : of or relating to keeping good relations between the governments of different countries **2** : not causing bad feelings — **dip·lo·mat·i·cal·ly** *adv*

dip·per *n* : ¹LADLE

dire *adj* **1** : causing horror or worry : DREADFUL **2** : very great

¹di·rect *vb* **di·rect·ed; di·rect·ing** **1** : to cause to point or move in a particular direction **2** : to cause to focus on **3** : to show or tell the way **4** : to put an address on **5** : ¹ORDER 2, COMMAND **6** : to manage or control the making or activities of

²direct *adj* **1** : going from one point to another without turning or stopping : STRAIGHT **2** : coming straight from a cause or source **3** : going straight to the point **4** : being in an unbroken family line — **di·rect·ness** *n*

³direct *adv* : DIRECTLY 1

direct current *n* : an electric current flowing in one direction only

di·rec·tion *n* **1** : the path along which something moves, lies, or points **2** : an order or instruction to be followed **3** : instructions on how to get somewhere **4** : SUPERVISION, MANAGEMENT

di·rect·ly *adv* **1** : in a straight course or line **2** : straight to or from a source : without interference **3** : IMMEDIATELY 2

direct object *n* : a word that represents the main goal or the result of the action of a verb

di·rec·tor *n* **1** : a person who manages something **2** : a person in charge of making a movie or play

di·rec·to·ry *n, pl* **di·rec·to·ries** : a book containing an alphabetical list of names, addresses, and telephone numbers

di·ri·gi·ble *n* : AIRSHIP

dirk *n* : a long dagger with a straight blade

dirt *n* **1** : ²SOIL 1 **2** : a substance (as mud or dust) that makes things unclean

¹dirty *adj* **dirt·i·er; dirt·i·est** **1** : not clean **2** : UNFAIR, MEAN **3** : not pleasant but usually necessary **4** : being vulgar : not decent **5** : showing dislike or anger — **dirt·i·ness** *n*

²dirty *adv* : in an unfair or dishonest way

³dirty *vb* **dirt·ied; dirty·ing** : to make or become unclean

dis- *prefix* **1** : do the opposite of **2** : deprive of **3** : opposite or absence of **4** : not

dis·abil·i·ty *n, pl* **dis·abil·i·ties** : a condition (as one present at birth or caused by injury) that damages or limits a person's abilities : the state of being disabled

dis·able *vb* **dis·abled; dis·abling** : to make unable or incapable

dis·abled *adj* : not having the ability to do certain mental or physical tasks (as because of illness, injury, or a condition present at birth) that a person is typically capable of doing

dis·ad·van·tage *n* : a state or condition that favors someone else

dis·ad·van·ta·geous *adj* : making it harder for a person or thing to succeed or do something

dis·agree *vb* **dis·agreed; dis·agree·ing 1** : to have different ideas or opinions **2** : to be unlike each other : be different **3** : to make ill

dis·agree·able *adj* **1** : UNPLEASANT **2** : difficult to get along with

dis·agree·ment *n* **1** : failure to agree **2** : ARGUMENT 1

dis·ap·pear *vb* **dis·ap·peared; dis·ap·pearing 1** : to stop being visible : pass out of sight **2** : to stop existing

dis·ap·pear·ance *n* : the act of passing out of sight or existence

dis·ap·point *vb* **dis·ap·point·ed; dis·ap·point·ing** : to fail to satisfy the hope or expectation of

dis·ap·point·ment *n* **1** : unhappiness from the failure of something hoped for or expected to happen **2** : someone or something that fails to satisfy hopes or expectations

dis·ap·prov·al *n* : the feeling of not liking or agreeing with something or someone

dis·ap·prove *vb* **dis·ap·proved; dis·ap·proving** : to dislike or be against someone or something

dis·arm *vb* **dis·armed; dis·arm·ing 1** : to take weapons from **2** : to reduce the size and strength of the armed forces of a country **3** : to make harmless **4** : to end dislike or mistrust : win over — **dis·ar·ma·ment** *n*

dis·ar·ray *n* : a confused or messy condition

dis·as·sem·ble *vb* **dis·as·sem·bled; dis·as·sem·bling** : to take apart

di·sas·ter *n* : something (as a flood or a tornado) that happens suddenly and causes much suffering or loss

di·sas·trous *adj* **1** : causing great suffering or loss **2** : very bad

dis·band *vb* **dis·band·ed; dis·band·ing** : to break up and stop being a group

dis·be·lief *n* : refusal or inability to believe

dis·be·lieve *vb* **dis·be·lieved; dis·be·liev·ing** : to think not to be true or real

dis·burse *vb* **dis·bursed; dis·burs·ing** : to pay out — **dis·burse·ment** *n*

disc *variant of* DISK

¹dis·card *vb* **dis·card·ed; dis·card·ing 1** : to get rid of as useless or unwanted **2** : to throw down an unwanted card from a hand of cards

²dis·card *n* : something thrown away or rejected

dis·cern *vb* **dis·cerned; dis·cern·ing** : to see, recognize, or understand something

¹dis·charge *vb* **dis·charged; dis·charg·ing 1** : to allow to leave or get off **2** : to dismiss from service **3** : to free of a load or burden : UNLOAD **4** : ¹SHOOT 2 **5** : to cause to shoot out of **6** : to pour forth fluid or other contents **7** : to get rid of by paying or doing

²dis·charge *n* **1** : the release of someone from a place **2** : the release from a duty or debt **3** : a certificate of release or payment **4** : the act of firing a person from a job **5** : an end of a person's military service **6** : an act of firing off **7** : something that flows out

dis·ci·ple *n* **1** : a person who accepts and helps to spread the teachings of another **2** : APOSTLE

dis·ci·plin·ary *adj* : relating to the correction or punishment of bad behavior

¹dis·ci·pline *n* **1** : PUNISHMENT 1 **2** : strict training that corrects or strengthens **3** : habits and ways of acting that are gotten through practice **4** : control that is gained by insisting that rules be followed

²discipline *vb* **dis·ci·plined; dis·ci·plin·ing 1** : to punish as a way to bring about good behavior **2** : to train in self-control or obedience **3** : to bring under control

disc jockey *n* : someone who plays recorded music on the radio or at a party

dis·claim *vb* **dis·claimed; dis·claim·ing** : to deny being part of or responsible for

dis·close *vb* **dis·closed; dis·clos·ing** : to make known : REVEAL

dis·clo·sure *n* **1** : an act of making known **2** : something made known

dis·col·or *vb* **dis·col·ored; dis·col·or·ing** : to change in color especially for the worse

dis·col·or·a·tion *n* **1** : change of color **2** : a spot that is changed in color

dis·com·fort *n* : the condition of being uncomfortable

dis·con·cert *vb* **dis·con·cert·ed; dis·con·cert·ing** : to make confused and a little upset

dis·con·nect *vb* **dis·con·nect·ed; dis·con·nect·ing** : to undo or break the connection of

dis·con·so·late *adj* : too sad to be cheered up — **dis·con·so·late·ly** *adv*

¹dis·con·tent *n* : the condition of being dissatisfied

²discontent *adj* : not satisfied

dis·con·tent·ed *adj* : not satisfied

dis·con·tin·ue *vb* **dis·con·tin·ued; dis·con·tinu·ing** : to bring to an end : STOP

dis·cord *n* : lack of agreement or harmony : CONFLICT

dis·cor·dant *adj* : being in disagreement

¹dis·count *n* : an amount taken off a regular price

²dis·count *vb* **dis·count·ed; dis·count·ing 1** : to lower the amount of a bill, debt, or price **2** : to think of as not important or serious

dis·cour·age *vb* **dis·cour·aged; dis·cour·ag·ing 1** : to make less determined, hopeful, or confident **2** : to make less likely to happen **3** : to try to persuade not to do something — **dis·cour·age·ment** *n*

¹dis·course *n* **1** : CONVERSATION **2** : a long talk or essay about a subject

²dis·course *vb* **dis·coursed; dis·cours·ing** : to talk especially for a long time

dis·cour·te·ous *adj* : not polite : RUDE

dis·cour·te·sy *n, pl* **dis·cour·te·sies 1** : rude behavior **2** : a rude act

dis·cov·er *vb* **dis·cov·ered; dis·cov·er·ing** : to find out, see, or learn of especially for the first time : FIND — **dis·cov·er·er** *n*

dis·cov·ery *n, pl* **dis·cov·er·ies 1** : an act of finding out or learning of for the first time **2** : something found or learned of for the first time

¹dis·cred·it *vb* **dis·cred·it·ed; dis·cred·it·ing 1** : to cause to seem dishonest or untrue **2** : to harm the reputation of

²discredit *n* : loss of good name or respect

dis·creet *adj* : careful not to attract attention or let out private information — **dis·creet·ly** *adv*

dis·crep·an·cy *n* : a difference between things that are expected to be the same

dis·crete *adj* : ²SEPARATE 3, DISTINCT

dis·cre·tion *n* **1** : care in not attracting attention or letting out private information **2** : the power to decide what to do

dis·crim·i·nate *vb* **dis·crim·i·nat·ed; dis·crim·i·nat·ing 1** : to unfairly treat a person or group differently from other people or groups **2** : to be able to tell the difference between things

dis·crim·i·na·tion *n* **1** : the practice of unfairly treating a person or group differently from other people or groups of people **2** : the ability to see differences

dis·crim·i·na·to·ry *adj* : showing discrimination : being unfair

dis·cus *n, pl* **dis·cus·es** : an object that is shaped like a disk and hurled for distance in a track-and-field event

dis·cuss *vb* **dis·cussed; dis·cuss·ing 1** : to talk about **2** : to argue or consider fully and openly

dis·cus·sion *n* : conversation for the purpose of understanding or debating a question or subject

¹dis·dain *n* : a feeling of dislike for someone or something considered not good enough — **dis·dain·ful** *adj* — **dis·dain·ful·ly** *adv*

²disdain *vb* **dis·dained; dis·dain·ing 1** : to feel dislike for something or someone usually for not being good enough **2** : to refuse because of feelings of dislike

dis·ease *n* : a change in a living body (as of a person or plant) that prevents it from functioning normally : SICKNESS

dis·eased *adj* : having a sickness

dis·em·bark *vb* **dis·em·barked; dis·em·bark·ing** : to leave or remove from a ship or airplane

dis·en·fran·chise *vb* **dis·en·fran·chised; dis·en·fran·chis·ing** : to deprive of the right to vote

dis·en·tan·gle *vb* **dis·en·tan·gled; dis·en·tan·gling** : UNTANGLE

dis·fa·vor *n* **1** : DISAPPROVAL **2** : the condition of being disliked

dis·fig·ure *vb* **dis·fig·ured; dis·fig·ur·ing** : to spoil the looks of

dis·fig·ure·ment *n* : something that spoils the appearance of a person or thing

dis·fran·chise *vb* **dis·fran·chised; dis·fran·chis·ing** : DISENFRANCHISE — **dis·fran·chise·ment** *n*

¹dis·grace *vb* **dis·graced; dis·grac·ing** : to bring shame to

²disgrace *n* **1** : the condition of being looked down on : loss of respect **2** : a cause of shame

dis·grace·ful *adj* : bringing or deserving shame — **dis·grace·ful·ly** *adv*

dis·grun·tled *adj* : GROUCHY

¹dis·guise *vb* **dis·guised; dis·guis·ing 1** : to change the looks or sound of to avoid being recognized **2** : to keep from revealing

²disguise *n* **1** : clothing worn to avoid being recognized **2** : an outward appearance that hides what something really is

¹dis·gust *n* : a strong feeling of dislike or annoyance for something considered sickening or bad

²disgust *vb* **dis·gust·ed; dis·gust·ing** : to cause to feel strong dislike or annoyance by being sickening or bad — **dis·gust·ed·ly** *adv*

dis·gust·ing *adj* : very sickening or bad

dish *n* **1** : a usually round shallow container used for cooking or serving food **2 dish·es** *pl* : all items (as plates and silverware) used for cooking and eating food **3** : the food in a container for serving or eating **4** : food that is prepared in a particular way **5** : a round shallow object

dis·heart·en *vb* **dis·heart·ened; dis·heart·ens** : DISCOURAGE 1

di·shev·eled *or* **di·shev·elled** *adj* : MESSY 1

dis·hon·est *adj* : not honest or trustworthy — **dis·hon·est·ly** *adv*

dis·hon·es·ty *n* : the quality of being untruthful : lack of honesty

¹dis·hon·or *n* **1** : loss of honor or good name **2** : a cause of disgrace

²dishonor *vb* **dis·hon·ored; dis·hon·ors** : to bring shame on : DISGRACE

dis·hon·or·able *adj* : SHAMEFUL — **dis·hon·or·ably** *adv*

dis·il·lu·sion *vb* **dis·il·lu·sioned; dis·il·lu·sions** : to cause to stop having a mistaken belief that something is good, valuable, or true — **dis·il·lu·sion·ment** *n*

dis·in·fect *vb* **dis·in·fect·ed; dis·in·fect·ing** : to cleanse of germs that might cause disease

dis·in·fec·tant *n* : something that kills germs

dis·in·her·it *vb* **dis·in·her·it·ed; dis·in·her·it·ing** : to take away the legal right to receive money or property from at death

dis·in·te·grate *vb* **dis·in·te·grat·ed; dis·in·te·grat·ing** : to separate or break up into small parts or pieces

dis·in·te·gra·tion *n* : the act or process of breaking into small pieces : the condition of being broken into small pieces

dis·in·ter·est·ed *adj* **1** : not interested **2** : not influenced by personal feelings or concerns

dis·joint·ed *adj* : not clear and orderly — **dis·joint·ed·ly** *adv*

disk *or* **disc** *n* **1** : something that is or appears to be flat and round **2** *usually disc* : CD **3** : a round, thin, flat plate coated with a magnetic substance on which data for a computer is stored **4** *usually disc* : a phonograph record — **disk·like** *adj*

disk drive *n* : the part of a computer that moves data to and from a disk

disk·ette *n* : FLOPPY DISK

¹dis·like *n* : a strong feeling of not liking or approving

²dislike *vb* **dis·liked; dis·lik·ing** : to not like or approve of

dis·lo·cate *vb* **dis·lo·cat·ed; dis·lo·cat·ing** : to displace a bone from its normal connections with another bone

dis·lo·ca·tion *n* : the condition of being moved out of a normal location

dis·lodge *vb* **dis·lodged; dis·lodg·ing** : to force out of a place of resting, hiding, or defense

dis·loy·al *adj* : failing to support or be true

dis·loy·al·ty *n, pl* **dis·loy·al·ties** **1** : lack of

faithfulness or support **2** : an act that shows a lack of faithfulness or support

dis·mal *adj* : very gloomy

dis·man·tle *vb* **dis·man·tled; dis·man·tling** **1** : to take completely apart (as for storing or repair) **2** : to strip of furniture or equipment

¹dis·may *vb* **dis·mayed; dis·may·ing** : to feel worry, disappointment, fear, or shock

²dismay *n* : a feeling of fear, disappointment, shock, or worry

dis·miss *vb* **dis·missed; dis·miss·ing** **1** : to allow or cause to leave **2** : to remove from a job or position **3** : to decide not to think about

dis·miss·al *n* : the act of dismissing : the state or fact of being dismissed

dis·mount *vb* **dis·mount·ed; dis·mount·ing** : to get down from something (as a horse or bicycle)

dis·obe·di·ence *n* : an act of failing or refusing to behave as told or taught

dis·obe·di·ent *adj* : not behaving as told or taught — **dis·obe·di·ent·ly** *adv*

dis·obey *vb* **dis·obeyed; dis·obey·ing** : to refuse or fail to behave as told or taught

¹dis·or·der *vb* **dis·or·dered; dis·or·der·ing** : to disturb the regular or normal arrangement or functioning of

²disorder *n* **1** : a confused or messy state **2** : unruly behavior **3** : a physical or mental condition that is not normal or healthy

dis·or·der·ly *adj* **1** : not behaving quietly or well : UNRULY **2** : not neat or orderly

dis·or·ga·ni·za·tion *n* : lack of order

dis·or·ga·nized *adj* **1** : not having order **2** : not able to manage or plan things well

dis·own *vb* **dis·owned; dis·own·ing** : to refuse to accept any longer a relationship with or connection to

dis·par·age *vb* **dis·par·aged; dis·par·ag·ing** : to speak of as unimportant or bad : BELITTLE — **dis·par·age·ment** *n*

dis·pas·sion·ate *adj* : not influenced by strong feeling or personal involvement : CALM, IMPARTIAL — **dis·pas·sion·ate·ly** *adv*

¹dis·patch *vb* **dis·patched; dis·patch·ing** **1** : to send away quickly to a certain place or for a certain reason **2** : to get done quickly **3** : ¹KILL 1 — **dis·patch·er** *n*

²dispatch *n* **1** : MESSAGE 1 **2** : a news story sent in to a newspaper **3** : ¹SPEED 1

dis·pel *vb* **dis·pelled; dis·pel·ling** : to make go away

dis·pense *vb* **dis·pensed; dis·pens·ing** **1** : to give out in small amounts **2** : to give out as deserved **3** : to put up or prepare medicine in a form ready for use — **dispense with** : to do or get along without

dis·pens·er *n* : a container that gives out something in small amounts

dis·perse *vb* **dis·persed; dis·pers·ing** : to break up and scatter

dis·pir·it·ed *adj* : not cheerful or enthusiastic — **dispiritedly** *adv*

dis·place *vb* **dis·placed; dis·plac·ing 1** : to remove from the usual or proper place **2** : to take the place of : REPLACE **3** : to move out of position — **dis·place·ment** *n*

¹dis·play *vb* **dis·played; dis·play·ing 1** : to put (something) in plain sight **2** : to make clear the existence or presence of : show plainly

²display *n* **1** : a presentation of something **2** : an arrangement of something where it can be easily seen **3** : an electronic device (as a computer monitor) that shows information

dis·please *vb* **dis·pleased; dis·pleas·ing** : to cause to feel unhappy or unsatisfied

dis·plea·sure *n* : a feeling of dislike and irritation : DISSATISFACTION

dis·pos·able *adj* : made to be thrown away after use

dis·pos·al *n* **1** : The act of getting rid of **2** : right or power to use : CONTROL

dis·pose *vb* **dis·posed; dis·pos·ing** : to put in place : ARRANGE — **dispose of 1** : to finish with **2** : to get rid of

dis·posed *adj* **1** : having the desire or tendency to **2** : feeling or thinking in a particular way about

dis·po·si·tion *n* **1** : a person's usual attitude or mood **2** : TENDENCY 2, LIKING **3** : ARRANGEMENT 1

dis·pro·por·tion *n* : a marked difference in the size, number, or amount of something as compared to another thing

dis·prove *vb* **dis·proved; dis·prov·ing** : to show to be false or wrong

¹dis·pute *vb* **dis·put·ed; dis·put·ing 1** : to question or deny the truth or rightness of **2** : ARGUE 1 **3** : to fight over

²dispute *n* **1** : ¹DEBATE 3 **2** : ¹QUARREL 1

dis·qual·i·fy *vb* **dis·qual·i·fied; dis·qual·i·fy·ing** : to make or declare not fit to have, do, or take part in

¹dis·qui·et *vb* **dis·qui·et·ed; dis·qui·et·ing** : to make uneasy or worried

²disquiet *n* : an uneasy feeling

¹dis·re·gard *vb* **dis·re·gard·ed; dis·re·gard·ing** : to pay no attention to

²disregard *n* : the act of paying no attention to

dis·re·pair *n* : the condition of needing to be fixed

dis·rep·u·ta·ble *adj* : not respectable or honest

dis·re·spect *n* : lack of respect : DISCOUR-

TESY — **dis·re·spect·ful** *adj* — **dis·re·spect·ful·ly** *adv*

dis·rupt *vb* **dis·rupt·ed; dis·rupt·ing 1** : to cause disorder in **2** : to interrupt the normal course of — **dis·rup·tion** *n* — **dis·rup·tive** *adj*

dis·sat·is·fac·tion *n* : a feeling of unhappiness or disapproval

dis·sat·is·fy *vb* **dis·sat·is·fied; dis·sat·is·fy·ing** : to fail to give what is desired or expected : DISPLEASE

dis·sect *vb* **dis·sect·ed; dis·sect·ing** : to cut or take apart especially for examination

dis·sec·tion *n* : the act of cutting something or taking something apart for examination

dis·sen·sion *n* : difference in opinion

¹dis·sent *vb* **dis·sent·ed; dis·sent·ing** : DISAGREE 1 — **dis·sent·er** *n*

²dissent *n* : difference of opinion

dis·ser·vice *n* : a harmful, unfair, or unjust act

dis·sim·i·lar *adj* : DIFFERENT 1

dis·si·pate *vb* **dis·si·pat·ed; dis·si·pat·ing 1** : to cause to break up and disappear: DISPERSE **2** : to scatter or waste foolishly : SQUANDER

dis·si·pat·ed *adj* : indulging in bad, foolish, or harmful activities

dis·si·pa·tion *n* **1** : the act of causing to break up and disappear **2** : indulgence in too much pleasure

dis·solve *vb* **dis·solved; dis·solv·ing 1** : to become part of a liquid **2** : to bring to an end : TERMINATE **3** : to fade away as if by melting or breaking up **4** : to be overcome by a strong feeling

dis·so·nance *n* : an unpleasant combination of musical sounds

dis·suade *vb* **dis·suad·ed; dis·suad·ing** : to persuade or advise not to do something

dis·tance *n* **1** : how far from each other two points or places are **2** : a point or place that is far away **3** : the quality or state of not being friendly : RESERVE

dis·tant *adj* **1** : existing or happening at a place far away **2** : far away in time **3** : not closely related **4** : ¹COLD 5, UNFRIENDLY — **dis·tant·ly** *adv*

dis·taste *n* : ¹DISLIKE

dis·taste·ful *adj* : UNPLEASANT

dis·tend *vb* **dis·tend·ed; dis·tend·ing** : EXPAND 2, SWELL

dis·till *also* **dis·til** *vb* **dis·tilled; dis·till·ing** : to make (a liquid) pure by heating it until it becomes a gas and then cooling it until it becomes a liquid — **dis·till·er** *n*

dis·til·la·tion *n* : the process of heating a liquid until it gives off a gas and then cooling the gas until it becomes liquid

dis·tinct *adj* **1** : different from each other **2**

: easy to notice or understand — **dis·tinct·ly** adv

dis·tinc·tion n 1 : DIFFERENCE 1 2 : the act of seeing or pointing out a difference 3 : great worth : EXCELLENCE 4 : something that makes a person or thing special or different

dis·tinc·tive adj 1 : clearly marking a person or a thing as different from others 2 : having or giving a special look or way — **dis·tinc·tive·ly** adv

dis·tin·guish vb **dis·tin·guished; dis·tin·guish·ing** 1 : to recognize one thing from others by some mark or quality 2 : to hear or see clearly 3 : to know the difference 4 : to set apart as different or special

dis·tin·guish·able adj : possible to recognize or tell apart from others

dis·tin·guished adj : widely known and admired

dis·tort vb **dis·tort·ed; dis·tort·ing** 1 : to twist out of shape 2 : to change so as to make untrue or inaccurate

dis·tor·tion n : the act of twisting out of shape or making inaccurate : the state or fact of being twisted out of shape or made inaccurate

dis·tract vb **dis·tract·ed; dis·tract·ing** 1 : to draw a person's thoughts or attention to something else

dis·trac·tion n 1 : something that makes it hard to pay attention 2 : the act of having thoughts or attention drawn away : the state of drawing thoughts or attention away 3 : confusion of thoughts or feelings

dis·traught adj : very upset

¹dis·tress n 1 : physical or mental pain or suffering 2 : a state of danger or desperate need

²distress vb **dis·tressed; dis·tress·ing** : to cause to suffer — **distressing** adj

dis·trib·ute vb **dis·trib·ut·ed; dis·trib·ut·ing** 1 : to give out or to deliver to 2 : to divide among many or several 3 : to spread out so as to cover something

dis·tri·bu·tion n 1 : the act of giving out or delivering to or dividing among 2 : the way things are given out or delivered to or divided among 3 : something given out or delivered to or divided among

dis·trib·u·tive adj 1 : of or relating to the act of giving or spreading out 2 : producing the same answer when operating on the sum of several numbers as when operating on each and collecting the results

dis·trib·u·tor n : a person or company that supplies stores or businesses with goods

dis·trict n 1 : an area or section (as of a city or nation) set apart for some purpose 2 : an area or region with some special feature

¹dis·trust n : a lack of belief or confidence in : SUSPICION — **dis·trust·ful** adj

²distrust vb **dis·trust·ed; dis·trust·ing** : to have no belief or confidence in

dis·turb vb **dis·turbed; dis·turb·ing** 1 : to interfere with : INTERRUPT 2 : to change the position or arrangement of 3 : UPSET, WORRY 4 : to make confused or disordered

dis·tur·bance n 1 : the act of interrupting, changing the arrangement of, or upsetting : the state of being interrupted, changed in arrangement, or upset 2 : ²DISORDER 2, COMMOTION

dis·turbed adj : showing signs of mental or emotional illness

dis·use n : lack of use

dis·used adj : not used any more

¹ditch n : a long narrow channel or trench dug in the earth

²ditch vb **ditched; ditch·ing** 1 : to get rid of : DISCARD 2 : to end a relationship with

dith·er n : a very nervous or excited state

dit·ty n, pl **ditties** : a short simple song

¹dive vb **dived** or **dove**; **div·ing** 1 : to plunge into water headfirst 2 : to swim underwater especially while using special equipment 3 : SUBMERGE 1 4 : to fall fast 5 : to descend in an airplane at a steep angle 6 : to move forward suddenly into or at something — **div·er** n

²dive n 1 : an act of plunging headfirst into water 2 : an act of swimming underwater especially while using special equipment 3 : an act of submerging a submarine 4 : a quick drop (as of prices) 5 : a sudden movement forward into or at something

di·verse adj 1 : different from each other : UNLIKE 2 : made up of people or things that are different from each other

di·ver·si·fy vb **di·ver·si·fied; di·ver·si·fy·ing** : to change to include many different things

di·ver·sion n 1 : an act or instance of changing the direction or use of 2 : something that relaxes, distracts, or entertains

di·ver·si·ty n, pl **di·ver·si·ties** : the condition or fact of being different

di·vert vb **di·vert·ed; di·vert·ing** 1 : to turn from one path or use to another 2 : to turn the attention away : DISTRACT 3 : to give pleasure to : AMUSE

di·vide vb **di·vid·ed; di·vid·ing** 1 : to separate into two or more parts or pieces 2 : to give out in shares 3 : to be or make different in opinion or interest 4 : to subject to or perform mathematical division 5 : to branch off : FORK — **di·vid·er** n

div·i·dend n 1 : a number to be divided by another number 2 : an amount of a company's profits that is paid to the owners of its stock

div·i·na·tion *n* : the art or practice of using signs and omens or magic powers to foretell the future

¹di·vine *adj* **1** : of or relating to God or a god **2** : being in praise of God : RELIGIOUS, HOLY **3** : like a god **4** : very good — **di·vine·ly** *adv*

²divine *vb* **di·vined; di·vin·ing 1** : to discover or understand something by using intuition **2** : to foretell the future by using signs and omens or magic powers

di·vin·i·ty *n, pl* **di·vin·i·ties 1** : the quality or state of being God or a god **2** : a god or goddess **3** : the study of religion

di·vis·i·ble *adj* : possible to divide or separate

di·vi·sion *n* **1** : the act or process of dividing or separating : the state of being divided or separated **2** : the mathematical process of finding out how many times one number is contained in another **3** : something that divides, separates, or marks off **4** : one of the parts or groups that make up a whole **5** : a large military unit **6** : a level of competitors **7** : a group of plants that ranks above the class and below the kingdom and in scientific classification is typically equal to a phylum

di·vi·sor *n* : the number by which a dividend is divided

¹di·vorce *n* : a legal ending of a marriage

²divorce *vb* **di·vorced; di·vorc·ing** : to end a marriage legally : get a divorce

di·vulge *vb* **di·vulged; di·vulg·ing** : to make known to others : REVEAL, DISCLOSE

diz·zy *adj* **diz·zi·er; diz·zi·est 1** : having the feeling of spinning **2** : causing a feeling of spinning **3** : overwhelmed with emotion — **diz·zi·ness** *n*

DMD *abbr* doctor of dental medicine

DNA *n* : a complicated organic acid that carries genetic information in the chromosomes

¹do *vb* **did; done; do·ing; does 1** : to cause (as an act or action) to happen : PERFORM **2** : ²ACT 2, BEHAVE **3** : to make progress : SUCCEED **4** : to finish working on — used in the past participle **5** : to put forth : EXERT **6** : to work on, prepare, produce, or put in order **7** : to work at as a paying job **8** : to serve the purpose : SUIT **9** : to have an effect **10** : to travel at a speed of **11** — used as a helping verb (1) before the subject in a question , (2) in a negative statement , (3) for emphasis , and (4) as a substitute for a predicate that has already been stated — **do away with 1** : to get rid of **2** : ¹KILL 1

²do *n* : the first note of the musical scale

DOB date of birth

doc·ile *adj* : easily taught, led, or managed — **doc·ile·ly** *adv*

¹dock *vb* **docked; dock·ing 1** : to cut off the end of **2** : to take away a part of

²dock *n* **1** : an artificial basin for ships that has gates to keep the water in or out **2** : a waterway usually between two piers to receive ships **3** : a wharf or platform for loading or unloading materials

³dock *vb* **docked; dock·ing 1** : to haul or guide into a dock **2** : to come or go into a dock **3** : to join (as two spacecraft) mechanically while in space

¹doc·tor *n* : a person (as a physician or veterinarian) skilled and specializing in the art of healing

²doctor *vb* **doc·tored; doc·tor·ing 1** : to use remedies on or for **2** : to practice medicine

doc·trine *n* : something (as a rule or principle) that is taught, believed in, or considered to be true

¹doc·u·ment *n* **1** : a written or printed paper that gives information about or proof of something **2** : a computer file containing data entered by a user

²document *vb* **doc·u·ment·ed; doc·u·ment·ing 1** : to record (as on paper or in film) the details about **2** : to prove through usually written records

doc·u·men·ta·ry *n* : a film that tells the facts about something

¹dodge *n* **1** : a sudden movement to one side **2** : a trick done to avoid something

²dodge *vb* **dodged; dodg·ing 1** : to move suddenly aside or to and fro **2** : to avoid especially by moving quickly **3** : EVADE — **dodg·er** *n*

dodge ball *n* : a game in which players try to knock other players out of the game by hitting them with a ball

do·do *n, pl* **do·does** *or* **do·dos** : a large heavy bird unable to fly that once lived on some of the islands of the Indian Ocean

doe *n* : the female of an animal (as a deer or kangaroo) the male of which is called *buck*

do·er *n* : a person who tends to act rather than talk or think about things

does *present third person sing of* DO

doesn't : does not

doff *vb* **doffed; doff·ing** : to take off

¹dog *n* **1** : a domestic animal that eats meat and is closely related to the wolves **2** : any of the group of mammals (as wolves, foxes, and jackals) to which the domestic dog belongs **3** : PERSON 1 — **dog·like** *adj*

²dog *vb* **dogged; dog·ging 1** : to hunt, track, or follow like a hound **2** : PESTER **3** : cause problems for

dog·catch·er *n* : an official paid to catch and get rid of stray dogs

dog days *n pl* : the hot period between early July and early September

dog–eared *adj* : having a lot of pages with corners turned over

dog·fish *n* : a small shark often seen near shore

dog·ged *adj* : stubbornly determined — **dog·ged·ly** *adv*

dog·gy *or* **dog·gie** *n, pl* **doggies** : a usually small or young dog

dog·house *n* : a shelter for a dog — **in the doghouse** : in trouble over some wrongdoing

dog·ma *n* 1 : something firmly believed 2 : a belief or set of beliefs taught by a church

dog·sled *n* : a sled pulled by dogs

dog·wood *n* : a shrub or small tree with clusters of small flowers often surrounded by four showy leaves that look like petals

doi·ly *n, pl* **doilies** : a small often lacy cloth or paper used to protect the surface of furniture

do·ing *n* 1 : the act of performing : ACTION 2 : **doings** *pl* : things that are done or that go on

dol·drums *n pl* 1 : a spell of sadness 2 : a period of no activity or improvement 3 : a part of the ocean near the equator known for its calms

¹dole *n* 1 : an act of giving out food, clothing, or money to the needy 2 : something given out to the needy especially at regular times

²dole *vb* **doled; dol·ing** : to give out

dole·ful *adj* : very sad — **dole·ful·ly** *adv*

doll *n* 1 : a child's toy in the form of a baby or small person 2 : a kind or loveable person

dol·lar *n* : any of various coins or pieces of paper money (as of the United States or Canada) equal to 100 cents

dolly *n, pl* **dollies** 1 : DOLL 1 2 : a platform on a roller or on wheels for moving heavy things

dol·phin *n* 1 : a small whale with teeth and a long nose 2 : either of two large fish usually of warm seas that are often used for food

-dom *n suffix* 1 : the area ruled by 2 : state or fact of being 3 : the group having a certain office, occupation, interest, or character

do·main *n* 1 : land under the control of a ruler or a government 2 : a field of knowledge or activity 3 : DOMAIN NAME

domain name *n, pl* **domain names** : the characters (as Merriam-Webster.com) that form the main part of an Internet address

dome *n* 1 : a rounded top or roof that looks like half of a ball 2 : a rounded structure

domed *adj* : having a rounded shape like a dome

do·mes·tic *adj* 1 : relating to a household or a family 2 : relating to, made in, or done in a person's own country 3 : living with or under the care of human beings : TAME — **do·mes·ti·cal·ly** *adv*

do·mes·ti·cate *vb* **do·mes·ti·cat·ed; do·mes·ti·cat·ing** : to bring under the control of and make usable by humans

do·mi·cile *n* : a place where someone lives

dom·i·nance *n* : the state or fact of being in control of or having more power than another

dom·i·nant *adj* 1 : controlling or being more powerful or important than all others 2 : being or produced by a form of a gene that prevents or hides the effect of another form

dom·i·nate *vb* **dom·i·nat·ed; dom·i·nat·ing** : to have a commanding position or controlling power over

do·min·ion *n* 1 : ruling or controlling power : SOVEREIGNTY 2 : a territory under the control of a ruler : DOMAIN

dom·i·no *n, pl* **dom·i·noes** *or* **dom·i·nos** : one of a set of flat oblong dotted pieces used in playing a game (**dominoes**)

don *vb* **donned; don·ning** : to put on

do·nate *vb* **do·nat·ed; do·nat·ing** : to give as a way of helping people in need : CONTRIBUTE

do·na·tion *n* : something given to help those in need

done *past participle of* DO

don·key *n, pl* **donkeys** : an animal related to but smaller than the horse that has short hair in mane and tail and very large ears

do·nor *n* : a person who makes a donation

don't : do not

¹doo·dle *vb* **doo·dled; doo·dling** : to scribble, sketch, or make designs on paper often while thinking about something else

²doodle *n* : a scribble, design, or sketch done often while thinking about something else

¹doom *n* 1 : terrible or unhappy ending or happening 2 : DEATH 1

²doom *vb* **doomed; doom·ing** : to make sure that something bad will happen

dooms·day *n* : the day the world ends or is destroyed

door *n* 1 : a usually swinging or sliding frame or barrier by which an entrance (as into a house) is closed and opened 2 : a part of a piece of furniture that swings or slides open or shut 3 : DOORWAY

door·bell *n* : a bell or set of chimes that is rung usually by pushing a button beside an outside door

door·man *n, pl* **door·men** : a person whose job is to help people at the door of a building

door·step *n* : a step or a series of steps in front of an outside door

door·way *n* : the opening or passage that a door closes

dope *n* **1** : an illegal drug **2** : a stupid person **3** : INFORMATION

dop·ey *adj* **dop·i·er; dop·i·est** **1** : lacking alertness and activity : SLUGGISH **2** : STUPID 2

dorm *n* : DORMITORY

dor·mant *adj* : not active for the time being

dor·mer *n* **1** : a window placed upright in a sloping roof or the structure containing it

dor·mi·to·ry *n, pl* **dor·mi·to·ries** **1** : a building at a school with rooms where students live **2** : a large room for several people to sleep

dor·mouse *n, pl* **dor·mice** : a small European animal that resembles a mouse but has a bushy tail, lives mostly in trees, and is active at night

dor·sal *adj* : relating to or being on or near the surface of the body that in humans is the back but in most animals is the upper surface

do·ry *n, pl* **dories** : a boat with a flat bottom, high sides that flare out, and a sharp bow

¹dose *n* : a measured amount to be used at one time

²dose *vb* **dosed; dos·ing** : to give medicine to

¹dot *n* **1** : a small point, mark, or spot **2** : a certain point in time **3** : a short click forming a letter or part of a letter (as in telegraphy)

²dot *vb* **dot·ted; dot·ting** : to mark with or as if with small spots

dote *vb* **dot·ed; dot·ing** : to give a lot of love or attention to

doth *present third person sing of do, archaic*

¹dou·ble *adj* **1** : being twice as great or as many **2** : made up of two parts or members **3** : having two very different aspects **4** : made for two **5** : extra large in size or amount

²double *vb* **dou·bled; dou·bling** **1** : to make or become twice as great or as many : multiply by two **2** : to fold usually in the middle **3** : to bend over at the waist **4** : CLENCH 2 **5** : to turn sharply and go back over the same path **6** : to have another use or job

³double *adv* **1** : two times the amount **2** : two together

⁴double *n* **1** : something that is twice the usual size or amount **2** : a hit in baseball that allows the batter to reach second base **3** : someone or something that is very like another — **on the double** : very quickly

double bass *n* : an instrument of the violin family that is the largest member and has the deepest tone

dou·ble–cross *vb* **dou·ble–crossed; dou-**

ble–cross·ing : BETRAY 2 — **dou·ble–cross·er** *n*

dou·ble–head·er *n* : two games played one right after the other on the same day

dou·ble–joint·ed *adj* : having a joint that permits unusual freedom of movement of the parts that are joined

double play *n* : a play in baseball by which two base runners are put out

dou·blet *n* : a close-fitting jacket worn by men in Europe especially in the 16th century

dou·ble–talk *n* : language that seems to make sense but is actually a mixture of sense and nonsense

dou·bly *adv* : to two times the amount or degree

¹doubt *vb* **doubt·ed; doubt·ing** **1** : to be uncertain about **2** : to lack confidence in **3** : to consider unlikely

²doubt *n* **1** : a feeling of being uncertain **2** : a reason for disbelief **3** : the condition of being undecided **4** : a lack of trust

doubt·ful *adj* **1** : undecided in opinion **2** : not likely to be true **3** : not likely to be good **4** : not certain in outcome — **doubt·ful·ly** *adv*

doubt·less *adv* **1** : without doubt **2** : in all probability

dough *n* **1** : a thick mixture usually mainly of flour and liquid that is baked **2** : MONEY 1

dough·nut *n* : a small ring of sweet dough fried in fat

dour *adj* : looking or being serious and unfriendly

douse *vb* **doused; dous·ing** **1** : to stick into water **2** : to throw a liquid on **3** : to put out : EXTINGUISH

¹dove *n* : a bird that is related to the pigeon but usually of somewhat smaller size

²dove *past of* DIVE

dowdy *adj* **dowd·i·er; dowd·i·est** **1** : not neatly or well dressed or cared for **2** : not stylish

dow·el *n* : a pin or peg used for fastening together two pieces of wood

¹down *adv* **1** : toward or in a lower position **2** : to a lying or sitting position **3** : toward or to the ground, floor, or bottom **4** : below the horizon **5** : to or toward the south **6** : in or into the stomach **7** : as a down payment **8** : on paper **9** : to a lower level or rate **10** : to a weaker or worse condition **11** : from a past time **12** : to or in a state of less activity **13** : in a way that limits movement

²down *prep* **1** : from a higher to a lower point of something **2** : along the course or path of

³down *vb* **downed; down·ing** **1** : to go or

cause to go or come to the ground **2** : EAT 1
3 : ¹DEFEAT 2

⁴down *adj* **1** : in a low position **2** : directed
or going downward **3** : at a lower level **4**
: having a lower score **5** : SAD 1 **6** : not
working **7** : finished or completed **8**
: learned completely

⁵down *n* : a low or falling period

⁶down *n* : a high area of land with low hills
and no trees — usually used in pl.

⁷down *n* **1** : soft fluffy feathers **2** : small soft
hairs

down·beat *n* : the first beat of a measure of
music

down·cast *adj* **1** : SAD 1 **2** : directed down

down·fall *n* : a sudden fall (as from power,
happiness, or a high position) or the cause of
such a fall — **down·fall·en** *adj*

¹down·grade *n* : a downward slope (as of a
road)

²downgrade *vb* **down·grad·ed; down·grad·
ing** : to lower in grade, rank, position, or
standing

down·heart·ed *adj* : SAD 1

¹down·hill *adv* **1** : toward the bottom of a hill
2 : toward a worse condition

²down·hill *adj* **1** : sloping downward **2**
: having to do with skiing down mountains

down·load *vb* **down·load·ed; down·load·ing**
: to move from a usually larger computer
system to another computer system

down payment *n* : a part of a price paid
when something is bought with an agreement to pay the rest later

down·pour *n* : a heavy rain

¹down·right *adv* : REALLY 2, VERY

²downright *adj* : ²OUTRIGHT 1, ABSOLUTE

¹down·stairs *adv* : down the stairs : on or to
a lower floor

²down·stairs *adj* : situated on a lower floor
or on the main or first floor

³down·stairs *n pl* : the lower floor of a building — usually used as singular

down·stream *adv* : in the direction a stream
is flowing

¹down·town *n* : the main or central part of a
city or town

²down·town *adv* : to or toward the main or
central part of a city or town

¹down·ward *or* **down·wards** *adv* : from a
higher place, amount, or level to a lower one

²downward *adj* : going or moving from a
higher place, amount, or level to a lower one

down·wind *adv or adj* : in the direction the
wind is blowing

downy *adj* **down·i·er; down·i·est** **1** : like
small soft feathers **2** : covered or filled with
small soft feathers or hairs

dow·ry *n, pl* **dowries** : property that in some

cultures a woman gives to her husband in
marriage

doz. *abbr* dozen

¹doze *vb* **dozed; doz·ing** : to sleep lightly —
doze off : to fall asleep

²doze *n* : a light sleep

doz·en *n, pl* **dozens** *or* **dozen** : a group of
twelve

Dr. *abbr* doctor

drab *adj* **drab·ber; drab·best** **1** : not bright
or interesting : DULL **2** : grayish brown in
color — **drab·ly** *adv* — **drab·ness** *n*

¹draft *n* **1** : a version of something written or
drawn (as an essay, document, or plan) that
has or will have more than one version **2** : a
current of air **3** : a device to regulate an air
supply (as in a fireplace) **4** : the act of
pulling or hauling : the thing or amount
pulled **5** : the act or an instance of drinking
or inhaling : the portion drunk or inhaled at
one time **6** : the act of drawing out liquid (as
from a cask) : a portion of liquid drawn out
7 : the depth of water a ship needs in order to
float **8** : the practice of ordering people into
military service **9** : the practice of choosing
someone to play on a professional sports
team **10** : an order made by one person or
organization to another to pay money to a
third person or organization

²draft *adj* **1** : used for pulling loads **2** : not
in final form **3** : ready to be drawn from a
container

³draft *vb* **draft·ed; draft·ing** **1** : to write or
draw a version of something (as an essay or
plan) that usually needs more work **2** : to
choose someone to do something **3** : to pick
especially for required military service

drafty *adj* **draft·i·er; draft·i·est** : having usually cool air moving through

¹drag *n* **1** : something used for pulling along
(as a device used underwater to catch something) **2** : something without wheels (as a
heavy sled for carrying loads) that is pulled
along or over a surface **3** : something that
slows down motion **4** : a dull or unpleasant
event, person, or thing

²drag *vb* **dragged; drag·ging** **1** : to pull
slowly or heavily **2** : to move with slowness
or difficulty **3** : to move or cause to move
along on the ground **4** : to bring by or as if
by force **5** : to pass or cause to pass slowly
6 : to hang or lag behind **7** : to search or
fish by pulling something (as a net) under
water

drag·net *n* **1** : a net that is pulled along the
bottom of a body of water in order to catch
or find something **2** : a series of actions by
police for catching a criminal

drag·on *n* : an imaginary animal usually pictured as a huge serpent or lizard with wings and large claws

drag·on·fly *n, pl* **drag·on·flies** : a large insect with a long slender body and four wings

drag race *n* : a race between vehicles to see who can increase speed most quickly over a short distance

¹**drain** *vb* **drained; drain·ing 1** : to remove (liquid) from something by letting it flow away or out **2** : to slowly make or become dry or empty **3** : to flow into, away from, or out of something **4** : to slowly disappear **5** : to tire out

²**drain** *n* **1** : something used to remove a liquid **2** : something that slowly empties of or uses up

drain·age *n* : the act or process of removing a liquid

drain·pipe *n* : a pipe for removing water

drake *n* : a male duck

dra·ma *n* **1** : a written work that tells a story through action and speech and is acted out : a usually serious play, movie, or television production **2** : the art or profession of creating or putting on plays **3** : an exciting or emotional situation or event

dra·mat·ic *adj* **1** : having to do with drama **2** : attracting attention **3** : sudden and extreme — **dra·mat·i·cal·ly** *adv*

dra·ma·tist *n* : PLAYWRIGHT

dra·ma·tize *vb* **dram·a·tized; dram·a·tiz·ing 1** : to make into a play, movie, or other show **2** : to present in a way that attracts attention — **dra·ma·ti·za·tion** *n*

drank *past and past participle of* DRINK

¹**drape** *vb* **draped; drap·ing 1** : to decorate or cover with or as if with folds of cloth **2** : to arrange or hang in flowing lines

²**drape** *n, pl* **drapes** : DRAPERY 1

drap·ery *n, pl* **drap·er·ies 1** : long heavy curtains **2** : a decorative fabric hung in loose folds

dras·tic *adj* : severe in effect : HARSH — **dras·ti·cal·ly** *adv*

draught *chiefly British variant of* DRAFT

¹**draw** *vb* **drew; drawn; draw·ing 1** : to cause to move by pulling **2** : to create a picture of by making lines on a surface **3** : to bring or pull out **4** : to move in a particular direction **5** : to bend (a bow) by pulling back the string **6** : to move or go slowly or steadily **7** : ATTRACT 2 **8** : to get as a response **9** : to bring or get from a source **10** : INHALE 1 **11** : to let air flow through **12** : WITHDRAW **13** : to take or get at random **14** : to think of after considering information **15** : to write out in proper form — **draw on 1** : to make use of something **2** : to come closer — **draw out 1** : to make last longer

2 : to cause to talk freely — **draw up 1** : to bring or come to a stop **2** : to straighten up

²**draw** *n* **1** : the act or the result of pulling out **2** : a tie game or contest **3** : something or someone that attracts people

draw·back *n* : an unwanted feature or characteristic

draw·bridge *n* : a bridge that moves up, down, or to the side to allow boats or vehicles to pass

draw·er *n* **1** : a box that slides in and out of a piece of furniture and is used for storage **2 drawers** *pl* : UNDERPANTS

draw·ing *n* **1** : a picture created by making lines on a surface **2** : the act or art of creating a picture, plan, or sketch by making lines on a surface **3** : an act or instance of picking something at random

drawing room *n* : a formal room for entertaining company

¹**drawl** *vb* **drawled; drawl·ing** : to speak slowly with vowel sounds that are longer than usual

²**drawl** *n* : a way of speaking with vowel sounds that are longer than usual

drawn *adj* : looking very thin and tired especially from worry, pain, or illness

draw·string *n* : a string at the top of a bag or on clothing that can be pulled to close or tighten

¹**dread** *vb* **dread·ed; dread·ing 1** : to fear or dislike greatly **2** : to be very unwilling to face

²**dread** *n* : great fear especially of something that will or might happen

³**dread** *adj* : causing great fear or anxiety

dread·ful *adj* **1** : causing fear **2** : very unpleasant

dread·ful·ly *adv* **1** : VERY **2** : very badly

¹**dream** *n* **1** : a series of thoughts or visions that occur during sleep **2** : ¹DAYDREAM **3** : something very pleasing **4** : a goal that is wished for

²**dream** *vb* **dreamed** *or* **dreamt; dream·ing 1** : to have a series of thoughts or visions while sleeping **2** : to spend time having daydreams **3** : to think of as happening or possible — **dream·er** *n* — **dream up** : to think of or invent

dreamy *adj* **dream·i·er; dream·i·est 1** : appearing to be daydreaming **2** : seeming like a dream **3** : quiet and relaxing — **dream·i·ly** *adv*

drea·ry *adj* **drea·ri·er; drea·ri·est** : dull and depressing — **drea·ri·ly** *adv* — **drea·ri·ness** *n*

¹**dredge** *vb* **dredged; dredg·ing** : to dig or gather with or as if with a device dragged along the bottom of a body of water — **dredg·er** *n*

²dredge *n* **1** : a heavy iron frame with a net attached to be dragged along the bottom of a body of water **2** : a machine or boat used in dragging along the bottom of a body of water **3** : a machine for removing earth usually by buckets on an endless chain or by a suction tube

dregs *n pl* **1** : solids that sink to the bottom of a liquid **2** : the worst or most useless part

drench *vb* **drenched; drench·ing** : to make completely wet

¹dress *vb* **dressed; dress·ing** **1** : to put clothes on **2** : to put on clothes in a particular way **3** : to wear formal or fancy clothes **4** : to apply medicine or bandages to **5** : to trim or decorate for display **6** : to prepare for cooking or eating — **dress up** **1** : to put on formal or fancy clothes **2** : to put on a costume

²dress *n* **1** : a piece of clothing for a woman or girl that has a top part that covers the upper body and that is connected to a skirt covering the lower body **2** : CLOTHING

³dress *adj* : proper for a formal event

¹dress·er *n* : a piece of furniture that has drawers for storing clothes and that sometimes has a mirror

²dresser *n* : a person who dresses in a certain way

dress·ing *n* **1** : a sauce put on a salad **2** : a seasoned mixture used as a stuffing **3** : material (as ointment or gauze) used to cover an injury **4** : the act of putting on clothes

dressy *adj* **dress·i·er; dress·i·est** **1** : requiring fancy clothes **2** : proper for formal events

drew *past of* DRAW

¹drib·ble *vb* **drib·bled; drib·bling** **1** : to fall or let fall in small drops : TRICKLE **2** : to let saliva or other liquid drip or trickle from the mouth **3** : to move forward by bouncing, tapping, or kicking

²dribble *n* **1** : a trickling flow **2** : the act of moving a ball or puck forward by bouncing, kicking, or tapping it

drier *variant of* DRYER

¹drift *n* **1** : the slow movement of something carried by wind or water **2** : a pile of something that has been blown by the wind **3** : a course something appears to be taking **4** : the meaning of something said or implied

²drift *vb* **drift·ed; drift·ing** **1** : to move slowly on wind or water **2** : to be piled up by wind or water **3** : to move along or change without effort or purpose — **drift·er** *n*

drift·wood *n* : wood carried by water

¹drill *vb* **drilled; drill·ing** **1** : to make holes in with a drill **2** : to teach by repeating a lesson or exercise again and again — **drill·er** *n*

²drill *n* **1** : a tool for making holes in hard

substances **2** : the training of soldiers (as in marching) **3** : instruction in a subject or physical training that is practiced repeatedly

³drill *n* : a special machine for making holes or furrows and planting seeds in them

⁴drill *vb* **drilled; drill·ing** : to sow seeds with or as if with a special machine

drily *variant of* DRYLY

¹drink *vb* **drank; drunk; drink·ing** **1** : to swallow liquid **2** : to absorb a liquid **3** : to drink alcoholic beverages **4** : to take in through the senses — **drink·er** *n*

²drink *n* **1** : a liquid safe for swallowing **2** : an amount of liquid swallowed **3** : alcoholic beverages

drink·able *adj* : suitable or safe for drinking

¹drip *vb* **dripped; drip·ping** **1** : to fall in drops **2** : to let fall drops of liquid **3** : to have or show a large amount of something

²drip *n* **1** : the act of falling in drops **2** : a drop of liquid that falls **3** : the sound made by falling drops

¹drive *vb* **drove; driv·en; driv·ing** **1** : to direct the movement of **2** : to go or carry in a vehicle **3** : to move using force **4** : to push in with force **5** : to set or keep in motion or operation **6** : to carry through **7** : to force to work or to act **8** : to bring into a particular condition — **driv·er** *n*

²drive *n* **1** : a trip in a vehicle **2** : DRIVEWAY **3** : an often scenic public road **4** : an organized effort to achieve a goal **5** : a strong natural need or desire **6** : energy and determination to succeed **7** : an act of leading animals in a group to another place **8** : the means for making a machine or machine part move **9** : a device in a computer that can read information off and copy information onto disks or tape

drive–in *n* : a restaurant or theater that serves customers while they stay in their vehicles

drive–through *adj* : DRIVE-UP

drive–up *adj* : set up to allow customers to be served while they stay in their vehicles

drive·way *n* : a private road leading from the street to a house or garage

¹driz·zle *n* : a fine misty rain

²drizzle *vb* **driz·zled; driz·zling** : to rain in very small drops

droll *adj* **droller; droll·est** : having an odd or amusing quality

drom·e·dary *n, pl* **drom·e·dar·ies** : the camel of western Asia and northern Africa that has only one hump

¹drone *n* : a male bee

²drone *vb* **droned; dron·ing** : to make or to speak with a low dull tone or hum

³drone *n* : a low dull tone or hum

¹drool *vb* **drooled; drool·ing** : to let saliva drip from the mouth

²drool *n* : saliva that drips from the mouth

¹droop *vb* **drooped; droop·ing 1** : to sink, bend, or hang down **2** : to become sad or weak

²droop *n* : the condition of hanging or bending down

¹drop *n* **1** : a small amount of liquid that falls in a rounded shape **2 drops** *pl* : liquid medicine measured by drops **3** : something (as a small round candy) that is shaped like a liquid drop **4** : a small amount **5** : the distance of a fall **6** : a decrease in amount or quality **7** : an act of delivering something : a place where something is left to be picked up

²drop *vb* **dropped; drop·ping 1** : to fall or let fall often by accident **2** : to go down suddenly **3** : to go or make lower **4** : to become less or make less **5** : LOSE 4 **6** : DISAPPEAR 1 **7** : to stop or let end **8** : QUIT **9** : to make a brief visit **10** : to deliver with a quick stop **11** : SEND 1 — **drop off** : to fall asleep

drop–down *adj* : PULL-DOWN

drop·let *n* : a tiny drop

drop·out *n* : a person who quits school or a training program

drop·per *n* : a short tube with a rubber bulb used to measure out liquids by drops

drought *n* : a long period of time during which there is very little or no rain

¹drove *n* : a large group of animals or people moving or acting together

²drove *past of* DRIVE

drown *vb* **drowned; drown·ing 1** : to die or cause to die from being underwater and unable to breathe **2** : to cover with a liquid **3** : to overpower especially with noise **4** : to make helpless or overwhelmed

¹drowse *vb* **drowsed; drows·ing** : to sleep lightly

²drowse *n* : a light sleep : DOZE

drowsy *adj* **drows·i·er; drows·i·est 1** : ready to fall asleep **2** : causing sleepiness — **drows·i·ly** *adv* — **drows·i·ness** *n*

drub *vb* **drubbed; drub·bing 1** : to beat severely **2** : to defeat completely

drudge *n* : a person who does hard or dull work

drudg·ery *n, pl* **drudg·er·ies** : hard or dull work

¹drug *n* **1** : a substance used as a medicine or in making medicines **2** : a substance (as cocaine or marijuana) that may harm or addict a user

²drug *vb* **drugged; drug·ging 1** : to poison with or as if with a drug **2** : to make sleepy or unconscious with drugs

drug·gist *n* : a person who prepares and sells drugs and medicines : PHARMACIST

drug·store *n* : a retail store where medicines and often other items are sold : PHARMACY

¹drum *n* **1** : a musical instrument usually consisting of a metal or wooden round frame with flat ends covered by tightly stretched skin **2** : a tapping sound : a sound of or like a drum **3** : an object shaped like a cylinder

²drum *vb* **drummed; drum·ming 1** : to beat or play a drum **2** : to make a tapping sound : make a sound like a drum **3** : to beat or tap in a rhythmic way **4** : to gather together or create by hard work **5** : to drive or force by steady or repeated effort — **drum·mer** *n*

drum major *n* : the marching leader of a band or drum corps

drum ma·jor·ette *n* : a girl who is the marching leader of a band or drum corps

drum·stick *n* **1** : a stick for beating a drum **2** : the lower section of the leg of a bird eaten for food

¹drunk *past participle of* DRINK

²drunk *adj* **drunk·er; drunk·est 1** : being so much under the influence of alcohol that normal thinking and acting become difficult or impossible **2** : controlled by a strong feeling

³drunk *n* : DRUNKARD

drunk·ard *n* : a person who is often drunk

drunk·en *adj* **1** : ²DRUNK 1 **2** : resulting from being drunk — **drunk·en·ly** *adv* — **drunk·en·ness** *n*

¹dry *adj* **dri·er; dri·est 1** : not wet or moist **2** : having little or no rain **3** : not being in or under water **4** : having little natural moisture **5** : no longer liquid or sticky **6** : containing no liquid **7** : not giving milk **8** : not producing desired results **9** : not producing a wet substance from the body **10** : funny but expressed in a serious way **11** : UNINTERESTING **12** : not sweet — **dry·ly** *or* **dri·ly** *adv* — **dry·ness** *n*

²dry *vb* **dried; dry·ing** : to remove or lose any moisture

dry cell *n* : a small cell producing electricity by means of chemicals in a sealed container

dry–clean *vb* **dry-cleaned; dry-clean·ing** : to clean (fabrics) with chemicals instead of water

dry cleaner *n* : a person whose business is cleaning fabrics with chemicals instead of water

dry cleaning *n* **1** : the cleaning of fabrics with a substance other than water **2** : something that has been cleaned by a dry cleaner

dry·er *also* **dri·er** *n* : a device for removing moisture by using heat or air

dry ice *n* : solidified carbon dioxide used chiefly to keep something very cold

DST *abbr* daylight saving time

du·al *adj* **1** : having two different parts or aspects **2** : having two like parts

¹dub *vb* **dubbed; dub·bing 1** : to make a knight of **2** : ²NAME 1, NICKNAME

²dub *vb* **dubbed; dub·bing** : to add (a different language or sound effects) to a film or broadcast

du·bi·ous *adj* **1** : causing doubt : UNCERTAIN **2** : feeling doubt **3** : QUESTIONABLE 1 — **du·bi·ous·ly** *adv*

duch·ess *n* **1** : the wife or widow of a duke **2** : a woman who has the same rank as a duke

¹duck *n* : a swimming bird that has a broad flat bill and is smaller than the related goose and swan

²duck *vb* **ducked; duck·ing 1** : to push under water for a moment **2** : to lower the head or body suddenly **3** : to avoid by moving quickly **4** : to avoid a duty, question, or responsibility

duck·bill *n* : PLATYPUS

duck·ling *n* : a young duck

duct *n* : a pipe, tube, or vessel that carries something

duct tape *n* : a wide sticky usually silver tape made of cloth

dud *n* **1** : a complete failure **2** : a bomb or missile that fails to explode **3 duds** *pl* : CLOTHING

dude *n* **1** : a person from the eastern United States in the West **2** : ¹MAN 1, GUY

¹due *adj* **1** : required or expected to happen or be done **2** : owed or deserved **3** : in a proper or necessary amount — **due to** : because of

²due *n* **1** : something that should be given **2 dues** *pl* : a regular or legal charge or fee

³due *adv* : DIRECTLY 1

¹du·el *n* **1** : a fight between two persons especially that is fought by agreement with weapons in front of other people **2** : a contest between two opponents

²duel *vb* **du·eled** *or* **du·elled; du·el·ing** *or* **du·el·ling** : to take part in an agreed-upon fight with weapons

du·et *n* **1** : a piece of music for two performers **2** : two people performing music together

dug *past and past participle of* DIG

dug·out *n* **1** : a low shelter facing a baseball diamond and containing the players' bench **2** : a shelter dug in a hillside or in the ground **3** : a boat made by hollowing out a log

duke *n* : a man of the highest rank of the British nobility

¹dull *adj* **dull·er; dull·est 1** : not sharp in edge or point : BLUNT **2** : not shiny or bright **3** : not interesting : BORING **4** : not clear and

ringing **5** : not sharp or intense **6** : slightly grayish **7** : CLOUDY 1, OVERCAST **8** : slow in understanding things : not smart **9** : without energy or spirit **10** : slow in action : SLUGGISH — **dull·ness** *n* — **dul·ly** *adv*

²dull *vb* **dulled; dull·ing** : to make or become less sharp, bright, or intense

du·ly *adv* : in a due or appropriate manner, time, or degree

dumb *adj* **dumb·er; dumb·est 1** : lacking the power of human speech **2** *often offensive* : lacking the ability to speak **3** : temporarily unable to speak (as from shock or surprise) **4** : STUPID 1, FOOLISH — **dumb·ly** *adv*

dumb·found *vb* **dumb·found·ed; dumb·found·ing** : to make speechless with surprise

dum·my *n, pl* **dummies 1** : something shaped like a human **2** : a doll used in a ventriloquist's act **3** : a stupid person

¹dump *vb* **dumped; dump·ing 1** : to let fall in a heap **2** : to get rid of

²dump *n* **1** : a place for getting rid of trash **2** : a place for storage of military materials or the materials stored **3** : a messy or shabby place

dump·ling *n* **1** : a small amount of dough cooked by boiling or steaming **2** : a dessert of fruit wrapped in dough

dumps *n pl* : a sad mood

dumpy *adj* **dump·i·er; dump·i·est** : having a short and round body

dun *n* : a slightly brownish dark gray

dunce *n* : a stupid person

dune *n* : a hill or ridge of sand piled up by the wind

dung *n* : solid waste matter from an animal

dun·ga·ree *n* **1** : a heavy cotton cloth : DENIM **2 dungarees** *pl* : clothes made of denim

dun·geon *n* : a dark usually underground prison

dunk *vb* **dunked; dunk·ing 1** : to dip into liquid **2** : to jump and push the ball down through the basket in basketball

duo *n, pl* **du·os 1** : two people who are usually seen together **2** : DUET

¹dupe *n* : a person who has been or is easily deceived or cheated

²dupe *vb* **duped; dup·ing** : ²TRICK

du·plex *n* : a house with two separate living spaces

¹du·pli·cate *adj* : exactly the same as another

²du·pli·cate *vb* **du·pli·cat·ed; du·pli·cat·ing** : to make an exact copy of

³du·pli·cate *n* : a thing that is exactly like another

du·pli·ca·tion *n* **1** : the act or process of copying **2** : the state of being copied

du·ra·bil·i·ty *n* : ability to last or to stand hard or continued use

du·ra·ble *adj* : able to last a long time

du·ra·tion *n* : the time during which something exists or lasts

dur·ing *prep* **1** : throughout the course of **2** : at some point in the course of

dusk *n* : the time when the sky is getting dark at night

dusky *adj* **dusk·i·er; dusk·i·est 1** : somewhat dark in color **2** : somewhat dark : DIM

¹dust *n* **1** : fine dry powdery particles (as of earth) : a fine powder that often builds up on furniture **2** : a fine powder made from a particular substance or from something that has disintegrated **3** : the surface of the ground

²dust *vb* **dust·ed; dust·ing 1** : to make free of dust : brush or wipe away dust **2** : to sprinkle with or as if with fine particles — **dust·er** *n*

dust·pan *n* : a flat pan shaped like a shovel into which dirt from the floor is swept

dust storm *n* : a very strong wind carrying dust across a dry region

dusty *adj* **dust·i·er; dust·i·est 1** : filled or covered with dust **2** : resembling dust

¹Dutch *adj* : of or relating to the Netherlands, its people, or their language

²Dutch *n* **1 Dutch** *pl* : the people of the Netherlands **2** : the language of the people of the Netherlands

du·ti·ful *adj* : doing or showing the willingness to do what is expected or required — **du·ti·ful·ly** *adv*

du·ty *n, pl* **duties 1** : something a person feels he or she ought to do because it is morally right **2** : something a person is required to do by law **3** : an action done as part of a job or position **4** : the time during which a person must do his or her job **5** : active military service **6** : a tax especially on imports into a country

DVD *n* : a plastic disk that is used to store information (as computer data or a movie) and is read using a laser

¹dwarf *n, pl* **dwarfs** *also* **dwarves 1** : a person, animal, or plant much smaller than normal size **2** : a creature in legends that is usually pictured as a small person who is skilled at some craft

²dwarf *vb* **dwarfed; dwarf·ing** : to cause to appear smaller

³dwarf *adj* : of less than the usual size

dwell *vb* **dwelt** *or* **dwelled; dwell·ing 1** : to live in a place : RESIDE **2** : to keep the attention directed — **dwell·er** *n*

dwell·ing *n* : a shelter in which a person or an animal lives

dwin·dle *vb* **dwin·dled; dwin·dling** : to make or become less or smaller

¹dye *n* : a substance used to change the color of something

²dye *vb* **dyed; dye·ing** : to change the color of something using a substance

dying *present participle of* DIE

dy·nam·ic *adj* : always active, energetic, or changing

¹dy·na·mite *n* : an explosive used in blasting

²dynamite *vb* **dy·na·mit·ed; dy·na·mit·ing** : to blow up with dynamite

dy·na·mo *n, pl* **dy·na·mos 1** : GENERATOR **2** : an energetic person

dy·nas·ty *n, pl* **dy·nas·ties** : a series of rulers of the same family

dys·en·tery *n* : a disease marked especially by severe often bloody diarrhea

dys·lex·ia *n* : a learning disability in which a person usually has a problem in reading, spelling, and writing — **dys·lex·ic** *adj*

E

e *n, pl* **e's** *or* **es** *often cap* **1** : the fifth letter of the English alphabet **2** : a grade that shows a student's work is failing **3** : a musical note referred to by the letter E

E *abbr* **1** east **2** eastern **3** excellent

ea. *abbr* each

¹each *adj* : every one of two or more individuals considered separately

²each *pron* : each one

³each *adv* : to or for each : APIECE

each other *pron* : each of two or more in a shared action or relationship

ea·ger *adj* : very excited and interested — **ea·ger·ly** *adv* — **ea·ger·ness** *n*

ea·gle *n* : a large bird of prey noted for keen sight and powerful flight

ea·glet *n* : a young eagle

-ean — see -AN

¹ear *n* **1** : the organ of hearing and balance of vertebrates that in most mammals is made up of an outer part that collects sound, a middle part that carries sound, and an inner part that receives sound and sends nerve signals to the brain **2** : the outer part of the ear **3** : the sense of hearing **4** : willing or sympathetic attention — **eared** *adj*

²ear *n* : the seed-bearing head of a cereal grass

ear·ache *n* : an ache or pain in the ear

ear·drum *n* : the membrane that separates the outer and middle parts of the ear and vibrates when sound waves strike it

earl *n* : a member of the British nobility who ranks below a marquess and above a viscount

¹**ear·ly** *adv* **ear·li·er; ear·li·est** 1 : at or near the beginning of a period of time 2 : before the usual or expected time

²**early** *adj* **ear·li·er; ear·li·est** : occurring near the beginning or before the usual time

ear·muff *n* : one of a pair of coverings joined by a flexible band and worn to protect the ears from cold or noise

earn *vb* **earned; earn·ing** 1 : to get for work done 2 : to deserve as a result of labor or service

ear·nest *adj* : not light or playful — **ear·nest·ly** *adv* — **ear·nest·ness** *n*

earn·ings *n pl* : money received as wages or gained as profit

ear·phone *n* : a device that converts electrical energy into sound and is worn over the opening of the ear or inserted into it

ear·ring *n* : an ornament worn on the ear

ear·shot *n* : the range within which a person's voice can be heard

earth *n* 1 *often cap* : the planet that we live on 2 : land as distinguished from sea and air 3 : ²SOIL 1

earth·en *adj* : made of earth or of baked clay

earth·en·ware *n* : things (as dishes) made of baked clay

earth·ly *adj* 1 : having to do with or belonging to the earth 2 : IMAGINABLE, POSSIBLE

earth·quake *n* : a shaking or trembling of a portion of the earth

earth·worm *n* : a worm that has a long body made up of similar segments and lives in damp soil

earthy *adj* **earth·i·er; earth·i·est** 1 : of or like earth 2 : open and direct 3 : not polite : CRUDE

ear·wax *n* : a yellowish brown waxy substance made by glands in the canal of the outer part of the ear

ear·wig *n* : an insect with long slender feelers and a part at the end of its body that pinches and is used for self-defense

¹**ease** *n* 1 : freedom from pain or trouble : comfort of body or mind 2 : lack of difficulty 3 : freedom from any feeling of difficulty or embarrassment

²**ease** *vb* **eased; eas·ing** 1 : to free from discomfort or worry : RELIEVE 2 : to make less tight : LOOSEN 3 : to move very carefully

ea·sel *n* : a frame for supporting an artist's painting

eas·i·ly *adv* 1 : without difficulty 2 : without doubt : by far

¹**east** *n* 1 : the direction of sunrise : the compass point opposite to west 2 *cap* : regions or countries east of a certain point

²**east** *adj* : placed toward, facing, or coming from the east

³**east** *adv* : to or toward the east

Eas·ter *n* : a Christian holy day that celebrates the Resurrection

east·er·ly *adv or adj* 1 : toward the east 2 : from the east

east·ern *adj* 1 : lying toward or coming from the east 2 *often cap* : of, relating to, or like that of the East

east·ward *adv or adj* : toward the east

¹**easy** *adj* **eas·i·er; eas·i·est** 1 : not hard to do or get : not difficult 2 : not hard to please 3 : free from pain, trouble, or worry 4 : COMFORTABLE 1 5 : showing ease : NATURAL

²**easy** *adv* 1 : EASILY 2 : slowly and carefully or calmly 3 : without much punishment

eat *vb* **ate; eat·en; eat·ing** 1 : to chew and swallow food 2 : to take a meal 3 : to destroy as if by eating : CORRODE — **eat·er** *n*

eat·able *adj* : fit to be eaten : EDIBLE

eave *n* : the lower edge of a roof that sticks out past the wall — usually used in pl.

eaves·drop *vb* **eaves·dropped; eaves·dropping** : to listen secretly to private conversation

¹**ebb** *n* 1 : the flowing out of the tide 2 : a point reached after things have gotten worse

²**ebb** *vb* **ebbed; ebb·ing** 1 : to flow out or away : RECEDE 2 : ¹DECLINE 2, WEAKEN

¹**eb·o·ny** *n, pl* **eb·o·nies** : a hard heavy blackish wood that comes from tropical trees

²**ebony** *adj* 1 : made of or like ebony 2 : very dark or black

¹**ec·cen·tric** *adj* 1 : acting or thinking in a strange way 2 : not of the usual or normal kind

²**eccentric** *n* : a person who behaves strangely

¹**echo** *n, pl* **ech·oes** : the repetition of a sound caused by the reflection of sound waves

²**echo** *vb* **ech·oed; echo·ing** 1 : to send back or repeat a sound 2 : to repeat another's words

éclair *n* : a long thin pastry filled with whipped cream or custard

¹**eclipse** *n* 1 : a complete or partial hiding of the sun caused by the moon's passing between the sun and the earth 2 : a darkening of the moon caused by its entering the shadow of the earth 3 : the hiding of any heavenly body by another

²eclipse *vb* **eclipsed; eclips·ing 1 :** to cause an eclipse of **2 :** to be or do much better than : OUTSHINE

eco·log·i·cal *adj* : of or relating to the science of ecology or the patterns of relationships between living things and their environment

ecol·o·gist *n* : a person specializing in ecology

ecol·o·gy *n* **1 :** a branch of science concerned with the relationships between living things and their environment **2 :** the pattern of relationships between living things and their environment

eco·nom·ic *adj* **1 :** of or relating to the study of economics **2 :** relating to or based on the making, selling, and using of goods and services

eco·nom·i·cal *adj* **1 :** using what is available carefully and without waste : FRUGAL **2 :** operating with little waste — **eco·nom·i·cal·ly** *adv*

eco·nom·ics *n pl* : the science concerned with the making, selling, and using of goods and services — used as singular or plural

econ·o·mize *vb* **econ·o·mized; econ·o·miz·ing 1 :** to be thrifty **2 :** to use less of : SAVE

econ·o·my *n, pl* **econ·o·mies 1 :** the way in which goods and services are made, sold, and used in a country or area **2 :** the careful use of money and goods : THRIFT

eco·sys·tem *n* : the whole group of living and nonliving things that make up an environment and affect each other

ec·sta·sy *n, pl* **ec·sta·sies** : very great happiness or delight

ec·stat·ic *adj* : very happy or excited

ec·ze·ma *n* : a skin disease in which the skin is red and itchy and has scaly or crusty patches

¹-ed *vb suffix or adj suffix* **1** — used to form the past participle of verbs **2 :** having : showing **3 :** having the characteristics of

²-ed *vb suffix* — used to form the past tense of verbs

¹ed·dy *n, pl* **eddies** : a current of air or water running against the main current or in a circle

²eddy *vb* **ed·died; ed·dy·ing :** to move in a circle : to form an eddy

¹edge *n* **1 :** the line where a surface ends : MARGIN, BORDER **2 :** the cutting side of a blade — **edged** *adj* — **on edge :** NERVOUS 2, TENSE

²edge *vb* **edged; edg·ing 1 :** to give a border to **2 :** to move slowly and gradually

edge·wise *adv* : SIDEWAYS 2

ed·i·ble *adj* : fit or safe to eat

edict *n* : a command or law given or made by an authority (as a ruler)

ed·i·fice *n* : a large or impressive building

ed·it *vb* **ed·it·ed; ed·it·ing 1 :** to correct, revise, and get ready for publication : collect and arrange material to be printed **2 :** to be in charge of the publication of something (as an encyclopedia or a newspaper) that is the work of many writers

edi·tion *n* **1 :** the form in which a book is published **2 :** the whole number of copies of a book, magazine, or newspaper published at one time **3 :** one of several issues of a newspaper for a single day

ed·i·tor *n* : a person whose job is to correct and revise writing so it can be published

¹ed·i·to·ri·al *adj* : of or relating to an editor or editing

²editorial *n* : a newspaper or magazine article that gives the opinions of its editors or publishers

ed·u·cate *vb* **ed·u·cat·ed; ed·u·cat·ing 1 :** to provide schooling for **2 :** to develop the mind and morals of especially by formal instruction : TEACH **3 :** to provide with necessary information — **ed·u·ca·tor** *n*

ed·u·cat·ed *adj* **1 :** having an education and especially a good education **2 :** based on some knowledge

ed·u·ca·tion *n* **1 :** the act or process of teaching or of being taught **2 :** knowledge, skill, and development gained from study or training **3 :** the study of the methods and problems of teaching

ed·u·ca·tion·al *adj* **1 :** having to do with education **2 :** offering information or something of value in learning

¹-ee *n suffix* **1 :** person who receives or benefits from a specified thing or action **2 :** person who does a specified thing

²-ee *n suffix* **1 :** a certain and especially a small kind of **2 :** one like or suggesting

eel *n* : a long fish that looks like a snake and has smooth slimy skin

-eer *n suffix* : person who is concerned with or conducts or produces as a profession

ee·rie *adj* **ee·ri·er; ee·ri·est** : causing fear and uneasiness : STRANGE

ef·face *vb* **ef·faced; ef·fac·ing :** to blot out completely

¹ef·fect *n* **1 :** an event, condition, or state of affairs that is produced by a cause : INFLUENCE **2 :** the act of making a certain impression **3 :** EXECUTION 2, OPERATION **4 effects** *pl* : personal property or possessions **5 :** something created in film, television, or radio to imitate something real — **in effect :** in actual fact

²effect *vb* **ef·fect·ed; ef·fect·ing :** to make happen : bring about

ef·fec·tive *adj* **1** : producing or able to produce a desired effect **2** : IMPRESSIVE **3** : being in operation — **ef·fec·tive·ly** *adv* — **ef·fec·tive·ness** *n*

ef·fec·tu·al *adj* : producing or able to produce a desired effect — **ef·fec·tu·al·ly** *adv*

ef·fi·cien·cy *n, pl* **ef·fi·cien·cies** : the ability to do something or produce something without waste

ef·fi·cient *adj* : capable of bringing about a desired result with little waste (as of time or energy) — **ef·fi·cient·ly** *adv*

ef·fort *n* **1** : hard physical or mental work : EXERTION **2** : a serious attempt : TRY **3** : something produced by work

ef·fort·less *adj* : showing or needing little or no effort — **ef·fort·less·ly** *adv*

e.g. *abbr* for example — abbreviation for Latin *exempli gratia*, which means "for example"

¹egg *n* **1** an oval or rounded body surrounded by a shell or membrane by which some animals (as birds, fish, insects, and reptiles) reproduce and from which the young hatches out **2** : EGG CELL **3** : the contents of the egg of a bird and especially a chicken that is eaten as food

²egg *vb* **egged; egg·ing** : to urge or encourage to do usually something foolish or dangerous

egg cell *n* : a female reproductive cell of animals and plants that can unite with a sperm cell to form a new individual

egg·nog *n* : a drink made of eggs beaten with sugar, milk or cream, and often alcoholic liquor

egg·plant *n* : an oval vegetable with a usually glossy purplish skin and white flesh

egg·shell *n* : the shell of an egg

egret *n* : a heron with usually white feathers

¹Egyp·tian *adj* : of or relating to Egypt or the Egyptians

²Egyptian *n* **1** : a person who is born or lives in Egypt **2** : the language of the ancient Egyptians

ei·der *n* : a large duck of northern seas with very soft down

¹eight *n* **1** : one more than seven : two times four : 8 **2** : the eighth in a set or series

²eight *adj* : being one more than seven

¹eigh·teen *n* : one more than 17 : three times six : 18

²eighteen *adj* : being one more than 17

¹eigh·teenth *adj* : coming right after 17th

²eighteenth *n* : number 18 in a series

¹eighth *adj* : coming right after seventh

²eighth *n* **1** : number eight in a series **2** : one of eight equal parts

¹eight·i·eth *adj* : coming right after 79th

²eightieth *n* : number 80 in a series

¹eighty *adj* : eight times ten : 80

²eighty *n* : being eight times ten

¹ei·ther *adj* **1** : ¹EACH **2** : being one or the other

²either *pron* : the one or the other

³either *conj* — used before words or phrases the last of which follows "or" to show that they are choices or possibilities

⁴either *adv* : ALSO — used after a negative statement

ejac·u·late *vb* **ejac·u·lat·ed; ejac·u·lat·ing** : EXCLAIM

eject *vb* **eject·ed; eject·ing** : to force or push out

eke out *vb* **eked out; ek·ing out** **1** : to get with great effort **2** : to add to bit by bit

¹elab·o·rate *adj* : made or done with great care or with much detail — **elab·o·rate·ly** *adv*

²elab·o·rate *vb* **elab·o·rat·ed; elab·o·rat·ing** **1** : to give more details about **2** : to work out in detail

elapse *vb* **elapsed; elaps·ing** : to slip past : go by

¹elas·tic *adj* : capable of returning to original shape or size after being stretched, pressed, or squeezed together

²elastic *n* **1** : RUBBER BAND **2** : material that can be stretched

elas·tic·i·ty *n* : the quality or state of being easily stretched

elate *vb* **elat·ed; elat·ing** : to fill with joy or pride

ela·tion *n* : the quality or state of being filled with joy or pride

¹el·bow *n* **1** : the joint or the region of the joint of the arm or of the same part of an animal's front legs **2** : a part (as of a pipe) bent like an elbow

²elbow *vb* **el·bowed; el·bow·ing** **1** : to jab with an elbow **2** : to push or force a way with or as if with the elbows

¹el·der *n* : ELDERBERRY 1

²elder *adj* : being older than another person

³elder *n* **1** : a person who is older **2** : a person having authority because of age and experience **3** : an official in some churches

el·der·ber·ry *n, pl* **el·der·ber·ries** **1** : a shrub or small tree with clusters of small white flowers and a black or red berrylike fruit **2** : the fruit of the elderberry

el·der·ly *adj* : somewhat old

el·dest *adj* : being oldest of a group of people

¹elect *vb* **elect·ed; elect·ing** : to select by vote **2** : to make a choice

²elect *adj* : chosen for office but not yet holding office

elec·tion *n* : an act of choosing or the fact of being chosen especially by vote

elec·tive *adj* : chosen or filled by election

electr- *or* **electro-** *prefix* **1** : electricity **2** : electric **3** : electric and

elec·tric *adj* **1** *or* **elec·tri·cal** : of or relating to electricity or its use **2** : heated, moved, made, or run by electricity **3** : giving off sounds through an electronic amplifier **4** : having a thrilling effect — **elec·tri·cal·ly** *adv*

electric eel : a large South American eel-shaped fish with organs that can give an electric shock

elec·tri·cian *n* : a person who installs, operates, or repairs electrical equipment

elec·tric·i·ty *n* **1** : an important form of energy that is found in nature but that can be artificially produced by rubbing together two unlike things (as glass and silk), by the action of chemicals, or by means of a generator **2** : electric current

elec·tri·fy *vb* **elec·tri·fied; elec·tri·fy·ing** **1** : to charge with electricity **2** : to equip for use of or supply with electric power **3** : THRILL 1

elec·tro·cute *vb* **elec·tro·cut·ed; elec·tro·cut·ing** : to kill by an electric shock — **elec·tro·cu·tion** *n*

elec·trode *n* : a conductor (as a metal or carbon) used to make electrical contact with a part of an electrical circuit that is not metallic

elec·trol·y·sis *n* : the producing of chemical changes by passage of an electric current through a liquid

elec·tro·lyte *n* **1** : a substance (as an acid or salt) that when dissolved (as in water) conducts an electric current **2** : a substance (as sodium or calcium) that is an ion in the body regulating the flow of nutrients into and waste products out of cells

elec·tro·lyt·ic *adj* : of or relating to electrolysis or an electrolyte

elec·tro·mag·net *n* : a piece of iron encircled by a coil of wire through which an electric current is passed to magnetize the iron

elec·tro·mag·net·ic *adj* : of or relating to a magnetic field produced by an electric current

electromagnetic wave *n* : a wave (as a radio wave or wave of light) that travels at the speed of light and consists of a combined electric and magnetic effect

elec·tron *n* : a very small particle that has a negative charge of electricity and travels around the nucleus of an atom

elec·tron·ic *adj* **1** : relating to or using the principles of electronics **2** : operating by means of or using a computer — **elec·tron·i·cal·ly** *adv*

electronic mail *n* : [1]E-MAIL

elec·tron·ics *n* : a science that deals with the giving off, action, and effects of electrons in vacuums, gases, and semiconductors and with devices using such electrons

electron tube *n* : a device in which conduction of electricity by electrons takes place through a vacuum or a gas within a sealed container and which has various uses (as in radio and television)

el·e·gance *n* **1** : gracefulness of style or movement **2** : tasteful luxury

el·e·gant *adj* : showing good taste : having or showing beauty and refinement — **el·e·gant·ly** *adv*

el·e·ment *n* **1** : any of more than 100 substances that cannot by ordinary chemical means be separated into different substances **2** : one of the parts of which something is made up **3** : the simplest principles of a subject of study **4** : a member of a mathematical set **5** : the state or place natural to or suited to a person or thing **6 elements** *pl* : the forces of nature

el·e·men·ta·ry *adj* **1** : relating to the beginnings or simplest principles of a subject **2** : relating to or teaching the basic subjects of education

el·e·phant *n* : a huge typically gray mammal of Africa or Asia with the nose drawn out into a long trunk and two large curved tusks

el·e·vate *vb* **el·e·vat·ed; el·e·vat·ing** : to lift up : RAISE

el·e·va·tion *n* **1** : height especially above sea level : ALTITUDE **2** : a raised place (as a hill) **3** : the act of raising : the condition of being raised

el·e·va·tor *n* **1** : a floor or little room that can be raised or lowered for carrying people or goods from one level to another **2** : a device (as an endless belt) for raising material **3** : GRAIN ELEVATOR

[1]eleven *n* **1** : one more than ten : 11 **2** : the eleventh in a set or series

[2]eleven *adj* : being one more than ten

[1]elev·enth *adj* : coming right after tenth

[2]eleventh *n* : number eleven in a series

elf *n, pl* **elves** : an often mischievous fairy

elf·in *adj* : relating to elves

el·i·gi·ble *adj* : qualified to be chosen, to participate, or to receive

elim·i·nate *vb* **elim·i·nat·ed; elim·i·nat·ing** : to get rid of : do away with

elim·i·na·tion *n* **1** : the act or process of excluding or getting rid of **2** : a getting rid of waste from the body

elk *n* **1** : a large deer of North America, Europe, and Asia with curved antlers having many branches **2** : the moose of Europe and Asia

el·lipse *n* : a shape that looks like a flattened circle

el·lip·ti·cal *or* **el·lip·tic** *adj* : having the shape of an ellipse

elm *n* : a tall shade tree with a broad rather flat top and spreading branches

el·o·cu·tion *n* : the art of reading or speaking clearly and effectively in public

elon·gate *vb* **elon·gat·ed; elon·gat·ing** : to make or grow longer

elope *vb* **eloped; elop·ing** : to run away to be married — **elope·ment** *n*

el·o·quence *n* **1** : speaking or writing that is forceful and convincing **2** : the ability to speak or write with force and in a convincing way

el·o·quent *adj* **1** : having or showing clear and forceful expression **2** : clearly showing some feeling or meaning — **el·o·quent·ly** *adv*

¹else *adv* **1** : in a different way or place or at a different time **2** : if the facts are or were different : if not

²else *adj* **1** : being other and different **2** : being in addition

else·where *adv* : in or to another place

elude *vb* **elud·ed; elud·ing** : to avoid or escape by being quick, skillful, or tricky

elu·sive *adj* **1** : hard to find or capture **2** : hard to understand or define

elves *pl of* ELF

em- — see EN-

¹e–mail *n* **1** : a system for sending messages between computers **2** : a message sent electronically from one computer to another

²e–mail *vb* **e–mailed; e–mail·ing** : to send e-mail or as e-mail

em·a·nate *vb* **em·a·nat·ed; em·a·nat·ing** **1** : to come out from a source **2** : to give off or out

eman·ci·pate *vb* **eman·ci·pat·ed; eman·ci·pat·ing** : to set free from control or slavery : LIBERATE — **eman·ci·pa·tor** *n*

eman·ci·pa·tion *n* : an act of setting someone free from control or slavery

em·balm *vb* **em·balmed; em·balm·ing** : to treat a dead body so as to preserve it from decay — **em·balm·er** *n*

em·bank·ment *n* : a raised bank or wall to carry a roadway or hold back water

em·bar·go *n, pl* **em·bar·goes** : an order of a government forbidding ships engaged in trade from leaving its ports

em·bark *vb* **em·barked; em·bark·ing** **1** : to go on or put on board a ship or an airplane **2** : to begin a project or task

em·bar·rass *vb* **em·bar·rassed; em·bar·rass·ing** : to cause to feel confused and foolish in front of other people

em·bar·rass·ment *n* **1** : something that causes a person or group to feel foolish **2** : the condition of feeling foolish in front of others

em·bas·sy *n, pl* **em·bas·sies** **1** : a group of people led by an ambassador who represent their country in a foreign county **2** : the building where an ambassador lives or works

em·bed *vb* **em·bed·ded; em·bed·ding** : to enclose in or as if in a surrounding substance

em·bel·lish *vb* **em·bel·lished; em·bel·lish·ing** : DECORATE 1 — **em·bel·lish·ment** *n*

em·ber *n* : a glowing piece of coal or wood in the ashes from a fire

em·bez·zle *vb* **em·bez·zled; em·bez·zling** : to steal (money or property) despite being entrusted to take care of it

em·bit·ter *vb* **em·bit·tered; em·bit·ter·ing** : to make sad and angry : make bitter

em·blem *n* : an object or an image used to suggest a thing that cannot be pictured

em·body *vb* **em·bod·ied; em·body·ing** **1** : to give form to **2** : to represent in visible form **3** : to make something a body or system or part of a body or system

em·boss *vb* **em·bossed; em·boss·ing** : to decorate with a raised pattern or design

¹em·brace *vb* **em·braced; em·brac·ing** **1** : to hold in the arms : HUG **2** : to surround on all sides **3** : to accept readily or gladly **4** : INCLUDE

²embrace *n* : an act of holding in the arms : HUG

em·broi·der *vb* **em·broi·dered; em·broi·der·ing** **1** : to make with needlework **2** : to decorate with needlework **3** : to make more interesting by exaggerating or adding details

em·broi·dery *n, pl* **em·broi·der·ies** **1** : needlework done to decorate cloth **2** : the act or art of embroidering

em·bryo *n, pl* **em·bry·os** **1** : an unborn human or animal in the earliest stages of growth when its basic structures are being formed **2** : a tiny young plant inside a seed

¹em·er·ald *n* : a gemstone of a rich green color

²emerald *adj* : brightly or richly green

emerge *vb* **emerged; emerg·ing** **1** : to come out or into view **2** : to become known

emer·gen·cy *n, pl* **emer·gen·cies** : an unexpected situation that requires immediate action

emergency room *n* : a room in a hospital with doctors, nurses, and medical equipment for treating people who need medical care immediately

em·ery *n, pl* **em·er·ies** : a mineral used as a powder for polishing and grinding

em·i·grant *n* : a person who leaves one country or region to live in another

em·i·grate *vb* **em·i·grat·ed; em·i·grat·ing** : to leave one country or region to live in another

em·i·gra·tion *n* : the act of leaving one region or country to live in another

em·i·nence *n* **1** : the condition of being well-known and respected **2** : a piece of high ground : HILL

em·i·nent *adj* : successful, well-known, and respected

em·is·sary *n, pl* **em·is·sar·ies** : a person sent on a mission to represent someone else

emis·sion *n* **1** : the act of giving off **2** : something that is given off

emit *vb* **emit·ted; emit·ting** : to send out from a source

emo·tion *n* : strong feeling (as anger, love, joy, or fear) often accompanied by a physical reaction

emo·tion·al *adj* **1** : relating to a person's feelings **2** : likely to show or express feelings **3** : expressing strong feelings — **emo·tion·al·ly** *adv*

em·pa·thize *vb* **em·pa·thized; em·pa·thiz·ing** : to share the same feelings as another person : to feel empathy

em·pa·thy *n* : the understanding and sharing of the emotions and experiences of another person

em·per·or *n* : a man who rules an empire

em·pha·sis *n, pl* **em·pha·ses** **1** : a forcefulness in the way something is said or written that gives it special attention or importance **2** : special force given to one or more words or syllables in speaking or reading **3** : special attention or importance given to something

em·pha·size *vb* **em·pha·sized; em·pha·siz·ing** : to give special attention or importance to

em·phat·ic *adj* : spoken or done forcefully — **em·phat·ic·al·ly** *adv*

em·phy·se·ma *n* : a disease in which the lungs become stretched and inefficient

em·pire *n* **1** : a group of territories or peoples under one ruler **2** : a country whose ruler is called an emperor

¹em·ploy *vb* **em·ployed; em·ploy·ing** **1** : to give a job to : use the services of **2** : to make use of

²employ *n* : the state of being hired for a job by

em·ploy·ee *n* : a person who is paid to work for another

em·ploy·er *n* : a person or business that pays others for their services

em·ploy·ment *n* **1** : the act of using something **2** : JOB 1, OCCUPATION **3** : the act of hiring a person to do work

em·pow·er *vb* **em·pow·ered; em·pow·er·ing** : to give authority or legal power to

em·press *n* **1** : a woman who rules an empire **2** : the wife of an emperor

¹emp·ty *adj* **emp·ti·er; emp·ti·est** **1** : containing nothing **2** : not occupied or lived in : VACANT **3** : not sincere or meaningful — **emp·ti·ness** *n*

²empty *vb* **emp·tied; emp·ty·ing** **1** : to remove the contents of **2** : to remove all of (something) from a container **3** : to become unoccupied **4** : to flow into

emp·ty–hand·ed *adj* **1** : not carrying or bringing anything **2** : having gotten or gained nothing

EMT *n, pl* **EMTs** *or* **EMT's** : a person that is trained to give emergency medical care to a patient before and on the way to a hospital

emu *n* : a large fast-running Australian bird that cannot fly

em·u·late *vb* **em·u·lat·ed; em·u·lat·ing** : to try hard to be like or do better than : IMITATE

em·u·la·tion *n* : an attempt to be like or do better than others

emul·si·fy *vb* **emul·si·fied; emul·si·fy·ing** : to combine two liquids to make an emulsion

emul·sion *n* : two liquids mixed together so that tiny drops of one liquid are scattered throughout the other

en- *also* **em-** *prefix* **1** : put or go into or onto **2** : cause to be **3** : provide with — in all senses usually *em-* before *b, m,* or *p*

¹-en *also* **-n** *adj suffix* : made of : consisting of

²-en *vb suffix* **1** : become or cause to be **2** : cause or come to have

en·able *vb* **en·abled; en·abling** : to give strength, power, or ability to : make able

en·act *vb* **en·act·ed; en·act·ing** **1** : to perform or act out **2** : to make into law — **en·act·ment** *n*

¹enam·el *vb* **enam·eled** *or* **enam·elled; enam·el·ing** *or* **enam·el·ling** : to cover or decorate with a smooth hard glossy coating

²enamel *n* **1** : a glassy substance used to coat the surface of metal, glass, and pottery **2** : the hard outer surface of the teeth **3** : a paint that dries to form a hard glossy coat

en·camp·ment *n* **1** : the act of making a camp **2** : ¹CAMP 1

en·case *vb* **en·cased; en·cas·ing** : to cover or surround : enclose in or as if in a case

-ence *n suffix* **1** : action or process **2** : quality or state

en·chant *vb* **en·chant·ed; en·chant·ing** **1** : to put under a spell by or as if by magic : BEWITCH **2** : to please greatly : DELIGHT — **en·chant·ment** *n*

en·chant·ing *adj* : very attractive : CHARMING

en·chant·ress *n* : a woman who casts magic spells : WITCH, SORCERESS

en·cir·cle *vb* **en·cir·cled; en·cir·cling** **1** : to make a circle around : SURROUND **2** : to go completely around

en·close *vb* **en·closed; en·clos·ing** **1** : to close in : SURROUND **2** : to hold in : CONFINE **3** : to put in the same package or envelope with something else

en·clo·sure *n* **1** : the act of closing in or surrounding **2** : a space that is closed in **3** : the act of including with a letter or package **4** : something included with a letter or package

en·com·pass *vb* **en·com·passed; en·com·pass·ing** **1** : to cover or surround : ENCIRCLE **2** : INCLUDE

en·core *n* **1** : a demand by an audience for a performance to continue or be repeated **2** : a further appearance or performance given in response to applause

¹en·coun·ter *vb* **en·coun·tered; en·coun·ter·ing** **1** : to meet face-to-face or by chance **2** : to experience or face often unexpectedly

²encounter *n* **1** : a meeting face-to-face and often by chance **2** : an often unexpected experience

en·cour·age *vb* **en·cour·aged; en·cour·ag·ing** **1** : make more determined, hopeful, or confident : HEARTEN **2** : to give help or support to : AID — **en·cour·ag·ing·ly** *adv*

en·cour·age·ment *n* **1** : something that gives hope, determination, or confidence **2** : the act of giving hope or confidence to

en·croach *vb* **en·croached; en·croach·ing** **1** : to take over the rights or property of another little by little or in secret **2** : to go beyond the usual or proper limits

en·crust *vb* **en·crust·ed; en·crust·ing** : to cover with or as if with a crust

en·cum·ber *vb* **en·cum·bered; en·cum·ber·ing** **1** : to weigh down : BURDEN **2** : to cause problems or delays for : HINDER

-en·cy *n suffix, pl* **-en·cies** : quality or state

en·cy·clo·pe·dia *n* : a book or a set of books containing information on all branches of learning in articles arranged alphabetically by subject

¹end *n* **1** : the part near the boundary of an area **2** : the point where something stops or ceases to exist **3** : the first or last part of a thing **4** : DEATH 1, DESTRUCTION **5** : ¹PURPOSE, GOAL **6** : a player in football positioned at the end of the line of scrimmage **7** : a part of an undertaking

²end *vb* **end·ed; end·ing** : to bring or come to an end : STOP, FINISH — **end up** : to reach or come to a place, condition, or situation unexpectedly

en·dan·ger *vb* **en·dan·gered; en·dan·ger·ing** : to expose to possible harm : RISK

en·dan·gered *adj* : close to becoming extinct : dying out

en·dear *vb* **en·deared; en·dear·ing** : to make beloved or admired

en·dear·ment *n* : a word or an act that shows love or affection

¹en·deav·or *vb* **en·deav·ored; en·deav·or·ing** : to make an effort : try hard

²endeavor *n* : a serious effort or attempt

end·ing *n* : the final part : END

end·less *adj* : lasting or taking a long time — **end·less·ly** *adv*

en·do·crine gland *n* : any of several glands (as the thyroid or pituitary gland) that release hormones directly into the blood

en·dorse *vb* **en·dorsed; en·dors·ing** **1** : to show support or approval for **2** : to sign the back of to receive payment — **en·dorse·ment** *n*

en·dow *vb* **en·dowed; en·dow·ing** **1** : to provide with money for support **2** : to provide with something freely or naturally

en·dow·ment *n* **1** : the act of providing money for support **2** : money provided for support

end·point *n* : either of two points that mark the ends of a line segment or a point that marks the end of a ray

en·dur·ance *n* : the ability to put up with strain, suffering, or hardship

en·dure *vb* **en·dured; en·dur·ing** **1** : to continue to exist over a long time : LAST **2** : to experience without giving in **3** : to put up with

en·e·my *n, pl* **en·e·mies** **1** : a person who hates another : a person who attacks or tries to harm another **2** : a country or group of people with which another country or group is at war or a person belonging to such a country or group **3** : something that harms or threatens

en·er·get·ic *adj* : having or showing the ability to be active — **en·er·get·i·cal·ly** *adv*

en·er·gize *vb* **en·er·gized; en·er·giz·ing** : to give the ability to be active to : give energy to

en·er·gy *n, pl* **en·er·gies** **1** : ability to be active : strength of body or mind to do things or to work **2** : strong action or effort **3** : usable power or the resources (as oil) used to produce usable power

en·fold *vb* **en·fold·ed; en·fold·ing** **1** : to wrap up **2** : ¹EMBRACE 1

en·force *vb* **en·forced; en·forc·ing** **1** : to make happen **2** : to carry out or make effective — **en·force·ment** *n*

Eng. *abbr* **1** England **2** English

en·gage *vb* **en·gaged; en·gag·ing** **1** : to catch and keep fixed (as someone's attention) **2** : to take part in or cause to take part in something **3** : to enter into contest or battle with **4** : to arrange for the services or use of : EMPLOY **5** : MESH

en·gaged *adj* **1** : busy with an activity **2** : promised to be married

en·gage·ment *n* **1** : the act of becoming engaged to be married : the state of being engaged to be married **2** : EMPLOYMENT 3 **3** : APPOINTMENT **4** : a fight between armed forces : BATTLE

en·gag·ing *adj* : attractive or interesting

en·gine *n* **1** : a mechanical tool or device **2** : a machine for driving or operating something especially by using the energy of steam, gasoline, or oil **3** : LOCOMOTIVE

¹en·gi·neer *n* **1** : a person who designs and builds machinery or technical equipment : a person who studies or works in a branch of engineering **2** : a person who runs or is in charge of a railroad engine or other machinery or technical equipment

²engineer *vb* **en·gi·neered; en·gi·neer·ing 1** : to plan, build, or manage as an engineer **2** : to plan out in a skillful or clever way : CONTRIVE

en·gi·neer·ing *n* : the application of science to the goal of creating useful machines (as automobiles) or structures (as roads and dams)

¹En·glish *adj* : of or relating to England, its people, or the English language

²English *n* **1** : the language of England, the United States, and some other countries now or at one time under British rule **2 English** *pl* : the people of England **3** : English language or literature as a subject in school

English horn *n* : a woodwind instrument that is similar to an oboe but is longer and has a deeper tone

en·grave *vb* **en·graved; en·grav·ing 1** : to cut or carve (as letters or designs) on a hard surface **2** : to cut (as letters or designs) on or into **3** : to print from a cut surface — **en·grav·er** *n*

en·grav·ing *n* **1** : the art of cutting something especially into the surface of wood, stone, or metal **2** : a print made from a cut surface

en·gross *vb* **en·grossed; en·gross·ing** : to take the attention of completely

en·gulf *vb* **en·gulfed; en·gulf·ing 1** : to flow over and cover or surround **2** : to be overwhelmed by

en·hance *vb* **en·hanced; en·hanc·ing** : to make greater or better

enig·ma *n* : someone or something that is hard to understand

en·joy *vb* **en·joyed; en·joy·ing 1** : to get pleasure from **2** : to have the use or benefit of

en·joy·able *adj* : providing pleasure

en·joy·ment *n* **1** : the action or condition of getting pleasure or satisfaction from something **2** : something that gives pleasure

en·large *vb* **en·larged; en·larg·ing** : to make or grow larger : EXPAND

en·large·ment *n* **1** : an act of making or growing larger **2** : the state of having been made or having grown larger **3** : a larger copy of a photograph

en·light·en *vb* **en·light·ened; en·light·en·ing** : to give knowledge or understanding to

en·list *vb* **en·list·ed; en·list·ing 1** : to join the armed forces as a volunteer **2** : to get the help of — **en·list·ment** *n*

en·list·ed *adj* : serving in the armed forces in a rank below a commissioned officer or warrant officer

en·liv·en *vb* **en·liv·ened; en·liv·en·ing** : to put life or spirit into

en·mi·ty *n, pl* **en·mi·ties** : hatred especially when shared : ILL WILL

enor·mous *adj* : unusually great in size, number, or degree — **enor·mous·ly** *adv*

¹enough *adj* : equal to the needs or demands

²enough *adv* : in the amount necessary or to the degree necessary

³enough *pron* : a number or amount that provides what is needed

enquire *chiefly British variant of* INQUIRE

en·rage *vb* **en·raged; en·rag·ing** : to fill with rage : ANGER

en·rich *vb* **en·riched; en·rich·ing 1** : to make rich or richer **2** : to improve the quality of food by adding vitamins and minerals **3** : to make more fertile

en·roll *vb* **en·rolled; en·roll·ing 1** : to include (as a name) on a roll or list **2** : to take in as a member **3** : to become a member : JOIN

en·roll·ment *n* **1** : the act of becoming a member or being made a member **2** : the number of members

en route *adv* : on or along the way

en·sem·ble *n* : a group of people or things making up a complete unit

en·sign *n* **1** : a flag flown as the symbol of nationality **2** : a commissioned officer of the lowest rank in the navy or coast guard

en·slave *vb* **en·slaved; en·slav·ing** : to make a slave of

en·sue *vb* **en·sued; en·su·ing** : to come after in time or as a result : FOLLOW

en·sure *vb* **en·sured; en·sur·ing** : to make sure, certain, or safe : GUARANTEE

en·tan·gle *vb* **en·tan·gled; en·tan·gling 1** : to make tangled or confused **2** : to catch in a tangle

en·ter *vb* **en·tered; en·ter·ing 1** : to come or go in or into **2** : to stab into : PIERCE **3** : to put into a list or book : write down **4** : to put in or into **5** : to become a member of **6** : to become a participant in or take an interest in **7** : enroll in : begin attending

en·ter·prise *n* **1** : a project or undertaking that is difficult, complicated, or risky **2** : willingness to engage in daring or difficult action **3** : a business organization or activity

en·ter·pris·ing *adj* : bold and energetic in trying or experimenting

en·ter·tain *vb* **en·ter·tained; en·ter·tain·ing 1** : to host a social event **2** : to have as a guest **3** : to perform for or provide amusement for **4** : to have in mind

en·ter·tain·er *n* : a person who performs for public entertainment

en·ter·tain·ment *n* **1** : the act of amusing or entertaining **2** : something (as a show) that is a form of amusement or recreation

en·thrall *vb* **en·thralled; en·thrall·ing** : to hold the attention of completely

en·throne *vb* **en·throned; en·thron·ing 1** : to place on a throne **2** : to seat or put in a place to indicate authority or value

en·thu·si·asm *n* : strong feeling in favor of something

en·thu·si·ast *n* : a person who is very excited about or interested in something

en·thu·si·as·tic *adj* : feeling strong excitement about something : full of enthusiasm

en·thu·si·as·ti·cal·ly *adv* : with strong excitement

en·tice *vb* **en·ticed; en·tic·ing** : to attract by raising hope or desire : TEMPT

en·tire *adj* : complete in all parts or respects — **en·tire·ly** *adv*

en·tire·ty *n* : the whole or total amount

en·ti·tle *vb* **en·ti·tled; en·ti·tling 1** : to give a title to **2** : to give a right or claim to

en·trails *n pl* : the internal parts of an animal

¹en·trance *n* **1** : the act of going in **2** : a door, gate, or way for going in **3** : permission to join, participate in, or attend

²en·trance *vb* **en·tranced; en·tranc·ing 1** : to put into a trance **2** : to fill with delight and wonder

en·trap *vb* **en·trapped; en·trap·ping** : to catch in or as if in a trap

en·treat *vb* **en·treat·ed; en·treat·ing** : to ask in a serious and urgent way

en·treaty *n, pl* **en·treat·ies** : a serious and urgent request

en·trust *vb* **en·trust·ed; en·trust·ing 1** : to give care of something to **2** : to give to another with confidence

en·try *n, pl* **en·tries 1** : the act of going in : ENTRANCE **2** : the right to go in or join **3** : a place (as a hall or door) through which entrance is made **4** : the act of making a written record of something **5** : something

written down as part of a list or a record **6** : a person or thing taking part in a contest

en·twine *vb* **en·twined; en·twin·ing** : to twist or twine together or around

enu·mer·ate *vb* **enu·mer·at·ed; enu·mer·at·ing 1** : ¹COUNT 1 **2** : to name one after another : LIST

enun·ci·ate *vb* **enun·ci·at·ed; enun·ci·at·ing 1** : to make known publicly **2** : to pronounce words or parts of words

enun·ci·a·tion *n* : clearness of pronunciation

en·vel·op *vb* **en·vel·oped; en·vel·op·ing** : to put a covering completely around : wrap up or in

en·ve·lope *n* : a flat usually paper container (as for a letter)

en·vi·ous *adj* : feeling or showing unhappiness over someone else's good fortune and a desire to have the same — **en·vi·ous·ly** *adv*

en·vi·ron·ment *n* **1** : a person's physical surroundings **2** : the surrounding conditions or forces (as soil, climate, and living things) that influence a plant's or animal's characteristics and ability to survive **3** : the social and cultural conditions that affect the life of a person or community

en·voy *n* **1** : a representative sent by one government to another **2** : MESSENGER

¹en·vy *n, pl* **envies 1** : a feeling of unhappiness over another's good fortune together with a desire to have the same good fortune **2** : a person or a thing that is envied

²envy *vb* **en·vied; en·vy·ing** : to feel unhappiness over the good fortune of (someone) and desire the same good fortune : feel envy toward or because of

en·zyme *n* : a substance produced by body cells that helps bring about or speed up bodily chemical activities (as the digestion of food) without being destroyed in so doing

eon *variant of* AEON

¹ep·ic *n* **1** : a long poem that tells the story of a hero's deeds

²epic *adj* **1** : telling a great and heroic story **2** : heroic or impressive because of great size or effort

¹ep·i·dem·ic *n* **1** : a rapidly spreading outbreak of disease **2** : something harmful that spreads or develops rapidly

²epidemic *adj* : spreading widely and affecting many people at the same time

epi·der·mis *n* **1** : a thin outer layer of skin covering the dermis **2** : any of various thin outer layers of plants or animals

ep·i·lep·sy *n* : a disorder of the nervous system that causes people to have seizures

ep·i·neph·rine *n* : a hormone that causes blood vessels to narrow and the blood pressure to increase

ep·i·sode *n* **1** : an event or one of a series of

events that stands out clearly **2** : one in a series of connected stories or performances

ep·i·taph *n* : a brief statement on a tombstone in memory of a dead person

ep·och *n* : a period that is important or memorable

¹equal *adj* **1** : exactly the same in number, amount, degree, rank, or quality **2** : the same for each person **3** : having enough strength, ability, or means — **equal·ly** *adv*

²equal *vb* **equaled** *or* **equalled; equal·ing** *or* **equal·ling** : to be the same in number, amount, degree, rank, or quality as

³equal *n* : someone or something that is as good or valuable as another

equal·i·ty *n, pl* **equal·i·ties** : the condition or state of being the same in number, amount, degree, rank, or quality

equal·ize *vb* **equal·ized; equal·iz·ing** : to make even or equal

equa·tion *n* **1** : a statement of the equality of two mathematical expressions **2** : an expression representing a chemical reaction by means of chemical symbols

equa·tor *n* : an imaginary circle around the earth everywhere equally distant from the north pole and the south pole

equa·to·ri·al *adj* : relating to or lying near the equator

eques·tri·an *adj* : relating to the act of riding horses

equi·lat·er·al *adj* : having all sides or faces equal

equi·lib·ri·um *n* **1** : a state of balance between opposing forces or actions **2** : the normal balanced state of the body that is maintained by the inner part of the ear and allows a person or animal to stand or move without falling

equi·nox *n* : either of the two times each year (as in spring around March 21 and in fall around September 23) when the sun's center crosses the equator and day and night are everywhere of equal length

equip *vb* **equipped; equip·ping** : to provide with necessary supplies or features

equip·ment *n* : supplies or tools needed for a special purpose

¹equiv·a·lent *adj* : alike or equal in number, value, or meaning

²equivalent *n* : something like or equal to something else in number, value, or meaning

¹-er *adj suffix or adv suffix* — used to form the comparative degree of adjectives and adverbs of one syllable and of some adjectives and adverbs of two or more syllables

²-er *also* **-ier** *or* **-yer** *n suffix* **1** : a person whose work or business is connected with **2** : a person or thing belonging to or associated

with **3** : a native of : resident of **4** : a person or thing that has **5** : a person or thing that produces **6** : a person or thing that performs a specified action **7** : a person or thing that is a suitable object of a specified action **8** : a person or thing that is

era *n* **1** : a period of time starting from some special date or event or known for a certain feature **2** : an important period of history

erad·i·cate *vb* **erad·i·cat·ed; erad·i·cat·ing** : to destroy completely

erase *vb* **erased; eras·ing** **1** : to cause to disappear by rubbing or scraping **2** : to remove marks from **3** : to remove recorded matter from — **eras·er** *n*

era·sure *n* **1** : an act of erasing **2** : something erased

¹ere *prep* : ²BEFORE 2

²ere *conj* : ³BEFORE 3

¹erect *adj* : straight up and down

²erect *vb* **erect·ed; erect·ing** **1** : to put up by fitting together materials or parts **2** : to set or place straight up — **erec·tor** *n*

er·mine *n* : a weasel of northern regions having a winter coat of white fur with a tail tipped in black

erode *vb* **erod·ed; erod·ing** : to wear away : destroy by wearing away

ero·sion *n* : the act of wearing away or eroding : the state of being eroded

err *vb* **erred; err·ing** : to make a mistake

er·rand *n* **1** : a short trip made to do or get something **2** : the purpose of a short trip

er·rant *adj* **1** : wandering in search of adventure **2** : straying from a proper course

er·rat·ic *adj* : not following a regular, usual, or expected course

er·ro·ne·ous *adj* : INCORRECT 1

er·ror *n* : a failure to be correct or accurate : MISTAKE

erupt *vb* **erupt·ed; erupt·ing** : to burst forth or cause to burst forth

erup·tion *n* : an act of bursting forth

-ery *n suffix, pl* **-er·ies** **1** : qualities considered as a group : character : -NESS **2** : art : practice **3** : place of doing, keeping, producing, or selling **4** : collection **5** : state or condition

¹-es *n pl suffix* — used to form the plural of most nouns that end in *s* , *z* , *sh* , *ch* , or a final *y* that changes to *i* and of some nouns ending in *f* that changes to *v*

²-es *vb suffix* — used to form the third person singular present of most verbs that end in *s* , *z* , *sh* , *ch* , or a final *y* that changes to *i*

es·ca·la·tor *n* : a moving stairway for going from one floor of a building to another

es·ca·pade *n* : a daring or reckless adventure

¹es·cape *vb* **es·caped; es·cap·ing** **1** : to get away : get free or clear **2** : to keep free of

: AVOID **3** : to fail to be noticed or remembered by **4** : to leak out

²es·cape n **1** : the act of getting away **2** : a way of getting away

¹es·cort n **1** : a person or group that accompanies someone to give protection or show courtesy **2** : the man who goes with a woman to a social event

²es·cort vb **es·cort·ed; es·cort·ing** : to accompany someone to protect or show courtesy

¹-ese adj suffix : of, relating to, or coming from a certain place or country

²-ese n suffix, pl **-ese 1** : native or resident of a specified place or country **2** : language of a particular place, country, or nationality

Es·ki·mo n, pl **Es·ki·mos** sometimes offensive : a member of a group of peoples of Alaska, northern Canada, Greenland, and eastern Siberia

ESL abbr English as a second language

esoph·a·gus n, pl **esoph·a·gi** : a muscular tube that leads from the mouth through the throat to the stomach

esp. abbr especially

es·pe·cial adj : more then usual : SPECIAL — **es·pe·cial·ly** adv

es·pi·o·nage n : the practice of spying : the use of spies

es·py vb **es·pied; es·py·ing** : to catch sight of

-ess n suffix : female

es·say n : a usually short piece of writing dealing with a subject from a personal point of view

es·say·ist n : a writer of essays

es·sence n **1** : the basic part of something **2** : a substance made from a plant or drug and having its special qualities **3** : ¹PERFUME 1

¹es·sen·tial adj **1** : extremely important or necessary **2** : forming or belonging to the basic part of something — **es·sen·tial·ly** adv

²essential n : something that is basic or necessary

-est adj suffix or adv suffix — used to form the superlative of adjectives and adverbs of one syllable and of some adjectives and adverbs of two or more syllables

es·tab·lish vb **es·tab·lished; es·tab·lish·ing 1** : to bring into being : FOUND **2** : to put beyond doubt : PROVE

es·tab·lish·ment n **1** : the act of founding or of proving **2** : a place where people live or do business

es·tate n **1** : the property of all kinds that a person leaves at death **2** : a mansion on a large piece of land **3** : ¹STATE 1

¹es·teem n : respect and affection

²esteem vb **es·teemed; es·teem·ing** : to think favorably of

¹es·ti·mate vb **es·ti·mat·ed; es·ti·mat·ing** : to give or form a general idea of (as the value, size, or cost of something)

²es·ti·mate n **1** : an opinion or judgment especially of the value or quality of something **2** : an approximation of the size or cost of something

es·ti·ma·tion n **1** : the act of making a judgment especially of value, size, or cost **2** : OPINION 2

es·tu·ary n, pl **es·tu·ar·ies** : an arm of the sea at the lower end of a river

et al. abbr and others — abbreviation for Latin et alia, which means "and others"

etc. abbr et cetera

et cet·era : and others of the same kind : and so forth : and so on

etch vb **etched; etch·ing** : to produce designs or figures on metal or glass by using acid to eat into the surface

etch·ing n **1** : the art or process of producing drawings or pictures by printing from etched plates **2** : a picture made from an etched plate

eter·nal adj **1** : lasting forever : having no beginning and no end **2** : continuing without interruption : seeming to last forever

eter·ni·ty n, pl **eter·ni·ties 1** : time without end **2** : the state after death **3** : a period of time that seems endless

-eth — see -TH

ether n : a light flammable liquid used to dissolve fats and especially in the past as an anesthetic

ethe·re·al adj **1** : suggesting heaven or the heavens **2** : very delicate : AIRY

eth·i·cal adj **1** : involving questions of right and wrong : relating to ethics **2** : following accepted rules of behavior

eth·ics n pl **1** : a branch of philosophy dealing with what is morally right or wrong **2** : the rules of moral behavior governing an individual or a group — used as singular or plural

eth·nic adj : of or relating to groups of people with common characteristics and customs — **eth·ni·cal·ly** adv

et·i·quette n : the rules governing the proper way to behave or to do something

-ette n suffix **1** : little one **2** : female

et·y·mol·o·gy n, pl **et·y·mol·o·gies** : the history of a word shown by tracing it or its parts back to the earliest known forms and meanings both in its own language and any other language from which it may have been taken

eu·ca·lyp·tus n, pl **eu·ca·lyp·ti** or **eu·ca·lyp·tus·es** : a tree mainly of Australia that is widely grown for its timber, gums, and oils

eu·gle·na n : a tiny green single-celled organism that lives in freshwater and moves about by means of a flagellum

eu·ro *n, pl* **euros** : a coin or bill used by many countries of the European Union

¹Eu·ro·pe·an *adj* : of or relating to Europe or the people of Europe

²European *n* : a native or resident of Europe

evac·u·ate *vb* **evac·u·at·ed; evac·u·at·ing 1** : to leave or cause to leave a place of danger **2** : to make empty : empty out **3** : to discharge waste matter from the body

evade *vb* **evad·ed; evad·ing** : to get away from or avoid meeting directly

eval·u·ate *vb* **eval·u·at·ed; eval·u·at·ing** : to judge the value or condition of

eval·u·a·tion *n* : the act or result of judging the condition or value of

evan·ge·list *n* : a Christian preacher who tries to change or increase religious feelings

evap·o·rate *vb* **evap·o·rat·ed; evap·o·rat·ing 1** : to change into vapor **2** : to remove some of the water from something (as by heating) **3** : to disappear without being seen to go

evap·o·ra·tion *n* : the process of changing from a liquid to a vapor

eve *n* **1** : EVENING **2** : the evening or day before a special day **3** : the period just before an important event

¹even *adj* **1** : having a flat, smooth, or level surface **2** : being on the same line or level **3** : staying the same over a period of time **4** : equal in size, number, or amount **5** : not giving an advantage to one side : FAIR **6** : possible to divide by two — **even·ly** *adv* — **even·ness** *n*

²even *adv* **1** — used to stress a highly unlikely condition or instance **2** : to a greater extent or degree : STILL **3** : so much as **4** : INDEED **5** : at the very time

³even *vb* **evened; even·ing** : to make or become smooth or equal

eve·ning *n* : the final part of the day and early part of the night

evening star *n* : a bright planet (as Venus) seen in the western sky after sunset

event *n* **1** : something important or notable that happens **2** : a social occasion (as a party) **3** : the fact of happening **4** : a contest in a program of sports

event·ful *adj* **1** : full of important happenings **2** : very important

even·tu·al *adj* : coming at some later time — **even·tu·al·ly** *adv*

ev·er *adv* **1** : at any time **2** : in any way **3** : ALWAYS 1

ev·er·glade *n* : a swampy grassland

¹ev·er·green *n* : a plant (as a pine or a laurel) having leaves that stay green through more than one growing season

²evergreen *adj* : having leaves that stay green through more than one growing season

ev·er·last·ing *adj* **1** : lasting forever : ETERNAL **2** : going on for a long time

ev·ery *adj* **1** : including each of a group or series without leaving out any **2** : at regularly spaced times or distances

ev·ery·body *pron* : every person

ev·ery·day *adj* : used or suitable for every day : ORDINARY

ev·ery·one *pron* : every person

ev·ery·thing *pron* : all that exists or is important

ev·ery·where *adv* : in or to every place

evict *vb* **evict·ed; evict·ing** : to force (someone) to leave a place

ev·i·dence *n* **1** : a sign which shows that something exists or is true : INDICATION **2** : material presented to a court to help find the truth about something

ev·i·dent *adj* : clear to the sight or to the mind : PLAIN — **ev·i·dent·ly** *adv*

¹evil *adj* **1** : morally bad : WICKED **2** : causing harm : tending to injure

²evil *n* **1** : something that brings sorrow, trouble, or destruction **2** : the fact of suffering or wrongdoing **3** : bad behavior or moral state : WICKEDNESS

evoke *vb* **evoked; evok·ing** : to bring to mind

evo·lu·tion *n* **1** : the theory that the various kinds of existing animals and plants have come from kinds that existed in the past **2** : the process of development of an animal or a plant

evolve *vb* **evolved; evolv·ing** : to change or develop gradually

ewe *n* : a female sheep

ex- *prefix* : former

¹ex·act *adj* : completely correct or precise : ACCURATE — **ex·act·ly** *adv* — **ex·act·ness** *n*

²exact *vb* **ex·act·ed; ex·act·ing** : to demand and get by force or threat

ex·act·ing *adj* : expecting a lot from a person

ex·ag·ger·ate *vb* **ex·ag·ger·at·ed; ex·ag·ger·at·ing** : to describe as larger or greater than what is true

ex·ag·ger·a·tion *n* **1** : the act of describing as larger or greater than what is true **2** : a statement that has been enlarged beyond what is true

ex·alt *vb* **ex·alt·ed; ex·alt·ing 1** : to raise to a higher level **2** : to praise highly

ex·am *n* : EXAMINATION

ex·am·i·na·tion *n* **1** : the act of checking closely and carefully **2** : a test given to determine progress, fitness, or knowledge

ex·am·ine *vb* **ex·am·ined; ex·am·in·ing 1** : to

example 150

look at or check carefully **2** : to question closely

ex·am·ple *n* **1** : something to be imitated : MODEL **2** : a sample of something taken to show what the whole is like : INSTANCE **3** : a problem to be solved to show how a rule works **4** : something that is a warning to others

ex·as·per·ate *vb* **ex·as·per·at·ed; ex·as·per·at·ing** : to make angry

ex·as·per·a·tion *n* : extreme annoyance : ANGER

ex·ca·vate *vb* **ex·ca·vat·ed; ex·ca·vat·ing 1** : to expose to view by digging away a covering **2** : to hollow out : form a hole in **3** : to make by hollowing out **4** : to dig out and remove

ex·ca·va·tion *n* **1** : the act of excavating **2** : a hollow place formed by excavating

ex·ceed *vb* **ex·ceed·ed; ex·ceed·ing 1** : to be greater than **2** : to go or be beyond the limit of

ex·ceed·ing·ly *adv* : to a very great degree

ex·cel *vb* **ex·celled; ex·cel·ling** : to do better than others : SURPASS

ex·cel·lence *n* : high quality

ex·cel·lent *adj* : very good of its kind — **ex·cel·lent·ly** *adv*

¹ex·cept *prep* **1** : not including **2** : other than : BUT

²except *conj* : if it were not for the fact that : ONLY

³except *vb* **ex·cept·ed; ex·cept·ing** : to leave out from a number or a whole : EXCLUDE

ex·cep·tion *n* **1** : someone or something that is not included **2** : a case to which a rule does not apply **3** : an objection or a reason for objecting

ex·cep·tion·al *adj* **1** : being unusual **2** : better than average : SUPERIOR — **ex·cep·tion·al·ly** *adv*

¹ex·cess *n* **1** : a state of being more than enough **2** : the amount by which something is or has too much

²excess *adj* : more than is usual or acceptable

ex·ces·sive *adj* : being too much — **ex·ces·sive·ly** *adv*

¹ex·change *n* **1** : an act of giving or taking of one thing in return for another : TRADE **2** : a place where goods or services are exchanged **3** : the act of giving and receiving between two groups

²exchange *vb* **ex·changed; ex·chang·ing** : to give or take one thing in return for another : TRADE, SWAP

ex·cit·able *adj* : easily excited

ex·cite *vb* **ex·cit·ed; ex·cit·ing 1** : to stir up feeling in **2** : to increase the activity of

ex·cit·ed *adj* : very enthusiastic and eager — **ex·cit·ed·ly** *adv*

ex·cite·ment *n* **1** : something that stirs up feelings of great enthusiasm and interest **2** : a feeling of great enthusiasm and interest : the state of being excited

ex·cit·ing *adj* : producing excitement

ex·claim *vb* **ex·claimed; ex·claim·ing** : to speak or cry out suddenly or with strong feeling

ex·cla·ma·tion *n* : a sharp or sudden cry or expression of strong feeling

exclamation point *n* : a punctuation mark ! used to show force in speaking or strong feeling

ex·clam·a·to·ry *adj* : containing or using exclamation

ex·clude *vb* **ex·clud·ed; ex·clud·ing** : to shut out : keep out

ex·clu·sion *n* : the act of shutting or keeping out : the state of being shut or kept out

ex·clu·sive *adj* **1** : excluding or trying to exclude others **2** : ⁴SOLE 2 **3** : ENTIRE, COMPLETE — **ex·clu·sive·ly** *adv*

ex·crete *vb* **ex·cret·ed; ex·cret·ing** : to separate and give off cellular waste matter from the body usually as urine or sweat

ex·cre·tion *n* **1** : the act or process of separating and giving off cellular waste matter from the body **2** : waste material given off from the body

ex·cre·to·ry *adj* : of or relating to excretion : used in excreting

ex·cur·sion *n* **1** : a brief trip for pleasure **2** : a trip at special reduced rates

ex·cus·able *adj* : possible to excuse

¹ex·cuse *vb* **ex·cused; ex·cus·ing 1** : to make apology for **2** : to overlook or pardon as of little importance **3** : to let off from doing something **4** : to be an acceptable reason for

²ex·cuse *n* **1** : a reason given for having done something wrong **2** : something that is an acceptable reason for or justifies **3** : a reason for doing something

ex·e·cute *vb* **ex·e·cut·ed; ex·e·cut·ing 1** : to kill according to a legal order **2** : to put into effect : CARRY OUT, PERFORM **3** : to make according to a design

ex·e·cu·tion *n* **1** : the act of killing someone as a legal penalty **2** : the act of doing or performing something

¹ex·ec·u·tive *adj* **1** : fitted for or relating to the managing or directing of things **2** : relating to the carrying out of the law and the conduct of public affairs

²executive *n* **1** : a person who manages or directs **2** : the executive branch of a government

ex·em·pli·fy *vb* **ex·em·pli·fied; ex·em·pli·fy·ing** : to serve as an example of

¹ex·empt *adj* : free or released from some requirement that other persons must meet or deal with

²exempt *vb* **ex·empt·ed; ex·empt·ing** : to release from a requirement that others must meet

ex·emp·tion *n* : freedom from having to do something that other people are required to do

¹ex·er·cise *n* **1** : the act of putting into use, action, or practice **2** : bodily activity for the sake of improving physical fitness **3** : a school lesson or other task performed to develop skill : practice work : DRILL **4 exercises** *pl* : a program of songs, speeches, and announcements of awards and honors

²exercise *vb* **ex·er·cised; ex·er·cis·ing 1** : to put into use : EXERT **2** : to take part in bodily activity for the sake of improving physical fitness **3** : to use again and again to train or develop

ex·ert *vb* **ex·ert·ed; ex·ert·ing 1** : to put forth (as strength) : bring into use **2** : to make an effort

ex·er·tion *n* **1** : the act of putting into use **2** : use of strength or ability

ex·hale *vb* **ex·haled; ex·hal·ing 1** : to breathe out **2** : to send forth : give off

¹ex·haust *vb* **ex·haust·ed; ex·haust·ing 1** : to tire out : FATIGUE **2** : to use up completely **3** : to try out all of

²exhaust *n* **1** : the gas that escapes from an engine **2** : a system of pipes through which exhaust escapes

ex·haus·tion *n* **1** : the condition of being very tired **2** : the act of using up completely

¹ex·hib·it *vb* **ex·hib·it·ed; ex·hib·it·ing 1** : to show by outward signs : REVEAL **2** : to put on display

²exhibit *n* **1** : an article or collection shown in an exhibition **2** : an object or document presented as evidence in a court of law

ex·hi·bi·tion *n* **1** : the act of showing **2** : a public showing (as of athletic skill or works of art)

ex·hil·a·rate *vb* **ex·hil·a·rat·ed; ex·hil·a·rat·ing** : to make cheerful or excited

ex·hort *vb* **ex·hort·ed; ex·hort·ing** : to try to influence by words or advice : urge strongly

¹ex·ile *n* **1** : the situation of a person who is forced to leave his or her own country **2** : the period of time someone is forced to live away from his or her country **3** : a person who is forced to leave his or her own country

²exile *vb* **ex·iled; ex·il·ing** : to force (someone) to leave his or her own country

ex·ist *vb* **ex·ist·ed; ex·ist·ing 1** : to have actual being : be real **2** : to be found : OCCUR **3** : to continue to live

ex·is·tence *n* **1** : the fact or the condition of being or of being real **2** : the state of being alive : LIFE

¹ex·it *n* **1** : the act of going out of or away from a place : DEPARTURE **2** : a way of getting out of a place

²exit *vb* **ex·it·ed; ex·it·ing** : LEAVE 5, DEPART

ex·o·dus *n* : the departure of a large number of people at the same time

ex·or·bi·tant *adj* : more than what is fair, reasonable, or expected

exo·sphere *n* : the outermost region of the atmosphere

ex·ot·ic *adj* **1** : very different, strange, or unusual **2** : introduced from another country : not native

ex·pand *vb* **ex·pand·ed; ex·pand·ing 1** : to grow or increase in size, number, or amount **2** : to open wide : UNFOLD **3** : to take up or cause to take up more space **4** : to speak or write about in greater detail

ex·panse *n* : a wide area or stretch

ex·pan·sion *n* : the act of growing or increasing : ENLARGEMENT

ex·pect *vb* **ex·pect·ed; ex·pect·ing 1** : to think that something probably will be or happen **2** : to await the arrival of **3** : to consider to be obliged **4** : to consider reasonable, due, or necessary

ex·pec·tant *adj* **1** : looking forward to or waiting for something **2** : awaiting the birth of a child

ex·pec·ta·tion *n* **1** : the state of looking forward to or waiting for something **2** : something expected

ex·pe·di·ent *adj* : providing a quick and easy way to accomplish something — **ex·pe·di·ent·ly** *adv*

ex·pe·di·tion *n* **1** : a journey for a particular purpose **2** : a group of people traveling for exploration or adventure

ex·pel *vb* **ex·pelled; ex·pel·ling 1** : to force to leave **2** : to force out

ex·pend *vb* **ex·pend·ed; ex·pend·ing 1** : to pay out : SPEND **2** : to use up

ex·pen·di·ture *n* **1** : the act of spending (as money, time, or energy) **2** : something that is spent

ex·pense *n* **1** : something spent or required to be spent : COST **2** : a cause for spending

ex·pen·sive *adj* : COSTLY 1

¹ex·pe·ri·ence *n* **1** : the process of living through an event or events **2** : the skill or knowledge gained by actually doing a thing **3** : something that one has actually done or lived through

²**experience** vb **ex·pe·ri·enced; ex·pe·ri·enc·ing** : to undergo or live through : have experience of

ex·pe·ri·enced adj : made skillful or wise from having lived through or undergone something

¹**ex·per·i·ment** n : a trial or test made to find out about something

²**ex·per·i·ment** vb **ex·per·i·ment·ed; ex·per·i·ment·ing** : to try or test a new way, idea, or activity : to make experiments

ex·per·i·men·tal adj : relating to, based on, or used for experiment

¹**ex·pert** adj : showing special skill or knowledge gained from experience or training — **ex·pert·ly** adv

²**ex·pert** n : a person with special skill or knowledge of a subject

ex·per·tise n : the skill or knowledge of an expert

ex·pi·ra·tion n **1** : the end of something that lasts for a certain period of time **2** : the act of breathing out

ex·pire vb **ex·pired; ex·pir·ing 1** : to come to an end **2** : ¹DIE 1 **3** : to breathe out : EXHALE

ex·plain vb **ex·plained; ex·plain·ing 1** : to make clear : CLARIFY **2** : to give the reasons for or cause of

ex·pla·na·tion n **1** : the act or process of making clear or giving reasons for **2** : a statement that makes something clear or gives reasons for something

ex·plan·a·to·ry adj : giving explanation

ex·plic·it adj : so clear in statement that there is no doubt about the meaning

ex·plode vb **ex·plod·ed; ex·plod·ing 1** : to burst or cause to burst with violence and noise **2** : to suddenly show or say with great emotion

¹**ex·ploit** n : an exciting or daring act

²**ex·ploit** vb **ex·ploit·ed; ex·ploit·ing 1** : to get the value or use out of **2** : to take unfair advantage of

ex·plo·ra·tion n : the act or an instance of searching through or into

ex·plore vb **ex·plored; ex·plor·ing 1** : to search through or into : study closely **2** : to go into or through for purposes of discovery or adventure — **ex·plor·er** n

ex·plo·sion n **1** : a sudden and noisy bursting (as of a bomb) : the act of exploding **2** : a sudden outburst of feeling

¹**ex·plo·sive** adj **1** : able to cause explosion **2** : tending to show anger easily : likely to explode — **ex·plo·sive·ly** adv

²**explosive** n : a substance that is used to cause an explosion

ex·po·nent n : a numeral written above and to the right of a number to show how many times the number is to be used as a factor

¹**ex·port** vb **ex·port·ed; ex·port·ing** : to send a product to another country to sell it

²**ex·port** n **1** : something that is sent to another country to be sold **2** : the act of sending a product to another country to be sold

ex·pose vb **ex·posed; ex·pos·ing 1** : to leave without protection, shelter, or care : subject to a harmful condition **2** : to cause to be affected or influenced by something **3** : to let light strike the photographic film or plate in taking a picture **4** : to make known : REVEAL

ex·po·si·tion n **1** : an explanation of something **2** : a public exhibition

ex·po·sure n **1** : the fact or condition of being subject to some effect or influence **2** : the condition that results from being unprotected especially from severe weather (as extreme cold) **3** : an act of making something public **4** : the act of letting light strike a photographic film or the time during which light strikes a film **5** : a section of a roll of film for one picture **6** : position with respect to direction

ex·pound vb **ex·pound·ed; ex·pound·ing** : EXPLAIN 1, INTERPRET

¹**ex·press** vb **ex·pressed; ex·press·ing 1** : to make known especially in words **2** : to represent by a sign or symbol **3** : to send by a quick method of delivery

²**express** adj **1** : clearly stated **2** : of a certain sort **3** : sent or traveling at high speed

³**express** vb **1** : a system for the quick transportation of goods **2** : a vehicle (as a train or elevator) run at special speed with few or no stops

ex·pres·sion n **1** : the act or process of making known especially in words **2** : a meaningful word or saying **3** : the look on someone's face **4** : a way of speaking, singing, or playing that shows mood or feeling

ex·pres·sive adj **1** : showing emotions : full of expression **2** : making something known — **ex·pres·sive·ly** adv

ex·press·ly adv : for the stated purpose : ESPECIALLY

ex·press·way n : a highway for rapid traffic

ex·pul·sion n : the act of forcing to leave : the state of being forced to leave

ex·qui·site adj **1** : finely made or done **2** : very pleasing (as through beauty) **3** : INTENSE 1, EXTREME

ex·tend vb **ex·tend·ed; ex·tend·ing 1** : to hold out **2** : to stretch out or across something **3** : to make longer **4** : ¹STRETCH 2 **5** : ENLARGE

ex·ten·sion n **1** : the act of making something longer or greater **2** : an increase in length or time **3** : a part forming an addition or enlargement

ex·ten·sive adj : including or affecting many things

ex·tent n **1** : the distance or range that is covered or affected by something **2** : the point, degree, or limit to which something reaches or extends

¹ex·te·ri·or *adj* : EXTERNAL

²exterior *n* **1** : an external part or surface **2** : the way someone appears

ex·ter·mi·nate *vb* **ex·ter·mi·nat·ed; ex·ter·mi·nat·ing** : to get rid of completely : wipe out — **ex·ter·mi·na·tion** *n*

ex·ter·nal *adj* : situated on or relating to the outside : OUTSIDE

ex·tinct *adj* **1** : no longer active **2** : no longer existing

ex·tinc·tion *n* : the state of being, becoming, or making extinct

ex·tin·guish *vb* **ex·tin·guished; ex·tin·guish·ing 1** : to cause to stop burning **2** : to cause to die out — **ex·tin·guish·er** *n*

ex·tol *vb* **ex·tolled; ex·tol·ling** : to praise highly : GLORIFY

¹ex·tra *adj* : being more than what is usual, expected, or due

²extra *adv* : beyond the usual size, amount, or extent

³extra *n* **1** : something additional **2** : an added charge **3** : a special edition of a newspaper **4** : a person hired for a group scene (as in a movie)

extra- *prefix* : outside : beyond

¹ex·tract *vb* **ex·tract·ed; ex·tract·ing 1** : to remove by pulling **2** : to get out by pressing, distilling, or by a chemical process **3** : to choose and take out for separate use

²ex·tract *n* **1** : a selection from a writing **2** : a product obtained by pressing, distilling, or a chemical process

ex·trac·tion *n* **1** : the act of pulling out **2** : ORIGIN 2, DESCENT

ex·tra·cur·ric·u·lar *adj* : relating to activities (as athletics) that are offered by a school but are not part of the course of study

ex·traor·di·nary *adj* : so unusual as to be remarkable — **ex·traor·di·nari·ly** *adv*

ex·trav·a·gance *n* **1** : the wasteful or careless spending of money **2** : something that is wasteful especially of money **3** : the quality or fact of being wasteful especially of money

ex·trav·a·gant *adj* **1** : going beyond what is reasonable or suitable **2** : wasteful especially of money — **ex·trav·a·gant·ly** *adv*

¹ex·treme *adj* **1** : very great **2** : farthest away **3** : more demanding or dangerous than normal — **ex·treme·ly** *adv*

²extreme *n* **1** : something as far as possible from a center or from its opposite **2** : the greatest possible degree : MAXIMUM

ex·trem·i·ty *n, pl* **ex·trem·i·ties 1** : the farthest limit, point, or part **2** : an end part (as a foot) of a limb of the body **3** : an extreme degree (as of emotion)

ex·tri·cate *vb* **ex·tri·cat·ed; ex·tri·cat·ing** : to free from a trap or difficulty

ex·u·ber·ant *adj* : filled with energy and enthusiasm — **ex·u·ber·ance** *n*

ex·ult *vb* **ex·ult·ed; ex·ult·ing** : to feel or show great happiness : REJOICE

ex·ul·tant *adj* : very happy and excited — **ex·ul·tant·ly** *adv*

-ey — see -Y

¹eye *n* **1** : the organ of seeing that in vertebrates is a round organ filled with a jellylike material, is located in a bony cavity in the skull, and has a lens which focuses light on the retina **2** : the eye along with its surrounding parts (as the eyelids) **3** : the colored surface of the iris **4** : the ability to see **5** : the ability to recognize or appreciate **6** : ²GLANCE **7** : close attention : WATCH **8** : JUDGMENT 1 **9** : something like or suggesting an eye **10** : the center of something — **eyed** *adj* — **eye·less** *adj*

²eye *vb* **eyed; eye·ing** *or* **ey·ing** : to look at : watch closely

eye·ball *n* : the whole eye

eye·brow *n* : the arch or ridge over the eye : the hair on the ridge over the eye

eye·drop·per *n* : DROPPER

eye·glass *n* **1** : a glass lens used to help a person to see clearly **2 eyeglasses** *pl* : GLASS 3

eye·lash *n* : one of the hairs that grow along the top of the eyelid

eye·let *n* **1** : a small hole (as in cloth or leather) for a lace or rope **2** : GROMMET

eye·lid *n* : the thin movable fold of skin and muscle that can be closed over the eyeball

eye·piece *n* : the lens or combination of lenses at the eye end of an optical instrument (as a microscope or telescope)

eye·sight *n* : ¹SIGHT 4, VISION

eye·sore *n* : something that looks ugly

eye·tooth *n, pl* **eye·teeth** : a canine tooth of the upper jaw

F

f *n, pl* **f's** *or* **fs** *often cap* **1** : the sixth letter of the English alphabet **2** : a grade that shows a student's work is failing **3** : a musical note referred to by the letter F

f. *abbr* female

F *abbr* **1** Fahrenheit **2** false

fa *n* : the fourth note of the musical scale

fa·ble *n* **1** : a story that is not true **2** : a story in which animals speak and act like people and which is usually meant to teach a lesson

fab·ric *n* **1** : CLOTH 1 **2** : the basic structure

fab·u·lous *adj* **1** : extremely good **2** : very

great in amount or size **3** : told in or based on fable — **fab·u·lous·ly** *adv*

fa·cade *n* : the face or front of a building

¹face *n* **1** : the front part of the head **2** : an expression of the face **3** : outward appearance **4** : a funny or silly expression **5** : an expression showing displeasure **6** : ¹RESPECT 1 **7** : a front, upper, or outer surface **8** : one of the flat surfaces that bound a solid

²face *vb* **faced; fac·ing 1** : to have the front or face toward **2** : to cover the front or surface of **3** : to oppose with determination

face–off *n* **1** : a method of beginning play (as in hockey or lacrosse) in which the puck or ball is dropped between two opposing players **2** : a clashing of forces or ideas

fac·et *n* : one of the small flat surfaces on a cut gem

fa·ce·tious *adj* : intended or trying to be funny — **fa·ce·tious·ly** *adv*

face–to–face *adv or adj* : within each other's presence

fa·cial *adj* : of or relating to the face

fa·cil·i·tate *vb* **fa·cil·i·tat·ed; fa·cil·i·tat·ing** : to make easier

fa·cil·i·ty *n, pl* **fa·cil·i·ties 1** : something built for a particular purpose **2** : something that makes an action, operation, or activity easier **3** : ease in doing something

fac·sim·i·le *n, pl* **fac·sim·i·les 1** : an exact copy **2** : a system of sending and reproducing printed matter or pictures by means of signals sent over telephone lines

fact *n* **1** : something that really exists or has occurred **2** : a true piece of information — **in fact** : in truth : ACTUALLY

¹fac·tor *n* **1** : something that helps produce a result **2** : any of the numbers that when multiplied together form a product

²factor *vb* **fac·tored; fac·tor·ing 1** : to be considered in making a judgment **2** : to find the factors of a number

fac·to·ry *n, pl* **fac·to·ries** : a place where products are manufactured

fac·tu·al *adj* : relating to or based on facts — **fac·tu·al·ly** *adv*

fac·ul·ty *n, pl* **fac·ul·ties 1** : ability to do something : TALENT **2** : one of the powers of the mind or body **3** : the teachers in a school or college

fad *n* : something that is very popular for a short time

fade *vb* **fad·ed; fad·ing 1** : to lose or cause to lose brightness of color **2** : to dry up : WITHER **3** : to grow dim or faint

Fahr·en·heit *adj* : relating to or having a temperature scale on which the boiling point of water is at 212 degrees above the zero of the

scale and the freezing point is at 32 degrees above zero

¹fail *vb* **failed; fail·ing 1** : to be unsuccessful **2** : to grade as not passing **3** : to stop functioning **4** : to be or become absent or not enough **5** : to become bankrupt **6** : ¹NEGLECT 2 **7** : DISAPPOINT, DESERT **8** : to lose strength : WEAKEN **9** : to fall short **10** : to die away

²fail *n* : FAILURE 2

fail·ing *n* : a weakness or flaw in a person's character, behavior, or ability

fail·ure *n* **1** : a lack of success **2** : the act of neglecting or forgetting to do or perform **3** : an instance of not working properly **4** : a loss of the ability to work normally **5** : someone or something that has not succeeded **6** : an instance of falling short **7** : BANKRUPTCY

¹faint *adj* **faint·er; faint·est 1** : not clear or plain : DIM **2** : weak or dizzy and likely to collapse **3** : lacking strength — **faint·ly** *adv* — **faint·ness** *n*

²faint *vb* **faint·ed; faint·ing** : to suddenly lose consciousness

³faint *n* : an act or condition of suddenly losing consciousness

faint·heart·ed *adj* : COWARDLY 1

¹fair *adj* **fair·er; fair·est 1** : not favoring one over another **2** : observing the rules **3** : neither good nor bad **4** : not stormy or cloudy **5** : not dark **6** : attractive in appearance : BEAUTIFUL **7** : being within the foul lines — **fair·ness** *n*

²fair *adv* : according to the rules

³fair *n* **1** : a large public event at which farm animals and products are shown and entertainment, amusements, and food are provided **2** : an event at which people gather to buy, sell, or get information **3** : a sale of articles for charity

fair·ground *n* : an area set aside for fairs, circuses, or exhibitions

fair·ly *adv* **1** : in a just and proper manner **2** : very close to **3** : for the most part : RATHER

fair·way *n* : the mowed part of a golf course between a tee and a green

¹fairy *n, pl* **fair·ies** : an imaginary magical creature who has the form of a tiny human being

²fairy *adj* : relating to or like a fairy

fairy·land *n* **1** : an imaginary place where fairies live **2** : a beautiful or magical place

fairy tale *n* : a simple children's story about magical creatures

faith *n* **1** : strong belief or trust **2** : belief in God **3** : a system of religious beliefs : RELIGION **4** : loyalty to duty or to a person or thing

faith·ful *adj* **1** : firm in devotion or support **2**

: RELIABLE **3** : true to the facts : ACCURATE — **faith·ful·ly** *adv* — **faith·ful·ness** *n*

faith·less *adj* : not worthy of trust : DISLOYAL

¹fake *adj* : not true or real

²fake *n* : a person or thing that is not really what is pretended

³fake *vb* **faked; fak·ing** **1** : ¹PRETEND 2 **2** : to change or treat in a way that gives a false effect **3** : to imitate in order to deceive

fal·con *n* **1** : a hawk trained for use in hunting small game **2** : any of several small hawks with long wings and swift flight

fal·con·ry *n* : the sport of hunting with a falcon

¹fall *vb* **fell; fall·en; fall·ing** **1** : to come or go down freely by the force of gravity **2** : to come as if by falling **3** : to become lower (as in degree or value) **4** : to topple from an upright position **5** : to collapse wounded or dead **6** : to become captured **7** : to occur at a certain time **8** : to pass from one condition of body or mind to another — **fall back** : ²RETREAT 1 — **fall short** : to fail to be as good or successful as expected

²fall *n* **1** : the act or an instance of going or coming down by the force of gravity **2** : AUTUMN **3** : a thing or quantity that falls **4** : a loss of greatness : DOWNFALL **5** : WATERFALL — usually used in pl. **6** : a decrease in size, amount, or value **7** : the distance something falls

fal·la·cy *n, pl* **fal·la·cies** **1** : a false or mistaken idea **2** : false reasoning

fall·out *n* **1** : the usually radioactive particles falling through the atmosphere as a result of a nuclear explosion **2** : the bad result of something

fal·low *adj* : not tilled or planted

fallow deer *n* : a small European deer with broad antlers and a pale yellowish coat spotted with white in summer

¹false *adj* **fals·er; fals·est** **1** : not true, genuine, or honest **2** : not faithful or loyal **3** : not based on facts or sound judgment **4** : CARELESS 2 — **false·ly** *adv*

²false *adv* : in a dishonest or misleading manner

false·hood *n* **1** : ³LIE **2** : the habit of lying

fal·si·fy *vb* **fal·si·fied; fal·si·fy·ing** : to change in order to deceive

fal·si·ty *n, pl* **fal·si·ties** **1** : ³LIE **2** : the quality or state of being not true or genuine

fal·ter *vb* **fal·tered; fal·ter·ing** **1** : to move unsteadily : WAVER **2** : to hesitate in speech **3** : to hesitate in purpose or action

fame *n* : the fact or condition of being known or recognized by many people

famed *adj* : known widely and well : FAMOUS

fa·mil·ial *adj* : relating to or typical of a family

fa·mil·iar *adj* **1** : often seen, heard, or experienced **2** : closely acquainted : INTIMATE **3** : having a good knowledge of **4** : INFORMAL 1 **5** : too friendly or bold

fa·mil·iar·i·ty *n, pl* **fa·mil·iar·i·ties** **1** : close friendship : INTIMACY **2** : good knowledge of something **3** : INFORMALITY

fa·mil·iar·ize *vb* **fa·mil·iar·ized; fa·mil·iar·iz·ing** : to make knowledgeable about

fam·i·ly *n, pl* **fam·i·lies** **1** : a social group made up of parents and their children **2** : a group of people who come from the same ancestor **3** : a group of people living together : HOUSEHOLD **4** : a group of things sharing certain characteristics **5** : a group of related living things (as plants or animals) that ranks above the genus and below the order in scientific classification

fam·ine *n* : a very great shortage of food that affects many people over a wide area

fam·ish *vb* **fam·ished; fam·ish·ing** : STARVE

fam·ished *adj* : very hungry

fa·mous *adj* : very well-known

fa·mous·ly *adv* : very well

¹fan *n* **1** : a machine or device that is used for producing a current of air **2** : something having a semicircular shape — **fan·like** *adj*

²fan *vb* **fanned; fan·ning** **1** : to direct a current of air upon with a fan **2** : to strike out in baseball

³fan *n* : an enthusiastic follower or admirer

¹fa·nat·ic *adj* : very or overly enthusiastic or devoted

²fanatic *n* : a very enthusiastic supporter or admirer

fan·ci·ful *adj* **1** : showing free use of the imagination **2** : coming from imagination rather than reason — **fan·ci·ful·ly** *adv*

¹fan·cy *adj* **fan·ci·er; fan·ci·est** **1** : not plain or ordinary **2** : being above the average (as in quality or price) **3** : done with great skill and grace — **fan·ci·ly** *adv* — **fan·ci·ness** *n*

²fancy *n, pl* **fan·cies** **1** : IMAGINATION 1 **2** : LIKING **3** : IDEA 2, NOTION

³fancy *vb* **fan·cied; fan·cy·ing** **1** : to have a liking for **2** : IMAGINE 1

fang *n* **1** : one of the long sharp teeth by which an animal seizes and holds its prey **2** : one of the usually two long hollow or grooved teeth by which a poisonous snake injects its poison — **fanged** *adj*

fan·ny *n* : a person's rear

fan·tas·tic *adj* **1** : produced by or like something produced by the imagination **2** : extremely good **3** : barely believable — **fan·tas·ti·cal·ly** *adv*

fan·ta·sy *n, pl* **fan·ta·sies** **1** : IMAGINATION 1 **2** : something produced by the imagination

¹**far** *adv* **far·ther** *or* **fur·ther; far·thest** *or* **fur·thest 1 :** at or to a great distance in space or time **2 :** to a great extent : MUCH **3 :** to or at a definite distance or point **4 :** to an advanced point — **by far :** by a great extent or degree

²**far** *adj* **far·ther** *or* **fur·ther; far·thest** *or* **fur·thest 1 :** very distant in space or time **2 :** the more distant of two **3 :** ¹LONG 2

far·away *adj* **1 :** ¹REMOTE 1, DISTANT **2 :** appearing as if lost in a daydream

farce *n* **:** something that is ridiculous

¹**fare** *vb* **fared; far·ing :** to get along : SUCCEED

²**fare** *n* **1 :** the money a person pays to travel (as on a bus) **2 :** a person paying a fare **3 :** FOOD 1

¹**fare·well** *n* **:** ²GOOD-BYE

²**fare·well** *adj* **:** relating to a time or act of leaving : FINAL

far·fetched *adj* **:** not likely to be true

¹**farm** *n* **1 :** a piece of land used for raising crops or animals **2 :** an area of water where fish or shellfish are grown

²**farm** *vb* **farmed; farm·ing 1 :** to use for raising crops or animals **2 :** to work on or run a farm — **farm·er** *n*

farm·hand *n* **:** a farm worker

farm·ing *n* **:** the occupation or business of running a farm

farm·yard *n* **:** the yard around or enclosed by farm buildings

far–off *adj* **:** distant in time or space

far–reach·ing *adj* **:** having a wide range, influence, or effect

far·sight·ed *adj* **1 :** able to see distant things more clearly than near ones **2 :** able to judge how something will work out in the future — **far·sight·ed·ness** *n*

¹**far·ther** *adv* **1 :** at or to a greater distance or more advanced point **2 :** more completely

²**farther** *adj* **:** more distant

¹**far·thest** *adj* **:** most distant

²**farthest** *adv* **1 :** to or at the greatest distance in space or time **2 :** to the most advanced point

fas·ci·nate *vb* **fas·ci·nat·ed; fas·ci·nat·ing 1 :** to seize and hold the attention of **2 :** to attract greatly

fas·ci·nat·ing *adj* **:** extremely interesting or charming

fas·ci·na·tion *n* **:** a great interest in or attraction to something

fas·cism *n, often cap* **:** a political system headed by a dictator in which the government controls business and labor and opposition is not permitted

fas·cist *n, often cap* **:** a person who supports or practices fascism

¹**fash·ion** *n* **1 :** the popular style of a thing at a certain time or among a certain group **2 :** MANNER 2, WAY

²**fashion** *vb* **fash·ioned; fash·ion·ing :** to give shape or form to

fash·ion·able *adj* **:** following the current fashion or style — **fash·ion·ably** *adv*

¹**fast** *adj* **fast·er; fast·est 1 :** moving, operating, or acting quickly **2 :** taking a short time **3 :** indicating ahead of the correct time **4 :** firmly placed **5 :** not likely to fade **6 :** totally loyal

²**fast** *adv* **fast·er; fast·est 1 :** with great speed **2 :** to the full extent : SOUND **3 :** in a firm or fixed way

³**fast** *vb* **fast·ed; fast·ing 1 :** to go without eating **2 :** to eat in small amounts or only certain foods

⁴**fast** *n* **1 :** the act of going without food **2 :** a time when no food is eaten

fas·ten *vb* **fas·tened; fas·ten·ing 1 :** to attach or join by or as if by pinning, tying, or nailing **2 :** to make firm and secure **3 :** to become fixed or joined — **fas·ten·er** *n*

fas·ten·ing *n* **:** something that holds another thing shut or in the right position

fast food *n* **:** food that is prepared and served quickly — **fast–food** *adj*

fast–for·ward *vb* **fast–for·ward·ed; fast–forward·ing :** to advance a recording (as of music or video) at a faster rate than normal

fas·tid·i·ous *adj* **:** hard to please : very particular

¹**fat** *adj* **fat·ter; fat·test 1 :** having much body fat **2 :** ¹THICK 1 **3 :** richly rewarding or profitable **4 :** swollen up — **fat·ness** *n*

²**fat** *n* **1 :** animal or plant tissue containing much greasy or oily material **2 :** any of numerous compounds of carbon, hydrogen, and oxygen that make up most of animal or plant fat and that are important to nutrition as sources of energy **3 :** a solid fat as distinguished from an oil **4 :** the best or richest part

fa·tal *adj* **1 :** causing death : MORTAL **2 :** causing ruin or failure — **fa·tal·ly** *adv*

fa·tal·i·ty *n, pl* **fa·tal·i·ties :** a death resulting from a disaster or accident

fate *n* **1 :** a power beyond human control that is believed to determine what happens : DESTINY **2 :** something that happens as though determined by fate : FORTUNE **3 :** final outcome

fate·ful *adj* **:** having serious results

¹**fa·ther** *n* **1 :** a male parent **2** *cap* **:** GOD 1 **3 :** ANCESTOR 1 **4 :** a person who cares for another as a father might **5 :** a person who invents or begins something **6 :** PRIEST — used especially to address a priest or as a priest's title — **fa·ther·hood** *n* — **fa·ther·less** *adj*

²**father** *vb* **fa·thered; fa·ther·ing 1 :** to become the father of **2 :** to care for as a father **3 :** to be the founder, producer, or author of

fa·ther–in–law *n, pl* **fa·thers–in–law :** the father of a person's husband or wife

fa·ther·land *n* **:** the land of a person's birth

fa·ther·ly *adj* **:** of or like a father

¹**fath·om** *n* **:** a unit of length equal to six feet (about 1.8 meters) used chiefly in measuring the depth of water

²**fathom** *vb* **fath·omed; fath·om·ing 1 :** to understand the reason for something **2 :** to measure the depth of water by means of a special line

¹**fa·tigue** *n* **1 :** a state of being very tired **2 fa·tigues** *pl* **:** the uniform worn by members of the military for physical labor

²**fatigue** *vb* **fa·tigued; fa·tigu·ing :** to tire by work or exertion

fat·ten *vb* **fat·tened; fat·ten·ing :** to make or become fat

fat·ty *adj* **fat·ti·er; fat·ti·est :** containing or like fat

fau·cet *n* **:** a fixture for controlling the flow of a liquid (as from a pipe or cask)

fault *n* **1 :** a weakness in character **:** FAILING **2 :** responsibility for something wrong **3 :** FLAW, IMPERFECTION **4 :** a crack in the earth's crust along which movement occurs — **at fault :** responsible for something wrong

fault·less *adj* **:** ¹PERFECT 1

faulty *adj* **fault·i·er; fault·i·est :** having a fault, flaw, or weakness **:** IMPERFECT

faun *n* **:** a Roman god of country life represented as part goat and part man

fau·na *n* **:** the animal life typical of a region, period, or special environment

¹**fa·vor** *n* **1 :** an act of kindness **2 :** APPROVAL 1, LIKING **3 :** a preference for one side over another **4 :** a small gift or decorative item — **in favor of 1 :** wanting or approving of **2 :** in support of

²**favor** *vb* **fa·vored; fa·vor·ing 1 :** to prefer especially unfairly **2 :** to approve of **3 :** to present with **4 :** to make possible or easier **5 :** to look like

fa·vor·able *adj* **1 :** showing approval **2 :** tending to help — **fa·vor·ably** *adv*

¹**fa·vor·ite** *n* **:** a person or a thing that is liked more than others

²**favorite** *adj* **:** most liked

fa·vor·it·ism *n* **:** the unfair treatment of some people better than others

¹**fawn** *n* **1 :** a young deer **2 :** a light grayish brown

²**fawn** *vb* **fawned; fawn·ing 1 :** to show affection — used especially of a dog **2 :** to try

to win favor by acting as if someone is superior

¹**fax** *n* **1 :** FACSIMILE 2 **2 :** a machine used to send or receive material by facsimile **3 :** something sent or received by facsimile

²**fax** *vb* **faxed; fax·ing :** to send material by facsimile

faze *vb* **fazed; faz·ing :** to cause to hesitate or feel fear

FBI *abbr* Federal Bureau of Investigation

¹**fear** *vb* **feared; fear·ing :** to be afraid of **:** feel fear

²**fear** *n* **:** a strong unpleasant feeling caused by being aware of danger or expecting something bad to happen

fear·ful *adj* **1 :** causing fear **2 :** filled with fear **3 :** showing or caused by fear — **fear·ful·ly** *adv* — **fear·ful·ness** *n*

fear·less *adj* **:** not afraid **:** BRAVE — **fear·less·ly** *adv* — **fear·less·ness** *n*

fear·some *adj* **:** very frightening

fea·si·ble *adj* **:** possible to do or accomplish

¹**feast** *n* **1 :** a fancy meal **2 :** a holy day observed by members of a religion

²**feast** *vb* **feast·ed; feast·ing 1 :** to eat well **2 :** ²DELIGHT 1

feat *n* **:** an act showing courage, strength, or skill

¹**feath·er** *n* **:** one of the light horny growths that make up the outer covering of a bird — **feath·ered** *adj*

²**feather** *vb* **feath·ered; feath·er·ing 1 :** to provide or decorate with feathers **2 :** to grow or form feathers

feath·ery *adj* **1 :** like a feather or tuft of feathers **2 :** covered with feathers

¹**fea·ture** *n* **1 :** a part (as the nose or the mouth) of the face **2 :** something especially noticeable **3 :** MOVIE 1 **4 :** a special story in a newspaper or magazine

²**feature** *vb* **fea·tured; fea·tur·ing 1 :** to have as a characteristic **2 :** to give special prominence to **3 :** to play an important part

Feb. *abbr* February

Feb·ru·ary *n* **:** the second month of the year

fe·ces *n pl* **:** body waste that passes out from the intestine

fed·er·al *adj* **:** relating to a nation formed by the union of several parts

fed·er·a·tion *n* **:** a union of organizations or states

fee *n* **1 :** an amount of money that must be paid **2 :** a charge for services

fee·ble *adj* **fee·bler; fee·blest 1 :** lacking in strength or endurance **2 :** not effective or sufficient — **fee·ble·ness** *n* — **fee·bly** *adv*

¹**feed** *vb* **fed; feed·ing 1 :** to give food to or give as food **2 :** to take food into the body **:** EAT **3 :** to supply with something nec-

essary (as to growth or operation) — **feed-er** *n*

²**feed** *n* : food especially for livestock

feed·back *n* : helpful information or criticism given to someone to indicate what can be done to improve something

¹**feel** *vb* **felt; feel·ing 1 :** to be aware of through physical contact **2 :** to examine or search for by touching **3 :** to be conscious of **4 :** to seem especially to the touch **5 :** to sense a physical, mental, or emotional state **6 :** to have sympathy **7 :** BELIEVE 4, THINK — **feel like :** to have an urge or desire to

²**feel** *n* **1 :** SENSATION 2, FEELING **2 :** the quality of something as learned through or as if through touch

feel·er *n* : a long flexible structure (as an insect's antenna) that is an organ of touch

feel·ing *n* **1 :** the sense by which a person knows whether things are hard or soft, hot or cold, heavy or light **2 :** a sensation of temperature or pressure **3 :** a state of mind **4 feelings** *pl* : the state of a person's emotions **5 :** an opinion, belief, or expectation

feet *pl of* FOOT

feign *vb* **feigned; feign·ing :** ¹PRETEND 2

¹**feint** *n* : a pretended blow or attack at one point or in one direction to take attention away from the point or direction the attack or blow is really coming from

²**feint** *vb* **feint·ed; feint·ing :** to make a feint

fe·lic·i·ty *n* : great happiness

¹**fe·line** *adj* **1 :** of or relating to the domestic cat or a related animal (as a lion) **2 :** like or like that of a cat

²**feline** *n* : CAT

¹**fell** *vb* **felled; fell·ing :** to cut or knock down

²**fell** *past of* FALL

¹**fel·low** *n* **1 :** a male person **2 :** COMPANION 1, COMRADE

²**fellow** *adj* : belonging to the same group or class

fel·low·ship *n* **1 :** friendly relationship existing among persons **2 :** a group with similar interests

fel·on *n* : ²CRIMINAL

fel·o·ny *n*, *pl* **fel·o·nies :** a very serious crime

¹**felt** *n* : a soft heavy cloth made by rolling and pressing fibers together

²**felt** *past and past participle of* FEEL

fem. *abbr* feminine

¹**fe·male** *adj* **1 :** of, relating to, or being the sex that bears young or lays eggs **2 :** having a pistil but no stamens **3 :** of or characteristic of women or girls

²**female** *n* **1 :** a woman or a girl **2 :** a person or animal that can bear young or lay eggs **3** : a plant with a pistil but no stamens

fem·i·nine *adj* **1 :** ¹FEMALE 1 **2 :** ¹FEMALE 3

fem·i·nism *n* **1 :** the belief that women and men should have equal rights and opportunities **2 :** organized activity on behalf of women's rights and interests — **fem·i·nist** *n or adj*

fe·mur *n*, *pl* **fe·murs** *or* **fem·o·ra :** the long leg bone that extends from the hip to the knee

¹**fence** *n* : a barrier (as of wood or wire) to prevent escape or entry or to mark a boundary

²**fence** *vb* **fenced; fenc·ing 1 :** to enclose with a fence **2 :** to fight with swords **:** to practice the sport of fencing — **fenc·er** *n*

fenc·ing *n* : the sport of having a pretended fight with blunted swords

fend *vb* **fend·ed; fend·ing 1 :** to drive away or repel **2 :** to get along without help

fend·er *n* : the part of a motor vehicle or bicycle that covers a wheel

fe·ral *adj* : having escaped from the care of people and become wild

¹**fer·ment** *vb* **fer·ment·ed; fer·ment·ing :** to go through a chemical change that results in the production of alcohol

²**fer·ment** *n* **1 :** something (as yeast) that causes fermentation **2 :** an excited state

fer·men·ta·tion *n* : a chemical breaking down of a substance (as sugar) that is controlled by an enzyme, usually does not require oxygen, and typically results in the production of alcohol and carbon dioxide

fern *n* : a plant that produces spores instead of seeds and no flowers and whose leaves are usually divided into many parts — **fern-like** *adj*

fe·ro·cious *adj* : FIERCE 1, SAVAGE — **fe·ro·cious·ly** *adv*

fe·roc·i·ty *n*, *pl* **fe·roc·i·ties :** the quality or state of being fierce or savage

¹**fer·ret** *n* : a domesticated animal with usually white or light brown or gray fur that originates from the European polecat

²**ferret** *vb* **fer·ret·ed; fer·ret·ing :** to find by eager searching

Fer·ris wheel *n* : an amusement park ride consisting of a large vertical wheel that is moved by a motor and has seats around its rim

¹**fer·ry** *vb* **fer·ried; fer·ry·ing 1 :** to carry by boat over a body of water **2 :** to cross a body of water by a ferryboat **3 :** to transport for a short distance

²**ferry** *n*, *pl* **fer·ries 1 :** FERRYBOAT **2 :** a place where persons or things are ferried

fer·ry·boat *n* : a boat used to carry passengers, vehicles, or goods

fer·tile *adj* **1 :** producing many plants or crops **2 :** producing many ideas **3 :** capable of developing and growing

fer·til·i·ty *n* : the condition of being fertile

fer·til·iza·tion *n* **1** : an act or process of making fertile **2** : the joining of an egg cell and a sperm cell to form the first stage of an embryo

fer·til·ize *vb* **fer·til·ized; fer·til·iz·ing** : to make fertile or more fertile

fer·til·iz·er *n* : material added to soil to make it more fertile

fer·vent *adj* : felt very strongly — **fer·vent·ly** *adv*

fer·vor *n* : strong feeling or expression

fes·ter *vb* **fes·tered; fes·ter·ing** : to become painfully red and sore and usually full of pus

fes·ti·val *n* **1** : a time or event of celebration **2** : a program of cultural events or entertainment

fes·tive *adj* **1** : having to do with a feast or festival **2** : very merry and joyful

fes·tiv·i·ty *n, pl* **fes·tiv·i·ties** **1** : festive activity **2** : celebration and enjoyment

¹fes·toon *n* : a chain or strip hanging between two points as decoration

²festoon *vb* **fes·tooned; fes·toon·ing** : to hang or form festoons or other decorations on

fetch *vb* **fetched; fetch·ing** **1** : to go after and bring back **2** : to bring as a price : sell for

fetch·ing *adj* : very attractive

¹fet·ter *n* **1** : a chain for the feet **2** : something that holds back : RESTRAINT

²fetter *vb* **fet·tered; fet·ter·ing** **1** : to chain the feet of **2** : to keep from moving or acting freely

fe·tus *n* : an animal not yet born or hatched but more developed than an embryo

¹feud *n* : a long bitter quarrel between two people, families, or groups

²feud *vb* **feud·ed; feud·ing** : to carry on a long bitter quarrel

feu·dal *adj* : relating to feudalism

feu·dal·ism *n* : a social system existing in medieval Europe in which people worked and fought for nobles who gave them protection and land in return

fe·ver *n* **1** : a body temperature that is higher than normal **2** : a disease involving fever

fe·ver·ish *adj* **1** : having a fever **2** : characteristic of or relating to a fever **3** : showing great emotion or activity : HECTIC — **fe·ver·ish·ly** *adv*

¹few *pron* : not many people or things

²few *adj* **few·er; few·est** : not many but some

³few *n* : a small number of people or things

few·er *pron* : a smaller number

fez *n, pl* **fez·zes** : a round red felt hat that usually has a tassel but no brim

fi·an·cé *pron* : a man that a woman is engaged to be married to

fi·an·cée *n* : a woman that a man is engaged to be married to

fi·as·co *n, pl* **fi·as·coes** : a complete failure

¹fib *n* : a lie about something unimportant

²fib *vb* **fibbed; fib·bing** : to tell a lie about something unimportant — **fib·ber** *n*

fi·ber *n* **1** : a thread or a structure or object resembling a thread **2** : plant material that cannot be digested

fi·ber·glass *n* : glass in the form of fibers used in various products (as filters and insulation)

fiber op·tics *n pl* : thin transparent fibers of glass or plastic that transmit light throughout their length

fi·brous *adj* : containing, made of, or like fibers

fib·u·la *n, pl* **fib·u·lae** *or* **fib·u·las** : the outer and smaller of the two bones between the knee and ankle

–fication *n suffix* : the act or process of or the result of

fick·le *adj* : changing often : not reliable — **fick·le·ness** *n*

fic·tion *n* **1** : something told or written that is not fact **2** : a made-up story **3** : works of literature that are not true stories

fic·tion·al *adj* : not real or true : MADE-UP

fic·ti·tious *adj* : not real

¹fid·dle *n* : VIOLIN

²fiddle *vb* **fid·dled; fid·dling** **1** : to play on a fiddle **2** : to move the hands or fingers restlessly **3** : to spend time in aimless activity **4** : to change or handle in a useless way **5** : to handle in a harmful or foolish way : TAMPER — **fid·dler** *n*

fi·del·i·ty *n* **1** : LOYALTY **2** : ACCURACY

fidg·et *vb* **fidg·et·ed; fidg·et·ing** : to move in a restless or nervous way

fidg·ety *adj* : nervous and restless

fief *n* : an estate of land given to a vassal by a feudal lord

¹field *n* **1** : a piece of open, cleared, or cultivated land **2** : a piece of land put to a special use or giving a special product **3** : an area of activity or influence **4** : a background on which something is drawn, painted, or mounted

²field *adj* : relating to a field

³field *vb* **field·ed; field·ing** : to catch or stop and throw a ball

field day *n* : a day of outdoor sports, activities, and athletic competitions

field·er *n* : a baseball player other than the pitcher or catcher on the team that is not at bat

field glasses *n pl* : binoculars without prisms

field goal *n* : a score in football made by kicking the ball through the goal during ordinary play

field hockey *n* : hockey played on a field

field trip *n* : a visit to a place (such as a museum) made by students to learn about something

fiend *n* **1** : DEMON 1, DEVIL **2** : a very wicked or cruel person **3** : ²FANATIC — **fiend·ish** *adj* — **fiend·ish·ly** *adv*

fierce *adj* **fierc·er; fierc·est 1** : likely to attack **2** : having or showing very great energy or enthusiasm **3** : wild or threatening in appearance **4** : characterized by extreme force, intensity, or anger — **fierce·ly** *adv* — **fierce·ness** *n*

fi·ery *adj* **fi·er·i·er; fi·er·i·est 1** : marked by fire **2** : hot or glowing like a fire **3** : full of spirit **4** : easily angered

fi·es·ta *n* : a celebration especially in Spain and Latin America that commemorates a saint

fife *n* : a small musical instrument like a flute that produces a shrill sound

¹fif·teen *adj* : being one more than 14

²fifteen *n* : one more than 14 : three times five : 15

¹fif·teenth *adj* : coming right after 14th

²fifteenth *n* : number 15 in a series

¹fifth *adj* : coming right after fourth

²fifth *n* **1** : number five in a series **2** : one of five equal parts

¹fif·ti·eth *adj* : coming right after 49th

²fiftieth *n* : number 50 in a series

¹fif·ty *adj* : being five times ten

²fifty *n* : five times ten : 50

fig *n* : a sweet fruit that is oblong or shaped like a pear and is often eaten dried

¹fight *vb* **fought; fight·ing 1** : to struggle in battle or in physical combat **2** : to argue angrily : QUARREL **3** : to try hard **4** : to struggle against — **fight·er** *n*

²fight *n* **1** : a meeting in battle or in physical combat **2** : ¹QUARREL 1 **3** : strength or desire for fighting

fig·u·ra·tive *adj* : expressing one thing in terms normally used for another — **fig·u·ra·tive·ly** *adv*

¹fig·ure *n* **1** : a symbol (as 1, 2, 3) that stands for a number : NUMERAL **2 figures** *pl* : ARITHMETIC 2 **3** : value or price expressed in figures **4** : the shape or outline of something or someone **5** : the shape of the body especially of a person **6** : an illustration in a printed text **7** : ¹PATTERN 1 **8** : a well-known or important person

²figure *vb* **fig·ured; fig·ur·ing 1** : CALCULATE 1 **2** : BELIEVE 4, DECIDE — **figure on 1** : to make plans based on **2** : to rely on **3** : to have in mind — **figure out 1** : to dis-

cover or solve by thinking **2** : to find a solution for

fig·ure·head *n* **1** : a carved figure on the bow of a ship **2** : a person who is called the head of something but who has no real power

figure of speech *n, pl* **figures of speech** : an expression (as a simile or a metaphor) that uses words in other than a plain or literal way

fil·a·ment *n* **1** : a fine thread **2** : a fine wire (as in a light bulb) that is made to glow by the passage of an electric current **3** : the stalk of a plant stamen that bears the anther

fil·bert *n* : the hazel or its nut

filch *vb* **filched; filch·ing** : to steal in a sneaky way

¹file *n* : a tool with sharp ridges or teeth for smoothing or rubbing down hard substances

²file *vb* **filed; fil·ing** : to rub, smooth, or cut away with a file

³file *vb* **filed; fil·ing 1** : to arrange in an orderly way **2** : to enter or record officially

⁴file *n* **1** : a device (as a folder, case, or cabinet) for storing papers or records in an orderly way **2** : a collection of papers or records kept in a file **3** : a collection of data treated as a unit by a computer

⁵file *n* : a row of persons or things arranged one behind the other

⁶file *vb* **filed; fil·ing** : to walk in a row

fil·ial *adj* : relating to or suitable for a son or daughter

fil·i·gree *n* : decoration made of fine wire

Fil·i·pi·no *n* **1** : a person born or living in the Philippines **2** : the language of the Philippines

¹fill *vb* **1** : to make or become full **2** : to use up all the space or time in **3** : to spread through **4** : to stop up : PLUG **5** : to do the duties of **6** : to hire a person for **7** : to supply according to directions **8** : to succeed in meeting or satisfying — **fill in 1** : to insert information **2** : to provide information **3** : to take another's place — **fill out 1** : to increase in size and fullness **2** : to complete by providing information

²fill *n* **1** : all that is wanted **2** : material for filling something

fill·er *n* : a material used for filling

fil·let *n* : a piece of boneless meat or fish

fill·ing *n* : a substance used to fill something else

filling station *n* : GAS STATION

fil·ly *n, pl* **fillies** : a young female horse

¹film *n* **1** : a roll of material prepared for taking pictures **2** : MOVIE 1 **3** : a thin coating or layer

²film *vb* **filmed; film·ing 1** : to make a movie **2** : to photograph on a film

filmy *adj* **film·i·er; film·i·est** : very thin and light

¹fil·ter *n* **1** : a device or a mass of material (as sand or paper) with tiny openings through which a gas or liquid is passed to remove something **2** : a transparent material that absorbs light of some colors and is used for changing light (as in photography)

²filter *vb* **fil·tered; fil·ter·ing 1** : to pass through a filter **2** : to remove by means of a filter

filth *n* : disgusting dirt

filthy *adj* **filth·i·er; filth·i·est** : extremely dirty — **filth·i·ness** *n*

fil·tra·tion *n* : the process of filtering

fin *n* **1** : any of the thin parts that stick out from the body of a water animal and especially a fish and are used in moving or guiding the body through the water **2** : something shaped like an animal's fin

¹fi·nal *adj* **1** : coming or happening at the end **2** : not to be changed — **fi·nal·ly** *adv*

²final *n* **1** : the last match or game of a tournament **2** : a final examination in a course

fi·na·le *n* : the close or end of something (as a musical work)

fi·nal·i·ty *n* : the condition of being final or complete

fi·nal·ize *vb* **fi·nal·ized; fi·nal·iz·ing** : to put in a final or finished form

¹fi·nance *n* **1 finances** *pl* : money available to a government, business, or individual **2** : the system that includes the circulation of money, the providing of banks and credit, and the making of investments

²finance *vb* **fi·nanced; fi·nanc·ing** : to provide money for

fi·nan·cial *adj* : having to do with money or finance — **fi·nan·cial·ly** *adv*

fin·an·cier *n* : a specialist in finance and especially in the financing of businesses

finch *n* : a songbird (as a sparrow, bunting, or canary) with a short bill used for eating seeds

¹find *vb* **found; find·ing 1** : to come upon by chance **2** : to come upon or get by searching, study, or effort **3** : to make a decision about **4** : to know by experience **5** : to gain or regain the use of **6** : to become aware of being in a place, condition, or activity — **find·er** *n* — **find fault** : to criticize in an unfavorable way — **find out** : to learn by studying, watching, or searching

²find *n* : a usually valuable item or person found

find·ing *n* **1** : the decision of a court **2** : the results of an investigation

¹fine *n* : a sum of money to be paid as a punishment

²fine *vb* **fined; fin·ing** : to punish by requiring payment of a sum of money

³fine *adj* **fin·er; fin·est 1** : very good in quality or appearance **2** : SATISFACTORY **3** : very small or thin **4** : made up of very small pieces — **fine·ly** *adv* — **fine·ness** *n*

⁴fine *adv* : very well

fin·ery *n, pl* **fin·er·ies** : stylish or showy clothes and jewelry

¹fin·ger *n* **1** : one of the five divisions of the end of the hand including the thumb **2** : something that resembles a finger **3** : the part of a glove into which a finger goes

²finger *vb* **fin·gered; fin·ger·ing** : to touch with the fingers : HANDLE

fin·ger·nail *n* : the hard covering at the end of a finger

¹fin·ger·print *n* : the unique pattern of marks made by pressing the tip of a finger on a surface

²fingerprint *vb* **fin·ger·print·ed; fin·ger·print·ing** : to obtain fingerprints in order to identify a person

fin·icky *adj* : very hard to please : FUSSY

¹fin·ish *vb* **fin·ished; fin·ish·ing 1** : to bring or come to an end : COMPLETE **2** : to use up completely **3** : to end a competition in a certain position **4** : to put a final coat or surface on

²finish *n* **1** : ¹END 2, CONCLUSION **2** : the final treatment or coating of a surface or the appearance given by such a treatment

finish line *n* : a line marking the end of a racecourse

fi·nite *adj* : having definite limits

¹fink 1 : a person who is disliked **2** : a person who tattles

²fink *vb* **finked; fink·ing** : to tell on : TATTLE

Finn *n* : a person born or living in Finland

finned *adj* : having fins

¹Finn·ish *adj* : relating to Finland, its people, or the Finnish language

²Finnish *n* : the language of the Finns

fiord *variant of* FJORD

fir *n* : a tall evergreen tree related to the pine that yields useful lumber

¹fire *n* **1** : the light and heat and especially the flame produced by burning **2** : fuel that is burning in a controlled setting (as in a fireplace) **3** : the destructive burning of something (as a building) **4** : the shooting of weapons **5** : ENTHUSIASM — **on fire** : actively burning — **under fire 1** : exposed to the firing of enemy guns **2** : under attack

²fire *vb* **fired; fir·ing 1** : ¹SHOOT 2 **2** : to dismiss from employment **3** : EXCITE 1, STIR **4** : to subject to great heat **5** : to set off : EXPLODE **6** : to set on fire

fire alarm *n* : an alarm sounded to signal that a fire has broken out

fire·arm *n* : a small weapon from which shot or a bullet is discharged by gunpowder

fire·crack·er *n* : a paper tube containing an explosive to be set off for amusement

fire drill *n* : a practice drill in getting out of a building in case of fire

fire engine *n* : a truck equipped to fight fires

fire escape *n* : a stairway that provides a way of escape from a building in case of fire

fire extinguisher *n* : something (as a container filled with chemicals) used to put out a fire

fire·fight·er *n* : a person whose job is to put out fires — **fire·fight·ing** *n*

fire·fly *n, pl* **fire·flies** : a small beetle producing a soft light

fire·house *n* : FIRE STATION

fire·man *n, pl* **fire·men** 1 : FIREFIGHTER 2 : a person who tends a fire (as in a large furnace)

fire·place *n* : a structure with a hearth on which an open fire can be built (as for heating)

fire·proof *adj* : not easily burned : made safe against fire

fire·side *n* 1 : a place near the hearth 2 : ¹HOME 1

fire station *n* : a building housing fire engines and usually firefighters

fire·wood *n* : wood cut for fuel

fire·work *n* 1 : a device that makes a display of light or noise by the burning of explosive or flammable materials 2 **fireworks** *pl* : a display of fireworks

¹firm *adj* 1 : having a solid compact texture 2 : STRONG 1, VIGOROUS 3 : not likely to be changed 4 : not easily moved or shaken : FAITHFUL 5 : showing certainty or determination — **firm·ly** *adv* — **firm·ness** *n*

²firm *vb* **firmed; firm·ing** 1 : to make or become hard or solid 2 : to make more secure or strong 3 : to put into final form

³firm *n* : BUSINESS 2

¹first *adj* : coming before all others in time, order, or importance

²first *adv* 1 : before any other 2 : for the first time

³first *n* 1 : number one in a series 2 : something or someone that comes before all others 3 : the winning place in a competition — **at first** : in the beginning

first aid *n* : care or treatment given to an ill or injured person in an emergency

first-class *adj* 1 : relating to the best group in a classification 2 : EXCELLENT

first·hand *adj or adv* : coming right from the original source

first lieutenant *n* : a commissioned officer in the army, air force, or marine corps ranking above a second lieutenant

first person *n* : a set of words or forms (as pronouns or verb forms) referring to the person speaking or writing them

first–rate *adj* : EXCELLENT

first sergeant *n* 1 : a noncommissioned officer serving as the chief assistant to a military commander 2 : a noncommissioned officer ranking above a sergeant first class in the army or above a gunnery sergeant in the marine corps

firth *n* : a narrow arm of the sea

¹fish *n, pl* **fish** *or* **fish·es** 1 : any of a large group of vertebrate animals that live in water, breathe with gills, and usually have fins and scales 2 : an animal that lives in water — usually used in combination — **fish·like** *adj*

²fish *vb* **fished; fish·ing** 1 : to catch or try to catch fish 2 : to search for something by or as if by groping

fish·er·man *n, pl* **fish·er·men** : a person who fishes

fish·ery *n, pl* **fish·er·ies** 1 : the business of catching, processing, and selling fish 2 : a place for catching fish

fish·hook *n* : a hook used for catching fish

fishy *adj* **fish·i·er; fish·i·est** 1 : of or like fish 2 : causing doubt or suspicion : QUESTIONABLE

fis·sion *n* 1 : a method of reproduction in which a living cell or body divides into two or more parts each of which grows into a whole new individual 2 : the process of splitting an atomic nucleus with the release of large amounts of energy

fis·sure *n* : a narrow opening or crack

fist *n* : the hand with the fingers bent tight into the palm

¹fit *adj* **fit·ter; fit·test** 1 : good enough : suitable for 2 : physically healthy 3 : made ready — **fit·ness** *n*

²fit *n* : a sudden attack or outburst

³fit *vb* **fit·ted; fit·ting** 1 : to be the right shape or size 2 : to bring to the right shape or size 3 : to find room or time for 4 : to go into a particular place 5 : to be suitable for or to 6 : EQUIP

⁴fit *n* : the way something fits

fit·ful *adj* : not regular or steady — **fit·ful·ly** *adv*

¹fit·ting *adj* : ¹APPROPRIATE, SUITABLE — **fit·ting·ly** *adv*

²fitting *n* : a small part that goes with something larger

¹five *adj* : being one more than four

²five *n* 1 : one more than four : 5 2 : the fifth in a set or series

¹fix *vb* **fixed; fix·ing** 1 : ¹REPAIR 1, MEND 2 : to make firm or secure 3 : to hold or direct steadily 4 : to set definitely : ESTABLISH 5

: to get ready : PREPARE **6** : to cause to chemically change into an available and useful form — **fix·er** *n*

²fix *n* **1** : an unpleasant or difficult position **2** : something that solves a problem

fixed *adj* **1** : not changing : SET **2** : firmly placed — **fix·ed·ly** *adv*

fixed star *n* : a star so distant that its motion can be measured only by very careful observations over long periods

fix·ture *n* : something (as a light or sink) attached as a permanent part

¹fizz *vb* **fizzed; fizz·ing** : to make a hissing or bubbling sound

²fizz *n* **1** : a hissing or bubbling sound **2** : a bubbling drink

fiz·zle *vb* **fiz·zled; fiz·zling** : to fail after a good start

fjord *or* **fiord** *n* : a narrow inlet of the sea between cliffs or steep slopes

FL *abbr* Florida

Fla. *abbr* Florida

flab·ber·gast *vb* **flab·ber·gast·ed; flab·ber·gast·ing** : to greatly surprise : ASTONISH

flab·by *adj* **flab·bi·er; flab·bi·est** : not hard and firm : SOFT — **flab·bi·ness** *n*

¹flag *n* : a piece of cloth with a special design or color that is used as a symbol (as of a nation) or as a signal

²flag *vb* **flagged; flag·ging** : to signal to stop

³flag *vb* **flagged; flag·ging** : to become weak

fla·gel·lum *n, pl* **fla·gel·la** : a long whiplike structure that sticks out from a cell and by which some tiny organisms (as bacteria) move

flag·man *n, pl* **flag·men** : a person who signals with a flag

flag·on *n* : a container for liquids usually having a handle, spout, and lid

flag·pole *n* : a pole on which to raise a flag

fla·grant *adj* : so bad as to be impossible to overlook — **fla·grant·ly** *adv*

flag·ship *n* : the ship carrying the commander of a group of ships and flying a flag that tells the commander's rank

flag·staff *n, pl* **flag·staffs** : FLAGPOLE

¹flail *vb* **flailed; flail·ing** **1** : to wave the arms or legs wildly **2** : to swing something with a violent motion

²flail *n* : a tool for threshing grain by hand

flair *n* **1** : natural ability **2** : ¹STYLE 4

¹flake *n* : a small thin flat piece

²flake *vb* **flaked; flak·ing** : to form or separate into small thin flat pieces

flaky *adj* **flak·i·er; flak·i·est** : tending to break apart into small thin flat pieces — **flak·i·ness** *n*

flam·boy·ant *adj* : having a noticeable or showy quality — **flam·boy·ant·ly** *adv*

¹flame *n* **1** : the glowing gas that makes up part of a fire **2** : a state of burning brightly **3** : strongly felt emotion

²flame *vb* **flamed; flam·ing** : to burn with or as if with a flame

flame·throw·er *n* : a weapon that shoots a burning stream of fuel

fla·min·go *n, pl* **fla·min·gos** *or* **fla·min·goes** : a large pale pink to reddish waterbird with very long neck and legs and a broad bill bent downward at the end

flam·ma·ble *adj* : capable of being easily set on fire and of burning quickly

¹flank *n* **1** : the area on the side of an animal between the ribs and the hip **2** : ¹SIDE 3 **3** : the right or left side of a formation (as of soldiers)

²flank *vb* **flanked; flank·ing** **1** : to be located at the side of **2** : to attack or threaten the side of

flan·nel *n* : a soft cloth made of wool or cotton

¹flap *n* **1** : something broad and flat or flexible that hangs loose **2** : the motion or sound made by something broad and flexible (as a sail or wing) moving back and forth **3** : an upset or worried state of mind

²flap *vb* **flapped; flap·ping** : to move with a beating or fluttering motion

flap·jack *n* : PANCAKE

¹flare *vb* **flared; flar·ing** **1** : to burn with an unsteady flame **2** : to shine or burn suddenly or briefly **3** : to become angry or active **4** : to spread outward

²flare *n* **1** : a sudden blaze of light **2** : a blaze of light used to signal, light up something, or attract attention **3** : a device or material used to produce a flare **4** : a sudden outburst **5** : a spreading outward : a part that spreads outward

¹flash *vb* **flashed; flash·ing** **1** : to shine or give off bright light suddenly **2** : to appear quickly or suddenly **3** : to come or pass very suddenly **4** : to show briefly

²flash *n* **1** : a sudden burst of or as if of light **2** : a very short time

³flash *adj* : beginning suddenly and lasting only a short time

flash·light *n* : a small portable electric light that runs on batteries

flashy *adj* **flash·i·er; flash·i·est** : GAUDY, SHOWY

flask *n* : a container like a bottle with a flat or rounded body

¹flat *adj* **flat·ter; flat·test** **1** : having a smooth level surface **2** : spread out on or along a surface **3** : having a broad smooth surface and little thickness **4** : very clear and definite **5** : not changing in amount **6** : not showing active business **7** : ¹DULL 3 **8** : having lost air **9** : no longer having bubbles **10** : lower than the true musical pitch **11** : lower by a half step in music **12** : not shiny — **flat·ly** adv

²flat n **1** : a level area of land : PLAIN **2** : a flat part or surface **3** : a note or tone that is a half step lower than the note named **4** : a sign ♭ meaning that the pitch of a musical note is to be lower by a half step **5** : a tire that has lost air

³flat adv **1** : on or against a flat surface **2** : without any time more or less : EXACTLY **3** : below the true musical pitch

flat·boat n : a large boat with a flat bottom and square ends

flat·car n : a railroad car without sides or a roof that is used to carry freight

flat·fish n : a fish (as the flounder) that has a flat body and swims on its side with both eyes on the upper side

flat·out adj **1** : ²OUT-RIGHT 1 **2** : greatest possible

flat out adv **1** : in a very clear manner **2** : at top speed

flat·pan·el adj : relating to a thin flat video display

flat·ten vb **flat·tened; flat·ten·ing** : to make or become flat

flat·ter vb **flat·tered; flat·ter·ing 1** : to praise but not sincerely **2** : to cause to feel pleased by showing respect or admiration **3** : to show as favorably as possible **4** : to make look more attractive — **flat·ter·er** n

flat·tery n, pl **flat·ter·ies** : praise that is not deserved or meant

flaunt vb **flaunt·ed; flaunt·ing 1** : to wave or flutter in a showy way **2** : to show in a way that attracts attention

¹fla·vor n **1** : the quality of something that affects the sense of taste **2** : a substance added to food to give it a desired taste

²flavor vb **fla·vored; fla·vor·ing** : to give or add something to produce a taste — **fla·vored** adj

fla·vor·ing n : ¹FLAVOR 2

flaw n : a small fault or weakness — **flaw·less** adj

flax n : a plant with blue flowers that is grown for its fiber from which rope and linen is made and for its seed from which oil and livestock feed are obtained

flax·en adj : having a light yellow color

flax·seed n : the seed of flax from which linseed oil comes

flay vb **flayed; flay·ing 1** : to strip off the skin or surface of **2** : to beat severely

flea n : a small bloodsucking insect that has no wings and a hard body

¹fleck vb **flecked; fleck·ing** : to mark with small streaks or spots

²fleck n **1** : ¹SPOT 2, MARK **2** : a small bit

fledg·ling n : a young bird that has just grown the feathers needed to fly

flee vb **fled; flee·ing** : to run away or away from

¹fleece n : the woolly coat of an animal and especially a sheep

²fleece vb **fleeced; fleec·ing** : to rob or cheat by trickery

fleecy adj **fleec·i·er; fleec·i·est** : covered with, made of, or similar to fleece

¹fleet n **1** : a group of warships under one commander **2** : a country's navy **3** : a group of ships or vehicles that move together or are owned by one company

²fleet adj **fleet·er; fleet·est** : very swift — **fleet·ly** adv

fleet·ing adj : passing by quickly

flesh n **1** : the soft parts of an animal's or person's body **2** : the part of an animal that is eaten : MEAT **3** : a soft edible plant part

fleshy adj **flesh·i·er; flesh·i·est 1** : like or consisting of flesh **2** : ¹FAT 1

flew past of FLY

flex vb **flexed; flex·ing 1** : to bend especially again and again **2** : to move or tense (a muscle)

flex·i·bil·i·ty n : the quality or state of being easy to bend

flex·i·ble adj **1** : possible or easy to bend **2** : easily changed

¹flick n : a light snapping stroke

²flick vb **flicked; flick·ing** : to strike or move with a quick motion

¹flick·er vb **flick·ered; flick·er·ing 1** : to burn unsteadily **2** : to appear briefly **3** : to move quickly

²flicker n **1** : a quick small movement **2** : a quick movement of light

³flicker n : a large North American woodpecker

fli·er or **fly·er** n **1** : a person or thing that flies **2** usually **flyer** : a printed sheet containing information or advertising that is given to many people

¹flight n **1** : an act of passing through the air by the use of wings **2** : a passing through the air or space **3** : a trip by an airplane or spacecraft **4** : a group of similar things flying through the air together **5** : an extraordinary display **6** : a series of stairs from one level or floor to the next

²flight n : the act of running away

flight·less adj : unable to fly

flighty adj **flight·i·er; flight·i·est 1** : easily excited or frightened : SKITTISH **2** : not steady or serious

flim·sy adj **flim·si·er; flim·si·est** : not strong or solid

flinch vb **flinched; flinch·ing** : to draw back from or as if from pain or fear

¹fling *vb* **flung; fling·ing 1** : to throw hard or without care **2** : to move forcefully

²fling *n* **1** : an act of throwing hard or without care **2** : a time of freedom for pleasure **3** : a brief try

flint *n* : a very hard stone that produces a spark when struck by steel

flint·lock *n* : an old-fashioned firearm using a piece of flint for striking a spark to fire the charge

¹flip *vb* **flipped; flip·ping** : to move or turn by or as if by tossing

²flip *n* **1** : a quick turn, toss, or movement **2** : a somersault in the air

flip·pant *adj* : not respectful or serious — **flip·pant·ly** *adv*

flip·per *n* **1** : a broad flat limb (as of a seal or whale) used for swimming **2** : a flat rubber shoe with the front widened into a paddle for use in swimming

¹flirt *vb* **flirt·ed; flirt·ing** : to show a romantic interest in someone just for fun

²flirt *n* : a person who flirts a lot

flit *vb* **flit·ted; flit·ting** : to move, pass, or fly quickly from one place or thing to another

¹float *n* **1** : something that rests in or on the surface of a liquid **2** : an inflated support for a person in water **3** : a light object that holds up the baited end of a fishing line **4** : a platform anchored near a shore for the use of swimmers or boats **5** : a structure that holds up an airplane in water **6** : a soft drink with ice cream floating in it **7** : a vehicle with a platform used to carry an exhibit in a parade

²float *vb* **float·ed; float·ing 1** : to rest on the surface of a liquid **2** : to be carried along by or as if by moving water or air **3** : to cause to rest on or be carried by water

¹flock *n* **1** : a group of animals living or kept together **2** : a group someone watches over **3** : a large number

²flock *vb* **flocked; flock·ing** : to gather or move in a crowd

floe *n* : a sheet or mass of floating ice

flog *vb* **flogged; flog·ging** : to beat severely with a rod or whip

¹flood *n* **1** : a huge flow of water that rises and spreads over the land **2** : the flowing in of the tide **3** : a very large number or amount

²flood *vb* **flood·ed; flood·ing 1** : to cover or become filled with water **2** : to fill as if with a flood

flood·light *n* : a light that shines brightly over a wide area

flood·plain *n* : low flat land along a stream that is flooded when the stream overflows

flood·wa·ter *n* : the water of a flood

¹floor *n* **1** : the part of a room on which people stand **2** : the lower inside surface of a hollow structure **3** : the area of ground at the bottom of something **4** : a story of a building

²floor *vb* **floored; floor·ing 1** : to cover or provide with a floor **2** : to knock down

floor·ing *n* **1** : ¹FLOOR 1 **2** : material for floors

¹flop *vb* **flopped; flop·ping 1** : to flap about **2** : to drop or fall limply **3** : ¹FAIL 1

²flop *n* **1** : the act or sound of flapping about or falling limply **2** : FAILURE 1

flop·py *adj* **flop·pi·er; flop·pi·est** : being soft and flexible

floppy disk *n* : a small flexible plastic disk with a magnetic coating on which computer data can be stored

flo·ra *n* : the plant life typical of a region, period, or special environment

flo·ral *adj* : of or relating to flowers

flor·id *adj* **1** : very fancy or flowery in style **2** : having a reddish color

flo·rist *n* : a person who sells flowers and houseplants

¹floss *n* **1** : DENTAL FLOSS **2** : soft thread used in embroidery **3** : fluffy material full of fibers

²floss *vb* **flossed; floss·ing** : to use dental floss on

flo·til·la *n* : a fleet of usually small ships

¹flounce *vb* **flounced; flounc·ing 1** : to move with exaggerated motions **2** *chiefly British* : to walk in a way that shows anger

²flounce *n* : a strip of fabric or ruffle attached by one edge — **flouncy** *adj*

¹floun·der *n* : a flatfish used for food

²flounder *vb* **floun·dered; floun·der·ing 1** : to struggle to move or get footing **2** : to behave or do something in a clumsy way

flour *n* : finely ground wheat or other food product

¹flour·ish *vb* **flour·ished; flour·ish·ing 1** : to grow well : THRIVE **2** : to do well : enjoy success **3** : to make sweeping movements with

²flourish *n* **1** : a fancy bit of decoration added to something **2** : a sweeping motion

flout *vb* **flout·ed; flout·ing** : to ignore in an open and disrespectful way

¹flow *vb* **flowed; flow·ing 1** : to move in or as if in a stream **2** : to glide along smoothly **3** : to hang loose and waving

²flow *n* **1** : an act of moving in or as if in a stream **2** : the rise of the tide **3** : a smooth even movement : STREAM **4** : an amount or mass of something moving in a stream

¹flow·er *n* **1** : a plant part that produces seed **2** : a small plant grown chiefly for its showy flowers **3** : the state of bearing flowers **4** : the best part or example — **flow·ered** *adj* — **flow·er·less** *adj*

²flower *vb* **flow·ered; flow·er·ing** : ²BLOOM 1

flower head *n* : a tight cluster of small flowers that are arranged so that the whole looks like a single flower

flowering plant *n* : a seed plant whose seeds are produced in the ovary of a flower

flow·ery *adj* **flow·er·i·er; flow·er·i·est** 1 : full of or covered with flowers 2 : full of fancy words

flown *past participle of* FLY

flu *n* 1 : INFLUENZA 2 : any of several virus diseases something like a cold

fluc·tu·ate *vb* **fluc·tu·at·ed; fluc·tu·at·ing** : to change continually and especially up and down

flue *n* : an enclosed passage for smoke or air

flu·en·cy *n* : the ability to speak easily and well

flu·ent *adj* 1 : able to speak easily and well 2 : smooth and correct — **flu·ent·ly** *adv*

¹fluff *n* : something light and soft

²fluff *vb* **fluffed; fluff·ing** : to make or become fuller, lighter, or softer

fluffy *adj* **fluff·i·er; fluff·i·est** 1 : having, covered with, or similar to down 2 : being or looking light and soft

¹flu·id *adj* 1 : capable of flowing like a liquid or gas 2 : having a graceful or flowing style or appearance — **flu·id·ly** *adv*

²fluid *n* : something that tends to flow and take the shape of its container

fluid ounce *n* : a unit of liquid capacity equal to 1/16 of a pint (about 29.6 milliliters)

flung *past and past participle of* FLING

flunk *vb* **flunked; flunk·ing** : ¹FAIL 1

fluo·res·cent *adj* 1 : giving out visible light when exposed to external radiation 2 : producing visible light by means of a fluorescent coating 3 : extremely bright or glowing

fluo·ri·date *vb* **fluo·ri·dat·ed; fluo·ri·dat·ing** : to add a fluoride to

fluo·ride *n* : a compound of fluorine

fluo·rine *n* : a yellowish flammable irritating gaseous chemical element

flur·ry *n, pl* **flur·ries** 1 : a gust of wind 2 : a brief light snowfall 3 : a brief outburst

¹flush *vb* **flushed; flush·ing** : to cause to leave a hiding place

²flush *n* 1 : an act of pouring water over or through 2 : ²BLUSH 1

³flush *vb* **flushed; flush·ing** 1 : ¹BLUSH 1 2 : to pour water over or through

⁴flush *adj* : even or level with another surface

⁵flush *adv* : so as to be even or level with another surface

¹flus·ter *vb* **flus·tered; flus·ter·ing** : to make nervous and confused : UPSET

²fluster *n* : a state of nervous confusion

flute *n* : a woodwind instrument in the form

of a slender tube open at one end that is played by blowing across a hole near the closed end

¹flut·ter *vb* **flut·tered; flut·ter·ing** 1 : to move the wings rapidly without flying or in making short flights 2 : to move with a quick flapping motion 3 : to move about excitedly

²flutter *n* 1 : an act of moving or flapping quickly 2 : a state of excitement

¹fly *vb* **flew; flown; fly·ing** 1 : to move in or pass through the air with wings 2 : to move through the air or before the wind 3 : to float or cause to float, wave, or soar in the wind 4 : to run away : FLEE 5 : to pass or move swiftly 6 : to operate or travel in an aircraft 7 : to become suddenly emotional

²fly *n, pl* **flies** 1 : a flap of material to cover a fastening in a garment 2 : a layer of fabric that goes over the top of a tent 3 : a baseball hit very high

³fly *n, pl* **flies** 1 : a winged insect 2 : any of a large group of mostly stout-bodied two-winged insects (as the housefly) 3 : a fishhook made to look like an insect

fly·catch·er *n* : a small bird that eats flying insects

flyer *variant of* FLIER

flying fish *n* : a fish with large fins that let it jump from the water and move for a distance through the air

fly·way *n* : a route regularly followed by migratory birds

¹foal *n* : a young animal of the horse family especially when less than one year old

²foal *vb* **foaled; foal·ing** : to give birth to a baby horse

¹foam *n* : a mass of tiny bubbles that forms in or on the surface of a liquid

²foam *vb* **foamed; foam·ing** : to produce or form a mass of tiny bubbles

foamy *adj* **foam·i·er; foam·i·est** : covered with or looking like foam — **foam·i·ness** *n*

fo·cal *adj* 1 : of, relating to, or having a focus 2 : having central or great importance

¹fo·cus *n, pl* **fo·ci** *also* **fo·cus·es** 1 : a point at which rays (as of light, heat, or sound) meet after being reflected or bent : the point at which an image is formed 2 : the distance from a lens or mirror to a focus 3 : an adjustment that gives clear vision 4 : a center of activity or interest

²focus *vb* **fo·cused** *also* **fo·cussed; fo·cus·ing** *also* **fo·cus·sing** 1 : to bring or come to a focus 2 : to adjust the focus of 3 : to direct or cause to direct at

fod·der *n* : coarse dry food (as cornstalks) for livestock

foe *n* : an enemy of a person or a country

¹fog *n* 1 : tiny drops of water floating in the

air at or near the ground **2** : a confused state of mind

²fog *vb* **fogged; fog·ging** : to cover or become covered with tiny drops of water

fog·gy *adj* **fog·gi·er; fog·gi·est** **1** : filled with fog **2** : unsure or confused

fog·horn *n* : a loud horn sounded in foggy weather to give warning

foi·ble *n* : an unimportant weakness or failing

¹foil *vb* **foiled; foil·ing** : to prevent from achieving a goal

²foil *n* : a very thin sheet of metal

³foil *n* : a fencing sword having a light flexible blade with a blunt point

¹fold *n* : an enclosure for sheep

²fold *vb* **fold·ed; fold·ing** **1** : to lay one part over or against another part **2** : to clasp together **3** : ¹EMBRACE 1

³fold *n* **1** : an act or the result of laying one part over or against another **2** : a part laid over another part **3** : a bend produced in a rock layer by pressure

-fold *suffix* **1** : multiplied by a specified number : times — used in adjectives and adverbs **2** : having so many parts

fold·er *n* **1** : a folded cover or large envelope for loose papers **2** : a folded printed sheet **3** : a part of a computer operating system used to organize files

fo·li·age *n* : the leaves of a plant

¹folk *or* **folks** *n pl* **1** : persons of a certain kind or group **2 folks** *pl* : people in general **3 folks** *pl* : family members and especially parents

²folk *adj* : created by the common people

folk·lore *n* : traditional customs, beliefs, stories, and sayings

folk·sing·er *n* : a person who sings songs (**folk songs**) created by and long sung among the common people

folk·tale *n* : a story made up and handed down by the common people

fol·low *vb* **fol·lowed; fol·low·ing** **1** : to go or come after or behind **2** : to come after in time or place **3** : to go on the track of **4** : to go along or beside **5** : to be led or guided by : OBEY **6** : to result from **7** : to work in or at something as a way of life **8** : to watch or pay attention to **9** : UNDERSTAND — **fol·low·er** *n* — **follow suit 1** : to play a card that belongs to the same group (as hearts) as the one first played **2** : to do the same thing someone else has just done — **follow through** : to complete something started — **follow up** : to take additional similar or related action

¹fol·low·ing *adj* : coming just after

²following *n* : a group of fans or supporters

³following *prep* : right after

fol·ly *n, pl* **follies 1** : lack of good sense **2** : a foolish act or idea

fond *adj* **fond·er; fond·est** **1** : having a liking or love **2** : AFFECTIONATE, LOVING **3** : strongly wished for — **fond·ly** *adv* — **fond·ness** *n*

fon·dle *vb* **fon·dled; fon·dling** : to touch or handle in a tender or loving manner

font *n* **1** : a basin to hold water for baptism **2** : SOURCE 1

food *n* **1** : the material that people and animals eat : material containing carbohydrates, fats, proteins, and supplements (as minerals and vitamins) that is taken in by and used in the living body for growth and repair and as a source of energy for activities **2** : inorganic substances (as nitrate and carbon dioxide) taken in by green plants and used to build organic nutrients **3** : organic materials (as sugar and starch) formed by plants and used in their growth and activities **4** : solid food as distinguished from drink

food chain *n* : a sequence of organisms in which each depends on the next and usually lower member as a source of food

food·stuff *n* : a substance that is used as food

food web *n* : the whole group of interacting food chains in a community

¹fool *n* **1** : a person without good sense or judgment **2** : JESTER

²fool *vb* **fooled; fool·ing** **1** : to speak or act in a playful way or in fun : JOKE **2** : ²TRICK **3** : to spend time in an aimless way **4** : to play with or handle something carelessly

fool·har·dy *adj* : foolishly adventurous : RECKLESS

fool·ish *adj* : showing or resulting from lack of good sense — **fool·ish·ly** *adv* — **fool·ish·ness** *n*

fool·proof *adj* : done, made, or planned so well that nothing can go wrong

¹foot *n, pl* **feet 1** : the end part of the leg of an animal or person : the part of an animal on which it stands or moves **2** : a unit of length equal to twelve inches (about .3 meter) **3** : the lowest or end part of something — **on foot** : by walking

²foot *vb* **foot·ed; foot·ing** **1** : ¹WALK 1 **2** : ¹PAY 2

foot·ball *n* **1** : a game played with an oval ball on a large field by two teams of eleven players that move the ball by kicking, passing, or running with it **2** : the ball used in football

foot·ed *adj* **1** : having a foot or feet **2** : having such or so many feet

foot·fall *n* : the sound of a footstep

foot·hill *n* : a hill at the bottom of higher hills

foot·hold *n* : a place where the foot may be put (as for climbing)

foot·ing *n* 1 : a firm position or placing of the feet 2 : FOOTHOLD 3 : position as compared to others 4 : social relationship

foot·lights *n pl* : a row of lights set across the front of a stage floor

foot·man *n, pl* **foot·men** : a male servant who performs various duties (as letting visitors in and serving food)

foot·note *n* : a note at the bottom of a page

foot·path *n* : a path for walkers

foot·print *n* : a track left by a foot

foot·step *n* 1 : a step of the foot 2 : the distance covered by a step 3 : FOOTPRINT 4 : the sound of a foot taking a step 5 : way of life or action

foot·stool *n* : a low stool for the feet

foot·work *n* : the skill with which the feet are moved

¹for *prep* 1 : by way of getting ready 2 : toward the goal or purpose of 3 : in order to reach 4 : as being 5 : because of 6 — used to show who or what is to receive something 7 : in order to help, serve, or defend 8 : directed at : AGAINST 9 : in exchange as equal to 10 : with regard to : CONCERNING 11 : taking into account 12 : through the period of 13 : to a distance of 14 : suitable to 15 : in favor of 16 : in place of or on behalf of 17 : ²AFTER 5

²for *conj* : BECAUSE

¹for·age *n* : food (as grass) for browsing or grazing animals

²forage *vb* **for·aged; for·ag·ing** 1 : to nibble or eat grass or other plants 2 : ¹SEARCH 1

for·bear *vb* **for·bore; for·borne; for·bear·ing** 1 : to hold back 2 : to be patient when annoyed or troubled

for·bid *vb* **for·bade; for·bid·den; for·bid·ding** : to order not to do something

for·bid·ding *adj* : tending to frighten or discourage

¹force *n* 1 : power that has an effect on something 2 : the state of existing and being enforced 3 : a group of people available for a particular purpose 4 : power or violence used on a person or thing 5 : an influence (as a push or pull) that tends to produce a change in the speed or direction of motion of something

²force *vb* **forced; forc·ing** 1 : to make someone or something do something 2 : to get, make, or move by using physical power 3 : to break open using physical power 4 : to speed up the development of

force·ful *adj* : having much strength : VIGOROUS — **force·ful·ly** *adv* — **force·ful·ness** *n*

for·ceps *n, pl* **forceps** : an instrument for grasping, holding, or pulling on things especially in delicate operations (as by a jeweler or surgeon)

forc·ible *adj* 1 : got, made, or done by physical power 2 : showing a lot of strength or energy — **forc·ibly** *adv*

¹ford *n* : a shallow place in a body of water that may be crossed by wading

²ford *vb* **ford·ed; ford·ing** : to cross by wading

¹fore *adv* : in or toward the front

²fore *adj* : being or coming before in time, place, or order

³fore *n* : ¹FRONT 1

⁴fore *interj* — used by a golfer to warn someone within range of a hit ball

fore- *prefix* 1 : earlier : beforehand 2 : at the front : in front 3 : front part of something specified

fore–and–aft *adj* : being in line with the length of a ship

fore·arm *n* : the part of the arm between the elbow and the wrist

fore·bear *n* : ANCESTOR 1

fore·bod·ing *n* : a feeling that something bad is going to happen

¹fore·cast *vb* **forecast; fore·cast·ing** : to predict often after thought and study of available evidence — **fore·cast·er** *n*

²forecast *n* : a prediction of something in the future

fore·cas·tle *n* 1 : the forward part of the upper deck of a ship 2 : quarters for the crew in the forward part of a ship

fore·fa·ther *n* : ANCESTOR 1

fore·fin·ger *n* : INDEX FINGER

fore·foot *n, pl* **fore·feet** : one of the front feet of an animal with four feet

fore·front *n* : the most important part or position

forego *variant of* FORGO

fore·go·ing *adj* : going before : already mentioned

fore·gone conclusion *n* : something felt to be sure to happen

fore·ground *n* : the part of a picture or scene that seems to be nearest to and in front of the person looking at it

fore·hand *n* : a stroke in sports played with a racket made with the palm of the hand turned in the direction in which the hand is moving

fore·head *n* : the part of the face above the eyes

for·eign *adj* 1 : located outside of a place or country and especially outside of a person's own country 2 : belonging to a place or country other than the one under consideration 3 : relating to or having to do with other nations 4 : not normally belonging or wanted where found

for·eign·er *n* : a person who is from a foreign country

fore·leg *n* : a front leg of an animal

fore·limb *n* : an arm, fin, wing, or leg that is located toward the front of the body

fore·man *n, pl* **fore·men** : the leader of a group of workers

fore·mast *n* : the mast nearest the bow of the ship

¹fore·most *adj* : first in time, place, or order : most important

²foremost *adv* : in the first place

fore·noon *n* : MORNING

fore·run·ner *n* : someone or something that comes before especially as a sign of the coming of another

fore·see *vb* **fore·saw; fore·seen; fore·see·ing** : to see or know about beforehand

fore·shad·ow *vb* **fore·shad·owed; fore·shad·ow·ing** : to give a hint of beforehand

fore·sight *n* 1 : the ability to see what will or might happen in the future 2 : care for the future : PRUDENCE

for·est *n* : a growth of trees and underbrush covering a large area — **for·est·ed** *adj*

fore·stall *vb* **fore·stalled; fore·stall·ing** : to keep out, interfere with, or prevent by steps taken in advance

forest ranger *n* : a person in charge of managing and protecting part of a public forest

for·est·ry *n* : the science and practice of caring for forests — **for·est·er** *n*

fore·tell *vb* **fore·told; fore·tell·ing** : to tell of a thing before it happens

fore·thought *n* : careful thinking or planning for the future

for·ev·er *adv* 1 : for a limitless time 2 : at all times

fore·warn *vb* **fore·warned; fore·warn·ing** : to warn in advance

forewent *past of* FORGO

fore·word *n* : PREFACE

¹for·feit *vb* **for·feit·ed; for·feit·ing** : to lose or lose the right to as punishment for a fault, error, or crime

²forfeit *n* : something or the right to something lost as punishment for a fault, error, or crime

¹forge *vb* **forged; forg·ing** 1 : to shape and work metal by heating and hammering 2 : to bring into existence 3 : to produce something that is not genuine : COUNTERFEIT — **forg·er** *n*

²forge *n* : a furnace or a place with a furnace where metal is shaped by heating and hammering

³forge *vb* **forged; forg·ing** : to move forward slowly but steadily

forg·ery *n, pl* **forg·er·ies** 1 : the crime of falsely making or changing a written paper or signing someone else's name 2 : something that is falsely made or copied

for·get *vb* **for·got; for·got·ten** *or* **for·got; for·get·ting** 1 : to be unable to think of or remember 2 : to fail by accident to do (something) : OVERLOOK

for·get·ful *adj* : forgetting easily — **for·get·ful·ness** *n*

for·get–me–not *n* : a small low plant with bright blue flowers

for·give *vb* **for·gave; for·giv·en; for·giv·ing** : to stop feeling angry at or hurt by

for·give·ness *n* : the act of ending anger at

for·giv·ing *adj* : willing or ready to excuse an error or offense

for·go *also* **fore·go** *vb* **for·went; for·gone; for·go·ing** : to give up the use or enjoyment of

¹fork *n* 1 : an implement having a handle and two or more prongs for taking up (as in eating), pitching, or digging 2 : a forked part or tool 3 : the place where something divides or branches 4 : one of the parts into which something divides or branches

²fork *vb* **forked; fork·ing** 1 : to divide into branches 2 : to pitch or lift with a fork

forked *adj* : having one end divided into two or more branches

for·lorn *adj* : sad from being left alone — **for·lorn·ly** *adv*

¹form *n* 1 : ¹SORT 1, KIND 2 : the shape and structure of something 3 : a printed sheet with blank spaces for information 4 : a way of doing something 5 : one of the different pronunciations, spellings, or inflections a word may have 6 : a mold in which concrete is placed to set

²form *vb* **formed; form·ing** 1 : to give form or shape to 2 : DEVELOP 5 3 : to come or bring together in making 4 : to take shape : come into being

¹for·mal *adj* 1 : following established form, custom, or rule 2 : acquired by attending classes in a school 3 : requiring proper clothing and manners 4 : suitable for a proper occasion — **for·mal·ly** *adv*

²formal *n* : a social gathering that requires proper clothing and behavior

for·mal·i·ty *n, pl* **for·mal·i·ties** 1 : the quality or state of being formal 2 : an established way of doing something

¹for·mat *n* : the general organization or arrangement of something

²format *vb* **for·mat·ted; for·mat·ting** 1 : to organize or arrange in a certain way 2 : to prepare for storing computer data

for·ma·tion *n* 1 : a creation or development of something 2 : something that is formed or created 3 : an arrangement of something

for·mer *adj* : coming before in time

for·mer·ly *adv* : at an earlier time

for·mi·da·ble *adj* **1** : causing fear or awe **2** : offering serious difficulties **3** : large or impressive in size or extent — **for·mi·da·bly** *adv*

form·less *adj* : having no regular form or shape

for·mu·la *n* **1** : a direction giving amounts of the substances for the preparation of something (as a medicine) **2** : an established form or method **3** : a milk mixture or substitute for feeding a baby **4** : a general fact or rule expressed in symbols **5** : an expression in symbols giving the makeup of a substance

for·mu·late *vb* **for·mu·lat·ed; for·mu·lat·ing** : to create, invent, or produce by careful thought and effort

for·sake *vb* **for·sook; for·sak·en; for·sak·ing** : to give up or leave entirely

for·syth·ia *n* : a bush often grown for its bright yellow flowers that appear in early spring

fort *n* : a strong or fortified place

forte *n* : something in which a person shows special ability

forth *adv* **1** : onward in time, place, or order **2** : out into view

forth·com·ing *adj* **1** : being about to appear **2** : ready or available when needed

forth·right *adj* : going straight to the point clearly and firmly — **forth·right·ly** *adv*

forth·with *adv* : without delay : IMMEDIATELY

¹for·ti·eth *adj* : coming right after 39th

²fortieth *n* : number 40 in a series

for·ti·fi·ca·tion *n* **1** : the act of making stronger or enriching **2** : something built to strengthen or protect

for·ti·fy *vb* **for·ti·fied; for·ti·fy·ing** **1** : to make strong **2** : to add material to (something) to stengthen or improve it

for·ti·tude *n* : strength of mind that lets a person meet danger, pain, or hardship with courage

fort·night *n* : two weeks

for·tress *n* : a place that is protected against attack

for·tu·nate *adj* **1** : bringing a good result **2** : having good luck : LUCKY — **for·tu·nate·ly** *adv*

for·tune *n* **1** : a large sum of money **2** : what happens to a person : good or bad luck **3** : what is to happen to one in the future **4** : WEALTH

for·tune–tell·er *n* : a person who claims to foretell future events

¹for·ty *adj* : being four times ten

²forty *n* : four times ten : 40

for·ty–nin·er *n* : a person in the California gold rush of 1849

fo·rum *n* **1** : the marketplace or public place of an ancient Roman city serving as the center for public business **2** : a place or opportunity for discussion

¹for·ward *adj* **1** : near, at, or belonging to the front part **2** : moving, tending, or leading to a position in front **3** : lacking proper modesty or reserve

²forward *or* **for·wards** *adv* : to or toward what is in front

³forward *vb* **for·ward·ed; for·ward·ing** **1** : to send on or ahead **2** : to help onward : ADVANCE

⁴forward *n* : a player at or near the front of his or her team or near the opponent's goal

fos·sil *n* : a trace or print or the remains of a plant or animal of a past age preserved in earth or rock

¹fos·ter *adj* : giving, receiving, or offering parental care even though not related by blood or legal ties

²foster *vb* **fos·tered; fos·ter·ing** **1** : to give parental care to **2** : to help the growth and development of

fought *past and past participle of* FIGHT

¹foul *adj* **foul·er; foul·est** **1** : disgusting in looks, taste, or smell **2** : full of or covered with something that pollutes **3** : being vulgar or insulting **4** : being wet and stormy **5** : very unfair **6** : very unpleasant or bad **7** : breaking a rule in a game or sport **8** : being outside the foul lines

²foul *n* **1** : a ball in baseball that is batted outside the foul lines **2** : an act of breaking the rules in a game or sport

³foul *vb* **fouled; foul·ing** **1** : to make or become foul or filthy **2** : to make a foul in a game

foul line *n* : either of two straight lines running from the rear corner of home plate through first and third base to the boundary of a baseball field

¹found *past and past participle of* FIND

²found *vb* **found·ed; found·ing** : to begin or create : ESTABLISH

foun·da·tion *n* **1** : the support upon which something rests **2** : the act of beginning or creating

¹found·er *n* : a person who creates or establishes something

²foun·der *vb* **found·ered; found·er·ing** : ¹SINK 1

found·ry *n, pl* **foundries** : a building or factory where metal goods are made

fount *n* : SOURCE 1

foun·tain *n* **1** : an artificial stream or spray of water (as for drinking or ornament) or the device from which it comes **2** : SOURCE 1 **3** : a spring of water coming from the earth

fountain pen *n* : a pen with ink inside that is fed as needed to the writing point

¹four *adj* : being one more than three

²four *n* **1** : one more than three : two times two : 4 **2** : the fourth in a set or series

four·fold *adj* : being four times as great or as many

four·score *adj* : ²EIGHTY

four·some *adj* : a group of four persons or things

¹four·teen *adj* : being one more than 13

²fourteen *n* : one more than 13 : two times seven : 14

¹four·teenth *adj* : coming right after 13th

²fourteenth *n* : number 14 in a series

¹fourth *adj* : coming right after third

²fourth *n* **1** : number four in a series **2** : one of four equal parts

Fourth of July *n* : INDEPENDENCE DAY

fowl *n, pl* **fowl** *or* **fowls** **1** : BIRD **2** : a common domestic rooster or hen **3** : the meat of a domestic fowl used as food

fox *n* **1** : a wild animal closely related to the wolf that has a sharp snout, pointed ears, and a long bushy tail **2** *cap* : a member of an American Indian people formerly living in what is now Wisconsin

foxy *adj* **fox·i·er; fox·i·est** : very clever

foy·er *n* **1** : a lobby especially in a theater **2** : an entrance hall

fr. *abbr* from

Fr. *abbr* father

fra·cas *n* : a noisy quarrel : BRAWL

frac·tion *n* **1** : a number (as $\frac{1}{2}$, $\frac{2}{3}$, $\frac{17}{100}$) that indicates one or more equal parts of a whole or group and that may be considered as indicating also division of the number above the line by the number below the line **2** : a part of a whole : FRAGMENT

frac·tion·al *adj* **1** : of, relating to, or being a fraction **2** : fairly small

¹frac·ture *n* : the result of breaking : damage or an injury caused by breaking

²fracture *vb* **frac·tured; frac·tur·ing** : ¹BREAK 2

frag·ile *adj* : easily broken or hurt : DELICATE

frag·ment *n* : a broken or incomplete part

fra·grance *n* : a sweet or pleasant smell

fra·grant *adj* : sweet or pleasant in smell — **fra·grant·ly** *adv*

frail *adj* : very delicate or weak

frail·ty *n, pl* **frailties** **1** : the quality or state of being weak **2** : a weakness of character

¹frame *vb* **framed; fram·ing** **1** : to enclose in or as if in a frame **2** : to express in words **3** : to make appear guilty

²frame *n* **1** : the structure of an animal and especially a human body : PHYSIQUE **2** : an arrangement of parts that give form or support to something **3** : an open case

or structure for holding or enclosing something

³frame *adj* : having a wooden frame

frame of mind *n* : a particular state or mood

frame·work *n* : a basic supporting part or structure

franc *n* : any of various coins or bills used or once used in countries where French is widely spoken

Fran·co- *prefix* **1** : French and **2** : French

frank *adj* : free in or characterized by freedom in expressing feelings and opinions — **frank·ly** *adv* — **frank·ness** *n*

frank·furt·er *or* **frank·furt** *n* : a cooked sausage : HOT DOG

frank·in·cense *n* : a fragrant plant gum that is burned for its sweet smell

fran·tic *adj* : wildly excited

fran·ti·cal·ly *adv* : in a frantic way

fra·ter·nal *adj* **1** : having to do with brothers **2** : made up of members banded together like brothers

fraternal twin *n* : either of a pair of twins that are produced from different fertilized eggs and may not have the same sex or appearance

fra·ter·ni·ty *n, pl* **fra·ter·ni·ties** : a club of boys or men (as in a college)

fraud *n* **1** : TRICKERY, DECEIT **2** : an act of deceiving : TRICK **3** : a person who pretends to be what he or she is not

fraud·u·lent *adj* : based on or done by deceit — **fraud·u·lent·ly** *adv*

fraught *adj* : full of some quality

¹fray *n* : ²FIGHT 1, BRAWL

²fray *vb* **frayed; fray·ing** : to wear into shreds

fraz·zle *n* : a tired or nervous condition

¹freak *n* : a strange, abnormal, or unusual person, thing, or event — **freak·ish** *adj* — **freaky** *adj*

²freak *adj* : not likely

¹freck·le *n* : a small brownish spot on the skin

²freckle *vb* **freck·led; freck·ling** : to mark or become marked with freckles or spots

¹free *adj* **fre·er** ; **fre·est** **1** : given without charge **2** : having liberty : not being a slave or prisoner **3** : not controlled by a harsh ruler or harsh laws **4** : not physically held by something **5** : not having or suffering from something unpleasant, unwanted, or painful **6** : not held back by fear or uncertainly : OPEN **7** : not blocked : CLEAR **8** : not required to be doing something **9** : not used or occupied **10** not combined — **free·ly** *adv*

²free *vb* **freed; free·ing** : to let go or set free : RELEASE

³free *adv* **1** : in a free manner : FREELY **2** : without charge

freed·man *n, pl* **freed·men** : a person freed from slavery

free·dom *n* **1** : the condition of having liberty **2** : ability to move or act as desired **3** : release from something unpleasant **4** : the quality of being very frank : CANDOR **5** : a political right

free·hand *adj or adv* : done without mechanical aids

free·man *n, pl* **free·men** : a free person : a person who is not a slave

free·stand·ing *adj* : standing alone free of attachment or support

free·way *n* : an expressway that can be used without paying tolls

free will *n* : a person's own choice or decision

¹freeze *vb* **froze; fro·zen; freez·ing 1** : to harden into or be hardened into a solid (as ice) by loss of heat **2** : to be uncomfortably cold **3** : to damage by cold **4** : to clog or become clogged by ice **5** : to become completely still

²freeze *n* **1** : a period of freezing weather : cold weather **2** : the state of being frozen

freez·er *n* : a compartment or room used to freeze food or keep it frozen

freezing point *n* : the temperature at which a liquid becomes solid

¹freight *n* **1** : goods or cargo carried by a ship, train, truck, or airplane **2** : the carrying (as by truck) of goods from one place to another **3** : the amount paid (as to a shipping company) for carrying goods **4** : a train that carries freight

²freight *vb* **freight·ed; freight·ing** : to send by train, truck, airplane, or ship

freight·er *n* : a ship or airplane used to carry freight

¹French *adj* : of or relating to France, its people, or the French language

²French *n* **1 French** *pl* : the people of France **2** : the language of the French people ·

french fry *n, often cap 1st F* : a strip of potato fried in deep fat

French horn *n* : a circular brass musical instrument with a large opening at one end and a mouthpiece shaped like a small funnel

fren·zied *adj* : very excited and upset

fren·zy *n, pl* **frenzies** : great and often wild or disorderly activity

fre·quen·cy *n, pl* **fre·quen·cies 1** : frequent repetition **2** : rate of repetition

¹fre·quent *vb* **fre·quent·ed; fre·quent·ing** : to visit often

²fre·quent *adj* : happening often — **fre·quent·ly** *adv*

fresh *adj* **fresh·er; fresh·est 1** : not salt **2** : PURE 1, BRISK **3** : not frozen, canned, or pickled **4** : not stale, sour, or spoiled **5** : not dirty or rumpled **6** : ¹NEW 4 **7** : newly made or received **8** : rude and disrespectful — **fresh·ly** *adv* — **fresh·ness** *n*

fresh·en *vb* **fresh·ened; fresh·en·ing** : to make or become fresh

fresh·man *n, pl* **fresh·men** : a first year student in high school or college

fresh·wa·ter *adj* : relating to or living in fresh water

¹fret *vb* **fret·ted; fret·ting** : ¹WORRY 3

²fret *n* : an irritated or worried state

fret·ful *adj* : irritated and worried — **fret·ful·ly** *adv*

Fri. *abbr* Friday

fri·ar *n* : a member of a Roman Catholic religious order for men

fric·tion *n* **1** : the rubbing of one thing against another **2** : resistance to motion between bodies in contact **3** : disagreement among persons or groups

Fri·day *n* : the sixth day of the week

friend *n* **1** : a person who has a strong liking for and trust in another person **2** : a person who is not an enemy **3** : a person who helps or supports something — **friend·less** *adj*

friend·ly *adj* **friend·li·er; friend·li·est 1** : having or showing the kindness and warmth of a friend **2** : being other than an enemy **3** : easy or suitable for — **friend·li·ness** *n*

friend·ship *n* **1** : the state of being friends **2** : a warm and kind feeling or attitude

frieze *n* : a band or stripe (as around a building) used as a decoration

frig·ate *n* **1** : a square-rigged warship **2** : a modern warship that is smaller than a destroyer

fright *n* **1** : sudden terror : great fear **2** : something that frightens or is ugly or shocking

fright·en *vb* **fright·ened; fright·en·ing** : to make afraid : TERRIFY — **fright·en·ing·ly** *adv*

fright·ful *adj* **1** : causing fear or alarm **2** : SHOCKING 1, OUTRAGEOUS — **fright·ful·ly** *adv*

frig·id *adj* **1** : freezing cold **2** : not friendly

frill *n* **1** : ²RUFFLE **2** : something added mostly for show

frilly *adj* **frill·i·er; frill·i·est** : having ruffles

¹fringe *n* **1** : a border or trimming made by or made to look like the loose ends of the cloth **2** : a narrow area along the edge

²fringe *vb* **fringed; fring·ing 1** : to decorate with a fringe **2** : to go along or around

frisk *vb* **frisked; frisk·ing 1** : to move around in a lively or playful way **2** : to search a person quickly for something that may be hidden

frisky *adj* **frisk·i·er; frisk·i·est :** PLAYFUL 1, LIVELY

¹frit·ter *n* **:** a small amount of fried batter often containing fruit or meat

²fritter *vb* **frit·tered; frit·ter·ing :** to waste on unimportant things

fri·vol·i·ty *n, pl* **fri·vol·i·ties :** a lack of seriousness

friv·o·lous *adj* **1 :** of little importance : TRIV-IAL **2 :** lacking in seriousness

frizzy *adj* **frizz·i·er; frizz·i·est :** very curly

fro *adv* **:** in a direction away

frock *n* **:** a woman's or girl's dress

frog *n* **1 :** a tailless animal that is an amphibian with smooth moist skin and webbed feet that spends more of its time in water than the related toad **2 :** an ornamental fastening for a garment

¹frol·ic *vb* **frol·icked; frol·ick·ing :** to play about happily : ROMP

²frolic *n* **:** ¹FUN 1

frol·ic·some *adj* **:** very lively and playful

from *prep* **1** — used to show a starting point **2** — used to show a point of separation **3** — used to show a material, source, or cause

frond *n* **:** a large leaf (as of a palm or fern) or leaflike structure (as of a seaweed) with many divisions

¹front *n* **1 :** the forward part or surface **2 :** a region in which active warfare is taking place **3 :** the boundary between bodies of air at different temperatures — **in front of :** directly before or ahead of

²front *vb* **front·ed; front·ing :** ²FACE 1

³front *adj* **:** situated at the front

fron·tal *adj* **:** of or directed at a front

¹fron·tier *n* **1 :** a border between two countries **2 :** the edge of the settled part of a country

²frontier *adj* **:** of, living in, or situated in the frontier

fron·tiers·man *n, pl* **fron·tiers·men :** a person living on the frontier

¹frost *n* **1 :** a covering of tiny ice crystals on a cold surface formed from the water vapor in the air **2 :** temperature cold enough to cause freezing

²frost *vb* **frost·ed; frost·ing 1 :** to cover with frosting **2 :** to cover or become covered with frost

frost·bite *n* **:** slight freezing of a part of the body (as the feet or hands) or the damage to body tissues caused by such freezing

frost·ing *n* **1 :** ICING **2 :** a dull finish on glass

frosty *adj* **frost·i·er; frost·i·est 1 :** covered with frost **2 :** cold enough to produce frost

¹froth *n* **:** bubbles formed in or on liquids

²froth *vb* **frothed; froth·ing :** to produce or form bubbles in or on a liquid

frothy *adj* **froth·i·er; froth·i·est :** full of or made up of small bubbles

¹frown *vb* **frowned; frown·ing 1 :** to have a serious facial expression (as in anger or thought) **2 :** to look with disapproval

²frown *n* **:** a serious facial expression that shows anger, unhappiness, or deep thought

froze *past of* FREEZE

frozen *past participle of* FREEZE

fru·gal *adj* **1 :** careful in spending or using supplies **2 :** simple and without unnecessary things — **fru·gal·ly** *adv*

¹fruit *n* **1 :** a pulpy or juicy plant part (as rhubarb, a strawberry, or an orange) that is often eaten as a dessert and is distinguished from a vegetable **2 :** a product of fertilization in a seed plant that consists of the ripened ovary of a flower with its included seeds **3 :** ²RESULT 1, PRODUCT — **fruit·ed** *adj*

²fruit *vb* **fruit·ed; fruit·ing :** to bear or cause to bear fruit

fruit·cake *n* **:** a rich cake containing nuts, dried or candied fruits, and spices

fruit·ful *adj* **1 :** very productive **2 :** bringing results — **fruit·ful·ly** *adv*

fruit·less *adj* **1 :** not bearing fruit **2 :** UN-SUCCESSFUL — **fruit·less·ly** *adv*

fruity *adj* **fruit·i·er; fruit·i·est :** relating to or suggesting fruit

frus·trate *vb* **frus·trat·ed; frus·trat·ing 1 :** to cause to feel angry or discouraged **2 :** to prevent from succeeding **3 :** ¹DEFEAT 2

frus·trat·ing *adj* **:** causing feelings of disappointment and defeat

frus·tra·tion *n* **:** DISAPPOINTMENT 1, DEFEAT

¹fry *vb* **fried; fry·ing :** to cook in fat

²fry *n, pl* **fries :** FRENCH FRY

³fry *n, pl* **fry :** a recently hatched or very young fish — usually used in pl.

ft. *abbr* **1** feet **2** foot **3** fort

fudge *n* **:** a soft creamy candy

¹fu·el *n* **:** a substance (as oil or gasoline) that can be burned to produce heat or power

²fuel *vb* **fu·eled** *or* **fu·elled; fu·el·ing** *or* **fu·el·ling :** to supply with or take on fuel

¹fu·gi·tive *adj* **:** running away or trying to escape

²fugitive *n* **:** a person who is running away

¹-ful *adj suffix* **1 :** full of **2 :** characterized by **3 :** having the qualities of **4 :** tending or given to

²-ful *n suffix* **:** number or quantity that fills or would fill

ful·crum *n, pl* **fulcrums** *or* **ful·cra :** the support on which a lever turns in lifting something

ful·fill *or* **ful·fil** *vb* **ful·filled; ful·fill·ing 1 :** to make real **2 :** SATISFY 4 — **ful·fill·ment** *n*

¹full *adj* **1 :** containing as much or as many as possible or normal **2 :** ¹COMPLETE 1 **3 :** not limited in any way **4 :** plump and rounded in outline **5 :** having much material — **full·ness** *n*

²full *adv* **1 :** ²VERY 1 **2 :** COMPLETELY

³full *n* **1 :** the highest state, extent, or degree **2 :** the complete amount

full·back *n* **1 :** a football player who runs with the ball and blocks **2 :** a player in games like soccer and field hockey who is usually positioned near the goal

full–grown *adj* **:** having reached full growth or development

full moon *n* **:** the moon with its whole disk lighted

full–time *adj* **:** working or involving the full number of hours considered normal or standard

ful·ly *adv* **1 :** COMPLETELY **2 :** at least

¹fum·ble *vb* **fum·bled; fum·bling 1 :** to feel about for or handle something in a clumsy way **2 :** to lose hold of the ball in football

²fumble *n* **:** an act of losing hold of the ball in football

¹fume *n* **:** a disagreeable smoke, vapor, or gas — usually used in pl.

²fume *vb* **fumed; fum·ing 1 :** to give off a disagreeable smoke, vapor, or gas **2 :** to be angry **3 :** to say something in an angry way

¹fun *n* **1 :** someone or something that provides amusement or enjoyment **2 :** a good time **:** AMUSEMENT **3 :** words or actions to make someone or something an object of ridicule

²fun *adj* **1 :** providing fun **2 :** full of fun

¹func·tion *n* **1 :** the action for which a person or thing is designed or used **:** PURPOSE **2 :** a large important ceremony or social affair

²function *vb* **func·tioned; func·tion·ing :** to serve a certain purpose **:** WORK

function key *n* **:** any of a set of keys on a computer keyboard with special functions

fund *n* **1 :** a sum of money for a special purpose **2 funds** *pl* **:** available money **3 :** ¹STOCK 1, SUPPLY

¹fun·da·men·tal *adj* **:** being or forming a foundation **:** BASIC, ESSENTIAL — **fun·da·men·tal·ly** *adv*

²fundamental *n* **:** a basic part

fu·ner·al *n* **:** the ceremonies held for a dead person (as before burial)

fun·gal *or* **fun·gous** *adj* **:** of, relating to, or caused by a fungus

fun·gi·cide *n* **:** a substance used to kill fungi — **fun·gi·cid·al** *adj*

fun·gus *n, pl* **fun·gi** *also* **fun·gus·es :** any member of the kingdom of living things (as mushrooms, molds, and rusts) that have no chlorophyll, must live in or on plants, animals, or decaying material, and were formerly considered plants

funk *n* **:** a sad or worried state

fun·nel *n* **1 :** a utensil usually shaped like a hollow cone with a tube extending from the point and used to catch and direct a downward flow **2 :** a large pipe for the escape of smoke or for ventilation (as on a ship)

fun·nies *n pl* **:** comic strips or a section of a newspaper containing comic strips

¹fun·ny *adj* **fun·ni·er; fun·ni·est 1 :** causing laughter **:** full of humor **2 :** STRANGE 2

²funny *adv* **:** in an odd or peculiar way

fur *n* **1 :** the hairy coat of a mammal especially when fine, soft, and thick **2 :** a piece of the pelt of an animal **3 :** an article of clothing made with fur — **furred** *adj*

fu·ri·ous *adj* **1 :** very angry **2 :** very active or fast **3 :** very powerful or violent — **fu·ri·ous·ly** *adv*

furl *vb* **furled; furl·ing :** to wrap or roll close to or around something

fur·long *n* **:** a unit of length equal to 220 yards (about 201 meters)

fur·lough *n* **:** a leave of absence from duty

fur·nace *n* **:** an enclosed structure in which heat is produced (as for heating a house or melting metals)

fur·nish *vb* **fur·nished; fur·nish·ing 1 :** to provide with furniture **2 :** to provide with what is needed **3 :** to supply to someone or something

fur·nish·ings *n pl* **:** articles of furniture for a room or building

fur·ni·ture *n* **:** movable articles used to furnish a room

¹fur·row *n* **1 :** a trench made by or as if by a plow **2 :** a narrow groove **:** WRINKLE

²furrow *vb* **fur·rowed; fur·row·ing :** to make wrinkles or grooves in

fur·ry *adj* **fur·ri·er; fur·ri·est 1 :** covered with fur **2 :** like fur

¹fur·ther *adv* **1 :** ¹FARTHER 1 **2 :** ²BESIDES, ALSO **3 :** to a greater degree or extent

²further *vb* **fur·thered; fur·ther·ing :** to help forward **:** PROMOTE

³further *adj* **1 :** ²FARTHER **2 :** going or extending beyond **:** ADDITIONAL

fur·ther·more *adv* **:** MOREOVER

fur·thest *adv or adj* **:** FARTHEST

fur·tive *adj* **:** done in a sneaky or sly manner — **fur·tive·ly** *adv*

fu·ry *n, pl* **furies 1 :** violent anger **:** RAGE **2 :** wild and dangerous force

¹fuse *vb* **fused; fus·ing 1 :** to change into a liquid or to a plastic state by heat **2 :** to unite by or as if by melting together

²fuse *n* **:** a device having a metal wire or strip

that melts and interrupts an electrical circuit when the current becomes too strong

³fuse *n* **1** : a cord that is set afire to ignite an explosive by carrying fire to it **2** : a device for setting off a bomb or torpedo

fu·se·lage *n* : the part of an airplane that holds the crew, passengers, and cargo

fu·sion *n* **1** : an act of fusing or melting together **2** : union by or as if by melting **3** : union of atomic nuclei to form heavier nuclei resulting in the release of enormous quantities of energy

¹fuss *n* **1** : unnecessary activity or excitement often over something unimportant **2** : ²PROTEST 1 **3** : a great show of interest

²fuss *vb* **fussed; fuss·ing** : to get excited or upset especially over something unimportant

fussy *adj* **fuss·i·er; fuss·i·est 1** : inclined to complain or whine **2** : hard to please **3** : overly decorated and complicated

fu·tile *adj* : having no result or effect — **fu·tile·ly** *adv*

fu·til·i·ty *n* : the quality or state of being ineffective

¹fu·ture *adj* : coming after the present

²future *n* **1** : the period of time that is to come **2** : the chance of future success

fuzz *n* : fine light hairs or fibers

fuzzy *adj* **fuzz·i·er; fuzz·i·est 1** : covered with or looking like short fine hairs or fibers **2** : not clear — **fuzz·i·ness** *n*

-fy *vb suffix* **-fied; -fy·ing 1** : make : form into **2** : provide with the characteristics of

G

g *n, pl* **g's** *or* **gs** *often cap* **1** : the seventh letter of the English alphabet **2** : the musical note referred to by the letter G **3** : a unit of force equal to the force of gravity on a body

g. *abbr* gram

G *abbr* good

Ga., GA *abbr* Georgia

¹gab *vb* **gabbed; gab·bing** : to talk in a relaxed way about unimportant things : CHAT

²gab *n* : talk about unimportant things

gab·ar·dine *n* : a firm cloth with a hard smooth finish

¹gab·ble *vb* **gab·bled; gab·bling** : to talk in a fast or foolish way or in a way that is hard to understand

²gabble *n* : talk that is fast or foolish or hard to understand

gab·by *adj* **gab·bi·er; gab·bi·est** : fond of talking a lot : TALKATIVE

ga·ble *n* : the triangular part of an outside wall of a building formed by the sides of a sloping roof — **ga·bled** *adj*

gad *vb* **gad·ded; gad·ding** : to wander or roam from place to place

gad·about *n* : a person who goes to many different places for enjoyment

gad·fly *n, pl* **gad·flies 1** : a large biting fly **2** : a person who annoys others especially with constant criticism

gad·get *n* : a small useful device that is often interesting, unfamiliar, or unusual

¹gag *vb* **gagged; gag·ging 1** : to stop from speaking or crying out by or as if by covering or blocking the mouth **2** : to vomit or feel like vomiting **3** : CHOKE 2

²gag *n* **1** : something covering or blocking the mouth especially to prevent speaking or

crying out **2** : something said or done to make other people laugh

gage *variant of* GAUGE

gag·gle *n* **1** : a group of animals and especially a flock of geese **2** : a group of people

gai·ety *n, pl* **gai·eties 1** : happy and lively activity : MERRYMAKING **2** : bright spirits or manner

gai·ly *adv* **1** : in a merry or lively way **2** : in a bright or showy way

¹gain *n* **1** : something valuable or desirable that is obtained or acquired : PROFIT **2** : an increase in amount, size, or degree

²gain *vb* **gained; gain·ing 1** : to get or win often by effort **2** : to get or acquire in a natural or gradual way **3** : to increase in **4** : to get to : REACH **5** : to get an advantage : PROFIT

gain·ful *adj* : producing gain : making money

gait *n* : a way of walking or running

gal. *abbr* gallon

¹ga·la *n* : a large showy celebration

²gala *adj* : being or resembling a large showy celebration

ga·lac·tic *adj* : of or relating to a galaxy

gal·axy *n, pl* **gal·ax·ies 1** : MILKY WAY GALAXY **2** : one of the very large groups of stars, gas, and dust that make up the universe

gale *n* **1** : a strong wind **2** : a wind of from about 32 to 63 miles per hour (about 51 to 101 kilometers per hour) **3** : an outburst of amusement

ga·le·na *n* : a bluish gray mineral that is the ore from which lead is obtained

¹gall *n* **1** : extreme boldness or rudeness **2**

: bile especially when obtained from an animal for use in the arts or medicine

²gall *n* : a sore spot (as on a horse's back) caused by rubbing

³gall *vb* **galled; gall·ing 1** : to make sore by rubbing **2** : to annoy or make angry

⁴gall *n* : an abnormal swelling or growth on a twig or leaf

gal·lant *adj* **1** : showing courage : very brave **2** : CHIVALROUS 2 **3** : very polite to women **4** : splendid or stately **5** : showy in dress or in the way of acting — **gal·lant·ly** *adv*

gal·lant·ry *n* **1** : courageous behavior : BRAVERY **2** : polite attention shown to women

gall·blad·der *n* : a small sac in which bile from the liver is stored

gal·le·on *n* : a large sailing ship used by the Spanish from the 1400s to the 1700s

gal·lery *n, pl* **gal·ler·ies 1** : a long narrow room or hall **2** : an indoor structure (as in a theater or church) built out from one or more walls **3** : a room or building in which people look at works of art **4** : the highest balcony of seats in a theater or the people who sit there **5** : a passage (as in wood) made by an animal and especially an insect

gal·ley *n, pl* **galleys 1** : a large low ship of olden times moved by oars and sails **2** : the kitchen especially of a ship or an airplane

gal·li·vant *vb* **gal·li·vant·ed; gal·li·vant·ing** : to travel from place to place doing things for pleasure

gal·lon *n* : a unit of liquid capacity equal to four quarts (about 3.8 liters)

¹gal·lop *vb* **gal·loped; gal·lop·ing 1** : to run or cause to run at a gallop **2** : to ride on a galloping horse

²gallop *n* **1** : the fast springing way an animal with four feet and especially a horse runs when all four of its feet leave the ground at the same time **2** : a ride or run on a galloping horse

gal·lows *n, pl* **gallows** *or* **gal·lows·es** : a structure from which criminals are hanged

ga·lore *adj* : in large amounts — used after the word it modifies

ga·losh *n* : a high shoe worn over another shoe to keep the foot dry especially in snow or wet weather — usually used in pl.

gal·va·nize *vb* **gal·va·nized; gal·va·niz·ing 1** : to excite about something so that action is taken **2** : to coat with zinc for protection

¹gam·ble *vb* **gam·bled; gam·bling 1** : to play a game in which something (as money) can be won or lost : BET **2** : to take a chance — **gam·bler** *n*

²gamble *n* : something that could produce a good or bad result : RISK

gam·bol *vb* **gam·boled** *or* **gam·bolled; gam-**

bol·ing *or* **gam·bol·ling** : to run or play happily : FROLIC

¹game *n* **1** : a contest or sport played according to rules with the players in direct opposition to each other **2** : the manner of playing in a game or contest **3** : playful activity : something done for amusement **4** : animals hunted for sport or for food **5** : the meat from animals hunted for food

²game *adj* **gam·er; gam·est 1** : willing or ready to do something **2** : full of spirit or eagerness **3** : relating to or being animals that are hunted

game·keep·er *n* : a person in charge of the breeding and protection of game animals or birds on private land

game·ly *adv* : with spirit and courage

gam·ing *n* : the practice of gambling

gam·ma ray *n* : a ray that is like an X-ray but of higher energy and that is given off especially by a radioactive substance

gamy *adj* **gam·i·er; gam·i·est** : having the flavor or smell of meat from wild animals especially when slightly spoiled

¹gan·der *n* : a male goose

²gander *n* : a look or glance

gang *n* **1** : a group of people working or going about together **2** : a group of people acting together to do something illegal **3** : a group of friends

gan·gli·on *n, pl* **gan·glia** : a mass of nerve cells especially outside the brain or spinal cord

gan·gly *adj* **gan·gli·er; gan·gli·est** : tall, thin, and awkward

gang·plank *n* : a movable bridge from a ship to the shore

gan·grene *n* : death of body tissue when the blood supply is cut off

gang·ster *n* : a member of a gang of criminals

gang up *vb* **ganged up; gang·ing up** : to join together as a group especially to attack, oppose, or criticize

gang·way *n* **1** : a passage into, through, or out of an enclosed space **2** : GANGPLANK

gan·net *n* : a large bird that eats fish and spends much time far from land

gan·try *n, pl* **gantries 1** : a structure over railroad tracks for holding signals **2** : a movable structure for preparing a rocket for launching

gap *n* **1** : an opening made by a break or rupture **2** : an opening between mountains **3** : a hole or space where something is missing

¹gape *vb* **gaped; gap·ing 1** : to stare with the mouth open in surprise or wonder **2** : to open or part widely

²**gape** *n* : an act or instance of opening or staring with the mouth open

ga·rage *n* **1** : a building or part of a building where vehicles are kept when not in use **2** : a shop where vehicles are repaired

¹**garb** *n* : style or kind of clothing

²**garb** *vb* **garbed; garb·ing** : CLOTHE 1

gar·bage *n* **1** : material (as waste food) that has been thrown out **2** : something that is worthless, useless, or untrue

gar·ble *vb* **gar·bled; gar·bling** : to change or twist the meaning or sound of

¹**gar·den** *n* **1** : a piece of ground in which fruits, flowers, or vegetables are grown **2** : a public area for the showing of plants

²**garden** *vb* **gar·dened; gar·den·ing** : to make or work in a garden

gar·den·er *n* : a person who works in a garden especially for pay

gar·de·nia *n* : a large white or yellowish flower with a fragrant smell

gar·gan·tuan *adj* : extremely large or great : HUGE

¹**gar·gle** *vb* **gar·gled; gar·gling** : to rinse the throat with a liquid kept in motion by air forced through it from the lungs

²**gargle** *n* **1** : a liquid used for rinsing the throat and mouth **2** : a sound like that of gargling

gar·goyle *n* : a strange or frightening human or animal figure that sticks out from the roof of a building and often serves as a waterspout

gar·ish *adj* : too bright or showy : GAUDY — **gar·ish·ly** *adv*

¹**gar·land** *n* : a wreath or rope of material (as leaves or flowers)

²**garland** *vb* **gar·land·ed; gar·land·ing** : to form into or decorate with a garland

gar·lic *n* : a plant related to the onion and grown for its bulbs that have a strong smell and taste and are used to flavor foods

gar·ment *n* : an article of clothing

gar·ner *vb* **gar·nered; gar·ner·ing** **1** : to collect or gather **2** : to acquire or earn

gar·net *n* : a deep red mineral used as a gem

¹**gar·nish** *vb* **gar·nished; gar·nish·ing** : to add decorations or seasoning (as to food)

²**garnish** *n* : something used to add decoration or flavoring (as to food)

gar·ret *n* : a room or unfinished part of a house just under the roof

¹**gar·ri·son** *n* **1** : a military camp, fort, or base **2** : the soldiers stationed at a garrison

²**garrison** *vb* **gar·ri·soned; gar·ri·son·ing** **1** : to station troops in **2** : to send (troops) to live in and defend

gar·ru·lous *adj* : very talkative

gar·ter *n* : a band worn to hold up a stocking or sock

garter snake *n* : any of numerous harmless American snakes with stripes along the back

¹**gas** *n, pl* **gas·es** **1** : a substance (as oxygen or hydrogen) having no fixed shape and tending to expand without limit **2** : NATURAL GAS **3** : a gas or a mixture of gases used to make a person unconscious (as for an operation) **4** : a substance that poisons the air or makes breathing difficult **5** : GASOLINE **6** : a gaseous product of digestion or the discomfort caused by it

²**gas** *vb* **gassed; gas·sing; gas·ses** **1** : to poison with gas **2** : to supply with gas

gas·eous *adj* **1** : having the form of gas **2** : of or relating to gas

¹**gash** *n* : a long deep cut

²**gash** *vb* **gashed; gash·ing** : to make a long deep cut in

gas mask *n* : a mask connected to a chemical air filter and used to protect the face and lungs from harmful gases

gas·o·line *n* : a flammable liquid made especially from natural gas found in the earth and from petroleum and used mostly as an automobile fuel

¹**gasp** *vb* **gasped; gasp·ing** **1** : to breathe in suddenly and loudly with the mouth open because of surprise, shock, or pain **2** : to breathe with difficulty : PANT **3** : to utter with quick difficult breaths

²**gasp** *n* **1** : the act of breathing in suddenly or with difficulty **2** : something gasped

gas station *n* : a place for servicing motor vehicles especially with gasoline and oil

gas·tric juice *n* : an acid liquid made by the stomach that helps to digest food

gate *n* **1** : an opening in a wall or fence **2** : a part of a barrier (as a fence) that opens and closes like a door **3** : a door, valve, or other device for controlling the flow of water or other fluids **4** : an area at an airport where passengers arrive and leave

gate·house *n* : a small building near a gate

gate·keep·er *n* : a person who guards a gate

gate·way *n* **1** : an opening for a gate **2** : a passage into or out of a place or condition

¹**gath·er** *vb* **gath·ered; gath·er·ing** **1** : to pick up and collect **2** : to choose and collect **3** : to come together in a group or around a center of attraction **4** : to gain little by little **5** : to bring or call forth (as strength or courage) from within **6** : to get an idea : CONCLUDE **7** : to draw together in or as if in folds

²**gather** *n* : the result of gathering cloth : PUCKER

gath·er·ing *n* : an occasion when people come together as a group

gaudy *adj* **gaud·i·er; gaud·i·est** : too bright and showy

¹**gauge** *also* **gage** *n* **1** : a measurement (as the distance between the rails of a railroad or the size of a shotgun barrel's inner diameter) according to some standard **2** : an instrument for measuring, testing, or registering

²**gauge** *also* **gage** *vb* **gauged** *also* **gaged**; **gaug·ing** *also* **gag·ing** **1** : to measure exactly **2** : to make a judgment about

gaunt *adj* **gaunt·er**; **gaunt·est** : very thin and bony (as from illness or hunger)

gaunt·let *n* **1** : a glove made of small metal plates and worn with a suit of armor **2** : a glove with a wide cuff that protects the wrist and part of the arm

gauze *n* **1** : a thin fabric that allows light to pass through it **2** : loosely woven cotton used as a bandage

gauzy *adj* **gauz·i·er**; **gauz·i·est** : thin and transparent like gauze

gave *past of* GIVE

gav·el *n* : a mallet with which the person in charge raps to get people's attention in a meeting or courtroom

gawk *vb* **gawked**; **gawk·ing** : to stare stupidly

gawky *adj* **gawk·i·er**; **gawk·i·est** : awkward and clumsy

gay *adj* **gay·er**; **gay·est** **1** : HAPPY : MERRY **2** : cheerful and lively **3** : brightly colored

¹**gaze** *vb* **gazed**; **gaz·ing** : to fix the eyes in a long steady look

²**gaze** *n* : a long steady look

ga·ze·bo *n, pl* **ga·ze·bos** : a small building (as in a garden or park) that is usually open on the sides

ga·zelle *n* : a swift graceful antelope of Africa and Asia

ga·zette *n* **1** : NEWSPAPER **2** : a journal giving official information

gaz·et·teer *n* : a geographical dictionary

ga·zil·lion *n* : an extremely large number — **gazillion** *adj*

GB *abbr* gigabyte

¹**gear** *n* **1** : EQUIPMENT **2** : a group of parts that has a specific function in a machine **3** : a toothed wheel : COGWHEEL **4** : the position the gears of a machine are in when they are ready to work **5** : one of the adjustments in a motor vehicle that determine the direction of travel and the relative speed between the engine and the motion of the vehicle **6** : working order or condition

²**gear** *vb* **geared**; **gear·ing** **1** : to make ready for operation **2** : to be or make suitable

gear·shift *n* : a mechanism by which gears are connected and disconnected

gecko *n, pl* **geck·os** *or* **geck·oes** : a small tropical lizard that eats insects and is usually active at night

gee *interj* — used to show surprise, enthusiasm, or disappointment

geese *pl of* GOOSE

Gei·ger counter *n* : an instrument for detecting the presence of cosmic rays or radioactive substances

¹**gel** *n* : a thick jellylike substance

²**gel** *vb* **gelled**; **gel·ling** : to change into a thick jellylike substance

gel·a·tin *n* **1** : a gummy or sticky protein obtained by boiling animal tissues and used especially as food **2** : an edible jelly made with gelatin

ge·lat·i·nous *adj* : resembling gelatin or jelly

gem *n* **1** : a usually valuable stone cut and polished for jewelry **2** : something prized as being beautiful or perfect

Gem·i·ni *n* **1** : a constellation between Taurus and Cancer usually pictured as twins sitting together **2** : the third sign of the zodiac or a person born under this sign

gem·stone *n* : a stone that when cut and polished can be used in jewelry

gen. *abbr* general

gen·der *n* : the state of being male or female : SEX

gene *n* : a unit of DNA that is usually located on a chromosome and that controls the development of one or more traits and is the basic unit by which genetic information is passed from parent to offspring

ge·ne·al·o·gy *n, pl* **ge·ne·al·o·gies** **1** : a line of ancestors of a person or family or a history of such a line of ancestors **2** : the study of family lines of ancestors

genera *pl of* GENUS

¹**gen·er·al** *adj* **1** : having to do with the whole : applying to more than just a small area or group **2** : not specific or detailed **3** : involving or including many or most people **4** : not specialized — **in general** : for the most part

²**general** *n* : a military officer ranking above a colonel

gen·er·al·iza·tion *n* **1** : the act of forming conclusions from a small amount of information **2** : a general statement : a conclusion based on only a small number of items or instances

gen·er·al·ize *vb* **gen·er·al·ized**; **gen·er·al·iz·ing** : to draw or state a general conclusion from a number of different instances

gen·er·al·ly *adv* **1** : for the most part **2** : in most cases : USUALLY

gen·er·ate *vb* **gen·er·at·ed**; **gen·er·at·ing** : to cause to come into being

gen·er·a·tion *n* **1** : those being a single step in a line originating from one ancestor **2** : a group of individuals born and living at about the same time **3** : the act or process of producing or creating something

gen·er·a·tor *n* : a machine that produces electricity

gen·er·os·i·ty *n* **1** : willingness to give or to share **2** : an act of unselfish giving

gen·er·ous *adj* **1** : freely giving or sharing **2** : providing more than enough of what is needed : ABUNDANT — **gen·er·ous·ly** *adv*

ge·net·ic *adj* : of or relating to genes or genetics

genetic code *n* : the arrangement of chemical groups within the genes which specify particular kinds of amino acids used to make proteins

ge·net·i·cist *n* : a person specializing in genetics

ge·net·ics *n* : the scientific study of how the characteristics of living things are controlled by genes

ge·nial *adj* : cheerful and pleasant — **ge·nial·ly** *adv*

ge·nie *n* : a magic spirit believed to take human form and serve the person who calls it

gen·i·tal *adj* : of or relating to reproduction or the sexual organs

ge·nius *n* **1** : a very smart or gifted person **2** : great natural ability **3** : a very clever or smart quality

gent *n* : ¹MAN 1, FELLOW

gen·teel *adj* **1** : relating to the upper classes **2** : having an elegant, tasteful, or polite quality

gen·tian *n* : a plant with smooth leaves and usually blue flowers

¹gen·tile *n, often cap* : a person who is not Jewish

²gentile *adj, often cap* : of or relating to people not Jewish

gen·til·i·ty *n* **1** : high social status **2** : a quality of elegance and politeness

gen·tle *adj* **gen·tler; gen·tlest 1** : having or showing a kind and quiet nature : not harsh, stern, or violent **2** : not hard or forceful **3** : not strong or harsh in quality or effect **4** : not steep or sharp — **gen·tle·ness** *n*

gen·tle·folk *n pl* : GENTRY

gen·tle·man *n, pl* **gen·tle·men 1** : a man with very good manners **2** : a man of any social position — used especially in polite speech or when speaking to a group of men **3** : a man of high social status — **gen·tle·man·ly** *adj*

gen·tle·wom·an *n, pl* **gen·tle·wom·en 1** : a woman of good birth and position **2** : a woman with very good manners : LADY

gen·tly *adv* : in a gentle manner

gen·try *n* : people of high social status

gen·u·flect *vb* **gen·u·flect·ed; gen·u·flect·ing**

: to kneel on one knee and rise again as an act of deep respect (as in a church)

gen·u·ine *adj* **1** : actual, real, or true : not false or fake **2** : sincere and honest — **gen·u·ine·ly** *adv*

ge·nus *n, pl* **gen·era** : a group of related living things (as plants or animals) that ranks below the family in scientific classification and is made up of one or more species

geo- *prefix* **1** : earth : soil **2** : geographical

geo·chem·is·try *n* : a science that deals with the chemical composition of and chemical changes in the earth's crust

ge·ode *n* : a stone with a hollow space inside lined with crystals or mineral matter

geog. *abbr* **1** geographic **2** geographical **3** geography

geo·graph·ic *or* **geo·graph·i·cal** *adj* : of or relating to geography

ge·og·ra·phy *n* **1** : a science that deals with the location of living and nonliving things on earth and the way they affect one another **2** : the natural features of an area

geo·log·ic *or* **geo·log·i·cal** *adj* : of or relating to geology

ge·ol·o·gist *n* : a person specializing in geology

ge·ol·o·gy *n* **1** : a science that deals with the history of the earth and its life especially as recorded in rocks **2** : the geologic features (as mountains or plains) of an area

geo·mag·net·ic *adj* : of or relating to the magnetism of the earth

geo·met·ric *adj* **1** : of or relating to geometry **2** : consisting of points, lines, and angles

ge·om·e·try *n* : a branch of mathematics that deals with points, lines, angles, surfaces, and solids

ge·ra·ni·um *n* : a plant often grown for its bright flowers

ger·bil *n* : a small Old World leaping desert animal that is a rodent and is often kept as a pet

germ *n* **1** : a source from which something develops **2** : a microorganism (as a bacterium) that causes disease **3** : a bit of living matter (as a cell) capable of forming a new individual or one of its parts

¹Ger·man *n* **1** : a person born or living in Germany **2** : the language spoken mainly in Germany, Austria, and parts of Switzerland

²German *adj* : of or relating to Germany, the Germans, or the German language

ger·ma·ni·um *n* : a white hard brittle element used as a semiconductor

German shepherd *n* : a large dog of German origin that is often used in police work and as a guide dog for the blind

germ cell *n* : a cell (as an egg or sperm cell)

that contributes to the formation of a new individual

ger·mi·nate *vb* **ger·mi·nat·ed; ger·mi·nat·ing** : to begin to grow : SPROUT

ger·mi·na·tion *n* : a beginning of development (as of a seed)

ges·tic·u·late *vb* **ges·tic·u·lat·ed; ges·tic·u·lat·ing** : to make gestures especially when speaking

¹ges·ture *n* **1** : a movement of the body (as the hands and arms) that expresses an idea or a feeling **2** : something said or done that shows a particular feeling

²gesture *vb* **ges·tured; ges·tur·ing** : to make or direct with a gesture

get *vb* **got; got** *or* **got·ten; get·ting** **1** : to gain possession of (as by receiving, earning, buying, or winning) **2** : to obtain by request or as a favor **3** : to come to have **4** : ¹CATCH 5 **5** : ARRIVE 1 **6** : GO 1, MOVE **7** : BECOME 1 **8** : to cause to be **9** : PREPARE 2 **10** : IRRITATE 1 **11** : ¹HIT 1 **12** : to find out by calculation **13** : to hear correctly **14** : UNDERSTAND 1 **15** : PERSUADE — **get ahead** : to achieve success (as in business) — **get along 1** : to approach old age **2** : to stay friendly **3** : to manage with little — **get around 1** : to become known by many people **2** : to avoid having to deal with **3** : to do or give attention to eventually — **get at 1** : to reach with or as if with the hand **2** : to deal with **3** : to say or suggest in an indirect way — **get away** : to avoid being caught — **get away with** : to not be punished for — **get back at** : to get revenge on — **get by 1** : to manage with little **2** : to do well enough to avoid failure — **get even** : to get revenge — **get into** : to become deeply interested in — **get it** : to receive punishment — **get off 1** : to start out on a journey **2** : to escape punishment or harm — **get on 1** : to approach old age **2** : to start or continue doing **3** : to stay friendly — **get out 1** : ¹ESCAPE 1 **2** : to become known — **get over 1** : to stop feeling unhappy about **2** : to recover from — **get up 1** : to arise from bed **2** : ¹STAND 1 **3** : to find the ability — **get wind of** : to become aware of : hear about

get·away *n* **1** : ²ESCAPE 1 **2** : a place suitable for vacation **3** : a usually short vacation

get–to·geth·er *n* : an informal social gathering

get·up *n* : ¹OUTFIT 1, COSTUME

gey·ser *n* : a spring that now and then shoots up hot water and steam

ghast·ly *adj* **ghast·li·er; ghast·li·est 1** : very shocking or horrible **2** : like a ghost : PALE

ghet·to *n, pl* **ghettos** *or* **ghettoes** : a part of

a city in which members of a particular group live in poor conditions

ghost *n* : the spirit of a dead person thought of as living in an unseen world or as appearing to living people

ghost·ly *adj* **ghost·li·er; ghost·li·est** : of, relating to, or like a ghost

ghost town *n* : a town where all the people have left

ghoul *n* **1** : an evil being of legend that robs graves and feeds on dead bodies **2** : someone whose activities suggest those of a ghoul : an evil or frightening person

GI *n* : a member of the United States armed forces

¹gi·ant *n* **1** : an imaginary person of great size and strength **2** : a person or thing that is very large, successful, or powerful

²giant *adj* : much larger than ordinary : HUGE

giant panda *n* : PANDA 2

giant sequoia *n* : an evergreen tree of California that has needles for leaves and can sometimes grow to over 270 feet (about 82 meters) in height

gib·ber·ish *n* : confused meaningless talk

gib·bon *n* : a small tailless ape of southeastern Asia that has long arms and legs and lives mostly in trees

¹gibe *or* **jibe** *vb* **gibed; gib·ing** : to speak or tease with words that are insulting or scornful : JEER

²gibe *or* **jibe** *n* : an insulting or scornful remark : JEER

gib·lets *n pl* : the edible inner organs (as the heart and liver) of a bird (as a turkey)

gid·dy *adj* **gid·di·er; gid·di·est 1** : having a feeling of whirling or spinning about : DIZZY **2** : causing dizziness **3** : playful and silly **4** : feeling and showing great happiness and joy — **gid·di·ness** *n*

gift *n* **1** : a special ability : TALENT **2** : something given : PRESENT

gift·ed *adj* : having great natural ability

gig *n* **1** : a long light boat for a ship's captain **2** : a light carriage having two wheels and pulled by a horse

giga·byte *n* : a unit of computer information storage capacity equal to 1,073,741,824 bytes

gi·gan·tic *adj* : extremely large or great (as in size, weight, or strength)

¹gig·gle *vb* **gig·gled; gig·gling** : to laugh with repeated short high sounds that sound childlike

²giggle *n* : a light silly laugh

Gi·la monster *n* : a large black and orange poisonous lizard of the southwestern United States

gild *vb* **gild·ed** *or* **gilt; gild·ing** : to cover with a thin coating of gold

¹**gill** *n* : a unit of liquid capacity equal to a quarter of a pint (about 120 milliliters)

²**gill** *n* : an organ (as of a fish) for taking oxygen from water

¹**gilt** *n* : gold or something resembling gold applied to a surface

²**gilt** *n* : a young female pig

gim·let *n* : a small pointed tool for making holes

gim·mick *n* : a method or trick that is designed to get people's attention or to sell something

¹**gin** *n* : COTTON GIN

²**gin** *vb* **ginned; gin·ning** : to separate seeds from cotton in a cotton gin

³**gin** *n* : a strong alcoholic liquor flavored with juniper berries

gin·ger *n* : a hot spice obtained from the root of a tropical plant and used especially to season foods

ginger ale *n* : a soft drink flavored with ginger

gin·ger·bread *n* : a dark cake flavored with ginger and molasses

gin·ger·ly *adv* : with great caution or care

gin·ger·snap *n* : a thin hard cookie flavored with ginger

ging·ham *n* : a cotton cloth that is often plaid or checked

gi·raffe *n* : a spotted mammal of Africa with a very long neck that feeds mostly on the leaves of trees and is the tallest of living animals on land

gird *vb* **gird·ed** *or* **girt ; gird·ing** 1 : to encircle or fasten with or as if with a belt or cord 2 : to prepare for conflict or for some difficult task

gird·er *n* : a horizontal main supporting beam

¹**gir·dle** *n* 1 : something (as a belt or sash) that encircles or binds 2 : a tight undergarment worn below the waist by women

²**girdle** *vb* **gir·dled; gir·dling** 1 : to bind with or as if with a girdle, belt, or sash : ENCIRCLE 2 : to strip a ring of bark from a tree trunk

girl *n* 1 : a female child or young woman 2 : a female servant 3 : GIRLFRIEND 2

girl·friend *n* 1 : a female friend 2 : a regular female companion of a boy or man

girl·hood *n* : the state or time of being a girl

girl·ish *adj* : having the characteristics of a girl

Girl Scout *n* : a member of the Girl Scouts of the United States of America

girth *n* 1 : the measure or distance around something 2 : a band put around the body of an animal to hold something (as a saddle) on its back

gist *n* : the main point of a matter

¹**give** *vb* **gave; giv·en; giv·ing** 1 : to hand over to be kept : PRESENT 2 : to cause to have 3 : to let someone or something have 4 : to offer for consideration or acceptance 5 : ²UTTER 6 : FURNISH 2, PROVIDE 7 : ¹PAY 1 8 : to deliver by some bodily action 9 : to yield as a product : PRODUCE 10 : to yield slightly — **give in** : to stop trying to fight — **give out** 1 : TELL 4 2 : to stop working — **give up** 1 : to let go of 2 : QUIT — **give way** 1 : to break down : COLLAPSE 2 : to be unable to resist

²**give** *n* : the ability to be bent or stretched

giv·en *adj* 1 : being likely to have or do something 2 : decided on beforehand

given name *n* : a first name

giz·zard *n* : a large muscular part of the digestive tract (as of a bird) in which food is churned and ground into small bits

gla·cial *adj* 1 : of or relating to glaciers 2 : very cold 3 : very slow

gla·cier *n* : a large body of ice moving slowly down a slope or over a wide area of land

glad *adj* **glad·der; glad·dest** 1 : being happy and joyful 2 : bringing or causing joy 3 : very willing — **glad·ly** *adv* — **glad·ness** *n*

glad·den *vb* **glad·dened; glad·den·ing** : to make glad

glade *n* : a grassy open space in a forest

glad·i·a·tor *n* : a man in ancient Rome who took part in fights as public entertainment

glad·i·o·lus *n, pl* **glad·i·o·li** *or* **gladiolus** *also* **glad·i·o·lus·es** : a plant with long stiff pointed leaves and stalks of brightly colored flowers

glam·or·ous *adj* : very exciting and attractive

glam·our *n* : romantic, exciting, and often misleading attractiveness

¹**glance** *vb* **glanced; glanc·ing** 1 : to strike at an angle and fly off to one side 2 : to give a quick look

²**glance** *n* : a quick look

gland *n* : a cluster of cells or an organ in the body that produces a substance (as saliva, sweat, or bile) to be used by the body or given off from it

glan·du·lar *adj* : of or relating to glands

¹**glare** *vb* **glared; glar·ing** 1 : to shine with a harsh bright light 2 : to look fiercely or angrily

²**glare** *n* 1 : a harsh bright light 2 : a fierce or angry look

glar·ing *adj* 1 : so bright as to be harsh 2 : very noticeable

glass *n* 1 : a hard brittle usually transparent substance commonly made from sand heated with chemicals 2 : a drinking container made of glass 3 **glasses** *pl* : a pair of glass or plastic lenses held in a frame and used to help a person see clearly or to protect the eyes 4 : the contents of a glass

glass·blow·ing *n* : the art of shaping a mass of melted glass by blowing air into it through a tube

glass·ful *n* : the amount a glass will hold

glass·ware *n* : articles made of glass

glassy *adj* **glass·i·er; glass·i·est 1** : smooth and shiny like glass **2** : not shiny or bright

¹glaze *vb* **glazed; glaz·ing 1** : to cover with a smooth or glossy coating **2** : to become dull

²glaze *n* : a glassy surface or coating

¹gleam *n* **1** : a faint, soft, or reflected light **2** : a bright or shining look **3** : a short or slight appearance

²gleam *vb* **gleamed; gleam·ing 1** : to shine with a soft light **2** : to give out gleams of light

glean *vb* **gleaned; glean·ing 1** : to gather from a field what is left by the harvesters **2** : to gather (as information) little by little with patient effort

glee *n* : great joy : DELIGHT — **glee·ful** *adj* — **glee·ful·ly** *adv*

glen *n* : a narrow hidden valley

glib *adj* **glib·ber; glib·best** : speaking or spoken carelessly and often insincerely — **glib·ly** *adv*

¹glide *vb* **glid·ed; glid·ing** : to move with a smooth continuous motion

²glide *n* : the act or action of moving with a smooth continuous motion

glid·er *n* : an aircraft without an engine that glides on air currents

¹glim·mer *vb* **glim·mered; glim·mer·ing** : to shine faintly and unsteadily

²glimmer *n* **1** : a faint unsteady light **2** : a faint suggestion **3** : a small amount

¹glimpse *vb* **glimpsed; glimps·ing** : to catch a quick view of

²glimpse *n* : a short hurried look

¹glint *vb* **glint·ed; glint·ing** : to shine with tiny bright flashes

²glint *n* : a brief flash

glis·ten *vb* **glis·tened; glis·ten·ing** : to shine with a soft reflected light

glitch *n* : a usually minor problem

¹glit·ter *vb* **glit·tered; glit·ter·ing** : to sparkle brightly

²glitter *n* : sparkling brightness — **glit·tery** *adj*

gloat *vb* **gloat·ed; gloat·ing** : to talk or think about something with mean or selfish satisfaction

glob·al *adj* **1** : in or having to do with the whole earth **2** : shaped like a globe

global warming *n* : a warming of the earth's atmosphere and oceans that is thought to be a result of air pollution

globe *n* **1** : a round object : BALL, SPHERE **2** : EARTH 1 **3** : a round model of the earth used like a map

glob·ule *n* : a small round mass

glock·en·spiel *n* : a portable musical instrument with a series of metal bars played with hammers

gloom *n* **1** : partial or complete darkness **2** : a sad mood

gloomy *adj* **gloom·i·er; gloom·i·est 1** : partly or completely dark **2** : SAD 1, BLUE **3** : causing feelings of sadness **4** : not hopeful or promising — **gloom·i·ly** *adv*

glo·ri·fy *vb* **glo·ri·fied; glo·ri·fy·ing 1** : to honor or praise as divine : WORSHIP **2** : to give honor and praise to **3** : to show in a way that looks good

glo·ri·ous *adj* **1** : having or deserving praise or admiration **2** : having great beauty or splendor **3** : DELIGHTFUL — **glo·ri·ous·ly** *adv*

¹glo·ry *n, pl* **glories 1** : praise, honor, and admiration given to a person by others **2** : something that brings honor, praise, or fame **3** : BRILLIANCE, SPLENDOR

²glory *vb* **glo·ried; glo·ry·ing** : to rejoice proudly : be proud or boastful

¹gloss *n* **1** : brightness from a smooth surface : SHEEN **2** : a falsely attractive surface appearance

²gloss *vb* **glossed; glos·sing 1** : to shine the surface of **2** : to explain as if unimportant

glos·sa·ry *n, pl* **glos·sa·ries** : a list that provides definitions for the difficult or unusual words used in a book

glossy *adj* **gloss·i·er; gloss·i·est** : smooth and shining on the surface

glove *n* : a covering for the hand having a separate section for each finger — **gloved** *adj*

¹glow *vb* **glowed; glow·ing 1** : to shine with or as if with great heat **2** : to shine with steady light **3** : to have a warm reddish color (as from exercise) **4** : to look happy, excited, or healthy

²glow *n* **1** : light such as comes from something that is very hot but not flaming **2** : brightness or warmth of color **3** : a feeling of physical warmth (as from exercise) **4** : a warm and pleasant feeling

glow·er *vb* **glow·ered; glow·er·ing** : to stare angrily : SCOWL

glow·worm *n* : an insect or insect larva that gives off light

glu·cose *n* : a sugar in plant saps and fruits that is the usual form in which carbohydrate is taken in by the animal body and used as a source of energy

¹glue *n* : a substance used to stick things tightly together — **glu·ey** *adj*

²glue *vb* **glued; glu·ing** : to stick with or as if with glue

glum *adj* **glum·mer; glum·mest** : gloomy and sad — **glum·ly** *adv*

¹glut *vb* **glut·ted; glut·ting** **1** : to make very full **2** : to flood with goods so that supply is greater than demand

²glut *n* : too much of something

glu·ti·nous *adj* : like glue : STICKY

glut·ton *n* : a person or animal that overeats — **glut·ton·ous** *adj*

glut·tony *n*, *pl* **glut·ton·ies** : the act or habit of eating or drinking too much

gly·co·gen *n* : a white tasteless starchy substance that is the main form in which glucose is stored in the body

gm *abbr* gram

gnarled *adj* : being full of knots, twisted, and rugged

gnarly *adj* **gnarl·i·er; gnarl·i·est** : GNARLED

gnash *vb* **gnashed; gnash·ing** : to strike or grind (the teeth) together

gnat *n* : a very small two-winged fly

gnaw *vb* **gnawed; gnaw·ing** : to bite so as to wear away : bite or chew upon

gnome *n* : an imaginary dwarf believed to live inside the earth and guard treasure

gnu *n*, *pl* **gnu** *or* **gnus** : WILDEBEEST

go *vb* **went; gone; go·ing; goes** **1** : to move or travel from one place to or toward another **2** : to move away : LEAVE **3** : to lead in a certain direction **4** : to be sent **5** : to become lost, used, or spent **6** : to pass by : ELAPSE **7** : to continue its course or action : RUN **8** : to be able to fit in or through a space **9** : to make its own special sound **10** : to be suitable : MATCH **11** : to reach some state — **go off** **1** : EXPLODE 1 **2** : to begin to make a usual noise **3** : to proceed as expected — **go on** **1** : to continue as time passes **2** : to continue talking — **go out** **1** : to leave home **2** : to stop burning — **go through** : ²EXPERIENCE

¹goad *n* **1** : a pointed rod used to keep an animal moving **2** : something that urges or forces someone to act

²goad *vb* **goad·ed; goad·ing** : to urge or force a person or an animal to act

goal *n* **1** : ¹PURPOSE **2** : an area or object into which a ball or puck must be driven in various games in order to score **3** : a scoring of one or more points by driving a ball or puck into a goal **4** : the point at which a race or journey is to end **5** : an area to be reached safely in certain games

goal·ie *n* : GOALKEEPER

goal·keep·er *n* : a player who defends a goal

goal line *n* : a line that must be crossed to score a goal

goal·post *n* : one of two upright posts often with a crossbar that serve as the goal in various games

goal·tend·er *n* : GOALKEEPER

goat *n* : an animal that has hollow horns that curve backward, is related to the sheep, and is often raised for its milk, wool, and meat — **goat·like** *adj*

goa·tee *n* : a small beard trimmed to a point

goat·herd *n* : a person who tends goats

goat·skin *n* : the skin of a goat or leather made from it

gob *n* : ¹LUMP 1

¹gob·ble *vb* **gob·bled; gob·bling** : to eat fast or greedily

²gobble *vb* **gob·bled; gob·bling** : to make the call of a turkey or a similar sound

³gobble *n* : the loud harsh call of a turkey

go–be·tween *n* : a person who acts as a messenger or peacemaker

gob·let *n* : a drinking glass with a foot and stem

gob·lin *n* : an ugly and often evil imaginary creature

god *n* **1** *cap* : the Being worshipped as the creator and ruler of the universe **2** : a being believed to have more than human powers **3** : an object worshipped as divine

god·child *n*, *pl* **god·chil·dren** : a person for whom another person acts as sponsor at baptism

god·daugh·ter *n* : a girl or woman for whom another person acts as sponsor at baptism

god·dess *n* : a female god

god·fa·ther *n* : a boy or man who is sponsor for someone at baptism

god·like *adj* : like or suitable for God or a god

god·ly *adj* **god·li·er; god·li·est** : DEVOUT 1, PIOUS

god·moth·er *n* : a girl or woman who is sponsor for someone at baptism

god·par·ent *n* : a sponsor at baptism

god·send *n* : some badly needed thing that comes unexpectedly

god·son *n* : a boy or man for whom another person acts as sponsor at baptism

God·speed *n* : a wish for success given to a person who is going away

goes *present third person sing of* GO

go–get·ter *n* : a person determined to succeed

gog·gle *vb* **gog·gled; gog·gling** : to stare with bulging or rolling eyes

gog·gles *n pl* : protective glasses set in a flexible frame (as of plastic) that fits snugly against the face

go·ings–on *n pl* : things that happen

goi·ter *n* : a swelling on the front of the neck caused by enlargement of the thyroid gland

gold *n* **1** : a soft yellow metallic chemical element used especially in coins and jewelry **2** : gold coins **3** : a medal awarded as the first prize in a competition **4** : a deep yellow

gold·en *adj* **1** : like, made of, or containing gold **2** : having the deep yellow color of gold **3** : very good or desirable **4** : very prosperous and happy

gold·en·rod *n* : a plant with tall stiff stems topped with clusters of tiny yellow flowers

gold·finch *n* **1** : a small European bird with a yellow patch on each wing **2** : a small mostly yellow American bird

gold·fish *n* : a small usually golden yellow or orange fish often kept in aquariums or ponds

gold·smith *n* : a person who makes or sells items of gold

golf *n* : a game played by hitting a small ball with special clubs into each of nine or 18 holes in as few strokes as possible

golf·er *n* : a person who plays golf

gon·do·la *n* **1** : a long narrow boat used in the canals of Venice, Italy **2** : a railroad freight car with no top **3** : an enclosure that hangs from a balloon or cable and carries passengers or instruments

¹gone *past participle of* GO

²gone *adj* **1** : no longer present **2** : no longer existing **3** : ¹DEAD 1

gon·er *n* : someone or something with no chance of surviving or succeeding

gong *n* : a metallic disk that produces a harsh ringing tone when struck

¹good *adj* **bet·ter** ; **best** **1** : better than average **2** : SKILLFUL **3** : behaving well **4** : PLEASANT 1, ENJOYABLE **5** : HEALTHFUL **6** : of a favorable character or tendency **7** : suitable for a use : SATISFACTORY **8** : DESIRABLE 1, ATTRACTIVE **9** : showing good sense or judgment **10** : closely following a standard of what is correct or proper **11** : RELIABLE **12** : HELPFUL, KIND **13** : being honest and upright **14** : being at least the amount mentioned **15** : CONSIDERABLE — **as good as** : ALMOST

²good *n* **1** : WELFARE 1, BENEFIT **2** : the good part of a person or thing **3** : something right or good **4 goods** *pl* : products that are made for sale **5 goods** *pl* : personal property

¹good–bye *or* **good–by** *interj* — used to express good wishes to someone who is leaving

²good–bye *or* **good–by** *n* : a remark made when someone is leaving

good–heart·ed *adj* : kind and generous — **good–heart·ed·ly** *adv*

good–hu·mored *adj* : GOOD-NATURED — **good–hu·mored·ly** *adv*

good·ly *adj* **good·li·er; good·li·est** **1** : of pleasing appearance **2** : LARGE, CONSIDERABLE

good–na·tured *adj* : having or showing a pleasant disposition — **good–na·tured·ly** *adv*

good·ness *n* **1** : the quality or state of being good **2** : excellence of morals and behavior

good–sized *adj* : fairly large

good–tem·pered *adj* : not easily angered or upset

good·will *n* : kind feelings or attitude

goody *n, pl* **good·ies** **1** : something especially good to eat **2** : something that is very attractive or desirable

goo·ey *adj* **goo·i·er; goo·i·est** : wet and sticky

¹goof *n* **1** : a stupid or silly person **2** : ²BLUNDER

²goof *vb* **goofed; goof·ing** **1** : to spend time foolishly **2** : to spend time doing silly or playful things **3** : to make a blunder

goofy *adj* **goof·i·er; goof·i·est** : ¹SILLY 1

goose *n, pl* **geese** **1** : a waterbird with webbed feet that is related to the smaller duck and the larger swan **2** : a female goose **3** : the meat of a goose used as food

goose·ber·ry *n, pl* **goose·ber·ries** : the sour berry of a thorny bush related to the currant

goose bumps *n pl* : a roughness of the skin caused by cold, fear, or a sudden feeling of excitement

goose·flesh *n* : GOOSE BUMPS

goose pimples *n pl* : GOOSE BUMPS

go·pher *n* **1** : a burrowing animal that is about the size of a large rat and has strong claws on the forefeet and a large fur-lined pouch on the outside of each cheek **2** : a striped ground squirrel of North American prairies **3** : a burrowing land tortoise of the southern United States

¹gore *n* **1** : blood from a wound or cut **2** : violence and bloodshed

²gore *vb* **gored; gor·ing** : to pierce or wound with a pointed object (as a horn or spear)

¹gorge *n* : a narrow steep-walled canyon or part of a canyon

²gorge *vb* **gorged; gorg·ing** : to eat greedily

gor·geous *adj* : very beautiful — **gor·geous·ly** *adv* — **gor·geous·ness** *n*

go·ril·la *n* : a very large ape of the forests of central Africa that lives mostly on the ground

gory *adj* **gor·i·er; gor·i·est** **1** : covered with blood **2** : having or showing much violence and bloodshed

gos·ling *n* : a young goose

gos·pel *n* **1** *often cap* : the teachings of Jesus

Christ and the apostles **2** : something told or accepted as being absolutely true

gos·sa·mer *n* : a film of cobwebs floating in the air

¹gos·sip *n* **1** : a person who repeats stories about other people **2** : talk or rumors involving the personal lives of other people

²gossip *vb* **gos·siped; gos·sip·ing** : to talk about the personal lives of other people

got *past and past participle of* GET

gotten *past participle of* GET

¹gouge *n* **1** : a chisel with a curved blade for scooping or cutting holes **2** : a hole or groove made by cutting or scraping

²gouge *vb* **gouged; goug·ing** : to make a hole or groove in something by cutting or scraping

gourd *n* : an inedible fruit with a hard rind and many seeds that grows on a vine, is related to the pumpkin and melon, and is often used for decoration or for making objects (as bowls)

gour·met *n* : a person who appreciates fine food and drink

gov. *abbr* governor

gov·ern *vb* **gov·erned; gov·ern·ing** **1** : ²RULE 1 **2** : to influence the actions and conduct of : CONTROL **3** : to serve as a rule for

gov·ern·ess *n* : a woman who teaches and trains a child especially in a private home

gov·ern·ment *n* **1** : control and direction of public business (as of a city or a nation) **2** : a system of control : an established form of political rule **3** : the people making up a governing body

gov·ern·men·tal *adj* : of or relating to government or the government

gov·er·nor *n* : a person who governs and especially the elected head of a state of the United States

gov·er·nor·ship *n* **1** : the office or position of governor **2** : the term of office of a governor

govt. *abbr* government

gown *n* **1** : a dress suitable for special occasions **2** : a loose robe

¹grab *vb* **grabbed; grab·bing** : to grasp or seize suddenly

²grab *n* : a sudden attempt to grasp or seize

¹grace *n* **1** : a short prayer at a meal **2** : beauty and ease of movement **3** : pleasant, controlled, and polite behavior **4** : GOODWILL, FAVOR **5** : the condition of being in favor

²grace *vb* **graced; grac·ing** **1** : to do credit to : HONOR **2** : to make more attractive : ADORN

grace·ful *adj* : showing grace or beauty in form or action — **grace·ful·ly** *adv*

gra·cious *adj* **1** : being kind and courteous

2 : GRACEFUL — **gra·cious·ly** *adv* — **gra·cious·ness** *n*

grack·le *n* : a large blackbird with shiny feathers that show changeable green, purple, and bronze colors

¹grade *n* **1** : a division of a school course representing a year's work **2** : the group of pupils in a school grade **3** : a mark or rating especially in school **4** : a position in a scale of rank, quality, or order **5** : a class of things that are of the same rank, quality, or order **6** : the degree of slope (as of a road)

²grade *vb* **grad·ed; grad·ing** **1** : to give a grade to as an indication of achievement **2** : to give a rating to **3** : to arrange in grades according to some quality **4** : to make level or evenly sloping

grad·er *n* **1** : a student in a specified grade **2** : a person who assigns grades **3** : a machine used for leveling earth

grade school *n* : a school including the first six or the first eight grades

grad·u·al *adj* : moving or happening by steps or degrees — **grad·u·al·ly** *adv*

¹grad·u·ate *n* : a person who has completed the required course of study in a college or school

²grad·u·ate *vb* **grad·u·at·ed; grad·u·at·ing** : to finish a course of study : become a graduate

grad·u·a·tion *n* **1** : the act or process of finishing a course of study **2** : COMMENCEMENT 1

Graeco- — see GRECO-

graf·fi·ti *n* : writing or drawing made on a public structure without permission

¹graft *n* **1** : a plant that has a twig or bud from another plant attached to it so they are joined and grow together **2** : something (as a piece of skin or a plant bud) that is joined to something similar so as to grow together **3** : something (as money or advantage) gotten in a dishonest way and especially by betraying a public trust

²graft *vb* **graft·ed; graft·ing** **1** : to attach a twig or bud from one plant to another plant so they are joined and grow together **2** : to join one thing to another as if by grafting **3** : to gain dishonestly — **graft·er** *n*

grain *n* **1** : the edible seed of some grasses (as wheat, corn, or oats) or a few other plants (as buckwheat) **2** : plants that produce grain **3** : a small hard particle **4** : a tiny amount **5** : a unit of weight equal to 0.0648 gram **6** : the arrangement of fibers in wood — **grained** *adj*

grain elevator *n* : a tall building for storing grain

gram *n* : a unit of mass in the metric system equal to 1/1000 kilogram

-gram *n suffix* : drawing : writing : record

gram·mar *n* **1** : the rules of how words are used in a language **2** : speech or writing judged according to the rules of grammar

gram·mat·i·cal *adj* : of, relating to, or following the rules of grammar — **gram·mat·i·cal·ly** *adv*

gra·na·ry *n, pl* **gra·na·ries** : a building in which grain is stored

grand *adj* **grand·er; grand·est** **1** : higher in rank than others : FOREMOST **2** : great in size **3** : COMPREHENSIVE, INCLUSIVE **4** : IMPRESSIVE **5** : very good — **grand·ly** *adv*

grand·child *n, pl* **grand·chil·dren** : a child of a person's son or daughter

grand·daugh·ter *n* : a daughter of a person's son or daughter

gran·deur *n* : impressive greatness

grand·fa·ther *n* **1** : the father of someone's father or mother **2** : ANCESTOR

grandfather clock *n* : a tall clock standing directly on the floor

gran·di·ose *adj* : overly grand or exaggerated

grand·ma *n* : GRANDMOTHER 1

grand·moth·er *n* **1** : the mother of someone's father or mother **2** : a female ancestor

grand·pa *n* : GRANDFATHER 1

grand·par·ent *n* : a parent of someone's father or mother

grand·son *n* : a son of someone's son or daughter

grand·stand *n* : a usually roofed structure at a racecourse or stadium for spectators

gran·ite *n* : a very hard rock that is used for buildings and for monuments

gran·ny *n, pl* **gran·nies** : GRANDMOTHER 1

gra·no·la *n* : a mixture of oats and other ingredients (as raisins, coconut, or nuts) that is eaten especially for breakfast or as a snack

¹grant *vb* **grant·ed; grant·ing** **1** : to agree to do, give, or allow **2** : to give as a favor or right **3** : to give legally or formally **4** : to admit to or agree with

²grant *n* **1** : the act of giving or agreeing to **2** : something given

grape *n* : a juicy berry that has a smooth green, dark red, or purple skin and grows in clusters on a woody vine (**grapevine**)

grape·fruit *n* : a large fruit with a yellow skin that is related to the orange and lemon

¹graph *n* : a diagram that by means of dots and lines shows a system of relationships between things

²graph *vb* **graphed; graph·ing** : to show something using a graph

-graph *n suffix* **1** : something written **2** : instrument for making or sending records

¹graph·ic *adj* **1** : being written, drawn, printed, or engraved **2** : described in very

clear detail **3** : of or relating to the pictorial arts or to printing

²graphic *n* **1** : a picture, map, or graph used for illustration **2 graphics** *pl* : a pictorial image or series of images displayed on a computer screen

graph·ite *n* : a soft black form of carbon used in making lead pencils and as a lubricant

-g·ra·phy *n suffix, pl* **-g·ra·phies** : writing or picturing in a special way, by a special means, or of a special thing

grapple *vb* **grap·pled; grap·pling** **1** : to seize or hold with an instrument (as a hook) **2** : to seize and struggle with another **3** : to deal with

¹grasp *vb* **grasped; grasp·ing** **1** : to seize and hold with or as if with the hand **2** : to make the motion of seizing **3** : UNDERSTAND 1

²grasp *n* **1** : a grip of the hand **2** : ²CONTROL 1, HOLD **3** : the power of seizing and holding : REACH **4** : ¹UNDERSTANDING 1

grasp·ing *adj* : GREEDY 1

grass *n* **1** : any of a large group of green plants with jointed stems, long slender leaves, and stalks of clustered flowers **2** : plants eaten by grazing animals **3** : land (as a lawn) covered with growing grass — **grass·like** *adj*

grass·hop·per *n* : a common leaping insect that feeds on plants

grass·land *n* : land covered with herbs (as grass and clover) rather than shrubs and trees

grassy *adj* **grass·i·er; grass·i·est** : like or covered with grass

¹grate *vb* **grat·ed; grat·ing** **1** : to break into small pieces by rubbing against something rough **2** : to grind or rub against something with a harsh noise **3** : to have an irritating effect

²grate *n* **1** : a frame containing parallel or crossed bars (as in a window) **2** : a frame of iron bars to hold a fire

grate·ful *adj* **1** : feeling or showing thanks **2** : providing pleasure or comfort — **grate·ful·ly** *adv*

grat·er *n* : a device with a rough surface for grating

grat·i·fi·ca·tion *n* **1** : the act of giving pleasure or satisfaction to : the state of being pleased or satisfied **2** : something that pleases or satisfies

grat·i·fy *vb* **grat·i·fied; grat·i·fy·ing** **1** : to give pleasure or satisfaction to **2** : to do or give whatever is wanted by

grat·ing *n* : ²GRATE 1

grat·i·tude *n* : a feeling of appreciation or thanks

¹grave *n* : a hole in the ground for burying a dead body

²grave *adj* **grav·er; grav·est 1** : very serious : IMPORTANT **2** : serious in appearance or manner — **grave·ly** *adv*

grav·el *n* : small pieces of rock and pebbles larger than grains of sand

grav·el·ly *adj* **1** : containing or made up of gravel **2** : sounding rough

grave·stone *n* : a monument on a grave

grave·yard *n* : CEMETERY

grav·i·tate *vb* **grav·i·tat·ed; grav·i·tat·ing** : to move or be drawn toward something

grav·i·ta·tion *n* **1** : GRAVITY 1 **2** : movement to or toward something

grav·i·ty *n, pl* **grav·i·ties 1** : a force of attraction that tends to draw particles or bodies together **2** : the attraction of bodies by the force of gravity toward the center of the earth **3** : great seriousness

gra·vy *n, pl* **gravies** : a sauce made from the juice of cooked meat

¹gray *also* **grey** *adj* **gray·er** *also* **grey·er; gray·est** *also* **grey·est 1** : of a color that is a blend of black and white **2** : having gray hair **3** : lacking cheer or brightness — **gray·ness** *n*

²gray *also* **grey** *n* : a color that is a blend of black and white

³gray *also* **grey** *vb* **grayed** *also* **greyed; gray·ing** *also* **grey·ing** : to make or become gray

gray·ish *adj* : somewhat gray

¹graze *vb* **grazed; graz·ing 1** : to eat grass **2** : to supply with grass or pasture

²graze *vb* **grazed; graz·ing 1** : to rub lightly in passing : barely touch **2** : to scrape by rubbing against something

³graze *n* : a scrape or mark caused by scraping against something

¹grease *n* **1** : a substance obtained from animal fat by melting **2** : oily material **3** : a thick lubricant

²grease *vb* **greased; greas·ing** : to coat or lubricate with an oily material

grease·paint *n* : actors' makeup

greasy *adj* **greas·i·er; greas·i·est 1** : covered with an oily material **2** : like or full of fat

great *adj* **great·er; great·est 1** : very large in size : HUGE **2** : large in amount **3** : LONG 3 **4** : much beyond the ordinary **5** : IMPORTANT 1, DISTINGUISHED **6** : very talented or successful **7** : very good — **great·ly** *adv*

great–grand·child *n, pl* **great–grand·children** : a grandson (**great–grandson**) or granddaughter (**great–granddaughter**) of someone's son or daughter

great–grand·par·ent *n* : a grandfather (**great–grandfather**) or grandmother (**great–grandmother**) of someone's father or mother

grebe *n* : a swimming and diving bird related to the loons

Gre·cian *adj* : ²GREEK

Gre·co- *or* **Grae·co-** *prefix* **1** : Greece : Greeks **2** : Greek and

greed *n* : selfish desire for more than is needed

greedy *adj* **greed·i·er; greed·i·est 1** : having or showing a selfish desire for more than is needed **2** : having a strong appetite for food or drink : very hungry **3** : very eager to have something — **greed·i·ly** *adv*

¹Greek *n* **1** : a person born or living in Greece **2** : the language of the Greeks

²Greek *adj* : of or relating to Greece, its people, or the Greek language

¹green *adj* **green·er; green·est 1** : of the color of grass : colored green **2** : covered with green plant growth **3** : made of green plants or of the leafy parts of plants **4** : not ripe **5** : not fully processed, treated, or seasoned **6** : lacking training or experience **7** : JEALOUS 2 **8** : supporting the protection of or helping to protect the environment

²green *n* **1** : a color between blue and yellow : the color of growing grass **2 greens** *pl* : leafy parts of plants used for food **3** : a grassy plain or plot

green bean *n* : a young long green pod of a bean plant eaten as a vegetable

green·ery *n, pl* **green·er·ies** : green plants or foliage

green·horn *n* : a person who is new at something

green·house *n* : a building with clear walls and roof (as of glass) for growing plants

greenhouse effect *n* : warming of the lower atmosphere of the earth that occurs when radiation from the sun is absorbed by the earth and then given off again and absorbed by carbon dioxide and water vapor in the atmosphere

green·ish *adj* : somewhat green

green thumb *n* : a talent for growing plants

greet *vb* **greet·ed; greet·ing 1** : to speak to in a friendly polite way upon arrival : WELCOME **2** : to respond to in a certain way **3** : to present itself to — **greet·er** *n*

greet·ing *n* **1** : an expression of pleasure on meeting or seeing someone **2** : an expression of good wishes

gre·gar·i·ous *adj* **1** : enjoying the company of other people **2** : tending to live in a flock, herd, or community rather than alone

gre·nade *n* : a small bomb designed to be thrown by hand or fired (as by a rifle)

grew *past of* GROW

grey *variant of* GRAY

grey·hound *n* : a tall swift dog with a smooth coat and good eyesight

grid *n* **1** : a network of horizontal and perpendicular lines (as for locating places on a map) **2** : a frame with bars running across it that is used to cover an opening **3** : a group of electrical conductors that form a network

grid·dle *n* : a flat surface or pan for cooking food

grid·iron *n* **1** : a grate for cooking food over a fire **2** : a football field

grief *n* **1** : very deep sorrow **2** : a cause of sorrow **3** : things that cause problems **4** : an unfortunate happening

griev·ance *n* : a reason for complaining

grieve *vb* **grieved; griev·ing** **1** : to feel or show grief **2** : to cause grief to

griev·ous *adj* **1** : causing suffering or pain **2** : SERIOUS 2, GRAVE

grif·fin *or* **grif·fon** *also* **gryph·on** *n* : an imaginary animal that is half eagle and half lion

¹grill *vb* **grilled; grill·ing** **1** : to cook or be cooked on a frame of bars over fire **2** : to question intensely

²grill *n* **1** : a frame of bars on which food is cooked over a fire **2** : a cooking device equipped with a frame of bars **3** : a dish of grilled or broiled food **4** : a usually casual restaurant

grille *or* **grill** *n* : an often ornamental arrangement of bars forming a barrier or screen

grim *adj* **grim·mer; grim·mest** **1** : ¹SAVAGE 2, CRUEL **2** : harsh in action or appearance : STERN **3** : GLOOMY 3, DISMAL **4** : showing firmness and seriousness **5** : FRIGHTFUL 1 — **grim·ly** *adv*

¹gri·mace *n* : a twisting of the face (as in disgust or pain)

²grimace *vb* **gri·maced; gri·mac·ing** : to twist the face

grime *n* : dirt rubbed into a surface

grimy *adj* **grim·i·er; grim·i·est** : ¹DIRTY 1

¹grin *vb* **grinned; grin·ning** : to smile broadly showing teeth

²grin *n* : a broad smile that shows teeth

¹grind *vb* **ground ; grind·ing** **1** : to make or be made into powder or small pieces by rubbing **2** : to wear down, polish, or sharpen by friction **3** : to rub together with a scraping noise **4** : to operate or produce by or as if by turning a crank

²grind *n* **1** : an act of sharpening or reducing to powder **2** : steady hard work

grind·stone *n* : a flat round stone that turns to sharpen or shape things

¹grip *vb* **gripped; grip·ping** **1** : to grab or hold tightly **2** : to hold the interest of

²grip *n* **1** : a strong grasp **2** : strength in holding : POWER **3** : UNDERSTANDING 1 **4** : SELF-CONTROL **5** : ¹HANDLE

¹gripe *vb* **griped; grip·ing** : COMPLAIN

²gripe *n* : COMPLAINT 1

grippe *n* : a disease like or the same as influenza

gris·ly *adj* **gris·li·er; gris·li·est** : HORRIBLE 1, GRUESOME

grist *n* : grain to be ground or that is already ground

gris·tle *n* : CARTILAGE — **gris·tly** *adj*

grist·mill *n* : a mill for grinding grain

¹grit *n* **1** : rough hard bits especially of sand **2** : strength of mind or spirit

²grit *vb* **grit·ted; grit·ting** : ¹GRIND 3, GRATE

grits *n pl* : coarsely ground hulled grain

grit·ty *adj* **grit·ti·er; grit·ti·est** **1** : containing or like rough hard bits especially of sand **2** : showing toughness and courage **3** : harshly realistic

griz·zled *adj* **1** : streaked or mixed with gray **2** : having gray hair

grizzly bear *n* : a large powerful brown bear of western North America

¹groan *vb* **groaned; groan·ing** **1** : to make or say with a moan **2** : to creak under a strain

²groan *n* : a low moaning sound

gro·cer *n* : a person who sells food and household supplies

gro·cery *n, pl* **gro·cer·ies** **1** *groceries pl* : food and household supplies sold at a store **2** : a store that sells food and household supplies

grog·gy *adj* **grog·gi·er; grog·gi·est** : weak, dazed, and unsteady

groin *n* : the fold or area where the abdomen joins the thigh

grom·met *n* : a metal or plastic ring to strengthen or protect a small hole

¹groom *n* **1** : a man who has just been or is about to be married **2** : a person in charge of horses

²groom *vb* **groomed; groom·ing** **1** : to make neat and attractive **2** : to prepare for a purpose

¹groove *n* **1** : a long narrow cut in a surface **2** : ¹ROUTINE 1

²groove *vb* **grooved; groov·ing** : to make a long narrow cut in

grope *vb* **groped; grop·ing** **1** : to move along by feeling with the hands **2** : to seek by or as if by feeling around

gros·beak *n* : a finch with a strong conical bill

¹gross *adj* **gross·er; gross·est** **1** : noticeably bad : GLARING **2** : DISGUSTING **3** : consisting of a whole before anything is subtracted **4** : showing poor manners : VULGAR

²**gross** n : the whole before anything is deducted

³**gross** n, pl **gross** : twelve dozen

gro·tesque adj : unnatural in an odd or ugly way

grot·to n, pl **grottoes** 1 : ¹CAVE, CAVERN 2 : an artificial structure like a cave

¹**grouch** n : a person who is irritable or complains a lot

²**grouch** vb **grouched; grouch·ing** : COMPLAIN

grouchy adj **grouch·i·er; grouch·i·est** : tending to be irritable or to complain a lot

¹**ground** n 1 : the surface of the earth 2 : ²SOIL 1, EARTH 3 : the bottom of a body of water 4 : an area of land 5 : an area used for some purpose 6 **grounds** pl : the land around and belonging to a building 7 : BACKGROUND 1 8 : a reason for a belief, action, or argument 9 : an area of knowledge 10 : a level of achievement or success 11 **grounds** pl : material in a liquid that settles to the bottom

²**ground** vb **ground·ed; ground·ing** 1 : to provide a reason for 2 : to instruct in basic knowledge or understanding 3 : to run or cause to run aground 4 : to connect electrically with the ground 5 : to prevent (a plane or pilot) from flying 6 : to prohibit from taking part in certain activities as punishment

³**ground** past and past participle of GRIND

ground·hog n : WOODCHUCK

ground·less adj : having no real reason

ground·work n : something upon which further work or progress is based

¹**group** n 1 : a number of persons or things considered as a unit 2 : a number of persons or things that are considered related in some way 3 : a small band

²**group** vb **grouped; group·ing** : to arrange in, put into, or form a unit or group

¹**grouse** n, pl **grouse** : a brownish bird mostly of wooded areas that feeds especially on the ground and is sometimes hunted for food or sport

²**grouse** vb **groused; grous·ing** : COMPLAIN

grove n : a small forest or group of planted trees

grov·el vb **grov·eled** or **grov·elled; grov·el·ing** or **grov·el·ling** 1 : to kneel, lie, or crawl on the ground (as in fear) 2 : to act toward someone in a weak or humble way

grow vb **grew; grown; grow·ing** 1 : to spring up and develop to maturity 2 : to be able to live and develop 3 : to be related in some way by reason of growing 4 : ¹INCREASE, EXPAND 5 : BECOME 1 6 : to cause to grow : RAISE — **grow·er** n — **grow on** : to

become more appealing over time — **grow up** : to become an adult

growing pains n pl : pains that occur in the legs of growing children but have not been proven to be caused by growth

¹**growl** vb **growled; growl·ing** 1 : to make a deep threatening sound 2 : to make a low rumbling noise 3 : to complain or say in an angry way

²**growl** n 1 : a deep threatening sound (as of an animal) 2 : a grumbling or muttered complaint

grown adj : having reached full growth : MATURE

¹**grown–up** adj : ¹ADULT

²**grown–up** n : an adult person

growth n 1 : a stage or condition in increasing, developing, or maturing 2 : a natural process of increasing in size or developing 3 : a gradual increase 4 : something (as a covering of plants) produced by growing

¹**grub** vb **grubbed; grub·bing** 1 : to root out by digging 2 : to work hard

²**grub** n 1 : a soft thick wormlike larva (as of a beetle) 2 : FOOD 1

grub·by adj **grub·bi·er; grub·bi·est** : ¹DIRTY 1

¹**grudge** vb **grudged; grudg·ing** : BEGRUDGE

²**grudge** n : a feeling of anger or dislike towards someone that lasts a long time

gru·el n : a thin porridge

gru·el·ing or **gru·el·ling** adj : calling for great effort

grue·some adj : causing horror or disgust

gruff adj **gruff·er; gruff·est** : rough in speech or manner — **gruff·ly** adv

¹**grum·ble** vb **grum·bled; grum·bling** 1 : to complain in a low voice 2 : ¹RUMBLE

²**grumble** n 1 : the act of complaining in a low voice 2 : ²RUMBLE

grumpy adj **grump·i·er; grump·i·est** : GROUCHY, CROSS — **grump·i·ly** adv

¹**grunt** vb **grunt·ed; grunt·ing** : to make a short low sound

²**grunt** n : a short low sound (as of a pig)

gryphon variant of GRIFFIN

GSA abbr Girl Scouts of America

GSUSA abbr Girl Scouts of the United States of America

gt. abbr great

GU abbr Guam

¹**guar·an·tee** n 1 : a promise that something will be or will happen as stated 2 : something given as a promise of payment : SECURITY

²**guarantee** vb **guar·an·teed; guar·an·tee·ing** 1 : to make a promise about the condition or occurrence of something 2 : to

promise to be responsible for the debt or duty of another person

guar·an·tor *n* : a person who gives a guarantee

¹guard *n* **1** : a person or a body of persons that guards against injury or danger **2** : the act or duty of keeping watch **3** : a device giving protection

²guard *vb* **guard·ed; guard·ing 1** : to protect from danger : DEFEND **2** : to watch over so as to prevent escape **3** : to keep careful watch for in order to prevent

guard·ed *adj* : CAUTIOUS

guard·house *n* **1** : a building used as a headquarters by soldiers on guard duty **2** : a military jail

guard·ian *n* **1** : a person who guards or looks after something : CUSTODIAN **2** : a person who legally has the care of another person or of another person's property — **guard·ian·ship** *n*

guards·man *n, pl* **guards·men** : a member of a national guard, coast guard, or other similar military body

gua·va *n* : the sweet yellow fruit of a tropical American tree

gu·ber·na·to·ri·al *adj* : relating to a governor

guer·ril·la *or* **gue·ril·la** *n* : a member of a group carrying on warfare but not part of a regular army

¹guess *vb* **guessed; guess·ing 1** : to form an opinion or give an answer about from little or no information **2** : to solve correctly mainly by chance **3** : THINK 2, SUPPOSE — **guess·er** *n*

²guess *n* : an opinion or answer that is reached with little information or by chance

guess·work *n* : work done or results gotten by guessing

guest *n* **1** : a person invited to visit or stay in someone's home **2** : a person invited to a special place or event **3** : a customer at a hotel, motel, inn, or restaurant

¹guf·faw *n* : a burst of loud laughter

²guffaw *vb* **guf·fawed; guf·faw·ing** : to laugh noisily

guid·ance *n* : help, instruction, or assistance

¹guide *n* : someone or something (as a book) that leads, directs, or shows the right way

²guide *vb* **guid·ed; guid·ing 1** : to show the way to **2** : to direct or control the course of **3** : ¹DIRECT 6, INSTRUCT

guide·book *n* : a book of information for travelers

guide dog *n* : a dog trained to lead a person who is blind

guide·line *n* : a rule about how something should be done

guide·post *n* : a post with signs giving directions for travelers

guide word *n* : either of the terms at the head of a page of an alphabetical reference work (as a dictionary) usually showing the first and last entries on the page

guild *n* : an association of people with common interests or aims

guile *n* : the use of clever and often dishonest methods

¹guil·lo·tine *n* : a machine for cutting off a person's head with a heavy blade that slides down two grooved posts

²guillotine *vb* **guil·lo·tined; guil·lo·tin·ing** : to cut off a person's head with a guillotine

guilt *n* **1** : responsibility for having done something wrong and especially something against the law **2** : a feeling of shame or regret as a result of bad conduct — **guilt·less** *adj*

guilty *adj* **guilt·i·er; guilt·i·est 1** : responsible for having done wrong **2** : suffering from or showing bad feelings about having done wrong — **guilt·i·ly** *adv*

guin·ea *n* : an old British gold coin

guinea fowl *n* : a dark gray African bird that is sometimes raised for food

guinea pig *n* : a small stocky South American animal that is a rodent with short ears and a very short tail and is often kept as a pet

guise *n* **1** : a style of dress **2** : outward appearance

gui·tar *n* : a musical instrument with six strings played by plucking or strumming

gulch *n* : a small narrow valley with steep sides

gulf *n* **1** : a part of an ocean or sea that extends into the land **2** : a deep split or gap in the earth **3** : a wide separation

gull *n* : a waterbird with webbed feet that is usually gray and white in color and has a thick strong bill

gul·let *n* : THROAT 2, ESOPHAGUS

gull·ible *adj* : easily fooled or cheated

gul·ly *n, pl* **gullies** : a trench worn in the earth by running water

¹gulp *vb* **gulped; gulp·ing 1** : to swallow in a hurry or in large amounts at a time **2** : to breathe in deeply **3** : to keep back as if by swallowing **4** : to say in a nervous way

²gulp *n* **1** : the act of swallowing or breathing deeply **2** : a large swallow

¹gum *n* : the flesh at the roots of the teeth

²gum *n* **1** : CHEWING GUM **2** : a sticky substance obtained from plants that hardens on drying **3** : a substance like a plant gum (as in stickiness)

³gum *vb* **gummed; gum·ming 1** : to smear, stick together, or clog with or as if with gum **2** : to cause not to work properly

gum·bo *n, pl* **gum·bos** : a rich soup usually thickened with okra

gum·drop *n* : a candy usually made from corn syrup and gelatin

gum·my *adj* **gum·mi·er; gum·mi·est** : consisting of or covered with gum or a sticky or chewy substance

gump·tion *n* : COURAGE

¹**gun** *n* **1** : a weapon that fires bullets or shells **2** : CANNON **3** : something like a gun in shape or function **4** : a discharge of a gun

²**gun** *vb* **gunned; gun·ning** : to open the throttle of quickly so as to increase speed

gun·boat *n* : a small armed ship for use near a coast

gun·fire *n* : the firing of guns

gunk *n* : a dirty, greasy, or sticky substance — **gunky** *adj*

gun·man *n, pl* **gun·men** : a criminal armed with a gun

gun·ner *n* : a person who operates a gun

gun·nery *n* : the use of guns

gunnery sergeant *n* : a noncommissioned officer in the marines ranking above a staff sergeant

gun·pow·der *n* : an explosive powder used in guns and blasting

gun·shot *n* **1** : a shot from a gun **2** : the distance that can be reached by a gun

gun·wale *n* : the upper edge of a ship's side

gup·py *n, pl* **guppies** : a small tropical fish often kept as an aquarium fish

¹**gur·gle** *vb* **gur·gled; gur·gling** **1** : to flow in a bubbling current **2** : to sound like a liquid flowing with a bubbling current

²**gurgle** *n* : a sound of or like liquid flowing with a bubbling current

¹**gush** *vb* **gushed; gush·ing** **1** : to flow or pour out in large amounts **2** : to act or speak in a very affectionate or enthusiastic way

²**gush** *n* : a sudden free pouring out

gust *n* **1** : a sudden brief rush of wind **2** : a sudden outburst

gusty *adj* **gust·i·er; gust·i·est** : WINDY

¹**gut** *n* **1** : the inner parts of an animal **2** : a person's stomach : BELLY **3** : the digestive tract or a part of it (as the intestine) **4** : the inner parts **5** : CATGUT **6 guts** *pl* : COURAGE

²**gut** *vb* **gut·ted; gut·ting** **1** . to remove the inner organs from **2** : to destroy the inside of

gut·ter *n* **1** : a trough along the eaves of a house to catch and carry off water **2** : a low area (as at the side of a road) to carry off surface water

¹**guy** *n* **1** : ¹FELLOW 1 **2** : PERSON 1

²**guy** *n* : a rope, chain, rod, or wire (**guy wire**) attached to something to steady it

guz·zle *vb* **guz·zled; guz·zling** : to drink greedily

gym *n* : GYMNASIUM

gym·na·si·um *n* : a room or building for sports events or exercise

gym·nast *n* : a person who is skilled in gymnastics

gym·nas·tic *adj* : of or relating to gymnastics

gym·nas·tics *n pl* : physical exercises for developing skill, strength, and control in the use of the body or a sport in which such exercises are performed — used as a singular

Gyp·sy *n, pl* **Gyp·sies** : a member of a group of people coming from India to Europe long ago and living a wandering way of life

gypsy moth *n* : a moth whose caterpillar does great damage to trees by eating the leaves

gy·rate *vb* **gy·rat·ed; gy·rat·ing** : to move back and forth with a circular motion — **gy·ra·tion** *n*

gy·ro·scope *n* : a wheel mounted to spin rapidly so that its axis is free to turn in various directions

H

h *n, pl* **h's** *or* **hs** *often cap* : the eighth letter of the English alphabet

ha *or* **hah** *interj* — used to show surprise or joy

hab·it *n* **1** : usual way of behaving **2** : clothing worn for a special purpose **3** : a way of acting or doing that has become fixed by being repeated often **4** : characteristic way of growing

hab·it·able *adj* : suitable or fit to live in

hab·i·tat *n* : the place where a plant or animal grows or lives in nature

hab·i·ta·tion *n* **1** : the act of living in a place **2** : a place to live

ha·bit·u·al *adj* **1** : occurring regularly or repeatedly : being or done by habit **2** : doing or acting by force of habit **3** : ¹REGULAR 2 — **ha·bit·u·al·ly** *adv*

ha·ci·en·da *n* : a large estate especially in a Spanish-speaking country

¹**hack** *vb* **hacked; hack·ing** **1** : to cut with repeated chopping blows **2** : to cough in a short broken way **3** : to write computer programs for enjoyment **4** : to gain access to a computer illegally

²**hack** *n* : a short broken cough

³**hack** *n* **1** : a horse let out for hire or used for varied work **2** : a person who works for pay

at a routine writing job **3** : a person who does work that is not good or original and especially a writer who is not very good

hack·er *n* **1** : HACK 3 **2** : an expert at programming and solving problems with a computer **3** : a person who illegally gains access to a computer system

hack·les *n pl* : hairs (as on the neck of a dog) that can be made to stand up

hack·ney *n, pl* **hack·neys** : a horse for ordinary riding or driving

hack·saw *n* : a saw with small teeth used for cutting hard materials (as metal)

had *past and past participle of* HAVE

had·dock *n, pl* **haddock** *or* **haddocks** : a fish of the northern Atlantic Ocean that is related to the cod and is often used for food

Ha·des *n* : the underground dwelling place of the dead in Greek mythology

hadn't : had not

haf·ni·um *n* : a metallic chemical element

hag *n* **1** : WITCH 1 **2** : an ugly old woman

hag·gard *adj* : having a hungry, tired, or worried look

hag·gle *vb* **hag·gled; hag·gling** : to argue especially over a price — **hag·gler** *n*

hah *variant of* HA

ha–ha *interj* — used to show amusement or scorn

hai·ku *n, pl* **haiku** : a Japanese poem or form of poetry without rhyme having three lines with the first and last lines having five syllables and the middle having seven

¹hail *n* **1** : small lumps of ice and snow that fall from the clouds sometimes during thunderstorms **2** : ¹VOLLEY 1

²hail *vb* **hailed; hail·ing** **1** : to fall as hail **2** : to pour down like hail

³hail *vb* **hailed; hailing** **1** : GREET 1, WELCOME **2** : to call out to — **hail from** : to come from

hail·stone *n* : a lump of hail

hail·storm *n* : a storm that brings hail

hair *n* **1** : a threadlike growth from the skin of a person or animal **2** : a covering or growth of hairs **3** : something (as a growth on a leaf) like an animal hair **4** : a very small distance or amount — **haired** *adj* — **hair·less** *adj* — **hair·like** *adj*

hair·cut *n* : the act, process, or result of cutting the hair

hair·do *n, pl* **hairdos** : a way of arranging a person's hair

hair·dress·er *n* : a person who styles or cuts hair — **hair·dress·ing** *n*

hair·pin *n* : a pin in the shape of a U for holding the hair in place

hair–rais·ing *adj* : causing terror, excitement, or great surprise

hair·style *n* : HAIRDO

hairy *adj* **hair·i·er; hair·i·est** : covered with hair — **hair·i·ness** *n*

¹hale *adj* : strong and healthy

²hale *vb* **haled; hal·ing** : to force to go

¹half *n, pl* **halves** **1** : one of two equal parts into which something can be divided **2** : a part of something that is about equal to the remainder **3** : one of a pair

²half *adj* **1** : being one of two equal parts **2** : amounting to about a half : PARTIAL

³half *adv* **1** : to the extent of half **2** : not completely

half·back *n* **1** : a football player who runs with the ball and blocks **2** : a player positioned behind the forward line in some games (as soccer)

half brother *n* : a brother by one parent only

half·dol·lar *n* **1** : a coin representing 50 cents **2** : the sum of 50 cents

half·heart·ed *adj* : lacking enthusiasm or interest — **half·heart·ed·ly** *adv*

half–knot *n* : a knot in which two rope ends are wrapped once around each other and which is used to start other knots

half–life *n, pl* **half–lives** : the time required for half of the atoms of a radioactive substance to change composition

half sister *n* : a sister by one parent only

half·time *n* : a period of rest between the halves of a game (as basketball)

¹half·way *adv* : at or to half the distance

²halfway *adj* **1** : midway between two points **2** : PARTIAL 1

half–wit *n* : a very stupid person — **half–witted** *adj*

hal·i·but *n, pl* **halibut** *or* **halibuts** : a very large saltwater flatfish often used for food

hall *n* **1** : a passage in a building that leads to rooms : CORRIDOR **2** : an entrance room **3** : AUDITORIUM **4** : a large building used for public purposes **5** : a building or large room set apart for a special purpose

hal·le·lu·jah *interj* — used to express praise, joy, or thanks

hal·low *vb* **hal·lowed; hal·low·ing** : to set apart for holy purposes : treat as sacred

Hal·low·een *n* : October 31 celebrated especially by wearing costumes and trick-or-treating

hal·lu·ci·na·tion *n* : the seeing of objects or the experiencing of feelings that are not real but are usually the result of mental disorder or the effect of a drug

hal·lu·ci·no·gen *n* : a drug that causes hallucinations — **hal·lu·ci·no·gen·ic** *adj*

hall·way *n* : HALL 1, CORRIDOR

ha·lo *n, pl* **halos** *or* **haloes** **1** : a bright circle around the head of a person (as in a painting) that signifies holiness **2** : a circle of light around the sun or moon caused by tiny ice crystals in the air

¹halt *vb* **halt·ed; halt·ing 1 :** to stop or cause to stop marching or traveling **2 :** ²END

²halt *n :* ¹END 2

hal·ter *n* **1 :** a set of straps placed around an animal's head so the animal can be led or tied **2 :** an article of clothing worn on a woman's upper body and held in place by straps around the neck and back

halve *vb* **halved; halv·ing 1 :** to divide into two equal parts **2 :** to reduce to one half

halves *pl of* HALF

hal·yard *n :* a rope for raising or lowering a sail

ham *n* **1 :** a cut of meat consisting of a thigh of pork **2 :** an operator of an amateur radio station **3 :** a showy performer

ham·burg·er *or* **ham·burg** *n* **1 :** a sandwich made of a patty of ground beef in a split bun **2 :** ground beef

ham·let *n :* a small village

¹ham·mer *n* **1 :** a tool consisting of a head fastened to a handle and used for pounding something (as a nail) **2 :** something like a hammer in shape or action **3 :** a heavy metal ball with a flexible handle thrown for distance in a track-and-field contest (**hammer throw**)

²hammer *vb* **ham·mered; ham·mer·ing 1 :** to strike with a hammer **2 :** to fasten or build (as by nailing) with a hammer **3 :** to hit something hard and repeatedly **4 :** to beat hard — **hammer out :** to produce or bring about by persistent effort

ham·mer·head *n :* a shark that has a wide flattened head with the eyes spaced widely apart

ham·mock *n :* a swinging bed made of fabric or netting attached on either end to an upright object (as a tree)

¹ham·per *vb* **ham·pered; ham·per·ing :** to keep from moving or acting freely

²hamper *n :* a large basket usually with a cover

ham·ster *n :* a stocky rodent with a short tail and large cheek pouches

¹hand *n* **1 :** the body part at the end of the human arm that includes the fingers and thumb **2 :** a bodily structure (as the hind foot of an ape) like the human hand in function or form **3 :** a pointer on a clock or watch **4 :** ²HELP 1, ASSISTANCE **5 :** ²CONTROL 1 **6 :** one side of a problem **7 :** an outburst of applause **8 :** the cards held by a player in a card game **9 :** a hired worker **:** LABORER **10 :** a promise of marriage **11 :** HANDWRITING **12 :** ABILITY 1 **13 :** a unit of measure equal to four inches (about ten centimeters) **14 :** a part or share in doing something — **at hand :** near in time or place

— **by hand :** without the use of automation **:** using the hands — **in hand :** in someone's possession or control — **on hand 1 :** available for use **2 :** ³PRESENT 2 — **out of hand :** out of control

²hand *vb* **hand·ed; hand·ing :** to give or pass with the hand

hand·bag *n :* a bag used for carrying money and small personal articles

hand·ball *n :* a game played by hitting a small ball against a wall or board with the hand

hand·bill *n :* a printed sheet (as of advertising) distributed by hand

hand·book *n :* a book of facts usually about one subject

hand·car *n :* a small railroad car that is made to move by hand or by a small motor

¹hand·cuff *n :* a metal ring that can be locked around a person's wrist — usually used in pl.

²handcuff *vb* **hand·cuffed; hand·cuff·ing :** to put handcuffs on

hand·ed *adj :* using a particular hand or number of hands

hand·ful *n, pl* **handfuls** *or* **hands·ful 1 :** as much or as many as the hand will grasp **2 :** a small amount or number

¹hand·i·cap *n* **1 :** a disadvantage that makes progress or success difficult **2 :** a contest in which someone more skilled is given a disadvantage and someone less skilled is given an advantage **3 :** the disadvantage or advantage given in a contest

²handicap *vb* **hand·i·capped; hand·i·cap·ping :** to put at a disadvantage

hand·i·craft *n* **1 :** an activity or craft (as weaving or pottery making) that requires skill with the hands **2 :** an article made by skillful use of the hands

hand·i·ly *adv :* in a handy manner **:** EASILY

hand·i·work *n :* work done by the hands

hand·ker·chief *n, pl* **hand·ker·chiefs :** a small usually square piece of cloth used for wiping the face, nose, or eyes

¹han·dle *n :* the part by which something (as a dish or tool) is picked up or held — **han·dled** *adj*

²handle *vb* **han·dled; han·dling 1 :** to touch, feel, hold, or move with the hand **2 :** to manage or control especially with the hands **3 :** MANAGE 1, DIRECT **4 :** to deal with or act on **5 :** to deal or trade in **6 :** to put up with — **han·dler** *n*

han·dle·bars *n pl :* a bar (as on a bicycle) that has a handle at each end and is used for steering

hand·made *adj :* made by hand rather than by machine

hand–me–downs *n pl :* used clothes

hand·out *n* : something (as food, clothing, or money) given to a poor person

hand·rail *n* : a rail to be grasped by the hand for support

hands down *adv* : without question : EASILY

hand·shake *n* : a clasping of hands by two people (as in greeting)

hand·some *adj* **hand·som·er; hand·som·est 1** : having a pleasing and impressive appearance **2** : CONSIDERABLE **3** : more than enough — **hand·some·ly** *adv*

hand·spring *n* : a movement in which a person turns the body forward or backward in a full circle from a standing position and lands first on the hands and then on the feet

hand·stand *n* : an act of balancing on the hands with the body and legs straight up

hand–to–hand *adj* : involving bodily contact

hand·writ·ing *n* : a person's writing

handy *adj* **hand·i·er; hand·i·est 1** : very useful or helpful **2** : within easy reach **3** : clever or skillful especially with the hands

¹hang *vb* **hung** *also* **hanged; hang·ing 1** : to fasten or be fastened to something without support from below **2** : to kill or be killed by suspending (as from a gallows) by a rope tied around the neck **3** : to cause to droop — **hang around 1** : to be or stay (somewhere) in an idle or casual way **2** : to spend time in an idle or casual way — **hang on 1** : to hold or grip something tightly **2** : to wait or stop briefly — **hang up 1** : to place on a hook or hanger **2** : to end a telephone connection

²hang *n* **1** : the way in which a thing hangs **2** : skill to do something

han·gar *n* : a shelter for housing and repairing aircraft

hang·er *n* : a device on which something hangs

hang·man *n, pl* **hang·men** : a person who hangs criminals

hang·nail *n* : a bit of skin hanging loose at the side or base of a fingernail

hang·out *n* : a favorite place for spending time

han·ker *vb* **han·kered; han·ker·ing** : to have a great desire

han·som *n* : a light covered carriage that has two wheels and a driver's seat elevated at the rear

Ha·nuk·kah *also* **Cha·nu·kah** *n* : a Jewish holiday lasting eight days in November or December and marked by the lighting of candles

hap·haz·ard *adj* : marked by lack of plan, order, or direction — **hap·haz·ard·ly** *adv*

hap·less *adj* : ¹UNFORTUNATE 1

hap·pen *vb* **hap·pened; hap·pen·ing 1** : to take place **2** : to occur or come about by chance **3** : to do or be by chance **4** : to come especially by way of injury or harm

hap·pen·ing *n* : something that occurs

hap·py *adj* **hap·pi·er; hap·pi·est 1** : feeling or showing pleasure : GLAD **2** : enjoying one's condition : CONTENT **3** : JOYFUL **4** : FORTUNATE 1, LUCKY **5** : being suitable for something — **hap·pi·ly** *adv* — **hap·pi·ness** *n*

hap·py–go–lucky *adj* : free from care

ha·rangue *n* : a scolding speech or writing

ha·rass *vb* **ha·rassed; ha·rass·ing 1** : to annoy again and again **2** : to make repeated attacks against an enemy — **ha·rass·ment** *n*

¹har·bor *n* **1** : a part of a body of water (as a sea or lake) so protected as to be a place of safety for ships : PORT **2** : a place of safety and comfort : REFUGE

²harbor *vb* **har·bored; har·bor·ing 1** : to give shelter to **2** : to have or hold in the mind

¹hard *adj* **hard·er; hard·est 1** : not easily cut, pierced, or divided : not soft **2** : difficult to do or to understand **3** : DILIGENT, ENERGETIC **4** : difficult to put up with : SEVERE **5** : sounding as the letter c in *cold* and the letter g in *geese* **6** : carried on with steady and earnest effort **7** : UNFEELING 2 **8** : high in alcoholic content **9** : containing substances that prevent lathering with soap — **hard·ness** *n*

²hard *adv* **hard·er; hard·est 1** : with great effort or energy **2** : in a forceful way **3** : with pain, bitterness, or resentment

hard copy *n* : a copy of information (as from computer storage) produced on paper in normal size

hard disk *n* **1** : a rigid metal disk used to store computer data **2** : HARD DRIVE

hard drive *n* : a data storage device of a computer containing one or more hard disks

hard·en *vb* **hard·ened; hard·en·ing 1** : to make or become hard or harder **2** : to make or become hardy or strong **3** : to make or become stubborn or unfeeling

hard·head·ed *adj* **1** : STUBBORN 1 **2** : using or showing good judgment

hard·heart·ed *adj* : showing or feeling no pity : UNFEELING

hard·ly *adv* : only just : BARELY

hard·ship *n* : something (as a loss or injury) that is hard to bear

hard·ware *n* **1** : things (as tools, cutlery, or parts of machines) made of metal **2** : equipment or parts used for a particular purpose

hard·wood *n* **1** : the usually hard wood of a tree (as a maple or oak) with broad leaves as distinguished from the wood of a tree (as a pine) with leaves that are needles **2** : a tree that produces hardwood

har·dy *adj* **har·di·er; har·di·est 1** : able to withstand weariness, hardship, or severe weather **2** : BOLD 1, BRAVE — **har·di·ly** *adv* — **har·di·ness** *n*

hare *n* : a gnawing animal that resembles the related rabbit but is usually larger and tends to live by itself

hare-brained *adj* : FOOLISH

hark *vb* **harked; hark·ing** : LISTEN 1 — **hark back** : to recall or cause to recall something earlier

¹harm *n* : physical or mental damage : INJURY

²harm *vb* **harmed; harm·ing** : to cause hurt, injury, or damage to

harm·ful *adj* : causing or capable of causing harm : INJURIOUS — **harm·ful·ly** *adv*

harm·less *adj* : not harmful — **harm·less·ly** *adv*

har·mon·i·ca *n* : a small musical instrument held in the hand and played by the mouth

har·mo·ni·ous *adj* **1** : showing agreement in action or feeling **2** : combining so as to produce a pleasing result **3** : having a pleasant sound : MELODIOUS — **har·mo·ni·ous·ly** *adv*

har·mo·nize *vb* **har·mo·nized; har·mo·niz·ing 1** : to play or sing in harmony **2** : to go together in a pleasing way : be in harmony

har·mo·ny *n, pl* **har·mo·nies 1** : the playing of musical tones together in chords **2** : a pleasing arrangement of parts **3** : AGREEMENT 1, ACCORD

¹har·ness *n* : the straps and fastenings placed on an animal so it can be controlled or prepared to pull a load

²harness *vb* **har·nessed; har·ness·ing 1** : to put straps and fastenings on **2** : to put to work : UTILIZE

¹harp *n* : a musical instrument consisting of a triangular frame set with strings that are plucked by the fingers

²harp *vb* **harped; harp·ing** : to call attention to something over and over again

¹har·poon *n* : a barbed spear used especially for hunting whales and large fish

²harpoon *vb* **har·pooned; har·poon·ing** : to strike with a barbed spear

harp·si·chord *n* : a keyboard instrument similar to a piano with strings that are plucked

¹har·row *n* : a piece of farm equipment that has metal teeth or disks for breaking up and smoothing soil

²harrow *vb* **har·rowed; har·row·ing 1** : to drag a harrow over (plowed ground) **2** : ²DISTRESS

har·row·ing *adj* : very distressing or painful

har·ry *vb* **har·ried; har·ry·ing** : HARASS

harsh *adj* **harsh·er; harsh·est 1** : causing physical discomfort **2** : having an unpleasant or harmful effect often because of great force or intensity **3** : severe or cruel : not kind or lenient — **harsh·ly** *adv* — **harsh·ness** *n*

¹har·vest *n* **1** : the gathering of a crop **2** : the season when crops are gathered **3** : a ripe crop

²harvest *vb* **har·vest·ed; har·vest·ing 1** : to gather in a crop **2** : to gather or collect for use

har·vest·er *n* **1** : a person who gathers crops or other natural products **2** : a machine for harvesting field crops

has *present third person sing of* HAVE

¹hash *n* **1** : cooked meat and vegetables chopped together and browned **2** : ¹MESS 1

²hash *vb* **hashed; hash·ing 1** : to talk about : DISCUSS **2** : to chop into small pieces

hasn't : has not

hasp *n* : a fastener (as for a door) consisting of a hinged metal strap that fits over a metal loop and is held by a pin or padlock

¹has·sle *n* **1** : something that annoys or bothers **2** : an argument or fight

²hassle *vb* **has·sled; has·sling** : to annoy continuously : HARASS

has·sock *n* : a firm stuffed cushion used as a seat or leg rest

haste *n* **1** : quickness of motion or action : SPEED **2** : hasty action

has·ten *vb* **has·tened; has·ten·ing** : to move or cause to move or act fast : HURRY

hasty *adj* **hast·i·er; hast·i·est 1** : done or made in a hurry **2** : made, done, or decided without proper care and thought — **hast·i·ly** *adv*

hat *n* : a covering for the head having a crown and usually a brim

¹hatch *n* **1** : an opening in the deck of a ship or in the floor or roof of a building **2** : a small door or opening (as in an airplane) **3** : the cover for such an opening

²hatch *vb* **hatched; hatch·ing 1** : to come out of an egg **2** : to break open and give forth young **3** : to develop usually in secret

hatch·ery *n, pl* **hatch·er·ies** : a place for hatching eggs

hatch·et *n* : a small ax with a short handle

hatch·way *n* : a hatch usually having a ladder or stairs

¹hate *n* : deep and bitter dislike

²hate *vb* **hat·ed; hat·ing** : to feel great dislike toward — **hate someone's guts** : to hate someone very much

hate·ful *adj* **1** : full of hate **2** : very bad or evil : causing or deserving hate

ha·tred *n* : ¹HATE

hat·ter *n* : a person who makes, sells, or cleans and repairs hats

haugh·ty *adj* **haugh·ti·er; haugh·ti·est** : hav-

ing or showing a proud and superior attitude
— **haugh·ti·ly** *adv* — **haugh·ti·ness** *n*

¹haul *vb* **hauled; haul·ing 1 :** to pull or drag
with effort **2 :** to transport in a vehicle

²haul *n* **1 :** the act of pulling or hauling **2**
: an amount collected **3 :** the distance or
route traveled or over which a load is moved

haunch *n* **1 :** HINDQUARTER **2 :** the upper
part of a person's thigh together with the
back part of the hip

¹haunt *vb* **haunt·ed; haunt·ing 1 :** to visit or
live in as a ghost **2 :** to visit often **3 :** to
come to mind frequently

²haunt *n* **:** a place often visited

have *vb, past & past participle* **had** ; *present
participle* **hav·ing** ; *present third person
sing* **has 1 :** to hold or own **2 :** to possess as
a characteristic **3 :** to eat or drink **4 :** to consist of or contain **5 :** to be affected by **6 :** to
plan, organize, and run (an event) **7 :** to give
birth to **8 :** to cause to be **9 :** to stand in
some relationship to **10 :** to perform a function or engage in an activity **11 :** EXPERI-
ENCE **12 :** to hold in the mind **13 :** OBTAIN,
GAIN, GET **14 :** to cause to **15 :** ¹PERMIT 1
16 : ²TRICK **17 —** used as a helping verb
with the past participle of another verb **18**
: to be forced or feel obliged **19 :** ²EXERCISE
1, USE — **had better** *or* **had best :** would be
wise to — **have to do with 1 :** to be about
2 : to be involved in or responsible for

ha·ven *n* **:** a safe place

haven't : have not

hav·er·sack *n* **:** a bag worn over one shoulder
for carrying supplies

hav·oc *n* **1 :** wide destruction **2 :** great confusion and lack of order

Ha·wai·ian *n* **1 :** a person born or living in
Hawaii **2 :** the language of the Hawaiians

¹hawk *n* **:** a bird of prey that has a strong
hooked bill and sharp curved claws and is
smaller than most eagles

²hawk *vb* **hawked; hawk·ing :** to offer for
sale by calling out — **hawk·er** *n*

³hawk *vb* **hawked; hawking :** to make a
harsh coughing sound in clearing the throat

haw·ser *n* **:** a large rope for towing or tying
up a ship

haw·thorn *n* **:** a thorny shrub or small tree
with shiny leaves, white, pink, or red flowers, and small red fruits

¹hay *n* **:** any of various herbs (as grasses) cut
and dried for use as food for animals

²hay *vb* **hayed; hay·ing :** to cut plants for hay

hay fever *n* **:** an allergy to pollen that is usually marked by sneezing, a runny or stuffed
nose, and itchy and watering eyes

hay·loft *n* **:** a loft in a barn or stable for storing hay

hay·mow *n* **:** HAYLOFT

hay·stack *n* **:** a large pile of hay stored outdoors

hay·wire *adj* **1 :** working badly or in an odd
way **2 :** emotionally or mentally out of control **:** CRAZY

¹haz·ard *n* **:** a source of danger

²hazard *vb* **haz·ard·ed; haz·ard·ing :** to offer
something (such as a guess or an opinion) at
the risk of being wrong

haz·ard·ous *adj* **:** DANGEROUS 1

haze *n* **:** fine dust, smoke, or fine particles of
water in the air

ha·zel *n* **1 :** a shrub or small tree that bears an
edible nut **2 :** a color that combines light
brown with green and gray

ha·zel·nut *n* **:** the nut of a hazel

hazy *adj* **haz·i·er; haz·i·est 1 :** partly hidden
or darkened by dust, smoke, or fine particles
of water in the air **2 :** not clear in thought or
meaning **:** VAGUE

H–bomb *n* **:** HYDROGEN BOMB

he *pron* **1 :** that male one **2 :** that person or
one — used in a general way when the sex
of the person is unknown

¹head *n* **1 :** the part of the body containing
the brain, eyes, ears, nose, and mouth **2**
: ¹MIND 1 **3 :** control of the mind or feelings
4 : the side of a coin or medal usually
thought of as the front **5 :** DIRECTOR 1,
LEADER **6 :** each person among a number **7**
pl **head :** a unit of number **8 :** something
like a head in position or use **9 :** the place
where a stream begins **10 :** a tight mass of
plant parts (as leaves or flowers) **11 :** a part
of a machine, tool, or weapon that performs
the main work **12 :** a place of leadership or
honor **13 :** CLIMAX, CRISIS — **over someone's head :** beyond someone's understanding

²head *adj* **1 :** ²CHIEF 1 **2 :** located at the
front **3 :** coming from in front

³head *vb* **head·ed; head·ing 1 :** to be the
leader of **2 :** to go or cause to go in a certain
direction **3 :** to be first or get in front of **4**
: to provide with or form a head

head·ache *n* **1 :** pain in the head **2 :** something that annoys or confuses

head·band *n* **:** a band worn on or around the
head

head·board *n* **:** a vertical board at the head of
a bed

head·dress *n* **:** a covering or ornament for
the head

head·ed *adj* **:** having such a head or so many
heads

head·first *adv* **:** with the head in front

head·gear *n* **:** something worn on the head

head·ing *n* **:** something (as a title or an address) at the top or beginning (as of a letter)

head·land *n* : a point of high land sticking out into the sea

head·light *n* : a light at the front of a vehicle

head·line *n* : a title of an article in a newspaper

¹**head·long** *adv* **1** : HEADFIRST **2** : without waiting to think things through

²**headlong** *adj* **1** : ¹RASH, IMPULSIVE **2** : plunging headfirst

head·mas·ter *n* : a man who heads the staff of a private school

head·mis·tress *n* : a woman who heads the staff of a private school

head–on *adv or adj* : with the front hitting or facing an object

head·phone *n* : an earphone held over the ear by a band worn on the head

head·quar·ters *n pl* : a place from which something is controlled or directed — used as singular or plural

head·stall *n* : an arrangement of straps or rope that fits around the head of an animal and forms part of a bridle or halter

head·stand *n* : the act of standing on the head with support from the hands

head start *n* : an advantage given at the beginning (as to a school child or a runner)

head·stone *n* : a stone that marks a grave

head·strong *adj* : very stubborn

head·wait·er *n* : the head of the staff of a restaurant

head·wa·ters *n pl* : the beginning and upper part of a stream

head·way *n* **1** : movement in a forward direction (as of a ship) **2** : ¹PROGRESS 2

heal *vb* **healed; heal·ing** : to make or become healthy or well again — **heal·er** *n*

health *n* **1** : the condition of being free from illness or disease **2** : the overall condition of the body

health·ful *adj* : good for the health

healthy *adj* **health·i·er; health·i·est** **1** : being sound and well : not sick **2** : showing good health **3** : aiding or building up health **4** : rather large in extent or amount — **health·i·ly** *adv*

¹**heap** *n* **1** : a large messy pile **2** : a large number or amount

²**heap** *vb* **heaped; heap·ing** **1** : to make into a pile : throw or lay in a heap **2** : to provide in large amounts **3** : to fill to capacity

hear *vb* **heard; hear·ing** **1** : to take in through the ear **2** : to have the power of hearing **3** : to gain knowledge of by hearing **4** : to listen to with care and attention — **hear·er** *n*

hear·ing *n* **1** : the act or power of taking in sound through the ear : the sense by which a person hears **2** : EARSHOT **3** : a chance to be heard or known **4** : a meeting at which arguments or testimony is heard

hearing aid *n* : an electronic device worn in or behind the ear of a person with poor hearing to make sounds louder

hear·ken *vb* **hear·kened; hear·ken·ing** : LISTEN 1

hear·say *n* : something heard from another : RUMOR

hearse *n* : a vehicle for carrying a dead person to the grave

heart *n* **1** : a hollow muscular organ of the body that expands and contracts to move blood through the arteries and veins **2** : something shaped like a heart **3** : a part near the center or deep into the interior **4** : the most essential part **5** : human feelings **6** : courage or enthusiasm — **by heart** : so as to be able to repeat from memory

heart·ache *n* : ¹SORROW 1

heart·beat *n* : a single contracting and expanding of the heart

heart·break *n* : very great or deep grief

heart·break·ing *adj* : causing great sorrow

heart·bro·ken *adj* : overcome by sorrow

heart·en *vb* **heart·ened; heart·en·ing** : to give new hope or courage to

heart·felt *adj* : deeply felt : SINCERE

hearth *n* **1** : an area (as of brick) in front of a fireplace **2** : the floor of a fireplace

hearth·stone *n* : a stone forming a hearth

heart·i·ly *adv* **1** : with sincerity or enthusiasm **2** : COMPLETELY

heart·less *adj* : UNFEELING 2, CRUEL

heart·sick *adj* : very sad

heart·wood *n* : the usually dark wood in the center of a tree

hearty *adj* **heart·i·er; heart·i·est** **1** : friendly and enthusiastic **2** : strong, healthy, and active **3** : having a good appetite **4** : large and plentiful — **heart·i·ness** *n*

¹**heat** *vb* **heat·ed; heat·ing** : to make or become warm or hot

²**heat** *n* **1** : a condition of being hot : WARMTH **2** : hot weather **3** : a form of energy that causes an object to rise in temperature **4** : strength of feeling or force of action **5** : a single race in a contest that includes two or more races

heat·ed *adj* **1** : HOT 1 **2** : ANGRY — **heat·ed·ly** *adv*

heat·er *n* : a device for heating

heath *n* **1** : a low, woody, and often evergreen plant that grows chiefly on poor wet soil **2** : a usually open level area of land on which heaths can grow

¹**hea·then** *adj* **1** : relating to people who do not know about or worship the God of the Bible **2** : UNCIVILIZED 1

²**heathen** *n, pl* **heathens** *or* **heathen** **1** : a

person who does not know about and worship the God of the Bible : PAGAN **2** : an uncivilized person

heath·er *n* : an evergreen heath of northern and mountainous areas with pink flowers and needlelike leaves

¹**heave** *vb* **heaved** *or* **hove** ; **heav·ing** **1** : to raise with an effort **2** : HURL, THROW **3** : to utter with an effort **4** : to rise and fall again and again **5** : to be thrown or raised up

²**heave** *n* **1** : an effort to lift or raise **2** : a forceful throw **3** : an upward motion (as of the chest in breathing or of waves in motion)

heav·en *n* **1** : SKY 1 — usually used in pl. **2** *often cap* : a place where good people are believed in some religions to be rewarded with eternal life after death **3** *cap* : GOD 1 **4** : a place or condition of complete happiness

heav·en·ly *adj* **1** : occurring or situated in the sky **2** : ¹DIVINE 1 **3** : entirely delightful

heav·i·ly *adv* **1** : with or as if with weight **2** : in a slow and difficult way **3** : very much

heavy *adj* **heavi·er; heavi·est 1** : having great weight **2** : unusually great in amount, force, or effect **3** : made with thick strong material **4** : dense and thick **5** : hard to put up with **6** : sad or troubled **7** : having little strength or energy — **heavi·ness** *n*

¹**He·brew** *adj* : of or relating to the Hebrew peoples or the Hebrew language

²**Hebrew** *n* **1** : a member of any of a group of peoples of the ancient kingdom of Israel decended from Jacob of the Bible **2** : the language of the ancient Hebrews or a later form of it

hec·tic *adj* : filled with excitement, activity, or confusion

hecto- *prefix* : hundred

hec·to·me·ter *n* : a unit of length in the metric system equal to 100 meters

he'd : he had : he would

¹**hedge** *n* : a fence or boundary made up of a thick growth of shrubs or low trees

²**hedge** *vb* **hedged; hedg·ing 1** : to surround or protect with a thick growth of shrubs or low trees **2** : to avoid giving a direct or exact answer or promise

hedge·hog *n* **1** : a mammal of Europe, Asia, and Africa that eats insects, has sharp spines mixed with the hair on its back, and is able to roll itself up into a ball when threatened **2** : PORCUPINE

hedge·row *n* : a row of shrubs or trees around a field

¹**heed** *vb* **heed·ed; heed·ing** : to pay attention to : MIND

²**heed** *n* : ATTENTION 1 — **heed·ful** *adj*

heed·less *adj* : not careful or attentive : CARELESS — **heed·less·ly** *adv*

¹**heel** *n* **1** : the back part of the human foot behind the arch and below the ankle **2** : the part of an animal's limb corresponding to a person's heel **3** : a part (as of a stocking or shoe) that covers or supports the human heel **4** : one of the crusty ends of a loaf of bread **5** : a rear, low, or bottom part **6** : a mean selfish person

²**heel** *vb* **heeled; heel·ing** : to lean to one side

heft *vb* **heft·ed; heft·ing** : to lift something up

hefty *adj* **heft·i·er; heft·i·est 1** : HEAVY 1 **2** : very forceful

heif·er *n* : a young cow

height *n* **1** : the distance from the bottom to the top of something standing upright **2** : distance upward **3** : the highest point or greatest degree

height·en *vb* **height·ened; height·en·ing** : to make greater : INCREASE

Heim·lich maneuver *n* : the use of upward pressure to the area directly above the navel of a choking person to force out an object blocking the trachea

heir *n* **1** : a person who inherits or has the right to inherit property after the death of its owner **2** : a person who has legal claim to a title or a throne when the person holding it dies

heir·ess *n* : a girl or a woman who is an heir

heir·loom *n* : a piece of personal property handed down in a family from one generation to another

held *past and past participle of* HOLD

he·li·cop·ter *n* : an aircraft supported in the air by horizontal propellers

he·li·port *n* : a place for a helicopter to land and take off

he·li·um *n* : a very light gaseous chemical element that is found in various natural gases, will not burn, and is used in balloons

hell *n* **1** : a place where evil people are believed in some religions to suffer after death **2** : a place or state of misery or wickedness

he'll : he shall : he will

hell·ish *adj* : extremely bad

hel·lo *interj* — used as a greeting or to express surprise

helm *n* **1** : a lever or wheel for steering a ship **2** : a position of control

hel·met *n* : a protective covering for the head

¹**help** *vb* **helped; help·ing 1** : to provide with what is useful in achieving an end **2** : to give relief from pain or disease **3** : PREVENT 1 **4** : ¹SERVE 1 — **help·er** *n*

²**help** *n* **1** : an act or instance of helping : AID **2** : the fact of being useful or helpful **3** : the ability to be helped **4** : a person or a thing that helps **5** : a body of hired helpers

help·ful *adj* : providing help — **help·ful·ly** *adv*

help·ing *n* : a serving of food

helping verb *n* : a verb (as *am, may,* or *will*) that is used with another verb to express person, number, mood, or tense

help·less *adj* : without help or defense — **help·less·ly** *adv* — **help·less·ness** *n*

hel·ter–skel·ter *adv* **1** : in a confused and reckless manner **2** : in great disorder

¹hem *n* : a border of a cloth article made by folding back an edge and sewing it down

²hem *vb* **hemmed; hem·ming 1** : to finish with or make a hem **2** : SURROUND 1

hemi- *prefix* : half

hemi·sphere *n* **1** : one of the halves of the earth as divided by the equator or by a meridian **2** : a half of a sphere **3** : either the left or the right half of the cerebrum — **hemi·spher·ic** *or* **hemi·spher·i·cal** *adj*

hem·lock *n* **1** : an evergreen tree related to the pine **2** : a poisonous plant with small white flowers and leaves divided into many parts

he·mo·glo·bin *n* : a protein of red blood cells that contains iron and carries oxygen from the lungs to the tissues and carbon dioxide from the tissues to the lungs

hem·or·rhage *n* : a large loss of blood

hemp *n* : a tall Asian plant grown for its tough woody fiber that is used especially in making rope and for its flowers and leaves that yield drugs (as marijuana)

hen *n* **1** : a female domestic fowl **2** : a female bird

hence *adv* **1** : from this place **2** : from this time **3** : as a result : THEREFORE

hence·forth *adv* : from this time on

hench·man *n, pl* **hench·men** : a trusted follower or supporter and especially one who performs unpleasant or illegal tasks

hep·a·ti·tis *n* : a disease which is caused by a virus and in which the liver is damaged and there is yellowing of the skin and fever

hepta- *or* **hept-** *prefix* : seven

hep·ta·gon *n* : a closed geometric figure having seven angles and seven sides

¹her *adj* : relating to or belonging to a certain woman, girl, or female animal

²her *pron, objective case of* SHE

¹her·ald *n* **1** : an official messenger **2** : a person who brings news or announces something

²herald *vb* **her·ald·ed; her·ald·ing 1** : to give notice of : ANNOUNCE **2** : FORETELL

her·ald·ry *n* : the art or science of tracing and recording family history and creating coats of arms

herb *n* **1** : a plant with soft stems that die down at the end of the growing season **2** : a

plant or plant part used in medicine or in seasoning foods

her·bi·vore *n* : an animal that feeds on plants

her·biv·o·rous *adj* : feeding on plants

¹herd *n* : a number of animals of one kind kept or living together

²herd *vb* **herd·ed; herd·ing** : to gather and move as a group — **herd·er** *n*

herds·man *n, pl* **herds·men** : a person who owns or watches over a flock or herd

¹here *adv* **1** : in or at this place **2** : at this time : happening now **3** : to or into this place : HITHER

²here *n* : this place

here·abouts *or* **here·about** *adv* : near or around this place

¹here·af·ter *adv* **1** : after this **2** : in some future time or state

²hereafter *n* **1** : ²FUTURE 1 **2** : life after death

here·by *adv* : by means of this

he·red·i·tary *adj* **1** : capable of being passed from parent to offspring **2** : received or passing from an ancestor to an heir

he·red·i·ty *n, pl* **he·red·i·ties** : the passing on of characteristics (as the color of the eyes or hair) from parents to offspring

here·in *adv* : in this

her·e·sy *n, pl* **her·e·sies 1** : the holding of religious beliefs opposed to church doctrine : such a belief **2** : belief or opinion opposed to a generally accepted view

her·e·tic *n* : a person who believes or teaches something opposed to accepted beliefs (as of a church)

here·to·fore *adv* : up to this time

here·up·on *adv* : right after this

here·with *adv* : with this

her·i·tage *n* : the traditions, achievements, and beliefs that are part of the history of a group of people

her·mit *n* : a person who lives apart from others especially for religious reasons

hermit crab *n* : a small crab that lives in the empty shells of mollusks (as snails)

he·ro *n, pl* **heroes 1** : a person admired for great deeds or fine qualities **2** : a person who shows great courage **3** : the chief male character in a story, play, or poem

he·ro·ic *adj* **1** : of or relating to heroism or heroes **2** : COURAGEOUS, DARING — **he·ro·ical·ly** *adv*

her·o·in *n* : a very harmful illegal drug that is highly addictive and is made from morphine

her·o·ine *n* **1** : a woman admired for great deeds or fine qualities **2** : the chief female character in a story, poem, or play

her·o·ism *n* **1** : behavior showing great courage especially for a noble purpose **2** : the qualities of a hero

her·on *n* : a wading bird that has long legs, a long neck, a long thin bill, and large wings

her·ring *n* : a fish of the northern Atlantic Ocean that is often used for food

hers *pron* : that which belongs to her

her·self *pron* : her own self

he's : he is : he has

hes·i·tan·cy *n* : the quality or state of being unwilling to do something because of doubt or nervousness

hes·i·tant *adj* : feeling or showing unwillingness to do something because of doubt or nervousness — **hes·i·tant·ly** *adv*

hes·i·tate *vb* **hes·i·tat·ed; hes·i·tat·ing 1** : to pause before doing something **2** : to be unwilling to do something because of doubt or nervousness — **hes·i·ta·tion** *n*

hew *vb* **hewed** *or* **hewn** ; **hew·ing 1** : to chop down **2** : to shape by cutting with an ax

hex *n* : a harmful spell : JINX

hexa- *or* **hex-** *prefix* : six

hexa·gon *n* : a closed geometric figure having six angles and six sides — **hex·ag·o·nal** *adj*

hey *interj* — used to call attention or to express surprise or joy

hey·day *n* : the time of greatest strength, popularity, or success

hi *interj* — used especially as a greeting

HI *abbr* Hawaii

hi·ber·nate *vb* **hi·ber·nat·ed; hi·ber·nat·ing** : to pass all or part of the winter in an inactive state in which the body temperature drops and breathing slows — **hi·ber·na·tor** *n*

hi·ber·na·tion *n* : the act of passing all or part of the winter in an inactive state

¹hic·cup *n* : a gulping sound caused by sudden movements of muscles active in breathing

²hiccup *vb* **hic·cuped** *also* **hic·cupped; hic·cup·ing** *also* **hic·cup·ping** : to make a gulping sound caused by sudden movements of muscles active in breathing

hick·o·ry *n, pl* **hick·o·ries** : a tall tree related to the walnuts that has strong tough wood and bears an edible nut (**hickory nut**) in a hard shell

¹hide *vb* **hid ; hid·den** *or* **hid; hid·ing 1** : to put or stay out of sight **2** : to keep secret **3** : to screen from view

²hide *n* : the skin of an animal

hide–and–go–seek *n* : HIDE-AND-SEEK

hide–and–seek *n* : a game in which one player covers his or her eyes and after giving the others time to hide goes looking for them

hide·away *n* : ¹RETREAT 3, HIDEOUT

hid·eous *adj* : very ugly or disgusting : FRIGHTFUL — **hid·eous·ly** *adv*

hide·out *n* : a secret place for hiding (as from the police)

hi·ero·glyph·ic *n* : any of the symbols in the picture writing of ancient Egypt

hig·gle·dy–pig·gle·dy *adv or adj* : in a messy way : TOPSY-TURVY

¹high *adj* **high·er; high·est 1** : extending to a great distance above the ground **2** : having a specified elevation : TALL **3** : of greater degree, size, amount, or cost than average **4** : having great force **5** : pitched or sounding above some other sound **6** : very serious **7** : of the best quality **8** : rich in quality

²high *adv* **higher; highest** : at or to a high place or degree

³high *n* **1** : a high point or level **2** : a region of high barometric pressure **3** : the arrangement of gears in an automobile giving the highest speed of travel **4** : the space overhead : SKY

high·brow *n* : a person of great learning or culture

high five *n* : a show of celebration by two people slapping each other's hands in the air

high–hand·ed *adj* : having or showing no regard for the rights, concerns, or feelings of others

high·land *n* : high or hilly country

¹high·light *n* : a very interesting event or detail

²highlight *vb* **high·light·ed; high·light·ing 1** : EMPHASIZE **2** : to be an interesting event or detail **3** : to mark with a highlighter **4** : to cause (something on a computer screen) to be displayed in a way that stands out

high·light·er *n* : a pen with a wide felt tip and brightly colored ink for marking text on a page so that it stands out clearly

high·ly *adv* **1** : to a high degree : very much **2** : with much approval

high·ness *n* **1** : the quality or state or being high **2** — used as a title for a person of very high rank

high–rise *adj* : having many stories

high school *n* : a school usually including the ninth to twelfth or tenth to twelfth grades

high seas *n pl* : the part of a sea or ocean that is away from land

high–spir·it·ed *adj* : LIVELY 1

high–strung *adj* : very sensitive or nervous

high tech *n* : technology involving the production or use of advanced or sophisticated devices — **high–tech** *adj*

high tide *n* : the tide when the water is at its greatest height

high·way *n* : a main road

high·way·man *n, pl* **high·way·men** : a man who robbed travelers on a road in past centuries

hi·jack *vb* **hi·jacked; hi·jack·ing 1** : to stop

and steal or steal from a moving vehicle **2** : to take control of (an aircraft) by force — **high·jack·er** *n*

¹hike *vb* **hiked; hik·ing** : to take a long walk especially for pleasure or exercise — **hik·er** *n*

²hike *n* : a long walk especially for pleasure or exercise

hi·lar·i·ous *adj* : very funny — **hi·lar·i·ous·ly** *adv*

hi·lar·i·ty *n* : noisy fun or laughter

hill *n* **1** : a usually rounded elevation of land lower than a mountain **2** : a surface that slopes **3** : a heap or mound of something

hill·bil·ly *n, pl* **hill·bil·lies** : a person from a backwoods area

hill·ock *n* : a small hill

hill·side *n* : the part of a hill between the top and the foot

hill·top *n* : the highest part of a hill

hilly *adj* **hill·i·er; hill·i·est** : having many hills

hilt *n* : a handle especially of a sword or dagger

him *pron, objective case of* HE

him·self *pron* : his own self

hind *adj* : being at the end or back : REAR

hin·der *vb* **hin·dered; hin·der·ing** : to make slow or difficult

hind·quar·ter *n* : the back half of a side of the body or carcass of a four-footed animal

hin·drance *n* : someone or something that makes a situation more difficult

hind·sight *n* : understanding of something only after it has happened

Hin·du *n* : a person who follows Hinduism

Hin·du·ism *n* : a set of cultural and religious beliefs and practices that originated in India

¹hinge *n* : a jointed piece on which a door, gate, or lid turns or swings

²hinge *vb* **hinged; hing·ing** **1** : to attach by or provide with hinges **2** : DEPEND 2

¹hint *n* **1** : information that helps a person guess an answer or do something more easily **2** : a small amount : TRACE

²hint *vb* **hint·ed; hint·ing** : to suggest something without plainly asking or saying it

hin·ter·land *n* : a region far from cities

hip *n* : the part of the body that curves out below the waist on each side

hip–hop *n* **1** : rap music **2** : the culture associated with rap music

hip·pie *or* **hip·py** *n, pl* **hippies** : a usually young person who rejects the values and practices of society and opposes violence and war

hip·po *n, pl* **hip·pos** : HIPPOPOTAMUS

hip·po·pot·a·mus *n, pl* **hip·po·pot·a·mus·es** *or* **hip·po·pot·a·mi** : a large African animal with thick hairless brownish gray skin, a big

head, and short legs that eats plants and spends most of its time in rivers

hire *vb* **hired; hir·ing** **1** : ¹EMPLOY 1 **2** : to get the temporary use of in return for pay **3** : to take a job

¹his *adj* : relating to or belonging to a certain man, boy, or male animal

²his *pron* : that which belongs to him

¹His·pan·ic *adj* : of or relating to people of Latin-American origin

²Hispanic *n* : a person of Latin-American origin

¹hiss *vb* **hissed; hiss·ing** **1** : to make a sound like a long \s\ **2** : to show dislike or disapproval by hissing **3** : to say (something) in a loud or angry whisper

²hiss *n* : a sound like a long \s\ sometimes used as a sign of dislike or disapproval

hist. *abbr* **1** historian **2** historical **3** history

his·to·ri·an *n* : a person who studies or writes about history

his·tor·ic *adj* : famous in history

his·tor·i·cal *adj* **1** : relating to or based on history **2** : known to be true — **his·tor·i·cal·ly** *adv*

his·to·ry *n, pl* **his·to·ries** **1** : events of the past and especially those relating to a particular place or subject **2** : a branch of knowledge that records and explains past events **3** : a written report of past events **4** : an established record of past events

¹hit *vb* **hit; hit·ting** **1** : to strike or be struck by (someone or something) forcefully **2** : to cause or allow (something) to come into contact with something **3** : to affect or be affected by in a harmful or damaging way **4** : OCCUR 1 **5** : to come upon by chance **6** : to arrive at — **hit·ter** *n*

²hit *n* **1** : a blow striking an object aimed at **2** : something very successful **3** : a batted baseball that enables the batter to reach base safely **4** : a match in a computer search

hit–and–run *adj* : being or involving a driver who does not stop after being in an automobile accident

¹hitch *vb* **hitched; hitch·ing** **1** : to fasten by or as if by a hook or knot **2** : HITCHHIKE **3** : to pull or lift (something) with a quick movement

²hitch *n* **1** : an unexpected stop or problem **2** : a jerky movement or pull **3** : a knot used for a temporary fastening

hitch·hike *vb* **hitch·hiked; hitch·hik·ing** : to travel by getting free rides in passing vehicles — **hitch·hik·er** *n*

hith·er *adv* : to this place

hith·er·to *adv* : up to this time

HIV *n* : a virus that causes AIDS by destroying large numbers of cells that help the human body fight infection

hive *n* **1** : a container for housing honeybees **2** : the usually aboveground nest of bees **3** : a colony of bees **4** : a place filled with busy people

hives *n pl* : an allergic condition in which the skin breaks out in large red itching patches

¹hoard *n* : a supply usually of something of value stored away or hidden

²hoard *vb* **hoard·ed; hoard·ing** : to gather and store away — **hoard·er** *n*

hoarse *adj* **hoars·er; hoars·est 1** : harsh in sound **2** : having a rough voice — **hoarse·ly** *adv* — **hoarse·ness** *n*

hoary *adj* **hoar·i·er; hoar·i·est 1** : very old **2** : having gray or white hair

¹hoax *vb* **hoaxed; hoax·ing** : to trick into thinking something is true or real when it isn't

²hoax *n* **1** : an act meant to fool or deceive **2** : something false passed off as real

¹hob·ble *vb* **hob·bled; hob·bling** : to walk slowly and with difficulty

²hobble *n* : a slow and difficult way of walking

hob·by *n, pl* **hobbies** : an interest or activity engaged in for pleasure

hob·by·horse *n* : a stick that has an imitation horse's head and that a child pretends to ride

hob·gob·lin *n* **1** : a mischievous elf **2** : BOGEY 2

ho·bo *n, pl* **hoboes** : ¹VAGRANT

hock *n* **1** : a small piece of meat from the leg of a pig **2** : the part of the rear leg of a four-footed animal that is like a human ankle

hock·ey *n* : a game played on ice or in a field by two teams who try to drive a puck or ball through a goal by hitting it with a stick

hodge·podge *n* : a disorderly mixture

¹hoe *n* : a tool with a long handle and a thin flat blade used for weeding and cultivating

²hoe *vb* **hoed; hoe·ing** : to weed or loosen the soil around plants with a hoe

¹hog *n* **1** : a usually large adult pig **2** : a greedy or dirty person

²hog *vb* **hogged; hog·ging** : to take or use in a way that keeps others from having or using

ho·gan *n* : a Navajo Indian dwelling made of logs and mud with a door traditionally facing east

hog·gish *adj* : very selfish or greedy — **hog·gish·ly** *adv*

hogs·head *n* **1** : a very large cask **2** : a unit of liquid measure equal to 63 gallons (about 238 liters)

¹hoist *vb* **hoist·ed; hoist·ing** : to lift up especially with a pulley

²hoist *n* : a device used for lifting heavy loads

¹hold *vb* **held ; hold·ing 1** : to have or keep

a grip on **2** : to take in and have within : CONTAIN **3** : ¹SUPPORT 1 **4** : to carry on by group action **5** : to have as a position of responsibility **6** : to continue in the same way or state : LAST **7** : to remain fast or fastened **8** : to have or keep possession or control of **9** : to have in mind **10** : to limit the movement or activity of : RESTRAIN **11** : to continue in a condition or position **12** : to continue moving on (a course) without change **13** : to make accept a legal or moral duty **14** : CONSIDER 3, REGARD — **hold·er** *n* — **hold out 1** : to continue to be present or exist **2** : to refuse to yield or agree — **hold up 1** : ²DELAY 2 **2** : to rob while threatening with a weapon

²hold *n* **1** : the act or way of holding : GRIP **2** : a note or rest in music kept up longer than usual

³hold *n* **1** : the part of a ship below the decks in which cargo is stored **2** : the cargo compartment of an airplane

hold·up *n* **1** : robbery by an armed robber **2** : ¹DELAY

hole *n* **1** : an opening into or through something **2** : a hollowed out place **3** : DEN 1, BURROW

hole up *vb* **holed up; hol·ing up** : to take shelter

hol·i·day *n* **1** : a special day of celebration during which schools and businesses are often closed **2** : VACATION

ho·li·ness *n* **1** : the quality or state of being holy **2** — used as a title for persons of high religious position

¹hol·ler *vb* **hol·lered; hol·ler·ing** : to cry out : SHOUT

²holler *n* : ²SHOUT, CRY

¹hol·low *adj* **hol·low·er; hol·low·est 1** : having a space inside : not solid **2** : curved inward : SUNKEN **3** : suggesting a sound made in an empty place **4** : not sincere — **hol·low·ly** *adv*

²hollow *n* **1** : a low spot in a surface **2** : a small valley **3** : an empty space within something

³hollow *vb* **hol·lowed; hol·low·ing** : to make or become hollow

hol·ly *n, pl* **hollies** : an evergreen tree or shrub that has shiny leaves with prickly edges and red berries

hol·ly·hock *n* : a plant with large rounded leaves and tall stalks of bright showy flowers

ho·lo·caust *n* **1** : a complete destruction especially by fire **2** *often cap* : the killing of civilians and especially Jews by the Nazis during World War II

ho·lo·gram *n* : a three-dimensional picture made by laser light reflected onto a photographic substance without the use of a camera

hol·ster *n* : a usually leather case in which a pistol is carried or worn

ho·ly *adj* **ho·li·er; ho·li·est** **1** : set apart for the service of God or of a divine being : SACRED **2** : being a deity **3** — used in exclamations to indicate surprise or excitement

holy day *n* : a day set aside for special religious observance

hom- *or* **homo-** *prefix* : one and the same : similar : alike

hom·age *n* **1** : a feudal ceremony in which a person pledges loyalty to a lord and becomes a vassal **2** : ¹RESPECT 1

¹home *n* **1** : the house or apartment where a person lives **2** : the place where a person was born or grew up **3** : HABITAT **4** : a place for the care of people unable to care for themselves **5** : a family living together **6** : ¹HOUSE 1 **7** : the goal or point to be reached in some games — **at home** : relaxed and comfortable

²home *adv* **1** : to or at home **2** : to the final place or limit

home·com·ing *n* : a return home

home·land *n* : the country a person comes from

home·less *adj* : having no home or permanent residence — **home·less·ness** *n*

home·like *adj* : like a home (as in comfort and kindly warmth)

home·ly *adj* **home·li·er; home·li·est** **1** : not pretty or handsome **2** : suggesting home life

home·made *adj* : made in the home

home·mak·er *n* : a person who manages a household especially as a wife and mother — **home·mak·ing** *n*

home page *n* : the page of a World Wide Web site that is seen first and that usually contains links to the other pages of the site or to other sites

home plate *n* : the base that a baseball runner must touch to score

hom·er *n* : HOME RUN

home·room *n* : a classroom where students of the same class report at the start of each day

home run *n* : a hit in baseball that enables the batter to go around all the bases and score

home·school *vb* **home·schooled; home·school·ing** : to teach school subjects to at home

home·school·er *n* **1** : a person who teaches school subjects to children at home **2** : a child who is taught school subjects at home

home·sick *adj* : longing for home and family — **home·sick·ness** *n*

home·spun *adj* **1** : made at home **2** : made

of a loosely woven fabric originally made from yarn spun at home **3** : not fancy : SIMPLE

¹home·stead *n* **1** : a home and the land around it **2** : a piece of land gained from United States public lands by living on and farming it

²homestead *vb* **home·stead·ed; home·stead·ing** : to acquire or settle on public land for use as a homestead — **home·stead·er** *n*

home·town *n* : the city or town where a person was born or grew up

home·ward *or* **home·wards** *adv or adj* : toward home

home·work *n* : work (as school lessons) to be done at home

hom·ey *adj* **hom·i·er; hom·i·est** : HOMELIKE

ho·mi·cide *n* : a killing of one human being by another

hom·ing pigeon *n* : a racing pigeon trained to return home

hom·i·ny *n* : kernels of corn that have the outer covering removed by processing and that are eaten cooked as a cereal or vegetable

homo- — see HOM-

ho·mog·e·nize *vb* **ho·mog·e·nized; ho·mog·e·niz·ing** : to reduce the particles within a liquid (as milk or paint) to the same size and spread them evenly in the liquid

ho·mo·graph *n* : one of two or more words spelled alike but different in meaning or origin or pronunciation

hom·onym *n* **1** : HOMOPHONE **2** : HOMOGRAPH **3** : one of two or more words spelled and pronounced alike but different in meaning

ho·mo·phone *n* : one of two or more words pronounced alike but different in meaning or origin or spelling

hone *vb* **honed; hon·ing** : to sharpen with or as if with a fine abrasive stone

hon·est *adj* **1** : not engaging in or involving cheating, stealing, or lying **2** : not marked by lies or trickery : STRAIGHTFORWARD **3** : being just what is indicated : REAL, GENUINE

hon·est·ly *adv* **1** : without cheating or lying : in an honest manner **2** : in a real and sincere way **3** — used to stress the truth or sincerity of what is being said **4** — used to show annoyance or disapproval

hon·es·ty *n* : the quality or state of being truthful and fair

hon·ey *n* **1** : a sweet sticky material made by bees from the nectar of flowers and stored by them in a honeycomb for food **2** : ¹DARLING 1

hon·ey·bee *n* : a bee whose honey is used by people as food

hon·ey·comb *n* : a mass of wax cells built by honeybees in their nest to contain young bees and stores of honey

hon·ey·dew melon *n* : a pale melon with greenish sweet flesh and smooth skin

¹hon·ey·moon *n* **1** : a trip taken by a recently married couple **2** : a period of harmony especially just after marriage

²honeymoon *vb* **hon·ey·mooned; hon·ey·moon·ing** : to go on a trip right after marrying — **hon·ey·moon·er** *n*

hon·ey·suck·le *n* : a climbing vine or a bush with fragrant white, yellow, or red flowers

¹honk *vb* **honked; honk·ing** : to make a sound like the cry of a goose

²honk *n* **1** : the cry of a goose **2** : a loud sound like the cry of a goose

¹hon·or *n* **1** : good character as judged by other people : REPUTATION **2** : outward respect : RECOGNITION **3** : PRIVILEGE **4** — used especially as a title for an official of high rank **5** : a person whose character and accomplishments bring respect or fame **6** : evidence or a symbol of great respect **7** : high moral standards of behavior

²honor *vb* **hon·ored; hon·or·ing** **1** : ²RESPECT 1 **2** : to recognize and show admiration for publicly **3** : to live up to or fulfill the requirements of

hon·or·able *adj* **1** : bringing about or deserving honor **2** : observing ideas of honor or reputation **3** : having high moral standards of behavior : ETHICAL, UPRIGHT — **hon·or·ably** *adv*

hon·or·ary *adj* : given or done as an honor

hon·our *chiefly British variant of* HONOR

hood *n* **1** : a covering for the head and neck and sometimes the face **2** : the movable covering for an automobile engine **3** : a cover that is used especially to protect or shield something — **hood·ed** *adj*

-hood *n suffix* **1** : state : condition : quality : nature **2** : instance of a specified state or quality **3** : individuals sharing a specified state or character

hood·lum *n* : a tough and violent criminal : THUG

hood·wink *vb* **hood·winked; hood·wink·ing** : to mislead by trickery

hoof *n, pl* **hooves** *or* **hoofs** **1** : a covering of tough material that protects the ends of the toes of some animals (as horses, oxen, or pigs) **2** : a foot (as of a horse) covered by a hoof — **hoofed** *adj*

¹hook *n* **1** : a curved device (as a piece of bent metal) for catching, holding, or pulling something **2** : something curved or bent like a hook — **by hook or by crook** : in any way : fairly or unfairly

²hook *vb* **hooked; hook·ing** **1** : to bend in the shape of a hook **2** : to catch or fasten with a hook **3** : CONNECT 1

hooked *adj* **1** : shaped like or provided with a hook **2** : fascinated by or fond of something

hook·worm *n* : a small worm that lives in the intestines and makes people sick by sucking their blood

hooky *also* **hook·ey** *n* : TRUANT

hoop *n* **1** : a circular figure or object **2** : a circular band used for holding together the strips that make up the sides of a barrel or tub **3** : a circle or series of circles of flexible material (as wire) used for holding a woman's skirt out from the body

hoo·ray *also* **hur·rah** *or* **hur·ray** *interj* — used to express joy, approval, or encouragement

¹hoot *vb* **hoot·ed; hoot·ing** **1** : to utter a loud shout or laugh **2** : to make the noise of an owl or a similar cry **3** : to express by hoots

²hoot *n* **1** : the sound made by an owl **2** : a loud laugh or shout **3** : the least bit

¹hop *vb* **hopped; hop·ping** **1** : to move by short quick jumps **2** : to jump on one foot **3** : to jump over **4** : to get on, in, or aboard by or as if by hopping **5** : to make a quick trip especially by air

²hop *n* **1** : a short quick jump especially on one leg **2** : a short trip especially by air

³hop *n* **1** : a twining vine whose greenish flowers look like small cones **2** **hops** *pl* : the dried flowers of the hop plant used chiefly in making beer and ale

¹hope *vb* **hoped; hop·ing** : to desire especially with expectation that the wish will be granted

²hope *n* **1** : desire together with the expectation of getting what is wanted **2** : a chance or likelihood for something desired **3** : something wished for **4** : someone or something that may be able to help

hope·ful *adj* **1** : full of hope **2** : giving hope : PROMISING — **hope·ful·ly** *adv*

hope·less *adj* **1** : having no hope **2** : offering no hope — **hope·less·ly** *adv* — **hope·less·ness** *n*

Ho·pi *n, pl* **Hopi** *or* **Ho·pis** **1** : a member of an American Indian people of northeastern Arizona **2** : the language of the Hopi people

hop·per *n* **1** : someone or something that hops **2** : an insect that moves by leaping **3** : a container used for pouring material (as grain or coal) into a machine or a bin **4** : a railroad car for materials that are transported in large quantities

hop·scotch *n* : a game in which a player tosses a stone into sections of a figure drawn on the ground and hops through the figure and back to pick up the stone

horde *n* : MULTITUDE, SWARM

ho·ri·zon *n* **1** : the line where the earth or sea seems to meet the sky **2** : the limit of a person's outlook or experience

¹hor·i·zon·tal *adj* : lying flat or level : parallel to the horizon — **hor·i·zon·tal·ly** *adv*

²horizontal *n* : something (as a line or plane) that is parallel to the horizon

hor·mone *n* : any of various chemical substances produced by body cells and released especially into the blood and having a specific effect on cells or organs of the body usually at a distance from the place of origin

horn *n* **1** : one of the hard bony growths on the head of many hoofed animals (as cattle, goats, or sheep) **2** : the tough material of which horns and hooves are composed **3** : a brass musical instrument (as a trumpet or French horn) **4** : a usually electrical device that makes a noise like that of a horn **5** : something shaped like or made from a horn **6** : a musical or signaling instrument made from an animal's horn — **horned** *adj* — **horn·less** *adj*

horned toad *n* : a small harmless lizard with a wide flattened body like a toad and hard pointed growths on the skin

hor·net *n* : a large wasp that can give a severe sting

horn of plenty *n, pl* **horns of plenty** : CORNUCOPIA

horny *adj* **horn·i·er; horn·i·est 1** : made of horn **2** : hard and rough

horo·scope *n* **1** : a diagram of the positions of the planets and signs of the zodiac used in astrology **2** : a prediction based on astrology

hor·ren·dous *adj* : very bad

hor·ri·ble *adj* **1** : causing horror : TERRIBLE **2** : very unpleasant — **hor·ri·bly** *adv*

hor·rid *adj* **1** : HORRIBLE **2** : very unpleasant : DISGUSTING

hor·ri·fy *vb* **hor·ri·fied; hor·ri·fy·ing** : to cause to feel great fear, dread, or shock

hor·ror *n* **1** : great fear, dread, or shock **2** : a quality or thing that causes horror

horse *n* **1** : a large hoofed animal that feeds especially on grasses and is used as a work animal and for riding **2** : a frame that supports something (as wood while being cut) **3** : a piece of gymnasium equipment used for vaulting exercises — **from the horse's mouth** : from the original source

¹horse·back *n* : the back of a horse

²horseback *adv* : on horseback

horse chestnut *n* : a shiny large brown nut that is unfit to eat and is the fruit of a tall tree native to Europe

horse·fly *n, pl* **horse·flies** : a large swift two-winged fly the females of which suck blood from animals

horse·hair *n* **1** : the hair of a horse especially from the mane or tail **2** : a cloth made from horsehair

horse·man *n, pl* **horse·men 1** : a horseback rider **2** : a person skilled in handling horses — **horse·man·ship** *n*

horse·play *n* : rough play

horse·pow·er *n* : a unit of power that equals the work done in lifting 550 pounds one foot in one second

horse·rad·ish *n* : a sharp-tasting relish made from the root of a tall white-flowered plant

horse·shoe *n* **1** : a protective iron plate that is nailed to the rim of a horse's hoof **2** : something shaped like a horseshoe **3** **horseshoes** *pl* : a game in which horseshoes are tossed at a stake in the ground

horse·tail *n* : a primitive plant that produces spores and has small leaves resembling scales

horse·whip *vb* **horse·whipped; horse·whipping** : to beat severely with a whip made to be used on a horse

horse·wom·an *n, pl* **horse·wom·en** : a woman skilled in riding on horseback or in handling horses

hors·ey *also* **horsy** *adj* **hors·i·er; hors·i·est** : of or relating to horses or horsemen and horsewomen

¹hose *n, pl* **hose** *or* **hos·es 1** *pl* **hose** : STOCKING 1, SOCK **2** : a flexible tube for carrying fluid

²hose *vb* **hosed; hos·ing** : to spray, water, or wash with a hose

ho·siery *n* : clothing (as stockings or socks) that is worn on the legs and feet

hos·pi·ta·ble *adj* **1** : friendly and generous to guests and visitors **2** : willing to deal with something new — **hos·pi·ta·bly** *adv*

hos·pi·tal *n* : a place where the sick and injured are given medical care

hos·pi·tal·i·ty *n* : friendly and generous treatment of guests

hos·pi·tal·ize *vb* **hos·pi·tal·ized; hos·pi·tal·iz·ing** : to place in a hospital for care and treatment — **hos·pi·tal·iza·tion** *n*

¹host *n* **1** : a person who receives or entertains guests **2** : a living animal or plant on or in which a parasite lives

²host *vb* **host·ed; host·ing** : to serve as host to or at

³host *n* : MULTITUDE

⁴host *n, often cap* : the bread used in Christian Communion

hos·tage *n* : a person who is captured by

someone who demands that certain things be done before the captured person is freed

hos·tel *n* : a place providing inexpensive lodging usually for young travelers

host·ess *n* : a woman who receives or entertains guests

hos·tile *adj* **1** : belonging to or relating to an enemy **2** : UNFRIENDLY

hos·til·i·ty *n, pl* **hos·til·i·ties 1** : an unfriendly or hostile state, attitude, or action **2** *hostilities pl* : acts of warfare

hot *adj* **hot·ter; hot·test 1** : having a high temperature **2** : having or causing the sensation of an uncomfortably high degree of body heat **3** : having a spicy or peppery flavor **4** : currently popular **5** : close to something sought **6** : easily excited **7** : marked by or causing anger or strong feelings **8** : very angry **9** : recently stolen **10** : recently made or received **11** : RADIOACTIVE — **hot·ly** *adv* — **hot·ness** *n*

hot·cake *n* : PANCAKE

hot dog *n* : a frankfurter cooked and then served in a long split roll

ho·tel *n* : a place that provides lodging and meals for the public : INN

hot·head *n* : a person who is easily excited or angered — **hot·head·ed** *adj*

hot·house *n* : a heated building enclosed by glass for growing plants

hot·line *n* : a direct telephone line for getting help in an emergency

hot plate *n* : a small portable appliance for heating or cooking

hot rod *n* : an automobile rebuilt for high speed and fast acceleration

hot water *n* : a difficult or distressing situation

¹hound *n* : a dog with drooping ears that is used in hunting and follows game by the sense of smell

²hound *vb* **hound·ed; hound·ing** : to hunt, chase, or annoy without ceasing

hour *n* **1** : one of the 24 divisions of a day : 60 minutes **2** : the time of day **3** : a fixed or particular time **4** : the distance that can be traveled in an hour

hour·glass *n* : a device for measuring time in which sand takes an hour to run from the upper into the lower part of a glass container

¹hour·ly *adv* : at or during every hour

²hourly *adj* **1** : occurring every hour **2** : figured by the hour

¹house *n, pl* **hous·es 1** : a place built for people to live in **2** : something (as a nest or den) used by an animal for shelter **3** : a building in which something is kept **4** : ¹HOUSEHOLD **5** : a body of persons assembled to make the laws for a country **6** : a business firm **7** : the audience in a theater or concert hall **8** : FAMILY 2 — **on the house** : free of charge

²house *vb* **housed; hous·ing 1** : to provide with living quarters or shelter **2** : CONTAIN 2

house·boat *n* : a roomy pleasure boat fitted for use as a place to live

house·boy *n* : a boy or man hired to do housework

house·fly *n, pl* **house·flies** : a two-winged fly that is common in houses and may carry disease germs

¹house·hold *n* : all the people in a family or group who live together in one house

²household *adj* **1** : of or relating to a house or a household **2** : FAMILIAR 1

house·hold·er *n* : a person who lives in a dwelling alone or as the head of a household

house·keep·er *n* : a person employed to take care of a house

house·keep·ing *n* : the care and management of a house or the rooms of a hotel

house·maid *n* : a woman or girl hired to do housework

house·moth·er *n* : a woman who acts as hostess, supervisor, and often housekeeper in a residence for young people

House of Representatives *n* : the lower house of a legislature (as the United States Congress)

house·plant *n* : a plant grown or kept indoors

house·top *n* : ¹ROOF 1

house·warm·ing *n* : a party to celebrate moving into a new home

house·wife *n, pl* **house·wives** : a married woman in charge of a household

house·work *n* : the labor involved in housekeeping

hous·ing *n* **1** : dwellings provided for a number of people **2** : something that covers or protects

hove *past and past participle of* HEAVE

hov·el *n* : a small poorly built usually dirty house

hov·er *vb* **hov·ered; hov·er·ing 1** : to fly or float in the air without moving far in any direction **2** : to stay near a place

¹how *adv* **1** : in what way : by what means **2** : for what reason **3** : to what degree, number, or amount **4** : in what state or condition — **how about** : what do you say to or think of — **how come** : ¹WHY — **how do you do** : HELLO

²how *conj* : in what manner or condition

how·ev·er *adv* **1** : to whatever degree or extent **2** : in whatever way **3** : in spite of that

¹howl *vb* **howled; howl·ing 1** : to make a loud long mournful cry or sound **2** : to cry out loudly (as with pain or amusement)

²howl *n* **1** : a loud long mournful sound

made by dogs and related animals (as wolves) **2** : a long loud cry (as of distress, disappointment, or rage)

hr. *abbr* hour

H.S. *abbr* high school

ht. *abbr* height

HTML *n* : a computer language that is used to create pages on the World Wide Web that can include text, pictures, sound, video, and hyperlinks to other Web pages

hub *n* **1** : the center of a wheel, propeller, or fan **2** : a center of activity

hub·bub *n* : UPROAR

huck·le·ber·ry *n, pl* **huck·le·ber·ries** : a dark edible berry like a blueberry but with hard rather large seeds

huck·ster *n* : PEDDLER, HAWKER

¹hud·dle *vb* **hud·dled; hud·dling** **1** : to crowd, push, or pile together **2** : to get together to talk something over **3** : to sit or lie in a curled or bent position

²huddle *n* **1** : a closely packed group **2** : a private meeting or conference **3** : a brief gathering of football players to hear instructions for the next play

hue *n* **1** : ¹COLOR 1 **2** : a shade of a color

¹huff *vb* **huffed; huff·ing** **1** : to give off puffs (as of air or steam) **2** : to do or say in a way that shows anger

²huff *n* : a fit of anger or temper

huffy *adj* **huff·i·er; huff·i·est** : easily offended or angered : PETULANT — **huff·i·ly** *adv*

¹hug *vb* **hugged; hug·ging** **1** : to clasp in the arms : EMBRACE **2** : to keep close to

²hug *n* : ²EMBRACE

huge *adj* **hug·er; hug·est** : great in size or degree : VAST — **huge·ly** *adv*

hulk *n* **1** : a person or thing that is bulky or clumsy **2** : an abandoned wreck or shell of something (as a ship)

hulk·ing *adj* : very large or heavy

¹hull *n* **1** : the outside covering of a fruit or seed **2** : the frame or body of a ship or boat

²hull *vb* **hulled; hull·ing** : to remove the outer covering of (a fruit or seed)

hul·la·ba·loo *n, pl* **hul·la·ba·loos** : a confused noise : UPROAR, COMMOTION

¹hum *vb* **hummed; hum·ming** **1** : to utter a sound like a long \m\ **2** : to make the buzzing noise of a flying insect **3** : to make musical tones with closed lips **4** : to give forth a low murmur of sounds **5** : to be very busy or active

²hum *n* **1** : a low continuous noise **2** : musical tones voiced without words

¹hu·man *adj* **1** : of, being, or characteristic of people as distinct from animals **2** : having the form or characteristics of people

²human *n* : HUMAN BEING — **hu·man·like** *adj*

human being *n* : a man, woman, or child : PERSON

hu·mane *adj* : having sympathy and consideration for people or animals — **hu·mane·ly** *adv*

¹hu·man·i·tar·i·an *n* : a person who works to improve the lives and living conditions of other people

²humanitarian *adj* : relating to or characteristic of people who work to improve the lives and living conditions of other people

hu·man·i·ty *n, pl* **hu·man·i·ties** **1** : the quality or state of being human **2** : the human race **3** *humanities pl* : studies (as literature, history, and art) concerned primarily with human culture **4** : KINDNESS 1, SYMPATHY

hu·man·ly *adv* : within the range of human ability

¹hum·ble *adj* **hum·bler; hum·blest** **1** : not regarding others as inferior : not overly proud : MODEST **2** : expressed in a way that does not show too much pride **3** : low in rank or condition — **hum·bly** *adv*

²humble *vb* **hum·bled; hum·bling** **1** : to make modest **2** : to easily and unexpectedly defeat

hum·bug *n* **1** : FRAUD 3 **2** : NONSENSE 1

hum·ding·er *n* : something striking or extraordinary

hum·drum *adj* : not interesting

hu·mer·us *n, pl* **humeri** : the long bone of the upper arm or forelimb that extends from the shoulder to the elbow

hu·mid *adj* : MOIST

hu·mid·i·fy *vb* **hu·mid·i·fied; hu·mid·i·fy·ing** : to make (as the air of a room) more moist — **hu·mid·i·fi·er** *n*

hu·mid·i·ty *n, pl* **hu·mid·i·ties** : the degree of wetness especially of the atmosphere

hu·mil·i·ate *vb* **hu·mil·i·at·ed; hu·mil·i·at·ing** : to cause (someone) to feel very ashamed or foolish

hu·mil·i·a·tion *n* **1** : the state of being made to feel ashamed or foolish **2** : an instance of being made to feel ashamed or foolish

hu·mil·i·ty *n* : the quality of being humble

hum·ming·bird *n* : a tiny brightly colored American bird whose wings make a humming sound in flight

hum·mock *n* : a rounded mound of earth : KNOLL

¹hu·mor *n* **1** : the amusing quality of something **2** : the ability to see or tell the amusing quality of things **3** : state of mind : MOOD — **hu·mor·less** *adj*

²humor *vb* **hu·mored; hu·mor·ing** : to give in to the wishes of

hu·mor·ist *n* : a person who writes or talks in a humorous way

hu·mor·ous *adj* : full of humor : FUNNY — **hu·mor·ous·ly** *adv*

hu·mour *chiefly British variant of* HUMOR

hump *n* 1 : a rounded bulge or lump (as on the back of a camel) 2 : a difficult part (as of a task) — **humped** *adj*

hump·back *n* 1 : a humped or crooked back 2 : HUMPBACK WHALE — **hump·backed** *adj*

humpback whale *n* : a large whale that is black above and white below and has very long flippers

hu·mus *n* : the dark rich part of earth formed from decaying plant or animal material

¹**hunch** *vb* **hunched; hunch·ing** 1 : to bend the body into an arch or hump 2 : to draw up close together or into an arch

²**hunch** *n* : a strong feeling about what will happen

hunch·back *n* 1 : HUMPBACK 1 2 : a person with a humped or crooked back

¹**hun·dred** *n* 1 : ten times ten : 100 2 : a very large number

²**hundred** *adj* : being 100

¹**hun·dredth** *adj* : coming right after 99th

²**hundredth** *n* : number 100 in a series

hung *past and past participle of* HANG

¹**hun·ger** *n* 1 : a desire or a need for food 2 : a strong desire

²**hunger** *vb* **hun·gered; hun·ger·ing** 1 : to feel a desire or need for food 2 : to have a strong desire

hun·gry *adj* **hun·gri·er; hun·gri·est** 1 : feeling or showing hunger 2 : having a strong desire — **hun·gri·ly** *adv*

hunk *n* : a large lump or piece

hun·ker *vb* **hun·kered; hun·ker·ing** : ¹CROUCH — **hunker down** : to settle in for a long time

¹**hunt** *vb* **hunt·ed; hunt·ing** 1 : to chase after in order to capture or kill 2 : to try to find — **hunting** *n*

²**hunt** *n* 1 : an instance or the practice of chasing to capture or kill 2 : an act of searching

hunt·er *n* 1 : a person who hunts wild animals 2 : a dog or horse used or trained for hunting 3 : a person who searches for something

hunts·man *n, pl* **hunts·men** : HUNTER 1

¹**hur·dle** *n* 1 : a barrier to be jumped in a race 2 **hurdles** *pl* : a race in which runners must jump over barriers 3 : OBSTACLE

²**hurdle** *vb* **hur·dled; hur·dling** 1 : to leap over while running 2 : OVERCOME 1

hurl *vb* **hurled; hurl·ing** : to throw with force

hurrah, hurray *variants of* HOORAY

hur·ri·cane *n* : a tropical cyclone with winds of 74 miles (119 kilometers) per hour or greater usually accompanied by rain, thunder, and lightning

hur·ried *adj* 1 : going or working with speed : FAST 2 : done in a hurry — **hur·ried·ly** *adv*

¹**hur·ry** *vb* **hur·ried; hur·ry·ing** 1 : to carry or cause to go with haste 2 : to move or act with haste 3 : to speed up

²**hurry** *n* : a need to act or move more quickly than usual : RUSH

¹**hurt** *vb* **hurt; hurt·ing** 1 : to feel or cause pain 2 : to do harm to : DAMAGE 3 : to cause to be sad 4 : to make poorer or more difficult

²**hurt** *n* 1 : an injury or wound to the body 2 : mental or emotional pain

³**hurt** *adj* : physically or emotionally injured

hurt·ful *adj* : causing injury or suffering

hur·tle *vb* **hur·tled; hur·tling** : to move or fall with great speed or force

¹**hus·band** *n* : a male partner in a marriage

²**husband** *vb* **hus·band·ed; hus·band·ing** : to manage with thrift : use carefully

hus·band·ry *n* 1 : the management or wise use of resources : THRIFT 2 : the raising and management of plants or animals for food

¹**hush** *vb* **hushed; hush·ing** : to make or become quiet, calm, or still : SOOTHE

²**hush** *n* : ¹QUIET

hush–hush *adj* : ¹SECRET 1, CONFIDENTIAL

¹**husk** *n* : the outer covering of a fruit or seed

²**husk** *vb* **husked; husk·ing** : to remove the outer covering from (a fruit or seed) — **husk·er** *n*

¹**hus·ky** *adj* **hus·ki·er; hus·ki·est** : HOARSE 2 — **hus·ki·ly** *adv* — **hus·ki·ness** *n*

²**husky** *n, pl* **huskies** : a strong dog with a thick coat often used to pull sleds in arctic regions

³**husky** *adj* **hus·ki·er; hus·ki·est** 1 : STRONG 1, BURLY 2 : larger than average — **hus·ki·ness** *n*

¹**hus·tle** *vb* **hus·tled; hus·tling** 1 : to push, crowd, or force forward roughly 2 : to move or work rapidly and tirelessly

²**hustle** *n* : energetic activity

hut *n* : a small roughly made and often temporary dwelling

hutch *n* 1 : a low cupboard usually having open shelves on top 2 : a pen or coop for an animal

hy·a·cinth *n* : a plant often grown for its stalks of fragrant flowers shaped like bells

¹**hy·brid** *n* 1 : an animal or plant whose parents differ in some hereditary characteristic or belong to different groups (as breeds or species) 2 : something that is of mixed origin or composition

²**hybrid** *adj* : of mixed origin : of or relating to a hybrid

hydr- *or* **hydro-** *prefix* **1** : water **2** : hydrogen

hy·drant *n* : a pipe with a spout through which water may be drawn

hy·drau·lic *adj* **1** : operated, moved, or brought about by means of water **2** : operated by liquid forced through a small hole or through a tube — **hy·drau·li·cal·ly** *adv*

hy·dro·car·bon *n* : a substance containing only carbon and hydrogen

hy·dro·chlo·ric acid *n* : a strong acid formed by dissolving in water a gas made up of hydrogen and chlorine

hy·dro·elec·tric *adj* : relating to or used in the making of electricity by waterpower

hy·dro·gen *n* : a colorless, odorless, and tasteless flammable gas that is the lightest of the chemical elements

hydrogen bomb *n* : a bomb whose great power is due to the sudden release of energy when the central portions of hydrogen atoms unite

hydrogen peroxide *n* : a liquid chemical containing hydrogen and oxygen and used for bleaching and as an antiseptic

hy·dro·plane *n* : a speedboat whose hull is completely or partly raised as it glides over water

hy·e·na *n* : a large doglike mammal of Asia and Africa that lives on flesh

hy·giene *n* **1** : a science that deals with the bringing about and keeping up of good health **2** : conditions or practices (as of cleanliness) necessary for health

hy·gien·ic *adj* : of, relating to, or leading toward health or hygiene

hy·gien·ist *n* : a person skilled in hygiene and especially in a specified branch of hygiene

hy·grom·e·ter *n* : an instrument for measuring the humidity of the air

hymn *n* : a song of praise especially to God

hym·nal *n* : a book of hymns

hyper- *prefix* : excessively

hy·per·ac·tive *adj* : extremely or overly active

hy·per·link *n* : an electronic link that allows a computer user to move directly from a marked place in a hypertext document to another in the same or a different document — **hyperlink** *vb*

hy·per·sen·si·tive *adj* : very sensitive

hy·per·ten·sion *n* : a medical condition marked by abnormally high blood pressure

hy·per·text *n* : an arrangement of the information in a computer database that allows the user to get other information by clicking on text displayed on the screen

hy·per·ven·ti·late *vb* **hy·per·ven·ti·lat·ed; hy-** **per·ven·ti·lat·ing** : to breathe very quickly and deeply

hy·pha *n, pl* **hy·phae** : one of the fine threads that make up the body of a fungus

¹**hy·phen** *n* : a mark - used to divide or to compound words or word elements

²**hyphen** *vb* **hy·phened; hy·phen·ing** : HY-PHENATE

hy·phen·ate *vb* **hy·phen·at·ed; hy·phen·at·ing** : to connect or mark with a hyphen

hyp·no·sis *n* : a state which resembles sleep but is produced by a person who can then make suggestions to which the person in this state can respond

hyp·not·ic *adj* **1** : of or relating to hypnosis **2** : having an effect like that of hypnosis

hyp·no·tism *n* : the act or practice of producing a state like sleep in a person in which he or she will respond to suggestions made by the hypnotist

hyp·no·tist *n* : a person who hypnotizes others

hyp·no·tize *vb* **hyp·no·tized; hyp·no·tiz·ing** : to affect by or as if by hypnotism

hy·poc·ri·sy *n, pl* **hy·poc·ri·sies** : the quality of acting in a way that goes against claimed beliefs or feelings

hyp·o·crite *n* : a person who acts in a way that goes against what he or she claims to believe or feel — **hyp·o·crit·i·cal** *adj*

hy·po·der·mic needle *n* **1** : ¹NEEDLE 5 **2** : a small syringe used with a hollow needle to inject material (as a vaccine) into or beneath the skin

hypodermic syringe *n* : HYPODERMIC NEEDLE 2

hy·pot·e·nuse *n* : the side of a right triangle that is opposite the right angle

hy·poth·e·sis *n, pl* **hy·poth·e·ses** : something not proved but assumed to be true for purposes of argument or further study or investigation

hy·po·thet·i·cal *adj* **1** : involving or based on a hypothesis **2** : imagined as an example for further thought — **hy·po·thet·i·cal·ly** *adv*

hys·te·ria *n* : a state in which emotions (as fear or joy) are so strong that a person acts in an uncontrolled way

hys·ter·i·cal *adj* **1** : feeling or showing extreme and uncontrolled emotion **2** : very funny — **hys·ter·i·cal·ly** *adv*

hys·ter·ics *n pl* : an outburst of uncontrollable laughing or crying — used as singular or plural

I

i *n, pl* **i's** *or* **is** *often cap* **1** : the ninth letter of the English alphabet **2** : the number one in Roman numerals

I *pron* : the person speaking or writing

Ia., IA *abbr* Iowa

-ial *adj suffix* : ¹-AL

-ian — see -AN

ibex *n, pl* **ibex** *or* **ibex·es** : a wild goat that lives mostly in high mountains of Europe, Asia, and northeastern Africa and has large horns that curve backward

-ibility — see -ABILITY

ibis *n, pl* **ibis** *or* **ibis·es** : a tall bird related to the herons with long legs and a slender bill that curves down

-ible — see -ABLE

-ic *adj suffix* **1** : of, relating to, or having the form of : being **2** : coming from, consisting of, or containing **3** : in the manner of **4** : making use of **5** : characterized by : exhibiting **6** : affected with

-ical *adj suffix* : -IC

¹ice *n* **1** : frozen water **2** : a sheet of frozen water **3** : a substance like ice **4** : a frozen dessert usually made with sweetened fruit juice

²ice *vb* **iced; ic·ing 1** : to coat or become coated with ice **2** : to chill with ice **3** : to cover with icing

ice age *n* : a period of time during which much of the earth is covered with glaciers

ice·berg *n* : a large mass of ice that has broken away from a glacier and is floating in the ocean

ice·bound *adj* : surrounded or blocked by ice

ice·box *n* : REFRIGERATOR

ice·break·er *n* **1** : a ship equipped to make and keep open a channel through ice **2** : something said or done that helps people relax and begin talking in a social situation

ice cap *n* : a large more or less level glacier flowing outward in all directions from its center

ice–cold *adj* : very cold

ice cream *n* : a frozen food containing sweetened and flavored cream or butterfat

ice hockey *n* : hockey played on ice

ice–skate *vb* **ice–skat·ed; ice–skat·ing** : to skate on ice — **ice skat·er** *n*

ice skate *n* : a shoe with a special blade on the bottom that is used for skating on ice

ici·cle *n* : a hanging piece of ice formed from dripping water as it freezes

ic·ing *n* : a sweet coating for baked goods (as cakes)

icon *n* **1** : a widely known symbol **2** : a person who is very successful or admired **3** : a religious image usually painted on a small wooden panel **4** : a small picture or symbol on a computer screen that represents a function that the computer can perform

-ics *n pl suffix* **1** : study : knowledge : skill : practice **2** : characteristic actions or qualities

ICU *abbr* intensive care unit

icy *adj* **ic·i·er; ic·i·est 1** : covered with, full of, or being ice **2** : very cold **3** : UN-FRIENDLY — **ic·i·ly** *adv*

ID *abbr* **1** Idaho **2** identification

I'd : I had : I would

idea *n* **1** : a thought or plan about what to do **2** : something imagined or pictured in the mind **3** : an understanding of something **4** : a central meaning or purpose **5** : an opinion or belief

¹ide·al *adj* : having no flaw : PERFECT — **ide·al·ly** *adv*

²ideal *n* **1** : a standard of perfection, beauty, or excellence **2** : someone who deserves to be imitated or admired

iden·ti·cal *adj* **1** : being one and the same **2** : being exactly alike or equal — **iden·ti·cal·ly** *adv*

identical twin *n* : either one of a pair of twins of the same sex that come from a single fertilized egg and are physically similar

iden·ti·fi·ca·tion *n* **1** : an act of finding out the identity of **2** : something that shows or proves identity

iden·ti·fy *vb* **iden·ti·fied; iden·ti·fy·ing 1** : to find out or show the identity of **2** : to feel empathy for **3** : to think of as joined or associated with

iden·ti·ty *n, pl* **iden·ti·ties 1** : the set of qualities and beliefs that make one person or group different from others : INDIVIDUALITY **2** : the fact of being the same person or thing as claimed **3** : the fact or condition of being exactly alike : SAMENESS

id·i·o·cy *n, pl* **id·i·o·cies 1** : the condition of being very stupid or foolish **2** : something very stupid or foolish

id·i·om *n* : an expression that cannot be understood from the meanings of its separate words but must be learned as a whole

id·i·o·syn·cra·sy *n, pl* **id·i·o·syn·cra·sies** : an unusual way of behaving or thinking that is characteristic of a person

id·i·ot *n* : a silly or foolish person

id·i·ot·ic *adj* : FOOLISH

¹idle *adj* **idler ; idlest 1** : not working or in

use **2** : LAZY 1 **3** : not based on anything
real or serious — **idle·ness** *n* — **idly** *adv*

²idle *vb* **idled; idling 1** : to spend time doing
nothing **2** : to run without being connected
for doing useful work

idol *n* **1** : an image worshipped as a god **2** : a
much loved or admired person or thing

idol·ize *vb* **idol·ized; idol·iz·ing** : to love or
admire greatly : make an idol of

i.e. *abbr* that is — abbreviation for Latin *id
est*, which means "that is"

-ie *also* **-y** *n suffix, pl* **-ies** : little one

-ier — see **²-ER**

if *conj* **1** : in the event that **2** : WHETHER 1 **3**
— used to introduce a wish

-ify *vb suffix* **-ified; -ify·ing** : -FY

ig·loo *n, pl* **igloos** : a house often made of
blocks of snow and shaped like a dome

ig·ne·ous *adj* : formed by hardening of
melted mineral material within the earth

ig·nite *vb* **ig·nit·ed; ig·nit·ing 1** : to set on
fire : LIGHT **2** : to catch fire

ig·ni·tion *n* **1** : the act of causing something
to start burning **2** : the process or means (as
an electric spark) of causing the fuel in an
engine to burn so that the engine begins
working **3** : a device that is used to start a
motor vehicle

ig·no·min·i·ous *adj* : DISGRACEFUL

ig·no·rance *n* : a lack of knowledge, understanding, or education : the state of being ignorant

ig·no·rant *adj* **1** : having little or no knowledge : not educated **2** : not knowing : UN-
AWARE **3** : resulting from or showing lack of
knowledge — **ig·no·rant·ly** *adv*

ig·nore *vb* **ig·nored; ig·nor·ing** : to pay no attention to

igua·na *n* : a large tropical American lizard
with a ridge of tall scales along its back

IL *abbr* Illinois

il- — see IN-

¹ill *adj* **worse; worst 1** : not in good health
: SICK **2** : not normal or sound **3** : meant to
do harm : EVIL **4** : causing suffering or distress **5** : not helpful **6** : not kind or friendly
7 : not right or proper

²ill *adv* **worse; worst 1** : with displeasure or
anger **2** : in a harsh or unkind way **3**
: SCARCELY 1, HARDLY **4** : in a bad or faulty
way

³ill *n* **1** : the opposite of good **2** : a sickness
or disease **3** : ²TROUBLE 2

Ill. *abbr* Illinois

I'll : I shall : I will

il·le·gal *adj* : not allowed by the laws or rules
— **il·le·gal·ly** *adv*

il·leg·i·ble *adj* : impossible or very hard to
read — **il·leg·i·bly** *adv*

il·le·git·i·mate *adj* : not accepted by the law as
rightful

il·lic·it *adj* : not permitted : UNLAWFUL

il·lit·er·a·cy *n* : the state or condition of being
unable to read or write

¹il·lit·er·ate *adj* : unable to read or write

²illiterate *n* : a person who is unable to read
or write

ill–man·nered *adj* : not polite

ill–na·tured *adj* : having or showing an unfriendly nature

ill·ness *n* **1** : an unhealthy condition of the
body or mind **2** : a specific sickness or disease

il·log·i·cal *adj* : not using or following good
reasoning — **il·log·i·cal·ly** *adv*

ill–tem·pered *adj* : having or showing a bad
temper

il·lu·mi·nate *vb* **il·lu·mi·nat·ed; il·lu·mi·nat·
ing 1** : to supply with light : light up **2** : to
make clear : EXPLAIN

il·lu·mi·na·tion *n* : the action of lighting
something : the state of being lighted

ill–use *vb* **ill–used; ill–us·ing** : to treat badly

il·lu·sion *n* **1** : something that is false or un-
real but seems to be true or real **2** : a mistaken idea

il·lu·so·ry *adj* : based on something that is not
true or real : DECEPTIVE

il·lus·trate *vb* **il·lus·trat·ed; il·lus·trat·ing 1**
: to supply with pictures or diagrams meant
to explain or decorate **2** : to make clear by
using examples **3** : to serve as an example

il·lus·tra·tion *n* **1** : a picture or diagram that
explains or decorates **2** : an example or instance used to make something clear **3** : the
action of illustrating : the condition of being
illustrated

il·lus·tra·tive *adj* : serving as an example

il·lus·tra·tor *n* : an artist who makes illustra-
tions (as for books)

il·lus·tri·ous *adj* : admired and respected because of greatness or achievement : EMI-
NENT

ill will *n* : unfriendly feeling

im- — see IN-

I'm : I am

im·age *n* **1** : a picture or reflection of something produced by a device (as a mirror or
lens) **2** : someone who looks very much like
another **3** : the thought of how something
looks **4** : a representation (as a picture or
statue) of something **5** : an idea of what
someone or something is like

im·ag·ery *n* : pictures or photographs of
something

imag·in·able *adj* : possible to imagine

imag·i·nary *adj* : existing only in the imagination : not real

imag·i·na·tion *n* **1** : the act, process, or power

of forming a mental picture of something not present and especially of something one has not known or experienced **2** : creative ability **3** : a creation of the mind

imag·i·na·tive *adj* **1** : relating to or showing imagination **2** : having a lively imagination

imag·ine *vb* **imag·ined; imag·in·ing 1** : to form a mental picture of : use the imagination **2** : THINK 1

imag·in·ings *n pl* : products of the imagination

im·be·cile *n* : IDIOT, FOOL

im·i·tate *vb* **im·i·tat·ed; im·i·tat·ing 1** : to follow as a pattern, model, or example **2** : to be or appear like : RESEMBLE **3** : to copy exactly : MIMIC

¹im·i·ta·tion *n* **1** : the act of copying someone or something **2** : ¹COPY 1

²imitation *adj* : made to look like something else and especially something valuable

im·i·ta·tive *adj* : made or done to be like something or someone else

im·mac·u·late *adj* **1** : perfectly clean **2** : having no flaw or error — **im·mac·u·late·ly** *adv*

im·ma·te·ri·al *adj* : not important : INSIGNIFICANT

im·ma·ture *adj* **1** : not yet fully grown or ripe **2** : acting in or exhibiting a childish manner — **im·ma·ture·ly** *adv*

im·mea·sur·able *adj* : very great in size or amount — **im·mea·sur·ably** *adv*

im·me·di·ate *adj* **1** : happening without any delay **2** : occurring or existing now **3** : having importance now **4** : not far away in time or space **5** : being next in line or nearest in relationship **6** : having nothing between

im·me·di·ate·ly *adv* **1** : with nothing between **2** : right away

im·mense *adj* : very great in size or amount : HUGE — **im·mense·ly** *adv*

im·men·si·ty *n, pl* **im·men·si·ties** : extremely great size, amount, or extent

im·merse *vb* **im·mersed; im·mers·ing 1** : to plunge into something (as a fluid) that surrounds or covers **2** : to become completely involved with

im·mi·grant *n* : a person who comes to a country to live there

im·mi·grate *vb* **im·mi·grat·ed; im·mi·grat·ing** : to come into a foreign country to live

im·mi·gra·tion *n* : an act or instance of coming into a foreign country to live

im·mi·nent *adj* : being about to happen

im·mo·bile *adj* : unable to move or be moved

im·mo·bi·lize *vb* **im·mo·bi·lized; im·mo·bi·liz·ing** : to keep from moving : make immovable

im·mod·est *adj* **1** : not proper in thought,

conduct, or dress **2** : being vain or showing vanity

im·mor·al *adj* : not following principles of right and wrong : WICKED, BAD

im·mo·ral·i·ty *n, pl* **im·mo·ral·i·ties** : the quality or state of being without principles of right and wrong

¹im·mor·tal *adj* : living or lasting forever

²immortal *n* **1** : a being that lives forever : a god or goddess **2** : a person of lasting fame

im·mor·tal·i·ty *n* **1** : the quality or state of living forever : endless life **2** : lasting fame or glory

im·mov·able *adj* **1** : impossible to move : firmly fixed in place **2** : not able to be changed or persuaded

im·mune *adj* **1** : having a high degree of resistance to an illness or disease **2** : of, relating to, or involving the body's immune system **3** : not influenced or affected by something **4** : not subject to something : EXEMPT

immune system *n* : the system of the body that fights infection and disease and that includes especially the white blood cells and antibodies and the organs that produce them

im·mu·ni·ty *n, pl* **im·mu·ni·ties 1** : freedom from an obligation or penalty to which others are subject **2** : the power to resist infection whether natural or acquired (as by vaccination)

im·mu·ni·za·tion *n* : treatment (as with a vaccine) to produce immunity to a disease

im·mu·nize *vb* **im·mu·nized; im·mu·niz·ing** : to make immune especially by vaccination

imp *n* **1** : a small demon **2** : a mischievous child

¹im·pact *n* **1** : a striking of one body against another : COLLISION **2** : a strong effect

²im·pact *vb* **im·pact·ed; im·pact·ing 1** : to have a strong and often bad effect on **2** : to hit with great force

im·pair *vb* **im·paired; im·pair·ing** : to make less (as in quantity, value, or strength) or worse : DAMAGE

im·pale *vb* **im·paled; im·pal·ing** : to pierce with something pointed

im·part *vb* **im·part·ed; im·part·ing 1** : to give or grant from or as if from a supply **2** : to make known

im·par·tial *adj* : not favoring one side over another : FAIR — **im·par·tial·ly** *adv*

im·par·tial·i·ty *n* : the quality or state of being fair and just

im·pass·able *adj* : impossible to pass, cross, or travel

im·pas·sioned *adj* : showing very strong feeling

im·pas·sive *adj* : not feeling or showing emotion — **im·pas·sive·ly** *adv*

im·pa·tience *n* **1** : the quality of not wanting to put up with or wait for something or someone : lack of patience **2** : restless or eager desire

im·pa·tient *adj* **1** : not wanting to put up with or wait for something or someone **2** : showing a lack of patience **3** : restless and eager — **im·pa·tient·ly** *adv*

im·peach *vb* **im·peached; im·peach·ing** : to charge a public official formally with misconduct in office

im·pec·ca·ble *adj* : free from fault or error

im·pede *vb* **im·ped·ed; im·ped·ing** : to interfere with the movement or progress of

im·ped·i·ment *n* **1** : something that interferes with movement or progress **2** : a condition that makes it difficult to speak normally

im·pel *vb* **im·pelled; im·pel·ling** : to urge or force into action

im·pend·ing *adj* : happening or likely to happen soon

im·pen·e·tra·ble *adj* **1** : impossible to pass through or see through **2** : impossible to understand

im·per·a·tive *adj* **1** : expressing a command, request, or strong encouragement **2** : URGENT 1

im·per·cep·ti·ble *adj* : not noticeable by the senses or by the mind : very small or gradual — **im·per·cep·ti·bly** *adv*

im·per·fect *adj* : having a fault of some kind : not perfect — **im·per·fect·ly** *adv*

im·per·fec·tion *n* **1** : the quality or state of having faults or defects : lack of perfection **2** : a small flaw or fault

im·pe·ri·al *adj* : of or relating to an empire or its ruler

im·per·il *vb* **im·per·iled** *or* **im·per·illed; im·per·il·ing** *or* **im·per·il·ling** : to place in great danger

im·per·son·al *adj* **1** : not caring about individual persons or their feelings **2** : not showing or involving personal feelings

im·per·son·ate *vb* **im·per·son·at·ed; im·per·son·at·ing** : to pretend to be another person

im·per·son·a·tion *n* : the act of pretending to be another person

im·per·ti·nence *n* : the quality or state of being very rude or disrespectful

im·per·ti·nent *adj* : very rude : having or showing a lack of respect

im·per·turb·able *adj* : hard to disturb or upset : very calm

im·per·vi·ous *adj* **1** : not letting something enter or pass through **2** : not bothered or affected by something

im·pet·u·ous *adj* : acting or done quickly and without thought : IMPULSIVE

imp·ish *adj* : playful and mischievous — **imp·ish·ly** *adv*

im·pla·ca·ble *adj* : impossible to please, satisfy, or change

im·plant *vb* **im·plant·ed; im·plant·ing** : to set securely or deeply

¹im·ple·ment *n* : an object (as a tool) intended for a certain use

²im·ple·ment *vb* **im·ple·ment·ed; im·ple·ment·ing** : to begin to do or use something

im·pli·cate *vb* **im·pli·cat·ed; im·pli·cat·ing** : to show to be connected or involved

im·pli·ca·tion *n* **1** : the fact or state of being involved in or connected to something **2** : a possible future effect or result **3** : something that is suggested

im·plic·it *adj* **1** : understood though not put clearly into words **2** : not affected by doubt : ABSOLUTE — **im·plic·it·ly** *adv*

im·plore *vb* **im·plored; im·plor·ing** : to make a very serious or emotional request to or for — **im·plor·ing·ly** *adv*

im·ply *vb* **im·plied; im·ply·ing** : to express indirectly : suggest rather than say plainly

im·po·lite *adj* : not polite — **im·po·lite·ly** *adv*

¹im·port *vb* **im·port·ed; im·port·ing** : to bring (as goods) into a country usually for selling

²im·port *n* **1** : IMPORTANCE **2** : something brought into a country

im·por·tance *n* : the quality or state of being important

im·por·tant *adj* **1** : having serious meaning or worth **2** : having power or authority — **im·por·tant·ly** *adv*

im·por·ta·tion *n* : the act or practice of bringing into a country

im·por·tune *vb* **im·por·tuned; im·por·tun·ing** : to beg or urge in a repeated or annoying way

im·pose *vb* **im·posed; im·pos·ing** **1** : to establish or apply as a charge or penalty **2** : to force someone to accept or put up with **3** : to ask for more than is fair or reasonable : take unfair advantage

im·pos·ing *adj* : impressive because of size, dignity, or magnificence

im·pos·si·bil·i·ty *n, pl* **im·pos·si·bil·i·ties** **1** : something that cannot be done or occur **2** : the quality or state of being impossible

im·pos·si·ble *adj* **1** : incapable of being or of occurring : not possible **2** : very difficult **3** : very bad or unpleasant — **im·pos·si·bly** *adv*

im·pos·tor *n* : a person who deceives others by pretending to be someone else

im·pos·ture *n* : the act of deceiving others by pretending to be someone else

im·po·tence *n* : the quality or state of lacking power or strength

im·po·tent *adj* : lacking in power, ability, or strength

im·pound *vb* **im·pound·ed; im·pound·ing**
: to shut up in or as if in an enclosed place

im·pov·er·ish *vb* **im·pov·er·ished; im·pov·er·ish·ing 1** : to make poor **2** : to use up the strength or richness of

im·prac·ti·ca·ble *adj* : difficult to put into practice or use

im·prac·ti·cal *adj* **1** : not suitable for a situation : not practical **2** : not capable of dealing sensibly with matters that require action

im·pre·cise *adj* : not clear or exact

im·preg·na·ble *adj* : not able to be captured by attack : UNCONQUERABLE

im·press *vb* **im·pressed; im·press·ing 1** : to produce by stamping, pressing, or printing **2** : to affect strongly or deeply and especially favorably **3** : to give a clear idea of

im·pres·sion *n* **1** : something (as a design) made by pressing or stamping a surface **2** : the effect that something or someone has on a person's thoughts or feelings **3** : an idea or belief that is usually uncertain **4** : an imitation of a famous person done for entertainment

im·pres·sion·able *adj* : easy to impress or influence

im·pres·sive *adj* : having the power to impress the mind or feelings especially in a positive way — **im·pres·sive·ly** *adv*

¹im·print *vb* **im·print·ed; im·print·ing 1** : to make a mark by pressing again a surface : STAMP **2** : to fix firmly in the mind or memory

²im·print *n* : a mark made by pressing against a surface

im·pris·on *vb* **im·pris·oned; im·pris·on·ing** : to put in prison

im·pris·on·ment *n* : the act of putting in prison : the state of being put or kept in prison

im·prob·a·bil·i·ty *n* : the quality or state of being unlikely

im·prob·a·ble *adj* : not likely : not probable — **im·prob·a·bly** *adv*

im·promp·tu *adj* : not prepared ahead of time : made or done without preparation

im·prop·er *adj* : not proper, right, or suitable — **im·prop·er·ly** *adv*

improper fraction *n* : a fraction whose numerator is equal to or larger than the denominator

im·prove *vb* **im·proved; im·prov·ing** : to make or become better

im·prove·ment *n* **1** : the act or process of making something better **2** : increased value or excellence **3** : an addition or change that makes something better or more valuable

im·pro·vi·sa·tion *n* **1** : the act or art of speaking or performing without practicing or preparing ahead of time **2** : something that is improvised

im·pro·vise *vb* **im·pro·vised; im·pro·vis·ing 1** : to speak or perform without preparing ahead of time **2** : to make, invent, or arrange by using whatever is available

im·pu·dence *n* : behavior or speech that is bold and disrespectful

im·pu·dent *adj* : bold and disrespectful : very rude — **im·pu·dent·ly** *adv*

im·pulse *n* **1** : a force that starts a body into motion **2** : the motion produced by a starting force **3** : a strong sudden desire to do something **4** : NERVE IMPULSE

im·pul·sive *adj* **1** : acting or tending to act suddenly and without careful thought **2** : resulting from a sudden impulse — **im·pul·sive·ly** *adv*

im·pure *adj* **1** : not pure : UNCLEAN, DIRTY **2** : mixed with something else that is usually not as good

im·pu·ri·ty *n, pl* **im·pu·ri·ties 1** : the quality or state of being impure **2** : something that is or makes something else impure

¹in *prep* **1** : located or positioned within **2** : INTO 1 **3** : DURING **4** : WITH 7 **5** — used to show a state or condition **6** — used to show manner or purpose **7** : INTO 2

²in *adv* **1** : to or toward the inside **2** : to or toward some particular place **3** : ¹NEAR 1 **4** : into the midst of something **5** : to or at its proper place **6** : on the inner side : WITHIN **7** : present and available for use — **in for** : sure to experience

³in *adj* **1** : being inside or within **2** : headed or bound inward **3** : FASHIONABLE

in. *abbr* inch

IN *abbr* Indiana

¹in- *or* **il-** *or* **im-** *or* **ir-** *prefix* : not : NON-, UN- — usually *il-* before *l* , *im-* before *b, m,* or *p* , *ir-* before *r* and *in-* before other sounds

²in- *or* **il-** *or* **im-** *or* **ir-** *prefix* **1** : in : within : into : toward : on — usually *il-* before *l* , *im-* before *b, m,* or *p* , *ir-* before *r* , and *in-* before other sounds **2** : EN- 2

in·abil·i·ty *n* : the condition of being unable to do something : lack of ability

in·ac·ces·si·bil·i·ty *n* : the quality or state of being hard or impossible to reach or get hold of

in·ac·ces·si·ble *adj* : hard or impossible to reach or get hold of

in·ac·cu·ra·cy *n, pl* **in·ac·cu·ra·cies 1** : lack of correctness or exactness **2** : ERROR, MISTAKE

in·ac·cu·rate *adj* : not correct or exact — **in·ac·cu·rate·ly** *adv*

in·ac·tion *n* : lack of action or activity

in·ac·tive *adj* : not active or in use

in·ac·tiv·i·ty *n* : the state or condition of not acting or moving : lack of activity

in·ad·e·qua·cy *n*, *pl* **in·ad·e·qua·cies** : the condition of being not enough or not good enough

in·ad·e·quate *adj* : not enough or not good enough

in·ad·ver·tent *adj* : not intended or deliberate : ACCIDENTAL — **in·ad·ver·tent·ly** *adv*

in·ad·vis·able *adj* : not wise to do : not advisable

in·alien·able *adj* : impossible to take away or give up

inane *adj* : silly and pointless

in·an·i·mate *adj* : not living

in·ap·pro·pri·ate *adj* : not right or suited for some purpose or situation — **in·ap·pro·pri·ate·ly** *adv*

in·ar·tic·u·late *adj* **1** : not able to express ideas or feelings clearly and easily **2** : not understandable as spoken words

in·as·much as *conj* : considering that : BE-CAUSE

in·at·ten·tion *n* : failure to pay attention

in·at·ten·tive *adj* : not paying attention — **in·at·ten·tive·ly** *adv*

in·au·di·ble *adj* : impossible to hear — **in·au·di·bly** *adv*

in·au·gu·ral *adj* : occuring as part of an inauguration

in·au·gu·rate *vb* **in·au·gu·rat·ed; in·au·gu·rat·ing** **1** : to introduce into office with suitable ceremonies **2** : to celebrate the opening of **3** : to bring about the beginning of

in·au·gu·ra·tion *n* : an act or ceremony of introducing into office

in·born *adj* : existing from the time someone is born : natural or instinctive

in·breed *vb* **in·bred** ; **in·breed·ing** : to breed with closely related individuals

inc. *abbr* **1** incomplete **2** incorporated

in·can·des·cent *adj* : white or glowing with great heat

incandescent lamp *n* : LIGHT BULB

in·ca·pa·ble *adj* : not able to do something

¹in·cense *n* : material used to produce a strong and pleasant smell when burned

²in·cense *vb* **in·censed; in·cens·ing** : to make very angry

in·cen·tive *n* : something that makes a person try or work hard or harder

in·ces·sant *adj* : going on and on : not stopping or letting up — **in·ces·sant·ly** *adv*

¹inch *n* : a unit of length equal to $\frac{1}{36}$ yard (2.54 centimeters)

²inch *vb* **inched; inch·ing** : to move a little bit at a time

inch·worm *n* : a small caterpillar that is a larva of moths and moves by bringing for-

ward the hind part of the body and then extending forward the front part of the body

in·ci·dent *n* : an often unimportant happening that may form a part of a larger event

in·ci·den·tal *adj* : happening as an unimportant part of something else

in·ci·den·tal·ly *adv* **1** : as a matter of less interest or importance **2** — used to introduce a statement that provides additional information or changes the subject

in·cin·er·ate *vb* **in·cin·er·at·ed; in·cin·er·at·ing** : to burn to ashes

in·cin·er·a·tor *n* : a furnace or a container for burning waste materials

in·cise *vb* **in·cised; in·cis·ing** : to cut into : CARVE, ENGRAVE

in·ci·sion *n* : an act of cutting into something or the cut or wound that results

in·ci·sor *n* : a tooth (as any of the four front teeth of the human upper or lower jaw) for cutting

in·cite *vb* **in·cit·ed; in·cit·ing** : to stir up usually harmful or violent action or feeling

in·clem·ent *adj* : STORMY 1

in·cli·na·tion *n* **1** : an act or the action of bending or leaning **2** : a usually favorable feeling toward something **3** : ²SLANT, TILT

¹in·cline *vb* **in·clined; in·clin·ing** **1** : to cause to bend or lean **2** : ²SLOPE, LEAN

²in·cline *n* : ¹SLOPE 2

in·clined *adj* **1** : having a desire **2** : having a tendency **3** : having a slope

in·clude *vb* **in·clud·ed; in·clud·ing** : to take in or have as part of a whole

in·clu·sion *n* **1** : an act taking in as part of a whole : the state of being taken in as part of a whole **2** : something taken in as part of a whole

in·clu·sive *adj* **1** : covering everything or all important points **2** : including the stated limits and all in between

in·cog·ni·to *adv or adj* : with someone's identity kept secret

in·co·her·ence *n* : the quality or state of not being connected in a clear or logical way

in·co·her·ent *adj* : not connected in a clear or logical way — **in·co·her·ent·ly** *adv*

in·come *n* : a gain usually measured in money that comes in from labor, business, or property

income tax *n* : a tax on the income of a person or business

in·com·ing *adj* : arriving at a destination

in·com·pa·ra·ble *adj* : better than any other — **in·com·pa·ra·bly** *adv*

in·com·pat·i·ble *adj* : not able to live or work together in harmony : not suited for each other — **in·com·pat·i·bly** *adv*

in·com·pe·tence *n* : the inability to do a good job

in·com·pe·tent *adj* : not able to do a good job
— **in·com·pe·tent·ly** *adv*

in·com·plete *adj* : not finished : not complete
— **in·com·plete·ly** *adv*

in·com·pre·hen·si·ble *adj* : impossible to understand — **in·com·pre·hen·si·bly** *adv*

in·con·ceiv·able *adj* : impossible to imagine or believe

in·con·gru·ous *adj* : not harmonious, suitable, or proper

in·con·sid·er·ate *adj* : careless of the rights or feelings of others

in·con·sis·ten·cy *n, pl* **in·con·sis·ten·cies** **1** : the quality or state of not being in agreement or not being regular **2** : something that is not in agreement or not regular

in·con·sis·tent *adj* **1** : not being in agreement **2** : not staying the same in thoughts or practices

in·con·spic·u·ous *adj* : not easily seen or noticed — **in·con·spic·u·ous·ly** *adv*

¹in·con·ve·nience *n* **1** : trouble or difficulty : lack of convenience **2** : something that causes trouble or difficulty

²inconvenience *vb* **in·con·ve·nienced; in·con·ve·nienc·ing** : to cause difficulties for

in·con·ve·nient *adj* : causing trouble or difficulty : not convenient — **in·con·ve·nient·ly** *adv*

in·cor·po·rate *vb* **in·cor·po·rat·ed; in·cor·po·rat·ing** **1** : to join or unite closely into a single mass or body **2** : to make a corporation of

in·cor·rect *adj* **1** : not accurate or true : not correct : WRONG **2** : not proper — **in·cor·rect·ly** *adv*

¹in·crease *vb* **in·creased; in·creas·ing** : to make or become greater

²in·crease *n* : an addition or enlargement in size, extent, or quantity

in·creas·ing·ly *adv* : more and more

in·cred·i·ble *adj* **1** : too strange or unlikely to be believed **2** : extremely or amazingly good, great, or large — **in·cred·i·bly** *adv*

in·cred·u·lous *adj* : feeling or showing disbelief : SKEPTICAL — **in·cred·u·lous·ly** *adv*

in·crim·i·nate *vb* **in·crim·i·nat·ed; in·crim·i·nat·ing** : to make (someone) appear guilty of or responsible for something

in·cu·bate *vb* **in·cu·bat·ed; in·cu·bat·ing** **1** : to sit upon eggs to hatch them by warmth **2** : to keep under conditions good for hatching or development

in·cu·ba·tion *n* **1** : the act or process of incubating **2** : the period of time between infection with germs and the appearance of symptoms of illness or disease

in·cu·ba·tor *n* **1** : a device that provides enough heat to hatch eggs artificially **2** : a device to help the growth of tiny newborn babies

in·cum·bent *n* : the holder of an office or position

in·cur *vb* **in·curred; in·cur·ring** : to experience as a result of a person's own actions

in·cur·able *adj* : impossible to cure — **in·cur·ably** *adv*

Ind. *abbr* **1** Indian **2** Indiana

in·debt·ed *adj* : being in debt : owing something — **in·debt·ed·ness** *n*

in·de·cen·cy *n, pl* **in·de·cen·cies** **1** : offensive quality : lack of decency **2** : an act or word that is offensive

in·de·cent *adj* : not decent : COARSE, VULGAR

in·de·ci·sion *n* : difficulty in making a decision

in·de·ci·sive *adj* **1** : not decisive or final **2** : finding it hard to make decisions — **in·de·ci·sive·ly** *adv*

in·deed *adv* : TRULY

in·de·fen·si·ble *adj* : impossible to defend

in·def·i·nite *adj* **1** : not certain in amount or length **2** : not clear in meaning or details — **in·def·i·nite·ly** *adv*

indefinite article *n* : either of the articles *a* or *an* used to show that the following noun refers to any person or thing of the kind named

in·del·i·ble *adj* **1** : impossible to erase, remove, or blot out **2** : making marks not easily removed — **in·del·i·bly** *adv*

in·del·i·cate *adj* : not polite or proper : COARSE — **in·del·i·cate·ly** *adv*

in·dent *vb* **in·dent·ed; in·dent·ing** : to set in from the margin

in·den·ta·tion *n* **1** : a blank or empty space at the beginning of a written or printed line or paragraph **2** : a cut or dent in something

in·de·pen·dence *n* : the quality or state of not being under the control of, reliant on, or connected with someone or something else

Independence Day *n* : July 4 observed by Americans as a legal holiday in honor of the adoption of the Declaration of Independence in 1776

¹in·de·pen·dent *adj* **1** : not under the control or rule of another **2** : not connected with something else : SEPARATE **3** : not depending on anyone else for money to live on **4** : thinking freely : not looking to others for guidance — **in·de·pen·dent·ly** *adv*

²independent *n* : an independent person

in·de·scrib·able *adj* : impossible to describe — **in·de·scrib·ably** *adv*

in·de·struc·ti·ble *adj* : impossible to destroy

¹in·dex *n, pl* **in·dex·es** *or* **in·di·ces** **1** : a list of names or topics (as in a book) given in alphabetical order and showing where each is

to be found **2** : POINTER 1 **3** : ¹SIGN 3, INDI-
CATION

²index *vb* **in·dexed; in·dex·ing 1** : to provide
(as a book) with an index **2** : to list in an
index

index finger *n* : the finger next to the thumb

¹In·di·an *n* **1** : a person born or living in India
2 : AMERICAN INDIAN

²Indian *adj* **1** : of or relating to India or its
peoples **2** : of or relating to the American
Indians or their languages

Indian corn *n* **1** : ¹CORN **2** : corn that is of a
variety having seeds of various colors (as
reddish brown, dark purple, and yellow) and
is typically used for ornamental purposes

Indian pipe *n* : a waxy white leafless woodland herb with a single drooping flower

Indian summer *n* : a period of mild weather
in late autumn or early winter

in·di·cate *vb* **in·di·cat·ed; in·di·cat·ing 1** : to
point out or point to **2** : to state or express
briefly

in·di·ca·tion *n* **1** : the act of pointing out or
stating briefly **2** : something that points out
or suggests something

in·dic·a·tive *adj* **1** : pointing out or showing
something **2** : of or relating to the verb form
that is used to state a fact that can be known
or proved

in·di·ca·tor *n* **1** : a sign that shows or suggests the condition or existence of something **2** : a pointer on a dial or scale **3**
: ¹DIAL 3, GAUGE

indices *pl of* INDEX

in·dict *vb* **in·dict·ed; in·dict·ing** : to formally
charge with an offense or crime — **in·dict·
ment** *n*

in·dif·fer·ence *n* : lack of interest or concern

in·dif·fer·ent *adj* **1** : not interested or concerned about something **2** : neither good
nor bad — **in·dif·fer·ent·ly** *adv*

in·di·gest·ible *adj* : not capable of being broken down and used by the body as food : not
easy to digest

in·di·ges·tion *n* : discomfort caused by slow
or painful digestion

in·dig·nant *adj* : filled with or expressing
anger caused by something unjust or unworthy — **in·dig·nant·ly** *adv*

in·dig·na·tion *n* : anger caused by something
unjust or unworthy

in·dig·ni·ty *n, pl* **in·dig·ni·ties 1** : an act that
injures a person's dignity or self-respect **2**
: treatment that shows a lack of respect

in·di·go *n, pl* **in·di·gos** *or* **in·di·goes 1** : a
blue dye made artificially or obtained especially formerly from plants (**indigo plants**)
2 : a deep purplish blue

in·di·rect *adj* **1** : not straight or direct **2** : not
straightforward **3** : not having a plainly

seen connection — **in·di·rect·ly** *adv* — **in·di·
rect·ness** *n*

indirect object *n* : an object that represents
the person or thing that receives what is
being given or done

in·dis·creet *adj* : not having or showing good
judgment : revealing things that should not
be revealed — **in·dis·creet·ly** *adv*

in·dis·cre·tion *n* **1** : lack of good judgment
or care in acting or saying things **2** : a
thoughtless or careless act or remark

in·dis·crim·i·nate *adj* : not done in a careful
way : wrongly causing widespread harm

in·dis·pens·able *adj* : extremely important or
necessary : ESSENTIAL

in·dis·posed *adj* **1** : slightly ill **2** : not willing

in·dis·put·able *adj* : impossible to question or
doubt — **in·dis·put·ably** *adv*

in·dis·tinct *adj* : not easily seen, heard, or
recognized — **in·dis·tinct·ly** *adv*

in·dis·tin·guish·able *adj* : impossible to recognize as different

¹in·di·vid·u·al *adj* **1** : relating to a single
member of a group **2** : intended for one person **3** : ¹PARTICULAR 1, SEPARATE **4** : having a special quality : DISTINCTIVE — **in·di·
vid·u·al·ly** *adv*

²individual *n* **1** : a single member of a group
2 : a single human being

in·di·vid·u·al·i·ty *n* : the qualities that make
one person or thing different from all others

in·di·vis·i·ble *adj* : impossible to divide or
separate — **in·di·vis·i·bly** *adv*

in·doc·tri·nate *vb* **in·doc·tri·nat·ed; in·doc·
tri·nat·ing** : to teach especially the ideas,
opinions, or beliefs of a certain group

in·do·lence *n* : the quality of being lazy

in·do·lent *adj* : LAZY 1, IDLE

in·dom·i·ta·ble *adj* : impossible to defeat

in·door *adj* : done, used, or belonging within
a building

in·doors *adv* : in or into a building

in·du·bi·ta·ble *adj* : being beyond question or
doubt — **in·du·bi·ta·bly** *adv*

in·duce *vb* **in·duced; in·duc·ing 1** : to cause
to do something **2** : to bring about **3** : to
produce (as an electric current) by induction

in·duce·ment *n* : something that causes
someone to do something

in·duct *vb* **in·duct·ed; in·duct·ing 1** : to take
in as a member of a military service **2** : to
place in office **3** : to officially introduce
(someone) as a member

in·duc·tion *n* **1** : the act or process of placing
someone in a new job or position **2** : the
production of an electrical or magnetic
effect through the influence of a nearby
magnet, electrical current, or electrically
charged body

in·dulge *vb* **in·dulged; in·dulg·ing 1 :** to give in to the desires of **2 :** to give in to a desire for something

in·dul·gence *n* **1 :** the practice of allowing enjoyment of whatever is desired **2 :** an act of doing what is desired **3 :** something that a person enjoys or desires

in·dul·gent *adj* **:** feeling or showing a willingness to allow enjoyment of whatever is wanted : LENIENT — **in·dul·gent·ly** *adv*

in·dus·tri·al *adj* **1 :** of, relating to, or engaged in industry **2 :** having highly developed industries — **in·dus·tri·al·ly** *adv*

in·dus·tri·al·ist *n* **:** a person who owns or engages in the management of an industry

in·dus·tri·al·i·za·tion *n* **:** the process of developing industries : the state of having industry developed

in·dus·tri·al·ize *vb* **in·dus·tri·al·ized; in·dus·tri·al·iz·ing :** to develop industries

in·dus·tri·ous *adj* **:** working hard and steadily — **in·dus·tri·ous·ly** *adv*

in·dus·try *n, pl* **in·dus·tries 1 :** businesses that provide a certain product or service **2 :** manufacturing activity **3 :** the habit of working hard and steadily

-ine *adj suffix* **:** of, relating to, or like

in·ed·i·ble *adj* **:** not fit for eating

in·ef·fec·tive *adj* **:** not having the desired effect — **in·ef·fec·tive·ly** *adv*

in·ef·fec·tu·al *adj* **:** not producing the proper or desired effect — **in·ef·fec·tu·al·ly** *adv*

in·ef·fi·cien·cy *n, pl* **in·ef·fi·cien·cies :** the state or an instance of being ineffective or inefficient

in·ef·fi·cient *adj* **1 :** not effective : INEFFECTUAL **2 :** not capable of bringing about a desired result with little waste — **in·ef·fi·cient·ly** *adv*

in·elas·tic *adj* **:** not elastic

in·el·i·gi·ble *adj* **:** not qualified to be chosen or used

in·ept *adj* **1 :** not suited to the occasion **2 :** lacking in skill or ability — **in·ept·ly** *adv* — **in·ept·ness** *n*

in·equal·i·ty *n, pl* **in·equal·i·ties :** the quality of being unequal or uneven : lack of equality

in·ert *adj* **:** unable or slow to move or react — **in·ert·ness** *n*

in·er·tia *n* **1 :** a property of matter by which it remains at rest or in motion in the same straight line unless acted upon by some external force **2 :** a tendency not to move or change

in·es·cap·able *adj* **:** INEVITABLE

in·ev·i·ta·bil·i·ty *n* **:** the quality or state of being sure to happen

in·ev·i·ta·ble *adj* **:** sure to happen : CERTAIN — **in·ev·i·ta·bly** *adv*

in·ex·act *adj* **:** INACCURATE

in·ex·cus·able *adj* **:** not to be excused — **in·ex·cus·ably** *adv*

in·ex·haust·ible *adj* **:** plentiful enough not to give out or be used up

in·ex·o·ra·ble *adj* **:** RELENTLESS — **in·ex·o·ra·bly** *adv*

in·ex·pen·sive *adj* **:** [1]CHEAP 1

in·ex·pe·ri·ence *n* **:** lack of experience

in·ex·pe·ri·enced *adj* **:** having little or no experience

in·ex·pli·ca·ble *adj* **:** impossible to explain or account for — **in·ex·pli·ca·bly** *adv*

in·ex·press·ible *adj* **:** being beyond the power to express : INDESCRIBABLE — **in·ex·press·ibly** *adv*

in·fal·li·ble *adj* **1 :** not capable of being wrong **2 :** certain to succeed : SURE — **in·fal·li·bly** *adv*

in·fa·mous *adj* **1 :** having an evil reputation **2 :** [1]EVIL 1, BAD — **in·fa·mous·ly** *adv*

in·fa·my *n, pl* **in·fa·mies 1 :** an evil reputation **2 :** an evil or terrible act

in·fan·cy *n, pl* **in·fan·cies 1 :** the first stage of a child's life : early childhood **2 :** a beginning or early period of existence

[1]in·fant *n* **1 :** a child in the first period of life : BABY **2 :** [2]MINOR

[2]infant *adj* **1 :** of or relating to infancy **2 :** intended for young children

in·fan·tile *adj* **:** CHILDISH 2

in·fan·try *n, pl* **in·fan·tries :** a branch of an army composed of soldiers trained to fight on foot

in·fat·u·at·ed *adj* **:** having a foolish or very strong love or admiration

in·fat·u·a·tion *n* **:** the state of having a foolish or very strong love or admiration

in·fect *vb* **in·fect·ed; in·fect·ing 1 :** to pass on or introduce a germ, illness, or disease to : to cause sickness in **2 :** to cause to share similar feelings

in·fec·tion *n* **1 :** the act or process of passing on or introducing a germ, illness, or disease to : the state of being infected **2 :** any disease caused by germs

in·fec·tious *adj* **1 :** passing from one to another in the form of a germ **2 :** easily spread to others

in·fer *vb* **in·ferred; in·fer·ring 1 :** to arrive at as a conclusion based on known facts **2 :** [1]GUESS 1 **3 :** [2]HINT, SUGGEST

in·fer·ence *n* **1 :** the act or process of reaching a conclusion about something from known facts **2 :** a conclusion or opinion reached based on known facts

[1]in·fe·ri·or *adj* **1 :** situated lower down (as in place or importance) **2 :** of little or less importance, value, or merit **3 :** of poor quality

[2]inferior *n* **:** a less important person or thing

in·fe·ri·or·i·ty *n* **1 :** the state of being of lower importance, value, or quality **2** : a sense of being less important or valuable

in·fer·nal *adj* **1** : very bad or unpleasant **2** : of or relating to hell

in·fer·tile *adj* : not fertile

in·fest *vb* **in·fest·ed; in·fest·ing** : to spread or swarm in or over in a harmful manner

in·fi·del *n* : a person who does not believe in a certain religion

in·field *n* **1** : the diamond-shaped part of a baseball field inside the bases and home plate **2** : the players in the infield

in·field·er *n* : a baseball player who plays in the infield

in·fi·nite *adj* **1** : having no limits of any kind **2** : seeming to be without limits — **in·fi·nite·ly** *adv*

in·fin·i·tes·i·mal *adj* : extremely small

in·fin·i·tive *n* : a verb form serving as a noun or as a modifier and at the same time taking objects and adverbial modifiers

in·fin·i·ty *n, pl* **in·fin·i·ties** **1** : the quality of being without limits **2** : a space, quantity, or period of time that is without limit

in·firm *adj* : weak or frail in body

in·fir·ma·ry *n, pl* **in·fir·ma·ries** : a place for the care and housing of sick people

in·fir·mi·ty *n, pl* **in·fir·mi·ties** : the condition of being weak or frail (as from age or illness)

in·flame *vb* **in·flamed; in·flam·ing** **1** : to make more active, excited, angry, or violent **2** : to cause to redden or grow hot (as from anger) **3** : to make or become sore, red, and swollen

in·flam·ma·ble *adj* **1** : FLAMMABLE **2** : easily inflamed : EXCITABLE

in·flam·ma·tion *n* : a bodily response to injury or disease in which heat, redness, and swelling are present

in·flam·ma·to·ry *adj* **1** : tending to excite anger or disorder **2** : causing or having inflammation

in·flat·able *adj* : possible to fill with air or gas

in·flate *vb* **in·flat·ed; in·flat·ing** **1** : to swell or fill with air or gas **2** : to cause to increase beyond proper limits

in·fla·tion *n* **1** : an act of filling with air or gas : the state of being filled with air or gas **2** : a continual rise in the price of goods and services

in·flect *vb* **in·flect·ed; in·flect·ing** **1** : to change a word by inflection **2** : to change the pitch of the voice

in·flec·tion *n* **1** : a change in the pitch of a person's voice **2** : a change in a word that shows a grammatical difference (as of number, person, or tense)

in·flex·i·ble *adj* **1** : not easily bent or twisted

2 : not easily influenced or persuaded **3** : not easily changed

in·flict *vb* **in·flict·ed; in·flict·ing** **1** : to give by or as if by striking **2** : to cause to be put up with

in·flo·res·cence *n* : the arrangement of flowers on a stalk

¹in·flu·ence *n* **1** : the act or power of causing an effect or change without use of direct force or authority **2** : a person or thing that has an indirect but usually important effect

²influence *vb* **in·flu·enced; in·flu·enc·ing** : to affect or change in an indirect but usually important way

in·flu·en·tial *adj* : having the power to cause change : having influence

in·flu·en·za *n* : a very contagious virus disease like a severe cold with fever

in·form *vb* **in·formed; in·form·ing** **1** : to let a person know something **2** : to give information so as to accuse or cause suspicion — **in·form·er** *n*

in·for·mal *adj* **1** : not requiring serious or formal behavior or dress **2** : suitable for ordinary or everyday use — **in·for·mal·ly** *adv*

in·for·mal·i·ty *n, pl* **in·for·mal·i·ties** : the quality or state of being informal

in·form·ant *n* : a person who gives information especially to accuse or cause suspicion about someone

in·for·ma·tion *n* : knowledge obtained from investigation, study, or instruction

information superhighway *n* : INTERNET

in·for·ma·tive *adj* : giving knowledge or information : INSTRUCTIVE

in·frac·tion *n* : VIOLATION

in·fra·red *adj* : being, relating to, or producing rays like light but lying outside the visible spectrum at its red end

in·fre·quent *adj* **1** : seldom happening : RARE **2** : not placed, made, or done at frequent intervals — **in·fre·quent·ly** *adv*

in·fringe *vb* **in·fringed; in·fring·ing** **1** : to fail to obey or act in agreement with : VIOLATE **2** : to go further than is right or fair to another : ENCROACH — **in·fringe·ment** *n*

in·fu·ri·ate *vb* **in·fu·ri·at·ed; in·fu·ri·at·ing** : to make furious : ENRAGE

in·fuse *vb* **in·fused; in·fus·ing** **1** : to put in as if by pouring **2** : to steep without boiling — **in·fu·sion** *n*

¹-ing *n suffix* **1** : action or process **2** : product or result of an action or process **3** : something used in or connected with making or doing

²-ing *vb suffix or adj suffix* — used to form the present participle and sometimes to form adjectives that do not come from a verb

in·ge·nious *adj* : showing ingenuity : CLEVER — **in·ge·nious·ly** *adv*

in·ge·nu·ity *n, pl* **in·ge·nu·ities** : skill or cleverness in discovering, inventing, or planning

in·gen·u·ous *adj* : showing innocence and childlike honesty — **in·gen·u·ous·ly** *adv*

in·got *n* : a mass of metal cast into a shape that is easy to handle or store

in·gra·ti·ate *vb* **in·gra·ti·at·ed; in·gra·ti·at·ing** : to gain favor for by effort

in·gra·ti·at·ing *adj* **1** : PLEASING **2** : intended to gain someone's favor — **in·gra·ti·at·ing·ly** *adv*

in·grat·i·tude *n* : lack of gratitude

in·gre·di·ent *n* : one of the substances that make up a mixture

in·hab·it *vb* **in·hab·it·ed; in·hab·it·ing** : to live or dwell in

in·hab·i·tant *n* : a person or animal that lives in a place

in·ha·la·tion *n* : the act or an instance of breathing or drawing in by breathing

in·hale *vb* **in·haled; in·hal·ing** **1** : to draw in by breathing **2** : to breathe in

in·hal·er *n* : a device used for breathing medicine into the lungs

in·her·ent *adj* : belonging to or being a part of the nature of a person or thing — **in·her·ent·ly** *adv*

in·her·it *vb* **in·her·it·ed; in·her·it·ing** **1** : to get by legal right from a person at his or her death **2** : to get by heredity

in·her·i·tance *n* **1** : the act of getting by legal right from a person at his or her death or through heredity **2** : something gotten by legal right from a person at his or her death

in·hib·it *vb* **in·hib·it·ed; in·hib·it·ing** : to prevent or hold back from doing something

in·hos·pi·ta·ble *adj* : not friendly or generous : not showing hospitality — **in·hos·pi·ta·bly** *adv*

in·hu·man *adj* **1** : lacking pity or kindness **2** : unlike what might be expected by a human

in·hu·mane *adj* : not kind or humane

in·hu·man·i·ty *n, pl* **in·hu·man·i·ties** : a cruel act or attitude

in·iq·ui·ty *n, pl* **in·iq·ui·ties** : an evil or unfair act

¹ini·tial *n* **1** : the first letter of a name **2** : a large letter beginning a text or a paragraph

²initial *adj* : occurring at or marking the beginning — **ini·tial·ly** *adv*

³initial *vb* **ini·tialed** *or* **ini·tialled; ini·tial·ing** *or* **ini·tial·ling** : to mark with the first letter or letters of a name

ini·ti·ate *vb* **ini·ti·at·ed; ini·ti·at·ing** **1** : to set going : BEGIN **2** : to admit into a club by special ceremonies **3** : to teach (someone) the basic facts about something

ini·ti·a·tion *n* **1** : the act or an instance of initiating : the process of being initiated **2** : the

ceremonies with which a person is admitted into a club

ini·tia·tive *n* **1** : a first step or movement **2** : energy shown in getting action started

in·ject *vb* **in·ject·ed; in·ject·ing** **1** : to force a fluid (as a medicine) into by using a special needle **2** : to introduce as something needed or additional

in·jec·tion *n* : an act or instance of forcing a fluid (as a medicine) into a part of the body by using a special needle

in·junc·tion *n* : a court order commanding or forbidding the doing of some act

in·jure *vb* **in·jured; in·jur·ing** : to cause pain or harm to

in·ju·ri·ous *adj* : causing injury or harm

in·ju·ry *n, pl* **in·ju·ries** **1** : hurt, damage, or loss suffered **2** : an act that damages or hurts

in·jus·tice *n* **1** : unfair treatment : violation of a person's rights **2** : an act of unfair treatment

ink *n* : a liquid material used for writing or printing

ink–jet *adj* : relating to or being a printer in which droplets of ink are sprayed onto the paper

in·kling *n* : a vague notion : HINT

ink·stand *n* : a small stand for holding ink and pens

ink·well *n* : a container for ink

inky *adj* **ink·i·er; ink·i·est** **1** : consisting of or like ink **2** : soiled with or as if with ink

in·laid *adj* **1** : set into a surface in a decorative pattern **2** : decorated with a design or material set into a surface

¹in·land *adj* : of or relating to the part of a country away from the coast

²inland *n* : the part of a country away from the coast or boundaries

³inland *adv* : into or toward the area away from a coast

in–law *n* : a relative by marriage and especially the mother or father of a person's husband or wife

¹in·lay *vb* **in·laid** ; **in·lay·ing** : to set into a surface for decoration or strengthening

²in·lay *n* : inlaid work : material used in inlaying

in·let *n* **1** : a small or narrow bay **2** : an opening through which air, gas, or liquid can enter something

in–line skate *n* : a roller skate whose wheels are set in a line one behind the other

in·mate *n* : a person confined in an institution (as a hospital or prison)

in·most *adj* : INNERMOST

inn *n* : a house that provides a place to sleep and food for travelers

in·ner *adj* **1** : located farther in **2** : of or relating to the mind or spirit

inner ear *n* : the inner part of the ear that is
located in a bony cavity and plays a key role
in hearing and keeping the body properly
balanced

in·ner·most *adj* : farthest inward

in·ning *n* : a division of a baseball game that
consists of a turn at bat for each team

inn·keep·er *n* : the person who runs an inn

in·no·cence *n* : the quality or state of being
free from sin or guilt

in·no·cent *adj* **1** : free from sin : PURE **2**
: free from guilt or blame **3** : free from evil
influence or effect : HARMLESS — **in·no·
cent·ly** *adv*

in·noc·u·ous *adj* : not harmful — **in·noc·u·
ous·ly** *adv*

in·no·va·tion *n* **1** : a new idea, method, or device : NOVELTY **2** : the introduction of
something new

in·nu·mer·a·ble *adj* : too many to be counted

in·oc·u·late *vb* **in·oc·u·lat·ed; in·oc·u·lat·ing**
: to inject a material (as a vaccine) into to
protect against or treat a disease

in·oc·u·la·tion *n* : an act or instance of inject-
ing a material (as a vaccine) into to protect
against or treat a disease

in·of·fen·sive *adj* : not likely to offend or
bother anyone

in·op·por·tune *adj* : INCONVENIENT

¹in·put *n* **1** : something (as power, a signal,
or data) that is put into a machine or system
2 : the point at which an input is made **3**
: the act of or process of putting in

²input *vb* **in·put·ted** *or* **input; in·put·ting** : to
enter (as data) into a computer

in·quest *n* : an official investigation especially into the cause of a death

in·quire *vb* **in·quired; in·quir·ing 1** : to ask
or ask about **2** : to make an investigation **3**
: to ask a question — **in·quir·er** *n* — **in·quir·
ing·ly** *adv*

in·qui·ry *n, pl* **in·qui·ries 1** : the act of asking
a question or seeking information **2** : a request for information **3** : a thorough examination

in·quis·i·tive *adj* **1** : in search of information
2 : overly curious — **in·quis·i·tive·ly** *adv*

in·sane *adj* **1** : not normal or healthy in mind
2 : used by or for people who are insane **3**
: very foolish or unreasonable — **in·sane·ly**
adv

in·san·i·ty *n* : the condition of being abnormal
or unhealthy in mind

in·sa·tia·ble *adj* : impossible to satisfy

in·scribe *vb* **in·scribed; in·scrib·ing 1** : to
write, engrave, or print as a lasting record **2**
: to write, engrave, or print something on or
in

in·scrip·tion *n* : words or a name inscribed on
a surface

in·sect *n* **1** : any of a group of small and
often winged animals that are arthropods
having six jointed legs and a body formed of
a head, thorax, and abdomen **2** : an animal
(as a spider or a centipede) similar to the
true insects — not used technically

in·sec·ti·cide *n* : a chemical used to kill insects

in·se·cure *adj* **1** : not safe or secure **2** : not
confident

in·se·cu·ri·ty *n* : the quality or state of being
not safe or not confident

in·sen·si·ble *adj* **1** : not able to feel **2** : not
aware of or caring about something

in·sen·si·tive *adj* **1** : lacking feeling : not
sensitive **2** : not caring or showing concern
about the problems or feelings of others —
in·sen·si·tive·ly *adv*

in·sen·si·tiv·i·ty *n* : lack of feeling

in·sep·a·ra·ble *adj* : impossible to separate

¹in·sert *vb* **in·sert·ed; in·sert·ing** : to put in or
into

²in·sert *n* : something that is or is meant to be
inserted

in·ser·tion *n* **1** : the act or process of putting
in or into **2** : ²INSERT

¹in·set *n* : a smaller thing that is inserted into
a larger thing

²inset *vb* **in·set** *or* **in·set·ted; in·set·ting**
: ¹INSERT 2

¹in·side *n* **1** : an inner side, surface, or space
: INTERIOR **2** : the inner parts of a person or
animal — usually used in pl.

²inside *adv* **1** : on the inner side **2** : in or
into the interior

³inside *adj* **1** : relating to or being on or near
the inside **2** : relating or known to a certain
few people

⁴inside *prep* **1** : to or on the inside of **2** : before the end of : WITHIN

inside out *adv* **1** : in such a way that the
inner surface becomes the outer **2** : in or
into a confused or disorganized state

in·sid·er *n* : a person having information not
generally available

in·sight *n* **1** : the ability to understand a person or a situation very clearly **2** : the understanding of the truth of a situation

in·sig·nia *n, pl* **insignia** *or* **in·sig·ni·as** : an
emblem of a certain office, authority, or
honor

in·sig·nif·i·cance *n* : the quality or state of
being unimportant

in·sig·nif·i·cant *adj* : not important — **in·sig·
nif·i·cant·ly** *adv*

in·sin·cere *adj* : not expressing or showing
true feelings : not sincere or honest — **in·
sin·cere·ly** *adv*

in·sin·cer·i·ty *n* : lack of honesty in showing feelings

in·sin·u·ate *vb* **in·sin·u·at·ed; in·sin·u·at·ing** 1 : ²HINT, IMPLY 2 : to bring or get in little by little or in a secret way

in·sip·id *adj* 1 : having little taste or flavor : TASTELESS 2 : not interesting or challenging : DULL

in·sist *vb* **in·sist·ed; in·sist·ing** 1 : to place special stress or great importance 2 : to make a demand

in·sis·tence *n* : the quality or state of being demanding about something

in·sis·tent *adj* : demanding that something happen or that someone act in a certain way — **in·sis·tent·ly** *adv*

in·so·lence *n* : lack of respect for rank or authority

in·so·lent *adj* : showing lack of respect for rank or authority — **in·so·lent·ly** *adv*

in·sol·u·ble *adj* 1 : having no solution or explanation 2 : difficult or impossible to dissolve

in·som·nia *n* : difficulty in sleeping

in·spect *vb* **in·spect·ed; in·spect·ing** 1 : to examine closely 2 : to view and examine in an official way

in·spec·tion *n* : the act of examining closely or officially

in·spec·tor *n* : a person who makes inspections

in·spi·ra·tion *n* 1 : the act or power of arousing the mind or the emotions 2 : a clever idea 3 : something that moves someone to act, create, or feel an emotion

in·spire *vb* **in·spired; in·spir·ing** 1 : to move or guide by divine influence 2 : to move (someone) to act, create, or feel emotions : AROUSE 3 : to cause something to occur or to be created or done

in·sta·bil·i·ty *n* : the quality or state of being unstable

in·stall *vb* **in·stalled; in·stall·ing** 1 : to put in office with ceremony 2 : to put in place for use or service

in·stal·la·tion *n* 1 : the act of putting something in place for use : the state of being put in place for use 2 : something put in place for use

¹in·stall·ment *n* : INSTALLATION 1

²installment *n* : one of several parts of something (as a book) presented over a period of time

in·stance *n* 1 : a particular occurrence of something : EXAMPLE 2 : a certain point or situation in a process or series of events

¹in·stant *n* : a very short time : MOMENT

²instant *adj* 1 : happening or done right away 2 : partially prepared by the manufacturer to make final preparation easy

in·stan·ta·neous *adj* : happening or done very quickly : happening in an instant — **in·stan·ta·neous·ly** *adv*

in·stant·ly *adv* : without delay : IMMEDIATELY

in·stead *adv* : as a substitute

in·stead of *prep* : in place of : as a substitute for

in·step *n* : the arched middle part of the human foot between the ankle and the toes

in·sti·gate *vb* **in·sti·gat·ed; in·sti·gat·ing** : to cause to happen or begin

in·still *vb* **in·stilled; in·still·ing** : to put into the mind little by little

in·stinct *n* 1 : an act or course of action in response to a stimulus that is automatic rather than learned 2 : a way of knowing something without learning or thinking about it 3 : a natural ability

in·stinc·tive *adj* : of or relating to instinct : resulting from instinct — **in·stinc·tive·ly** *adv*

¹in·sti·tute *vb* **in·sti·tut·ed; in·sti·tut·ing** 1 : to begin or establish 2 : to give a start to

²institute *n* 1 : an organization for the promotion of a cause 2 : a place for study usually in a special field

in·sti·tu·tion *n* 1 : the beginning or establishment of something 2 : an established custom, practice, or law 3 : an established organization

in·struct *vb* **in·struct·ed; in·struct·ing** 1 : to give knowledge to : TEACH 2 : to give information to 3 : to give directions or commands to

in·struc·tion *n* 1 **instructions** *pl* : a specific rule or command 2 **instructions** *pl* : an outline of how something is to be done 3 : the act or practice of teaching

in·struc·tive *adj* : helping to give knowledge or information

in·struc·tor *n* : TEACHER

in·stru·ment *n* 1 : a tool or device for doing a particular kind of work 2 : a device used to produce music 3 : a way of getting something done 4 : a legal document (as a deed) 5 : a device that measures something (as altitude or temperature)

in·stru·men·tal *adj* 1 : acting to get something done 2 : relating to or done with an instrument 3 : played on an instrument rather than sung

in·sub·or·di·nate *adj* : not obeying authority : DISOBEDIENT

in·sub·or·di·na·tion *n* : failure to obey authority

in·sub·stan·tial *adj* : not large or important

in·suf·fer·able *adj* : impossible to bear — **in·suf·fer·ably** *adv*

in·suf·fi·cient *adj* : not enough : not sufficient — **in·suf·fi·cient·ly** *adv*

in·su·late *vb* **in·su·lat·ed; in·su·lat·ing 1 :** to separate from others : ISOLATE **2 :** to separate a conductor of electricity, heat, or sound from other conductors by means of something that does not allow the passage of electricity, heat, or sound

in·su·la·tion *n* **1 :** material that is used to stop the passage of electricity, heat, or sound from one conductor to another **2 :** the act of insulating : the state of being insulated

in·su·la·tor *n* : a material (as rubber or glass) that is a poor conductor of electricity, heat, or sound

in·su·lin *n* : a hormone made by the pancreas that helps the cells in the body take up glucose from the blood and that is used to treat diabetes

¹**in·sult** *vb* **in·sult·ed; in·sult·ing :** to treat or speak to with disrespect

²**in·sult** *n* : an act or statement showing disrespect

in·sur·ance *n* **1 :** an agreement by which a person pays a company and the company promises to pay money if the person becomes injured or dies or to pay for the value of property lost or damaged **2 :** the amount for which something is insured **3 :** the business of insuring persons or property

in·sure *vb* **in·sured; in·sur·ing 1 :** to give or get insurance on or for **2 :** to make certain — **in·sur·er** *n*

in·sur·gent *n* : a person who revolts : REBEL

in·sur·rec·tion *n* : an act or instance of rebelling against a government

in·tact *adj* : not broken or damaged : not touched especially by anything that harms

in·take *n* **1 :** the act of taking in **2 :** something taken in **3 :** a place where liquid or air is taken into something (as a pump)

in·tan·gi·ble *adj* **1 :** not capable of being touched **2 :** not having physical substance

in·te·ger *n* : a number that is a natural number (as 1, 2, or 3), the negative of a natural number (as −1, −2, −3), or 0

in·te·gral *adj* : very important and necessary : needed to make something complete

in·te·grate *vb* **in·te·grat·ed; in·te·grat·ing 1 :** to form into a whole : UNITE **2 :** to make a part of a larger unit **3 :** DESEGREGATE

integrated circuit *n* : a tiny group of electronic devices and their connections that is produced in or on a small slice of material (as silicon)

in·te·gra·tion *n* **1 :** the act or process of uniting different things **2 :** the practice of uniting people from different races in an attempt to give people equal rights

in·teg·ri·ty *n* **1 :** total honesty and sincerity **2 :** the condition of being free from damage or defect

in·tel·lect *n* **1 :** the ability to think and understand **2 :** a person with great powers of thinking and reasoning

¹**in·tel·lec·tu·al** *adj* **1 :** of or relating to thought or understanding **2 :** interested in serious study and thought **3 :** requiring study and thought — **in·tel·lec·tu·al·ly** *adv*

²**intellectual** *n* : a person who takes pleasure in serious study and thought

in·tel·li·gence *n* **1 :** the ability to learn and understand **2 :** secret information collected about an enemy or a possible enemy

in·tel·li·gent *adj* **1 :** having or showing serious thought and good judgment **2 :** able to learn and understand — **in·tel·li·gent·ly** *adv*

in·tel·li·gi·ble *adj* : possible to understand — **in·tel·li·gi·bly** *adv*

in·tem·per·ance *n* : lack of self-control (as in satisfying an appetite)

in·tem·per·ate *adj* **1 :** not moderate or mild **2 :** having or showing a lack of self-control (as in the use of alcoholic beverages)

in·tend *vb* **in·tend·ed; in·tend·ing :** to have in mind as a purpose or goal : PLAN

in·tense *adj* **1 :** very great in degree : EXTREME **2 :** done with great energy, enthusiasm, or effort **3 :** having very strong feelings — **in·tense·ly** *adv*

in·ten·si·fy *vb* **in·ten·si·fied; in·ten·si·fy·ing :** to make or become stronger or more extreme

in·ten·si·ty *n, pl* **in·ten·si·ties 1 :** strength or force **2 :** the degree or amount of a quality or condition

¹**in·ten·sive** *adj* **1 :** involving special effort or concentration **2 :** giving emphasis

²**intensive** *n* : a word that emphasizes or stresses something

intensive care *n* : constant observation and treatment of very ill patients in a special unit of a hospital

¹**in·tent** *n* **1 :** what someone plans to do or accomplish : PURPOSE **2 :** MEANING 2

²**intent** *adj* **1 :** showing concentration or great attention **2 :** showing great determination — **in·tent·ly** *adv*

in·ten·tion *n* **1 :** a determination to act in a particular way **2 :** an aim or plan

in·ten·tion·al *adj* : done in a deliberate way : not accidental — **in·ten·tion·al·ly** *adv*

in·ter *vb* **in·terred; in·ter·ring :** BURY 2

inter- *prefix* **1 :** between : among : together **2 :** mutual : mutually **3 :** located, occurring, or carried on between

in·ter·act *vb* **in·ter·act·ed; in·ter·act·ing 1 :** to talk or do things with other people **2 :** to act upon or together with something else

in·ter·ac·tion *n* **1 :** the act of talking or doing things with other people **2 :** the action or influence of things on one another

in·ter·ac·tive *adj* : designed to be used in a way that involves the frequent participation of a user — **in·ter·ac·tive·ly** *adv*

in·ter·cede *vb* **in·ter·ced·ed; in·ter·ced·ing 1** : to try to help settle differences between unfriendly individuals or groups **2** : to plead for the needs of someone else

in·ter·cept *vb* **in·ter·cept·ed; in·ter·cept·ing 1** : to take, seize, or stop before reaching an intended destination **2** : to catch (a football) passed by a member of the opposing team

¹in·ter·change *vb* **in·ter·changed; in·ter·chang·ing** : to put each in the place of the other : EXCHANGE

²in·ter·change *n* **1** : an act or instance of sharing or exchanging things **2** : an area where highways meet and it is possibe to move from one to the other without stopping

in·ter·change·able *adj* : capable of being used in place of each other — **in·ter·change·ably** *adv*

in·ter·com *n* : a communication system with a microphone and loudspeaker at each end

in·ter·course *n* : dealings between persons or groups

in·ter·de·pen·dence *n* : the quality or state of depending on one another

in·ter·de·pen·dent *adj* : depending on one another

¹in·ter·est *n* **1** : a feeling of concern or curiosity about or desire to be involved with something **2** : a quality that makes something more appealing or interesting **3** : something that a person enjoys learning about or doing **4** : something that provides help or benefit to a person or group **5** : the money paid by a borrower for the use of borrowed money **6** : the profit made on money that is invested **7** : a right, title, or legal share in something **8 interests** *pl* : a group financially interested in an industry or business

²interest *vb* **in·ter·est·ed; in·ter·est·ing 1** : to persuade to become involved in **2** : to arouse and hold the concern, curiosity, or attention of

in·ter·est·ed *adj* : wanting to learn more about or become involved with something

in·ter·est·ing *adj* : holding the attention : not dull or boring — **in·ter·est·ing·ly** *adv*

in·ter·fere *vb* **in·ter·fered; in·ter·fer·ing 1** : to get in the way of as an obstacle **2** : to become involved in the concerns of others when such involvement is not wanted

in·ter·fer·ence *n* **1** : something that gets in the way as an obstacle **2** : involvement in the concerns of others when such involvement is not wanted

in·ter·im *n* : a period of time between events

¹in·te·ri·or *adj* **1** : being or occurring inside

something : INNER **2** : far from the border or shore : INLAND

²interior *n* **1** : the inner part of something **2** : the inland part

interj *abbr* interjection

in·ter·ject *vb* **in·ter·ject·ed; in·ter·ject·ing** : to put between or among other things

in·ter·jec·tion *n* **1** : a word or cry (as "ouch") expressing sudden or strong feeling **2** : the act of inserting or including something

in·ter·lace *vb* **in·ter·laced; in·ter·lac·ing** : to unite by or as if by lacing together

in·ter·lock *vb* : to connect or lock together

in·ter·lop·er *n* : a person present in a situation or place where he or she is not wanted

in·ter·lude *n* **1** : a period of time or event that comes between others **2** : an entertainment between the acts of a play **3** : a musical composition between parts of a longer composition or of a drama

in·ter·mar·riage *n* : marriage between members of different groups

in·ter·mar·ry *vb* **in·ter·mar·ried; in·ter·mar·ry·ing** : to marry a member of a different group

in·ter·me·di·ary *n, pl* **in·ter·me·di·ar·ies** : GO-BETWEEN

¹in·ter·me·di·ate *adj* : being or occurring in the middle of a series or between extremes — **in·ter·me·di·ate·ly** *adv*

²intermediate *n* : someone or something that is in the middle of a series or between extremes

in·ter·ment *n* : BURIAL

in·ter·mi·na·ble *adj* : having or seeming to have no end — **in·ter·mi·na·bly** *adv*

in·ter·min·gle *vb* **in·ter·min·gled; in·ter·min·gling** : to mix together

in·ter·mis·sion *n* : a pause or short break (as between acts of a play)

in·ter·mit·tent *adj* : starting, stopping, and starting again — **in·ter·mit·tent·ly** *adv*

¹in·tern *vb* **in·terned; in·tern·ing** : to force to stay within a place (as a prison) especially during a war — **in·tern·ment** *n*

²in·tern *n* : a student or recent graduate in a special field of study (as medicine or teaching) who works for a period of time to gain practical experience — **in·tern·ship** *n*

in·ter·nal *adj* **1** : being within something : INNER **2** : occurring or located within the body **3** : existing or occurring within a country — **in·ter·nal·ly** *adv*

in·ter·na·tion·al *adj* **1** : involving two or more nations : occurring between nations **2** : active or known in many nations — **in·ter·na·tion·al·ly** *adv*

In·ter·net *n* : a communications system that connects computers and databases all over the world

in·ter·pose *vb* **in·ter·posed; in·ter·pos·ing 1** : to put between two or more things **2** : to introduce between parts of a conversation

in·ter·pret *vb* **in·ter·pret·ed; in·ter·pret·ing 1** : to explain the meaning of **2** : to understand in a particular way **3** : to bring out the meaning of

in·ter·pret·er *n* : a person who turns spoken words of one language into a different language

in·ter·pre·ta·tion *n* **1** : the way something is explained or understood **2** : a particular way of performing something (as a dramatic role)

in·ter·pre·tive *adj* : designed or serving to explain the meaning of something

in·ter·ra·cial *adj* : of or involving members of different races

in·ter·re·late *vb* **in·ter·re·lat·ed; in·ter·re·lat·ing** : to bring into or have a connection with each other

in·ter·ro·gate *vb* **in·ter·ro·gat·ed; in·ter·ro·gat·ing** : to question thoroughly

in·ter·ro·ga·tion *n* : the act of questioning thoroughly

in·ter·rog·a·tive *adj* : having the form or force of a question

in·ter·rupt *vb* **in·ter·rupt·ed; in·ter·rupt·ing 1** : to stop or hinder by breaking in **2** : to break the sameness or course of

in·ter·rup·tion *n* : an act of stopping or hindering by breaking in

in·ter·scho·las·tic *adj* : existing or carried on between schools

in·ter·sect *vb* **in·ter·sect·ed; in·ter·sect·ing** : to cut or divide by passing through or across : CROSS

in·ter·sec·tion *n* **1** : the act or process of crossing or passing across **2** : the place or point where two or more things (as streets) meet or cross each other **3** : the set of mathematical elements common to two or more sets

in·ter·sperse *vb* **in·ter·spersed; in·ter·spers·ing 1** : to put (something) here and there among other things **2** : to put things at various places in or among

in·ter·state *adj* : existing or occurring between two or more states

in·ter·stel·lar *adj* : existing or taking place among the stars

in·ter·twine *vb* **in·ter·twined; in·ter·twin·ing** : to twist or weave together

in·ter·val *n* **1** : a period of time between events or states **2** : a space between things **3** : the difference in pitch between two tones

in·ter·vene *vb* **in·ter·vened; in·ter·ven·ing 1** : to come or occur between events, places, or points of time **2** : to interfere with something so as to stop, settle, or change

in·ter·ven·tion *n* : the act or fact of taking action about something in order to have an effect on its outcome

¹in·ter·view *n* **1** : a meeting at which people talk to each other in order to ask questions and get information **2** : an account of an interview

²interview *vb* **in·ter·viewed; in·ter·view·ing** : to question and talk with to get information — **in·ter·view·er** *n*

in·ter·weave *vb* **in·ter·wove; in·ter·wo·ven; in·ter·weav·ing 1** : to twist or weave together **2** : to blend together

in·tes·ti·nal *adj* : of, relating to, or affecting the intestine

in·tes·tine *n* : the lower part of the digestive canal that is a long tube made up of the small intestine and large intestine and in which most of the digestion and absorption of food occurs and through which waste material passes to be discharged

in·ti·ma·cy *n, pl* **in·ti·ma·cies 1** : a state marked by emotional closeness **2** : a quality suggesting closeness or warmth **3** : something that is very personal or private

¹in·ti·mate *vb* **in·ti·mat·ed; in·ti·mat·ing** : to say indirectly : hint at

²in·ti·mate *adj* **1** : very personal or private **2** : marked by very close association **3** : suggesting closeness or warmth : COZY — **in·ti·mate·ly** *adv*

³in·ti·mate *n* : a very close and trusted friend

in·tim·i·date *vb* **in·tim·i·dat·ed; in·tim·i·dat·ing** : to frighten especially by threats

in·tim·i·da·tion *n* : the act of making frightened by or as if by threats

in·to *prep* **1** : to the inside of **2** : to the state, condition, position, or form of **3** : so as to hit : AGAINST **4** : in the direction of **5** — used to indicate division

in·tol·er·a·ble *adj* : UNBEARABLE — **in·tol·er·a·bly** *adv*

in·tol·er·ance *n* **1** : the quality or state of being unable or unwilling to put up with **2** : an unwillingness to grant rights to other people

in·tol·er·ant *adj* **1** : not able or willing to put up with **2** : not willing to grant rights to some people

in·to·na·tion *n* : the rise and fall in pitch of the voice in speech

in·tox·i·cate *vb* **in·tox·i·cat·ed; in·tox·i·cat·ing 1** : to affect by alcohol or a drug especially so that normal thinking and acting becomes difficult or impossible : make drunk **2** : to make wildly excited or enthusiastic

in·tox·i·ca·tion *n* **1** : the condition of being

drunk **2** : an unhealthy state that is or is like a poisoning

in·tra·mu·ral *adj* : being or occurring within the limits of a school

intrans. *abbr* intransitive

in·tran·si·tive *adj* : not having or containing a direct object

in·trep·id *adj* : feeling no fear : BOLD

in·tri·ca·cy *n, pl* **in·tri·ca·cies 1** : the quality or state of being complex or having many parts **2** : something that is complex or has many parts

in·tri·cate *adj* **1** : having many closely combined parts or elements **2** : very difficult to follow or understand — **in·tri·cate·ly** *adv*

¹**in·trigue** *vb* **in·trigued; in·trigu·ing 1** : to arouse the interest or curiosity of **2** : ²PLOT 1, SCHEME

²**in·trigue** *n* : a secret and complex plot

in·tro·duce *vb* **in·tro·duced; in·tro·duc·ing 1** : to cause to be acquainted : make known **2** : to bring into practice or use **3** : to make available for sale for the first time **4** : to bring forward for discussion or consideration **5** : to put in : INSERT

in·tro·duc·tion *n* **1** : the part of a book that leads up to and explains what will be found in the main part **2** : the act of causing a person to meet another person **3** : the action of bringing into use, making available, or presenting for consideration or discussion **4** : something introduced or added

in·tro·duc·to·ry *adj* : serving to introduce : PRELIMINARY

in·trude *vb* **in·trud·ed; in·trud·ing 1** : to force in, into, or on especially where not right or proper **2** : to come or go in without an invitation or right — **in·trud·er** *n*

in·tru·sion *n* **1** : the act of going or forcing in without being wanted **2** : something that goes in or interferes without being wanted

in·tu·i·tion *n* **1** : the ability to know something without having proof **2** : something known without proof

In·u·it *n, pl* **Inuit** *or* **In·u·its 1** : a member of the Eskimo people of North America, Greenland, or Canada **2** : any of the languages of the Inuit people

in·un·date *vb* **in·un·dat·ed; in·un·dat·ing** : to cover with or as if with a flood

in·vade *vb* **in·vad·ed; in·vad·ing 1** : to enter by force to conquer or plunder **2** : to show lack of respect for — **in·vad·er** *n*

¹**in·val·id** *adj* : having no force or effect

²**in·va·lid** *n* : a person suffering from sickness or disability

in·val·i·date *vb* **in·val·i·dat·ed; in·val·i·dat·ing** : to weaken or destroy the effect of

in·valu·able *adj* : PRICELESS

in·vari·able *adj* : not changing or capable of change — **in·vari·ably** *adv*

in·va·sion *n* : an act of invading

in·vent *vb* **in·vent·ed; in·vent·ing 1** : to create or produce for the first time **2** : to think up : make up — **in·ven·tor** *n*

in·ven·tion *n* **1** : an original device or process **2** : ³LIE **3** : the act or process of inventing **4** : the ability to think of new ideas

in·ven·tive *adj* : CREATIVE

¹**in·ven·to·ry** *n, pl* **in·ven·to·ries 1** : a supply of goods **2** : a list of items (as goods on hand) **3** : the act or process of making a list of items

²**inventory** *vb* **in·ven·to·ried; in·ven·to·ry·ing** : to make a complete list of

in·verse *adj* **1** : opposite in order, nature, or effect **2** : being a mathematical operation that is opposite in effect to another operation — **in·verse·ly** *adv*

in·vert *vb* **in·vert·ed; in·vert·ing 1** : to turn inside out or upside down **2** : to reverse the order or position of

¹**in·ver·te·brate** *adj* : having no backbone

²**invertebrate** *n* : an animal (as a worm or a crab) that does not have a backbone

¹**in·vest** *vb* **in·vest·ed; in·vest·ing** : to give power or authority to

²**invest** *vb* **in·vest·ed; in·vest·ing 1** : to put out money in order to gain profit **2** : to put out (as effort) in support of a usually worthy cause — **in·ves·tor** *n*

in·ves·ti·gate *vb* **in·ves·ti·gat·ed; in·ves·ti·gat·ing** : to study by close examination and questioning — **in·ves·ti·ga·tor** *n*

in·ves·ti·ga·tion *n* : the act or process of studying by close examination and questioning

in·vest·ment *n* **1** : the act of putting out money in order to gain a profit **2** : a sum of money invested **3** : a property in which money is invested

in·vig·o·rate *vb* **in·vig·o·rat·ed; in·vig·o·rat·ing** : to give life and energy to

in·vin·ci·bil·i·ty *n* : the quality or state of being impossible to defeat

in·vin·ci·ble *adj* : impossible to defeat

in·vi·o·la·ble *adj* **1** : too sacred to be broken or denied **2** : impossible to harm or destroy by violence

in·vis·i·bil·i·ty *n* : the quality or state of being impossible to see

in·vis·i·ble *adj* : impossible to see — **in·vis·i·bly** *adv*

in·vi·ta·tion *n* **1** : a written or spoken request for someone to go somewhere or do something **2** : the act of inviting

in·vite *vb* **in·vit·ed; in·vit·ing 1** : to ask (someone) to go somewhere or do something **2** : [1]WELCOME 2 **3** : to tend to bring on

in·vit·ing *adj* : ATTRACTIVE — **in·vit·ing·ly** *adv*

in·voice *n* : a list of goods shipped usually showing the price and the terms of sale

in·voke *vb* **in·voked; in·vok·ing 1** : to ask for aid or protection (as in prayer) **2** : to call forth by magic **3** : to appeal to as an authority or for support

in·vol·un·tary *adj* **1** : not done consciously **2** : not done by choice — **in·vol·un·tari·ly** *adv*

in·volve *vb* **in·volved; in·volv·ing 1** : to draw into a situation : ENGAGE **2** : to take part in **3** : INCLUDE **4** : to be accompanied by **5** : to have or take the attention of completely — **in·volve·ment** *n*

in·volved *adj* : very complicated

in·vul·ner·a·ble *adj* **1** : impossible to injure or damage **2** : safe from attack

[1]**in·ward** *adj* **1** : toward the inside or center **2** : of or concerning the mind or spirit

[2]**inward** *or* **in·wards** *adv* **1** : toward the inside or center **2** : toward the mind or spirit

in·ward·ly *adv* **1** : in a way that is not openly shown or stated : PRIVATELY **2** : on the inside

io·dine *n* **1** : a chemical element found in seawater and seaweeds and used especially in medicine and photography **2** : a solution of iodine in alcohol used to kill germs

io·dize *vb* **io·dized; io·diz·ing** : to add iodine to

ion *n* : an atom or group of atoms that carries an electric charge

-ion *n suffix* **1** : act or process **2** : result of an act or process **3** : state or condition

ion·ize *vb* **ion·ized; ion·iz·ing** : to change into ions

ion·o·sphere *n* : the part of the earth's atmosphere beginning at an altitude of about 30 miles (50 kilometers) and extending outward that contains electrically charged particles

io·ta *n* : a tiny amount

IOU *n* : a written promise to pay a debt

-ious *adj suffix* : -OUS

IQ *n* : a number that represents a person's level of intelligence based on the score of a special test

ir- — see IN-

[1]**Iraqi** *n, pl* **Iraqis** : a person born or living in Iraq

[2]**Iraqi** *adj* : of or relating to Iraq or its people

iras·ci·ble *adj* : easily angered

irate *adj* : ANGRY

ire *n* : [2]ANGER, WRATH

ir·i·des·cence *n* : a shifting and constant change of colors producing rainbow effects

ir·i·des·cent *adj* : having iridescence

irid·i·um *n* : a hard brittle heavy metallic chemical element

iris *n* **1** : the colored part around the pupil of an eye **2** : a plant with long pointed leaves and large usually brightly colored flowers

[1]**Irish** *adj* : of or relating to Ireland, its people, or the Irish language

[2]**Irish** *n* **1** **Irish** *pl* : the people of Ireland **2** : a language of Ireland

irk *vb* **irked; irk·ing** : ANNOY

irk·some *adj* : causing annoyance

[1]**iron** *n* **1** : a heavy silvery white metallic chemical element that rusts easily, is strongly attracted by magnets, occurs in meteorites and combined in minerals, and is necessary for transporting oxygen in the blood **2** : a device that is heated and used for making cloth smooth **3** : a device that is heated to perform a task **4 irons** *pl* : handcuffs or chains used to bind or to hinder movement

[2]**iron** *adj* **1** : made of iron **2** : strong and healthy **3** : not giving in

[3]**iron** *vb* **ironed; iron·ing** : to press with a heated iron

iron·ic *also* **iron·i·cal** *adj* : relating to, containing, or showing irony — **iron·i·cal·ly** *adv*

iron·work *n* **1** : things made of iron **2 iron·works** *pl* : a mill where iron or steel is smelted or heavy iron or steel products are made

iro·ny *n, pl* **iro·nies 1** : the use of words that mean the opposite of what is really meant **2** : a result opposite to what was expected

Ir·o·quois *n, pl* **Ir·o·quois** : a member of any of the peoples of an American Indian confederacy that existed originally in central New York state

ir·ra·di·ate *vb* **ir·ra·di·at·ed; ir·ra·di·at·ing 1** : to cast rays of light on **2** : to treat by exposure to radiation (as X-rays)

ir·ra·di·a·tion *n* : exposure to radiation

ir·ra·tio·nal *adj* **1** : not able to reason **2** : not based on reason — **ir·ra·tio·nal·ly** *adv*

ir·rec·on·cil·able *adj* : impossible to bring into agreement or harmony

ir·re·deem·able *adj* : impossible to save or help

ir·re·fut·able *adj* : impossible to prove wrong : INDISPUTABLE

ir·reg·u·lar *adj* **1** : not following custom or rule **2** : not following the usual manner of inflection **3** : not straight, smooth, or even **4** : not continuous or coming at set times — **ir·reg·u·lar·ly** *adv*

ir·reg·u·lar·i·ty *n, pl* **ir·reg·u·lar·i·ties 1** : the quality or state of being unusual, uneven, or happening at different times **2** : something that is unusual, uneven, or happening at different times

ir·rel·e·vance *n* : the quality or state of having no relation or importance to what is being considered

ir·rel·e·vant *adj* : having no importance or relation to what is being considered

ir·rep·a·ra·ble *adj* : impossible to get back or to make right — **ir·rep·a·ra·bly** *adv*

ir·re·place·able *adj* : too valuable or too rare to be replaced

ir·re·press·ible *adj* : impossible to repress or control

ir·re·proach·able *adj* : not deserving of criticism : without fault

ir·re·sist·ible *adj* : impossible to resist — **ir·re·sist·ibly** *adv*

ir·res·o·lute *adj* : uncertain how to act or proceed — **ir·res·o·lute·ly** *adv*

ir·re·spec·tive of *prep* : without regard to

ir·re·spon·si·bil·i·ty *n* : the quality or state of not being responsible

ir·re·spon·si·ble *adj* : having or showing little or no sense of responsibility — **ir·re·spon·si·bly** *adv*

ir·re·triev·able *adj* : impossible to get back — **ir·re·triev·ably** *adv*

ir·rev·er·ence *n* : lack of respect

ir·rev·er·ent *adj* : not respectful — **ir·rev·er·ent·ly** *adv*

ir·re·vers·i·ble *adj* : impossible to change back to a previous condition : impossible to reverse

ir·rev·o·ca·ble *adj* : impossible to take away or undo — **ir·rev·o·ca·bly** *adv*

ir·ri·gate *vb* **ir·ri·gat·ed; ir·ri·gat·ing 1** : to supply (as land) with water by artificial means **2** : to clean with a flow of liquid

ir·ri·ga·tion *n* : an act or process of supplying with water or cleaning with a flow of liquid

ir·ri·ta·bil·i·ty *n* : the quality of easily becoming angry or annoyed

ir·ri·ta·ble *adj* : easily made angry or annoyed — **ir·ri·ta·bly** *adv*

ir·ri·tant *n* **1** : something that is annoying **2** : something that causes soreness or sensitivity

ir·ri·tate *vb* **ir·ri·tat·ed; ir·ri·tat·ing 1** : ANNOY **2** : to make sensitive or sore

ir·ri·ta·tion *n* **1** : the act of making annoyed or sore and sensitive : the state of being annoyed or sore and sensitive **2** : IRRITANT 1

is *present third person sing of* BE

-ish *adj suffix* **1** : of, relating to, or being **2** : characteristic of **3** : somewhat **4** : about (as an age or a time)

Is·lam *n* : a religion based on belief in Allah as the only God and in Muhammad the prophet of God — **Is·lam·ic** *adj*

is·land *n* **1** : an area of land surrounded by water and smaller than a continent **2** : something like an island in its isolation

is·land·er *n* : a person who lives on an island

isle *n* : a usually small island

is·let *n* : a small island

-ism *n suffix* **1** : act : practice : process **2** : manner of action or behavior like that of a specified person or thing **3** : state : condition **4** : teachings : theory : system

isn't : is not

iso·bar *n* : a line on a map to indicate areas having the same atmospheric pressure

iso·late *vb* **iso·lat·ed; iso·lat·ing** : to place or keep apart from others

iso·la·tion *n* : the act of keeping apart from others : the condition of being kept apart from others

isos·ce·les triangle *n* : a triangle having two sides of equal length

ISP *abbr* Internet service provider

[1]Is·rae·li *adj* : of or relating to the country of Israel or its people

[2]Israeli *n* : a person born or living in the country of Israel

Is·ra·el·ite *n* : a person born or living in the ancient kingdom of Israel

is·su·ance *n* : the act of making something available or distributing something : the act of issuing

[1]is·sue *n* **1** : something that is discussed or disputed **2** : the version of a newspaper or magazine that is published at a particular time **3** : the action of going, coming, or flowing out **4** : OFFSPRING, PROGENY **5** : a giving off (as of blood) from the body **6** : the act of bringing out, offering, or making available

[2]issue *vb* **is·sued; is·su·ing 1** : to go, come, or flow out **2** : to distribute officially **3** : to announce officially **4** : to send out for sale or circulation

-ist *n suffix* **1** : performer of a specified action : maker : producer **2** : a person who plays a specified musical instrument or operates a specified mechanical device **3** : a person who specializes in a specified art or science or skill **4** : a person who follows or favors a specified teaching, practice, system, or code of behavior

isth·mus *n* : a narrow strip of land separating two bodies of water and connecting two larger areas of land

[1]it *pron* **1** : the thing, act, or matter about which these words are spoken or written **2** : the whole situation **3** — used as a subject of a verb that expresses a condition or action without a doer

[2]it *n* : the player who has to do something special in a children's game

ital. *abbr* italic **2** italicized

[1]Ital·ian *n* **1** : a person born or living in Italy **2** : the language of the Italians

²**Ital·ian** *adj* : of or relating to Italy, its people, or the Italian language

¹**ital·ic** *adj* : of or relating to a type style with letters that slant to the right (as in " *italic* letters")

²**italic** *n* : a type style with letters that slant to the right : an italic letter or italic type

ital·i·cize *vb* **ital·i·cized; ital·i·ciz·ing 1** : to print in italics **2** : UNDERLINE 1

¹**itch** *vb* **itched; itch·ing** : to have or produce an unpleasant feeling that causes a desire to scratch

²**itch** *n* **1** : an unpleasant feeling that causes a desire to scratch **2** : a skin disorder in which an itch is present **3** : a restless usually constant desire

itchy *adj* **itch·i·er; itch·i·est** : having, feeling, or causing a desire to scratch

it'd : it had : it would

-ite *n suffix* **1** : native : resident **2** : descendant **3** : adherent : follower

item *n* **1** : a single thing in a list, account, or series **2** : a brief piece of news

item·ize *vb* **item·ized; item·iz·ing** : to set down one by one : LIST

itin·er·ant *adj* : traveling from place to place

-itis *n suffix* : inflammation of

it'll : it shall : it will

its *adj* : relating to or belonging to it or itself

it's 1 : it is **2** : it has

it·self *pron* : that identical one

-ity *n suffix, pl* **-ities** : quality : state : degree

I've : I have

-ive *adj suffix* : that does or tends to do a specified action

ivo·ry *n, pl* **ivo·ries 1** : a hard creamy-white material that forms the tusks of mammals (as an elephant) **2** : a creamy white color

ivy *n, pl* **ivies 1** : a climbing vine with evergreen leaves and black berries often found growing on buildings **2** : a climbing plant that resembles ivy

-i·za·tion *n suffix* : action : process : state

-ize *vb suffix* **-ized; -iz·ing 1** : cause to be or be like : form or cause to be formed into **2** : cause to experience a specified action **3** : saturate, treat, or combine with **4** : treat like **5** : engage in a specified activity

J

j *n, pl* **j's** *or* **js** *often cap* : the tenth letter of the English alphabet

¹**jab** *vb* **jabbed; jab·bing** : to poke quickly or suddenly with or as if with something sharp

²**jab** *n* : a quick or sudden poke

¹**jab·ber** *vb* **jab·bered; jab·ber·ing** : to talk too fast or not clearly enough to be understood

²**jabber** *n* : CHATTER

¹**jack** *n* **1** : a device for lifting something heavy a short distance **2** : a playing card with the picture of a young man **3** : a small six-pointed usually metal object used in a children's game (**jacks**) **4** : a socket used with a plug to connect one electric circuit with another

²**jack** *vb* **jacked; jack·ing** : to move or lift with a special device

jack·al *n* : a wild dog of Africa and Asia like but smaller than a wolf

jack·ass *n* **1** : a donkey and especially a male donkey **2** : a stupid person

jack·daw *n* : a black and gray European bird related to but smaller than a crow

jack·et *n* **1** : a short coat **2** : an outer cover or casing

jack–in–the–box *n, pl* **jack–in–the–box·es** *or* **jacks–in–the–box** : a small box out of which a toy figure springs when the lid is raised

jack–in–the–pul·pit *n, pl* **jack–in–the–pulpits** *or* **jacks–in–the–pul·pit** : a plant that grows in moist shady woods and has a stalk of tiny yellowish flowers protected by a leaf bent over like a hood

¹**jack·knife** *n, pl* **jack·knives** : a knife that has a folding blade or blades and can be put in a pocket

²**jackknife** *vb* **jack·knifed; jack·knif·ing** : to double up like a jackknife

jack–of–all–trades *n, pl* **jacks–of–all–trades** : a person who can do several kinds of work fairly well

jack–o'–lan·tern *n* : a pumpkin with its insides scooped out and cut to look like a human face

jack·pot *n* **1** : a large amount of money to be won **2** : a large and often unexpected success or reward

jack·rab·bit *n* : a large hare of North America that has very long ears and long hind legs

jade *n* : a usually green mineral used for jewelry and carvings

jag·ged *adj* : having a sharply uneven edge or surface

jag·uar *n* : a large yellowish brown black-spotted animal of the cat family found chiefly from Mexico to Argentina

¹**jail** *n* : PRISON

²**jail** *vb* **jailed; jail·ing** : to shut up in or as if in a prison

jail·break *n* : escape from prison by force

jail·er *also* **jail·or** *n* : a person responsible for the operation of a prison

ja·lopy *n, pl* **ja·lop·ies** : a worn old automobile

¹jam *vb* **jammed; jam·ming 1** : to crowd, squeeze, or wedge into a tight position **2** : to put into action hard or suddenly **3** : to hurt by pressure **4** : to be or cause to be stuck or unable to work because a part is wedged tight **5** : to cause interference in (radio or television signals)

²jam *n* : a food made by boiling fruit with sugar until it is thick

³jam *n* **1** : a crowded mass of people or things that blocks something **2** : a difficult situation

jamb *n* : a vertical piece forming the side of an opening (as for a doorway)

jam·bo·ree *n* **1** : a large party or celebration **2** : a national or international camping assembly of Boy Scouts

Jan. *abbr* January

¹jan·gle *vb* **jan·gled; jan·gling** : to make or cause to make a sound like the harsh ringing of a bell

²jangle *n* : a harsh often ringing sound

jan·i·tor *n* : a person who takes care of a building (as a school)

Jan·u·ary *n* : the first month of the year

¹Jap·a·nese *adj* : of or relating to Japan, its people, or the Japanese language

²Japanese *n, pl* **Japanese 1** : a person born or living in Japan **2** : the language of the Japanese

Japanese beetle *n* : a small glossy green or brown Asian beetle now found in the United States that as a grub feeds on roots and as an adult eats leaves and fruits

¹jar *n* **1** : a usually glass or pottery container with a wide mouth **2** : the contents of a jar

²jar *vb* **jarred; jar·ring 1** : to shake or cause to shake hard **2** : to have a disagreeable effect

³jar *n* **1** : ²JOLT 1 **2** : ²SHOCK 1

jar·gon *n* **1** : the special vocabulary of an activity or group **2** : language that is not clear and is full of long words

jas·mine *n* : a usually climbing plant of warm regions with fragrant flowers

jas·per *n* : an opaque usually red, green, brown, or yellow stone used for making decorative objects

jaunt *n* : a short pleasure trip

jaun·ty *adj* **jaun·ti·er; jaun·ti·est** : lively in manner or appearance — **jaun·ti·ly** *adv* — **jaun·ti·ness** *n*

jav·e·lin *n* **1** : a light spear **2** : a slender rod thrown for distance in a track-and-field contest (**javelin throw**)

jaw *n* **1** : either of an upper or lower bony structure that supports the soft parts of the mouth and usually bears teeth on its edge and of which the lower part is movable **2** : a part of an invertebrate animal (as an insect) that resembles or does the work of a human jaw **3** : one of a pair of moving parts that open and close for holding or crushing something

jaw·bone *n* : JAW 1

jay *n* : a usually blue bird related to the crow that has a loud call

jay·walk *vb* **jay·walked; jay·walk·ing** : to cross a street in a place or in a way that is against traffic regulations — **jay·walk·er** *n*

jazz *n* : a type of American music with lively rhythms and melodies that are often made up by musicians as they play

jeal·ous *adj* **1** : feeling anger because of the belief that a loved one might be unfaithful **2** : feeling a mean anger toward someone because he or she is more successful **3** : CAREFUL 1, WATCHFUL — **jeal·ous·ly** *adv*

jeal·ou·sy *n, pl* **jeal·ou·sies 1** : a feeling of unhappiness and anger caused by a belief that a loved one might be unfaithful **2** : a feeling of unhappiness caused by wanting what someone else has

jeans *n pl* : pants made of denim

jeep *n* : a small motor vehicle used by the United States military for travel on rough surfaces

¹jeer *vb* **jeered; jeer·ing 1** : to speak or cry out in scorn **2** : to scorn or mock with taunts

²jeer *n* : a scornful remark or sound : TAUNT

Je·ho·vah *n* : GOD 1

jell *vb* **jelled; jell·ing 1** : to become as firm as jelly : SET **2** : to take shape

jel·lied *adj* : made into or as part of a jelly

jel·ly *n, pl* **jellies** : a soft springy food made from fruit juice boiled with sugar, from meat juices, or from gelatin — **jel·ly·like** *adj*

jelly bean *n* : a chewy bean-shaped candy

jel·ly·fish *n* : a free-swimming sea animal related to the corals that has a nearly transparent jellylike body shaped like a saucer and tentacles with stinging cells

jen·net *n* : a female donkey

jeop·ar·dize *vb* **jeop·ar·dized; jeop·ar·diz·ing** : to put in danger

jeop·ar·dy *n* : DANGER 1

¹jerk *vb* **jerked; jerk·ing 1** : to give a quick sharp pull or twist to **2** : to move in a quick motion

²jerk *n* **1** : a short quick pull or jolt **2** : a foolish person

jer·kin *n* : a short sleeveless jacket

jerky *adj* **jerk·i·er; jerk·i·est** : moving with sudden starts and stops

jer·sey *n, pl* **jerseys 1** : a knitted cloth (as of

cotton) used mostly for making clothing **2** : a shirt made of knitted fabric and especially one worn by a sports team

¹jest *n* **1** : a comic act or remark : JOKE **2** : a playful mood or manner

²jest *vb* **jest·ed; jest·ing** : to make comic remarks : JOKE

jest·er *n* : a person formerly kept in royal courts to amuse people

Je·sus *n* : JESUS CHRIST

Jesus Christ *n* : the founder of the Christian religion

¹jet *n* **1** : a rush of liquid, gas, or vapor through a narrow opening or a nozzle **2** : JET AIRPLANE **3** : a nozzle for a rush of gas or liquid **4** : JET ENGINE

²jet *adj* : of a very dark black color

³jet *n* **1** : a black mineral that is often used for jewelry **2** : a very dark black

⁴jet *vb* **jet·ted; jet·ting** : to come forcefully from a narrow opening

jet airplane *n* : an airplane powered by a jet engine

jet engine *n* : an engine in which fuel burns to produce a rush of heated air and gases that shoot out from the rear and drive the engine forward

jet plane *n* : JET AIRPLANE

jet–pro·pelled *adj* : driven forward or onward by a jet engine

jet·sam *n* : goods thrown overboard to lighten a ship in danger of sinking

jet stream *n* : high-speed winds blowing from a westerly direction several miles above the earth's surface

jet·ti·son *vb* **jet·ti·soned; jet·ti·son·ing** : to throw out especially from a ship or an airplane

jet·ty *n, pl* **jetties** **1** : a pier built to change the path of the current or tide or to protect a harbor **2** : a landing wharf

Jew *n* : a person who is a descendant of the ancient Hebrews or whose religion is Judaism

jew·el *n* **1** : GEM 1 **2** : an ornament of precious metal often set with gemstones and worn on the body **3** : a person who is greatly admired

jew·el·er *or* **jew·el·ler** *n* : a person who makes or buys and sells jewelry and related articles (as silverware)

jew·el·ry *n* : ornamental pieces (as rings or necklaces) worn on the body

Jew·ish *adj* : of or relating to Jews or Judaism

jib *n* : a three-cornered sail extending forward from the foremast

¹jibe *variant of* GIBE

²jibe *vb* **jibed; jib·ing** : to be in agreement

jif·fy *n, pl* **jiffies** : MOMENT 1

¹jig *n* **1** : a lively dance **2** : music for a lively dance **3** : a dishonest act

²jig *vb* **jigged; jig·ging** **1** : to dance a jig **2** : to move with quick sudden motions

jig·gle *vb* **jig·gled; jig·gling** : to move or cause to make a light clinking sound

jig·saw *n* : a machine saw used to cut curved and irregular lines or openwork patterns

jigsaw puzzle *n* : a puzzle of many small pieces of a picture that must be fitted together

jim·my *vb* **jim·mied; jim·my·ing** : to force open with or as if with a short crowbar

jim·son·weed *n* : a poisonous weedy plant with bad-smelling leaves and large white or purple flowers

¹jin·gle *vb* **jin·gled; jin·gling** : to make or cause to make a light clinking sound

²jingle *n* **1** : a light clinking sound **2** : a short catchy verse or song used to help sell a product

¹jinx *n, pl* **jinx·es** : something or someone that brings bad luck

²jinx *vb* **jinxed; jinx·ing** : to bring bad luck to

jit·ters *n pl* : extreme nervousness

jit·tery *adj* **1** : very nervous **2** : showing nervousness

job *n* **1** : work done regularly for pay **2** : a special duty or function **3** : a piece of work usually done on order at an agreed rate **4** : something produced by or as if by work — **job·less** *adj*

jock *n* : ATHLETE

jock·ey *n, pl* **jockeys** **1** : a professional rider in a horse race **2** : OPERATOR 1

¹jog *vb* **jogged; jog·ging** **1** : to go or cause to go at a slow run **2** : to run slowly (as for exercise) **3** : to give a slight shake or push to : NUDGE **4** : to make more alert — **jog·ger** *n*

²jog *n* **1** : a slow run **2** : a slight shake or push **3** : a slow jerky gait (as of a horse)

³jog *n* : a short change in direction

jog·gle *vb* **jog·gled; jog·gling** : to shake or cause to shake slightly

john·ny·cake *n* : a bread made of cornmeal, milk, flour, and eggs

join *vb* **joined; join·ing** **1** : to come into the company of **2** : to take part in a group activity **3** : to come, bring, or fasten together **4** : to become a member of **5** : to come or bring into close association **6** : to combine the elements of **7** : ADJOIN

¹joint *n* **1** : a point where two bones of the skeleton come together usually in a way that allows motion **2** : a place where two things or parts are joined **3** : a part of a plant stem where a leaf or branch develops **4** : a business establishment — **joint·ed** *adj*

²joint *adj* **1** : joined together **2** : done by or shared by two or more — **joint·ly** *adv*

joist *n* : any of the small timbers or metal beams laid crosswise in a building to support a floor or ceiling

¹joke *n* **1** : something said or done to cause laughter or amusement **2** : a very short story with a funny ending that is a surprise **3** : something not worthy of being taken seriously

²joke *vb* **joked; jok·ing 1** : to say or do something to cause laughter or amusement **2** : to make funny remarks

jok·er *n* **1** : a person who says or does things to make others laugh **2** : an extra card used in some card games

jok·ing·ly *adv* : in a manner that is not meant to be taken seriously

jol·li·ty *n* : the state of being happy and cheerful

¹jol·ly *adj* **jol·li·er; jol·li·est** : full of fun or joy

²jolly *adv* : ²VERY 1

¹jolt *vb* **jolt·ed; jolt·ing 1** : to move or cause to move with a sudden jerky motion **2** : to cause to be upset

²jolt *n* **1** : an abrupt jerky and usually powerful blow or movement **2** : a sudden shock or surprise

jon·quil *n* : a plant related to the daffodil but with fragrant yellow or white flowers with a short central tube

josh *vb* **joshed; josh·ing** : to make humorous remarks or tease in a good-natured way

jos·tle *vb* **jos·tled; jos·tling** : to push roughly

¹jot *n* : the least bit

²jot *vb* **jot·ted; jot·ting** : to write briefly or in a hurry

jounce *vb* **jounced; jounc·ing** : to move, fall, or bounce so as to shake

jour·nal *n* **1** : a brief record (as in a diary) of daily happenings **2** : a magazine that reports on things of special interest to a particular group **3** : a daily newspaper

jour·nal·ism *n* **1** : the business of collecting and editing news (as for newspapers, radio, or television) **2** : writing of general or popular interest

jour·nal·ist *n* : an editor or reporter of the news

¹jour·ney *n, pl* **jour·neys** : an act of traveling from one place to another

²journey *vb* **jour·neyed; jour·ney·ing** : to travel to a distant place

jour·ney·man *n, pl* **jour·ney·men** : a worker who has learned a trade and usually works for another person by the day

¹joust *vb* **joust·ed; joust·ing** : to take part in a combat on horseback with a lance

²joust *n* : a combat on horseback between two knights with lances

jo·vial *adj* : ¹JOLLY — **jo·vial·ly** *adv*

¹jowl *n* : loose flesh hanging from the lower jaw, cheeks, and throat

²jowl *n* **1** : an animal's jaw and especially the lower jaw **2** : CHEEK 1

joy *n* **1** : a feeling of pleasure or happiness that comes from success, good fortune, or a sense of well-being **2** : something that gives pleasure or happiness

joy·ful *adj* : feeling, causing, or showing pleasure or happiness — **joy·ful·ly** *adv* — **joy·ful·ness** *n*

joy·ous *adj* : JOYFUL — **joy·ous·ly** *adv* — **joy·ous·ness** *n*

joy·stick *n* : a control lever (as for a computer display or an airplane) capable of motion in two or more directions

Jr. *abbr* junior

ju·bi·lant *adj* : expressing great joy especially with shouting : noisily happy

ju·bi·la·tion *n* : the act of rejoicing : the state of being noisily happy

ju·bi·lee *n* **1** : a 50th anniversary **2** : a time of celebration

Ju·da·ism *n* : a religion developed among the ancient Hebrews that stresses belief in one God and faithfulness to the laws of the Torah

¹judge *vb* **judged; judg·ing 1** : to form an opinion after careful consideration **2** : to act with authority to reach a decision (as in a trial) **3** : THINK 1 **4** : to form an opinion of in comparison with others

²judge *n* **1** : a public official whose duty is to decide questions brought before a court **2** : a person appointed to decide in a contest or competition **3** : a person with the experience to give a meaningful opinion : CRITIC

judg·ment *or* **judge·ment** *n* **1** : a decision or opinion (as of a court) given after careful consideration **2** : an opinion or estimate formed by examining and comparing **3** : the ability for reaching a decision after careful consideration

ju·di·cial *adj* **1** : of courts or judges **2** : ordered or done by a court — **ju·di·cial·ly** *adv*

ju·di·cious *adj* : having, using, or showing good judgment : WISE — **ju·di·cious·ly** *adv*

ju·do *n* : a sport developed in Japan in which opponents try to throw or pin each other to the ground

jug *n* : a large deep usually earthenware or glass container with a narrow mouth and a handle

jug·gle *vb* **jug·gled; jug·gling 1** : to keep several things moving in the air at the same time **2** : to work or do (several things) at the same time — **jug·gler** *n*

juice *n* **1** : the liquid part that can be squeezed out of vegetables and fruit **2** : the liquid part of meat

juicy *adj* **juic·i·er; juic·i·est** : having much liquid — **juic·i·ness** *n*

Ju·ly *n* : the seventh month of the year

¹jum·ble *n* : a disorderly mass or pile

²jumble *vb* **jum·bled; jum·bling** : to mix in a confused mass

jum·bo *adj* : very large

¹jump *vb* **jumped; jump·ing** **1** : to spring into the air : LEAP **2** : to pass over or cause to pass over with or as if with a leap **3** : to make a sudden movement **4** : to make a sudden attack **5** : to have or cause a sudden sharp increase **6** : to make a hasty judgment — **jump the gun** **1** : to start in a race before the starting signal **2** : to do something before the proper time

²jump *n* **1** : an act or instance of leaping **2** : a sudden involuntary movement : START **3** : a sharp sudden increase **4** : an initial advantage

jum·per *n* **1** : someone or something that jumps **2** : a sleeveless dress worn usually with a blouse

jumping jack *n* : an exercise in which a person who is standing jumps to a position with legs and arms spread out and then jumps back to the original position

jump·suit *n* : a one-piece garment consisting of a shirt with attached pants or shorts

jumpy *adj* **jump·i·er; jump·i·est** : NERVOUS 2

jun *abbr* junior

jun·co *n*, *pl* **juncos** *or* **juncoes** : a small mostly gray North American bird usually having a pink bill

junc·tion *n* **1** : a place or point where two or more things meet **2** : an act of joining

junc·ture *n* : an important or particular point or stage in a process or activity

June *n* : the sixth month of the year

jun·gle *n* **1** : a thick or tangled growth of tropical plants **2** : a large area of land usually in a tropical region covered with a thick tangled growth of plants

jungle gym *n* : a structure of bars for children to climb on

¹ju·nior *adj* **1** : being younger — used to distinguish a son from a father with the same name **2** : lower in rank **3** : of or relating to students in the next-to-last year at a high school, college, or university

²junior *n* **1** : a person who is younger or lower in rank than another **2** : a student in the next-to-last year at a high school, college, or university

junior high school *n* : a school usually including seventh, eighth, and ninth grades

ju·ni·per *n* : an evergreen tree or shrub related to the pines but having tiny cones resembling berries

¹junk *n* **1** : things that have been thrown away or are of little value or use **2** : a poorly made product **3** : something of little meaning, worth, or significance

²junk *vb* **junked; junk·ing** : to get rid of as worthless : SCRAP

³junk *n* : an Asian sailing boat that is high in the front

junk food *n* : food that is high in calories but low in nutritional content

junky *adj* **junk·i·er; junk·i·est** : of poor quality

Ju·pi·ter *n* : the planet that is fifth in order of distance from the sun and is the largest of the planets with a diameter of about 89,000 miles (140,000 kilometers)

ju·ror *n* : a member of a jury

ju·ry *n*, *pl* **juries** **1** : a group of citizens chosen to hear and decide the facts of a case in a court of law **2** : a committee that judges and awards prizes (as at an exhibition)

¹just *adj* **1** : being what is deserved **2** : having a foundation in fact or reason : REASONABLE **3** : agreeing with a standard of correctness **4** : morally right or good — **just·ly** *adv*

²just *adv* **1** : to an exact degree or in an exact manner **2** : very recently **3** : by a very small amount : with nothing to spare **4** : by a very short distance **5** : nothing other than **6** : ²VERY 2

jus·tice *n* **1** : fair treatment **2** : ²JUDGE 1 **3** : the process or result of using laws to fairly judge people accused of crimes **4** : the quality of being fair or just

jus·ti·fi·ca·tion *n* **1** : the act or an instance of proving to be just, right, or reasonable **2** : sufficient reason to show that an action is correct or acceptable

jus·ti·fy *vb* **jus·ti·fied; jus·ti·fy·ing** : to prove or show to be just, right, or reasonable — **jus·ti·fi·able** *adj* — **jus·ti·fi·ably** *adv*

jut *vb* **jut·ted; jut·ting** : to extend or cause to extend above or beyond a surrounding area

jute *n* : a strong glossy fiber from a tropical plant used chiefly for making sacks and twine

¹ju·ve·nile *adj* **1** : not fully grown or developed **2** : of or designed for young people **3** : having or showing a lack of emotional maturity

²juvenile *n* : a young person : YOUTH

K

k *n, pl* **k's** *or* **ks** *often cap* **1** : the eleventh letter of the English alphabet **2** : THOUSAND **3** : KILOBYTE

kale *n* : a hardy cabbage with wrinkled leaves that do not form a head

ka·lei·do·scope *n* **1** : a tube that contains bits of colored glass or plastic and two mirrors at one end and that shows many different patterns as it is turned **2** : a changing pattern or scene

Kan. *abbr* Kansas

kan·ga·roo *n, pl* **kan·ga·roos** : a leaping mammal of Australia and nearby islands that feeds on plants and has long powerful hind legs, a thick tail used as a support in standing or walking, and in the female a pouch on the abdomen in which the young are carried

Kans. *abbr* Kansas

ka·o·lin *n* : a very pure white clay used in making porcelain

kar·a·o·ke *n* : a form of entertainment in which a device plays music to which a person sings along

kar·at *n* : a unit of fineness for gold

ka·ra·te *n* : an art of self-defense developed in Japan in which an attacker is defeated by kicks and punches

ka·ty·did *n* : a large green American grasshopper with males that make shrill noises

kay·ak *n* : a small boat that is pointed at both ends, holds one or two people, and is moved by a paddle with two blades

ka·zoo *n, pl* **ka·zoos** : a toy musical instrument which produces a buzzing tone when a person hums into the mouth hole

KB *abbr* kilobyte

keel *n* : a long heavy piece of wood or metal that runs along and usually sticks out from the center of the bottom of a ship

keel over *vb* **keeled over; keel·ing over** : to fall suddenly (as in a faint)

keen *adj* **1** : having a fine edge or point : SHARP **2** : having or showing mental sharpness **3** : very sensitive (as in seeing, smelling, or hearing) **4** : full of enthusiasm : EAGER **5** : seeming to cut or sting — **keen·ly** *adv* — **keen·ness** *n*

¹keep *vb* **kept; keep·ing** **1** : to remain or cause to remain in a given place, situation, or condition **2** : to put in a specified place for storage **3** : PROTECT **4** : to continue doing something **5** : to continue to have in possession or power **6** : to prevent from leaving : DETAIN **7** : to hold back **8** : to be faithful to : FULFILL **9** : to act properly in re-

lation to **10** : to take care of : TEND **11** : to have available for service or at one's disposal **12** : to preserve a record in **13** : to continue in an unspoiled condition **14** : ¹REFRAIN — **keep an eye on** : ¹WATCH 3

keep up **1** : to continue without interruption **2** : to stay even with others (as in a race) **3** : to stay well informed about something **4** : MAINTAIN 2

²keep *n* **1** : the strongest part of a castle in the Middle Ages **2** : the necessities of life — **for keeps** **1** : with the understanding that a person or group may keep what is won **2** : for a long time : PERMANENTLY

keep·er *n* : a person who watches, guards, or takes care of something

keep·ing *n* **1** : watchful attention : CARE **2** : a proper or fitting relationship : HARMONY

keep·sake *n* : something kept or given to be kept in memory of a person, place, or happening

keg *n* **1** : a small barrel holding 30 gallons (about 114 liters) **2** : the contents of a keg

kelp *n* : a large brown seaweed

ken·nel *n* **1** : a shelter for a dog **2** : a place where dogs or cats are bred or housed

kept *past and past participle of* KEEP

ker·chief *n, pl* **kerchiefs** : a square of cloth worn as a head covering or as a scarf

ker·nel *n* **1** : the inner softer part of a seed, fruit stone, or nut **2** : the whole grain or seed of a cereal plant **3** : a very small amount

ker·o·sene *n* : a thin oil obtained from petroleum and used as a fuel and solvent

ketch *n* : a fore-and-aft rigged ship with two masts

ketch·up *also* **cat·sup** *n* : a thick seasoned sauce made from tomatoes

ket·tle *n* **1** : a pot for boiling liquids **2** : TEAKETTLE

ket·tle·drum *n* : a large brass or copper drum that has a rounded bottom and can be varied in pitch

¹key *n* **1** : an instrument by which the bolt of a lock (as on a door) is turned or by which an engine is started **2** : a device having the form or function of a key **3** : the thing that is necessary or most important in doing something **4** : something (as a map legend) that gives an explanation : SOLUTION **5** : one of the levers with a flat surface that is pressed with a finger to activate a mechanism of a machine or instrument **6** : a system of seven musical tones arranged in relation to a keynote from which the system is named

²key *vb* **keyed; key·ing 1 :** to regulate the musical pitch of **2 :** to bring into harmony **3 :** to record or enter by operating the keys of a machine

³key *adj* **:** of great importance **:** most important

⁴key *n* **:** a low island or reef

key·board *n* **1 :** a row of keys by which a musical instrument (as a piano) is played **2 :** a portable electronic musical instrument with a row of keys like that of a piano **3 :** the whole arrangement of keys (as on a computer or typewriter)

key·hole *n* **:** a hole for receiving a key

key·note *n* **1 :** the first tone of a scale fundamental to harmony **2 :** the fundamental fact, idea, or mood

key·stone *n* **1 :** the wedge-shaped piece at the top of an arch that locks the other pieces in place **2 :** something on which other things depend for support

kg *abbr* kilogram

kha·ki *n* **1 :** a light yellowish brown cloth used especially for military uniforms **2 kha·kis** *pl* **:** a pair of pants made of khaki **3 :** a light yellowish brown

¹kick *vb* **kicked; kick·ing 1 :** to hit with the foot **2 :** to move the legs forcefully **3 :** to put an end to — **kick·er** *n* — **kick off 1 :** to start play in a game (as in football or soccer) by kicking the ball **2 :** BEGIN 1

²kick *n* **1 :** a blow with the foot **2 :** the act of hitting a ball with the foot **3 :** a feeling or source of pleasure **4 :** a usually sudden strong interest

kick·ball *n* **:** a game similar to baseball played with a large rubber ball that is kicked instead of hit with a bat

kick·off *n* **:** a kick that puts the ball into play (as in football or soccer)

kick·stand *n* **:** a metal bar or rod attached to a two-wheeled vehicle (as a bicycle) that is used to prop the vehicle up when it is not in use

¹kid *n* **1 :** CHILD **2 :** a young goat or a related animal **3 :** the flesh, fur, or skin of a young goat or related animal or something (as leather) made from one of these

²kid *vb* **kid·ded; kid·ding 1 :** to deceive or trick as a joke **2 :** ¹TEASE — **kid·der** *n*

kid·nap *vb* **kid·napped; kid·nap·ping :** to carry away a person by force or by fraud and against his or her will — **kid·nap·per** *n*

kid·ney *n, pl* **kid·neys :** either of a pair of organs near the backbone that give off waste from the body in the form of urine and in humans are bean-shaped

kidney bean *n* **:** the large usually dark red edible seed of a bean plant

¹kill *vb* **killed; kill·ing 1 :** to end the life of **:** SLAY **2 :** to put an end to **3 :** to use up **4 :** ¹DEFEAT **2 5 :** to cause to become very tired

²kill *n* **1 :** an act of taking the life of a person or animal **2 :** an animal whose life has been taken

kill·deer *n* **:** a grayish brown North American bird that has a high-pitched mournful call

¹kill·er *n* **:** someone or something that takes the life of a person or animal

²killer *adj* **1 :** very impressive or effective **2 :** very difficult **3 :** causing death or ruin

killer whale *n* **:** a toothed whale that is mostly black above and white below and feeds especially on fish, squid, birds, and sea mammals (as seals)

kill·joy *n* **:** a person who spoils the pleasure of others

kiln *n* **:** a furnace or oven in which something (as pottery) is hardened, burned, or dried

ki·lo *n, pl* **kilos :** KILOGRAM

kilo- *prefix* **:** thousand

ki·lo·byte *n* **:** a unit of computer information storage equal to 1024 bytes

ki·lo·gram *n* **:** a metric unit of weight equal to 1000 grams

ki·lo·me·ter *n* **:** a metric unit of length equal to 1000 meters

kilo·watt *n* **:** a unit of electrical power equal to 1000 watts

kilt *n* **:** a knee-length pleated skirt usually of tartan worn by men in Scotland

kil·ter *n* **:** proper condition

ki·mo·no *n, pl* **ki·mo·nos 1 :** a loose robe with wide sleeves that is traditionally worn with a broad sash as an outer garment by a Japanese person **2 :** a loose dressing gown worn chiefly by women

kin *n* **1 :** a person's relatives **2 :** KINSMAN

-kin *also* **-kins** *n suffix* **:** little

¹kind *n* **:** a group of persons or things that belong together or have something in common

²kind *adj* **kind·er; kind·est 1 :** wanting or liking to do good and to bring happiness to others **:** CONSIDERATE **2 :** showing or growing out of gentleness or goodness of heart

kin·der·gar·ten *n* **:** a school or a class for very young children — **kin·der·gart·ner** *n*

kind·heart·ed *adj* **:** having or showing a kind and sympathetic nature

kin·dle *vb* **kin·dled; kin·dling 1 :** to set on fire **:** LIGHT **2 :** to stir up **:** EXCITE

kin·dling *n* **:** material that burns easily and is used for starting a fire

¹kind·ly *adj* **kind·li·er; kind·li·est 1 :** ²KIND 1 **2 :** pleasant or wholesome in nature — **kind·li·ness** *n*

²kind·ly *adv* **1** : in a sympathetic manner **2** : in a willing manner **3** : in an appreciative manner **4** : in an obliging manner

kind·ness *n* **1** : the quality or state of being gentle and considerate **2** : a kind deed : FAVOR

kind of *adv* : to a moderate degree : SOMEWHAT

¹kin·dred *adj* : alike in nature or character

²kindred *n* **1** : a group of related individuals **2** : a person's relatives

ki·net·ic *adj* : relating to the motions of objects and the forces associated with them

kin·folk *n* : ²KINDRED 2

king *n* **1** : a male ruler of a country who usually inherits his position and rules for life **2** : a person or thing that is better or more important than all others **3** : the chief piece in the game of chess **4** : a playing card bearing the picture of a king **5** : a piece in checkers that has reached the opponent's back row

king·dom *n* **1** : a country whose ruler is a king or queen **2** : one of the three basic divisions (**animal kingdom, plant kingdom, mineral kingdom**) into which natural objects are commonly grouped **3** : a group of related living things (as plants, animals, or bacteria) that ranks above the phylum and division in scientific classification and is the highest and broadest group

king·fish·er *n* : a crested bird with a short tail, long sharp bill, and bright feathers

king·let *n* : a small active bird especially of wooded areas

king·ly *adj* **1** : suited to a king **2** : of a king

king–size *or* **king–sized** *adj* : unusually large

kink *n* **1** : a short tight twist or curl (as in a thread or hose) **2** : ¹CRAMP 1 **3** : an imperfection that makes something hard to use or work — **kinky** *adj*

-kins — see -KIN

kin·ship *n* : the quality or state of being related

kins·man *n, pl* **kins·men** : a relative usually by birth

kins·wom·an *n, pl* **kins·wom·en** : a woman who is a relative usually by birth

¹kiss *vb* **kissed; kiss·ing 1** : to touch with the lips as a mark of love or greeting **2** : to touch gently or lightly

²kiss *n* **1** : a loving touch with the lips **2** : a gentle touch or contact

kiss·er *n* **1** : a person who kisses **2** : a person's face

¹kit *n* **1** : a set of articles for personal use **2** : a set of tools or supplies **3** : a set of parts to be put together

²kit *n* : a young fur-bearing animal

kitch·en *n* : a room in which food is prepared and cooking is done

kitch·en·ette *n* : a small kitchen

kitchen garden *n* : a piece of land where vegetables are grown for household use

kite *n* **1** : a toy that consists of a light covered frame for flying in the air at the end of a long string **2** : a small hawk with long narrow wings and deeply forked tail that feeds mostly on insects and small reptiles

kith *n* : familiar friends and neighbors or relatives

kit·ten *n* : a young cat — **kit·ten·ish** *adj*

kit·ty *n, pl* **kitties** : CAT 1, KITTEN

ki·wi *n* **1** : a grayish-brown bird of New Zealand that is unable to fly **2** : KIWIFRUIT

ki·wi·fruit *n* : the fruit of a Chinese vine having a fuzzy brown skin and slightly tart green flesh

klutz *n* : a clumsy person

km *abbr* kilometer

knack *n* **1** : a natural ability : TALENT **2** : a clever or skillful way of doing something : TRICK

knap·sack *n* : a bag for carrying things on the shoulders or back

knave *n* **1** : RASCAL 2 **2** : ¹JACK 2

knead *vb* **knead·ed; knead·ing 1** : to work and press into a mass with or as if with the hands **2** : ²MASSAGE — **knead·er** *n*

knee *n* **1** : the joint or region in which the thigh and lower leg come together **2** : the part of a garment covering the knee **3** : ¹LAP

knee·cap *n* : a thick flat movable bone forming the front part of the knee

kneel *vb* **knelt** *or* **kneeled; kneel·ing** : to bend the knee : support the body on the knees

knell *n* **1** : a stroke or sound of a bell especially when rung slowly for a death, funeral, or disaster **2** : an indication of the end or failure of something

knew *past of* KNOW

knick·ers *n pl* : loose-fitting short pants gathered at the knee

knick·knack *n* : a small ornamental object

¹knife *n, pl* **knives 1** : a cutting instrument consisting of a sharp blade fastened to a handle **2** : a cutting blade in a machine

²knife *vb* **knifes; knifed; knif·ing** : to stab, slash, or wound with a knife

¹knight *n* **1** : a warrior of the Middle Ages who fought on horseback, served a king, held a special military rank, and swore to behave in a noble way **2** : a man honored for merit by a king or queen of England and ranking below a baronet **3** : one of the pieces in the game of chess — **knight·ly** *adj*

²knight *vb* **knight·ed; knight·ing** : to honor a

man for merit by granting him the title of knight

knight·hood *n* : the rank, dignity, or profession of a knight

knit *vb* **knit** *or* **knit·ted; knit·ting 1** : to form a fabric or garment by interlacing yarn or thread in connected loops with needles (**knitting needles**) **2** : ²WRINKLE **3** : to draw or come together closely as if knitted : unite firmly — **knit·ter** *n*

knob *n* **1** : a small rounded handle **2** : a rounded switch on an electronic device **3** : a rounded lump **4** : a rounded hill

knob·by *adj* **knob·bi·er; knob·bi·est 1** : covered with small rounded lumps **2** : forming rounded lumps

¹knock *vb* **knocked; knock·ing 1** : to strike in order to get someone's attention **2** : to bump against something without intending to **3** : to make a pounding noise **4** : to find fault with **5** : to hit forcefully — **knock down 1** : to strike to the ground with or as if with a sharp blow **2** : to take apart — **knock off** : to stop doing something — **knock over** : to cause to fall

²knock *n* **1** : a pounding noise **2** : a sharp blow **3** : a difficult or painful experience

knock·er *n* : a device made like a hinge and fastened to a door for use in knocking

knock–kneed *adj* : having the legs curved inward at the knees

knoll *n* : a small round hill

¹knot *n* **1** : a section of rope or string that has been tied together to form a lump or knob or to keep something secure **2** : ²TANGLE 1 **3** : a painful or uncomfortable area in a body part **4** : a cluster of persons or things **5** : the inner end of a woody branch enclosed in a plant stem or a section of this in sawed lumber **6** : one nautical mile per hour (about two kilometers per hour)

²knot *vb* **knot·ted; knot·ting 1** : to tie together in a way that cannot be easily untied **2** : to become tense or tight

knot·hole *n* : a hole in wood where a knot has come out

knot·ty *adj* **knot·ti·er; knot·ti·est 1** : full of lumps, knobs, tangles, or hard spots **2** : DIFFICULT 3

know *vb* **knew; known; know·ing 1** : to recognize the identity of **2** : to be aware of the truth of **3** : to have a practical understanding of **4** : to have information or knowledge **5** : to be or become aware **6** : to be acquainted or familiar with **7** : to have understanding of **8** : to recognize the nature of

know–how *n* : knowledge of how to get things done

know·ing *adj* **1** : having or showing special

knowledge, information, or intelligence **2** : shrewdly and keenly alert — **know·ing·ly** *adv*

know–it–all *n* : a person who always claims to know everything

knowl·edge *n* **1** : understanding and skill gained by experience **2** : the state of being aware of something or of having information **3** : range of information or awareness **4** : something learned and kept in the mind : LEARNING

knowl·edge·able *adj* : having or showing understanding and skill gained through experience or education

known *adj* : generally recognized

knuck·le *n* : the rounded lump formed by the ends of two bones (as of a finger) where they come together in a joint

ko·ala *n* : a tailless Australian animal with thick fur and big hairy ears, sharp claws for climbing, and a pouch like the kangaroo's for carrying its young

kohl·ra·bi *n* : a cabbage that does not form a head but has a fleshy roundish edible stem

Ko·mo·do dragon *n* : a lizard of Indonesia that is the largest of all known lizards and may grow to be 10 feet (3 meters) long

kook *n* : a person who acts in a strange or insane way — **kooky** *adj*

kook·a·bur·ra *n* : an Australian bird that has a call resembling loud laughter

Ko·ran *n* : a book of sacred writings accepted by Muslims as revealed to Muhammad by Allah

¹Ko·re·an *n* **1** : a person born or living in North Korea or South Korea **2** : the language of the Koreans

²Korean *adj* : of or relating to North Korea or South Korea, the Korean people, or their language

ko·sher *adj* **1** : accepted by Jewish law as fit for use **2** : selling or serving food that is accepted as fit for use according to Jewish law

krill *n* : tiny floating sea animals that resemble shrimp and are a chief food source of some whales

KS *abbr* Kansas

kud·zu *n* : a fast-growing Asian vine that is grown for hay and to control erosion and is often a serious weed in the southeastern United States

kum·quat *n* : a small citrus fruit that has a sweet rind and sour pulp and is used mostly in preserves

kung fu *n* : an art of self-defense without weapons that was developed in China

Kwan·zaa *n* : an African-American cultural festival held from December 26 to January 1

Ky., KY *abbr* Kentucky

L

l *n, pl* **l's** *or* **ls** *often cap* **1** : the twelfth letter of the English alphabet **2** : 50 in Roman numerals

L *abbr* **1** large **2** left **3** liter

la *n* : the sixth note of the musical scale

La., LA *abbr* Louisiana

lab *n* : LABORATORY

¹la·bel *n* **1** : a slip (as of paper or cloth) attached to something to identify or describe it **2** : a word or phrase that describes or names something or someone

²label *vb* **la·beled** *or* **la·belled; la·bel·ing** *or* **la·bel·ling** **1** : to put a word or words on (something) to identify or describe it **2** : to name or describe with or as if with a label

¹la·bor *n* **1** : usually hard physical or mental effort **2** : something that has to be done : TASK **3** : work for which someone is paid **4** : workers considered as a group **5** : the process by which or time during which a woman gives birth

²labor *vb* **la·bored; la·bor·ing** **1** : to work hard : TOIL **2** : to move slowly and with great effort

lab·o·ra·to·ry *n, pl* **lab·o·ra·to·ries** : a room or building in which scientific experiments and tests are done

Labor Day *n* : the first Monday in September observed as a legal holiday in honor of working people

la·bored *adj* : produced or done with effort or difficulty

la·bor·er *n* : a person who does physical work for pay

la·bo·ri·ous *adj* : requiring much effort — **la·bo·ri·ous·ly** *adv*

labor union *n* : an organization of workers formed to help them get better pay and working conditions

la·bour *chiefly British variant of* LABOR

lab·y·rinth *n* : a place that has many confusing paths and passages

¹lace *vb* **laced; lac·ing** : to fasten or join with or as if with a cord or string

²lace *n* **1** : a cord or string for pulling and holding together opposite edges (as of a shoe) **2** : a very delicate fabric made with patterns of holes

lac·er·ate *vb* **lac·er·at·ed; lac·er·at·ing** : to injure by cutting or tearing deeply or roughly

lac·er·a·tion *n* : a deep or jagged cut or tear of the flesh

¹lack *vb* **lacked; lack·ing** **1** : to be missing **2** : to need or be without something

²lack *n* : the fact or state of not having any or enough of something

¹lac·quer *n* : a material like varnish that dries quickly into a shiny layer (as on wood or metal)

²lacquer *vb* **lac·quered; lac·quer·ing** : to coat with lacquer

la·crosse *n* : a game played on a field using a long-handled stick with a shallow net for catching, throwing, and carrying the ball

lac·tose *n* : a sugar that is found in milk

lacy *adj* **lac·i·er; lac·i·est** : resembling or made of lace

lad *n* : BOY 1, YOUTH

lad·der *n* : a device used for climbing usually consisting of two long pieces of wood, rope, or metal joined at short distances by horizontal pieces on which a person may step

lad·die *n* : a young boy

lad·en *adj* : heavily loaded

¹la·dle *n* : a large and deep spoon with a long handle that is used especially for serving liquids

²ladle *vb* **la·dled; la·dling** : to take up and carry in a ladle

la·dy *n, pl* **la·dies** **1** : a woman of high social position **2** : a woman or girl who behaves in a polite way **3** : WOMAN 1 **4** : WIFE **5** : a British noblewoman — used as a title

la·dy·bird *n* : LADYBUG

la·dy·bug *n* : a small rounded beetle that is often brightly colored and spotted and feeds mostly on other insects (as aphids)

la·dy·like *adj* : suitable to a woman or girl who behaves in a polite way

la·dy·ship *n* : the rank of a lady — used as a title

lady's slipper *or* **lady slipper** *n* : a North American wild orchid with flowers resembling a slipper

¹lag *n* : a space of time between two events

²lag *vb* **lagged; lag·ging** : to move or advance slowly or more slowly than others

¹lag·gard *adj* : slow to act, move, or respond

²laggard *n* : a person who does not go or move as quickly as others

la·goon *n* : a shallow channel or pond near or connected to a larger body of water

laid *past and past participle of* LAY

lain *past participle of* LIE

lair *n* : the den or resting place of a wild animal

lake *n* : a large inland body of standing water

¹lamb *n* **1** : a young sheep usually less than one year old **2** : the meat of a lamb used as food

²lamb *vb* **lambed; lamb·ing** : to give birth to a lamb

lamb·kin *n* : a young lamb

¹lame *adj* **lam·er; lam·est** **1** : not able to get around without pain or difficulty **2** : injured or sore so that walking or movement is painful or difficult **3** : not very convincing or effective — **lame·ly** *adv* — **lame·ness** *n*

²lame *vb* **lamed; lam·ing** : to make or become unable to get around without pain and difficulty

¹la·ment *vb* **la·ment·ed; la·ment·ing** **1** : to mourn aloud : WAIL **2** : to express great sorrow or regret for

²lament *n* **1** : a crying out in great sorrow **2** : a sad song or poem

la·men·ta·ble *adj* : REGRETTABLE

lam·en·ta·tion *n* **1** : great sorrow **2** : an expression of great sorrow

lam·i·nat·ed *adj* : made of thin layers of material firmly joined together

lamp *n* : a device for producing light

lam·prey *n, pl* **lampreys** : a water animal that looks like an eel but has a sucking mouth with no jaws

¹lance *n* : a weapon with a long handle and a sharp steel head used by knights on horseback

²lance *vb* **lanced; lanc·ing** : to cut open with a small sharp instrument

lance corporal *n* : an enlisted person in the marine corps ranking above a private first class

¹land *n* **1** : the solid part of the surface of the earth **2** : an area of ground or soil of a particular kind **3** : a part of the earth's surface marked off by boundaries **4** : a country or nation **5** : the people of a country — **land·less** *adj*

²land *vb* **land·ed; land·ing** **1** : to go ashore or cause to go ashore from a ship **2** : to come down or bring down and settle on a surface **3** : to hit or come to a surface **4** : to be or cause to be in a particular place or condition **5** : to catch and bring in **6** : to succeed in getting

land·fill *n* **1** : a system of garbage and trash disposal in which waste is buried between layers of earth **2** : an area built up by such a landfill

land·hold·er *n* : LANDOWNER

land·ing *n* **1** : the act of returning to a surface after a flight or voyage **2** : a place for unloading or taking on passengers and cargo **3** : a level area at the top of a flight of stairs or between two flights of stairs

landing field *n* : a field where aircraft land and take off

landing strip *n* : AIRSTRIP

land·la·dy *n, pl* **land·la·dies** **1** : a woman who owns land or houses that she rents **2** : a woman who runs an inn or rooming house

land·locked *adj* **1** : shut in or nearly shut in by land **2** : kept from leaving fresh water by some barrier

land·lord *n* **1** : a person who owns land or houses and rents them to other people **2** : a person who runs an inn or rooming house

land·lub·ber *n* : a person who lives on land and knows little or nothing about the sea

land·mark *n* **1** : something (as a building, a large tree, or a statue) that is easy to see and can help a person find the way to a place near it **2** : a building of historical importance **3** : a very important event or achievement

land·mass *n* : a very large area of land

land mine *n* : a mine placed just below the surface of the ground and designed to be exploded by the weight of vehicles or troops passing over it

land·own·er *n* : a person who owns land

¹land·scape *n* **1** : a picture of natural scenery **2** : the land that can be seen in one glance

²landscape *vb* **land·scaped; land·scap·ing** : to improve the natural beauty of a piece of land

land·slide *n* **1** : the sudden and rapid downward movement of a mass of rocks or earth on a steep slope **2** : the material that moves in a landslide **3** : the winning of an election by a very large number of votes

lane *n* **1** : a narrow path or road (usually between fences, hedges, or buildings) **2** : a special route (as for ships) **3** : a strip of road used for a single line of traffic **4** : a long narrow wooden floor used for bowling **5** : a narrow course of a track or swimming pool in which a competitor must stay during a race

lan·guage *n* **1** : the words and expressions used and understood by a large group of people **2** : spoken or written words of a particular kind **3** : a means of expressing ideas or feelings **4** : a formal system of signs and symbols that is used to carry information **5** : the special words used by a certain group or in a certain field **6** : the study of languages

lan·guid *adj* **1** : having very little strength, energy, or spirit **2** : having a slow and relaxed quality — **lan·guid·ly** *adv*

lan·guish *vb* **lan·guished; lan·guish·ing** **1** : to be or become weak, dull, or listless **2** : to continue for a long time without activity or progress in an unpleasant or unwanted situation

lank *adj* **lank·er; lank·est** **1** : not well filled out : THIN **2** : hanging straight and limp in an unattractive way

lanky *adj* **lank·i·er; lank·i·est** : very tall and thin

lan·tern *n* : a usually portable lamp with a protective covering

lan·yard *n* **1** : a short rope or cord used as a fastening on ships **2** : a cord worn around the neck to hold something (as a knife or whistle) **3** : a strong cord with a hook at one end used in firing a cannon

¹lap *n* : the front part of a person between the hips and the knees when seated

²lap *vb* **lapped; lap·ping** : OVERLAP

³lap *n* **1** : a part of something that overlaps another part **2** : one time around or over a course (as of a racetrack or swimming pool) **3** : a stage in a trip

⁴lap *vb* **lapped; lap·ping** **1** : to scoop up food or drink with the tongue **2** : to splash gently

lap·dog *n* : a dog small enough to be held in a person's lap

la·pel *n* : the fold of the front of a coat or jacket below the collar

¹lapse *n* **1** : a slight error usually caused by lack of attention or forgetfulness **2** : a change that results in a worse condition **3** : a passage of time

²lapse *vb* **lapsed; laps·ing** **1** : to slip, pass, or fall gradually **2** : to come to an end : CEASE

lap·top *n* : a small portable computer that can run on battery power and has the main parts (as keyboard and display screen) combined into a single unit

lar·board *n* : ³PORT

lar·ce·ny *n, pl* **lar·ce·nies** : the unlawful taking of personal property without the owner's consent : THEFT

larch *n* : a tree related to the pine that sheds its needles each fall

lard *n* : a soft white fat from fatty tissue of the hog

lar·der *n* : a place where food is kept

large *adj* **larg·er; larg·est** : more than most others of a similar kind in amount or size : BIG — **large·ness** *n* — **at large** **1** : not captured or locked up **2** : as a group or a whole **3** : representing a whole state or district

large intestine *n* : the wide lower part of the intestine from which water is absorbed and in which feces are formed

large·ly *adv* : MOSTLY, CHIEFLY

lar·i·at *n* : a long light rope used to catch livestock or tie up grazing animals

¹lark *n* : a usually brownish bird of Europe and Asia that has a pleasant song

²lark *n* : something done for fun or adventure

lark·spur *n* : a tall plant that is often grown for its stalks of showy blue, purple, pink, or white flowers

lar·va *n, pl* **lar·vae** **1** : a young wingless form (as a grub or caterpillar) of many insects that hatches from an egg **2** : an early form of any animal (as a frog) that at birth or hatching is very different from its parents

lar·yn·gi·tis *n* : swelling and irritation of the larynx in which the voice becomes hoarse or weak and the throat sore

lar·ynx *n, pl* **la·ryn·ges** *or* **lar·ynx·es** : the upper part of the trachea that contains the vocal cords

la·sa·gna *n* : layers of broad flat noodles baked with a sauce usually of tomatoes, cheese, and meat or vegetables

la·ser *n* : a device that produces a very powerful beam of light

laser printer *n* : a printer for computer output that produces high-quality images formed by a laser

¹lash *vb* **lashed; lash·ing** **1** : to hit with a whip **2** : to move forcefully from side to side **3** : to hit with force **4** : to make a sudden and angry attack against

²lash *n* **1** : a blow with a whip or switch **2** : the flexible part of a whip **3** : EYELASH

³lash *vb* **lashed; lashing** : to tie or tie down with a rope or chain

lash·ing *n* : something used for tying, wrapping, or fastening

lass *n* : GIRL 1

lass·ie *n* : a young girl

¹las·so *vb* **las·soed; las·so·ing** : to catch with a rope having a slipknot

²lasso *n, pl* **lassos** *or* **lassoes** : a rope with a slipknot that is used for catching animals

¹last *vb* **last·ed; last·ing** **1** : to go on **2** : to stay in good condition **3** : to be enough for the needs of **4** : to be able to continue in a particular condition

²last *adv* **1** : after any others in time or order **2** : most recently

³last *adj* **1** : following all the rest : FINAL **2** : most recent **3** : lowest in rank or position **4** : most unlikely

⁴last *n* : a person or thing that is last — **at last** *or* **at long last** : after a long period of time : FINALLY

last·ing *adj* : continuing for a long while

last·ly *adv* : at the end

¹latch *n* : a movable piece that holds a door, gate, or window closed

²latch *vb* **latched; latch·ing** : to close or fasten with a latch

¹late *adj* **lat·er; lat·est** **1** : coming or occurring after the usual or proper time **2** : coming or occurring toward the end **3** : having died or recently left a certain position **4** : RECENT 2 — **late·ness** *n*

²late *adv* **lat·er; lat·est** **1** : after the usual or proper time **2** : near the end of something — **of late** : LATELY

late·com·er *n* : a person who arrives late

late·ly *adv* : not long ago : RECENTLY

la·tent *adj* : present but not visible or active

lat·er·al *adj* : being on or directed toward the side — **lat·er·al·ly** *adv*

la·tex *n* **1** : a milky plant juice that is the source of rubber **2** : a mixture of water and tiny particles of rubber or plastic used especially in paints

lath *n, pl* **laths** : a thin strip of wood used (as in a wall) as a base for plaster

lathe *n* : a machine in which a piece of material (as wood) is held and turned while being shaped by a tool

¹lath·er *n* **1** : the foam made by stirring soap and water together **2** : foam from sweating (as on a horse)

²lather *vb* **lath·ered; lath·er·ing** **1** : to spread soapy foam over **2** : to form a foam

¹Lat·in *adj* **1** : of or relating to the language of the ancient Romans **2** : of or relating to the countries or people of Latin America

²Latin *n* **1** : the language of the ancient Romans **2** : a member of a people whose language and customs have descended from the ancient Romans **3** : a person born or living in Latin America

La·ti·na *n* : a woman or girl born or living in Latin America or of Latin-American origin living in the United States

Lat·in–Amer·i·can *adj* : of or relating to Latin America or its people

Latin American *n* : a person born or living in Latin America

La·ti·no *n, pl* **Latinos** : a person born or living in Latin America or of Latin-American origin living in the United States

lat·i·tude *n* **1** : the distance north or south of the equator measured in degrees **2** : a region marked by its distance north or south of the equator **3** : freedom to act or speak as desired

lat·ter *adj* **1** : coming or occurring near the end **2** : relating to or being the last thing or person mentioned

lat·tice *n* **1** : a structure made of thin strips of wood or metal that cross each other **2** : a window or gate having a lattice

¹laugh *vb* **laughed; laugh·ing** : to show amusement, joy, or scorn by smiling and making sounds (as chuckling) in the throat

²laugh *n* : the act or sound of laughing

laugh·able *adj* : causing or likely to cause laughter or scorn — **laugh·ably** *adv*

laugh·ing·ly *adv* : with laughter

laugh·ing·stock *n* : a person or thing that is made fun of

laugh·ter *n* : the action or sound of laughing

¹launch *vb* **launched; launch·ing** **1** : to throw or spring forward : HURL **2** : to send off especially with force **3** : to set afloat **4** : to give a start to : BEGIN

²launch *n* : an act of launching

³launch *n* : a small open or partly covered motorboat

launch·pad *n* : a nonflammable platform from which a rocket can be launched

laun·der *vb* **laun·dered; laun·der·ing** : to wash or wash and iron clothes or household linens — **laun·der·er** *n*

laun·dry *n, pl* **laundries** **1** : clothes or household linens that need to be washed or that have been washed **2** : a place where clothes and household linens are washed and dried

lau·rel *n* **1** : a small evergreen European tree with shiny pointed leaves used in ancient times to crown victors (as in sports) **2** : a tree or shrub (as the American **mountain laurel**) that resembles the European laurel **3** : a crown of laurel used as a mark of honor

la·va *n* : melted rock coming from a volcano or after it has cooled and hardened

lav·a·to·ry *n, pl* **lav·a·to·ries** **1** : a small sink (as in a bathroom) **2** : a room for washing that usually has a toilet **3** : TOILET 3

lav·en·der *n* **1** : a European mint with narrow leaves and stalks of small sweet-smelling pale violet flowers **2** : a pale purple

¹lav·ish *adj* **1** : giving or involving a large amount : EXTRAVAGANT **2** : spent, produced, or given in large amounts — **lav·ish·ly** *adv*

²lavish *vb* **lav·ished; lav·ish·ing** : to spend, use, or give in large amounts

law *n* **1** : a rule of conduct or action that a nation or a group of people agrees to follow **2** : a whole collection of established rules **3** : a rule or principle that always works the same way under the same conditions **4** : a bill passed by a legislature **5** : ²POLICE 1 **6** : the profession of a lawyer

law–abid·ing *adj* : obeying the law

law·break·er *n* : a person who breaks the law

law·ful *adj* **1** : permitted by law **2** : recognized by law — **law·ful·ly** *adv*

law·less *adj* **1** : having no laws : not based on or controlled by law **2** : uncontrolled by law : UNRULY — **law·less·ness** *n*

law·mak·er *n* : someone who takes part in writing and passing laws : LEGISLATOR — **law·mak·ing** *adj or n*

lawn *n* : ground (as around a house) covered with grass that is kept mowed

lawn mower *n* : a machine used to mow the grass on lawns

lawn tennis *n* : TENNIS

law·suit *n* : a process by which a dispute between people or organizations is decided in court

law·yer *n* : a person whose profession is to handle lawsuits for people or to give advice about legal rights and duties

lax *adj* **1** : not firm or tight : LOOSE **2** : not stern or strict — **lax·ness** *n*

¹**lax·a·tive** *adj* : tending to relieve constipation

²**laxative** *n* : a medicine that relieves constipation

¹**lay** *vb* **laid** ; **lay·ing** **1** : to put or set down **2** : to bring down (as with force) **3** : to produce an egg **4** : BURY 1 **5** : to place in position on or along a surface **6** : PREPARE 1, ARRANGE **7** : to bring into contact with **8** : to place a burden, charge, or penalty — **lay down** : to declare forcefully — **lay eyes on** : to catch sight of : SEE — **lay in** : to store for later use — **lay off** **1** : to stop employing often temporarily **2** : to let alone — **lay out** **1** : to plan in detail **2** : to arrange in a particular pattern or design **3** : to explain in detail — **lay up** **1** : to store up **2** : to disable or confine with illness or injury

²**lay** *n* : the way a thing lies in relation to something else

³**lay** *past of* LIE

¹**lay·er** *n* **1** : one thickness of something laid over another **2** : a person who lays something **3** : a bird that lays eggs

²**layer** *vb* **lay·ered; lay·er·ing** : to form or arrange one thickness of something over another

lay·man *n, pl* **lay·men** **1** : a person who is not a member of the clergy **2** : a person who is not a member of a certain profession

lay·out *n* : the design or arrangement of something

lay·per·son *n* : LAYMAN 1

laze *vb* **lazed; laz·ing** : to spend time relaxing

la·zy *adj* **la·zi·er; la·zi·est** **1** : not liking or willing to act or work **2** : not having much activity **3** : moving slowly : SLUGGISH — **la·zi·ly** *adv* — **la·zi·ness** *n*

lb *abbr* pound — abbreviation for Latin *libra*, which means "pound"

leach *vb* **leached; leach·ing** : to remove or remove from by the action of a liquid passing through a substance

¹**lead** *vb* **led** ; **lead·ing** **1** : to guide on a way often by going ahead **2** : to be at the head or front part of **3** : to direct or guide the actions of **4** : to be best, first, or ahead **5** : to go through : LIVE **6** : to reach or go in a certain direction

²**lead** *n* **1** : position at the front **2** : the

amount or distance that a person or thing is ahead **3** : the main role in a movie or play **4** : something serving as an indication or clue **5** : the first part of a news story

³**lead** *n* **1** : a heavy soft gray metallic element that is easily bent and shaped **2** : a long thin piece of graphite used in pencils **3** : AMMUNITION

lead·en *adj* **1** : made of lead **2** : feeling heavy and difficult to move **3** : of a dull gray color

lead·er *n* : someone or something that leads or is able to lead — **lead·er·ship** *n*

¹**leaf** *n, pl* **leaves** **1** : one of the usually flat green parts that grow from a plant stem and that functions mainly in making food by photosynthesis **2** : FOLIAGE **3** : a single sheet of a book containing a page on each side **4** : a part that can be added to or removed from a table top — **leaf·less** *adj* — **leaf·like** *adj*

²**leaf** *vb* **leafed; leaf·ing** **1** : to grow leaves **2** : to turn the pages of a book

leaf·let *n* **1** : a printed and often folded sheet of paper that is usually given to people at no cost **2** : one of the divisions of a leaf which is made up of two or more smaller parts **3** : a young or small leaf

leaf·stalk *n* : a slender plant part that supports a leaf

leafy *adj* **leaf·i·er; leaf·i·est** : having, covered with, or resembling leaves

¹**league** *n* **1** : a group of nations working together for a common purpose **2** : an association of persons or groups with common interests or goals **3** : an unofficial association or agreement **4** : a class or category of a certain quality or type

²**league** *n* : any of several old units of distance from about 2.4 to 4.6 miles (3.9 to 7.4 kilometers)

¹**leak** *vb* **leaked; leak·ing** **1** : to enter or escape or let enter or escape through an opening usually by accident **2** : to let a substance or light in or out through an opening **3** : to make or become known

²**leak** *n* **1** : a crack or hole that accidentally lets something pass in or out **2** : the accidental or secret passing of information **3** : an act or instance of leaking

leak·age *n* : the act or process of entering or escaping through a crack or hole : LEAK

leaky *adj* **leak·i·er; leak·i·est** : letting fluid in or out through a crack or hole

¹**lean** *vb* **leaned; lean·ing** **1** : to bend or tilt from an upright position **2** : to bend and rest on **3** : DEPEND 1 **4** : to tend or move toward in opinion, taste, or desire

²**lean** *adj* **lean·er; lean·est** **1** : having too little flesh : SKINNY **2** : having little body fat

3 : containing very little fat **4** : not large or plentiful — **lean·ness** *n*

lean–to *n, pl* **lean·tos** **1** : a building that has a roof with only one slope and is usually joined to another building **2** : a rough shelter that has a roof with only one slope and is held up by posts, rocks, or trees

¹leap *vb* **leaped** *or* **leapt; leap·ing** **1** : to jump or cause to jump from a surface **2** : to move, act, or pass quickly — **leap·er** *n*

²leap *n* **1** : an act of springing up or over : JUMP **2** : a place that is jumped over or from **3** : the distance that is jumped

leap·frog *n* : a game in which one player bends down and another player leaps over the first player

leap year *n* : a year of 366 days with February 29 as the extra day

learn *vb* **learned** *also* **learnt; learn·ing** **1** : to get knowledge of or skill in by study, instruction, or experience **2** : MEMORIZE **3** : to become able through practice **4** : to come to realize and understand **5** : to find out **6** : to gain knowledge — **learn·er** *n*

learned *adj* : having or showing knowledge or learning

learn·ing *n* **1** : the act of a person who gains knowledge or skill **2** : knowledge or skill gained from teaching or study

learning disability *n* : any of various conditions (as dyslexia) that make learning difficult — **learning disabled** *adj*

¹lease *n* **1** : an agreement by which a person exchanges property (as a car or house) for a period of time in return for payment or services **2** : a piece of property that is leased

²lease *vb* **leased; leas·ing** : to give or get the use of (property) in return for payment or services

¹leash *n* : a line for holding or controlling an animal

²leash *vb* **leashed; leash·ing** : to put on a line for holding or controlling

¹least *adj, superlative of* ¹LITTLE : smallest in size or degree

²least *n* : the smallest or lowest amount or degree — **at least** **1** : not less or fewer than **2** : in any case

³least *adv, superlative of* ²LITTLE : in or to the smallest degree

least common denominator *n* : the least common multiple of the denominators of two or more fractions

least common multiple *n* : the smallest number that is a multiple of each of two or more numbers

leath·er *n* : animal skin that is prepared for use

leath·ery *adj* : like leather

¹leave *vb* **left** ; **leav·ing** **1** : to go away from

2 : to cause to remain behind on purpose or without meaning to **3** : to cause or allow to be or remain in a certain condition **4** : to cause to remain as a trace, mark, or sign **5** : to have as a remainder **6** : to allow to be under another's control **7** : to cause to be available **8** : to give by will **9** : to give up **10** : DELIVER 1

²leave *n* **1** : permitted absence from duty or work **2** : the act of going away and saying good-bye **3** : PERMISSION

leaved *adj* : having leaves

leav·en *vb* **leav·ened; leav·en·ing** : to cause to rise by adding something (as baking powder) that produces a gas

leaves *pl of* LEAF

leav·ings *n pl* : things remaining

¹lec·ture *n* **1** : a talk or speech that teaches something **2** : a serious talk or scolding

²lecture *vb* **lec·tured; lec·tur·ing** **1** : to give a talk or speech that teaches something **2** : to give a serious or angry talk to — **lec·tur·er** *n*

led *past and past participle of* LEAD

LED *n* : an electronic device that emits light when power is supplied to it

ledge *n* **1** : a piece projecting from a top or an edge like a shelf **2** : a flat surface that sticks out from a wall of rock

¹lee *n* **1** : a protecting shelter **2** : the side (as of a ship) sheltered from the wind

²lee *adj* : of or relating to the side sheltered from the wind

leech *n* **1** : a bloodsucking worm related to the earthworm **2** : a person who stays around other people and uses them for personal gain

leek *n* : a vegetable having leaves and thick stems which taste like a mild onion

¹leer *vb* **leered; leer·ing** : to look with an unpleasant, mean, or eager glance

²leer *n* : an unpleasant, mean, or eager glance

leery *adj* : SUSPICIOUS 2, WARY

¹lee·ward *n* : the side that is sheltered from the wind

²leeward *adj* : located on the side that is sheltered from the wind

¹left *adj* **1** : located on the same side of the body as the heart **2** : located nearer to the left side of the body than to the right — **left** *adv*

²left *n* : the left side : a part or location on or toward the left side

³left *past and past participle of* LEAVE

left–hand *adj* **1** : located on the left side **2** : LEFT-HANDED

left–hand·ed *adj* **1** : using the left hand better or more easily than the right **2** : done or made with or for the left hand

left·over *n* : something (as food) left over

lefty *n, pl* **left·ies** : a left-handed person

leg *n* **1** : one of the limbs of an animal or person that support the body and are used in walking and running **2** : the part of the leg between the knee and the foot **3** : something like a leg in shape or use **4** : the part of a garment that covers the leg **5** : a stage or part of a journey

leg·a·cy *n, pl* **leg·a·cies** **1** : property (as money) left to a person by a will **2** : something (as memories or knowledge) that comes from the past or a person of the past

le·gal *adj* **1** : of or relating to law or lawyers **2** : based on law **3** : allowed by law or rules — **le·gal·ly** *adv*

le·gal·ize *vb* **le·gal·ized; le·gal·iz·ing** : to make allowable by law — **le·gal·iza·tion** *n*

leg·end *n* **1** : an old story that is widely believed but cannot be proved to be true **2** : a person or thing that is very famous for having special qualities or abilities **3** : a list of symbols used (as on a map)

leg·end·ary *adj* **1** : told about in legends **2** : very famous because of special qualities or abilities

leg·ged *adj* : having legs especially of a certain kind or number

leg·ging *n* : an outer covering for the leg usually of cloth or leather

leg·i·ble *adj* : clear enough to be read — **leg·i·bly** *adv*

le·gion *n* **1** : a group of from 3000 to 6000 soldiers that made up the chief army unit in ancient Rome **2** : ARMY 1 **3** : a very great number

leg·is·late *vb* **leg·is·lat·ed; leg·is·lat·ing** : to make laws

leg·is·la·tion *n* **1** : the action of making laws **2** : the laws that are made

leg·is·la·tive *adj* **1** : having the power or authority to make laws **2** : of or relating to the action or process by which laws are made

leg·is·la·tor *n* : a person who makes laws and is a member of a legislature

leg·is·la·ture *n* : a body of persons having the power to make and change laws

le·git·i·mate *adj* **1** : accepted by the law as rightful : LAWFUL **2** : being right or acceptable — **le·git·i·mate·ly** *adv*

leg·less *adj* : having no legs

le·gume *n* : any of a large group of plants (as peas, beans, and clover) with fruits that are pods which split into two parts and root nodules containing bacteria that fix nitrogen

lei·sure *n* : free time — **at leisure** *or* **at someone's leisure** **1** : in a way that is not hurried **2** : when there is free time available **3** : not busy

lei·sure·ly *adj* : UNHURRIED

lem·on *n* **1** : an oval yellow fruit with a sour juice that is related to the orange and grows on a small spiny tree **2** : something unsatisfactory : DUD

lem·on·ade *n* : a drink made of lemon juice, sugar, and water

lend *vb* **lent ; lend·ing** **1** : ²LOAN **2** : to give usually for a time **3** : to add something that improves or makes more attractive — **lend·er** *n*

length *n* **1** : the measured distance from one end to the other of the longer or longest side of an object **2** : a measured distance **3** : amount of time something takes **4** : a piece of something that is long **5** : the sound of a vowel or syllable as it is affected by the time needed to pronounce it — **at length** **1** : very fully **2** : at the end : FINALLY

length·en *vb* **length·ened; length·en·ing** : to make or become longer

length·ways *adv* : LENGTHWISE

length·wise *adj or adv* : in the direction of the length

lengthy *adj* **length·i·er; length·i·est** : very long

le·nient *adj* : being kind and patient : not strict — **le·nient·ly** *adv*

lens *n* **1** : a clear curved piece of material (as glass) used to bend the rays of light to form an image **2** : a clear part of the eye behind the pupil and iris that focuses rays of light on the retina to form clear images

len·til *n* : the flattened round edible seed of a plant originally of southwestern Asia

Leo *n* **1** : a constellation between Cancer and Virgo imagined as a lion **2** : the fifth sign of the zodiac or a person born under this sign

leop·ard *n* : a large animal of the cat family found in Asia and Africa that has a brownish buff coat with black spots and is an excellent climber

leop·ard·ess *n* : a female leopard

le·o·tard *n* : a tight one-piece garment worn by a dancer or acrobat

le·sion *n* : an abnormal spot or area of the body caused by sickness or injury

¹less *adj, comparative of* ¹LITTLE **1** : being fewer **2** : not so much : a smaller amount of

²less *adv, comparative of* ²LITTLE : not so much or so well

³less *n* **1** : a smaller number or amount **2** : something that is not as important

⁴less *prep* : ¹MINUS 1

-less *adj suffix* **1** : not having **2** : not able to be acted on or to act in a specified way

less·en *vb* **less·ened; less·en·ing** : to make or become fewer or smaller in amount

¹less·er *adj* : of smaller size or importance

²lesser *adv* : ²LESS

les·son *n* **1** : something learned or taught **2**

: a single class or part of a course of instruction

lest *conj* : for fear that

let *vb* **let; let·ting** **1** : to allow or permit to **2** : to allow to go or pass **3** : to cause to : MAKE **4** : ²RENT 2 **5** — used as a warning — **let alone** : to leave undisturbed — **let down** : DISAPPOINT — **let go** **1** : to relax or release a grip **2** : to dismiss from employment **3** : to fail to take care of — **let on** : to admit or reveal — **let up** **1** : to slow down **2** : ¹STOP 4, CEASE

-let *n suffix* **1** : small one **2** : something worn on

let·down *n* : DISAPPOINTMENT 2

let's : let us

¹let·ter *n* **1** : one of the marks that are symbols for speech sounds in writing or print and that make up the alphabet **2** : a written or printed communication (as one sent through the mail) **3 letters** *pl* : LITERATURE 2 **4** : the strict or outward meaning **5** : the initial of a school awarded to a student usually for athletic achievement

²letter *vb* **let·tered; let·ter·ing** : to mark with symbols for speech sounds

letter carrier *n* : a person who delivers mail

let·ter·head *n* : the name and address of an organization that is printed at the top of a piece of paper used as official stationery

let·ter·ing *n* : symbols for speech sounds written on something

let·tuce *n* : a garden plant that has large crisp leaves eaten especially in salads

leu·ke·mia *n* : a serious disease in which too many white blood cells are formed

le·vee *n* : a bank built along a river to prevent flooding

¹lev·el *n* **1** : a horizontal line or surface usually at a named height **2** : a step or stage in height, position, or rank **3** : a device used (as by a carpenter) to find a horizontal line or surface

²level *vb* **lev·eled** *or* **lev·elled; lev·el·ing** *or* **lev·el·ling** : to make or become horizontal, flat, or even

³level *adj* **1** : having a flat even surface **2** : ¹HORIZONTAL **3** : of the same height or rank : EVEN **4** : steady and cool in judgment

¹le·ver *n* **1** : a bar used to pry or move something **2** : a stiff bar for lifting a weight at one point of its length by pressing or pulling at a second point while the bar turns on a support **3** : a bar or rod used to run or adjust something

²lever *vb* **le·vered; le·ver·ing** : to raise or move with a bar

lev·i·tate *vb* **lev·i·tat·ed; lev·i·tat·ing** : to rise or make rise up in the air

¹levy *n, pl* **lev·ies** : something (as taxes) collected by authority of the law

²levy *vb* **lev·ied; levy·ing** : to collect legally

li·a·ble *adj* **1** : LIKELY 1 **2** : judged by law to be responsible for something **3** : not sheltered or protected (as from danger or accident)

li·ar *n* : a person who tells lies

¹li·bel *n* : the publication of a false statement that hurts a person's reputation

²libel *vb* **li·beled** *or* **li·belled; li·bel·ing** *or* **li·bel·ling** : to hurt a person's reputation by publishing a false statement — **li·bel·er** *or* **li·bel·ler** *n*

lib·er·al *adj* **1** : not stingy : GENEROUS **2** : not strict **3** : BROAD 4 — **lib·er·al·ly** *adv*

lib·er·ate *vb* **lib·er·at·ed; lib·er·at·ing** : to set free

lib·er·ty *n, pl* **lib·er·ties** **1** : the state of being free : FREEDOM **2** : freedom to do as desired **3** : the state of not being busy : LEISURE **4** : a political right **5** : an action that is too free — **at liberty** : able to act or speak freely

Li·bra *n* **1** : a constellation between Virgo and Scorpio imagined as a pair of scales **2** : the seventh sign of the zodiac or a person born under this sign

li·brar·i·an *n* : a person in charge of a library

li·brary *n, pl* **li·brar·ies** **1** : a place where literary or reference materials (as books, manuscripts, recordings, or films) are kept for use but are not for sale **2** : a collection of literary or reference materials

lice *pl of* LOUSE

¹li·cense *or* **li·cence** *n* **1** : permission to do something granted especially by qualified authority **2** : a paper, card, or tag showing legal permission **3** : freedom of action that is carried too far

²license *also* **licence** *vb* **li·censed** *also* **li·cenced; li·cens·ing** *also* **li·cenc·ing** : to grant formal permission

li·chen *n* : a plantlike organism made up of an alga and a fungus growing together

¹lick *vb* **licked; lick·ing** **1** : to pass the tongue over **2** : to touch or pass over like a tongue **3** : to hit again and again : BEAT **4** : to get the better of : DEFEAT — **lick·ing** *n*

²lick *n* **1** : the act of passing the tongue over **2** : a small amount **3** : a place (**salt lick**) where salt is found or provided for animals

lick·e·ty–split *adv* : at top speed

lic·o·rice *n* **1** : the dried root of a European plant or a juice from it used in medicine and in candy **2** : candy flavored with licorice

lid *n* **1** : a movable cover **2** : EYELID — **lid·ded** *adj* — **lid·less** *adj*

¹lie *vb* **lay ; lain ; ly·ing** **1** : to stretch out or be stretched out **2** : to be spread flat so as to cover **3** : to be located or placed **4** : to be or stay

²lie *vb* **lied; ly·ing** : to say something that is not true in order to deceive someone

³lie *n* : something said or done in the hope of deceiving : an untrue statement

liege *n* : a lord in the time of the Middle Ages

lieu·ten·ant *n* **1** : an official who acts for a higher official **2** : FIRST LIEUTENANT **3** : SECOND LIEUTENANT **4** : a commissioned officer in the navy or coast guard ranking above a lieutenant junior grade

lieutenant junior grade *n* : a commissioned officer in the navy or coast guard ranking above an ensign

life *n, pl* **lives 1** : the state characterized by the ability to get and use energy, reproduce, grow, and respond to change : the quality that plants and animals lose when they die **2** : the period during which a person or thing is alive or exists **3** : all the experiences that make up the existence of a person : the course of existence **4** : existence as a living being **5** : a way of living **6** : the time when something can be used or enjoyed **7** : energy and spirit **8** : BIOGRAPHY

life belt *n* : a life preserver worn like a belt

life·boat *n* : a sturdy boat (as one carried by a ship) for use in an emergency

life buoy *n* : a life preserver in the shape of a ring

life·guard *n* : a person employed at a beach or swimming pool to protect swimmers from drowning

life jacket *n* : a life preserver in the form of a vest

life·less *adj* **1** : having no living things **2** : dead or appearing to be dead **3** : lacking spirit, interest, or energy

life·like *adj* : very like something that is alive

life·long *adj* : continuing through life

life preserver *n* : a device (as a life jacket or life buoy) designed to save a person from drowning by keeping the person afloat

life raft *n* : a small usually rubber boat for use by people forced into the water when a larger boat sinks

life·sav·er *n* : someone or something that provides greatly needed help

life–size *or* **life–sized** *adj* : of natural size : having the same size as the original

life·style *n* : the usual way of life of a person, group, or society

life·time *n* : LIFE 2

life vest *n* : LIFE JACKET

¹lift *vb* **lift·ed; lift·ing 1** : to raise from a lower to a higher position, rate, or amount **2** : to rise from the ground **3** : to move upward and disappear or become scattered

²lift *n* **1** : the action or an instance of picking up and raising **2** : an improved mood or condition **3** : a ride in a vehicle **4** *chiefly British* : ELEVATOR 1 **5** : an upward force (as on an airplane wing) that opposes the pull of gravity

lift-off *n* : a vertical takeoff (as by a rocket)

lig·a·ment *n* : a tough band of tissue that holds bones together or keeps an organ in place in the body

¹light *n* **1** : the bright form of energy given off by something (as the sun) that makes it possible to see **2** : a source (as a lamp) of light **3** : DAYLIGHT 1 **4** : public knowledge **5** : understanding that comes from information someone has provided

²light *adj* **light·er; light·est 1** : having light : BRIGHT **2** : not dark or deep in color

³light *vb* **lit** *or* **light·ed; light·ing 1** : to make or become bright **2** : to burn or cause to burn

⁴light *adj* **1** : having little weight : not heavy **2** : less in amount or force than usual **3** : not hard to bear, do, pay, or digest **4** : active in motion **5** : free from care : HAPPY **6** : not dense and thick **7** : intended mainly to entertain — **light·ly** *adv* — **light·ness** *n*

⁵light *adv* : with little baggage

⁶light *vb* **lit** *or* **light·ed; light·ing 1** : ²PERCH, SETTLE **2** : to come by chance

light bulb *n* : a lamp in which a glow is produced by the heating of a wire by an electric current

¹light·en *vb* **light·ened; light·en·ing** : to make or become lighter, brighter, or clearer — **light·en·er** *n*

²lighten *vb* **lightened; lightening 1** : to make or become less heavy **2** : to make less sad or serious — **light·en·er** *n*

light·face *n* : a type having thin lines

light·heart·ed *adj* : free from worry — **light·heart·ed·ly** *adv* — **light·heart·ed·ness** *n*

light·house *n* : a tower that produces a powerful glow to guide sailors at night or in poor visibility

light·ing *n* : supply of light or of lights

light·ning *n* : the flashing of light caused by the passing of electricity from one cloud to another or between a cloud and the earth

lightning bug *n* : FIREFLY

light·weight *adj* : having less than the usual or expected weight

light–year *n* : a unit of length in astronomy equal to the distance that light travels in one year or about 5.88 trillion miles (9.46 trillion kilometers)

lik·able *or* **like·able** *adj* : having pleasant or attractive qualities : easily liked

¹like *vb* **liked; lik·ing 1** : ENJOY 1 **2** : to feel toward : REGARD **3** : CHOOSE 3, PREFER

²like *n* : LIKING, PREFERENCE

³**like** *adj* : SIMILAR, ALIKE

⁴**like** *prep* **1** : similar or similarly to **2** : typical of **3** : likely to **4** : such as **5** : close to

⁵**like** *n* : ³EQUAL, COUNTERPART

⁶**like** *conj* **1** : AS IF **2** : in the same way that : AS **3** : such as

-like *adj suffix* : resembling or characteristic of

like·li·hood *n* : PROBABILITY 1

¹**like·ly** *adj* **1** : very possibly going to happen **2** : seeming to be the truth : BELIEVABLE **3** : giving hope of turning out well : PROMISING

²**likely** *adv* : without great doubt

lik·en *vb* **lik·ened; lik·en·ing** : to describe as similar to : COMPARE

like·ness *n* **1** : the state of being similar : RESEMBLANCE **2** : a picture of a person : PORTRAIT

like·wise *adv* **1** : in similar manner **2** : ALSO

lik·ing *n* : a feeling of being pleased with someone or something

li·lac *n* **1** : a bush having clusters of fragrant pink, purple, or white flowers **2** : a medium purple

lilt *vb* **lilt·ed; lilt·ing** : to sing or play in a lively cheerful manner

lily *n, pl* **lil·ies** : a plant (as the **Easter lily** or the **tiger lily**) that grows from a bulb and has a leafy stem and showy funnel-shaped flowers

lily of the valley *n, pl* **lilies of the valley** : a small plant related to the lilies that has usually two leaves and a stalk of fragrant flowers shaped like bells

li·ma bean *n* : the edible seed of a bean plant that is usually pale green or white

limb *n* **1** : any of the paired parts (as an arm, wing, or leg) of an animal that stick out from the body and are used mostly in moving and grasping **2** : a large branch of a tree — **limbed** *adj* — **limb·less** *adj*

¹**lim·ber** *adj* : bending easily

²**limber** *vb* **lim·bered; lim·ber·ing** : to make or become limber

¹**lime** *n* : a small greenish yellow fruit that is related to the lemon and orange

²**lime** *n* : a white substance made by heating limestone or shells and used in making plaster and cement and in farming

³**lime** *vb* **limed; lim·ing** : to treat or cover with a white substance made from limestone or shells

lime·light *n* : the center of public attention

lim·er·ick *n* : a funny poem with five lines

lime·stone *n* : a rock formed chiefly from animal remains (as shells or coral) that is used in building and gives lime when burned

¹**lim·it** *n* **1** : a point beyond which it is impossible to go **2** : an amount or number that is the lowest or highest allowed **3** : a boundary line

²**limit** *vb* **lim·it·ed; lim·it·ing** : to place a control on the size or extent of something

lim·i·ta·tion *n* **1** : an act or instance of controlling the size or extent of something **2** : something that controls size or extent

lim·it·ed *adj* : small in number

lim·it·less *adj* : having no boundaries : very numerous or large

lim·ou·sine *n* : a large luxurious automobile often driven by a chauffeur

¹**limp** *vb* **limped; limp·ing** : to walk in a slow or uneven way because of an injury to a foot or leg

²**limp** *n* : a slow or uneven way of walking caused by an injury to a leg or foot

³**limp** *adj* : not firm or stiff — **limp·ly** *adv*

lim·pid *adj* : perfectly clear

lin·den *n* : a shade tree with heart-shaped leaves and drooping clusters of yellowish white flowers

¹**line** *n* **1** : a long thin cord or rope **2** : a long narrow mark **3** : an arrangement of people or things in a row **4** : a row of letters, words, or musical notes across a page or column **5** : the boundary or limit of a place **6** : FAMILY 2 **7** : a way of behaving or thinking **8** : ¹OUTLINE 1, CONTOUR **9** : an area of activity or interest **10** : the position of military forces who are facing the enemy **11** : a pipe carrying a fluid (as steam, water, or oil) **12** : an outdoor wire carrying electricity or a telephone signal **13 lines** *pl* : the words of a part in a play **14** : the path along which something moves or is directed **15** : the track of a railway **16** : AGREEMENT 1, HARMONY **17** : a system of transportation **18** : the football players whose positions are along the line of scrimmage **19** : a geometric element produced by moving a point **20** : a plan for making or doing something

²**line** *vb* **lined; lin·ing** **1** : to indicate with or draw a long narrow mark **2** : to place or be placed in a row along — **line up 1** : to gather or arrange in a row or rows **2** : to put into alignment

³**line** *vb* **lined; lin·ing** : to cover the inner surface of

lin·eage *n* **1** : the ancestors from whom a person is descended **2** : people descended from the same ancestor

lin·ear *adj* **1** : made up of, relating to, or like a line : STRAIGHT **2** : involving a single dimension

lin·en *n* **1** : smooth strong cloth or yarn made from flax **2** : household articles (as tablecloths or sheets) or clothing that were once often made of linen

line of scrimmage *n* : an imaginary line in

football parallel to the goal lines and running through the place where the ball is laid before each play begins

liner *n* : something that covers or is used to cover the inner surface of another thing

line segment *n* : SEGMENT 3

line-up *n* **1** : a list of players taking part in a game (as baseball) **2** : a row of persons arranged especially for police identification

-ling *n suffix* **1** : one associated with **2** : young, small, or minor one

lin-ger *vb* **lin-gered; lin-ger-ing 1** : to be slow in leaving : DELAY **2** : to continue to exist as time passes

lin-guist *n* **1** : a person skilled in languages **2** : a person who specializes in the study of human speech

lin-guis-tics *n* : the study of human speech including the nature, structure, and development of language or of a language or group of languages

lin-i-ment *n* : a liquid medicine rubbed on the skin to ease pain

lin-ing *n* : material that covers an inner surface

¹link *n* **1** : a single ring of a chain **2** : something that connects : CONNECTION **3** : HYPERLINK

²link *vb* **linked; link-ing 1** : to physically join or connect **2** : to show or suggest a connection

linking verb *n* : an intransitive verb that connects a subject with a word or words in the predicate

li-no-leum *n* : a floor covering with a canvas back and a surface of hardened linseed oil and cork dust

lin-seed *n* : FLAXSEED

linseed oil *n* : a yellowish oil obtained from flaxseed

lint *n* **1** : loose bits of thread **2** : COTTON 1

lin-tel *n* : a horizontal piece or part across the top of an opening (as of a door) to carry the weight of the structure above it

li-on *n* : a large meat-eating animal of the cat family that has a brownish buff coat, a tufted tail, and in the male a shaggy mane and that lives in Africa and southern Asia

li-on-ess *n* : a female lion

lip *n* **1** : either of the two folds of flesh that surround the mouth **2** : the edge of a hollow container (as a jar) especially where it is slightly spread out **3** : an edge (as of a wound) like or of flesh **4** : an edge that sticks out — **lipped** *adj*

lip-stick *n* : a waxy solid colored cosmetic for the lips usually in stick form

liq-ue-fy *vb* **liq-ue-fied; liq-ue-fy-ing** : to make or become liquid

¹liq-uid *adj* **1** : flowing freely like water **2**

: neither solid nor gaseous **3** : clear and smooth or shining **4** : made up of or easily changed into cash

²liquid *n* : a substance that flows freely like water

liq-uor *n* : a strong alcoholic beverage

¹lisp *vb* **lisped; lisp-ing** : to pronounce the sounds \s\ and \z\ as \th\ and \th\

²lisp *n* : the act or habit of pronouncing the sounds \s\ and \z\ as \th\ and \th\

¹list *n* : a series of items written, mentioned, or considered one following another

²list *vb* **list-ed; list-ing** : to put in a series of items

³list *vb* **listed; listing** : to lean to one side

⁴list *n* : a leaning over to one side

lis-ten *vb* **lis-tened; lis-ten-ing 1** : to pay attention in order to hear **2** : to hear and consider seriously — **lis-ten-er** *n*

list-less *adj* : too tired or too little interested to want to do things — **list-less-ly** *adv* — **list-less-ness** *n*

lit *past and past participle of* LIGHT

li-ter *n* : a metric unit of liquid capacity equal to 1.057 quarts

lit-er-al *adj* **1** : following the ordinary or usual meaning of the words **2** : true to fact — **lit-er-al-ly** *adv* — **lit-er-al-ness** *n*

lit-er-ary *adj* : of or relating to literature

lit-er-ate *adj* **1** : able to read and write **2** : having gotten a good education

lit-er-a-ture *n* **1** : written works considered as having high quality and ideas of lasting and widespread interest **2** : written material

lithe *adj* : ¹LIMBER, SUPPLE

lith-o-sphere *n* : the outer part of the solid earth

lit-mus paper *n* : paper treated with coloring matter that turns red in the presence of an acid and blue in the presence of a base

¹lit-ter *n* **1** : the young born to an animal at a single time **2** : a messy collection of things scattered about : TRASH **3** : material used to soak up the urine and feces of animals **4** : a covered and curtained couch having poles and used for carrying a single passenger **5** : a stretcher for carrying a sick or wounded person

²litter *vb* **lit-tered; lit-ter-ing 1** : to throw or leave trash on the ground **2** : to cover in an untidy way

lit-ter-bug *n* : a person who carelessly scatters trash in a public area

¹lit-tle *adj* **lit-tler** *or* **less; lit-tlest** *or* **least 1** : small in size **2** : small in quantity **3** : ¹YOUNG 1 **4** : short in duration or extent **5** : small in importance **6** : ¹NARROW 3

²little *adv* **less; least 1** : in a very small quantity or degree — **little by little** : by small steps or amounts : GRADUALLY

³little *n* : a small amount or quantity

Little Dipper *n* : a group of seven stars in the northern sky arranged in a form like a dipper with the North Star forming the tip of the handle

little finger *n* : the shortest finger of the hand farthest from the thumb

lit·ur·gy *n, pl* **lit·ur·gies** : a religious rite or body of rites — **li·tur·gi·cal** *adj*

¹live *vb* **lived; liv·ing 1** : to be alive **2** : to continue in life **3** : DWELL 1 **4** : to spend life — **live it up** : to live with great enthusiasm and excitement — **live up to** : to be good enough to satisfy expectations

²live *adj* **1** : having life : ALIVE **2** : broadcast at the time of production **3** : charged with an electric current **4** : burning usually without flame **5** : not exploded

live·li·hood *n* : ²LIVING 3

live·long *adj* : during all of

live·ly *adj* **live·li·er; live·li·est 1** : full of life : ACTIVE **2** : showing or resulting from active thought **3** : full of spirit or feeling : ANIMATED — **live·li·ness** *n*

liv·en *vb* **liv·ened; liv·en·ing** : to make or become lively — often used with *up*

live oak *n* : any of several American oaks that have evergreen leaves

liv·er *n* : a large gland in the body that has a rich blood supply, secretes bile, and helps in storing some nutrients and in forming some body wastes

liv·er·ied *adj* : wearing a special uniform

liv·er·wort *n* : a flowerless plant that resembles a moss

liv·ery *n, pl* **liv·er·ies 1** : a special uniform worn by the servants of a wealthy household **2** : the business of keeping horses and vehicles for hire : a place (**livery stable**) that keeps horses and vehicles for hire

lives *pl of* LIFE

live·stock *n* : animals (as cows, horses, and pigs) kept or raised especially on a farm and for profit

live wire *n* : an alert active person

liv·id *adj* **1** : very angry **2** : pale as ashes **3** : discolored by bruising

¹liv·ing *adj* **1** : not dead : ALIVE **2** : true to life

²living *n* **1** : the condition of being alive **2** : conduct or manner of life **3** : what a person has to have to meet basic needs

living room *n* : a room in a house for general family use

liz·ard *n* : a reptile with movable eyelids, ears that are outside the body, and usually four legs

lla·ma *n* : a South American hoofed animal that has a long neck, is related to the camel, and is sometimes used to carry loads and as a source of wool

lo *interj* — used to call attention or to show wonder or surprise

¹load *n* **1** : something lifted up and carried : BURDEN **2** : the quantity of material put into a device at one time **3** : a large number or amount **4** : a mass or weight supported by something **5** : something that causes worry or sadness **6** : a charge for a firearm

²load *vb* **load·ed; load·ing 1** : to put a load in or on **2** : to supply abundantly **3** : to put something into a device so it can be used — **load·er** *n*

¹loaf *n, pl* **loaves 1** : a usually oblong mass of bread **2** : a dish (as of meat) baked in an oblong form

²loaf *vb* **loafed; loaf·ing** : to spend time idly or lazily — **loaf·er** *n*

loam *n* : a soil having the appropriate amount of silt, clay, and sand for good plant growth

loamy *adj* **loam·i·er; loam·i·est** : made up of or like rich soil

¹loan *n* **1** : money given with the understanding that it will be paid back **2** : something given for a time to a borrower **3** : permission to use something for a time

²loan *vb* **loaned; loan·ing** : to give to another for temporary use with the understanding that the same or a like thing will be returned

loath *also* **loth** *adj* : not willing

loathe *vb* **loathed; loath·ing** : to dislike greatly

loathing *n* : very great dislike

loath·some *adj* : very unpleasant : OFFENSIVE

loaves *pl of* LOAF

¹lob *vb* **lobbed; lob·bing** : to send (as a ball) in a high arc by hitting or throwing easily

²lob *n* : an act of throwing or hitting (as a ball) in a high arc

lob·by *n, pl* **lobbies** : a hall or entry especially when large enough to serve as a waiting room

lobe *n* : a rounded part — **lobed** *adj*

lob·ster *n* : a large edible sea animal that is a crustacean with five pairs of legs of which the first pair usually has large claws

¹lo·cal *adj* : of, in, or relating to a particular place — **lo·cal·ly** *adv*

²local *n* **1** : a public vehicle (as a bus or train) that makes all or most stops on its run **2** : a branch (as of a lodge or labor union) in a particular place

local area network *n* : a computer network that covers a small area (as an office building or a home)

lo·cal·i·ty *n, pl* **lo·cal·i·ties** : a place and its surroundings

lo·cal·ize *vb* **lo·cal·ized; lo·cal·iz·ing** : to keep or be kept in a certain area

lo·cate *vb* **lo·cat·ed; lo·cat·ing** 1 : to find the position of 2 : to settle or establish in a particular place

lo·ca·tion *n* 1 : the act or process of establishing in or finding a particular place 2 : ¹PLACE 3, POSITION

¹lock *n* : a small bunch of hair or of fiber (as cotton or wool)

²lock *n* 1 : a fastening (as for a door) in which a bolt is operated (as by a key) 2 : the device for exploding the charge or cartridge of a firearm 3 : an enclosure (as in a canal) with gates at each end used in raising or lowering boats as they pass from level to level

³lock *vb* **locked; lock·ing** 1 : to fasten with or as if with a lock 2 : to shut in or out by or as if by means of a lock 3 : to make unable to move by linking parts together

lock·er *n* : a cabinet, compartment, or chest for personal use or for storing frozen food at a low temperature

locker room *n* : a room where sports players change clothes and store equipment in lockers

lock·et *n* : a small ornamental case usually worn on a chain

lock·jaw *n* : TETANUS

lock·smith *n* : a worker who makes or repairs locks

lock·up *n* : PRISON

lo·co·mo·tion *n* : the act or power of moving from place to place

lo·co·mo·tive *n* : a vehicle that moves under its own power and is used to haul cars on a railroad

lo·cust *n* 1 : a grasshopper that moves in huge swarms and eats up the plants in its path 2 : CICADA 3 : a tree with hard wood, leaves with many leaflets, and drooping flower clusters

lode·stone *n* 1 : a magnetic rock

¹lodge *vb* **lodged; lodg·ing** 1 : to provide a temporary living or sleeping space for 2 : to use a place for living or sleeping 3 : to become stuck or fixed 4 : ³FILE 2

²lodge *n* 1 : a house set apart for residence in a special season or by an employee on an estate 2 : a den or resting place of an animal 3 : the meeting place of a social organization

lodg·er *n* : a person who lives in a rented room in another's house

lodging *n* 1 : a temporary living or sleeping place 2 **lodgings** *pl* : a room or rooms in the house of another person rented as a place to live

loft *n* 1 : an upper room or upper story of a building 2 : a balcony in a church 3 : an upper part of a barn

lofty *adj* **loft·i·er; loft·i·est** 1 : rising to a great height 2 : of high rank or admirable quality 3 : showing a proud and superior attitude — **loft·i·ly** *adv* — **loft·i·ness** *n*

¹log *n* 1 : a large piece of a cut or fallen tree 2 : a long piece of a tree trunk ready for sawing 3 : the record of a ship's voyage or of an aircraft's flight 4 : a record of performance, events, or daily activities

²log *vb* **logged; log·ging** 1 : to engage in cutting trees for timber 2 : to make an official record of — **log on** : to connect to a computer or network

log·ger·head *n* : a very large sea turtle found in the warmer parts of the Atlantic Ocean

log·ic *n* 1 : a proper or reasonable way of thinking about something : sound reasoning 2 : a science that deals with the rules and processes used in sound thinking and reasoning

log·i·cal *adj* 1 : according to a proper or reasonable way of thinking 2 : according to what is reasonably expected — **log·i·cal·ly** *adv*

-logy *n suffix* : area of knowledge : science

loin *n* 1 : the part of the body between the hip and the lower ribs 2 : a piece of meat (as beef) from the loin of an animal

loi·ter *vb* **loi·tered; loi·ter·ing** 1 : to hang around somewhere for no good reason 2 : to dawdle on the way to somewhere — **loi·ter·er** *n*

loll *vb* **lolled; loll·ing** 1 : to hang loosely : DROOP 2 : to lie around lazily

lol·li·pop *or* **lol·ly·pop** *n* : a round piece of hard candy on the end of a stick

lone *adj* 1 : having no companion 2 : situated by itself

lone·ly *adj* **lone·li·er; lone·li·est** 1 : LONE 1 2 : not often visited 3 : sad from being alone : LONESOME 4 : producing sad feelings from being alone — **lone·li·ness** *n*

lone·some *adj* 1 : sad from being without companions 2 : not often visited or traveled over

¹long *adj* **lon·ger; lon·gest** 1 : of great length from end to end : not short 2 : lasting for some time : not brief 3 : being more than the usual length 4 : having a stated length (as in distance or time) 5 : of, relating to, or being one of the vowel sounds \ā, ē, ī, ō, ü\ and sometimes \ä\ and \o\

²long *adv* 1 : for or during a long time 2 : for the whole length of 3 : at a distant point of time

³long *n* : a long time

⁴long *vb* **longed; long·ing** : to wish for something very much

long division *n* : division in arithmetic

that involves several steps that are written out

long·hand *n* : HANDWRITING

long·horn *n* : a cow with very long horns that was once common in the southwestern United States

long–horned *adj* : having long horns or antennae

long·house *n* : a long dwelling especially of the Iroquois for several families

long·ing *n* : an eager desire — **long·ing·ly** *adv*

lon·gi·tude *n* : distance measured in degrees east or west of an imaginary line that runs from the north pole to the south pole and passes through Greenwich, England

lon·gi·tu·di·nal *adj* : placed or running lengthwise — **lon·gi·tu·di·nal·ly** *adv*

long–lived *adj* : living or lasting for a long time

long–range *adj* **1** : involving a long period of time **2** : capable of traveling or being used over great distances

long–wind·ed *adj* : using or having too many words

¹look *vb* **looked; look·ing** **1** : to use the power of vision : SEE **2** : to direct the attention or eyes **3** : SEEM 1 **4** : to have an appearance that is suitable **5** : ²FACE 1 — **look after** : to take care of — **look down on** : to regard as bad or inferior — **look out** : to be careful — **look up** **1** : to search for in a reference book **2** : to get better — **look up to** : RESPECT 1

²look *n* **1** : an act of looking **2** : the expression on a person's face or in a person's eyes **3 looks** *pl* : physical appearance **4** : appearance that suggests what something is or means

looking glass *n* : ¹MIRROR 1

look·out *n* **1** : a careful watch for something expected or feared **2** : a high place from which a wide view is possible **3** : a person who keeps watch

¹loom *n* : a frame or machine for weaving cloth

²loom *vb* **loomed; loom·ing** **1** : to come into sight suddenly and often with a large, strange, or frightening appearance **2** : to be about to happen

loon *n* : a large diving bird that eats fish and has a black head and a black back spotted with white

¹loop *n* **1** : an almost oval form produced when something flexible and thin (as a wire or a rope) crosses over itself **2** : something (as a figure or bend) suggesting a flexible loop

²loop *vb* **looped; loop·ing** **1** : to make a circle or loop in **2** : to form a circle or loop

loop·hole *n* : a way of avoiding something

¹loose *adj* **loos·er; loos·est** **1** : not tightly fixed or fastened **2** : not pulled tight **3** : not tied up or shut in **4** : not brought together in a bundle or binding **5** : having parts that are not held or squeezed tightly together **6** : not exact or precise — **loose·ly** *adv* — **loose·ness** *n*

²loose *vb* **loosed; loos·ing** **1** : to make less tight **2** : to set free

loose–leaf *adj* : arranged so that pages can be put in or taken out

loos·en *vb* **loos·ened; loos·en·ing** : to make or become less tight or firmly fixed

¹loot *n* : something stolen or taken by force

²loot *vb* **loot·ed; loot·ing** : ¹PLUNDER — **loot·er** *n*

¹lope *n* : an effortless way of moving with long smooth steps

²lope *vb* **loped; lop·ing** : to go or run in an effortless way with long smooth steps

lop·sid·ed *adj* : uneven in position, size, or amount

¹lord *n* **1** : a person having power and authority over others **2** *cap* : GOD 1 **3** *cap* : JESUS CHRIST **4** : a British nobleman or bishop — used as a title

²lord *vb* **lord·ed; lord·ing** : to act in a proud or bossy way toward others

lord·ship *n* : the rank or dignity of a lord — used as a title

lore *n* : common or traditional knowledge or belief

lose *vb* **lost; los·ing** **1** : to be unable to find or have at hand **2** : to become deprived of **3** : to become deprived of by death **4** : to fail to use : WASTE **5** : to fail to win **6** : to fail to keep — **los·er** *n*

loss *n* **1** : the act or fact of losing something **2** : harm or distress that comes from losing something or someone **3** : something that is lost **4** : failure to win — **at a loss** : unsure of how to proceed

lost *adj* **1** : unable to find the way **2** : unable to be found **3** : not used, won, or claimed **4** : no longer possessed or known **5** : fully occupied **6** : not capable of succeeding

lot *n* **1** : an object used in deciding something by chance or the use of such an object to decide something **2** : FATE 2 **3** : a piece or plot of land **4** : a large number or amount

loth *variant of* LOATH

lo·tion *n* : a creamy liquid preparation used on the skin especially for healing or as a cosmetic

lot·tery *n*, *pl* **lot·ter·ies** : a way of raising money in which many tickets are sold and a few of these are drawn to win prizes

lo·tus *n* : any of various water lilies

¹loud *adj* **1** : not low, soft, or quiet in sound

: NOISY **2** : not quiet or calm in expression **3** : too bright or showy to be pleasing — **loud·ly** *adv* — **loud·ness** *n*

²loud *adv* : in a loud manner

loud·speak·er *n* : an electronic device that makes sound louder

¹lounge *vb* **lounged; loung·ing** : to stand, sit, or lie in a relaxed manner

²lounge *n* **1** : a comfortable room where one can relax **2** : a long chair or couch

louse *n, pl* **lice 1** : a small, wingless, and usually flat insect that lives on the bodies of warm-blooded animals **2** : an insect or related arthropod that resembles a body louse and feeds on plant juices or decaying matter

lousy *adj* **lous·i·er; lous·i·est 1** : BAD 1 **2** : deserving disgust or contempt

lov·able *adj* : deserving to be loved : having attractive or appealing qualities

¹love *n* **1** : strong and warm affection (as of a parent for a child) **2** : a great liking **3** : a beloved person

²love *vb* **loved; lov·ing 1** : to feel strong affection for **2** : to like very much — **lov·er** *n*

love·ly *adj* **love·li·er; love·li·est 1** : very attractive or beautiful **2** : very pleasing — **love·li·ness** *n*

lov·ing *adj* : feeling or showing love or great care — **lov·ing·ly** *adv*

¹low *vb* **lowed; low·ing** : to make the sound of a cow : MOO

²low *n* : the mooing of a cow

³low *adj* **low·er; low·est 1** : not high or tall **2** : lying or going below the usual level **3** : not loud : SOFT **4** : deep in pitch **5** : not cheerful : SAD **6** : less than usual (as in quantity or value) **7** : less than enough **8** : not strong **9** : not favorable : POOR — **low·ness** *n*

⁴low *n* **1** : a point or level that is the least in degree, size, or amount **2** : a region of reduced barometric pressure **3** : the arrangement of gears in an automobile that gives the slowest speed of travel

⁵low *adv* **low·er; low·est** : so as to be low

¹low·er *adj* **1** : located below another or others of the same kind **2** : located toward the bottom part of something **3** : placed below another or others in rank or order **4** : less advanced or developed

²lower *vb* **low·ered; low·er·ing 1** : to move to a level or position that is below or less than an earlier one **2** : to let or pull down **3** : to make or become less (as in value, amount, or volume) **4** : to reduce the height of

low·er·case *adj* : having the form a, b, c, rather than A, B, C — **lowercase** *n*

lowest common denominator *n* : LEAST COMMON DENOMINATOR

lowest common multiple *n* : LEAST COMMON MULTIPLE

low·land *n* : low flat country

lowly *adj* **low·li·er; low·li·est** : of low rank or importance: HUMBLE

loy·al *adj* : having or showing true and constant support for someone or something — **loy·al·ly** *adv*

loy·al·ty *n, pl* **loy·al·ties** : the quality or state of being true and constant in support of someone or something

loz·enge *n* : a small candy often containing medicine

LSD *n* : a dangerous drug that causes hallucinations

Lt. *abbr* lieutenant

ltd. *abbr* limited

lu·bri·cant *n* : something (as oil or grease) that makes a surface smooth or slippery

lu·bri·cate *vb* **lu·bri·cat·ed; lu·bri·cat·ing** : to apply oil or grease to in order to make smooth or slippery

lu·bri·ca·tion *n* : the act or process of making something smooth or slippery

lu·cid *adj* **1** : having or showing the ability to think clearly **2** : easily understood — **lu·cid·ly** *adv*

luck *n* **1** : something that happens to a person by or as if by chance **2** : the accidental way things happen **3** : good fortune

luck·i·ly *adv* : by good luck

lucky *adj* **luck·i·er; luck·i·est 1** : helped by luck : FORTUNATE **2** : happening because of good luck **3** : thought of as bringing good luck

lu·di·crous *adj* : funny because of being ridiculous : ABSURD — **lu·di·crous·ly** *adv*

lug *vb* **lugged; lug·ging** : to pull or carry with great effort

lug·gage *n* : suitcases for a traveler's belongings : BAGGAGE

luke·warm *adj* **1** : slightly warm **2** : not very interested or eager

¹lull *vb* **lulled; lull·ing** : to make or become sleepy or less watchful

²lull *n* : a period of calm or inactivity

lul·la·by *n, pl* **lul·la·bies** : a song for helping a baby or child fall asleep

¹lum·ber *vb* **lum·bered; lum·ber·ing** : to move in a slow or awkward way

²lumber *n* : timber especially when sawed into boards

lum·ber·jack *n* : a person whose job is cutting down trees for wood

lum·ber·yard *n* : a place where lumber is kept for sale

lu·mi·nous *adj* : giving off light — **lu·mi·nous·ly** *adv*

¹lump *n* **1** : a small piece or chunk **2** : a

swelling or growth **3** : a tight feeling in the throat caused by emotion

²lump *vb* **lumped; lump·ing 1** : to group together **2** : to form into lumps

³lump *adj* : not divided into parts

lumpy *adj* **lump·i·er; lump·i·est** : having or full of lumps

lu·nar *adj* **1** : of or relating to the moon **2** : measured by the revolutions of the moon

¹lu·na·tic *adj* : INSANE 1

²lunatic *n* **1** : an insane person **2** : a person who behaves very foolishly

¹lunch *n* **1** : a light meal especially when eaten in the middle of the day **2** : food prepared for lunch

²lunch *vb* **lunched; lunch·ing** : to eat lunch

lun·cheon *n* **1** : ¹LUNCH 1 **2** : a formal lunch

lunch·room *n* : a room (as in a school) where lunch may be eaten

lung *n* : either of two organs in the chest that are like bags and are the main breathing structure in animals that breathe air

¹lunge *n* : a sudden movement forward

²lunge *vb* **lunged; lung·ing** : to move or reach forward in a sudden forceful way

lung·fish *n* : a fish that breathes with structures like lungs as well as with gills

lu·pine *n* : a plant related to the clovers that has tall spikes of showy flowers

¹lurch *n* : a sudden swaying, tipping, or jerking movement

²lurch *vb* **lurched; lurch·ing** : to move with a sudden swaying, tipping, or jerking motion

¹lure *n* **1** : something that attracts or tempts **2** : an artificial bait for catching fish

²lure *vb* **lured; lur·ing** : to tempt by offering pleasure or gain

lu·rid *adj* **1** : causing shock or disgust **2** : glowing with an overly bright color — **lu·rid·ly** *adv*

lurk *vb* **lurked; lurk·ing** : to hide in or about a place

lus·cious *adj* **1** : having a delicious taste or smell **2** : delightful to hear, see, or feel

lush *adj* **1** : characterized by full and healthy growth **2** : covered with a thick growth of healthy plants **3** : LUXURIOUS 1 — **lush·ly** *adv* — **lush·ness** *n*

lust *n* : a strong longing

lus·ter *or* **lus·tre** *n* : the shiny quality of a surface that reflects light

lus·trous *adj* : having a shiny quality

lusty *adj* **lust·i·er; lust·i·est** : full of strength and energy

lute *n* : a musical instrument with a pear-shaped body and usually paired strings played with the fingers

lux·u·ri·ant *adj* **1** : having heavy and thick growth **2** : LUXURIOUS 1

lux·u·ri·ous *adj* **1** : very fine and comfortable : having an appealing rich quality **2** : feeling or showing a desire for fine and expensive things — **lux·u·ri·ous·ly** *adv*

lux·u·ry *n, pl* **lux·u·ries 1** : very rich, pleasant, and comfortable surroundings **2** : something desirable but expensive or hard to get **3** : something adding to pleasure or comfort but not absolutely necessary

¹-ly *adj suffix* **1** : like : similar to **2** : happening in each specified period of time : every

²-ly *adv suffix* **1** : in a specified manner **2** : from a specified point of view

lye *n* : a dangerous compound that is used in cleaning and in making soap

lying *present participle of* LIE

lymph *n* : a clear liquid like blood without the red blood cells that nourishes the tissues and carries off wastes

lym·phat·ic *adj* : relating to or carrying lymph

lymph node *n* : one of the small rounded bits of tissue in the body through which lymph passes to be filtered

lym·pho·cyte *n* : any of the white blood cells of the immune system that play a role in recognizing and destroying foreign cells, particles, or substances that have invaded the body

lynx *n, pl* **lynx** *or* **lynx·es** : any of several wildcats with rather long legs, a short tail, and often ears with tufts of long hairs at the tip

lyre *n* : a stringed musical instrument like a harp used by the ancient Greeks

¹lyr·ic *n* **1** : the words of a song — often used in pl. **2** : a poem that expresses feelings in a way that is like a song

²lyric *adj* : expressing personal emotion in a way that is like a song

M

m *n, pl* **m's** *or* **ms** *often cap* **1** : the 13th letter of the English alphabet **2** : 1000 in Roman numerals

m. *abbr* **1** male **2** meter **3** mile

ma *n, often cap* : ¹MOTHER 1

MA *abbr* Massachusetts

ma'am *n* : MADAM

mac·ad·am *n* : a road surface made of small closely packed broken stone

ma·caque *n* : a monkey mostly found in Asia that often has a short tail

mac·a·ro·ni *n* : pasta in the shape of little curved tubes

ma·caw *n* : a large parrot of Central and

South America with a long tail, a harsh voice, and bright feathers

¹mace *n* : a spice made from the dried outer covering of the nutmeg

²mace *n* **1** : a decorated pole carried by an official as a sign of authority **2** : a heavy spiked club used as a medieval weapon

ma·chete *n* : a large heavy knife used for cutting sugarcane and underbrush and as a weapon

ma·chine *n* **1** : a device with moving parts that does some desired work when it is provided with power **2** : VEHICLE 2

machine gun *n* : a gun that fires bullets continuously and rapidly

ma·chin·ery *n* **1** : a group of devices with moving parts that are used to perform specific jobs **2** : the working parts of a device used to perform a particular job **3** : the people and equipment by which something is done

machine shop *n* : a workshop in which metal articles are put together

ma·chin·ist *n* : a person who makes or works on machines

mack·er·el *n, pl* **mackerel** *or* **mackerels** : a fish of the North Atlantic that is green above with blue bars and silvery below and is often used as food

mack·i·naw *n* : a short heavy woolen coat

ma·cron *n* : a mark ¯ placed over a vowel to show that the vowel is long

mad *adj* **mad·der; mad·dest 1** : ANGRY **2** : INSANE 1 **3** : done or made without thinking **4** : INFATUATED **5** : having rabies **6** : marked by intense and often disorganized activity — **mad·ly** *adv* — **mad·ness** *n* — **like mad** : with a great amount of energy or speed

mad·am *n, pl* **mes·dames** — used without a name as a form of polite address to a woman

ma·dame *n, pl* **mes·dames** *or* **ma·dames** — used as a title that means *Mrs.* for a married woman who is not of an English-speaking nationality

mad·cap *adj* : RECKLESS, WILD

mad·den *vb* **mad·dened; mad·den·ing** : to make angry

mad·den·ing *adj* : very annoying

made *past and past participle of* MAKE

made–up *adj* : created from the imagination

mad·house *n* : a place or scene of complete confusion or noisy excitement

mad·man *n, pl* **mad·men** : a man who is or acts as if insane

mag·a·zine *n* **1** : a publication issued at regular intervals (as weekly or monthly) **2** : a storehouse or warehouse for military supplies **3** : a container in a gun for holding cartridges

ma·gen·ta *n* : a deep purplish red

mag·got *n* : a legless grub that is the larva of a fly (as a housefly)

¹mag·ic *n* **1** : the power to control natural forces possessed by certain persons (as wizards and witches) in folk tales and fiction **2** : the art or skill of performing tricks or illusions for entertainment **3** : a power that seems mysterious **4** : something that charms

²magic *adj* **1** : having or seeming to have the power to make impossible things happen **2** : of or relating to the power to make impossible things happen **3** : giving a feeling of enchantment

mag·i·cal *adj* : ²MAGIC

ma·gi·cian *n* : a person skilled in performing tricks or illusions

mag·is·trate *n* **1** : a chief officer of government **2** : a local official with some judicial power

mag·ma *n* : molten rock within the earth

mag·na·nim·i·ty *n* : the quality of being generous and noble

mag·nan·i·mous *adj* : generous and noble — **mag·nan·i·mous·ly** *adv*

mag·ne·sium *n* : a silvery white metallic chemical element that is lighter than aluminum and is used in lightweight alloys

mag·net *n* : a piece of material (as of iron, steel, or alloy) that is able to attract iron

mag·net·ic *adj* **1** : acting like a magnet **2** : of or relating to the earth's magnetism **3** : having a great power to attract people

magnetic field *n* : the portion of space near a magnetic object within which magnetic forces can be detected

magnetic needle *n* : a narrow strip of magnetized steel that is free to swing around to show the direction of the earth's magnetism

magnetic pole *n* **1** : either of the poles of a magnet **2** : either of two small regions of the earth which are located near the north and south poles and toward which a compass needle points

magnetic tape *n* : a thin ribbon of plastic coated with a magnetic material on which information (as sound) may be stored

mag·ne·tism *n* **1** : a magnet's power to attract **2** : the power to attract others : personal charm

mag·ne·tize *vb* **mag·ne·tized; mag·ne·tiz·ing** : to cause to be magnetic

mag·nif·i·cence *n* : impressive beauty or greatness

mag·nif·i·cent *adj* : very beautiful or impressive — **mag·nif·i·cent·ly** *adv*

mag·ni·fy *vb* **mag·ni·fied; mag·ni·fy·ing 1** : to enlarge in fact or appearance **2** : to cause to seem greater or more important : EXAGGERATE

magnifying glass *n* : a lens that makes something seen through it appear larger than it actually is

mag·ni·tude *n* : greatness of size or importance

mag·no·lia *n* : a tree or tall shrub having showy white, pink, yellow, or purple flowers that appear in early spring

mag·pie *n* : a noisy black-and-white bird related to the jays

Ma·hi·can *or* **Mo·hi·can** *n, pl* **Ma·hi·can** *or* **Ma·hi·cans** *or* **Mo·hi·can** *or* **Mo·hi·cans 1** : a member of an American Indian people of northeastern New York **2** : the language of the Mahican people

ma·hog·a·ny *n, pl* **ma·hog·a·nies** : a strong reddish brown wood that is used especially for furniture and is obtained from several tropical trees

maid *n* **1** : ¹MAIDEN **2** : a female servant

¹**maid·en** *n* : an unmarried girl or woman

²**maiden** *adj* **1** : UNMARRIED **2** : ¹FIRST

maid·en·hair fern *n* : a fern with slender stems and delicate feathery leaves

maiden name *n* : a woman's last name before she is married

maid of honor *n, pl* **maids of honor** : a woman who stands with the bride at a wedding

¹**mail** *n* **1** : letters and packages sent from one person to another through the post office **2** : the system used for sending and delivering letters and packages **3** : ¹E-MAIL 2

²**mail** *vb* **mailed; mail·ing** : to send letters and packages through the post office

³**mail** *n* : a fabric made of metal rings linked together and used as armor

mail·box *n* **1** : a public box in which to place outgoing letters **2** : a private box (as on a house) for the delivery of incoming letters

mail carrier *n* : LETTER CARRIER

mail·man *n, pl* **mail·men** : LETTER CARRIER

maim *vb* **maimed; maim·ing** : to injure badly or cripple by violence

¹**main** *adj* : first in size, rank, or importance : CHIEF — **main·ly** *adv*

²**main** *n* **1** : the chief part : essential point **2** : a principal line, tube, or pipe of a utility system **3** : HIGH SEAS **4** : physical strength : FORCE

main·land *n* : a continent or the largest part of a continent as distinguished from an offshore island or islands

main·mast *n* : the principal mast of a sailing ship

main·sail *n* : the principal sail on the mainmast

main·spring *n* : the principal spring in a mechanical device (as a watch or clock)

main·stay *n* **1** : the large strong rope from the maintop of a ship usually to the foot of the foremast **2** : a chief support

main·tain *vb* **main·tained; main·tain·ing 1** : to carry on : CONTINUE **2** : to keep in a particular or desired state **3** : to insist to be true **4** : to provide for : SUPPORT

main·te·nance *n* **1** : the act of keeping or providing for : the state of being kept or provided for **2** : UPKEEP

main·top *n* : a platform around the head of a mainmast

maize *n* : ¹CORN

Maj. *abbr* major

ma·jes·tic *adj* : very impressive and beautiful or dignified — **ma·jes·ti·cal·ly** *adv*

maj·es·ty *n, pl* **maj·es·ties 1** — used as a title for a king, queen, emperor, or empress **2** : the quality or state of being impressive and dignified **3** : royal dignity or authority

¹**ma·jor** *adj* **1** : great or greater in number, quantity, rank, or importance **2** : of or relating to a musical scale of eight notes with half steps between the third and fourth and between the seventh and eighth notes and with whole steps between all the others

²**major** *n* : a commissioned officer in the army, air force, or marine corps ranking above a captain

ma·jor·i·ty *n, pl* **ma·jor·i·ties 1** : a number greater than half of a total **2** : a group or party that makes up the greater part of a whole body of people **3** : the amount by which a number is more than half the total **4** : the age at which a person has the full rights of an adult

¹**make** *vb* **made ; mak·ing 1** : to form or put together out of material or parts **2** : to cause to exist or occur **3** : to prepare food or drink **4** : to cause to be or become **5** : COMPEL 1 **6** : to arrange the blankets and sheets on (a bed) so that the mattress is covered **7** : to combine to produce **8** : GET 1, GAIN **9** : ¹REACH 2 **10** : ¹DO 1, PERFORM **11** : to act so as to be — **mak·er** *n* — **make believe** : to act as if something known to be imaginary is real or true — **make fun of** : to cause to be the target of laughter in an unkind way — **make good** : FULFILL 1, COMPLETE — **make out 1** : to write out **2** : UNDERSTAND 1 **3** : IDENTIFY 1 **4** : ¹FARE — **make up 1** : to create from the imagination **2** : ²FORM 3, COMPOSE **3** : to do something to correct or repay a wrong **4** : to become friendly again **5** : to put on makeup **6** : DECIDE

²**make** *n* : ¹BRAND 2

[1]**make–be·lieve** *n* : something that is imagined to be real or true

[2]**make–believe** *adj* : not real : IMAGINARY

make·shift *adj* : serving as a temporary substitute

make·up *n* **1** : any of various cosmetics (as lipstick or powder) **2** : the way the parts or elements of something are put together or joined **3** : materials used in changing a performer's appearance (as for a play or other entertainment)

mal- *prefix* **1** : bad : badly **2** : abnormal : abnormally

mal·ad·just·ed *adj* : not able to deal with other people in a normal or healthy way

mal·a·dy *n, pl* **mal·a·dies** : a disease or disorder of the body or mind

ma·lar·ia *n* : a serious disease with chills and fever that is spread by the bite of a mosquito

[1]**male** *n* **1** : a man or a boy **2** : a person or animal that produces germ cells (as sperm) that fertilize the eggs of a female **3** : a plant with stamens but no pistil

[2]**male** *adj* **1** : of, relating to, or being the sex that fertilizes the eggs of a female **2** : bearing stamens but no pistil **3** : of or characteristic of men or boys

ma·lev·o·lent *adj* : having or showing a desire to cause harm to another person

mal·for·ma·tion *n* : something that is badly or wrongly formed

mal·ice *n* : a desire to cause harm to another person

ma·li·cious *adj* : feeling or showing a desire to cause harm to another person — **ma·li·cious·ly** *adv*

[1]**ma·lign** *adj* : MALICIOUS

[2]**malign** *vb* **ma·ligned; ma·lign·ing** : to say evil things about : SLANDER

ma·lig·nant *adj* **1** : MALICIOUS **2** : likely to cause death : DEADLY — **ma·lig·nant·ly** *adv*

mall *n* **1** : a large building or group of buildings containing a variety of shops **2** : a public area for pedestrians

mal·lard *n* : a common wild duck of the northern hemisphere that is the ancestor of the domestic ducks

mal·lea·ble *adj* : capable of being extended or shaped with blows from a hammer

mal·let *n* **1** : a hammer with a barrel-shaped head of wood or soft material **2** : a club with a short thick head and a long thin handle

mal·low *n* : a tall plant with usually large white, rose, or purplish flowers with five petals

mal·nu·tri·tion *n* : a condition of weakness and poor health that results from not eating enough food or from eating food without the proper nutrients

malt *n* **1** : grain and especially barley soaked in water until it has sprouted **2** : MALTED MILK

malt·ed milk *n* : a beverage made by dissolving a powder made from dried milk and cereals in milk

mal·treat *vb* **mal·treat·ed; mal·treat·ing** : to treat in a rough or unkind way : ABUSE

ma·ma *also* **mam·ma** *or* **mom·ma** *n* : [1]MOTHER 1

mam·mal *n* : a warm-blooded animal (as a dog, mouse, bear, whale, or human being) with a backbone that feeds its young with milk produced by the mother and has skin usually more or less covered with hair

[1]**mam·moth** *n* : a very large hairy extinct elephant with long tusks that curve upward

[2]**mammoth** *adj* : very large : HUGE

[1]**man** *n, pl* **men** **1** : an adult male human being **2** : a human being : PERSON **3** : the human race : MANKIND **4** : [1]HUSBAND **5** : an adult male servant or employee **6** : one of the pieces with which various games (as chess and checkers) are played **7** : a member of the group to which human beings belong including both modern humans and extinct related forms

[2]**man** *vb* **manned; man·ning** : to work at or do the work of operating

Man. *abbr* Manitoba

man·age *vb* **man·aged; man·ag·ing** **1** : to look after and make decisions about **2** : to succeed in doing : accomplish what is desired — **man·age·able** *adj*

man·age·ment *n* **1** : the act of looking after and making decisions about something **2** : the people who look after and make decisions about something

man·ag·er *n* **1** : a person who is in charge of a business or part of a business **2** : a person who directs the training and performance of a sports team

man·a·tee *n* : a mainly tropical water-dwelling mammal that eats plants and has a broad rounded tail

man·da·rin *n* **1** : a public official of the Chinese Empire **2** *cap* : the chief dialect of China

man·date *n* **1** : an order from a higher court to a lower court **2** : a command or instruction from an authority **3** : the instruction given by voters to their elected representatives

man·da·tory *adj* : required by law or by a command

man·di·ble *n* **1** : a lower jaw often with its soft parts **2** : either the upper or lower part of the bill of a bird **3** : either of a pair of mouth parts of some invertebrates (as an insect) that are usually used for biting

man·do·lin *n* : a musical instrument with four pairs of strings played by plucking

mane *n* : long heavy hair growing about the neck and head of some animals (as a horse or lion) — **maned** *adj*

¹**ma·neu·ver** *n* **1** : skillful action or management **2** : a training exercise by armed forces **3** : a planned movement of troops or ships

²**maneuver** *vb* **ma·neu·vered; ma·neu·ver·ing** **1** : to guide skillfully **2** : to move troops or ships where they are needed — **ma·neu·ver·abil·i·ty** *n* — **ma·neu·ver·able** *adj*

man·ga·nese *n* : a grayish white brittle metallic chemical element that resembles iron

mange *n* : a contagious skin disease usually of domestic animals in which there is itching and loss of hair

man·ger *n* : an open box in which food for farm animals is placed

man·gle *vb* **man·gled; man·gling** **1** : to injure badly by cutting, tearing, or crushing **2** : to spoil while making or performing

man·go *n, pl* **man·goes** *or* **man·gos** : a tropical fruit with yellowish red skin and juicy mildly tart yellow flesh

mangy *adj* **mang·i·er; mang·i·est** **1** : affected with mange **2** : SHABBY 1 **3** : SEEDY 2

man·hole *n* : a covered hole (as in a street) large enough to let a person pass through

man·hood *n* **1** : qualities (as strength and courage) believed to be typical of men **2** : the state of being an adult human male **3** : adult human males

ma·nia *n* : extreme enthusiasm

ma·ni·ac *n* **1** : a person who is or behaves as if insane **2** : a person who is extremely enthusiastic about something

¹**man·i·cure** *n* : a treatment for the care of the hands and fingernails

²**manicure** *vb* **man·i·cured; man·i·cur·ing** : to give a beauty treatment to the hands and fingernails

man·i·cur·ist *n* : a person whose job is the treatment of hands and fingernails

¹**man·i·fest** *adj* : easy to detect or recognize : OBVIOUS

²**manifest** *vb* **man·i·fest·ed; man·i·fest·ing** : to show plainly

man·i·fes·ta·tion *n* **1** : the act of showing plainly **2** : something that makes clear : EVIDENCE

man·i·fold *adj* : of many and various kinds

ma·nip·u·late *vb* **ma·nip·u·lat·ed; ma·nip·u·lat·ing** **1** : to operate, use, or move with the hands or by mechanical means **2** : to manage skillfully and especially with intent to deceive

man·kind *n* **1** : human beings **2** : men as distinguished from women

man·ly *adj* **man·li·er; man·li·est** : having or showing qualities (as strength or courage) often felt to be proper for a man — **man·li·ness** *n*

man–made *adj* : made by people rather than nature

man·na *n* **1** : food which according to the Bible was supplied by a miracle to the Israelites in the wilderness **2** : a usually sudden and unexpected source of pleasure or gain

man·ne·quin *n* : a form representing the human figure used especially for displaying clothes

man·ner *n* **1** : the way something is done or happens **2** : a way of acting **3 manners** *pl* : behavior toward or in the presence of other people **4** : ¹SORT 1

man·nered *adj* : having manners of a specified kind

man·ner·ism *n* : a habit (as of looking or moving in a certain way) that occurs commonly in a person's behavior

man·ner·ly *adj* : showing good manners

man–of–war *n, pl* **men–of–war** : WARSHIP

man·or *n* : a large estate

man·sion *n* : a large fine house

man·slaugh·ter *n* : the unintentional but unlawful killing of a person

man·ta ray *n* : a very large ray of warm seas that has fins that resemble wings

man·tel *n* : a shelf above a fireplace

man·tel·piece *n* **1** : a shelf above a fireplace along with side pieces **2** : MANTEL

man·tis *n, pl* **man·tis·es** *also* **man·tes** : PRAYING MANTIS

man·tle *n* **1** : a loose sleeveless outer garment **2** : something that covers or wraps **3** : the part of the earth's interior beneath the crust and above the central core **4** : a fold of the body wall of a mollusk that produces the shell material

¹**man·u·al** *adj* **1** : of or relating to hard physical work **2** : operated by the hands **3** : of or with the hands — **man·u·al·ly** *adv*

²**manual** *n* : HANDBOOK

¹**man·u·fac·ture** *vb* **man·u·fac·tured; man·u·fac·tur·ing** **1** : to make from raw materials by hand or machinery **2** : to create using the imagination often in order to deceive — **man·u·fac·tur·er** *n*

²**manufacture** *n* **1** : the making of products by hand or machinery **2** : PRODUCTION 2

ma·nure *n* : material (as animal wastes) used to fertilize land

man·u·script *n* **1** : a document written by hand especially before the development of printing **2** : the original copy of a writer's work before it is printed

¹many *adj* **more ; most 1** : amounting to a large number **2** : being one of a large but not definite number

²many *pron* : a large number of people or things

³many *n* : a large number

¹map *n* **1** : a picture or chart that shows the features of an area **2** : a picture or chart of the sky showing the position of stars and planets

²map *vb* **mapped; map·ping 1** : to make a map of **2** : to plan in detail

ma·ple *n* : a tree having deeply notched leaves and hard pale wood and including some whose sap is evaporated to a sweet syrup (**maple syrup**) and a brownish sugar (**maple sugar**)

mar *vb* **marred; mar·ring** : to ruin the beauty or perfection of : SPOIL

Mar. *abbr* March

ma·ra·ca *n* : a musical rhythm instrument made of a dried gourd with seeds or pebbles inside that is usually played in pairs by shaking

mar·a·thon *n* **1** : a long-distance running race **2** : a long hard contest

ma·raud *vb* **ma·raud·ed; ma·raud·ing** : to roam about and raid in search of things to steal — **ma·raud·er** *n*

mar·ble *n* **1** : a type of limestone that is capable of taking a high polish and is used in architecture and sculpture **2** : a little ball (as of glass) used in a children's game (**marbles**)

¹march *vb* **marched; march·ing 1** : to move or cause to move along with a steady regular step especially with others **2** : to make steady progress — **march·er** *n*

²march *n* **1** : the action of moving along with a steady regular step especially with others **2** : an organized walk by a large group of people to support or protest something **3** : the distance covered in marching **4** : a regular and organized way that soldiers walk **5** : a musical piece in a lively rhythm with a strong beat that is suitable to march to

March *n* : the third month of the year

mar·chio·ness *n* **1** : the wife or widow of a marquess **2** : a woman who holds the rank of a marquess in her own right

mare *n* : an adult female horse or related animal (as a zebra or donkey)

mar·ga·rine *n* : a food product made usually from vegetable oils and skim milk and used as a spread or for cooking

mar·gin *n* **1** : the part of a page or sheet outside the main body of print or writing **2** : ¹BORDER 2 **3** : an extra amount (as of time

or money) allowed for use if needed **4** : a measurement of difference

mari·gold *n* : a plant grown for its usually yellow, orange, or brownish red flowers

mar·i·jua·na *n* : dried leaves and flowers of the hemp plant smoked as a drug

ma·ri·na *n* : a dock or basin providing a place to anchor motorboats and yachts

¹ma·rine *adj* **1** : of or relating to the sea **2** : of or relating to the navigation of the sea : NAUTICAL **3** : of or relating to soldiers in the United States Marine Corps

²marine *n* **1** : a soldier of the United States Marine Corps **2** : the ships of a country

mar·i·ner *n* : SEAMAN 1, SAILOR

mar·i·o·nette *n* : a puppet moved by attached strings

mar·i·tal *adj* : of or relating to marriage

mar·i·time *adj* **1** : of or relating to ocean navigation or trade **2** : bordering on or living near the sea

¹mark *n* **1** : a blemish (as a scratch or stain) made on a surface **2** : a written or printed symbol **3** : something that shows that something else exists : SIGN, INDICATION **4** : something aimed at : TARGET **5** : a grade or score showing the quality of work or conduct **6** : something designed or serving to record position **7** : the starting line of a race

²mark *vb* **marked; mark·ing 1** : to indicate a location **2** : to set apart by a line or boundary **3** : to make a shape, symbol, or word on **4** : to decide and show the value or quality of : GRADE **5** : to be an important characteristic of **6** : to take notice of — **mark·er** *n*

marked *adj* **1** : having notes or information written on it **2** : NOTICEABLE **3** : showing identification

¹mar·ket *n* **1** : a public place where people gather to buy and sell things **2** : a store where foods are sold to the public **3** : a region in which something can be sold **4** : an opportunity for selling something

²market *vb* **mar·ket·ed; mar·ket·ing** : to sell or promote the sale of

mar·ket·place *n* : a location where public sales are held

mark·ing *n* **1** : a shape, symbol, or word on something **2** : the arrangement or pattern of contrasting colors on an animal

marks·man *n, pl* **marks·men** : a person who shoots well — **marks·man·ship** *n*

mar·ma·lade *n* : a jam containing pieces of fruit and fruit rind

mar·mo·set *n* : a small monkey of South and Central America with soft fur and a bushy tail

mar·mot *n* : a stocky burrowing animal with short legs and a bushy tail that is related to the squirrels

¹**ma·roon** *vb* **ma·rooned; ma·roon·ing** : to abandon in a place that is difficult to escape from

²**maroon** *n* : a dark red

mar·quess *n* : a British nobleman ranking below a duke and above an earl

mar·quis *n* : MARQUESS

mar·quise *n* : MARCHIONESS

mar·riage *n* **1** : the state of being united in a legal relationship as husband and wife **2** : the act of getting married

mar·row *n* : BONE MARROW

mar·ry *vb* **mar·ried; mar·ry·ing 1** : to take for husband or wife **2** : to become joined in marriage **3** : to join in marriage **4** : to give (as a child) in marriage

Mars *n* : the planet that is fourth in order of distance from the sun, is known for its redness, and has a diameter of about 4200 miles (6800 kilometers)

marsh *n* : an area of soft wet land with grasses and related plants

¹**mar·shal** *n* **1** : a person who arranges and directs ceremonies **2** : an officer of the highest rank in some military forces **3** : a federal official having duties similar to those of a sheriff **4** : the head of a division of a city government

²**marshal** *vb* **mar·shaled** *or* **mar·shalled; mar·shal·ing** *or* **mar·shal·ling** : to arrange in order

marsh·mal·low *n* : a soft spongy sweet food made from corn syrup, sugar, and gelatin

marshy *adj* **marsh·i·er; marsh·i·est** : like or containing soft wet land

mar·su·pi·al *n* : a mammal (as a kangaroo or opossum) that does not develop a true placenta and usually has a pouch on the female's abdomen in which the young develop and are carried

mart *n* : a trading place : MARKET

mar·ten *n* : a slender animal related to the weasel that has soft gray or brown fur and often climbs trees

mar·tial *adj* : having to do with or suitable for war

martial art *n* : any of several forms of combat and self-defense (as karate or judo) that are widely practiced as sports

mar·tin *n* **1** : a European swallow with a forked tail **2** : any of several birds (as the North American **purple martin**) resembling or related to the true martin

Mar·tin Lu·ther King Day *n* : the third Monday in January observed as a legal holiday in the United States

¹**mar·tyr** *n* : a person who suffers greatly or dies rather than give up his or her religion or principles

²**martyr** *vb* **mar·tyred; mar·tyr·ing** : to put to death for refusing to give up a belief

¹**mar·vel** *n* : something that causes wonder or astonishment

²**marvel** *vb* **mar·veled** *or* **mar·velled; mar·vel·ing** *or* **mar·vel·ling** : to feel astonishment or wonder

mar·vel·ous *or* **mar·vel·lous** *adj* **1** : causing wonder or astonishment **2** : of the finest kind or quality — **mar·vel·ous·ly** *adv*

masc. *abbr* masculine

mas·cot *n* : a person, animal, or object adopted as the symbol of a group (as a school or sports team) and believed to bring good luck

mas·cu·line *adj* **1** : of the male sex **2** : characteristic of or relating to men : MALE

¹**mash** *vb* **mashed; mash·ing** : to make into a soft mass

²**mash** *n* **1** : a mixture of ground feeds used for feeding livestock **2** : a mass of something made soft by beating or crushing **3** : a wet mixture of crushed malt or grain used to make alcoholic drinks

¹**mask** *n* **1** : a cover for the face or part of the face used for disguise or protection **2** : something that disguises or conceals

²**mask** *vb* **masked; mask·ing** : CONCEAL, DISGUISE

ma·son *n* : a person who builds or works with stone or brick

ma·son·ry *n, pl* **ma·son·ries 1** : something built of stone or brick **2** : the work done using stone or brick **3** : the art, trade, or occupation of a mason

masque *n* : an old form of dramatic entertainment in which the actors wore masks

¹**mas·quer·ade** *n* **1** : a party (as a dance) at which people wear masks and costumes **2** : the act of pretending to be something different

²**masquerade** *vb* **mas·quer·ad·ed; mas·quer·ad·ing 1** : to wear a disguise **2** : to pretend to be something different : POSE — **mas·quer·ad·er** *n*

¹**mass** *n* **1** : a large quantity or number **2** : an amount of something that holds or clings together **3** : large size : BULK **4** : the principal part : main body **5 masses** *pl* : the body of ordinary or common people

²**mass** *vb* **massed; mass·ing** : to collect into a large body

³**mass** *n, often cap* : a religious service in which communion is celebrated

Mass. *abbr* Massachusetts

¹**mas·sa·cre** *n* : the violent and cruel killing of a large number of people

²**massacre** *vb* **mas·sa·cred; mas·sa·cring** : to kill a large number of people in a violent and cruel manner

¹mas·sage *n* : a soothing treatment of the body done by rubbing, kneading, and tapping

²massage *vb* **mas·saged; mas·sag·ing** : to give a soothing treatment to (the body) by rubbing, stroking, or pressing with the hands

mas·sive *adj* : very large, heavy, and solid

mast *n* : a long pole that rises from the bottom of a ship and supports the sails and rigging — **mast·ed** *adj*

¹mas·ter *n* **1** : someone having authority over another person, an animal, or a thing **2** : a male teacher **3** : an artist or performer of great skill **4** — used as a title for a young boy too young to be called *mister*

²master *vb* **mas·tered; mas·ter·ing 1** : to get control of **2** : to become skillful at

mas·ter·ful *adj* **1** : tending to take control : displaying authority **2** : having or showing great skill

mas·ter·ly *adj* : showing exceptional knowledge or skill

mas·ter·piece *n* : something done or made with exceptional skill

master sergeant *n* : a noncommissioned officer in the army ranking above a sergeant first class or in the air force ranking above a technical sergeant or in the marines ranking above a gunnery sergeant

mas·tery *n* **1** : complete control **2** : a very high level of skill or knowledge

mast·head *n* : the top of a ship's mast

mas·ti·cate *vb* **mas·ti·cat·ed; mas·ti·cat·ing** : ¹CHEW

mas·tiff *n* : a very large powerful dog with a smooth coat

¹mat *n* **1** : a piece of material used as a floor or seat covering or in front of a door to wipe the shoes on **2** : a decorative piece of material used under dishes or vases **3** : a pad or cushion for gymnastics or wrestling **4** : something made up of many tangled strands

²mat *vb* **mat·ted; mat·ting** : to form into a tangled mass

mat·a·dor *n* : a bullfighter who plays the most important human part in a bullfight

¹match *n* **1** : a person or thing that is equal to or as good as another **2** : a contest between two individuals or teams **3** : a thing that is exactly like another thing **4** : two people or things that go well together **5** : MARRIAGE 1

²match *vb* **matched; match·ing 1** : to be the same or suitable to one another **2** : to choose something that is the same as another or goes with it **3** : to place in competition **4** : to be as good as

³match *n* : a short slender piece of material

tipped with a mixture that produces fire when scratched

match·book *n* : a small folder containing rows of paper matches

match·less *adj* : having no equal : better than any other of the same kind

¹mate *n* **1** : COMPANION 1, COMRADE **2** *chiefly British* : ¹CHUM, FRIEND — often used as a familiar form of address **3** : either member of a breeding pair of animals **4** : an officer on a ship used to carry passengers or freight who ranks below the captain **5** : either member of a married couple **6** : either of two objects that go together

²mate *vb* **mat·ed; mat·ing 1** : to join as married partners **2** : to come or bring together for breeding

¹ma·te·ri·al *adj* **1** : of, relating to, or made of matter : PHYSICAL **2** : of or relating to a person's bodily needs or wants **3** : having real importance — **ma·te·ri·al·ly** *adv*

²material *n* **1** : the elements, substance, or parts of which something is made or can be made **2** : equipment needed for doing something

ma·te·ri·al·ize *vb* **ma·te·ri·al·ized; ma·te·ri·al·iz·ing 1** : to appear suddenly **2** : to become actual fact **3** : to cause to take on a physical form

ma·ter·nal *adj* **1** : of or relating to a mother **2** : related through the mother — **ma·ter·nal·ly** *adv*

ma·ter·ni·ty *n* : the state of being a mother

math *n* : MATHEMATICS

math·e·mat·i·cal *adj* **1** : of or relating to numbers, quantities, measurements, and the relations between them : of or relating to mathematics **2** : ¹EXACT — **math·e·mat·i·cal·ly** *adv*

math·e·ma·ti·cian *n* : a specialist in mathematics

math·e·mat·ics *n* : the science that studies and explains numbers, quantities, measurements, and the relations between them

mat·i·nee *or* **mat·i·née** *n* : a musical or dramatic performance in the afternoon

ma·tri·arch *n* : a woman who is the head of a family, group, or state

mat·ri·mo·ni·al *adj* : of or relating to marriage

mat·ri·mo·ny *n* : MARRIAGE 1

ma·tron *n* **1** : a married woman usually of high social position **2** : a woman who is in charge of women or children (as in a school or police station)

¹mat·ter *n* **1** : something to be dealt with or considered **2** : PROBLEM 2, DIFFICULTY **3** : the substance things are made of : something that takes up space and has weight **4** : material substance of a certain kind or function **5** : PUS **6** : a small quantity or amount — **as a matter of fact** : ACTUALLY — **no matter** : it makes no difference — **no matter what** : regardless of the costs or consequences

²**matter** *vb* **mat·tered; mat·ter·ing** : to be of importance

mat·ter–of–fact *adj* : sticking to or concerned with fact and usually not showing emotion — **mat·ter–of–fact·ly** *adv*

mat·ting *n* : rough fabric used as a floor covering

mat·tress *n* : a springy pad for use on a bed

¹**ma·ture** *adj* **1** : fully grown or developed : ADULT, RIPE **2** : having or showing the qualities of an adult person

²**mature** *vb* **ma·tured; ma·tur·ing** : to reach full development

ma·tu·ri·ty *n* : the condition of being fully developed

¹**maul** *n* : a heavy hammer used especially for driving wedges or posts

²**maul** *vb* **mauled; maul·ing 1** : to attack and injure by biting, cutting, or tearing flesh **2** : to handle roughly

mauve, *n* : a medium purple, violet, or lilac

maxi- *prefix* : very long or large

max·il·la *n, pl* **max·il·lae 1** : an upper jaw especially of a mammal **2** : either of the pair of mouth parts next behind the mandibles of an arthropod (as an insect or a crustacean)

max·im *n* : a short saying (as "live and let live") expressing a general truth or rule of conduct

¹**max·i·mum** *n, pl* **max·i·ma** *or* **maximums** : the highest value : greatest amount

²**maximum** *adj* : as great as possible in amount or degree

³**maximum** *adv* : at the most

may *helping verb, past* **might** ; *present sing & pl* **may 1** : have permission to **2** : be in some degree likely to **3** — used to express a wish **4** — used to express purpose

May *n* : the fifth month of the year

may·be *adv* : possibly but not certainly

mayn't : may not

may·on·naise *n* : a creamy dressing usually made of egg yolk, oil, and vinegar or lemon juice

may·or *n* : an official elected to serve as head of a city, town, or borough

maze *n* : a confusing arrangement of paths or passages

MB *abbr* **1** Manitoba **2** megabyte

Md., MD *abbr* Maryland

M.D. *abbr* doctor of medicine

me *pron, objective case of* I

Me., ME *abbr* Maine

mead·ow *n* : usually moist and low grassland

mead·ow·lark *n* : a songbird that has brownish upper parts and a yellow breast

mea·ger *or* **mea·gre** *adj* **1** : not enough in quality or amount **2** : having little flesh : THIN

¹**meal** *n* **1** : the food eaten or prepared for eating at one time **2** : the act or time of eating

²**meal** *n* : coarsely ground seeds of a cereal grass and especially of corn

mealy *adj* **meal·i·er; meal·i·est** : soft, dry, and crumbly — **meal·i·ness** *n*

¹**mean** *vb* **meant ; mean·ing 1** : to represent or have as a definite explanation or idea : SIGNIFY **2** : to be an indication of **3** : to have in mind as a purpose : INTEND **4** : to intend for a particular use **5** : to have importance to

²**mean** *adj* **mean·er; mean·est 1** : deliberately unkind **2** : STINGY 1 **3** : low in quality, worth, or dignity **4** : EXCELLENT — **mean·ly** *adv* — **mean·ness** *n*

³**mean** *adj* : occurring or being in a middle position : AVERAGE

⁴**mean** *n* **1** : a middle point or something (as a place, time, number, or rate) that falls at or near a middle point : MODERATION **2** : ARITHMETIC MEAN **3 means** *pl* : something that helps a person to get what he or she wants **4 means** *pl* : WEALTH 1 — **by all means** : CERTAINLY 1 — **by any means** : in any way — **by means of** : through the use of — **by no means** : certainly not

me·an·der *vb* **me·an·dered; me·an·der·ing 1** : to follow a winding course **2** : to wander without a goal or purpose

mean·ing *n* **1** : the idea that is represented by a word, phrase, or statement **2** : the idea a person intends to express by something said or done **3** : the reason or explanation for something **4** : the quality of communicating something or of being important

mean·ing·ful *adj* : having a meaning or purpose — **mean·ing·ful·ly** *adv*

mean·ing·less *adj* : having no meaning or importance

¹**mean·time** *n* **1** : the time between events or points of time **2** : a time during which more than one thing is being done

²**meantime** *adv* : in the time between events or points of time or during which more than one thing is being done

¹**mean·while** *n* : ¹MEANTIME

²**meanwhile** *adv* **1** : ²MEANTIME **2** : at the same time

mea·sles *n pl* **1** : a contagious disease in which there are fever and red spots on the skin **2** : any of several diseases (as **German measles**) resembling true measles — used as singular or plural

mea·sly *adj* **mea·sli·er; mea·sli·est :** so small or unimportant as to be rejected with scorn

mea·sur·able *adj* **:** capable of having the size, extent, amount, or significance determined — **mea·sur·ably** *adv*

¹mea·sure *n* **1 :** EXTENT 2, DEGREE, AMOUNT **2 :** the size, capacity, or quantity of something that has been determined **3 :** something (as a yardstick or cup) used in determining size, capacity, or quantity **4 :** a unit used in determining size, capacity, or quantity **5 :** a system of determining size, capacity, or quantity **6 :** the notes and rests between bar lines on a musical staff **7 :** a way of accomplishing something — **for good measure :** as an extra

²measure *vb* **mea·sured; mea·sur·ing 1 :** to find out the size, extent, or amount of **2 :** to separate out a fixed amount **3 :** ¹ESTIMATE **4 :** to bring into comparison **5 :** to give a determination of size, capacity, or quantity **:** INDICATE **6 :** to have as its size, capacity, or quantity — **measure up :** to satisfy needs or requirements

mea·sure·ment *n* **1 :** the act of determining size, capacity, or quantity **2 :** the extent, size, capacity, or amount of something as has been determined

meat *n* **1 :** the flesh of an animal used as food — often does not include the flesh of fish or seafood **2 :** solid food as distinguished from drink **3 :** the part of something that can be eaten **4 :** the most important part **:** SUBSTANCE — **meat·less** *adj*

meat·ball *n* **:** a small round lump of chopped or ground meat

me·chan·ic *n* **:** a person who makes or repairs machines

me·chan·i·cal *adj* **1 :** of or relating to machinery **2 :** made or operated by a machine **3 :** done or produced as if by a machine — **me·chan·i·cal·ly** *adv*

me·chan·ics *n pl* **1 :** a science dealing with the action of forces on objects **2 :** the way something works or things are done — used as singular or plural

mech·a·nism *n* **1 :** a piece of machinery **2 :** the parts by which a machine operates **3 :** the parts or steps that make up a process or activity

mech·a·nize *vb* **mech·a·nized; mech·a·niz·ing 1 :** to cause to be done by machines rather than humans or animals **2 :** to equip with machinery

med·al *n* **:** a piece of metal often in the form of a coin with a design and words in honor of a special event, a person, or an achievement

me·dal·lion *n* **1 :** a large medal **2 :** a decoration shaped like a large medal

med·dle *vb* **med·dled; med·dling :** to be overly interested or involved in someone else's business

med·dle·some *adj* **:** intruding in another person's business in an inconsiderate and annoying way

me·dia *n* **:** the system and organizations of communication through which information is spread to a large number of people — used as singular or plural

med·i·cal *adj* **:** of or relating to the science or practice of medicine or to the treatment of disease — **med·i·cal·ly** *adv*

med·i·cate *vb* **med·i·cat·ed; med·i·cat·ing 1 :** to treat with medicine **2 :** to add medicinal material to

med·i·ca·tion *n* **:** MEDICINE 1

me·dic·i·nal *adj* **:** used or likely to prevent, cure, or relieve disease — **me·dic·i·nal·ly** *adv*

med·i·cine *n* **1 :** something (as a pill or liquid) used to prevent, cure, or relieve a disease **2 :** a science dealing with the prevention, cure, or relief of disease

medicine dropper *n* **:** DROPPER 2

medicine man *n* **:** a person especially among American Indian groups believed to have magic powers to cure illnesses and keep away evil spirits

me·di·eval *also* **me·di·ae·val** *adj* **:** of or relating to the Middle Ages

me·di·o·cre *adj* **:** neither good nor bad **:** ORDINARY

med·i·tate *vb* **med·i·tat·ed; med·i·tat·ing 1 :** to consider carefully **:** PLAN **2 :** to spend time in quiet thinking **:** REFLECT

med·i·ta·tion *n* **:** the act or an instance of planning or thinking quietly

Med·i·ter·ra·nean *adj* **:** of or relating to the Mediterranean Sea or to the lands or peoples surrounding it

¹me·di·um *n, pl* **me·di·ums** *or* **me·dia 1 :** something that is between or in the middle **2 :** the thing by which or through which something is done **3 :** the substance in which something lives or acts **4** *pl usually* **media :** a form or system of communication, information, or entertainment **5 :** a person through whom other persons try to communicate with the spirits of the dead

²medium *adj* **:** intermediate in amount, quality, position, or degree

med·ley *n, pl* **medleys 1 :** MIXTURE 2, JUMBLE **2 :** a musical selection made up of a series of different songs or parts of different compositions

me·dul·la ob·lon·ga·ta *n* **:** the part of the brain that joins the spinal cord and is concerned especially with control of involuntary activities (as breathing and beating of the heart) necessary for life

meek *adj* **meek·er; meek·est** : having or showing a quiet, gentle, and humble nature — **meek·ly** *adv* — **meek·ness** *n*

¹meet *vb* **met; meet·ing 1** : to get to know : become acquainted **2** : to come upon or across **3** : to be at a place to greet or keep an appointment **4** : to approach from the opposite direction **5** : to touch and join or cross **6** : to experience something **7** : to hold a gathering or assembly **8** : to be sensed by **9** : to deal with **10** : to fulfill the requirements of : SATISFY

²meet *n* : a meeting for sports competition

meet·ing *n* **1** : the act of persons or things that come together **2** : a gathering of people for a particular purpose

meet·ing·house *n* : a building used for public assembly and especially for Protestant worship

mega·byte *n* : a unit of computer information storage capacity equal to 1,048,576 bytes

mega·phone *n* : a device shaped like a cone that is used to direct the voice and increase its loudness

¹mel·an·choly *adj* : SAD 1

²melancholy *n* : a sad or gloomy mood

¹mel·low *adj* **1** : fully ripe or mature **2** : made mild by age **3** : being clear, full, and pure : not harsh **4** : very calm and relaxed — **mel·low·ness** *n*

²mellow *vb* **mel·lowed; mel·low·ing** : to make or become mild or relaxed especially over time

me·lod·ic *adj* : MELODIOUS

me·lo·di·ous *adj* : having a pleasant musical sound — **me·lo·di·ous·ly** *adv*

melo·dra·mat·ic *adj* : extremely or overly emotional

mel·o·dy *n, pl* **mel·o·dies 1** : pleasing arrangement of sounds **2** : a series of musical notes or tones arranged in a definite pattern of pitch and rhythm **3** : the main part in a musical composition

mel·on *n* : a usually large fruit (as a watermelon or cantaloupe) that grows on a vine and has juicy sweet flesh and a hard rind

melt *vb* **melt·ed; melt·ing 1** : to change from a solid to a liquid usually through the action of heat **2** : to grow less : DISAPPEAR **3** : to make or become gentle : SOFTEN **4** : to lose clear outline

melting point *n* : the temperature at which a solid melts

mem·ber *n* **1** : someone or something that is part of a group **2** : a part (as an arm or leg) of a person or animal **3** : a part of a structure

mem·ber·ship *n* **1** : the state or fact of belonging to a group **2** : the whole number of individuals that make up a group

mem·brane *n* : a thin soft flexible layer especially of animal or plant tissue

mem·bra·nous *adj* : made of or like membrane

me·men·to *n, pl* **me·men·tos** *or* **me·men·toes** : something that serves as a reminder

mem·o·ra·ble *adj* : worth remembering : not easily forgotten — **mem·o·ra·bly** *adv*

mem·o·ran·dum *n, pl* **mem·o·ran·dums** *or* **mem·o·ran·da 1** : an informal report or message **2** : a written reminder

¹me·mo·ri·al *n* : something by which the memory of a person or an event is kept alive : MONUMENT

²memorial *adj* : serving to honor the memory of a person or event

Memorial Day *n* : a legal holiday in remembrance of war dead observed on the last Monday in May in most states of the United States

mem·o·rize *vb* **mem·o·rized; mem·o·riz·ing** : to learn by heart

mem·o·ry *n, pl* **mem·o·ries 1** : the power or process of remembering **2** : the store of things learned and kept in the mind **3** : the act of remembering and honoring **4** : something remembered **5** : the time within which past events are remembered **6** : a device or part in a computer which can receive and store information for use when wanted **7** : capacity for storing information

men *pl of* MAN

¹men·ace *n* **1** : DANGER 2 **2** : an annoying person

²menace *vb* **men·aced; men·ac·ing** : to threaten harm to

me·nag·er·ie *n* : a collection of wild animals kept especially to be shown to the public

¹mend *vb* **mend·ed; mend·ing 1** : IMPROVE, CORRECT **2** : to put into good shape or working order again **3** : to improve in health : HEAL — **mend·er** *n*

²mend *n* : a place where something has been fixed so that it is usable again — **on the mend** : getting better

men·folk *or* **men·folks** *n pl* : the men of a family or community

men·ha·den *n, pl* **menhaden** : a fish of the Atlantic coast of the United States that is related to the herring and is a source of oil and fertilizer

me·nial *adj* : of or relating to boring or unpleasant work that does not require special skill

men–of–war *pl of* MAN-OF-WAR

me·no·rah *n* : a holder for candles used in Jewish worship

men·stru·a·tion *n* : a discharge of bloody fluid from the uterus that usually happens each month

-ment *n suffix* **1** : result, goal, or method of a specified action **2** : action : process **3** : place of a specified action **4** : state : condition

men·tal *adj* **1** : of or relating to the mind **2** : done in the mind **3** : intended for the care of persons affected by a disorder of the mind — **men·tal·ly** *adv*

men·tal·i·ty *n* **1** : mental ability **2** : a particular way of thinking : OUTLOOK

men·thol *n* : a white crystalline soothing substance from oils of mint

¹**men·tion** *n* : a short statement calling attention to something or someone

²**mention** *vb* **men·tioned; men·tion·ing** : to refer to or speak about briefly

menu *n* **1** : a list of dishes that may be ordered in a restaurant **2** : the dishes or kinds of food served at a meal **3** : a list shown on a computer screen from which a user can select an operation for the computer to perform

¹**me·ow** *n* : the cry of a cat

²**meow** *vb* **me·owed; me·ow·ing** : to make the cry of a cat

mer·can·tile *adj* : of or relating to merchants or trade

¹**mer·ce·nary** *n, pl* **mer·ce·nar·ies** : a soldier paid by a foreign country to fight in its army

²**mercenary** *adj* **1** : doing something only for the pay or reward **2** : greedy for money

mer·chan·dise *n* : goods that are bought and sold

mer·chant *n* **1** : a person who buys and sells goods especially on a large scale or with foreign countries **2** : STOREKEEPER 1

merchant marine *n* **1** : the trading ships of a nation **2** : the people who work in trading ships

mer·ci·ful *adj* : having or showing mercy or compassion — **mer·ci·ful·ly** *adv*

mer·ci·less *adj* : having no mercy or pity — **mer·ci·less·ly** *adv*

mer·cu·ry *n* **1** : a heavy silvery white poisonous metallic chemical element that is liquid at ordinary temperatures **2** : the column of mercury in a thermometer or barometer **3** *cap* : the planet that is nearest the sun and has a diameter of about 3000 miles (4700 kilometers)

mer·cy *n, pl* **mer·cies** **1** : kind and forgiving treatment of someone (as a wrongdoer or an opponent) **2** : kindness or help given to an unfortunate person **3** : a kind sympathetic disposition : willingness to forgive, spare, or help **4** : a blessing as an act of divine love **5** : a fortunate happening — **at the mercy of** : completely without protection from

mere *adj, superlative* **mer·est** : nothing more than

mere·ly *adv* : nothing else than : JUST

merge *vb* **merged; merg·ing** : to be or cause to be combined or blended into a single unit

merg·er *n* : the combination of two or more businesses into one

me·rid·i·an *n* **1** : any imaginary semicircle on the earth's surface reaching from the north pole to the south pole **2** : a representation of a meridian on a map or globe numbered according to degrees of longitude

me·ringue *n* : a light mixture of beaten egg whites and sugar used especially as a topping for pies or cakes

me·ri·no *n, pl* **me·ri·nos** **1** : a sheep of a breed that produces a heavy fleece of white fine wool **2** : a fine wool and cotton yarn

¹**mer·it** *n* **1** : the condition or fact of deserving reward or punishment **2** : ²WORTH 1, VALUE **3** : a quality worthy of praise : VIRTUE

²**merit** *vb* **mer·it·ed; mer·it·ing** : to be worthy of or have a right to

mer·i·to·ri·ous *adj* : deserving reward or honor : PRAISEWORTHY

mer·maid *n* : an imaginary sea creature usually shown with a woman's head and body and a fish's tail

mer·man *n, pl* **mer·men** : an imaginary sea creature usually shown with a man's head and body and a fish's tail

mer·ri·ment *n* : laughter and enjoyment

mer·ry *adj* **mer·ri·er; mer·ri·est** **1** : full of joy and good cheer **2** : full of festive celebration and enjoyment — **mer·ri·ly** *adv*

mer·ry–go–round *n* : a round platform that spins and has seats and figures of animals on which people sit for a ride

mer·ry·mak·er *n* : a person taking part in joyful celebration

mer·ry·mak·ing *n* : fun and enjoyment : joyful celebration

me·sa *n* : a hill with a flat top and steep sides

mesdames *pl of* MADAM, MADAME *or* MRS.

¹**mesh** *n* **1** : a material of open texture with evenly spaced holes **2** : one of the spaces formed by the threads of a net or the wires of a sieve or screen **3** : the coming or fitting together (as of the teeth of two sets of gears)

²**mesh** *vb* **meshed; mesh·ing** : to fit or join together

mes·mer·ize *vb* **mes·mer·ized; mes·mer·iz·ing** : to hold the complete attention of : FASCINATE

Mes·o·zo·ic *n* : an era of geological history which extends from the Paleozoic to the Cenozoic and in which dinosaurs are present and the first birds, mammals, and flowering plants appear

mes·quite *n* : a spiny shrub or small tree of the southwestern United States and Mexico

¹mess *n* **1** : a dirty or untidy state **2** : something in a dirty or untidy state **3** : a difficult situation **4** : a group of people (as military personnel) who regularly eat together **5** : a place (as in the military) where meals are served

²mess *vb* **messed; mess·ing 1** : to make dirty or untidy **2** : to make mistakes in or mix up **3** : to become confused or make an error **4** : to use or do in an aimless way **5** : to handle in a careless way **6** : to deal with in a way that may cause anger or trouble

mes·sage *n* **1** : the exchange of information in writing, in speech, or by signals **2** : an underlying theme or idea

mes·sen·ger *n* : a person who carries a message or does an errand

Messrs. *pl of* MR.

messy *adj* **mess·i·er; mess·i·est 1** : not clean or tidy **2** : causing or making a mess **3** : not careful or precise — **mess·i·ness** *n*

met *past and past participle of* MEET

met·a·bol·ic *adj* : of or relating to metabolism

me·tab·o·lism *n* : the processes by which a living organism uses food to obtain energy and build tissue and disposes of waste material

met·al *n* **1** : a substance (as gold, tin, copper, or bronze) that has a more or less shiny appearance, is a good conductor of electricity and heat, and usually can be made into a wire or hammered into a thin sheet **2** : METTLE

me·tal·lic *adj* **1** : relating to, being, or resembling a metal **2** : containing or made of metal **3** : having a harsh sound

met·al·lur·gi·cal *adj* : of or relating to metallurgy

met·al·lur·gy *n* : the science of obtaining metals from their ores and preparing them for use

meta·mor·phic *adj* : formed by the action of pressure, heat, and water that results in a more compact form

meta·mor·pho·sis *n, pl* **meta·mor·pho·ses 1** : a great change in appearance or character **2** : the process of great and usually rather sudden change in the form and habits of some animals during transformation from an immature stage (as a caterpillar or tadpole) to an adult stage (as a butterfly or frog)

met·a·phor *n* : a figure of speech comparing two unlike things without using *like* or *as*

mete *vb* **met·ed; met·ing** : to distribute as deserved

me·te·or *n* : one of the small pieces of matter in the solar system that enter the earth's at-

mosphere where friction may cause them to glow and form a streak of light

me·te·or·ic *adj* **1** : of or relating to a meteor **2** : like a meteor in speed or in sudden and temporary success

me·te·or·ite *n* : a meteor that reaches the surface of the earth

me·te·o·rol·o·gist *n* : a person who specializes in meteorology

me·te·o·rol·o·gy *n* : a science that deals with the atmosphere, weather, and weather forecasting

¹me·ter *n* **1** : a planned rhythm in poetry that is usually repeated **2** : the repeated pattern of musical beats in a measure

²meter *n* : a measure of length on which the metric system is based and which is equal to about 39.37 inches

³meter *n* : an instrument for measuring and sometimes recording the amount of something

-meter *n suffix* : instrument for measuring

meth·od *n* **1** : a certain way of doing something **2** : careful arrangement

me·thod·i·cal *adj* **1** : done or arranged in a planned way : using a careful and orderly procedure **2** : following a planned and orderly way of doing something especially out of habit — **me·thod·i·cal·ly** *adv*

me·tic·u·lous *adj* : showing extreme or excessive care in thinking about or dealing with small details

met·ric *adj* : of, relating to, or based on the metric system

met·ri·cal *adj* : of or relating to poetic or musical meter

metric system *n* : a system of weights and measures in which the meter is the unit of length and the kilogram is the unit of weight

metric ton *n* : a unit of weight equal to 1000 kilograms

met·ro·nome *n* : a device that ticks in a regular pattern to help a musician play a piece of music at the proper speed

me·trop·o·lis *n* **1** : the chief or capital city of a country, state, or region **2** : a large or important city

met·ro·pol·i·tan *adj* : of, relating to, or like that of a large city

met·tle *n* : strength of spirit : COURAGE

¹mew *vb* **mewed; mew·ing** : to make a sound like a meow

²mew *n* : ¹MEOW

Mex. *abbr* **1** Mexican **2** Mexico

¹Mex·i·can *adj* : of or relating to Mexico or its people

²Mexican *n* : a person born or living in Mexico

mg *abbr* milligram

mi *n* : the third note of the musical scale

mi. *abbr* **1** mile **2** miles

MI *abbr* Michigan

mi·ca *n* : a mineral that easily breaks into very thin transparent sheets

mice *pl of* MOUSE

Mich. *abbr* Michigan

micr- *or* **micro-** *prefix* **1** : small : tiny **2** : millionth

mi·crobe *n* : a very tiny and often harmful living thing : MICROORGANISM

mi·cro·com·put·er *n* : PERSONAL COMPUTER

mi·cro·film *n* : a film on which something (as printing) is recorded in a much smaller size

mi·crom·e·ter *n* **1** : an instrument used with a telescope or microscope for measuring very small distances **2** : an instrument having a rod moved by fine screw threads and used for making exact measurements

mi·cro·or·gan·ism *n* : a living thing (as a bacterium) that can only be seen with a microscope

mi·cro·phone *n* : an instrument in which sound is changed into an electrical signal for transmitting or recording (as in radio or television)

mi·cro·pro·ces·sor *n* : a computer processor contained on an integrated-circuit chip

mi·cro·scope *n* : an instrument with one or more lenses used to help a person to see something very small by making it appear larger

mi·cro·scop·ic *adj* **1** : of, relating to, or conducted with the microscope **2** : so small as to be visible only through a microscope : very tiny — **mi·cro·scop·i·cal·ly** *adv*

¹mi·cro·wave *n* **1** : a radio wave between one millimeter and one meter in wavelength **2** : MICROWAVE OVEN

²microwave *vb* **mi·cro·waved; mi·cro·wav·ing** : to cook or heat in a microwave oven

microwave oven *n* : an oven in which food is cooked by the heat produced as a result of penetration of the food by microwaves

¹mid *adj* : being the part in the middle

²mid *prep* : AMID

mid·air *n* : a region in the air some distance above the ground

mid·day *n* : NOON

¹mid·dle *adj* **1** : equally distant from the ends : CENTRAL **2** : being at neither extreme : halfway between two opposite states or conditions

²middle *n* : the part, point, or position that is equally distant from the ends or opposite sides : CENTER

middle age *n* : the period of life from about 45 to about 64 years of age — **mid·dle–aged** *adj*

Middle Ages *n pl* : the period of European history from about A.D. 500 to about 1500

middle class *n* : a social class between that of the wealthy and the poor

Middle English *n* : the English language of the 12th to 15th centuries

middle finger *n* : the long finger that is the middle one of the five fingers of the hand

middle school *n* : a school usually including grades five to eight or six to eight

midge *n* : a very small fly : GNAT

¹midg·et *n, sometimes offensive* : a person who is much smaller than normal

²midget *adj* : much smaller than usual or normal

mid·night *n* : twelve o'clock at night

mid·rib *n* : the central vein of a leaf

mid·riff *n* : the middle part of the human body between the chest and the waist

mid·ship·man *n, pl* **mid·ship·men** : a person who is training to become an officer in the navy

¹midst *n* **1** : the middle or central part **2** : a position among the members of a group **3** : the condition of being surrounded

²midst *prep* : AMID

mid·stream *n* : the part of a stream farthest from each bank

mid·sum·mer *n* **1** : the middle of summer **2** : the summer solstice

¹mid·way *adv or adj* : in the middle of the way or distance : HALFWAY

²mid·way *n* : an area at a fair, carnival, or amusement park for food stands, games, and rides

mid·wife *n* : a woman who helps other women during childbirth

mid·win·ter *n* **1** : the middle of winter **2** : the winter solstice

mien *n* : a person's appearance or way of acting that shows mood or personality

¹might *past of* MAY — used as a helping verb to show that something is possible but not likely

²might *n* : power that can be used (as by a person or group)

might·i·ly *adv* **1** : very forcefully **2** : very much

mightn't : might not

¹mighty *adj* **might·i·er; might·i·est** **1** : having great power or strength **2** : done by or showing great power or strength **3** : great in size or effect

²mighty *adv* : ²VERY 1

mi·grant *n* : a person or animal that migrates

mi·grate *vb* **mi·grat·ed; mi·grat·ing** **1** : to move from one country or region to another **2** : to pass from one region to another on a regular basis

mi·gra·tion *n* : the act or an instance of moving from one place to another often on a regular basis

mi·gra·to·ry *adj* **1** : moving from one place to another **2** : of or relating to migration

mike *n* : MICROPHONE

mild *adj* **mild·er; mild·est 1** : gentle in personality or behavior **2** : not strong or harsh in action or effect **3** : not sharp, spicy, or bitter **4** : not extreme or severe — **mild·ly** *adv* — **mild·ness** *n*

¹mil·dew *n* **1** : a thin whitish growth produced by a fungus especially on decaying material or on living plants **2** : a fungus producing mildew

²mildew *vb* **mil·dewed; mil·dew·ing** : to become affected with mildew

mile *n* **1** : a measure of distance (**statute mile**) equal to 5280 feet (1609 meters) **2** : a measure of distance (**geographical mile** or **nautical mile**) used in air and sea travel equal to about 6076 feet (1852 meters)

mile·age *n* **1** : distance in miles **2** : distance covered or traveled in miles **3** : the average number of miles a car or truck will travel on a gallon of fuel **4** : an amount of money given for traveling expenses at a certain rate per mile

mile·stone *n* **1** : a stone by the side of a road showing the distance in miles to a given place **2** : an important point in progress or development

¹mil·i·tary *adj* **1** : of or relating to soldiers, the army, or war **2** : carried on by soldiers : supported by armed force

²military *n, pl* **military** : members of the armed forces

mi·li·tia *n* : a group of citizens with some military training who are called into service only in emergencies

¹milk *n* **1** : a whitish liquid produced and given off by the breasts or udder of a female mammal as food for her young **2** : milk from an animal and especially a cow used as food by people **3** : a liquid that looks like milk

²milk *vb* **milked; milk·ing** : to draw milk from (as by pressing)

milk·man *n, pl* **milk·men** : a person who sells or delivers milk

milk shake *n* : a drink made of milk, a flavoring syrup, and ice cream that is shaken or mixed thoroughly

milk tooth *n, pl* **milk teeth** : one of the first and temporary teeth of which humans grow 20

milk·weed *n* : a plant with milky juice and clusters of flowers

milky *adj* **milk·i·er; milk·i·est 1** : like milk especially in color **2** : containing or full of milk

Milky Way *n* **1** : a broad band of light that stretches across the sky and is caused by the light of a very great number of faint stars **2** : MILKY WAY GALAXY

Milky Way galaxy *n* : the galaxy of which the sun and the solar system are a part and which contains the stars that make up the Milky Way

¹mill *n* **1** : a building with machinery for grinding grain into flour **2** : a machine or device that prepares a material for use by grinding or crushing **3** : a factory using machines to make a product from raw material

²mill *vb* **milled; mill·ing 1** : to subject to processing in a mill **2** : to move about in a circle or in disorder

³mill *n* : one tenth of a cent

mil·len·ni·um *n, pl* **mil·len·nia** *or* **mil·len·ni·ums 1** : a period of 1000 years **2** : a 1000th anniversary or its celebration — **mil·len·ni·al** *adj*

mill·er *n* : a person who works in or runs a mill that grinds grain into flour

mil·let *n* : a grass with small whitish seeds that are used as food for people, livestock, and birds

milli- *prefix* : thousandth

mil·li·gram *n* : a unit of weight equal to 1/1000 gram

mil·li·li·ter *n* : a unit of capacity equal to 1/1000 liter

mil·li·me·ter *n* : a unit of length equal to 1/1000 meter

mil·li·ner *n* : a person who makes, decorates, or sells women's hats

¹mil·lion *n* **1** : one thousand thousands : 1,000,000 **2** : a very large number

²million *adj* **1** : being 1,000,000 **2** : being very great in number

mil·lion·aire *n* : a person having a million dollars or more

¹mil·lionth *adj* : being last in a series of a million

²millionth *n* : number 1,000,000 in a series

mil·li·pede *n* : an animal that is an arthropod with a long roundish body somewhat like that of a centipede but with two pairs of legs on most of its many body sections

mill·stone *n* : either of two large circular stones used for grinding grain

mime *n* **1** : the art of showing a character or telling a story using body movements and gestures without words **2** : a person who performs mime

mim·eo·graph *n* : a machine for making copies of typed, written, or drawn matter using a stencil

¹mim·ic *n* : a person or animal that imitates something or someone

²mimic *vb* **mim·icked; mim·ick·ing 1** : to imitate very closely **2** : to make fun of by imitating

mim·ic·ry *n* : a type of protection from predators in which one animal resembles the coloring, form, or behavior of another animal that is harmful or bad-tasting

min. *abbr* minute

min·a·ret *n* : a tall slender tower of a mosque with a balcony from which the people are called to prayer

mince *vb* **minced; minc·ing** **1** : to cut or chop into very small pieces **2** : to act or speak in an unnaturally dainty way **3** : to phrase comments in such a way as to not cause offense

mince·meat *n* : a finely chopped mixture (as of raisins, apples, spices, and sometimes meat) that is especially used in pies

¹mind *n* **1** : the part of a person that thinks, reasons, feels, understands, and remembers **2** : MEMORY 1 **3** : INTENTION 1 **4** : a person's view or opinion about something

²mind *vb* **mind·ed; mind·ing** **1** : to pay attention to **2** : OBEY 1 **3** : to be bothered by **4** : to object to : DISLIKE **5** : to take charge of **6** : to be careful about

mind·ed *adj* **1** : having a particular kind of mind **2** : greatly interested or concerned about something

mind·ful *adj* : keeping in mind : AWARE

mind·less *adj* : using or requiring little attention or thought

¹mine *pron* : that which belongs to me

²mine *n* **1** : a pit or tunnel from which minerals (as coal, gold, or diamonds) are taken **2** : an explosive device placed in the ground or water and set to explode when disturbed (as by an enemy soldier, vehicle, or ship) **3** : a rich source of supply

³mine *vb* **mined; min·ing** **1** : to dig or work in a mine **2** : to obtain from a mine **3** : to place explosive mines in or under — **min·er** *n*

¹min·er·al *n* **1** : a naturally occurring solid substance (as diamond, gold, or quartz) that is not of plant or animal origin **2** : a naturally occurring substance (as ore, coal, salt, or petroleum) obtained from the ground usually for humans to use

²mineral *adj* **1** : of or relating to minerals **2** : containing gases or mineral salts

mineral kingdom *n* : a basic group of natural objects that includes objects consisting of matter that does not come from plants and animals

min·gle *vb* **min·gled; min·gling** **1** : to bring or combine together or with something else **2** : to move among others within a group

mini- *prefix* : very short or small

¹min·i·a·ture *n* **1** : a copy of something that is much smaller than the original **2** : a very small portrait especially on ivory or metal

²miniature *adj* : very small : represented on a small scale

min·i·mize *vb* **min·i·mized; min·i·miz·ing** : to make as small as possible

¹min·i·mum *n, pl* **min·i·mums** *or* **min·i·ma** : the lowest value : the least amount

²minimum *adj* : being the least or lowest possible

min·ing *n* : the process or business of digging in mines to obtain minerals

¹min·is·ter *n* **1** : a person who performs religious ceremonies especially in Protestant church services **2** : a government official at the head of a section of government activities **3** : a person who represents his or her government in a foreign country

²minister *vb* **min·is·tered; min·is·ter·ing** : to give help or care

min·is·try *n, pl* **min·is·tries** **1** : the office or duties of a religious minister **2** : a group of religious ministers : CLERGY **3** : a section of a government headed by a minister

mink *n, pl* **mink** *or* **minks** **1** : a small animal related to the weasel that has partly webbed feet, lives around water, and feeds on smaller animals (as frogs, crabs, and mice) **2** : the soft thick usually brown fur of a mink

Minn. *abbr* Minnesota

min·now *n* **1** : a small freshwater fish (as a shiner) related to the carp **2** : a fish that looks like a true minnow

¹mi·nor *adj* **1** : not great in size, importance, or seriousness **2** : of or relating to a musical scale having the third tone lowered a half step

²minor *n* : a person too young to have the full rights of an adult

mi·nor·i·ty *n, pl* **mi·nor·i·ties** **1** : the state of not being old enough to have the full rights of an adult **2** : a number less than half of a total **3** : a group that makes up a smaller part of a larger group **4** : a part of a population that is in some ways (as in race or religion) different from others

min·strel *n* **1** : a musical entertainer in the Middle Ages **2** : a member of a group of entertainers who performed black American melodies and jokes with blackened faces in the 19th and early 20th centuries

¹mint *n* **1** : a fragrant plant (as catnip or peppermint) with square stems **2** : a piece of candy flavored with mint

²mint *n* **1** : a place where coins are made from metals **2** : a great amount especially of money

³mint *vb* **mint·ed; mint·ing** : to make coins out of metal : COIN

min·u·end *n* : a number from which another number is to be subtracted

min·u·et *n* : a slow graceful dance

¹mi·nus *prep* **1** : with the subtraction of : LESS **2** : ¹WITHOUT 2

²minus *adj* **1** : having a value that is below zero **2** : located in the lower part of a range

mi·nus·cule *adj* : very small

minus sign *n* : a sign – used especially in mathematics to indicate subtraction (as in 8–6=2) or a quantity less than zero (as in –15°)

¹min·ute *n* **1** : a unit of time equal to 60 seconds : the 60th part of an hour **2** : MOMENT 1 **3** : one of 60 equal parts into which a degree can be divided for measuring angles **4 minutes** *pl* : a brief record of what was said and done during a meeting

²mi·nute *adj* **mi·nut·er; mi·nut·est 1** : very small : TINY **2** : marked by or paying attention to small details — **mi·nute·ly** *adv*

min·ute·man *n, pl* **min·ute·men** : a member of a group of armed men who favored independence of the American colonies and who were ready to fight at a minute's notice immediately before and during the American Revolution

mir·a·cle *n* **1** : an extraordinary event taken as a sign of the power of God **2** : something (as an event or accomplishment) that is very outstanding, unusual, or wonderful

mi·rac·u·lous *adj* : being or being like a miracle : very wonderful or amazing — **mi·rac·u·lous·ly** *adv*

mi·rage *n* : an illusion sometimes seen at sea, in the desert, or over hot pavement that looks like a pool of water or a mirror in which distant objects are glimpsed

¹mire *n* : heavy deep mud

²mire *vb* **mired; mir·ing** : to stick or cause to become stuck in or as if in heavy deep mud

¹mir·ror *n* **1** : a piece of glass that reflects images **2** : something that gives a true likeness or description

²mirror *vb* **mir·rored; mir·ror·ing** : to reflect in or as if in a mirror

mirth *n* : happiness and laughter : merry behavior

mis- *prefix* **1** : in a way that is bad or wrong **2** : bad : wrong **3** : opposite or lack of

mis·ad·ven·ture *n* : an unfortunate or unpleasant event

mis·be·have *vb* **mis·be·haved; mis·be·hav·ing** : to behave badly

mis·cal·cu·late *vb* **mis·cal·cu·lat·ed; mis·cal·cu·lat·ing** : to make a mistake in figuring or estimating

mis·car·ry *vb* **mis·car·ried; mis·car·ry·ing** : to go wrong : FAIL

mis·cel·la·neous *adj* : consisting of many things of different sorts

mis·chief *n* **1** : behavior or activity that annoys or bothers but is not meant to cause serious harm **2** : injury or damage caused by a person

mis·chie·vous *adj* **1** : causing or likely to cause minor injury or harm **2** : showing a spirit of irresponsible fun or playfulness **3** : harming or intended to do harm — **mis·chie·vous·ly** *adv*

mis·con·duct *n* : bad behavior

mis·count *vb* **mis·count·ed; mis·count·ing** : to incorrectly determine the total of

mis·cre·ant *n* : VILLAIN, RASCAL

mis·deed *n* : a bad action

mis·de·mean·or *n* **1** : a crime less serious than a felony **2** : MISDEED

mis·di·rect *vb* **mis·di·rect·ed; mis·di·rect·ing** : to send to the wrong place

mi·ser *n* : a stingy person who lives poorly in order to store away money

mis·er·a·ble *adj* **1** : very unhappy or distressed **2** : causing great discomfort **3** : very unsatisfactory — **mis·er·a·bly** *adv*

mi·ser·ly *adj* : STINGY

mis·ery *n, pl* **mis·er·ies** : great suffering or unhappiness

mis·fit *n* **1** : something that is the wrong shape or size or is inappropriate **2** : a person who does not seem to belong in a particular group or situation

mis·for·tune *n* **1** : bad luck **2** : an unfortunate situation or event

mis·giv·ing *n* : a feeling of distrust or doubt especially about what is going to happen

mis·guid·ed *adj* : having or resulting from mistaken ideas or values

mis·hap *n* : an unfortunate accident

mis·judge *vb* **mis·judged; mis·judg·ing** : to make a wrong or unfair judgment or estimate of

mis·lay *vb* **mis·laid; mis·lay·ing** : to put in a place later forgotten : LOSE

mis·lead *vb* **mis·led; mis·lead·ing** : to cause (someone) to believe something that is not true

mis·place *vb* **mis·placed; mis·plac·ing 1** : to put (something) where it doesn't belong **2** : MISLAY

mis·print *n* : a mistake in a word that has been printed

mis·pro·nounce *vb* **mis·pro·nounced; mis·pro·nounc·ing** : to say or make the sounds of incorrectly

mis·pro·nun·ci·a·tion *n* : the act or state of saying or making the sounds of incorrectly

mis·read *vb* **mis·read; mis·read·ing 1** : to incorrectly pronounce or understand something written **2** : MISUNDERSTAND

mis·rep·re·sent *vb* **mis·rep·re·sent·ed; mis·rep·re·sent·ing** : to give a false or misleading idea of

¹miss *vb* **missed; miss·ing** 1 : to fail to hit, catch, reach, or get 2 : ¹ESCAPE 2 3 : to fail to arrive in time for 4 : to feel or notice the absence of 5 : to fail to take 6 : to fail to be present for 7 : to fail to hear or see

²miss *n* : failure to hit or catch

³miss *n* 1 *cap* — used as a title before the name of an unmarried woman 2 : young lady — used without a name as a form of polite address to a girl or young woman

Miss. *abbr* Mississippi

mis·shap·en *adj* : badly shaped

mis·sile *n* : an object (as a stone, arrow, bullet, or rocket) that is dropped, thrown, shot, or launched usually so as to strike something at a distance

miss·ing *adj* 1 : ¹ABSENT 1 2 : LOST 4

mis·sion *n* 1 : a task that is assigned or begun 2 : a task that is regarded as a very important duty 3 : a group of missionaries 4 : a group of people sent by a government to represent it in a foreign country 5 : a place where the work of missionaries is carried on

¹mis·sion·ary *n, pl* **mis·sion·ar·ies** : a person sent to a place to spread a religious faith

²missionary *adj* : relating to efforts to gain new religious followers or to people sent to spread a religion

mis·sive *n* : ¹LETTER 2

mis·spell *vb* **mis·spelled; mis·spell·ing** : to spell in an incorrect way

mis·step *n* 1 : a wrong movement 2 : ²MISTAKE 2, SLIP

¹mist *n* : very tiny drops of water floating in the air or falling as fine rain

²mist *vb* **mist·ed; mist·ing** 1 : to cover or become covered with tiny drops of water 2 : to become wet with tears 3 : to rain very lightly

¹mis·take *vb* **mis·took; mis·tak·en; mis·tak·ing** 1 : MISUNDERSTAND 2 : to fail to recognize correctly

²mistake *n* 1 : a wrong judgment or action 2 : something that is incorrect

mis·tak·en *adj* 1 : being in error : judging wrongly 2 : ²WRONG 2, INCORRECT — **mis·tak·en·ly** *adv*

mis·ter *n* 1 *cap* — used sometimes in writing instead of the usual *Mr.* 2 : SIR 1

mis·tle·toe *n* : a plant with waxy white berries that grows on the branches and trunks of trees

mis·treat *vb* **mis·treat·ed; mis·treat·ing** : to handle, use, or act toward in a harsh way : ABUSE

mis·tress *n* 1 : a female teacher 2 : a

woman who has control or authority over another person, an animal, or a thing

¹mis·trust *n* : ¹DISTRUST

²mistrust *vb* **mis·trust·ed; mis·trust·ing** 1 : ²DISTRUST, SUSPECT 2 : to lack confidence in

misty *adj* **mist·i·er; mist·i·est** 1 : full of very tiny drops of water 2 : clouded by tears 3 : VAGUE 3, INDISTINCT — **mist·i·ly** *adv*

mis·un·der·stand *vb* **mis·un·der·stood; mis·un·der·stand·ing** : to fail to get the meaning of : fail to understand

mis·un·der·stand·ing *n* 1 : a failure to get the meaning of : a failure to understand 2 : ARGUMENT 1, QUARREL

¹mis·use *vb* **mis·used; mis·us·ing** 1 : to put into action or service in a wrong way 2 : ²ABUSE 1, MISTREAT

²mis·use *n* : incorrect or improper handling

mite *n* 1 : a tiny animal that is related to and resembles the spider and often lives as a parasite on plants and other animals 2 : a very small person, thing, or amount — **a mite** : ²SOMEWHAT

mi·to·chon·dri·on *n, pl* **mi·to·chon·dria** : one of the parts found in the cytoplasm of a cell outside the nucleus that provides the cell with energy released from the breakdown of nutrients

mi·to·sis *n, pl* **mi·to·ses** : a process of cell division in which two new nuclei are formed each containing the original number of chromosomes

mitt *n* 1 : MITTEN 2 : a baseball catcher's or first baseman's glove

mit·ten *n* : a covering for the hand and wrist having a separate division for the thumb only

¹mix *vb* **mixed; mix·ing** 1 : to make into one thing by stirring together : BLEND 2 : to become one thing through blending 3 : to make by combining different things 4 : to bring together 5 : to feel or act friendly toward — **mix·er** *n* — **mix up** 1 : CONFUSE 1 2 : to put in the wrong place with other things 3 : to involve or cause to be involved with a bad situation or group

²mix *n* 1 : MIXTURE 2 2 : a prepared combination of ingredients for making a food

mixed *adj* 1 : made up of two or more kinds 2 : made up of both females and males 3 : made up of parts that are very different from one another

mixed number *n* : a number (as $1\frac{2}{3}$) made up of a whole number and a fraction

mix·ture *n* 1 : the act of combining 2 : something combined or being combined 3 : two or more substances combined together in such a way that each remains unchanged 4 : a combination of different things

mix–up *n* : an instance of confusion

miz·zen *n* **1** : a fore-and-aft sail set on the mizzenmast **2** : MIZZENMAST

miz·zen·mast *n* : the mast behind or next behind the mainmast

ml *abbr* milliliter

mm *abbr* millimeter

MN *abbr* Minnesota

mo. *abbr* month

MO *abbr* Missouri

¹moan *n* **1** : a long low sound showing pain or grief **2** : a long low sound

²moan *vb* **moaned; moan·ing 1** : to utter a long low sound **2** : COMPLAIN

moat *n* : a deep wide ditch around the walls of a castle or fort that is usually filled with water

¹mob *n* **1** : a rowdy excited crowd **2** : the people of a society who are poor and uneducated

²mob *vb* **mobbed; mob·bing** : to crowd about in an aggressive, excited, or annoying way

¹mo·bile *adj* **1** : easily moved : MOVABLE **2** : changing quickly in expression

²mo·bile *n* : an artistic structure whose parts can be moved especially by air currents

mo·bi·lize *vb* **mo·bi·lized; mo·bi·liz·ing** : to assemble (as military forces) and make ready for action

moc·ca·sin *n* **1** : a soft shoe with no heel and the sole and sides made of one piece **2** : WATER MOCCASIN

¹mock *vb* **mocked; mock·ing 1** : to treat with scorn : RIDICULE **2** : ²MIMIC 2

²mock *adj* : not real : MAKE-BELIEVE

mock·ery *n, pl* **mock·er·ies 1** : ¹RIDICULE **2** : a bad imitation : FAKE

mock·ing·bird *n* : a songbird of the southern United States noted for its imitations of other birds

¹mode *n* **1** : a particular form or variety of something **2** : a way of doing something

²mode *n* : a popular fashion or style

¹mod·el *n* **1** : a small but exact copy of a thing **2** : a pattern or figure of something to be made **3** : a person who sets a good example **4** : a person who poses for an artist or photographer **5** : a person who wears and displays garments that are for sale **6** : a special type of a product

²model *adj* **1** : worthy of being imitated **2** : being a miniature copy

³model *vb* **mod·eled** *or* **mod·elled; mod·el·ing** *or* **mod·el·ling 1** : to plan or shape after a pattern **2** : to make a model of **3** : to act or serve as a model

mo·dem *n* : a device that changes electrical signals from one form to another and is used especially to send or receive computer data over a telephone line

¹mod·er·ate *adj* **1** : neither too much nor too little **2** : neither very good nor very bad **3** : not expensive : REASONABLE **4** : not extreme or excessive — **mod·er·ate·ly** *adv*

²mod·er·ate *vb* **mod·er·at·ed; mod·er·at·ing** : to make or become less extreme or severe

mod·er·a·tion *n* **1** : the act of avoiding extreme behavior or belief **2** : the condition of being reasonable and not extreme

mod·ern *adj* **1** : of or characteristic of the present time or times not long past **2** : of a style or way of thinking that is new and different **3** : having a style that is newer and different from older, more traditional styles **4** : of the period from about 1500 to the present

mod·ern·ize *vb* **mod·ern·ized; mod·ern·iz·ing** : to make or become new and different or suitable for the present time

mod·est *adj* **1** : not overly proud or confident : not boastful **2** : limited in size or amount **3** : not showy **4** : decent in thought, conduct, and dress — **mod·est·ly** *adv*

mod·es·ty *n* : the quality of being decent or not boastful

mod·i·fi·ca·tion *n* **1** : the act or process of changing parts of something **2** : a slightly changed form

mod·i·fi·er *n* : a word (as an adjective or adverb) used with another word to limit its meaning

mod·i·fy *vb* **mod·i·fied; mod·i·fy·ing 1** : to make changes in **2** : to lower or reduce in amount or scale **3** : to limit in meaning : QUALIFY

mod·ule *n* : a part of a space vehicle that can work alone

mo·hair *n* : a fabric or yarn made from the long silky hair of an Asian goat

Mo·hawk *n, pl* **Mohawk** *or* **Mo·hawks 1** : a member of an American Indian people of central New York **2** : the language of the Mohawk people

Mo·he·gan *or* **Mo·hi·can** *n, pl* **Mo·he·gan** *or* **Mo·he·gans** *or* **Mohican** *or* **Mo·hi·cans** : a member of an American Indian people of southeastern Connecticut

moist *adj* : slightly wet : DAMP — **moist·ness** *n*

moist·en *vb* **moist·ened; moist·en·ing** : to make damp

mois·ture *n* : a small amount of liquid that makes something slightly wet

mo·lar *n* : a large tooth near the back of the mouth with a broad surface used for grinding

mo·las·ses *n* : a thick brown syrup that is made from raw sugar

¹mold *n* **1 :** a hollow form in which something is shaped **2 :** something shaped in a mold

²mold *vb* **mold·ed; mold·ing 1 :** to work and press into shape **2 :** to shape in a hollow form **3 :** to influence or affect the character of

³mold *n* **1 :** an often fuzzy surface growth of fungus on damp or decaying material **2 :** a fungus that forms mold

⁴mold *vb* **mold·ed; mold·ing :** to become moldy

⁵mold *n* **:** light rich crumbly earth that contains decaying material

mold·ing *n* **:** a strip of material having a design and used as a decoration (as on a wall or the edge of a table)

moldy *adj* **mold·i·er; mold·i·est :** covered with or containing mold

¹mole *n* **:** a small usually brown spot on the skin

²mole *n* **:** a small burrowing animal with soft fur and very small eyes

mo·lec·u·lar *adj* **:** of or relating to a molecule

mol·e·cule *n* **:** the smallest portion of a substance having the properties of the substance

mole·hill *n* **:** a little ridge of dirt pushed up by a mole as it burrows underground

mo·lest *vb* **mo·lest·ed; mo·lest·ing :** to disturb or injure by interfering

mol·li·fy *vb* **mol·li·fied; mol·li·fy·ing :** to soothe in temper or disposition

mol·lusk *n* **:** an animal (as a clam, snail, or octopus) that lives mostly in water and has a soft body usually enclosed in a shell containing calcium

molt *vb* **molt·ed; molt·ing :** to shed outer material (as hair, shell, or horns) that will be replaced by a new growth

mol·ten *adj* **:** melted especially by very great heat

mo·lyb·de·num *n* **:** a white metallic chemical element used in some steel to give greater strength and hardness

mom *n* **:** ¹MOTHER 1

mo·ment *n* **1 :** a very brief time **2 :** present time **3 :** IMPORTANCE

mo·men·tary *adj* **:** lasting only a very brief time — **mo·men·tar·i·ly** *adv*

mo·men·tous *adj* **:** very important

mo·men·tum *n* **:** the force that a moving body has because of its weight and motion

momma *variant of* MAMA

mom·my *n, pl* **mom·mies :** ¹MOTHER 1

Mon. *abbr* Monday

mon- *or* **mono-** *prefix* **:** one : single : alone

mon·arch *n* **1 :** a person who reigns over a kingdom or an empire **2 :** MONARCH BUTTERFLY

monarch butterfly *n* **:** a large orange and black American butterfly

mon·ar·chy *n, pl* **mon·ar·chies 1 :** a state or country having a king or queen **2 :** a form of government headed by a king or queen

mon·as·tery *n, pl* **mon·as·ter·ies :** a place where a community of monks lives and works

mo·nas·tic *adj* **:** of or relating to monks or monasteries

Mon·day *n* **:** the second day of the week

mo·ner·an *n* **:** any member of the kingdom of living things (as bacteria) consisting of a single simple cell that lacks a nucleus

mon·e·tary *adj* **:** of or relating to money

mon·ey *n, pl* **moneys** *or* **mon·ies 1 :** something (such as coins or bills) used to buy goods and services and to pay people for their work **2 :** a person's wealth

money order *n* **:** a piece of paper like a check that can be bought (as at a post office) and that orders payment of a sum of money printed on it to the person named

mon·goose *n, pl* **mon·goos·es :** a long thin furry animal with sharp claws that eats small animals (as snakes and mice), eggs, and fruit

¹mon·grel *n* **:** an animal of mixed or uncertain origin

²mongrel *adj* **:** of mixed or uncertain origin

¹mon·i·tor *n* **1 :** a video screen used for display (as of television pictures or computer information) **2 :** a student in a school picked for a special duty (as keeping order) **3 :** a person or thing that watches or checks something

²monitor *vb* **mon·i·tored; mon·i·tor·ing :** to watch or check for a special reason

monk *n* **:** a member of a religious group of men who promise to stay poor, obey the rules of their group, and not get married

¹mon·key *n, pl* **monkeys :** a furry animal of warm regions that has a long tail and that along with the apes is most closely related to humans

²monkey *vb* **mon·keyed; mon·key·ing 1 :** to spend time in an idle or aimless way **2 :** to handle secretly or in a careless or incorrect way

mon·key·shine *n* **:** PRANK — usually used in pl.

monkey wrench *n* **1 :** a wrench with one fixed and one adjustable jaw **2 :** something that disrupts

mono- — see MON-

mono·gram *n* **:** a design usually made by combining two or more of a person's initials

mono·plane *n* **:** an airplane with only one large wing that crosses the body

mo·nop·o·lize *vb* **mo·nop·o·lized; mo·nop·o·liz·ing** : to get or have complete control over

mo·nop·o·ly *n, pl* **mo·nop·o·lies** **1** : complete ownership or control of the entire supply of goods or a service in a certain market **2** : a person or group having complete control over something **3** : complete ownership or control of something

mono·syl·la·ble *n* : a word of one syllable

mo·not·o·nous *adj* : boring from always being the same — **mo·not·o·nous·ly** *adv*

mo·not·o·ny *n, pl* **mo·not·o·nies** : a boring lack of change

mon·soon *n* **1** : a wind in the Indian Ocean and southern Asia that blows from the southwest from April to October and from the northeast from October to April **2** : the rainy season that comes with the southwest monsoon

mon·ster *n* **1** : a strange or horrible creature **2** : something unusually large **3** : an extremely wicked or cruel person

mon·stros·i·ty *n, pl* **mon·stros·i·ties** : something that is large and ugly

mon·strous *adj* **1** : unusually large : ENORMOUS **2** : very bad or wrong **3** : having the qualities or appearance of a monster — **mon·strous·ly** *adv*

Mont. *abbr* Montana

month *n* : one of the twelve parts into which the year is divided

¹month·ly *adj* **1** : happening, done, or published every month **2** : figured in terms of one month **3** : lasting a month — **monthly** *adv*

²monthly *n, pl* **monthlies** : a magazine published every month

mon·u·ment *n* **1** : a structure (as a building, stone, or statue) made to keep alive the memory of a person or event **2** : something that serves as a good reminder or example

¹moo *vb* **mooed; moo·ing** : to make the sound of a cow : LOW

²moo *n, pl* **moos** : the low sound made by a cow

¹mood *n* : an emotional state of mind or feeling

²mood *n* : a set of forms of a verb that show whether the action or state expressed is to be thought of as a fact, a command, or a wish or possibility

moody *adj* **mood·i·er; mood·i·est** : often feeling or showing a gloomy or a bad frame of mind — **mood·i·ly** *adv* — **mood·i·ness** *n*

¹moon *n* **1** : the natural heavenly body that shines by reflecting light from the sun and revolves about the earth in about 29½ days **2** : SATELLITE 1

²moon *vb* **mooned; moon·ing** : ²DAYDREAM

moon·beam *n* : a ray of light from the moon

moon·light *n* : the light of the moon

moon·lit *adj* : lighted by the moon

moon·shine *n* **1** : MOONLIGHT **2** : alcoholic liquor produced illegally

moon·stone *n* : a partly transparent shining stone used as a gem

¹moor *n* : an area of open land that is too wet or too poor for farming

²moor *vb* **moored; moor·ing** : to fasten in place with cables, lines, or anchors

moor·ing *n* **1** : a place where a boat can be fastened so it will not float away **2** : a chain or line used to hold a boat in place

moor·land *n* : land consisting of ground that is too wet or too poor for farming

moose *n, pl* **moose** : a large animal with broad flattened antlers and humped shoulders that is related to the deer and lives in forests of Canada, the northern United States, Europe, and Asia

¹mop *n* **1** : a tool for cleaning floors made of a bundle of cloth or yarn or a sponge fastened to a long handle **2** : something that looks like a cloth or yarn mop

²mop *vb* **mopped; mop·ping** : to wipe or clean with or as if with a mop

mope *vb* **moped; mop·ing** : to be in a dull and sad state of mind

mo·raine *n* : a pile of earth and stones left by a glacier

¹mor·al *adj* **1** : concerned with or relating to what is right and wrong in human behavior **2** : able to teach a lesson of how people should behave **3** : ¹GOOD 13, VIRTUOUS **4** : able to tell right from wrong — **mor·al·ly** *adv*

²moral *n* **1** : the lesson to be learned from a story or experience **2 morals** *pl* : ways of behaving : moral conduct **3 morals** *pl* : teachings or rules of right behavior

mo·rale *n* : the condition of the mind or feelings (as in relation to enthusiasm, spirit, or hope) of an individual or group

mo·ral·i·ty *n, pl* **mo·ral·i·ties** **1** : the quality or fact of being in agreement with ideals of right behavior **2** : beliefs about what kind of behavior is good or bad

mo·rass *n* : MARSH, SWAMP

mo·ray eel *n* : an often brightly colored eel of warm seas with sharp teeth

mor·bid *adj* **1** : not healthy or normal **2** : having or showing an interest in unpleasant or gloomy things

¹more *adj* **1** : greater in amount, number, or size **2** : ¹EXTRA, ADDITIONAL

²more *adv* **1** : in addition **2** : to a greater extent — often used with an adjective or adverb to form the comparative

³more *n* **1** : a greater amount or number **2** : an additional amount

more·over *adv* : in addition to what has been said : BESIDES

Mor·mon *n* : a member of a Christian church that was founded by Joseph Smith in the United States in 1830

morn *n* : MORNING

morn·ing *n* : the early part of the day : the time from sunrise to noon

morning glory *n* : a vine that climbs by twisting around something and has large trumpet-shaped flowers that close in bright sunshine

morning star *n* : a bright planet (as Venus) seen in the eastern sky before or at sunrise

mo·ron *n* : a stupid or foolish person

mo·rose *adj* : very serious, unhappy, and quiet

mor·phine *n* : a habit-forming drug made from opium and used to relieve pain

mor·row *n* : the next day

Morse code *n* : a system of sending messages that uses long and short sounds or dots and dashes to represent letters and numbers

mor·sel *n* : a little piece (as of food)

¹mor·tal *adj* **1** : capable of causing death **2** : certain to die **3** : feeling great and lasting hatred **4** : very great or overpowering **5** : ¹HUMAN 1 — **mor·tal·ly** *adv*

²mortal *n* : a human being

¹mor·tar *n* **1** : a strong deep bowl in which substances are pounded or crushed with a pestle **2** : a short light cannon used to shoot shells high into the air

²mortar *n* : a building material made of lime and cement mixed with sand and water that is spread between bricks or stones so as to hold them together when it hardens

¹mort·gage *n* **1** : a transfer of rights to a piece of property (as a house) that is usually in return for a loan of money and that is canceled when the loan is paid **2** : the document recording such a transfer

²mortgage *vb* **mort·gaged; mort·gag·ing** : to transfer rights to a piece of property in a mortgage transaction

mor·ti·fy *vb* **mor·ti·fied; mor·ti·fy·ing** : to embarrass greatly

mo·sa·ic *n* : a decoration on a surface made by setting small pieces of glass, stone, or tile of different colors into another material to make patterns or pictures

Mos·lem *variant of* MUSLIM

mosque *n* : a building in which Muslims worship

mos·qui·to *n, pl* **mos·qui·toes** : a small fly the female of which punctures the skin of people and animals to suck their blood

moss *n* **1** : a plant that has no flowers and grows as a small leafy stem in patches like cushions clinging to rocks, bark, or damp ground **2** : a plant or plantlike organism (as a lichen) resembling moss

mossy *adj* **moss·i·er; moss·i·est** : like or covered with moss

¹most *adj* **1** : the majority of : almost all **2** : greatest in amount or extent

²most *adv* **1** : to the greatest or highest level or extent — often used with an adjective or adverb to form the superlative **2** : VERY

³most *n* : the greatest amount, number, or part

most·ly *adv* : for the greatest part

mote *n* : a small particle : SPECK

mo·tel *n* : a building or group of buildings for travelers to stay in which the rooms are usually reached directly from an outdoor parking area

moth *n, pl* **moths** : an insect that usually flies at night and has mostly feathery antennae and stouter body, duller coloring, and smaller wings than the related butterflies

¹moth·er *n* **1** : a female parent **2** : a nun in charge of a convent **3** : ¹CAUSE 1, ORIGIN — **moth·er·hood** *n* — **moth·er·less** *adj*

²mother *adj* **1** : of or having to do with a mother **2** : being in a relation suggesting that of a mother to others

³mother *vb* **moth·ered; moth·er·ing** : to be or act as a mother to

moth·er·board *n* : the main circuit board especially of a small computer

moth·er–in–law *n, pl* **mothers–in–law** : the mother of someone's husband or wife

moth·er·ly *adj* **1** : of or characteristic of a mother **2** : like a mother

Mother Nature *n* : nature represented as a woman thought of as the guiding force behind natural events

moth·er–of–pearl *n* : a hard pearly material that lines the shell of some mollusks (as mussels) and is often used for ornamental objects and buttons

¹mo·tion *n* **1** : an act or process of changing place or position : MOVEMENT **2** a movement of the body or its parts **3** : a formal plan or suggestion for action offered according to the rules of a meeting — **mo·tion·less** *adj*

²motion *vb* **mo·tioned; mo·tion·ing** : to direct or signal by a movement or sign

motion picture *n* **1** : a series of pictures projected on a screen rapidly one after another so as to give the appearance of a continuous picture in which the objects move **2** : MOVIE 1

mo·ti·vate *vb* **mo·ti·vat·ed; mo·ti·vat·ing** : to give or be a reason for doing something

¹mo·tive *n* : a reason for doing something

²motive *adj* : causing motion

mot·ley *adj* : composed of various often unlike kinds or parts

¹mo·tor *n* : a machine that produces motion or power for doing work

²motor *adj* **1** : of, relating to, or designed for use in an automobile **2** : equipped with or driven by a motor **3** : causing or controlling movement

³motor *vb* **mo·tored; mo·tor·ing** : ¹DRIVE 2

mo·tor·bike *n* : a small usually lightweight motorcycle

mo·tor·boat *n* : an often small boat driven by a motor

mo·tor·cade *n* : a line of motor vehicles traveling as a group

mo·tor·car *n* : AUTOMOBILE

mo·tor·cy·cle *n* : a motorized vehicle for one or two passengers that has two wheels

mo·tor·ist *n* : a person who travels by automobile

mo·tor·ized *adj* **1** : having a motor **2** : using motor vehicles for transportation

motor scooter *n* : a motorized vehicle having two or three wheels like a child's scooter but having a seat

motor vehicle *n* : a motorized vehicle (as an automobile or motorcycle) not operated on rails

mot·tled *adj* : having spots or blotches of different colors

mot·to *n, pl* **mottoes 1** : a phrase or word inscribed on something (as a coin or public building) to suggest its use or nature **2** : a short expression of a guiding rule of conduct

¹mound *n* **1** : a small hill or heap of dirt or stones **2** : ¹HEAP 1, PILE **3** : the slightly raised ground on which a baseball pitcher stands

²mound *vb* **mound·ed; mound·ing** : to make a pile or heap of

¹mount *n* : a high hill : MOUNTAIN — used especially before a proper name

²mount *vb* **mount·ed; mount·ing 1** : to go up : CLIMB **2** : to get up onto something **3** : to increase rapidly in amount **4** : to prepare for use or display by fastening in position on a support **5** : to organize and carry out

³mount *n* **1** : a frame or support that holds something **2** : a horse used for riding

moun·tain *n* **1** : a raised area of land higher than a hill **2** : a great mass or huge number

moun·tain·eer *n* **1** : a person who lives in the mountains **2** : a mountain climber

mountain goat *n* : a goatlike animal of the mountains of western North America with a thick white coat and slightly curved black horns

mountain lion *n* : COUGAR

moun·tain·ous *adj* **1** : having many mountains **2** : like a mountain in size : HUGE

moun·tain·side *n* : the side of a mountain

moun·tain·top *n* : the highest part of a mountain

mount·ing *n* : a frame or support that holds something

mourn *vb* **mourned; mourn·ing** : to feel or show grief or sorrow especially over someone's death — **mourn·er** *n*

mourn·ful *adj* **1** : full of sorrow or sadness **2** : causing sorrow — **mourn·ful·ly** *adv* — **mourn·ful·ness** *n*

mourn·ing *n* **1** : the act of feeling or expressing sorrow **2** : an outward sign (as black clothes or an arm band) of grief for a person's death

mourning dove *n* : a dove of the United States named from its mournful cry

mouse *n, pl* **mice 1** : a very small furry gnawing animal that is a rodent with a pointed snout and long slender tail **2** : a person without spirit or courage **3** *pl also* **mous·es** : a small movable device that is connected to a computer and used to move the cursor and select functions on the screen — **mouse·like** *adj*

mouse pad *n* : a thin flat pad (as of rubber) on which a computer mouse is used

mous·er *n* : a cat good at catching mice

moustache *variant of* MUSTACHE

¹mouth *n, pl* **mouths 1** : the opening through which food passes into the body and which in humans is surrounded on the outside by the lips and contains the tongue and teeth **2** : an opening that is like a mouth **3** : the place where a stream enters a larger body of water

²mouth *vb* **mouthed; mouth·ing 1** : to form with the lips without speaking **2** : to repeat without being sincere or without understanding

mouthed *adj* : having a mouth especially of a specified kind

mouth·ful *n* **1** : as much as the mouth will hold **2** : the amount put into the mouth at one time **3** : a word or phrase that is very long or difficult to say

mouth·piece *n* : the part put to, between, or near the lips

mov·able *or* **move·able** *adj* **1** : possible to move **2** : changing date from year to year

¹move *vb* **moved; mov·ing 1** : to go from one place to another **2** : to change the place or position of : SHIFT **3** : to set in motion **4** : to cause to act : PERSUADE **5** : to affect the feelings of **6** : to change position **7** : to change residence **8** : to suggest according to the rules in a meeting

²move *n* **1** : the action of changing position,

place, or residence **2** : the act of moving a piece in a game **3** : the turn of a player to move **4** : an action taken to accomplish something

move·ment *n* **1** : the act or process of moving and especially changing place or position : an instance of moving **2** : a program or series of acts working toward a desired end **3** : a mechanical arrangement (as of wheels) for causing a particular motion (as in a clock or watch) **4** : a section of a longer piece of music **5** : an emptying of waste matter from the bowels

mov·er *n* : a person or company that moves the belongings of others (as from one home to another)

mov·ie *n* **1** : a story represented in motion pictures **2** : a showing of a movie — often used in pl.

mov·ing *adj* **1** : changing place or position **2** : causing feelings of sadness or sympathy **3** : used for transporting belongings from one place to another — **mov·ing·ly** *adv*

moving picture *n* : MOTION PICTURE 1

¹mow *n* : the part of a barn where hay or straw is stored

²mow *vb* **mowed**; **mowed** *or* **mown**; **mow·ing** **1** : to cut down with a blade or machine **2** : to cut the standing plant cover from **3** : to cause to fall in a violent way — **mow·er** *n*

mpg *abbr* miles per gallon

mph *abbr* miles per hour

Mr. *n, pl* **Messrs.** — used as a title before a man's name

Mrs. *n, pl* **Mes·dames** — used as a title before a married woman's name

Ms. *n* — often used instead of *Miss* or *Mrs.*

MS *abbr* Mississippi

mt. *abbr* **1** mount **2** mountain

MT *abbr* Montana

¹much *adj* **more** ; **most** **1** : great in amount or extent **2** : great in importance **3** : more than enough

²much *adv* **more; most** **1** : to a great or high level or extent **2** : just about : NEARLY

³much *n* **1** : a great amount or part **2** : something important or impressive

mu·ci·lage *n* : a water solution of a gum or similar substance used especially to stick things together

muck *n* **1** : MUD, MIRE **2** : soft moist barnyard manure **3** : DIRT 2, FILTH

mu·cous *adj* : containing or producing mucus

mu·cus *n* : a slippery thick sticky substance that coats, protects, and moistens the linings of body passages and spaces (as of the nose, lungs, and intestines)

mud *n* : soft wet earth or dirt

¹mud·dle *vb* **mud·dled**; **mud·dling** **1** : to be or cause to be confused or bewildered **2** : to mix up in a confused manner **3** : to think or proceed in a confused way

²muddle *n* : a state of confusion

¹mud·dy *adj* **mud·di·er**; **mud·di·est** **1** : filled or covered with mud **2** : looking like mud **3** : not clear or bright : DULL **4** : being mixed up

²muddy *vb* **mud·died**; **mud·dy·ing** **1** : to soil or stain with or as if with mud **2** : to make cloudy or dull (as in color)

¹muff *n* : a soft thick cover into which both hands can be placed to protect them from cold

²muff *vb* **muffed**; **muff·ing** : to make a mistake in doing or handling

muf·fin *n* : a bread made of batter containing eggs and baked in a small cup-shaped container

muf·fle *vb* **muf·fled**; **muf·fling** **1** : to deaden the sound of **2** : to wrap up so as to hide or protect

muf·fler *n* **1** : a scarf for the neck **2** : a device to deaden the noise of an engine (as of an automobile)

mug *n* : a large drinking cup with a handle

mug·gy *adj* **mug·gi·er**; **mug·gi·est** : being very warm and humid — **mug·gi·ness** *n*

Mu·ham·mad *n* : the founder of Islam

mul·ber·ry *n, pl* **mul·ber·ries** : a tree that bears edible usually purple fruit like berries and has leaves on which silkworms can be fed

¹mulch *n* : a material (as straw or bark) spread over the ground especially to protect the roots of plants from heat or cold, to keep soil moist, and to control weeds

²mulch *vb* **mulched**; **mulch·ing** : to cover with mulch

mule *n* **1** : an animal that is an offspring of a donkey and a horse **2** : a stubborn person

mul·ish *adj* : STUBBORN 1 — **mul·ish·ly** *adv*

mull *vb* **mulled**; **mull·ing** : to think about slowly and carefully : PONDER

mulled *adj* : mixed with sugar and spice and served warm

mul·let *n* : any of various chiefly saltwater fishes some mostly gray (**gray mullets**) and others red or golden (**red mullets**) that are often used as food

multi- *prefix* **1** : many : much **2** : more than two **3** : many times over

mul·ti·col·ored *adj* : having, made up of, or including many colors

mul·ti·cul·tur·al *adj* : relating to or made up of several different cultures

mul·ti·me·dia *adj* : using or composed of more than one form of communication or expression

¹**mul·ti·ple** *adj* : being or consisting of more than one

²**multiple** *n* : the number found by multiplying one number by another

mul·ti·pli·cand *n* : a number that is to be multiplied by another number

mul·ti·pli·ca·tion *n* : a short way of finding out what would be the result of adding one number the number of times indicated by a second number

mul·ti·pli·er *n* : a number by which another number is multiplied

mul·ti·ply *vb* **mul·ti·plied; mul·ti·ply·ing 1** : to increase in number : make or become more numerous **2** : to find the product of by means of multiplication

mul·ti·tude *n* : a great number of people or things

¹**mum** *adj* : SILENT 4

²**mum** *chiefly British variant of* MOM

¹**mum·ble** *vb* **mum·bled; mum·bling** : to speak softly so that words are not clear

²**mumble** *n* : speech that is not clear enough to be understood

mum·my *n, pl* **mummies** : a dead body preserved for burial in the manner of the ancient Egyptians

mumps *n pl* : a contagious disease marked especially by fever and swelling of the glands around the lower jaw — used as singular or plural

munch *vb* **munched; munch·ing** : to eat or chew especially with a crunching sound

mu·nic·i·pal *adj* : of or relating to the government of a town or city

mu·nic·i·pal·i·ty *n, pl* **mu·nic·i·pal·i·ties** : a town or city having its own local government

mu·ni·tion *n* : military equipment and supplies for fighting : AMMUNITION

mural *n* : a usually large painting on a wall

¹**mur·der** *n* : the intentional and unlawful killing of a human being

²**murder** *vb* **mur·dered; mur·der·ing 1** : to kill (someone) intentionally and unlawfully **2** : to spoil or ruin by performing or using badly — **mur·der·er** *n*

mur·der·ous *adj* **1** : intending or capable of causing murder : DEADLY **2** : very hard to bear or withstand

murk *n* : darkness or fog that is hard to see through

murky *adj* **murk·i·er; murk·i·est 1** : very dark or foggy **2** : CLOUDY 2 **3** : not clearly expressed or understood

¹**mur·mur** *n* **1** : a low faint sound **2** : a quiet expression of an opinion or feeling

²**murmur** *vb* **mur·mured; mur·mur·ing 1** : to make a low faint sound **2** : to say in a voice too quiet to be heard clearly

mus·cle *n* **1** : a tissue of the body consisting of long cells that can contract and produce motion **2** : an organ of the body that is a mass of muscle tissue attached at either end (as to bones) so that it can make a body part move **3** : strength of the muscles

mus·cle–bound *adj* : having large muscles that do not move and stretch easily

mus·cu·lar *adj* **1** : of, relating to, or done by the muscles **2** : having large and strong muscles

muse *vb* **mused; mus·ing** : to think about carefully or thoroughly : PONDER

mu·se·um *n* : a building in which objects of interest or value are displayed

¹**mush** *n* **1** : cornmeal boiled in water or milk **2** : something that is soft and wet and often shapeless

²**mush** *vb* **mushed; mush·ing** : to travel across snow with a sled pulled by dogs

¹**mush·room** *n* : a part of a fungus that bears spores, grows above ground, and suggests an umbrella in shape

²**mushroom** *vb* **mush·roomed; mush·room·ing** : to appear or develop suddenly or increase rapidly

mushy *adj* **mush·i·er; mush·i·est 1** : soft and wet **2** : overly romantic or sentimental

mu·sic *n* **1** : an arrangement of sounds having melody, rhythm and usually harmony **2** : the art of producing pleasing or expressive combinations of tones especially with melody, rhythm, and usually harmony **3** : a musical composition set down on paper **4** : a pleasing sound

¹**mu·si·cal** *adj* **1** : having to do with music or the writing or performing of music **2** : pleasing like music **3** : fond of or talented in music **4** : set to music — **mu·si·cal·ly** *adv*

²**musical** *n* : a movie or play that tells a story with both speaking and singing

music box *n* : a box that contains a mechanical device which uses gears like those of a clock to play a tune when the box is open

mu·si·cian *n* : a person who writes, sings, or plays music with skill and especially as a profession

musk *n* : a strong-smelling material that is used in perfumes and is obtained from a gland of an Asian deer (**musk deer**) or is prepared artificially

mus·ket *n* : a firearm that is loaded through the muzzle and that was once used by soldiers trained to fight on foot

mus·ke·teer *n* : a soldier armed with a musket

musk·mel·on *n* : a small round to oval melon (as a cantaloupe) with sweet usually green or orange flesh

musk ox *n* : a shaggy animal like an ox found in Greenland and northern North America

musk·rat *n, pl* **muskrat** *or* **musk·rats** : a North American animal that is a rodent living in or near water and having webbed hind feet, a long scaly tail, and glossy usually dark brown fur

musky *adj* **musk·i·er; musk·i·est** : having an odor of or resembling musk

Mus·lim *n* : a person whose religion is Islam

mus·lin *n* : a cotton fabric of plain weave

¹muss *n* : a state of disorder : MESS

²muss *vb* **mussed; muss·ing** : to make messy or untidy

mus·sel *n* **1** : a saltwater shellfish that has a long dark shell in two parts and is sometimes used as food **2** : a freshwater clam of the United States with shells from which mother-of-pearl is obtained

¹must *helping verb, present and past all persons* **must 1** : to be commanded, requested, or urged to **2** : to be required to **3** : to be very likely to

²must *n* : something that is or seems to be required or necessary

mus·tache *also* **mous·tache** *n* : the hair growing on the human upper lip

mus·tang *n* : a small hardy wild horse of the western United States that is descended from horses brought in by the Spaniards

mus·tard *n* : a sharp-tasting yellow powder that is prepared from the seeds of a plant related to the cabbage and is used especially as a seasoning for foods

¹mus·ter *n* **1** : a formal gathering of military troops for inspection **2** : an act of careful examination or consideration to determine whether something is acceptable or good enough

²muster *vb* **mus·tered; mus·ter·ing 1** : to call together (as troops) for roll call or inspection **2** : to bring into being or action

mustn't : must not

musty *adj* **must·i·er; must·i·est** : smelling of dampness, decay, or lack of fresh air

¹mu·tant *adj* : resulting from genetic mutation

²mutant *n* : a plant, animal, or microorganism resulting from genetic mutation

mu·tate *vb* **mu·tat·ed; mu·tat·ing** : to undergo genetic mutation

mu·ta·tion *n* : a change in a gene or the resulting new trait it produces in an individual

¹mute *adj* **mut·er; mut·est 1** : unable or unwilling to speak **2** : felt or expressed without the use of words

²mute *n* **1** : a person who cannot or does not speak **2** : a device on a musical instrument that deadens, softens, or muffles its tone

³mute *vb* **mut·ed; mut·ing** : to soften or reduce the sound of

mu·ti·late *vb* **mu·ti·lat·ed; mu·ti·lat·ing 1** : to destroy or cut off a necessary part (as a limb) : MAIM **2** : to ruin by damaging or changing

mu·ti·neer *n* : a person who takes part in a mutiny

mu·ti·nous *adj* **1** : involved in turning against a person in charge (as the captain of a ship) **2** : feeling or showing a desire to disobey

¹mu·ti·ny *n, pl* **mu·ti·nies 1** : a turning of a group (as of sailors) against a person in charge **2** : refusal to obey those in charge

²mutiny *vb* **mu·ti·nied; mu·ti·ny·ing** : to try to take control away from a person in charge

mutt *n* : a dog that is a mix of usually undetermined breeds

mut·ter *vb* **mut·tered; mut·ter·ing 1** : to speak in a low voice with lips partly closed **2** : to complain in a low voice : GRUMBLE

mut·ton *n* : the meat of an adult sheep

mu·tu·al *adj* **1** : given and received in equal amount **2** : having the same relation to one another **3** : shared by two or more at the same time — **mu·tu·al·ly** *adv*

¹muz·zle *n* **1** : the nose and mouth of an animal (as a dog) **2** : a covering for the mouth of an animal to prevent it from biting or eating **3** : the open end of a gun from which the bullet comes out when the gun is fired

²muzzle *vb* **muz·zled; muz·zling 1** : to put a muzzle on **2** : to keep from free expression of ideas or opinions

my *adj* : belonging or relating to me or myself

my·nah *or* **my·na** *n* : an Asian bird that is related to the starling and can be trained to mimic words

¹myr·i·ad *n* : a very large number of things

²myriad *adj* : many in number : extremely numerous

myrrh *n* : a sticky brown fragrant material obtained from African and Arabian trees and used especially in perfumes or formerly in incense

myr·tle *n* **1** : an evergreen shrub of southern Europe with fragrant flowers **2** : ¹PERIWINKLE

my·self *pron* : my own self — **by myself** : ALONE

mys·te·ri·ous *adj* : strange, unknown, or hard to understand or explain — **mys·te·ri·ous·ly** *adv* — **mys·te·ri·ous·ness** *n*

mys·tery *n, pl* **mys·ter·ies 1** : something that has not been or cannot be explained **2** : a piece of fiction about solving a crime

mys·tic *adj* **1** : MYSTICAL **2** : relating to magic **3** : MYSTERIOUS

narrow

mys·ti·cal *adj* : having a spiritual meaning that is difficult to see or understand

mys·ti·fy *vb* **mys·ti·fied; mys·ti·fy·ing** : to confuse or bewilder completely

myth *n* **1** : a story often describing the adventures of beings with more than human powers that attempts to explain mysterious events (as the changing of the seasons) or that explains a religious belief or practice **2** : such stories as a group **3** : a person or thing existing only in the imagination **4** : a popular belief that is not true

myth·i·cal *adj* **1** : based on or told of in a myth **2** : IMAGINARY

my·thol·o·gy *n, pl* **my·thol·o·gies** : a collection of myths

N

n *n, pl* **n's** *or* **ns** *often cap* : the 14th letter of the English alphabet

n *abbr* noun

N *abbr* **1** north **2** northern

-n — see -EN

nab *vb* **nabbed; nab·bing** : ¹ARREST 1

na·cho *n, pl* **nachos** : a tortilla chip topped with melted cheese and often additional toppings

¹nag *vb* **nagged; nag·ging 1** : to annoy by repeated complaining, scolding, or urging **2** : to annoy continually or again and again

²nag *n* : an old and usually worn-out horse

na·iad *n, pl* **na·iads** *or* **na·ia·des** : a nymph believed in ancient times to be living in lakes, rivers, and springs

¹nail *n* **1** : a tough covering protecting the upper end of each finger and toe **2** : a slender pointed piece of metal driven into or through something for fastening

²nail *vb* **nailed; nail·ing** : to fasten with or as if with a nail

na·ive *or* **na·ïve** *adj* **na·iv·er; na·iv·est 1** : showing lack of experience or knowledge **2** : being simple and sincere — **na·ive·ly** *adv*

na·ked *adj* **1** : having no clothes on : NUDE **2** : lacking a usual or natural covering **3** : not in its case or without a covering **4** : stripped of anything misleading : PLAIN **5** : not aided by an artificial device — **na·ked·ly** *adv* — **na·ked·ness** *n*

¹name *n* **1** : a word or combination of words by which a person or thing is known **2** : REPUTATION 2 **3** : a word or phrase used to describe and insult someone

²name *vb* **named; nam·ing 1** : to choose a word or words by which something will be known : give a name to **2** : to refer to by the word by which a person or thing is known : call by name **3** : to appoint to a job of authority **4** : to decide on **5** : ²MENTION **6** : to choose to be

³name *adj* : well known because of wide distribution

name·less *adj* **1** : having no name **2** : not marked with a name **3** : ¹UNKNOWN, ANONYMOUS **4** : not to be described

name·ly *adv* : that is to say

name·sake *n* : a person who has the same name as someone else

nan·ny *n, pl* **nannies** : a child's nurse

nanny goat *n* : a female goat

¹nap *n* : a short sleep especially during the day

²nap *vb* **napped; nap·ping 1** : to sleep briefly especially during the day **2** : to be unprepared

³nap *n* : a hairy or fluffy surface (as on cloth)

nape *n* : the back of the neck

naph·tha *n* : any of various usually flammable liquids prepared from coal or petroleum and used especially to dissolve substances

nap·kin *n* : a small piece of cloth or paper used when eating to wipe the lips or fingers and protect the clothes

nar·cis·sus *n, pl* **narcissus** *or* **nar·cis·sus·es** *or* **nar·cis·si** : a daffodil with flowers that have short trumpet-shaped tubes

¹nar·cot·ic *n* : an addicting drug that in small doses dulls the senses, relieves pain, and brings on sleep but in larger doses has dangerous effects and that includes some (as morphine) that are used in medicine and others (as heroin) that are used illegally

²narcotic *adj* : of, relating to, or being a narcotic

nar·rate *vb* **nar·rat·ed; nar·rat·ing** : to tell in full detail — **nar·ra·tor** *n*

nar·ra·tion *n* **1** : the act or process or an instance of telling in full detail **2** : ¹NARRATIVE

¹nar·ra·tive *n* : something (as a story) that is told in full detail

²narrative *adj* : having the form of a story

¹nar·row *adj* **nar·row·er; nar·row·est 1** : of slender or less than usual width **2** : limited in size or extent **3** : not broad or open in mind or views **4** : barely successful : CLOSE — **nar·row·ly** *adv* — **nar·row·ness** *n*

²narrow *vb* **nar·rowed; nar·row·ing 1** : to make or become less wide **2** : to limit in number : become fewer

³narrow *n* : a narrow passage connecting two bodies of water — usually used in pl.

nar·row–mind·ed *adj* : [1]NARROW 3, INTOLER-
ANT — **nar·row–mind·ed·ly** *adv* — **narrow–mind·ed·ness** *n*

nar·whal *n* : an arctic marine animal that is
related to dolphins and whales and in the
male has a long twisted ivory tusk

na·sal *adj* 1 : of or relating to the nose 2
: uttered with the nose passage open — **na·
sal·ly** *adv*

nas·tur·tium *n* : an herb with roundish leaves
and red, yellow, or white flowers

nas·ty *adj* **nas·ti·er; nas·ti·est** 1 : [2]MEAN 1 2
: very unpleasant 3 : very serious : HARM-
FUL 4 : very dirty : FILTHY 5 : INDECENT —
nas·ti·ly *adv* — **nas·ti·ness** *n*

na·tion *n* 1 : COUNTRY 1 2 : a community of
people made up of one or more nationalities
usually with its own territory and government 3 : NATIONALITY 3

[1]**na·tion·al** *adj* : of or relating to an entire
country — **na·tion·al·ly** *adv*

[2]**national** *n* : a citizen of a particular country

National Guard *n* : a part of the United States
military whose members are recruited by
each state, equipped by the federal government, and can be used by either the state or
the country

na·tion·al·ism *n* : devotion to the interests of
a certain country and belief that it is better
and more important than other countries

na·tion·al·ist *n* : a person who believes that
his or her country is better and more important than other countries

na·tion·al·i·ty *n, pl* **na·tion·al·i·ties** 1 : the
fact or state of belonging to a particular
country 2 : the state of being a separate
country 3 : a group of people having a common history, tradition, culture, or language

na·tion·al·ize *vb* **na·tion·al·ized; na·tion·al·iz-
ing** : to place under government control

na·tion·wide *adj* : extending throughout an
entire country

[1]**na·tive** *adj* 1 : born in a certain place or
country 2 : belonging to a person because
of place of birth 3 : living or growing naturally in a certain region 4 : grown, produced, or coming from a certain place 5
: NATURAL 3

[2]**native** *n* 1 : a person who was born in or
comes from a particular place 2 : a kind of
plant or animal that originally grew or lived
in a particular place

Native American *n* : a member of any of the
first groups of people to live in North and
South America and especially in the United
States

Na·tiv·i·ty *n, pl* **Na·tiv·i·ties** : the birth of Jesus
Christ

nat·ty *adj* **nat·ti·er; nat·ti·est** : very neat, trim,
and stylish — **nat·ti·ly** *adv*

nat·u·ral *adj* 1 : found in or produced by nature 2 : being or acting as expected : NOR-

MAL 3 : present or existing at birth : born in
a person or animal 4 : having qualities or
skills without training or effort 5 : occurring in the normal course of life 6 : being
simple and sincere 7 : LIFELIKE 8 : not
raised or lowered in musical pitch using a
sharp or flat

natural gas *n* : a flammable gas mixture
from below the earth's surface that is used
especially as a fuel

nat·u·ral·ist *n* : a person who studies nature
and especially plants and animals as they
live in nature

nat·u·ral·i·za·tion *n* : the act or process of making or becoming a citizen

nat·u·ral·ize *vb* **nat·u·ral·ized; nat·u·ral·iz·ing**
1 : to become or allow to become a citizen 2
: to become or cause to become established
as if native

nat·u·ral·ly *adv* 1 : without anything added
or changed : by natural character 2 : in the
normal or expected way 3 : because of a
quality present at birth 4 : in a way that is
relaxed and normal

natural number *n* : the number 1 or any
number obtained by adding 1 to it one or
more times

natural resource *n* : something (as water, a
mineral, forest, or kind of animal) that is
found in nature and is valuable to humans

na·ture *n* 1 : the physical world and everything in it 2 : natural scenery or surroundings 3 : the basic character of a person or
thing 4 : natural feelings : DISPOSITION,
TEMPERAMENT 5 : [1]SORT 1, TYPE

[1]**naught** *also* **nought** *pron* : [1]NOTHING 1

[2]**naught** *also* **nought** *n* : ZERO 1, CIPHER

naugh·ty *adj* **naugh·ti·er; naugh·ti·est** : behaving in a bad or improper way — **naugh-
ti·ly** *adv* — **naugh·ti·ness** *n*

nau·sea *n* 1 : a disturbed and unpleasant
condition of the stomach : the feeling of
being about to vomit 2 : deep disgust
: LOATHING

nau·se·ate *vb* **nau·se·at·ed; nau·se·at·ing**
: to cause to feel nausea — **nau·se·at·ing** *adj*
— **nau·se·at·ing·ly** *adv*

nau·seous *adj* 1 : suffering from nausea 2
: causing nausea

nau·ti·cal *adj* : of or relating to sailors, navigation, or ships

Na·va·jo *also* **Na·va·ho** *n, pl* **Na·va·jos** *also*
Na·va·hos 1 : a member of an American In-
dian people of northern New Mexico and
Arizona 2 : the language of the Navajo people

na·val *adj* : of or relating to a navy or warships

nave *n* : the long central main part of a
church

na·vel *n* : a hollow or bump in the middle of

the stomach that marks the place where the umbilical cord was attached

nav·i·ga·ble *adj* **1** : deep enough and wide enough to permit passage of ships **2** : possible to steer — **nav·i·ga·bil·i·ty** *n*

nav·i·gate *vb* **nav·i·gat·ed; nav·i·gat·ing 1** : to travel by water **2** : to sail or travel over, on, or through **3** : to steer a course in a ship or aircraft **4** : to steer or direct the course of (as a boat) **5** : to find information on the Internet or a Web site

nav·i·ga·tion *n* **1** : the act or practice of steering, directing the course of, or finding a way through **2** : the science of figuring out the position and course of a ship or aircraft — **nav·i·ga·tion·al** *adj*

nav·i·ga·tor *n* : an officer on a ship or aircraft responsible for directing its course

na·vy *n, pl* **navies 1** : the complete military organization of a nation for warfare at sea **2** : a dark blue

¹**nay** *adv* : ¹NO 2

²**nay** *n, pl* **nays 1** : ³NO 2 **2** : ³NO 3

Na·zi *n* : a member of a political party controlling Germany from 1933 to 1945

NB *abbr* New Brunswick

NC *abbr* North Carolina

ND, N. Dak. *abbr* North Dakota

NE *abbr* **1** Nebraska **2** northeast

Ne·an·der·thal *or* **Ne·an·der·tal** *n* : an ancient human who lived 30,000 to 200,000 years ago

¹**near** *adv* **near·er; near·est 1** : at, within, or to a short distance or time **2** : ALMOST, NEARLY

²**near** *prep* : close to

³**near** *adj* **near·er; near·est 1** : closely related or associated **2** : not far away in distance or time **3** : coming close : NARROW **4** : being the closer of two — **near·ness** *n*

⁴**near** *vb* **neared; near·ing** : to come near : APPROACH

near·by *adv or adj* : close at hand

near·ly *adv* **1** : in a close manner or relationship **2** : almost but not quite **3** : to the least extent

near·sight·ed *adj* : able to see things that are close more clearly than distant ones — **near·sight·ed·ness** *n*

neat *adj* **neat·er; neat·est 1** : showing care and a concern for order **2** : skillful in a fascinating or entertaining way — **neat·ly** *adv* — **neat·ness** *n*

Neb., Nebr. *abbr* Nebraska

neb·u·la *n, pl* **neb·u·lae** *or* **neb·u·las 1** : any of many clouds of gas or dust seen in the sky among the stars **2** : GALAXY 2

neb·u·lous *adj* : not clear : VAGUE

¹**nec·es·sary** *adj* : needing to be had or done : ESSENTIAL — **nec·es·sar·i·ly** *adv*

²**necessary** *n, pl* **nec·es·sar·ies** : something that is needed

ne·ces·si·tate *vb* **ne·ces·si·tat·ed; ne·ces·si·tat·ing** : to make necessary : REQUIRE

ne·ces·si·ty *n, pl* **ne·ces·si·ties 1** : the state of things that forces certain actions **2** : very great need **3** : the state of being in need : POVERTY **4** : something that is badly needed

neck *n* **1** : the part of the body between the head and the shoulders **2** : the section of a garment covering or nearest to the part connecting the head with the body **3** : something that is long and narrow or that connects two larger parts — **necked** *adj* — **neck and neck** : so nearly equal (as in a race or election) that one cannot be said to be ahead of the other

neck·er·chief *n, pl* **neck·er·chiefs** : a square of cloth worn folded around the neck like a scarf

neck·lace *n* : a piece of jewelry (as a string of beads) worn around the neck

neck·line *n* : the outline of the neck opening of a garment

neck·tie *n* : a narrow length of material worn under the collar and tied in front

nec·tar *n* : a sweet liquid produced by plants and used by bees in making honey

nec·tar·ine *n* : a peach with a smooth skin

née *or* **nee** *adj* — used to identify a woman by her maiden name

¹**need** *vb* **need·ed; need·ing 1** : to suffer from the lack of something important to life or health **2** : to be necessary **3** : to be without : REQUIRE

²**need** *n* **1** : something that must be done : OBLIGATION **2** : a lack of something necessary, useful, or desired **3** : something necessary or desired

need·ful *adj* : ¹NECESSARY

¹**nee·dle** *n* **1** : a small slender pointed usually steel tool used for sewing **2** : a slender pointed piece of metal or plastic (used for knitting) **3** : a leaf (as of a pine) shaped like a needle **4** : a pointer on a dial **5** : a slender hollow instrument that has a sharp point and by which material is put into or taken from the body through the skin — **nce·dle·like** *adj*

²**needle** *vb* **nee·dled; nee·dling** : ¹TEASE, TAUNT

nee·dle·point *n* : embroidery done on canvas usually in simple even stitches across counted threads

need·less *adj* : UNNECESSARY — **need·less·ly** *adv*

nee·dle·work *n* **1** : things made by embroidery, knitting, or needlepoint **2** : the activity or art of making things by embroidery, knitting, or needlepoint

needn't : need not

needy *adj* **need·i·er; need·i·est** : very poor — **need·i·ness** *n*

ne'er *adv* : NEVER

ne'er–do–well *n* : a worthless person who will not work

¹neg·a·tive *adj* **1** : emphasizing the bad side of a person, situation, or thing **2** : not positive **3** : less than zero and shown by a minus sign **4** : being the part toward which the electric current flows from the outside circuit **5** : of, being, or relating to electricity of which the electron is the unit and which is produced in a hard rubber rod that has been rubbed with wool **6** : having more electrons than protons — **neg·a·tive·ly** *adv* — **neg·a·tiv·i·ty** *n*

²negative *n* **1** : a part of something which is harmful or bad **2** : an expression (as the word *no*) that denies or says the opposite **3** : the side that argues or votes against something **4** : a photographic image on film from which a final picture is made

¹ne·glect *vb* **ne·glect·ed; ne·glect·ing 1** : to fail to give the right amount of attention to **2** : to fail to do or look after especially because of carelessness

²neglect *n* **1** : lack of attention or care to something or someone **2** : the state of not being looked after or given attention

ne·glect·ful *adj* : not looking after or giving attention to : NEGLIGENT

neg·li·gee *n* : a woman's loose robe made of thin material

neg·li·gence *n* : failure to take proper or normal care of something or someone

neg·li·gent *adj* : failing to take proper or normal care of something or someone — **neg·li·gent·ly** *adv*

neg·li·gi·ble *adj* : so small or unimportant as to deserve little or no attention

ne·go·tia·ble *adj* **1** : able to be discussed in order to reach an agreement **2** : able to be successfully dealt with or traveled over

ne·go·ti·ate *vb* **ne·go·ti·at·ed; ne·go·ti·at·ing 1** : to have a discussion with another in order to settle something **2** : to arrange for by discussing **3** : to be successful in getting around, through, or over — **ne·go·ti·a·tor** *n*

ne·go·ti·a·tion *n* : the act or process of having a discussion in order to reach an agreement

Ne·gro *n, pl* **Ne·groes** *sometimes offensive* : a member of a race of people native to Africa and classified according to certain physical characteristics (as dark skin)

¹neigh *vb* **neighed; neigh·ing** : to make the long loud cry of a horse

²neigh *n* : the long loud cry of a horse

¹neigh·bor *n* **1** : a person living near another **2** : a person, animal, or thing located near some other person, animal, or thing

²neighbor *vb* **neigh·bored; neigh·bor·ing** : to be near or next to — **neigh·bor·ing** *adj*

neigh·bor·hood *n* **1** : a residential section of a city **2** : the people living near one another **3** : a place or region near : VICINITY **4** : an amount, size, or range that is close to

neigh·bor·ly *adj* : familiar and helpful : FRIENDLY — **neigh·bor·li·ness** *n*

¹nei·ther *conj* **1** : not either **2** : also not

²neither *pron* : not the one and not the other

³neither *adj* : not either

ne·on *n* : a colorless gaseous chemical element found in very small amounts in the air and used in electric lamps

neo·phyte *n* **1** : BEGINNER, NOVICE **2** : a new convert

neph·ew *n* : a son of a person's brother or sister

Nep·tune *n* : the planet that is eighth in order of distance from the sun and has a diameter of about 31,000 miles (50,000 kilometers)

nep·tu·ni·um *n* : a radioactive chemical element similar to uranium

nerd *n* **1** : a person who is socially awkward, unattractive, or not fashionable **2** : a person who is extremely interested in technical or intellectual subjects — **nerdy** *adj*

nerve *n* **1** : a bundle of nerve fibers that carries messages in the form of nerve impulses to or away from the brain and spinal cord **2** : COURAGE, BOLDNESS **3** : rude or disrespectful boldness **4 nerves** *pl* : feelings of worry **5** : the sensitive soft inner part of a tooth — **nerve·less** *adj*

nerve cell *n* : a cell of the nervous system with fibers that carrry nerve impulses

nerve fiber *n* : any of the threadlike extensions (as axons or dendrites) of a nerve cell that carry nerve impulses

nerve impulse *n* : an electrical signal carried by nerve cells which relays information from the body's sense organs to the brain and spinal cord or instructions from the brain and spinal cord to a body part (as a muscle or gland)

ner·vous *adj* **1** : having or showing feelings of worry, fear, or anxiety **2** : easily becoming worried, frightened, or anxious **3** : of, relating to, or made up of nerves or nerve cells — **ner·vous·ly** *adv* — **ner·vous·ness** *n*

nervous system *n* : a system of the body that in vertebrates includes the brain, spinal cord, nerves, and sense organs and receives, interprets, and responds to stimuli from inside and outside the body

nervy *adj* **nerv·i·er; nerv·i·est 1** : showing calm courage **2** : showing or acting with disrespectful boldness

-ness *n suffix* : state : condition

¹nest *n* **1** : a shelter made by an animal and especially a bird for its eggs and young **2** : a place where some animals live and usually lay eggs **3** : a cozy place : HOME **4** : those living in a nest

²nest *vb* **nest·ed; nest·ing** : to build or live in a nest

nes·tle *vb* **nes·tled; nes·tling 1** : to lie close and snug : CUDDLE **2** : to be located snugly or in a place not easily noticed

nest·ling *n* : a young bird not yet able to leave the nest

¹net *n* **1** : a device made of strands that weave in and out with open spaces between and used to hold or catch something **2** : a fabric made of strands of thread, cord, rope, or wire that weave in and out with much open space **3** : the object placed between players in some games (as tennis) **4** : the area that serves as the goal in some games (as soccer and hockey) **5** *often cap* : INTERNET **6** : NETWORK 1 **7** : something that traps and is difficult to escape from

²net *vb* **net·ted; net·ting 1** : to cover with or as if with a net **2** : to catch in or as if in a net

³net *adj* : remaining after all charges or expenses have been subtracted

⁴net *vb* **net·ted; net·ting** : to gain or produce as profit : CLEAR

net·ting *n* **1** : ¹NET 1 **2** : ¹NET 2

net·tle *n* : a tall plant with hairs on the leaves that when touched can cause a painful skin rash

net·work *n* **1** : an arrangement of things forming a pattern with spaces between **2** : a system of computers connected by communications lines **3** : a group of connected radio or television stations

neu·ron *n* : NERVE CELL

neu·ter *vb* **neu·tered; neu·ter·ing** : to remove the sex glands and especially the testes from : CASTRATE

¹neu·tral *n* **1** : a person or group that does not favor either side in a quarrel, contest, or war **2** : a grayish color or color that is not bright **3** : a position of gears (as in the transmission of a motor vehicle) in which they are not in contact

²neutral *adj* **1** : not favoring either side in a quarrel, contest, or war **2** : of or relating to a country that doesn't favor either side in a dispute **3** : not strong in opinion or feeling **4** : having a color that is not bright : GRAYISH **5** : neither acid nor basic **6** : not electrically charged

neu·tral·i·ty *n* : the quality or state of not favoring one side or the other

neu·tral·i·za·tion *n* : the act or process of making chemically neutral : the state of being chemically neutral

neu·tral·ize *vb* **neu·tral·ized; neu·tral·iz·ing 1** : to make chemically neutral **2** : to make ineffective

neu·tron *n* : a particle that has a mass nearly equal to that of the proton but no electrical charge and that is present in all atomic nuclei except those of hydrogen

Nev. *abbr* Nevada

nev·er *adv* **1** : not ever : at no time **2** : not to any extent or in any way

nev·er·more *adv* : never again

nev·er·the·less *adv* : even so : HOWEVER

¹new *adj* **new·er; new·est 1** : recently bought, acquired, or rented **2** : taking the place of one that came before **3** : recently discovered or learned **4** : beginning as a repeating of a previous thing **5** : being in a position, place, or state the first time **6** : having recently come into existence **7** : not used by anyone previously **8** : not accustomed . — **new·ness** *n*

²new *adv* : NEWLY, RECENTLY

new·born *adj* **1** : recently born **2** : made new or strong again

new·com·er *n* **1** : someone or something recently arrived **2** : BEGINNER

new·el *n* : a post at the bottom or at a turn of a stairway

new·fan·gled *adj* : of the newest style : NOVEL

new·ly *adv* : not long ago : RECENTLY

new·ly·wed *n* : a person recently married

new moon *n* **1** : the moon's phase when its dark side is toward the earth **2** : the thin curved outline of the moon seen shortly after sunset for a few days after the new moon

news *n* **1** : a report of recent events or unknown information **2** : information or recent events reported in a newspaper or magazine or on a broadcast **3** : a broadcast of information on recent events **4** : an event that is interesting enough to be reported

news·boy *n* : a boy or man who delivers or sells newspapers

news·cast *n* : a radio or television broadcast of information on recent events

news·girl *n* : a girl or woman who delivers or sells newspapers

news·man *n, pl* **news·men** : a person who gathers or reports information on recent events

news·pa·per *n* : a paper that is printed and sold usually every day or weekly and that contains information on recent events, articles of opinion, features, and advertising

news·reel *n* : a short motion picture made in the past about events at that time

news·stand *n* : a place where newspapers and magazines are sold

news·wom·an *n, pl* **news·wom·en** : a woman who gathers or reports information on recent events

New World *n* : the lands in the western hemisphere and especially North and South America

newt *n* : a small salamander that lives mostly in water

New Year's Day *n* : January 1 observed as a legal holiday in many countries

¹next *adj* : coming just before or after

²next *adv* **1** : in the nearest place, time, or order following **2** : at the first time after this

³next *n* : a person or thing that immediately follows another person or thing

next–door *adj* : located in the next building, apartment, or room

next door *adv* : in or to the nearest building, apartment, or room

¹next to *prep* **1** : BESIDE 1 **2** : following right after

²next to *adv* : very nearly

Nez Percé *or* **Nez Perce** *pl* **Nez Percé** *or* **Nez Perc·és** *or* **Nez Perce** *or* **Nez Perc·es** **1** : a member of an American Indian people of Idaho, Washington, and Oregon **2** : the language of the Nez Percé people

NH *abbr* New Hampshire

nib *n* **1** : a pointed object (as the bill of a bird) **2** : the point of a pen

¹nib·ble *vb* **nib·bled; nib·bling** : to bite or chew gently or bit by bit

²nibble *n* : a very small amount

nice *adj* **nic·er; nic·est** **1** : PLEASING, PLEASANT **2** : kind, polite, and friendly **3** : of good quality **4** : done very well **5** : well behaved — **nice·ly** *adv* — **nice·ness** *n*

ni·ce·ty *n, pl* **ni·ce·ties** **1** : something dainty, delicate, or of especially good quality **2** : a fine detail that is considered part of polite or proper behavior

niche *n* **1** : an open hollow space in a wall (as for a statue) **2** : a place, job, or use for which a person or a thing is best fitted

¹nick *n* **1** : a small cut or chip in a surface **2** : the last moment

²nick *vb* **nicked; nick·ing** : to make a small cut or chip in

nick·el *n* **1** : a hard silvery white metallic chemical element that can be highly polished, resists weathering, and is used in alloys **2** : a United States coin worth five cents

nick·er *vb* **nick·ered; nick·er·ing** : ¹NEIGH, WHINNY

¹nick·name *n* **1** : a usually descriptive name used in addition to a person's given name **2** : a familiar form of a proper name

²nickname *vb* **nick·named; nick·nam·ing** : to give a usually descriptive name to that is additional to a given name

nic·o·tine *n* : a poisonous substance found in small amounts in tobacco

niece *n* : a daughter of a person's brother or sister

nif·ty *adj* **nif·ti·er; nif·ti·est** : very unusual and attractive

nig·gling *adj* : PETTY 1

¹nigh *adv* **1** : near in time or place **2** : ALMOST, NEARLY

²nigh *adj* : ³CLOSE 1, NEAR

night *n* **1** : the time between dusk and dawn when there is no sunlight **2** : the early part of the night : NIGHTFALL **3** : the darkness of night

night·club *n* : a place of entertainment open at night usually serving food and alcoholic beverages and having music for dancing

night crawl·er *n* : EARTHWORM

night·fall *n* : the coming of night

night·gown *n* : a loose garment worn in bed

night·hawk *n* : a bird that is active at twilight and feeds on insects caught in flight

night·in·gale *n* : a reddish brown European bird noted for the sweet song of the male usually heard at night

¹night·ly *adj* : happening or done at night or every night

²nightly *adv* : every night

night·mare *n* **1** : a frightening dream **2** : a horrible experience — **night·mar·ish** *adj*

night·shirt *n* : a long loose shirt worn in bed

night·stick *n* : a police officer's club

night·time *n* : NIGHT 1

nil *n* : nothing at all : ZERO

nim·ble *adj* **nim·bler; nim·blest** **1** : quick and light in motion : AGILE **2** : quick in understanding and learning : CLEVER — **nim·ble·ness** *n* — **nim·bly** *adv*

nim·bus *n, pl* **nim·bi** *or* **nim·bus·es** : a rain cloud

¹nine *adj* : being one more than eight

²nine *n* **1** : one more than eight : three times three : 9 **2** : the ninth in a set or series

¹nine·teen *adj* : being one more than 18

²nineteen *n* : one more than 18 : 19

¹nine·teenth *adj* : coming right after 18th

²nineteenth *n* : number 19 in a series

¹nine·ti·eth *adj* : coming right after 89th

²ninetieth *n* : number 90 in a series

¹nine·ty *adj* : being nine times ten

²ninety *n* : nine times ten : 90

nin·ja *n, pl* **ninja** *also* **nin·jas** : a person trained in ancient Japanese martial arts who works as a spy and assassin especially in the past

¹ninth *adj* : coming right after eighth

²ninth *n* **1** : number nine in a series **2** : one of nine equal parts

¹nip *vb* **nipped; nip·ping** **1** : to bite or pinch lightly **2** : to injure or make numb with cold **3** : to remove or cut off by or as if by pinching **4** : to move quickly — **nip (something)**

in the bud : to stop (something) right away so it does not become a problem

²nip *n* : a light bite or pinch

³nip *n* : a small amount of liquor

nip and tuck *adj or adv* : so close that the lead shifts rapidly from one contestant to another

nip·ple *n* **1** : the part of the breast or chest from which a baby or young animal sucks milk **2** : something (as the mouthpiece of a baby's bottle) like a nipple

nip·py *adj* **nip·pi·er; nip·pi·est** : CHILLY

nit *n* : the egg of a louse

ni·trate *n* : a substance that is made from or similar in composition to nitric acid

ni·tric acid *n* : a strong liquid acid that contains hydrogen, nitrogen, and oxygen and is used in making fertilizers, explosives, and dyes

ni·tro·gen *n* : a colorless odorless gaseous chemical element that makes up 78 percent of the atmosphere and forms a part of all living tissues

nitrogen cycle *n* : a continuous series of natural processes by which nitrogen passes from air to soil to living things and back into the air

nitrogen fix·a·tion *n* : the changing of nitrogen into an available and useful form especially by bacteria (**nitrogen–fixing bacteria**)

ni·tro·glyc·er·in *or* **ni·tro·glyc·er·ine** *n* : an oily liquid explosive from which dynamite is made

NJ *abbr* New Jersey

NL *abbr* Newfoundland and Labrador

NM, N. Mex. *abbr* New Mexico

¹no *adv* **1** : not at all : not any **2** : not so — used to express disagreement or refusal **3** — used to express surprise, doubt, or disbelief

²no *adj* **1** : not any **2** : hardly any : very little **3** : not a

³no *n, pl* **noes** *or* **nos 1** : an act or instance of refusing or denying by the use of the word *no* : DENIAL **2** : a vote or decision against something **3** *noes or nos pl* : persons voting against something

no. *abbr* **1** north **2** number

no·bil·i·ty *n, pl* **no·bil·i·ties 1** : the quality or state of having a fine or admirable qualities **2** : high social rank **3** : the class or a group of people of high birth or rank

¹no·ble *adj* **no·bler; no·blest 1** : having or showing very fine or admirable qualities **2** : of very high birth or rank **3** : grand in appearance — **no·ble·ness** *n* — **no·bly** *adv*

²noble *n* : a person of high birth or rank

no·ble·man *n, pl* **no·ble·men** : a man of high birth or rank

no·ble·wom·an *n, pl* **no·ble·wom·en** : a woman of high birth or rank

¹no·body *pron* : no person : not anybody

²nobody *n, pl* **no·bod·ies** : a person of no importance

noc·tur·nal *adj* **1** : happening at night **2** : active at night

¹nod *vb* **nod·ded; nod·ding 1** : to bend the head up and down one or more times **2** : to move up and down **3** : to tip the head in a certain direction — **nod off** : to fall asleep

²nod *n* : the action of bending the head up and down

node *n* : a thickened spot or part (as of a plant stem where a leaf develops)

nod·ule *n* : a small roundish lump or mass

no·el *n* **1** : a Christmas carol **2** *cap* : the Christmas season

noes *pl of* NO

nog·gin *n* : a person's head

¹noise *n* **1** : a loud or unpleasant sound **2** : ³SOUND 1 — **noise·less** *adj* — **noise·less·ly** *adv*

²noise *vb* **noised; nois·ing** : to spread by rumor or report

noise·mak·er *n* : a device used to make noise especially at parties

noisy *adj* **nois·i·er; nois·i·est 1** : making a lot of noise **2** : full of noise — **nois·i·ly** *adv* — **nois·i·ness** *n*

¹no·mad *n* **1** : a member of a people having no permanent home but moving from place to place usually in search of food or to graze livestock **2** : a person who moves often

²nomad *adj* : NOMADIC

no·mad·ic *adj* **1** : characteristic of or being a nomad or group of nomads **2** : roaming about from place to place

nom·i·nal *adj* **1** : existing as something in name only **2** : very small — **nom·i·nal·ly** *adv*

nom·i·nate *vb* **nom·i·nat·ed; nom·i·nat·ing** : to choose as a candidate for election, appointment, or honor

nom·i·na·tion *n* : the act or an instance of choosing as a candidate for election, appointment, or honor

nom·i·na·tive *adj* : being or belonging to the case of a noun or pronoun that is usually the subject of a verb

nom·i·nee *n* : someone or something that has been chosen as a candidate for election, appointment, or honor

non- *prefix* : not

non·cha·lance *n* : the state of being relaxed and free from concern or excitement

non·cha·lant *adj* : showing or having a relaxed manner free from concern or excitement — **non·cha·lant·ly** *adv*

non·com·bat·ant *n* **1** : a member (as a chaplain) of the armed forces whose duties do not include fighting **2** : a person who is not in the armed forces : CIVILIAN

non·com·mis·sioned officer *n* : an officer in the army, air force, or marine corps appointed from among the enlisted persons

non·com·mit·tal *adj* : not revealing thoughts or decisions

non·con·form·ist *n* : a person who does not behave according to generally accepted standards or customs

non·de·script *adj* : having no special or interesting characteristics : not easily described

¹**none** *pron* : not any : not one

²**none** *adv* **1** : not at all **2** : in no way

non·en·ti·ty *n, pl* **non·en·ti·ties** : someone or something of no importance

¹**non·es·sen·tial** *adj* : not necessary

²**nonessential** *n* : something that is not necessary

none·the·less *adv* : NEVERTHELESS

non·fic·tion *n* : writing that is about facts or real events

non·flam·ma·ble *adj* : not easily set on fire

non·liv·ing *adj* : not living

non·par·ti·san *adj* : not supporting one party or side over another

non·per·ish·able *adj* : able to be stored for a long time without spoiling

non·plussed *adj* : so surprised or confused as to be at a loss as to what to say, think, or do

non·poi·son·ous *adj* : not poisonous

non·prof·it *adj* : not existing or done to make a profit

non·re·new·able *adj* : not restored or replaced by natural processes in a short period of time

¹**non·res·i·dent** *adj* : not living in a certain place

²**nonresident** *n* : a person who does not live in a certain place

non·sec·tar·i·an *adj* : not limited to a particular religious group

non·sense *n* : foolish or meaningless words, ideas, or actions

non·sen·si·cal *adj* : making no sense : ABSURD

non·smok·er *n* : a person who does not smoke tobacco

non·smok·ing *adj* : reserved for the use of nonsmokers

non·stan·dard *adj* : different from or lower in quality than what is typical

non·stop *adv or adj* : without a stop

noo·dle *n* : a thin often flat strip of fresh or dried dough (as of flour and egg) that is usually boiled

nook *n* **1** : an inner corner **2** : a sheltered or hidden place

noon *n* : the middle of the day : twelve o'clock in the daytime

noon·day *n* : NOON, MIDDAY

no one *pron* : ¹NOBODY

noon·time *n* : NOON

noose *n* : a loop that passes through a knot at the end of a line so that it gets smaller when the other end of the line is pulled

nor *conj* : and not

norm *n* **1** : ¹AVERAGE 2 **2** : a common practice

¹**nor·mal** *adj* **1** : of the regular or usual kind **2** : healthy in body or mind — **nor·mal·ly** *adv*

²**normal** *n* : the usual form, state, level, or amount : AVERAGE

nor·mal·cy *n* : NORMALITY

nor·mal·i·ty *n* : the quality or state of being of the regular or usual kind

Nor·man *n* **1** : one of the Scandinavians who conquered Normandy in the tenth century **2** : one of the people of mixed Norman and French ancestry who conquered England in 1066

Norse *n* **1** *pl* **Norse** : the people of Scandinavia **2** *pl* **Norse** : the people of Norway **3** : any of the languages of the Norse people

¹**north** *adv* : to or toward the north

²**north** *adj* : placed toward, facing, or coming from the north

³**north** *n* **1** : the direction to the left of someone facing east : the compass point opposite to south **2** *cap* : regions or countries north of a point that is mentioned or understood

¹**North American** *n* : a person born or living in North America

²**North American** *adj* : of or relating to North America or the North Americans

north·bound *adj* : going north

¹**north·east** *adv* : to or toward the direction between north and east

²**northeast** *adj* : placed toward, facing, or coming from the northeast

³**northeast** *n* **1** : the direction between north and east **2** *cap* : regions or countries northeast of a point that is mentioned or understood

north·east·er·ly *adv or adj* **1** : from the northeast **2** : toward the northeast

north·east·ern *adj* **1** *often cap* : of, relating to, or like that of the Northeast **2** : lying toward or coming from the northeast

north·er·ly *adj or adv* **1** : from the north **2** : toward the north

north·ern *adj* **1** *often cap* : of, relating to, or like that of the North **2** ; lying toward or coming from the north

northern lights *n pl* : AURORA BOREALIS

north·land *n, often cap* : land in the north : the north of a country or region

north pole *n* **1** *often cap N&P* : the most northern point of the earth : the northern end of the earth's axis **2** : the end of a magnet that points toward the north when the magnet is free to swing

North Star *n* : the star toward which the northern end of the earth's axis most closely points

north·ward *adv or adj* : toward the north

¹north·west *adv* : to or toward the direction between north and west

²northwest *adj* : placed toward, facing, or coming from the northwest

³northwest *n* **1** : the direction between north and west **2** *cap* : regions or countries northwest of a point that is mentioned or understood

north·west·er·ly *adv or adj* **1** : from the northwest **2** : toward the northwest

north·west·ern *adj* **1** *often cap* : of, relating to, or like that of the Northwest **2** : lying toward or coming from the northwest

¹Nor·we·gian *adj* : of or relating to Norway, its people, or the Norwegian language

²Norwegian *n* **1** : a person who is born or lives in Norway **2** : the language of the Norwegians

nos *pl of* NO

¹nose *n* **1** : the part of the face or head that contains the nostrils **2** : the sense or organ of smell **3** : the front end or part of something **4** : an ability to discover — **nosed** *adj*

²nose *vb* **nosed; nos·ing 1** : to search for or find by smelling **2** : to touch or rub with the nose : NUZZLE **3** : to search for especially in an unwelcome way : PRY **4** : to move ahead slowly or carefully

nose-bleed *n* : a bleeding at the nose

nose cone *n* : a protective cone forming the forward end of an airplane, rocket, or missile

nose-dive *n* **1** : a downward plunge (as of an airplane) **2** : a sudden sharp drop (as in prices)

nose–dive *vb* **nose–dived; nose–div·ing** : to plunge or drop suddenly or sharply

nos·tal·gia *n* : a longing for something past

nos·tal·gic *adj* : having, showing, or characterized by a longing for something past

nos·tril *n* : either of the outer openings of the nose through which people and many animals breathe

nosy *or* **nos·ey** *adj* **nos·i·er; nos·i·est** : wanting to know about someone else's business

not *adv* **1** — used to make a word or group of words negative **2** — used to stand for the negative of a group of words that comes before

¹no·ta·ble *adj* **1** : deserving special notice : REMARKABLE **2** : very successful or respected : DISTINGUISHED — **no·ta·bly** *adv*

²notable *n* : a famous person

no·ta·rize *vb* **no·ta·rized; no·ta·riz·ing** : to sign as a notary public to show that a document is authentic

no·ta·ry public *n, pl* **notaries public** *or* **notary publics** : a public official who witnesses the making of a document (as a will) and signs it to show that it is authentic

no·ta·tion *n* **1** : the act of noting **2** : ²NOTE 5 **3** : a system of signs, marks, or figures used to give a certain kind of information

¹notch *n* **1** : a cut in the shape of a V in an edge or surface **2** : a narrow pass between mountains **3** : DEGREE 1, STEP

²notch *vb* **notched; notch·ing** : to make V-shaped cuts in

¹note *vb* **not·ed; not·ing 1** : to notice or observe with care **2** : to record in writing **3** : to make special mention of

²note *n* **1** : a musical sound : TONE **2** : a symbol in music that by its shape and position on the staff shows the pitch of a tone and the length of time it is to be held **3** : the musical call or song of a bird **4** : a quality that shows a feeling **5** : something written down often to aid the memory **6** : a printed comment in a book that helps explain part of the text **7** : DISTINCTION 3 **8** : a short written message or letter **9** : careful notice **10** : frame of mind : MOOD **11** : a piano key **12** : a written promise to pay a debt

note·book *n* : a book of blank pages for writing in

not·ed *adj* : well-known and highly regarded

note·wor·thy *adj* : worthy of attention : REMARKABLE

¹noth·ing *pron* **1** : not anything : no thing **2** : someone or something of no interest, value, or importance

²nothing *adv* : not at all : in no way

³nothing *n* **1** : something that does not exist : empty space **2** : ZERO 1 **3** : someone or something of little or no worth or importance — **noth·ing·ness** *n* — **for nothing 1** : for no reason **2** : for no money

¹no·tice *n* **1** : WARNING, ANNOUNCEMENT **2** : an indication that an agreement will end at a specified time **3** : ATTENTION 1, HEED **4** : a written or printed announcement **5** : a short piece of writing that gives an opinion (as of a book or play)

²notice *vb* **no·ticed; no·tic·ing** : to become aware of : pay attention to

no·tice·able *adj* : deserving notice : likely to attract attention — **no·tice·ably** *adv*

no·ti·fi·ca·tion *n* **1** : the act or an instance of giving notice or information **2** : something written or printed that gives notice

no·ti·fy *vb* **no·ti·fied; no·ti·fy·ing** : to give notice to : INFORM

no·tion *n* **1** : IDEA 2 **2** : WHIM **3 notions** *pl* : small useful articles (as buttons, needles, and thread)

no·to·ri·e·ty *n* : the state of being widely known especially for some bad characteristic

no·to·ri·ous *adj* : widely known especially for some bad characteristic — **no·to·ri·ous·ly** *adv*

¹not·with·stand·ing *prep* : in spite of

²notwithstanding *adv* : NEVERTHELESS

nou·gat *n* : a candy consisting of a sugar paste with nuts or fruit pieces

nought *variant of* NAUGHT

noun *n* : a word or phrase that is the name of something (as a person, place, or thing) and that is used in a sentence especially as subject or object of a verb or as object of a preposition

nour·ish *vb* **nour·ished; nour·ish·ing** : to cause to grow or live in a healthy state especially by providing with enough good food or nutrients — **nour·ish·ing** *adj*

nour·ish·ment *n* : something (as food) that causes growth or health

Nov. *abbr* November

¹nov·el *adj* : new and different from what is already known

²novel *n* : a long story usually about imaginary characters and events

nov·el·ist *n* : a writer of novels

nov·el·ty *n, pl* **nov·el·ties 1** : something new or unusual **2** : the quality or state of being new or unusual **3** : a small unusual ornament or toy

No·vem·ber *n* : the eleventh month of the year

nov·ice *n* **1** : a person who has no previous experience with something : BEGINNER **2** : a new member of a religious community who is preparing to take the vows of religion

¹now *adv* **1** : at this time **2** : immediately before the present time **3** : in the time immediately to follow **4** — used to express command or introduce an important point **5** : SOMETIMES **6** : in the present circumstances **7** : at the time referred to — **now and then** : from time to time : OCCASIONALLY

²now *conj* : in view of the fact that : SINCE

³now *n* : the present time

now·a·days *adv* : at the present time

¹no·where *adv* **1** : not in or at any place **2** : to no place **3** : not at all

²nowhere *n* : a place that does not exist

nox·ious *adj* : causing harm

noz·zle *n* : a short tube often used on the end of a hose or pipe to direct or speed up a flow of fluid

NS *abbr* Nova Scotia

NT *abbr* Northwest Territories

-n't *adv suffix* : not

NU *abbr* Nunavut

nub *n* **1** : a small rounded part that sticks out from something **2** : a small piece or end that remains after something has been removed or worn away

nub·by *adj* **nub·bi·er; nub·bi·est** : having small knobs or lumps

nu·cle·ar *adj* **1** : of, relating to, or being a nucleus (as of a cell) **2** : of or relating to the nucleus of the atom **3** : produced by a nuclear reaction **4** : of, relating to, or being a weapon whose destructive power comes from an uncontrolled nuclear reaction **5** : relating to or powered by nuclear energy

nu·cle·us *n, pl* **nu·clei 1** : a usually round part of most cells that is enclosed in a double membrane, controls the activities of the cell, and contains the chromosomes **2** : the central part of an atom that comprises nearly all of the atomic mass and that consists of protons and neutrons **3** : a central point, group, or mass

nude *adj* **nud·er; nud·est** : not wearing clothes : NAKED

¹nudge *vb* **nudged; nudg·ing 1** : to touch or push gently **2** : to attract the attention of by touching or pushing gently (as with the elbow)

²nudge *n* : a slight push

nu·di·ty *n* : the state of having no clothes on

nug·get *n* **1** : a solid lump especially of precious metal **2** : a small usually rounded piece of food

nui·sance *n* : an annoying or troublesome person, thing, or situation

null *adj* : having no legal force : not binding

¹numb *adj* **1** : unable to feel anything especially because of cold **2** : unable to think, feel, or react normally (as because of great fear, surprise, or sadness) — **numb·ly** *adv* — **numb·ness** *n*

²numb *vb* **numbed; numb·ing** : to make or become unable to feel pain or touch

¹num·ber *n* **1** : the total of persons, things, or units taken together : AMOUNT **2** : a total that is not specified **3** : a unit belonging to a mathematical system and subject to its rules **4** : a word, symbol, or letter used to represent a mathematical number : NUMERAL **5** : a certain numeral for telling one person or thing from another or from others **6** : a quality of a word form that shows whether the word is singular or plural **7** : one of a series **8** : a song or dance usually that is part of a larger performance

²number *vb* **num·bered; num·ber·ing 1** : ¹COUNT 1 **2** : INCLUDE **3** : to limit to a certain number **4** : to give a number to **5** : to add up to or have a total of

num·ber·less *adj* : too many to count

number line *n* : a line in which points are matched to numbers

nu·mer·al *n* : a symbol or group of symbols representing a number

nu·mer·a·tor *n* : the part of a fraction that is above the line

nu·mer·i·cal *adj* : of or relating to numbers : stated in numbers — **nu·mer·i·cal·ly** *adv*

nu·mer·ous *adj* : consisting of a large number : MANY

nun *n* : a woman belonging to a religious community and living according to vows

nun·nery *n, pl* **nun·ner·ies** : CONVENT

nup·tial *adj* : of or relating to marriage or a wedding

nup·tials *n pl* : WEDDING

¹nurse *n* **1** : a person skilled or trained in caring for sick or injured people **2** : a woman employed for the care of a young child

²nurse *vb* **nursed; nurs·ing 1** : to feed at the breast : SUCKLE **2** : to take care of (as a young child or a sick person) **3** : to treat with special care or attention

nurse·maid *n* : ¹NURSE 2

nurs·ery *n, pl* **nurs·er·ies 1** : the room where a baby sleeps **2** : a place where small children are temporarily cared for in their parent's absence **3** : a place where plants (as trees or shrubs) are grown and usually sold

nursery rhyme *n* : a short rhyme for children that often tells a story

nursery school *n* : a school for children usually under five years old

¹nur·ture *n* **1** : the way a person or animal was raised : UPBRINGING **2** : something (as food) that is essential to healthy growth and development

²nurture *vb* **nur·tured; nur·tur·ing 1** : to provide with things (as food and protection)

essential to healthy growth and development **2** : to further the development of

nut *n* **1** : a dry fruit or seed with a firm inner kernel and a hard shell **2** : the often edible kernel of a nut **3** : a small piece of metal with a hole through it that can be screwed onto a bolt for tightening or holding something **4** : a foolish or crazy person **5** : a person who is very interested in or enthusiastic about something — **nut·like** *adj*

nut·crack·er *n* : a device used for cracking the shells of nuts

nut·hatch *n* : a small bird that creeps on tree trunks and branches and eats insects

nut·meg *n* : a spice made from the ground seeds of a small tropical evergreen tree

nu·tri·ent *n* : a substance that is needed for healthy growth, development, and functioning

nu·tri·ment *n* : something that nourishes

nu·tri·tion *n* : the act or process of nourishing or being nourished : the processes by which a living thing takes in and uses nutrients

nu·tri·tion·al *adj* : relating to, providing, or involved in the proper intake of nutrients

nu·tri·tious *adj* : providing nutrients : NOURISHING

nu·tri·tive *adj* **1** : NUTRITIONAL **2** : NUTRITIOUS

nuts *adj* **1** : enthusiastic about or interested in something **2** : CRAZY 1

nut·shell *n* : the shell of a nut — **in a nutshell** : very briefly

nut·ty *adj* **nut·ti·er; nut·ti·est 1** : not showing good sense **2** : having a flavor like that of nuts

nuz·zle *vb* **nuz·zled; nuz·zling** : to push or rub with the nose

NV *abbr* Nevada

NW *abbr* northwest

NY *abbr* New York

ny·lon *n* : a strong man-made material used in the making of fabrics and plastics

nymph *n* **1** : one of many goddesses in old legends represented as beautiful young women living in the mountains, forests, and waters **2** : an immature insect that differs from the adult chiefly in being of smaller size and having undeveloped wings

O

o *n, pl* **o's** *or* **os** *often cap* **1** : the 15th letter of the English alphabet **2** : ZERO 1

O *variant of* OH

O. *abbr* Ohio

oaf *n* : a stupid or awkward person — **oaf·ish** *adj*

oak *n* : a tree or shrub that produces acorns and has tough wood much used for furniture and flooring

oak·en *adj* : made of oak

oar *n* : a long pole that is flat and wide at one end and is used for rowing or steering a boat

oar·lock *n* : a usually U-shaped device for holding an oar in place

oars·man *n, pl* **oars·men** : a person who rows a boat

oa·sis *n, pl* **oa·ses** : a fertile or green spot in a desert

oat *n* **1** : a cereal grass grown for its loose clusters of seeds that are used for human food and animal feed **2 oats** *pl* : a crop or the seeds of the oat

oath *n, pl* **oaths** **1** : a solemn promise to tell the truth or do a specific thing **2** : an obscene or impolite word used to express anger or frustration

oat·meal *n* **1** : oat seeds that have had the outer covering removed and are ground into meal or flattened into flakes **2** : a hot cereal made from meal or flakes of oats

obe·di·ence *n* : the act of obeying : willingness to obey

obe·di·ent *adj* : willing to do as told by someone in authority : willing to obey — **obe·di·ent·ly** *adv*

obe·lisk *n* : a four-sided pillar that becomes narrower toward the top and ends in a pyramid

obese *adj* : very fat — **obe·si·ty** *n*

obey *vb* **obeyed; obey·ing** **1** : to follow the commands or guidance of **2** : to comply with : carry out

obit·u·ary *n, pl* **obit·u·ar·ies** : a notice of a person's death (as in a newspaper)

obj. *abbr* **1** object **2** objective

¹ob·ject *n* **1** : something that may be seen or felt **2** : PURPOSE, AIM **3** : something that arouses feelings in an observer **4** : a noun or a term behaving like a noun that receives the action of a verb or completes the meaning of a preposition

²ob·ject *vb* **ob·ject·ed; ob·ject·ing** **1** : to offer or mention as a reason for a feeling of disapproval **2** : to oppose something firmly and usually with words

ob·jec·tion *n* **1** : an act of showing disapproval or great dislike **2** : a reason for or a feeling of disapproval

ob·jec·tion·able *adj* : arousing disapproval or great dislike : OFFENSIVE

¹ob·jec·tive *adj* **1** : dealing with facts without allowing personal feelings to confuse them **2** : being or belonging to the case of a noun or pronoun that is an object of a transitive verb or a preposition **3** : being outside of the mind and independent of it — **ob·jec·tive·ly** *adv*

²objective *n* : PURPOSE, GOAL

ob·li·gate *vb* **ob·li·gat·ed; ob·li·gat·ing** : to make (someone) do something by law or because it is right

ob·li·ga·tion *n* **1** : something a person must

do because of the demands of a promise or contract **2** : something a person feels he or she must do : DUTY **3** : a feeling of being indebted for an act of kindness

oblige *vb* **obliged; oblig·ing** **1** : ²FORCE 1, COMPEL **2** : to do a favor for or do something as a favor **3** : to earn the gratitude of

oblig·ing *adj* : willing to do favors — **oblig·ing·ly** *adv*

oblique *adj* : having a slanting position or direction : neither perpendicular nor parallel — **oblique·ly** *adv*

oblit·er·ate *vb* **oblit·er·at·ed; oblit·er·at·ing** : to remove, destroy, or hide completely

obliv·i·on *n* **1** : the state of forgetting or having forgotten or of being unaware or unconscious **2** : the state of being forgotten

obliv·i·ous *adj* : not being conscious or aware — **obliv·i·ous·ly** *adv*

¹ob·long *adj* : different from a square, circle, or sphere by being longer in one direction than the other

²oblong *n* : a figure or object that is larger in one direction than the other

ob·nox·ious *adj* : very disagreeable : HATEFUL — **ob·nox·ious·ly** *adv*

oboe *n* : a woodwind instrument with two reeds that is pitched higher than the bassoon and has a distinctive bright sound

ob·scene *adj* : very shocking to a person's sense of what is moral or decent

ob·scen·i·ty *n, pl* **ob·scen·i·ties** **1** : the quality or state of being shocking to a person's sense of what is moral or decent **2** : something that is shocking to a person's sense of what is moral or decent

¹ob·scure *adj* **1** : not easy to see : FAINT **2** : hidden from view **3** : not easily understood or clearly expressed **4** : not outstanding or famous

²obscure *vb* **ob·scured; ob·scur·ing** : to make difficult to see or understand

ob·scu·ri·ty *n, pl* **ob·scu·ri·ties** **1** : the state of being difficult to see or understand **2** : the state of being unknown or forgotten **3** : something that is difficult to understand

ob·serv·able *adj* : NOTICEABLE — **ob·serv·ably** *adv*

ob·ser·vance *n* **1** : an established practice or ceremony **2** : an act of following a custom, rule, or law

ob·ser·vant *adj* : quick to take notice : WATCHFUL, ALERT — **ob·ser·vant·ly** *adv*

ob·ser·va·tion *n* **1** : an act or the power of seeing or taking notice of something **2** : the gathering of information by noting facts or occurrences **3** : an opinion formed or expressed after watching or noticing **4** : the fact of being watched and studied

ob·ser·va·to·ry *n, pl* **ob·ser·va·to·ries** : a

place that has instruments for making observations (as of the stars)

ob·serve *vb* **ob·served; ob·serv·ing 1 :** to watch carefully **2 :** to act in agreement with **:** OBEY **3 :** CELEBRATE 1 **4 :** ²REMARK, SAY — **ob·serv·er** *n*

ob·sess *vb* **ob·sessed; ob·sess·ing :** to occupy the thoughts of completely or abnormally

ob·ses·sion *n* **:** a persistent abnormally strong interest in or concern about someone or something

ob·sid·i·an *n* **:** a smooth dark rock formed by the cooling of lava

ob·so·lete *adj* **:** no longer in use **:** OUT-OF-DATE

ob·sta·cle *n* **:** something that stands in the way or opposes **:** HINDRANCE

ob·sti·nate *adj* **1 :** sticking stubbornly to an opinion or purpose **2 :** difficult to deal with or get rid of — **ob·sti·nate·ly** *adv*

ob·struct *vb* **ob·struct·ed; ob·struct·ing 1 :** to block or make passage through difficult **2 :** to be or come in the way of **:** HINDER **3 :** to make (something) difficult to see

ob·struc·tion *n* **1 :** an act of blocking or hindering **:** the state of having something that blocks or hinders **2 :** something that gets in the way **:** OBSTACLE

ob·tain *vb* **ob·tained; ob·tain·ing :** to gain or get hold of with effort

ob·tain·able *adj* **:** possible to get

ob·tuse *adj* **1 :** measuring more than a right angle **2 :** not able to understand something obvious

ob·vi·ous *adj* **:** easily found, seen, or understood — **ob·vi·ous·ly** *adv* — **ob·vi·ous·ness** *n*

¹oc·ca·sion *n* **1 :** a special event **2 :** the time of an event **3 :** a suitable opportunity **:** a good chance

²occasion *vb* **oc·ca·sioned; oc·ca·sion·ing :** to bring about

oc·ca·sion·al *adj* **:** happening or met with now and then — **oc·ca·sion·al·ly** *adv*

oc·cu·pan·cy *n, pl* **oc·cu·pan·cies :** the act of using, living in, or taking possession of a place

oc·cu·pant *n* **:** a person who uses, lives in, or possesses a place

oc·cu·pa·tion *n* **1 :** a person's business or profession **2 :** the act of using or taking possession and control of a place

oc·cu·pa·tion·al *adj* **:** relating to a person's business or profession — **oc·cu·pa·tion·al·ly** *adv*

oc·cu·py *vb* **oc·cu·pied; oc·cu·py·ing 1 :** to fill up (an extent of time or space) **2 :** to take up the attention or energies of **3 :** to live in

as an owner or tenant **4 :** to take or hold possession of **5 :** to perform the functions of

oc·cur *vb* **oc·curred; oc·cur·ring 1 :** to come by or as if by chance **:** HAPPEN **2 :** to come into the mind **3 :** to be found or met with **:** APPEAR

oc·cur·rence *n* **1 :** something that happens **2 :** the action or process of happening

ocean *n* **1 :** the whole body of salt water that covers nearly three fourths of the earth **2 :** one of the large bodies of water into which the larger body that covers the earth is divided

oce·an·ic *adj* **:** of or relating to the ocean

ocean·og·ra·phy *n* **:** a science that deals with the ocean

oce·lot *n* **:** a medium-sized American wildcat that is yellowish brown or grayish and blotched with black

o'·clock *adv* **:** according to the clock

Oct. *abbr* October

octa- *or* **octo-** *also* **oct-** *prefix* **:** eight

oc·ta·gon *n* **:** a flat geometric figure with eight angles and eight sides

oc·tag·o·nal *adj* **:** having eight sides

oc·tave *n* **1 :** a space of eight steps between musical notes **2 :** a tone or note that is eight steps above or below another note or tone

Oc·to·ber *n* **:** the tenth month of the year

oc·to·pus *n, pl* **oc·to·pus·es** *or* **oc·to·pi :** a marine animal that has a soft rounded body with eight long flexible arms about its base which have sucking disks able to seize and hold things (as prey)

oc·u·lar *adj* **:** of or relating to the eye or eyesight

odd *adj* **odd·er; odd·est 1 :** not usual or common **:** STRANGE **2 :** not usual, expected, or planned **3 :** not capable of being divided by two without leaving a remainder **4 :** not one of a pair or a set **5 :** being or having a number that cannot be divided by two without leaving a remainder **6 :** some more than the number mentioned — **odd·ly** *adv* — **odd·ness** *n*

odd·ball *n* **:** a person who behaves strangely

odd·i·ty *n, pl* **odd·i·ties 1 :** something strange **2 :** the quality or state of being strange

odds *n pl* **1 :** a difference in favor of one thing over another **2 :** conditions that make something difficult **3 :** DISAGREEMENT 1

odds and ends *n pl* **:** things left over **:** miscellaneous things

ode *n* **:** a lyric poem that expresses a noble feeling with dignity

odi·ous *adj* **:** causing hatred or strong dislike **:** worthy of hatred

odom·e·ter *n* **:** an instrument for measuring the distance traveled (as by a vehicle)

odor *n* : a particular smell — **odor·less** *adj*

o'er *adv or prep* : OVER

of *prep* **1** — used to join an amount or a part with the whole which includes it **2** : belonging to, relating to, or connected with **3** : CONCERNING **4** : that is **5** : made from **6** : that has : WITH **7** — used to show what has been taken away **8** — used to indicate the reason for **9** : living in **10** : that involves **11** — used to indicate what an amount or number refers to **12** — used to indicate the point from which someone or something is located **13** — used to indicate the object affected by an action

¹off *adv* **1** : from a place or position **2** : from a course : ASIDE **3** : so as not to be supported, covering or enclosing, or attached **4** : so as to be discontinued or finished **5** : away from work

²off *prep* **1** : away from the surface or top of **2** : at the expense of **3** : released or freed from **4** : below the usual level of **5** : away from

³off *adj* **1** : not operating or flowing **2** : not attached to or covering **3** : started on the way **4** : not taking place **5** : not correct : WRONG **6** : not as good as usual **7** : provided for **8** : small in degree : SLIGHT **9** : away from home or work

off. *abbr* office

of·fend *vb* **of·fend·ed; of·fend·ing 1** : to hurt the feelings of or insult **2** : to do wrong

of·fend·er *n* : a person who does wrong

of·fense *or* **of·fence** *n* **1** : something done that hurts feelings or insults **2** : WRONGDOING, SIN **3** : the act of hurting feelings or insulting **4** : a team or the part of a team that attempts to score in a game **5** : an act of attacking : ASSAULT

¹of·fen·sive *adj* **1** : causing displeasure or resentment **2** : of or relating to the attempt to score in a game or contest **3** : made for or relating to an attack — **of·fen·sive·ly** *adv* — **of·fen·sive·ness** *n*

²offensive *n* : ²ATTACK 1 — **on the offensive** : in a situation that calls for opposing action

¹of·fer *vb* **of·fered; of·fer·ing 1** : to present (something) to be accepted or rejected **2** : to declare willingness **3** : to present for consideration : SUGGEST **4** : to make by effort **5** : to present as an act of worship

²offer *n* **1** : an act of presenting (something) to be accepted or rejected **2** : an act of declaring willingness **3** : a price suggested by someone prepared to buy : BID

of·fer·ing *n* **1** : something presented for acceptance **2** : a contribution to the support of a church **3** : a sacrifice given as part of worship

off·hand *adv or adj* : without previous thought or preparation

of·fice *n* **1** : a place where business is done or a service is supplied **2** : a special duty or position and especially one of authority in government

of·fice·hold·er *n* : a person who has been elected or appointed to a public position

of·fi·cer *n* **1** : a person given the responsibility of enforcing the law **2** : a person who holds a position of authority **3** : a person who holds a commission in the military

¹of·fi·cial *n* : a person who holds a position of authority in an organization or government

²official *adj* **1** : relating to a position of authority **2** : having authority to perform a duty **3** : coming from or meeting the requirements of an authority **4** : proper for a person in office — **of·fi·cial·ly** *adv*

of·fi·ci·ate *vb* **of·fi·ci·at·ed; of·fi·ci·at·ing 1** : to perform a ceremony or duty **2** : to act as an officer : PRESIDE

off·ing *n* : the near future or distance

off·lim·its *adj* : not to be entered or used

off·line *adj or adv* : not connected to or directly controlled by a computer system

offset *vb* **offset; off·set·ting** : to make up for

off·shoot *n* : a branch of a main stem of a plant

¹off·shore *adj* **1** : coming or moving away from the shore **2** : located off the shore

²off·shore *adv* : from the shore : at a distance from the shore

off·spring *n, pl* **offspring** *also* **off·springs** : the young of a person, animal, or plant

off·stage *adv or adj* : off or away from the stage

oft *adv* : OFTEN

of·ten *adv* : many times : FREQUENTLY

of·ten·times *adv* : OFTEN

ogle *vb* **ogled; ogling** : to look at in a way that suggests unusual interest or desire

ogre *n* **1** : an ugly giant of fairy tales and folklore who eats people **2** : a person or object that is frightening or causes strong feelings of dislike

oh *also* **O** *interj* **1** — used to express an emotion (as surprise or pain) **2** — used in direct address

OH *abbr* Ohio

¹oil *n* **1** : any of numerous greasy usually liquid substances from plant, animal, or mineral sources that do not dissolve in water and are used especially as lubricants, fuels, and food **2** : PETROLEUM **3** : paint made of pigments and oil **4** : a painting done in oils

²oil *vb* **oiled; oil·ing** : to rub on or lubricate with a greasy substance

oil·cloth *n* : material treated with a greasy

substance so as to be waterproof and used for shelf and table coverings

oily *adj* **oil·i·er; oil·i·est** : covered with or containing a greasy substance — **oil·i·ness** *n*

oint·ment *n* : a thick greasy medicine for use on the skin

Ojib·wa *or* **Ojib·way** *or* **Ojib·we** *n, pl* **Ojibwa** *or* **Ojib·was** *or* **Ojibway** *or* **Ojib·ways** *or* **Ojibwe** *or* **Ojib·wes 1** : a member of an American Indian people originally of Michigan **2** : the language of the Ojibwa people

¹OK *or* **okay** *adv or adj* : all right

²OK *or* **okay** *n* : APPROVAL

³OK *or* **okay** *vb* **OK'd** *or* **okayed; OK'·ing** *or* **okay·ing** : APPROVE 2, AUTHORIZE

⁴OK *abbr* Oklahoma

oka·pi *n* : an animal of the African forests related to the giraffe

Okla. *abbr* Oklahoma

okra *n* : the green pods of a garden plant that are used as a vegetable especially in soups and stews

¹old *adj* **1** : having lived a long time **2** : showing the effects of time or use **3** : having existed for a specified length of time **4** : dating from the distant past : ANCIENT **5** : having lasted or been such for a long time **6** : FORMER

²old *n* : a distant or earlier time

old·en *adj* : of an earlier period

Old English *n* : the language of England from the earliest documents in the seventh century to about 1100

old–fash·ioned *adj* **1** : from or like that of an earlier time **2** : using or preferring ways and traditions of the past

Old French *n* : the French language from the ninth to the thirteenth century

Old Glory *n* : the flag of the United States

old maid *n* **1** : an elderly unmarried woman **2** : a very neat fussy person **3** : a card game in which cards are matched in pairs and the player holding the extra queen at the end loses

old–time *adj* : from or like that of an earlier or distant period

old–tim·er *n* **1** : a person who has been part of an organization (as a business) for a long time **2** : an old person

old–world *adj* : having old-fashioned charm

Old World *n* : the lands in the eastern hemisphere and especially Europe but not including Australia

ol·fac·to·ry *adj* : of or relating to smelling or the sense of smell

ol·ive *n* **1** : the oily fruit of an evergreen tree that is eaten both ripe and unripe and is the source of an edible oil (**olive oil**) **2** : a yellowish green color

Olym·pic *adj* : of or relating to the Olympic Games

Olympic Games *n pl* : a series of international athletic contests held as separate winter and summer events in a different country every four years

om·e·let *or* **om·e·lette** *n* : beaten eggs cooked without stirring until firm and folded in half often with a filling

omen *n* : a happening believed to be a sign or warning of a future event

om·i·nous *adj* : considered a sign of evil or trouble to come — **om·i·nous·ly** *adv*

omis·sion *n* **1** : something left out **2** : the act of leaving out : the state of being left out

omit *vb* **omit·ted; omit·ting 1** : to leave out : fail to include **2** : to leave undone : NEGLECT

om·ni·bus *n, pl* **om·ni·bus·es** : BUS

om·nip·o·tent *adj* : having power or authority without limit : ALMIGHTY — **om·nip·o·tence** *n*

om·ni·vore *n* : an animal that feeds on plants and other animals

om·niv·o·rous *adj* : feeding on plants and animals

¹on *prep* **1** : in contact with and supported by **2** — used to indicate means of being carried **3** — used to indicate the location of something **4** — used to indicate the focus of a certain action **5** : AGAINST 4 **6** : near or connected with **7** : ¹TO 1 **8** : sometime during **9** : in the state or process of **10** : ²ABOUT 3 **11** : by means of

²on *adv* **1** : into operation or a position allowing operation **2** : in or into contact with a surface **3** : forward in time, space, or action **4** : from one to another

³on *adj* **1** : being in operation **2** : placed so as to allow operation **3** : taking place **4** : having been planned

ON *abbr* Ontario

¹once *adv* **1** : one time only **2** : at some time in the past : FORMERLY **3** : at any one time : EVER — **once and for all** : now and for the last time — **once in a while** : from time to time

²once *n* : one single time — **at once 1** : at the same time **2** : IMMEDIATELY 2

³once *conj* : as soon as : WHEN

once–over *n* : a quick glance or examination

on·com·ing *adj* : coming nearer

¹one *adj* **1** : being a single unit or thing **2** : being a certain unit or thing **3** : being the same in kind or quality **4** : not specified

²one *n* **1** : the number denoting a single unit : 1 **2** : the first in a set or series **3** : a single person or thing

³**one** *pron* **1** : a single member or individual **2** : any person

one another *pron* : EACH OTHER

Onei·da *n, pl* **Oneida** *or* **Onei·das** **1** : a member of an American Indian people originally of New York **2** : the language of the Oneida people

oner·ous *adj* : being difficult and unpleasant to do or to deal with

one·self *pron* : a person's own self

one–sid·ed *adj* **1** : done or occurring on one side only **2** : having one side more developed : LOPSIDED **3** : favoring or dominated by one side

one–time *adj* : FORMER

one–way *adj* : moving or allowing movement in one direction only

on·go·ing *adj* : being in progress or movement

on·ion *n* : the roundish edible bulb of a plant related to the lily that has a sharp odor and taste and is used as a vegetable and to season foods

online *adj or adv* : connected to, directly controlled by, or available through a computer system

on·look·er *n* : SPECTATOR

¹**on·ly** *adj* **1** : alone in or of a class or kind : SOLE **2** : best without doubt

²**only** *adv* **1** : no more than **2** : no one or nothing other than **3** : in no other situation, time, place, or condition except **4** : in the end **5** : as recently as

³**only** *conj* : except that

on·o·mato·poe·ia *n* : the forming of a word (as "buzz" or "hiss") in imitation of a natural sound

on·rush *n* : a strong fast movement forward

on·set *n* **1** : BEGINNING 1 **2** : ²ATTACK 1

on·slaught *n* : a violent attack

Ont. *abbr* Ontario

on·to *prep* : to a position on or against

¹**on·ward** *adv* : toward or at a point lying ahead in space or time : FORWARD

²**onward** *adj* : directed or moving forward

oo·dles *n pl* : a great quantity

¹**ooze** *n* : soft mud : SLIME

²**ooze** *vb* **oozed; ooz·ing** : to flow or leak out slowly

opal *n* : a mineral with soft changeable colors that is used as a gem

opaque *adj* **1** : not letting light through : not transparent **2** : not reflecting light : DULL

¹**open** *adj* **1** : not shut or blocked : not closed **2** : not sealed, locked, or fastened **3** : easy to enter, get through, or see **4** : ready to consider appeals or ideas **5** : not drawn together : spread out **6** : not enclosed or covered **7** : not secret : PUBLIC **8** : to be used, entered, or taken part in by all **9** : not decided or settled — **open·ly** *adv* — **open·ness** *n*

²**open** *vb* **opened; open·ing** **1** : to change or move from a shut condition **2** : to clear by or as if by removing something in the way **3** : to make or become ready for use **4** : to give access **5** : BEGIN 1, START — **open·er** *n*

³**open** *n* : space that is not enclosed or covered : OUTDOORS

open air *n* : space that is not enclosed or covered — **open–air** *adj*

open–and–shut *adj* : ¹PLAIN 3, OBVIOUS

open·heart·ed *adj* **1** : FRANK **2** : GENEROUS 1

open house *n* **1** : friendly and welcoming treatment to anyone who comes **2** : an event in which an organization (as a school) invites the public to see the things that happen there

open·ing *n* **1** : a place that is not enclosed or covered : CLEARING **2** : an act of making or becoming ready for use **3** : BEGINNING **4** : ¹OCCASION 3 **5** : a job opportunity

open·work *n* : something made or work done so as to show spaces through the fabric or material

op·era *n* : a play in which the entire text is sung with orchestral accompaniment

op·er·ate *vb* **op·er·at·ed; op·er·at·ing** **1** : to work or cause to work in a proper or particular way **2** : MANAGE 1 **3** : to perform surgery : do an operation on

operating system *n* : a program or series of programs that controls the operation of a computer and directs the processing of the user's programs

op·er·a·tion *n* **1** : a set of actions for a particular purpose **2** : a medical procedure that involves cutting into a living body in order to repair or remove a damaged or diseased part **3** : the process of putting military forces into action **4** : the state of working or being able to work **5** : a method or manner of working **6** : a process (as addition or multiplication) of getting one mathematical expression from others according to a rule **7** : a single step performed by a computer in carrying out a program

op·er·a·tion·al *adj* : ready for use

op·er·a·tor *n* **1** : a person who manages or controls something **2** : a person in charge of a telephone switchboard **3** : a person who is skillful at achieving things by persuasion or deception

op·er·et·ta *n* : a funny play set to music with speaking, singing, and dancing scenes

opin·ion *n* **1** : a belief based on experience and on certain facts but not amounting to sure knowledge **2** : a judgment about a person or thing **3** : a statement by an expert after careful study

opin·ion·at·ed *adj* : having and expressing very strong ideas and opinions about things

opi·um *n* : a bitter brownish narcotic drug that is the dried juice of a poppy of Europe and Asia

opos·sum *n* : an American animal related to the kangaroo that has a long pointed snout, lives both on the ground and in trees, and is active at night

op·po·nent *n* : a person or thing that takes an opposite position in a contest, fight, or controversy

op·por·tu·ni·ty *n, pl* **op·por·tu·ni·ties** **1** : a favorable combination of circumstances, time, and place **2** : a chance for greater success

op·pose *vb* **op·posed; op·pos·ing** **1** : to disagree with or disapprove of **2** : to compete against **3** : to provide contrast to **4** : to offer resistance to : try to stop or defeat

¹op·po·site *adj* **1** : being at the other end, side, or corner **2** : being as different as possible **3** : being in a position to contrast with or cancel out

²opposite *n* : either of two persons or things that are as different as possible

³opposite *adv* : on the other side of someone or something : across from

⁴opposite *prep* : across from (someone or something)

op·po·si·tion *n* **1** : the state of disagreeing with or disapproving of **2** : the action of resisting **3** : a group of people that disagree with, disapprove of, or resist someone or something

op·press *vb* **op·pressed; op·press·ing** **1** : to control or rule in a harsh or cruel way **2** : to cause to feel burdened in spirit — **op·press·or** *n*

op·pres·sion *n* : cruel or unjust use of power or authority

op·pres·sive *adj* **1** : cruel or harsh without just cause **2** : very unpleasant or uncomfortable — **op·pres·sive·ly** *adv*

op·tic *adj* : of or relating to seeing or the eye

op·ti·cal *adj* **1** : relating to the science of optics **2** : relating to seeing : VISUAL **3** : involving the use of devices that are sensitive to light to get information for a computer

optical fiber *n* : a single fiber used in fiber optics

optical illusion *n* : something that looks different from what it actually is

op·ti·cian *n* : a person who prepares lenses for and sells eyeglasses

op·tics *n* : a science that deals with the nature and properties of light and the changes that it undergoes and produces

op·ti·mism *n* : a feeling or belief that good things will happen

op·ti·mist *n* : a person who habitually expects good things to happen

op·ti·mis·tic *adj* : expecting good things to happen : HOPEFUL — **op·ti·mis·ti·cal·ly** *adv*

op·ti·mum *adj* : most desirable or satisfactory

op·tion *n* **1** : the power or right to choose **2** : something that can be chosen **3** : a right to buy or sell something at a specified price during a specified period

op·tion·al *adj* : left to choice : not required

op·tom·e·trist *n* : a person who examines the eyes and prescribes glasses or exercise to improve the eyesight

op·u·lent *adj* : having or showing much wealth

or *conj* — used between words or phrases that are choices

OR *abbr* Oregon

¹-or *n suffix* : someone or something that does a specified thing

²-or *n suffix* : condition : activity

or·a·cle *n* **1** : a person (as a priestess in ancient Greece) through whom a god is believed to speak **2** : the place where a god speaks through a person **3** : an answer given by a person through whom a god speaks

oral *adj* **1** : ²SPOKEN 1 **2** : of, involving, or given by the mouth — **oral·ly** *adv*

or·ange *n* **1** : a color between red and yellow : the color of a carrot **2** : a sweet juicy citrus fruit with orange colored rind that grows on an evergreen tree with shining leaves and fragrant white flowers

orang·utan *n* : a large ape of Borneo and Sumatra that lives in trees, eats mostly fruit, leaves, and other plant matter, and has very long arms, long reddish brown hair, and a nearly hairless face

ora·tion *n* : an important speech given on a special occasion

or·a·tor *n* : a public speaker noted for skill and power in speaking

or·a·to·ry *n* **1** : the art of making speeches **2** : the style of language used in important speeches

orb *n* : something in the shape of a ball (as a planet or the eye)

¹or·bit *n* : the path taken by one body circling around another body

²orbit *vb* **or·bit·ed; or·bit·ing** **1** : to move in an orbit around : CIRCLE **2** : to send up so as to move in an orbit

or·ca *n* : KILLER WHALE

or·chard *n* : a place where fruit trees are grown

or·ches·tra *n* **1** : a group of musicians who perform instrumental music using mostly stringed instruments **2** : the front part of the main floor in a theater — **or·ches·tral** *adj*

or·chid *n* : a plant with usually showy flowers with three petals of which the middle petal is enlarged and differs from the others in shape and color

or·dain *vb* **or·dained; or·dain·ing 1** : [2]DECREE **2** : to make a person a Christian minister or priest by a special ceremony

or·deal *n* : a severe test or experience

[1]**or·der** *vb* **or·dered; or·der·ing 1** : to put into a particular grouping or sequence : ARRANGE **2** : to give a command to or for

[2]**order** *n* **1** : a certain rule or regulation : COMMAND **2** : the arrangement of objects or events in space or time **3** : the way something should be **4** : the state of things when law or authority is obeyed **5** : good working condition **6** : a statement of what a person wants to buy **7** : goods or items bought or sold **8** : a group of people united (as by living under the same religious rules or by loyalty to common needs or duties) **9 orders** *pl* : the office of a person in the Christian ministry **10** : a group of related living things (as plants or animals) that ranks above the family and below the class in scientific classification **11** : a written direction to pay a sum of money — **in order that** : so that — **in order to** : for the purpose of

[1]**or·der·ly** *adj* **1** : having a neat arrangement : TIDY **2** : obeying commands or rules : well-behaved

[2]**orderly** *n, pl* **order·lies 1** : a soldier who works for an officer especially to carry messages **2** : a person who does cleaning and general work in a hospital

or·di·nal *n* : ORDINAL NUMBER

ordinal number *n* : a number that is used to show the place (as first, fifth, 22nd) taken by an element in a series

or·di·nance *n* : a law or regulation especially of a city or town

or·di·nar·i·ly *adv* : in the usual course of events : USUALLY

[1]**or·di·nary** *adj* **1** : to be expected : NORMAL, USUAL **2** : neither good nor bad : AVERAGE **3** : not very good : MEDIOCRE

[2]**ordinary** *n* : the conditions or events that are usual or normal

ord·nance *n* **1** : military supplies (as guns, ammunition, trucks, and tanks) **2** : ARTILLERY 1

ore *n* : a mineral mined to obtain a substance (as gold) that it contains

Ore., Oreg. *abbr* Oregon

or·gan *n* **1** : a musical instrument played by means of one or more keyboards and having pipes sounded by compressed air **2** : a part of a person, plant, or animal that is special-ized to perform a particular function **3** : a way of getting something done

or·gan·ic *adj* **1** : relating to or obtained from living things **2** : relating to carbon compounds : containing carbon **3** : being, involving, or producing food grown or made without the use of artificial chemicals

or·gan·ism *n* : a living thing made up of one or more cells and able to carry on the activities of life (as using energy, growing, or reproducing)

or·gan·ist *n* : a person who plays an organ

or·ga·ni·za·tion *n* **1** : the act or process of arranging **2** : the state or way of being arranged **3** : a group of people united for a common purpose

or·ga·nize *vb* **or·ga·nized; or·ga·niz·ing 1** : to arrange by effort and planning **2** : to put in a certain order **3** : to make separate parts into one united whole — **or·ga·niz·er** *n*

ori·ent *vb* **ori·ent·ed; ori·ent·ing 1** : to set or arrange in a position especially so as to be lined up with certain points of the compass **2** : to make familiar with an existing situation or environment **3** : to direct toward the interests of a particular group — **ori·en·ta·tion** *n*

ori·en·tal *adj, often cap* **1** *sometimes offensive* : [1]ASIAN **2** : relating to or from the region that includes the countries of eastern Asia (as China, Japan, South Korea, and North Korea)

ori·ga·mi *n* : the art of folding paper into three-dimensional figures or designs without cutting the paper or using glue

or·i·gin *n* **1** : basic source or cause **2** : a person's ancestry **3** : the rise or beginning from a source

[1]**orig·i·nal** *adj* **1** : of or relating to the source or beginning : FIRST **2** : not copied from anything else : not translated : NEW **3** : able to think up new things : CREATIVE — **orig·i·nal·ly** *adv*

[2]**original** *n* : something that is produced by an artist or writer and from which a copy or translation can be made

orig·i·nal·i·ty *n* : the quality or state of being creative or new and different

orig·i·nate *vb* **orig·i·nat·ed; orig·i·nat·ing 1** : to bring into being : INVENT, INITIATE **2** : to come into being — **orig·i·na·tor** *n*

ori·ole *n* **1** : an American songbird related to the blackbird that has a bright orange and black male **2** : a yellow and black bird of Europe and Asia related to the crow

[1]**or·na·ment** *n* : something that adds beauty : DECORATION

[2]**or·na·ment** *vb* **or·na·ment·ed; or·na·ment·ing** : DECORATE 1

¹**or·na·men·tal** *adj* : serving to add beauty : DECORATIVE

²**ornamental** *n* : a plant grown for its beauty

or·na·men·ta·tion *n* **1** : the act or process of decorating : the state of being decorated **2** : something that adds beauty

or·nate *adj* : decorated in a fancy way — **or·nate·ly** *adv* — **or·nate·ness** *n*

or·nery *adj* **or·neri·er; or·neri·est** : becoming angry or annoyed easily

¹**or·phan** *n* : a child whose parents are dead

²**orphan** *vb* **or·phaned; or·phan·ing** : to leave without parents : cause to become an orphan

or·phan·age *n* : a place where children who have lost their parents live and are cared for

or·tho·don·tist *n* : a dentist who adjusts badly placed or crooked teeth especially through the use of braces

or·tho·dox *adj* **1** : approved as measuring up to some standard : CONVENTIONAL **2** : closely following the established beliefs of a religion

¹**-ory** *n suffix, pl* **-ories** : place of or for

²**-ory** *adj suffix* : of, relating to, or associated with

Osage *n, pl* **Osag·es** *or* **Osage 1** : a member of an American Indian people of Missouri **2** : the language of the Osage people

os·cil·late *vb* **os·cil·lat·ed; os·cil·lat·ing** : to swing or move back and forth between two points

os·mo·sis *n* : a passing of material and especially water through a membrane (as of a living cell) that will not allow all kinds of molecules to pass

os·prey *n, pl* **ospreys** : a large hawk that feeds chiefly on fish

os·ten·si·ble *adj* : seeming to be true : APPARENT — **os·ten·si·bly** *adv*

os·ten·ta·tious *adj* : attracting or fond of attracting attention by showing off wealth or cleverness

os·tra·cize *vb* **os·tra·cized; os·tra·ciz·ing** : to shut out of a group

os·trich *n* : a very large bird of Africa that often weighs as much as 300 pounds (140 kilograms) and runs very fast but cannot fly

¹**oth·er** *adj* **1** : being the one (as of two or more) left **2** : ¹SECOND 1 **3** : ¹EXTRA, ADDITIONAL **4** : different or separate from those already mentioned

²**other** *n* : a remaining or different one

³**other** *pron* : another thing

oth·er·wise *adv* **1** : in another way **2** : in different circumstances **3** : in other ways **4** : if not : or else

ot·ter *n* : a web-footed animal that lives mostly in the water, feeds on fish, and has dark brown fur

ouch *interj* — used especially to express sudden pain

ought *helping verb* **1** — used to show duty **2** — used to show what it would be wise to do **3** — used to show what is naturally expected **4** — used to show what is correct

oughtn't : ought not

ounce *n* **1** : a unit of weight equal to $\frac{1}{16}$ pound (about 28 grams) **2** : a unit of liquid capacity equal to $\frac{1}{16}$ pint (about 30 milliliters)

our *adj* : relating to or belonging to us : caused by, produced by, or participated in by us

ours *pron* : that which belongs to us

our·selves *pron* : our own selves

-ous *adj suffix* : full of : having : resembling

oust *vb* **oust·ed; oust·ing** : to force or drive out (as from office or from possession of something)

oust·er *n* : the act or an instance of forcing out or of being forced out

¹**out** *adv* **1** : in a direction away from the inside, center, or surface **2** : away from home, business, or the usual or proper place **3** : so as to be used up, completed, or discontinued **4** : so as to be missing or moved from the usual or proper place **5** : in or into the open **6** : ALOUD **7** : beyond control or possession **8** : so as to be or make unsuccessful in reaching base in baseball

²**out** *prep* **1** : outward through **2** : outward on or along — **out of 1** : from the inside to the outside of : not in **2** : beyond the limits or range of **3** : because of **4** : in a group of **5** : ¹WITHOUT 2 **6** : FROM 3

³**out** *adj* **1** : no longer in power or use **2** : no longer continuing or taking place **3** : not confined : not concealed or covered **4** : ¹ABSENT 1 **5** : located outside or at a distance **6** : being no longer at bat and not successful in reaching base **7** : no longer in fashion **8** : OUT-OF-BOUNDS

⁴**out** *n* : the act of causing a baseball player to be unsuccessful in reaching base

out- *prefix* : in a manner that goes beyond

out–and–out *adj* : THOROUGH 1, ABSOLUTE

out·board motor *n* : a small gasoline engine with an attached propeller that can be fastened to the back end of a small boat

out·break *n* : a sudden occurrence or increase of something

out·build·ing *n* : a building (as a shed or stable) separate from a main building

out·burst *n* **1** : a sudden expression of strong feeling **2** : a sudden increase of activity or growth

outcast *n* : a person who is not accepted by society

out·class *vb* **out·classed; out·class·ing** : to be or do much better than : SURPASS

out·come *n* : [2]RESULT 1

out·cry *n, pl* **out·cries** 1 : a loud and excited shout 2 : a strong protest

out·dat·ed *adj* : not modern or current

out·dis·tance *vb* **out·dis·tanced; out·dis·tanc·ing** : to go far ahead of (as in a race)

out·do *vb* **out·did; out·done; out·do·ing; out·does** : to do better than : SURPASS

out·door *adj* 1 : used, being, or done outside 2 : preferring to spend time in the open air

[1]**out·doors** *adv* : outside a building : in or into the open air

[2]**outdoors** *n* : the open air

out·er *adj* : located on the outside or farther out

out·er·most *adj* : farthest out

outer space *n* : the region beyond earth's atmosphere and especially beyond the solar system

out·field *n* : the part of a baseball field beyond the infield and between the foul lines

out·field·er *n* : a baseball player who plays in the outfield

[1]**out·fit** *n* 1 : a set of clothing worn together 2 : the equipment for a special use 3 : a group of persons working together or associated in the same activity

[2]**outfit** *vb* **out·fit·ted; out·fit·ting** : to supply with equipment for a special purpose : EQUIP — **out·fit·ter** *n*

out·go *n, pl* **outgoes** : EXPENDITURE 2

out·go·ing *adj* 1 : FRIENDLY 1 2 : leaving a place 3 : retiring from a place or position

out·grow *vb* **out·grew; out·grown; out·grow·ing** 1 : to grow too large or too old for 2 : to grow faster than

out·growth *n* : something that grows out of or develops from something else

out·ing *n* : a brief usually outdoor trip for pleasure

out·land·ish *adj* : very strange or unusual : BIZARRE

out·last *vb* **out·last·ed; out·last·ing** : to last longer than

[1]**out·law** *n* : a person who has broken the law and is hiding or fleeing to avoid punishment

[2]**outlaw** *vb* **out·lawed; out·law·ing** : to make illegal

out·lay *n* : an amount of money spent

out·let *n* 1 : a place or opening for letting something out 2 : a way of releasing or expressing a feeling or impulse 3 : a device (as in a wall) into which the prongs of an electrical plug are inserted for making connection with an electrical circuit

[1]**out·line** *n* 1 : a line that traces or forms the outer limits of an object or figure and shows its shape 2 : a drawing or picture or style of drawing in which only the outer edges of an object or figure are shown 3 : an often numbered or lettered list of the important parts of something (as an essay) 4 : a short treatment of a subject

[2]**outline** *vb* **out·lined; out·lin·ing** 1 : to draw or trace the outer edges of 2 : to list or describe the main features or parts of

out·live *vb* **out·lived; out·liv·ing** : to live or last longer than

out·look *n* 1 : a view from a certain place 2 : a way of thinking about or looking at things 3 : conditions that seem to lie ahead

out·ly·ing *adj* : being far from a central point : REMOTE

out·mod·ed *adj* : no longer in style or in use

out·num·ber *vb* **out·num·bered; out·num·ber·ing** : to be more than in number

out–of–bounds *adv or adj* : outside the limits of the playing area in a game or sport

out–of–date *adj* : not modern or current

out–of–doors *n* : [2]OUTDOORS

out of doors *adv* : [1]OUTDOORS

out·post *n* 1 : a guard placed at a distance from a military force or camp 2 : the place occupied by such a guard 3 : an outlying settlement

out·pour·ing *n* : an act of expressing or giving freely

[1]**out·put** *n* 1 : something produced 2 : the information produced by a computer

[2]**output** *vb* **out·put·ted** *or* **out·put; out·put·ting** : to produce something

[1]**out·rage** *n* 1 : angry feelings caused by a hurtful, unjust, or insulting act 2 : an act that is hurtful or unjust or shows disrespect for a person's feelings

[2]**outrage** *vb* **out·raged; out·rag·ing** 1 : to cause to feel anger or strong resentment 2 : to cause to suffer great insult

out·ra·geous *adj* 1 : extremely annoying, insulting, or shameful 2 : very strange or unusual

[1]**out·right** *adv* 1 : COMPLETELY 2 : without holding back 3 : quickly and entirely

[2]**outright** *adj* 1 : complete and total : very clear or obvious 2 : done, made, or given with no restrictions or exceptions

out·run *vb* **out·ran; out·run; out·run·ning** : to run or move faster than

out·sell *vb* **out·sold; out·sell·ing** : to sell or be sold more than

out·set *n* : BEGINNING 1, START

out·shine *vb* **out·shone; out·shin·ing** 1 : to shine brighter than 2 : to do better than : OUTDO

[1]**out·side** *n* 1 : an outer side or surface 2 : the greatest amount or limit : MOST

[2]**outside** *adj* 1 : of, relating to, or being on

the outside **2** : not belonging to a place or group **3** : barely possible

³outside *adv* : ¹OUTDOORS

⁴outside *prep* **1** : on or to the outside of **2** : beyond the limits of

out·sid·er *n* : a person who does not belong to a particular group

out·size *adj* : unusually large

out·skirts *n pl* : the area that lies away from the center of a city or town

out·smart *vb* **out·smart·ed; out·smart·ing** : to beat or trick by being more clever than

out·spo·ken *adj* : talking in a free and honest way : BLUNT — **out·spo·ken·ly** *adv* — **out·spo·ken·ness** *n*

out·spread *adj* : spread out completely

out·stand·ing *adj* **1** : standing out especially because of excellence **2** : UNPAID — **out·stand·ing·ly** *adv*

out·stay *vb* **out·stayed; out·stay·ing** : OVERSTAY

out·stretched *adj* : stretched out

out·strip *vb* **out·stripped; out·strip·ping 1** : to go faster or farther than **2** : to do better than

¹out·ward *adj* **1** : moving or turned toward the outside or away from a center **2** : showing on the outside

²outward *or* **out·wards** *adv* : away from a center

out·ward·ly *adv* : on the outside : in outward appearance

out·weigh *vb* **out·weighed; out·weigh·ing** : to be greater than in weight or importance

out·wit *vb* **out·wit·ted; out·wit·ting** : OUTSMART

ova *pl of* OVUM

¹oval *n* : something having the shape of an egg or ellipse

²oval *adj* : having the shape of an egg or ellipse : ELLIPTICAL

ova·ry *n, pl* **ova·ries 1** : one of the usually two organs in the body of female animals in which eggs are produced **2** : the larger rounded lower part of the pistil of a flower that contains the ovules in which the seeds are formed

ova·tion *n* : an expression of approval or enthusiasm made by clapping or cheering

ov·en *n* : a heated chamber (as in a stove) for baking, heating, or drying

¹over *adv* **1** : across a barrier or space **2** : in a direction down or forward and down **3** : across the brim **4** : so as to bring the underside up **5** : from one person or side to another **6** : to someone's home **7** : beyond a limit **8** : more than needed **9** : once more : AGAIN **10** : ¹OVERNIGHT 1 — **over and over** : many times

²over *prep* **1** : above in place : higher than **2**
: above in power or value **3** : in front of **4** : more than **5** : down upon **6** : all through or throughout **7** : on or along the surface of **8** : on or to the other side of : ACROSS **9** : down from the top or edge of **10** : having to do with

³over *adj* **1** : being more than needed or expected **2** : brought or come to an end

over- *prefix* : more than usual, normal, or proper

¹over·all *adv* : as a whole : in most ways

²overall *adj* : including everyone or everything

over·alls *n pl* : loose pants usually with shoulder straps and a piece in front to cover the chest

over·bear·ing *adj* : acting in a proud or bossy way toward other people

over·board *adv* **1** : over the side of a ship into the water **2** : to extremes of enthusiasm

over·bur·den *vb* **over·bur·dened; over·bur·den·ing** : to burden too heavily

over·cast *adj* : covered with or darkened by clouds

over·charge *vb* **over·charged; over·charg·ing** : to charge too much money

over·coat *n* : a heavy coat worn over indoor clothing

over·come *vb* **over·came; overcome; over·com·ing 1** : to win a victory over : CONQUER **2** : to gain control of through great effort **3** : to cause to lose physical ability or emotional control

over·crowd *vb* **over·crowd·ed; over·crowd·ing** : to cause to be too crowded

over·do *vb* **over·did; over·done; over·do·ing 1** : to do too much of **2** : to use too much of **3** : to cook too long

over·dose *n* : too large a dose (as of a drug)

over·dress *vb* **over·dressed; over·dress·ing** : to dress in clothes too fancy for an occasion

over·due *adj* **1** : not paid when due **2** : delayed beyond an expected time **3** : more than ready

over·eat *vb* **over·ate; over·eat·en; over·eat·ing** : to eat too much — **over·eat·er** *n*

over·es·ti·mate *vb* **over·es·ti·mat·ed; over·es·ti·mat·ing** : to estimate too highly

¹over·flow *vb* **over·flowed; over·flow·ing 1** : to flow over the top of **2** : to flow over bounds **3** : to fill or become filled beyond capacity **4** : to fill a space up and spread beyond its limits

²over·flow *n* **1** : a flowing over **2** : something that flows over or fills a space and spreads beyond its limits

over·grown *adj* **1** : grown too big **2** : covered with plants that have grown in an uncontrolled way

¹over·hand *adj* : made with the hand brought forward and down from above the shoulder

²overhand *adv* : with an overhand movement

¹over·hang *vb* **over·hung; over·hang·ing** : to stick out or hang over

²overhang *n* : a part that overhangs

¹over·haul *vb* **over·hauled; over·haul·ing 1** : to examine thoroughly and make necessary repairs or improvements on **2** : to catch up with : OVERTAKE

²over·haul *n* : an instance of overhauling

¹over·head *adv* : above someone's head : in the sky or space above someone

²over·head *adj* : placed in the space above someone

³over·head *n* : the general expenses (as for rent or heat) of a business

over·hear *vb* **over·heard; over·hear·ing** : to hear something by accident without the speaker's knowledge

over·heat *vb* **over·heat·ed; over·heat·ing** : to heat too much : become too hot

over·joyed *adj* : filled with great joy

¹over·land *adv* : by land rather than by water

²overland *adj* : going by land rather than by water

over·lap *vb* **over·lapped; over·lap·ping** : to place or be placed so that a part of one covers a part of another

¹over·lay *vb* **over·laid; over·lay·ing** : to lay or spread over or across

²over·lay *n* : a usually thin covering that is laid over or across something

over·load *vb* **over·load·ed; over·load·ing** : to put too great a load on or in

over·look *vb* **over·looked; over·look·ing 1** : to look down upon or provide a view of from above **2** : to fail to see : MISS **3** : to pay no attention to : IGNORE

over·ly *adv* : by too much : to an excessive degree

¹over·night *adv* **1** : during or through the night **2** : very quickly or suddenly

²overnight *adj* **1** : done or lasting through the night **2** : staying for the night **3** : for use on short trips **4** : happening very quickly or suddenly

over·pass *n* **1** : a crossing (as of two highways or a highway and a railroad) at different levels usually by means of a bridge **2** : the upper level of an overpass

over·pop·u·la·tion *n* : the condition of having too many people living in a certain area

over·pow·er *vb* **over·pow·ered; over·pow·er·ing 1** : to overcome by greater force : DEFEAT **2** : to affect by being too strong

over·rate *vb* **over·rat·ed; over·rat·ing** : to value or praise too highly

over·re·act *vb* **over·re·act·ed; over·re·act·ing** : to respond with an emotion that is too

strong or an action that is extreme or unnecessary

over·ride *vb* **over·rode; over·rid·den; over·rid·ing** : to push aside as less important

over·ripe *adj* : passed beyond ripeness toward decay

over·rule *vb* **over·ruled; over·rul·ing 1** : to decide against **2** : to set aside a decision or ruling made by someone having less authority

over·run *vb* **over·ran; overrun; over·run·ning 1** : to take over and occupy by force **2** : to run or go past **3** : to spread over so as to cover

¹over·seas *adv* : to or in a foreign country that is across the sea

²overseas *adj* : involving, occurring in, or intended for lands across the sea

over·see *vb* **over·saw; over·seen; over·see·ing** : to be in charge of : SUPERVISE

over·seer *n* : a person who supervises something

over·shad·ow *vb* **over·shad·owed; over·shad·ow·ing 1** : to cast a shadow over : DARKEN **2** : to be or become more important than

over·shoe *n* : a shoe (as of rubber) worn over another for protection

over·shoot *vb* **over·shot; over·shoot·ing** : to miss by going beyond

over·sight *n* **1** : the act or duty of overseeing : watchful care **2** : an error or something forgotten through carelessness or haste

over·sim·pli·fy *vb* **over·sim·pli·fied; over·sim·pli·fy·ing** : to cause (something) to seem simpler than it is

over·size *or* **over·sized** *adj* : larger than the usual or normal size

over·sleep *vb* **over·slept; over·sleep·ing** : to sleep beyond the usual time or beyond the time set for getting up

over·state *vb* **over·stat·ed; over·stat·ing** : to put in too strong terms : EXAGGERATE

over·stay *vb* **over·stayed; over·stay·ing** : to stay beyond or longer than

over·step *vb* **over·stepped; over·step·ping** : to step over or beyond : EXCEED

over·sup·ply *n, pl* **over·sup·plies** : a supply that is too large

overt *adj* : not secret or hidden

over·take *vb* **over·took; over·tak·en; over·tak·ing 1** : to catch up with and often pass **2** : to come upon or happen to suddenly or without warning

¹over·throw *vb* **over·threw; over·thrown; over·throw·ing 1** : OVERTURN 1 **2** : to cause the fall or end of : DESTROY

²over·throw *n* : an act of causing the fall or end of : the state of being overthrown : DEFEAT

over·time *n* **1** : time spent working that is more than one usually works in a day or a week **2** : extra time added to a game when the score is tied at the end of the normal playing time

over·ture *n* **1** : something first offered or suggested with the hope of reaching an agreement **2** : a piece of music played at the beginning of an opera or musical play

over·turn *vb* **over·turned; over·turn·ing 1** : to turn over or upside down **2** : to reverse or cancel something previously decided or ordered

over·view *n* : a short explanation or description : SUMMARY

over·weight *adj* : weighing more than is normal, necessary, or allowed

over·whelm *vb* **over·whelmed; over·whelming 1** : to overcome completely (as with great force or emotion) **2** : to cover over completely : SUBMERGE

over·whelm·ing *adj* **1** : very great or strong **2** : very difficult or confusing

¹**over·work** *vb* **over·worked; over·work·ing 1** : to work or cause to work too much or too hard **2** : to use too much or too often

²**overwork** *n* : too much work

over·wrought *adj* : very excited or upset

ovule *n* : a tiny structure in the ovary of a flower and on the scale of a cone that contains an egg cell and can develop into a seed following fertilization

ovum *n, pl* **ova** : EGG CELL

owe *vb* **owed; ow·ing 1** : to be obligated to pay, give, or return **2** : to be in debt to **3** : to have as a result

owing to *prep* : because of

owl *n* : a large bird with big head and eyes, hooked bill, and strong claws that is active at night and feeds on small animals — **owl·ish** *adj*

owl·et *n* : a young or small owl

¹**own** *adj* — used to show the fact that something belongs to or relates to a particular person or thing and no other

²**own** *vb* **owned; own·ing 1** : to have or hold as property **2** : to admit that something is true

own·er *n* : a person who owns something

own·er·ship *n* : the state or fact of owning something

ox *n, pl* **ox·en** *also* **ox 1** : one of our common domestic cattle or a closely related animal (as a yak) **2** : an adult castrated male ox used especially for hauling loads

ox·bow *n* : a bend in a river in the shape of a U

ox·cart *n* : a cart pulled by oxen

ox·i·da·tion *n* : the process of oxidizing

ox·ide *n* : a compound of oxygen with another element or group of elements

ox·i·dize *vb* **ox·i·dized; ox·i·diz·ing** : to combine or become combined with oxygen

ox·y·gen *n* : a chemical element found in the air as a colorless odorless tasteless gas that is necessary for life

oys·ter *n* : a shellfish that lives on stony bottoms (**oyster beds**) in shallow seawater, has a rough grayish shell made up of two hinged parts, and is often used for food

oz. *abbr* **1** ounce **2** ounces

ozone *n* : a faintly blue form of oxygen that is present in the air in small quantities

ozone layer *n* : a layer of the earth's upper atmosphere that is characterized by high ozone content which blocks most of the sun's ultraviolet radiation from entering the lower atmosphere

P

p *n, pl* **p's** *or* **ps** *often cap* : the sixteenth letter of the English alphabet

p. *abbr* page

pa *n* : ¹FATHER 1

Pa., PA *abbr* Pennsylvania

¹**pace** *n* **1** : the speed of moving forward or ahead **2** : the speed at which something is done or happens **3** : a horse's gait in which the legs on the same side move at the same time **4** : a single step or its length

²**pace** *vb* **paced; pac·ing 1** : to walk back and forth across **2** : to walk with slow steps **3** : to measure by steps **4** : to set or regulate the speed at which something is done or happens

pa·cif·ic *adj* **1** *cap* : relating to the Pacific Ocean **2** : ³CALM 1, PEACEFUL **3** : making peace : PEACEABLE

pac·i·fy *vb* **pac·i·fied; pac·i·fy·ing** : to make peaceful or quiet : CALM, SOOTHE

¹**pack** *n* **1** : a bundle arranged for carrying especially on the back of a person or animal **2** : a group of like persons or things

²**pack** *vb* **packed; pack·ing 1** : to put into a container or bundle **2** : to put things into **3** : to crowd into so as to fill full : CRAM **4** : to send away — **pack·er** *n*

pack·age *n* **1** : a bundle made up for mailing or transporting **2** : a container that covers or holds something **3** : something that comes in a container

pack·et *n* : a small package

pact *n* : AGREEMENT 2, TREATY

¹pad *n* **1** : a tablet of writing or drawing paper **2** : something soft used for protection or comfort : CUSHION **3** : one of the cushioned parts of the underside of the feet of some animals (as a dog) **4** : a floating leaf of a water plant (as a water lily) **5** : a piece of material that holds ink used in inking rubber stamps

²pad *vb* **pad·ded; pad·ding** : to move with quiet steps

³pad *vb* **pad·ded; pad·ding 1** : to stuff or cover with soft material **2** : to make longer by adding words

pad·ding *n* : soft material used to cover or line a surface

¹pad·dle *vb* **pad·dled; pad·dling 1** : to move or drive forward with an instrument like an oar or with short quick movements of hands and feet **2** : to stir, mix, or beat with a paddle

²paddle *n* **1** : an instrument like an oar used in moving and steering a small boat (as a canoe) **2** : an implement having a broad flat end and used for beating, mixing, or hitting **3** : one of the broad boards at the outer edge of a waterwheel or a paddle wheel

³paddle *vb* **paddled; paddling** : to move or splash about in the water

paddle wheel *n* : a wheel with broad boards near its outer edge used to make a boat move

pad·dock *n* **1** : an enclosed area where animals are put to eat grass or to exercise **2** : an enclosed area where racehorses are saddled and paraded

pad·dy *n, pl* **paddies** : wet land in which rice is grown

¹pad·lock *n* : a removable lock with a curved piece that snaps into a catch

²padlock *vb* **pad·locked; pad·lock·ing** : to fasten with a removable lock

¹pa·gan *n* : ²HEATHEN 1

²pagan *adj* : of or relating to heathens or their worship : HEATHEN

¹page *n* **1** : one side of a printed or written sheet of paper **2** : a large section of computer memory **3** : the information found at a single World Wide Web address

²page *n* **1** : a person employed (as by a hotel or the United States Congress) to carry messages or run errands **2** : a boy being trained to be a knight in the Middle Ages

³page *vb* **paged; pag·ing** : to send for or contact someone by a public announcement or by using a pager

pag·eant *n* **1** : a grand and fancy public ceremony and display **2** : an entertainment made up of scenes based on history or legend **3** : a contest in which a group of women or girls are judged

pag·er *n* : a small electronic device that beeps, vibrates, or flashes when it receives a signal

pa·go·da *n* : a tower of several stories built as a temple or memorial in eastern or southeastern Asia

paid *past and past participle of* PAY

pail *n* **1** : a usually round container with a handle : BUCKET **2** : PAILFUL

pail·ful *n, pl* **pail·fuls** : the amount a bucket holds

¹pain *n* **1** : physical suffering that accompanies a bodily disorder (as a disease or an injury) **2** : a very unpleasant feeling (as a prick or an ache) that is caused especially by something harmful **3** : suffering of the mind or emotions : GRIEF **4 pains** *pl* : great care or effort **5** : someone or something annoying — **pain·ful** *adj* — **pain·ful·ly** *adv* — **pain·less** *adj*

²pain *vb* **pained; pain·ing 1** : to cause physical or mental suffering in or to **2** : to give or feel physical or mental suffering

pains·tak·ing *adj* : taking or showing great care — **pains·tak·ing·ly** *adv*

¹paint *vb* **paint·ed; paint·ing 1** : to cover a surface with or as if with paint **2** : to make a picture or design by using paints **3** : to describe clearly — **paint·er** *n*

²paint *n* : a mixture of coloring matter with a liquid that forms a dry coating when spread on a surface

paint·brush *n* : a tool with bristles that is used to apply paint

paint·ing *n* **1** : a work of art made with paint **2** : the art or occupation of creating pictures with paint

¹pair *n, pl* **pairs** *or* **pair 1** : two things that match or are meant to be used together **2** : a thing having two similar parts that are connected **3** : two people who are connected in some way or do something together

²pair *vb* **paired; pair·ing 1** : to put in or join in a group of two **2** : to form a group of two : MATCH

Pai·ute *n* **1** : a member of an American Indian people originally of Utah, Arizona, Nevada, and California **2** : either of the two languages of the Paiute people

pa·ja·mas *n pl* : clothes usually consisting of pants and top that are worn for sleeping

pal *n* : a close friend

pal·ace *n* **1** : the home of a ruler **2** : a large or splendid house

pal·at·able *adj* : pleasant to the taste

pal·ate *n* **1** : the top area of the inside of the mouth made up of a bony front part (**hard palate**) and a soft flexible back part (**soft palate**) **2** : the sense of taste

¹pale *adj* **pal·er; pal·est 1** : having very light

skin **2** : having a lighter skin color than normal because of sickness or fear **3** : not bright or brilliant **4** : light in color or shade — **pale·ness** n

²**pale** vb **paled; pal·ing 1** : to lose color **2** : to make or become less adequate, impressive, or intense

Pa·leo·zo·ic n : an era of geological history ending about 280 million years ago which came before the Mesozoic and in which vertebrates and land plants first appeared

pal·ette n **1** : a thin board or tablet on which a painter puts and mixes colors **2** : the set of colors that an artist is using

pal·in·drome n : a word, phrase, sentence, or number that reads the same backward or forward

pal·i·sade n **1** : a fence made of poles to protect against attack **2** : a line of steep cliffs

¹**pall** vb **palled; pall·ing** : to become dull

²**pall** n **1** : a heavy cloth covering for a coffin, hearse, or tomb **2** : something that makes things gloomy or depressing

pall·bear·er n : a person who helps to carry the coffin at a funeral

pal·let n **1** : a mattress of straw **2** : a hard temporary bed

pal·lid adj : ¹PALE 1

pal·lor n : paleness of face

¹**palm** n : a tropical tree, shrub, or vine with a usually tall stem or trunk topped with large leaves that are shaped like feathers or fans

²**palm** n **1** : the under part of the hand between the fingers and the wrist **2** : a measure of length based on the width of a palm

³**palm** vb **palmed; palm·ing** : to hide in the hand — **palm off** : to get rid of or pass on in a dishonest way

pal·met·to n, pl **pal·met·tos** or **pal·met·toes** : a low-growing palm with leaves shaped like fans

pal·o·mi·no n, pl **pal·o·mi·nos** : a horse with a light golden coat and a cream or white mane and tail

pal·pi·tate vb **pal·pi·tat·ed; pal·pi·tat·ing** : ¹THROB 1

pal·sy n **1** : PARALYSIS **2** : an uncontrollable trembling of the body or a part of the body

pal·try adj **pal·tri·er; pal·tri·est** : of little amount, value, or importance

pam·pas n pl : wide treeless plains of South America

pam·per vb **pam·pered; pam·per·ing** : to treat (someone or something) with great care and attention

pam·phlet n : a short publication without a binding : BOOKLET

¹**pan** n **1** : a usually shallow open container used for cooking **2** : a shallow open tray or container

²**pan** vb **panned; pan·ning** : to wash earthy material so as to collect bits of metal (as gold) — **pan out** : to give a good result : SUCCEED

pan·cake n : a flat cake made of thin batter and cooked on both sides on a griddle

pan·cre·as n : a large gland near the stomach that produces insulin and a fluid (**pancreatic juice**) with enzymes that aid digestion

pan·cre·at·ic adj : of or relating to the pancreas

pan·da n **1** : RED PANDA **2** : a large black-and-white animal of central and western China that feeds mostly on the leaves and stems of the bamboo and is related to the bear

pan·de·mo·ni·um n : wild uproar

pane n : a sheet of glass (as in a window)

¹**pan·el** n **1** : a usually rectangular section of something (as a door or a wall) **2** : a piece of material (as plywood) made to form part of a surface (as of a wall) **3** : a board into which instruments or controls are set **4** : a group of people appointed for some service **5** : a group of people taking part in a discussion or answering questions for an audience

²**panel** vb **pan·eled** or **pan·elled; pan·el·ing** or **pan·el·ling** : to cover or decorate with sections of material (as wood)

pan·el·ing n : sections of material (as wood) joined in a continuous surface and used to cover a wall or ceiling

pang n : a sudden sharp feeling of physical pain or emotion

¹**pan·ic** n : a sudden overpowering fear often without reasonable cause

²**panic** vb **pan·icked; pan·ick·ing** : to feel or cause to feel sudden overpowering fear

pan·icky adj : feeling or overcome with sudden fear

pan·o·rama n : a clear complete view in every direction

pan·sy n, pl **pansies** : a garden plant related to the violets that has large velvety colorful flowers

¹**pant** vb **pant·ed; pant·ing** : to breathe hard or quickly

²**pant** n : a hard or quick breath

pan·ta·loons n pl : PANTS

pan·ther n **1** : LEOPARD **2** : COUGAR **3** : JAGUAR

pant·ie or **panty** n, pl **pant·ies** : a woman's or child's undergarment with short legs or no legs

¹**pan·to·mime** n **1** : the act of showing or explaining something through movements of the body and face instead of by talking **2** : a show in which a story is told by using ex-

pressions on the face and movements of the body instead of words

²pantomime *vb* **pan·to·mimed; pan·to·mim·ing :** to tell through movements rather than words

pan·try *n, pl* **pan·tries :** a small room where mainly food is kept

pants *n pl* **:** a piece of clothing usually reaching from the waist to the ankle and covering each leg separately

pa·pa *n* **:** ¹FATHER 1

papaw *variant of* PAWPAW

pa·pa·ya *n* **:** a yellow fruit that has a sweet flesh and many black seeds and grows on a tropical American tree

¹pa·per *n* **1 :** a material made from fibers (as of wood or cloth) and in the form of thin sheets or a sheet or piece of such material **2 :** a piece of paper having something written or printed on it **:** DOCUMENT **3 :** NEWSPAPER **4 :** a piece of written schoolwork **5 :** WALLPAPER

²paper *adj* **:** made of paper

³paper *vb* **pa·pered; pa·per·ing :** to cover with wallpaper

pa·per·back *n* **:** a book with a flexible paper binding

paper clip *n* **:** a piece of bent wire used to hold sheets of paper together

pa·per·work *n* **:** the documents that are a requirement for or a routine part of something

pa·pery *adj* **:** very thin or dry

pa·pier–mâ·ché *n* **:** material made of paper mixed with glue and other substances that hardens as it dries

pa·pri·ka *n* **:** a mild red spice made from dried peppers

pa·py·rus *n, pl* **pa·py·rus·es** *or* **pa·py·ri 1 :** a tall African plant related to the grasses that grows especially in Egypt **2 :** a material like paper used by ancient people to write on

par *n* **1 :** an equal level **2 :** the score set for each hole of a golf course **3 :** a usual or average level

par·a·ble *n* **:** a simple story that teaches a moral lesson

¹para·chute *n* **:** a piece of equipment usually made of cloth and attached to someone or something for making a safe jump or drop from an airplane

²parachute *vb* **para·chut·ed; para·chut·ing :** to transport or come down by parachute

¹pa·rade *n* **1 :** a public celebration that includes people moving in order down a street by walking or riding in vehicles or on floats **2 :** the formation of troops before an officer for inspection **3 :** great show or display

²parade *vb* **pa·rad·ed; pa·rad·ing 1 :** to march in an orderly group **2 :** to show off

par·a·dise *n* **1 :** a place, state, or time of great beauty or happiness **2 :** HEAVEN 2 **3 :** the place where Adam and Eve first lived according to the Bible

par·a·dox *n* **1 :** a statement that seems to say opposite things and yet is perhaps true **2 :** a person or thing having qualities that seem to be opposite

par·af·fin *n* **:** a white waxy substance obtained from wood, coal, or petroleum and used in coating and sealing and in candles

para·graph *n* **:** a part of a piece of writing that is made up of one or more sentences and has to do with one topic or gives the words of one speaker

par·a·keet *n* **:** a small parrot that has a long tail and is sometimes kept as a caged bird

¹par·al·lel *adj* **:** lying or moving in the same direction but always the same distance apart

²parallel *n* **1 :** a line or surface that lies at or moves in the same direction as another but is always the same distance from it **2 :** one of the imaginary circles on the earth's surface running in the same direction as the equator and marking latitude **3 :** a way in which things are similar **4 :** EQUAL

³parallel *vb* **par·al·leled; par·al·lel·ing 1 :** to move, run, or extend in the same direction with but always at the same distance from **2 :** to be similar or equal to

par·al·lel·o·gram *n* **:** a plane figure with four sides whose opposite sides are parallel and equal

pa·ral·y·sis *n, pl* **pa·ral·y·ses :** loss of the ability to move all or part of the body (as from disease or injury)

par·a·lyze *vb* **par·a·lyzed; par·a·lyz·ing 1 :** to cause to be unable to move all or part of the body **2 :** to destroy or decrease something's energy or ability to act

par·a·me·cium *n, pl* **par·a·me·cia** *also* **par·a·me·ciums :** a tiny living thing found in water that is a single cell shaped like a slipper and moves by means of cilia

para·med·ic *n* **:** a person specially trained to care for a patient before or during the trip to a hospital

par·a·mount *adj* **:** highest in importance or greatness

para·noid *adj* **:** having unreasonable feelings of suspicion, distrust, and persecution

par·a·pet *n* **1 :** a low wall or fence at the edge of a platform, roof, or bridge **2 :** a wall of earth or stone to protect soldiers

¹para·phrase *vb* **para·phrased; para·phras·ing :** to give the meaning of in different words

²paraphrase *n* **:** a way of stating something again by giving the meaning in different words

para·pro·fes·sion·al *n* : a person trained to assist a professional person (as a teacher)

par·a·site *n* **1** : a living thing (as a flea, worm, or fungus) that lives in or on another living thing and gets food and sometimes shelter from it and usually causes harm to it **2** : a person who lives at the expense of another

par·a·sit·ic *adj* : relating to or having the habit of a parasite : caused by parasites

par·a·sol *n* : a light umbrella used as a protection against the sun

para·troop·er *n* : a soldier trained and equipped to parachute from an airplane

¹par·cel *n* **1** : PACKAGE 1 **2** : a plot of land

²parcel *vb* **par·celed** *or* **par·celled; par·cel·ing** *or* **par·cel·ling** : to divide and give out by parts

parcel post *n* : a mail service that handles packages

parch *vb* **parched; parch·ing** : to dry or make dry from heat and lack of moisture

parch·ment *n* **1** : the skin of a sheep or goat prepared so that it can be written on **2** : strong tough paper used in baking and in wrapping food

¹par·don *n* **1** : forgiveness for wrong or rude behavior **2** : the act of freeing from legal punishment

²pardon *vb* **par·doned; par·don·ing 1** : to free from penalty for a fault or crime **2** : to allow (a wrong act) to pass without punishment : FORGIVE

pare *vb* **pared; par·ing 1** : to cut or shave off the outside or the ends of **2** : to reduce as if by cutting

par·ent *n* **1** : a father or mother of a child **2** : an animal or plant that produces offspring

par·ent·age *n* : a line of ancestors

pa·ren·tal *adj* : of or as expected from a mother and father

pa·ren·the·sis *n, pl* **pa·ren·the·ses** : one of a pair of marks ( ) used to enclose a word or group of words or to group mathematical terms to be dealt with as a unit — **par·en·thet·i·cal** *adj*

par·ish *n* **1** : a section of a church district under the care of a priest or minister **2** : the people who attend a particular church **3** : a division in the state of Louisiana that is similar to a county in other states

parish house *n* : a building for the educational and social activities of a church

pa·rish·io·ner *n* : a member of a particular church

¹park *n* **1** : an area of land set aside for recreation or for its beauty **2** : an enclosed field for ball games

²park *vb* **parked; park·ing** : to stop a vehicle and leave it for a while

par·ka *n* : a warm windproof jacket with a hood

park·way *n* : a broad landscaped highway

¹par·ley *n, pl* **parleys** : a discussion with an enemy

²parley *vb* **par·leyed; par·ley·ing** : to hold a discussion of terms with an enemy

par·lia·ment *n* : an assembly that is the highest legislative body of a country (as the United Kingdom)

par·lor *n* **1** : a room for receiving guests and for conversation **2** : a usually small place of business

pa·ro·chi·al school *n* : a private school that is run by a religious body

pa·role *n* : an early release of a prisoner

par·rot *n* : a brightly colored tropical bird that has a strong hooked bill and is sometimes trained to imitate human speech

¹par·ry *vb* **par·ried; par·ry·ing 1** : to turn aside an opponent's weapon or blow **2** : to avoid by a skillful answer

²parry *n, pl* **par·ries** : an act or instance of skillfully avoiding something

pars·ley *n, pl* **pars·leys** : a garden plant that has small leaves used to season or decorate various foods

pars·nip *n* : the long white root of a garden plant that is cooked as a vegetable

par·son *n* : ¹MINISTER 1

par·son·age *n* : a house provided by a church for its pastor to live in

¹part *n* **1** : one of the sections into which something is divided **2** : some of something **3** : a general area **4** : a piece of a machine **5** : one of the sides or aspects **6** : the role of a character in a play **7** : a line along which the hair is divided **8** : a person's share or duty **9** : the music for a voice or instrument **10** : a voice or instrument **11** : a piece of a plant or animal body — **for the most part** : with few exceptions : on the whole

²part *vb* **part·ed; part·ing 1** : to leave each other **2** : to separate the hair by combing on each side of a line **3** : to give up possession of **4** : to hold apart **5** : to come apart **6** : to divide into parts

part. *abbr* participle

par·take *vb* **par·took; par·tak·en; par·tak·ing** : to take a share or part

par·tial *adj* **1** : not complete **2** : favoring one side of a question over another **3** : fond or too fond of someone or something — **par·tial·ly** *adv*

par·ti·al·i·ty *n* : the quality or state of favoring one side over another

par·tic·i·pant *n* : a person who takes part in something

par·tic·i·pate *vb* **par·tic·i·pat·ed; par·tic·i·pat·ing** : to join with others in doing something

par·tic·i·pa·tion *n* : the act of joining with others in doing something

par·ti·ci·ple *n* : a form of a verb that is used to indicate a past or ongoing action and that can be used like an adjective

par·ti·cle *n* : a very small bit or amount of something

¹**par·tic·u·lar** *adj* **1** : relating to one person or thing **2** : not usual : SPECIAL **3** : having strong opinions about what is acceptable **4** : being one of several **5** : concerned about details — **par·tic·u·lar·ly** *adv* — **in particular 1** : that can be specifically named **2** : more specially than others : ESPECIALLY

²**particular** *n* : a single fact or detail

part·ing *n* : an act of leaving someone

par·ti·san *n* : a person who strongly supports something or someone — **par·ti·san·ship** *n*

¹**par·ti·tion** *n* : a wall or screen that separates one area from another

²**partition** *vb* **par·ti·tioned; par·ti·tion·ing** : to divide into separate shares, parts, or areas

part·ly *adv* : somewhat but not completely

part·ner *n* **1** : a person who does or shares something with another **2** : either one of a married couple **3** : Someone who plays with another person on the same side in a game **4** : one of two or more people who run a business together

part·ner·ship *n* : an arrangement in which people engage in an activity or business with one another or share something with each other

part of speech *n, pl* **parts of speech** : a class of words (as adjectives, adverbs, conjunctions, interjections, nouns, prepositions, pronouns, or verbs) identified according to the kinds of ideas they express and the work they do in a sentence

partook *past of* PARTAKE

par·tridge *n, pl* **partridge** *or* **par·tridg·es** : a plump grayish brown bird that lives mostly on the ground and is sometimes hunted for food or sport

part–time *adj* : involving fewer than the usual hours

par·ty *n, pl* **par·ties 1** : a social gathering or the entertainment provided for it **2** : a person or group concerned in some action **3** : a group of people who take one side of a question or share a set of beliefs

¹**pass** *vb* **passed; pass·ing 1** : ¹MOVE 1, PROCEED **2** : to go away **3** : to go by or move past **4** : to go or allow to go across, over, or through **5** : to transfer or throw to another person **6** : to go successfully through an examination or inspection **7** : to cause or permit to elapse **8** : HAPPEN 1 **9** : to move from one place or condition to another **10** : to be or cause to be approved **11** : to be or cause to be identified or recognized **12** : ¹DIE 1 — **pass·er** *n* — **pass away** : ¹DIE 1 — **pass out** : to become unconscious : FAINT — **pass up** : to let go by : REFUSE

²**pass** *n* **1** : an opening or way for going along or through **2** : a gap in a mountain range

³**pass** *n* **1** : the act or an instance of moving **2** : the act or an instance of throwing or transferring (as a ball) to another person **3** : a written permit to go or come **4** : SITUATION 1

pass·able *adj* **1** : fit to be traveled on **2** : barely good enough — **pass·ably** *adv*

pas·sage *n* **1** : a space or path by which something or someone can go through **2** : a brief part of a speech or written work **3** : the act or process of going from one place or condition to another **4** : the act of approving a law **5** : a right or permission to go as a passenger

pas·sage·way *n* : a space, road, or way by which a person or thing may move

pas·sen·ger *n* : someone riding on or in a vehicle

passenger pigeon *n* : a North American wild pigeon once common but now extinct

pass·er·by *n, pl* **pass·ers·by** : someone who goes by

¹**pass·ing** *adj* **1** : going by or past **2** : lasting only for a short time **3** : showing haste or lack of attention **4** : used for going past **5** : showing satisfactory work in a test or course of study

²**passing** *n* **1** : the act of going by or going away **2** : DEATH 1

pas·sion *n* **1** : a strong feeling or emotion **2** : an object of someone's love, liking, or desire **3** : strong liking or desire : LOVE

pas·sion·ate *adj* **1** : showing or affected by strong feeling **2** : easily caused to feel strong emotions — **pas·sion·ate·ly** *adv*

pas·sive *adj* **1** : not taking an active part **2** : showing that the person or thing represented by the subject is acted on by the verb **3** : offering no resistance — **pas·sive·ly** *adv*

Pass·over *n* : a Jewish holiday celebrated in March or April in honor of the freeing of the Hebrews from slavery in Egypt

pass·port *n* : a government document needed to enter or leave a country

pass·word *n* : a secret word, phrase, or group of numbers that a person must know to be allowed to enter a place or use a computer system

¹**past** *adj* **1** : of or relating to a time that has gone by **2** : relating to a verb tense that expresses a time gone by **3** : no longer serving

²past *prep* **1** : ²BEYOND 1 **2** : going close to and then beyond

³past *n* **1** : a former time **2** : life or history of a time gone by

⁴past *adv* : so as to pass by or beyond

pas·ta *n* **1** : a dough of flour, eggs, and water made in different shapes and dried or used fresh **2** : a dish of cooked pasta

¹paste *n* **1** : a mixture of flour or starch and water used for sticking things together **2** : a soft smooth thick mixture

²paste *vb* **past·ed; past·ing** : to stick on or together with an adhesive mixture

paste·board *n* : CARDBOARD

¹pas·tel *n* **1** : a soft pale color **2** : a crayon made by mixing ground coloring matter with a watery solution of a gum **3** : a drawing made with pastels

²pastel *adj* **1** : made with pastels **2** : light and pale in color

pas·teur·i·za·tion *n* : the process of heating a liquid to a temperature to kill germs and then rapidly cooling it

pas·teur·ize *vb* **pas·teur·ized; pas·teur·iz·ing** : to keep a liquid (as milk) for a time at a temperature high enough to kill many harmful germs and then cool it rapidly — **pas·teur·iz·er** *n*

pas·time *n* : something (as a hobby) that helps to make time pass pleasantly

pas·tor *n* : a minister or priest in charge of a church

pas·to·ral *adj* **1** : of or relating to peaceful scenes of the countryside **2** : of or relating to the pastor of a church

past participle *n* : a word that expresses completed action and is one of the principal parts of a verb

past·ry *n, pl* **past·ries 1** : sweet baked goods (as pies) made mainly of flour and fat **2** : a piece of sweet baked goods

past tense *n* : a verb tense used to express an action or state having already taken place or existed

pas·ture *n* **1** : plants (as grass) for feeding grazing animals **2** : land on which animals graze

¹pat *vb* **pat·ted; pat·ting** : to tap or stroke gently with the open hand

²pat *n* **1** : a light tap with the open hand or a flat instrument **2** : the sound of a pat or tap **3** : a small flat piece (as of butter)

³pat *adj* **pat·ter; pat·test 1** : learned perfectly **2** : exactly suitable **3** : not changing

pat. *abbr* patent

¹patch *n* **1** : a piece of cloth used to mend or cover a torn or worn place **2** : a small piece or area different from what is around it

²patch *vb* **patched; patch·ing** : to mend or

cover with a piece of cloth — **patch up** : to resolve by agreement

patch·work *n* **1** : pieces of cloth of different colors and shapes sewed together **2** : something made up of different parts

pa·tel·la *n, pl* **pa·tel·lae** *or* **pa·tel·las** : KNEECAP

¹pat·ent *adj* **1** : OBVIOUS, EVIDENT **2** : relating to or concerned with patents

²pat·ent *n* : a document that gives the inventor of something the right to be the only one to make or sell the invention for a certain number of years

³pat·ent *vb* **pat·ent·ed; pat·ent·ing** : to obtain the legal right to be the only one to make or sell an invention

pa·ter·nal *adj* **1** : of or like that of a father : FATHERLY **2** : related through the father — **pa·ter·nal·ly** *adv*

path *n, pl* **paths 1** : a track made by traveling on foot **2** : the way or track in which something moves or in which something will be encountered **3** : a way of life or thought

pa·thet·ic *adj* : causing feelings of pity, tenderness, or sorrow — **pa·thet·i·cal·ly** *adv*

path·way *n* : PATH 1

pa·tience *n* : the ability to remain calm when dealing with a difficult or annoying situation, task, or person

¹pa·tient *adj* : able to or showing the ability to remain calm when dealing with a difficult or annoying situation, task, or person — **pa·tient·ly** *adv*

²patient *n* : a person under medical care or treatment

pa·tio *n, pl* **pa·ti·os** : an open area next to a house that is usually paved

pa·tri·arch *n* **1** : a man who heads a family, group, or government **2** : a respected old man

pa·tri·ot *n* : a person who loves his or her country and strongly supports it

pa·tri·ot·ic *adj* : having or showing love that a person feels for his or her country

pa·tri·ot·ism *n* : love that a person feels for his or her country

¹pa·trol *n* **1** : the action of going around an area to make sure that it is safe **2** : a person or group going around an area to make sure that it is safe **3** : a part of a Boy Scout or Girl Scout troop

²patrol *vb* **pa·trolled; pa·trol·ling** : to go around an area for the purpose of watching or protecting

pa·trol·man *n, pl* **pa·trol·men** : a police officer who has a regular beat

pa·tron *n* **1** : a person who gives generous support or approval **2** : CUSTOMER

pa·tron·age *n* **1** : the help or business given

by a supporter **2** : a group of customers (as of a shop or theater) **3** : the control by officials of giving out jobs, contracts, and favors

pa·tron·ize *vb* **pa·tron·ized; pa·tron·iz·ing 1** : to act as a supporter of **2** : to be a customer of **3** : to treat (a person) as if he or she were not as good or less important

patron saint *n* : a saint to whom a church or society is dedicated

¹pat·ter *vb* **pat·tered; pat·ter·ing 1** : to strike again and again with light blows **2** : to run with quick light steps

²patter *n* : a series of quick light sounds

¹pat·tern *n* **1** : the form or figures used in decoration : DESIGN **2** : a model or guide for making something **3** : the regular and repeated way in which something is done **4** : something worth copying : MODEL — **pat·terned** *adj*

²pattern *vb* **pat·terned; pat·tern·ing 1** : to make or develop by following an example **2** : to have a design

pat·ty *n, pl* **pat·ties** : a small flat cake of chopped food

pau·per *n* : a very poor person

¹pause *n* **1** : a temporary stop **2** : a sign ◠ above a musical note or rest to show that the note or rest is to be held longer

²pause *vb* **paused; paus·ing** : to stop for a time : make a temporary stop

pave *vb* **paved; pav·ing** : to make a hard surface on (as with concrete or asphalt) —
pave the way : to make it easier for something to happen or for someone to do something

pave·ment *n* **1** : a hard surface of concrete or asphalt **2** : material used in making a hard surface

pa·vil·ion *n* **1** : a very large tent **2** : a building usually with open sides that is used as a place for entertainment or shelter in a park or garden

pav·ing *n* : PAVEMENT

¹paw *n* : the foot of a four-footed animal (as a lion, dog, or cat) that has claws

²paw *vb* **pawed; paw·ing 1** : to touch or hit with a paw **2** : to beat or scrape with a hoof **3** : to touch or handle in a clumsy or rude way

¹pawn *n* **1** : the piece of least value in the game of chess **2** : a person who has little power and is controlled by a more powerful person or group

²pawn *vb* **pawned; pawn·ing** : to leave as a guarantee of repayment for a loan

pawn·bro·ker *n* : a person who lends money in exchange for personal property that can be sold if the money is not repaid

paw·paw *also* **pa·paw** *n* **1** : PAPAYA **2** : the

greenish or yellow edible fruit of a North American tree with purple flowers

¹pay *vb* **paid; pay·ing 1** : to give (as money) in return for services received or for something bought **2** : to give money for (something owed) **3** : to get even with **4** : to give or offer freely **5** : to have a worthwhile result : be worth the effort or pains required — **pay·er** *n* — **pay off 1** : to give all of what is owed **2** : to have a good result — **pay up** : to pay in full especially debts that are due

²pay *n* **1** : the act of giving money for something bought or used or for what is owed : PAYMENT **2** : SALARY

pay·able *adj* : that may, can, or must be paid

pay·check *n* : a check given or received as wages or salary

pay·ment *n* **1** : the act of giving money for something bought or for a service used **2** : money given to pay a debt

pay·roll *n* **1** : a list of persons who receive pay **2** : the amount of money necessary to pay the employees of a business

PC *n, pl* **PCs** *or* **PC's** : PERSONAL COMPUTER

PE *abbr* Prince Edward Island

pea *n, pl* **peas 1** : a round green seed that is eaten as a vegetable and comes from the pods of a climbing garden plant **2** : a plant (as the sweet pea) resembling or related to the garden plant that produces peas

peace *n* **1** : freedom or a period of freedom from public disturbance or war **2** : a quiet and calm state of mind **3** : agreement and harmony among people **4** : an agreement to end a war

peace·able *adj* **1** : PEACEFUL 1 **2** : PEACEFUL 3

peace·ful *adj* **1** : not easily moved to argue or fight **2** : full of or enjoying quiet, calm, or freedom from disturbance **3** : not involving fighting — **peace·ful·ly** *adv* — **peace·ful·ness** *n*

peace·mak·er *n* : a person who settles an argument or stops a fight

peace pipe *n* : a decorated pipe of the American Indians used for certain ceremonies

peach *n* **1** : a fruit that is related to the plum and has a sweet juicy yellow or whitish pulp, hairy skin, and a large rough pit **2** : a pale yellowish pink color

pea·cock *n* : the male of a very large Asian pheasant that can lift up its very long colorful tail and spread it apart like a fan

peak *n* **1** : a prominent mountain **2** : the pointed top of a hill or mountain **3** : a sharp or pointed end **4** : the highest point of development

¹peaked *adj* : having a point or a prominent end

²peak·ed *adj* : looking pale and sick

¹peal *n* **1** : the sound of bells **2** : a loud sound : a series of loud sounds

²peal *vb* **pealed; peal·ing** : to make a loud sound and especially the sound of bells.

pea·nut *n* : a nutlike edible seed related to the pea that comes from the tough underground pods of a widely grown plant and that are eaten whole or crushed to form a spread (**peanut butter**) or produce oil for cooking (**peanut oil**)

pear *n* : a fruit with pale green or brownish skin and white sweet juicy flesh that is usually larger at the end opposite the stem

pearl *n* **1** : a smooth rounded shiny usually white body that is formed within the shell of some mollusks (as an oyster) usually around an irritating particle which has gotten into the shell **2** : MOTHER-OF-PEARL **3** : something like a pearl in shape, color, or value

pearly *adj* **pearl·i·er; pearl·i·est** : resembling a pearl in color, shape, or luster

peas·ant *n* : a farmer or farm worker of low social class

peat *n* : a blackish or dark brown material that is the remains of plants partly decayed in water and is dug and dried for use as fuel

peat moss *n* : a spongy brownish moss of wet areas that is often the chief plant making up peat

peb·ble *n* : a small rounded stone

pe·can *n* : an oval edible nut related to the walnut that usually has a thin shell and is the fruit of a tall tree of the central and southern United States

pec·ca·ry *n, pl* **pec·ca·ries** : a mostly tropical American animal that gathers in herds, is active at night, and looks like but is smaller than the related pig

¹peck *vb* **pecked; peck·ing 1** : to strike or pick up with the beak or a sharp instrument (as a pick) **2** : to make by striking with the beak or a sharp instrument

²peck *n* **1** : a unit of capacity equal to one quarter of a bushel **2** : a great deal : a large quantity

³peck *n* **1** : the act of striking with the bill or with a sharp instrument **2** : a mark made by striking with the bill or with a sharp instrument

pe·cu·liar *adj* **1** : of or limited to only one person, thing, or place **2** : different from the usual : ODD — **pe·cu·liar·ly** *adv*

pe·cu·li·ar·i·ty *n, pl* **pe·cu·li·ar·i·ties 1** : something odd or individual **2** : the quality or state of being odd or individual

¹ped·al *n* : a lever worked by the foot or feet

²pedal *vb* **ped·aled** *also* **ped·alled; ped·al·**ing *also* **ped·al·ling** : to use or work levers with a foot or feet

ped·dle *vb* **ped·dled; ped·dling** : to go about especially from house to house with goods for sale

ped·dler *also* **ped·lar** *n* : someone who goes about trying to sell things

ped·es·tal *n* **1** : a support or foot of an upright structure (as a column, statue, or lamp) **2** : a position of high regard

pe·des·tri·an *n* : a person who is walking

pe·di·a·tri·cian *n* : a doctor who specializes in the care of babies and children

ped·i·cure *n* : a treatment of the feet, toes, and toenails for beauty or comfort

ped·i·gree *n* **1** : a table or list showing the line of ancestors of a person or animal **2** : a line of ancestors

pe·dom·e·ter *n* : an instrument that measures the distance a person covers in walking

¹peek *vb* **peeked; peek·ing 1** : to look in a sneaky or cautious way **2** : to take a quick glance

²peek *n* : a quick or sly look

¹peel *vb* **peeled; peel·ing 1** : to strip off the skin or bark of **2** : to strip or tear off **3** : to come off smoothly or in bits — **peel·er** *n*

²peel *n* : an outer covering and especially the skin of a fruit

¹peep *vb* **peeped; peep·ing 1** : to look through or as if through a small hole or a crack : PEEK **2** : to look quickly **3** : to show slightly

²peep *n* **1** : a quick or sneaky look **2** : the first appearance

³peep *vb* **peeped; peeping** : to make a short high sound such as a young bird makes — **peep·er** *n*

⁴peep *n* : a short high sound

¹peer *vb* **peered; peer·ing 1** : to look curiously or carefully **2** : to come slightly into view : peep out

²peer *n* **1** : a person of the same rank or kind : EQUAL **2** : a member of one of the five ranks (duke, marquis, earl, viscount, and baron) of the British nobility

peer·less *adj* : having no equal

pee·vish *adj* : complaining a lot : IRRITABLE — **pee·vish·ly** *adv* — **pee·vish·ness** *n*

pee·wee *n* : someone or something that is small

¹peg *n* **1** : a small stick or rod (as of wood or metal) used especially to fasten things together or to hang things on **2** : a piece driven into the ground to mark a boundary or to hold something **3** : a level in approval or esteem

²peg *vb* **pegged; peg·ging 1** : to mark or fasten with a small stick or rod driven into a surface **2** : to work hard

PEI *abbr* Prince Edward Island

pel·i·can *n* : a large bird with webbed feet and a very large bill having a pouch on the lower part used to scoop in fish for food

pel·la·gra *n* : a disease caused by a diet containing too little protein and too little of a necessary vitamin

pel·let *n* **1** : a little ball (as of food or medicine) **2** : a piece of small shot **3** : a wad of undigested material (as bones and fur) that was thrown up by a bird of prey (as an owl)

pell–mell *adv* : in a confused or hurried way

¹**pelt** *n* : a skin of an animal especially with its fur or wool

²**pelt** *vb* **pelt·ed; pelt·ing 1** : to hit with repeated blows **2** : to repeatedly throw (something) at **3** : to beat or pound against something again and again

pel·vis *n* : the bowl-shaped part of the skeleton that includes the hip bones and the lower bones of the backbone

¹**pen** *n* : an instrument for writing with ink

²**pen** *vb* **penned; pen·ning** : to write especially with a pen

³**pen** *n* : a small enclosure especially for animals

⁴**pen** *vb* **penned; pen·ning** : to shut in a small enclosure

pe·nal *adj* : relating to or used for punishment

pe·nal·ize *vb* **pe·nal·ized; pe·nal·iz·ing** : to give a penalty to

pen·al·ty *n, pl* **pen·al·ties 1** : punishment for doing something wrong **2** : a disadvantage given for breaking a rule in a sport or game

pen·ance *n* : an act showing sorrow or regret for sin

pence *pl of* PENNY

¹**pen·cil** *n* : a device for writing or drawing consisting of a stick of black or colored material enclosed in wood, plastic, or metal

²**pencil** *vb* **pen·ciled** *or* **pen·cilled; pen·cil·ing** *or* **pen·cil·ling** : to write, mark, or draw with a pencil

pen·dant *n* : a piece of jewelry hanging on a chain or cord that is worn around the neck

¹**pend·ing** *prep* : while waiting for

²**pending** *adj* : not yet decided

pen·du·lum *n* : a weight hung from a point so as to swing freely back and forth under the action of gravity

pen·e·trate *vb* **pen·e·trat·ed; pen·e·trat·ing 1** : to pass into or through **2** : to see into or through

pen·e·tra·tion *n* **1** : the act or process of piercing **2** : keen understanding

pen·guin *n* : a short-legged seabird that cannot fly, uses its stiff wings for swimming, and is found in the colder regions of the southern hemisphere

pen·i·cil·lin *n* : an antibiotic that is produced by a mold and is used against disease-causing bacteria

pen·in·su·la *n* : a piece of land extending out into a body of water

pe·nis *n, pl* **pe·nis·es** *also* **pe·nes** : a male organ in mammals through which urine and sperm leave the body

pen·i·tence *n* : deep sadness that a person feels for his or her sins or faults

¹**pen·i·tent** *adj* : feeling or showing sadness for a person's own sins or faults

²**penitent** *n* : a person who feels or shows sorrow for sins or faults

pen·i·ten·tia·ry *n, pl* **pen·i·ten·tia·ries** : PRISON

pen·knife *n, pl* **pen·knives** : a small jackknife

pen·man·ship *n* : style or quality of handwriting

Penn., Penna. *abbr* Pennsylvania

pen name *n* : a false name that an author uses on his or her work

pen·nant *n* **1** : a narrow pointed flag used for identification, signaling, or decoration **2** : a flag that serves as the emblem of a championship

pen·ni·less *adj* : very poor : having no money

pen·ny *n, pl* **pennies 1** : CENT **2** *or pl* **pence** : a coin of the United Kingdom equal to ¹/₁₀₀ pound

pen pal *n* : a friend known only through letter writing

¹**pen·sion** *n* : a sum paid regularly to a person who has retired from work

²**pension** *vb* **pen·sioned; pen·sion·ing** : to grant or give a regularly paid sum to (a person who has retired from work)

pen·sive *adj* : lost in serious or sad thought
— **pen·sive·ly** *adv*

pent *adj* : kept inside : not released

penta- *or* **pent-** *prefix* : five

pen·ta·gon *n* : a flat geometric figure having five angles and five sides

pen·tath·lon *n* : an athletic contest in which each person participates in five different events

pent·house *n* : an apartment on the top floor or roof of a building

pe·on *n* : a person who does hard or dull work for very little money

pe·o·ny *n, pl* **pe·o·nies** : a plant that is widely grown for its large showy white, pink, or red flowers

¹**peo·ple** *n, pl* **people** *or* **peoples 1** : all persons considered together **2** : a group of human beings who have something in common — often used in compounds instead of *persons* **3** : a body of persons making up a race, tribe, or nation

²people *vb* **peo·pled; peo·pling 1** : to fill with human beings or a certain type of human beings **2** : to dwell on or in

¹pep *n* : brisk energy or liveliness

²pep *vb* **pepped; pep·ping** : to make more lively or energetic

¹pep·per *n* **1** : a black or white spice that has a sharp flavor and comes from the dried ground-up fruit of an Indian climbing shrub **2** : a usually green, red, or yellow vegetable that has a sharp or mildly sweet flavor and grows on a bushy garden plant

²pepper *vb* **pep·pered; pep·per·ing 1** : to season with or as if with pepper **2** : to hit with or as if with a shower of blows or objects

pep·per·mint *n* **1** : a mint plant with small usually purple flowers that yields an oil used especially to flavor candies **2** : a candy flavored with peppermint

pep·per·o·ni *n* : a spicy dry Italian sausage

pep·py *adj* **pep·pi·er; pep·pi·est** : full of brisk energy or liveliness

pep·sin *n* : an enzyme that starts the digestion of proteins in the stomach

per *prep* **1** : to or for each **2** : as directed by

per an·num *adv* : by the year : in or for each year : ANNUALLY

per cap·i·ta *adv or adj* : by or for each person

per·ceive *vb* **per·ceived; per·ceiv·ing 1** : to become aware of through the senses and especially through sight **2** : to recognize or realize **3** : to think of as

¹per·cent *adj or adv* : out of every hundred : measured by the number of units as compared with one hundred

²percent *n, pl* **percent** : a part or fraction of a whole expressed in hundredths

per·cent·age *n* **1** : a part of a whole expressed in hundredths **2** : a share of profits

per·cep·ti·ble *adj* : possible to detect

per·cep·tion *n* **1** : a judgment resulting from awareness or understanding **2** : the ability to understand (as meanings and ideas) **3** : understanding or awareness gained through the use of the senses

¹perch *n* **1** : a place where birds roost **2** : a raised seat or position

²perch *vb* **perched; perch·ing** : to sit or rest on a raised seat or position

³perch *n, pl* **perch** *or* **perch·es 1** : a common yellow and greenish brown fish of North America that is sometimes caught for food or sport **2** : any of various fish related to or resembling the North American perch

per·chance *adv* : PERHAPS

per·co·late *vb* **per·co·lat·ed; per·co·lat·ing 1** : to trickle or cause to trickle through something porous : OOZE **2** : to prepare (coffee) by passing hot water through ground coffee

beans again and again — **per·co·la·tion** *n* — **per·co·la·tor** *n*

per·cus·sion *n* : the musical instruments (as drums, cymbals, and maracas) that are played by striking or shaking

¹pe·ren·ni·al *adj* **1** : present all through the year **2** : living from year to year **3** : never ending : CONSTANT **4** : happening again and again

²perennial *n* : a plant that lives from year to year

¹per·fect *adj* **1** : having no mistake or flaw **2** : satisfying all requirements **3** : thoroughly skilled or trained : meeting the highest standards **4** : TOTAL 3 — **per·fect·ly** *adv*

²per·fect *vb* **per·fect·ed; per·fect·ing** : to improve (something) so that it has no flaws

per·fec·tion *n* **1** : a quality or condition that cannot be improved **2** : the act of improving something so that it has no flaws **3** : excellence or skill without flaw

per·fo·rate *vb* **per·fo·rat·ed; per·fo·rat·ing** : to make a hole or many holes through

per·form *vb* **per·formed; per·form·ing 1** : to carry out : DO **2** : to do something needing special skill **3** : to give a public presentation for entertainment — **per·form·er** *n*

per·for·mance *n* **1** : the carrying out of an action **2** : a public entertainment

¹per·fume *n* **1** : a liquid used to make a person smell nice **2** : a pleasant smell : FRAGRANCE

²per·fume *vb* **per·fumed; per·fum·ing** : to add a usually pleasant odor to : have the odor of

per·haps *adv* : possibly but not certainly : MAYBE

per·il *n* **1** : the state of being in great danger **2** : a cause or source of danger

per·il·ous *adj* : DANGEROUS 1 — **per·il·ous·ly** *adv*

pe·rim·e·ter *n* **1** : the whole outer boundary of a figure or area **2** : the length of the boundary of a figure

pe·ri·od *n* **1** : a punctuation mark . used chiefly to mark the end of a declarative sentence or an abbreviation **2** : a portion of time set apart by some quality **3** : a portion of time that forms a stage in history **4** : one of the divisions of a school day **5** : a single occurrence of menstruation

pe·ri·od·ic *adj* : occurring regularly over a period of time

¹pe·ri·od·i·cal *adj* **1** : PERIODIC **2** : published regularly — **pe·ri·od·i·cal·ly** *adv*

²periodical *n* : something (as a magazine) published regularly (as every month)

peri·scope *n* : an instrument containing lenses and mirrors by which a person (as on a submarine) can get a view that would otherwise be blocked

per·ish *vb* **per·ished; per·ish·ing** : to become destroyed : DIE

per·ish·able *adj* : likely to spoil or decay

¹per·i·win·kle *n* : an evergreen plant that spreads along the ground and has blue or white flowers

²periwinkle *n* : a small snail that lives along rocky seashores

perk *vb* **perked; perk·ing 1** : to make or become more lively or cheerful **2** : to make fresher in appearance **3** : to lift in a quick, alert, or bold way

perky *adj* **perk·i·er; perk·i·est** : being lively and cheerful

per·ma·nence *n* : the quality or state of lasting forever or for a long time

per·ma·nent *adj* : lasting or meant to last for a long time : not temporary — **per·ma·nent·ly** *adv*

per·me·able *adj* : having pores or openings that let liquids or gases pass through

per·me·ate *vb* **per·me·at·ed; per·me·at·ing 1** : to pass through something that has pores or small openings or is in a loose form **2** : to spread throughout

per·mis·sion *n* : the approval of a person in authority

¹per·mit *vb* **per·mit·ted; per·mit·ting 1** : to allow to happen or do : give permission **2** : to make possible : give an opportunity

²per·mit *n* : a statement of permission (as a license or pass)

per·ni·cious *adj* : causing great damage or harm

per·ox·ide *n* : HYDROGEN PEROXIDE

¹per·pen·dic·u·lar *adj* **1** : exactly vertical **2** : being at right angles to a line or surface — **per·pen·dic·u·lar·ly** *adv*

²perpendicular *n* : a line, surface, or position at right angles to another line, surface, or position

per·pe·trate *vb* **per·pe·trat·ed; per·pe·trat·ing** : to bring about or carry out : COMMIT — **per·pe·tra·tor** *n*

per·pet·u·al *adj* **1** : lasting forever or for a very long time **2** : occurring continually : CONSTANT — **per·pet·u·al·ly** *adv*

per·pet·u·ate *vb* **per·pet·u·at·ed; per·pet·u·at·ing** : to cause to last a long time

per·plex *vb* **per·plexed; per·plex·ing** : to make unable to understand : CONFUSE

per·plexed *adj* : unable to understand something clearly or to think clearly

per·plex·i·ty *n, pl* **per·plex·i·ties 1** : a puzzled or anxious state of mind **2** : something that puzzles

per·se·cute *vb* **per·se·cut·ed; per·se·cut·ing** : to treat continually in a cruel and harmful way

per·se·cu·tion *n* **1** : the act of continually treating in a cruel and harmful way **2** : the state of being continually treated in a cruel and harmful way

per·se·ver·ance *n* : the act or power of continuing to do something in spite of difficulties

per·se·vere *vb* **per·se·vered; per·se·ver·ing** : to keep trying to do something in spite of difficulties

per·sim·mon *n* : an orange roundish sweet fruit that grows on a tree of the southeastern United States and Asia and may be very sour when unripe

per·sist *vb* **per·sist·ed; per·sist·ing 1** : to keep on doing or saying something : continue stubbornly **2** : to last on and on : continue to exist or occur

per·sist·ence *n* **1** : the act or fact of stubbornly continuing to do something **2** : the act or fact of continuing to exist longer than usual

per·sist·ent *adj* : continuing to act or exist longer than usual — **per·sist·ent·ly** *adv*

per·son *n* **1** : a human being considered as an individual — sometimes used in compounds especially to avoid *man* in words that apply to both sexes **2** : the body of a human being

per·son·able *adj* : pleasing in appearance or manner

per·son·age *n* : an important or famous person

per·son·al *adj* **1** : of, relating to, or belonging to an individual human being : not public : not general **2** : made or done by a particular individual and not by someone acting for him or her **3** : of the body **4** : relating to someone's private matters **5** : intended for or given to one particular individual **6** : relating to a particular individual or his or her qualities often in a way that is hurtful — **per·son·al·ly** *adv*

personal computer *n* : a computer designed for an individual user

per·son·al·i·ty *n, pl* **per·son·al·i·ties 1** : the qualities (as moods or habits) that make one human being different from others **2** : a human being's pleasing or interesting qualities **3** : a famous person

personal pronoun *n* : a pronoun (as *I, you, it,* or *they*) used instead of a noun that names a definite person or thing

per·son·i·fy *vb* **per·son·i·fied; per·son·i·fy·ing** : to think of or represent as a person

per·son·nel *n* : a group of people employed in a business or an organization

per·spec·tive *n* **1** : the angle or direction in

which a person looks at an object **2** : POINT OF VIEW **3** : the ability to understand what is important and what isn't **4** : an accurate rating of what is important and what isn't **5** : the art of painting or drawing a scene so that objects in it seem to have their right shape and to be the right distance apart

per·spi·ra·tion *n* **1** : the act or process of perspiring **2** : salty liquid given off from skin glands

per·spire *vb* **per·spired; per·spir·ing** : to give off salty liquid through the skin

per·suade *vb* **per·suad·ed; per·suad·ing** : to win over to a belief or way of acting : CONVINCE

per·sua·sion *n* **1** : the act of convincing **2** : the power to convince **3** : a way of believing : BELIEF

per·sua·sive *adj* : able or likely to convince — **per·sua·sive·ly** *adv* — **per·sua·sive·ness** *n*

pert *adj* **1** : rude and disrespectful : FRESH **2** : PERKY

per·tain *vb* **per·tained; per·tain·ing 1** : to relate to a person or thing **2** : to belong to as a part, quality, or function

per·ti·nent *adj* : relating to the subject that is being thought about or discussed : RELEVANT

per·turb *vb* **per·turbed; per·turb·ing** : to disturb in mind : trouble greatly

pe·rus·al *n* : the act of reading or reading through carefully

pe·ruse *vb* **pe·rused; pe·rus·ing 1** : READ 1 **2** : to read through carefully

per·vade *vb* **per·vad·ed; per·vad·ing** : to spread through all parts of : PERMEATE

per·verse *adj* **1** : stubborn in being against what is right or sensible **2** : wrong especially in a way that is strange or offensive

pes·ky *adj* **pesk·i·er; pesk·i·est** : TROUBLESOME 1

pe·so *n, pl* **pesos 1** : a bill or coin used in one of several Spanish-speaking countries of North and South America **2** : a bill or coin used in the Philippines

pes·si·mism *n* : a feeling or belief that things are usually bad or that bad things will happen

pes·si·mist *n* : a person who habitually expects bad things to happen or thinks things are bad

pes·si·mis·tic *adj* **1** : tending to think that bad things will happen **2** : having the belief that evil is more common than good

pest *n* **1** : NUISANCE **2** : a plant or animal that is harmful to humans or property **3** : PESTILENCE

pes·ter *vb* **pes·tered; pes·ter·ing** : to bother again and again

pes·ti·cide *n* : a substance used to destroy pests (as insects or weeds)

pes·ti·lence *n* : a contagious usually fatal disease that spreads quickly

pes·tle *n* : a tool shaped like a small club for crushing substances in a mortar

¹**pet** *n* **1** : a tame animal kept as a companion rather than for work **2** : a person who is treated with special kindness or consideration

²**pet** *adj* **1** : kept or treated as a pet **2** : showing fondness **3** : ²FAVORITE

³**pet** *vb* **pet·ted; pet·ting** : to stroke or pat gently or lovingly

pet·al *n* : one of the often brightly colored leaflike outer parts of a flower

pet·i·ole *n* : the slender stem of a leaf

pe·tite *adj* : having a small trim figure

¹**pe·ti·tion** *n* **1** : an earnest appeal **2** : a formal written request made to an authority

²**petition** *vb* **pe·ti·tioned; pe·ti·tion·ing** : to make an often formal request to or for — **pe·ti·tion·er** *n*

pe·trel *n* : a small seabird with long wings that flies far from land

pet·ri·fy *vb* **pet·ri·fied; pet·ri·fy·ing 1** : to change plant or animal matter into stone or something like stone **2** : to frighten very much

pe·tro·leum *n* : a raw oil that is obtained from wells drilled in the ground and that is the source of gasoline, kerosene, and other oils used for fuel

pet·ti·coat *n* : a skirt worn under a dress or outer skirt

petting zoo *n* : a collection of farm animals or gentle exotic animals for children to pet and feed

pet·ty *adj* **pet·ti·er; pet·ti·est 1** : small and of no importance **2** : showing or having a mean narrow-minded attitude — **pet·ti·ness** *n*

petty officer *n* : an officer in the navy or coast guard appointed from among the enlisted people

pet·u·lance *n* : an irritable temper

pet·u·lant *adj* : often in a bad mood : CROSS

pe·tu·nia *n* : a plant grown for its brightly colored flowers that are shaped like funnels

pew *n* : one of the benches with backs and sometimes doors set in rows in a church

pe·wee *n* : a small grayish or greenish brown bird that eats flying insects

pew·ter *n* **1** : a metallic substance made mostly of tin sometimes mixed with copper or antimony that is used in making utensils (as pitchers and bowls) **2** : utensils made of pewter

pg. *abbr* page

pH *n* : a measure of the acidity or alkalinity of a substance

phan·tom *n* : an image or figure that can be sensed (as with the eyes or ears) but that is not real

pha·raoh *n, often cap* : a ruler of ancient Egypt

phar·ma·cist *n* : a person whose job is preparing medicines according to a doctor's prescription

phar·ma·cy *n, pl* **phar·ma·cies** : a place where medicines are prepared and sold by a pharmacist : DRUGSTORE

phar·ynx *n, pl* **pha·ryn·ges** *also* **phar·ynx·es** : a tube extending from the back of the nasal passages and mouth to the esophagus that is the passage through which air passes to the larynx and food to the esophagus

phase *n* 1 : a step or part in a series of events or actions : STAGE 2 : the way that the moon or a planet looks to the eye at any time in its series of changes with respect to how it shines

pheas·ant *n* : a large brightly colored bird with a long tail that is related to the chicken and is sometimes hunted for food or sport

phe·nom·e·nal *adj* : very remarkable : EXTRAORDINARY

phe·nom·e·non *n, pl* **phe·nom·e·na** *or* **phe·nom·e·nons** 1 phenomena *pl* : an observable fact or event 2 : a rare or important fact or event 3 phenomenons *pl* : an extraordinary or exceptional person or thing

¹-phil *or* **-phile** *n suffix* : a person who loves or is strongly attracted to

²-phil *or* **-phile** *adj suffix* : having a fondness for or strong attraction to

phil·an·throp·ic *adj* : for or relating to the act of giving money and time to help needy people : CHARITABLE

phi·lan·thro·pist *n* : a person who gives generously to help other people

phi·lan·thro·py *n, pl* **phi·lan·thro·pies** 1 : desire and active effort to help other people 2 : something done or given to help needy people 3 : an organization giving or supported by charitable gifts

phil·o·den·dron *n* : a plant often grown for its showy usually shiny leaves

phi·los·o·pher *n* 1 : a person who studies ideas about knowledge, right and wrong, reasoning, and the value of things 2 : a person who takes misfortunes with calmness and courage

phil·o·soph·i·cal *also* **phil·o·soph·ic** *adj* 1 : of or relating to the study of basic ideas about knowledge, right and wrong, reasoning, and the value of things 2 : showing wisdom and calm when faced with misfortune — **phil·o·soph·i·cal·ly** *adv*

phi·los·o·phy *n, pl* **phi·los·o·phies** 1 : the study of the basic ideas about knowledge, right and wrong, reasoning, and the value of things 2 : a specific set of ideas of a person or a group 3 : a set of ideas about how to do something or how to live

phlox *n, pl* **phlox** *or* **phlox·es** : a plant grown for its showy clusters of usually white, pink, or purplish flowers

pho·bia *n* : an unreasonable, abnormal, and lasting fear of something

phoe·be *n* : a small grayish brown bird that eats flying insects

phoe·nix *n* : a legendary bird which was thought to live for 500 years, burn itself to death, and rise newborn from the ashes

phon- *or* **phono-** *prefix* : sound : voice : speech

¹phone *n* : ¹TELEPHONE

²phone *vb* **phoned; phon·ing** : ²TELEPHONE

pho·neme *n* : one of the smallest units of speech that distinguish one utterance from another

pho·net·ic *adj* : of or relating to spoken language or speech sounds

pho·nics *n* : a method of teaching beginners to read and pronounce words by learning the usual sound of letters, letter groups, and syllables

pho·no·graph *n* : an instrument that reproduces sounds recorded on a grooved disk

¹pho·ny *also* **pho·ney** *adj* **pho·ni·er; pho·ni·est** : not real or genuine

²phony *also* **phoney** *n, pl* **pho·nies** *also* **pho·neys** 1 : a person who is not sincere 2 : something that is not real or genuine

phos·pho·rus *n* : a white or yellowish wax-like chemical element that gives a faint glow in moist air

pho·to *n, pl* **photos** : ¹PHOTOGRAPH

¹pho·to·copy *n* : a copy of usually printed material made using a process in which an image is formed by the action of light on an electrically charged surface

²photocopy *vb* **pho·to·cop·ied; pho·to·copy·ing** : to make a photocopy of — **pho·to·copi·er** *n*

¹pho·to·graph *n* : a picture taken by a camera

²photograph *vb* **pho·to·graphed; pho·to·graph·ing** : to take a picture of with a camera — **pho·tog·ra·pher** *n*

pho·to·graph·ic *adj* : obtained by or used in photography

pho·tog·ra·phy *n* : the making of pictures by means of a camera that directs the image of an object onto a surface that is sensitive to light

pho·to·syn·the·sis *n* : the process by which green plants and a few other organisms (as some protists) form carbohydrates from carbon dioxide and water in the presence of light — **pho·to·syn·thet·ic** *adj*

¹**phrase** *n* **1** : a group of two or more words that express a single idea but do not form a complete sentence **2** : a brief expression that is commonly used

²**phrase** *vb* **phrased; phras·ing** : to express in words

phy·lum *n, pl* **phy·la** : a group of related living things (as animals or plants) that ranks above the class and below the kingdom in scientific classification

phys ed *n* : PHYSICAL EDUCATION

phys·i·cal *adj* **1** : of the body : BODILY **2** : existing in a form that can be touched or seen **3** : of or relating to physics — **phys·i·cal·ly** *adv*

physical education *n* : instruction in the care and development of the body

phy·si·cian *n* : a specialist in healing human disease : a doctor of medicine

phys·i·cist *n* : a person specializing in physics

phys·ics *n* : a science that deals with the facts about matter and motion and includes the subjects of mechanics, heat, light, electricity, sound, and the atomic nucleus

phys·i·o·log·i·cal *or* **phys·i·o·log·ic** *adj* : of or relating to the processes and activities that keep living things alive

phys·i·ol·o·gist *n* : a person specializing in physiology

phys·i·ol·o·gy *n* **1** : a branch of biology that deals with the processes and activities that keep living things alive **2** : the processes and activities by which a living thing or any part of it functions

phy·sique *n* : the size and shape of a person's body

pi *n, pl* **pis** **1** : the symbol π representing the ratio of the circumference of a circle to its diameter **2** : the ratio itself having a value of about 3.1416

pi·a·nist *n* : a person who plays the piano

pi·a·no *n, pl* **pianos** : a keyboard instrument having steel wire strings that make a sound when struck by hammers covered with felt

pic·co·lo *n, pl* **pic·co·los** : a high-pitched instrument resembling a small flute

¹**pick** *vb* **picked; pick·ing** **1** : to gather one by one **2** : to remove bit by bit **3** : to remove unwanted material from between or inside **4** : CHOOSE 1, SELECT **5** : to walk along slowly and carefully **6** : to eat sparingly or in a finicky manner **7** : to steal from **8** : to start (a fight) with someone deliberately **9** : to pluck with the fingers or with a pick **10** : to unlock without a key — **pick·er** *n* — **pick on** : to single out for mean treatment — **pick up** **1** : to take hold of and lift

2 : to clean up : TIDY **3** : to stop for and take along **4** : LEARN 1 **5** : to get without great effort or by chance **6** : to get by buying **7** : to begin again after a temporary stop **8** : to bring within range of hearing **9** : to gain or get back speed or strength

²**pick** *n* **1** : a heavy tool with a wooden handle and a blade pointed at one or both ends for loosening or breaking up soil or rock **2** : a slender pointed instrument **3** : a thin piece of metal or plastic used to pluck the strings of a musical instrument **4** : the act or opportunity of choosing **5** : ¹CHOICE 3 **6** : the best ones

pick·ax *n* : ²PICK 1

pick·er·el *n, pl* **pickerel** *or* **pick·er·els** : a freshwater fish that resembles but is smaller than the related pike

¹**pick·et** *n* **1** : a pointed stake or slender post (as for making a fence) **2** : a soldier or a group of soldiers assigned to stand guard **3** : a person standing or marching near a place (as a factory or store) as part of a strike or protest

²**picket** *vb* **pick·et·ed; pick·et·ing** : to stand or march near a place as part of a strike or protest

¹**pick·le** *n* **1** : a piece of food and especially a cucumber that has been preserved in a solution of salt water or vinegar **2** : a mixture of salt and water or vinegar for keeping foods : BRINE **3** : a difficult or very unpleasant situation

²**pickle** *vb* **pick·led; pick·ling** : to soak or keep in a solution of salt water or vinegar

pick·pock·et *n* : a thief who steals from pockets and purses

pick·up *n* : a light truck with an open body and low sides

picky *adj* **pick·i·er; pick·i·est** : hard to please

¹**pic·nic** *n* **1** : an outdoor party with food taken along and eaten in the open **2** : a pleasant or carefree experience

²**picnic** *vb* **pic·nicked; pic·nick·ing** : to go on a picnic

pic·to·graph *n* **1** : an ancient or prehistoric drawing or painting on a rock wall **2** : a diagram showing information by means of pictures

pic·to·ri·al *adj* **1** : of or relating to pictures **2** : having or using pictures

¹**pic·ture** *n* **1** : an image of something or someone formed on a surface (as by drawing, painting, printing, or photography) **2** : an idea of what someone or something might look like or be like **3** : a perfect example of something **4** : MOVIE 1 **5** : an image on the screen of a television set

²**picture** *vb* **pic·tured; pic·tur·ing** **1** : to show or represent in a drawing, painting, or

photograph **2** : to form an idea or mental image of : IMAGINE **3** : to describe in a particular way

picture graph n : PICTOGRAPH 2

pic·tur·esque adj : suggesting a painted scene in being very pretty or charming

pie n : a food consisting of a pastry crust and a filling (as of fruit or meat)

pie·bald adj : spotted with two colors and especially black and white

¹piece n **1** : a part cut, torn, or broken from something **2** : one of a group, set, or mass of things **3** : a portion marked off **4** : a single item or example **5** : a definite amount or size in which something is made or sold **6** : something made or written **7** : a movable object used in playing a board game **8** : ¹COIN 1 — **in one piece** : not broken, hurt, or damaged

²piece vb **pieced; piec·ing** : to join into a whole : connect the parts or pieces of

piece·meal adv : one piece at a time : little by little

pier n **1** : a support for a bridge **2** : a structure built out into the water as a place for boats to dock or for people to walk or to protect or form a harbor

pierce vb **pierced; pierc·ing** **1** : to make a hole in or through or as if in or through **2** : to force or make a way into or through

pierc·ing adj **1** : able to penetrate **2** : loud and high-pitched

pi·e·ty n, pl **pieties** : devotion to God : the state or fact of being pious

pig n **1** : a hoofed stout-bodied animal with a short tail and legs, thick bristly skin, and a long flattened snout **2** : a domestic pig developed from the wild boar and raised for meat **3** : a person who has a disagreeable or offensive habit or behavior (as being dirty, rude, or greedy) **4** : a metal cast (as of iron) poured directly from the smelting furnace into a mold

pi·geon n : a bird with a plump body, short legs, and smooth feathers and especially one that is a variety of the rock dove and is found in cities throughout the world

pi·geon–toed adj : having the toes and front of the foot turned inward

pig·gy·back adv or adj : on the back or shoulders

piggy bank n : a container for keeping coins that is often in the shape of a pig

pig·head·ed adj : very stubborn

pig·let n : a baby pig

pig·ment n **1** : a substance that gives color to other materials **2** : natural coloring matter in animals and plants

pig·pen n **1** : a place where pigs are kept **2** : a dirty or messy place

pig·sty n : PIGPEN

pig·tail n : a tight braid of hair

¹pike n, pl **pike** or **pikes** : a long slender freshwater fish with a large mouth

²pike n : a long wooden pole with a steel point once used as a weapon by soldiers

³pike n : TURNPIKE, ROAD

¹pile n : a large stake or pointed post (as of wood or steel) driven into the ground to support a foundation

²pile n **1** : a large number of things that are put one on top of another **2** : a great amount **3** : REACTOR

³pile vb **piled; pil·ing** **1** : to lay or place one on top of another : STACK **2** : to heap in large amounts **3** : to move or push forward in a crowd or group

⁴pile n : a soft surface of fine short raised threads or fibers

pil·fer vb **pil·fered; pil·fer·ing** : to steal small amounts or articles of small value

pil·grim n **1** : a person who travels to a holy place as an act of religious devotion **2** cap : one of the English colonists who founded the first permanent settlement in New England at Plymouth in 1620

pil·grim·age n : a journey made by a pilgrim

pil·ing n : a supporting structure made of large stakes or pointed posts driven into the ground

pill n : medicine or a food supplement in the form of a small rounded mass to be swallowed whole

¹pil·lage n : the act of robbing by force especially during a war

²pillage vb **pil·laged; pil·lag·ing** : to rob by force especially during a war

pil·lar n **1** : a large post that supports something (as a roof) **2** : a single column built as a monument **3** : a supporting or important member or part **4** : something that resembles a column in shape

pil·lo·ry n, pl **pil·lo·ries** : a device once used for punishing someone in public consisting of a wooden frame with holes in which the head and hands can be locked

pil·low n : a bag filled with soft or springy material used as a cushion usually for the head of a person lying down

pil·low·case n : a removable covering for a pillow

¹pi·lot n **1** : a person who flies an aircraft **2** : a person who steers a ship **3** : a person especially qualified to guide ships into and out of a port or in dangerous waters

²pilot vb **pi·lot·ed; pi·lot·ing** **1** : to fly (an airplane) **2** : to steer or guide (a boat)

pi·mien·to also **pi·men·to** n, pl **pi·mien·tos** also **pi·men·tos** : a mildly sweet pepper with thick flesh

pim·ple *n* : a small red swelling of the skin often containing pus — **pim·pled** *adj* — **pim·ply** *adj*

¹pin *n* **1** : a small pointed piece of wire with a rounded head used especially for fastening pieces of cloth **2** : something (as an ornament or badge) fastened to the clothing by a pin **3** : a slender pointed piece (as of wood or metal) usually having the shape of a cylinder used to fasten articles together or in place **4** : one of ten pieces set up as the target in bowling

²pin *vb* **pinned; pin·ning 1** : to fasten or join with a pin **2** : to prevent or be prevented from moving

pin·a·fore *n* : a sleeveless garment with a low neck worn as an apron or a dress

pi·ña·ta *n* : a decorated container filled with treats (as candy and toys) and hung up to be broken open by a blindfolded person with a stick

pin·cer *n* **1 pincers** *pl* : a tool with two handles and two jaws for holding or gripping small objects **2** : a part (as the claw of a lobster) resembling a pair of pincers

¹pinch *vb* **pinched; pinch·ing 1** : to squeeze between the finger and thumb or between the jaws of an instrument **2** : to squeeze painfully **3** : to break off by squeezing with the thumb and fingers **4** : to cause to look thin or shrunken — **pinch pennies** : to be thrifty or stingy

²pinch *n* **1** : a time of emergency **2** : an act of squeezing skin between the thumb and fingers **3** : as much as may be picked up between the finger and the thumb : a very small amount

pinch hitter *n* **1** : a baseball player who is sent in to bat for another **2** : a person who does another's work in an emergency

pin·cush·ion *n* : a small cushion in which pins may be stuck when not in use

¹pine *n* : an evergreen tree that has narrow needles for leaves, cones, and a wood that ranges from very soft to hard

²pine *vb* **pined; pin·ing 1** : to become thin and weak because of sadness or worry **2** : to long for very much

pine·ap·ple *n* : a large fruit that grows on a tropical plant and has a thick skin and sweet juicy yellow flesh

pin·feath·er *n* : a new feather just breaking through the skin of a bird

pin·ion *vb* **pin·ioned; pin·ion·ing 1** : to restrain by tying the arms to the body **2** : to tie up or hold tightly **3** : to prevent a bird from flying especially by cutting off the end of one wing

¹pink *n* : a plant with narrow leaves that is grown for its showy pink, red, or white flowers

²pink *n* : a pale red color

³pink *adj* : colored a pale red

pink·eye *n* : a contagious infection that causes the eye and inner part of the eyelid to become red and sore

pin·kie *or* **pin·ky** : LITTLE FINGER

pink·ish *adj* : somewhat pink

pin·na·cle *n* **1** : the peak of a mountain **2** : the highest point of development or achievement **3** : a slender tower generally coming to a narrow point at the top

pin·point *vb* **pin·point·ed; pin·point·ing** : to locate or find out exactly

pint *n* : a unit of liquid capacity equal to one half quart or 16 ounces (about .47 liter)

pin·to *n, pl* **pintos** : a horse or pony that has patches of white and another color

pin·wheel *n* : a toy with fanlike blades at the end of a stick that spin in the wind

¹pi·o·neer *n* **1** : a person who is one of the first to settle in an area **2** : a person who begins or helps develop something new and prepares the way for others to follow

²pioneer *vb* **pi·o·neered; pi·o·neer·ing 1** : to explore or open up ways or regions for others to follow **2** : to begin something new or take part in the early development of something

pi·ous *adj* : showing devotion to God

¹pipe *n* **1** : a long tube or hollow body for carrying a substance (as water, steam, or gas) **2** : a musical instrument or part of a musical instrument consisting of a tube (as of wood or metal) played by blowing or having air passed through it **3** : BAGPIPE — usually used in pl. **4** : a tube with a small bowl at one end for smoking tobacco or for blowing bubbles

²pipe *vb* **piped; pip·ing 1** : to move by means of pipes **2** : to play on a pipe — **pip·er** *n* — **pipe down** : to stop talking or making noise — **pipe up** : to start talking : say something

pipe·line *n* : a line of connected pipes with pumps and control devices for carrying liquids or gases over a long distance

pip·ing *n* **1** : a quantity or system of pipes **2** : the music of a pipe **3** : a high-pitched sound or call **4** : a narrow fold of material used to decorate edges or seams

pique *vb* **piqued; piqu·ing 1** : to stir up : EXCITE **2** : to make annoyed or angry

pi·ra·cy *n, pl* **pi·ra·cies 1** : robbery of a ship at sea **2** : the use of another's work or invention without permission

pi·ra·nha *n* : a small South American freshwater fish that has very sharp teeth, often occurs in groups, and may attack human beings and animals in the water

pi·rate *n* : a robber of ships at sea : a person who commits piracy

pis *pl of* PI

Pi·sces *n* **1** : a constellation between Aquarius and Aries imagined as two fish **2** : the twelfth sign of the zodiac or a person born under this sign

pis·ta·chio *n, pl* **pis·ta·chios** : the greenish edible seed of a small Asian tree

pis·til *n* : the part in the center of a flower that is made up of the stigma, style, and ovary and produces the seed

pis·tol *n* : a small gun made to be aimed and fired with one hand

pis·ton *n* : a disk or short cylinder that slides back and forth inside a larger cylinder and is moved by steam in steam engines and by the explosion of fuel in automobiles

¹pit *n* **1** : a cavity or hole in the ground usually made by digging **2** : an area set off from and often sunken below surrounding areas **3** : a small hole or dent on a surface **4 pits** *pl* : something very bad — **pit·ted** *adj*

²pit *vb* **pit·ted; pit·ting 1** : to make small holes or dents in **2** : to set against another in a fight or contest

³pit *n* : a hard seed or stone of a fruit (as a peach or cherry)

⁴pit *vb* **pit·ted; pit·ting** : to remove the pit from

pi·ta *n* : a thin flat bread that can be opened to form a pocket for holding food

¹pitch *vb* **pitched; pitch·ing 1** : to set up and fix firmly in place **2** : to throw usually toward a certain point **3** : to throw a baseball or softball to a batter **4** : to plunge or fall forward **5** : ²SLOPE, SLANT **6** : to fix or set at a certain highness or lowness **7** : to move in such a way that one end falls while the other end rises — **pitch in** : to contribute to a common task or goal

²pitch *n* **1** : highness or lowness of sound **2** : amount of slope **3** : an up-and-down movement **4** : the throw of a baseball or softball to a batter **5** : the amount or level of something (as a feeling) — **pitched** *adj*

³pitch *n* **1** : a dark sticky substance left over from distilling tar and used in making roofing paper, in waterproofing seams, and in paving **2** : resin from various evergreen trees (as the pine)

pitch–black *adj* : extremely dark or black

pitch·blende *n* : a dark mineral that is a source of radium and uranium

pitch–dark *adj* : extremely dark

¹pitch·er *n* : a container usually with a handle and a lip or spout used for holding and pouring out liquids

²pitcher *n* : the player who throws the ball to the batter in baseball or softball

pitch·fork *n* : a tool having a long handle and two or three metal prongs that is used especially for lifting and tossing hay or straw

pit·e·ous *adj* : PITIFUL — **pit·e·ous·ly** *adv*

pit·fall *n* **1** : a covered or camouflaged pit used to capture animals or people **2** : a danger or difficulty that is hidden or is not easily recognized

pith *n* **1** : the loose spongy tissue forming the center of the stem in most plants **2** : the important part

piti·able *adj* : PITIFUL

piti·ful *adj* **1** : deserving or causing feelings of pity **2** : deserving or causing a feeling of dislike or disgust by not being sufficient or good enough — **piti·ful·ly** *adv*

piti·less *adj* : having no pity : CRUEL

pi·tu·i·tary gland *n* : a gland at the base of the brain that produces several hormones of which one affects growth

¹pity *n* **1** : a feeling of sadness or sympathy for the suffering or unhappiness of others **2** : something that causes regret or disappointment

²pity *vb* **pit·ied; pity·ing** : to feel sadness and sympathy for

¹piv·ot *n* **1** : a shaft or pin with a pointed end on which something turns **2** : the action or an instance of turning around on a point

²pivot *vb* **piv·ot·ed; piv·ot·ing** : to turn on or as if on a pivot : turn around on a central point

pix·el *n* : any of the small parts that make up an image (as on a computer or television screen)

pix·ie *also* **pixy** *n, pl* **pix·ies** : a mischievous elf or fairy

piz·za *n* : a dish made of flattened bread dough topped usually with tomato sauce and cheese and often meat and vegetables and baked

pk. *abbr* **1** park **2** peck

pkg. *abbr* package

pl. *abbr* plural

plac·ard *n* : a large notice or poster for announcing or advertising something

pla·cate *vb* **pla·cat·ed; pla·cat·ing** : to calm the anger of

¹place *n* **1** : an available seat or space : ROOM **2** : a region or space not specified **3** : a particular portion of a surface : SPOT **4** : a point in a speech or a piece of writing **5** : a building or area used for a special purpose **6** : a certain area or region of the world **7** : a piece of land with a house on it **8** : position in a scale or series in comparison with another or others **9** : usual space or use **10**

: the position of a figure in a numeral **11** : a public square **12** : a short street

²place *vb* **placed; plac·ing 1** : to put in or as if in a certain space or position **2** : to give an order for **3** : to appoint to a job or find a job for **4** : to identify by connecting with a certain time, place, or happening

place·hold·er *n* : a symbol (as *x*, Δ, *) used in mathematics in the place of a numeral

place·kick *n* : a kick in football made with the ball held in place on the ground

pla·cen·ta *n* : the organ in most mammals by which the fetus is joined to the uterus of the mother and is nourished

place value *n* : the value of the location of a digit in a number

plac·id *adj* : calm and peaceful

pla·gia·rism *n* : an act of copying the ideas or words of another person without giving credit to that person

¹plague *n* **1** : something that causes much distress **2** : a disease that causes death and spreads quickly to a large number of people **3** : BUBONIC PLAGUE

²plague *vb* **plagued; plagu·ing 1** : to affect with disease or trouble **2** : to cause worry or distress to

plaid *n* **1** : a pattern consisting of rectangles formed by crossed lines of various widths **2** : TARTAN — **plaid** *adj*

¹plain *adj* **plain·er; plain·est 1** : having no pattern or decoration **2** : not handsome or beautiful **3** : not hard to do or understand **4** : without anything having been added **5** : open and clear to the sight **6** : FRANK **7** : of common or average accomplishments or position : ORDINARY — **plain·ly** *adv* — **plain·ness** *n*

²plain *n* : a large area of level or rolling treeless land

³plain *adv* : without any question : to a complete degree

plain·tive *adj* : showing or suggesting sadness : MOURNFUL

¹plait *n* : a flat braid (as of hair)

²plait *vb* **plait·ed; plait·ing 1** : ¹BRAID **2** : to make by braiding

¹plan *n* **1** : a method or scheme of acting, doing, or arranging **2** : a drawing or diagram showing the parts or outline of something

²plan *vb* **planned; plan·ning 1** : to form a diagram of or for : arrange the parts or details of ahead of time **2** : to have in mind : INTEND

¹plane *n* **1** : AIRPLANE **2** : a surface in which if any two points are chosen a straight line joining them lies completely in that surface **3** : a level of thought, existence, or development **4** : a level or flat surface

²plane *adj* : ¹HORIZONTAL, FLAT

³plane *n* : a tool that smooths wood by shaving off thin strips

⁴plane *vb* **planed; plan·ing 1** : to smooth or level off with a tool made for smoothing **2** : to remove with or as if with a tool for smoothing wood

plan·et *n* : any large heavenly body that orbits a star (as the sun)

plan·e·tar·i·um *n* : a building in which there is a device for projecting the images of heavenly bodies on a ceiling shaped like a dome

plan·e·tary *adj* **1** : of or relating to a planet **2** : having a motion like that of a planet

plank *n* : a heavy thick board

plank·ton *n* : the tiny floating plants and animals of a body of water

¹plant *vb* **plant·ed; plant·ing 1** : to place in the ground to grow **2** : to fill with seeds or plants **3** : to set firmly in the ground **4** : to place firmly **5** : to introduce as a thought or idea **6** : to place (someone or something) secretly

²plant *n* **1** : any member of the kingdom of many-celled mostly photosynthetic living things (as mosses, ferns, grasses, and trees) that lack a nervous system or sense organs and the ability to move about and that have cellulose cell walls **2** : the buildings and equipment of an industrial business or an institution — **plant·like** *adj*

plan·tain *n* : the greenish fruit of a kind of banana plant that is eaten cooked and is larger, less sweet, and more starchy than the ordinary banana

plan·ta·tion *n* **1** : a large area of land where crops are grown and harvested **2** : a settlement in a new country or region

plant·er *n* **1** : someone or something that plants crops **2** : a person who owns or runs a plantation **3** : a container in which plants are grown

plant kingdom *n* : a basic group of natural objects that includes all living and extinct plants

plant louse *n* : APHID

plaque *n* **1** : a flat thin piece (as of metal) with writing on it that serves as a memorial of something **2** : a sticky usually colorless thin film on the teeth that is formed by and contains bacteria

plas·ma *n* : the watery part of blood, lymph, or milk

¹plas·ter *n* : a paste (as of lime, sand, and water) that hardens when it dries and is used for coating walls and ceilings

²plaster *vb* **plas·tered; plas·ter·ing 1** : to cover or smear with or as if with a paste used for coating **2** : to paste or fasten on especially so as to cover

plaster of par·is *n, often cap 2nd P* : a white powder that mixes with water to form a paste that hardens quickly and is used for casts and molds

¹plas·tic *adj* **1** : made of plastic **2** : capable of being molded or modeled

²plastic *n* : any of various manufactured materials that can be molded into objects or formed into films or fibers

¹plate *n* **1** : a shallow usually round dish **2** : a main course of a meal **3** : a thin flat piece of material **4** : HOME PLATE **5** : a piece of metal on which something is engraved or molded **6** : an illustration often covering a full page of a book **7** : a sheet of glass coated with a chemical sensitive to light for use in a camera

²plate *vb* **plat·ed; plat·ing** : to cover with a thin layer of metal (as gold or silver)

pla·teau *n, pl* **plateaus** *or* **pla·teaux** : a broad flat area of high land

plate·let *n* : one of the tiny colorless disk-shaped bodies of the blood that assist in blood clotting

plat·form *n* **1** : a level usually raised surface **2** : a raised floor or stage for performers or speakers **3** : a statement of the beliefs and rules of conduct for which a group stands **4** : an arrangement of computer components that uses a particular operating system

plat·i·num *n* : a heavy grayish white metallic chemical element

pla·toon *n* : a part of a military company usually made up of two or more squads

platoon sergeant *n* : a noncommissioned officer in the army ranking above a staff sergeant

plat·ter *n* : a large plate used especially for serving meat

platy·pus *n* : a small water-dwelling mammal of Australia that lays eggs and has webbed feet, dense fur, and a bill that resembles that of a duck

plau·si·ble *adj* : seeming to be reasonable — **plau·si·bly** *adv*

¹play *vb* **played; play·ing** **1** : to do activities for enjoyment **2** : to take part in a game of **3** : to compete against in a game **4** : to produce music or sound with **5** : to perform the music of **6** : to act or present on the stage or screen **7** : PRETEND 1 **8** : to perform (as a trick) for fun **9** : ²ACT 2, BEHAVE **10** : to handle something idly : TOY **11** : to affect something by performing a function **12** : to move swiftly or lightly

²play *n* **1** : a story performed on stage **2** : the action of or a particular action in a game **3** : exercise or activity for enjoyment **4** : a person's turn to take part in a game **5** : quick or light movement **6** : freedom of

motion **7** : a way of acting : CONDUCT **8** : the state of being active

play·act·ing *n* : the performance of make-believe roles

play·er *n* **1** : a person who participates in a game **2** : a person who produces sound on a musical instrument **3** : a device that reproduces sounds or video images that have been recorded (as on magnetic tape or a hard drive)

play·ful *adj* **1** : full of energy and a desire for fun **2** : not serious : HUMOROUS — **play·ful·ly** *adv* — **play·ful·ness** *n*

play·ground *n* : an area used for games and playing

play·house *n* **1** : a small house for children to play in **2** : THEATER 1

playing card *n* : any of a set of cards marked to show rank and suit (**spades**, **hearts**, **diamonds**, or **clubs**) and used in playing various games

play·mate *n* : a friend with whom a child plays

play·off *n* : a game or series of games to determine a championship or to break a tie

play·pen *n* : a small enclosure in which a baby is placed to play

play·thing *n* : ¹TOY 1

play·wright *n* : a writer of plays

pla·za *n* : a public square in a city or town

plea *n* **1** : an earnest appeal **2** : something offered as a defense or excuse

plead *vb* **plead·ed** *or* **pled; plead·ing** **1** : to ask for in a serious and emotional way : BEG **2** : to offer as a defense, an excuse, or an apology **3** : to argue for or against : argue in court **4** : to answer to a criminal charge

pleas·ant *adj* **1** : giving pleasure : AGREEABLE **2** : having pleasing manners, behavior, or appearance — **pleas·ant·ly** *adv*

¹please *vb* **pleased; pleas·ing** **1** : to make happy or satisfied **2** : to be willing : LIKE, CHOOSE

²please *adv* — used to show politeness or emphasis in requesting or accepting

pleas·ing *adj* : giving pleasure : AGREEABLE — **pleas·ing·ly** *adv*

plea·sur·able *adj* : PLEASANT 1

plea·sure *n* **1** : a feeling of enjoyment or satisfaction **2** : recreation or enjoyment **3** : something that pleases or delights **4** : a particular desire

¹pleat *vb* **pleat·ed; pleat·ing** : to arrange in folds made by doubling material over on itself

²pleat *n* : a fold (as in cloth) made by doubling material over on itself

¹pledge *n* **1** : a promise or agreement that must be kept **2** : something handed over to another to ensure that the giver will keep his or her promise or agreement **3** : a promise to give money

²pledge *vb* **pledged; pledg·ing 1** : to promise to give **2** : to cause (someone) to promise something **3** : to give as assurance of a promise (as of repayment of a loan)

plen·ti·ful *adj* **1** : present in large numbers or amount : ABUNDANT **2** : giving or containing a large number or amount — **plen·ti·ful·ly** *adv*

plen·ty *n* : a full supply : more than enough

pleu·ri·sy *n* : a sore swollen state of the membrane that lines the chest often with fever, painful breathing, and coughing

plex·us *n*, *pl* **plex·us·es** : a network usually of nerves or blood vessels

pli·able *adj* **1** : possible to bend without breaking **2** : easily influenced

pli·ant *adj* : PLIABLE

pli·ers *n pl* : small pincers with long jaws used for bending or cutting wire or handling small things

plight *n* : a bad condition or state : PREDICAMENT

plod *vb* **plod·ded; plod·ding** : to move or travel slowly but steadily — **plod·der** *n*

¹plop *vb* **plopped; plop·ping 1** : to move with or make a sound like that of something dropping into water **2** : to sit or lie down heavily **3** : to place or drop heavily

²plop *n* : a sound like something dropping into water

¹plot *n* **1** : a secret usually evil scheme **2** : the plan or main story of a play or novel **3** : a small area of ground

²plot *vb* **plot·ted; plot·ting 1** : to plan or scheme secretly usually to do something bad **2** : to make a plan of — **plot·ter** *n*

plough *chiefly British variant of* PLOW

plo·ver *n* : a small shorebird having a shorter and stouter bill than the related sandpiper

¹plow *n* **1** : a farm machine used to dig into, break up, and turn over soil **2** : a device (as a snowplow) used to spread or clear away matter on the ground

²plow *vb* **plowed; plow·ing 1** : to dig into, break up, or turn over soil with a plow **2** : to move through or continue with force or determination

plow·share *n* : the part of a plow that cuts into the earth

ploy *n*, *pl* **ploys** : a trick used to make someone do something or get an advantage

pls. *abbr* please

¹pluck *vb* **plucked; pluck·ing 1** : to pull off : PICK **2** : to remove something (as a hair or feather) with a quick pull **3** : to seize and remove quickly : SNATCH **4** : to pull at (a string) and let go

²pluck *n* **1** : a sharp pull : TUG **2** : COURAGE, SPIRIT

plucky *adj* **pluck·i·er; pluck·i·est** : showing courage : BRAVE

¹plug *n* **1** : a device usually on a cord used to make an electrical connection by putting it into another part (as a socket) **2** : a piece (as of wood or metal) used to stop up or fill a hole

²plug *vb* **plugged; plug·ging 1** : to connect to an electric circuit **2** : to stop or make tight with something that fills a hole **3** : to keep steadily at work or in action

plum *n* **1** : a fruit related to the peach and cherry that usually has smooth purple or reddish skin, sweet juicy flesh, and a stony pit **2** : a dark reddish purple **3** : a choice or desirable thing : PRIZE

plum·age *n* : the feathers of a bird

¹plumb *n* : a small weight attached to a line and used to show depth or a straight vertical line

²plumb *vb* **plumbed; plumb·ing** : to measure or test with a plumb

³plumb *adv* **1** : exactly straight up and down **2** : COMPLETELY

plumb·er *n* : a person who installs or repairs plumbing

plumb·ing *n* **1** : a system of pipes and fixtures for supplying and carrying off water in a building **2** : the installation or repair of part or all of such a system of pipes and fixtures

plume *n* **1** : a large or showy feather of a bird **2** : an ornamental feather or tuft of feathers (as on a hat) **3** : something shaped like a large feather — **plumed** *adj*

plum·met *vb* **plum·met·ed; plum·met·ing** : to fall straight down

¹plump *adj* **plumper; plumpest** : having a pleasingly full rounded shape — **plump·ness** *n*

²plump *vb* **plumped; plump·ing 1** : to drop or fall heavily or suddenly **2** : to come out in favor of something

³plump *adv* : DIRECTLY 1

⁴plump *vb* **plumped; plump·ing** : to make or become rounded or filled out

¹plun·der *vb* **plun·dered; plun·der·ing** : to rob or steal especially openly and by force (as during war)

²plunder *n* : something stolen by force : LOOT

¹plunge *vb* **plunged; plung·ing 1** : to leap or dive suddenly **2** : to thrust or force quickly **3** : to suddenly enter or cause to enter a certain situation or state **4** : to drop suddenly downward or forward and downward

²plunge *n* : a sudden dive, rush, or leap

plung·er *n* : a part that moves up and down usually inside a tube or cylinder to push something out

plunk *vb* **plunked; plunk·ing 1 :** to lie or sit down suddenly or heavily **2 :** to drop or place heavily or carelessly **3 :** to make a sound on (an instrument) by pulling the strings or keys

¹plu·ral *adj* : relating to or being a word form used to show more than one

²plural *n* : a form of a word used to show that more than one person or thing is meant

¹plus *adj* : falling high in a certain range

²plus *prep* : increased by : with the addition of

¹plush *adj* **plush·er; plush·est 1 :** made of a thick soft fabric **2 :** very rich and fine

²plush *n* : a fabric like a very thick soft velvet

plus sign *n* : a sign + used in mathematics to show addition (as in 8+6=14) or a quantity greater than zero (as in +10°)

Plu·to *n* : a celestial object that orbits the sun at an average distance of 3.7 million miles (5.9 million kilometers) and has a diameter of about 1500 miles (2300 kilometers) and is often considered one of the planets

plu·to·ni·um *n* : a radioactive metallic chemical element formed from neptunium and used for releasing atomic energy

¹ply *vb* **plied; ply·ing 1 :** to use something steadily or forcefully **2 :** to keep supplying **3 :** to work at

²ply *n, pl* **plies :** one of the folds, layers, or threads of which something (as yarn or plywood) is made up

ply·wood *n* : a strong board made by gluing together thin sheets of wood under heat and pressure

p.m., P.M. *abbr* afternoon — abbreviation for Latin *post meridiem*, which means "after noon"

pneu·mat·ic *adj* **1 :** moved or worked by the pressure of air **2 :** made to hold or be inflated with compressed air

pneu·mo·nia *n* : a serious illness affecting the lungs that is marked especially by fever, cough, and difficulty in breathing

P.O. *abbr* post office

¹poach *vb* **poached; poach·ing :** to cook slowly in liquid

²poach *vb* **poached; poaching :** to hunt or fish unlawfully

pock *n* : a small swelling like a pimple on the skin (as in smallpox) or the mark it leaves

¹pock·et *n* **1 :** a small bag sewn into a piece of clothing for carrying small articles **2 :** a place or thing that is different from the larger place or thing that it is part of **3 :** a condition of the air (as a down current) that causes an airplane to drop suddenly **4 :** a bag at the corner or side of a pool table

²pocket *vb* **pock·et·ed; pock·et·ing 1 :** to put something in a pocket **2 :** to keep often dishonestly

³pocket *adj* : POCKET-SIZE

pock·et·book *n* **1 :** HANDBAG **2 :** the amount of money that someone has to spend

pock·et·knife *n, pl* **pock·et·knives :** a small knife that has one or more blades that fold into the handle

pock·et–size *adj* : small enough to fit in a pocket

pock·mark *n* **1 :** the mark left by a pock **2 :** a small hole or dent — **pock·marked** *adj*

pod *n* : a fruit (as a pea or bean) that is dry when ripe and splits open to free its seeds

po·di·um *n* **1 :** a raised platform especially for the conductor of an orchestra **2 :** a stand with a slanted surface (as for holding papers or a book) that a person can stand behind or near when giving a speech

po·em *n* : a piece of writing often having figurative language and lines that have rhythm and sometimes rhyme

po·et *n* : a writer of poems

po·et·ic *or* **po·et·i·cal** *adj* : of, relating to, or like that of poets or poetry

po·et·ry *n* **1 :** writing that usually involves figurative language and lines that have rhythm and sometimes rhyme : VERSE **2 :** the writings of a poet

po·go stick *n* : a pole with a strong spring at the bottom and two rests for the feet on which a person stands and bounces

poin·set·tia *n* : a tropical plant with showy usually red leaves that grow like petals around its small greenish yellow flowers

¹point *n* **1 :** a separate or particular detail : ITEM **2 :** an individual quality : CHARAC-TERISTIC **3 :** the chief idea or meaning **4 :** PURPOSE, AIM **5 :** a geometric element that has a position but no dimensions and is pictured as a small dot **6 :** a particular place or position **7 :** a particular stage or moment **8 :** the usually sharp end (as of a sword, pin, or pencil) **9 :** a piece of land that sticks out **10 :** a dot in writing or printing **11 :** one of the 32 marks indicating direction on a compass **12 :** a unit of scoring in a game — **point·ed** *adj* — **pointy** *adj*

²point *vb* **point·ed; point·ing 1 :** to show the position or direction of something especially by extending a finger in a particular direction **2 :** to direct someone's attention to **3 :** ¹AIM 1, DIRECT **4 :** to give a sharp end to

point–blank *adv* : in a very clear and direct way

point·ed·ly *adv* : in a way that very clearly expresses a particular meaning or thought

point·er *n* **1** : something that points or is used for pointing **2** : a helpful hint **3** : a large dog with long ears and short hair that is trained to direct its head and body in the direction of an animal that is being hunted

point·less *adj* : having no meaning or purpose

point of view *n, pl* **points of view** : a way of looking at or thinking about something

¹poise *vb* **poised; pois·ing 1** : to hold or make steady by balancing **2** : to remain in position without moving **3** : to be or become ready for something

²poise *n* **1** : the state of being balanced **2** : a natural self-confident manner

¹poi·son *n* : a substance that by its chemical action can injure or kill a living thing

²poison *vb* **poi·soned; poi·son·ing 1** : to injure or kill with poison **2** : to put poison on or in

poison ivy *n* **1** : a usually climbing plant that has leaves with three leaflets and can cause an itchy painful rash when touched **2** : a skin rash caused by poison ivy

poison oak *n* : a bush related to poison ivy that can cause an itchy painful rash when touched

poi·son·ous *adj* : containing poison : having or causing an effect of poison

poison sumac *n* : a shrub or small tree related to poison ivy that can cause an itchy painful rash when touched

¹poke *vb* **poked; pok·ing 1** : to push something usually thin or sharp into or at **2** : to make by stabbing or piercing **3** : to thrust or stick out or cause to thrust or stick out **4** : to search through or look around often without purpose **5** : to move slowly or lazily

²poke *n* : a quick push with something pointed

¹pok·er *n* : a metal rod used for stirring a fire

²po·ker *n* : a card game in which players bet on the value of their cards

poky *or* **pok·ey** *adj* **pok·i·er; pok·i·est 1** : so slow as to be annoying **2** : small and cramped

po·lar *adj* **1** : of or relating to the north pole or south pole or nearby regions **2** : coming from or being like a polar region **3** : of or relating to a pole of a magnet

polar bear *n* : a large creamy-white bear of arctic regions

¹pole *n* : a long straight thin piece of material (as wood or metal)

²pole *n* **1** : either end of the imaginary line on which the earth or another planet turns **2** : either of the two ends of a magnet

Pole *n* : a person born or living in Poland

pole·cat *n, pl* **pole·cats** *or* **polecat 1** : a brown or black European animal related to the weasel **2** : SKUNK

pole vault *n* : a track-and-field event in which each athlete uses a pole to jump over a high bar

¹po·lice *vb* **po·liced; po·lic·ing** : to keep order in or among

²police *n, pl* **police 1** : the department of government that keeps order and enforces law, investigates crimes, and makes arrests **2 police** *pl* : members of a police force

police dog *n* : a dog trained to help police

po·lice·man *n, pl* **po·lice·men** : a man who is a police officer

police officer *n* : a member of a police force

po·lice·wom·an *n, pl* **po·lice·wom·en** : a woman who is a police officer

¹pol·i·cy *n, pl* **pol·i·cies** : a set of guidelines or rules that determine a course of action

²policy *n, pl* **pol·i·cies** : a document that contains the agreement made by an insurance company with a person whose life or property is insured

po·lio *n* : a once common disease often affecting children and sometimes causing paralysis

po·lio·my·eli·tis *n* : POLIO

¹pol·ish *vb* **pol·ished; pol·ish·ing 1** : to make smooth and shiny usually by rubbing **2** : to improve in manners, condition, or style — **pol·ish·er** *n* — **polish off** : to finish completely

²polish *n* **1** : a smooth and shiny surface **2** : a substance for making a surface smooth and shiny **3** : good manners : REFINEMENT

¹Pol·ish *adj* : of or relating to Poland, the Poles, or Polish

²Polish *n* : the language of the Poles

po·lite *adj* **po·lit·er; po·lit·est** : showing courtesy or good manners — **po·lite·ly** *adv* — **po·lite·ness** *n*

po·lit·i·cal *adj* : relating to the government or the way government is carried on — **po·lit·i·cal·ly** *adv*

pol·i·ti·cian *n* : a person who is active in government usually as an elected official

pol·i·tics *n pl* **1** : the activities, actions, and policies that are used to gain and hold power in a government or to influence a government **2** : a person's opinions about the management of government — used as singular or plural

pol·ka *n* : a lively dance for couples or the music for it

pol·ka dot *n* : a dot in a pattern of evenly spaced dots (as on fabric)

¹poll *n* **1** : the casting or recording of the votes or opinions of a number of persons **2**

: the place where votes are cast — usually used in pl.

²poll *vb* **polled; poll·ing** : to question in order to get information or opinions about something

pol·lack *or* **pol·lock** *n, pl* **pollack** *or* **pollock** : either of two fishes of the northern Atlantic Ocean and the northern Pacific Ocean that are related to the cod and are often used for food

pol·len *n* : the very tiny grains produced by the stamens of a flower or special sacs of a male cone that fertilize the seeds and usually appear as fine yellow dust

pol·li·nate *vb* **pol·li·nat·ed; pol·li·nat·ing** : to transfer or carry pollen from a stamen to a pistil of a flower or from a male cone to a female cone

pol·li·na·tion *n* : the transfer of pollen from a stamen to a pistil of a flower or from a male cone to a female cone

pol·lut·ant *n* : a substance that makes something (as air or water) impure and often unsafe

pol·lute *vb* **pol·lut·ed; pol·lut·ing** : to spoil or make impure especially with waste made by humans — **pol·lut·er** *n*

pol·lu·tion *n* : the action of making something impure and often unsafe or unsuitable for use : the state of being polluted

pol·ly·wog *or* **pol·li·wog** *n* : TADPOLE

po·lo *n* : a game played by teams of players on horseback who use long-handled mallets to hit a wooden ball into a goal

poly- *prefix* : many : much : MULTI-

poly·es·ter *n* : a synthetic fiber used especially in clothing

poly·gon *n* : a flat geometric figure having three or more straight sides

poly·mer *n* : a chemical compound that is made of small molecules that are arranged in a simple repeating structure to form a larger molecule

pol·yp *n* : a small sea animal (as a coral) having a tubelike body closed and attached to something (as a rock) at one end and opening at the other with a mouth surrounded by tentacles

pome·gran·ate *n* : a reddish fruit that has a thick leathery skin and many seeds in a pulp of tart flavor and that grows on a tropical Asian tree

pom·mel *n* : a rounded knob on the handle of a sword or at the front of a saddle

pomp *n* : a show of wealth and splendor

pom–pom *n* **1** : a small fluffy ball used as decoration especially on clothing **2** : a usually brightly colored fluffy ball waved by cheerleaders

pomp·ous *adj* : having or showing an atti-

tude of someone who thinks he or she is better than other people — **pomp·ous·ly** *adv*

pon·cho *n, pl* **ponchos** : a garment that is like a blanket with a hole in the middle for the head

pond *n* : a body of water usually smaller than a lake

pon·der *vb* **pon·dered; pon·der·ing** : to think over carefully

pon·der·ous *adj* **1** : very heavy **2** : slow or clumsy because of weight and size **3** : unpleasantly dull — **pon·der·ous·ly** *adv*

pon·toon *n* : a large hollow container filled with air and used to make something (as a boat, plane, or bridge) float

po·ny *n, pl* **ponies** : a small horse

pony express *n, often cap P & E* : a rapid postal system that operated across the western United States in 1860–61 by changing horses and riders along the way

po·ny·tail *n* : long hair that is pulled together and banded usually at the back of the head

poo·dle *n* : a small or medium-sized dog with a thick curly coat of solid color

¹pool *n* **1** : a small deep body of usually fresh water **2** : something like a pool (as in shape or depth) **3** : a small body of standing liquid : PUDDLE **4** : SWIMMING POOL

²pool *n* **1** : a game of billiards played on a table with six pockets **2** : people, money, or things come together or put together for some purpose

³pool *vb* **pooled; pool·ing** : to contribute to a common fund or effort

pooped *adj* : very tired

poor *adj* **poor·er; poor·est** **1** : having little money or few possessions **2** : less than enough **3** : worthy of pity **4** : low in quality or condition : not satisfactory — **poor·ly** *adv*

¹pop *vb* **popped; pop·ping** **1** : to burst or cause to burst with a short loud sound **2** : to cause to open suddenly **3** : to go, come, or appear suddenly or unexpectedly **4** : to put into or onto quickly or suddenly **5** : to stick out **6** : to shoot with a gun

²pop *n* **1** : a short loud sound **2** : SODA POP

pop·corn *n* **1** : corn whose kernels burst open when exposed to high heat to form white or yellowish puffy pieces **2** : the kernels after popping

pope *n, often cap* : the head of the Roman Catholic Church

pop·lar *n* : a tree that has rough bark and a white substance resembling cotton around its seeds

pop·py *n, pl* **pop·pies** : a plant with a hairy stem and showy usually red, yellow, or white flowers

pop·u·lace *n* **1** : the common people **2** : the

people who live in a country or area : POPU-
LATION

pop·u·lar *adj* **1** : of or relating to most of the
people in a country or area **2** : enjoyed or
approved by many people **3** : frequently encountered or widely accepted — **pop·u·lar-
ly** *adv*

pop·u·lar·i·ty *n* : the quality or state of being
liked, enjoyed, accepted, or practiced by a
large number of people

pop·u·late *vb* **pop·u·lat·ed; pop·u·lat·ing** : to
fill or provide with people, animals, or
things

pop·u·la·tion *n* **1** : the whole number of people living in a country, city, or area **2** : a
group of people or animals living in a certain place

pop·u·lous *adj* : having a large population

por·ce·lain *n* : a hard white product of baked
clay used especially for dishes, tile, and decorative objects

porch *n* : a covered entrance to a building
usually with a separate roof

por·cu·pine *n* : a gnawing slow-moving animal that is a large rodent and has stiff sharp
quills among its hairs

¹**pore** *vb* **pored; por·ing** : to read with great
attention : STUDY

²**pore** *n* : a tiny opening (as in the skin or in
the soil)

pork *n* : the meat of a pig used for food

po·rous *adj* **1** : full of small holes **2** : capable of absorbing liquids

por·poise *n* **1** : a small whale with teeth that
resembles a dolphin but has a blunt rounded
snout : DOLPHIN 1

por·ridge *n* : a soft food made by boiling
partly ground grain or a vegetable (as peas)
in water or milk until it thickens

¹**port** *n* **1** : a town or city with a harbor where
ships load or unload cargo **2** : a place (as a
harbor) where ships can find shelter from a
storm

²**port** *n* **1** : an opening (as in machinery) for
gas, steam, or water to go in or out **2** : PORT-
HOLE

³**port** *n* : the left side of a ship or airplane
looking forward

por·ta·ble *adj* : easy or possible to carry or
move about

por·tal *n* : a large or fancy door or gate

port·cul·lis *n* : a heavy iron gate that can be
lowered to prevent entrance (as to a castle)

por·tend *vb* **por·tend·ed; por·tend·ing** : to
give a sign or warning of beforehand

por·tent *n* : a sign or warning of something
usually bad that is going to happen : OMEN

por·ten·tous *adj* : giving a sign or warning of
something usually bad that is going to happen

por·ter *n* **1** : a person whose job is to carry
baggage (as at a hotel) **2** : a person whose
job is helping passengers on a train

port·fo·lio *n, pl* **port·fo·li·os 1** : a flat case for
carrying papers or drawings **2** : a collection
of art (as paintings) presented together in a
folder

port·hole *n* : a small window in the side of a
ship or airplane

por·ti·co *n, pl* **por·ti·coes** *or* **por·ti·cos** : a
row of columns supporting a roof at the en-
trance of a building

¹**por·tion** *n* **1** : a part or share of a whole **2**
: SERVING

²**portion** *vb* **por·tioned; por·tion·ing** : to divide into parts : DISTRIBUTE

port·ly *adj* **port·li·er; port·li·est** : having a
round and heavy body : somewhat fat

por·trait *n* : a picture of a person usually
showing the face

por·tray *vb* **por·trayed; por·tray·ing 1** : to
make a portrait of **2** : to describe in words
or words and images **3** : to play the role of

por·tray·al *n* : the act or result of showing in
a portrait or describing in words or images

¹**Por·tu·guese** *adj* : of or relating to Portugal,
its people, or the Portuguese language

²**Portuguese** *n, pl* **Portuguese 1** : a person
born or living in Portugal **2** : the language
of Portugal and Brazil

¹**pose** *vb* **posed; pos·ing 1** : to hold or
cause to hold a special position of the body
2 : to be or create **3** : to ask (a question) **4**
: to pretend to be someone or something else

²**pose** *n* **1** : a position of the body held for a
special purpose **2** : a pretended attitude

¹**po·si·tion** *n* **1** : the way in which something
or someone is placed or arranged **2** : a way
of looking at or considering things **3** : the
place where a person or thing is or should be
4 : the situation that someone or something
is in **5** : the rank or role a person has in an
organization or in society **6** : JOB 1

²**position** *vb* **po·si·tioned; po·si·tion·ing** : to
put in a particular place or arrangement

¹**pos·i·tive** *adj* **1** : fully confident : CERTAIN
2 : having a real or beneficial effect or result
3 : beyond doubt : UNQUESTIONABLE **4**
: showing acceptance or approval **5** : thinking of good qualities or possibilities : OPTI-
MISTIC **6** : being greater than zero and often
shown by a plus sign **7** : being or relating to
electricity of a kind that is produced in a
glass rod rubbed with silk **8** : having more
protons than electrons **9** : being the part
from which the electric current flows to the
external circuit **10** : showing the presence
of what is looked for or suspected to be present **11** : relating to or having the form of an

adjective or adverb that shows no degree of comparison — **pos·i·tive·ly** *adv*

²**positive** *n* **1** : a good or useful feature or quality **2** : the degree or a form of an adjective or adverb that shows no comparison

poss. *abbr* possessive

pos·se *n* : a group of people gathered together to make a search and especially in the past to search for a criminal

pos·sess *vb* **pos·sessed; pos·sess·ing 1** : to have and hold as property : OWN **2** : to have as a characteristic or quality **3** : to enter into and control firmly — **pos·ses·sor** *n*

pos·ses·sion *n* **1** : the act or state of possessing or holding as property **2** : something that is held by someone as property

¹**pos·ses·sive** *adj* **1** : being or belonging to the case of a noun or pronoun that shows possession **2** : showing the desire to possess or control : unwilling to share

²**possessive** *n* : a word or form of a word that shows possession

pos·si·bil·i·ty *n, pl* **pos·si·bil·i·ties 1** : a chance that something may or may not happen or exist : the state or fact of being possible **2** : something that may happen

pos·si·ble *adj* **1** : able to be done **2** : able to happen or exist **3** : able or suited to be or to become

pos·si·bly *adv* **1** : by any possibility **2** : by nothing more than chance : PERHAPS

pos·sum *n* : OPOSSUM

¹**post** *n* : a piece of material (as metal or wood) placed firmly in an upright position and used especially as a support or marker

²**post** *vb* **post·ed; post·ing 1** : to fasten (as a notice or sign) to a suitable place (as a wall or bulletin board) **2** : to make known publicly as if by putting up a notice **3** : to forbid persons from entering or using by putting up warning notices

³**post** *vb* **post·ed; post·ing 1** : to ride or travel quickly **2** : to send by mail **3** : to make aware of recent news about something

⁴**post** *n* **1** : the place where a soldier or guard is stationed **2** : a place where a body of troops is stationed **3** : a place or office to which a person is appointed **4** : TRADING POST

⁵**post** *vb* **post·ed; post·ing** : to station in a given place

post- *prefix* : after : later : following : behind

post·age *n* : a fee for sending a letter or package by mail

post·al *adj* : relating to the post office or the sending and delivery of mail

postal card *n* **1** : a blank card with a postage stamp printed on it **2** : POSTCARD 1

postal service *n* : a government department in charge of handling the mail

post·card *n* **1** : a card on which a message may be sent by mail without an envelope and that often has a picture on one side **2** : POSTAL CARD 1

post·er *n* : a usually large sheet with writing or pictures on it that is displayed as a notice, advertisement, or for decoration

pos·ter·i·ty *n* : all future generations

post·man *n, pl* **post·men** : LETTER CARRIER

post·mark *n* : a mark put on a piece of mail especially for canceling the postage stamp

post·mas·ter *n* : a person in charge of a post office

post·mis·tress *n* : a woman in charge of a post office

post office *n* **1** : POSTAL SERVICE **2** : a place where mail is received, handled, and sent out

post·paid *adv* : with postage paid by the sender

post·pone *vb* **post·poned; post·pon·ing** : to put off until a later time — **post·pone·ment** *n*

post·script *n* : a note added at the end of a letter, article, or book

pos·ture *n* : the way in which the body is positioned when sitting or standing : the general way of holding the body

po·sy *n, pl* **posies 1** : a small bunch of flowers **2** : ¹FLOWER 1

¹**pot** *n* **1** : a deep usually rounded container **2** : the amount a pot will hold

²**pot** *vb* **pot·ted; pot·ting** : to put or pack in a pot

pot·ash *n* : potassium or a compound of potassium

po·tas·si·um *n* : a silvery soft light metallic chemical element found especially in minerals

po·ta·to *n, pl* **po·ta·toes** : the thick edible usually rounded underground tuber of a widely grown South American plant that is eaten as a vegetable

potato chip *n* : a thin slice of potato fried crisp

po·tent *adj* **1** : very effective : STRONG **2** : having power or authority

¹**po·ten·tial** *adj* : existing as a possibility : capable of becoming real — **po·ten·tial·ly** *adv*

²**potential** *n* **1** : the chance or possibility that something will develop and become real **2** : an ability or quality that can lead to success or excellence : PROMISE

pot·hole *n* : a deep round hole (as in a road)

po·tion *n* : a drink that is meant to have a special or magical effect on someone

pot·luck *n* : a meal to which people bring food to share

pot·ter *n* : a person who makes pottery

pot·tery *n, pl* **pot·ter·ies** **1** : the art or craft of making objects (as dishes and vases) out of clay **2** : objects made from clay that is shaped while moist and hardened by heat

pouch *n* **1** : a small bag that can be closed (as with a string) **2** : a bag for carrying goods or valuables **3** : a pocket of folded skin especially for carrying the young (as on the abdomen of a kangaroo) or for carrying food (as in the cheek of a hamster) **4** : a structure of the body in the form of a bag

poul·tice *n* : a soft and heated preparation usually containing medicine that is spread on cloth and placed on the skin to heal a sore or relieve pain

poul·try *n* : birds (as chickens, turkeys, ducks, and geese) raised for their meat or eggs

pounce *vb* **pounced; pounc·ing** **1** : to suddenly jump toward and seize something with or as if with claws **2** : to act, approach, or attack suddenly or without hesitation

¹pound *n* **1** : a measure of weight equal to sixteen ounces (about .45 kilogram) **2** : any of several units of money (as of the United Kingdom or Egypt)

²pound *n* : a place where stray animals are kept

³pound *vb* **pound·ed; pound·ing** **1** : to crush or break into very small pieces by beating **2** : to hit with force again and again **3** : to move with heavy and loud steps **4** : ¹THROB 1

pour *vb* **poured; pour·ing** **1** : to flow or cause to flow in or as if in a stream **2** : to rain hard **3** : to move or come continuously

¹pout *vb* **pout·ed; pout·ing** **1** : to show displeasure by pushing out the lips **2** : ¹SULK

²pout *n* : a facial expression that shows displeasure and is made by pushing out the lips

pov·er·ty *n* : the condition of being poor : lack of money or possessions

¹pow·der *vb* **pow·dered; pow·der·ing** **1** : to sprinkle or cover with or as if with fine particles of something **2** : to reduce or change to powder

²powder *n* **1** : a dry substance made up of fine particles **2** : something (as a food, medicine, or cosmetic) made in or changed to the form of a powder **3** : GUNPOWDER

powder horn *n* : a cow or ox horn made into a container for carrying gunpowder

pow·dery *adj* **1** : made of or like powder **2** : easily crumbled **3** : covered or sprinkled with or as if with powder

¹pow·er *n* **1** : possession of control, authority, or influence over others **2** : a nation that has influence among other nations **3** : the ability to act or produce an effect **4** : the right to do something **5** : physical might : STRENGTH **6** : the number of times as shown by an exponent that a number is used as a factor to obtain a product **7** : force or energy used to do work **8** : the rate of speed at which work is done **9** : the number of times an optical instrument (as a microscope) magnifies the object viewed

²power *vb* **pow·ered; pow·er·ing** : to supply with a form of energy

pow·er·ful *adj* : full of or having power, strength, or influence — **pow·er·ful·ly** *adv*

pow·er·house *n* **1** : POWER PLANT **2** : a person or thing having unusual strength or energy

pow·er·less *adj* : without power, strength, authority, or influence

power plant *n* : a building in which electric power is generated

pow·wow *n* **1** : an American Indian ceremony or social gathering **2** : a meeting for discussion

pp. *abbr* pages

PQ *abbr* Province of Quebec

pr. *abbr* pair

PR *abbr* Puerto Rico

prac·ti·ca·ble *adj* : possible to do or put into practice

prac·ti·cal *adj* **1** : of or relating to real action rather than ideas or thought **2** : capable of being put to use : reasonable to do or use **3** : tending to act according to reason and logic

practical joke *n* : a joke involving an act rather than words : a trick played on someone — **practical joker** *n*

prac·ti·cal·ly *adv* **1** : ALMOST **2** : in a way that is reasonable or logical

¹prac·tice *vb* **prac·ticed; prac·tic·ing** **1** : to do or work at often so as to learn well or improve **2** : to do or perform often or usually **3** : to engage in or work at as a profession

²practice *n* **1** : the act of doing something again and again in order to learn or improve **2** : a regular event at which something is done again and again to increase skill **3** : actual performance : USE **4** : a usual way of doing something **5** : continuous work in a profession

prai·rie *n* : a large area of level or rolling grassland

prairie chicken *n* : a grouse of the prairies of the central United States

prairie dog *n* : a burrowing animal of the prairies of the central and western United States that is related to the squirrel and lives in large colonies

prairie schooner *n* : a long covered wagon used by pioneers to cross the prairies

¹**praise** *vb* **praised; prais·ing** **1** : to express approval of **2** : to glorify (God or a saint)

²**praise** *n* **1** : an expression of approval **2** : ¹WORSHIP 1

praise·wor·thy *adj* : deserving praise

prance *vb* **pranced; pranc·ing** **1** : to move by taking high steps **2** : to walk or move in a lively and proud way

prank *n* : a mischievous act : PRACTICAL JOKE

¹**prat·tle** *vb* **prat·tled; prat·tling** : to talk a great deal about unimportant or uninteresting things

²**prattle** *n* : uninteresting or unimportant talk

pray *vb* **prayed; pray·ing** **1** : to speak to God especially to give thanks or ask for something **2** : to hope or wish very much for **3** : to ask earnestly : BEG

prayer *n* **1** : words spoken to God **2** : the act of praying to God **3** : a strong hope or wish **4** : a set form of words used in praying **5** : a religious service that is mostly prayers

praying mantis *n* : a large usually green insect that feeds on other insects which are held in the raised front legs

pre- *prefix* **1** : earlier than : before **2** : beforehand **3** : in front of : front

preach *vb* **preached; preach·ing** **1** : to give a sermon **2** : to urge publicly

preach·er *n* **1** : a person who gives sermons **2** : ¹MINISTER 1

pre·am·ble *n* : an introduction (as to a law) that often gives the reasons for what follows

pre·car·i·ous *adj* : not safe, strong, or steady — **pre·car·i·ous·ly** *adv*

pre·cau·tion *n* : something done beforehand to prevent harm or trouble or bring about good results

pre·cede *vb* **pre·ced·ed; pre·ced·ing** : to be or go before in importance, position, or time

pre·ce·dent *n* : something that can be used as a rule or example to be followed in the future

pre·ced·ing *adj* : existing or happening before in time or place : PREVIOUS

pre·cinct *n* **1** : any of the sections into which a town or city is divided for a particular purpose (as voting or police protection) **2** : a surrounding or enclosed area

pre·cious *adj* **1** : very valuable **2** : greatly loved or valued

prec·i·pice *n* : a very steep side of a mountain or cliff

pre·cip·i·tate *vb* **pre·cip·i·tat·ed; pre·cip·i·tat·ing** **1** : to cause to happen suddenly or unexpectedly **2** : to change from a vapor to a liquid or solid and fall as rain or snow **3** : to separate from a solution

pre·cip·i·ta·tion *n* : water that falls to the earth as hail, mist, rain, sleet, or snow

pre·cise *adj* **1** : exactly stated or explained **2** : very exact : ACCURATE **3** : being exactly the one mentioned or indicated and no other — **pre·cise·ly** *adv*

pre·ci·sion *n* : the quality or state of being precise or exact : ACCURACY

pre·co·cious *adj* : showing qualities or abilities of an adult at an unusually early age — **pre·co·cious·ly** *adv*

pred·a·tor *n* : an animal that lives mostly by killing and eating other animals

pred·a·to·ry *adj* : living by killing and eating other animals

pre·de·ces·sor *n* : a person who held a job or position before someone else

pre·dic·a·ment *n* : a bad situation

¹**pred·i·cate** *n* : the part of a sentence or clause that tells what is said about the subject

²**predicate** *adj* : completing the meaning of a linking verb

pre·dict *vb* **pre·dict·ed; pre·dict·ing** : to say that (something) will or might happen in the future

pre·dic·tion *n* **1** : an act of saying what will or might happen in the future **2** : a statement about what will or might happen in the future

pre·dom·i·nance *n* : the quality or state of being greater than others in number, frequency, strength, influence, or authority

pre·dom·i·nant *adj* : greater than others in number, frequency, strength, influence, or authority

pre·dom·i·nate *vb* **pre·dom·i·nat·ed; pre·dom·i·nat·ing** : to be greater than others in number, frequency, strength, influence, or authority

preen *vb* **preened; preen·ing** **1** : to smooth and clean with the bill **2** : to make a person's own appearance neat and tidy

pre·fab·ri·cat·ed *adj* : made of parts that are made at a factory and can be put together later

pref·ace *n* : a section at the beginning that introduces a book or a speech

pre·fer *vb* **pre·ferred; pre·fer·ring** : to like better than another or others

pref·er·a·ble *adj* : better or more desireable — **pref·er·a·bly** *adv*

pref·er·ence *n* **1** : a choosing of or special liking for one person or thing rather than another or others **2** : the power or chance to choose : CHOICE **3** : a person or thing that is liked or wanted more than another

pre·fix *n* : a letter or group of letters that comes at the beginning of a word and has its own meaning

preg·nan·cy *n, pl* **preg·nan·cies** : the state of being pregnant

preg·nant *adj* **1** : carrying one or more unborn offspring in the body **2** : full of meaning

pre·hen·sile *adj* : capable of grasping something by wrapping around it

pre·his·tor·ic *adj* : relating to or existing in the time before written history began

¹prej·u·dice *n* **1** : a liking or dislike for one rather than another especially without good reason **2** : a feeling of unfair dislike directed against an individual or a group because of some characteristic (as race or religion) **3** : injury or damage to a person's rights

²prejudice *vb* **prej·u·diced; prej·u·dic·ing 1** : to cause to have an unfair dislike of **2** : to cause damage to (as a person's rights)

prej·u·diced *adj* : having or showing an unfair dislike of a person or group because of some characteristic (as race or religion)

¹pre·lim·i·nary *n, pl* **pre·lim·i·nar·ies** : something that comes before the main or final part

²preliminary *adj* : coming before the main or full part

pre·lude *n* **1** : something that comes before and prepares for the main or more important parts **2** : a short piece of music played at the beginning of something (as an opera or church service)

pre·ma·ture *adj* : happening, coming, or done before the usual or proper time : too early — **pre·ma·ture·ly** *adv*

pre·med·i·tate *vb* **pre·med·i·tat·ed; pre·med·i·tat·ing** : to think about and plan beforehand

¹pre·mier *adj* : first in importance, excellence, or rank

²premier *n* : PRIME MINISTER

¹pre·miere *n* : a first showing or performance

²premiere *vb* **pre·miered; pre·mier·ing** : to have a first showing or performance

prem·ise *n* **1** : a statement or idea taken to be true and on which an argument or reasoning may be based **2 premises** *pl* : a piece of land with the buildings on it

pre·mi·um *n* **1** : a reward for a special act **2** : an amount above the regular or stated price **3** : the amount paid for a contract of insurance **4** : a high or extra value

pre·mo·lar *n* : a double-pointed tooth that comes between the canines and molars

pre·mo·ni·tion *n* : a feeling that something is going to happen

pre·oc·cu·pied *adj* : thinking about or worrying about one thing a great deal

prep *abbr* preposition

prep·a·ra·tion *n* **1** : the act or process of making or getting ready beforehand **2** : something done to make or get ready **3** : something made for a special purpose

pre·par·a·to·ry *adj* : preparing or serving to prepare for something

pre·pare *vb* **pre·pared; pre·par·ing 1** : to make or get ready beforehand **2** : to put together the elements of

pre·pay *vb* **pre·paid** ; **pre·pay·ing** : to pay or pay for beforehand

prep·o·si·tion *n* : a word or group of words that combines with a noun or pronoun to form a phrase that usually acts as an adverb, adjective, or noun

prep·o·si·tion·al *adj* : relating to or containing a preposition

pre·pos·ter·ous *adj* : making little or no sense : FOOLISH

pre·req·ui·site *n* : something that is needed beforehand : REQUIREMENT

pres. *abbr* **1** present **2** president

¹pre·school *adj* : relating to the time in a child's life that comes before attendance at school

²preschool *n* : a school for children usually under five years old who are too young for kindergarten

pre·school·er *n* : a child of preschool age

pre·scribe *vb* **pre·scribed; pre·scrib·ing 1** : to order or direct the use of as a remedy **2** : to lay down as a rule of action : ORDER

pre·scrip·tion *n* **1** : a written direction or order for the preparing and use of a medicine **2** : a medicine that is ordered by a doctor as a remedy

pres·ence *n* **1** : the fact or condition of being in a certain place **2** : position close to a person **3** : a person's appearance or manner

presence of mind *n* : ability to think clearly and act quickly in an emergency

¹pres·ent *n* : something given : GIFT

²pres·ent *vb* **pre·sent·ed; pre·sent·ing 1** : to give with ceremony **2** : to make a gift to **3** : to bring before the public **4** : to introduce one person to another **5** : to appear in a particular place **6** : to offer to view : SHOW, DISPLAY **7** : to come into or cause to come into being

³pres·ent *adj* **1** : not past or future : now going on **2** : being at a certain place and not elsewhere **3** : pointing out or relating to time that is not past or future

⁴pres·ent *n* : the time right now

pre·sent·able *adj* : having a satisfactory or pleasing appearance

pre·sen·ta·tion *n* **1** : an act of showing, describing, or explaining something to a group of people **2** : an act of giving a gift or award **3** : something given

pres·ent·ly *adv* **1** : before long : SOON **2** : at the present time : NOW

present participle *n* : the form of a verb that

in English is formed with the suffix *-ing* and that expresses present action

present tense *n* : a verb tense that expresses action or state in the present time and is used of what is true at the time of speaking or is always true

pres·er·va·tion *n* : the effort of keeping from injury, loss, or decay

pre·ser·va·tive *n* : a substance added to food to keep it from spoiling

¹pre·serve *vb* **pre·served; pre·serv·ing 1** : to keep or save from injury, loss, or ruin : PROTECT **2** : to prepare (as by canning or pickling) fruits or vegetables to be kept for future use **3** : MAINTAIN 2, CONTINUE — **pre·serv·er** *n*

²preserve *n* **1** : fruit cooked in sugar or made into jam or jelly — often used in pl. **2** : an area where land and animals are protected

pre·side *vb* **pre·sid·ed; pre·sid·ing** : to be in charge

pres·i·den·cy *n, pl* **pres·i·den·cies 1** : the office of president **2** : the term during which a president holds office

pres·i·dent *n* **1** : the head of the government and chief executive officer of a modern republic **2** : the chief officer of a company, organization, or society

pres·i·den·tial *adj* : of or relating to a president or the presidency

¹press *vb* **pressed; press·ing 1** : to push steadily against **2** : to ask or urge strongly **3** : to move forward forcefully **4** : to squeeze so as to force out the juice or contents **5** : to flatten out or smooth by bearing down upon especially by ironing

²press *n* **1** : ²CROWD 1, THRONG **2** : a machine that uses pressure to shape, flatten, squeeze, or stamp **3** : the act of pressing : PRESSURE **4** : a printing or publishing business **5** : the newspapers and magazines of a country **6** : news reporters and broadcasters **7** : PRINTING PRESS **8** : CLOSET 2

press·ing *adj* : needing immediate attention

pres·sure *n* **1** : the action of pushing steadily against **2** : a force or influence that cannot be avoided **3** : the force with which one body presses against another **4** : the need to get things done

pres·tige *n* : importance or respect gained through success or excellence

pres·to *adv or adj* : suddenly as if by magic

pre·sum·ably *adv* : it seems likely : PROBABLY

pre·sume *vb* **pre·sumed; pre·sum·ing 1** : to undertake without permission or good reason : DARE **2** : to suppose to be true without proof

pre·sump·tion *n* **1** : behavior or attitude

going beyond what is proper **2** : a strong reason for believing something to be so **3** : something believed to be so but not proved

pre·sump·tu·ous *adj* : going beyond what is proper — **pre·sump·tu·ous·ly** *adv* — **pre·sump·tu·ous·ness** *n*

pre·tend *vb* **pre·tend·ed; pre·tend·ing 1** : to make believe **2** : to put forward as true something that is not true — **pre·tend·er** *n*

pre·tense *or* **pre·tence** *n* **1** : an act or appearance that looks real but is false **2** : an effort to reach a certain condition or quality

pre·ten·tious *adj* : trying to appear better or more important than is really the case — **pre·ten·tious·ly** *adv* — **pre·ten·tious·ness** *n*

¹pret·ty *adj* **pret·ti·er; pret·ti·est** : pleasing to the eye or ear especially because of being graceful or delicate — **pret·ti·ly** *adv* — **pret·ti·ness** *n*

²pretty *adv* : in some degree : FAIRLY

pret·zel *n* : a brown cracker that is salted and is often shaped like a loose knot

pre·vail *vb* **pre·vailed; pre·vail·ing 1** : to succeed in convincing **2** : to be or become usual, common, or widespread **3** : to win against opposition

prev·a·lence *n* : the state of happening, being accepted, or being practiced often or over a wide area

prev·a·lent *adj* : accepted, practiced, or happening often or over a wide area

pre·vent *vb* **pre·vent·ed; pre·vent·ing 1** : to keep from happening **2** : to hold or keep back — **pre·vent·able** *adj*

pre·ven·tion *n* : the act or practice of keeping something from happening

pre·ven·tive *adj* : used for keeping something from happening

pre·view *n* : an instance of showing something (as a movie) before others get to see it

pre·vi·ous *adj* : going before in time or order : PRECEDING — **pre·vi·ous·ly** *adv*

¹prey *n* **1** : an animal that is hunted or killed by another animal for food **2** : a person that is helpless and unable to escape attack : VICTIM

²prey *vb* **preyed; prey·ing 1** : to hunt and kill for food **2** : to have a harmful effect

¹price *n* **1** : the quantity of one thing given or asked for something else : the amount of money paid or to be paid **2** : the cost at which something is gotten or done **3** : a reward for the apprehension of a criminal

²price *vb* **priced; pric·ing 1** : to determine the amount something costs **2** : to find out how much something costs

price·less *adj* : more valuable than any amount of money : not to be bought for any amount of money

¹prick *n* **1** : an act of piercing with a small sharp point **2** : a feeling of pain that accompanies a piercing of the skin with a sharp point **3** : a sudden strong feeling

²prick *vb* **pricked; prick·ing 1** : to point upward **2** : to pierce slightly with a sharp point **3** : to have or to cause a feeling of or as if of being pierced with a sharp point

prick·er *n* : ¹PRICKLE 1, THORN

¹prick·le *n* **1** : a small sharp point (as a thorn) **2** : a slight stinging pain

²prickle *vb* **prick·led; prick·ling** : ²PRICK 3

prick·ly *adj* **prick·li·er; prick·li·est 1** : having small sharp points **2** : having or causing slight stinging pain

prickly pear *n* : a cactus with flat branching spiny stems and a sweet fruit shaped like a pear

¹pride *n* **1** : a reasonable and justifiable feeling of being worthwhile : SELF-RESPECT **2** : a feeling of being better than others **3** : a sense of pleasure that comes from some act or possession **4** : someone or something that makes someone proud

²pride *vb* **prid·ed; prid·ing** : to feel self-esteem

priest *n* : a person who has the authority to lead or perform religious ceremonies

priest·ess *n* : a woman who has the authority to lead or perform religious ceremonies

prim *adj* **prim·mer; prim·mest** : very formal and proper — **prim·ly** *adv*

pri·mar·i·ly *adv* : more than anything else : MAINLY

¹pri·ma·ry *adj* **1** : first in time or development **2** : most important : MAIN **3** : not made or coming from something else : BASIC **4** : relating to or being the heaviest of three levels of stress in pronunciation

²primary *n, pl* **pri·ma·ries** : an election in which members of a political party nominate candidates for office

primary color *n* : one of the colors red, yellow, or blue which can be mixed together to make other colors

pri·mate *n* : any of a group of mammals that includes humans together with the apes and monkeys and a few related forms

¹prime *n* : the period in life when a person is best in health, looks, or strength

²prime *adj* : first in importance, rank, or quality

³prime *vb* **primed; prim·ing 1** : to put a first color or coating on (an unpainted surface) **2** : to put into working order by filling **3** : to make (someone or something) ready

prime minister *n* : the chief officer of the government in some countries

prime number *n* : a number (as 2, 3, or 5) that results in a whole number from division only when it is divided by itself or by 1

prim·er *n* **1** : a small book for teaching children to read **2** : a book or other writing that introduces a subject

pri·me·val *adj* : belonging to the earliest time : PRIMITIVE

prim·i·tive *adj* **1** : of or belonging to very early times **2** : of or belonging to an early stage of development

primp *vb* **primped; primp·ing** : to dress or arrange in a careful or fussy manner

prim·rose *n* : a small plant with large leaves and showy often yellow or pink flowers

prince *n* **1** : MONARCH 1 **2** : the son of a monarch **3** : a nobleman of very high or the highest rank

prince·ly *adj* **1** : suitable for a prince **2** : very large or impressive

prin·cess *n* : a daughter or granddaughter of a monarch : a female member of a royal family

¹prin·ci·pal *adj* : highest in rank or importance : CHIEF — **prin·ci·pal·ly** *adv*

²principal *n* **1** : the head of a school **2** : a leading or most important person or thing **3** : a sum of money that is placed to earn interest, is owed as a debt, or is used as a fund

prin·ci·pal·i·ty *n, pl* **prin·ci·pal·i·ties** : a small territory that is ruled by a prince

principal parts *n pl* : the infinitive, the past tense, and the past and present participles of an English verb

prin·ci·ple *n* **1** : a general or basic truth on which other truths or theories can be based **2** : a rule of conduct based on beliefs of what is right and wrong **3** : a law or fact of nature which makes possible the working of a machine or device

¹print *n* **1** : a mark made on the surface of something **2** : FOOTPRINT **3** : printed matter **4** : printed letters **5** : a picture, copy, or design taken from an engraving or photographic negative **6** : cloth upon which a design is stamped

²print *vb* **print·ed; print·ing 1** : to write in separate letters **2** : PUBLISH 1 **3** : to make a copy of by pressing paper against an inked surface (as type or an engraving) **4** : to make a picture from a photographic negative — **print out** : to produce a paper copy of from a computer

print·er *n* **1** : a person or company whose business is making copies of text and images **2** : a machine that produces text and images on paper

print·ing *n* **1** : the art, practice, or business of making copies of text and images **2** : writing that uses separate letters

printing press *n* : a machine that makes copies of text and images

print·out *n* : a printed copy produced by a computer

¹pri·or *n* : a monk who is head of a religious house

²prior *adj* **1** : being or happening before something else **2** : being more important than something else — **prior to** : ²BEFORE 2

pri·or·ess *n, pl* **pri·or·ess·es** : a nun who is head of a religious house

pri·or·i·ty *n, pl* **pri·or·i·ties** : a condition of being more important than other things

pri·o·ry *n, pl* **pri·o·ries** : a religious house under the leadership of a prior or prioress

prism *n* : a transparent object that usually has three sides and bends light so that it breaks up into rainbow colors

pris·on *n* : a place where criminals are locked up

pris·on·er *n* : a person who has been captured or locked up

pri·va·cy *n* **1** : the state of being out of the sight and hearing of other people **2** : freedom from intrusion

¹pri·vate *adj* **1** : having to do with or for the use of a single person or group : not public **2** : not holding any public office **3** : ¹SECRET 1 — **pri·vate·ly** *adv*

²private *n* : an enlisted person of the lowest rank in the marine corps or of either of the two lowest ranks in the army

pri·va·teer *n* **1** : a privately owned armed ship permitted by its government to make war on ships of an enemy country **2** : a sailor on a privateer

private first class *n* : an enlisted person in the army or marine corps ranking above a private

priv·et *n* : a shrub with small white flowers that is often used for hedges

priv·i·lege *n* **1** : a right or liberty granted as a favor or benefit especially to some and not others **2** : an opportunity that is special and pleasant

priv·i·leged *adj* : having more things and a better chance in life than most people

privy *n, pl* **priv·ies** : a small building without plumbing used as a toilet

¹prize *n* **1** : something won or to be won in a contest **2** : something unusually valuable or eagerly sought

²prize *adj* **1** : outstanding of its kind **2** : awarded as a prize **3** : awarded a prize

³prize *vb* **prized; priz·ing** : to value highly : TREASURE

⁴prize *n* : something taken (as in war) by force especially at sea

prize·fight·er *n* : a professional boxer

¹pro *n, pl* **pros** : an argument or evidence in favor of something

²pro *adv* : in favor of something

³pro *n or adj* : PROFESSIONAL

pro- *prefix* : approving : in favor of

prob·a·bil·i·ty *n, pl* **prob·a·bil·i·ties** **1** : the chance of happening **2** : something likely **3** : a measure of how likely a given event is

prob·a·ble *adj* : reasonably sure but not certain of happening or being true : LIKELY

prob·a·bly *adv* : very likely

pro·ba·tion *n* **1** : the condition of being closely watched and evaluated for a period of time or the period of time during which this happens **2** : the early release of a prisoner on certain conditions

¹probe *n* **1** : a slender instrument for examining a cavity (as a deep wound) **2** : a careful investigation

²probe *vb* **probed; prob·ing** **1** : to examine with or as if with an instrument **2** : to investigate thoroughly

prob·lem *n* **1** : something to be worked out or solved **2** : a person or thing that is hard to understand or deal with

pro·bos·cis *n* : a long flexible hollow body part (as the trunk of an elephant)

pro·ce·dure *n* : an action or series of actions for doing or accomplishing something

pro·ceed *vb* **pro·ceed·ed; pro·ceed·ing** **1** : to go forward or onward : ADVANCE **2** : to begin and continue with an action or process **3** : to go or act by an orderly method **4** : to come from a source

pro·ceed·ings *n pl* : things that are said or done

pro·ceeds *n pl* : money or profit made

¹pro·cess *n* **1** : a series of actions, motions, or operations leading to some result **2** : a series of changes that occur naturally

²process *vb* **pro·cessed; pro·cess·ing** **1** : to change by a special treatment **2** : to take care of according to a routine **3** : to take in and organize for use

pro·ces·sion *n* : a group of individuals moving along in an orderly often ceremonial way

pro·ces·sor *n* **1** : a person or machine that changes something by a special treatment or takes care of something according to a routine **2** : COMPUTER **3** : the part of a computer that operates on data

pro·claim *vb* **pro·claimed; pro·claim·ing** : to announce publicly : DECLARE

proc·la·ma·tion *n* **1** : the act of making something known publicly or officially **2** : an official formal announcement

pro·cras·ti·nate *vb* **pro·cras·ti·nat·ed; pro·cras·ti·nat·ing** : to keep putting off something that should be done

pro·cure *vb* **pro·cured; pro·cur·ing** : OBTAIN

¹**prod** *vb* **prod·ded; prod·ding** **1** : to poke with something **2** : to stir or encourage a person or animal to action

²**prod** *n* **1** : something used for stirring an animal to action **2** : an act of poking **3** : a sharp urging or reminder

¹**prod·i·gal** *adj* : carelessly wasteful

²**prodigal** *n* : somebody who wastes money carelessly

prod·i·gy *n, pl* **prod·i·gies** **1** : an unusually talented child **2** : an amazing event or action : WONDER

¹**pro·duce** *vb* **pro·duced; pro·duc·ing** **1** : to bring forth : YIELD **2** : ¹MANUFACTURE 1 **3** : to bring to view : EXHIBIT **4** : to prepare (as a play) for public presentation — **pro·duc·er** *n*

²**pro·duce** *n* : fresh fruits and vegetables

prod·uct *n* **1** : the number resulting from the multiplication of two or more numbers **2** : something resulting from manufacture, labor, thought, or growth

pro·duc·tion *n* **1** : something prepared for public presentation **2** : the act of manufacturing **3** : the amount brought forth

pro·duc·tive *adj* **1** : having the power to yield in large amounts **2** : producing well

prof. *abbr* professor

¹**pro·fane** *adj* : showing disrespect for God or holy things

²**profane** *vb* **pro·faned; pro·fan·ing** : to treat (something sacred) with great disrespect

pro·fan·i·ty *n, pl* **pro·fan·i·ties** : language that is offensive or disrespectful

pro·fess *vb* **pro·fessed; pro·fess·ing** **1** : to declare openly **2** : PRETEND 2

pro·fes·sion *n* **1** : an occupation (as medicine, law, or teaching) that is not mechanical or agricultural and that requires special education **2** : an act of publicly declaring or claiming **3** : the people working in an occupation

¹**pro·fes·sion·al** *adj* **1** : relating to an occupation : of or as an expert **2** : taking part in an activity (as a sport) in order to make money **3** : participated in by people who are paid to compete **4** : having or showing a quality appropriate in a profession — **pro·fes·sion·al·ly** *adv*

²**professional** *n* **1** : a person who does a job that requires special education or skill **2** : a person who is paid to participate in a sport or activity

pro·fes·sor *n* : a teacher especially of the highest rank at a college or university

prof·fer *vb* **prof·fered; prof·fer·ing** : ¹OFFER 1

pro·fi·cient *adj* : very good at doing something — **pro·fi·cient·ly** *adv*

pro·file *n* **1** : something (as a head or a

mountain) seen or drawn from the side **2** : a level of activity that draws attention

¹**prof·it** *n* **1** : the gain after all the expenses are subtracted from the total amount received **2** : the gain or benefit from something — **prof·it·less** *adj*

²**profit** *vb* **prof·it·ed; prof·it·ing** **1** : to get some good out of something : GAIN **2** : to be of use to (someone)

prof·it·able *adj* : producing a benefit or monetary gain — **prof·it·ably** *adv*

pro·found *adj* **1** : having or showing great knowledge and understanding **2** : very deeply felt — **pro·found·ly** *adv*

pro·fuse *adj* : very plentiful — **pro·fuse·ly** *adv*

pro·fu·sion *n* : a plentiful supply : PLENTY

prog·e·ny *n, pl* **prog·e·nies** : human descendants or animal offspring

¹**pro·gram** *n* **1** : a brief statement or written outline (as of a concert, play, ceremony, or religious service) **2** : PERFORMANCE 2 **3** : a plan of action **4** : a set of step-by-step instructions that tell a computer to do something with data

²**program** *vb* **pro·grammed** ; **pro·gram·ming** : to give (a computer) a set of instructions : provide with a program

pro·gram·mer *n* : a person who creates and tests programs for computers

¹**prog·ress** *n* **1** : the act of moving toward a goal **2** : gradual improvement — **in progress** : happening at the present time

²**pro·gress** *vb* **pro·gressed; pro·gress·ing** **1** : to move forward in place or time : ADVANCE **2** : to move toward a higher, better, or more advanced stage

pro·gres·sion *n* **1** : the act of advancing or moving forward **2** : a continuous and connected series (as of acts, events, or steps)

pro·gres·sive *adj* **1** : of, relating to, or showing advancement **2** : taking place gradually or step-by-step **3** : favoring gradual political change and social improvement by action of the government — **pro·gres·sive·ly** *adv*

pro·hib·it *vb* **pro·hib·it·ed; pro·hib·it·ing** **1** : to forbid by authority **2** : to make impossible

pro·hi·bi·tion *n* **1** : the act of making something illegal or impossible **2** : the forbidding by law of the sale or manufacture of alcoholic liquids for use as beverages

¹**proj·ect** *n* **1** : a plan or scheme to do something **2** : a task or problem in school that requires work over a period of time and is often displayed or presented **3** : a group of houses or apartment buildings built according to a single plan

²**pro·ject** *vb* **pro·ject·ed; pro·ject·ing 1** : to stick out **2** : to cause to fall on a surface **3** : to send or throw forward

pro·jec·tile *n* : something (as a bullet or rocket) thrown or shot especially from a weapon

pro·jec·tion *n* **1** : something that sticks out **2** : the act or process of causing to appear on a surface (as by means of motion pictures or slides)

pro·jec·tor *n* : a machine for producing images on a screen

pro·lif·ic *adj* **1** : very inventive or productive **2** : producing young or fruit in large numbers

pro·long *vb* **pro·longed; pro·long·ing** : to make longer than usual or expected

prom *n* : a usually formal dance given by a high school or college class

prom·e·nade *n* **1** : a walk or ride for pleasure or to be seen **2** : a place for walking

prom·i·nence *n* **1** : the state of being important, famous, or noticeable **2** : something (as a mountain) that is conspicuous

prom·i·nent *adj* **1** : important or well-known **2** : attracting attention (as by size or position) : CONSPICUOUS **3** : sticking out beyond the surface — **prom·i·nent·ly** *adv*

¹**prom·ise** *n* **1** : a statement by a person that he or she will do or not do something **2** : a cause or ground for hope

²**promise** *vb* **prom·ised; prom·is·ing 1** : to state that something will or will not be done **2** : to give reason to expect

prom·is·ing *adj* : likely to turn out well or be good

prom·on·to·ry *n, pl* **prom·on·to·ries** : a high point of land sticking out into the sea

pro·mote *vb* **pro·mot·ed; pro·mot·ing 1** : to move up in position or rank **2** : to help (something) to grow or develop

pro·mo·tion *n* **1** : the act of moving up in position or rank **2** : the act of helping something happen, develop, or increase

¹**prompt** *vb* **prompt·ed; prompt·ing 1** : to lead to do something **2** : to be the cause of **3** : to remind of something forgotten or poorly learned — **prompt·er** *n*

²**prompt** *adj* **prompt·er; prompt·est 1** : quick and ready to act **2** : being on time : PUNCTUAL **3** : done at once : given without delay — **prompt·ly** *adv* — **prompt·ness** *n*

pron *abbr* pronoun

prone *adj* **1** : likely to be or act a certain way **2** : lying with the front of the body facing downward

prong *n* **1** : one of the sharp points of a fork **2** : a slender part that sticks out (as a point of an antler)

prong·horn *n* : an animal that resembles an antelope and lives mostly in the grasslands and deserts of western North America

pro·noun *n* : a word used as a substitute for a noun

pro·nounce *vb* **pro·nounced; pro·nounc·ing 1** : to use the voice to make the sounds of **2** : to say correctly **3** : to state in an official or solemn way

pro·nounced *adj* : very noticeable

pro·nounce·ment *n* : an official or solemn statement

pro·nun·ci·a·tion *n* : the act or way of saying a word or words

¹**proof** *n* **1** : evidence of truth or correctness **2** : a printing (as from type) prepared for study and correction **3** : a test print made from a photographic negative **4** : ¹TEST 2

²**proof** *adj* : able to keep out something that could be harmful — usually used in compounds

proof·read *vb* **proof·read; proof·read·ing** : to read over and fix mistakes in (written or printed matter) — **proof·read·er** *n*

¹**prop** *vb* **propped; prop·ping 1** : to keep from falling or slipping by providing a support under or against **2** : to give help, encouragement, or support to

²**prop** *n* : something that supports

³**prop** *n* : an object used by a performer or actor or used to create a certain effect in a play or movie

pro·pa·gan·da *n* : an organized spreading of often false ideas or the ideas spread in such a way

prop·a·gate *vb* **prop·a·gat·ed; prop·a·gat·ing 1** : to have or cause to have offspring : MULTIPLY **2** : to cause (as an idea or belief) to spread out and affect a greater number or wider area

prop·a·ga·tion *n* : the act or process of causing to multiply or spread out

pro·pel *vb* **pro·pelled; pro·pel·ling** : to push or cause to move usually forward or onward

pro·pel·ler *n* : a device having a hub fitted with blades that is made to turn rapidly by an engine and that causes a ship, power boat, or airplane to move

pro·pen·si·ty *n* : a natural tendency to do or favor something

prop·er *adj* **1** : correct according to social or moral rules **2** : APPROPRIATE, SUITABLE **3** : strictly accurate : CORRECT **4** : referring to one individual only **5** : considered in its true or basic meaning

proper fraction *n* : a fraction in which the numerator is smaller than the denominator

prop·er·ly *adv* **1** : in a fit or suitable way **2** : according to fact

proper noun *n* : a noun that names a particular person, place, or thing

prop·er·ty *n, pl* **prop·er·ties 1 :** something (as land or money) that is owned **2 :** a special quality of a thing

proph·e·cy *n, pl* **proph·e·cies 1 :** something foretold : PREDICTION **2 :** the ability to predict what will happen in the future

proph·e·sy *vb* **proph·e·sied; proph·e·sy·ing** : FORETELL, PREDICT

proph·et *n* **1 :** someone who declares publicly a message that he or she believes has come from God or a god **2 :** a person who predicts the future

pro·phet·ic *adj* **1 :** of or relating to a prophet or prophecy **2 :** serving to foretell

pro·por·tion *n* **1 :** the size, number, or amount of one thing or group of things as compared to that of another thing or group of things **2 :** a balanced or pleasing arrangement **3 :** a statement of the equality of two ratios (as $\frac{4}{2} = \frac{10}{5}$) **4 :** a fair or just share **5 :** size, shape, or extent of something

pro·por·tion·al *adj* **:** having a direct relationship to something in size, number, or amount — **pro·por·tion·al·ly** *adv*

pro·pos·al *n* **1 :** an act of stating or putting forward something for consideration **2 :** something suggested : PLAN **3 :** an offer of marriage

pro·pose *vb* **pro·posed; pro·pos·ing 1 :** to make a suggestion to be thought over and talked about : SUGGEST **2 :** to make plans : INTEND **3 :** to make an offer of marriage **4 :** to suggest (someone) for filling a place or position

prop·o·si·tion *n* **1 :** something suggested for discussion and thought **2 :** a statement to be proved, explained, or discussed

pro·pri·e·tor *n* **:** a person who owns something : OWNER

pro·pri·e·ty *n, pl* **pro·pri·e·ties 1 :** correctness in manners or behavior **2 :** the quality or state of being proper **3** *proprieties pl* **:** the rules of correct behavior

pro·pul·sion *n* **1 :** the act or process of propelling **2 :** the force that moves something forward

pros *pl of* PRO

prose *n* **1 :** the ordinary language that people use in speaking or writing **2 :** writing without the repeating rhythm that is used in poetry

pros·e·cute *vb* **pros·e·cut·ed; pros·e·cut·ing 1 :** to carry on a legal action against an accused person to prove his or her guilt **2 :** to follow up to the end : keep at

pros·e·cu·tion *n* **1 :** the act of carrying on a legal action against a person accused of a crime in court **2 :** the lawyers in a criminal case trying to prove that the accused person is guilty

pros·e·cu·tor *n* **:** a lawyer in a criminal case who tries to prove that the accused person is guilty

¹pros·pect *n* **1 :** something that is waited for or expected : POSSIBILITY **2 :** someone or something that is likely to be successful : a likely candidate **3 :** a wide view

²prospect *vb* **pros·pect·ed; pros·pect·ing** : to explore especially for mineral deposits

pro·spec·tive *adj* **1 :** likely to become **2** : likely to come about

pros·pec·tor *n* **:** a person who explores a region in search of valuable minerals (as metals or oil)

pros·per *vb* **pros·pered; pros·per·ing 1 :** to become successful usually by making money **2 :** ¹FLOURISH 1, THRIVE

pros·per·i·ty *n* **:** the state of being successful usually by making money

pros·per·ous *adj* **1 :** having or showing success or financial good fortune **2 :** strong and healthy in growth

¹pros·trate *adj* **1 :** lying with the face turned toward the ground **2 :** lacking strength or energy

²prostrate *vb* **pros·trat·ed; pros·trat·ing 1** : lie on the ground with the face down **2 :** to bring to a weak and powerless condition

pro·tect *vb* **pro·tect·ed; pro·tect·ing :** keep from being harmed especially by covering or shielding : GUARD

pro·tec·tion *n* **1 :** the act of shielding from harm : the state of being shielded from harm **2 :** a person or thing that shields from harm

pro·tec·tive *adj* **:** giving or meant to keep from harm — **pro·tec·tive·ly** *adv* — **pro·tec·tive·ness** *n*

pro·tec·tor *n* **:** a person or thing that shields from harm or is intended to shield from harm

pro·tein *n* **:** a nutrient found in food (as meat, milk, eggs, and beans) that is made up of many amino acids joined together, is a necessary part of the diet, and is essential for normal cell structure and function

¹pro·test *vb* **pro·test·ed; pro·test·ing 1** : to complain strongly about : object to **2** : to declare positively : ASSERT — **pro·test·er** *n*

²pro·test *n* **1 :** a complaint or objection against an idea, an act, or a way of doing things **2 :** an event in which people gather to show disapproval of something

¹Prot·es·tant *n* **:** a member of one of the Christian churches that separated from the Roman Catholic Church in the 16th century ~

²**Protestant** *adj* : of or relating to Protestants

pro·tist *n* : any member of the kingdom of mostly single-celled organisms (as protozoans and algae) that have a nucleus and sometimes form colonies

pro·ton *n* : a very small particle that exists in the nucleus of every atom and has a positive charge of electricity

pro·to·plasm *n* : the usually colorless and jellylike living part of cells

pro·to·zo·an *n* : a single-celled organism (as an amoeba or paramecium) that is a protist and is capable of movement

pro·tract *vb* **pro·tract·ed; pro·tract·ing** : to make longer : draw out in time or space

pro·trac·tor *n* : an instrument used for drawing and measuring angles

pro·trude *vb* **pro·trud·ed; pro·trud·ing** : to stick out or cause to stick out

proud *adj* **proud·er; proud·est** **1** : having great self-respect or dignity **2** : having a feeling of pleasure or satisfaction especially with a person's own achievements or with someone else's achievements : very pleased **3** : having or showing a feeling of being better than others : HAUGHTY — **proud·ly** *adv*

prove *vb* **proved; proved** *or* **prov·en** ; **prov·ing** **1** : to show the truth or existence of something with facts **2** : to turn out to be **3** : to check the correctness of **4** : to test by experiment or by a standard

prov·erb *n* : a short well-known saying containing a wise thought : MAXIM, ADAGE

pro·ver·bi·al *adj* **1** : of a proverb **2** : commonly spoken of — **pro·ver·bi·al·ly** *adv*

pro·vide *vb* **pro·vid·ed; pro·vid·ing** **1** : to give something that is needed **2** : to supply something : supply (someone) with something **3** : to make as a condition — **pro·vid·er** *n*

pro·vid·ed *conj* : IF 1

prov·i·dence *n* **1** *often cap* : help or care from God or heaven **2** *cap* : God as the guide and protector of all human beings **3** : PRUDENCE, THRIFT

prov·ince *n* **1** : a part of a country having a government of its own (as one of the divisions of Canada) **2 provinces** *pl* : the part or parts of a country far from the capital or chief city **3** : an area of activity or authority

pro·vin·cial *adj* **1** : of, relating to, or coming from a province **2** : lacking in social graces or sophistication **3** : having narrow or limited concerns or interests

¹**pro·vi·sion** *n* **1** : a stock or store of supplies and especially of food — usually used in pl. **2** : the act of supplying **3** : ¹CONDITION 2 **4** : something done beforehand

²**provision** *vb* **pro·vi·sioned; pro·vi·sion·ing** : to supply with things that are needed

prov·o·ca·tion *n* : something that causes anger or action

pro·voc·a·tive *adj* : serving or likely to cause a reaction (as interest, curiosity, or anger) — **pro·voc·a·tive·ly** *adv*

pro·voke *vb* **pro·voked; pro·vok·ing** **1** : to cause to become angry **2** : to bring about

prow *n* : the bow of a ship

prow·ess *n* **1** : great bravery especially in battle **2** : very great ability

prowl *vb* **prowled; prowl·ing** : to move about quietly and secretly in hunting or searching — **prowl·er** *n*

proxy *n, pl* **prox·ies** **1** : authority to act for another or a paper giving such authority **2** : a person with authority to act for another

prude *n* : a person who cares too much about proper speech and conduct — **prud·ish** *adj*

pru·dence *n* : careful good judgment that allows someone to avoid danger or risks

pru·dent *adj* : wise and careful in action or judgment — **pru·dent·ly** *adv*

¹**prune** *n* : a dried plum

²**prune** *vb* **pruned; prun·ing** **1** : to cut off dead or unwanted parts of a bush or tree **2** : to cut out useless or unwanted parts (as unnecessary words in something written)

¹**pry** *vb* **pried; pry·ing** **1** : to raise or open with a lever **2** : to get at with great difficulty

²**pry** *vb* **pried; pry·ing** : to be nosy about something

pry·ing *adj* : rudely nosy

P.S. *abbr* **1** postscript **2** public school

psalm *n* **1** : a sacred song or poem **2** *cap* : one of the hymns that make up the Old Testament Book of Psalms

psy·chi·a·trist *n* : a doctor specializing in psychiatry

psy·chi·a·try *n* : a branch of medicine dealing with problems of the mind, emotions, or behavior

psy·cho·log·i·cal *adj* : of or relating to psychology or the mind

psy·chol·o·gist *n* : a person specializing in psychology

psy·chol·o·gy *n* : the science that studies the mind and behavior

pt. *abbr* **1** pint **2** point

PTA *abbr* Parent-Teacher Association

ptero·dac·tyl *n* : a very large extinct flying reptile that lived at the same time as the dinosaurs

PTO *abbr* Parent-Teacher Organization

pub *n* : an establishment where alcoholic drinks are served

pu·ber·ty *n* : the age at or period during which the body of a boy or girl matures and becomes capable of reproducing

¹**pub·lic** *adj* **1** : open to all **2** : of or relating to the people as a whole **3** : known to many people : not kept secret **4** : of, relating to, or working for a government or community **5** : WELL-KNOWN, PROMINENT — **pub·lic·ly** *adv*

²**public** *n* **1** : the people as a whole **2** : a group of people having common interests

pub·li·ca·tion *n* **1** : the act or process of producing (a printed work) and selling it to the public **2** : a printed work (as a book or magazine) made for sale or distribution

pub·lic·i·ty *n* **1** : attention that is given to someone or something by the media **2** : something that attracts the interest of the public

pub·li·cize *vb* **pub·li·cized; pub·li·ciz·ing** : to give publicity to

public school *n* : a free school paid for by taxes and run by a local government

pub·lish *vb* **pub·lished; pub·lish·ing** **1** : to bring printed works (as books) before the public usually for sale **2** : to print (as in a magazine or newspaper) **3** : to make widely known — **pub·lish·er** *n*

puck *n* : a rubber disk used in hockey

¹**puck·er** *vb* **puck·ered; puck·er·ing** : to draw or cause to draw up into folds or wrinkles

²**pucker** *n* : a fold or wrinkle in a normally even surface

pud·ding *n* : a soft creamy dessert

pud·dle *n* : a very small pool of liquid

pudgy *adj* **pudg·i·er; pudg·i·est** : being short and plump : CHUBBY

pueb·lo *n, pl* **pueb·los** **1** : an American Indian village of Arizona or New Mexico made up of groups of stone or adobe houses with flat roofs **2** *cap* : a member of any of several American Indian peoples of Arizona or New Mexico

¹**Puer·to Ri·can** *adj* : of or relating to Puerto Rico or Puerto Ricans

²**Puerto Rican** *n* : a person born or living in Puerto Rico

¹**puff** *vb* **puffed; puff·ing** **1** : to breathe hard : PANT **2** : to send out small whiffs or clouds (as of smoke) **3** : to swell up or become swollen with or as if with air

²**puff** *n* **1** : a quick short instance of sending or letting out air, smoke, or steam **2** : a slight swelling **3** : a soft pad for putting powder on the skin **4** : a light pastry

puf·fin *n* : a black-and-white seabird that has a short thick neck and a large bill marked with several colors

puffy *adj* **puff·i·er; puff·i·est** **1** : somewhat swollen **2** : soft, light, and rounded **3** : BREATHLESS 1 **4** : blowing in puffs

pug *n* : a small muscular dog having a curled tail and a flattened face with wrinkles

pug nose *n* : a usually short nose turning up at the end

puke *vb* **puked; puk·ing** : ²VOMIT

¹**pull** *vb* **pulled; pull·ing** **1** : to use force on so as to cause movement toward the force **2** : to separate from a firm or a natural attachment **3** : ¹MOVE 1 **4** : to draw apart : TEAR, REND **5** : to move (something) up or down **6** : to operate by drawing toward **7** : to stretch repeatedly — **pull through** : to survive a difficult or dangerous period

²**pull** *n* **1** : the act or an instance of grasping and causing to move **2** : a device for making something move **3** : a force that draws one body toward another

pull–down *adj* : appearing on a computer screen below a selected item

pul·let *n* : a young hen

pul·ley *n, pl* **pulleys** : a wheel over which a belt, rope, or chain is pulled to lift or lower a heavy object

pull·over *n* : a garment (as a sweater) that is put on by being pulled over the head

pulp *n* **1** : the soft juicy or moist part of a fruit or vegetable **2** : the part of a fruit or vegetable that is left after the liquid has been squeezed from it **3** : a material prepared usually from wood or rags and used in making paper **4** : the soft sensitive tissue inside a tooth **5** : a seriously injured or damaged state

pul·pit *n* **1** : a raised place in which a clergyman stands while preaching or conducting a religious service **2** : the profession of preachers

pul·sate *vb* **pul·sat·ed; pul·sat·ing** : to have or show strong regular beats

pulse *n* **1** : a strong regular beating or throbbing **2** : the beat resulting from the regular widening of an artery in the body as blood flows through it

pul·ver·ize *vb* **pul·ver·ized; pul·ver·iz·ing** : to beat or grind into a powder or dust

pu·ma *n* : COUGAR

pum·ice *n* : a very light porous volcanic glass that is used in powder form for smoothing and polishing

pum·mel *vb* **pum·meled** *also* **pum·melled; pum·mel·ing** *also* **pum·mel·ling** : to strike again and again

¹**pump** *n* : a device for raising, moving, or compressing liquids or gases

²**pump** *vb* **pumped; pump·ing** **1** : to raise, move, or compress by using a pump **2** : to fill by using a pump **3** : to draw, force, or drive onward in the manner of a pump **4** : to question again and again to find out something **5** : to move (something) up and down or in and out quickly and repeatedly **6** : to

remove (a liquid or gas) from by using a pump

pum·per·nick·el *n* : a dark rye bread

pump·kin *n* : a large round orange fruit that grown on a vine, is related to the squash and cucumber, and is used for food or decoration

¹**pun** *n* : a form of joking in which a person uses a word in two senses

²**pun** *vb* **punned; pun·ning** : to make a joke by using a word in two senses

¹**punch** *vb* **punched; punch·ing 1** : to strike with the fist **2** : to sharply press or poke **3** : to make (a hole) by pressing into or through something **4** : to make a hole in with a punch

²**punch** *n* : a drink usually containing different fruit juices

³**punch** *n* : a blow with or as if with the fist

⁴**punch** *n* : a tool for piercing, stamping, or cutting

punc·tu·al *adj* : arriving or acting at the right time : not late

punc·tu·ate *vb* **punc·tu·at·ed; punc·tu·at·ing** : to add punctuation marks to writing

punc·tu·a·tion *n* **1** : the act of adding punctuation marks to writing **2** : a system of using punctuation marks

punctuation mark *n* : any one of the marks (as a period, comma, or question mark) used in writing to make the meaning clear and separate parts (as clauses and sentences)

¹**punc·ture** *n* **1** : an act of piercing with something pointed **2** : a hole or wound made by piercing with something pointed

²**puncture** *vb* **punc·tured; punc·tur·ing 1** : to pierce with something pointed **2** : to weaken or damage as if by piercing a hole in

pun·gent *adj* : having a strong or sharp taste or smell — **pun·gent·ly** *adv*

pun·ish *vb* **pun·ished; pun·ish·ing 1** : to make suffer for a fault or crime **2** : to make someone suffer for (as a crime)

pun·ish·able *adj* : deserving to be punished

pun·ish·ment *n* **1** : the act of making a wrongdoer suffer : the state or fact of being made to suffer for wrongdoing **2** : the penalty for a wrong or crime

punk *n* : a rude and violent young man

¹**punt** *vb* **punt·ed; punt·ing** : to drop and kick a ball before it hits the ground — **punt·er** *n*

²**punt** *n* : an act or instance of dropping and kicking a ball before it hits the ground

pu·ny *adj* **pu·ni·er; pu·ni·est 1** : small and weak in size or power **2** : not very impressive or effective

pup *n* **1** : PUPPY **2** : a young animal

pu·pa *n, pl* **pu·pae** *or* **pupas** : an insect (as a bee, moth, or beetle) in an intermediate inactive stage of its growth in which it is enclosed in a cocoon or case

¹**pu·pil** *n* : a child in school or under the care of a teacher

²**pupil** *n* : the opening in the iris through which light enters the eye

pup·pet *n* **1** : a doll moved by hand or by strings or wires **2** : someone or something (as a government) whose acts are controlled by another

pup·py *n, pl* **puppies** : a young dog

¹**pur·chase** *vb* **pur·chased; pur·chas·ing** : to get by paying money : BUY

²**purchase** *n* **1** : an act of buying **2** : something bought **3** : a firm hold or grasp or a safe place to stand

pure *adj* **pur·er; pur·est 1** : not mixed with anything else : free from everything that might injure or lower the quality **2** : free from sin : INNOCENT, CHASTE **3** : nothing other than : ABSOLUTE — **pure·ly** *adv*

pure·bred *adj* : bred from ancestors of a single breed for many generations

¹**purge** *vb* **purged; purg·ing 1** : to get rid of **2** : to rid of unwanted things or people

²**purge** *n* **1** : an act or instance of ridding of what is unwanted **2** : the removal of members thought to be treacherous or disloyal

pu·ri·fi·ca·tion *n* : an act or instance of freeing from impurities or of being freed from impurities

pu·ri·fy *vb* **pu·ri·fied; pu·ri·fy·ing** : to make pure : free from impurities

pu·ri·tan *n* **1** *cap* : a member of a 16th and 17th century Protestant group in England and New England opposing formal customs of the Church of England **2** : a person who practices, preaches, or follows a stricter moral code than most people

pu·ri·ty *n* **1** : freedom from dirt or impurities **2** : freedom from sin or guilt

pur·ple *n* : a color between red and blue

pur·plish *adj* : somewhat purple

pur·pose *n* : something set up as a goal to be achieved : INTENTION, AIM — **on purpose** : PURPOSELY

pur·pose·ful *adj* : having a clear intention or aim — **pur·pose·ful·ly** *adv* — **pur·pose·ful·ness** *n*

pur·pose·ly *adv* : with a clear or known aim

¹**purr** *vb* **purred; purr·ing** : to make the low murmuring sound of a contented cat or a similar sound

²**purr** *n* : the low murmuring sound of a contented cat or a similar sound

¹**purse** *n* **1** : a bag or pouch for money **2** : HANDBAG **3** : the amount of money that a person, organization, or government has available for use **4** : a sum of money offered as a prize or collected as a present

²purse *vb* **pursed; purs·ing :** to form into a tight circle or line

pur·sue *vb* **pur·sued; pur·su·ing 1 :** to follow after in order to catch or destroy : CHASE **2 :** to follow up or proceed with **3 :** to try to get or do over a period of time — **pur·su·er** *n*

pur·suit *n* **1 :** the act of chasing, following, or trying to obtain **2 :** ACTIVITY 2, OCCUPATION

pus *n* **:** a thick yellowish substance that is produced when a part of the body or a wound becomes infected

¹push *vb* **pushed; push·ing 1 :** to press against with force so as to drive or move away **2 :** to force forward, downward, or outward **3 :** to go or make go ahead **4 :** to pressure to do something or work hard at something

²push *n* **1 :** a sudden thrust : SHOVE **2 :** a steady applying of force in a direction away from the body from which it comes

push button *n* **:** a small button or knob that when pushed operates something usually by closing an electric circuit

push·cart *n* **:** a cart pushed by hand

push·over *n* **1 :** an opponent that is easy to defeat **2 :** someone who is easy to persuade or influence **3 :** something easily done

push–up *n* **:** an exercise performed while lying with the face down by raising and lowering the body with the straightening and bending of the arms

pushy *adj* **push·i·er; push·i·est :** too aggressive : FORWARD

pussy willow *n* **:** a willow with large furry flower clusters

put *vb* **put; put·ting 1 :** to place in or move into a particular position **2 :** to bring into a specified state or condition **3 :** to cause to undergo something **4 :** to give expression to **5 :** to devote to or urge to an activity **6 :** to think of as worthy of : ATTRIBUTE **7 :** to begin a voyage — **put away :** to take in food and drink — **put down 1 :** to bring to an end by force **2 :** CRITICIZE — **put forward :** PROPOSE 1 — **put in 1 :** to ask for **2 :** to spend time in a place or activity — **put off**

: to hold back to a later time : DEFER — **put on 1 :** to dress in **2 :** PRETEND 2 **3 :** ¹PRODUCE 4 — **put out 1 :** EXTINGUISH 1 **2 :** IRRITATE 1, ANNOY **3 :** ¹MAKE 1 **4 :** to cause to be out (in baseball) **5 :** to make use of — **put together 1 :** to create as a whole : CONSTRUCT **2 :** to consider as a single unit — **put up 1 :** ¹BUILD 1 **2 :** to make (as food) ready for later use **3 :** to give or get shelter and often food **4 :** to make by action or effort — **put up to :** to urge or cause to do something wrong or unexpected — **put up with :** to stand for : TOLERATE

put·out *n* **:** ⁴OUT

pu·trid *adj* **1 :** ROTTEN 1 **2 :** coming from or suggesting something rotten

put·ter *vb* **put·tered; put·ter·ing :** to act or work without much purpose

¹put·ty *n, pl* **putties :** a soft sticky substance that hardens as it dries and is used for holding glass in a window frame or filling holes

²putty *vb* **put·tied; put·ty·ing :** to seal up with putty

¹puz·zle *vb* **puz·zled; puz·zling 1 :** CONFUSE 1, PERPLEX **2 :** to solve by thought or by clever guessing

²puzzle *n* **1 :** a question, problem, or device intended to test skill or cleverness **2 :** JIGSAW PUZZLE **3 :** something that perplexes : MYSTERY

puz·zle·ment *n* **:** the state of being perplexed

pyg·my *adj* **:** smaller than the usual size

pyr·a·mid *n* **1 :** a large structure built especially in ancient Egypt that usually has a square base and four triangular sides meeting at a point and that contains tombs **2 :** a shape or structure with a polygon for its base and three or more triangles for its sides which meet to form the top

pyre *n* **:** a heap of wood for burning a dead body

py·thon *n* **:** a large nonpoisonous snake of Africa, Asia, and Australia that squeezes and suffocates its prey

Q

q *n, pl* **q's** *or* **qs** *often cap* **:** the 17th letter of the English alphabet

QC *abbr* Quebec

qt. *abbr* quart

¹quack *vb* **quacked; quack·ing :** to make the cry of a duck

²quack *n* **:** a cry made by a duck

³quack *n* **:** a person who pretends to have medical knowledge and skill

⁴quack *adj* **1 :** relating to or being a person who pretends to have medical knowledge and skill **2 :** pretending to cure disease

quadri- *or* **quadr-** *or* **quadru-** *prefix* **1 :** four **2 :** fourth

quad·ri·lat·er·al *n* : a flat geometric figure of four sides and four angles

quad·ru·ped *n* : an animal having four feet

¹qua·dru·ple *vb* **qua·dru·pled; qua·dru·pling** : to make or become four times as great or many

²quadruple *adj* **1** : having four units or parts **2** : being four times as great or as many

qua·dru·plet *n* : one of four offspring born at one birth

quag·mire *n* **1** : soft spongy wet ground that shakes or gives way under the foot **2** : a difficult situation

¹quail *n, pl* **quail** *or* **quails** : a small plump bird (as a bobwhite) that feeds mostly on the ground and is sometimes hunted for food or sport

²quail *vb* **quailed; quail·ing** : to lose courage : draw back in fear

quaint *adj* **quaint·er; quaint·est** : pleasingly old-fashioned or unfamiliar — **quaint·ly** *adv* — **quaint·ness** *n*

¹quake *vb* **quaked; quak·ing** **1** : to shake usually from shock or lack of stability **2** : to tremble or shudder usually from cold or fear

²quake *n* : EARTHQUAKE

qual·i·fi·ca·tion *n* **1** : a special skill, knowledge, or ability that makes someone suitable for a particular job or activity **2** : a condition or requirement that must be met **3** : something that is added to a statement to limit or change its meaning

qual·i·fy *vb* **qual·i·fied; qual·i·fy·ing** **1** : to give the training, skill, or ability needed for a special purpose **2** : to have or show the skill or ability needed for a special purpose or event **3** : to narrow down or make less general in meaning

¹qual·i·ty *n, pl* **qual·i·ties** **1** : what sets a person or thing apart : CHARACTERISTIC **2** : how good or bad something is **3** : a high standard : EXCELLENCE

²quality *adj* : very good : EXCELLENT

qualm *n* : a feeling of doubt or uncertainty especially in matters of right and wrong

quan·da·ry *n, pl* **quan·da·ries** : a state of doubt or confusion

quan·ti·ty *n, pl* **quan·ti·ties** **1** : ²AMOUNT, NUMBER **2** : a large number or amount

¹quar·an·tine *n* **1** : isolation of people, animals, or things (as plants) out of a certain area to prevent the spread of disease or pests **2** : a period during which a person or animal with a contagious disease is isolated **3** : a place (as a hospital) where a person or animal with a contagious disease is isolated

²quarantine *vb* **quar·an·tined; quar·an·tin·ing** : to put or hold in isolation to prevent the spread of disease or pests

¹quar·rel *n* **1** : an angry argument or disagreement **2** : a cause of disagreement or complaint

²quarrel *vb* **quar·reled** *or* **quar·relled; quar·rel·ing** *or* **quar·rel·ling** **1** : to argue angrily **2** : to find fault

quar·rel·some *adj* : usually ready to disagree or argue

¹quar·ry *n, pl* **quar·ries** : an animal or bird hunted as game or prey

²quarry *n, pl* **quar·ries** : an open pit usually for obtaining building stone, slate, or limestone

³quarry *vb* **quar·ried; quar·ry·ing** **1** : to dig or take from or as if from a quarry **2** : to make a quarry in

quart *n* : a measure of liquid capacity that equals two pints (about .95 liter)

¹quar·ter *n* **1** : one of four equal parts into which something can be divided **2** : a United States coin worth 25 cents **3** : someone or something (as a place, direction, or group) not clearly identified **4** : a particular division or district of a city **5 quarters** *pl* : a dwelling place **6** : MERCY 1

²quarter *vb* **quar·tered; quar·ter·ing** **1** : to divide into four usually equal parts **2** : to provide with lodgings or shelter

³quarter *adj* : consisting of or equal to one fourth of

quar·ter·back *n* : a football player who leads a team's attempts to score usually by passing the ball to other players

quarter horse *n* : a stocky muscular saddle horse capable of running fast for short distances

¹quar·ter·ly *adv* : four times a year

²quarterly *adj* : coming or happening four times a year

³quarterly *n, pl* **quar·ter·lies** : a magazine published four times a year

quar·ter·mas·ter *n* **1** : an army officer who provides clothing and supplies for troops **2** : an officer of a ship (as in the navy) in charge of navigation

quar·tet *also* **quar·tette** *n* **1** : a piece of music for four instruments or voices **2** : a group of four singers or musicians who perform together **3** : a group or set of four

quartz *n* : a common mineral often found in the form of colorless transparent crystals but sometimes (as in amethysts, agates, and jaspers) brightly colored

¹qua·ver *vb* **qua·vered; qua·ver·ing** : to sound in shaky or unsteady tones

²quaver *n* : a sound that trembles or is unsteady

quay *n* : a structure built along the bank of a waterway (as a river) for use as a landing for loading and unloading boats

quea·sy *adj* **quea·si·er; quea·si·est** **1**

: somewhat nauseated **2** : full of doubt : UN-EASY — **quea·si·ness** *n*

queen *n* **1** : a woman who rules a country or kingdom **2** : the wife or widow of a king **3** : a woman or girl who is highly respected or well-known within a field **4** : the most powerful piece in the game of chess **5** : a playing card bearing the figure of a queen **6** : a fully developed adult female insect (as a bee, ant, or termite) that lays eggs — **queen·ly** *adj*

queer *adj* **queer·er; queer·est** : oddly unlike the usual or normal — **queer·ly** *adv*

quell *vb* **quelled; quell·ing 1** : to stop or end by force **2** : ⁴QUIET, CALM

quench *vb* **quenched; quench·ing 1** : to end by satisfying **2** : to put out (as a fire)

quer·u·lous *adj* : having or showing a complaining attitude

¹que·ry *n, pl* **queries** : ¹QUESTION 1

²query *vb* **que·ried; que·ry·ing 1** : to put as a question **2** : to ask questions about especially in order to clear up a doubt **3** : to ask questions of

quest *n* **1** : an effort to find or do something **2** : a usually adventurous journey made in search of something

¹ques·tion *n* **1** : something asked **2** : a topic discussed or argued about **3** : OBJECTION 1 **4** : doubt or uncertainty about something **5** : POSSIBILITY 1, CHANCE

²question *vb* **ques·tioned; ques·tion·ing 1** : to ask questions of or about **2** : to have or express doubts about

ques·tion·able *adj* **1** : not certain or exact : DOUBTFUL **2** : not believed to be true, sound, or proper

question mark *n* : a punctuation mark ? used chiefly at the end of a sentence to indicate a direct question

ques·tion·naire *n* : a set of questions to be asked of a number of people usually in order to gather information or opinions

¹queue *n* **1** : PIGTAIL **2** : a waiting line

²queue *vb* **queued; queu·ing** *or* **queue·ing** : to form or wait in a line

¹quib·ble *vb* **quib·bled; quib·bling** : to argue or complain about small and unimportant things

²quibble *n* : a small and usually unimportant complaint, criticism, or argument

¹quick *adj* **quick·er; quick·est 1** : done or taking place in a very short period of time **2** : very swift : SPEEDY **3** : fast in learning or understanding : mentally alert **4** : easily stirred up — **quick·ly** *adv* — **quick·ness** *n*

²quick *n* **1** : a very tender area of flesh (as under a fingernail) **2** : someone's innermost feelings

³quick *adv* **quick·er; quick·est** : in a quick manner : FAST

quick·en *vb* **quick·ened; quick·en·ing 1** : to make or become faster : HASTEN **2** : to make or become stronger or more active

quick·sand *n* : a deep area of loose sand mixed with water into which heavy objects sink

quick·sil·ver *n* : MERCURY 1

quick–tem·pered *adj* : easily made angry

¹qui·et *n* : the quality or state of being calm or without noise

²quiet *adj* **qui·et·er; qui·et·est 1** : free from noise or uproar **2** : marked by little or no motion or activity : CALM **3** : not disturbed : PEACEFUL **4** : tending not to talk or show excitement much **5** : not shown in an obvious way **6** : away from public view : SECLUDED — **qui·et·ly** *adv* — **qui·et·ness** *n*

³quiet *adv* : in a quiet manner : QUIETLY

⁴quiet *vb* **qui·et·ed; qui·et·ing** : to make or become calmer or less noisy

quill *n* **1** : a large stiff feather of a bird's wing or tail **2** : the hollow tubelike part of a feather **3** : a hollow sharp spine of a porcupine or hedgehog **4** : a pen made from a feather

¹quilt *n* : a bed cover made of two layers of cloth with a filling of wool, cotton, or down held together by patterned stitching

²quilt *vb* **quilt·ed; quilt·ing** : to stitch or sew together as in making a quilt

quince *n* : a hard sour yellow fruit that resembles an apple, grows on a shrubby Asian tree, and is used especially in jams and jellies

qui·nine *n* : a bitter drug obtained from cinchona bark and used to treat malaria

quin·tet *n* **1** : a piece of music for five instruments or voices **2** : a group of five singers or musicians who perform together **3** : a group or set of five

quin·tu·plet *n* **1** : one of five offspring born at one birth **2** : a combination of five of a kind

quirk *n* **1** : an odd or unusual characteristic or habit **2** : something strange that happens by chance

quirky *adj* **quirk·i·er; quirk·i·est** : unusual especially in an interesting way

quit *vb* **quit; quit·ting** : to leave or stop doing something

quite *adv* **1** : beyond question or doubt : COMPLETELY **2** : to a considerable extent

quit·ter *n* : a person who gives up too easily

¹quiv·er *n* : a case for carrying arrows

²quiver *vb* **quiv·ered; quiv·er·ing** : to move with a slight trembling motion

³quiver *n* : the act or instance of trembling

¹quiz *n, pl* **quiz·zes** : a short test

²quiz *vb* **quizzed; quiz·zing** : to ask a lot of questions of

quiz·zi·cal *adj* : showing doubt, puzzlement or curiosity — **quiz·zi·cal·ly** *adv*

quoit *n* : a ring (as of rope) tossed at a peg in a game (**quoits**)

quo·rum *n* : the smallest number of people who must be present at a meeting in order for business to be carried on

quo·ta *n* **1** : a limit on the number or amount of people or things that are allowed **2** : a share assigned to each member of a group **3** : a specific amount or number of things that is expected to be achieved

quo·ta·tion *n* : material (as a sentence or passage from a book) that is repeated exactly by someone else

quotation mark *n* : one of a pair of punctuation marks " " or ' ' used chiefly to indicate the beginning and end of a quotation

¹quote *vb* **quot·ed; quot·ing** : to repeat (someone else's words) exactly

²quote *n* : QUOTATION

quo·tient *n* : the number obtained by dividing one number by another

R

r *n, pl* **r's** *or* **rs** *often cap* : the 18th letter of the English alphabet

r. *abbr* right

R *abbr* regular

R. *abbr* rabbi

rab·bi *n, pl* **rab·bis** : a person educated in Jewish law and able to lead a Jewish congregation

rab·bit *n* : a short-tailed mammal that has soft fur and long ears and hind legs and digs burrows

rab·ble *n* **1** : a crowd that is noisy and hard to control : MOB **2** : a group of people looked down upon as ignorant and hard to handle

ra·bid *adj* **1** : very angry : FURIOUS **2** : having or expressing a very extreme opinion about or interest in something **3** : affected with rabies — **ra·bid·ly** *adv*

ra·bies *n* : a deadly disease of the nervous system that affects animals and can be passed on to people by the bite of an infected animal

rac·coon *n* : a small North American animal that is mostly gray with black around the eyes, has a bushy tail with black rings, is active mostly at night, and eats small animals, fruits, eggs, and insects

¹race *vb* **raced; rac·ing** **1** : to go, move, function, or drive at top speed **2** : to take part in a contest of speed **3** : to cause an engine of a motor vehicle in neutral to run fast

²race *n* **1** : a contest of speed **2** : a contest involving progress toward a goal **3** : a strong or rapid current of water

³race *n* **1** : any one of the groups that human beings can be divided into based on shared distinctive physical traits **2** : a group of individuals who share a common culture or history **3** : a major group of living things

race·course *n* : a place where races are held

race·horse *n* : a horse bred or kept for racing

rac·er *n* **1** : a person, animal, or vehicle that participates in or is used for participation in races **2** : a long slender active snake (as the blacksnake)

race·track *n* : a usually oval course on which races are run

ra·cial *adj* : of, relating to, or based on race — **ra·cial·ly** *adv*

rac·ism *n* **1** : belief that certain races of people are by birth and nature superior to others **2** : discrimination or hatred based on race

rac·ist *adj* : based on or showing racism — **racist** *n*

¹rack *n* : a frame or stand for storing or displaying things

²rack *vb* **racked; rack·ing** **1** : to cause to suffer torture, pain, or sorrow **2** : to force to think hard

¹rack·et *n* **1** : a loud confused noise **2** : a dishonest scheme for obtaining money

²racket *or* **rac·quet** *n* : a piece of sports equipment consisting of a handle and a frame with strings stretched tightly across it

rack·e·teer *n* : a person who gets money or advantages by using force or threats

ra·dar *n* : a radio device for detecting the position of things in the distance and the direction of moving objects (as distant airplanes or ships)

ra·di·ance *n* : warm or vivid brightness

ra·di·ant *adj* **1** : giving out or reflecting rays of light **2** : glowing with love, confidence, or joy **3** : transmitted by radiation

radiant energy *n* : energy sent out in the form of electromagnetic waves

ra·di·ate *vb* **ra·di·at·ed; ra·di·at·ing** **1** : to send out rays : SHINE **2** : to come forth in the form of rays **3** : to go out in a direct line from a center **4** : to spread around from or as if from a center **5** : to show very clearly

ra·di·a·tion *n* **1** : the process of giving off energy in the form of waves or particles **2**

: something that is radiated (as light or X-rays)

ra·di·a·tor *n* : a device to heat air (as in a room) or to cool an object (as an automobile engine) by heating the surrounding air

¹rad·i·cal *adj* **1** : very new and different from the usual or ordinary : EXTREME **2** : of or relating to people who favor rapid and sweeping changes in laws and government — **rad·i·cal·ly** *adv*

²radical *n* : a person who favors rapid and sweeping changes especially in laws and government

radii *pl of* RADIUS

¹ra·dio *n, pl* **ra·di·os** **1** : the process that is used for sending or receiving signals by means of electromagnetic waves without a connecting wire **2** : a device that receives signals sent by radio **3** : programs that are broadcast by radio **4** : a device used to both send and receive messages by radio **5** : the radio broadcasting industry

²radio *adj* **1** : of or relating to radio waves **2** : of, relating to, or used in radio broadcasting

³radio *vb* **ra·di·oed; ra·di·o·ing** : to communicate or send a message to by radio

ra·dio·ac·tive *adj* : caused by or exhibiting radioactivity

ra·dio·ac·tiv·i·ty *n* **1** : the giving off of rays of energy or particles by the breaking apart of atoms of certain elements (as uranium) **2** : the rays or particles that are given off when atoms break apart

radio wave *n* : an electromagnetic wave used in radio, television, or radar communication

rad·ish *n* : a small roundish crisp root that has a sharp flavor and is usually eaten raw as a vegetable

ra·di·um *n* : a strongly radioactive element found in very small quantities in various minerals (as pitchblende) and used in the treatment of cancer

ra·di·us *n, pl* **ra·dii** **1** : a straight line extending from the center of a circle to the outside edge or from the center of a sphere to the surface **2** : an area that extends in all directions from a place **3** : the bone on the thumb side of the arm between the wrist and the elbow

¹raf·fle *n* : a contest for a prize in which people buy tickets and which is won by the person whose ticket is picked at a drawing

²raffle *vb* **raf·fled; raf·fl·ing** : to give (something) as a prize in a raffle

¹raft *n* : a flat structure (as a group of logs fastened together) for support or transportation on water

²raft *n* : a large amount or number

raf·ter *n* : one of the usually sloping timbers that support a roof

rag *n* **1** : a worn piece of cloth **2 rags** *pl* : shabby or very worn clothing

rag·a·muf·fin *n* : a poorly clothed and often dirty child

¹rage *n* **1** : very strong and uncontrolled anger : FURY **2** : a fit of anger **3** : violent action (as of wind or sea) **4** : FAD

²rage *vb* **raged; rag·ing** **1** : to feel or show extreme or uncontrolled anger **2** : to continue out of control

rag·ged *adj* **1** : having a rough or uneven edge or outline **2** : very worn-out : TATTERED **3** : wearing very worn-out clothes **4** : done in an uneven way — **rag·ged·ly** *adv* — **rag·ged·ness** *n*

rag·gedy *adj* **1** : RAGGED 2 **2** : RAGGED 3

rag·tag *adj* : not well organized or put together

rag·time *n* : music that has a lively melody and a steady rhythm like a march

rag·weed *n* : a common weed with pollen that irritates the eyes and noses of some people

¹raid *n* : a sudden attack or invasion

²raid *vb* **raid·ed; raid·ing** **1** : to enter (a place) to look for something or someone or to steal or take something **2** : to make a sudden attack — **raid·er** *n*

¹rail *n* **1** : a bar extending from one support to another and serving as a guard or barrier **2** : a bar of steel forming a track for wheeled vehicles **3** : RAILROAD 1

²rail *vb* **railed; rail·ing** : to provide with a railing

³rail *n* : a small or medium-sized wading bird related to the crane that has very long toes for walking on the soft mud of marshes

⁴rail *vb* **railed; rail·ing** : to scold or complain in harsh or bitter language

rail·ing *n* **1** : a barrier (as a fence) made up of vertical bars and their supports **2** : material for making rails

rail·lery *n* : an act or instance of making fun of someone in a good-natured way

rail·road *n* **1** : a permanent road that has parallel steel rails that make a track for train cars **2** : a company that owns and operates trains

rail·way *n* : RAILROAD 1

rai·ment *n* : CLOTHING

¹rain *n* **1** : water falling in drops from the clouds **2** : a fall of water in drops from the clouds **3** : rainy weather **4** : a heavy fall of objects

²rain *vb* **rained; rain·ing** **1** : to fall as water in drops from the clouds **2** : to send down rain **3** : to fall in large amounts **4** : to give

in large amounts — **rain cats and dogs**
: POUR 2

rain·bow *n* : an arc of colors that appears in
the sky opposite the sun and is caused by the
sun shining through rain, mist, or spray

rain·coat *n* : a coat of waterproof or water-resistant material

rain·drop *n* : a drop of rain

rain·fall *n* **1** : ¹RAIN 2 **2** : amount of precipi-
tation

rain forest *n* : a woodland with a high annual
rainfall and very tall trees and that is often
found in tropical regions

rain·proof *adj* : not letting in rain

rain·storm *n* : a storm of or with rain

rain·wa·ter *n* : water from rain

rainy *adj* **rain·i·er; rain·i·est** : having much
rain

¹**raise** *vb* **raised; rais·ing** **1** : to cause to rise
: LIFT **2** : COLLECT 1 **3** : to look after the
growth and development of : GROW **4** : to
bring up a child : REAR **5** : to bring to notice
6 : ¹INCREASE **7** : to make louder **8** : to give
life to : AROUSE **9** : to set upright by lifting
or building **10** : PROMOTE 1, ELEVATE **11**
: to give rise to : PROVOKE **12** : to make light
and airy **13** : to cause to form on the skin —
rais·er *n*

²**raise** *n* : an increase in amount (as of pay)

rai·sin *n* : a sweet dried grape used for food

ra·ja *or* **ra·jah** *n* : an Indian prince

¹**rake** *n* : a garden tool with a long handle and
a bar with teeth or prongs at the end

²**rake** *vb* **raked; rak·ing** **1** : to gather, loosen,
or smooth thoroughly with or as if with a
rake **2** : to search through **3** : to sweep the
length of with gunfire

rak·ish *adj* : JAUNTY, DASHING

¹**ral·ly** *vb* **ral·lied; ral·ly·ing** **1** : to bring or
come together for a common purpose **2** : to
publicly support or oppose **3** : to rouse from
low spirits or weakness

²**rally** *n, pl* **rallies** **1** : a sudden improvement
in performance or condition **2** : a big meeting held to rouse enthusiasm

¹**ram** *vb* **rammed; ram·ming** **1** : to strike or
strike against with violence **2** : to force in,
down, or together by driving or pressing **3**
: ²FORCE 2

²**ram** *n* **1** : a male sheep **2** : BATTERING RAM

RAM *n* : a computer memory that provides
the main storage available to the user for
programs and data

Ram·a·dan *n* : the ninth month of the Islamic
calendar observed as sacred with fasting
practiced daily from sunrise to sunset

¹**ram·ble** *vb* **ram·bled; ram·bling** **1** : to go
aimlessly from place to place : WANDER **2**
: to talk or write without a clear purpose or

point **3** : to grow or extend in many directions

²**ramble** *n* : a long stroll with no particular
destination

ram·bunc·tious *adj* : not under control in a
way that is playful or full of energy

ram·i·fi·ca·tion *n* : something that is the result
of something else

ramp *n* : a sloping passage or roadway connecting different levels

ram·page *n* : a period or instance of violent
action or behavior

ram·pant *adj* : existing or growing greatly
and quickly

ram·part *n* : a broad bank or wall raised as a
protective barrier

ram·rod *n* : a rod for forcing the charge down
the barrel in a firearm that is loaded through
the muzzle

ram·shack·le *adj* : ready to fall down

ran *past of* RUN

¹**ranch** *n* **1** : a large farm for the raising of
livestock (as cattle) **2** : a farm devoted to a
special crop

²**ranch** *vb* **ranched; ranch·ing** : to live or
work on a large farm where livestock are
raised — **ranch·er** *n*

ran·cid *adj* : having a strong disagreeable
smell or taste from no longer being fresh

ran·cor *n* : deep hatred

ran·cor·ous *adj* : showing deep hatred

ran·dom *adj* : lacking a clear plan, purpose,
or pattern — **ran·dom·ly** *adv* — **ran·dom·
ness** *n*

ran·dom–ac·cess *adj* : permitting access to
stored data in any order the user desires

random–access memory *n* : RAM

rang *past of* ³RING

¹**range** *n* **1** : a series of things in a line **2**
: the distance over which someone or something can be seen, heard, or reached **3** : a
cooking stove **4** : open land over which
livestock may roam and feed **5** : a variety of
choices within a scale **6** : the distance a gun
will shoot **7** : a place where shooting is
practiced

²**range** *vb* **ranged; rang·ing** **1** : to arrange in
a particular place or order **2** : to roam over
or through **3** : to come within an upper and
a lower limit

rang·er *n* **1** : FOREST RANGER **2** : a soldier
specially trained in close-range fighting and
in raiding tactics

rangy *adj* **rang·i·er; rang·i·est** : tall and slender

¹**rank** *n* **1** : ²ROW 1, SERIES **2** : a line of soldiers standing side by side **3 ranks** *pl* : the
body of enlisted persons in an army **4** : position within a group **5** : high social position
6 : official grade or position

²rank *adj* **1 :** strong and active in growth **2 :** OUTRIGHT **3 :** having an unpleasant smell

³rank *vb* **ranked; rank·ing 1 :** to take or have a certain position in a group **2 :** to arrange in a classification **3 :** to arrange in lines or in a formation

ran·kle *vb* **ran·kled; ran·kling :** to cause anger, irritation, or bitterness

ran·sack *vb* **ran·sacked; ran·sack·ing :** to search through in a way that causes disorder or damage

¹ran·som *n* **1 :** something paid or demanded for the freedom of a captured person **2 :** the act of freeing from captivity by paying a price

²ransom *vb* **ran·somed; ran·som·ing :** to free from captivity or punishment by paying a price

rant *vb* **rant·ed; rant·ing :** to talk loudly and wildly

¹rap *vb* **rapped; rap·ping :** to give a quick sharp blow

²rap *n* **1 :** a sharp blow or knock **2 :** the blame or punishment for something

³rap *vb* **rapped; rap·ping 1 :** to talk freely and informally **2 :** to perform rap music

⁴rap *n* **1 :** an informal talk : CHAT **2 :** a type of music that usually has a fast rhythm and in which words are spoken instead of sung

ra·pa·cious *adj* **1 :** very greedy **2 :** PREDATORY — **ra·pa·cious·ly** *adv* — **ra·pa·cious·ness** *n*

¹rape *n* **:** a plant related to the mustard that is grown for animals to graze on, for its seeds which are fed to birds, and as a source of oil

²rape *vb* **raped; rap·ing :** to have sexual intercourse with by force

³rape *n* **:** the crime of forcing someone to have sexual intercourse

rap·id *adj* **:** very fast — **rap·id·ly** *adv*

ra·pid·i·ty *n* **:** the quality or state of being rapid

rap·ids *n pl* **:** a part of a river where the current flows very fast usually over rocks

ra·pi·er *n* **:** a straight sword with a narrow blade having two sharp edges

rap·per *n* **:** a person who performs rap music

rap·port *n* **:** a friendly relationship

rapt *adj* **:** showing complete delight or interest

rap·tor *n* **:** BIRD OF PREY

rap·ture *n* **:** a strong feeling of joy, delight, or love

¹rare *adj* **rar·er; rar·est 1 :** very uncommon **2 :** very fine : EXCELLENT **3 :** not thick or compact : THIN

²rare *adj* **rar·er; rar·est :** cooked so that the inside is still red

rare·ly *adv* **:** not often : SELDOM

rar·i·ty *n, pl* **rar·i·ties 1 :** the quality, state, or fact of being rare **2 :** something that is uncommon

ras·cal *n* **1 :** a usually young mischievous person **2 :** a mean or dishonest person

¹rash *adj* **:** done or made quickly and without thought of the likely result — **rash·ly** *adv* — **rash·ness** *n*

²rash *n* **1 :** a breaking out of the skin with red spots (as from illness or an allergic reaction) **2 :** a series of bad things that happen in a short time

¹rasp *vb* **rasped; rasp·ing 1 :** to say with or make a harsh sound **2 :** to rub with or as if with a rough object or substance

²rasp *n* **1 :** a harsh sound or sensation **2 :** a coarse file used for shaping or smoothing

rasp·ber·ry *n, pl* **rasp·ber·ries :** a sweet juicy red, black, or purple berry of a prickly plant

raspy *adj* **:** having a harsh sound

¹rat *n* **1 :** a gnawing animal with brown, black, white, or grayish fur that looks like but is larger than a mouse **2 :** a person who betrays friends

²rat *vb* **rat·ted; rat·ting :** to betray a friend

¹rate *n* **1 :** a price or charge set according to a scale or standard **2 :** the amount of something measured in units of something else or in comparison with others — **at any rate :** in any case

²rate *vb* **rat·ed; rat·ing 1 :** to be placed in comparison with others : RANK **2 :** CONSIDER 3, REGARD **3 :** to have a right to : DESERVE

rath·er *adv* **1 :** ²SOMEWHAT **2 :** more willingly **3 :** more correctly or truly **4 :** INSTEAD

rat·i·fi·ca·tion *n* **:** the act or process of giving legal approval to

rat·i·fy *vb* **rat·i·fied; rat·i·fy·ing :** to give legal approval to (as by a vote)

rat·ing *n* **:** a position within a grading system

ra·tio *n, pl* **ra·tios :** the relationship in number or quantity between two or more things

¹ra·tion *n* **1 :** a food allowance for one day **2 rations** *pl* **:** ¹PROVISION 1 **3 :** the amount each person is allowed by an authority

²ration *vb* **ra·tioned; ra·tion·ing 1 :** to control the amount an individual can use **2 :** to use sparingly

ra·tio·nal *adj* **1 :** having the ability to reason **2 :** based on or showing reason — **ra·tio·nal·ly** *adv*

ra·tio·nale *n* **:** a basic explanation or reason for something

ra·tio·nal·ize *vb* **ra·tio·nal·ized; ra·tio·nal·iz·ing :** to find an excuse for something that seems reasonable or believable

rational number *n* **:** a number that can be expressed as a whole number or the quotient of two whole numbers

rat·ter *n* : a dog or cat that catches rats

¹**rat·tle** *vb* **rat·tled; rat·tling 1** : to make or cause to make a rapid series of short sharp sounds **2** : to move with a clatter **3** : to speak or say quickly or without stopping **4** : to disturb the calmness of : UPSET

²**rattle** *n* **1** : a series of short sharp sounds **2** : a toy that makes a rattling sound **3** : a part at the end of a rattlesnake's tail that makes a buzzing rattle when shaken

rat·tler *n* : RATTLESNAKE

rat·tle·snake *n* : a poisonous American snake with a rattle at the end of its tail

rat·ty *adj* **rat·ti·er; rat·ti·est** : in bad condition : SHABBY

rau·cous *adj* **1** : loud and harsh **2** : behaving in a rough and noisy way — **rau·cous·ly** *adv*

¹**rav·age** *n* : destructive action or effect

²**ravage** *vb* **rav·aged; rav·ag·ing** : to attack or act upon with great violence

rave *vb* **raved; rav·ing 1** : to talk wildly or as if crazy **2** : to talk with great enthusiasm

rav·el *vb* **rav·eled** *or* **rav·elled; rav·el·ing** *or* **rav·el·ling** : UNRAVEL 1

¹**ra·ven** *n* : a large shiny black bird that is larger than the related crow

²**raven** *adj* : shiny and black like a raven's feathers

rav·en·ous *adj* : very hungry — **rav·en·ous·ly** *adv*

ra·vine *n* : a small narrow valley with steep sides that is larger than a gully and smaller than a canyon

rav·ish *vb* **rav·ished; rav·ish·ing 1** : to seize and take away by force **2** : to fill with joy or delight

rav·ish·ing *adj* : very beautiful

raw *adj* **raw·er; raw·est 1** : not cooked **2** : having the skin scraped or roughened **3** : being in or nearly in the natural state : not treated or prepared **4** : not trained or experienced **5** : unpleasantly damp or cold **6** : lacking a normal or usual finish — **raw·ness** *n*

raw·hide *n* : cattle skin before it has been made into leather

¹**ray** *n* **1** : one of the lines of light that appear to be given off by a bright object **2** : a thin beam of radiant energy (as light) **3** : light cast in rays **4** : a tiny bit : PARTICLE **5** : any of a group of lines that spread out from the same center **6** : a straight line extending from a point in one direction only **7** : a slender plant or animal structure

²**ray** *n* : a flat broad fish (as a skate or stingray) related to the shark that has its eyes on the top of its head and often winglike fins

ray·on *n* : a cloth made with fibers produced chemically from cellulose

raze *vb* **razed; raz·ing** : to destroy completely by knocking down or breaking to pieces : DEMOLISH

ra·zor *n* : a sharp cutting instrument used to shave off hair

razz *vb* **razzed; razz·ing** : to make fun of : TEASE

rd. *abbr* **1** : road **2** : rod

re *n* : the second note of the musical scale

re- *prefix* **1** : again **2** : back : backward

¹**reach** *vb* **reached; reach·ing 1** : to extend the arm far enough to touch or grab **2** : to arrive at : COME **3** : to extend or stretch to **4** : to communicate with **5** : to grow, develop, or increase

²**reach** *n* **1** : the distance within which something can be touched or grabbed **2** : the act of stretching especially to take hold of something **3** : the probability that something can be achieved **4** : an unbroken stretch (as of a river) **5** : ability to stretch (as an arm) so as to touch something

re·act *vb* **re·act·ed; re·act·ing 1** : to act or behave in response to something **2** : to oppose a force or influence — usually used with *against* **3** : to go through a chemical reaction

re·ac·tion *n* **1** : behavior or attitude in response to something **2** : a response of the body to a stimulus **3** : a chemical change that is brought about by the action of one substance on another and results in a new substance being formed

re·ac·tor *n* : a device using atomic energy to produce heat

read *vb* **read; read·ing 1** : to understand language through written symbols for speech sounds **2** : to speak aloud written or printed words **3** : to learn from information provided in writing or printing **4** : to discover something about by looking at certain characteristics or behavior **5** : to show by letters or numbers **6** : to explain what something is **7** : to interpret stored data (as on a computer drive or optical disk)

read·able *adj* : able to be read easily

read·er *n* **1** : a person who reads or has the ability to read **2** : a book for learning or practicing reading

read·i·ly *adv* **1** : quickly and easily **2** : without hesitation or complaint

read·ing *n* **1** : the act of reading **2** : something read or available to be read **3** : the number or fact shown on an instrument

read–only memory *n* : ROM

read·out *n* **1** : information from an automatic device (as a computer) that is recorded (as on a disk) or presented in a form that can be seen **2** : an electronic device that presents information in a form that can be seen

¹**ready** *adj* **read·i·er; read·i·est** **1** : prepared for use or action **2** : likely to do something **3** : WILLING 1 **4** : needing or wanting something as soon as possible **5** : showing ease and promptness **6** : available right away : HANDY — **read·i·ness** *n*

²**ready** *vb* **read·ied; ready·ing** : to prepare for use or action

ready–made *adj* : made beforehand in large numbers

¹**re·al** *adj* **1** : not imaginary : ACTUAL **2** : not artificial : GENUINE

²**real** *adv* : ²VERY 1

real estate *n* : property consisting of buildings and land

re·al·ism *n* : willingness to face facts or to give in to what is necessary

re·al·is·tic *adj* **1** : true to life or nature **2** : ready to see things as they really are and to deal with them sensibly — **re·al·is·ti·cal·ly** *adv*

re·al·i·ty *n, pl* **re·al·i·ties** **1** : the way things actually are **2** : someone or something that is real or actually exists

re·al·i·za·tion *n* **1** : the state of understanding or becoming aware of something **2** : the act of accomplishing something planned or hoped for

re·al·ize *vb* **re·al·ized; re·al·iz·ing** **1** : to be aware of : UNDERSTAND **2** : to bring into being : ACCOMPLISH **3** : to get as a result of effort : GAIN

re·al·ly *adv* **1** : in fact **2** : without question

realm *n* **1** : KINGDOM 1 **2** : field of activity or influence

real time *n* : the actual time during which something takes place — **real–time** *adj*

re·al·ty *n* : REAL ESTATE

ream *n* **1** : a quantity of paper that may equal 480, 500, or 516 sheets **2 reams** *pl* : a great amount

reap *vb* **reaped; reap·ing** **1** : to cut (as grain) or clear (as a field) with a sickle, scythe, or machine **2** : ²HARVEST 1 **3** : to get as a result

reap·er *n* : a worker or machine that harvests crops

re·ap·pear *vb* **re·ap·peared; re·ap·pear·ing** : to appear again after not being seen for a while

¹**rear** *vb* **reared; rear·ing** **1** : to rise up on the hind legs **2** : to bring up **3** : to rise high **4** : to take care of the breeding and raising of

²**rear** *n* **1** : the space or position at the back **2** : the part (as of an army) or area farthest from the enemy **3** : the human buttocks

³**rear** *adj* : being at the back

re·ar·range *vb* **re·ar·ranged; re·ar·rang·ing** : to arrange again usually in a different way

¹**rea·son** *n* **1** : a statement given to explain a belief or an act **2** : a fact that makes something right or fair to do **3** : ¹CAUSE 1 **4** : the power to think and understand in a logical way **5** : a fair and sensible way of thinking about something

²**reason** *vb* **rea·soned; rea·son·ing** **1** : to think in a logical way **2** : to talk with another in a sensible way so as to influence his or her actions or opinions **3** : to state or ask logically

rea·son·able *adj* **1** : fair and sensible **2** : not too expensive **3** : fairly or moderately good — **rea·son·able·ness** *n* — **rea·son·ably** *adv*

re·as·sure *vb* **re·as·sured; re·as·sur·ing** : to make (someone) feel less afraid, upset, or doubtful

re·as·sur·ance *n* : something that is said or done to make someone feel less afraid, upset, or doubtful

rebate *n* : the return of part of a payment or of an amount owed

¹**reb·el** *n* **1** : a person who opposes or fights against a government **2** : a person who does not obey authority or follow usual standards

²**re·bel** *vb* **re·belled; re·bel·ling** **1** : to be or fight against authority and especially the authority of a person's government **2** : to feel or show anger, strong dislike, or disapproval

³**reb·el** *adj* : opposing or fighting against a government or ruler

re·bel·lion *n* **1** : open opposition to authority **2** : an open fight by citizens against their government

re·bel·lious *adj* **1** : taking part in rebellion **2** : fighting against or refusing to obey authority — **re·bel·lious·ly** *adv* — **re·bel·lious·ness** *n*

re·birth *n* **1** : a period in which something becomes popular again **2** : a period of new life or growth

re·born *adj* : born again

¹**re·bound** *vb* **re·bound·ed; re·bound·ing** **1** : to bounce back after hitting something **2** : to get over a disappointment **3** : to catch a basketball after a player has thrown it at the basket and has not scored a point

²**re·bound** *n* **1** : the action of bouncing back after hitting something **2** : an immediate reaction to a loss or disappointment **3** : the act of catching a basketball after a player has thrown it at the basket and missed

¹**re·buff** *vb* **re·buffed; re·buff·ing** : to refuse (something) in a sharp or rude way

²**rebuff** *n* : a sharp or rude refusal of something (as an offer)

re·build *vb* **re·built; re·build·ing** **1** : to make important repairs to or changes in **2** : to construct again

¹re·buke *vb* **re·buked; re·buk·ing** : to criticize severely

²rebuke *n* : an expression of strong disapproval

re·bus *n* : a riddle or puzzle made up of letters, pictures, and symbols whose names sound like the syllables and words of a phrase or sentence

re·but *vb* **re·but·ted; re·but·ting** : to prove to be wrong by argument or by proof

¹re·call *vb* **re·called; re·call·ing 1** : to bring back to mind : REMEMBER **2** : to ask or order to come back

²re·call *n* **1** : the ability to remember or an instance of remembering **2** : a command to return

re·cap·ture *vb* **re·cap·tured; re·cap·tur·ing 1** : to regain possession of **2** : to experience again

rec'd. *abbr* received

re·cede *vb* **re·ced·ed; re·ced·ing 1** : to move back or away **2** : to become smaller or weaker

re·ceipt *n* **1** : a written statement saying that money or goods have been received **2** : RECIPE **3** : the act of receiving **4 receipts** *pl* : something received

re·ceive *vb* **re·ceived; re·ceiv·ing 1** : to take or get something that is given, paid, or sent **2** : ²EXPERIENCE **3** : to accept as a visitor or member : WELCOME **4** : to change incoming radio waves into sounds or pictures

re·ceiv·er *n* **1** : a device for changing electricity or radio waves into light or sound **2** : a football player who catches passes thrown toward the opponent's goal

re·cent *adj* **1** : of or relating to a time not long past **2** : having lately appeared to come into being : NEW, FRESH — **re·cent·ly** *adv*

re·cep·ta·cle *n* : something used to receive and hold smaller objects

re·cep·tion *n* **1** : the act or manner of welcoming **2** : a social gathering to celebrate something or welcome someone **3** : the ability to receive a radio or television broadcast **4** : the act of catching a pass thrown toward the opponent's goal

re·cep·tion·ist *n* : an office employee who deals with callers or visitors

re·cep·tive *adj* : willing to consider new ideas

re·cep·tor *n* : a cell that receives a stimulus (as light or heat) and activates an associated nerve to send a message to the brain and that may be grouped into a sense organ (as a taste bud)

¹re·cess *n* **1** : a brief period for relaxation between work periods **2** : a secret or hidden place **3** : a hollow cut or built into a surface (as a wall) **4** : a brief time off from the activity of a court

²recess *vb* **re·cessed; re·cess·ing 1** : to put into a hollow space **2** : to interrupt for or take a brief time off

re·ces·sion *n* : a period of reduced business activity

re·ces·sive *adj* : being or produced by a form of a gene whose effect can be hidden by a dominant gene and which can produce a noticeable effect only when two copies of the gene are present

rec·i·pe *n* : a set of instructions for making something (as a food dish) by combining various things

re·cip·i·ent *n* : someone who receives something

re·cip·ro·cal *n* : one of a pair of numbers (as 9 and ⅑, ⅔ and 3⁄2) whose product is one

re·cit·al *n* **1** : a public performance of music or dance given by one or more people **2** : an act of describing something usually in great detail

rec·i·ta·tion *n* **1** : the act or an instance of saying something out loud **2** : the act of saying something in a particular order

re·cite *vb* **re·cit·ed; re·cit·ing 1** : to repeat from memory **2** : to tell about in detail

reck·less *adj* : showing lack of caution : engaging in wild careless behavior — **reck·less·ly** *adv* — **reck·less·ness** *n*

reck·on *vb* **reck·oned; reck·on·ing 1** : to believe that something is true or possible **2** : CALCULATE 1 **3** : to regard or think of as : CONSIDER

re·claim *vb* **re·claimed; re·claim·ing 1** : to get back (something that was lost or taken away) **2** : to restore to an original state **3** : to obtain from a waste product or by-product

rec·la·ma·tion *n* : the act or process of recovering : the state of being recovered

re·cline *vb* **re·clined; re·clin·ing 1** : to lie down or sit back usually in a relaxed way **2** : to lean backward

rec·og·ni·tion *n* **1** : the act of knowing and remembering upon seeing **2** : the act of accepting the existence, truth, or importance of something **3** : special attention or notice

rec·og·nize *vb* **rec·og·nized; rec·og·niz·ing 1** : to know and remember upon seeing **2** : to be willing to accept **3** : to take approving notice of

¹re·coil *vb* **re·coiled; re·coil·ing 1** : to draw back **2** : to spring back to or as if to a starting position

²recoil *n* : a sudden backward movement or springing back (as of a gun just fired)

rec·ol·lect *vb* **rec·ol·lect·ed; rec·ol·lect·ing** : to call to mind : REMEMBER

rec·ol·lec·tion *n* **1** : the act or power of remembering : MEMORY **2** : something remembered

rec·om·mend *vb* **rec·om·mend·ed; rec·om·mend·ing 1** : to present or support as worthy or fit **2** : to make a suggestion : ADVISE **3** : to make acceptable

rec·om·men·da·tion *n* **1** : the act of presenting or supporting as worthy or fit **2** : a thing or course of action suggested as suitable or appropriate **3** : something (as a letter) that explains why a person is appropriate or qualified

¹rec·om·pense *vb* **rec·om·pensed; rec·om·pens·ing** : to pay for or pay back

²recompense *n* : something given in return for damage or suffering

rec·on·cile *vb* **rec·on·ciled; rec·on·cil·ing 1** : to make friendly again **2** : to settle by agreement : ADJUST **3** : to make agree **4** : to cause to give in or accept

rec·on·cil·i·a·tion *n* : the act of becoming friendly again (as after a disagreement)

re·con·di·tion *vb* **re·con·di·tioned; re·con·di·tion·ing** : to restore to good condition

re·con·nais·sance *n* : a survey (as of enemy territory) to get information

re·con·sid·er *vb* **re·con·sid·ered; re·con·sid·er·ing** : to think carefully about again especially with the possibility of change or reversal

re·con·sid·er·a·tion *n* : the act of thinking carefully about again especially with the possibility of change or reversal

re·con·struct *vb* **re·con·struct·ed; re·con·struct·ing** : to make or form again : REBUILD

¹re·cord *vb* **re·cord·ed; re·cord·ing 1** : to set down in writing **2** : to show a measurement of **3** : to change sound or visual images into a form (as on an optical disk or hard drive) that can be listened to or watched at a later time

²rec·ord *n* **1** : something written to give proof of something or tell about past events **2** : something that recalls or tells about past events **3** : a performance or achievement that is the best of its kind **4** : the known or recorded facts about a person or thing **5** : something on which sound or visual images have been recorded — **of record** : made known in public documents — **on record** : published in official documents

³rec·ord *adj* : outstanding among other like things

re·cord·er *n* **1** : a person or device that records **2** : a musical instrument like a long hollow whistle with eight holes for the fingers

re·cord·ing *n* : ²RECORD 4

¹re·count *vb* **re·count·ed; re·count·ing** : to tell all about : NARRATE

²re·count *vb* **re·count·ed; re·count·ing** : to count again

³re·count *n* : a counting again (as of election votes)

re·course *n* : someone or something that can be turned to for help or protection

re·cov·er *vb* **re·cov·ered; re·cov·er·ing 1** : to get back : REGAIN **2** : to regain or return to a normal or usual state (as of health or composure **3** : to make up for

re·cov·ery *n, pl* **re·cov·er·ies** : the act or process of regaining or returning to a normal or usual state

rec·re·a·tion *n* : something done for fun and relaxation

¹re·cruit *vb* **re·cruit·ed; re·cruit·ing 1** : to enlist as a member of the armed forces **2** : to get the services of

²recruit *n* **1** : a newly enlisted member of the armed forces **2** : a newcomer to a group or field of activity

rect·an·gle *n* : a flat geometric four-sided figure with right angles and with opposite sides parallel

rect·an·gu·lar *adj* : shaped like a rectangle

rec·ti·fy *vb* **rec·ti·fied; rec·ti·fy·ing** : to set or make right

rec·tor *n* : PASTOR

rec·tum *n, pl* **rec·tums** *also* **rec·ta** : the last part of the large intestine

re·cu·per·ate *vb* **re·cu·per·at·ed; re·cu·per·at·ing** : to regain health or strength

re·cu·per·a·tion *n* : a recovery of health or strength

re·cur *vb* **re·curred; re·cur·ring** : to occur or appear again

re·cur·rence *n* : the state of occurring or appearing again or time after time

re·cur·rent *adj* : happening or appearing again and again

re·cy·cla·ble *adj* : able to be recycled

re·cy·cle *vb* **re·cy·cled; re·cy·cling** : to process (as paper, glass, or cans) in order to regain or reuse materials

¹red *adj* **red·der; red·dest 1** : of the color of blood : colored red **2** : flushed with emotion (as embarrassment) — **red·ness** *n*

²red *n* **1** : the color of blood or of the ruby **2** : something red in color

red·bird *n* : any of several birds (as a cardinal) with mostly red feathers

red blood cell *n* : a tiny reddish cell of the blood that contains hemoglobin and carries oxygen from the lungs to the tissues

red·breast *n* : a bird (as a robin) with a reddish breast

red cell *n* : RED BLOOD CELL

red-coat *n* : a British soldier especially in America during the Revolutionary War

red·den *vb* **red·dened; red·den·ing** : to make or become red

red·dish *adj* : somewhat red

re·deem *vb* **1** : to make up for **2** : to buy, get, or win back **3** : to make good : FULFILL **4** : to exchange for something of value **5** : to free from sin — **re·deem·er** *n*

re·demp·tion *n* **1** : the act of making up for **2** : an exchange for something of value **3** : the act of saving from sin

red–hand·ed *adv or adj* : in the act of doing something wrong

red·head *n* : a person having reddish hair

red·head·ed *adj* : having reddish hair or a red head

red–hot *adj* **1** : glowing red with heat **2** : very active or successful **3** : extremely popular

re·di·rect *vb* **re·di·rect·ed; re·di·rect·ing** : to change the course or direction of

re·dis·cov·er *vb* **re·dis·cov·ered; re·dis·cov·er·ing** : to discover again

red–let·ter *adj* : of special importance : MEMORABLE

re·do *vb* **re·did; re·done; re·do·ing** : to do over or again

re·dou·ble *vb* **re·dou·bled; re·dou·bling** : to greatly increase the size or amount of

red panda *n* : a long-tailed animal that is related to and resembles the raccoon, has long reddish brown fur, and is found from the Himalayas to southern China

re·dress *vb* **re·dressed; re·dress·ing** : to set right : REMEDY

red tape *n* : usually official rules and regulations that seem unnecessary and prevent things from being done quickly and easily

re·duce *vb* **re·duced; re·duc·ing** **1** : to make smaller or less **2** : to bring to a usually worse state **3** : to lower in grade or rank **4** : to change to a simpler form **5** : to lose weight by dieting

re·duc·tion *n* **1** : the act of making something smaller or less : the state of being made smaller or less **2** : the amount by which something is made smaller or less

red·wood *n* : a very tall tree of California that bears cones and has light durable brownish red wood

reed *n* **1** : a tall slender grass that grows in wet areas **2** : a stem or a growth or mass of reeds **3** : a thin flexible piece of cane, plastic, or metal fastened to the mouthpiece of an instrument (as a clarinet) or over an air opening in an instrument (as an accordion) and made to vibrate by an air current

reef *n* : a chain of rocks or coral or a ridge of sand at or near the surface of water

¹reek *n* : a strong or unpleasant smell

²reek *vb* **reeked; reek·ing** : to have a strong or unpleasant smell

¹reel *n* **1** : a device that can be turned round and round to wind up something flexible **2** : a quantity of something wound on a reel

²reel *vb* **reeled; reel·ing** **1** : to wind on a reel **2** : to pull by the use of a reel — **reel off** : to say or recite rapidly or easily

³reel *vb* **reeled; reel·ing** **1** : to whirl or spin around **2** : to be in a confused or dizzy state **3** : to fall back suddenly (as after being hit) **4** : to walk or move unsteadily : STAGGER

⁴reel *n* : a lively folk dance

re·elect *vb* **re·elect·ed; re·elect·ing** : to elect for another term

re·en·act *vb* **re·en·act·ed; re·en·act·ing** : to repeat the actions of (an earlier event)

re·en·ter *vb* **re·en·tered; re·en·ter·ing** : to enter again

re·es·tab·lish *vb* **re·es·tab·lished; re·es·tab·lish·ing** : to establish again : bring back into existence

ref *n* : ¹REFEREE 1

re·fer *vb* **re·ferred; re·fer·ring** **1** : to look at for information **2** : to send or direct to some person or place for treatment, aid, information, or decision **3** : to call attention **4** : to mention (something) in talking or writing

¹ref·er·ee *n* **1** : a sports official with final authority for conducting a game **2** : a person who is asked to settle a disagreement

²referee *vb* **ref·er·eed; ref·er·ee·ing** : to act or be in charge of as referee

ref·er·ence *n* **1** : the act of looking at or in something for information **2** : a relation to or concern with something **3** : the act or an instance of mentioning **4** : a work (as a dictionary) that contains useful information **5** : something that refers a reader to another source of information **6** : a person who can be asked for information about another person's character or ability **7** : a written statement about someone's character or ability

ref·er·en·dum *n, pl* **ref·er·en·da** *or* **ref·er·en·dums** : the practice of voting on an issue

¹re·fill *vb* **re·filled; re·fill·ing** : to fill or become filled again

²re·fill *n* : a new or fresh supply of something

re·fine *vb* **re·fined; re·fin·ing** **1** : to bring to a pure state **2** : to make better : IMPROVE

re·fined *adj* **1** : having or showing good taste or training **2** : freed from impurities : PURE

re·fine·ment *n* **1** : the act or process of improving something or bringing something to a pure state **2** : excellence of manners or tastes **3** : a small change meant to improve something

re·fin·ery *n, pl* **re·fin·er·ies** : a building and equipment where something (as oil or metal) is made pure and ready for use

re·fin·ish *vb* **re·fin·ished; re·fin·ish·ing** : to give (as furniture) a new surface

re·fit *vb* **re·fit·ted; re·fit·ting** : to make ready for use again

re·flect *vb* **re·flect·ed; re·flect·ing** **1** : to bend or throw back (waves of light, sound, or heat) **2** : to give back an image or likeness of in the manner of a mirror **3** : to make known **4** : to cause to be thought of in a specified way or in a bad way **5** : to think seriously and carefully about

re·flec·tion *n* **1** : the return of light or sound waves from a surface **2** : an image produced by or as if by a mirror **3** : something that brings blame or disgrace **4** : careful thought **5** : an opinion formed or a remark made after careful thought

re·flec·tor *n* : a shiny surface for reflecting light or heat

re·flex *n* **1** : an action or movement that is made automatically without thinking as a reaction to a stimulus **2 re·flex·es** *pl* : the natural ability to react quickly

re·for·est *vb* **re·for·est·ed; re·for·est·ing** : to renew forest growth by planting seeds or young trees

re·for·es·ta·tion *n* : the act of renewing forest growth by planting seeds or young trees

¹re·form *vb* **re·formed; re·form·ing** **1** : to make better or improve by removal of faults **2** : to stop engaging in bad habits or behavior — **re·form·er** *n*

²reform *n* : the improvement of something by removing faults or problems

ref·or·ma·tion *n* : the act of changing something or someone for the better

re·fract *vb* **re·fract·ed; re·fract·ing** : to make (light) bend when it passes through at an angle

re·frac·tion *n* : the bending of a ray when it passes at an angle from one medium into another in which its speed is changed (as when light passes from air into water)

re·frac·to·ry *adj* **1** : resisting control or authority : STUBBORN **2** : capable of enduring very high temperatures

¹re·frain *vb* **re·frained; re·frain·ing** : to keep from giving in to a desire or impulse

²refrain *n* : a phrase or verse repeated regularly in a poem or song

re·fresh *vb* **re·freshed; re·fresh·ing** : to bring back to an original state or normal condition (as by restoring energy or making more active) — **re·fresh·er** *n*

re·fresh·ment *n* : something (as food or drink) that refreshes — often used in pl.

re·frig·er·ate *vb* **re·frig·er·at·ed; re·frig·er·at·ing** : to make or keep cold or cool especially by placing in a refrigerator

re·frig·er·a·tor *n* : a device or room for keeping articles (as food) cool

re·fu·el *vb* **re·fu·eled; re·fu·el·ing** : to provide with or take on more fuel

ref·uge *n* **1** : shelter or protection from danger or distress **2** : a place that provides shelter or protection

ref·u·gee *n* : a person who flees for safety (as from war) usually to a foreign country

¹re·fund *vb* **re·fund·ed; re·fund·ing** : return (money) as repayment

²re·fund *n* : an amount of money that is returned as repayment

re·fus·al *n* : the act of showing unwillingness to do, give, or allow something

¹re·fuse *vb* **re·fused; re·fus·ing** **1** : to express unwillingness to accept : turn down (something) **2** : to express or show unwillingness to do, give, or allow something

²ref·use *n* : TRASH 1, RUBBISH

re·fute *vb* **re·fut·ed; re·fut·ing** : to say or prove that something is wrong or untrue

reg. *abbr* **1** region **2** regular

re·gain *vb* **re·gained; re·gain·ing** **1** : to gain or get again : get back **2** : to get back to : reach again

re·gal *adj* : relating to or suitable for a king or queen : ROYAL — **re·gal·ly** *adv*

re·gale *vb* **re·galed; re·gal·ing** : to give pleasure or amusement to

¹re·gard *n* **1** : CONSIDERATION 2 **2** : a feeling of respect **3 regards** *pl* : friendly greetings **4** : a point to be considered **5** : ²LOOK 1 — **in regard to** : in relation to — **with regard to** : in relation to

²regard *vb* **re·gard·ed; re·gard·ing** **1** : to think of in a particular way : CONSIDER **2** : to look at **3** : to give consideration to

re·gard·ing *prep* : relating to : ABOUT

re·gard·less *adv* : in spite of something that might be a problem

regardless of *prep* : in spite of

re·gat·ta *n* : a race or a series of races between sailboats, speedboats, or rowing boats

re·gen·er·ate *vb* **re·gen·er·at·ed; re·gen·er·at·ing** : to grow (as a lost body part) once more

re·gent *n* : a person who temporarily governs a kingdom in place of a monarch

re·gime *n* **1** : a form or system of government **2** : REGIMEN

reg·i·men *n* : a systematic course of action

reg·i·ment *n* : a military unit made up usually of a number of battalions

re·gion *n* **1** : an area having no definite

boundaries **2** : a broad geographic area **3** : VICINITY 2

re·gion·al *adj* : of, relating to, or characteristic of a certain geographic area

¹reg·is·ter *n* **1** : an official list or book for keeping records of something **2** : a mechanical device (as a cash register) that records items **3** : a device for regulating ventilation or the flow of heated air from a furnace

²register *vb* **reg·is·tered; reg·is·ter·ing 1** : to enter or enroll in an official list or book of public records **2** : to record automatically **3** : to show by expression and bodily movements **4** : to make known officially and publicly **5** : to be recognized or remembered **6** : to get special protection for (something mailed) by paying extra postage

reg·is·tra·tion *n* **1** : the act of entering on an official list **2** : a document showing that something is registered

reg·is·try *n, pl* **reg·is·tries** : a place where registration takes place

¹re·gret *vb* **re·gret·ted; re·gret·ting** : to be sorry for

²regret *n* **1** : sadness or disappointment caused especially by something beyond a person's control **2** : an expression of sorrow or disappointment **3 regrets** *pl* : a note politely refusing to accept an invitation

re·gret·ful *adj* : feeling or showing regret — **re·gret·ful·ly** *adv*

re·gret·ta·ble *adj* : causing sorrow or disappointment — **re·gret·ta·bly** *adv*

re·group *vb* **re·grouped; re·group·ing 1** : to form into another group

reg·u·lar *adj* **1** : steady in practice or occurrence : happening on or as if on a schedule **2** : following established usages or rules **3** : ¹NORMAL 1 **4** : following the usual manner of inflection **5** : having all sides equal and all angles equal — **reg·u·lar·ly** *adv*

reg·u·lar·i·ty *n* : the quality or state of happening on or as if on a schedule

reg·u·late *vb* **reg·u·lat·ed; reg·u·lat·ing 1** : to bring under the control of authority : make rules concerning **2** : to control the time, amount, degree, or rate of **3** : to bring order or method to — **reg·u·la·tor** *n*

reg·u·la·tion *n* **1** : a rule or law telling how something is to be done **2** : the act of controlling or bringing under control

re·gur·gi·tate *vb* **re·gur·gi·tat·ed; re·gur·gi·tat·ing** : to bring food that has been swallowed back to and out of the mouth

re·hears·al *n* : a private performance or practice session in preparation for a public appearance

re·hearse *vb* **re·hearsed; re·hears·ing** : to practice in private in preparation for a public performance

¹reign *n* **1** : the authority or rule of a monarch **2** : the time during which a monarch rules

²reign *vb* **reigned; reign·ing 1** : to rule as a monarch **2** : to be usual or widespread **3** : to be the best or most powerful

re·im·burse *vb* **re·im·bursed; re·im·burs·ing** : to pay back : REPAY — **re·im·burse·ment** *n*

¹rein *n* **1** : a line or strap that is attached at either end of the bit of a bridle and is used to control an animal — usually used in pl. **2** : an influence that slows, limits, or holds back **3** : controlling or guiding power

²rein *vb* **reined; rein·ing** : to check, control, or stop by or as if by reins

re·in·car·na·tion *n* : rebirth of the soul in a new body after death

rein·deer *n, pl* **reindeer** : CARIBOU

re·in·force *vb* **re·in·forced; re·in·forc·ing 1** : to strengthen with new supplies or more people **2** : to strengthen by adding more material for support

re·in·force·ment *n* **1** : people or things (as supplies) sent to help or support **2** : the act of making something stronger or able to last longer

re·in·state *vb* **re·in·stat·ed; re·in·stat·ing** : to place again in a former position or condition — **re·in·state·ment** *n*

re·it·er·ate *vb* **re·it·er·at·ed; re·it·er·at·ing** : to repeat something said or done

¹re·ject *vb* **re·ject·ed; re·ject·ing** : to refuse to accept, believe, or consider

²re·ject *n* : a person or thing not accepted as good enough for some purpose

re·jec·tion *n* : the act of not accepting, believing, or considering something : the state of being rejected

re·joice *vb* **re·joiced; re·joic·ing** : to feel or show joy or happiness

re·join *vb* **re·joined; re·join·ing 1** : to join again : return to **2** : to reply often in a sharp or critical way

re·join·der *n* : ²REPLY

re·kin·dle *vb* **re·kin·dled; re·kin·dling** : to cause to be active again

¹re·lapse *n* **1** : a return of illness after a period of improvement **2** : a return to a former and undesirable state or condition

²re·lapse *vb* **re·lapsed; re·laps·ing** : to return to a former state or condition (as of illness or bad behavior) after a change for the better

re·late *vb* **re·lat·ed; re·lat·ing 1** : to give an account of : NARRATE **2** : to show or have a relationship to or between : CONNECT

re·lat·ed *adj* **1** : sharing some connection **2** : connected by common ancestry or by marriage **3** : connected by a usually distant common ancestor and typically sharing similar characteristics

re·la·tion *n* **1** : CONNECTION **2**, RELATIONSHIP **2** : a related person : RELATIVE **3** : REFERENCE **2**, RESPECT **4 relations** *pl* : the interaction between two or more people, groups, or countries

re·la·tion·ship *n* **1** : the state of being related or connected **2** : connection by common ancestry or marriage **3** : the state of interaction between two or more people, groups, or countries

¹rel·a·tive *n* : a person connected with another by ancestry or marriage

²relative *adj* **1** : existing in comparison to something else **2** : RELEVANT — **rel·a·tive·ly** *adv*

re·lax *vb* **re·laxed; re·lax·ing 1** : to make or become loose or less tense **2** : to make or become less severe or strict **3** : to become calm and free from stress **4** : to seek rest or enjoyment

re·lax·a·tion *n* **1** : the act or fact of being or becoming rested, calm, or less tense or severe **2** : a way of becoming rested or calm and free from stress

¹re·lay *n* **1** : a race between teams in which each team member covers a certain part of the course **2** : the act of passing something from one person to the next **3** : a fresh supply (as of horses or people) arranged to relieve others

²re·lay *vb* **re·layed; re·lay·ing** : to pass along by stages

¹re·lease *vb* **re·leased; re·leas·ing 1** : to set free or let go of **2** : to allow to escape **3** : to relieve from a duty, responsibility, or burden **4** : to give up or hand over to someone else **5** : to permit to be published, sold, or shown

²release *n* **1** : the act of setting free or letting go **2** : the act of allowing something to escape **3** : a discharge from an obligation or responsibility **4** : relief or rescue from sorrow, suffering, or trouble **5** : a device for holding or releasing a mechanism **6** : the act of making something available to the public **7** : something (as a new product or song) that is made available to the public

re·lent *vb* **re·lent·ed; re·lent·ing 1** : to become less severe, harsh, or strict **2** : to give in after first resisting or refusing

re·lent·less *adj* : showing no lessening of severity, intensity, or strength — **re·lent·less·ly** *adv* — **re·lent·less·ness** *n*

rel·e·vance *n* : relation to the matter at hand

rel·e·vant *adj* : having something to do with the matter at hand

re·li·abil·i·ty *n* : the quality or state of being fit to be trusted or relied on

re·li·able *adj* : fit to be trusted or relied on: DEPENDABLE — **re·li·ably** *adv*

re·li·ance *n* : the act or state of depending on someone or something

rel·ic *n* **1** : something left behind after decay or disappearance **2** : an object that is considered holy because of its connection with a saint or martyr

re·lief *n* **1** : the feeling of happiness that occurs when something unpleasant or distressing stops or does not happen **2** : removal or lessening of something painful or troubling **3** : something that interrupts in a welcome way **4** : release from a post or from performance of a duty **5** : WELFARE **2** **6** : raising of figures or designs from the background **7** : elevations of a land surface

re·lieve *vb* **re·lieved; re·liev·ing 1** : to free partly or wholly from a burden, pain, or distress **2** : to bring about the removal or lessening of **3** : to release from a post or duty **4** : to break the sameness of — **re·liev·er** *n*

re·li·gion *n* **1** : the belief in and worship of God or gods **2** : a system of religious beliefs and practices

re·li·gious *adj* **1** : believing in God or gods and following the practices of a religion **2** : of or relating to religion **3** : very devoted and faithful — **re·li·gious·ly** *adv*

re·lin·quish *vb* **re·lin·quished; re·lin·quish·ing** : to let go of : give up

¹rel·ish *n* **1** : great enjoyment **2** : a highly seasoned food eaten with other food to add flavor

²relish *vb* **rel·ished; rel·ish·ing 1** : to be pleased by : ENJOY **2** : to like the taste of

re·live *vb* **re·lived; re·liv·ing** : to experience again (as in the imagination)

re·luc·tance *n* : the quality or state of showing doubt or unwillingness

re·luc·tant *adj* : showing doubt or unwillingness — **re·luc·tant·ly** *adv*

re·ly *vb* **re·lied; re·ly·ing** : to trust in or depend on

re·main *vb* **re·mained; re·main·ing 1** : to stay in the same place **2** : to stay after others have gone **3** : to continue to be **4** : to be left after others have been removed, subtracted, or destroyed **5** : to be something yet to be done or considered

re·main·der *n* **1** : a group or part that is left **2** : the number left after a subtraction **3** : the number left over from the dividend after division that is less than the divisor

re·mains *n pl* **1** : whatever is left over or behind **2** : a dead body

re·make *vb* **re·made; re·mak·ing** : to make again or in a different form

¹re·mark *n* **1** : a brief comment **2 remarks** *pl* : a short speech

²remark *vb* **re·marked; re·mark·ing :** to make a comment **:** express as an observation

re·mark·able *adj* **:** worthy of being or likely to be noticed especially as being unusual — **re·mark·ably** *adv*

re·match *n* **:** a second meeting between the same contestants

re·me·di·al *adj* **:** intended to make something better

¹rem·e·dy *n, pl* **rem·e·dies** **1 :** a medicine or treatment that cures or relieves **2 :** something that corrects a problem

²remedy *vb* **rem·e·died; rem·e·dy·ing :** to provide or serve as a cure or solution for

re·mem·ber *vb* **re·mem·bered; re·mem·ber·ing** **1 :** to bring to mind or think of again **2 :** to keep in mind **3 :** to pass along greetings from

re·mem·brance *n* **1 :** the act of thinking about again **2 :** MEMORY 4 **3 :** something that is done to honor the memory of a person or event **4 :** something (as a souvenir) that brings to mind a past experience

re·mind *vb* **re·mind·ed; re·mind·ing :** to cause to remember — **re·mind·er** *n*

rem·i·nisce *vb* **rem·i·nisced; rem·i·nisc·ing :** to talk or think about things in the past

rem·i·nis·cence *n* **1 :** the act of recalling or telling of a past experience **2 reminis·cences** *pl* **:** a story of a person's memorable experiences

rem·i·nis·cent *adj* **:** being a reminder of something else

re·miss *adj* **:** careless in the performance of work or duty

re·mis·sion *n* **:** a period of time during a serious illness when there are few or no symptoms

re·mit *vb* **re·mit·ted; re·mit·ting** **1 :** to send money (as in payment) **2 : ²**PARDON 2

re·mit·tance *n* **:** money sent in payment

rem·nant *n* **:** something that remains or is left over

re·mod·el *vb* **re·mod·eled** *or* **re·mod·elled; re·mod·el·ing** *or* **re·mod·el·ling :** to change the structure or appearance of

re·mon·strate *vb* **re·mon·strat·ed; re·mon·strat·ing : ¹**PROTEST 1

re·morse *n* **:** deep regret for doing or saying something wrong — **re·morse·ful** *adj* — **re·morse·less** *adj*

¹re·mote *adj* **re·mot·er; re·mot·est** **1 :** far off in place or time **2 :** SECLUDED 1 **3 :** small in degree **4 :** distant in manner **:** ALOOF **5 :** not closely connected or related — **re·mote·ly** *adv* — **re·mote·ness** *n*

²remote *n* **:** REMOTE CONTROL 1

remote control *n* **1 :** a device for controlling something from a distance **2 :** control (as by a radio signal) of operation from a distant point

re·mov·able *adj* **:** possible to be taken off or gotten rid of

re·mov·al *n* **:** the act of moving away or getting rid of **:** the fact of being moved away or gotten rid of

re·move *vb* **re·moved; re·mov·ing** **1 :** to move by lifting or taking off or away **2 :** to get rid of **3 :** to dismiss from a job or office

re·mov·er *n* **:** something (as a chemical) used in getting rid of a substance

re·nais·sance *n* **1** *cap* **:** the period of European history between the 14th and 17th centuries marked by a fresh interest in ancient art and literature and by the beginnings of modern science **2 :** the act of changing in a positive way **:** a period during which things are improving

re·name *vb* **re·named; re·nam·ing :** to give a new name to

rend *vb* **rent ; rend·ing :** to tear apart by force

ren·der *vb* **ren·dered; ren·der·ing** **1 :** to cause to be or become **2 :** to furnish or give to another **3 :** to officially report **4 :** to obtain by heating **5 :** PERFORM 3

ren·dez·vous *n, pl* **ren·dez·vous** **1 :** a place agreed on for a meeting **2 :** a planned meeting

ren·di·tion *n* **:** an act or a result of performing

ren·e·gade *n* **1 :** a person who deserts a faith, cause, or party **2 :** a person who does not obey rules

re·nege *vb* **re·neged; re·neg·ing :** to go back on a promise or agreement

re·new *vb* **re·newed; re·new·ing** **1 :** to make or become new, fresh, or strong again **2 :** to make, do, or begin again **3 :** to put in a fresh supply of **4 :** to continue in force for a new period

re·new·able *adj* **:** capable of being replaced by natural processes

re·new·al *n* **1 :** the act of continuing in force for a new period **2 :** the state of being made new, fresh, or strong again **3 :** something renewed

re·nounce *vb* **re·nounced; re·nounc·ing** **1 :** to give up, abandon, or resign usually by a public declaration **2 :** to refuse to follow, obey, or recognize any longer

ren·o·vate *vb* **ren·o·vat·ed; ren·o·vat·ing :** to put in good condition again — **ren·o·va·tor** *n*

re·nown *n* **:** the state of being widely and favorably known

re·nowned *adj* **:** widely and favorably known

¹rent *n* **:** money paid for the use of another's property — **for rent :** available for use at a price

²**rent** *vb* **rent·ed; rent·ing 1 :** to pay money in exchange for the use of someone else's property **2 :** to give the possession and use of in return for an agreed upon amount of money **3 :** to be available for use at a price

³**rent** *past and past participle of* REND

¹**rent·al** *n* **:** an amount paid or collected as rent

²**rental** *adj* **:** relating to or available for rent

rent·er *n* **:** a person who pays money for the use of something (as a place to live)

re·open *vb* **re·opened; re·open·ing :** to open again

re·or·ga·nize *vb* **re·or·ga·nized; re·or·ga·niz·ing :** to organize differently

rep. *abbr* representative

¹**re·pair** *vb* **re·paired; re·pair·ing 1 :** to put back in good condition **:** FIX **2 :** to make up for

²**repair** *n* **1 :** the act or process of putting back in good condition **2 :** ¹CONDITION 4

rep·a·ra·tion *n* **1 :** the act of making up for a wrong **2 :** something paid by a country losing a war to the winner to make up for damages done in the war

re·past *n* **:** ¹MEAL

re·pay *vb* **re·paid; re·pay·ing 1 :** to pay back **2 :** to do or give something in return

re·pay·ment *n* **:** the act or an instance of paying back

re·peal *vb* **re·pealed; re·peal·ing :** to do away with especially by legislative action

¹**re·peat** *vb* **re·peat·ed; re·peat·ing 1 :** to state or tell again **2 :** to say from memory **:** RECITE **3 :** to make or do again

²**repeat** *n* **1 :** the act of happening or being done again **2 :** something happening or being done again

re·peat·ed *adj* **:** done or happening again and again — **re·peat·ed·ly** *adv*

re·pel *vb* **re·pelled; re·pel·ling 1 :** to drive back **2 :** to push away **3 :** to keep out **:** RESIST **4 :** ²DISGUST

re·pel·lent *n* **:** a substance used to keep off pests (as insects)

re·pent *vb* **re·pent·ed; re·pent·ing :** to acknowledge regret for having done something wrong

re·pen·tance *n* **:** the action or process of acknowledging regret for having done something wrong

re·pen·tant *adj* **:** feeling or showing regret for something said or done — **re·pen·tant·ly** *adv*

re·per·cus·sion *n* **:** a widespread, indirect, or unexpected effect of something said or done

rep·er·toire *n* **:** a list or supply of plays, operas, or pieces that a company or person is prepared to perform

rep·er·to·ry *n, pl* **rep·er·to·ries :** REPERTOIRE

rep·e·ti·tion *n* **1 :** the act or an instance of stating or doing again **2 :** something stated or done again

re·place *vb* **re·placed; re·plac·ing 1 :** to put back in a former or proper place **2 :** to take the place of **3 :** to put something new in the place of

re·place·ment *n* **1 :** the act of putting back, taking the place of, or substituting **:** the state of being put back or substituted **2 :** ¹SUBSTITUTE

re·plen·ish *vb* **re·plen·ished; re·plen·ish·ing :** to make full or complete once more

re·plete *adj* **:** well supplied

rep·li·ca *n* **:** a very exact copy

¹**re·ply** *vb* **re·plied; re·ply·ing :** to say or do in answer **:** RESPOND

²**reply** *n, pl* **re·plies :** something said, written, or done in answer

¹**re·port** *n* **1 :** a usually complete description or statement **2 :** a written or spoken statement that may or may not be true **3 :** REPUTATION 1 **4 :** an explosive noise

²**report** *vb* **re·port·ed; re·port·ing 1 :** to give a written or spoken description of something **2 :** to make known to the proper authorities **3 :** to complain about (someone) for misconduct **4 :** to make a statement that may or may not be true **5 :** to prepare or present an account of something (as for television or a newspaper) **6 :** to show up — **re·port·er** *n*

report card *n* **:** a written statement of a student's grades

¹**re·pose** *vb* **re·posed; re·pos·ing :** to lay or lie at rest

²**repose** *n* **1 :** a state of resting **2 :** freedom from disturbance or excitement **:** CALM

rep·re·hen·si·ble *adj* **:** deserving criticism or condemnation

rep·re·sent *vb* **rep·re·sent·ed; rep·re·sent·ing 1 :** to present a picture, image, or likeness of **:** PORTRAY **2 :** to be a sign or symbol of **3 :** to act for or in place of

rep·re·sen·ta·tion *n* **1 :** one (as a picture or symbol) that is a sign or portrayal of something else **2 :** the act of doing something on behalf of another or others **:** the state of doing something on behalf of another or others (as in a legislative body)

¹**rep·re·sen·ta·tive** *adj* **1 :** serving to portray **2 :** carried on by people elected to act for others **3 :** being a typical example of the thing mentioned

²**representative** *n* **1 :** a typical example (as of a group or class) **2 :** a person who acts for others (as in a legislature and especially in the House of Representatives of the United States or of a state)

re·press *vb* **re·pressed; re·press·ing :** to hold in check by or as if by pressure

¹**re·prieve** *vb* **re·prieved; re·priev·ing 1 :** to delay something (as the punishment of a prisoner sentenced to die) **2 :** to give relief to

²**reprieve** *n* **1 :** the act of postponing something **2 :** a temporary relief

¹**rep·ri·mand** *n* **:** a severe or formal criticism : CENSURE

²**reprimand** *vb* **rep·ri·mand·ed; rep·ri·mand·ing :** to criticize (a person) severely or formally

re·pri·sal *n* **:** an act in return for harm done by another : an act of revenge

¹**re·proach** *vb* **re·proached; re·proach·ing : :** to find fault with : BLAME

²**reproach** *n* **1 :** something that deserves blame or disgrace **2 :** an expression of disapproval — **re·proach·ful** *adj* — **re·proach·ful·ly** *adv*

re·pro·duce *vb* **re·pro·duced; re·pro·duc·ing 1 :** to produce another living thing of the same kind **2 :** to imitate closely **3 :** to make a copy of

re·pro·duc·tion *n* **1 :** the process by which living things produce offspring **2 :** the act or process of copying something **3 :** ¹COPY 1

re·pro·duc·tive *adj* **:** relating to or concerned with the production of offspring

re·proof *n* **:** blame or criticism for a fault

re·prove *vb* **re·proved; re·prov·ing :** to express blame or disapproval of : SCOLD

rep·tile *n* **:** a cold-blooded animal (as snake, lizard, turtle, or alligator) that breathes air and usually has the skin covered with scales or bony plates

re·pub·lic *n* **:** a country with elected representatives and an elected chief of state who is not a monarch and who is usually a president

¹**re·pub·li·can** *n* **1 :** a person who favors a form of government having elected representatives **2** *cap* **:** a member of the Republican party of the United States

²**republican** *adj* **1 :** being a form of government having elected representatives **2 :** relating to a major political party in the United States that is associated with business interests and favors a limited government role in economic matters

re·pu·di·ate *vb* **re·pu·di·at·ed; re·pu·di·at·ing 1 :** to refuse to have anything to do with **2 :** to refuse to believe or approve of

¹**re·pulse** *vb* **re·pulsed; re·puls·ing 1 :** to drive or beat back : REPEL **2 :** to reject in a rude or unfriendly way : SNUB **3 :** to cause dislike or disgust in

²**repulse** *n* **1 :** ²REBUFF, SNUB **2 :** the action of driving back an attacker

re·pul·sive *adj* **:** causing disgust — **re·pul·sive·ly** *adv* — **re·pul·sive·ness** *n*

rep·u·ta·ble *adj* **:** having a good reputation

rep·u·ta·tion *n* **1 :** overall quality or character as seen or judged by people in general **2 :** notice by other people of some quality or ability

¹**re·pute** *vb* **re·put·ed; re·put·ing :** CONSIDER 3

²**repute** *n* **1 :** REPUTATION 1 **2 :** good reputation : HONOR

¹**re·quest** *n* **1 :** the act of asking for something **2 :** something asked for **3 :** the condition of being asked for

²**request** *vb* **re·quest·ed; re·quest·ing 1 :** to ask something of someone **2 :** to ask for

re·qui·em *n* **1 :** a mass for a dead person **2 :** a musical service or hymn in honor of dead people

re·quire *vb* **re·quired; re·quir·ing 1 :** to have a need for **2 :** ¹ORDER 2, COMMAND

re·quire·ment *n* **:** something that is necessary

¹**req·ui·site** *adj* **:** needed for reaching a goal or achieving a purpose

²**requisite** *n* **:** REQUIREMENT

re·read *vb* **re·read ; re·read·ing :** to read again

res. *abbr* residence

¹**res·cue** *vb* **res·cued; res·cu·ing :** to free from danger : SAVE — **res·cu·er** *n*

²**rescue** *n* **:** an act of freeing someone or something from danger

¹**re·search** *n* **:** careful study and investigation for the purpose of discovering and explaining new knowledge — **re·search·er** *n*

²**research** *vb* **re·searched; re·search·ing :** to search or investigate thoroughly

re·sem·blance *n* **:** the quality or state of being similar to another

re·sem·ble *vb* **re·sem·bled; re·sem·bling :** to be like or similar to

re·sent *vb* **re·sent·ed; re·sent·ing :** to feel annoyance or anger at

re·sent·ful *adj* **:** full of angry displeasure

re·sent·ment *n* **:** a feeling of angry displeasure at a real or imagined wrong, insult, or injury

res·er·va·tion *n* **1 :** an act of setting something aside for future use **2 :** an arrangement to have something (as seating in a restaurant) held for someone's use **3 :** something (as land) set aside for a special use **4 :** an area of land set aside for American Indians to live **5 :** something that limits

¹**re·serve** *vb* **re·served; re·serv·ing 1 :** to arrange to have set aside and held for someone's use **2 :** to keep in store for special use **3 :** to keep from using until a future time **4 :** to hold over to a future time or place

²**reserve** *n* **1 reserves** *pl* **:** military forces

held back or available for later use **2** : an area of land set apart **3** : caution in words and behavior **4** : something stored for future use **5** : an act of setting something aside for future use

re·served *adj* **1** : cautious in words and actions **2** : kept or set apart for future or special use

res·er·voir *n* : a place where something (as water) is kept in store for future use

re·set *vb* **re·set; re·set·ting** : to set again

re·side *vb* **re·sid·ed; re·sid·ing** **1** : to live permanently and continuously : DWELL **2** : to have its place : EXIST

res·i·dence *n* **1** : the act or fact of living in a place **2** : a building used for a home **3** : the time during which a person lives in a place

¹res·i·dent *n* : a person who lives in a place

²resident *adj* **1** : living in a place for some length of time **2** : serving in a full-time position

res·i·den·tial *adj* **1** : used as a residence or by residents **2** : suitable for or containing residences

res·i·due *n* : whatever remains after a part is taken, set apart, or lost

re·sign *vb* **re·signed; re·sign·ing** **1** : to give up (a job or position) by a formal or official act **2** : to prepare to accept something unpleasant

res·ig·na·tion *n* **1** : an act of giving something up formally or officially **2** : a letter or written statement that gives notice of giving something up **3** : the feeling of a person who is prepared to accept something unpleasant

re·signed *adj* : showing acceptance of something unpleasant

res·in *n* **1** : a yellowish or brownish substance obtained from the gum or sap of some trees (as the pine) and used in varnishes and medicine **2** : any of various manufactured products that are similar to natural resins in properties and are used especially as plastics

re·sist *vb* **re·sist·ed; re·sist·ing** **1** : to fight against : OPPOSE **2** : to avoid doing or having something **3** : to withstand the force or effect of

re·sis·tance *n* **1** : an act or instance of opposing **2** : the ability to withstand the force or effect of **3** : an opposing or slowing force **4** : the opposition offered by a substance to the passage through it of an electric current

re·sis·tant *adj* : capable of withstanding the force or effect of

res·o·lute *adj* : firmly determined — **res·o·lute·ly** *adv*

res·o·lu·tion *n* **1** : something decided on **2** : firmness of purpose : DETERMINATION **3**

: the act of solving **4** : the solution to a problem **5** : a statement of the feelings, wishes, or decisions of a group

¹re·solve *vb* **re·solved; re·solv·ing** **1** : to find an answer to : SOLVE **2** : to reach a firm decision about something **3** : to decide by a formal resolution and vote

²resolve *n* : firmness of purpose : DETERMINATION

res·o·nance *n* : a long loud, clear, and deep quality of sound

res·o·nant *adj* : making a long loud, clear, and deep sound — **res·o·nant·ly** *adv*

¹re·sort *n* **1** : someone or something that is looked to for help **2** : a place where people go on vacation

²resort *vb* **re·sort·ed; re·sort·ing** : to seek aid, relief, or advantage

re·sound *vb* **re·sound·ed; re·sound·ing** **1** : to become filled with sound : REVERBERATE **2** : to sound loudly

re·sound·ing *adj* **1** : producing resonant sound **2** : leaving no doubt

re·source *n* **1 resources** *pl* : a usable stock or supply (as of money or products) **2** : NATURAL RESOURCE **3** : the ability to meet and deal with situations

re·source·ful *adj* : clever in dealing with problems — **re·source·ful·ness** *n*

¹re·spect *n* **1** : high or special regard : ESTEEM **2** : thoughtfulness or consideration **3 respects** *pl* : an expression of regard or courtesy **4** : ¹DETAIL 2 **5** : relation to or concern with something specified

²respect *vb* **re·spect·ed; re·spect·ing** **1** : to consider worthy of high regard : ESTEEM **2** : to pay attention to

re·spect·able *adj* **1** : decent or correct in conduct : PROPER **2** : fit to be seen : PRESENTABLE **3** : deserving high regard **4** : fair in size or quantity — **re·spect·ably** *adv*

re·spect·ful *adj* : showing high regard or courtesy — **re·spect·ful·ly** *adv*

re·spect·ing *prep* : CONCERNING

re·spec·tive *adj* : not the same or shared : SEPARATE — **re·spec·tive·ly** *adv*

res·pi·ra·tion *n* **1** : the act or process of breathing : the inhaling of oxygen and the exhaling of carbon dioxide **2** : the process by which cells use oxygen to break down sugar and obtain energy

res·pi·ra·tor *n* **1** : a device covering the mouth or nose especially to prevent the breathing in of harmful substances (as dust or fumes) **2** : a device used for helping a person to breathe

res·pi·ra·to·ry *adj* : of, relating to, or concerned with breathing or the parts of the body involved in breathing

respiratory system *n* : a system of the body

used in breathing that in human beings consists of the nose, nasal passages, pharynx, larynx, trachea, bronchial tubes, and lungs

re·spire *vb* **re·spired; re·spir·ing** : BREATHE 1

res·pite *n* **1** : a short delay **2** : a period of rest or relief

re·splen·dent *adj* : shining brightly : SPLENDID — **re·splen·dent·ly** *adv*

re·spond *vb* **re·spond·ed; re·spond·ing 1** : to say something in return **2** : to react in a way that shows some action was successful

re·sponse *n* **1** : an act or instance of replying : ANSWER **2** : words said or sung by the people or choir in a religious service **3** : a reaction of a living being (as to a drug)

re·spon·si·bil·i·ty *n, pl* **re·spon·si·bil·i·ties 1** : the quality or state of being in charge of someone or something **2** : the quality of being dependable **3** : something or someone for which someone has charge

re·spon·si·ble *adj* **1** : getting the credit or blame for acts or decisions **2** : RELIABLE **3** : needing a dependable person — **re·spon·si·bly** *adv*

re·spon·sive *adj* **1** : showing interest **2** : quick to respond in a sympathetic way — **re·spon·sive·ly** *adv* — **re·spon·sive·ness** *n*

¹rest *vb* **rest·ed; rest·ing 1** : to relax, sleep, or refrain from taking part in work or an activity **2** : to refrain from using for a short time **3** : to sit or lie fixed or supported **4** : DEPEND **2 5** : to lie dead **6** : to fix or be fixed in trust or confidence

²rest *n* : something that is left over : REMAINDER

³rest *n* **1** : a state of inactivity during which the body and mind become refreshed **2** : freedom from activity or work **3** : a state of not moving or not doing anything **4** : a place for stopping or refraining from activity **5** : a silence in music **6** : a symbol in music that stands for a certain period of silence in a measure **7** : something used for support

res·tau·rant *n* : a public eating place

rest·ful *adj* : giving a feeling of peace or relaxation : QUIET

res·tive *adj* : showing impatience, nervousness, or discomfort

rest·less *adj* **1** : not relaxed or calm **2** : having or giving no rest — **rest·less·ly** *adv* — **rest·less·ness** *n*

res·to·ra·tion *n* **1** : an act of returning something to its original condition : the result of having been returned to the original condition **2** : something (as a building) that has been returned to its original condition

re·store *vb* **re·stored; re·stor·ing 1** : to put or bring back to an earlier or original state **2**

: to put back into use or service **3** : to give back

re·strain *vb* **re·strained; re·strain·ing 1** : to keep from doing something **2** : to keep back : CURB

re·straint *n* **1** : the act of stopping or holding back : the state of being stopped or held back **2** : a force or influence that stops or holds back **3** : control over thoughts or feelings

re·strict *vb* **re·strict·ed; re·strict·ing** : to keep within bounds : set limits to

re·stric·tion *n* **1** : something (as a law or rule) that limits **2** : an act of limiting : the condition of being limited

re·stric·tive *adj* : serving or likely to keep within bounds

rest·room *n* : a room with a toilet and sink

¹re·sult *vb* **re·sult·ed; re·sult·ing 1** : to come about as an effect **2** : to end as an effect

²result *n* **1** : something that comes about as an effect or end **2** : a good effect

re·sume *vb* **re·sumed; re·sum·ing 1** : to begin again **2** : to take or occupy again

re·sump·tion *n* : the act of starting again

res·ur·rect *vb* **res·ur·rect·ed; res·ur·rect·ing 1** : to bring back to life **2** : to bring to view or into use again

res·ur·rec·tion *n* **1** : an instance of coming back into use or importance **2** *cap* : the rising of Jesus Christ from the dead **3** *often cap* : the act of rising again to life of all human dead before the final judgment

re·sus·ci·tate *vb* **re·sus·ci·tat·ed; re·sus·ci·tat·ing** : to bring back from apparent death or unconsciousness

re·sus·ci·ta·tion *n* : the act of bringing back from apparent death or unconsciousness

¹re·tail *vb* **re·tailed; re·tail·ing** : to sell in small amounts to people for their own use — **re·tail·er** *n*

²retail *n* : the sale of products or goods in small amounts to people for their own use

³retail *adj* : relating to or engaged in selling products in small amounts to people for their own use

re·tain *vb* **re·tained; re·tain·ing 1** : to keep or continue to use **2** : to hold safe or unchanged

re·tal·i·ate *vb* **re·tal·i·at·ed; re·tal·i·at·ing** : to get revenge by returning like for like

re·tal·i·a·tion *n* : the act or an instance of getting revenge

re·tard *vb* **re·tard·ed; re·tard·ing** : to slow down : DELAY

retch *vb* **retched; retch·ing** : to vomit or try to vomit

re·ten·tion *n* **1** : the act of continuing to possess, control, or hold **2** : the power or ability to keep or hold something

ret·i·na *n, pl* **retinas** *also* **ret·i·nae** : the membrane that lines the back part of the eyeball, contains the rods and cones, and converts the images received by the lens into signals that are transmitted to the brain

re·tire *vb* **re·tired; re·tir·ing** **1** : to give up a job permanently : quit working **2** : to go away especially to be alone **3** : to go to bed **4** : to withdraw from use or service **5** : to get away from action or danger : RETREAT — **re·tire·ment** *n*

re·tired *adj* : not working at active duties or business

re·tir·ing *adj* : ¹SHY 2, RESERVED

¹re·tort *vb* **re·tort·ed; re·tort·ing** **1** : to reply usually angrily or sharply **2** : to reply with an argument against

²retort *n* : a quick, clever, or angry reply

re·trace *vb* **re·traced; re·trac·ing** : to go over once more

re·tract *vb* **re·tract·ed; re·tract·ing** **1** : to pull back or in **2** : to take back (as an offer or statement) : WITHDRAW

¹re·treat *n* **1** : an act of going back or away especially from something dangerous, difficult, or disagreeable **2** : a military signal for turning away from the enemy **3** : a place of privacy or safety **4** : a period of time in which a person goes away to pray, think quietly, or study

²retreat *vb* **re·treat·ed; re·treat·ing** **1** : to move back or away especially from something dangerous, difficult, or disagreeable **2** : to go to a place of privacy or safety

ret·ri·bu·tion *n* : PUNISHMENT 1

re·trieve *vb* **re·trieved; re·triev·ing** **1** : to get and bring back **2** : to find and bring back killed or wounded game

re·triev·er *n* : a dog that has a water-resistant coat and is skilled in retrieving game

ret·ro·spect *n* : a looking back on things past

¹re·turn *vb* **re·turned; re·turn·ing** **1** : to come or go back again **2** : to bring, give, send, or put back **3** : REPAY 1 **4** : to respond in the same way **5** : to make an official report of **6** : ¹YIELD 4, PRODUCE

²return *n* **1** : the act of coming or going back to a place or condition **2** : RECURRENCE **3** : the act of returning something (as to a former condition or owner) **4** : something given in payment or exchange **5** : a report of the results of voting **6** : a statement of income to be taxed **7** : the profit from labor, investment, or business

³return *adj* **1** : happening or done for the second time **2** : used for returning

re·union *n* **1** : an act of coming or bringing together again after being apart **2** : an organized gathering of people who have not been together for some time

re·unite *vb* **re·unit·ed; re·unit·ing** : to come or bring together again after being apart

re·use *vb* **re·used; re·us·ing** : to use again

rev *vb* **revved; rev·ving** : to increase the number of revolutions per minute of (a motor)

Rev. *abbr* reverend

re·veal *vb* **re·vealed; re·veals** **1** : to make known **2** : to show clearly

rev·eil·le *n* : a signal sounded at about sunrise on a bugle to call soldiers or sailors to duty

¹rev·el *vb* **rev·eled** *or* **rev·elled; rev·el·ing** *or* **rev·el·ling** : to take great pleasure

²revel *n* : a noisy or merry celebration

rev·e·la·tion *n* : a secret or surprising fact that is made known

rev·el·ry *n, pl* **rev·el·ries** : wild and noisy celebration

¹re·venge *vb* **re·venged; re·veng·ing** : to cause harm or injury in return for

²revenge *n* **1** : an act or instance of causing harm or injury in return for a wrong **2** : a desire to cause harm or injury in return for a wrong **3** : a chance for getting satisfaction

rev·e·nue *n* **1** : money that is made by or paid to a business or organization **2** : money collected by a government (as through taxes)

re·ver·ber·ate *vb* **re·ver·ber·at·ed; re·ver·ber·at·ing** : to continue in or as if in a series of echoes

re·vere *vb* **re·vered; re·ver·ing** : to have great respect for

rev·er·ence *n* : honor and respect often mixed with love and awe

rev·er·end *adj* **1** : worthy of honor and respect **2** — used as a title for a member of the clergy

rev·er·ent *adj* : very respectful — **rev·er·ent·ly** *adv*

rev·er·ie *n, pl* **rev·er·ies** : the state of being lost in thought especially about pleasant things

re·ver·sal *n* : a change to an opposite or former state, condition, view, or direction

¹re·verse *adj* **1** : opposite to a previous, normal, or usual condition **2** : opposite to the front

²reverse *vb* **re·versed; re·vers·ing** **1** : to turn completely around or upside down or inside out **2** : to change the order or position of **3** : to change or cause to change to an opposite or former state, condition, or view **4** : to go or cause to go in the opposite direction

³reverse *n* **1** : something opposite to something else : CONTRARY **2** : an act or instance of changing to an opposite or former state, condition, view, or direction **3** : the back part of something **4** : a gear that reverses something

re·vert *vb* **re·vert·ed; re·vert·ing** : to come or go back

¹re·view *n* **1** : a look at or examination of **2** : a piece of writing about the quality of something (as a book, performance, or product) **3** : a fresh study of material studied before **4** : a formal inspection of troops by officers of high rank or an important person

²review *vb* **re·viewed; re·view·ing 1** : to look at or study again **2** : to look at or examine carefully **3** : to report on or evaluate the quality of **4** : to make an official inspection of (as troops) — **re·view·er** *n*

re·vile *vb* **re·viled; re·vil·ing** : to speak to or about in an insulting way

re·vise *vb* **re·vised; re·vis·ing** : to make changes that correct or improve

re·viv·al *n* **1** : a return of interest in **2** : a new production of an older play or movie **3** : a return of strength or importance **4** : a meeting or series of meetings led by a preacher to stir up religious feelings or to make converts

re·vive *vb* **re·vived; re·viv·ing 1** : to bring back or come back to life, consciousness, freshness, or activity **2** : to bring back into use or popularity

re·voke *vb* **re·voked; re·vok·ing** : to take away or cancel

¹re·volt *vb* **re·volt·ed; re·volt·ing 1** : to rebel against a ruler or government **2** : to be or cause to be disgusted or shocked

²revolt *n* : violent action against a ruler or government : REBELLION

rev·o·lu·tion *n* **1** : the action by a heavenly body of going round in a fixed course **2** : a spinning motion around a center or axis : ROTATION **3** : a single complete turn (as of a wheel) **4** : a sudden, extreme, or complete change (as in manner of living or working) **5** : the overthrow of a ruler or government by violent action

rev·o·lu·tion·ary *adj* **1** : relating to or involving rebellion against a ruler or government **2** : being or bringing about a big or important change **3** *cap* : of or relating to the American Revolution

rev·o·lu·tion·ize *vb* **rev·o·lu·tion·ized; rev·o·lu·tion·iz·ing** : to change greatly or completely

re·volve *vb* **re·volved; re·volv·ing 1** : to move in an orbit **2** : ROTATE 1

re·volv·er *n* : a pistol having a revolving cylinder holding several bullets all of which may be shot without loading again

re·vue *n* : a show in a theater consisting usually of short and often funny sketches and songs

re·vul·sion *n* : a strong feeling of dislike or disgust

¹re·ward *vb* **re·ward·ed; re·ward·ing 1** : to give something (as money) to in return for a service or accomplishment **2** : to give something in return for

²reward *n* : something (as money) given or offered in return for a service or accomplishment

re·wind *vb* **re·wound; re·wind·ing** : to reverse the winding or direction of play of

re·word *vb* **re·word·ed; re·word·ing** : to state in different words

re·write *vb* **re·wrote; re·writ·ten; re·writ·ing** : to write over again especially in a different way

rhea *n* : a tall flightless South American bird that resembles but is smaller than the ostrich

rheu·mat·ic fever *n* : a serious disease especially of children that causes fever, pain and swelling of joints, and sometimes heart damage

rheu·ma·tism *n* : a condition in which muscles or joints are painful

rhine·stone *n* : a small imitation gem used in jewelry or for decoration

rhi·no *n, pl* **rhino** *or* **rhi·nos** : RHINOCEROS

rhi·noc·er·os *n, pl* **rhi·noc·er·os·es** *also* **rhi·noceros** : a large plant-eating mammal of Africa and Asia with short legs, thick gray to brown skin with little hair, and one or two heavy upright horns on the snout

rho·do·den·dron *n* : a shrub with leathery evergreen leaves and showy clusters of flowers

rhom·bus *n* : a parallelogram whose sides are equal in length

rhu·barb *n* : the thick juicy pink or red stems of a garden plant that have a tart flavor and are used cooked especially in jams and desserts

¹rhyme *n* **1** : close similarity in the final sounds of two or more words or lines of writing **2** : a piece of writing (as a poem) whose lines end in similar sounds

²rhyme *vb* **rhymed; rhym·ing 1** : to end with the same sound **2** : to have lines that end with the same sound **3** : to cause lines or words to end with a similar sound

rhythm *n* : a regular repeated pattern of beats, sounds, activity, or movements

rhyth·mic *or* **rhyth·mi·cal** *adj* : having a regular repeated pattern of beats, sounds, activity, or movements — **rhyth·mi·cal·ly** *adv*

RI *abbr* Rhode Island

rib *n* **1** : one of the curved bones of the chest that are joined to the backbone and help to stiffen the body wall and protect the organs **2** : a piece of meat from an animal (as a cow or pig) that includes a rib and is used as food **3** : something (as a piece of wire supporting the fabric of an umbrella) that is like a rib in shape or use **4** : one of the parallel ridges in a knitted or woven fabric — **ribbed** *adj*

rib·bon *n* **1** : a narrow strip of usually colorful fabric used especially for decoration or to tie things **2** : a ribbon that is given as an award **3** : TATTER 1, SHRED — usually used in pl.

rib cage *n* : the bony enclosing wall of the chest consisting of the ribs and their connecting parts

rice *n* : the small seeds of a tall cereal grass widely grown in warm wet regions that are the chief food in many parts of the world

rich *adj* **1** : having a lot of money and possessions : WEALTHY **2** : ¹VALUABLE 1, EXPENSIVE **3** : well supplied : ABUNDANT **4** : FERTILE 1 **5** : containing much sugar, fat, or seasoning **6** : deep and pleasing in color or tone — **rich·ly** *adv* — **rich·ness** *n*

rich·es *n pl* : things that make someone rich

rick·ets *n* : a disease especially of children in which the bones are soft and deformed and which is caused by lack of vitamin D

rick·ety *adj* : in poor condition and likely to break

rick·shaw *also* **rick·sha** *n* : a small carriage with two wheels that is pulled by one person and was used originally in Japan

ric·o·chet *vb* **ric·o·cheted; ric·o·chet·ing** : to bounce off at an angle

rid *vb* **rid** *also* **rid·ded; rid·ding** : to free from something : RELIEVE

¹rid·dle *n* **1** : a puzzling question to be solved or answered by guessing **2** : someone or something that is hard to understand

²riddle *vb* **rid·dled; rid·dling** **1** : to pierce with many holes **2** : to fill with something unpleasant or unwanted

¹ride *vb* **rode; rid·den; rid·ing** **1** : to travel or move by sitting or standing on or in **2** : to sit on and control so as to be carried along **3** : to be supported or carried on **4** : to travel over a surface **5** : to endure without great harm or damage **6** : DEPEND 2 — **rid·er** *n*

²ride *n* **1** : a trip on horseback or by vehicle **2** : a mechanical device (as a merry-go-round) that moves around while people sit or stand on it for entertainment **3** : a way of getting from one place to another

ridge *n* **1** : a range of hills or mountains or its upper part **2** : a raised strip **3** : the line made where two sloping surfaces come together — **ridged** *adj*

¹rid·i·cule *n* : the act of making fun of someone or something in a cruel or harsh way : mean or unkind comments or behavior

²ridicule *vb* **rid·i·culed; rid·i·cul·ing** : to make fun of in a cruel or harsh way

ri·dic·u·lous *adj* : causing or deserving ridicule : very silly or unreasonable — **ri·dic·u·lous·ly** *adv*

¹rif·fle *vb* **rif·fled; rif·fling** **1** : to move lightly **2** : to look through quickly

²riffle *n* **1** : a shallow area of a stream bed that causes ripples **2** : ²RIPPLE 1

riff·raff *n* : a group of people who are not considered respectable or honest

¹ri·fle *vb* **ri·fled; ri·fling** **1** : to search through quickly and roughly often to steal something **2** : ¹STEAL 1

²rifle *n* : a gun that has a long barrel with spiral grooves on its inside

rift *n* **1** : an opening made by splitting or separation : CLEFT **2** : a break in friendly relations

¹rig *vb* **rigged; rig·ging** **1** : to build or set up usually quickly and for temporary use **2** : to provide (as a ship) with rigging **3** : CLOTHE 1, DRESS **4** : to provide with gear

²rig *n* **1** : the shape, number, and arrangement of sails and masts of a ship that sets it apart from other types of ships **2** : equipment or machinery for a certain purpose

rig·ging *n* : lines and chains used on a ship to help support the masts and sails

¹right *adj* **1** : following or in accordance with what is just, good, or proper **2** : ACCURATE, CORRECT **3** : SUITABLE, APPROPRIATE **4** : located on the side of the body away from the heart **5** : located nearer to the right side of the body than to the left **6** : being or meant to be the side on top, in front, or on the outside **7** : in a normal or healthy state or condition **8** : ¹STRAIGHT 1 — **right·ly** *adv* — **right·ness** *n*

²right *n* **1** : the ideal of what is just, good, or proper **2** : something to which a person has a just claim **3** : the cause of truth or justice **4** : the right side : a part or location that is on or toward the right side

³right *adv* **1** : according to what is just, good, or proper **2** : in the exact location, position, or moment : PRECISELY **3** : in a direct line or course : STRAIGHT **4** : according to truth or fact **5** : in a suitable, proper, or desired way **6** : all the way **7** : without delay : IMMEDIATELY **8** : on or to the right **9** : in a complete way — **right away** : without delay : IMMEDIATELY

⁴right *vb* **right·ed; right·ing** **1** : to make better or more just **2** : to adjust or restore to a proper state or condition **3** : to bring or bring back to an upright position **4** : to become upright

right angle *n* : an angle formed by two lines

that are perpendicular to each other : an angle of 90 degrees

righ·teous *adj* **1** : doing or being what is just or proper **2** : caused by an insult to what is believed to be just or proper — **righ·teous·ly** *adv* — **righ·teous·ness** *n*

right·ful *adj* : LAWFUL 2, PROPER — **right·ful·ly** *adv*

right–hand *adj* **1** : located on the right side **2** : RIGHT-HANDED 1 **3** : relied on most of all

right–hand·ed *adj* **1** : using the right hand better or more easily than the left **2** : done or made with or for the right hand

right–of–way *n, pl* **rights–of–way 1** : the legal right to pass over someone else's land **2** : the right of some traffic to go before other traffic

right triangle *n* : a triangle having a right angle

righty *n, pl* **right·ies** : a right-handed person

rig·id *adj* **1** : not flexible : STIFF **2** : STRICT 2, SEVERE — **rig·id·ly** *adv*

rig·ma·role *n* **1** : a long and usually meaningless or uninteresting story **2** : a complicated and often unnecessary procedure

rig·or *n* : a harsh condition (as of discipline)

rig·or·ous *adj* **1** : very strict **2** : hard to endure because of extreme conditions : HARSH — **rig·or·ous·ly** *adv*

rile *vb* **riled; ril·ing** : to make angry : IRRITATE

rill *n* : a very small stream

¹rim *n* **1** : an outer edge especially of something curved **2** : the part of a wheel that the tire is mounted on — **rimmed** *adj*

²rim *vb* **rimmed; rim·ming** : to form a rim around

rime *n* : ¹FROST 1

rind *n* : a tough outer layer

¹ring *n* **1** : a circular band used for holding, fastening, or connecting **2** : a circular band usually of precious metal worn especially on the finger as jewelry **3** : something circular in shape **4** : an often circular space for shows or contests **5** : a group of people who work together for dishonest purposes **6** : ANNUAL RING — **ringed** *adj*

²ring *vb* **ringed; ring·ing** : to place or form a ring around

³ring *vb* **rang; rung; ring·ing 1** : to make or cause to make a clear vibrating sound **2** : to announce by or as if by striking a bell **3** : to sound loudly **4** : to fill or be filled with the sound of something **5** : to be filled with a humming sound **6** : to seem to be a certain way **7** : to call for especially by ringing a bell

⁴ring *n* **1** : a clear sound made by or as if by vibrating metal **2** : a continuous or repeat-ing loud sound **3** : something that suggests a certain quality **4** : a telephone call

ring finger *n* : the third finger especially of the left hand when counting the index finger as the first

ring·lead·er *n* : a leader especially of a group of people who cause trouble

ring·let *n* : a long curl of hair

ring·worm *n* : a fungus infection that causes red ring-shaped patches to appear on the skin

rink *n* : a place for ice-skating or roller-skating

¹rinse *vb* **rinsed; rins·ing 1** : to wash lightly with water **2** : to remove (something) with clean water

²rinse *n* **1** : an act of washing with a liquid and especially with clean water **2** : a liquid used for rinsing

¹ri·ot *n* **1** : violent and uncontrolled public behavior by a group of people **2** : a colorful display **3** : someone or something that is very funny

²riot *vb* **ri·ot·ed; ri·ot·ing** : to take part in violent and uncontrolled public behavior

¹rip *vb* **ripped; rip·ping 1** : to cut or tear open : split apart **2** : to remove quickly (as by tearing) — **rip·per** *n*

²rip *n* : a usually long tear

ripe *adj* **rip·er; rip·est 1** : fully grown and developed **2** : of advanced years **3** : ¹READY 1 — **ripe·ness** *n*

rip·en *vb* **rip·ened; rip·en·ing** : to make or become ripe

¹rip·ple *vb* **rip·pled; rip·pling 1** : to move or cause to move in small waves **2** : to pass or spread over or through

²ripple *n* **1** : a very small wave on the surface of a liquid **2** : something that passes or spreads through

¹rise *vb* **rose ; ris·en ; ris·ing 1** : to get up from lying, kneeling, or sitting **2** : to get up from sleeping in a bed **3** : to go or move up **4** : to swell in size or volume **5** : to increase in amount or number **6** : to become encouraged or grow stronger **7** : to appear above the horizon **8** : to gain a higher rank or position **9** : to come into being **10** : to successfully deal with a difficult situation **11** : to return from death **12** : to launch an attack or revolt — **ris·er** *n*

²rise *n* **1** : an increase in amount, number, or volume **2** : upward movement **3** : the act of gaining a higher rank or position **4** : BEGINNING 1, ORIGIN **5** : an upward slope **6** : a spot higher than surrounding ground **7** : an angry reaction

¹risk *n* **1** : possibility of loss or injury **2** : something or someone that may cause loss or injury

²risk *vb* **risked; risk·ing 1 :** to expose to danger **2 :** to take the risk or danger of

risky *adj* **risk·i·er; risk·i·est :** DANGEROUS 1

rite *n* **:** an act performed in a ceremony

rit·u·al *n* **:** a ceremony or series of acts that is always performed the same way

¹ri·val *n* **:** someone or something that tries to defeat or be more successful than another

²rival *adj* **:** being equally good

³rival *vb* **ri·valed** *or* **ri·valled; ri·val·ing** *or* **ri·val·ling :** to be as good as or almost as good as

ri·val·ry *n, pl* **ri·val·ries :** the state of trying to defeat or be more successful than another **:** COMPETITION

riv·er *n* **1 :** a natural stream of water larger than a brook or creek **2 :** a large stream or flow

¹riv·et *n* **:** a bolt with a head that is passed through two or more pieces and is hammered into place

²rivet *vb* **riv·et·ed; riv·et·ing 1 :** to fasten with rivets **2 :** to attract and hold (as someone's attention) completely **3 :** to make (someone) unable to move because of fear or shock

riv·u·let *n* **:** a small stream

roach *n* **:** COCKROACH

road *n* **1 :** a hard flat surface for vehicles, persons, and animals to travel on **2 :** a way to achieve something

road·run·ner *n* **:** a long-tailed bird that is found in dry regions of the southwestern United States and is able to run very fast

road·side *n* **:** the strip of land beside a road

road·way *n* **:** the part of a road used by vehicles

roam *vb* **roamed; roam·ing :** to go from place to place with no fixed purpose or direction

¹roan *adj* **:** of a dark color (as black or brown) mixed with white

²roan *n* **:** an animal (as a horse) with a dark-colored coat mixed with white

¹roar *vb* **roared; roar·ing 1 :** to make a long loud sound **2 :** to laugh loudly **3 :** to say loudly **4 :** to move with a loud noise

²roar *n* **:** a long shout, bellow, or loud noise

roar·ing *adj* **:** very active or strong

¹roast *vb* **roast·ed; roast·ing 1 :** to cook with dry heat (as in an oven) **2 :** to be or make very hot — **roast·er** *n*

²roast *adj* **:** cooked with dry heat

³roast *n* **1 :** a piece of meat suitable for cooking with dry heat **2 :** an outdoor party at which food is cooked over an open fire

rob *vb* **robbed; rob·bing 1 :** to unlawfully take something away from a person or place in secrecy or by force, threat, or trickery **2**

: to keep from getting something due, expected, or desired — **rob·ber** *n*

rob·bery *n, pl* **rob·ber·ies :** the act or practice of taking something unlawfully

¹robe *n* **1 :** a long loose or flowing garment **2 :** a loose garment worn especially after bathing or while relaxing at home

²robe *vb* **robed; rob·ing :** to dress especially in a robe

rob·in *n* **1 :** a large North American songbird with a grayish back and dull reddish breast **2 :** a small European songbird with an orange throat and breast

ro·bot *n* **1 :** a machine that looks and acts like a human being **2 :** a machine that can do the work of a person automatically or under the control of a computer

ro·bust *adj* **:** strong and healthy — **ro·bust·ly** *adv*

¹rock *vb* **rocked; rock·ing 1 :** to move gently back and forth or side to side **2 :** to cause (something) to shake violently

²rock *n* **1 :** solid mineral deposits **2 :** a mass of stone

³rock *n* **1 :** a rocking movement **2 :** popular music played on instruments that are amplified electronically

rock and roll *or* **rock 'n' roll** *n* **:** ³ROCK 2

rock dove *n* **1 :** a bluish gray dove of Europe and Asia that nests on rocky cliffs **2 :** a variety of the rock dove that is now found in cities throughout the world

rock·er *n* **1 :** ROCKING CHAIR **2 :** a curving piece of wood or metal on which an object (as a cradle or rocking chair) rocks

¹rock·et *n* **1 :** a firework that is driven through the air by the gases produced by a burning substance **2 :** a jet engine that is driven by gases produced by a burning substance **3 :** a bomb, missile, or vehicle that is driven by gases produced by a burning substance

²rocket *vb* **rock·et·ed; rock·et·ing 1 :** to rise swiftly **2 :** to travel rapidly in or as if in a rocket

rock·ing chair *n* **:** a chair mounted on rockers

rock·ing horse *n* **:** a toy horse mounted on rockers

rock salt *n* **:** common salt in large crystals

rocky *adj* **rock·i·er; rock·i·est :** full of or consisting of rocks

rod *n* **1 :** a light flexible pole often with line and a reel attached used in fishing **2 :** a stick or bundle of twigs used in whipping a person **3 :** a straight slender stick or bar **4 :** a measure of length equal to 16½ feet (about 5 meters) **5 :** a cell of the retina of the eye that is shaped like a rod and is sensitive to faint light

rode *past of* RIDE

ro·dent *n* : a usually small mammal (as a squirrel, rat, mouse, or beaver) with sharp front teeth used in gnawing

ro-deo *n, pl* **ro·de·os** : an exhibition that features cowboy skills (as riding and roping)

roe *n* : the eggs of a fish especially while still held together in a membrane

rogue *n* **1** : a dishonest or evil person **2** : a pleasantly mischievous person

rogu·ish *adj* : showing mischievousness — **rogu·ish·ly** *adv*

role *n* **1** : a character assigned or taken on **2** : a part played by an actor or singer **3** : ¹FUNCTION 1

role model *n* : a person whose behavior in a certain function is imitated by others

¹roll *vb* **rolled; roll·ing 1** : to move or cause to move by turning over and over on a surface **2** : to shape or become shaped in rounded form **3** : to sound with a full echoing tone or with a continuous beating sound **4** : to flow in or as if in a continuous stream **5** : to move or cause to move in a circular manner **6** : to go by : PASS **7** : to move with a side-to-side sway **8** : to make smooth, even, or firm with a roller **9** : to move on rollers or wheels — **roll around** : to happen again

²roll *n* **1** : something or a quantity of something that is rolled up or rounded as if rolled **2** : a small piece of baked bread dough **3** : a writing that may be rolled up : SCROLL **4** : an official list of names

³roll *n* **1** : a sound produced by rapid strokes on a drum **2** : a heavy echoing sound **3** : a movement or action that involves turning over and over or circling around

roll·er *n* **1** : a turning cylinder over or on which something is moved or which is used to press, shape, or smooth something **2** : a rod on which something (as a map or hair) is rolled up **3** : a small wheel **4** : a long heavy wave on the sea

roller coaster *n* : an amusement park ride that is an elevated railway with sharp curves and steep slopes over which cars travel

roller–skate *vb* **roller–skat·ed; roller–skat·ing** : to ride on roller skates

roller skate *n* : a skate that has wheels instead of a runner

rolling pin *n* : a cylinder (as of wood) used to roll out dough

ROM *n* : a usually small computer memory that contains special-purpose information (as a program) which cannot be changed

¹Ro·man *n* **1** : a person born or living in Rome **2** : a citizen of an ancient empire centered on Rome **3** *not cap* : upright letters or type

²Roman *adj* **1** : of or relating to Rome or the

Romans **2** *not cap* : of or relating to a type style with upright characters (as in "these letters")

Roman Catholic *adj* : belonging to or relating to the Christian church led by the pope

ro·mance *n* **1** : an attraction or appeal to the emotions **2** : a love story **3** : a love affair **4** : an old tale of knights and noble ladies **5** : an adventure story

Ro·mance *adj* : relating to or being the languages (as French, Italian, and Spanish) that are descended from Latin

Roman numeral *n* : a numeral in a system of figures based on the ancient Roman system

ro·man·tic *adj* **1** : stressing or appealing to the emotions or imagination **2** : involving or showing feelings of love **3** : not realistic : IMPRACTICAL **4** : suitable for a love story — **ro·man·ti·cal·ly** *adv*

¹romp *vb* **romped; romp·ing** : to play in a rough and noisy way

²romp *n* : rough and noisy play : FROLIC

romp·er *n* : a young child's one-piece garment having legs that can be unfastened around the inside — usually used in pl.

¹roof *n, pl* **roofs 1** : the upper covering part of a building **2** : something like a roof in form, position, or purpose — **roofed** *adj*

²roof *vb* **roofed; roof·ing** : to cover with a roof

roof·ing *n* : material for a roof

¹rook *n* : a crow of Europe and Asia that nests and sleeps in groups usually in the tops of trees

²rook *vb* **rooked; rook·ing** : ¹CHEAT 2, SWINDLE

³rook *n* : one of the pieces in the game of chess

rook·ie *n* : BEGINNER, RECRUIT

¹room *n* **1** : a divided part of the inside of a building **2** : a bedroom in a home or hotel **3** : the people in a room **4** : available space **5** : a suitable opportunity

²room *vb* **roomed; room·ing** : to provide with or live in lodgings

room·er *n* : LODGER

rooming house *n* : a house having furnished rooms for rent to lodgers

room·mate *n* : one of two or more people sharing a room or dwelling

roomy *adj* **room·i·er; room·i·est** : SPACIOUS — **room·i·ness** *n*

¹roost *n* : a place where birds rest or sleep

²roost *vb* **roost·ed; roost·ing** : to settle down for rest or sleep

roost·er *n* : an adult male chicken

¹root *n* **1** : the leafless underground part of a plant that absorbs water and minerals, stores food, and holds the plant in place **2** : the part of something by which it is attached **3**

: SOURCE 1 **4** : the ancestors of a person or group of people **5** : a special relationship **6** : ¹CORE 3 **7** : a word or part of a word from which other words are obtained by adding a prefix or suffix — **root·ed** *adj*

²**root** *vb* **root·ed; root·ing 1** : to form or cause to form roots **2** : to attach by or as if by roots — **root out** : to remove by or as if by pulling out the roots

³**root** *vb* **rooted; rooting** : to turn up or dig with or as if with the snout

⁴**root** *vb* **rooted; rooting** : to wish for the success of — **root·er** *n*

root beer *n* : a sweet drink flavored with extracts of roots and herbs

¹**rope** *n* **1** : a strong thick cord of strands (as of fiber or wire) twisted or braided together **2** : a number of similar things held together on a string

²**rope** *vb* **roped; rop·ing 1** : to bind, fasten, or tie with a cord **2** : to set off or divide by a cord **3** : ¹LASSO — **rop·er** *n*

ro·sa·ry *n, pl* **ro·sa·ries** : a string of beads used in counting prayers

¹**rose** *past of* RISE

²**rose** *n* **1** : a showy and usually fragrant white, yellow, pink, or red flower that grows on a prickly shrub **2** : a medium pink

rose·mary *n* : a fragrant mint with needlelike leaves used as a seasoning in cooking

ro·sette *n* : a badge or ornament of ribbon gathered in the shape of a rose

rose·wood *n* : a reddish or purplish wood streaked with black that is used especially for making furniture and musical instruments

Rosh Ha·sha·nah *n* : the Jewish New Year observed as a religious holiday in September or October

ros·in *n* : a hard brittle yellow to dark red substance obtained especially from pine trees and used in varnishes and on violin bows

ros·ter *n* : an orderly list of people belonging to some group

ros·trum *n, pl* **ros·tra** *or* **rostrums** : a stage or platform for public speaking

rosy *adj* **ros·i·er; ros·i·est 1** : having a pink color **2** : PROMISING, HOPEFUL

¹**rot** *vb* **rot·ted; rot·ting 1** : to undergo decay **2** : to go to ruin

²**rot** *n* **1** : the process of decaying : the state of being decayed **2** : something that has decayed or is decaying

ro·ta·ry *adj* **1** : turning on an axis like a wheel **2** : having a rotating part

ro·tate *vb* **ro·tat·ed; ro·tat·ing 1** : to turn about an axis or a center **2** : to go from one person to another or others in a cycle **3** : to pass in a series

ro·ta·tion *n* **1** : the act of turning about an axis **2** : the system of growing different crops in the same field usually in a regular order

rote *n* : the act of repeating over and over often without attention to meaning

ro·tor *n* **1** : the part of an electrical machine that turns **2** : a system of spinning horizontal blades that support a helicopter in the air

rot·ten *adj* **1** : having rotted **2** : morally bad **3** : of poor quality **4** : very unpleasant

ro·tund *adj* **1** : somewhat round **2** : ¹PLUMP

rouge *n* : a cosmetic used to give a red color to cheeks or lips

¹**rough** *adj* **1** : uneven in surface **2** : having many bumps and jolts **3** : not calm **4** : being harsh or violent **5** : difficult or unpleasant to deal with **6** : coarse or rugged in nature or look **7** : having a harsh sound **8** : not complete or exact — **rough·ly** *adv* — **rough·ness** *n*

²**rough** *n* **1** : uneven ground covered with high grass, brush, and stones **2** : something in a crude or unfinished state

³**rough** *vb* **roughed; rough·ing 1** : to handle violently : BEAT **2** : to make or shape coarsely or unevenly — **rough it** : to live without ordinary comforts

rough·age *n* **1** : FIBER 2 **2** : food (as bran) containing much indigestible material acting as fiber

rough·en *vb* **rough·ened; rough·en·ing** : to make or become rough

rough·neck *n* : a rough aggressive person

¹**round** *adj* **round·er; round·est 1** : having every part of the surface or circumference the same distance from the center : shaped like a circle or ball **2** : shaped like a cylinder **3** : ¹PLUMP **4** : having curves rather than angles **5** : ¹COMPLETE 1, FULL **6** : nearly correct or exact **7** : LARGE **8** : moving in or forming a circle — **round·ish** *adj* — **round·ness** *n*

²**round** *adv* : ¹AROUND

³**round** *n* **1** : a regularly covered route **2** : something (as a circle or globe) that is round **3** : one shot fired by a soldier or a gun **4** : a series or cycle of repeated actions or events **5** : a song in which three or four singers sing the same melody and words one after another at intervals **6** : a period of applause **7** : an indirect path **8** : ammunition for one shot **9** : one of the parts into which a contest or game is divided **10** : a cut of beef especially between the rump and the lower leg

⁴**round** *vb* **round·ed; round·ing 1** : to go or pass around **2** : to express as a round number **3** : to bring to completion **4** : to make or become round — **round up 1** : to collect

(as cattle) by circling in vehicles or on horseback and forcing them in **2** : to gather in or bring together

⁵round *prep* : ²AROUND

round·about *adj* : not direct

round·house *n, pl* **round·hous·es** : a circular building where locomotives are kept or repaired

round trip *n* : a trip to a place and back usually over the same route

round·up *n* **1** : the act of gathering together animals on the range by circling them in vehicles or on horseback and driving them in **2** : the act of gathering together scattered persons or things **3** : ²SUMMARY

round·worm *n* : a worm that has a round body with no segments and is sometimes a serious parasite of people and animals

rouse *vb* **roused; rous·ing 1** : ¹AWAKE 1 **2** : to stir up : EXCITE

¹rout *vb* **rout·ed; rout·ing 1** : to cause to run away **2** : to defeat completely

²rout *n* **1** : an easy or lopsided defeat **2** : wild confusion or disorderly retreat

¹route *n* : a regular, chosen, or assigned course of travel

²route *vb* **rout·ed; rout·ing** : to send or transport by a selected course

¹rou·tine *n* **1** : a usual order and way of doing something **2** : a series of things that are repeated as part of a performance

²routine *adj* **1** : done very often **2** : done or happening in a standard or usual way — **rou·tine·ly** *adv*

rove *vb* **roved; rov·ing** : to wander without definite plan or direction — **rov·er** *n*

¹row *vb* **rowed; row·ing 1** : to move a boat by using oars **2** : to travel or carry in a rowboat

²row *n* **1** : a series of persons or things lined up in an orderly arrangement **2** : ¹WAY 1, STREET

³row *n* : noisy disturbance or quarrel

⁴row *n* : an act or instance of using oars to move a boat

row·boat *n* : a boat made to be moved by oars

¹row·dy *adj* **row·di·er; row·di·est** : rough or noisy — **row·di·ness** *n*

²rowdy *n, pl* **rowdies** : a person who behaves coarsely or roughly

roy·al *adj* **1** : of or relating to a king or queen : REGAL **2** : fit for a king or queen — **roy·al·ly** *adv*

roy·al·ty *n, pl* **roy·al·ties 1** : the status or power of a king or queen or his or her family **2** : members of the royal family of a king or queen **3** : a share of a product or profit (as of a mine) claimed by the owner for allowing another to use the property **4** : payment

made to the owner of a patent or copyright for the use of it

rpm *abbr* revolutions per minute

RR *abbr* railroad

R.S.V.P. *abbr* please reply — abbreviation for French *répondez s'il vous plaît*, which means "please reply"

rt. *abbr* right

rte. *abbr* route

¹rub *vb* **rubbed; rub·bing 1** : to move along the surface of something with pressure **2** : to move back and forth against something in a way that causes pain or damage **3** : to scour, polish, or smear by pressure and friction — **rub elbows with** : to meet and talk with in a friendly way — **rub in** : to keep reminding someone of (something unpleasant) — **rub off** : to come off a surface and often stick to another surface by rubbing — **rub the wrong way** : to cause to be angry : IRRITATE

²rub *n* **1** : the act of rubbing **2** : something that causes a problem

rub·ber *n* **1** : an elastic substance obtained from the milky juice of some tropical plants **2** : something (as an overshoe) made of rubber **3** : something used in rubbing **4** : a synthetic substance like rubber **5** : a flat white rectangle on which a baseball pitcher stands

rubber band *n* : a continuous band made of rubber for holding things together : ELASTIC

rubber stamp *n* : a stamp with a printing face of rubber

rub·bery *adj* : weak, shaky, and unstable

rub·bish *n* **1** : TRASH 1 **2** : NONSENSE

rub·ble *n* : rough broken pieces of stone or brick from buildings

ru·ble *n* : a Russian coin or bill

ru·by *n, pl* **rubies 1** : a gemstone of a deep red color **2** : a deep purplish red

ruck·sack *n* : KNAPSACK

ruck·us *n* : a noisy disturbance or quarrel

rud·der *n* : a movable flat piece attached at the rear of a ship or aircraft for steering

rud·dy *adj* **rud·di·er; rud·di·est** : having a healthy reddish color

rude *adj* **rud·er; rud·est 1** : IMPOLITE **2** : not refined or cultured **3** : roughly made — **rude·ly** *adv* — **rude·ness** *n*

ru·di·ment *n* : a basic principle

ru·di·men·ta·ry *adj* **1** : ELEMENTARY, SIMPLE **2** : not fully developed

rue *vb* **rued; ru·ing** : to feel sorrow or regret for

rue·ful *adj* **1** : exciting pity or sympathy **2** : MOURNFUL 1, REGRETFUL

ruff *n* **1** : a large round collar of pleated fabric worn by men and women in the 16th and 17th centuries **2** : a fringe of long hairs or feathers growing around or on the neck of an animal

ruf·fi·an *n* : a violent and cruel person

¹ruf·fle *vb* **ruf·fled; ruf·fling 1** : to move or lift so as to disturb the smoothness of **2** : ²TROUBLE 1, VEX

²ruffle *n* : a strip of fabric gathered or pleated on one edge

rug *n* : a piece of thick heavy fabric usually with a nap or pile used especially as a floor covering

rug·ged *adj* **1** : having a rough uneven surface **2** : STRONG 3, TOUGH **3** : involving hardship — **rug·ged·ly** *adv* — **rug·ged·ness** *n*

¹ru·in *vb* **ru·ined; ru·in·ing 1** : to reduce to wreckage **2** : to damage beyond repair **3** : to have a very bad effect on the quality of (something) **4** : ³BANKRUPT

²ruin *n* **1** : complete collapse or destruction **2 ruins** *pl* : the remains of something destroyed **3** : the situation in which someone experiences loss of money, social status, or position — **in ruins** : nearly or completely destroyed

ru·in·ous *adj* : causing or likely to cause collapse or destruction — **ru·in·ous·ly** *adv*

¹rule *n* **1** : a guide or principle for conduct or action **2** : an accepted or usual method, custom, or habit **3** : the exercise of authority or control : GOVERNMENT **4** : RULER 2

²rule *vb* **ruled; rul·ing 1** : to exercise authority over : GOVERN **2** : ¹CONTROL 1, DIRECT **3** : to be supreme or outstanding in **4** : to give or state as a considered decision **5** : to mark with lines drawn along the straight edge of a ruler

rul·er *n* **1** : a person (as a king or queen) having supreme power over a nation **2** : a straight strip (as of plastic, wood, or metal) with a smooth edge that is marked off in units and used for measuring or as a guide in drawing straight lines

rul·ing *n* : an official decision (as by a judge)

rum *n* : an alcoholic liquor made from sugarcane or molasses

¹rum·ble *vb* **rum·bled; rum·bling** : to make or move with a low heavy continuous sound

²rumble *n* : a low heavy rolling sound

ru·mi·nant *n* : a hoofed animal (as a cow or sheep) that chews its cud and has a stomach with usually four chambers — **ruminant** *adj*

ru·mi·nate *vb* **ru·mi·nat·ed; ru·mi·nat·ing** : to think carefully and deeply : MEDITATE

¹rum·mage *vb* **rum·maged; rum·mag·ing** : to search especially by moving and looking through the contents of a place or container

²rummage *n* : a mixed up collection of different articles

rum·my *n* : a card game in which each player tries to lay down cards in groups of three or more

¹ru·mor *n* : information or a story that is passed from one person to another but has not been proven to be true and has no known source

²rumor *vb* **ru·mored; ru·mor·ing** : to spread information or a story that has not been proven to be true

rump *n* **1** : the back part of an animal's body where the hips and thighs join **2** : a cut of beef between the loin and the round

rum·ple *vb* **rum·pled; rum·pling** : to make (something) messy or wrinkled

rum·pus *n* : a noisy disturbance or quarrel

¹run *vb* **ran ; run; run·ning 1** : to go at a pace faster than a walk **2** : to go rapidly or hurriedly **3** : to take to flight **4** : to pass over, across, or through **5** : ²FUNCTION **6** : to cause to function **7** : EXTEND 1 **8** : to move freely about **9** : ¹FLOW 1 **10** : to be in charge of : MANAGE **11** : to do something by or as if by running **12** : to take part in a race **13** : to move on or as if on wheels **14** : to go back and forth often according to a fixed schedule **15** : to migrate or move in schools **16** : to continue in force **17** : to pass into a specified condition **18** : to spread into another area **19** : to give off liquid **20** : to tend to develop a specified feature or quality **21** : to slip through or past **22** : to cause to penetrate **23** : to cause to go **24** : to take on **25** : to print or broadcast **26** : to be a candidate for office **27** : to occur again and again — **run away** : to leave home secretly without intending to return — **run into** : to meet by chance — **run off** : to leave in a hurry — **run out 1** : to come to an end **2** : to become used up — **run out of** : to use up the available supply of — **run over** : ¹OVERFLOW 1

²run *n* **1** : an act or the action of running **2** : a score made in baseball by a base runner reaching home plate **3** : an enclosure for animals where they may feed and exercise **4** : the usual or normal kind **5** : a continuous series especially of similar things **6** : sudden heavy demands from depositors, creditors, or customers **7** : the quantity of work turned out in a continuous operation **8** : the distance covered in a period of continuous traveling **9** : a regular course or trip **10** : freedom of movement **11** : a way, track, or path frequented by animals **12** : ¹SLOPE 1 **13** : a spot in knitted fabric that has unraveled

¹run·away *n* **1** : someone who leaves a place (as home) secretly without intending to return **2** : a horse that is running out of control

²runaway *adj* **1** : having left a place secretly with no intention of returning **2** : escaping from control

run–down *adj* **1** : in poor condition **2** : in poor health

¹rung *past participle of* ³RING

²rung *n* **1** : a rounded part placed as a crosspiece between the legs of a chair **2** : one of the crosspieces of a ladder

run–in *n* : an angry argument

run·ner *n* **1** : a person or animal that runs **2** : a thin piece or part on or in which something slides **3** : MESSENGER **4** : a slender creeping branch of a plant that roots at the end or at the joints to form new plants **5** : a long narrow carpet (as for a hall)

run·ner–up *n, pl* **run·ners–up** : the competitor in a contest who finishes second

run·ny *adj* **run·ni·er; run·ni·est** : giving off or likely to give off liquid

runt *n* : an unusually small person or animal

run·way *n* **1** : a path beaten by animals in going to and from feeding grounds **2** : a paved strip of ground on a landing field for the landing and takeoff of aircraft

ru·pee *n* : any of various coins (as of India or Pakistan)

¹rup·ture *n* **1** : a break in peaceful or friendly relations **2** : a breaking or tearing apart of body tissue **3** : a crack or break in something

²rupture *vb* **rup·tured; rup·tur·ing** **1** : to part by violence : BREAK **2** : to produce a break or tear in **3** : to have or develop a break or tear

ru·ral *adj* : relating to the country, country people or life, or agriculture

ruse *n* : ¹TRICK 3, ARTIFICE

¹rush *vb* **rushed; rush·ing** **1** : to move forward or act very quickly or in a way that shows eagerness or the need to hurry **2** : to perform in a short time or at high speed **3** : to make (someone) act quickly **4** : to bring (someone) to a place quickly **5** : ¹ATTACK 1, CHARGE

²rush *n* **1** : a quick strong forward motion **2** : a burst of activity or speed **3** : an eager mi-

gration of people usually to a new place in search of wealth

³rush *n* : a grasslike marsh plant with hollow stems used in chair seats and mats

⁴rush *adj* : demanding special speed

¹Rus·sian *adj* : of or relating to Russia, its people, or the Russian language

²Russian *n* **1** : a person born or living in Russia **2** : a language of the Russians

¹rust *n* **1** : a reddish coating formed on metal (as iron) when it is exposed especially to moist air **2** : a plant disease caused by fungi that makes spots on plants **3** : a fungus that causes a rust

²rust *vb* **rust·ed; rust·ing** : to make or become rusty

¹rus·tic *adj* **1** : relating to or suitable for the country **2** : ¹PLAIN 7, SIMPLE **3** : made from rough wood

²rustic *n* : a person living or raised in the country

¹rus·tle *vb* **rus·tled; rus·tling** **1** : to make or cause to make a quick series of small sounds **2** : to steal (as cattle) from the range — **rus·tler** *n*

²rustle *n* : a quick series of small sounds

rusty *adj* **rust·i·er; rust·i·est** **1** : affected by rust **2** : less skilled and slow through lack of practice or use — **rust·i·ness** *n*

¹rut *n* **1** : a track worn by a wheel or by habitual passage **2** : ¹ROUTINE 1

²rut *vb* **rut·ted; rut·ting** : to make a track in

ru·ta·ba·ga *n* : a turnip with a large yellow root

ruth·less *adj* : having no pity : CRUEL — **ruth·less·ly** *adv* — **ruth·less·ness** *n*

-ry *n suffix, pl* **-ries** : -ERY

rye *n* : a hardy cereal grass grown especially for its edible seeds that are used in flour and animal feeds

S

s *n, pl* **s's** *or* **ss** *often cap* **1** : the 19th letter of the English alphabet **2** : a grade rating a student's work as satisfactory

S *abbr* **1** satisfactory **2** small **3** south **4** southern

¹-s *n pl suffix* — used to form the plural of most nouns that do not end in *s, z, sh, ch, x,* or *y* following a consonant and with or without an apostrophe to form the plural of abbreviations, numbers, letters, and symbols used as nouns

²-s *adv suffix* — used to form adverbs showing usual or repeated action or state

³-s *vb suffix* — used to form the third person singular present of most verbs that do not end in *s, z, sh, ch, x,* or *y* following a consonant

-'s *n suffix or pron suffix* — used to form the possessive of singular nouns, of plural nouns not ending in *s*, and of some pronouns

Sab·bath *n* : a day of the week that is regularly observed as a day of rest and worship

sa·ber *or* **sa·bre** *n* : a long sword with a curved blade

sa·ber–toothed cat *n* : SABER-TOOTHED TIGER

saber–toothed tiger *n* : a very large extinct cat of prehistoric times with long sharp curved upper canine teeth

sa·ble *n* **1** : the color black **2** : a meat-eating animal of northern Europe and Asia that is related to the weasel and has soft brown fur

¹sab·o·tage *n* : deliberate destruction of or damage to property

²sabotage *vb* **sab·o·taged; sab·o·tag·ing** : to damage or destroy on purpose : to engage in sabotage

sac *n* : a part of a plant or animal resembling a bag and often containing a liquid or air — **sac·like** *adj*

sa·chem *n* : a North American Indian chief

¹sack *n* **1** : ¹BAG 1 **2** : a sack and its contents

²sack *vb* **sacked; sack·ing** **1** : to put into a sack **2** : to fire from a job or position

³sack *vb* **sacked; sack·ing** : to loot after capture : PLUNDER

sack·ing *n* : a strong rough cloth (as burlap) from which sacks are made

sac·ra·ment *n* : a Christian religious act or ceremony that is considered especially sacred

sa·cred *adj* **1** : HOLY 1 **2** : RELIGIOUS 2 **3** : deserving to be respected and honored

¹sac·ri·fice *n* **1** : the act or ceremony of making an offering to God or a god especially on an altar **2** : something offered as a religious act **3** : an act of giving up something especially for the sake of someone or something else **4** : something given up especially for the sake of helping others

²sacrifice *vb* **sac·ri·ficed; sac·ri·fic·ing** **1** : to offer or kill as a religious act **2** : to give up (something) especially for the sake of something or someone else

sad *adj* **sad·der; sad·dest** **1** : feeling or showing sorrow or unhappiness **2** : causing sorrow or unhappiness — **sad·ly** *adv* — **sad·ness** *n*

sad·den *vb* **sad·dened; sad·den·ing** : to make or become sad

¹sad·dle *n* **1** : a padded and leather-covered seat for a rider on horseback **2** : something like a saddle in shape, position, or use

²saddle *vb* **sad·dled; sad·dling** **1** : to put a saddle on **2** : to put a load on : BURDEN

saddle horse *n* : a horse suited for or trained for riding

sa·fa·ri *n* : a trip to see or hunt animals especially in Africa

¹safe *adj* **saf·er; saf·est** **1** : free or secure from harm or danger **2** : giving protection or security against harm or danger **3** : HARMLESS **4** : unlikely to be wrong or cause disagreement **5** : not likely to take risks : CAREFUL **6** : successful in reaching a base in baseball — **safe·ly** *adv*

²safe *n* : a metal box with a lock that is used for keeping something (as money) safe

¹safe·guard *n* : something that protects and gives safety

²safeguard *vb* **safe·guard·ed; safe·guard·ing** : to make or keep safe or secure

safe·keep·ing *n* : the act of keeping safe : protection from danger or loss

safe·ty *n* : freedom from danger or harm : the state of being safe

safety belt *n* : SEAT BELT

safety pin *n* : a pin that is bent back to form a spring and has a guard that covers the point

saf·fron *n* **1** : an orange spice that is made from the dried stigmas of a crocus and is used to color or flavor foods **2** : an orange to orange yellow

¹sag *vb* **sagged; sag·ging** **1** : to sink, settle, or hang below the natural or right level **2** : to become less firm or strong

²sag *n* : a part or area that sinks or hangs below the natural or right level

sa·ga *n* **1** : a story of heroic deeds **2** : a long and often complicated story

sa·ga·cious *adj* : quick and wise in understanding and judging

¹sage *adj* : WISE — **sage·ly** *adv*

²sage *n* : a very wise person

³sage *n* **1** : a mint with grayish green leaves used especially to flavor foods **2** : SAGEBRUSH

sage·brush *n* : a plant of the western United States that grows as a low shrub and has a bitter juice and strong smell

sag·gy *adj* : hanging down too much : not firm

Sag·it·tar·i·us *n* **1** : a constellation between Scorpio and Capricorn imagined as a centaur **2** : the ninth sign of the zodiac or a person born under this sign

sa·gua·ro *n, pl* **sa·gua·ros** : a giant cactus of the southwestern United States and Mexico

said *past and past participle of* SAY

¹sail *n* **1** : a sheet of strong cloth (as canvas) used to catch enough wind to move boats through the water or over ice **2** : the sails of a ship **3** : a trip in a ship or boat moved especially by the wind

²sail *vb* **sailed; sail·ing** **1** : to travel on a boat moved especially by the wind **2** : to travel on or by water **3** : to control the motion of (a ship or boat) while traveling on water **4** : to move or proceed in a quick and smooth way

sail·boat *n* : a boat equipped with sails

sail·fish *n* : a fish with a large fin like a sail on its back

sail·or *n* : a person who works on or controls a boat or ship as part of the crew

saint *n* **1** : a good and holy person and especially one who in the Christian church is declared to be worthy of special honor **2** : a person who is very good, helpful, or patient

Saint Ber·nard *n* : a very large powerful dog originally of the Swiss Alps and used in the past to find and help lost travelers

saint·ly *adj* : like a saint or like that of a saint — **saint·li·ness** *n*

sake *n* **1** : PURPOSE **2** : WELFARE 1, BENEFIT

sal·able *or* **sale·able** *adj* : good enough to sell

sal·ad *n* **1** : a mixture of raw usually green leafy vegetables (as lettuce) combined with other vegetables (as tomato and cucumber) and served with a dressing **2** : a mixture of small pieces of food (as meat, fish, pasta, fruit, or vegetables) usually combined with a dressing

sal·a·man·der *n* : a small animal with smooth moist skin that is related to the frog but looks like a lizard

sa·la·mi *n* : a large highly seasoned sausage of pork and beef that is usually eaten cold

sal·a·ry *n, pl* **sal·a·ries** : a fixed amount of money paid at regular times for work done

sale *n* **1** : an exchange of goods or property for money **2** : the state of being available for purchase **3** : an event at which goods are sold at lowered prices

sales·clerk *n* : a person who works in a store selling goods

sales·man *n, pl* **sales·men** : a person who sells goods or services in a particular geographic area, in a store, or by telephone

sales·per·son *n* : SALESMAN

sales tax *n* : a tax paid by the buyer on goods bought

sales·wom·an *n, pl* **sales·wom·en** : a woman who sells goods or services in a particular geographic area, in a store, or by telephone

sa·li·va *n* : a watery fluid that moistens chewed food and contains enzymes which break down starch and that is secreted into the mouth from three pairs of glands near the mouth

sal·i·vary *adj* : of, relating to, or producing saliva

sal·low *adj* : slightly yellow in a way that does not look healthy

¹**sal·ly** *n, pl* **sallies** **1** : a sudden attack especially by besieged soldiers **2** : a clever and funny remark

²**sally** *vb* **sal·lied; sal·ly·ing** **1** : to rush out **2** : to set out (as from home)

salm·on *n* : a fish with reddish or pinkish flesh that is often caught for sport or food and lives most of its life in the ocean but swims up rivers or streams as an adult to deposit or fertilize eggs

sa·lon *n* : a business that offers customers beauty treatments

sa·loon *n* : a place where alcoholic drinks are sold and drunk : BAR

sal·sa *n* **1** : a spicy sauce of tomatoes, onions, and hot peppers **2** : popular music of Latin American origin with characteristics of jazz and rock

¹**salt** *n* **1** : a colorless or white substance that consists of sodium and chlorine and is used in seasoning foods, preserving meats and fish, and in making soap and glass **2** : a compound formed by the combination of an acid and a base or a metal

²**salt** *vb* **salt·ed; salt·ing** : to flavor or preserve with salt

³**salt** *adj* : containing salt : SALTY

salt·wa·ter *adj* : relating to or living in salt water

salty *adj* **salt·i·er; salt·i·est** : of, tasting of, or containing salt

sa·lu·ta·tion *n* **1** : an act or action of greeting **2** : a word or phrase used as a greeting at the beginning of a letter

¹**sa·lute** *vb* **sa·lut·ed; sa·lut·ing** **1** : to give a sign of respect to (as a military officer) especially by a movement of the right hand to the forehead **2** : to show or express respect for : HONOR

²**salute** *n* **1** : the position taken or the movement made when bringing the right hand to the forehead in a sign of respect (as for a military officer) **2** : an act or ceremony that is a show of respect or honor

¹**sal·vage** *n* **1** : the act of saving a ship or its cargo **2** : the saving or rescuing of possessions in danger of being lost (as from fire) **3** : something that is saved (as from a wreck)

²**salvage** *vb* **sal·vaged; sal·vag·ing** : to recover (something usable) especially from wreckage or ruin

sal·va·tion *n* **1** : the saving of a person from sin or evil **2** : something that saves from danger or difficulty

¹**salve** *n* : a healing or soothing ointment

²**salve** *vb* **salved; salv·ing** : to quiet or soothe with or as if with a salve

¹**same** *adj* **1** : not another : IDENTICAL **2** : UNCHANGED **3** : very much alike

²**same** *pron* : something identical with or like another

same·ness *n* **1** : the quality or state of being identical or like another **2** : MONOTONY

¹**sam·ple** *n* **1** : a part or piece that shows the quality or character of the whole **2** : a small amount of something that is given to people to try

²**sample** *vb* **sam·pled; sam·pling** : to judge the quality or character of by trying or examining a small part or amount

san·a·to·ri·um *n, pl* **san·a·to·ri·ums** *or* **san·a·to·ria** : a place for the care and treatment usually of people recovering from illness or having a disease likely to last a long time

¹**sanc·tion** *n* **1** : official approval or permission **2** : an action (as the ending of financial aid) taken by one or more nations to make another nation comply with a law or rule

²**sanction** *vb* **sanc·tioned; sanc·tion·ing** : to officially accept or allow

sanc·tu·ary *n, pl* **sanc·tu·ar·ies** **1** : a holy or sacred place **2** : a building or room for religious worship **3** : a place that provides safety or protection **4** : the protection from danger or a difficult situation that is provided by a safe place

¹**sand** *n* **1** : loose material in grains produced by the natural breaking up of rocks **2** : a soil made up mostly of sand

²**sand** *vb* **sand·ed; sand·ing** **1** : to sprinkle with sand **2** : to smooth or clean with sandpaper — **sand·er** *n*

san·dal *n* : a shoe consisting of a sole that is held in place by straps

san·dal·wood *n* : the fragrant yellowish wood of an Asian tree

sand·bag *n* : a bag filled with sand and used as a weight (as on a balloon) or as part of a wall or dam

sand·bar *n* : a ridge of sand formed in water by tides or currents

sand·box *n* : a large low box for holding sand especially for children to play in

sand dollar *n* : a flat round sea urchin

sand·pa·per *n* : paper that has rough material (as sand) glued on one side and is used for smoothing and polishing

sand·pip·er *n* : a small shorebird with long slender legs and bill

sand·stone *n* : rock made of sand held together by a natural cement (as of calcium carbonate)

sand·storm *n* : a desert storm with strong wind that blows clouds of sand

¹**sand·wich** *n* : two or more slices of bread or a split roll with a filling (as meat or cheese) between them

²**sandwich** *vb* **sand·wiched; sand·wich·ing** : to fit in between two or more things or people

sandy *adj* **sand·i·er; sand·i·est** **1** : full of or

covered with sand **2** : of a yellowish gray color

sane *adj* **san·er; san·est** **1** : having a healthy and sound mind **2** : very sensible

sang *past of* SING

san·i·tar·i·um *n, pl* **san·i·tar·i·ums** *or* **san·i·tar·ia** : SANATORIUM

san·i·tary *adj* **1** : relating to health or hygiene **2** : free from filth, infection, or other dangers to health

san·i·ta·tion *n* : the act or process of making or keeping things free from filth, infection, or other dangers to health

san·i·ty *n* : the state of having a healthy and sound mind

sank *past of* SINK

San·ta Claus *n* : the spirit of Christmas as represented by a plump jolly old man with a white beard who is dressed in a red suit and delivers presents to good children

¹**sap** *n* : a watery juice that circulates through a plant and carries food and nutrients

²**sap** *vb* **sapped; sap·ping** : to weaken or use up little by little

sap·ling *n* : a young tree

sap·phire *n* : a clear bright blue gemstone

sap·py *adj* **sap·pi·er; sap·pi·est** : sad or romantic in a foolish or exaggerated way

sap·wood *n* : young wood through which sap travels that is found just beneath the bark of a tree and is usually lighter in color than the heartwood

sar·casm *n* : the use of words that normally mean one thing to mean just the opposite usually to hurt someone's feelings or show scorn

sar·cas·tic *adj* **1** : showing sarcasm **2** : being in the habit of using sarcasm — **sar·cas·ti·cal·ly** *adv*

sar·dine *n* : a young or very small fish often preserved in oil and used for food

sa·ri *n* : a piece of clothing worn mainly by women of southern Asia that is a long light cloth wrapped around the body and head or shoulder

sar·sa·pa·ril·la *n* : a sweetened carbonated beverage that tastes somewhat like root beer

¹**sash** *n* : a broad band of cloth worn around the waist or over the shoulder

²**sash** *n* **1** : a frame for a pane of glass in a door or window **2** : the movable part of a window

Sask. *abbr* Saskatchewan

¹**sass** *n* : a rude or disrespectful reply

²**sass** *vb* **sassed; sass·ing** : to speak to in a rude or disrespectful way

sas·sa·fras *n* : a tall tree of eastern North America whose dried root bark was formerly used in medicine or as a flavoring

sassy *adj* **sass·i·er; sass·i·est** : having or showing a rude lack of respect

sat *past and past participle of* SIT

Sat. *abbr* Saturday

Sa·tan *n* : DEVIL 1

satch·el *n* : a small bag (as for carrying clothes or books) that often has a shoulder strap

sat·el·lite *n* **1** : a smaller body that revolves around a planet **2** : an object or vehicle sent out from the earth to revolve around the earth, moon, sun, or a planet

satellite dish *n* : a bowl-shaped antenna for receiving transmissions (as of television programs) from a satellite orbiting the earth

sat·in *n* : a cloth with a smooth shiny surface

sat·ire *n* **1** : humor that is used to make fun of and often show the weaknesses of someone or something **2** : something (as a book or movie) that uses satire

sat·is·fac·tion *n* **1** : a feeling of happiness or content with something : the condition of being satisfied **2** : something that makes a person happy, pleased, or content

sat·is·fac·to·ry *adj* : good enough for a particular purpose : causing satisfaction — **sat·is·fac·to·ri·ly** *adv*

sat·is·fy *vb* **sat·is·fied; sat·is·fy·ing 1** : to make happy or contented **2** : to meet the needs of **3** : CONVINCE **4** : to do what has been agreed upon

sat·u·rate *vb* **sat·u·rat·ed; sat·u·rat·ing** : to soak completely

Sat·ur·day *n* : the seventh day of the week

Sat·urn *n* : the planet that is sixth in distance from the sun and has a diameter of about 75,000 miles (120,000 kilometers)

sauce *n* **1** : a usually thick liquid poured over or mixed with food **2** : boiled or canned fruit

sauce·pan *n* : a small deep cooking pan with a handle

sau·cer *n* : a small shallow dish often with a slightly lower center for holding a cup

saucy *adj* **sauc·i·er; sauc·i·est 1** : being rude and disrespectful : SASSY **2** : stylish in dress or appearance — **sauc·i·ly** *adv*

sau·er·kraut *n* : finely cut cabbage soaked in a salty mixture

saun·ter *vb* **saun·tered; saun·ter·ing** : to walk in a slow relaxed way : STROLL

sau·sage *n* **1** : spicy ground meat (as pork) usually stuffed in casings **2** : a roll of sausage in a casing

¹sav·age *adj* **1** : not tamed : WILD **2** : being cruel and brutal : FIERCE — **sav·age·ly** *adv*

²savage *n* **1** : a person belonging to a group with a low level of civilization **2** : a cruel or violent person

sav·age·ry *n, pl* **sav·age·ries 1** : an uncivi-

lized condition or character **2** : an act of cruelty or violence

sa·van·na *also* **sa·van·nah** *n* : land of warm regions (as Africa) that is covered with grass and only a few shrubs and trees

¹save *vb* **saved; sav·ing 1** : to free or keep from danger or harm **2** : to keep from being ruined : PRESERVE **3** : to put aside for later use **4** : to put aside money **5** : to keep from being spent, wasted, or lost **6** : to make unnecessary

²save *prep* : ¹EXCEPT 2

sav·ing *n* **1** : something that is not spent, wasted, or lost **2 savings** *pl* : money put aside (as in a bank)

sav·ior *or* **sav·iour** *n* **1** : a person who saves someone or something from danger or harm **2** *cap* : JESUS CHRIST

¹sa·vor *n* : the taste or smell of something

²savor *vb* **sa·vored; sa·vor·ing 1** : to taste or smell with pleasure **2** : to delight in : ENJOY

sa·vo·ry *adj* : pleasing to the taste or smell

¹saw *past of* SEE

²saw *n* : a tool or machine with a blade having sharp teeth that is used for cutting hard material (as wood or metal)

³saw *vb* **sawed; sawed** *or* **sawn; saw·ing** : to cut or shape with a saw

⁴saw *n* : a common saying : PROVERB

saw·dust *n* : tiny bits (as of wood) which fall from something being sawed

saw·horse *n* : a frame or rack on which wood is rested while being sawed

saw·mill *n* : a mill or factory having machinery for sawing logs

saw–toothed *adj* : having an edge or outline like the teeth of a saw

sax·o·phone *n* : a woodwind instrument usually in the form of a curved metal tube with keys used to change pitch and a mouthpiece with a single reed

¹say *vb* **said; say·ing 1** : to express in words **2** : to state as an opinion or decision : DECLARE **3** : ¹REPEAT 2, RECITE **4** : INDICATE 2, SHOW **5** : to consider as a possibility or example

²say *n* **1** : an expression of opinion **2** : the power to decide or help decide

say·ing *n* : PROVERB

SC *abbr* South Carolina

scab *n* : a crust mostly of hardened blood that forms over and protects a sore or wound as it heals

scab·bard *n* : a protective case or sheath for the blade of a sword or dagger

scab·by *adj* **scab·bi·er; scab·bi·est** : covered with scabs

sca·bies *n, pl* **scabies** : an itch or mange

caused by mites living as parasites under the skin

scaf·fold *n* **1** : a raised platform built as a support for workers and their tools and materials **2** : a platform on which executions take place

scal·a·wag *or* **scal·ly·wag** *n* : RASCAL 1

¹scald *vb* **scald·ed; scald·ing 1** : to burn with or as if with hot liquid or steam **2** : to bring to a temperature just below the boiling point

²scald *n* : an injury caused by burning with hot liquid or steam

scald·ing *adj* : very hot

¹scale *n* **1** : either pan of a balance or the balance itself **2** : a device for weighing

²scale *n* **1** : one of the small stiff plates that cover much of the body of some animals (as fish and snakes) **2** : a thin layer or part suggesting a fish scale — **scaled** *adj* — **scale·less** *adj*

³scale *vb* **scaled; scal·ing 1** : to remove the scales of **2** : ²FLAKE

⁴scale *vb* **scaled; scal·ing 1** : to climb by or as if by a ladder **2** : to regulate or set according to a standard — often used with *down* or *up*

⁵scale *n* **1** : a series of musical tones going up or down in pitch in fixed steps **2** : a series of spaces marked off by lines and used for measuring distances or amounts **3** : a series of like things arranged in order (as according to size or degree) **4** : the size of a picture, plan, or model of a thing compared to the size of the thing itself **5** : a standard for measuring or judging **6** : the size or extent of something especially in comparison to something else

¹scal·lop *n* **1** : an edible shellfish that is a mollusk with a ribbed shell in two parts **2** : one of a series of half-circles that form a border on an edge (as of lace)

²scallop *vb* **scal·loped; scal·lop·ing 1** : to bake with crumbs, butter, and milk **2** : to embroider, cut, or edge with half-circles

¹scalp *n* : the part of the skin of the head usually covered with hair

²scalp *vb* **scalped; scalp·ing** : to remove the scalp from

scaly *adj* **scal·i·er; scal·i·est** : covered with scales or flakes

scamp *n* : RASCAL 1

¹scam·per *vb* **scam·pered; scam·per·ing** : to run or move quickly and often playfully about

²scamper *n* : a hurried and often playful run or movement

scan *vb* **scanned; scan·ning 1** : to examine or look over carefully **2** : to look through or over quickly **3** : to examine with a special device (as a scanner) especially to obtain information

scan·dal *n* **1** : something that angers or shocks people because rules or standards of behavior are violated **2** : talk that injures a person's good name

scan·dal·ous *adj* **1** : containing shocking information **2** : very bad or shocking

¹Scan·di·na·vian *n* : a person born or living in Scandinavia

²Scandinavian *adj* : of or relating to Scandinavia or its people

scan·ner *n* : a device that converts a printed image (as text or a photograph) into a form a computer can display or alter

scant *adj* **1** : barely enough **2** : not quite to a full amount, degree, or extent

scanty *adj* **scant·i·er; scant·i·est** : barely enough : lacking in size or quantity

¹scar *n* **1** : a mark left on the skin after a wound heals **2** : an ugly mark (as on furniture) showing damage **3** : the lasting effect (as a feeling of sadness) of some unhappy experience

²scar *vb* **scarred; scar·ring 1** : to mark or become marked with a scar **2** : to leave a lasting bad effect on

scar·ab *n* : a large dark beetle used in ancient Egypt as a symbol of eternal life

¹scarce *adj* **scarc·er; scarc·est** : not plentiful

²scarce *adv* : HARDLY, SCARCELY

scarce·ly *adv* **1** : only just : BARELY **2** : certainly not

scar·ci·ty *n, pl* **scar·ci·ties** : a very small supply : the condition of being scarce

¹scare *vb* **scared; scar·ing** : to become or cause to become frightened — **scare up** : to find or get with some difficulty

²scare *n* **1** : a sudden feeling of fear : FRIGHT **2** : a widespread state of alarm

scare·crow *n* : an object made to look like a person and set up to scare birds away from crops

scarf *n, pl* **scarves** *or* **scarfs 1** : a piece of cloth worn loosely on the shoulders, around the neck, or on the head **2** : a long narrow strip of cloth used as a cover (as on a bureau)

¹scar·let *n* : a bright red

²scarlet *adj* : colored bright red

scarlet fever *n* : a serious illness in which there is a sore throat, high fever, and red rash

scary *adj* **scar·i·er; scar·i·est** : causing fright

scat *vb* **scat·ted; scat·ting** : to go away quickly — often used as a command to frighten away an animal

scat·ter *vb* **scat·tered; scat·ter·ing 1** : to toss, sow, or place here and there **2** : to separate or cause to separate and go in different ways

scat·ter·brain *n* : a person who is unable to concentrate or think clearly — **scat·ter·brained** *adj*

scav·enge *vb* **scav·enged; scav·eng·ing** : to search through and collect usable items especially from what has been thrown away

scav·en·ger *n* **1** : a person who picks over junk or garbage for useful items **2** : an animal (as a vulture) that feeds on dead or decaying material

scene *n* **1** : a division of an act in a play **2** : a single interesting or important happening in a play or story **3** : the place of an event or action **4** : a view or sight that resembles a picture **5** : a display of anger or bad behavior

scen·ery *n* **1** : the painted scenes used on a stage and the furnishings that go with them **2** : pleasant outdoor scenes or views **3** : a person's usual surroundings

sce·nic *adj* **1** : having views of pleasant natural features **2** : relating to stage scenery

¹scent *n* **1** : an odor that is given off by someone or something **2** : power or sense of smell **3** : a course followed in search or pursuit of something **4** : ¹PERFUME 1

²scent *vb* **scent·ed; scent·ing** **1** : to become aware of or follow through the sense of smell **2** : to get a hint of **3** : to fill with an odor : PERFUME

scep·ter *n* : a rod carried by a ruler as a sign of authority

¹sched·ule *n* **1** : a plan of things that need to be done and the times they will be done **2** : a written or printed list of things and the time they will be done **3** : a list of the times set for certain events **4** : TIMETABLE

²schedule *vb* **sched·uled; sched·ul·ing** : to plan at a certain time

¹scheme *n* **1** : a secret plan : PLOT **2** : a plan of something to be done : PROJECT **3** : an organized design

²scheme *vb* **schemed; schem·ing** : to form a secret plan — **schem·er** *n*

schol·ar *n* **1** : a student in a school : PUPIL **2** : a person who knows a great deal about one or more subjects : a learned person

schol·ar·ly *adj* : like that of or suitable to learned persons

schol·ar·ship *n* **1** : money given to a student to help pay for further education **2** : serious academic study or research of a subject

scho·las·tic *adj* : relating to schools, students, or education

¹school *n* **1** : a place for teaching and learning **2** : a session of teaching and learning **3** : SCHOOLHOUSE **4** : the teachers and pupils of a school **5** : a group of persons who share the same opinions and beliefs

²school *vb* **schooled; school·ing** : TEACH 2, TRAIN

³school *n* : a large number of one kind of fish or water animals swimming together

school·bag *n* : a bag for carrying schoolbooks

school·book *n* : TEXTBOOK

school·boy *n* : a boy who goes to school

school·girl *n* : a girl who goes to school

school·house *n, pl* **school·hous·es** : a building used as a place for teaching and learning

school·ing *n* : EDUCATION 1

school·mas·ter *n* : a man who is in charge of a school or teaches in a school

school·mate *n* : a fellow student

school·mis·tress *n* : a woman who is in charge of a school or teaches in a school

school·room *n* : CLASSROOM

school·teach·er *n* : a person who teaches in a school

school·work *n* : lessons done at school or assigned to be done at home

school·yard *n* : the playground of a school

schoo·ner *n* : a ship usually having two masts with the mainmast located toward the center and the shorter mast toward the front

schwa *n* **1** : an unstressed vowel that is the usual sound of the first and last vowels of the English word *America* **2** : the symbol ə commonly used for a schwa and sometimes also for a similarly pronounced stressed vowel (as in *cut*)

sci. *abbr* science

sci·ence *n* **1** : knowledge about the natural world that is based on facts learned through experiments and observation **2** : an area of study that deals with the natural world (as biology or physics) **3** : a subject that is formally studied **4** : something that can be studied and learned

science fiction *n* : made-up stories about the influence of real or imagined science on society or individuals

sci·en·tif·ic *adj* **1** : relating to science or scientists **2** : using or applying the methods of science — **sci·en·tif·i·cal·ly** *adv*

sci·en·tist *n* : a person who studies, specializes in, or investigates a field of science and does scientific work

scis·sors *n pl* : a cutting instrument with two blades fastened together so that the sharp edges slide against each other — used as singular or plural

scoff *vb* **scoffed; scoff·ing** : to show great disrespect with mocking laughter or behavior

¹scold *vb* **scold·ed; scold·ing** : to find fault with or criticize in an angry way — **scold·ing** *n*

²scold *n* : a person who frequently criticizes and blames

¹scoop *n* **1** : the amount held by a scoop **2** : a kitchen utensil resembling a deep spoon and used for digging into and lifting out a soft substance **3** : a motion made with or as if with a scoop **4** : a large deep shovel for digging, dipping, or shoveling

²scoop *vb* **scooped; scoop·ing 1** : to take out or up with or as if with a dipping motion **2** : to make something (as a hole) by creating a hollow place

scoot *vb* **scoot·ed; scoot·ing** : to go suddenly and quickly

scoot·er *n* **1** : a vehicle consisting of a narrow rectangular base mounted between a front and a back wheel, guided by a handle attached to the front wheel, and moved by the rider pushing off with one foot **2** : MOTOR SCOOTER

scope *n* **1** : space or opportunity for action or thought **2** : the area or amount covered, reached, or viewed

scorch *vb* **scorched; scorch·ing 1** : to burn on the surface **2** : to dry or shrivel with or as if with intense heat **3** : to produce intense heat

¹score *n* **1** : a record of points made or lost (as in a game) **2** : the number of points earned for correct answers on a test **3** : a group of 20 things : TWENTY **4** : harm done by someone and kept in mind for later response **5** : DEBT 2 **6** : a line (as a scratch) made with or as if with something sharp **7** : ¹GROUND 8, REASON **8** : the written or printed form of a musical composition — **score·less** *adj*

²score *vb* **scored; scor·ing 1** : to make or cause to make a point or points in a game **2** : to cut or mark with a line, scratch, or notch **3** : ACHIEVE 1, WIN **4** : ²GRADE 1, MARK **5** : to set down in an account : RECORD **6** : to keep the score in a game

¹scorn *n* **1** : a strong feeling of disgust and anger **2** : an expression of disgust and anger

²scorn *vb* **scorned; scorn·ing** : to show disgust and anger for

scorn·ful *adj* : feeling or showing disgust and anger — **scorn·ful·ly** *adv*

Scor·pio *n* **1** : a constellation between Libra and Sagittarius imagined as a scorpion **2** : the eighth sign of the zodiac or a person born under this sign

scor·pi·on *n* : an animal related to the spiders that has a long jointed body ending in a slender tail with a poisonous stinger at the end

Scot *n* : a person born or living in Scotland

¹Scotch *adj* : ¹SCOTTISH

²Scotch *n pl* : ²SCOTTISH

scot–free *adj* : completely free from duty, harm, or punishment

¹Scot·tish *adj* : of or relating to Scotland or the Scottish people

²Scottish *n pl* : the people of Scotland

scoun·drel *n* : a mean or wicked person

¹scour *vb* **scoured; scour·ing 1** : to rub hard with a rough substance or object in order to clean **2** : to free or clear from impurities by or as if by rubbing

²scour *vb* **scoured; scouring** : to go or move swiftly about, over, or through in search of something

¹scourge *n* **1** : a cause of widespread or great suffering **2** : ²WHIP 1

²scourge *vb* **scourged; scourg·ing 1** : to cause trouble or suffering to : AFFLICT **2** : to whip severely : FLOG

¹scout *vb* **scout·ed; scout·ing 1** : to explore an area to find out information about it **2** : to search an area for someone or something

²scout *n* **1** : a person, group, boat, or plane that gathers information or searches an area **2** *often cap* : BOY SCOUT **3** *often cap* : GIRL SCOUT

scout·ing *n* **1** : the activity of gathering information or searching an area **2** *often cap* : the general activities of Boy Scout and Girl Scout groups

scout·mas·ter *n* : the leader of a troop of Boy Scouts

scow *n* : a large boat with a flat bottom and square ends that is used chiefly for loading and unloading ships and for carrying rubbish

¹scowl *vb* **scowled; scowl·ing 1** : to make a look that shows anger **2** : to say with an angry look

²scowl *n* : an angry look

scrag·gly *adj* **scrag·gli·er; scrag·gli·est** : of rough or uneven outline : UNKEMPT

scram *vb* **scrammed; scram·ming** : to go away at once — often used as a command

¹scram·ble *vb* **scram·bled; scram·bling 1** : to move or climb quickly and if necessary on hands and knees **2** : to cook the mixed whites and yolks of eggs by stirring them while frying **3** : to put in the wrong order **4** : to work hard to win or escape something

²scramble *n* : a disorderly rush

¹scrap *n* **1** : a small bit **2 scraps** *pl* : pieces of leftover food **3** : waste material (as metal) that can be made fit to use again

²scrap *vb* **scrapped; scrap·ping** : to abandon or throw away as worthless

³scrap *n* : ¹QUARREL 1, FIGHT

scrap·book *n* : a blank book in which clippings or pictures are kept

¹scrape *vb* **scraped; scrap·ing 1** : to remove by repeated strokes with something sharp or rough **2 :** to clean or smooth by rubbing **3 :** to rub or cause to rub so as to make a harsh noise **4 :** to hurt or roughen by dragging against a rough surface **5 :** to get with difficulty and a little at a time

²scrape *n* **1 :** a sound, mark, or injury made by something being dragged or rubbed against something else **2 :** a difficult or unpleasant situation — **3 :** the act of scraping

scrap·er *n* **:** a tool used to scrape something off a surface

¹scratch *vb* **scratched; scratch·ing 1 :** to scrape or rub lightly **2 :** to injure by scraping with something sharp **3 :** to make a scraping noise **4 :** to erase by scraping

²scratch *n* **:** a mark or injury made by scraping with something sharp

scratchy *adj* **scratch·i·er; scratch·i·est 1 :** likely to injure with something sharp **2 :** causing irritation **3 :** COARSE 1 **4 :** somewhat sore

¹scrawl *vb* **scrawled; scrawl·ing :** to write quickly and carelessly

²scrawl *n* **:** something written carelessly or without skill

scraw·ny *adj* **scraw·ni·er; scraw·ni·est :** poorly nourished **:** SKINNY

¹scream *vb* **screamed; scream·ing :** to cry out (as in fright) with a loud and high-pitched sound — **scream·er** *n*

²scream *n* **:** a long cry that is loud and high-pitched

¹screech *vb* **screeched; screech·ing 1 :** to make a high-pitched harsh sound **2 :** to utter with a high-pitched harsh sound **3 :** to cry out in a loud, high-pitched way (as in terror or pain) **4 :** to make a high-pitched harsh sound

²screech *n* **1 :** a high-pitched harsh cry **2 :** a high-pitched harsh sound

¹screen *n* **1 :** a frame that holds a usually wire netting and is used to let air in but keep pests (as insects) out **2 :** a curtain or wall used to hide or to protect **3 :** the flat surface on which movies are projected **4 :** the surface on which the image appears in an electronic display (as on a television set or computer terminal) **5 :** a network of wire set in a frame for separating finer parts from coarser parts (as of sand)

²screen *vb* **screened; screen·ing 1 :** to hide or protect with or as if with a curtain or wall **2 :** to separate or sift with a network of wire set in a frame **3 :** to look at carefully to select as suitable

screen saver *n* **:** a computer program that usually displays images on the screen of a computer that is on but not in use so as to prevent damage to the screen

¹screw *n* **1 :** a nail-shaped or rod-shaped piece of metal with a winding ridge around its length used for fastening and holding pieces together **2 :** the act of twisting **3 :** PROPELLER

²screw *vb* **screwed; screw·ing 1 :** to attach or fasten with a screw **2 :** to turn or twist on a winding ridge to attach **3 :** to twist out of shape **4 :** to increase in amount

screw·driv·er *n* **:** a tool for turning screws

screwy *adj* **screw·i·er; screw·i·est 1 :** oddly different and unfamiliar **2 :** CRAZY 1

¹scrib·ble *vb* **scrib·bled; scrib·bling :** to write quickly or carelessly — **scrib·bler** *n*

²scribble *n* **:** something written quickly or carelessly

scribe *n* **:** a person who copies writing (as in a book)

scrim·mage *n* **1 :** the action between two football teams when one attempts to move the ball down the field **2 :** a practice game between two teams or between two groups from the same team

script *n* **1 :** the written form of a play or movie or the lines to be said by a performer **2 :** HANDWRITING

scrip·ture *n* **1** *cap* **:** BIBLE 1 **2 :** writings sacred to a religious group

¹scroll *n* **:** a roll of paper or parchment on which something is written or engraved

²scroll *vb* **scrolled; scroll·ing :** to move words or images up or down a display screen as if by unrolling a scroll

¹scrub *vb* **scrubbed; scrub·bing :** to rub hard in washing

²scrub *n* **:** a thick growth of small or stunted shrubs or trees

³scrub *n* **:** the act, an instance, or a period of rubbing hard in washing

scrub·by *adj* **scrub·bi·er; scrub·bi·est :** covered with a thick growth of small or stunted shrubs or trees

scruff *n* **:** the loose skin on the back of the neck

scruffy *adj* **scruff·i·er; scruff·i·est :** dirty or shabby in appearance

scrump·tious *adj* **1 :** DELICIOUS **2 :** DELIGHTFUL

scrunch *vb* **scrunched; scrunch·ing 1 :** to cause (as facial features) to draw together **2 :** ¹CROUCH, HUNCH **3 :** to draw or squeeze together tightly **4 :** CRUMPLE 1 **5 :** ¹CRUSH 1

scru·ple *n* **1 :** a sense of right and wrong that keeps a person from doing something bad **2 :** a feeling of guilt from doing something bad

scru·pu·lous *adj* **:** careful in doing what is right and proper — **scru·pu·lous·ly** *adv*

scru·ti·nize *vb* **scru·ti·nized; scru·ti·niz·ing :** to examine very closely

scru·ti·ny *n* **:** a close inspection

scuba *n* : equipment used for breathing while swimming underwater

scuba diver *n* : a person who swims underwater with scuba gear

scuff *vb* **scuffed; scuff·ing** 1 : to scrape the feet while walking 2 : to mark or scratch by scraping

¹**scuf·fle** *vb* **scuf·fled; scuf·fling** 1 : to fight briefly and not very seriously 2 : SCUFF 1

²**scuffle** *n* 1 : a short fight that is not very serious 2 : the sound of shuffling

scull *n* : a boat driven by one or more pairs of short oars

sculpt *vb* **sculpt·ed; sculpt·ing** : ²SCULPTURE — **sculp·tor** *n*

¹**sculp·ture** *n* 1 : the action or art of making statues by carving or chiseling (as in wood or stone), by modeling (as in clay), or by casting (as in melted metal) 2 : a work of art produced by sculpture

²**sculpture** *vb* **sculp·tured; sculp·tur·ing** : to make (a work of art) by shaping (as stone, wood, or metal)

scum *n* 1 : a film of matter that rises to the top of a boiling or fermenting liquid 2 : a coating (as of algae) on the surface of still water 3 : a loathsome person

¹**scur·ry** *vb* **scur·ried; scur·ry·ing** : to move quickly

²**scurry** *n, pl* **scur·ries** : the act of moving quickly

¹**scur·vy** *n* : a disease caused by a lack of vitamin C in which the teeth loosen, the gums soften, and there is bleeding under the skin

²**scurvy** *adj* **scur·vi·er; scur·vi·est** : ²MEAN 1, CONTEMPTIBLE

¹**scut·tle** *vb* **scut·tled; scut·tling** : to run rapidly from view

²**scuttle** *n* : a pail or bucket for carrying coal

³**scuttle** *n* : a small opening with a lid or cover (as in the deck of a ship)

⁴**scuttle** *vb* **scut·tled; scut·tling** : to sink (a ship) by cutting holes through the bottom or sides

scythe *n* : a tool with a curved blade on a long curved handle that is used to mow grass or grain by hand

SD, S. Dak. *abbr* South Dakota

SE *abbr* southeast

sea *n* 1 : a body of salt water not as large as an ocean and often nearly surrounded by land 2 : OCEAN 1 3 : rough water 4 : something suggesting a sea's great size or depth

sea anemone *n* : a hollow sea animal that is related to the coral and has a cluster of tentacles around its mouth

sea·bird *n* : a bird (as a gull or puffin) that lives on or near the open ocean

sea·coast *n* : the shore of the sea

sea cucumber *n* : a sea animal that is related

to the starfish and has a flexible muscular body shaped like a cucumber

¹**sea·far·ing** *adj* : of or employed in sailing

²**seafaring** *n* : sailing on the sea as work or as recreation

sea·food *n* : saltwater fish and shellfish used as food

sea·go·ing *adj* : suitable or used for sea travel

sea·gull *n* : a gull that lives near the sea

sea horse *n* : a small fish with a head which looks like the head of a horse

¹**seal** *n* 1 : a sea mammal that swims with flippers, lives mostly in cold regions, bears young on land, feeds on fish and other sea animals (as squid), and is sometimes hunted for its fur, hide, or oil 2 : the soft fur of a seal

²**seal** *n* 1 : something that closes tightly 2 : the condition of having a tight seal 3 : an official mark stamped or pressed on something 4 : a device with a cut or raised design or figure that can be stamped or pressed into wax or paper 5 : a stamp that may be used to close a letter or package 6 : something (as a pledge) that makes safe or secure

³**seal** *vb* **sealed; seal·ing** 1 : to close tightly or completely to prevent anyone or anything from moving in or out 2 : to put an official mark on — **seal·er** *n*

sea level *n* : the surface of the sea halfway between the average high and low tides

sea lion *n* : a large seal of the Pacific Ocean

seal·skin *n* : ¹SEAL 2

seam *n* 1 : the fold, line, or groove made by sewing together or joining two edges or two pieces of material 2 : a layer in the ground of a mineral or metal

sea·man *n, pl* **sea·men** 1 : a person who helps in the handling of a ship at sea : SAILOR 2 : an enlisted person in the navy or coast guard ranking above a seaman apprentice

seaman apprentice *n* : an enlisted person in the navy or coast guard ranking above a seaman recruit

seaman recruit *n* : an enlisted person of the lowest rank in the navy or coast guard

seam·stress *n* : a woman who sews especially for a living

sea·plane *n* : an airplane that can rise from and land on water

sea·port *n* : a port, harbor, or town within reach of seagoing ships

sear *vb* **seared; sear·ing** 1 : to burn, mark, or injure with or as if with sudden heat 2 : to dry by or as if by heat : PARCH 3 : to quickly cook the surface by high heat

¹**search** *vb* **searched; search·ing** 1 : to go through or look around carefully and thoroughly in an effort to find something 2 : to

carefully look for someone or something **3**
: to look in the pockets or the clothing of
(someone) for something hidden

²search *n* : an act or instance of looking for
someone or something

search engine *n* : computer software used to
search data (as text or a database) for requested information

search·light *n* : a lamp for sending a beam of
bright light

sea·shell *n* : the shell of a sea animal

sea·shore *n* : the shore of a sea

sea·sick *adj* : sick in the stomach from the
pitching or rolling of a ship — **sea·sick-
ness** *n*

sea·side *n* : SEACOAST

¹sea·son *n* **1** : one of the four quarters into
which a year is commonly divided **2** : a period of time associated with something special

²season *vb* **sea·soned; sea·son·ing 1** : to
add flavor to (food) with spices and herbs **2**
: to make suitable for use (as by aging or
drying)

sea·son·al *adj* : happening, available, or used
at a certain season

sea·son·ing *n* : something added to food to
give it more flavor

sea star *n* : STARFISH

¹seat *n* **1** : something (as a chair) used to sit
in or on **2** : the part of something on which
a person sits **3** : the place on or at which a
person sits **4** : a place that serves as a capital or center — **seat·ed** *adj*

²seat *vb* **seat·ed; seat·ing 1** : to place in
or on a seat **2** : to have enough places to
sit for

seat belt *n* : a strap (as in an automobile or
airplane) designed to hold a person in a seat

sea urchin *n* : a small sea animal that is related to the starfish, lives on the sea bottom,
and is enclosed in a roundish shell covered
with spines that can move

sea·wall *n* : a bank or a wall to prevent sea
waves from eroding the shore

sea·wa·ter *n* : water in or from the sea

sea·weed *n* : an alga (as a kelp) that grows in
the sea

sea·wor·thy *adj* : fit or safe for a sea voyage

sec. *abbr* second

se·cede *vb* **se·ced·ed; se·ced·ing** : to end an
association with an organization (as a country)

se·clud·ed *adj* **1** : hidden from sight **2** : living or kept away from others

se·clu·sion *n* : the condition of being hidden
from sight or kept away from others

¹sec·ond *adj* **1** : being next after the first in
time or order **2** : next lower in rank, value,

or importance than the first **3** : another of
the same type

²second *n* **1** : a 60th part of a minute of time
or of a degree **2** : MOMENT 1, INSTANT

³second *vb* **sec·ond·ed; sec·ond·ing** : to
support a suggestion, motion, or nomination

⁴second *adv* : in the second place or rank

⁵second *n* : someone or something that is
second

sec·ond·ary *adj* **1** : second in rank, value, or
importance **2** : derived from or coming after
something original or primary **3** : relating to
secondary school **4** : relating to or being the
second of three levels of stress in pronunciation

secondary school *n* : a school for students
above elementary school level and below
college level

sec·ond·hand *adj* **1** : not new : having had a
previous owner **2** : selling used goods

second lieutenant *n* : a commissioned officer of the lowest rank in the army, air force,
or marine corps

second person *n* : a set of words or forms
(as pronouns or verb forms) referring to the
person the speaker or writer is addressing

sec·ond–rate *adj* : of ordinary or second
quality or value

se·cre·cy *n* **1** : the act of keeping things secret **2** : the quality or state of being secret or
hidden

¹se·cret *adj* **1** : hidden from the knowledge
of others **2** : done, made, or working in a
way that no other or only a few other people
know about — **se·cret·ly** *adv*

²secret *n* : something kept or planned to be
kept from others' knowledge

sec·re·tary *n, pl* **sec·re·tar·ies 1** : a person
who is employed to take care of records, letters, and routine work for another person **2**
: an officer of a business corporation or society who is in charge of the letters and
records and who keeps minutes of meetings
3 : a government official in charge of a department **4** : a writing desk with a top section for books

¹se·crete *vb* **se·cret·ed; se·cret·ing** : to produce and give off as a secretion

²secrete *vb* **se·cret·ed; se·cret·ing** : to put in
a hiding place

se·cre·tion *n* **1** : the act or process of giving
off a substance **2** : a substance formed in
and given off by a gland that usually performs a useful function in the body

se·cre·tive *adj* : tending to act in secret or
keep secrets

sect *n* : a group within a religion which has a
special set of teachings or a special way of
doing things

¹sec·tion *n* **1** : a division of a thing or place

2 : a part cut off or separated **3** : a part of a written work **4** : CROSS SECTION

²**section** *vb* **sec·tioned; sec·tion·ing** : to cut into parts

sec·tor *n* : a part of an area or of a sphere of activity

sec·u·lar *adj* **1** : not concerned with religion or the church **2** : not belonging to a religious order

¹**se·cure** *adj* **se·cur·er; se·cur·est 1** : free from danger or risk **2** : strong or firm enough to ensure safety **3** : free from worry or doubt : CONFIDENT **4** : ¹SURE 5, CERTAIN

²**secure** *vb* **se·cured; se·cur·ing 1** : to make safe **2** : to fasten or put something in a place to keep it from coming loose **3** : to get hold of : ACQUIRE

se·cu·ri·ty *n, pl* **se·cu·ri·ties 1** : the state of being safe : SAFETY **2** : freedom from worry or anxiety **3** : something given as a pledge of payment **4** : something (as a stock certificate) that is evidence of debt or ownership

se·dan *n* **1** : a closed automobile that has two or four doors and a permanent top and seats four or more people **2** : SEDAN CHAIR

sedan chair *n* : a chair made to hold one person and to be carried on two poles by two others

se·date *adj* : quiet and steady in manner or conduct — **se·date·ly** *adv*

sed·a·tive *n* : a medicine that calms or relaxes someone

sed·en·tary *adj* : doing much sitting : not physically active

sedge *n* : a plant that is like grass but has solid stems and grows in tufts in marshes

sed·i·ment *n* **1** : the material from a liquid that settles to the bottom **2** : material (as stones and sand) carried onto land or into water by water, wind, or a glacier

sed·i·men·ta·ry *adj* : relating to or formed from sediment

se·duce *vb* **se·duced; se·duc·ing** : to persuade (someone) to do something and especially to do something wrong

¹**see** *vb* **saw; seen; see·ing 1** : to have the power of sight **2** : to view with the eyes **3** : to have experience of **4** : to understand the meaning or importance of **5** : to come to know : DISCOVER **6** : to call on : VISIT **7** : to form a mental picture of **8** : to imagine as a possibility **9** : to make sure **10** : to attend to **11** : to meet with **12** : ACCOMPANY 1, ESCORT

²**see** *n* **1** : the city in which a bishop's church is located **2** : DIOCESE

¹**seed** *n* **1** : a tiny developing plant that is enclosed in a protective coat usually along with a supply of food and that is able to develop under suitable conditions into a plant

like the one that produced it **2** : a small structure (as a spore or a tiny dry fruit) other than a true seed by which a plant reproduces itself **3** : the descendants of one individual **4** : a source of development or growth : GERM — **seed·ed** *adj* — **seed·less** *adj*

²**seed** *vb* **seed·ed; seed·ing 1** : ²sow 2, PLANT **2** : to produce or shed seeds **3** : to take the seeds out of

seed·ling *n* **1** : a young plant grown from seed **2** : a young tree before it becomes a sapling

seed plant *n* : a plant that produces seed

seed·pod *n* : POD

seedy *adj* **seed·i·er; seed·i·est 1** : having or full of seeds **2** : poor in condition or quality

seek *vb* **sought ; seek·ing 1** : to try to find **2** : to try to win or get **3** : to make an attempt

seem *vb* **seemed; seem·ing 1** : to give the impression of being : APPEAR **2** — used to make a statement less forceful or more polite

seem·ing *adj* : APPARENT **3** — **seem·ing·ly** *adv*

seen *past participle of* SEE

seep *vb* **seeped; seep·ing** : to flow slowly through small openings

seer *n* : a person who predicts events

¹**see·saw** *n* **1** : a plank for children to play on that is balanced in the middle on a raised bar with one end going up while the other goes down **2** : a situation in which something keeps changing from one state to another and back again

²**seesaw** *vb* **see·sawed; see·saw·ing** : to keep changing from one state to another and back again

seethe *vb* **seethed; seeth·ing 1** : to feel or show great excitement or emotion (as anger) **2** : to move constantly and without order

seg·ment *n* **1** : any of the parts into which a thing is divided or naturally separates **2** : a part cut off from a figure (as a circle) by means of a line or plane **3** : a part of a straight line included between two points

seg·re·gate *vb* **seg·re·gat·ed; seg·re·gat·ing** : to separate a race, class, or group from the rest of society

seg·re·ga·tion *n* : the practice or policy of separating a race, class, or group from the rest of society

seis·mo·graph *n* : a device that measures and records vibrations of the earth

seize *vb* **seized; seiz·ing 1** : to take possession of by or as if by force **2** : to take hold of suddenly or with force **3** : to take or use eagerly or quickly

sei·zure *n* **1** : an act of taking suddenly or with force : the state of being taken suddenly or with force **2** : an abnormal state in which a person usually experiences convulsions and may become unconscious

sel·dom *adv* : not often : RARELY

¹se·lect *vb* **se·lect·ed; se·lect·ing** : to pick out from a group

²select *adj* **1** : chosen to include the best or most suitable individuals **2** : of special value or excellence

se·lec·tion *n* **1** : the act or process of choosing **2** : something that is chosen

se·lec·tive *adj* : careful to choose or include only the best or most suitable individuals

se·le·ni·um *n* : a gray powdery chemical element used chiefly in electronic devices

self *n, pl* **selves 1** : a person regarded as an individual apart from everyone else **2** : a special side of a person's character

self- *prefix* **1** : someone's or something's self **2** : of or by someone's or something's self **3** : to, with, for, or toward someone's or something's self

self–ad·dressed *adj* : addressed for return to the sender

self–cen·tered *adj* : SELFISH

self–con·fi·dence *n* : someone's confidence in himself or herself and in his or her own abilities

self–con·scious *adj* : feeling uncomfortably nervous or embarrassed when in the presence of or when being observed by other people — **self–con·scious·ly** *adv* — **self–con·scious·ness** *n*

self–con·trol *n* : someone's control over his or her own impulses, emotions, or actions

self–de·fense *n* : someone's act of defending himself or herself or his or her property

self–es·teem *n* : a feeling of satisfaction that someone has in himself or herself and his or her own abilities

self–ev·i·dent *adj* : clearly true and requiring no proof

self–gov·ern·ing *adj* : being governed by its own member or citizens

self–gov·ern·ment *n* : government by the people making up a group or community

self–im·por·tance *n* : an attitude showing that someone has an overly high opinion of his or her own importance

self–im·por·tant *adj* : having or showing the attitude of someone who has too high an opinion of his or her own importance : showing self-importance

self·ish *adj* : taking care of only a person's own needs and feelings without thought for others — **self·ish·ly** *adv* — **self·ish·ness** *n*

self·less *adj* : showing great concern for and willingness to give unselfishly to others — **self·less·ly** *adv* — **self·less·ness** *n*

self–pos·sessed *adj* : having or showing control of emotions or reactions

self–pro·pelled *adj* : containing within itself the means for its own movement

self–re·li·ance *n* : a feeling of trust that someone has in his or her own efforts and abilities

self–re·spect *n* : someone's proper regard for himself or herself as a human being

self–re·straint *n* : proper self-control over actions or emotions

self–righ·teous *adj* : having or showing the attitude of someone who strongly believes in the rightness of his or her own actions or opinions — **self–righ·teous·ness** *n*

self–same *adj* : exactly the same

self–ser·vice *n* : allowing or requiring customers to serve themselves without help from workers

self–suf·fi·cient *adj* : able to live or function without the help of others

self–worth *n* : SELF-ESTEEM

sell *vb* **sold ; sell·ing 1** : to exchange in return for money or something else of value **2** : to make available for sale **3** : to be sold or priced — **sell·er** *n* — **sell out 1** : to be bought until all are gone **2** : to betray a person or duty

selves *pl of* SELF

sem·a·phore *n* **1** : a device for sending signals that can be seen by the receiver **2** : a system of sending signals with two flags held one in each hand

sem·blance *n* : outward appearance

se·mes·ter *n* : either of two terms that make up a school year

semi- *prefix* **1** : half **2** : partly : not completely **3** : partial

semi·cir·cle *n* : half of a circle

semi·co·lon *n* : a punctuation mark ; that can be used to separate parts of a sentence which need clearer separation than would be shown by a comma, to separate main clauses which have no conjunction between, and to separate phrases and clauses containing commas

semi·con·duc·tor *n* : a solid substance that conducts electricity imperfectly

semi·fi·nal *n* : a match or game coming before the final round in a tournament

sem·i·nary *n, pl* **sem·i·nar·ies 1** : a private school at or above the high school level **2** : a school for the training of priests, ministers, or rabbis

Sem·i·nole *n, pl* **Sem·i·noles** *or* **Seminole** : a member of an American Indian people of Florida and Oklahoma

semi·sol·id *adj* : having the qualities of both a solid and a liquid

Sen. *abbr* senate, senator

sen·ate *n* **1** *cap* : the upper house of a legislature (as the United States Congress) **2** : a governing body

sen·a·tor *n* : a member of a Senate

send *vb* **sent; send·ing 1** : to cause to go **2** : to set in motion by physical force **3** : to cause to move in a particular direction or manner **4** : to cause someone to pass a message on or do an errand **5** : to give an order or request to come or go **6** : to bring into a certain condition — **send·er** *n*

Sen·e·ca *n, pl* **Seneca** *or* **Sen·e·cas 1** : a member of an American Indian people of western New York **2** : the language of the Seneca people

¹se·nior *n* **1** : a person older or higher in rank than someone else **2** : a student in the final year of high school or college **3** : an elderly person

²senior *adj* **1** : being older — often used to distinguish a father from a son with the same name **2** : higher in rank or office **3** : relating to students in the final year of high school or college

senior airman *n* : an enlisted person in the air force who ranks above airman first class but who has not been made sergeant

sen·sa·tion *n* **1** : awareness (as of noise or heat) or a mental process (as seeing or smelling) resulting from stimulation of a sense organ **2** : an indefinite awareness of a feeling or experience **3** : a state of excited interest or feeling **4** : a cause or object of excited interest

sen·sa·tion·al *adj* **1** : causing or meant to cause great interest **2** : very or unexpectedly excellent

¹sense *n* **1** : a specialized function or mechanism (as sight, taste, or touch) of the body that involves the action and effect of a stimulus on a sense organ **2** : awareness arrived at through or as if through the senses **3** : a particular sensation or kind of sensation **4** : the ability to make wise decisions **5** : an awareness or understanding of something **6** : a reason or excuse based on intelligence or good judgment **7** : a logical, sensible, or practical thing, act, or way of doing **8** : a meaning or one of a set of meanings a word, phrase, or story may have

²sense *vb* **sensed; sens·ing** : to be or become aware of

sense·less *adj* **1** : UNCONSCIOUS 2 **2** : STUPID 2 — **sense·less·ly** *adv*

sense organ *n* : a part of the body (as the eye or nose) that contains special cells that receive stimuli (as light) and activate associated nerves so that they carry impulses to the brain

sen·si·bil·i·ty *n, pl* **sen·si·bil·i·ties 1** : the ability to receive or feel sensations **2** : the ability to feel and understand emotions

sen·si·ble *adj* **1** : showing or containing good sense or judgment **2** : designed for a practical purpose rather than for appearance **3** : capable of feeling or perceiving — **sen·si·bly** *adv*

sen·si·tive *adj* **1** : easily or strongly affected, impressed, or hurt **2** : likely to affect, impress, or hurt **3** : understanding of the feelings of others **4** : capable of responding to stimulation **5** : readily affected or changed often in an unpleasant or negative way — **sen·si·tive·ly** *adv*

sen·si·tiv·i·ty *n* **1** : an awareness and understanding of the feelings of others **2** : the ability to express thoughts and feelings

sen·so·ry *adj* : of or relating to sensation or the senses

sen·su·al *adj* : relating to the pleasing of the senses

sent *past and past participle of* SEND

¹sen·tence *n* **1** : a group of words that makes a statement, asks a question, or expresses a command, wish, or exclamation **2** : punishment set by a court **3** : a mathematical statement (as an equation) in words or symbols

²sentence *vb* **sen·tenced; sen·tenc·ing** : to set the punishment of

sen·ti·ment *n* **1** : a thought or attitude influenced by feeling **2** : OPINION 1 **3** : tender feelings of affection

sen·ti·men·tal *adj* **1** : influenced strongly by feelings of affection or yearning **2** : primarily affecting the emotions

sen·ti·nel *n* : SENTRY

sen·try *n, pl* **sentries** : a person (as a soldier) on duty as a guard

Sep. *abbr* September

se·pal *n* : one of the specialized leaves that form the calyx of a flower

¹sep·a·rate *vb* **sep·a·rat·ed; sep·a·rat·ing 1** : to set or keep apart **2** : to make a distinction between **3** : to cease to be together : PART

²sep·a·rate *adj* **1** : set apart **2** : not shared : INDIVIDUAL **3** : existing independently from each other

sep·a·rate·ly *adv* : apart from others or another

sep·a·ra·tion *n* **1** : the act of setting or pulling apart : the state of being set or pulled apart **2** : a point or line at which something is divided **3** : a space between

Sept. *abbr* September

Sep·tem·ber *n* : the ninth month of the year

sep·tet *n* : a group or set of seven

sep·ul·chre *or* **sep·ul·cher** *n* : ¹GRAVE, TOMB

se·quel *n* **1** : a book or movie that continues a story begun in another **2** : an event that follows or comes afterward : RESULT

se·quence *n* **1** : the order in which things are or should be connected, related, or dated **2** : a group of things that come one after another

se·quin *n* : a bit of shiny metal or plastic used as an ornament usually on clothing

se·quoia *n* **1** : GIANT SEQUOIA **2** : REDWOOD

¹ser·e·nade *n* : music sung or played at night for a woman

²serenade *vb* **ser·e·nad·ed; ser·e·nad·ing** : to entertain (a woman) with music sung or played at night

se·rene *adj* **1** : being calm and quiet **2** : ¹CLEAR 2 — **se·rene·ly** *adv*

se·ren·i·ty *n* : the quality or state of being calm and peaceful

serf *n* : a servant or laborer of olden times who was treated as part of the land worked on and went along with the land if it was sold

serge *n* : a strong woolen cloth

ser·geant *n* **1** : a noncommissioned officer in the army or marine corps ranking above a corporal or in the air force ranking above an airman first class **2** : an officer in a police force

sergeant first class *n* : a noncommissioned officer in the army ranking above a staff sergeant

sergeant major *n* **1** : the chief noncommissioned officer at a military headquarters **2** : a noncommissioned officer in the marine corps ranking above a first sergeant

¹se·ri·al *adj* : arranged in or appearing in parts or numbers that follow a regular order

²serial *n* : a story appearing (as in a magazine or on television) in parts at regular intervals

se·ries *n, pl* **series** : a number of things or events arranged in order and connected by being alike in some way

se·ri·ous *adj* **1** : not joking or funny **2** : being such as to cause distress or harm **3** : thoughtful or quiet in appearance or manner **4** : requiring much thought or work — **se·ri·ous·ness** *n*

se·ri·ous·ly *adv* **1** : in an earnest way **2** : in a literal way **3** : to a large degree or extent

ser·mon *n* **1** : a speech usually by a priest, minister, or rabbi for the purpose of giving religious instruction **2** : a serious talk to a person about his or her conduct

ser·pent *n* : a usually large snake

ser·pen·tine *adj* : winding or turning one way and another

se·rum *n* : the clear liquid part that can be separated from coagulated blood and contains antibodies

ser·vant *n* : a person hired to perform household or personal services

¹serve *vb* **served; serv·ing** **1** : to help people to food or drink or set out helpings of food or drink **2** : to be of use : answer some purpose **3** : to be a servant **4** : to give the service and respect due **5** : to be in prison for or during (a period of time) **6** : to provide helpful services **7** : to be enough for **8** : to hold an office : perform a duty **9** : to perform a term of service **10** : to furnish with something needed or desired **11** : to put the ball or shuttlecock in play (as in tennis, volleyball, or badminton) — **serve someone right** : to be deserved

²serve *n* : an act of putting the ball or shuttlecock in play (as in tennis, volleyball, or badminton)

¹ser·vice *n* **1** : ²HELP 1, USE **2** : a religious ceremony **3** : the occupation or function of serving or working as a servant **4** : the work or action of helping customers **5** : a helpful or useful act : good turn **6** : a set of dishes or silverware **7** : an organization that provides something to the public **8** : a nation's armed forces **9** : an organization or business that supplies some public demand or provides maintenance and repair for something **10** : ²SERVE

²service *vb* **ser·viced; ser·vic·ing** : to work on in order to maintain or repair

ser·vice·able *adj* **1** : USEFUL 1 **2** : of adequate quality

ser·vice·man *n, pl* **ser·vice·men** : a man who is a member of the armed forces

service station *n* : GAS STATION

ser·vice·wom·an *n, pl* **ser·vice·wom·en** : a woman who is a member of the armed forces

ser·vile *adj* **1** : of or suitable to a slave **2** : very obedient and trying too hard to please

serv·ing *n* : a helping of food

ser·vi·tude *n* : the condition of being a slave or of having to obey another

ses·sion *n* **1** : a meeting or period devoted to a particular activity **2** : a single meeting (as of a court, lawmaking body, or school) **3** : a whole series of meetings **4** : the time during which a court, congress, or school meets

¹set *vb* **set; set·ting** **1** : to put or fix in a place or condition **2** : to cause to be, become, or do **3** : ¹START 4 **4** : to fix or decide on **5** : to furnish as a model **6** : to adjust or put in order for use **7** : to fix firmly **8** : to pass below the horizon : go down **9** : to begin some activity **10** : to cause to sit **11** : to arrange in a desired and especially a normal position **12** : to become or cause to become firm or solid **13** : to cover and warm eggs to hatch them **14** : to locate the plot of (a story) **15** : to provide (as words or verses) with music — **set aside** : to reserve for some purpose — **set eyes on** : to catch sight of : SEE — **set in** : to make its appearance : BEGIN — **set off 1** : to start a journey **2** : EXPLODE 1 **3** : to make noticeable **4** : to cause to start — **set out 1** : to begin on a course or journey **2** : to begin with a purpose — **set up 1** : to place or secure in position **2** : to put in operation

²**set** *n* **1** : a number of persons or things of the same kind that belong together, are used together, or occur together **2** : the act or action of going below the horizon **3** : an electronic apparatus **4** : a collection of mathematical elements **5** : a group of tennis games that make up a match **6** : the form or movement of the body or of its parts **7** : an artificial setting for a scene of a play or motion picture

³**set** *adj* **1** : fixed by authority **2** : not very willing to change **3** : ¹READY 1

set·back *n* : a slowing of progress : a temporary defeat

set·tee *n* : a long seat with a back

set·ter *n* **1** : a large dog that has long hair and is used in hunting birds **2** : one that sets

set·ting *n* **1** : the act of one that sets **2** : that in which something is set or mounted **3** : the background (as time and place) of the action of a story or play

¹**set·tle** *vb* **set·tled; set·tling 1** : to come to rest **2** : to make a home **3** : to make quiet : CALM **4** : DECIDE 1 **5** : to place so as to stay **6** : to sink gradually to a lower level **7** : to sink in a liquid **8** : to give attention to **9** : to fix by agreement **10** : to put in order **11** : to complete payment on **12** : to bring to an end **13** : to take up a stable life **14** : to be content with

²**settle** *n* : a long wooden bench with arms and a high solid back

set·tle·ment *n* **1** : a formal agreement that ends an argument or dispute **2** : final payment (as of a bill) **3** : the act or fact of establishing colonies **4** : a place or region newly settled **5** : a small village

set·tler *n* : a person who settles in a new region : COLONIST

¹**sev·en** *adj* : being one more than six

²**seven** *n* **1** : one more than six : 7 **2** : the seventh in a set or series

¹**sev·en·teen** *adj* : being one more than 16

²**seventeen** *n* : one more than 16 : 17

¹**sev·en·teenth** *adj* : coming right after 16th

²**seventeenth** *n* : number 17 in a series

¹**sev·enth** *adj* : coming right after sixth

²**seventh** *n* **1** : number seven in a series **2** : one of seven equal parts

¹**sev·en·ti·eth** *adj* : coming right after 69th

²**seventieth** *n* : number 70 in a series

¹**sev·en·ty** *adj* : being seven times ten

²**seventy** *n* : seven times ten : 70

sev·er *vb* **sev·ered; sev·er·ing** : to cut off

¹**sev·er·al** *adj* **1** : consisting of more than two but not very many **2** : separate or distinct from others : DIFFERENT

²**several** *pron* : a small number : more than two but not many

se·vere *adj* **se·ver·er; se·ver·est 1** : serious in feeling or manner **2** : hard to bear or deal with **3** : very strict : HARSH **4** : not using unnecessary ornament : PLAIN — **se·vere·ly** *adv*

se·ver·i·ty *n* : the quality or state of being severe

sew *vb* **sewed; sewn** *or* **sewed; sew·ing 1** : to join or fasten by stitches **2** : to work with needle and thread

sew·age *n* : waste materials carried off by sewers

¹**sew·er** *n* : a usually covered drain to carry off water and waste

²**sew·er** *n* : someone that sews

sew·er·age *n* **1** : the removal and disposal of waste materials by sewers **2** : a system of sewers

sew·ing *n* **1** : the act, method, or occupation of someone that works with needle and thread **2** : material being or to be worked with needle and thread

sex *n* **1** : either of two divisions into which many living things can be divided according to their roles in reproduction and which consist of males or females **2** : the state of being male or female **3** : sexual activity

sex·ism *n* : distinction and especially unjust distinction based on gender and made against one person or group (as women) in favor of another

sex·ist *adj* : based on or showing sexism — **sexist** *n*

sex·ton *n* : an official of a church who takes care of church buildings and property

sex·u·al *adj* **1** : of or relating to sex or the sexes **2** : of, relating to, or being the form of reproduction in which germ cells from two parents combine in fertilization to form a new individual — **sex·u·al·ly** *adv*

Sgt. *abbr* sergeant

shab·by *adj* **shab·bi·er; shab·bi·est 1** : faded and worn from use or wear **2** : in poor condition : DILAPIDATED **3** : dressed in worn clothes **4** : not fair or generous — **shab·bi·ly** *adv* — **shab·bi·ness** *n*

shack *n* : HUT, SHANTY

¹**shack·le** *n* **1** : a ring or band that prevents

free use of the legs or arms **2** : something that prevents free action

²shackle *vb* **shack·led; shack·ling 1** : to bind or fasten with a ring or band placed on the legs or arms **2** : to prevent free action

shad *n, pl* **shad** : a silvery ocean fish that swims up rivers to lay or fertilize eggs and is often used for food

¹shade *n* **1** : space sheltered from light or heat and especially from the sun **2** : partial darkness **3** : something that blocks off or cuts down light **4** : the darkness or lightness of a color **5** : a very small difference or amount **6** : GHOST, SPIRIT **7** : the darkening of some objects in a painting or drawing to suggest that they are in shade

²shade *vb* **shad·ed; shad·ing 1** : to shelter from light or heat **2** : to mark with or turn a darker color

¹shad·ow *n* **1** : the dark figure cast on a surface by a body that is between the surface and the light **2** : ¹SHADE **3** : PHANTOM **4** : a very little bit : ¹TRACE **5** : something that causes a bad feeling **6 shadows** *pl* : darkness caused by the setting of the sun

²shadow *vb* **shad·owed; shad·ow·ing 1** : to cast a shadow upon **2** : to follow and watch closely especially in a secret way

shad·owy *adj* **1** : full of shade **2** : INDISTINCT

shady *adj* **shad·i·er; shad·i·est 1** : sheltered from the sun's rays **2** : producing shade **3** : not right or honest

shaft *n* **1** : the long handle of a weapon, tool, or instrument **2** : one of two poles between which a horse is hitched to pull a wagon or carriage **3** : an arrow or its narrow stem **4** : a narrow beam of light **5** : a long narrow part or structure especially when round **6** : a mine opening made for finding or mining ore **7** : an opening or passage straight down through the floors of a building **8** : a bar to support rotating pieces of machinery or to give them motion

shag·gy *adj* **shag·gi·er; shag·gi·est** : covered with or made up of a long and tangled growth (as of hair)

¹shake *vb* **shook; shak·en; shak·ing 1** : to make or cause to make quick movements back and forth or up and down **2** : to tremble or make tremble : QUIVER **3** : to move from side to side **4** : to grasp and move up and down **5** : to get away from **6** : to make less firm : WEAKEN **7** : to cause to be, become, go, or move by or as if by using a quick back and forth motion

²shake *n* : a quick back and forth or up and down movement

shak·er *n* : a container used to mix the contents or sprinkle out some of the contents

shaky *adj* **shak·i·er; shak·i·est 1** : characterized by quivering : not firm **2** : likely to fail or be insufficient : UNSOUND — **shak·i·ly** *adv*

shale *n* : a rock with a fine grain formed from clay, mud, or silt

shall *helping verb, past* **should** ; *present sing & pl* **shall 1** : am or are going to or expecting to : WILL **2** : is or are forced to : MUST

¹shal·low *adj* **shal·low·er; shal·low·est 1** : not deep **2** : taking in small amounts of air **3** : showing little knowledge, thought, or feeling — **shal·low·ness** *n*

²shallow *n* : a shallow place in a body of water — usually used in pl.

¹sham *n* **1** : something that deceives : HOAX **2** : something that is claimed to be true or real but which is actually phony **3** : a decorative covering for a pillow

²sham *adj* : not real : FALSE

³sham *vb* **shammed; sham·ming** : to act in a deceiving way

sham·ble *vb* **sham·bled; sham·bling** : to walk in an awkward unsteady way

sham·bles *n pl* : a place or scene of disorder or destruction — used as singular or plural

¹shame *n* **1** : a painful emotion caused by having done something wrong or improper **2** : ability to feel shame **3** : ¹DISHONOR 1, DISGRACE **4** : something that brings disgrace or causes painful emotion or strong regret

²shame *vb* **shamed; sham·ing 1** : to make ashamed **2** : ²DISHONOR **3** : to force by causing to feel shame

shame·faced *adj* : seeming ashamed

shame·ful *adj* : bringing shame : DISGRACEFUL — **shame·ful·ly** *adv* — **shame·ful·ness** *n*

shame·less *adj* : having no shame — **shame·less·ly** *adv* — **shame·less·ness** *n*

¹sham·poo *n, pl* **sham·poos 1** : a cleaner made for washing the hair **2** : an act of washing the hair

²sham·poo *vb* **sham·pooed; sham·poo·ing** : to wash the hair and scalp

sham·rock *n* : a plant (as some clovers) that has leaves with three leaflets and is used as an emblem by the Irish

shank *n* **1** : the part of the leg between the knee and ankle **2** : a cut of meat from the usually upper part of the leg **3** : the part of a tool that connects the working part with a part by which it is held or moved

shan't : shall not

shan·ty *n, pl* **shanties** : a small roughly built shelter or dwelling

¹shape *vb* **shaped; shap·ing 1** : to give a certain form or shape to **2** : to plan out : DE-

VISE **3 :** to have great influence on the development of — **shap·er** *n* — **shape up 1 :** to develop in a particular way **2 :** to improve in behavior or condition

²**shape** *n* **1 :** outward appearance : the form or outline of something **2 :** definite arrangement and form **3 :** ¹CONDITION 3 **4 :** a physically fit condition — **shaped** *adj*

shape·less *adj* **1 :** having no fixed or definite shape **2 :** lacking a pleasing or usual shape or form

shape·ly *adj* **shape·li·er; shape·li·est :** having a pleasing shape or form

shard *n* **:** a sharp piece or fragment of something

¹**share** *n* **1 :** a portion belonging to, due to, or contributed by one person **2 :** the part given or belonging to one of a group of people owning something together **3 :** any of the equal parts into which a property or corporation is divided

²**share** *vb* **shared; shar·ing 1 :** to divide and distribute in portions **2 :** to use, experience, or enjoy with others **3 :** to have or take a part in **4 :** to have in common

share·crop *vb* **share·cropped; share·cropping :** to farm another's land for a share of the crop or profit — **share·crop·per** *n*

¹**shark** *n* **:** a large usually gray saltwater fish that has sharp teeth and a skeleton of cartilage

²**shark** *n* **:** a person who cheats others out of money

¹**sharp** *adj* **sharp·er; sharp·est 1 :** having a thin edge or fine point (as for cutting or piercing) **2 :** brisk and cold **3 :** very smart **4 :** ATTENTIVE 1 **5 :** having very good ability to see or hear **6 :** ENERGETIC, BRISK **7 :** showing anger or disapproval **8 :** causing distress : SEVERE **9 :** strongly affecting the senses **10 :** ending in a point or edge **11 :** involving a sudden and quick change **12 :** clear in outline or detail : DISTINCT **13 :** raised in pitch by a half step **14 :** higher than true pitch **15 :** STYLISH — **sharp·ly** *adv* — **sharp·ness** *n*

²**sharp** *adv* **1 :** at an exact time **2 :** at a higher than true pitch **3 :** in a stylish way

³**sharp** *n* **1 :** a musical note or tone that is a half step higher than the note named **2 :** a sign ♯ that tells that a note is to be made higher by a half step

sharp·en *vb* **sharp·ened; sharp·en·ing :** to make or become sharp or sharper — **sharp·en·er** *n*

shat·ter *vb* **shat·tered; shat·ter·ing 1 :** to break or fall to pieces **2 :** to destroy or damage badly

¹**shave** *vb* **shaved; shaved** *or* **shav·en; shav·ing 1 :** to cut or trim off a thin layer of

(as with a sharp blade) **2 :** to cut off very close to the skin **3 :** to make bare or smooth by cutting the hair from

²**shave** *n* **1 :** an act of making bare or smooth by cutting the hair from **2 :** a narrow escape

shav·ing *n* **:** a thin slice or strip sliced or trimmed off with a cutting tool

shawl *n* **:** a square or oblong piece of cloth used especially by women as a loose covering for the head or shoulders

she *pron* **:** that female one

sheaf *n, pl* **sheaves 1 :** a bundle of stalks and ears of grain **2 :** a group of things fastened together

shear *vb* **sheared; sheared** *or* **shorn; shear·ing 1 :** to cut the hair or wool from : CLIP **2 :** to cut or clip (as hair or wool) from something **3 :** to strip of as if by cutting **4 :** to cut or break sharply — **shear·er** *n*

shears *n pl* **:** a cutting tool like a pair of large scissors

sheath *n, pl* **sheaths 1 :** a case for a blade (as of a knife) **2 :** a covering that surrounds and usually protects something

sheathe *vb* **sheathed; sheath·ing 1 :** to put into a sheath **2 :** to cover with something that protects

sheath·ing *n* **:** material used as a protective covering

sheaves *pl of* SHEAF

¹**shed** *vb* **shed; shed·ding 1 :** to give off in drops **2 :** to get rid of **3 :** to give off or out **4 :** REPEL 3 **5 :** to lose or cast aside (a natural covering or part)

²**shed** *n* **:** a small simple building used especially for storage

she'd : she had : she would

sheen *n* **:** a bright or shining condition : LUSTER

sheep *n, pl* **sheep 1 :** an animal related to the goat that is often raised for meat or for its wool and skin **2 :** a weak helpless person who is easily led

sheep·fold *n* **:** a pen or shelter for sheep

sheep·herd·er *n* **:** a person in charge of a flock of sheep

sheep·ish *adj* **1 :** like a sheep (as in being meek or shy) **2 :** feeling or showing embarrassment especially over being discovered having done something wrong or foolish — **sheep·ish·ly** *adv*

sheep·skin *n* **:** the skin of a sheep or leather prepared from it

sheer *adj* **sheer·er; sheer·est 1 :** very thin or transparent **2 :** complete and total **:** ABSOLUTE **3 :** taken or acting apart from everything else **4 :** very steep

¹**sheet** *n* **1 :** a large piece of cloth used to cover something and especially to cover a

bed **2** : a usually rectangular piece of paper **3** : a broad continuous surface **4** : something that is very thin as compared with its length and width

²**sheet** *n* : a rope or chain used to adjust the angle at which the sail of a boat is set to catch the wind

sheikh *or* **sheik** *n* **1** : an Arab chief **2** : a leader of a Muslim group

shek·el *n* : a bill or coin used in Israel

shelf *n, pl* **shelves** **1** : a flat piece (as of wood or metal) set above a floor (as on a wall or in a bookcase) to hold things **2** : a flat area (as of rock)

¹**shell** *n* **1** : a stiff hard covering of an animal (as a turtle, oyster, or crab) **2** : the tough outer covering of an egg **3** : the outer covering of a nut, fruit, or seed especially when hard or tough **4** : something like a shell (as in shape, function, or material) **5** : a narrow light racing boat rowed by one or more persons **6** : a metal or paper case holding the explosive charge and the shot or object to be fired from a gun or cannon — **shelled** *adj*

²**shell** *vb* **shelled; shell·ing** **1** : to remove the shell or outer covering of **2** : to remove the kernels of grain from (as a cob of corn) **3** : to shoot shells at or upon

she'll : she shall : she will

¹**shel·lac** *n* : a varnish made from a material given off by an Asian insect dissolved usually in alcohol

²**shellac** *vb* **shel·lacked; shel·lack·ing** : to coat with shellac

shell·fish *n, pl* **shellfish** : an invertebrate animal (as a clam or lobster) that has a hard outer shell and lives in water

¹**shel·ter** *n* **1** : something that covers or protects **2** : a place that provides food and housing to those in need **3** : the condition of being protected

²**shelter** *vb* **shel·tered; shel·ter·ing** **1** : to provide with a place that covers or protects : be a shelter for **2** : to find and use a shelter for protection

shelve *vb* **shelved; shelv·ing** **1** : to place or store on a shelf **2** : to put off or aside : DEFER

shelves *pl of* SHELF

she·nan·i·gans *n pl* : funny or mischievous activity or behavior

¹**shep·herd** *n* : a person who takes care of and guards a flock of sheep

²**shepherd** *vb* **shep·herded; shep·herd·ing** **1** : to take care of and guard a flock of sheep **2** : to gather, lead, or move in the manner of a shepherd

shep·herd·ess *n* : a woman who takes care of and guards a flock of sheep

sher·bet *n* : a frozen dessert made of sweetened fruit juice and milk

sher·iff *n* : the officer of a county who is in charge of enforcing the law

she's : she is : she has

Shet·land pony *n* : a small stocky horse with a heavy coat and short legs

¹**shield** *n* **1** : a broad piece of armor carried (as by a soldier) for protection **2** : something that serves as a defense or protection

²**shield** *vb* **shield·ed; shield·ing** : to cover or screen (as from danger or harm) : provide with protection

¹**shift** *vb* **shift·ed; shift·ing** **1** : to change or make a change in place, position, or direction **2** : to go through a change **3** : to change the arrangement of gears transmitting power (as in an automobile) **4** : to get along without help : FEND

²**shift** *n* **1** : a change in place, position, or direction **2** : a change in emphasis or attitude **3** : a group of workers who work together during a scheduled period of time **4** : the scheduled period of time during which one group of workers is working **5** : GEARSHIFT

shift·less *adj* : LAZY

shifty *adj* **shift·i·er; shift·i·est** : not worthy of trust : causing suspicion

shil·ling *n* : an old British coin equal to ¹⁄₂₀ pound

¹**shim·mer** *vb* **shim·mered; shim·mer·ing** : to shine with a wavering light : GLIMMER

²**shimmer** *n* : a wavering light

shim·my *vb* **shim·mied; shim·my·ing** : to move the body from side to side

¹**shin** *n* : the front part of the leg below the knee

²**shin** *vb* **shinned; shin·ning** : SHINNY

¹**shine** *vb* **shone** *or* **shined; shin·ing** **1** : to give off light **2** : to be glossy : GLEAM **3** : to direct the light of **4** : to be outstanding **5** : to make bright by polishing

²**shine** *n* **1** : brightness from light given off or reflected **2** : fair weather : SUNSHINE **3** : ²POLISH 1

shin·er *n* : a small silvery American freshwater fish

¹**shin·gle** *n* **1** : a small thin piece of building material for laying in overlapping rows as a covering for the roof or sides of a building **2** : a small sign

²**shingle** *vb* **shin·gled; shin·gling** : to cover with shingles

shin·ny *vb* **shin·nied; shin·ny·ing** : to climb (as a pole) by grasping with arms and legs and moving upward by repeated jerks

shiny *adj* **shin·i·er; shin·i·est** : having a smooth bright appearance

¹**ship** *n* **1** : a large boat designed for travel by

sea **2** : AIRSHIP, AIRPLANE **3** : a vehicle for traveling beyond the earth's atmosphere

²ship *vb* **shipped; ship·ping 1** : to cause to be transported **2** : to put or receive on board for transportation by water **3** : to send (someone) to a place **4** : to take into a ship or boat **5** : to sign on as a crew member on a ship

-ship *n suffix* **1** : state : condition : quality **2** : office : rank : profession **3** : skill **4** : something showing a quality or state of being **5** : someone having a specified rank

ship·board *n* **1** : a ship's side **2** : ¹SHIP 1

ship·ment *n* **1** : the act of shipping **2** : a package or goods shipped

ship·ping *n* **1** : the act or business of a person who ships goods **2** : a group of ships in one place or belonging to one port or country

ship·shape *adj* : being neat and orderly : TIDY

¹ship·wreck *n* **1** : a ruined or destroyed ship **2** : the loss or destruction of a ship

²shipwreck *vb* **ship·wrecked; ship·wreck·ing 1** : to cause to experience destruction of a ship and usually be left stranded **2** : to ruin or destroy (a ship) by crashing ashore or sinking

ship·yard *n* : a place where ships are built or repaired

shirk *vb* **shirked; shirk·ing** : to avoid doing something especially because of laziness, fear, or dislike

shirt *n* : a piece of clothing for the upper part of the body usually with sleeves and often a collar

¹shiv·er *vb* **shiv·ered; shiv·er·ing** : to shake slightly (as from cold or fear)

²shiver *n* : a small shaking movement of the body (as from cold or emotion)

¹shoal *adj* **shoal·er; shoal·est** : ¹SHALLOW 1

²shoal *n* **1** : a place where a sea, lake, or river is shallow **2** : a mound or ridge of sand just below the surface of the water

³shoal *n* : ³SCHOOL

¹shock *n* : a bunch of sheaves of grain or stalks of corn set on end (as in a field)

²shock *n* **1** : a sudden strong unpleasant or upsetting feeling **2** : something that causes a sudden unpleasant or upsetting feeling **3** : a severe shake, jerk, or impact **4** : the effect of a charge of electricity passing through the body of a person or animal **5** : a serious bodily reaction that usually follows severe injury or large loss of blood

³shock *vb* **shocked; shock·ing 1** : to strike with surprise, horror, or disgust **2** : to affect by a charge of electricity **3** : to move to action especially by causing upset, surprise, or disgust

⁴shock *n* : a thick bushy mass

shock·ing *adj* **1** : causing surprise, horror, or disgust **2** : being intense or bright in color — **shock·ing·ly** *adv*

shod·dy *adj* **shod·di·er; shod·di·est** : poorly done or made — **shod·di·ness** *n*

¹shoe *n* **1** : an outer covering for the human foot usually having a thick and somewhat stiff sole and heel and a lighter upper part **2** : HORSESHOE 1

²shoe *vb* **shod** *also* **shoed; shoe·ing** : to put a shoe or horseshoe on : furnish with shoes

shoe·horn *n* : a curved piece (as of metal) to help in sliding the heel of the foot into a shoe

shoe·lace *n* : a lace or string for fastening a shoe

shoe·mak·er *n* : a person who makes or repairs shoes

shoe·string *n* : SHOELACE

shone *past and past participle of* SHINE

shoo *vb* **shooed; shoo·ing** : to wave, scare, or send away — often used as a command

shook *past of* SHAKE

¹shoot *vb* **shot; shoot·ing 1** : to let fly or cause to be driven forward with force **2** : to cause a projectile (as a bullet) to be driven out of **3** : to cause a weapon to discharge a projectile **4** : to strike with a projectile from a bow or gun **5** : to hit, throw, or kick (as a ball or puck) toward or into a goal **6** : to score by shooting **7** : ¹PLAY 2 **8** : to thrust forward swiftly **9** : to grow rapidly **10** : to go, move, or pass rapidly **11** : to direct at quickly and suddenly **12** : to stream out suddenly : SPURT **13** : to film or photograph **14** : to pass swiftly along or through — **shoot·er** *n*

²shoot *n* **1** : a stem or branch of a plant especially when young or just beginning to grow **2** : a hunting party or trip

shooting star *n* : a meteor appearing as a temporary streak of light in the night sky

¹shop *n* **1** : a place where goods are sold : a usually small store **2** : a worker's place of business **3** : a place in which workers are doing a particular kind of work

²shop *vb* **shopped; shop·ping** : to visit stores or shops for the purpose of looking over and buying goods — **shop·per** *n*

shop·keep·er *n* : STOREKEEPER 1

shop·lift *vb* **shop·lift·ed; shop·lift·ing** : to steal merchandise on display in stores — **shop·lift·er** *n*

¹shore *n* : the land along the edge of a body of water

²shore *vb* **shored; shor·ing** : to keep from sinking, sagging, or falling by placing a support under or against

shore·bird *n* : a bird (as a plover or sand-piper) that frequents the seashore

shore·line *n* : the line or strip of land where a body of water and the shore meet

shorn *past participle of* SHEAR

¹**short** *adj* **short·er; short·est** **1** : not long or tall **2** : not great in distance **3** : not lasting long : brief in time **4** : cut down to a brief length **5** : less than the usual or needed amount **6** : having less than what is needed : not having enough **7** : not reaching far enough **8** : easily stirred up **9** : rudely brief **10** : of, relating to, or being one of the vowel sounds \ə, a, e, i, ù\ and sometimes \ä\ and \ò\ — **short·ness** *n*

²**short** *adv* **1** : with suddenness **2** : to or at a point that is not as far as expected or desired

³**short** *n* **1** **shorts** *pl* : pants that reach to or almost to the knees **2** **shorts** *pl* : short underpants **3** : something (as a movie) shorter than the usual or regular length **4** : SHORT CIRCUIT

short·age *n* : a condition in which there is not enough of something needed : DEFICIT

short·cake *n* : a dessert made usually of rich biscuit dough baked and served with sweetened fruit

short circuit *n* : an electrical connection made between points in an electric circuit between which current does not normally flow

short·com·ing *n* : FAULT 1

short·cut *n* : a shorter, quicker, or easier way

short·en *vb* **shor·tened; shor·ten·ing** : to make or become short or shorter

short·en·ing *n* : a fat used in baking especially to make pastry flaky

short·horn *n* : a cow of a short-horned breed of beef and dairy cattle developed in England

short–lived *adj* : living or lasting only a short time

short·ly *adv* **1** : in or within a short time : SOON **2** : in a brief way that shows anger or disapproval

short–sight·ed *adj* **1** : made without thinking about what will happen in the future **2** : NEARSIGHTED

short·stop *n* : a baseball infielder whose position is between second and third base

Sho·shone *or* **Sho·sho·ni** *n, pl* **Sho·shones** *or* **Shoshoni** **1** : a member of a group of American Indian peoples originally of California, Idaho, Nevada, Utah, and Wyoming **2** : the language of the Shoshones

¹**shot** *n* **1** : the act of shooting **2** *pl* **shot** : a bullet, ball, or pellet for a gun or cannon **3** : ²ATTEMPT, TRY **4** : CHANCE **5** : the flight of a projectile or the distance it travels : RANGE **6** : a person who shoots **7** : a heavy metal ball thrown for distance in a track-and-field contest (**shot put**) **8** : an act of hitting, throwing, or kicking a ball or puck toward or into a goal **9** : an injection of something (as medicine) into the body **10** : PHOTOGRAPH

²**shot** *past and past participle of* SHOOT

shot·gun *n* : a gun with a long barrel used to fire shot at short range

should *past of* SHALL **1** : ought to **2** : happen to **3** — used as a more polite or less assured form of *shall*

¹**shoul·der** *n* **1** : the part of the body of a person or animal where the arm or foreleg joins the body **2** : the part of a piece of clothing that covers a person's shoulder **3** : a part that resembles a person's shoulder in shape **4** : the edge of a road

²**shoulder** *vb* **shoul·dered; shoul·der·ing** **1** : to push with the shoulder **2** : to accept as a burden or duty

shoulder blade *n* : the flat triangular bone of the back of the shoulder

shouldn't : should not

¹**shout** *vb* **shout·ed; shout·ing** : to make a sudden loud cry **2** : to say in a loud voice

²**shout** *n* : a sudden loud cry

¹**shove** *vb* **shoved; shov·ing** **1** : to push with steady force **2** : to push along or away carelessly or rudely

²**shove** *n* : a forceful push

¹**shov·el** *n* **1** : a tool with a long handle and broad scoop used to lift and throw loose material (as dirt or snow) **2** : as much as a shovel will hold

²**shovel** *vb* **shov·eled** *or* **shov·elled; shov·el·ing** *or* **shov·el·ling** **1** : to lift or throw with a shovel **2** : to dig or clean out with a shovel **3** : to move large amounts of into something quickly

¹**show** *vb* **showed; shown** *or* **showed; show·ing** **1** : to place in sight : DISPLAY **2** : REVEAL 2 **3** : to make known **4** : to give as appropriate treatment **5** : TEACH 1, INSTRUCT **6** : PROVE 1 **7** : to lead to a place : DIRECT **8** : to point out to **9** : to be easily seen or noticed — **show off** : to make an obvious display of a person's own abilities or possessions in order to impress others — **show up** : APPEAR 3

²**show** *n* **1** : a public performance intended to entertain people **2** : a television or radio program **3** : an event at which things of the same kind are put on display **4** : a display to make known a feeling or quality **5** : an appearance meant to deceive

show·boat *n* : a river steamboat used as a traveling theater

show·case *n* : a protective glass case in which things are displayed

¹show·er *n* **1** : a short fall of rain over a small area **2** : a large number of things that fall, are given off, or happen at the same time **3** : a bath in which water is sprayed on the body or a device for providing such a bath **4** : a party where gifts are given especially to a woman who is about to be married or have a baby

²shower *vb* **show·ered; show·er·ing 1** : to wet with fine spray or drops **2** : to fall in or as if in a shower **3** : to provide in great quantity **4** : to bathe in a shower

show·man *n, pl* **show·men** : a person having a special skill for presenting something in a dramatic way

show–off *n* : a person who tries to impress other people with his or her abilities or possessions

showy *adj* **show·i·er; show·i·est 1** : attracting attention : STRIKING **2** : given to or being too much outward display : GAUDY

shrank *past of* SHRINK

shrap·nel *n* : small metal pieces that scatter outwards from an exploding bomb, shell, or mine

¹shred *n* **1** : a long narrow piece torn or cut off : STRIP **2** : a small amount : BIT

²shred *vb* **shred·ded; shred·ding** : to cut or tear into small pieces

shrew *n* **1** : a small mouselike animal with a long pointed snout and tiny eyes that lives mostly on insects and worms **2** : an unpleasant bad-tempered woman

shrewd *adj* **shrewd·er; shrewd·est** : showing quick practical cleverness — **shrewd·ly** *adv* — **shrewd·ness** *n*

¹shriek *vb* **shrieked; shriek·ing 1** : to make a loud high-pitched cry **2** : to say in a loud high-pitched voice

²shriek *n* : a loud high-pitched cry or sound

¹shrill *vb* **shrilled; shrill·ing 1** : to make a high-pitched usually piercing sound **2** : to say in a loud high-pitched voice

²shrill *adj* **shrill·er; shrill·est** : having a high-pitched usually piercing sound — **shrill·ness** *n* — **shril·ly** *adv*

shrimp *n* **1** : a small shellfish of the sea that is related to the crabs and lobsters and is often used for food **2** : a very small or unimportant person or thing

shrine *n* **1** : a case or box for sacred relics (as the bones of saints) **2** : a place connected with a holy person or event where people worship **3** : a place that is considered sacred or regarded with great respect

shrink *vb* **shrank** *or* **shrunk; shrunk** *or* **shrunk·en; shrink·ing 1** : to make or become smaller **2** : to curl up or move back in or as if in fear or pain **3** : to refrain from

doing something especially because of difficulty or unpleasantness

shrink·age *n* : the amount by which something shrinks or becomes less

shriv·el *vb* **shriv·eled** *or* **shriv·elled; shriv·el·ing** *or* **shriv·el·ling** : to shrink and become dry and wrinkled

¹shroud *n* **1** : the cloth placed over or around a dead body **2** : something that covers or hides

²shroud *vb* **shroud·ed; shroud·ing** : to cover or hide with or as if with a shroud

shrub *n* : a woody plant that has several stems and is smaller than most trees

shrub·bery *n, pl* **shrub·ber·ies** : a group of shrubs or an area where shrubs are growing

¹shrug *vb* **shrugged; shrug·ging** : to raise and lower the shoulders usually to express doubt, uncertainty, or lack of interest

²shrug *n* : an act of raising and lowering the shoulders

¹shuck *n* : a covering shell or husk

²shuck *vb* **shucked; shuck·ing** : to remove the shell or husk from

¹shud·der *vb* **shud·dered; shud·der·ing 1** : to tremble especially with fear or horror or from cold **2** : to move or sound as if being shaken

²shudder *n* : an act or instance of trembling or shaking

¹shuf·fle *vb* **shuf·fled; shuf·fling 1** : to slide back and forth without lifting **2** : to walk or move by sliding or dragging the feet **3** : to mix up the order of (as playing cards) **4** : to push or move about or from place to place

²shuffle *n* **1** : a sliding or dragging walk **2** : an act of mixing up or moving so as to change the order or position **3** : a confusing jumble

shun *vb* **shunned; shun·ning** : to avoid purposely or by habit

shunt *vb* **shunt·ed; shunt·ing 1** : to turn or move off to one side or out of the way **2** : to switch (as a train) from one track to another

shut *vb* **shut; shut·ting 1** : to close or become closed **2** : to stop or cause to stop operation **3** : to confine by or as if by enclosing or by blocking the way out **4** : to close by bringing parts together — **shut out 1** : to keep (something) from entering **2** : to keep (an opponent) from scoring in a game — **shut up** : to stop talking

shut·out *n* : a game in which one side fails to score

shut·ter *n* **1** : a usually movable cover for the outside of a window **2** : a device in a camera that opens to let in light when a picture is taken

¹shut·tle *n* **1** : an instrument used in weaving to carry the thread back and forth from side to side through the threads that run lengthwise **2** : a vehicle (as a bus or train) that goes back and forth over a short route **3** : SPACE SHUTTLE

²**shuttle** *vb* **shut·tled; shut·tling** : to move or bring back and forth rapidly or often

shut·tle·cock *n* : a light cone-shaped object that is used in badminton

¹**shy** *adj* **shi·er** *or* **shy·er; shi·est** *or* **shy·est** **1** : not feeling comfortable meeting and talking to people **2** : easily frightened : TIMID **3** : showing a dislike of attention **4** : tending to avoid something or someone **5** : having less than a full or an expected amount or number — **shy·ly** *adv* — **shyness** *n*

²**shy** *vb* **shied; shy·ing 1** : to avoid or draw back in dislike or distaste **2** : to move quickly to one side in fright

sib·ling *n* : a brother or sister

sick *adj* **sick·er; sick·est 1** : affected with disease or illness : not well **2** : of, relating to, or intended for use in or during illness **3** : affected with or accompanied by nausea **4** : badly upset by strong emotion **5** : annoyed or bored of something from having too much of it **6** : filled with disgust or anger

sick·bed *n* : a bed on which a sick person lies

sick·en *vb* **sick·ened; sick·en·ing 1** : to make or become sick or ill **2** : to cause to feel disgusted or angry

sick·en·ing *adj* : causing sickness or disgust — **sick·en·ing·ly** *adv*

sick·le *n* : a tool with a sharp curved blade and a short handle used especially to cut grass and grain

sick·ly *adj* **sick·li·er; sick·li·est 1** : somewhat sick : often ailing **2** : caused by or associated with ill health **3** : SICKENING **4** : appearing as if sick

sick·ness *n* **1** : ill health : ILLNESS **2** : a specific disease **3** : NAUSEA 1

¹**side** *n* **1** : the right or left part of the body from the shoulder to the hip **2** : a place, space, or direction away from or beyond a central point or line **3** : a surface or line forming a border or face of an object **4** : an outer surface or part of something considered as facing in a certain direction **5** : either surface of a thin object **6** : a place next to something or someone **7** : an opinion or position viewed as opposite or different from another **8** : a group of people involved in a competition, dispute, or war **9** : a line of ancestors traced back from either parent

²**side** *adj* **1** : of or located on the side **2** : going toward or coming from the side **3** : related to something in a minor or unimportant way **4** : being in addition to a main portion

³**side** *vb* **sid·ed; sid·ing** : to agree with or support the opinions or actions of

side·arm *adv* : with the arm moving out to the side

side·board *n* : a piece of furniture for holding dishes, silverware, and table linen

side·burns *n pl* : hair growing on the side of the face in front of the ears

sid·ed *adj* : having sides often of a stated number or kind

side·line *n* **1** : a line marking the side of a playing field or court **2** : a business or a job done in addition to a person's regular occupation

¹**side·long** *adj* : made to one side or out of the corner of the eye

²**sidelong** *adv* : out of the corner of the eye

side·show *n* : a small show off to the side of a main show or exhibition (as of a circus)

side·step *vb* **side·stepped; side·step·ping 1** : to take a sideways step **2** : to avoid by a step to the side **3** : to avoid answering or dealing with

side·track *vb* **side·tracked; side·track·ing** : to turn aside from a main purpose or direction

side·walk *n* : a usually paved walk at the side of a street or road

side·ways *adv or adj* **1** : from one side **2** : with one side forward **3** : to one side

side·wise *adv or adj* : SIDEWAYS

sid·ing *n* **1** : a short railroad track connected with the main track **2** : material (as boards or metal pieces) used to cover the outside walls of frame buildings

si·dle *vb* **si·dled; si·dling** : to go or move with one side forward

siege *n* : the act of moving an army around a fortified place to capture it — **lay siege to** : to attack militarily

si·er·ra *n* : a range of mountains especially with jagged peaks

si·es·ta *n* : a nap or rest especially at midday

sieve *n* : a utensil with meshes or holes to separate finer particles from coarser ones or solids from liquids

sift *vb* **sift·ed; sift·ing 1** : to pass or cause to pass through a sieve **2** : to separate or separate out by or as if by passing through a sieve **3** : to test or examine carefully — **sift·er** *n*

¹**sigh** *vb* **sighed; sigh·ing 1** : to take or let out a long loud breath often as an expression of sadness or weariness **2** : to make a sound like sighing **3** : to say with a sigh

²**sigh** *n* : the act or a sound of taking or letting out a long loud breath

¹**sight** *n* **1** : the function, process, or power of seeing : the sense by which a person or animal becomes aware of the position, form,

and color of objects **2** : the act of seeing **3** : something that is seen : SPECTACLE **4** : something that is worth seeing **5** : something that is peculiar, funny, or messy **6** : the presence of an object within the field of vision **7** : the distance a person can see **8** : a device (as a small metal bead on a gun barrel) that aids the eye in aiming or in finding the direction of an object

²sight *vb* **sight·ed; sight·ing 1** : to get a look at : SEE **2** : to look at through or as if through a device that aids the eye in aiming or in finding the direction of an object

sight·less *adj* : lacking sight : BLIND

sight·see *vb* **sight·saw; sight·see·ing** : to go about seeing places and things of interest — **sight·se·er** *n*

¹sign *n* **1** : a motion, action, or movement of the hand that means something **2** : a public notice that advertises something or gives information **3** : something that indicates what is present or is to come **4** : a symbol (as + or ÷) indicating a mathematical operation **5** : one of the twelve parts of the zodiac

²sign *vb* **signed; sign·ing 1** : to put a signature on to show acceptance, agreement or responsibility **2** : to communicate by using sign language **3** : to represent or show by a motion, action, or movement **4** : to make or place a sign on — **sign up** : to sign someone's name in order to get, do, or take something

¹sig·nal *n* **1** : a sign, event, or word that serves to start some action **2** : a sound, a movement of part of the body, or an object that gives warning or a command **3** : a radio wave that transmits a message or effect (as in radio or television)

²signal *vb* **sig·naled** *or* **sig·nalled; sig·nal·ing** *or* **sig·nal·ling 1** : to notify by a motion, action, movement, or sound **2** : to communicate with motions, actions, movements, or sounds

³signal *adj* **1** : unusually great **2** : used for sending a message, warning, or command

sig·na·ture *n* **1** : the name of a person written by that person **2** : a sign or group of signs placed at the beginning of a staff in music to show the key (**key signature**) or the meter (**time signature**)

sign·board *n* : a board with a sign or notice on it

sig·nif·i·cance *n* **1** : MEANING 2 **2** : IMPORTANCE

sig·nif·i·cant *adj* **1** : having a special or hidden meaning **2** : IMPORTANT 1 **3** : large enough to be noticed

sig·ni·fy *vb* **sig·ni·fied; sig·ni·fy·ing 1** : ¹MEAN 1, DENOTE **2** : to show especially by a sign

: make known **3** : to have importance : MATTER

sign language *n* : a system of hand movements used for communication (as by people who are deaf)

sign·post *n* : a post with a sign (as for directing travelers)

si·lage *n* : fodder fermented (as in a silo) to produce a juicy feed for livestock

¹si·lence *n* **1** : the state of keeping or being silent **2** : the state of there being no sound or noise : STILLNESS

²silence *vb* **si·lenced; si·lenc·ing 1** : to stop the noise or speech of : cause to be silent **2** : SUPPRESS 1

si·lent *adj* **1** : not speaking **2** : not talkative **3** : free from noise or sound : STILL **4** : done or felt without being spoken **5** : making no mention **6** : not in operation **7** : not pronounced **8** : made without spoken dialogue — **si·lent·ly** *adv*

¹sil·hou·ette *n* **1** : ¹OUTLINE 1 **2** : a drawing, picture, or portrait of the outline of a person or object filled in with a solid usually black color

²silhouette *vb* **sil·hou·ett·ed; sil·hou·ett·ing** : to represent by an outline : show against a light background

sil·i·con *n* : a chemical element that next to oxygen is the most common element in the earth's crust and is used especially in electronic devices

silk *n* **1** : a fine fiber that is spun by many insect larvae usually to form their cocoon or by spiders to make their webs and that includes some kinds used for weaving cloth **2** : thread, yarn, or fabric made from silk **3** : the threadlike strands that are found over the kernels of an ear of corn

silk·en *adj* **1** : made of or with silk **2** : having a soft and smooth look or feel

silk·worm *n* : a yellowish caterpillar that is the larva of an Asian moth (**silk moth** or **silkworm moth**), is raised in captivity on mulberry leaves, and produces a strong silk that is the silk most used for thread or cloth

silky *adj* **silk·i·er; silk·i·est 1** : soft and smooth **2** : agreeably smooth

sill *n* **1** : a heavy horizontal piece (as of wood) that forms the bottom part of a window frame or a doorway **2** : a horizontal supporting piece at the base of a structure

sil·ly *adj* **sil·li·er; sil·li·est 1** : having or showing a lack of common sense : FOOLISH **2** : not serious or important **3** : playful and lighthearted — **sil·li·ness** *n*

si·lo *n, pl* **silos** : a covered trench, pit, or especially a tall round building in which silage is made and stored

¹silt *n* **1** : particles of small size left as sediment from water **2** : a soil made up mostly of silt and containing little clay

²silt *vb* **silt·ed; silt·ing** : to fill, cover, or block with silt

¹sil·ver *n* **1** : a soft white metallic chemical element that can be polished and is used for money, jewelry and ornaments, and table utensils **2** : coin made of silver **3** : SILVERWARE **4** : a medal made of silver that is given to someone who wins second place in a contest **5** : a medium gray

²silver *adj* **1** : made of, coated with, or yielding the soft white metallic chemical element silver **2** : having the medium gray color of silver

³silver *vb* **sil·vered; sil·ver·ing** : to coat with or as if with silver

sil·ver·smith *n* : a person who makes objects of silver

sil·ver·ware *n* : things (as knives, forks, and spoons) made of silver, silver-plated metal, or stainless steel

sil·very *adj* : shiny and medium gray

sim·i·lar *adj* : having qualities in common — **sim·i·lar·ly** *adv*

sim·i·lar·i·ty *n, pl* **sim·i·lar·i·ties** : the quality or state of being alike in some way or ways

sim·i·le *n* : a figure of speech comparing two unlike things using *like* or *as*

sim·mer *vb* **sim·mered; sim·mer·ing** **1** : to cook gently at or just below the boiling point **2** : to be on the point of bursting out with violence or anger

sim·per *vb* **sim·pered; sim·per·ing** : to smile or speak in a way that is not sincere or natural

sim·ple *adj* **sim·pler; sim·plest** **1** : not hard to understand or solve **2** : ¹EASY 1, STRAIGHTFORWARD **3** : lacking in education, experience, or intelligence **4** : not complex or fancy **5** : INNOCENT 1, MODEST **6** : not rich or important **7** : ABSOLUTE 2

simple machine *n* : one of the fundamental devices that all machines were formerly thought to be made from

sim·ple·ton *n* : a foolish or stupid person

sim·plic·i·ty *n, pl* **sim·plic·i·ties** **1** : the quality or state of being simple or plain and not complicated or difficult **2** : SINCERITY **3** : directness or clearness in speaking or writing

sim·pli·fy *vb* **sim·pli·fied; sim·pli·fy·ing** : to make simple or simpler : make easier

sim·ply *adv* **1** : in a clear way **2** : in a plain way **3** : in a sincere and direct way **4** : ²ONLY 1, MERELY **5** : in actual fact : REALLY, TRULY

si·mul·ta·neous *adj* : existing or taking place at the same time — **si·mul·ta·neous·ly** *adv*

¹sin *n* **1** : an action that breaks a religious law **2** : an action that is or is felt to be bad

²sin *vb* **sinned; sin·ning** : to do something that breaks a religious law or is felt to be bad — **sin·ner** *n*

¹since *adv* **1** : from a definite past time until now **2** : before the present time : AGO **3** : after a time in the past

²since *conj* **1** : in the period after **2** : BECAUSE

³since *prep* **1** : in the period after **2** : continuously from

sin·cere *adj* **sin·cer·er; sin·cer·est** **1** : HONEST 1, STRAIGHTFORWARD **2** : being what it seems to be : GENUINE — **sin·cere·ly** *adv*

sin·cer·i·ty *n* : freedom from fraud or deception : HONESTY

sin·ew *n* : TENDON

sin·ewy *adj* **1** : STRONG 1, POWERFUL **2** : full of tendons : TOUGH, STRINGY

sin·ful *adj* : being or full of sin : WICKED

sing *vb* **sang** *or* **sung; sung; sing·ing** **1** : to produce musical sounds with the voice **2** : to express in musical tones **3** : to make musical sounds **4** : ¹CHANT 2 **5** : to make a small high-pitched sound **6** : to speak with enthusiasm **7** : to do something with song — **sing·er** *n*

sing. *abbr* singular

singe *vb* **singed; singe·ing** : to burn lightly or on the surface : SCORCH

¹sin·gle *adj* **1** : being alone : being the only one **2** : being a separate whole : INDIVIDUAL **3** : not married **4** : made up of or having only one **5** : made for only one person

²single *vb* **sin·gled; sin·gling** : to select or distinguish (as one person or thing) from a number or group

³single *n* **1** : a separate individual person or thing **2** : a hit in baseball that enables the batter to reach first base

sin·gle–hand·ed *adj* **1** : done or managed by one person or with one hand **2** : working alone : lacking help — **single–handed** *adv* — **sin·gle–hand·ed·ly** *adv*

sin·gly *adv* : one by one : INDIVIDUALLY

sing·song *n* : a way of speaking in which the pitch of the voice rises and falls in a pattern — **singsong** *adj*

¹sin·gu·lar *adj* **1** : of, relating to, or being a word form used to show not more than one person or thing **2** : ¹SUPERIOR 2, EXCEPTIONAL **3** : of unusual quality **4** : STRANGE 2, ODD

²singular *n* : a form of a word used to show that only one person or thing is meant

sin·is·ter *adj* **1** : threatening evil, harm, or danger **2** : [1]EVIL 1, CORRUPT

[1]**sink** *vb* **sank** *or* **sunk; sunk; sink·ing 1** : to move or cause to move downward so as to be swallowed up **2** : to fall or drop to a lower level **3** : to penetrate or cause to penetrate **4** : to go into or become absorbed **5** : to become known or felt **6** : to lessen in amount **7** : to form by digging or boring **8** : to spend (money) unwisely **9** : to descend into a feeling of sadness or dread

[2]**sink** *n* : a wide bowl or basin attached to a wall or floor and having water faucets and a drain

sin·u·ous *adj* : having a wavy or winding form

si·nus *n* : any of several spaces in the skull mostly connected with the nostrils

Sioux *n, pl* **Sioux** : DAKOTA

[1]**sip** *vb* **sipped; sip·ping** : to take small drinks of

[2]**sip** *n* **1** : the act of taking a small drink **2** : a small amount taken by sipping

[1]**si·phon** *n* **1** : a bent pipe or tube through which a liquid can be drawn by air pressure up and over the edge of a container **2** : a tubelike part especially of a mollusk (as a clam) usually used to draw in or squirt out water

[2]**siphon** *vb* **si·phoned; si·phon·ing** : to draw off by or as if by a siphon

sir *n* **1** — used without a name as a form of polite address to a man **2** *cap* — used as a title before the given name of a knight or a baronet **3** *cap* — used without a name as a form of address at the beginning of a letter

[1]**sire** *n* **1** *often cap* : [1]FATHER 1 **2** : the male parent of a domestic animal **3** — used in the past to address a man of rank (as a king)

[2]**sire** *vb* **sired; sir·ing** : to become the father of

si·ren *n* : a device that makes a loud warning sound

sir·loin *n* : a cut of beef taken from the part just in front of the rump

si·sal *n* : a long strong white fiber made from the leaves of a Mexican plant and used to make rope and twine

sis·sy *n, pl* **sis·sies** : a fearful or cowardly person

sis·ter *n* **1** : a female person or animal related to another person or animal by having one or both parents in common **2** : a member of a religious society of women : NUN **3** : a woman related to another by a common tie or interest — **sis·ter·ly** *adj*

sis·ter·hood *n* **1** : the state of being a sister **2** : women joined in a group

sis·ter–in–law *n, pl* **sis·ters–in–law 1** : the sister of someone's husband or wife **2** : the wife of someone's brother

sit *vb* **sat; sit·ting 1** : to rest upon the part of the body where the hips and legs join : to rest on the buttocks or hindquarters **2** : to put the buttocks down on a surface **3** : to cause to be seated **4** : [2]PERCH **5** : to be located or stay in a place or position **6** : to provide seats for **7** : to hold a place as a member of an official group **8** : to hold a session **9** : to pose for a portrait or photograph **10** : BABYSIT

site *n* **1** : the place where something (as a town or event) is found or took place **2** : the space of ground a building rests upon **3** : WEB SITE

sit·ter *n* : BABY-SITTER

sit·ting *n* **1** : a period during which someone poses for a portrait or photograph **2** : SESSION 2 **3** : a time when a meal is served to a number of people

sitting room *n* : LIVING ROOM

sit·u·at·ed *adj* **1** : having its place **2** : being in such financial circumstances

sit·u·a·tion *n* **1** : the combination of surrounding conditions **2** : a state of affairs that is urgent or difficult **3** : [1]PLACE 3 **4** : position or place of employment : JOB

sit–up *n* : an exercise done by lying on the back and rising to a sitting position

[1]**six** *adj* : being one more than five

[2]**six** *n* **1** : one more than five : two times three : 6 **2** : the sixth in a set or series

six·pence *n* **1** : the sum of six pence **2** : an old British coin worth six pence

six–shoot·er *n* : a revolver having six chambers

[1]**six·teen** *adj* : being one more than 15

[2]**sixteen** *n* : one more than 15 : four times four : 16

[1]**six·teenth** *adj* : coming right after 15th

[2]**sixteenth** *n* : number 16 in a series

[1]**sixth** *adj* : coming right after fifth

[2]**sixth** *n* **1** : number six in a series **2** : one of six equal parts

[1]**six·ti·eth** *adj* : coming right after 59th

[2]**sixtieth** *n* : number 60 in a series

[1]**six·ty** *adj* : being six times ten

[2]**sixty** *n* : six times ten : 60

siz·able *or* **size·able** *adj* : fairly large

size *n* **1** : amount of space occupied by someone or something : how large or small someone or something is **2** : the number or amount of people or things **3** : one of a series of measures especially of manufactured articles (as clothing)

sized *adj* : having a specified size

siz·zle *vb* **siz·zled; siz·zling** : to make a hissing or sputtering noise in or as if in frying or burning

SK *abbr* Saskatchewan

¹**skate** *vb* **skat·ed; skat·ing 1 :** to glide along on skates **2 :** to slide or glide along — **skat·er** *n*

²**skate** *n* **1 :** a metal blade fitting the sole of the shoe or a shoe with a permanently attached metal blade used for gliding on ice **2 :** ROLLER SKATE

³**skate** *n* **:** a flat fish related to the sharks that has large and nearly triangular fins

¹**skate·board** *n* **:** a short board mounted on small wheels that is used for coasting and often for performing athletic stunts

²**skateboard** *vb* **skate·board·ed; skate·board·ing :** to ride or perform stunts on a skateboard — **skate·board·er** *n*

skein *n* **:** a quantity of yarn or thread arranged in a loose coil

skel·e·tal *adj* **:** of or relating to a skeleton

skel·e·ton *n* **1 :** a firm structure or framework of a living thing that in vertebrates (as fish, birds, or humans) is typically made of bone and supports the soft tissues of the body and protects the internal organs **2 :** FRAMEWORK

skep·tic *n* **:** a person who has or shows doubt about something

skep·ti·cal *adj* **:** having or showing doubt

¹**sketch** *n* **1 :** a rough outline or drawing showing the main features of something **2 :** a short written work (as a story or essay) **3 :** a short comic performance

²**sketch** *vb* **sketched; sketch·ing 1 :** to make a drawing, rough draft, or outline of **2 :** to describe or outline (something) briefly

sketchy *adj* **sketch·i·er; sketch·i·est 1 :** roughly outlined **2 :** lacking completeness or clearness

¹**ski** *n, pl* **skis :** one of a pair of narrow strips fastened one on each foot and used in gliding over snow or water

²**ski** *vb* **skied; ski·ing :** to glide on skis — **ski·er** *n*

¹**skid** *vb* **skid·ded; skid·ding 1 :** ¹SLIDE 1, SLIP **2 :** to slide sideways **3 :** to roll or slide on a platform of logs, planks, or rails

²**skid** *n* **1 :** a platform of logs, planks, or rails used to support a heavy object while it is being moved or stored **2 :** the act of sliding

skiff *n* **:** a small light rowboat

ski·ing *n* **:** the art or sport of gliding and jumping on skis

skill *n* **1 :** ability that comes from training or practice **2 :** a developed or acquired ability

skilled *adj* **1 :** having skill **2 :** requiring skill and training

skil·let *n* **:** a frying pan

skill·ful *adj* **1 :** having or showing ability **:** EXPERT **2 :** done or made with ability — **skill·ful·ly** *adv*

skim *vb* **skimmed; skim·ming 1 :** to clean a liquid of scum or floating substance **:** remove (as cream or film) from the top part of a liquid **2 :** to read or examine quickly and not thoroughly **3 :** to skip (a stone) along the surface of water **4 :** to pass swiftly or lightly over

skim milk *n* **:** milk from which the cream has been removed

skimp *vb* **skimped; skimp·ing :** to give too little or just enough attention or effort to or money for

skimpy *adj* **skimp·i·er; skimp·i·est :** very small in size or amount **:** SCANTY

¹**skin** *n* **1 :** the usually flexible outer layer of an animal body that in vertebrate animals is made up of two layers of cells forming an inner dermis and an outer epidermis **2 :** the hide of an animal **3 :** an outer or surface layer — **skin·less** *adj* — **skinned** *adj*

²**skin** *vb* **skinned; skin·ning 1 :** to strip, scrape, or rub off the skin of **2 :** to remove an outer layer from (as by peeling)

skin–dive *vb* **skin–dived; skin–div·ing :** to swim below the surface of water with a face mask and sometimes a portable breathing device — **skin diver** *n*

skin·ny *adj* **skin·ni·er; skin·ni·est :** very thin

¹**skip** *vb* **skipped; skip·ping 1 :** to move by taking short light steps and jumps **2 :** to pass over or omit an item, space, or step **3 :** to leap over lightly and nimbly **4 :** to fail to attend or do **5 :** to bound or cause to bound off one point after another **:** SKIM

²**skip** *n* **1 :** a light bounding step **2 :** a way of moving by hops and steps

skip·per *n* **:** the master of a ship and especially of a fishing, trading, or pleasure boat

¹**skir·mish** *n* **1 :** a minor fight in war **2 :** a minor argument

²**skirmish** *vb* **skir·mished; skir·mish·ing :** to take part in a fight or dispute

¹**skirt** *n* **1 :** a piece of clothing or part of a piece of clothing worn by women or girls that hangs from the waist down **2 :** a part or attachment serving as a rim, border, or edging

²**skirt** *vb* **skirt·ed; skirt·ing 1 :** ²BORDER 2 **2 :** to go or pass around or about the outer edge of **3 :** to avoid for fear of difficulty

skit *n* **:** a brief sketch in play form

skit·ter *vb* **skit·tered; skit·ter·ing :** to glide or skip lightly or quickly

skit·tish *adj* **:** easily frightened

skulk *vb* **skulked; skulk·ing :** to hide or move in a sly or sneaking way

skull *n* **:** the case of bone or cartilage that forms the skeleton of the head and face, encloses the brain, and supports the jaws

skunk *n* **:** a North American animal related to

the weasels that has coarse black-and-white fur and can squirt out a fluid with a very unpleasant smell

sky *n, pl* **skies 1** : the stretch of space over the earth **2** : [1]WEATHER, CLIMATE

sky·div·ing *n* : the sport of jumping from an airplane using a parachute

sky·lark *n* : a European lark noted for its song

sky·light *n* : a window or group of windows in a roof or ceiling

sky·line *n* **1** : the line where earth and sky seem to meet : HORIZON **2** : an outline against the sky

sky·scrap·er *n* : a very tall building

slab *n* : a flat thick piece or slice

[1]**slack** *adj* **1** : CARELESS 2, NEGLIGENT **2** : not energetic : SLOW **3** : not tight or firm **4** : not busy or active

[2]**slack** *vb* **slacked; slack·ing 1** : to make or become looser, slower, or less energetic **2** : to avoid work — **slack·er** *n*

[3]**slack** *n* **1** : a part (as of a rope or sail) that hangs loose without strain **2 slacks** *pl* : dressy pants **3** : a portion (as of work or resources) that is required but lacking **4** : additional relief from pressure — usually used with *cut*

slack·en *vb* **slack·ened; slack·en·ing 1** : to make slower or less energetic **2** : to make less tight or firm

slag *n* : the waste left after the melting of ores and the separation of the metal from them

slain *past participle of* SLAY

slake *vb* **slaked; slak·ing** : QUENCH 1

[1]**slam** *vb* **slammed; slam·ming 1** : to shut with noisy force : BANG **2** : to strike or beat hard **3** : to put or place with force **4** : to criticize harshly

[2]**slam** *n* **1** : a severe blow **2** : the noise made by a violent act of closing : BANG

[1]**slan·der** *vb* **slan·dered; slan·der·ing** : to make a false and damaging statement against

[2]**slander** *n* : a false statement that damages another person's reputation

slang *n* : very informal words used by a group of people

[1]**slant** *vb* **slant·ed; slant·ing** : to turn or incline diagonally from a straight line or level : SLOPE

[2]**slant** *n* : a direction, line, or surface that is not level or straight up and down : SLOPE

[3]**slant** *adj* : not level or straight up and down

slant·wise *adv or adj* : at a slant : in a slanting position

[1]**slap** *vb* **slapped; slap·ping 1** : to strike with or as if with the open hand **2** : to make a sound like that of slapping **3** : to put, place, or throw with careless haste or force

[2]**slap** *n* **1** : a quick sharp blow especially with the open hand **2** : a noise like that made by a blow with the open hand

[1]**slash** *vb* **slashed; slash·ing 1** : to cut or strike at with sweeping blows **2** : to reduce sharply

[2]**slash** *n* **1** : an act of cutting or striking with sweeping strokes **2** : a long cut or slit made with sweeping blows

slat *n* : a thin narrow strip of wood, plastic, or metal

slate *n* **1** : a fine-grained usually bluish gray rock that splits into thin layers or plates and is used mostly for roofing and blackboards **2** : a framed piece of slate used to write on

[1]**slaugh·ter** *n* **1** : the act of killing **2** : the act of killing and preparing animals for food **3** : destruction of many lives especially in battle

[2]**slaughter** *vb* **slaugh·tered; slaugh·ter·ing 1** : [2]BUTCHER 1 **2** : [2]MASSACRE

slaugh·ter·house *n, pl* **slaugh·ter·hous·es** : a building where animals are killed and prepared for food

Slav *n* : a native speaker of a Slavic language

[1]**slave** *n* **1** : a person who is owned by another person and can be sold at the owner's will **2** : a person who is strongly influenced and controlled by something **3** : DRUDGE

[2]**slave** *vb* **slaved; slav·ing** : to work very hard, for long hours, or under difficult conditions

slave·hold·er *n* : an owner of slaves

slav·ery *n* **1** : the state of being owned by another person : BONDAGE **2** : the custom or practice of owning slaves **3** : hard tiring labor : DRUDGERY

Slav·ic *adj* : of, relating to, or characteristic of the Slavs or their languages

slav·ish *adj* : following, copying, or accepting something or someone without questioning

slay *vb* **slew; slain; slay·ing** : [1]KILL 1 — **slay·er** *n*

[1]**sled** *n* **1** : a vehicle on runners for carrying loads especially over snow **2** : a small vehicle used mostly by children for sliding on snow and ice

[2]**sled** *vb* **sled·ded; sled·ding** : to ride or carry on a sled

sledge *n* : a strong heavy sled

sledge·ham·mer *n* : a large heavy hammer usually used with both hands

sleek *adj* **sleek·er; sleek·est 1** : smooth and glossy as if polished **2** : having a healthy well-groomed look **3** : straight and smooth in design or shape **4** : stylish and elegant

[1]**sleep** *vb* **slept; sleep·ing** : to rest with eyes closed in a temporary state of inactivity : be or lie in a state of sleep

²sleep *n* **1** : a natural temporary state of rest during which an individual becomes physically inactive and unaware of the surrounding environment and many bodily functions (as breathing) slow **2** : an inactive state (as hibernation) like true sleep **3** : DEATH 3 — **sleep·less** *adj* — **sleep·less·ness** *n*

sleep·er *n* **1** : someone that sleeps **2** : a railroad car with berths for sleeping

sleeping bag *n* : a large fabric bag that is warmly lined for sleeping outdoors or in a camp or tent

sleep·over *n* : an overnight stay at another's home

sleep·walk *vb* **sleep·walked; sleep·walk·ing** : to walk about while asleep — **sleep·walk·er** *n*

sleepy *adj* **sleep·i·er; sleep·i·est** **1** : ready to fall asleep : DROWSY **2** : not active, noisy, or busy — **sleep·i·ness** *n*

¹sleet *n* : frozen or partly frozen rain

²sleet *vb* **sleet·ed; sleet·ing** : to shower sleet

sleeve *n* **1** : the part of a piece of clothing covering the arm **2** : a part that fits over or around something like a sleeve — **sleeved** *adj* — **sleeve·less** *adj* — **up someone's sleeve** : held secretly in reserve

sleigh *n* : an open usually horse-drawn vehicle with runners for use on snow or ice

sleight of hand *n* : skill and quickness in the use of the hands especially in doing magic tricks

slen·der *adj* **slen·der·er; slen·der·est** **1** : gracefully thin **2** : narrow for its height or length **3** : very little

slept *past and past participle of* SLEEP

slew *past of* SLAY

¹slice *vb* **sliced; slic·ing** **1** : to cut with or as if with a knife **2** : to cut into thin flat pieces

²slice *n* : a thin flat piece cut from something

¹slick *vb* **slicked; slick·ing** : to make sleek or smooth

²slick *adj* **1** : having a smooth surface : SLIPPERY **2** : TRICKY **3** : having skill and cleverness

slick·er *n* : a long loose raincoat

¹slide *vb* **slid; slid·ing** **1** : to move or cause to move smoothly over a surface : GLIDE **2** : to move or pass smoothly and without much effort **3** : to get gradually worse over time

²slide *n* **1** : the act or motion of moving smoothly over a surface **2** : a movement to a lower or worse condition **3** : a surface down which a person or thing slides **4** : a loosened mass that moves swiftly : AVALANCHE **5** : a glass or plastic plate for holding an object to be examined under a microscope **6** : a transparent picture that can be projected on a screen **7** : something that operates or adjusts by sliding

¹slight *adj* **slight·er; slight·est** **1** : small of its kind or in amount **2** : thin and delicate **3** : not important : TRIVIAL **4** : FLIMSY, FRAIL — **slight·ly** *adv*

²slight *vb* **slight·ed; slight·ing** : to treat without proper respect or courtesy

³slight *n* **1** : an act or an instance of treating without proper respect or courtesy **2** : an instance of being treated without proper respect or courtesy

¹slim *adj* **slim·mer; slim·mest** **1** : SLENDER 1 **2** : very small

²slim *vb* **slimmed; slim·ming** : to make or become slender

slime *n* **1** : soft slippery mud **2** : a soft slippery material (as on the skin of a slug or catfish)

slimy *adj* **slim·i·er; slim·i·est** **1** : having a slippery feel or look **2** : covered with slime

¹sling *vb* **slung; sling·ing** **1** : to throw with a sudden sweeping motion : FLING **2** : to hurl with a sling

²sling *n* **1** : a device (as a short strap with a string attached at each end) for hurling stones **2** : a device (as a rope or chain) by which something is lifted or carried **3** : a bandage hanging from the neck to hold up the arm or hand

³sling *vb* **slung; sling·ing** **1** : to put in or move or support with a sling **2** : to hang from two points

sling·shot *n* : a forked stick with an elastic band attached for shooting small stones

slink *vb* **slunk; slink·ing** : to move or go by or as if by creeping especially so as not to be noticed (as in fear or shame)

¹slip *vb* **slipped; slip·ping** **1** : to move easily and smoothly **2** : to slide into or out of place or away from a support **3** : to slide on a slippery surface so as to lose balance **4** : to pass or let pass or escape without being noted, used, or done **5** : to move into or out of a place without being noticed **6** : to escape the attention or memory of **7** : to put on or take off a piece of clothing quickly and easily **8** : to make or become known by mistake **9** : to go from one state or condition to an often worse one **10** : to get away from — **slip up** : to make a mistake

²slip *n* **1** : the act or an instance of sliding down or out of place **2** : a secret or quick departure or escape **3** : a small mistake : BLUNDER **4** : a fall from some level or standard : DECLINE **5** : a place for a ship between two piers **6** : an undergarment for women made in dress or skirt length

³slip *n* **1** : a usually small piece of paper and

especially one used for some record **2** : a long narrow piece of material

slip·cov·er *n* : a cover (as for a sofa or chair)

slip·knot *n* : a knot made by tying the end of a line around the line itself to form a loop so that the size of the loop may be changed by slipping the knot

slip·per *n* : a light low shoe that is easily slipped on the foot and is made to be worn indoors

slip·pery *adj* **slip·per·i·er; slip·per·i·est 1** : having a surface smooth or wet enough to make holding onto or moving or standing on difficult **2** : not to be trusted : TRICKY

slip·shod *adj* : very careless

¹slit *n* : a long narrow cut or opening

²slit *vb* **slit; slit·ting** : to make a long narrow cut in : SLASH

slith·er *vb* **slith·ered; slith·er·ing** : ¹GLIDE

slith·ery *adj* : having a slippery surface, texture, or quality

¹sliv·er *n* **1** : a long slender piece of something cut or torn off : SPLINTER **2** : a small amount

²sliver *vb* **sliv·ered; sliv·er·ing** : to cut or form into long slender pieces

slob *n* **1** : a sloppy or lazy person **2** : an ordinary person

¹slob·ber *vb* **slob·bered; slob·ber·ing** : to let saliva or liquid dribble from the mouth

²slobber *n* : dripping saliva

slo·gan *n* : a word or phrase used by a party, a group, or a business to attract attention

sloop *n* : a sailing boat with one mast and a fore-and-aft mainsail and jib

¹slop *n* **1** : thin tasteless drink or liquid food **2** : food waste or gruel fed to animals **3** : body waste **4** : soft mud

²slop *vb* **slopped; slop·ping 1** : to spill or spill something on or over **2** : to feed slop to

¹slope *n* **1** : a piece of slanting ground (as a hillside) **2** : upward or downward slant

²slope *vb* **sloped; slop·ing** : to take a slanting direction

slop·py *adj* **slop·pi·er; slop·pi·est 1** : careless in work or in appearance **2** : wet enough to spatter easily : containing a lot of moisture

slosh *vb* **sloshed; slosh·ing 1** : to walk with trouble through water, mud, or slush **2** : to move with a splashing motion

¹slot *n* : a narrow opening, groove, or passage

²slot *vb* **slot·ted; slot·ting** : to cut a narrow opening, groove, or passage in

sloth *n* **1** : the quality or state of being lazy **2** : an animal of Central and South America that hangs with its back downward and moves slowly along the branches of trees on whose leaves, twigs, and fruits it feeds

¹slouch *n* **1** : a lazy worthless person **2** : a

way of standing, sitting, or walking with the head and shoulders bent forward

²slouch *vb* **slouched; slouch·ing** : to walk, stand, or sit lazily with the head and shoulders bent forward

slough *n* : a wet marshy or muddy place

slov·en·ly *adj* **1** : personally untidy **2** : very careless

¹slow *adj* **slow·er; slow·est 1** : moving, flowing, or going at less than the usual speed **2** : taking more time than is expected or desired **3** : not as smart or as quick to understand as most people **4** : not active **5** : indicating less than is correct **6** : not easily aroused or excited — **slow·ly** *adv* — **slow·ness** *n*

²slow *vb* **slowed; slow·ing** : to go or make go less than the usual speed

³slow *adv* **slow·er; slow·est** : in a slow way

slow·poke *n* : a very slow person

sludge *n* : a soft muddy mass resulting from sewage treatment

¹slug *n* : a wormlike animal living mostly on land that is a mollusk related to the snails but that has an undeveloped shell or none at all

²slug *n* **1** : BULLET **2** : a metal disk often used in place of a coin

³slug *n* : a hard blow especially with the fist

⁴slug *vb* **slugged; slug·ging** : to hit hard with the fist or with a bat

slug·gard *n* : a lazy person

slug·ger *n* : a boxer or baseball batter who hits hard

slug·gish *adj* : slow in movement or reaction — **slug·gish·ly** *adv*

¹sluice *n* **1** : a man-made channel for water with a gate for controlling its flow or changing its direction **2** : a device for controlling the flow of water **3** : a sloping trough for washing ore or for floating logs

²sluice *vb* **sluiced; sluic·ing 1** : to wash in a stream of water running through a sluice **2** : ³FLUSH 2, DRENCH

slum *n* : a very poor crowded dirty section especially of a city

¹slum·ber *vb* **slum·bered; slum·ber·ing** : ¹SLEEP 1

²slumber *n* : ²SLEEP 1

¹slump *vb* **slumped; slump·ing 1** : to drop or slide down suddenly : COLLAPSE **2** : ²SLOUCH **3** : to drop sharply

²slump *n* : a big or continued drop especially in prices, business, or performance

slung *past and past participle of* SLING

slunk *past and past participle of* SLINK

¹slur *n* : an insulting remark

²slur *vb* **slurred; slur·ring** : to speak in a way that is difficult to understand

³**slur** *n* : a way of talking that is difficult to understand

¹**slurp** *vb* **slurped; slurp·ing** : to eat or drink noisily or with a sucking sound

²**slurp** *n* : a sucking sound made while eating and drinking

slush *n* : partly melted snow

slushy *adj* **slush·i·er; slush·i·est** : covered with or resembling partly melted snow

sly *adj* **sli·er** *or* **sly·er; sli·est** *or* **sly·est 1** : both clever and tricky **2** : tending to keep secrets and hide intentions **3** : MISCHIEVOUS 2 — **sly·ly** *adv* — **sly·ness** *n* — **on the sly** : so as not to be seen or caught : SECRETLY

¹**smack** *vb* **smacked; smack·ing 1** : to make or give a noisy slap **2** : to close and open the lips noisily especially in eating **3** : to kiss usually loudly or hard

²**smack** *n* **1** : a noisy slap or blow **2** : a quick sharp noise made by the lips (as in enjoyment of some taste) **3** : a loud kiss

³**smack** *adv* : in a square and sharp manner : DIRECTLY

⁴**smack** *vb* **smacked; smacking** : to have a flavor, trace, or suggestion

⁵**smack** *n* : a slight taste, trace, or touch of something

¹**small** *adj* **small·er; small·est 1** : little in size **2** : few in numbers or members **3** : little in amount **4** : very young **5** : not very much **6** : UNIMPORTANT **7** : operating on a limited scale **8** : very soft and quiet **9** : not generous : MEAN **10** : made up of units of little worth **11** : ¹HUMBLE 3, MODEST **12** : lowered in pride **13** : being letters that are not capitals — **small·ness** *n*

²**small** *n* : a part smaller and usually narrower than the rest

small intestine *n* : the long narrow upper part of the intestine in which food is mostly digested and from which digested food is absorbed into the body

small·pox *n* : a sometimes deadly disease in which fever and skin rash occur and which is believed to have been wiped out worldwide by vaccination

¹**smart** *adj* **smart·er; smart·est 1** : quick to learn or do : BRIGHT **2** : showing good judgment : WISE **3** : FRESH 8 **4** : stylish and fashionable **5** : BRISK, SPIRITED — **smart·ly** *adv* — **smart·ness** *n*

²**smart** *vb* **smart·ed; smart·ing 1** : to cause or feel a sharp stinging pain **2** : to be upset

³**smart** *n* : a stinging pain usually in one spot

smart al·eck *n* : a person who likes to show off in a clever but rude or annoying way

¹**smash** *n* **1** : a violent blow **2** : the action or sound of shattering or hitting violently **3** : a striking success

²**smash** *vb* **smashed; smash·ing 1** : to break in pieces : SHATTER **2** : to hit or move violently **3** : to destroy completely

¹**smear** *vb* **smeared; smear·ing 1** : to spread or soil with something oily or sticky **2** : to spread over a surface **3** : to harm the reputation of (someone) with false statements

²**smear** *n* : a spot or streak made by or as if by an oily or sticky substance : SMUDGE

¹**smell** *vb* **smelled** *or* **smelt; smell·ing 1** : to become aware of the odor of by means of special cells located in the nose **2** : to detect by means or use of the sense of smell **3** : to have or give off an odor **4** : to sense as if by smelling

²**smell** *n* **1** : the sense by which a person or animal becomes aware of an odor **2** : the sensation gotten through the sense of smell : ODOR, SCENT

smelly *adj* **smel·li·er; smel·li·est** : having an odor and especially a bad odor

¹**smelt** *n, pl* **smelts** *or* **smelt** : a small silvery fish that is sometimes used for food

²**smelt** *vb* **smelt·ed; smelt·ing** : to melt (as ore) in order to separate the metal : REFINE

¹**smile** *vb* **smiled; smil·ing 1** : make the corners of the mouth turn up in an expression of amusement or pleasure **2** : to look with amusement or pleasure **3** : to express by a smile

²**smile** *n* : an expression in which the corners of the mouth turn upward especially to show amusement or pleasure

smirk *vb* **smirked; smirk·ing** : to smile in an insincere manner — **smirk** *n*

smite *vb* **smote; smit·ten; smit·ing 1** : to strike hard especially with the hand or a weapon **2** : to kill or injure

smith *n* **1** : a worker in metals **2** : BLACK-SMITH

smith·er·eens *n pl* : small broken pieces

smithy *n, pl* **smith·ies** : the workshop of someone who works in metals and especially of a blacksmith

smock *n* : a loose outer garment worn especially for protection of clothing

smog *n* : a fog made heavier and thicker by the action of sunlight on polluted air

¹**smoke** *n* **1** : the gas given off by burning materials (as coal, wood, or tobacco) made visible by particles of carbon floating in it **2** : the act of drawing in and blowing out the fumes of burning tobacco

²**smoke** *vb* **smoked; smok·ing 1** : to give out smoke **2** : to draw in and blow out the fumes of burning tobacco (as in a cigarette) **3** : to expose (as meat) to the fumes of burning materials to give flavor and keep from spoiling — **smok·er** *n*

smoke de·tec·tor *n* : a device that sounds an alarm automatically when it detects smoke

smoke·house *n, pl* **smoke·hous·es** : a building where meat or fish is smoked

smoke·stack *n* : a large chimney or a pipe for carrying away smoke (as on a factory or ship)

smoky *adj* **smok·i·er; smok·i·est 1** : giving off smoke especially in large amounts **2** : filled with or darkened by smoke **3** : having a flavor, taste, or appearance of smoke

smol·der *or* **smoul·der** *vb* **smol·dered** *or* **smoul·dered; smol·der·ing** *or* **smoul·der·ing 1** : to burn slowly usually with smoke and without flame **2** : to burn inwardly

¹smooth *adj* **smooth·er; smooth·est 1** : not rough or uneven in surface **2** : not hairy **3** : free from difficulties or things in the way **4** : moving or progressing without breaks, sudden changes, or shifts **5** : appearing to be friendly and flattering without really meaning it — **smooth·ly** *adv* — **smooth·ness** *n*

²smooth *vb* **smoothed; smooth·ing 1** : to remove bumps, lumps, or wrinkles : make smooth **2** : to free from trouble or difficulty

smote *past of* SMITE

smoth·er *vb* **smoth·ered; smoth·er·ing 1** : to kill or injure by keeping from getting air or by exposing to smoke or fumes : SUFFOCATE **2** : to become suffocated **3** : to keep from growing or developing by or as if by covering **4** : to keep from happening : SUPPRESS **5** : to cover thickly

¹smudge *n* **1** : a blurred spot or streak : SMEAR **2** : a smoky fire (as to drive away mosquitoes)

²smudge *vb* **smudged; smudg·ing** : to soil or blur by rubbing or smearing

smug *adj* **smug·ger; smug·gest** : showing a superior attitude — **smug·ly** *adv*

smug·gle *vb* **smug·gled; smug·gling 1** : to export or import secretly and unlawfully **2** : to take or bring secretly — **smug·gler** *n*

smut *n* **1** : something (as a particle of soot) that soils or blackens **2** : a destructive disease of plants (as cereal grasses) that is caused by a fungus **3** : a fungus that causes smut

¹snack *n* : a small amount of food eaten between meals

²snack *vb* **snacked; snack·ing** : to eat a small amount of food between meals

¹snag *n* **1** : a rough or broken part sticking out from something **2** : an unexpected difficulty **3** : a stump or stub of a tree branch especially when hidden under water

²snag *vb* **snagged; snag·ging 1** : to catch or damage on or as if on a part sticking up or

out **2** : to catch or capture by or as if by reaching out quickly and grabbing

snail *n* : a small slow-moving mollusk that has a spiral shell into which it can draw itself for safety and that can live either on land or in water

¹snake *n* **1** : a limbless reptile that has a long body with scales and feeds usually on large insects or small animals and birds **2** : a person who is mean or can't be trusted

²snake *vb* **snaked; snak·ing** : to crawl, wind, or move like a snake

snaky *adj* **snak·i·er; snak·i·est 1** : of or like a snake **2** : full of snakes

¹snap *vb* **snapped; snap·ping 1** : to break or break apart suddenly and often with a cracking noise **2** : to grasp or grasp at something suddenly with the mouth or teeth **3** : to speak or utter sharply or irritably **4** : to make or cause to make a sharp or crackling sound **5** : to close or fit in place with a quick movement **6** : to put into or remove from a position suddenly or with a cracking sound **7** : to act or be acted on with energy **8** : to grasp at something eagerly **9** : to get, take, or buy at once **10** : to close by means of snaps or fasteners **11** : to take a snapshot of **12** : to make a short sharp sound by quickly moving the middle finger against the thumb

²snap *n* **1** : a sudden short sharp sound **2** : an act of moving the middle finger against the thumb to make a short sharp sound **3** : something that is easy and presents no problems **4** : a sudden change in weather **5** : a catch or fastening that closes or locks with a click **6** : SNAPSHOT **7** : a short amount of time

³snap *adj* **1** : made suddenly or without careful thought **2** : closing with a click or by means of a device that snaps **3** : very easy

snap·drag·on *n* : a garden plant with stalks of usually white, pink, red, or yellow flowers with two lips

snap·per *n* **1** : SNAPPING TURTLE **2** : an active fish of warm seas that is caught for sport and food

snap·ping tur·tle *n* : a large American turtle that catches its prey with a snap of the powerful jaws

snap·py *adj* **snap·pi·er; snap·pi·est 1** : full of life : LIVELY **2** : briskly cold : CHILLY **3** : QUICK **4** : STYLISH, SMART **5** : clever and funny

snap·shot *n* : a photograph taken usually with an inexpensive hand-held camera

¹snare *n* **1** : a trap (as a noose) for catching small animals and birds **2** : something that traps or deceives

²snare *vb* **snared; snar·ing** : to catch or en-tangle by or as if by use of a trap for catching small animals

snare drum *n* : a small drum with two heads that has strings stretched across its lower head to produce a rattling sound

¹**snarl** *vb* **snarled; snarl·ing 1** : to growl with a showing of teeth **2** : to speak in an angry way

²**snarl** *n* : an angry growl

³**snarl** *n* **1** : a tangle usually of hairs or thread : KNOT **2** : a situation that makes movement difficult

⁴**snarl** *vb* **snarled; snarl·ing** : to get or become tangled

¹**snatch** *vb* **snatched; snatch·ing** : to take hold of or try to take hold of something quickly or suddenly

²**snatch** *n* **1** : something brief, hurried, or in small bits **2** : an act of taking hold of something quickly **3** : a brief period

¹**sneak** *vb* **sneaked** *or* **snuck; sneak·ing** : to move, act, bring, put, or take in a sly or secret way

²**sneak** *n* : a person who acts in a sly or secret way

sneak·er *n* : a sports shoe with a rubber sole

sneaky *adj* **sneak·i·er; sneak·i·est** : behaving in a sly or secret way or showing that kind of behavior

¹**sneer** *vb* **sneered; sneer·ing 1** : to smile or laugh while making a face that shows disrespect **2** : to speak or write in a disrespectful way

²**sneer** *n* : a disrespectful expression or remark

¹**sneeze** *vb* **sneezed; sneez·ing** : to force the breath out in a sudden and noisy way

²**sneeze** *n* : an act or instance of sneezing

¹**snick·er** *vb* **snick·ered; snick·er·ing** : to give a small and often mean or sly laugh

²**snicker** *n* : an act or sound of laughing in a mean or sly way

snide *adj* : unkind or insulting in an indirect way

¹**sniff** *vb* **sniffed; sniff·ing 1** : to smell by taking short breaths **2** : to draw air into the nose in short breaths loud enough to be heard **3** : to say with scorn

²**sniff** *n* **1** : the act or sound of drawing air into the nose in short breaths (as to smell something) **2** : an odor detected through the nose

snif·fle *vb* **snif·fled; snif·fling 1** : to sniff repeatedly **2** : to speak with sniffs

snif·fles *n pl* : a common cold in which the main symptom is a runny nose

¹**snig·ger** *vb* **snig·gered; snig·ger·ing** : ¹SNICKER

²**snigger** *n* : ²SNICKER

¹**snip** *n* **1** : a small piece that is clipped off **2** : an act or sound of clipping

²**snip** *vb* **snipped; snip·ping** : to cut or cut off with or as if with shears or scissors

¹**snipe** *n, pl* **snipes** *or* **snipe** : a bird that lives in marshes and has a long straight bill

²**snipe** *vb* **sniped; snip·ing 1** : to shoot from a hiding place (as at individual enemy soldiers) **2** : to criticize someone in a harsh or unfair way — **snip·er** *n*

¹**snitch** *vb* **snitched; snitch·ing** : ¹STEAL 1

²**snitch** *vb* **snitched; snitching** : INFORM 2, TATTLE

³**snitch** *n, pl* **snitch·es** : TATTLETALE

snob *n* : a person who looks down on or avoids those felt to be less important

snob·bish *adj* : being or characteristic of a snob

snob·by *adj* **snob·bi·er; snob·bi·est** : SNOBBISH

¹**snoop** *vb* **snooped; snoop·ing** : to look or search especially in a sneaking or nosy way — **snoop·er** *n*

²**snoop** *n* : a person who looks or searches in a sneaky or nosy way

snoot *n* : ¹NOSE 1

snooty *adj* **snoot·i·er; snoot·i·est** : rude and arrogant especially to people from a lower class

¹**snooze** *vb* **snoozed; snooz·ing** : to take a nap

²**snooze** *n* : a short sleep : NAP

¹**snore** *vb* **snored; snor·ing** : to breathe with a rough hoarse noise while sleeping

²**snore** *n* : an act or sound of breathing with a rough hoarse noise while sleeping

¹**snor·kel** *n* : a tube used by swimmers for breathing with the head underwater

²**snorkel** *vb* **snor·keled; snor·kel·ing** : to swim underwater using a tube for breathing

¹**snort** *vb* **snort·ed; snort·ing 1** : to force air through the nose with a rough harsh sound **2** : to say something with anger or scorn

²**snort** *n* : an act of or the rough harsh sound made by forcing air through the nose

snot·ty *adj* **snot·ti·er; snot·ti·est** : rude and arrogant

snout *n* **1** : the projecting part of an animal's face that includes the nose or nose and mouth **2** : a usually large and ugly human nose

¹**snow** *n* **1** : small white crystals of ice formed directly from the water vapor of the air **2** : a mass of snowflakes fallen to earth

²**snow** *vb* **snowed; snow·ing** : to fall or cause to fall in or as snow

snow·ball *n* : a round mass of snow pressed or rolled together

snow·bank *n* : a mound or pile of snow that results from clearing pavement

snow–blind *adj* : having the eyes red and swollen and unable to see from the effect of glare reflected from snow

snow·blow·er *n* : a machine in which rotating parts pick up snow and throw it aside

snow·board *n* : a board like a wide ski ridden in a surfing position over snow — **snow·board·er** *n* — **snow·board·ing** *n*

snow·bound *adj* : shut in or blocked by snow

snow·drift *n* : a bank of drifted snow

snow·fall *n* **1** : a fall of snow **2** : the amount of snow that falls in a single storm or in a certain period

snow·flake *n* : a single snow crystal : a small mass of snow crystals

snow·man *n, pl* **snow·men** : snow shaped to look like a person

snow·mo·bile *n* : a small motor vehicle designed for travel on snow

snow·plow *n* : any of various devices used for clearing away snow

¹**snow·shoe** *n* : a light frame of wood strung with a net (as of rawhide) and worn under a shoe to prevent sinking into soft snow

²**snowshoe** *vb* **snow·shoed; snow·shoe·ing** : to walk with snowshoes

snow·storm *n* : a storm of falling snow

snow·suit *n* : a one-piece or two-piece warm outer garment for a child

snow thrower *n* : SNOWBLOWER

snowy *adj* **snow·i·er; snow·i·est 1** : having or covered with snow **2** : white like snow

¹**snub** *vb* **snubbed; snub·bing** : to ignore or treat rudely on purpose

²**snub** *n* : an act or an instance of ignoring or treating rudely on purpose

snub–nosed *adj* : having a stubby and usually slightly turned-up nose

snuck *past and past participle of* SNEAK

¹**snuff** *n* : powdered tobacco that is chewed, placed against the gums, or drawn in through the nostrils

²**snuff** *vb* **snuffed; snuff·ing** : to draw through or into the nose with force

³**snuff** *vb* **snuffed; snuffing 1** : to cut or pinch off the burned end of the wick of a candle **2** : to put an end to

¹**snuf·fle** *vb* **snuf·fled; snuf·fling** : to breathe noisily through a nose that is partly blocked

²**snuffle** *n* : the sound made in breathing through a nose that is partly blocked

snug *adj* **snug·ger; snug·gest 1** : fitting closely and comfortably **2** : COMFORTABLE 1, COZY **3** : offering protection or a hiding place — **snug·ly** *adv*

snug·gle *vb* **snug·gled; snug·gling 1** : to curl up comfortably or cozily : CUDDLE **2** : to pull in close to someone

¹**so** *adv* **1** : in the way indicated **2** : in the same way : ALSO **3** : ¹THEN 2 **4** : to an indi-

cated extent or way **5** : to a great degree : VERY, EXTREMELY **6** : to a definite but not specified amount **7** : most certainly : INDEED **8** : THEREFORE

²**so** *conj* **1** : in order that **2** : and therefore

³**so** *pron* **1** : the same : THAT **2** : approximately that

so. *abbr* south

¹**soak** *vb* **soaked; soak·ing 1** : to lie covered with liquid **2** : to place in a liquid to wet or as if to wet thoroughly **3** : to make very wet **4** : to enter or pass through something by or as if by tiny holes : PERMEATE **5** : to draw in by or as if by absorption

²**soak** *n* **1** : the act or process of letting something stay in a liquid for a long time to soften or clean it **2** : a long bath

¹**soap** *n* : a substance that is used for washing

²**soap** *vb* **soaped; soap·ing** : to rub a cleaning substance over or into something

soap·stone *n* : a soft stone that has a soapy or greasy feeling

soapy *adj* **soap·i·er; soap·i·est 1** : covered with soap **2** : containing soap **3** : like soap

soar *vb* **soared; soar·ing 1** : to fly or glide through the air often at a great height **2** : to increase quickly **3** : to rise quickly **4** : to rise to a great height

¹**sob** *vb* **sobbed; sob·bing 1** : to cry noisily with short sudden breaths **2** : to say while crying noisily

²**sob** *n* : an act or the sound of crying loudly with short sudden breaths

¹**so·ber** *adj* **1** : not drinking too much : TEMPERATE **2** : not drunk **3** : having or showing a serious attitude : SOLEMN **4** : having a plain color **5** : carefully reasoned or considered : REALISTIC

²**sober** *vb* **so·bered; so·ber·ing 1** : to make or become less drunk **2** : to make or become serious or thoughtful

so–called *adj* : commonly or wrongly named

soc·cer *n* : a game played between two teams of eleven players in which a round inflated ball is moved toward a goal usually by kicking

so·cia·ble *adj* **1** : liking to be around other people : FRIENDLY **2** : involving or encouraging friendliness or pleasant companionship with other people

¹**so·cial** *adj* **1** : enjoying other people : SOCIABLE **2** : relating to interaction with other people especially for pleasure **3** : of or relating to human beings as a group **4** : living naturally in groups or communities **5** : relating to or based on rank in a particular society — **so·cial·ly** *adv*

²**social** *n* : a friendly gathering usually for a special reason

so·cial·ism *n* : a social system or theory in which the government owns and controls the means of production (as factories) and distribution of goods

so·cial·ist *n* : a person who supports socialism

social studies *n pl* : the studies (as civics, history, and geography) that deal with human relationships and the way society works

so·ci·ety *n, pl* **so·ci·et·ies** **1** : a community or group of people having common traditions, institutions, and interests **2** : all of the people of the world **3** : a group of persons with a common interest, belief, or purpose **4** : friendly association with others

¹sock *n, pl* **socks** : a knitted or woven covering for the foot usually reaching past the ankle and sometimes to the knee

²sock *vb* **socked; sock·ing :** ¹HIT 1, PUNCH

³sock *n* : ³PUNCH

sock·et *n* : a small opening or hollow part that forms a holder for something

sod *n* : the upper layer of the soil that is filled with roots (as of grass)

so·da *n* **1** : a powdery substance like salt used in washing and in making glass or soap **2** : BAKING SODA **3** : SODA WATER **4** : SODA POP **5** : a sweet drink made of soda water, flavoring, and often ice cream

soda pop *n* : a beverage containing soda water, flavoring, and a sweet syrup

soda water *n* : water with carbon dioxide added

sod·den *adj* : SOGGY

so·di·um *n* : a soft waxy silver-white chemical element occurring in nature in combined form (as in salt)

sodium bicarbonate *n* : BAKING SODA

sodium chlo·ride *n* : ¹SALT 1

so·fa *n* : a long upholstered seat usually with a back and arms

¹soft *adj* **soft·er; soft·est** **1** : not hard, solid, or firm **2** : smooth or pleasant to touch **3** : having a soothing or comfortable effect : not bright or glaring **4** : quiet in pitch or volume **5** : not strong or forceful : GENTLE **6** : involving little work or effort : EASY **7** : sounding like the *c* in *ace* and the *g* in *gem* **8** : easily affected by emotions : sympathetic and kind **9** : lacking in strength or fitness **10** : free from substances that prevent lathering of soap **11** : not containing alcohol — **soft·ness** *n*

²soft *adv* **softer; softest** : SOFTLY

soft·ball *n* **1** : a game like baseball played with a larger ball thrown underhand **2** : the ball used in softball

soft·en *vb* **soft·ened; soft·en·ing** **1** : to make or become soft or less firm **2** : to

make or become gentler or less harsh — **soft·en·er** *n*

soft·ly *adv* : in a soft way : quietly or gently

soft·ware *n* : the programs and related information used by a computer

soft·wood *n* : the wood of a tree (as a pine or spruce) that has needles as distinguished from the wood of a tree (as a maple) with broad leaves

sog·gy *adj* **sog·gi·er; sog·gi·est** : heavy with water or moisture

¹soil *vb* **soiled; soil·ing** : to make or become dirty

²soil *n* **1** : the loose surface material of the earth in which plants grow **2** : COUNTRY 2, LAND — **soil·less** *adj*

¹so·journ *n* : a temporary stay

²sojourn *vb* **so·journed; so·journ·ing :** to stay as a temporary resident

sol *n* : the fifth note of the musical scale

so·lace *n* **1** : comfort in times of sorrow or worry **2** : something that gives comfort

so·lar *adj* **1** : of or relating to the sun **2** : measured by the earth's course around the sun **3** : produced or made to work by the action of the sun's light or heat

solar system *n* : the sun and the planets, asteroids, comets, and meteors that revolve around it

sold *past and past participle of* SELL

¹sol·der *n* : a metal or a mixture of metals used when melted to join or repair surfaces of metal

²solder *vb* **sol·dered; sol·der·ing :** to join together or repair with solder

sol·dier *n* : a person in military service and especially an enlisted person who is in the army

¹sole *n* **1** : the bottom of the foot **2** : the bottom of a shoe, slipper, or boot

²sole *vb* **soled; sol·ing :** to put a new sole on

³sole *n* : a flatfish that has a small mouth and small eyes set close together and is often used for food

⁴sole *adj* **1** : ¹SINGLE 1, ONLY **2** : limited or belonging only to the person or group mentioned

sole·ly *adv* **1** : without another involved : ALONE **2** : ²ONLY 2

sol·emn *adj* **1** : very serious or formal in manner, behavior, or expression **2** : done or made seriously and thoughtfully — **sol·emn·ly** *adv*

so·lem·ni·ty *n, pl* **so·lem·ni·ties** **1** : a serious or formal ceremony **2** : formal dignity

so·lic·it *vb* **so·lic·it·ed; so·lic·it·ing** **1** : to come to with a request or plea **2** : to try to get by asking or pleading

¹sol·id *adj* **1** : not hollow **2** : not loose or spongy : COMPACT **3** : neither liquid nor gaseous **4** : made firmly and well **5** : being without a break, interruption, or change **6** : UNANIMOUS 1 **7** : RELIABLE, DEPENDABLE **8** : of one material, kind, or color — **sol·id·ly** *adv*

²**solid** *n* **1** : something (as a cube) that has length, width, and thickness **2** : a substance that keeps its size and shape : a solid substance

so·lid·i·fy *vb* **so·lid·i·fied; so·lid·i·fy·ing** : to make or become solid

sol·i·taire *n* : a card game played by one person alone

sol·i·tary *adj* **1** : all alone : without anyone or anything else **2** : seldom visited : LONELY **3** : growing or living alone : not one of a group or cluster

sol·i·tude *n* : the quality or state of being alone or away from others : SECLUSION

¹**so·lo** *n, pl* **solos 1** : a piece of music performed by one singer or musician **2** : an action done alone

²**solo** *adv or adj* : without another person : ALONE

³**solo** *vb* **so·loed; so·lo·ing** : to do something (as perform music or fly an airplane) alone or without an instructor

so·lo·ist *n* : a person who performs a solo

sol·stice *n* : the time of year when the sun passes overhead the farthest north (**summer solstice**, about June 22) or south (**winter solstice**, about December 22) of the equator

sol·u·ble *adj* **1** : capable of being dissolved in liquid **2** : capable of being solved or explained

so·lu·tion *n* **1** : the act or process of solving **2** : an answer to a problem : EXPLANATION **3** : the act or process by which a solid, liquid, or gas is dissolved in a liquid **4** : a liquid in which something has been dissolved

solve *vb* **solved; solv·ing** : to find the answer to or a solution for

sol·vent *n* : a usually liquid substance in which other substances can be dissolved or dispersed

som·ber *or* **som·bre** *adj* **1** : very sad or serious **2** : being dark and gloomy : DULL

som·bre·ro *n, pl* **som·bre·ros** : a tall hat with a very wide brim worn especially in Mexico

¹**some** *adj* **1** : not known, named, or specified **2** : being one, a part, or an unspecified number of something **3** : being of an amount or number that is not mentioned

²**some** *pron* : a certain number or amount

¹**-some** *adj suffix* : distinguished by a specified thing, quality, state, or action

²**-some** *n suffix* : group of so many members

¹**some·body** *pron* : a person who is not known, named, or specified

²**somebody** *n, pl* **some·bod·ies** : a person of importance

some·day *adv* : at some future time

some·how *adv* : in a way that is not known or certain

some·one *pron* : a person who is not known, named, or specified

¹**som·er·sault** *n* : a movement in which someone makes a complete turn by bringing the feet over the head

²**somersault** *vb* **som·er·sault·ed; som·er·sault·ing** : to perform a movement in which a person makes a complete turn by bringing the feet over the head

some·thing *pron* **1** : a thing that is not known or named **2** : a thing or amount that is clearly known but not named **3** : SOMEWHAT

some·time *adv* **1** : at a future time **2** : at a time not known or not specified

some·times *adv* : now and then : OCCASIONALLY

some·way *adv* : SOMEHOW

¹**some·what** *pron* : some amount or extent

²**somewhat** *adv* : to some extent

some·where *adv* **1** : in, at, or to a place not known or named **2** : rather close to

son *n* **1** : a male child or offspring **2** : a man or boy closely associated with or thought of as a child of something (as a country, race, or religion)

so·nar *n* : a device for detecting objects underwater using reflected sound waves

so·na·ta *n* : a musical composition for one or two instruments consisting of three or four separate sections in different forms and keys

song *n* **1** : a short musical composition of words and music **2** : the act or art of singing **3** : a series of usually musical sounds produced by an animal and especially a bird **4** : a small amount

song·bird *n* : a bird that produces a series of usually musical sounds

son·ic *adj* : using, produced by, or relating to sound waves

sonic boom *n* : a sound like an explosion that is made by an aircraft traveling faster than the speed of sound

son–in–law *n, pl* **sons–in–law** : the husband of a person's daughter

son·ny *n, pl* **son·nies** : a young boy — used mostly by an older person to address a boy

so·no·rous *adj* : loud, deep, or rich in sound : RESONANT

soon *adv* **soon·er; soon·est 1** : without delay : before long **2** : in a prompt way

: QUICKLY **3** : before long **4** : ¹EARLY 2 **5**
: by choice : WILLINGLY

soot *n* : a black powder formed when something is burned : the very fine powder that colors smoke

soothe *vb* **soothed; sooth·ing** **1** : to please by praise or attention **2** : RELIEVE 1 **3** : to calm down : COMFORT

sooth·say·er *n* : a person who claims to foretell events

sooty *adj* **soot·i·er; soot·i·est** **1** : covered with soot **2** : like soot in color

sop *vb* **sopped; sop·ping** **1** : to soak or dip in or as if in liquid **2** : to mop or soak up

so·phis·ti·cat·ed *adj* **1** : very complicated : COMPLEX **2** : having a lot of knowledge about the world especially through experience **3** : appealing to a person's intelligence

soph·o·more *n* : a student in his or her second year at a high school or college

so·pra·no *n, pl* **so·pra·nos** **1** : the highest part in harmony that has four parts **2** : the highest singing voice of women or boys **3** : a singer or an instrument having a soprano range or part

sor·cer·er *n* : a person who practices sorcery or witchcraft : WIZARD

sor·cer·ess *n* : a woman who practices sorcery or witchcraft : WITCH

sor·cery *n, pl* **sor·cer·ies** : the use of magic : WITCHCRAFT

sor·did *adj* **1** : very dirty : FILTHY **2** : of low moral quality

¹sore *adj* **sor·er; sor·est** **1** : very painful or sensitive : TENDER **2** : hurt or red and swollen so as to be or seem painful **3** : causing emotional distress **4** : ANGRY — **sore·ly** *adv* — **sore·ness** *n*

²sore *n* : a sore or painful spot on the body usually with the skin broken or bruised and often with infection

sor·ghum *n* **1** : a tall grass that is grown for forage and grain **2** : a sweet syrup from the juice of sorghum stems

so·ror·i·ty *n, pl* **so·ror·i·ties** : a club of girls or women especially at a college

¹sor·rel *n* **1** : a light reddish brown horse often with a white mane and tail **2** : a brownish orange to light brown

²sorrel *n* : any of several plants with sour juice

¹sor·row *n* **1** : sadness felt after a loss (as of someone or something loved) **2** : a cause of grief or sadness **3** : a feeling of regret

²sorrow *vb* **sor·rowed; sor·row·ing** : to feel or express sorrow : GRIEVE

sor·row·ful *adj* **1** : full of or showing sadness **2** : causing sadness

sor·ry *adj* **sor·ri·er; sor·ri·est** **1** : feeling sorrow or regret **2** : causing sorrow, pity, or scorn : PITIFUL

¹sort *n* **1** : a group of persons or things that have something in common : KIND **2** : PERSON 1, INDIVIDUAL **3** : general disposition : NATURE — **out of sorts** **1** : not feeling well **2** : easily angered : IRRITABLE

²sort *vb* **sort·ed; sort·ing** **1** : to separate and arrange according to kind or class **2** : ¹SEARCH 1

SOS *n* **1** : an international radio code distress signal used especially by ships and airplanes calling for help **2** : a call for help

¹so–so *adv* : fairly well

²so–so *adj* : neither very good nor very bad

sought *past and past participle of* SEEK

soul *n* **1** : the spiritual part of a person believed to give life to the body **2** : the essential or most important part of something **3** : a person who leads or stirs others to action : LEADER **4** : a person's moral and emotional nature **5** : human being : PERSON **6** : a style of music expressing deep emotion that was created by African-Americans

¹sound *adj* **1** : free from disease or weakness : HEALTHY **2** : solid and strong **3** : free from error **4** : showing good sense : WISE **5** : SEVERE 2 **6** : deep and undisturbed — **sound·ly** *adv* — **sound·ness** *n*

²sound *adv* : to the full extent

³sound *n* **1** : the sensation experienced through the sense of hearing : an instance or occurrence of this **2** : one of the noises that together make up human speech **3** : the suggestion carried or given by something heard or read **4** : hearing distance : EARSHOT — **sound·less** *adj* — **sound·less·ly** *adv*

⁴sound *vb* **sound·ed; sound·ing** **1** : to make or cause to make a sound or noise **2** : PRONOUNCE 1 **3** : to order, signal, or indicate by a sound **4** : to make known : PROCLAIM **5** : to make or give an impression especially when heard

⁵sound *n* : a long stretch of water that is wider than a strait and often connects two larger bodies of water or forms a channel between the mainland and an island

⁶sound *vb* **sound·ed; sound·ing** **1** : to measure the depth of (as by a weighted line dropped down from the surface) **2** : to try to find out the views or intentions of a person

sound·proof *adj* : capable of keeping sound from entering or escaping

sound wave *n* : a wave that is produced when a sound is made and is responsible for carrying the sound to the ear

soup *n* : a liquid food made by cooking vegetables, meat, or fish in a large amount of liquid

¹sour *adj* **sour·er; sour·est** **1** : having an

acid or tart taste **2** : having spoiled : not fresh **3** : suggesting decay **4** : not pleasant or friendly — **sour·ly** adv — **sour·ness** n

²sour vb **soured; sour·ing 1** : to make or become acid or tart in taste (as by spoiling) **2** : to lose or cause to lose interest or enthusiasm **3** : to harm or damage

source n **1** : a cause or starting point **2** : the beginning of a stream of water **3** : someone or something that supplies information **4** : someone or something that provides what is needed

sou·sa·phone n : a large circular tuba designed to rest on the player's shoulder and used chiefly in marching bands

¹south adv : to or toward the south

²south adj : placed toward, facing, or coming from the south

³south n **1** : the direction to the right of one facing east : the compass point opposite to north **2** cap : regions or countries south of a point that is mentioned or understood

¹South American n : a person born or living in South America

²South American adj : of or relating to South America or the South American people

south·bound adj : going south

¹south·east adv : to or toward the direction between south and east

²southeast adj : placed toward, facing, or coming from the southeast

³southeast n **1** : the direction between south and east **2** cap : regions or countries southeast of a point that is mentioned or understood

south·east·er·ly adv or adj **1** : from the southeast **2** : toward the southeast

south·east·ern adj **1** often cap : of, relating to, or like that of the Southeast **2** : lying toward or coming from the southeast

south·er·ly adj or adv **1** : from the south **2** : toward the south

south·ern adj **1** often cap : of, relating to, or like that of the South **2** : lying toward or coming from the south

south·paw n : a person (as a baseball pitcher) who is left-handed

south pole n, often cap S&P **1** : the most southern point of the earth : the southern end of the earth's axis **2** : the end of a magnet that points toward the south when the magnet is free to swing

south·ward adv or adj : toward the south

¹south·west adv : to or toward the direction between south and west

²southwest adj : placed toward, facing, or coming from the southwest

³southwest n **1** : the direction between south and west **2** cap : regions or countries

southwest of a point that is mentioned or understood

south·west·er·ly adv or adj **1** : from the southwest **2** : toward the southwest

south·west·ern adj **1** often cap : of, relating to, or like that of the Southwest **2** : lying toward or coming from the southwest

sou·ve·nir n : something that serves as a reminder

¹sov·er·eign n **1** : a person (as a king or queen) having the highest power and authority **2** : an old British gold coin

²sovereign adj **1** : highest in power or authority **2** : having independent authority **3** : of the most important kind

sov·er·eign·ty n, pl **sov·er·eign·ties 1** : supreme power especially over a political unit (as a country) **2** : a country's independent authority and right of self-control

¹sow n : an adult female pig

²sow vb **sowed; sown** or **sowed; sow·ing 1** : to plant or scatter (as seed) for growing **2** : to cover with or as if with scattered seed for growing **3** : to set in motion : cause to exist — **sow·er** n

sow bug n : WOOD LOUSE

soy·bean n : the edible seed of an Asian plant that is rich in protein

soy sauce n : a brown sauce made from soybeans and used especially in Chinese and Japanese cooking

¹space n **1** : a part of a distance, area, or volume that can be measured **2** : a certain place set apart or available **3** : the area without limits in which all things exist and move **4** : a period of time **5** : the region beyond the earth's atmosphere **6** : an empty place

²space vb **spaced; spac·ing** : to place or separate with some distance or time between

space·craft n, pl **spacecraft** : a vehicle for travel beyond the earth's atmosphere

space·ship n : SPACECRAFT

space shuttle n : a spacecraft designed to transport people and cargo between earth and space that can be used repeatedly

space station n : an artificial satellite designed to stay in orbit permanently and to be occupied by humans for long periods

space suit n : a suit that covers the entire body and is equipped to keep its wearer alive in space

spa·cious adj : having ample space

spade n : a digging tool with a long handle that has a flat blade which can be pushed into the ground with the foot

spa·ghet·ti n : pasta made in the shape of long thin strings

¹spam n : e-mail sent to a large number of addresses and usually containing advertising

²spam *vb* **spammed; spam·ming** : to send spam to — **spam·mer** *n*

¹span *n* **1** : a limited portion of time **2** : the spread (as of an arch or bridge) from one support to another **3** : the width of something from one side to another

²span *vb* **spanned; span·ning 1** : to reach or extend across **2** : to continue over a period of time

span·gle *n* : SEQUIN

Span·iard *n* : a person born or living in Spain

span·iel *n* : a small or medium-sized dog with a thick wavy coat, long drooping ears, and usually short legs

¹Span·ish *adj* : of or relating to Spain, its people, or the Spanish language

²Spanish *n* **1** : the language of Spain and the countries colonized by Spaniards **2 Spanish** *pl* : the people of Spain

spank *vb* **spanked; spank·ing** : to strike on the buttocks with the open hand

¹spank·ing *adj* : BRISK 1, LIVELY

²spanking *adv* : ¹VERY 1

¹spar *n* : a long rounded piece of wood or metal (as a mast) to which a sail is fastened

²spar *vb* **sparred; spar·ring 1** : to box or make boxing movements with the fists for practice or for fun **2** : to argue often in a playful way

¹spare *vb* **spared; spar·ing 1** : to keep from being punished or harmed : show mercy to **2** : to free from having to go through something difficult **3** : to keep from using or spending **4** : to give up especially as not really needed **5** : to have left over

²spare *adj* **spar·er; spar·est 1** : held in reserve (as for an emergency) **2** : being over what is needed **3** : somewhat thin **4** : SCANTY

³spare *n* **1** : a replacement or duplicate piece or part **2** : the knocking down of all ten bowling pins with the first two balls

spare·ribs *n pl* : a cut of pork ribs

spar·ing *adj* : careful in the use of money or supplies — **spar·ing·ly** *adv*

¹spark *n* **1** : a small bit of burning material **2** : a hot glowing bit struck from a mass (as by steel on flint) **3** : a short bright flash of electricity between two points **4** : ²SPARKLE 1 **5** : ¹TRACE 2

²spark *vb* **sparked; spark·ing 1** : to give off or cause to give off small bits of burning material or short bright flashes of electricity **2** : to set off

¹spar·kle *vb* **spar·kled; spar·kling 1** : to give off small flashes of light **2** : to be lively or bright

²sparkle *n* **1** : a little flash of light **2** : the quality of being bright or giving off small flashes of light

spar·kler *n* : a small firework that throws off very bright sparks as it burns

spark plug *n* : a device used in an engine to produce a spark that ignites a fuel mixture

spar·row *n* : a small songbird that has usually brownish or grayish feathers

sparrow hawk *n* : a small hawk

sparse *adj* **spars·er; spars·est** : not thickly grown or settled — **sparse·ly** *adv*

spasm *n* **1** : a sudden uncontrolled and often painful tightening of muscles **2** : a sudden, strong, and temporary effort, emotion, or outburst

spas·mod·ic *adj* : relating to or affected by spasm : involving spasms — **spas·mod·i·cal·ly** *adv*

¹spat *past and past participle of* SPIT

²spat *n* : a cloth or leather covering for the instep and ankle men once wore over shoes

³spat *n* : a brief unimportant quarrel

spa·tial *adj* : of or relating to space

¹spat·ter *vb* **spat·tered; spat·ter·ing 1** : to splash with drops or small bits of something wet **2** : to scatter by splashing

²spatter *n* **1** : the act or sound of something splashing in drops **2** : a drop or splash spattered on something : a spot or stain due to spattering

spat·u·la *n* **1** : a tool resembling a knife with a broad flexible blade that is used mostly for spreading or mixing soft substances **2** : a kitchen utensil with a long handle and a wide blade used for scraping batter from a bowl or for lifting and flipping food

¹spawn *vb* **spawned; spawn·ing** : to produce or deposit eggs

²spawn *n* : the eggs of a water animal (as an oyster or fish) that produces many small eggs

spay *vb* **spayed; spay·ing** : to remove the ovaries of (a female animal)

speak *vb* **spoke; spo·ken; speak·ing 1** : to utter words : TALK **2** : to utter in words **3** : to mention in speech or writing **4** : to use or be able to use in talking — **speak out** : to express an opinion openly — **speak up 1** : to speak loudly and clearly **2** : to express an opinion openly

speak·er *n* **1** : a person who speaks **2** : a person who conducts a meeting **3** : LOUDSPEAKER

¹spear *n* **1** : a weapon with a long straight handle and sharp head or blade used for throwing or jabbing **2** : an instrument with a sharp point and curved hooks used in stabbing fish

²spear *vb* **speared; spear·ing** : to strike or pierce with or as if with a spear

³spear *n* : a usually young blade or sprout (as of grass)

¹spear·head *n* **1** : the head or point of a spear **2** : the person, thing, or group that is the leading force (as in a development or an attack)

²spearhead *vb* **spear·head·ed; spear·head·ing** : to serve as leader of

spear·mint *n* : a common mint used for flavoring

spe·cial *adj* **1** : unusual and better in some way : EXTRAORDINARY **2** : liked very well **3** : different from others : UNIQUE **4** : ¹EXTRA **5** : meant for a particular purpose or occasion — **spe·cial·ly** *adv*

special education *n* : classes or instruction designed for students with special educational needs

spe·cial·ist *n* **1** : a person who studies or works at a special occupation or branch of learning **2** : an enlisted person in the army with a rank similar to that of corporal

spe·cial·ize *vb* **spe·cial·ized; spe·cial·iz·ing** **1** : to limit attention or energy to one business, subject, or study **2** : to change and develop so as to be suited for some particular use or living conditions

spe·cial·ty *n, pl* **spe·cial·ties** : something for which a person or place is known

spe·cies *n, pl* **species 1** : a group of similar living things that ranks below the genus in scientific classification and is made up of individuals able to produce offspring with one another **2** : a class of things of the same kind and with the same name : KIND, SORT

spe·cif·ic *adj* **1** : relating to or being an example of a certain kind of thing **2** : relating to a particular individual or situation **3** : clearly and exactly presented or stated — **spe·cif·ic·al·ly** *adv*

spec·i·fi·ca·tion *n* **1** : the act or process of mentioning exactly and clearly **2** : a single item exactly and clearly mentioned **3** : a description of work to be done or materials to be used — often used in pl.

spec·i·fy *vb* **spec·i·fied; spec·i·fy·ing 1** : to mention or name exactly and clearly **2** : to include in a description of work to be done or materials to be used

spec·i·men *n* **1** : something collected as a sample or for examination **2** : a notable example of something **3** : an example of a type of person

speck *n* **1** : a small spot or blemish **2** : a very small amount : BIT

¹speck·le *n* : a small mark (as of color)

²speckle *vb* **speck·led; speck·ling** : to mark or be marked with small spots

spec·ta·cle *n* **1** : an unusual or impressive public display (as a big parade) **2 spectacles** *pl* : EYEGLASSES **3** : an object of curiosity or contempt

spec·tac·u·lar *adj* : STRIKING, SHOWY

spec·ta·tor *n* : a person who looks on (as at a sports event)

spec·ter *or* **spec·tre** *n* **1** : GHOST **2** : something that haunts or bothers the mind

spec·trum *n, pl* **spec·tra** *or* **spec·trums** : the group of different colors including red, orange, yellow, green, blue, indigo, and violet seen when light passes through a prism and falls on a surface or when sunlight is affected by drops of water (as in a rainbow)

spec·u·late *vb* **spec·u·lat·ed; spec·u·lat·ing 1** : to think or wonder about something **2** : to come up with ideas or theories about something **3** : to engage in a risky but possibly very profitable business deal

spec·u·la·tion *n* **1** : ²GUESS **2** : the taking of a big risk in business in hopes of making a big profit

SpEd, SPED *abbr* special education

speech *n* **1** : the communication or expression of thoughts in spoken words **2** : something that is spoken : STATEMENT **3** : a public talk **4** : a form of communication (as a language or dialect) used by a particular group **5** : a way of speaking **6** : the ability to speak

speech·less *adj* : unable to speak especially because of a strong emotion

¹speed *n* **1** : quickness in movement or action **2** : rate of moving or doing

²speed *vb* **sped** *or* **speed·ed; speed·ing 1** : to move or cause to move fast : HURRY **2** : to go or drive at too high a rate of movement **3** : to increase the rate of an action or movement — **speed up** : to move more quickly

speed·boat *n* : a motorboat designed to go fast

speed bump *n* : a low ridge built across a roadway (as in a parking lot) to limit vehicle speed

speed·om·e·ter *n* : an instrument that measures speed

speedy *adj* **speed·i·er; speed·i·est** : moving or taking place fast — **speed·i·ly** *adv*

¹spell *vb* **spelled; spell·ing 1** : to name, write, or print in order the letters of a word **2** : to make up the letters of **3** : to have (such) a spelling **4** : to amount to : MEAN

²spell *n* **1** : a spoken word or group of words believed to have magic power : CHARM **2** : a very strong influence

³spell *n* **1** : a short period of time **2** : a stretch of a specified kind of weather **3** : a period of bodily or mental distress or disorder **4** : a person's turn at work or duty **5** : a period spent in a job or occupation

⁴spell *vb* **spelled; spelling** : to take the place of for a time : RELIEVE

spell·bound *adj* : having the interest or attention held by or as if by magic power

spell–check·er *n* : a computer program that shows the user any words that might be incorrectly spelled

spell·er *n* **1** : a person who spells words **2** : a book with exercises for teaching spelling

spell·ing *n* **1** : an exercise or the practice of forming words from letters **2** : the letters composing a word

spend *vb* **spent; spend·ing 1** : to use (money) to pay for something **2** : to cause or allow (as time) to pass **3** : to use wastefully : SQUANDER

spend·thrift *n* : a person who uses up money wastefully

spent *adj* **1** : used up **2** : drained of energy

sperm *n* : SPERM CELL

sperm cell *n* : a male reproductive cell of animals and plants that can unite with an egg cell to form a new individual cell

sperm whale *n* : a huge whale with a large head having a closed cavity that contains a mixture of wax and oil

spew *vb* **spewed; spew·ing** : to pour out

sphere *n* **1** : an object (as the moon) shaped like a ball **2** : a figure so shaped that every point on its surface is an equal distance from its center **3** : a field of influence or activity

spher·i·cal *adj* : relating to or having the form of a sphere

sphinx *n* : a mythical figure of ancient Egypt having the body of a lion and the head of a man, a ram, or a hawk

¹spice *n* **1** : a seasoning (as pepper or nutmeg) that comes from a dried plant part and that is usually a powder or seed **2** : something that adds interest

²spice *vb* **spiced; spic·ing** : to add something that gives flavor or interest

spick–and–span *or* **spic–and–span** *adj* **1** : quite new and unused **2** : very clean and neat

spicy *adj* **spic·i·er; spic·i·est 1** : flavored with or containing spice **2** : somewhat shocking or indecent — **spic·i·ness** *n*

spi·der *n* **1** : a wingless animal that is somewhat like an insect but has eight legs instead of six and a body divided into two parts instead of three and that often spins threads of silk into webs for catching prey **2** : a cast-iron frying pan

spi·der·web *n* : the silken web spun by most spiders and used as a resting place and a trap for prey

spig·ot *n* **1** : a plug used to stop the vent in a barrel **2** : FAUCET

¹spike *n* **1** : a very large nail **2** : something pointed like a nail **3** : one of the metal objects attached to the heel and sole of a shoe (as a baseball shoe) to prevent slipping

²spike *vb* **spiked; spik·ing 1** : to fasten with large nails **2** : to pierce or cut with or on a large nail **3** : to hit or throw (a ball) sharply downward **4** : to add alcohol or drugs to

³spike *n* **1** : a tight mass of grain **2** : a long usually rather narrow flower cluster in which the blossoms grow very close to a central stem

¹spill *vb* **spilled** *also* **spilt; spill·ing 1** : to cause or allow to fall, flow, or run out so as to be wasted or scattered **2** : to flow or run out, over, or off and become wasted or scattered **3** : to cause (blood) to flow by wounding **4** : to make known

²spill *n* **1** : an act of spilling **2** : a fall especially from a horse or vehicle **3** : something spilled

¹spin *vb* **spun; spin·ning 1** : to turn or cause to turn round and round rapidly : TWIRL **2** : to make yarn or thread from (fibers) **3** : to make (yarn or thread) from fibers **4** : to form threads or a web or cocoon by giving off a sticky fluid that quickly hardens **5** : to feel as if in a whirl **6** : to make up and tell using the imagination **7** : to move swiftly on wheels or in a vehicle **8** : to make, shape, or produce by or as if by whirling — **spin·ner** *n*

²spin *n* **1** : a rapid motion of turning around and around **2** : a short trip in or on a wheeled vehicle

spin·ach *n* : a garden plant with usually large dark green leaves that are eaten cooked or raw as a vegetable

spi·nal *adj* : of, relating to, or located near the backbone or the spinal cord

spinal column *n* : BACKBONE 1

spinal cord *n* : a thick bundle of nerves that extends from the brain down through the cavity of the backbone and connects with nerves throughout the body to carry information to and from the brain

spin·dle *n* **1** : a slender round rod or stick with narrowed ends by which thread is twisted in spinning and on which it is wound **2** : something (as an axle or shaft) which has a slender round shape and on which something turns

spin·dly *adj* : being thin and long or tall and usually feeble or weak

spine *n* **1** : BACKBONE 1 **2** : a stiff pointed part growing from the surface of a plant or animal

spine·less *adj* **1** : lacking spines **2** : having no backbone **3** : lacking spirit, courage, or determination

spin·et *n* **1** : a harpsichord with one keyboard and only one string for each note **2** : a small upright piano

spinning wheel *n* : a small machine driven by the hand or foot that is used to spin yarn or thread

spin·ster *n* : an unmarried woman past the usual age for marrying

spiny *adj* **spin·i·er; spin·i·est** : covered with spines

spiny lobster *n* : a sea animal that is related to and resembles the lobster

spi·ra·cle *n* : an opening on the body (as of an insect) used for breathing

¹spi·ral *adj* **1** : winding or circling around a center and gradually getting closer to or farther away from it **2** : circling around a center like the thread of a screw

²spiral *n* **1** : a single turn or coil in a spiral object **2** : something having a form that winds or circles around a center

³spiral *vb* **spi·raled** *or* **spi·ralled; spi·ral·ing** *or* **spi·ral·ling** : to move in or as if in a winding or circular path

spire *n* **1** : a pointed roof especially of a tower **2** : STEEPLE

spi·rea *or* **spi·raea** *n* : a shrub related to the rose that bears clusters of small white or pink flowers

¹spir·it *n* **1** : ¹MOOD **2** : a being (as a ghost) whose existence cannot be explained **3** : a lively or brisk quality **4** : a force within a human being thought to give the body life, energy, and power : SOUL **5** : an attitude or feeling **6** : PERSON 1 **7** : an alcoholic liquor — usually used in pl. **8** *cap* : the active presence of God in human life : the third person of the Trinity **9 spirits** *pl* : a solution in alcohol **10** : real meaning or intention — **spir·it·less** *adj*

²spirit *vb* **spir·it·ed; spir·it·ing** : to carry off secretly or mysteriously

spir·it·ed *adj* : full of courage or energy

¹spir·i·tu·al *adj* **1** : of, relating to, or consisting of spirit : not bodily or material **2** : of or relating to sacred or religious matters — **spir·i·tu·al·ly** *adv*

²spiritual *n* : a religious folk song developed especially among black people of the southern United States

¹spit *vb* **spit** *or* **spat; spit·ting** **1** : to force (saliva) from the mouth **2** : to force (something) from the mouth **3** : to express by or as if by spitting **4** : to give off usually briskly : EMIT **5** : to rain lightly or snow in flurries — **spit up** : ²VOMIT

²spit *n* **1** : SALIVA **2** : a foamy material given off by some insects **3** : perfect likeness

³spit *n* **1** : a thin pointed rod for holding meat over a fire **2** : a small point of land that runs out into a body of water

¹spite *n* : dislike or hatred for another person with a wish to torment, anger, or defeat — **in spite of** : without being prevented by

²spite *vb* **spit·ed; spit·ing** : ANNOY, ANGER

spite·ful *adj* : filled with or showing spite : MALICIOUS — **spite·ful·ly** *adv*

spitting image *n* : IMAGE 2

spit·tle *n* **1** : SALIVA **2** : ²SPIT 3

¹splash *vb* **splashed; splash·ing** **1** : to hit (something liquid or sloppy) and cause to move and scatter roughly **2** : to wet or soil by spattering with something wet (as water or mud) **3** : to move or strike with a splashing sound **4** : to spread or scatter like a splashed liquid

²splash *n* **1** : material that has been hit and made to scatter **2** : a spot or smear from or as if from liquid that has been hit and made to scatter **3** : the sound or action of liquid that has been hit and made to scatter

¹splat·ter *vb* **splat·tered; splat·ter·ing** : to splash against something in large drops

²splatter *n* : ²SPLASH 2

spleen *n* : an organ near the stomach that destroys worn-out red blood cells and produces some of the white blood cells

splen·did *adj* **1** : impressive in beauty, excellence, or magnificence **2** : having or showing splendor : BRILLIANT **3** : EXCELLENT — **splen·did·ly** *adv*

splen·dor *n* **1** : great brightness **2** : POMP, GLORY **3** : an impressive feature

¹splice *vb* **spliced; splic·ing** **1** : to unite (as two ropes) by weaving together **2** : to unite (as rails or pieces of film) by connecting the ends together

²splice *n* : the process of joining or a joint made by weaving or connecting the ends together

splint *n* **1** : a thin flexible strip of wood woven together with others in making a chair seat or basket **2** : a rigid device for keeping a broken or displaced bone in place while it heals

¹splin·ter *n* : a thin piece split or torn off lengthwise : SLIVER

²splinter *vb* **splin·tered; splin·ter·ing** : to break into slivers

¹split *vb* **split; split·ting** **1** : to divide lengthwise or by layers **2** : to separate into parts or groups **3** : to burst or break apart or in pieces **4** : to divide into shares or sections

²split *n* **1** : a product or result of dividing, separating, or breaking apart : CRACK **2** : the act or process of dividing, separating, or breaking apart : DIVISION **3** : an action or position in which a person's legs are extended in a straight line and in opposite directions

³split *adj* : divided by or as if by splitting

splurge *vb* **splurged; splurg·ing** : to spend lavishly or give in to indulgence

splut·ter *vb* **splut·tered; splut·ter·ing 1** : to make a noise as if spitting **2** : to speak or say in haste or confusion

¹spoil *vb* **spoiled** *or* **spoilt ; spoil·ing 1** : to damage the character of by allowing too many things or not correcting bad behavior **2** : to damage badly : RUIN **3** : to damage the quality or effect of **4** : to decay or lose freshness, value, or usefulness by being kept too long

²spoil *n* : stolen goods : PLUNDER

spoil·age *n* : the process or result of the decay of food

¹spoke *past of* SPEAK

²spoke *n* : one of the bars or rods extending from the hub of a wheel to the rim

¹spo·ken *past participle of* SPEAK

²spo·ken *adj* **1** : expressed in speech : ORAL **2** : used in speaking **3** : speaking in a specified manner

spokes·man *n, pl* **spokes·men** : a person who speaks for or represents someone or something

spokes·per·son *n* : SPOKESMAN

spokes·wom·an *n, pl* **spokes·wom·en** : a woman who speaks for or represents someone or something

¹sponge *n* **1** : a water animal that lives permanently attached to a solid surface (as the ocean bottom) and has a simple body of loosely connected cells with a skeleton supported by stiff fibers or hard particles **2** : a piece of springy material that forms the skeleton of sponges or is manufactured and is used for cleaning **3** : a pad of folded gauze used in surgery and medicine

²sponge *vb* **sponged; spong·ing 1** : to clean or wipe with a sponge **2** : to get something or live at the expense of another

spongy *adj* **spong·i·er; spong·i·est** : springy and absorbent

¹spon·sor *n* **1** : a person who takes the responsibility for some other person or thing **2** : a person who represents someone being baptized and takes responsibility for his or her spiritual development : GODPARENT **3** : a person or an organization that pays for or plans and carries out a project or activity **4** : a person who gives money to someone participating in an event for charity **5** : a person or an organization that pays the cost of a radio or television program — **spon·sor·ship** *n*

²sponsor *vb* **spon·sored; spon·sor·ing** : to act as sponsor for

spon·ta·ne·ous *adj* **1** : done, said, or produced freely and naturally **2** : acting or tak-

ing place without outside force or cause — **spon·ta·ne·ous·ly** *adv*

spontaneous combustion *n* : a bursting of material into flame from the heat produced within itself through chemical action

¹spook *vb* **spooked; spook·ing** : to make or become frightened

²spook *n* : GHOST, SPECTER

spooky *adj* **spook·i·er; spook·i·est 1** : scary and frightening **2** : suggesting the presence of ghosts

spool *n* : a small cylinder which has a rim or ridge at each end and a hole from end to end for a pin or spindle and on which material (as thread, wire, or tape) is wound

¹spoon *n* : an eating and cooking utensil consisting of a small shallow bowl with a handle

²spoon *vb* **spooned; spoon·ing** : to take up in or as if in a spoon

spoon·bill *n* : a wading bird having a bill which widens and flattens at the tip

spoon·ful *n, pl* **spoon·fuls** *also* **spoons·ful** : as much as a spoon can hold

spore *n* : a reproductive body that is produced by fungi and by some plants and microorganisms and consists of a single cell that is able to produce a new individual — **spored** *adj*

¹sport *n* **1** : physical activity (as running or an athletic game) engaged in for pleasure or exercise **2** : a person who shows good sportsmanship **3** : PASTIME, RECREATION **4** : ¹FUN 3

²sport *vb* **sport·ed; sport·ing** : to wear in a way that attracts attention

sports·man *n, pl* **sports·men** : a person who engages in or is interested in sports and especially outdoor sports (as hunting and fishing)

sports·man·ship *n* : fair play, respect for opponents, and gracious behavior in winning or losing

sports·wom·an *n, pl* **sports·wom·en** : a woman who engages in or is interested in sports and especially outdoor sports

sport–utility vehicle *n* : an automobile similar to a station wagon but built on a light truck frame

¹spot *n* **1** : a small part that is different from the main part **2** : an area soiled or marked (as by dirt) **3** : a particular place **4** : POSITION 3 **5** : FAULT — **spot·ted** *adj* — **on the spot 1** : right away **2** : at the place of action **3** : in difficulty or danger

²spot *vb* **spot·ted; spot·ting 1** : to mark or be marked with spots **2** : to single out : IDENTIFY

spot·less *adj* **1** : free from spot or blemish

2 : perfectly clean or pure — **spot·less·ly** *adv*

¹spot·light *n* **1** : a spot of light used to show up a particular area, person, or thing (as on a stage) **2** : public notice **3** : a lamp used to direct a narrow strong beam of light on a small area

²spotlight *vb* **spot·light·ed** *or* **spot·lit**; **spot·light·ing 1** : to light up with or as if with a spotlight **2** : to bring to public attention

spotted owl *n* : a rare brown owl with white spots and dark stripes that is found from British Columbia to southern California and central Mexico

spot·ty *adj* **spot·ti·er**; **spot·ti·est 1** : having spots **2** : not always the same especially in quality

spouse *n* : a married person : HUSBAND, WIFE

¹spout *vb* **spout·ed**; **spout·ing 1** : to shoot out (liquid) with force **2** : to speak with a long and quick flow of words so as to sound important **3** : to flow out with force : SPURT

²spout *n* **1** : a tube, pipe, or hole through which something (as rainwater) shoots out **2** : a sudden strong stream of fluid

¹sprain *n* : an injury that results from the sudden or severe twisting of a joint with stretching or tearing of ligaments

²sprain *vb* **sprained**; **sprain·ing** : to injure by a sudden or severe twist

sprang *past of* SPRING

¹sprawl *vb* **sprawled**; **sprawl·ing 1** : to lie or sit with arms and legs spread out **2** : to spread out unevenly

²sprawl *n* : the act or posture of spreading out

¹spray *vb* **sprayed**; **spray·ing 1** : to scatter or let fall in a fine mist **2** : to scatter fine mist on or into — **spray·er** *n*

²spray *n* **1** : liquid flying in fine drops like water blown from a wave **2** : a burst of fine mist **3** : a device for scattering fine drops of liquid or mist

³spray *n* : a green or flowering branch or a usually flat arrangement of these

¹spread *vb* **spread**; **spread·ing 1** : to stretch out : EXTEND **2** : to pass or cause to pass from person to person **3** : to open or arrange over a larger area **4** : to increase in size or occurrence **5** : to scatter or be scattered **6** : to give out over a period of time or among a group **7** : to put or have a layer of on a surface **8** : to cover something with **9** : to stretch or move apart **10** : to prepare for a meal : SET

²spread *n* **1** : the act or process of increasing in size, amount, or occurrence **2** : the distance between two points that are farthest to each side **3** : a noticeable display in a magazine or newspaper **4** : a food to be put over

the surface of bread or crackers **5** : a very fine meal : FEAST **6** : a cloth cover for a table or bed

spree *n* : an outburst of an activity

sprig *n* : a small shoot or twig

spright·ly *adj* **spright·li·er**; **spright·li·est** : full of spirit : LIVELY

¹spring *vb* **sprang** *or* **sprung**; **sprung**; **spring·ing 1** : to move suddenly upward or forward : LEAP **2** : to appear or grow quickly or suddenly **3** : to have (a leak) appear **4** : to move quickly by or as if by stretching and springing back **5** : to cause to operate suddenly **6** : to come into being : ARISE

²spring *n* **1** : the season between winter and summer including in the northern hemisphere usually the months of March, April, and May **2** : a twisted or coiled strip of material (as metal) that recovers its original shape when it is released after being squeezed or stretched **3** : the ability of something to return to its orginal shape when it is compressed or stretched **4** : a source of supply (as of water coming up from the ground) **5** : the act or an instance of leaping up or forward **6** : a bouncy or lively quality

spring·board *n* : a flexible board usually fastened at one end and used for jumping high in the air in gymnastics or diving

spring peep·er *n* : a small frog that makes a high peeping sound heard mostly in spring

spring·time *n* : the season of spring

springy *adj* **spring·i·er**; **spring·i·est 1** : able to return to an original shape when twisted or stretched **2** : having or showing a lively and energetic movement

¹sprin·kle *vb* **sprin·kled**; **sprin·kling 1** : to scatter in drops or particles **2** : to scatter over or in or among **3** : to rain lightly — **sprin·kler** *n*

²sprinkle *n* **1** : a light rain **2** : SPRINKLING

sprin·kling *n* : a very small number or amount

¹sprint *vb* **sprint·ed**; **sprint·ing** : to run at top speed especially for a short distance — **sprint·er** *n*

²sprint *n* **1** : a short run at top speed **2** : a race over a short distance

sprite *n* : ELF, FAIRY

sprock·et *n* : one of many points that stick up on the rim of a wheel (**sprocket wheel**) shaped so as to fit into the links of a chain

¹sprout *vb* **sprout·ed**; **sprout·ing** : to produce or cause to produce new growth

²sprout *n* : a young stem of a plant especially when coming directly from a seed or root

¹spruce *n* : an evergreen tree that has short

needles for leaves, drooping cones, and light soft wood

²spruce *vb* **spruced; spruc·ing :** to make (someone or something) neat or stylish in appearance

³spruce *adj* **spruc·er; spruc·est :** neat or stylish in appearance — **spruce·ly** *adv*

sprung *past and past participle of* SPRING

spry *adj* **spri·er** *or* **spry·er; spri·est** *or* **spry·est :** LIVELY 1, ACTIVE

spun *past and past participle of* SPIN

spunk *n* **:** COURAGE, SPIRIT

spunky *adj* **spunk·i·er; spunk·i·est :** full of spirit and courage

¹spur *n* **1 :** a pointed device fastened to the back of a rider's boot and used to urge a horse on **2 :** something that makes a person want to do something **:** INCENTIVE **3 :** a mass of jagged rock coming out from the side of a mountain **4 :** a short section of railway track coming away from the main line **5 :** a usually short pointed growth or projecting part (as a spine on the leg of a rooster) — **spurred** *adj* — **on the spur of the moment :** without thinking for a long time — often used as an adjective

²spur *vb* **spurred; spur·ring 1 :** to urge a horse on with spurs **2 :** INCITE

spurn *vb* **spurned; spurn·ing :** to reject with scorn

¹spurt *vb* **spurt·ed; spurt·ing :** to pour out or make pour out suddenly

²spurt *n* **:** a sudden pouring out

³spurt *n* **:** a brief burst of increased effort, activity, or development

¹sput·ter *vb* **sput·tered; sput·ter·ing 1 :** to spit noisily from the mouth **2 :** to speak in a hasty or explosive way in confusion or excitement **3 :** to make explosive popping sounds

²sputter *n* **:** the act or sound of sputtering

¹spy *vb* **spied; spy·ing 1 :** to watch secretly **2 :** to catch sight of **:** SEE

²spy *n, pl* **spies 1 :** a person who watches the movement or actions of others especially in secret **2 :** a person who tries secretly to get information especially about a country or organization for another country or organization

spy·glass *n* **:** a small telescope

squab *n* **:** a young pigeon especially when ready for use as food

¹squab·ble *n* **:** a noisy quarrel usually over something unimportant

²squabble *vb* **squab·bled; squab·bling :** to quarrel noisily for little or no reason

squad *n* **1 :** a small group of soldiers **2 :** a small group working or playing together

squad car *n* **:** CRUISER 2

squad·ron *n* **1 :** a group of soldiers, ships, or

aircraft moving and working together **2 :** a large group

squal·id *adj* **:** filthy or degraded from a lack of care or money

¹squall *vb* **squalled; squall·ing :** to let out a harsh cry or scream

²squall *n* **:** a harsh cry

³squall *n* **:** a sudden strong gust of wind often with rain or snow

squal·or *n* **:** the quality or state of being squalid

squan·der *vb* **squan·dered; squan·der·ing :** to spend foolishly **:** WASTE

¹square *n* **1 :** a flat geometric figure that has four equal sides and four right angles **2 :** something formed with four equal or roughly equal sides and four right angles **3 :** the product of a number or amount multiplied by itself **4 :** an open place or area where two or more streets meet **5 :** a tool having at least one right angle and two or more straight edges used to mark or test right angles

²square *adj* **squar·er; squar·est 1 :** having four equal sides and four right angles **2 :** being a unit of area consisting of a figure with four right angles and four sides of a given length **3 :** having a specified length in each of two equal dimensions **4 :** having outlines that suggest sharp corners rather than curves **5 :** forming a right angle **6 :** ¹JUST 4, FAIR **7 :** not owing anything **:** EVEN **8 :** large enough to satisfy — **square·ly** *adv*

³square *vb* **squared; squar·ing 1 :** to form with right angles, straight edges, and flat surfaces **2 :** to make straight **3 :** to multiply a number by itself **4 :** AGREE 4 **5 :** ²BALANCE 2, SETTLE

⁴square *adv* **:** in a direct, firm, or honest way

square dance *n* **:** a dance for four couples who form the sides of a square

square knot *n* **:** a knot made of two half-knots tied in opposite directions that does not come untied easily

square–rigged *adj* **:** having the principal sails extended on yards fastened in a horizontal position to the masts at their center

square root *n* **:** a number that when multiplied by itself equals a specified number

¹squash *vb* **squashed; squash·ing :** to beat or press into a soft or flat mass **:** CRUSH

²squash *n* **:** the fruit of a plant related to the gourd that comes in many varieties and is usually eaten as a vegetable

¹squat *vb* **squat·ted; squat·ting 1 :** to crouch by bending the knees fully so as to sit on or close to the heels **2 :** to settle without any right on land that someone else owns **3**

: to settle on government land in order to become its owner

²**squat** *adj* **squat·ter; squat·test 1** : low to the ground **2** : having a short thick body

³**squat** *n* : a position in which the knees are fully bent and the body sits on or close to the heels

¹**squawk** *vb* **squawked; squawk·ing 1** : to make a harsh short cry **2** : to complain or protest loudly or with strong feeling

²**squawk** *n* **1** : a harsh short cry **2** : a noisy complaint

¹**squeak** *vb* **squeaked; squeak·ing 1** : to make a short high-pitched cry or sound **2** : to barely get, win, or pass

²**squeak** *n* : a short high-pitched cry or sound

squeaky *adj* **squeak·i·er; squeak·i·est** : making or likely to make a short high-pitched cry or sound

¹**squeal** *vb* **squealed; squeal·ing 1** : to make a sharp long high-pitched cry or noise **2** : INFORM 2

²**squeal** *n* : a sharp high-pitched cry or noise

squea·mish *adj* : hesitant because of shock or disgust

¹**squeeze** *vb* **squeezed; squeez·ing 1** : to press together from the opposite sides or parts of : COMPRESS **2** : to get by squeezing **3** : to force or crowd in by compressing

²**squeeze** *n* : an act or instance of compressing

squid *n* : a sea mollusk that is related to the octopus and has a long thin soft body with eight short arms and two usually longer tentacles

¹**squint** *vb* **squint·ed; squint·ing 1** : to look or peer with the eyes partly closed **2** : to cause (an eye) to partly close

²**squint** *n* : the action or an instance of causing the eyes to partly close or of looking at something with the eyes partly closed

squire *n* **1** : a person who carries the shield or armor of a knight **2** : ¹ESCORT 1 **3** : an owner of a country estate

squirm *vb* **squirmed; squirm·ing** : to twist about because of nervousness or embarrassment or in an effort to move or escape

squir·rel *n* : a small gnawing animal that is a rodent usually with a bushy tail and soft fur and strong hind legs used especially for leaping among tree branches

¹**squirt** *vb* **squirt·ed; squirt·ing** : to shoot out liquid in a thin stream : SPURT

²**squirt** *n* : a small powerful stream of liquid : JET

Sr. *abbr* **1** senior **2** sister

st. *abbr* state

St. *abbr* **1** saint **2** street

¹**stab** *n* **1** : a wound produced by or as if by a pointed weapon **2** : ²THRUST 1 **3** : ²TRY, EFFORT

²**stab** *vb* **stabbed; stab·bing 1** : to wound or pierce with or as if with a pointed weapon **2** : ¹DRIVE 2, THRUST

sta·bil·i·ty *n, pl* **sta·bil·i·ties** : the condition of being reliable or unlikely to change suddenly or greatly

sta·bi·lize *vb* **sta·bi·lized; sta·bi·liz·ing** : to make or become unlikely to change suddenly or greatly — **sta·bi·liz·er** *n*

¹**sta·ble** *n* : a building in which horses are housed and cared for

²**stable** *vb* **sta·bled; sta·bling** : to put or keep in a stable

³**stable** *adj* **sta·bler; sta·blest 1** : not easily changed or affected **2** : not likely to change suddenly or greatly **3** : LASTING

stac·ca·to *adj* **1** : cut short so as not to sound connected **2** : played or sung with breaks between notes

¹**stack** *n* **1** : a neat pile of objects usually one on top of the other **2** : a large number or amount **3** : a large pile (as of hay) usually shaped like a cone **4** : CHIMNEY 1, SMOKESTACK **5** : a structure with shelves for storing books

²**stack** *vb* **stacked; stack·ing** : to arrange in or form a neat pile

sta·di·um *n, pl* **sta·di·ums** *or* **sta·dia** : a large usually outdoor structure with rows of seats for spectators at sports events

staff *n, pl* **staffs** *or* **staves 1** : a pole, stick, rod, or bar used as a support or as a sign of authority **2 staffs** *pl* : a group of persons serving as assistants to or employees under a chief **3** : the five parallel lines with their four spaces on which music is written **4** : something that is a source of strength **5 staffs** *pl* : a group of military officers who plan and manage for a commanding officer

staff sergeant *n* : a noncommissioned officer in the army, air force, or marine corps ranking above a sergeant

stag *n* : an adult male deer

¹**stage** *n* **1** : a raised floor (as for speaking or performing) **2** : a step forward in a journey, a task, a process, or a development : PHASE **3** : the theatrical profession or art **4** : a place where something important happens **5** : STAGECOACH

²**stage** *vb* **staged; stag·ing** : to produce or show to others on or as if on the stage

stage·coach *n* : a coach pulled by horses that runs on a schedule from place to place carrying passengers and mail

¹**stag·ger** *vb* **stag·gered; stag·ger·ing 1** : to move or cause to move unsteadily from side to side as if about to fall : REEL **2** : to cause

stagger

or feel great surprise or shock **3** : to arrange or be arranged in a zigzag but balanced way

²stagger *n* : a reeling or unsteady walk

stag·nant *adj* **1** : not flowing **2** : not active or brisk : DULL

stag·nate *vb* **stag·nat·ed; stag·nat·ing** : to be or become inactive or still

¹stain *vb* **stained; stain·ing** **1** : to soil or discolor especially in spots **2** : to use something (as a dye) to change the color of **3** : ¹CORRUPT 1 **4** : ¹DISGRACE

²stain *n* **1** : ¹SPOT 2, DISCOLORATION **2** : a mark of guilt or disgrace : STIGMA **3** : something (as a dye) used in staining — **stain·less** *adj*

stained glass *n* : pieces of colored glass used to make patterns in windows

stainless steel *n* : an alloy of steel and chromium that is resistant to stain, rust, and corrosion

stair *n* **1** : a series of steps or flights of steps for going from one level to another — often used in pl. **2** : one step of a stairway

stair·case *n* : a flight of steps with their supporting structure and railings

stair·way *n* : one or more flights of steps usually with connecting landings

¹stake *n* **1** : a pointed piece (as of wood) that is driven into the ground as a marker or a support for something **2** : a post to which a person is tied to be put to death by burning **3** : something that is put up to be won or lost in gambling **4** : the prize in a contest **5** : ¹SHARE 1, INTEREST — **at stake** : in a position to be lost if something goes wrong

²stake *vb* **staked; stak·ing** **1** : ²BET 1 **2** : to mark the limits of by stakes **3** : to fasten or support (as plants) with stakes **4** : to give money to in order to help (as with a project)

sta·lac·tite *n* : a deposit hanging from the roof or side of a cave in the shape of an icicle formed by the partial evaporation of dripping water containing minerals

sta·lag·mite *n* : a deposit like an upside down stalactite formed by the dripping of water containing minerals onto the floor of a cave

stale *adj* **stal·er; stal·est** **1** : having lost a good taste or quality through age **2** : used or heard so often as to be dull **3** : not so strong, energetic, or effective as before

¹stalk *n* **1** : a plant stem especially when not woody **2** : a slender supporting structure — **stalked** *adj*

²stalk *vb* **stalked; stalk·ing** **1** : to walk in a stiff or proud manner **2** : to hunt slowly and quietly — **stalk·er** *n*

¹stall *n* **1** : a compartment for one animal in a stable or barn **2** : a booth, stand, or counter where business may be carried on or articles may be displayed for sale **3** : a seat

in a church choir : a church pew **4** : a small enclosed private compartment

²stall *vb* **stalled; stall·ing** : to distract attention or make excuses to gain time

³stall *vb* **stalled; stall·ing** **1** : to stop or cause to stop usually by accident **2** : to put or keep in a stall

stal·lion *n* : a male horse

stal·wart *adj* : STURDY 1, RESOLUTE

sta·men *n* : the part of a flower that produces pollen and is made up of an anther and a filament

stam·i·na *n* : the ability or strength to keep doing something for a long time

¹stam·mer *vb* **stam·mered; stam·mer·ing** : to speak with involuntary stops and much repeating

²stammer *n* : an act or instance of speaking with involuntary stops and much repeating

¹stamp *vb* **stamped; stamp·ing** **1** : to bring the foot down hard and with noise **2** : to put an end to by or as if by hitting with the bottom of the foot **3** : to mark or cut out with a tool or device having a design **4** : to attach a postage stamp to **5** : CHARACTERIZE 1

²stamp *n* **1** : a small piece of paper or a mark attached to something to show that a tax or fee has been paid **2** : a device or instrument for marking with a design **3** : the mark made by stamping **4** : a sign of a special quality **5** : the act of bringing the foot down hard

¹stam·pede *n* **1** : a wild rush or flight of frightened animals or people **2** : a sudden foolish action or movement of a large number of people

²stampede *vb* **stam·ped·ed; stam·ped·ing** **1** : to run or cause to run away in fright or panic **2** : to act or cause to act together suddenly and without thought

stance *n* : way of standing : POSTURE

¹stand *vb* **stood; stand·ing** **1** : to be in or take an upright position on the feet **2** : to take up or stay in a specified position or condition **3** : to rest, remain, or set in a usually vertical position **4** : to be in a specified place **5** : to put up with : ENDURE **6** : to have an opinion **7** : to stay in effect **8** : UNDERGO **9** : to perform the duty of — **stand by 1** : to be or remain loyal or true to **2** : to be present **3** : to be or get ready to act — **stand for 1** : to be a symbol for : REPRESENT **2** : to put up with : PERMIT — **stand out** : to be easily seen or recognized — **stand up 1** : to stay in good condition **2** : to fail to keep an appointment with — **stand up for** : DEFEND 2 — **stand up to** : to face boldly

²stand *n* **1** : a structure containing rows of seats for spectators of a sport or spectacle **2**

: a stall or booth often outdoors for a small business **3** : ¹POSITION 2 **4** : a group of plants growing near one another **5** : an act of stopping or staying in one place **6** : a halt for defense or resistance **7** : a place or post which a person occupies : STATION **8** : a small structure (as a rack or table) on or in which something may be placed **9** : a raised area (as for speakers or performers)

¹stan·dard n **1** : something set up as a rule for measuring or as a model **2** : the personal flag of the ruler of a state **3** : an upright support **4** : a figure used as a symbol by an organized body of people

²standard adj **1** : used as or matching a model or rule to compare against **2** : regularly and widely used **3** : widely known and accepted to be of good and permanent value

stan·dard·ize vb **stan·dard·ized; stan·dard·iz·ing** : to make alike or matching a model

standard time n : the time established by law or by common usage over a region or country

¹stand·ing adj **1** : ¹ERECT **2** : done while standing **3** : not flowing : STAGNANT **4** : remaining at the same level or amount until canceled **5** : PERMANENT

²standing n **1** : length of existence or service **2** : ¹POSITION 5, STATUS

stand·point n : a way in which things are thought about : POINT OF VIEW

stand·still n : the condition of not being active or busy : STOP

stank past of STINK

stan·za n : a group of lines forming a division of a poem

¹sta·ple n **1** : a short thin wire with bent ends that is punched through papers and squeezed to hold them together or punched through thin material to fasten it to a surface **2** : a piece of metal shaped like a U with sharp points to be driven into a surface to hold something (as a hook, rope, or wire)

²staple vb **sta·pled; sta·pling** : to fasten with staples

³staple n **1** : a chief product of business or farming of a place **2** : something that is used widely and often **3** : the chief part of something

⁴staple adj **1** : much used, needed, or enjoyed usually by many people **2** : ¹PRINCIPAL, CHIEF

sta·pler n : a device that fastens using staples

¹star n **1** : any of the heavenly bodies except planets which are visible at night and look like fixed points of light **2** : a figure or object with five or more points that represents or suggests a star in the sky **3** : a very talented or popular performer **4** : a planet that is believed in astrology to influence some-

one's life **5** : the principal member of a theater or opera company

²star vb **starred; star·ring** **1** : to mark with a star or an asterisk as being special or very good **2** : to present in the role of a star **3** : to play the most important role **4** : to perform in an outstanding manner

³star adj **1** : being favored or very popular **2** : being of outstanding excellence

star·board n : the right side of a ship or airplane looking forward

¹starch n : a white odorless tasteless substance that is the chief form in which carbohydrates are stored in plants, is an important component of many foods (as rice and bread), and has various uses (as for stiffening clothes)

²starch vb **starched; starch·ing** : to stiffen with starch

starchy adj **starch·i·er; starch·i·est** : like or containing starch

¹stare vb **stared; star·ing** : to look at hard and long often with wide-open eyes

²stare n : the act or an instance of looking at hard and long

star·fish n : a sea animal that usually has five arms that spread out from a central disk and feeds mostly on mollusks

¹stark adj **stark·er; stark·est** **1** : ¹BARREN 2, DESOLATE **2** : clear and harsh **3** : very obvious

²stark adv : COMPLETELY

star·light n : the light given by the stars

star·ling n : a dark brown or greenish black European bird that is now common in the United States

star·lit adj : lighted by the stars

star·ry adj **star·ri·er; star·ri·est** **1** : full of stars **2** : shining like stars **3** : having parts arranged like a star

Stars and Stripes n pl : the flag of the United States — used as singular

¹start vb **start·ed; start·ing** **1** : to begin an activity **2** : to come or bring into being or action **3** : to begin to move toward a particular place or in a particular direction **4** : to cause to move, act, or operate **5** : to give a sudden twitch or jerk (as in surprise) **6** : to stick out or seem to stick out

²start n **1** : a sudden twitching or jerking movement **2** : a beginning of movement, action, or development **3** : a brief act, movement, or effort **4** : a place of beginning (as of a race)

start·er n : someone or something that starts something or causes something else to start

star·tle vb **star·tled; star·tling** **1** : to move or jump (as in surprise or fear) **2** : to frighten suddenly but slightly

star·tling *adj* : causing a moment of fright or surprise

star·va·tion *n* : suffering or death caused by lack of food : the condition of being starved

starve *vb* **starved; starv·ing** **1** : to suffer or die or cause to suffer or die from lack of food **2** : to suffer or cause to suffer from a lack of something other than food

¹stash *vb* **stashed; stash·ing** : to store in a usually secret place for future use

²stash *n* : an amount of something stored secretly for future use

¹state *n* **1** : manner or condition of being **2** : a body of people living in a certain territory under one government : the government of such a body of people **3** : one of the divisions of a nation having a federal government

²state *vb* **stat·ed; stat·ing** **1** : to express especially in words **2** : to set by rule, law, or authority

state·house *n* : the building where the legislature of a state meets

state·ly *adj* **state·li·er; state·li·est** : impressive in size or dignity — **state·li·ness** *n*

state·ment *n* **1** : something written or said in a formal way : something stated **2** : a brief record of a business account

state·room *n* : a private room on a ship or a train

states·man *n, pl* **states·men** : a usually wise, skilled, and respected government leader

¹stat·ic *n* : noise produced in a radio or television receiver by atmospheric or electrical disturbances

²static *adj* **1** : showing little change or action **2** : of or relating to charges of electricity (as those produced by friction) that do not flow

¹sta·tion *n* **1** : a regular stopping place (as on a bus, train, or subway line) : DEPOT **2** : a place for specialized observation or for a public service **3** : a collection of or the place that contains radio or television equipment for transmitting or receiving **4** : ¹POSITION 5, RANK **5** : the place or position where a person or thing stands or is assigned to stand or remain **6** : a post or area of duty

²station *vb* **sta·tioned; sta·tion·ing** : to assign to or set in a post or position : POST

sta·tion·ary *adj* **1** : having been set in a certain place or post : IMMOBILE **2** : not changing : STABLE

sta·tion·ery *n* : writing paper and envelopes

station wagon *n* : an automobile that is longer on the inside than a sedan and has one or more folding or removable seats but no separate luggage compartment

stat·ue *n* : an image or likeness (as of a person or animal) sculptured, modeled, or cast in a solid substance (as marble or bronze)

stat·ure *n* **1** : a person's height **2** : quality or fame gained (as by growth or development)

sta·tus *n* **1** : position or rank of a person or thing **2** : state of affairs : SITUATION

stat·ute *n* : LAW 4

staunch *adj* **staunch·er; staunch·est** **1** : strongly built : SUBSTANTIAL **2** : LOYAL, STEADFAST — **staunch·ly** *adv*

¹stave *n* **1** : one of the narrow strips of wood or iron plates that form the sides, covering, or lining of something (as a barrel) **2** : a wooden stick : STAFF

²stave *vb* **staved** *or* **stove; stav·ing** **1** : to break in the staves of **2** : to smash a hole in — **stave off** : to keep away : ward off

staves *pl of* STAFF

¹stay *vb* **stayed; stay·ing** **1** : to remain after others have gone **2** : to continue unchanged **3** : to stop going forward : PAUSE **4** : to live for a while **5** : to put a stop to : HALT

²stay *n* **1** : a period of living in a place **2** : the action of bringing to a stop : the state of being stopped

³stay *n* : a strong rope or wire used to steady or brace something (as a mast)

⁴stay *n* **1** : ²PROP, SUPPORT **2** : a thin firm strip (as of steel or plastic) used to stiffen a garment (as a corset) or part of a garment (as a shirt collar)

⁵stay *vb* **stayed; staying** : to hold up

stead *n* **1** : ADVANTAGE — used mostly in the phrase *stand someone in good stead* **2** : the place usually taken or duty carried out by the person or thing mentioned

stead·fast *adj* **1** : not changing : RESOLUTE **2** : LOYAL — **stead·fast·ly** *adv* — **stead·fast·ness** *n*

¹steady *adj* **steadi·er; steadi·est** **1** : firmly fixed in position **2** : direct or sure in action **3** : showing little change **4** : not easily upset **5** : RELIABLE — **stead·i·ly** *adv* — **stead·i·ness** *n*

²steady *vb* **stead·ied; steady·ing** : to make, keep, or become steady

steak *n* **1** : a thick slice of meat and especially beef **2** : a thick slice of a large fish (as salmon)

¹steal *vb* **stole; sto·len; steal·ing** **1** : to take and carry away (something that belongs to another person) without permission and with the intention of keeping **2** : to come or go quietly or secretly **3** : to draw attention away from others **4** : to take or get secretly or in a tricky way **5** : to reach the next base safely in baseball by running to it when the ball has not been hit in play **6** : to take (as a ball or puck) from another player **7** : to take something from a situation

²steal *n* **1** : the act or an instance of stealing **2** : ¹BARGAIN 2

stealth *n* : sly or secret action

stealthy *adj* **stealth·i·er; stealth·i·est** : done in a sly or secret manner — **stealth·i·ly** *adv*

¹steam *n* **1** : the vapor into which water is changed when heated to the boiling point **2** : steam or the heat or power produced by it when kept under pressure **3** : the mist formed when water vapor cools **4** : driving force : POWER

²steam *vb* **steamed; steam·ing 1** : to give off steam or vapor **2** : to rise or pass off as steam **3** : to move or travel by or as if by the power of steam **4** : to expose to steam (as for cooking)

steam·boat *n* : a boat powered by steam

steam engine *n* : an engine powered by steam

steam·er *n* **1** : a ship powered by steam **2** : a container in which something is steamed

steam·roll·er *n* : a machine that has wide heavy rollers for pressing down and smoothing roads

steam·ship *n* : STEAMER 1

steam shovel *n* : a power machine for digging

steamy *adj* **steam·i·er; steam·i·est 1** : hot and humid **2** : producing or covered with steam

steed *n* : a usually lively horse

¹steel *n* **1** : a hard and tough metal made by treating iron with great heat and mixing carbon with it **2** : an item (as a sword) made of steel

²steel *vb* **steeled; steel·ing** : to fill with courage or determination

³steel *adj* : made of steel

steely *adj* **steel·i·er; steel·i·est** : like steel (as in hardness, strength, or color)

¹steep *adj* **steep·er; steep·est 1** : having a very sharp slope : almost straight up and down **2** : too great or high — **steep·ly** *adv* — **steep·ness** *n*

²steep *vb* **steeped; steep·ing 1** : to soak in a hot liquid **2** : to fill with or involve deeply

stee·ple *n* **1** : a tall pointed structure usually built on top of a church tower **2** : a church tower

stee·ple·chase *n* **1** : a horse race across country **2** : a race on a course that has hedges, walls, and ditches to be crossed

¹steer *vb* **steered; steer·ing 1** : to make a vehicle move in a particular direction **2** : to guide or change the direction of something **3** : to follow a course of action

²steer *n* : a castrated bull usually raised for beef

steering wheel *n* : a wheel that allows a driver to control the direction of a vehicle

stego·sau·rus *n* : a large plant-eating dinosaur with bony plates along its back and tail and with spikes at the end of the tail

¹stem *n* **1** : the main stalk of a plant that develops buds and shoots and usually grows above ground **2** : a thin plant part (as a leafstalk) that supports another part **3** : the bow of a ship **4** : the basic part of a word to which prefixes or suffixes may be added **5** : something like a stalk or shaft — **from stem to stern** : in or to every part : THOROUGHLY

²stem *vb* **stemmed; stem·ming 1** : to make progress against **2** : to check or hold back the progress of

³stem *vb* **stemmed; stem·ming 1** : to develop as a consequence of **2** : to come from : DERIVE **3** : to remove the stem from

⁴stem *vb* **stemmed; stem·ming** : to stop or check by or as if by damming

stemmed *adj* : having a stem

¹sten·cil *n* **1** : a piece of material (as a sheet of paper or plastic) that has lettering or a design cut out and is used as a guide (as in painting or drawing) **2** : a pattern, design, or print produced with a stencil

²stencil *vb* **sten·ciled** *or* **sten·cilled; sten·cil·ing** *or* **sten·cil·ling 1** : to mark or paint with a stencil **2** : to produce with a stencil

¹step *n* **1** : a movement made by lifting one foot and putting it down in another spot **2** : a rest or place for the foot in going up or down : STAIR **3** : a combination of foot and body movements in a repeated pattern **4** : manner of walking **5** : FOOTPRINT **6** : the sound of a footstep **7** : the space passed over in one step **8** : a short distance **9** : the height of one stair **10 steps** *pl* : ¹COURSE 3 **11** : one of a series of actions taken to achieve something **12** : a stage in a process **13** : a level, grade, or rank in a scale or series **14** : the distance from one tone of a musical scale or one note on a musical staff to another that is one tone away (**half step**) or two tones away (**whole step**)

²step *vb* **stepped; step·ping 1** : to move in a particular way or direction by lifting one foot and putting it down in another spot **2** : ¹DANCE 1 **3** : to go on foot : WALK **4** : to move quickly **5** : to put or press the foot on or in **6** : to come or move as if at a step by the foot **7** : to measure by steps — **step up** : to increase the amount, speed, or intensity of

step–by–step *adj* : moving or happening by steps one after the other

step·fa·ther *n* : the husband of someone's mother after the death or divorce of his or her real father

step·lad·der *n* : a light freestanding ladder with broad flat steps and a hinged frame

step·moth·er *n* : the wife of someone's father after the death or divorce of his or her real mother

steppe *n* : land that is dry, rather level, mostly treeless, and covered with grass in regions (as parts of Asia and southeastern Europe) with usually hot summers and cold winters

step·ping—stone *n* **1** : a stone on which to step (as in crossing a stream) **2** : something that helps in progress or advancement

-ster *n suffix* **1** : someone who does or handles or operates **2** : someone who makes or uses **3** : someone who is associated with or takes part in **4** : someone who is

ste·reo *n, pl* **ste·re·os** : a sound system that reproduces the effect of listening to the original sound — **stereo** *adj*

¹ste·reo·type *n* : a fixed idea that many people have about a thing or a group that may often be untrue or only partly true

²ste·reo·type *vb* **ste·reo·typed; ste·reo·typ·ing** : to form a fixed and often untrue or only partly true idea about

ste·reo·typed *adj* : following a pattern or stereotype : lacking originality

ste·reo·typ·i·cal *adj* : based on or characteristic of a stereotype — **ste·reo·typ·i·cal·ly** *adv*

ster·ile *adj* **1** : not able to produce fruit, crops, or offspring : not fertile **2** : free from living germs

ster·il·ize *vb* **ster·il·ized; ster·il·iz·ing** : to make sterile and especially free from germs

¹ster·ling *n* **1** : British money **2** : sterling silver : articles made from sterling silver

²sterling *adj* **1** : of or relating to British sterling **2** : being or made of a specific alloy that is mostly silver with a little copper **3** : EXCELLENT

¹stern *adj* **stern·er; stern·est 1** : hard and severe in nature or manner : very strict and serious **2** : showing severe displeasure or disapproval **3** : firm and not changeable — **stern·ly** *adv*

²stern *n* : the rear end of a boat

ster·num *n, pl* **ster·nums** *or* **ster·na** : BREASTBONE

ste·roid *n* : any of various chemical compounds that include many hormones (as anabolic steroids)

stetho·scope *n* : a medical instrument used for listening to sounds produced in the body and especially those of the heart and lungs

¹stew *n* **1** : a dish of usually meat with vegetables prepared by slow boiling **2** : a state of excitement, worry, or confusion

²stew *vb* **stewed; stew·ing 1** : to boil slowly : SIMMER **2** : to become excited or worried

stew·ard *n* **1** : a manager of a very large home, an estate, or an organization **2** : a person employed to manage the supply and distribution of food and look after the needs of passengers (as on an airplane or ship)

stew·ard·ess *n* : a woman who looks after passengers (as on an airplane or ship)

¹stick *n* **1** : a cut or broken branch or twig **2** : a long thin piece of wood **3** : WALKING STICK 1 **4** : something like a stick in shape or use

²stick *vb* **stuck; stick·ing 1** : to push into or through **2** : to stab or pierce with something pointed **3** : to put in place by or as if by pushing **4** : to push out, up, into, or under **5** : to put in a specified place or position **6** : to remain in a place, situation, or environment **7** : to halt the movement or action of **8** : BAFFLE **9** : to burden with something unpleasant **10** : to fix or become fixed in place by or as if by gluing **11** : to cling or cause to cling **12** : to become blocked or jammed

stick·er *n* : something (as a slip of paper with glue on its back) that can be stuck to a surface

stick insect *n* : a wingless long-legged insect that has a long body resembling a stick

stick·le·back *n* : a small scaleless fish with sharp spines on its back

sticky *adj* **stick·i·er; stick·i·est 1** : tending to cling like glue : ADHESIVE **2** : coated with a substance that sticks to things **3** : MUGGY, HUMID **4** : tending to become blocked or jammed — **stick·i·ness** *n*

stiff *adj* **stiff·er; stiff·est 1** : not easily bent **2** : not easily moved **3** : firm and not changeable **4** : not friendly, relaxed, or graceful in manner **5** : POWERFUL, STRONG **6** : not flowing easily : THICK **7** : SEVERE **3 8** hard to do or deal with : DIFFICULT — **stiff·ly** *adv* — **stiff·ness** *n*

stiff·en *vb* **stiff·ened; stiff·en·ing 1** : to make or become stiff or stiffer **2** : to become tense and still

sti·fle *vb* **sti·fled; sti·fling 1** : to cause or have difficulty in breathing **2** : to keep in check by effort

stig·ma *n, pl* **stig·ma·ta** *or* **stig·mas 1** : a mark of disgrace or dishonor **2** : the upper part of the pistil of a flower which receives the pollen grains

stile *n* **1** : a step or set of steps for crossing a fence or wall **2** : TURNSTILE

sti·let·to *n, pl* **sti·let·tos** *or* **sti·let·toes** : a knife with a slender pointed blade

¹still *adj* **1** : having no motion **2** : making no sound : QUIET **3** : free from noise and commotion — **still·ness** *n*

²still *vb* **stilled; still·ing 1** : to make or become motionless or silent **2** : to calm or make less intense

³still *adv* **1** : without motion **2** : up to this or that time **3** : NEVERTHELESS **4** : ²EVEN **2** **5** : in addition

⁴still *n* : ¹QUIET, SILENCE

⁵still *n* : a device used in making alcoholic liquors

stilt *n* **1** : one of a pair of tall poles each with a high step or loop for the support of a foot used to lift the person wearing them above the ground in walking **2** : a stake or post used as one of the supports of a structure (as a building) above ground or water level

stilt·ed *adj* : not easy and natural

¹stim·u·lant *n* **1** : something (as a drug) that makes the body or one of its parts temporarily more active **2** : STIMULUS 1

²stimulant *adj* : stimulating or tending to stimulate

stim·u·late *vb* **stim·u·lat·ed; stim·u·lat·ing 1** : to make active or more active : AROUSE **2** : to act on as a bodily stimulus or stimulant

stim·u·la·tion *n* : an act or result of making more active

stim·u·lus *n, pl* **stim·u·li 1** : something that stirs or urges to action **2** : an influence that acts usually from outside the body to partly change bodily activity (as by exciting a receptor or sense organ)

¹sting *vb* **stung; sting·ing 1** : to prick painfully usually with a sharp or poisonous stinger **2** : to suffer or affect with sharp quick burning pain **3** : to hurt emotionally

²sting *n* **1** : an act of pricking painfully usually with a sharp or poisonous stinger **2** : a wound or burning pain caused by the pricking of the skin with a stinger **3** : emotional pain **4** : STINGER

sting·er *n* : a sharp part of an animal (as a bee or scorpion) that is used to wound and often poison prey or an enemy

sting·ray *n* : a flat fish with a sharp stinging spine on its long thin tail

stin·gy *adj* **stin·gi·er; stin·gi·est 1** : not generous **2** : very small in amount — **stin·gi·ness** *n*

¹stink *vb* **stank** *or* **stunk; stunk; stink·ing 1** : to give off or cause to have a strong unpleasant smell **2** : to be very bad or unpleasant

²stink *n* : a strong unpleasant smell

stink·bug *n* : a bug that gives off a bad smell

stinky *adj* **stink·i·er; stink·i·est** : having a strong unpleasant smell

¹stint *vb* **stint·ed; stint·ing** : to be stingy or sparing

²stint *n* **1** : an amount of work given **2** : a period of time spent at a particular activity

¹stir *vb* **stirred; stir·ring 1** : to make or cause to make a usually slight movement or change of position **2** : to make active **3** : to mix, dissolve, or move about by making a

circular movement in **4** : to cause to arise or take place

²stir *n* **1** : a state of upset or activity **2** : a slight movement **3** : the act of making circular movements in

stir·ring *adj* : MOVING 2

stir·rup *n* : either of a pair of small light frames or loops often of metal hung by straps from a saddle and used as a support for the foot of a horseback rider

¹stitch *n* **1** : one in-and-out movement of a threaded needle in sewing or in closing a wound : a portion of thread left after one such movement **2** : a single loop of thread or yarn around a tool (as a knitting needle or crochet hook) **3** : a type or style of stitching **4** : a sudden sharp pain especially in the side

²stitch *vb* **stitched; stitch·ing 1** : to fasten or join by sewing **2** : to make, mend, or decorate by or as if by sewing **3** : SEW 2

¹stock *n* **1** : the whole supply or amount on hand **2 stocks** *pl* : a wooden frame with holes to hold the feet or the feet and hands once used to punish a wrongdoer publicly **3** : the wooden part by which a rifle or shotgun is held against the shoulder during firing **4** : the source from which others descend : ANCESTRY **5** : farm animals : LIVESTOCK, CATTLE **6** : a part ownership in a business that can be traded independently **7** : liquid in which meat, fish, or vegetables have been simmered — **in stock** : on hand : in the store and available for purchase

²stock *vb* **stocked; stock·ing 1** : to provide with or get supplies especially for future use **2** : to get or keep a supply of

³stock *adj* **1** : kept regularly in supply especially for sale **2** : commonly used : STANDARD

stock·ade *n* **1** : a line of strong posts set in the ground to form a defense **2** : an enclosure usually formed by posts pounded into the ground

stock·bro·ker *n* : a person who handles orders to buy and sell stocks

stock·hold·er *n* : an owner of stock

stock·ing *n* **1** : a close-fitting usually knit covering for the foot and leg **2** : ¹SOCK

stock market *n* : a place where shares of stock are bought and sold

stocky *adj* **stock·i·er; stock·i·est** : short, broad, and sturdy in build

stock·yard *n* : a yard for keeping livestock about to be slaughtered or shipped

¹stole *past of* STEAL

²stole *n* : a long wide scarf worn across the shoulders

stolen *past participle of* STEAL

stol·id *adj* : having or showing little or no feeling — **stol·id·ly** *adv*

¹stom·ach *n* **1** : the pouch into which food passes from the esophagus for mixing and digestion before passing to the small intestine **2** : the part of the body that contains the stomach : ABDOMEN **3** : ²DESIRE 1, LIKING

²stomach *vb* **stom·ached; stom·ach·ing** : to bear patiently : put up with

stomp *vb* **stomped; stomp·ing** : to walk heavily or noisily : STAMP

¹stone *n* **1** : earth or mineral matter hardened in a mass : ROCK **2** : a piece of rock coarser than gravel **3** : GEM 1 **4** : a stony mass that sometimes forms in certain organs of the body **5** : the seed of a fruit (as a peach) in its hard case **6** *pl usually* **stone** : an English measure of weight equaling 14 pounds (about 6.3 kilograms)

²stone *vb* **stoned; ston·ing 1** : to throw stones at **2** : to remove the stony seeds of

³stone *adj* : relating to or made of stone

⁴stone *adv* : COMPLETELY, TOTALLY

Stone Age *n* : the oldest period in which human beings are known to have existed : the age during which stone tools were used

stony *adj* **ston·i·er; ston·i·est 1** : full of stones **2** : hard as or like stone **3** : INSENSITIVE 1, UNFEELING

stood *past and past participle of* STAND

stool *n* **1** : a seat without back or arms supported by three or four legs or by a central post **2** : FOOTSTOOL **3** : a mass of bodily waste discharged from the intestine

¹stoop *vb* **stooped; stoop·ing 1** : to bend down or over **2** : to stand or walk with the head and shoulders bent forward **3** : to do something that is petty, deceitful, or morally wrong

²stoop *n* : a forward bend of the head and shoulders

³stoop *n* : a porch, platform, or stairway at the entrance of a house or building

¹stop *vb* **stopped; stop·ping 1** : to cease moving especially temporarily or for a purpose **2** : to halt the movement or progress of **3** : to keep from doing something **4** : to come or bring (something) to an end **5** : to cease operating or functioning **6** : to close or block up or become closed or blocked up : PLUG **7** : to take time

²stop *n* **1** : ¹END 2, FINISH **2** : the act of bringing or coming to a halt : the state of being stopped **3** : a halt in a journey : STAY **4** : a stopping place **5** : something that delays, blocks, or brings to a halt **6** : STOPPER, PLUG **7** : a set of organ pipes of one tone quality : a control knob for such a set

stop·light *n* **1** : TRAFFIC LIGHT **2** : a light on

the rear of a motor vehicle that goes on when the driver presses the brake pedal

stop·over *n* : a stop made during a journey

stop·page *n* : ²STOP 2

stop·per *n* : something (as a cork or plug) used to close or block an opening

stop·watch *n* : a watch that can be started and stopped for exact timing (as of a race)

stor·age *n* **1** : space or a place for putting things for future use or for safekeeping **2** : the act of putting things somewhere especially for future use : the state of being stored

storage battery *n* : a battery that can be made capable of being used again by passing an electric current through it

¹store *vb* **stored; stor·ing 1** : to place or leave something in a location (as a warehouse, library, or computer memory) for later use, disposal, or safekeeping **2** : to bring together or collect as a supply **3** : to provide with what is needed : SUPPLY

²store *n* **1** : a place where goods are sold : SHOP **2** : a large quantity, supply, or number **3 stores** *pl* : something collected and kept for future use — **in store** : ¹READY 1

store·house *n, pl* **store·hous·es 1** : a building for storing goods **2** : a large supply or source

store·keep·er *n* **1** : an owner or manager of a store or shop **2** : a person in charge of supplies (as in a factory)

store·room *n* : a room for keeping things for future use

stork *n* : a large wading bird that has a long heavy bill and long legs and builds large nests usually in trees or on the top of roofs and poles

¹storm *n* **1** : a heavy fall of rain, snow, or sleet often with strong winds **2** : a serious disturbance of any element of nature **3** : a strong outburst **4** : a violent attack on a defended position

²storm *vb* **stormed; storm·ing 1** : to blow hard and rain, snow, or sleet heavily **2** : to make a sudden mass attack against **3** : to feel or express angry feelings : RAGE **4** : to rush about violently or angrily

stormy *adj* **storm·i·er; storm·i·est 1** : relating to or affected by a storm **2** : displaying anger and strong emotions

¹sto·ry *n, pl* **sto·ries 1** : a report about incidents or events : ACCOUNT **2** : a short often amusing tale **3** : a fictional tale shorter than a novel **4** : a widely told rumor **5** : ³LIE, FALSEHOOD

²sto·ry *also* **sto·rey** *n, pl* **sto·ries** *also* **sto·reys** : a set of rooms or an area making up one floor level of a building

stout *adj* **stout·er; stout·est 1** : of strong character : BRAVE, DETERMINED **2** : of a strong or lasting sort : STURDY, TOUGH **3** : having a large body with much fat **4** : wide and usually thick — **stout·ly** adv — **stout·ness** n

¹stove n : a device usually of iron or steel that burns fuel or uses electricity to provide heat (as for cooking or heating)

²stove past and past participle of STAVE

stove·pipe n **1** : a metal pipe to carry away smoke from a stove **2** : a tall silk hat

stow vb **stowed; stow·ing 1** : to put away : STORE **2** : ²LOAD 1 — **stow away** : to hide on a vehicle (as a ship) in order to travel without paying or being seen

stow·away n : a person who hides on a vehicle (as a ship) to travel without paying or being seen

strad·dle vb **strad·dled; strad·dling 1** : to stand, sit, or walk with the legs spread wide apart **2** : to stand, sit, or ride with a leg on either side of **3** : to seem to favor two opposite sides of

strag·gle vb **strag·gled; strag·gling 1** : to walk or move in a slow and disorderly way **2** : to move away or spread out from others of the same kind — **strag·gler** n

strag·gly adj **strag·gli·er; strag·gli·est** : growing, hanging, or arranged in an untidy or scattered way

¹straight adj **straight·er; straight·est 1** : following the same direction throughout its length : not having curves, bends, or angles **2** : being perfectly vertical or horizontal **3** : following one after the other in order **4** : not changing from an indicated pattern **5** : not straying from what is right or honest **6** : correctly ordered or arranged **7** : ²CORRECT 2 **8** : not showing any feeling especially of amusement — **straight·ness** n

²straight adv **1** : without delay or hesitation **2** : in a direct and uninterrupted course : without turning or curving aside **3** : in or into an upright position **4** : without interruption **5** : in a normal or correct way

straight·away adv : without delay : IMMEDIATELY

straight·en vb **straight·ened; straight·en·ing 1** : to make or become straight **2** : to put in order

straight·for·ward adj : being clear and honest : FRANK — **straight·for·ward·ly** adv

straight·way adv : STRAIGHTAWAY

¹strain n **1** : a group of closely related living things that look similar but possess one or more unique characteristics **2** : a quality or disposition that runs through a family or group **3** : a small amount : TRACE **4** : MELODY 2, TUNE

²strain vb **strained; strain·ing 1** : to stretch or be stretched, pulled, or used to the limit **2**

: to stretch beyond a proper limit **3** : to try very hard : make a great effort **4** : to injure or be injured by too much or too hard use or effort **5** : to press or pass through a strainer : FILTER **6** : to pour off liquid from by using a strainer

³strain n **1** : great worry and concern or physical effort **2** : something that causes great worry and concern or physical effort **3** : bodily injury resulting from too much use or from a wrench or twist that stretches muscles and ligaments **4** : a force that pulls or stretches something to its limit : STRESS

strained adj **1** : showing the effects of worry and concern **2** : not easy or natural **3** : not friendly or relaxed

strain·er n : a device (as a screen, sieve, or filter) to hold back solid pieces while a liquid passes through

strait n **1** : a narrow channel connecting two bodies of water **2** : a situation of difficulty or distress — often used in pl.

¹strand n : the land bordering a body of water : SHORE, BEACH

²strand vb **strand·ed; strand·ing 1** : to run, drive, or cause to drift from the water onto land **2** : to leave in a strange or unfavorable place especially without any way of leaving

³strand n **1** : one of the fibers, threads, strings, or wires twisted or braided to make a cord, rope, or cable **2** : something long or twisted like a rope

strange adj **strang·er; strang·est 1** : UNFAMILIAR 1 **2** : different from what is usual, normal, or expected **3** : not relaxed : UNEASY — **strange·ly** adv — **strange·ness** n

strang·er n **1** : a person in a new or unfamiliar place **2** : a person whom another person does not know or has not met

stran·gle vb **stran·gled; stran·gling 1** : to choke to death by squeezing the throat **2** : to die or suffer from or as if from being choked — **stran·gler** n

¹strap n : a narrow strip of flexible material used especially for fastening, holding together, or wrapping

²strap vb **strapped; strap·ping 1** : to fasten with or attach by means of a strap **2** : to whip with a strap

strap·ping adj : strong and healthy

strat·a·gem n : a clever trick or plan

stra·te·gic adj **1** : relating to or showing the use of a plan or method to achieve a goal **2** : useful or important in military strategy

strat·e·gy n, pl **strat·e·gies** : a carefully developed plan or method for achieving a goal or the skill in developing and undertaking such a plan or method

strato·sphere *n* : an upper portion of the atmosphere extending from about 6 miles (10 kilometers) to 30 miles (50 kilometers) upward where temperature changes little and clouds rarely form

stra·tum *n, pl* **stra·ta** : ¹LAYER 1

stra·tus *n, pl* **stra·ti** : a cloud extending over a large area at an altitude of from 2000 to 7000 feet (600 to 2100 meters)

straw *n* **1** : dry plant stems (as of grain after threshing) **2** : a slender tube for sucking up a beverage

straw·ber·ry *n, pl* **straw·ber·ries** : the juicy edible usually red fruit of a low-growing plant with white flowers and long slender runners

¹stray *n* : a domestic animal (as a cat or dog) that is lost or has no home

²stray *vb* **strayed; stray·ing 1** : to wander from a group or from the proper place : ROAM **2** : to go off from a direct or chosen route or the right course **3** : to become distracted from a topic or train of thought

³stray *adj* **1** : lost or having no home **2** : not in the proper or intended place **3** : occurring here and there : RANDOM

¹streak *n* **1** : a line or mark of a different color or texture from its background **2** : a narrow band of light **3** : an amount of a quality **4** : a short series of something — **streaked** *adj*

²streak *vb* **streaked; streak·ing 1** : to make or have a line or mark of color in or on **2** : to move swiftly : RUSH

¹stream *n* **1** : a body of water (as a brook or river) flowing on the earth **2** : a flow of liquid or gas **3** : a steady series (as of words or events) following one another

²stream *vb* **streamed; stream·ing 1** : to flow in or as if in a stream **2** : to give out a bodily fluid in large amounts **3** : to become wet with flowing liquid **4** : to trail out at full length **5** : to pour, enter, or arrive in large numbers

stream·er *n* **1** : a flag that floats or moves in the wind : PENNANT **2** : a long narrow strip (as of ribbon or paper) that is often hung for decoration **3 streamers** *pl* : AURORA BOREALIS

stream·lined *adj* **1** : designed or constructed to make motion through water or air easier or as if for this purpose **2** : made shorter, simpler, or more efficient

street *n* **1** : a public road especially in a city, town, or village **2** : the people living along a street

street·car *n* : a vehicle for carrying passengers that runs on rails and operates mostly on city streets

strength *n* **1** : the quality or state of being physically strong **2** : power to resist force **3** : ability to produce an effect **4** : degree of intensity **5** : power as measured in numbers **6** : a strong or positive quality **7** : the inner courage or determination that allows a person to face and deal with difficulties

strength·en *vb* **strength·ened; strength·en·ing** : to make, grow, or become stronger or more powerful

stren·u·ous *adj* **1** : showing or requiring much energy and effort **2** : very active : ENERGETIC — **stren·u·ous·ly** *adv*

strep throat *n* : a sore throat that is accompanied by fever and caused by a bacterium

¹stress *n* **1** : a force that tends to change the shape of an object **2** : something that causes physical or emotional tension : a state of tension resulting from a stress **3** : special importance given to something **4** : relative loudness or force of a part of a spoken word or a beat in music

²stress *vb* **stressed; stress·ing 1** : to subject to excessive use or to forces that cause a change in shape **2** : to cause or experience physical or emotional tension **3** : to pronounce (part of a word) with relative loudness or force **4** : to give special importance to : EMPHASIZE

stress mark *n* : a mark used to show what part or syllable of a written word should be stressed when spoken

¹stretch *vb* **stretched; stretch·ing 1** : to reach out : EXTEND, SPREAD **2** : to pull or draw out in length or width or both : EXPAND, ENLARGE **3** : to extend (as the body) in a flat position **4** : to extend the body or limbs **5** : to pull tight **6** : to cause to reach or continue **7** : EXAGGERATE **8** : to become extended without breaking **9** : to extend over a continuous period

²stretch *n* **1** : the act of extending or drawing out beyond ordinary or normal limits **2** : the ability to be pulled or drawn out in length or width or both **3** : the act or an instance of stretching the body or one of its parts **4** : a continuous extent in length, area, or time

stretch·er *n* : a device like a cot used for carrying sick or injured persons

strew *vb* **strewed; strewed** *or* **strewn; strew·ing 1** : SCATTER 1 **2** : to spread by scattering **3** : to cover by or as if by scattering something

strick·en *adj* **1** : showing the effect of disease, misfortune, or sorrow **2** : hit or wounded by or as if by an object that was shot or thrown

strict *adj* **strict·er; strict·est 1** : not to be avoided or ignored : requiring obedience **2** : strongly enforcing rules and discipline **3** : kept with great care : ABSOLUTE **4** : carefully observing something (as a rule or principle) **5** : EXACT 1, PRECISE — **strict·ly** *adv* — **strict·ness** *n*

¹stride *vb* **strode; strid·den; strid·ing** : to walk or run with long even steps

²stride *n* **1** : a long step or the distance covered by such a step **2** : a step forward : ADVANCE **3** : a way of walking

strife *n* : bitter and sometimes violent disagreement

¹strike *vb* **struck; struck** *also* **strick·en; strik·ing 1** : to touch, hit, or affect with force **2** : to come into contact or collision with **3** : to attack or seize suddenly **4** : GO 1, PROCEED **5** : to lower, take down, or take apart **6** : to make known by sounding : cause to sound **7** : to affect usually suddenly **8** : to produce by or as if by a blow **9** : to happen with damaging force or effect **10** : to cause to ignite by scratching **11** : to agree on the arrangements of **12** : to make an impression on **13** : to come to mind **14** : to produce on a musical instrument **15** : to remove or cancel with or as if with the stroke of a pen **16** : to come upon : DISCOVER **17** : to take on : ASSUME **18** : to stop work in order to force an employer to meet demands regarding conditions of work **19** : to produce by stamping — **strike out** : to be out in baseball by getting three strikes during a turn at bat — **strike up** : to cause to begin

²strike *n* **1** : an act or instance of striking **2** : a stopping of work by workers to force an employer to agree to demands **3** : an unhelpful or undesirable characteristic : DISADVANTAGE **4** : a baseball pitch that is not hit fair or that passes through a certain area over home plate (**strike zone**) without being hit and that counts against the batter **5** : the knocking down of all the pins with the first ball in bowling **6** : a discovery of a valuable mineral deposit **7** : a military attack

strike-out *n* : an out in baseball that results from a batter getting three strikes during a turn at bat

strik·ing *adj* : attracting attention : REMARKABLE — **strik·ing·ly** *adv*

¹string *n* **1** : a thin cord used to bind, fasten, or tie **2** : something that resembles a string **3** : the gut, wire, or plastic cord of a musical instrument that vibrates to produce a tone when touched **4 strings** *pl* : the stringed instruments of an orchestra **5** : a group, series, or line of things threaded on a string or arranged as if strung together **6** : a series of events which follow each other in time **7 strings** *pl* : requirements that are connected with something

²string *vb* **strung ; string·ing 1** : to provide with strings **2** : ²THREAD 4 **3** : to tie, hang, or fasten with string **4** : to set or stretch out in a line **5** : to remove the tough fibers of

string bass *n* : DOUBLE BASS

string bean *n* : a bean with a long slender pod that is cooked and eaten as a vegetable

stringed instrument *n* : a musical instrument (as a violin, guitar, or harp) sounded by plucking or striking or by drawing a bow across its tight strings

stringy *adj* **string·i·er; string·i·est** : containing, consisting of, or like string

¹strip *vb* **stripped; strip·ping 1** : to remove clothes : UNDRESS **2** : to remove a covering or surface layer from **3** : to make bare or clear **4** : to take away all duties, honors, or special rights **5** : to remove all the contents (as equipment or accessories) from **6** : to tear or damage the thread of (as a screw or bolt)

²strip *n* : a long narrow piece or area

¹stripe *vb* **striped; strip·ing** : to make stripes on

²stripe *n* **1** : a line or long narrow section differing in color or appearance from the background **2** : a piece of material often with a special design worn (as on a sleeve) to show military rank or length of service

striped *adj* : having stripes

strive *vb* **strove; striv·en** *or* **strived; striv·ing** : to try very hard

strode *past of* STRIDE

¹stroke *vb* **stroked; strok·ing** : to rub gently in one direction

²stroke *n* **1** : the act of striking : BLOW **2** : one of a series of repeated movements (as in swimming or rowing) **3** : a sudden serious illness caused by the breaking or blocking of an artery in the brain **4** : the sound of striking (as of a clock or bell) **5** : the hitting of a ball in a game (as golf or tennis) **6** : a sudden or unexpected example **7** : a single movement or the mark made by a single movement of a brush, pen, or tool **8** : a sudden action or process that results in something being struck **9** : effort by which something is done or the results of such effort

¹stroll *vb* **strolled; stroll·ing** : to walk in a leisurely manner

²stroll *n* : a leisurely walk

stroll·er *n* : a small carriage in which a baby can sit and be pushed around

strong *adj* **stron·ger; stron·gest 1** : having great power in the muscles **2** : HEALTHY 1 **3** : not easy to injure, overcome, or resist : SOLID **4** : ENTHUSIASTIC, ZEALOUS **5** : moving with speed and force **6** : having much of some quality : INTENSE **7** : having a great deal of power **8** : of a specified number **9** : PERSUASIVE **10** : well established

: FIRM **11** : having a powerful action or effect **12** : very noticeable — **strong·ly** adv
strong·hold n : FORTRESS
strove past of STRIVE
struck past and past participle of STRIKE
struc·tur·al adj : relating to or affecting the way in which something is built
struc·ture n **1** : something built, arranged, or organized in a definite way **2** : the manner in which something is built, arranged, or organized
¹strug·gle vb **strug·gled; strug·gling 1** : to make a great effort to do or achieve something or to overcome someone or something **2** : to move with difficulty or with great effort
²struggle n **1** : a difficult or violent effort **2** : ²FIGHT 1, CONTEST
strum vb **strummed; strum·ming** : to play on a stringed instrument by brushing the strings with the fingers
strung past and past participle of STRING
¹strut vb **strut·ted; strut·ting** : to walk in a confident and proud way
²strut n **1** : a stiff proud step or walk **2** : a bar or brace used to resist pressure in the direction of its length
¹stub n **1** : a short part remaining after the rest has been removed or used up **2** : a small part of a larger piece of printed paper (as a check or ticket) kept as a record of the purpose of the paper
²stub vb **stubbed; stub·bing** : to strike (as the toe) against an object
stub·ble n **1** : a short growth of beard **2** : the short ends of crops and especially cereal grasses remaining attached to the ground after harvest
stub·born adj **1** : refusing to change an opinion or course of action in spite of difficulty or urging **2** : PERSISTENT **3** : difficult to handle, manage, or treat — **stub·born·ly** adv — **stub·born·ness** n
stub·by adj **stub·bi·er; stub·bi·est** : short and thick like a stub
stuc·co n, pl **stuc·cos** or **stuc·coes** : a plaster for coating walls
stuck past and past participle of STICK
stuck–up adj : VAIN 2, CONCEITED
¹stud n **1** : one of the smaller vertical supports in the walls of a building to which the wall materials are fastened **2** : a removable device like a button used for fastening or as an ornament **3** : one of the metal cleats used on a snow tire to provide a better grip **4** : a small piece of jewelry that is attached through a hole in part of a person's body
²stud vb **stud·ded; stud·ding** : to cover or be covered with many small items

stu·dent n : a person who studies especially in school : PUPIL
stu·dio n, pl **stu·di·os 1** : the place where an artist, sculptor, or photographer works **2** : a place for the study of an art **3** : a place where movies are made **4** : a place from which radio or television programs are broadcast
stu·di·ous adj : very serious about studying — **stu·di·ous·ly** adv
¹study vb **stud·ied; study·ing 1** : to make an effort to learn about something by reading, investigating, or memorizing **2** : to give close attention to
²study n, pl **stud·ies 1** : the act of making an effort to learn by reading, practicing, or memorizing **2** : a careful investigation or examination of something **3** : a room especially for study, reading, or writing
¹stuff n **1** : materials, supplies, or equipment that people need or use **2** : writing, speech, sounds, actions, or ideas of little value **3** : something mentioned or understood but not named **4** : basic part of something : SUBSTANCE
²stuff vb **stuffed; stuff·ing 1** : to force into something : THRUST **2** : to fill by packing or crowding things in : CRAM **3** : OVEREAT, GORGE **4** : to fill with a stuffing **5** : to block up : CONGEST
stuff·ing n **1** : a mixture (as of bread crumbs and seasonings) used to stuff a food (as meat or a vegetable) **2** : material used in filling up something
stuffy adj **stuff·i·er; stuff·i·est 1** : needing fresh air **2** : stuffed or blocked up **3** : very formal and self-important
¹stum·ble vb **stum·bled; stum·bling 1** : to trip in walking, running, or dancing **2** : to walk unsteadily **3** : to speak or act in a clumsy manner **4** : to come unexpectedly or accidentally
²stumble n : an act or instance of tripping or walking unsteadily
¹stump n **1** : the part of a tree that remains in the ground after the tree is cut down **2** : the part of something (as a tooth or a pencil) that remains after the rest has been removed, lost, or worn away : STUB
²stump vb **stumped; stump·ing 1** : PERPLEX, BAFFLE **2** : to walk or walk over heavily, stiffly, or clumsily as if with a wooden leg
stun vb **stunned; stun·ning 1** : to make dizzy or senseless by or as if by a blow **2** : to affect with shock or confusion : fill with disbelief
stung past and past participle of STING
stunk past and past participle of STINK
stun·ning adj **1** : able or likely to make a

person senseless or confused **2** : unusually lovely or attractive : STRIKING

¹stunt *n* **1** : an unusual or difficult performance or act **2** : something done for the purpose of gaining attention or publicity

²stunt *vb* **stunt·ed; stunt·ing** : to hold back the normal growth of

stu·pe·fy *vb* **stu·pe·fied; stu·pe·fy·ing 1** : to make confused or unable to think clearly **2** : ASTONISH, ASTOUND

stu·pen·dous *adj* : amazing especially because of great size or height — **stu·pen·dous·ly** *adv*

stu·pid *adj* **stu·pid·er; stu·pid·est 1** : not intelligent : slow in understanding **2** : not sensible : FOOLISH **3** : not interesting or worthwhile — **stu·pid·ly** *adv*

stu·pid·i·ty *n, pl* **stu·pid·i·ties 1** : the quality or state of being foolish or slow in understanding **2** : a foolish thought, action, or remark

stu·por *n* : a condition of being not alert or able to think normally

stur·dy *adj* **stur·di·er; stur·di·est 1** : firmly built or made **2** : strong and healthy in body : ROBUST **3** : RESOLUTE — **stur·di·ly** *adv* — **sturd·i·ness** *n*

stur·geon *n* : a large fish that has tough skin and rows of bony plates and is often used for food

¹stut·ter *vb* **stut·tered; stut·ter·ing** : to speak or say with involuntary repetition or interruption of sounds

²stutter *n* : the act or an instance of speaking with involuntary repetition or interruption

¹sty *n, pl* **sties** : PIGPEN

²sty *or* **stye** *n, pl* **sties** *or* **styes** : a painful red swelling on the edge of an eyelid

¹style *n* **1** : a particular form or design of something **2** : a way of speaking or writing **3** : an individual way of behaving or doing something **4** : a method, manner, or quality that is felt to be very respectable, fashionable, or proper : FASHION **5** : an easy and graceful manner **6** : the narrow middle part of the pistil of a flower

²style *vb* **styled; styl·ing 1** : to design and make in a known or new style **2** : to give a special shape to someone's hair **3** : to identify by some descriptive term : CALL

styl·ish *adj* : having style : FASHIONABLE — **styl·ish·ly** *adv*

sty·lus *n, pl* **sty·li** *also* **sty·lus·es** : a pointed instrument used in ancient times for writing on wax tablets

¹sub *n* : ¹SUBSTITUTE

²sub *vb* **subbed; sub·bing** : to act as a substitute

³sub *n* : SUBMARINE

sub- *prefix* **1** : under : beneath : below **2**

: lower in importance or rank : lesser **3** : division or part of

sub·di·vide *vb* **sub·di·vid·ed; sub·di·vid·ing 1** : to divide the parts of into smaller parts **2** : to divide (a piece of land) into lots on which houses will be built

sub·di·vi·sion *n* **1** : the act of dividing into smaller parts **2** : one of the parts into which something is subdivided

sub·due *vb* **sub·dued; sub·du·ing 1** : to bring under control **2** : to overcome in battle

sub·dued *adj* : lacking in liveliness, intensity, or strength

sub·head *n* : a heading under which one of the divisions of a subject is listed

sub·head·ing *n* : SUBHEAD

¹sub·ject *n* **1** : the person or thing discussed : TOPIC **2** : an area of knowledge that is studied in school **3** : a person who owes loyalty to a monarch or state **4** : a person under the authority or control of another **5** : the word or group of words about which the predicate makes a statement **6** : a person or animal that is studied or experimented on

²subject *adj* **1** : owing obedience or loyalty to another **2** : possible or likely to be affected by **3** : depending on

³sub·ject *vb* **sub·ject·ed; sub·ject·ing 1** : to bring under control or rule **2** : to cause to put up with

sub·jec·tive *adj* : based mainly on opinions or feelings rather than on facts

sub·lime *adj* **1** : grand or noble in thought, expression, or manner **2** : beautiful or impressive enough to arouse a feeling of admiration and wonder

sub·ma·rine *n* : a naval ship designed to operate underwater

sub·merge *vb* **sub·merged; sub·merg·ing 1** : to put under or plunge into water **2** : to cover or become covered with or as if with water

sub·mis·sion *n* **1** : the act of putting forward something (as for consideration or comment) **2** : the condition of being humble or obedient **3** : the act of giving in to power or authority

sub·mis·sive *adj* : willing to give in to others — **sub·mis·sive·ly** *adv*

sub·mit *vb* **sub·mit·ted; sub·mit·ting 1** : to leave to the judgment or approval of someone else **2** : to yield to the authority, control, or choice of another **3** : to put forward as an opinion, reason, or idea

¹sub·or·di·nate *adj* **1** : being in a lower class or rank : INFERIOR **2** : yielding to or controlled by authority

subordinate

426

²sub·or·di·nate *n* : someone who has less power or authority than someone else

³sub·or·di·nate *vb* **sub·or·di·nat·ed; sub·or·di·nat·ing** : to treat as inferior in rank or importance

sub·scribe *vb* **sub·scribed; sub·scrib·ing 1** : to place an order for a publication or service which is delivered over a stated period **2** : to agree with or support — **sub·scrib·er** *n*

sub·scrip·tion *n* : an agreement to buy a publication or service for a stated period

sub·se·quent *adj* : following in time, order, or place — **sub·se·quent·ly** *adv*

sub·ser·vi·ent *adj* : SUBMISSIVE

sub·set *n* : a small division or portion

sub·side *vb* **sub·sid·ed; sub·sid·ing 1** : to become less strong or intense **2** : to become lower : SINK

sub·sist *vb* **sub·sist·ed; sub·sist·ing** : to continue living or being

sub·sis·tence *n* : the smallest amount (as of food and clothing) necessary to support life

sub·soil *n* : a layer of soil lying just under the topsoil

sub·stance *n* **1** : material of a certain kind **2** : the most basic or important part or quality **3** : material belongings : WEALTH

sub·stan·dard *adj* : lower in quality than expected

sub·stan·tial *adj* **1** : large in amount **2** : IMPORTANT **3** : firmly constructed **4** : ABUNDANT **5** : PROSPEROUS 1 **6** : made up of or relating to substance : MATERIAL

¹sub·sti·tute *n* : a person or thing that takes the place of another

²substitute *vb* **sub·sti·tut·ed; sub·sti·tut·ing 1** : to put in the place of another **2** : to take the place of another

sub·sti·tu·tion *n* : the act or process of putting in or taking the place of another

sub·ter·ra·nean *adj* : being, lying, or operating under the surface of the earth

sub·tle *adj* **sub·tler; sub·tlest 1** : difficult to perceive **2** : SHREWD, KEEN **3** : DELICATE 1 — **sub·tly** *adv*

sub·top·ic *n* : a topic (as in a composition) that is a division of a main topic

sub·tract *vb* **sub·tract·ed; sub·tract·ing** : to take away (as one part or number from another) : DEDUCT

sub·trac·tion *n* : the act or process of taking one number away from another

sub·urb *n* : a smaller community close to a city — **sub·ur·ban** *adj*

sub·way *n* : a usually electric underground railway

suc·ceed *vb* **suc·ceed·ed; suc·ceed·ing 1** : to achieve a desired result : be successful **2** : to turn out well **3** : to come after : FOLLOW

4 : to come next after another person in office or position

suc·cess *n* **1** : satisfactory completion of something **2** : the gaining of wealth, respect, or fame **3** : a person or thing that succeeds

suc·cess·ful *adj* **1** : resulting or ending well or in success **2** : gaining or having gained success — **suc·cess·ful·ly** *adv*

suc·ces·sion *n* **1** : a series of people or things that follow one after another **2** : the order, act, or right of succeeding to a throne, title, or property

suc·ces·sive *adj* : following in order and without interruption — **suc·ces·sive·ly** *adv*

suc·ces·sor *n* : a person who succeeds to a throne, title, property, or office

suc·cor *n* : ²HELP 1, RELIEF

suc·cu·lent *adj* : JUICY

suc·cumb *vb* **suc·cumbed; suc·cumb·ing 1** : to yield to force or pressure **2** : ¹DIE 1

¹such *adj* **1** : of a kind just specified or to be specified **2** : of the same class, type, or sort : SIMILAR **3** : so great : so remarkable

²such *pron* : that sort of person, thing, or group

suck *vb* **sucked; suck·ing 1** : to draw something (as liquid or air) into the mouth **2** : to draw liquid from by action of the mouth **3** : to allow to dissolve gradually in the mouth **4** : to put (as a thumb) into the mouth and draw on as if drawing liquid **5** : to take in by or as if by absorption or suction

suck·er *n* **1** : a person easily fooled or cheated **2** : a part of an animal's body used for sucking or for clinging by suction **3** : LOLLIPOP **4** : a freshwater fish related to the carp that has thick soft lips for sucking in food **5** : a new stem from the roots or lower part of a plant **6** : SUCKLING

suck·le *vb* **suck·led; suck·ling** : to feed from the breast or udder

suck·ling *n* : a young mammal still sucking milk from its mother

su·crose *n* : a sweet usually crystalline substance found in many plants that is obtained especially from sugarcane and sugar beets for use in sweetening foods and beverages

suc·tion *n* **1** : the act or process of sucking **2** : the process of drawing something into a space (as in a pump) by removing air from the space **3** : the force caused by suction

sud·den *adj* **1** : happening or coming quickly and unexpectedly **2** : met with unexpectedly **3** : HASTY 2 — **sud·den·ly** *adv* — **sud·den·ness** *n* — **all of a sudden** : sooner than was expected : SUDDENLY

suds *n pl* **1** : soapy water especially when foamy **2** : the foam on soapy water

sue *vb* **sued; su·ing** : to seek justice or right by bringing legal action

suede *n* : leather tanned and rubbed so that it is soft and has a nap

su·et *n* : the hard fat around the kidneys in beef and mutton from which tallow is made

suf·fer *vb* **suf·fered; suf·fer·ing** **1** : to feel or endure pain, illness, or injury **2** : to experience something unpleasant **3** : to bear loss or damage **4** : to become worse **5** : [1]PERMIT 1 — **suf·fer·er** *n*

suf·fer·ing *n* : pain experienced during an injury or loss

suf·fice *vb* **suf·ficed; suf·fic·ing** : to satisfy a need : be enough

suf·fi·cient *adj* : enough to achieve a goal or fill a need — **suf·fi·cient·ly** *adv*

suf·fix *n* : a letter or group of letters that comes at the end of a word and has a meaning of its own

suf·fo·cate *vb* **suf·fo·cat·ed; suf·fo·cat·ing** **1** : to kill by stopping the breathing of or by depriving of oxygen to breathe **2** : to die from being unable to breathe **3** : to be or become choked or smothered **4** : to suffer from lack of fresh air

suf·fo·ca·tion *n* : the act of killing by or dying from lack of air : the state of being killed by lack of air

suf·frage *n* : the right to vote

[1]**sug·ar** *n* **1** : a sweet material that consists essentially of sucrose obtained from sugarcane or sugar beets, is typically colorless or white when pure, and is commonly used to sweeten foods and beverages **2** : any of numerous soluble and usually sweet carbohydrates (as glucose or sucrose) that occur naturally especially in plants

[2]**sugar** *vb* **su·gared; su·gar·ing** : to mix, cover, or sprinkle with sugar

sugar beet *n* : a large beet with white roots that is grown as a source of sugar

sug·ar·cane *n* : a tall strong grass with jointed stems widely raised in tropical regions for the sugar it yields

sugar maple *n* : a maple tree of the northeastern United States with hard strong wood and a sweet sap that is used to make maple syrup and maple sugar

sug·ary *adj* **1** : containing a lot of sugar **2** : too sweetly sentimental

sug·gest *vb* **sug·gest·ed; sug·gest·ing** **1** : to put (as a thought or desire) into a person's mind **2** : to recommend as being worthy of accepting or doing **3** : to call to mind through close connection or association

sug·ges·tion *n* **1** : a thought or plan that is offered or proposed **2** : the act or process of putting a thought in someone's mind **3** : [1]HINT 2

sug·ges·tive *adj* **1** : giving a hint **2** : full of suggestions **3** : suggesting something improper or indecent

sui·cide *n* **1** : the act of someone who kills himself or herself purposely **2** : a person who kills himself or herself purposely

[1]**suit** *n* **1** : a set of clothing having matching top and bottom pieces **2** : a set of clothes or protective coverings worn for a special purpose or under particular conditions **3** : an action in court to settle a disagreement or enforce a right or claim **4** : all the playing cards of one kind (as spades, hearts, diamonds, or clubs) in a pack

[2]**suit** *vb* **suit·ed; suit·ing** **1** : to be suitable or satisfactory **2** : to make suitable : ADAPT **3** : to be proper for or pleasing with **4** : to meet the needs or desires of

suit·able *adj* : being fit or right for a use or group — **suit·abil·i·ty** *n* — **suit·ably** *adv*

suit·case *n* : a flat rectangular traveling bag

suite *n* **1** : a number of connected rooms (as in a hotel) **2** : a set of matched furniture for a room

suit·or *n* : a man who tries to get a woman to marry him

sul·fur *also* **sul·phur** *n* : a yellow chemical element that is found widely in nature and is used in making chemicals and paper

sul·fu·rous *also* **sul·phu·rous** *adj* : containing or suggesting sulfur

[1]**sulk** *vb* **sulked; sulk·ing** : to be angry or irritable about something but childishly refuse to talk about it

[2]**sulk** *n* **1** : the state of a person who is sullenly silent or irritable **2** : a sulky mood

[1]**sulky** *adj* **sulk·i·er; sulk·i·est** **1** : angry or upset by something but refusing to discuss it **2** : often angry or upset

[2]**sulky** *n, pl* **sulk·ies** : a light vehicle with two wheels, a seat for the driver only, and usually no body

sul·len *adj* **1** : not sociable : SULKY **2** : GLOOMY 1, DREARY — **sul·len·ly** *adv*

sul·tan *n* : a ruler especially of a Muslim state

sul·ta·na *n* : the wife, mother, sister, or daughter of a sultan

sul·try *adj* **sul·tri·er; sul·tri·est** : very hot and humid

[1]**sum** *n* **1** : the result obtained by adding numbers **2** : a problem in arithmetic **3** : a quantity of money **4** : the whole amount

[2]**sum** *vb* **summed; sum·ming** : to find the total number of by adding or counting — **sum up** : to tell again in a few words : SUMMARIZE

su·mac *also* **su·mach** *n* : a tree, shrub, or woody vine that has leaves with many leaflets and loose clusters of red or white berries

sum·ma·rize *vb* **sum·ma·rized; sum·ma·riz-**

ing : to tell in or reduce to a short statement of the main points

¹**sum·ma·ry** *adj* **1** : expressing or covering the main points briefly : CONCISE **2** : done without delay

²**summary** *n, pl* **sum·ma·ries** : a short statement of the main points (as in a book or report)

¹**sum·mer** *n* **1** : the season between spring and autumn which is in the northern hemisphere usually the months of June, July, and August **2** : one of the years of a person's lifetime

²**summer** *vb* **sum·mered; sum·mer·ing** : to pass the summer

sum·mer·time *n* : the summer season

sum·mery *adj* : relating to or typical of summer

sum·mit *n* : the highest point (as of a mountain) : TOP

sum·mon *vb* **sum·moned; sum·mon·ing 1** : to call or send for : CONVENE **2** : to order to appear before a court of law **3** : to call into being : AROUSE

sum·mons *n, pl* **sum·mons·es 1** : the act of calling or sending for **2** : a call by authority to appear at a place named or to attend to some duty **3** : a written order to appear in court

sump·tu·ous *adj* : very expensive or luxurious

¹**sun** *n* **1** : the heavenly body in our solar system whose light makes our day and around which the planets revolve **2** : SUNSHINE 1 **3** : a heavenly body like our sun

²**sun** *vb* **sunned; sun·ning** : to expose to or lie or sit in the rays of the sun

Sun. *abbr* Sunday

sun·bathe *vb* **sun·bathed; sun·bath·ing** : to sit or lie in the rays of the sun to get a tan

sun·beam *n* : a ray of sunlight

sun·block *n* : a preparation applied to the skin to prevent sunburn usually by blocking the sun's ultraviolet radiation

sun·bon·net *n* : a bonnet with a wide curving brim that shades the face and usually a ruffle at the back that protects the neck from the sun

¹**sun·burn** *n* : a sore red state of the skin caused by too much sunlight

²**sunburn** *vb* **sun·burned** *or* **sun·burnt; sun·burn·ing** : to burn or discolor by exposure to the sun

sun·dae *n* : a serving of ice cream with a topping (as fruit, syrup, whipped cream, nuts, or bits of candy)

Sun·day *n* : the first day of the week

Sunday school *n* : a school held on Sunday in a church for religious education

sun·di·al *n* : a device that shows the time of day by the position of the shadow cast onto a marked plate by an object with a straight edge

sun·down *n* : SUNSET 2

sun·dries *n pl* : various small articles or items

sun·dry *adj* : more than one or two : VARIOUS

sun·fish *n, pl* **sunfish** *or* **sun·fish·es** : a small and brightly colored North American freshwater fish related to the perch

sun·flow·er *n* : a tall plant often grown for its large flower heads with brown center and yellow petals or for its edible oily seeds

sung *past and past participle of* SING

sun·glass·es *n pl* : glasses worn to protect the eyes from the sun

sunk *past and past participle of* SINK

sunk·en *adj* **1** : fallen in : HOLLOW **2** : lying at the bottom of a body of water **3** : built or settled below the surrounding or normal level

sun·less *adj* : being without sunlight : DARK

sun·light *n* : SUNSHINE 1

sun·lit *adj* : lighted by the sun

sun·ny *adj* **sun·ni·er; sun·ni·est 1** : bright with sunshine **2** : MERRY 1, CHEERFUL

sun·rise *n* **1** : the apparent rise of the sun above the horizon **2** : the light and color of the rise of the sun above the horizon **3** : the time at which the sun rises

sun·screen *n* : a preparation applied to the skin to prevent sunburn usually by chemically absorbing the sun's ultraviolet radiation

sun·set *n* **1** : the apparent passing of the sun below the horizon **2** : the light and color of the passing of the sun below the horizon **3** : the time at which the sun sets

sun·shade *n* : something (as a parasol) used to protect from the sun's rays

sun·shine *n* **1** : the sun's light or direct rays : the warmth and light given by the sun's rays **2** : something that spreads warmth or happiness

sun·stroke *n* : an illness that is marked by high fever and weakness and is caused by exposure to too much sun

sun·tan *n* : a browning of skin from exposure to the sun

sun·up *n* : SUNRISE 2

sun·ward *adv or adj* : toward or facing the sun

sup *vb* **supped; sup·ping** : to eat the evening meal

su·per *adj* **1** : very great **2** : very good

super- *prefix* **1** : more than **2** : extremely : very

su·perb *adj* : outstandingly excellent, impressive, or beautiful

su·per·com·put·er *n* : a large very fast computer used especially for scientific computations

su·per·fi·cial *adj* **1** : of or relating to the surface or appearance only **2** : not thorough or complete — **su·per·fi·cial·ly** *adv*

su·per·flu·ous *adj* : going beyond what is enough or necessary : EXTRA

su·per·he·ro *n* : a fictional hero having extraordinary or superhuman powers

su·per·high·way *n* : an expressway for high-speed traffic

su·per·hu·man *adj* : going beyond normal human power, size, or ability

su·per·in·tend *vb* **su·per·in·tend·ed; su·per·in·tend·ing** : to have or exercise the charge of

su·per·in·ten·dent *n* : a person who looks after or manages something (as schools or a building)

¹su·pe·ri·or *adj* **1** : situated higher up : higher in rank, importance, numbers, or quality **2** : excellent of its kind : BETTER **3** : showing the feeling of being better or more important than others : ARROGANT

²superior *n* **1** : a person who is higher than another in rank, importance, or quality **2** : the head of a religious house or order

su·pe·ri·or·i·ty *n* : the state or fact of being better, more important, or higher in rank than others

¹su·per·la·tive *adj* **1** : being the form of an adjective or adverb that shows the greatest degree of comparison **2** : better than all others : SUPREME

²superlative *n* : the superlative degree or a superlative form in a language

su·per·mar·ket *n* : a store selling foods and household items

su·per·nat·u·ral *adj* : of or relating to something beyond or outside of nature or the visible universe

su·per·sede *vb* **su·per·sed·ed; su·per·sed·ing** : to take the place or position of

su·per·son·ic *adj* **1** : above the normal range of human hearing **2** : having a speed from one to five times that of sound

su·per·sti·tion *n* : a belief or practice resulting from ignorance, fear of the unknown, or trust in magic or chance

su·per·sti·tious *adj* : showing or influenced by superstition

su·per·vise *vb* **su·per·vised; su·per·vis·ing** : to coordinate and direct the activities of

su·per·vi·sion *n* : the act of overseeing : MANAGEMENT

su·per·vi·sor *n* **1** : a person who is in charge of others **2** : an officer in charge of a unit or an operation of a business, government, or school

sup·per *n* **1** : the evening meal especially

when dinner is eaten at midday **2** : refreshments served late in the evening especially at a social gathering

sup·plant *vb* **sup·plant·ed; sup·plant·ing** : to take the place of another

sup·ple *adj* **sup·pler ; sup·plest 1** : capable of bending or of being bent easily without stiffness, creases, or damage **2** : ADAPTABLE

¹sup·ple·ment *n* : something that supplies what is needed or adds to something else

²sup·ple·ment *vb* **sup·ple·ment·ed; sup·ple·ment·ing** : to add to : COMPLETE

sup·ple·men·ta·ry *adj* : added to something else : ADDITIONAL

sup·pli·cate *vb* **sup·pli·cat·ed; sup·pli·cat·ing** : to ask or beg in a humble way : BESEECH

sup·pli·ca·tion *n* : the act of asking or begging in a humble way

¹sup·ply *vb* **sup·plied; sup·ply·ing 1** : to provide for : SATISFY **2** : to make available : FURNISH

²supply *n, pl* **sup·plies 1** : the amount of something that is needed or can be gotten **2** : ²STORE 3 **3** : the act or process of providing something

¹sup·port *vb* **sup·port·ed; sup·port·ing 1** : to hold up or in position : serve as a foundation or prop for **2** : to take sides with : FAVOR **3** : to provide evidence for : VERIFY **4** : to pay the costs of : MAINTAIN **5** : to keep going : SUSTAIN **6** : to provide help or encouragement to — **sup·port·er** *n*

²support *n* **1** : the act of supporting : the condition of being supported **2** : someone or something that supports

sup·pose *vb* **sup·posed; sup·pos·ing 1** : to think of as true or as a fact for the sake of argument **2** : BELIEVE 2, THINK **3** : ¹GUESS 1

sup·posed *adj* **1** : forced, expected, or required **2** : believed or claimed to be true or real **3** : given permission — **sup·pos·ed·ly** *adv*

sup·press *vb* **sup·pressed; sup·press·ing 1** : to put down (as by authority or force) : SUBDUE **2** : to hold back : REPRESS

sup·pres·sion *n* : an act or instance of putting down or holding back : the state of being put down or held back

su·prem·a·cy *n, pl* **su·prem·a·cies** : the highest rank, power, or authority

su·preme *adj* **1** : highest in rank, power, or authority **2** : highest in degree or quality **3** : most extreme or great — **su·preme·ly** *adv*

Supreme Being *n* : GOD 1

supreme court *n, often cap* : the highest court of law in the United States or in many of its states

¹sure *adj* **sur·er; sur·est 1 :** having no doubt **: CERTAIN 2 :** true without question **3 :** firmly established **4 : RELIABLE, TRUSTWORTHY 5 :** bound to happen **6 :** bound as if by fate

²sure *adv* **1 : SURELY** 1 **2 : SURELY** 2

sure·ly *adv* **1 :** without doubt **2 :** beyond question **: REALLY 3 :** with confidence **: CONFIDENTLY**

¹surf *n* **1 :** the waves of the sea that splash on the shore **2 :** the sound, splash, and foam of breaking waves

²surf *vb* **surfed; surf·ing 1 :** to ride the incoming waves of the sea (as on a surfboard) **2 :** to scan a wide range of offerings (as on television or the Internet) for something that is interesting or fills a need

¹sur·face *n* **1 :** the outside or any one side of an object **2 :** the outside appearance

²surface *adj* **:** not deep or real

³surface *vb* **sur·faced; sur·fac·ing 1 :** to come to the surface **2 :** to become obvious **3 :** to give a new top layer to **:** make smooth (as by sanding or paving)

surf·board *n* **:** a long narrow board that floats and is ridden in surfing

surf·ing *n* **:** the sport of riding waves toward the shore usually while standing on a surfboard

¹surge *vb* **surged; surg·ing 1 :** to rise suddenly and greatly **2 :** to move suddenly and quickly in a particular direction

²surge *n* **1 :** a rush like that of a wave **2 :** a large wave

sur·geon *n* **:** a doctor who performs surgery

sur·gery *n, pl* **sur·ger·ies :** medical treatment (as of disease, injury, or physical abnormality) that involves cutting into the body usually to expose internal parts

sur·gi·cal *adj* **:** of, relating to, or associated with surgery or surgeons

sur·ly *adj* **sur·li·er; sur·li·est :** mean and rude **: UNFRIENDLY**

¹sur·mise *n* **:** a thought or idea based on very little evidence **: GUESS**

²surmise *vb* **sur·mised; sur·mis·ing :** to form an idea on very little evidence **: GUESS**

sur·mount *vb* **sur·mount·ed; sur·mount·ing 1 : OVERCOME** 1 **2 :** to get to the top of **3 :** to be at the top of

sur·name *n* **:** the name that comes at the end of someone's full name

sur·pass *vb* **sur·passed; sur·pass·ing 1 :** to be greater, better, or stronger than **: EXCEED 2 :** to go beyond the reach or powers of

¹sur·plus *n* **:** an amount left over **: EXCESS**

²surplus *adj* **:** left over **: EXTRA**

¹sur·prise *n* **1 :** something that is unexpected **2 : ASTONISHMENT, AMAZEMENT 3 :** an act or instance of coming upon without warning

²surprise *vb* **sur·prised; sur·pris·ing 1 :** to cause to feel wonder or amazement because of being unexpected **2 :** to come upon without warning **3 :** to attack without warning **:** capture by an unexpected attack

sur·pris·ing *adj* **:** causing astonishment **: UNEXPECTED — sur·pris·ing·ly** *adv*

¹sur·ren·der *vb* **sur·ren·dered; sur·ren·der·ing 1 :** to give up after a struggle **2 :** to let go of **: RELINQUISH**

²surrender *n* **1 :** the act of giving up after a struggle **2 :** the act of giving something over to the possession or control of someone else

sur·rey *n, pl* **surreys :** a pleasure carriage that has two wide seats and four wheels and is drawn by horses

sur·round *vb* **sur·round·ed; sur·round·ing 1 :** to enclose on all sides **: ENCIRCLE 2 :** to be closely related or connected to

sur·round·ings *n pl* **:** the circumstances, conditions, or things around an individual **: ENVIRONMENT**

¹sur·vey *vb* **sur·veyed; sur·vey·ing 1 :** to look over **: EXAMINE 2 :** to find out the size, shape, or boundaries of (as a piece of land) **3 :** to gather information from **:** ask questions of

²sur·vey *n, pl* **surveys 1 :** the action or an instance of gathering information or examining something **2 :** something that is examined **3 :** a history or description that covers a large subject briefly

sur·vey·ing *n* **1 :** the act or occupation of a person who determines the size, shape, or boundaries of a piece of land **2 :** a branch of mathematics that teaches how to measure the earth's surface and record these measurements accurately

sur·vey·or *n* **:** a person whose occupation is determining the size, shape, or boundries of pieces of land

sur·viv·al *n* **:** the continuation of life

sur·vive *vb* **sur·vived; sur·viv·ing 1 :** to remain alive **:** continue to exist **2 :** to live or exist longer than or past the end of **— sur·vi·vor** *n*

sus·cep·ti·ble *adj* **1 :** of such a nature as to permit **2 :** having little resistance (as to infection or damage) **3 :** easily affected or impressed by

¹sus·pect *vb* **sus·pect·ed; sus·pect·ing 1 :** to suppose to be true or likely **2 :** to have doubts of **: DISTRUST 3 :** to imagine to be guilty without proof

²sus·pect *n* **:** a person who is thought to be guilty of something

³sus·pect *adj* **:** thought of with suspicion

sus·pend *vb* **sus·pend·ed; sus·pend·ing 1 :** to force to give up some right or office for a time **2** : to hang especially so as to be free except at one point **3** : to stop or do away with for a time **4** : to stop operation or action for a time

sus·pend·er *n* : one of a pair of straps that are attached to pants or a skirt and go over the shoulders

sus·pense *n* : uncertainty, worry, or excitement in wondering about the result of something

sus·pen·sion *n* **1** : the act of stopping, removing, or making someone or something ineffective for a time **2** : the state of being stopped, removed, or made ineffective for a time **3** : the period during which someone or something is stopped, removed, or made ineffective **4** : the act of hanging : the state of being hung **5** : the system of springs that support the upper part of a vehicle on the axles

sus·pi·cion *n* **1** : an act or instance of suspecting or the state of being suspected **2** : a feeling that something is wrong : DOUBT

sus·pi·cious *adj* **1** : likely to arouse suspicion **2** : likely to distrust or be distrustful **3** : showing distrust

sus·tain *vb* **sus·tained; sus·tain·ing 1** : to provide with what is needed **2** : to keep up the spirits of **3** : to keep up : PROLONG **4** : to hold up the weight of **5** : ^{2}EXPERIENCE **6** : to allow or uphold as true, legal, or fair

sus·te·nance *n* **1** : ^{2}LIVING 3, SUBSISTENCE **2** : the act of supplying with the necessities of life **3** : ^{2}SUPPORT 2

SUV *n, pl* **SUVs** : SPORT-UTILITY VEHICLE

SW *abbr* southwest

^{1}**swab** *n* **1** : a yarn mop especially as used on a ship **2** : a wad of absorbent material usually wound around the end of a small stick and used for applying or removing material (as medicine or makeup)

^{2}**swab** *vb* **swabbed; swab·bing 1** : to clean with or as if with a mop **2** : to apply medication to with a wad of absorbent material

^{1}**swag·ger** *vb* **swag·gered; swag·ger·ing** : to walk with a proud strut

^{2}**swagger** *n* : an act or instance of walking with a proud strut

^{1}**swal·low** *n* : a small bird that has long wings and a forked tail and feeds on insects caught while in flight

^{2}**swallow** *vb* **swal·lowed; swal·low·ing 1** : to take into the stomach through the mouth and throat **2** : to perform the actions used in swallowing something **3** : to completely surround : ENGULF **4** : to accept or believe without question **5** : to keep from expressing or showing : REPRESS

^{3}**swallow** *n* **1** : an act of taking something

into the stomach through the mouth and throat : an act of swallowing **2** : an amount that can be swallowed at one time

swam *past of* SWIM

^{1}**swamp** *n* : wet spongy land often partly covered with water

^{2}**swamp** *vb* **swamped; swamp·ing 1** : to fill or cause to fill with water : sink after filling with water **2** : OVERWHELM 1

swampy *adj* **swamp·i·er; swamp·i·est** : consisting of or like a swamp

swan *n* : a usually white waterbird that has a long neck and large body and is related to but larger than the goose

^{1}**swap** *vb* **swapped; swap·ping** : to give in exchange : make an exchange : TRADE

^{2}**swap** *n* : ^{1}EXCHANGE 1, TRADE

^{1}**swarm** *n* **1** : a large number of bees that leave a hive together to form a new colony elsewhere **2** : a large number grouped together and usually in motion

^{2}**swarm** *vb* **swarmed; swarm·ing 1** : to form a swarm and leave the hive **2** : to move or gather in a large number **3** : to be filled with a great number : TEEM

swar·thy *adj* **swar·thi·er; swar·thi·est** : having a dark complexion

^{1}**swat** *vb* **swat·ted; swat·ting** : to hit with a quick hard blow

^{2}**swat** *n* : a hard blow

swath *or* **swathe** *n, pl* **swaths** *or* **swathes 1** : an area of grass or grain that has been cut or mowed **2** : a long broad strip or belt

^{1}**sway** *vb* **swayed; sway·ing 1** : to swing slowly back and forth or from side to side **2** : to change or cause to change between one point, position, or opinion and another

^{2}**sway** *n* **1** : the act of slowly swinging back and forth or from side to side **2** : a controlling influence or force : RULE

swear *vb* **swore; sworn; swear·ing 1** : to use bad or vulgar language : CURSE **2** : to make a statement or promise with sincerity or under oath : VOW **3** : to give an oath to **4** : to bind by an oath **5** : to be or feel certain

^{1}**sweat** *vb* **sweat** *or* **sweat·ed; sweat·ing 1** : to give off salty moisture through the pores of the skin : PERSPIRE **2** : to collect moisture on the surface **3** : to work hard enough to perspire

^{2}**sweat** *n* **1** : PERSPIRATION 2 **2** : moisture coming from or collecting in drops on a surface **3** : the condition of one perspiring

sweat·er *n* : a knitted or crocheted piece of clothing for the upper body

sweat gland *n* : a small gland of the skin that gives off perspiration

sweat·shirt *n* : a loose pullover or jacket without a collar and usually with long sleeves

sweaty *adj* **sweat·i·er; sweat·i·est** : wet with, stained by, or smelling of sweat

Swede *n* : a person born or living in Sweden

¹Swed·ish *adj* : of or relating to Sweden, the Swedes, or Swedish

²Swedish *n* : the language of the Swedes

¹sweep *vb* **swept; sweep·ing** 1 : to remove with a broom or brush 2 : to clean by removing loose dirt or small trash with a broom or brush 3 : to move over or across swiftly often with force or destruction 4 : to move or gather as if with a broom or brush 5 : to move the eyes or an instrument through a wide curve 6 : to touch a surface of quickly 7 : to drive along with steady force 8 : to become suddenly very popular throughout 9 : to achieve a complete or easy victory — **sweep·er** *n*

²sweep *n* 1 : a curving movement, course, or line 2 : an act or instance of cleaning with a broom or brush 3 : a wide stretch or curve of land 4 : something that sweeps or works with a sweeping motion 5 : a complete or easy victory 6 : ¹RANGE 2, SCOPE 7 : CHIMNEY SWEEP

¹sweep·ing *adj* 1 : moving or extending in a wide curve or over a wide area 2 : EXTENSIVE

²sweeping *n* 1 : an act of cleaning an area with a broom or brush 2 **sweepings** *pl* : things collected by sweeping

sweep·stakes *n pl* : a contest in which money or prizes are given to winners picked by chance (as by drawing names) — used as singular or plural

¹sweet *adj* **sweet·er; sweet·est** 1 : containing or tasting of sugar 2 : having a pleasant sound, smell, or appearance 3 : very gentle, kind, or friendly 4 : pleasing to the mind or feelings : AGREEABLE 5 : much loved : DEAR 6 : agreeable to oneself but not to others 7 : not sour, stale, or spoiled 8 : not salt or salted 9 : having a mild taste : not sharp — **sweet·ly** *adv* — **sweet·ness** *n* — **sweet on** : in love with

²sweet *n* 1 : something (as candy) that contains or tastes of sugar 2 : ¹DARLING 1, DEAR

sweet corn *n* : corn with kernels rich in sugar that is cooked and eaten as a vegetable while young

sweet·en *vb* **sweet·ened; sweet·en·ing** : to make or become sweet or sweeter

sweet·en·ing *n* 1 : the act or process of making sweet 2 : something that sweetens

sweet·heart *n* : a person whom one loves

sweet·meat *n* : a food (as a piece of candy or candied fruit) rich in sugar

sweet pea *n* : a climbing plant that is grown for its fragrant flowers of many colors

sweet potato *n* : the large sweet edible root of a tropical vine that is cooked and eaten as a vegetable

¹swell *vb* **swelled; swelled** *or* **swol·len; swell·ing** 1 : to enlarge in an abnormal way usually by pressure from within or by growth 2 : to grow or make bigger (as in size or value) 3 : to stretch upward or outward : BULGE 4 : to fill or become filled with emotion

²swell *n* 1 : a gradual increase in size, value, or volume 2 : a long rolling wave or series of waves in the open sea 3 : the condition of bulging 4 : a rounded elevation

³swell *adj* : EXCELLENT, FIRST-RATE

swell·ing *n* : a swollen lump or part

swel·ter *vb* **swel·tered; swel·ter·ing** : to suffer, sweat, or be faint from heat

swel·ter·ing *adj* : oppressively hot

swept *past and past participle of* SWEEP

¹swerve *vb* **swerved; swerv·ing** : to turn aside suddenly from a straight line or course

²swerve *n* : an act or instance of turning aside suddenly

¹swift *adj* **swift·er; swift·est** 1 : moving or capable of moving with great speed 2 : occurring suddenly — **swift·ly** *adv* — **swift·ness** *n*

²swift *adv* : in a swift manner

³swift *n* : a small usually black bird that is related to the hummingbirds but looks like a swallow

swig *n* : the amount drunk at one time : GULP

¹swill *vb* **swilled; swill·ing** : to eat or drink greedily

²swill *n* 1 : ¹SLOP 2 2 : GARBAGE 1, REFUSE

¹swim *vb* **swam; swum; swim·ming** 1 : to move through or in water by moving arms, legs, fins, or tail 2 : to cross by swimming 3 : to float on or in or be covered with or as if with a liquid 4 : to be dizzy : move or seem to move in a dizzying way — **swim·mer** *n*

²swim *n* : an act or period of swimming

swimming pool *n* : a tank (as of concrete or plastic) made for swimming

swim·suit *n* : a garment for swimming or bathing

¹swin·dle *vb* **swin·dled; swin·dling** : to get money or property from dishonestly : CHEAT

²swindle *n* : an act or instance of getting money or property from someone dishonestly

swin·dler *n* : a person who swindles

swine *n, pl* **swine** : a wild or domestic pig

¹**swing** *vb* **swung; swing·ing 1 :** to move rapidly in a sweeping curve **2 :** to turn on a hinge or pivot **3 :** to move with a curving motion **4 :** to turn or move quickly in a particular direction **5 :** to move back and forth or from side to side while hanging from a fixed point **6 :** to move back and forth in or on a swing **7 :** to manage or handle successfully

²**swing** *n* **1 :** a seat usually hung by overhead ropes and used to move back and forth **2 :** an act of moving something (as a bat) rapidly in a sweeping curve **3 :** a sweeping movement, blow, or rhythm **4 :** the distance through which something sways to and fro **5 :** a style of jazz marked by lively rhythm and played mostly for dancing

¹**swipe** *n* **:** a strong sweeping movement

²**swipe** *vb* **swiped; swip·ing 1 :** ¹STEAL 1 **2 :** to make a strong sweeping movement

¹**swirl** *vb* **swirled; swirl·ing :** to move with a spinning or twisting motion

²**swirl** *n* **1 :** a spinning mass or motion **:** EDDY **2 :** busy movement or activity **3 :** a twisting shape or mark

¹**swish** *vb* **swished; swish·ing :** to make, move, or strike with a soft sweeping or brushing sound

²**swish** *n* **1 :** a soft sweeping or brushing sound **2 :** a movement that produces a sweeping or brushing sound

¹**Swiss** *n, pl* **Swiss :** a person born or living in Switzerland

²**Swiss** *adj* **:** of or relating to Switzerland or the Swiss

¹**switch** *n* **1 :** a device for making, breaking, or changing the connections in an electrical circuit **2 :** a change from one thing to another **3 :** a narrow flexible whip, rod, or twig **4 :** an act of switching **5 :** a device for adjusting the rails of a track so that a train or streetcar may be turned from one track to another

²**switch** *vb* **switched; switch·ing 1 :** to turn, shift, or change by operating a device that makes, breaks, or changes the connections in an electrical circuit **2 :** to move quickly from side to side **3 :** to make a shift or change **4 :** to strike with or as if with a whip, rod, or twig

switch·board *n* **:** a panel for controlling the operation of a number of electric circuits

¹**swiv·el** *n* **:** a device joining two parts so that one or both can turn freely (as on a bolt or pin)

²**swivel** *vb* **swiv·eled** *or* **swiv·elled; swiv·el·ing** *or* **swiv·el·ling :** to turn on or as if on a swivel

swollen *past participle of* SWELL

¹**swoon** *vb* **swooned; swoon·ing :** ²FAINT

²**swoon** *n* **:** ³FAINT

¹**swoop** *vb* **swooped; swoop·ing :** to rush down or pounce suddenly

²**swoop** *n* **:** an act or instance of rushing down or pouncing suddenly

sword *n* **:** a weapon having a long blade usually with a sharp point and edge

sword·fish *n, pl* **swordfish** *or* **sword·fish·es :** a large ocean fish that has a long pointed bill formed by the bones of the upper jaw and is often used for food

swords·man *n, pl* **swords·men :** a person who fights with a sword

swore *past of* SWEAR

sworn *past participle of* SWEAR

swum *past participle of* SWIM

swung *past and past participle of* SWING

syc·a·more *n* **1 :** a fig tree of Egypt and the Middle East **2 :** a large tree of the United States with round hard fruits and bark that peels off in flakes

syl·lab·ic *adj* **:** relating to or being syllables

syl·lab·i·cate *vb* **syl·lab·i·cat·ed; syl·lab·i·cat·ing :** SYLLABIFY

syl·lab·i·ca·tion *n* **:** the forming of syllables **:** the dividing of words into syllables

syl·lab·i·fi·ca·tion *n* **:** SYLLABICATION

syl·lab·i·fy *vb* **syl·lab·i·fied; syl·lab·i·fy·ing :** to form or divide into syllables

syl·la·ble *n* **1 :** a unit of spoken language that consists of one or more vowel sounds alone or with one or more consonant sounds coming before or following **2 :** one or more letters (as *syl, la,* and *ble*) in a written word (as *syl·la·ble*) usually separated from the rest of the word by a centered dot or a hyphen and used as guides to the division of the word at the end of a line

sym·bol *n* **1 :** something that stands for something else **:** EMBLEM **2 :** a letter, character, or sign used instead of a word to represent a quantity, position, relationship, direction, or something to be done

sym·bol·ic *also* **sym·bol·i·cal** *adj* **:** of, relating to, or using symbols or symbolism

sym·bol·ism *n* **1 :** the use of symbols to represent an idea or quality **2 :** the meaning of a symbol

sym·bol·ize *vb* **sym·bol·ized; sym·bol·iz·ing :** to serve as a representation of

sym·met·ri·cal *or* **sym·met·ric** *adj* **:** having or showing symmetry

sym·me·try *n, pl* **sym·me·tries :** close agreement in size, shape, and position of parts that are on opposite sides of a dividing line or center **:** an arrangement involving regular and balanced proportions

sym·pa·thet·ic *adj* **1 :** feeling or showing care or understanding **2 :** feeling favorable — **sym·pa·thet·i·cal·ly** *adv*

sym·pa·thize *vb* **sym·pa·thized; sym·pa·thiz·ing** **1** : to feel or show pity or care and understanding for **2** : to be in favor of something

sym·pa·thy *n, pl* **sym·pa·thies** **1** : sorrow or pity for another **2** : readiness to favor or support **3** : a relationship between people or things in which whatever affects one similarly affects the other

sym·phon·ic *adj* : relating to a symphony

sym·pho·ny *n, pl* **sym·pho·nies** **1** : a usually long musical composition for a full orchestra **2** : a large orchestra of wind, string, and percussion instruments **3** : harmonious arrangement (as of sound or color)

symp·tom *n* **1** : a noticeable change in the body or its functions that indicates the presence of a disease or other disorder **2** : INDICATION 2, SIGN

syn. *abbr* synonym

syn·a·gogue *also* **syn·a·gog** *n* : a Jewish house of worship

syn·apse *n* : the point at which a nerve impulse passes from one nerve cell to another

syn·co·pa·tion *n* : an instance of temporarily accenting a normally weak beat in music to vary the rhythm

syn·o·nym *n* : a word having the same or almost the same meaning as another word in the same language

syn·on·y·mous *adj* : alike in meaning

syn·tax *n* : the way in which words are put together to form phrases, clauses, or sentences

syn·the·size *vb* **syn·the·sized; syn·the·siz·ing** : to produce from the combination of simpler materials

syn·thet·ic *adj* : produced artificially especially by chemical means : produced by human beings

sy·ringe *n* : a device used to force fluid into or withdraw it from the body or its cavities

syr·up *n* **1** : a thick sticky solution of sugar and water often containing flavoring or a medicine **2** : the juice of a fruit or plant with some of the water removed

sys·tem *n* **1** : a group of parts combined to form a whole that works or moves as a unit **2** : a body that functions as a whole **3** : a group of organs that together perform an important function in the body **4** : an orderly way of managing, controlling, organizing, or doing something

sys·tem·at·ic *adj* : using a system or a regular and orderly method — **sys·tem·at·i·cal·ly** *adv*

sys·tem·ic *adj* : of or relating to the body as a whole

T

t *n, pl* **t's** *or* **ts** *often cap* : the 20th letter of the English alphabet — **to a T** : just fine : EXACTLY

T *abbr* true

tab *n* **1** : a short flap or tag attached to something for filing, pulling, or hanging **2** : a careful watch

tab·by *n, pl* **tabbies** : a domestic cat with a striped and spotted coat

tab·er·na·cle *n* **1** : a place of worship **2** *often cap* : a tent used as a place of worship by the ancient Israelites during their wanderings in the wilderness with Moses

¹ta·ble *n* **1** : a piece of furniture having a smooth flat top on legs **2** : food to eat **3** : the people around a table **4** : short list **5** : an arrangement in rows or columns for reference

²table *vb* **ta·bled; ta·bling** **1** : TABULATE **2** : to put on a table

tab·leau *n, pl* **tab·leaux** *also* **tab·leaus** : a scene or event shown by a group of persons who remain still and silent

ta·ble·cloth *n* : a covering spread over a dining table before the places are set

ta·ble·land *n* : PLATEAU

ta·ble·spoon *n* **1** : a large spoon used mostly for dishing up food **2** : a unit of measure used in cooking equal to ½ fluid ounce (about 15 milliliters)

ta·ble·spoon·ful *n, pl* **tablespoonfuls** *also* **ta·ble·spoons·ful** **1** : as much as a tablespoon will hold **2** : TABLESPOON 2

tab·let *n* **1** : a thin flat slab used for writing, painting, or drawing **2** : a number of sheets of writing paper glued together at one edge **3** : a small usually round mass of material containing medicine

table tennis *n* : a game played on a table by two or four players who use paddles to hit a small hollow plastic ball back and forth over a net

ta·ble·ware *n* : utensils (as of china, glass, or silver) for use at the table

tab·u·late *vb* **tab·u·lat·ed; tab·u·lat·ing** : to count and record in an orderly way

tac·it *adj* : understood or made known without being put into words — **tac·it·ly** *adv*

¹tack *n* **1** : a small nail with a sharp point and usually a broad flat head **2** : the direction a

take

ship is sailing as shown by the position the sails are set in **3** : a course or method of action **4** : a temporary stitch used in sewing

²**tack** *vb* **tacked; tack·ing 1** : to fasten with tacks **2** : to attach or join loosely or quickly **3** : to change from one course to another in sailing **4** : to follow a zigzag course

¹**tack·le** *vb* **tack·led; tack·ling 1** : to seize and throw (a person) to the ground **2** : to begin working on

²**tackle** *n* **1** : a set of special equipment **2** : an arrangement of ropes and wheels for hoisting or pulling something heavy **3** : an act of seizing and throwing a person to the ground **4** : a football player positioned on the line of scrimmage

ta·co *n, pl* **tacos** : a corn tortilla usually folded and fried and filled with a spicy mixture (as of ground meat and cheese)

tact *n* : the ability to do or say things without offending other people

tact·ful *adj* : having or showing the ability to do or say things without offending other people — **tact·ful·ly** *adv* — **tact·ful·ness** *n*

tac·tic *n* : a planned action for some purpose

tac·tics *n pl* **1** : the science and art of arranging and moving troops or warships for best use **2** : a system or method for reaching a goal — used as singular or plural

tac·tile *adj* : relating to the sense of touch

tact·less *adj* : having or showing no tact — **tact·less·ly** *adv* — **tact·less·ness** *n*

tad·pole *n* : the larva of a frog or toad that has a long tail, breathes with gills, and lives in water

taf·fy *n, pl* **taffies** : a candy made usually of molasses or brown sugar boiled and pulled until soft

¹**tag** *n* : a small flap or tab fixed or hanging on something

²**tag** *vb* **tagged; tag·ging 1** : to follow closely and continually **2** : to put a tab or label on — **tag along** : to follow another's lead in going from one place to another

³**tag** *n* : a game in which one player who is it chases the others and tries to touch one of them to make that person it

⁴**tag** *vb* **tagged; tag·ging 1** : to touch in or as if in a game of tag **2** : to touch a runner in baseball with the ball and cause the runner to be out

¹**tail** *n* **1** : the rear part of an animal or a usually slender flexible growth that extends from this part **2** : something that in shape, appearance, or position is like an animal's tail **3** : the back, last, or lower part of something **4** : the side or end opposite the head — **tailed** *adj* — **tail·less** *adj*

²**tail** *vb* **tailed; tail·ing** : to follow closely to keep watch on

tail·gate *n* : a panel at the back end of a vehicle that can be lowered for loading and unloading

¹**tai·lor** *n* : a person whose business is making or making adjustments in clothes

²**tailor** *vb* **tai·lored; tai·lor·ing 1** : to make or make adjustments in (clothes) **2** : to change to fit a special need

tail·pipe *n* : the pipe carrying off the exhaust gases from the muffler of an engine in a car or truck

tail·spin *n* : a dive by an airplane turning in a circle

¹**taint** *vb* **taint·ed; taint·ing 1** : to rot slightly **2** : to affect slightly with something bad

²**taint** *n* : a trace of decay

¹**take** *vb* **took; tak·en; tak·ing 1** : to get hold of : GRASP **2** : to carry or go with from one place to another **3** : to get control of : CAPTURE **4** : to receive into the body **5** : to get possession or use of **6** : to begin to perform the responsibilities of : ASSUME **7** : to do the action of **8** : to use as a way of going from one place to another **9** : REQUIRE 1 **10** : to put up with : ENDURE **11** : to come upon **12** : to adopt or accept **13** : WIN 2 **14** : CHOOSE 1, SELECT **15** : to sit in or on **16** : to find out by testing or examining **17** : to save in some permanent form **18** : BELIEVE 2 **19** : to be guided by : FOLLOW **20** : to become affected suddenly **21** : UNDERSTAND 4, INTERPRET **22** : to react in a certain way **23** : SUBTRACT **24** : CONSIDER 1 **25** : to have effect : be successful **26** : to be formed or used with **27** : CAPTIVATE, DELIGHT — **tak·er** *n* — **take advantage of 1** : to make good use of **2** : to treat (someone) unfairly — **take after** : RESEMBLE — **take back** : to try to cancel (as something said) — **take care** : to be careful — **take care of** : to do what is needed : look after — **take charge** : to assume care or control — **take effect 1** : to go into existence or operation **2** : to have an intended or expected result — **take for granted** : to assume as true, real, or expected — **take hold** : to become attached or established — **take in 1** : to make smaller **2** : to receive as a guest **3** : to allow to join **4** : to receive and do at home for pay **5** : to have within its limits **6** : to go to **7** : to get the meaning of **8** : ¹CHEAT 2 — **take off 1** : to take away (a covering) : REMOVE **2** : DEDUCT **3** : to leave a surface in beginning a flight or leap — **take on 1** : to begin (a task) or struggle against (an opponent) **2** : to gain or show as or as if a part of oneself **3** : ¹EMPLOY 2 **4** : to make an unusual show of grief or anger — **take over** : to get control of — **take part** : to do or join in something together with others — **take place** : to

come about or occur : HAPPEN — **take up 1** : to get together from many sources **2** : to start something for the first time or after a pause **3** : to change by making tighter or shorter

²take n **1** : the number or quantity of animals or fish killed, captured, or caught **2** : money received

take·off n **1** : an act or instance of leaving the ground (as by an airplane) **2** : an imitation especially to mock the original **3** : a spot at which something leaves the ground

talc n : a soft mineral that has a soapy feel and is used especially in making talcum powder

tal·cum powder n : a usually perfumed powder for the body made of talc

tale n **1** : something told **2** : a story about an imaginary event **3** : ³LIE **4** : a piece of harmful gossip

tal·ent n **1** : unusual natural ability **2** : a special often creative or artistic ability **3** : a person or group of people having special abilities — **tal·ent·ed** adj

tal·is·man n, pl **tal·is·mans** : a ring or stone carved with symbols and believed to have magical powers : CHARM

¹talk vb **talked; talk·ing 1** : to express in speech : SPEAK **2** : to speak about : DISCUSS **3** : to cause or influence with words **4** : to use a certain language **5** : to exchange ideas by means of spoken words : CONVERSE **6** : to pass on information other than by speaking **7** : ²GOSSIP **8** : to reveal secret information — **talk·er** n — **talk over** : DISCUSS 1

²talk n **1** : the act or an instance of speaking with someone **2** : a way of speaking : LANGUAGE **3** : CONFERENCE **4** : ¹RUMOR **5** : the topic of comment or gossip **6** : an informal address

talk·a·tive adj : fond of talking — **talk·a·tive·ness** n

talk·ing–to n : an often wordy scolding

¹tall adj **tall·er; tall·est 1** : having unusually great height **2** : of a stated height **3** : made up — **tall·ness** n

²tall adv : so as to be or look tall

tal·low n : a white solid fat of cattle and sheep used mostly in making candles and soap

¹tal·ly n, pl **tallies 1** : a recorded count **2** : a score or point made (as in a game)

²tally vb **tal·lied; tal·ly·ing 1** : to keep a count of **2** : to make a tally : SCORE **3** : to match or agree : CORRESPOND

Tal·mud n : a collection of writings on Jewish law and custom and religious practice

tal·on n : the claw of a bird of prey — **tal·oned** adj

ta·ma·le n : seasoned ground meat rolled in cornmeal, wrapped in corn husks, and steamed

tam·bou·rine n : a small shallow drum with only one head and loose metal disks around the rim that is played by shaking or hitting with the hand

¹tame adj **tam·er; tam·est 1** : changed from the wild state so as to become useful and obedient to people : DOMESTIC **2** : not afraid of people **3** : not interesting : DULL — **tame·ly** adv

²tame vb **tamed; tam·ing** : to make or become gentle or obedient — **tam·er** n

tamp vb **tamped; tamp·ing** : to press down or in by hitting lightly

tam·per vb **tam·pered; tam·per·ing** : to interfere or change in a secret or incorrect way

¹tan vb **tanned; tan·ning 1** : to change animal hide into leather especially by soaking in a tannin solution **2** : to make or become brown in color **3** : ¹BEAT 1, THRASH

²tan adj **tan·ner; tan·nest** : of a light yellowish brown color

³tan n **1** : a brown color given to the skin by the sun or wind **2** : a light yellowish brown : the color of sand

tan·a·ger n : a brightly colored mostly tropical bird that feeds on insects and fruit

¹tan·dem n **1** : a carriage pulled by horses hitched one behind the other **2** : TANDEM BICYCLE

²tandem adv : one behind another

tandem bicycle n : a bicycle for two people sitting one behind the other

tang n : a sharp flavor or smell — **tangy** adj

tan·ger·ine n : a Chinese orange with a loose skin and sweet pulp

tan·gi·ble adj **1** : possible to touch or handle : MATERIAL **2** : easily seen or recognized — **tan·gi·bly** adv

¹tan·gle vb **tan·gled; tan·gling** : to twist or become twisted together into a mass that is hard to straighten out again

²tangle n **1** : a mass that is twisted together and hard to straighten **2** : a complicated or confused state

tank n **1** : an often large container for a liquid **2** : an enclosed combat vehicle that has heavy armor and guns and a tread which is an endless belt

tan·kard n : a tall cup with one handle and often a lid

tank·er n : a vehicle or ship with tanks for carrying a liquid

tan·ner n : a person who tans hides into leather

tan·nery n, pl **tan·ner·ies** : a place where hides are tanned

tan·nin n : a substance often made from oak bark or sumac and used in tanning animal hides, dyeing fabric and yarn, and making ink

tan·ta·lize *vb* **tan·ta·lized; tan·ta·liz·ing** : to tease or excite by or as if by showing, mentioning, or offering something desirable but keeping it out of reach

tan·trum *n* : an outburst of bad temper

¹tap *vb* **tapped; tap·ping** : to hit lightly — **tap·per** *n*

²tap *n* : a light blow or its sound

³tap *n* : FAUCET, SPIGOT — **on tap** : coming up

⁴tap *vb* **tapped; tap·ping** **1** : to let out or cause to flow by making a hole or by pulling out a plug **2** : to make a hole in to draw off a liquid **3** : to draw from or upon **4** : to connect into (a telephone wire) to listen secretly — **tap·per** *n*

tap–dance *vb* **tap–danced; tap–danc·ing** : to perform a tap dance — **tap–danc·er** *n*

tap dance *n* : a kind of dance featuring loud tapping sounds from shoes with metal plates on the heels and toes

¹tape *n* **1** : a narrow strip of material that is sticky on one side and is used to stick one thing to another **2** : MAGNETIC TAPE **3** : ¹VIDEOTAPE 2 **4** : TAPE RECORDING **5** : a narrow band of cloth or plastic

²tape *vb* **taped; tap·ing** **1** : to fasten, cover, or hold up with sticky tape **2** : to make a recording of

tape deck *n* : a device used to play back and often to record on magnetic tapes

tape measure *n* : a flexible piece of material marked off for measuring

¹ta·per *n* **1** : a slender candle **2** : a gradual lessening in thickness or width in a long object

²taper *vb* **ta·pered; ta·per·ing** **1** : to make or become gradually smaller toward one end **2** : to grow gradually less and less

tape recorder *n* : a device for recording on and playing back magnetic tapes

tape recording *n* : a recording made on magnetic tape

tap·es·try *n, pl* **tap·es·tries** : a heavy cloth that has designs or pictures woven into it and is used especially as a wall hanging — **tap·es·tried** *adj*

tape·worm *n* : a worm with a long flat body that lives as a parasite in the intestines of people and animals

tap·i·o·ca *n* : small pieces of starch from roots of a tropical plant used especially in puddings

ta·pir *n* : a large hoofed plant-eating animal of tropical America and southeastern Asia that has short thick legs, a short tail, and a long flexible snout

tap·root *n* : a main root of a plant that grows

straight down and gives off smaller side roots

taps *n pl* : the last bugle call at night blown as a signal to put out the lights — used as singular or plural

¹tar *n* **1** : a thick dark sticky liquid made from wood, coal, or peat **2** : a substance (as one formed by burning tobacco) that resembles tar

²tar *vb* **tarred; tar·ring** : to cover with or as if with tar

ta·ran·tu·la *n* : a large hairy spider of warm regions of North and South America whose bite may be painful but is usually not serious to humans except for a few South American species

tar·dy *adj* **tar·di·er; tar·di·est** : not on time : LATE — **tar·di·ness** *n*

tar·get *n* **1** : a mark or object to shoot at or attack **2** : a person or thing that is talked about, criticized, or laughed at **3** : a goal to be reached

tar·iff *n* **1** : a list of taxes placed by a government on goods coming into a country **2** : the tax or the rate of taxation set up in a tariff list

¹tar·nish *vb* **tar·nished; tar·nish·ing** **1** : to make or become dull, dim, or discolored **2** : to bring disgrace or ruin

²tarnish *n* : a surface coating formed during tarnishing

tarp *n* : TARPAULIN

tar·pau·lin *n* : a sheet of waterproof canvas

¹tar·ry *vb* **tar·ried; tar·ry·ing** **1** : to be slow in coming or going **2** : to stay in or at a place

²tar·ry *adj* : like or covered with tar

¹tart *adj* **tart·er; tart·est** **1** : pleasantly sharp or sour to the taste **2** : having an unkind quality — **tart·ly** *adv* — **tart·ness** *n*

²tart *n* : a small pie often with no top crust

tar·tan *n* : a woolen cloth with a plaid design originally made in Scotland

tar·tar *n* : a crust that forms on the teeth and consists of plaque that has become hardened by the deposit of calcium-containing salts

tar·tar sauce *or* **tar·tare sauce** *n* : a sauce made chiefly of mayonnaise and chopped pickles

task *n* : a piece of work that has been assigned, needs to be done, or presents a challenge

tas·sel *n* **1** : a hanging ornament (as on clothing) made of a bunch of cords of the same length fastened at one end **2** : the male flower cluster on the top of some plants and especially corn

¹taste *vb* **tast·ed; tast·ing** **1** : to find out the flavor of something by taking a little into the mouth **2** : to have a certain flavor **3** : to recognize by the sense of taste **4** : to eat or drink usually in small amounts **5** : ²EXPERI-ENCE — **tast·er** *n*

²taste *n* **1** : the sense by which sweet, sour, bitter, or salty flavors are detected through sense organs (**taste buds**) in the tongue **2** : the quality of something recognized by the sense of taste or by this together with smell and touch : FLAVOR **3** : a small amount tasted **4** : a personal liking **5** : the ability to choose and enjoy what is good or beautiful **6** : a sample of what something is like

taste·ful *adj* : having or showing the ability to choose what is good, beautiful, or proper — **taste·ful·ly** *adv*

taste·less *adj* **1** : having little flavor **2** : not having or showing the ability to choose what is good, beautiful, or proper — **taste·less·ly** *adv*

tasty *adj* **tast·i·er; tast·i·est** : pleasing to the taste — **tast·i·ness** *n*

tat·ter *n* **1** : a part torn and left hanging : SHRED **2 tatters** *pl* : ragged clothing

tat·tered *adj* **1** : torn in or worn to shreds **2** : dressed in ragged clothes

tat·tle *vb* **tat·tled; tat·tling** : to tell on someone — **tat·tler** *n*

tat·tle·tale *n* : a person who tells on someone

¹tat·too *vb* **tat·tooed; tat·too·ing** : to mark the body with a picture or pattern by using a needle to put color under the skin

²tattoo *n, pl* **tat·toos** : a picture or design made by putting color under the skin

taught *past and past participle of* TEACH

¹taunt *n* : a mean insulting remark

²taunt *vb* **taunt·ed; taunt·ing** : to make fun of or say insulting things to

Tau·rus *n* **1** : a constellation between Aries and Gemini imagined as a bull **2** : the second sign of the zodiac or a person born under this sign

taut *adj* **taut·er; taut·est 1** : tightly stretched **2** : very tense **3** : firm and not flabby — **taut·ly** *adv*

tav·ern *n* **1** : a place where beer and liquor are sold and drunk **2** : INN

taw·ny *adj* **taw·ni·er; taw·ni·est** : of a brownish orange color

¹tax *n* : money collected by the government from people or businesses for public use

²tax *vb* **taxed; tax·ing 1** : to require to pay money to a government for public use **2** : to cause a strain on

tax·able *adj* : subject to tax

tax·a·tion *n* **1** : the action of taxing **2** : money gotten from taxes

¹taxi *n, pl* **tax·is** : TAXICAB

²taxi *vb* **tax·ied; taxi·ing 1** : to run an airplane slowly along the ground under its own power **2** : to go by taxicab

taxi·cab *n* : a vehicle that carries passengers for a fare usually based on the distance traveled

taxi·der·my *n* : the practice or job of preparing, stuffing, and mounting the skins of animals

tax·on·o·my *n* : classification of living things (as plants and animals) using a system that is usually based on natural relationships

tax·pay·er *n* : a person who pays or is responsible for paying a tax

TB *n* : TUBERCULOSIS

T–ball *n* : baseball for young children in which the ball is batted from a tee rather than being pitched

tbs., tbsp. *abbr* tablespoon

tea *n* **1** : the dried leaves and leaf buds of a shrub widely grown in eastern and southern Asia **2** : a drink made by soaking tea in boiling water **3** : refreshments often including tea served in late afternoon **4** : a party at which tea is served **5** : a drink or medicine made by soaking plant parts (as dried roots)

teach *vb* **taught; teach·ing 1** : to help in learning how to do something : show how **2** : to guide the studies of **3** : to give lessons in **4** : to cause to know the unpleasant results of something

teach·er *n* : a person who passes on information or skill

teaching *n* **1** : the duties or profession of a teacher **2** : something taught

tea·cup *n* : a cup used with a saucer for hot drinks

teak *n* : the hard yellowish-brown wood of a tall Asian tree that resists decay

tea·ket·tle *n* : a covered pot that is used for boiling water and has a handle and spout

teal *n* : a small wild duck of America and Europe

¹team *n* **1** : a group of persons who work or play together **2** : two or more animals used to pull the same vehicle or piece of machinery

²team *vb* **teamed; team·ing** : to form a team

team·mate *n* : a person who belongs to the same team as someone else

team·ster *n* : a worker who drives a team or a truck

team·work *n* : the work of a group of persons acting together

tea·pot *n* : a pot for making and serving tea

¹tear *n* **1** : a drop of the salty liquid that moistens the eyes and the inner eyelids and that flows from the eyes when someone is crying **2** *pl* : an act of crying

²tear *vb* **tore; torn; tear·ing 1** : to pull into two or more pieces by force **2** : to wound or injure by or as if by tearing : LACERATE **3** : to remove by force **4** : to move powerfully or swiftly — **tear down** : to knock down and break into pieces

³tear *n* : damage from being torn

tear·drop *n* : ¹TEAR

tear·ful *adj* : flowing with, accompanied by, or causing tears — **tear·ful·ly** *adv*

¹tease *vb* **teased; teas·ing 1** : to make fun of **2** : to annoy again and again — **teas·er** *n*

²tease *n* **1** : the act of making fun of or repeatedly bothering a person or animal **2** : a person who makes fun of people usually in a friendly way

tea·spoon *n* **1** : a small spoon used especially for stirring drinks **2** : a unit of measure used in cooking equal to ⅙ fluid ounce or ⅓ tablespoon (about 5 milliliters)

tea·spoon·ful *n, pl* **teaspoonfuls** *also* **tea·spoons·ful 1** : as much as a teaspoon can hold **2** : TEASPOON

teat *n* : NIPPLE 1 — used mostly of domestic animals

tech·ni·cal *adj* **1** : having special knowledge especially of a mechanical or scientific subject **2** : relating to a practical or scientific subject **3** : according to a strict explanation of the rules or facts — **tech·ni·cal·ly** *adv*

tech·ni·cal·i·ty *n, pl* **tech·ni·cal·i·ties** : something that is understood only by a person with special training

tech·ni·cian *n* : a person skilled in the details or techniques of a subject, art, or job

tech·nique *n* **1** : the way in which basic physical movements or skills are used **2** : the ability to use basic physical movements and skills **3** : a way of doing something using special knowledge or skill

tech·no·log·i·cal *adj* : of or relating to technology

tech·nol·o·gist *n* : a person who specializes in technology

tech·nol·o·gy *n, pl* **tech·nol·o·gies 1** : the use of science in solving problems (as in industry or engineering) **2** : a method of or machine for doing something that is created by technology

ted·dy bear *n* : a stuffed toy bear

te·dious *adj* : tiring because of length or dullness — **te·dious·ly** *adv* — **te·dious·ness** *n*

tee *n* : a device (as a post or peg) on which a ball is placed to be hit or kicked in various sports

teem *vb* **teemed; teem·ing** : to be full of something

teen·age *or* **teen·aged** *adj* : being or relating to teenagers

teen·ag·er *n* : a person between the ages of 13 and 19

teens *n pl* : the years 13 through 19 in a person's life

tee·ny *adj* **tee·ni·er; tee·ni·est** : TINY

tee shirt *variant of* T-SHIRT

tee·ter *vb* **tee·tered; tee·ter·ing** : to move unsteadily back and forth or from side to side

tee·ter–tot·ter *n* : ¹SEESAW 1

teeth *pl of* TOOTH

teethe *vb* **teethed; teeth·ing** : to experience the growth of teeth through the gums

TEFL *abbr* teaching English as a foreign language

tele- *or* **tel-** *prefix* **1** : at a distance **2** : television **3** : using a telephone

tele·gram *n* : a message sent by telegraph

¹tele·graph *n* : an electric device or system for sending messages by a code over connecting wires

²telegraph *vb* **tele·graphed; tele·graph·ing 1** : to send by code over connecting wires **2** : to send a telegram to

tele·mar·ket·ing *n* : the act of selling goods or services by telephone

te·lep·a·thy *n* : a way of communicating thoughts directly from one mind to another without speech or signs

¹tele·phone *n* : a device for transmitting and receiving sounds over long distances

²telephone *vb* **tele·phoned; tele·phon·ing** : to speak to by telephone

¹tele·scope *n* : a piece of equipment shaped like a long tube that has lenses for viewing objects at a distance and especially for observing objects in outer space

²telescope *vb* **tele·scoped; tele·scop·ing** : to slide or force one part into another

tele·vise *vb* **tele·vised; tele·vis·ing** : to send (a program) by television

tele·vi·sion *n* **1** : an electronic system of sending images and sound over a wire or through space by devices that change light and sound into electrical signals and then change these back into light and sound **2** : a piece of equipment with a screen and speakers that reproduces images and sound **3** : programs that are broadcast by television

tell *vb* **told; tell·ing 1** : to let a person know something : to give information to **2** : ¹ORDER 2 **3** : to find out by observing **4** : ¹SAY 1 **5** : to describe in detail **6** : to make known **7** : to bring the bad behavior of to the attention of an authority **8** : ¹COUNT 1 **9** : to have a noticeable result **10** : to act as evidence

tell·er *n* **1** : a person who tells stories : NARRATOR **2** : a bank employee who receives and pays out money **3** : a person who counts votes

tell·tale *adj* : indicating or giving evidence of something

¹tem·per *n* **1** : characteristic state of feeling **2** : calmness of mind **3** : an angry mood **4** : a tendency to be easily angered **5** : the hardness or toughness of a substance (as metal)

²temper *vb* **tem·pered; tem·per·ing** **1** : to make less severe or extreme : SOFTEN **2** : to heat and cool a substance (as steel) until it is as hard, tough, or flexible as is wanted

tem·per·a·ment *n* : a person's attitude as it affects what he or she says or does

tem·per·a·men·tal *adj* **1** : likely to become angry or upset **2** : unpredictable in behavior or performance — **tem·per·a·men·tal·ly** *adv*

tem·per·ance *n* **1** : control over actions, thoughts, or feelings **2** : the use of little or no liquor

tem·per·ate *adj* **1** : keeping or held within limits : not extreme or excessive **2** : not drinking much liquor **3** : showing self-control **4** : having a mild climate that is not too hot or too cold

tem·per·a·ture *n* **1** : degree of hotness or coldness as measured on a scale **2** : abnormally high body heat : FEVER

tem·pest *n* **1** : a strong wind often accompanied by rain, hail, or snow **2** : UPROAR

tem·pes·tu·ous *adj* : very stormy

¹tem·ple *n* : a building for worship

²temple *n* : the flattened space on either side of the forehead

tem·po *n, pl* **tem·pi** *or* **tempos** : the rate of speed at which a musical composition is played or sung

tem·po·rary *adj* : not permanent — **tem·po·rar·i·ly** *adv*

tempt *vb* **tempt·ed; tempt·ing** : to consider or cause to consider doing something wrong or unwise — **tempt·er** *n*

temp·ta·tion *n* **1** : the act of considering or causing to consider doing something wrong or unwise **2** : a strong desire **3** : something that causes a strong desire

¹ten *adj* : being one more than nine

²ten *n* **1** : one more than nine : two times five : 10 **2** : the tenth in a set or series

te·na·cious *adj* **1** : PERSISTENT **2** : not easily pulled apart

te·nac·i·ty *n* : the quality or state of being persistent

¹ten·ant *n* : a person or business that rents property from its owner

²tenant *vb* **ten·ant·ed; ten·ant·ing** : to hold or live in as a renter

¹tend *vb* **tend·ed; tend·ing** **1** : to take care of **2** : to pay attention **3** : to manage the operation of

²tend *vb* **tended; tending** **1** : to be likely **2** : to move or turn in a certain direction

ten·den·cy *n, pl* **ten·den·cies** **1** : a leaning toward a particular kind of thought or action **2** : a way of doing something that is becoming more common : TREND

¹ten·der *adj* **ten·der·er; ten·der·est** **1** : not tough **2** : DELICATE 4 **3** : YOUNG 1 **4** : feeling or showing love **5** : very easily hurt — **ten·der·ly** *adv* — **ten·der·ness** *n*

²tender *vb* **ten·dered; ten·der·ing** **1** : to offer in payment **2** : to present for acceptance

³tender *n* **1** : ²OFFER 3 **2** : something (as money) that may be offered in payment

⁴tend·er *n* **1** : a boat that carries passengers or freight to a larger ship **2** : a car attached to a locomotive for carrying fuel or water

ten·der·heart·ed *adj* : easily affected with feelings of love, pity, or sorrow

ten·don *n* : a band of tough white fiber connecting a muscle to another part (as a bone)

ten·dril *n* **1** : a slender leafless winding stem by which some climbing plants attach themselves to a support **2** : something that winds like a plant's tendril

ten·e·ment *n* : a building divided into separate apartments for rent

Tenn. *abbr* Tennessee

ten·nis *n* : a game played on a level court by two or four players who use rackets to hit a ball back and forth across a low net dividing the court

ten·or *n* **1** : the next to the lowest part in harmony having four parts **2** : the highest male singing voice **3** : a singer or an instrument having a tenor range or part

¹tense *n* : a form of a verb used to show the time of the action or state

²tense *adj* **tens·er; tens·est** **1** : feeling or showing worry or nervousness : not relaxed **2** : marked by strain or uncertainty **3** : stretched tight — **tense·ly** *adv* — **tense·ness** *n*

³tense *vb* **tensed; tens·ing** **1** : to make or become worried or nervous **2** : to make (a muscle) hard and tight

ten·sion *n* **1** : the act of straining or stretching : the condition of being strained or stretched **2** : a state of worry or nervousness **3** : a state of unfriendliness

tent *n* : a portable shelter (as of canvas) stretched and supported by poles

ten·ta·cle *n* : one of the long thin flexible parts that stick out around the head or the mouth of an animal (as a jellyfish or sea anemone) and are used especially for feeling or grasping

ten·ta·tive *adj* **1** : not final **2** : showing caution or hesitation — **ten·ta·tive·ly** *adv*

tent caterpillar *n* : a caterpillar that lives in groups that spin a large silken web resembling a tent

¹tenth *adj* : coming right after ninth

²tenth *n* **1** : number ten in a series **2** : one of ten equal parts

te·pee *n* : a tent shaped like a cone and used as a home by some American Indians

tep·id *adj* : LUKEWARM 1

¹term *n* **1** : a word or expression that has an exact meaning in some uses or is limited to a subject or field **2** : a period of time fixed especially by law or custom **3 terms** *pl* : conditions that limit the nature and scope of something (as a treaty or a will) **4 terms** *pl* : relationship between people **5** : any one of the numbers in a series **6** : the numerator or denominator of a fraction

²term *vb* **termed; term·ing** : to call by a particular name

¹ter·mi·nal *adj* : relating to or forming an end

²terminal *n* **1** : either end of a transportation line or a passenger or freight station located at it **2** : a device (as in a computer system) used to put in, receive, and display information **3** : a device at the end of a wire or on a machine for making an electrical connection

ter·mi·nate *vb* **ter·mi·nat·ed; ter·mi·nat·ing** : END, CLOSE

ter·mi·na·tion *n* **1** : the end of something **2** : the act of ending something

ter·mi·nus *n, pl* **ter·mi·ni** *or* **ter·mi·nus·es 1** : an ending point **2** : the end of a travel route **3** : a station at the end of a travel route

ter·mite *n* : a chewing antlike insect of a light color that lives in large colonies and feeds on wood

tern *n* : a small slender seagull with black cap, white body, and narrow wings

¹ter·race *n* **1** : a level area next to a building **2** : a raised piece of land with the top leveled **3** : a row of houses on raised ground or a slope

²terrace *vb* **ter·raced; ter·rac·ing** : to form into a terrace or supply with terraces

ter·rain *n* : the features of the surface of a piece of land

ter·ra·pin *n* : a North American turtle that lives in or near fresh or somewhat salty water

ter·rar·i·um *n, pl* **ter·rar·ia** *or* **ter·rar·i·ums** : a usually glass container used for keeping plants or small animals (as turtles) indoors

ter·res·tri·al *adj* **1** : relating to the earth or its people **2** : living or growing on land

ter·ri·ble *adj* **1** : very great in degree **2** : very bad **3** : causing great fear — **ter·ri·bly** *adv*

ter·ri·er *n* : a usually small dog originally used by hunters to force animals from their holes

ter·rif·ic *adj* **1** : EXCELLENT **2** : very unusual : EXTRAORDINARY **3** : causing terror : TERRIBLE

ter·ri·fy *vb* **ter·ri·fied; ter·ri·fy·ing** : to cause (someone) to become very frightened

ter·ri·to·ri·al *adj* **1** : of or relating to a terri-

tory **2** : displaying behavior associated with defending an animal's territory

ter·ri·to·ry *n, pl* **ter·ri·to·ries 1** : a geographical area belonging to or under the rule of a government **2** : a part of the United States not included within any state but organized with a separate governing body **3** : REGION 1, DISTRICT **4** : an area that is occupied and defended by an animal or group of animals

ter·ror *n* **1** : a state of great fear **2** : a cause of great fear

ter·ror·ism *n* : the use of violence as a means of achieving a goal

ter·ror·ist *n* : someone who engages in terrorism

ter·ror·ize *vb* **ter·ror·ized; ter·ror·iz·ing 1** : to fill with fear **2** : to use terrorism against

terse *adj* **ters·er; ters·est** : being brief and to the point — **terse·ly** *adv*

¹test *n* **1** : a set of questions or problems by which a person's knowledge, intelligence, or skills are measured **2** : a means of finding out the nature, quality, or value of something

²test *vb* **test·ed; test·ing 1** : to measure a person's knowledge, intelligence, or skills **2** : to find out the nature, quality, or value of something

tes·ta·ment *n* **1** : either of two main parts (**Old Testament** and **New Testament**) of the Bible **2** : ²WILL 4

tes·ti·fy *vb* **tes·ti·fied; tes·ti·fy·ing** : to make a formal statement of something sworn to be true

tes·ti·mo·ny *n, pl* **tes·ti·mo·nies** : a statement made by a witness under oath especially in a court

tes·tis *n, pl* **tes·tes** : a male reproductive gland that produces sperm

test tube *n* : a plain tube of thin glass closed at one end and used especially in chemistry and biology

tet·a·nus *n* : a serious disease that is marked by spasms of the muscles especially of the jaws and that is caused by poison from a bacterium that usually enters the body through a wound

¹tether *vb* **teth·ered; teth·er·ing** : to fasten by a line that limits range of movement

²tether *n* : a line by which something is fastened so as to limit where it can go

Tex. *abbr* Texas

text *n* **1** : the actual words of an author's work **2** : the main body of printed or written matter on a page **3** : TEXTBOOK **4** : a passage from the Bible chosen as the subject of a sermon

text·book *n* : a book used in the study of a subject

tex·tile *n* : a woven or knit cloth

tex·ture *n* : the structure, feel, and appearance of something

-th *or* **-eth** *adj suffix* — used to form numbers that show the place of something in a series

than *conj* : when compared to the way in which, the extent to which, or the degree to which

thank *vb* **thanked; thank·ing** **1** : to express gratitude to **2** : to hold responsible

thank·ful *adj* **1** : feeling or showing thanks : GRATEFUL **2** : GLAD — **thank·ful·ly** *adv* — **thank·ful·ness** *n*

thank·less *adj* **1** : UNGRATEFUL **2** : not appreciated

thanks *n pl* **1** : GRATITUDE **2** : an expression of gratitude (as for something received) — **thanks to** **1** : with the help of **2** : because of

thanks·giv·ing *n* **1** *cap* : THANKSGIVING DAY **2** : a prayer or an expression of gratitude

Thanksgiving Day *n* : the fourth Thursday in November observed as a legal holiday for giving thanks

¹that *pron, pl* **those** **1** : the person or thing seen, mentioned, or understood **2** : the time, action, or event mentioned **3** : the one farther away **4** : the one : the kind

²that *conj* **1** — used to introduce a clause that modifies a noun or adjective **2** — used to introduce a clause that modifies an adverb or adverbial expression **3** — used to introduce a noun clause serving especially as the subject or object of a verb **4** : ²SO 1 **5** — used to introduce a clause naming a result **6** : BECAUSE

³that *adj, pl* **those** **1** : being the one mentioned, indicated, or understood **2** : being the one farther away

⁴that *pron* **1** : WHO 2, WHOM, WHICH **2** : in, on, or at which

⁵that *adv* : to the extent or degree shown (as by the hands)

¹thatch *n* : a plant material (as straw) for use as roofing

²thatch *vb* **thatched; thatch·ing** : to cover (a roof) with straw or other plant material

¹thaw *vb* **thawed; thaw·ing** **1** : to melt or cause to melt **2** : to grow less unfriendly or quiet in manner

²thaw *n* **1** : a period of weather warm enough to melt ice and snow **2** : the action, fact, or process of becoming less hostile or unfriendly

¹the *definite article* **1** : that or those mentioned, seen, or clearly understood **2** : that or those near in space, time, or thought **3** : ¹EACH **4** : that or those considered best, most typical, or most worth singling out **5**
: any one typical of or standing for the entire class named **6** : all those that are

²the *adv* **1** : than before **2** : to what extent : by how much **3** : to that extent : by that much

the·ater *or* **the·atre** *n* **1** : a building in which plays, motion pictures, or shows are presented **2** : the art or profession of producing plays **3** : plays or the performance of plays **4** : a place or area where some important action is carried on

the·at·ri·cal *adj* : for or relating to the presentation of plays

thee *pron, objective case of* THOU

theft *n* : the act of stealing

their *adj* : of or relating to them or themselves especially as owners or as agents or objects of an action

theirs *pron* : that which belongs to them

them *pron, objective case of* THEY

theme *n* **1** : a subject of a work of art, music, or literature **2** : a specific quality, characteristic, or concern **3** : a written exercise : ESSAY

theme park *n* : an amusement park in which the rides and buildings are based on a central subject

them·selves *pron* : their own selves

¹then *adv* **1** : at that time **2** : soon after that : NEXT **3** : in addition : BESIDES **4** : in that case **5** : as an expected result

²then *n* : that time

³then *adj* : existing or acting at that time

thence *adv* **1** : from that place **2** : from that fact

thence·forth *adv* : from that time on

the·ol·o·gy *n, pl* **the·ol·o·gies** : the study and explanation of religious faith, practice, and experience

the·o·ry *n, pl* **the·o·ries** **1** : an idea or opinion that is presented as true **2** : a general rule offered to explain a scientific phenomenon **3** : the general rules followed in a science or an art

ther·a·peu·tic *adj* : MEDICINAL

ther·a·pist *n* : a person specializing in treating disorders or injuries of the body or mind especially in ways that do not involve drugs and surgery

ther·a·py *n, pl* **ther·a·pies** : treatment of a disorder or injury of the body or mind

¹there *adv* **1** : in or at that place **2** : to or into that place **3** : in that situation or way **4** — used to show satisfaction, soothing, or defiance **5** — used to attract attention

²there *pron* — used to introduce a sentence in which the subject comes after the verb

³there *n* : that place

there·abouts *also* **there·about** *adv* **1** : near

that place or time **2** : near that number, degree, or amount

there·af·ter *adv* : after that

there·by *adv* : by that

there·fore *adv* : for that reason

there·in *adv* : in or into that place, time, or thing

there·of *adv* : of that or it

there·on *adv* : on that

there·to *adv* : to that

there·up·on *adv* **1** : on that thing **2** : for that reason **3** : immediately after that : at once

there·with *adv* : with that

ther·mal *adj* : of, relating to, or caused by heat

ther·mom·e·ter *n* : an instrument for measuring temperature

ther·mos *n* : a container (as a bottle or jar) that has a vacuum between an inner and an outer wall and is used to keep liquids hot or cold for several hours

ther·mo·stat *n* : a device that automatically controls temperature

the·sau·rus *n, pl* **the·sau·ri** *or* **the·sau·rus·es** : a book of words and their synonyms

these *pl of* THIS

the·sis *n, pl* **the·ses** **1** : a statement that a person wants to discuss or prove **2** : an essay presenting results of original research

they *pron* : those individuals : those ones

they'd : they had : they would

they'll : they shall : they will

they're : they are

they've : they have

thi·a·mine *also* **thi·a·min** *n* : a type of vitamin B that is used by the body to convert carbohydrates into energy and to maintain normal nerve function

¹thick *adj* **thick·er; thick·est** **1** : having great size from one surface to its opposite **2** : closely packed together **3** : heavily built **4** : not flowing easily **5** : measuring a certain amount in the smallest of three dimensions **6** : producing speech that is hard to understand **7** : STUPID 1 **8** : occurring in large numbers : NUMEROUS **9** : having haze, fog, or mist **10** : too intense to see in — **thick·ly** *adv*

²thick *n* **1** : the most crowded or active part **2** : the part of greatest thickness

thick·en *vb* **thick·ened; thick·en·ing** : to make or become thick — **thick·en·er** *n*

thick·et *n* : a thick usually small patch of bushes or low trees

thick·ness *n* **1** : the quality or state of being thick **2** : the smallest of three dimensions

thick·set *adj* : STOCKY

thief *n, pl* **thieves** : a person who steals : ROBBER

thieve *vb* **thieved; thiev·ing** : ¹STEAL 1, ROB

thiev·ery *n* : THEFT

thigh *n* : the part of a leg between the hip and the knee

thim·ble *n* : a cap or cover used in sewing to protect the finger that pushes the needle

¹thin *adj* **thin·ner; thin·nest** **1** : having little body fat **2** : having little size from one surface to its opposite : not thick **3** : having the parts not close together **4** : flowing very easily **5** : having less than the usual number **6** : not very convincing **7** : somewhat weak or high **8** : having less oxygen than normal — **thin·ly** *adv* — **thin·ness** *n*

²thin *vb* **thinned; thin·ning** : to make or become smaller in thickness or number

thine *pron, archaic* : YOURS — used as singular or plural

thing *n* **1** : an act or matter that is or is to be done **2** : something that exists and can be talked about **3** **things** *pl* : personal possessions **4** : ¹DETAIL 2 **5** **things** *pl* : existing conditions and circumstance **6** : EVENT 1 **7** : ¹DEED 1, ACHIEVEMENT, ACT **8** : a piece of clothing **9** : what is needed or wanted **10** : an action or interest especially that someone enjoys very much **11** : ²INDIVIDUAL 1 **12** : a spoken or written observation or point

think *vb* **thought; think·ing** **1** : to have as an opinion or belief **2** : to form or have in the mind **3** : REMEMBER 1 **4** : to use the power of the mind to understand, find out, or decide **5** : to consider for some time : PONDER **6** : to invent something by thinking **7** : to hold a strong feeling **8** : to have as a plan **9** : to care about — **think·er** *n*

thin·ner *n* : a liquid used to thin paint

¹third *adj* : coming right after second

²third *n* **1** : number three in a series **2** : one of three equal parts

third person *n* : a set of words or forms (as pronouns or verb forms) referring to people or things that are not being addressed directly

¹thirst *n* **1** : a feeling of dryness in the mouth and throat that accompanies a need for liquids **2** : the bodily condition that produces thirst **3** : a strong desire

²thirst *vb* **thirst·ed; thirst·ing** **1** : to feel a need for liquids **2** : to have a strong desire

thirsty *adj* **thirst·i·er; thirst·i·est** **1** : feeling a need for liquids **2** : needing moisture **3** : having a strong desire : EAGER — **thirst·i·ly** *adv*

¹thir·teen *adj* : being one more than twelve

²thirteen *n* : one more than twelve : 13

¹thir·teenth *adj* : coming right after twelfth

²thirteenth *n* : number 13 in a series

¹**thir·ti·eth** *adj* : coming right after 29th

²**thirtieth** *n* : number 30 in a series

¹**thir·ty** *adj* : being three times ten

²**thirty** *n* : three times ten : 30

¹**this** *pron, pl* **these** **1** : the one nearer **2** : the person, thing, or idea that is present or near in place, time, or thought or that has just been mentioned

²**this** *adj, pl* **these** **1** : being the one present, near in place, time, or thought or that has just been mentioned **2** : being the one nearer

³**this** *adv* **1** : to the degree suggested by something in the present situation **2** : to the extent shown (as with the hands)

this·tle *n* : a prickly plant that has usually purplish often showy heads of flowers

thith·er *adv* : to that place : THERE

thong *n* **1** : a strip of leather used especially for fastening something **2** : a sandal held on by straps that run across the foot and between the big and second toe

tho·rax *n, pl* **tho·rax·es** *or* **tho·ra·ces** **1** : the part of the body of a mammal that lies between the neck and the abdomen and contains the heart and lungs **2** : the middle of the three main divisions of the body of an insect

thorn *n* **1** : a hard sharp leafless point on the stem or branch of a plant (as a rose bush) **2** : a bush or tree that has thorns

thorny *adj* **thorn·i·er; thorn·i·est** **1** : full of or covered with thorns **2** : full of difficulties

thor·ough *adj* **1** : being such to the fullest degree : COMPLETE **2** : careful about little things — **thor·ough·ly** *adv* — **thor·ough·ness** *n*

¹**thor·ough·bred** *adj* : PUREBRED

²**thoroughbred** *n* **1** *cap* : a speedy horse of an English breed kept mainly for racing **2** : a purebred animal **3** : a very educated or skilled person

thor·ough·fare *n* **1** : a street or road open at both ends **2** : a main road

thor·ough·go·ing *adj* : THOROUGH 1

those *pl of* THAT

thou *pron, archaic* : YOU

¹**though** *conj* : ALTHOUGH

²**though** *adv* : HOWEVER 3, NEVERTHELESS

¹**thought** *past and past participle of* THINK

²**thought** *n* **1** : the act or process of thinking **2** : something (as an idea or opinion) formed in the mind **3** : serious attention

thought·ful *adj* **1** : considerate of others **2** : deep in thought **3** : showing careful thinking — **thought·ful·ly** *adv* — **thought·ful·ness** *n*

thought·less *adj* **1** : not considerate of others **2** : not careful and alert **3** : done without thinking — **thought·less·ly** *adv* — **thought·less·ness** *n*

¹**thou·sand** *n* **1** : ten times one hundred : 1000 **2** : a very large number

²**thousand** *adj* : being 1000

¹**thou·sandth** *adj* : coming right after 999th

²**thousandth** *n* : number 1000 in a series

thrash *vb* **thrashed; thrash·ing** **1** : to beat very hard **2** : to move about violently **3** : THRESH 1

thrash·er *n* : an American bird (as the common reddish brown **brown thrasher**) related to the mockingbird and noted for its song

¹**thread** *n* **1** : a thin fine cord formed by spinning and twisting short fibers into a continuous strand **2** : a thin fine line or strand of something **3** : the ridge or groove that winds around a screw **4** : a train of thought that connects the parts of something (as an argument or story) — **thread·like** *adj*

²**thread** *vb* **thread·ed; thread·ing** **1** : to put a thread in working position (as in a needle) **2** : to pass something through another thing **3** : to make a way through or between **4** : to put together on a thread : STRING

thread·bare *adj* **1** : worn so much that the thread shows : SHABBY **2** : not effective because of overuse

threat *n* **1** : the act of showing an intention to do harm **2** : someone or something that threatens

threat·en *vb* **threat·ened; threat·en·ing** **1** : to show an intention to do harm or something unwanted **2** : to give warning of by an indication — **threat·en·ing·ly** *adv*

¹**three** *adj* : being one more than two

²**three** *n* **1** : one more than two : 3 **2** : the third in a set or series

3–D *adj* : THREE-DIMENSIONAL 2

three–dimensional *adj* **1** : relating to or having the three dimensions of length, width, and height **2** : giving the appearance of depth or varying distances

three·fold *adj* : being three times as great or as many

three·score *adj* : ¹SIXTY

thresh *vb* **threshed; thresh·ing** **1** : to separate the seed from a harvested plant by beating **2** : THRASH 2

thresh·er *n* : THRESHING MACHINE

threshing machine *n* : a machine used to separate grain from harvested plants

thresh·old *n* **1** : the sill of a door **2** : a point or place of beginning or entering

threw *past of* THROW

thrice *adv* : three times

thrift *n* : careful management especially of money

thrifty *adj* **thrift·i·er; thrift·i·est** : carefully and wisely managing money

¹**thrill** *vb* **thrilled; thrill·ing** : to have or cause to have a sudden feeling of excitement or pleasure — **thrill·er** *n*

²**thrill** *n* **1** : a sudden strong feeling especially of excitement or happiness **2** : something that produces a feeling of excitement

thrive *vb* **thrived** *or* **throve; thrived** *also* **thriv·en; thriv·ing** : to grow or develop very well : FLOURISH

throat *n* **1** : the passage through the neck from the mouth to the stomach and lungs **2** : the front part of the neck on the outside

throaty *adj* **throat·i·er; throat·i·est** : uttered or produced in deep low tones

¹**throb** *vb* **throbbed; throb·bing 1** : to feel repeated pangs of pain **2** : to beat hard or fast **3** : to beat or rotate in a normal way

²**throb** *n* **1** : ²BEAT 2, PULSE **2** : pain that comes in repeated pangs

throne *n* **1** : the chair used by a monarch or bishop for ceremonies **2** : the position of king or queen

¹**throng** *n* : a large group of people : CROWD

²**throng** *vb* **thronged; throng·ing** : ¹CROWD 4

¹**throt·tle** *vb* **throt·tled; throt·tling 1** : to strangle or choke (someone) **2** : to reduce the speed of (an engine) by closing the throttle valve

²**throttle** *n* : a valve or a lever that controls the valve for regulating the flow of steam or fuel in an engine

¹**through** *prep* **1** : into at one side and out at the other side of **2** : from one side or end to another of **3** : by way of **4** : AMONG 1 **5** : by means of **6** : over the whole of **7** : during the whole of **8** : to and including **9** : into and out of

²**through** *adv* **1** : from one end or side to the other **2** : from beginning to end **3** : to completion **4** : in or to every part

³**through** *adj* **1** : having reached an end **2** : allowing free or continuous passage : DIRECT **3** : going from point of origin to destination without changes or transfers **4** : coming from and going to points outside a local zone

¹**through·out** *adv* **1** : EVERYWHERE **2** : from beginning to end

²**throughout** *prep* **1** : in or to every part of **2** : during the whole period of

throve *past of* THRIVE

¹**throw** *vb* **threw; thrown; throw·ing 1** : to send through the air with a quick forward motion of the arm **2** : to put suddenly in a certain position or condition **3** : to cause to fall **4** : to put on or take off in a hurry **5** : to move (the body or part of the body) in a cer-

tain way **6** : to move (as a window or switch) to an open or closed position **7** : to give by way of entertainment — **thrower** *n* — **throw away 1** : to get rid of : DISCARD **2** : SQUANDER, WASTE — **throw out 1** : to get rid of **2** : to remove from a place, position, or participation **3** : to give off **4** : to cause to project : EXTEND — **throw up** : ²VOMIT

²**throw** *n* **1** : an act of causing something to move with a motion of the arm **2** : the distance something is or may be sent with a motion of the arm

thrum *vb* **thrummed; thrum·ming** : to play a stringed instrument idly : STRUM

thrush *n* : a usually brown bird that has a spotted breast and a melodious song

¹**thrust** *vb* **thrust; thrust·ing 1** : to push with force : SHOVE **2** : PIERCE 1, STAB **3** : EXTEND **4** : to press the acceptance of on someone

²**thrust** *n* **1** : a push or jab with a pointed weapon **2** : a military attack **3** : a forward or upward push

thru·way *n* : EXPRESSWAY

Thu. *abbr* Thursday

¹**thud** *n* : a dull sound : THUMP

²**thud** *vb* **thud·ded; thud·ding** : to move, strike, or pound so as to make a dull sound

thug *n* : a violent person or criminal

¹**thumb** *n* **1** : the short thick finger next to the forefinger **2** : the part of a glove covering the thumb

²**thumb** *vb* **thumbed; thumb·ing 1** : to turn the pages of quickly with the thumb **2** : to seek or get (a ride) in a passing automobile by signaling with the thumb

thumb·tack *n* : a tack with a broad flat head for pressing into a board or wall with the thumb

¹**thump** *vb* **thumped; thump·ing 1** : to strike or beat with something thick or heavy so as to cause a dull sound **2** : to beat hard : POUND

²**thump** *n* **1** : a blow with something blunt or heavy **2** : the sound made by or as if by a blow with something blunt or heavy

¹**thun·der** *n* **1** : the loud sound that follows a flash of lightning **2** : a loud noise

²**thunder** *vb* **thun·dered; thun·der·ing 1** : to produce thunder **2** : to make a loud sound **3** : ¹ROAR 1, SHOUT

thun·der·bolt *n* : a flash of lightning and the thunder that follows it

thun·der·cloud *n* : a dark storm cloud that produces lightning and thunder

thun·der·head *n* : a rounded mass of dark cloud with white edges often appearing before a thunderstorm

thun·der·show·er *n* : a shower with thunder and lightning

thun·der·storm *n* : a storm with thunder and lightning

thun·der·struck *adj* : stunned as if struck by a thunderbolt

Thur., Thurs. *abbr* Thursday

Thurs·day *n* : the fifth day of the week

thus *adv* 1 : in this or that way 2 : to this degree or extent : SO 3 : because of this or that : THEREFORE

thwart *vb* **thwart·ed; thwart·ing** : to stop from happening or succeeding

thy *adj, archaic* : YOUR

thyme *n* : a mint with tiny fragrant leaves used especially in cooking

thy·roid *n* : a gland at the base of the neck that produces hormones which affect growth, development, and the rate at which the body uses energy

thy·self *pron, archaic* : YOURSELF

ti *n* : the seventh note of the musical scale

tib·ia *n, pl* **tib·i·ae** *also* **tib·i·as** : the inner and larger of the two bones between the knee and ankle

¹tick *n* 1 : a light rhythmic tap or beat (as of a clock) 2 : a small mark used chiefly to draw attention to something or to check an item on a list

²tick *vb* **ticked; tick·ing** 1 : to make a light rhythmic tap or a series of light rhythmic taps 2 : to mark, count, or announce by or as if by light rhythmic taps 3 : ²CHECK 4 4 : OPERATE 1, FUNCTION

³tick *n* : a tiny animal with eight legs that is related to the spider and attaches itself to humans and animals from which it sucks blood

¹tick·et *n* 1 : a document or token showing that a fare or a fee for admission or participation has been paid 2 : a summons or warning issued to a person who breaks a traffic law 3 : a list of candidates for nomination or election 4 : a slip or card recording a sale or giving information 5 : the correct or desirable thing

²ticket *vb* **tick·et·ed; tick·et·ing** 1 : to attach a tag to : LABEL 2 : to give a traffic ticket to

¹tick·le *vb* **tick·led; tick·ling** 1 : to have a tingling or prickling sensation 2 : to touch (a body part) lightly so as to cause laughter or jerky movements 3 : to excite or stir up agreeably 4 : AMUSE 2

²tickle *n* : a tingling or prickling sensation

tick·lish *adj* 1 : sensitive to tickling 2 : calling for careful handling

tid·al *adj* : of or relating to tides : flowing and ebbing like tides

tidal wave *n* 1 : a very high sea wave that sometimes follows an earthquake 2 : an unusual rise of water along a shore due to strong winds

tid·bit *n* 1 : a small tasty piece of food 2 : a small interesting but unimportant bit (as of news)

¹tide *n* 1 : the rising and falling of the surface of the ocean caused twice daily by the attraction of the sun and the moon 2 : something that rises and falls or rushes in a mass

²tide *vb* **tid·ed; tid·ing** : to help to overcome or put up with a difficulty

tide pool *n* : a pool of salt water that is left behind when the tide goes out and in which small sea animals (as snails, crabs, and barnacles) are often found

tid·ings *n pl* : NEWS 4

¹ti·dy *adj* **ti·di·er; ti·di·est** 1 : well ordered and cared for : NEAT 2 : LARGE, SUBSTANTIAL — **ti·di·ness** *n*

²tidy *vb* **ti·died; ti·dy·ing** : to make things neat

¹tie *n* 1 : NECKTIE 2 : an equality in number (as of votes or scores) 3 : a contest that ends with an equal score 4 : one of the cross supports to which railroad rails are fastened 5 : a connecting link : BOND 6 : a line, ribbon, or cord used for fastening, joining, or closing 7 : a part (as a beam or rod) holding two pieces together

²tie *vb* **tied; ty·ing** *or* **tie·ing** 1 : to fasten, attach, or close by means of a tie 2 : to form a knot or bow in 3 : to bring together firmly : UNITE 4 : to hold back from freedom of action 5 : to make or have an equal score with in a contest

tier *n* : a row, rank, or layer usually arranged in a series one above the other

tiff *n* : a minor quarrel

ti·ger *n* : a large Asian meat-eating animal of the cat family that is light brown with black stripes

¹tight *adj* **tight·er; tight·est** 1 : very closely packed or compressed 2 : fixed or held very firmly in place 3 : fitting too closely 4 : firmly stretched or drawn : TAUT 5 : difficult to get through or out of 6 : firm in control 7 : STINGY 1 8 : low in supply : SCARCE 9 : painfully or uncomfortably tense 10 : barely allowing enough time — **tight·ly** *adv* — **tight·ness** *n*

²tight *adv* 1 : in a firm, secure, or close manner 2 : in a deep and uninterrupted manner : SOUNDLY

tight·en *vb* **tight·ened; tight·en·ing** : to make or become tight

tight·rope *n* : a rope or wire stretched tight on which an acrobat performs

tights *n pl* : a garment closely fitted to the body and covering it usually from the waist down

tight·wad *n* : a stingy person

ti·gress *n* : a female tiger

til·de *n* : a mark ˜ placed especially over the letter *n* (as in Spanish *señor*) to indicate a sound that is approximately \nyə\

¹**tile** *n* **1** : a thin piece of material (as plastic, stone, or clay) used for roofs, walls, floors, or drains **2** : a small flat piece used in a game

²**tile** *vb* **tiled; til·ing** : to cover with tiles

¹**till** *prep or conj* : UNTIL

²**till** *vb* **tilled; till·ing** : to work by plowing, sowing, and raising crops on

³**till** *n* : a drawer for money

till·age *n* : the practice of working land by plowing, sowing, and raising crops on

¹**til·ler** *n* : a lever used to turn the rudder of a boat from side to side

²**tiller** *n* : someone or something that tills land

¹**tilt** *vb* **tilt·ed; tilt·ing** : to move or shift so as to slant or tip

²**tilt** *n* **1** : ²SLANT **2** : ¹SPEED 2

tim·ber *n* **1** : wood suitable for building or for carpentry **2** : a large squared piece of wood ready for use or forming part of a structure

tim·ber·land *n* : wooded land especially as a source of timber

tim·ber·line *n* : the upper limit beyond which trees do not grow (as on mountains)

¹**time** *n* **1** : a period during which an action, process, or condition exists or continues **2** : a point or period when something occurs : OCCASION **3** : one of a series of repeated instances or actions **4** : a moment, hour, day, or year as shown by a clock or calendar **5** : a set or usual moment or hour for something to occur **6** : a historical period : AGE **7** : conditions of a period — usually used in pl. **8 times** *pl* : added quantities or examples **9** : a person's experience during a certain period **10** : a part of the day when a person is free to do as he or she pleases **11** : rate of speed : TEMPO **12** : a system of determining time **13** : RHYTHM — **at times** : SOMETIMES — **for the time being** : for the present — **from time to time** : once in a while — **in time 1** : soon enough **2** : as time goes by : EVENTUALLY **3** : at the correct speed in music — **time after time** : over and over again — **time and again** : over and over again

²**time** *vb* **timed; tim·ing 1** : to arrange or set the point or rate at which something happens **2** : to measure or record the point at which something happens, the length of the period it takes for something to happen, or the rate at which certain actions take place — **tim·er** *n*

time capsule *n* : a container holding records or objects representative of a current culture that is put in a safe place for discovery in the future

time·keep·er *n* : an official who keeps track of the time in a sports contest

time·less *adj* : not restricted to a certain historical period

time·ly *adj* **time·li·er; time·li·est 1** : coming early or at the right time **2** : especially suitable to the time

time–out *n* **1** : a short period during a game in which play is stopped **2** : a quiet period used as a way to discipline a child

time·piece *n* : a device (as a clock or watch) to measure the passing of time

times *prep* : multiplied by

time·ta·ble *n* : a table telling when something (as a bus or train) is scheduled to leave or arrive

time zone *n* : a geographic region within which the same standard time is used

tim·id *adj* : feeling or showing a lack of courage or self-confidence : SHY — **tim·id·ly** *adv* — **tim·id·ness** *n*

tim·ing *n* : the time when something happens or is done especially when it is thought of as having a good or bad effect on the result

tim·o·rous *adj* : easily frightened : FEARFUL — **tim·o·rous·ly** *adv*

tin *n* **1** : a soft bluish white metallic chemical element used chiefly in combination with other metals or as a coating to protect other metals **2** : something (as a can or sheet) made from tinplate

tin·der *n* : material that burns easily and can be used as kindling

tin·foil *n* : a thin metal sheeting usually of aluminum or an alloy of tin and lead

¹**tinge** *n, pl* **ting·es** : a slight coloring, flavor, or quality

²**tinge** *vb* **tinged; tinge·ing** : to color or flavor slightly

¹**tin·gle** *vb* **tin·gled; tin·gling** : to feel or cause a prickling or thrilling sensation

²**tingle** *n* : a prickling or thrilling sensation or condition

tin·ker *vb* **tin·kered; tin·ker·ing** : to repair or adjust something in an unskilled or experimental manner

¹**tin·kle** *vb* **tin·kled; tin·kling** : to make or cause to make short high ringing or clinking sounds

²**tinkle** *n* : a short high ringing or clinking sound

tin·plate *n* : thin steel sheets covered with tin

tin·sel *n* **1** : a thread or strip of metal or plastic used for decoration **2** : something that seems attractive but is of little worth

tin·smith *n* : a worker in tin or sometimes other metals

¹tint *n* **1** : a slight or pale coloring **2** : a shade of a color

²tint *vb* **tint·ed; tint·ing** : to give a tint to : COLOR

ti·ny *adj* **ti·ni·er; ti·ni·est** : very small

¹tip *n* **1** : the usually pointed end of something **2** : a small piece or part serving as an end, cap, or point

²tip *vb* **tipped; tip·ping** **1** : to turn over **2** : to bend from a straight position : SLANT **3** : to raise and tilt forward

³tip *n* : a piece of useful or secret information

⁴tip *n* : a small sum of money given for a service

⁵tip *vb* **tipped; tip·ping** : to give a small sum of money for a service

⁶tip *vb* **tipped; tip·ping** **1** : to attach an end or point to **2** : to cover or decorate the tip of

¹tip·toe *n* : the position of being balanced on the balls of the feet and toes with the heels raised — usually used with *on*

²tiptoe *adv or adj* : on or as if on the balls of the feet and toes with the heels raised

³tiptoe *vb* **tip·toed; tip·toe·ing** : to walk on the balls of the feet and toes with the heels raised

¹tip·top *adj* : EXCELLENT, FIRST-RATE

²tiptop *n* : the highest point

¹tire *vb* **tired; tir·ing** **1** : to make or become weary **2** : to lose or cause to lose patience or attention : BORE

²tire *n* : a rubber cushion that usually contains compressed air and fits around a wheel (as of an automobile)

tired *adj* : needing rest : WEARY

tire·less *adj* : able to work or persist a long time without becoming tired — **tire·less·ly** *adv*

tire·some *adj* : causing boredom, annoyance, or impatience because of length or dullness

'tis : it is

tis·sue *n* **1** : a fine lightweight fabric **2** : a piece of soft absorbent paper **3** : a mass or layer of cells usually of one kind that perform a special function and form the basic structural material of an animal or plant body

ti·tan·ic *adj* : enormous in size, force, or power

ti·tle *n* **1** : the name given to something (as a book, song, or job) to identify or describe it **2** : a word or group of words attached to a person's name to show an honor, rank, or office **3** : a legal right to the ownership of property **4** : CHAMPIONSHIP

tit·mouse *n, pl* **tit·mice** : a small active usually gray bird that feeds mostly on seeds and insects

¹tit·ter *vb* **tit·tered; tit·ter·ing** : to laugh in a quiet and nervous way

²titter *n* : a nervous laugh

Tlin·git *n, pl* **Tlingit** *or* **Tlin·gits** **1** : a member of a group of American Indian peoples of the islands and coast of southern Alaska **2** : the language of the Tlingit people

TN *abbr* Tennessee

TNT *n* : an explosive used in artillery shells and bombs and in blasting

¹to *prep* **1** : in the direction of **2** : AGAINST **4**, ON **3** : as far as **4** : so as to become or bring about **5** : ²BEFORE 3 **6** : ¹UNTIL **7** : fitting or being a part of or response to **8** : along with **9** : in relation to or comparison with **10** : in agreement with **11** : within the limits of **12** : contained, occurring, or included in **13** — used to show the one or ones that an action is directed toward **14** : for no one except **15** : into the action of **16** — used to mark an infinitive

²to *adv* **1** : in a direction toward **2** : to a conscious state

toad *n* : a tailless leaping animal that is an amphibian and differs from the related frog by having rough dry skin and by living mostly on land

toad·stool *n* : a mushroom especially when poisonous or unfit for food

¹toast *vb* **toast·ed; toast·ing** **1** : to make (food) crisp, hot, and brown by heat **2** : to warm completely

²toast *n* **1** : sliced bread made crisp, hot, and brown by heat **2** : an act of drinking in honor of a person **3** : a person in whose honor other people drink **4** : a highly admired person

³toast *vb* **toast·ed; toast·ing** : to drink in honor of

toast·er *n* : an electrical appliance for making slices of bread crisp, hot, and brown

toasty *adj* **toast·i·er; toast·i·est** : comfortably warm

to·bac·co *n, pl* **to·bac·cos** : the usually large sticky leaves of a tall plant related to the potato that are dried and prepared for use in smoking or chewing or as snuff

to·bog·gan *n* : a long light sled made without runners and curved up at the front

¹to·day *adv* **1** : on this day **2** : at the present time

²today *n* : the present day, time, or age

tod·dler *n* : a small child

¹toe *n* **1** : one of the separate parts of the front end of a foot **2** : the front end or part of a foot or hoof **3** : the front end of something worn on the foot — **toed** *adj*

²toe *vb* **toed; toe·ing** : to touch, reach, or kick with the toes

toe·nail *n* : the hard covering at the end of a toe

to·fu *n* : a soft food product prepared from soybeans

to·ga *n* : the loose outer garment worn in public by citizens of ancient Rome

to·geth·er *adv* **1** : in or into one group, body, or place **2** : in touch or in partnership with **3** : with or near someone or something else **4** : at one time **5** : in or by combined effort **6** : in or into agreement **7** : considered as a whole **8** : in or into contact **9** : as a single unit or piece

¹toil *n* : long hard labor

²toil *vb* **toiled; toil·ing 1** : to work hard and long **2** : to go on with effort

toi·let *n* **1** : a device for getting rid of body waste that consists usually of a bowl that is flushed with water **2** : BATHROOM **3** : the act or process of getting dressed and groomed

toilet paper *n* : a thin soft sanitary absorbent paper usually in a roll for bathroom use

to·ken *n* **1** : an outer sign : PROOF **2** : a piece like a coin that has a special use **3** : an object used to suggest something that cannot be pictured **4** : SOUVENIR **5** : INDICATION 2

told *past and past participle of* TELL

tol·er·a·ble *adj* **1** : capable of being put up with **2** : fairly good — **tol·er·a·bly** *adv*

tol·er·ance *n* **1** : ability to put up with something harmful, bad, or annoying **2** : sympathy for or acceptance of feelings or habits which are different from someone's own

tol·er·ant *adj* : showing tolerance — **tol·er·ant·ly** *adv*

tol·er·ate *vb* **tol·er·at·ed; tol·er·at·ing 1** : to allow something to be or to be done without making a move to stop it **2** : to stand the action of

¹toll *n* **1** : a tax paid for a privilege (as the use of a highway or bridge) **2** : a charge paid for a service **3** : the cost in life or health

²toll *vb* **tolled; toll·ing 1** : to announce or call by the sounding of a bell **2** : to sound with slow strokes

³toll *n* : the sound of a bell ringing slowly

tom·a·hawk *n* : a light ax used as a weapon by North American Indians

to·ma·to *n, pl* **to·ma·toes** : the usually red juicy fruit of a plant related to the potato that is eaten raw or cooked as a vegetable

tomb *n* **1** : ¹GRAVE **2** : a house or burial chamber for dead people

tom·boy *n* : a girl who enjoys things that some people think are more suited to boys

tomb·stone *n* : GRAVESTONE

tom·cat *n* : a male cat

tome *n* : a big thick book

tom·fool·ery *n* : playful or foolish behavior

¹to·mor·row *adv* : on the day after today

²tomorrow *n* : the day after today

tom–tom *n* : a drum (as a traditional Asian, African, or American Indian drum) that is beaten with the hands

ton *n* : a measure of weight equal either to 2000 pounds (about 907 kilograms) (**short ton**) or 2240 pounds (about 1016 kilograms) (**long ton**) with the short ton being more frequently used in the United States and Canada

¹tone *n* **1** : an individual way of speaking or writing especially when used to express an emotion **2** : common character or quality **3** : quality of spoken or musical sound **4** : a sound on one pitch **5** : a shade of color **6** : a color that changes another **7** : a healthy state of the body or any of its parts

²tone *vb* **toned; ton·ing** : to give a healthy state to : STRENGTHEN — **tone down** : to soften or blend in color, appearance, or sound

tongs *n pl* : a tool for taking hold of or lifting something that consists usually of two movable pieces joined at one end or in the middle

tongue *n* **1** : a fleshy movable part of the mouth used in tasting, in taking and swallowing food, and by human beings in speaking **2** : a particular way or quality of speaking **3** : LANGUAGE 1 **4** : something that is long and fastened at one end

tongue–tied *adj* : unable to speak clearly or freely (as from shyness)

ton·ic *n* **1** : a medicine or preparation for improving the strength or health of mind or body **2** : SODA POP — used mostly in New England **3** : the first note of a scale

¹to·night *adv* : on this present night or the night following this present day

²tonight *n* : the present or the coming night

ton·nage *n* **1** : ships in terms of the total number of tons that are or can be carried **2** : total weight in tons shipped, carried, or mined

ton·sil *n* : either of a pair of masses of spongy tissue at the back of the mouth

ton·sil·li·tis *n* : a sore reddened state of the tonsils

too *adv* **1** : in addition : ALSO **2** : to a greater than wanted or needed degree **3** : ¹VERY 1

took *past of* TAKE

¹tool *n* **1** : an instrument (as a saw, file, knife, or wrench) used or worked by hand or machine to perform a task **2** : something that helps to gain an end **3** : a person used by another : DUPE

²tool *vb* **tooled; tool·ing 1** : to drive or ride in a vehicle **2** : to shape, form, or finish with a tool **3** : to equip a plant or industry with machines and tools for production

tool·box *n* : a box for storing or carrying tools

tool·shed *n* : a small building for storing tools

¹**toot** *vb* **toot·ed; toot·ing** **1** : to sound a short blast (as on a horn) **2** : to blow or sound an instrument (as a horn) especially in short blasts

²**toot** *n* : a short blast (as on a horn)

tooth *n, pl* **teeth** **1** : one of the hard bony structures set in sockets on the jaws of most vertebrates and used especially to chew and bite **2** : something like or suggesting an animal's tooth in shape, arrangement, or action **3** : one of the projections around the rim of a wheel that fit between the projections on another part causing the other part to move as the wheel turns — **tooth·less** *adj*

tooth·ache *n* : pain in or near a tooth

tooth·brush *n* : a brush for cleaning the teeth

toothed *adj* : having or showing teeth especially of a particular kind

tooth·paste *n* : a paste for cleaning the teeth

tooth·pick *n* : a pointed instrument for removing bits of food caught between the teeth

tooth·some *adj* : pleasing to the taste : DELICIOUS

toothy *adj* **tooth·i·er; tooth·i·est** : having or showing many usually large teeth

¹**top** *n* **1** : the highest point, level, or part of something **2** : the upper end, edge, or surface **3** : an upper piece, lid, or covering **4** : the highest position **5** : a garment worn on the upper part of the body **6** : the stalk and leaves of a plant and especially of one with roots that are used for food

²**top** *vb* **topped; top·ping** **1** : to cover with or be covered with **2** : to go over the top of **3** : to be better than or exceed **4** : to remove or cut the top of

³**top** *adj* : relating to or being at the top

⁴**top** *n* : a child's toy with a tapering point on which it can be made to spin

to·paz *n* : a clear yellow crystal that is used as a gem

top·coat *n* : a lightweight overcoat

top·ic *n* : the subject of something that is being discussed or has been written or thought about

topic sentence *n* : a sentence that states the main thought of a paragraph

top·knot *n* : a tuft of feathers or hair on the top of the head

top·mast *n* : the second mast above a ship's deck

top·most *adj* : highest of all

top·ple *vb* **top·pled; top·pling** : to fall or cause to fall from an upright position

top·sail *n* **1** : the sail next above the lowest sail on a mast in a square-rigged ship **2** : the sail above the large sail on a mast in a ship with a fore-and-aft rig

top·soil *n* : the rich upper layer of soil in which plants have most of their roots

top·sy–tur·vy *adv or adj* **1** : upside down **2** : in complete disorder

To·rah *n* **1** : the Jewish Bible and especially the first five books of writings **2** : a scroll containing the first five books of the Jewish Bible that is used in religious services

torch *n* **1** : a flaming light that is made of something which burns brightly and that is usually carried in the hand **2** : something that gives light or guidance **3** : a portable device for producing a hot flame

tore *past of* TEAR

¹**tor·ment** *vb* **tor·ment·ed; tor·ment·ing** **1** : to cause severe suffering of body or mind to **2** : VEX 1, HARASS

²**tor·ment** *n* **1** : extreme pain or distress of body or mind **2** : a cause of suffering in mind or body

torn *past participle of* TEAR

tor·na·do *n, pl* **tor·na·does** *or* **tor·na·dos** : a violent whirling wind accompanied by a cloud that is shaped like a funnel and moves overland in a narrow path

¹**tor·pe·do** *n, pl* **tor·pe·does** : a long narrow self-propelled underwater weapon used for blowing up ships

²**torpedo** *vb* **tor·pe·doed; tor·pe·do·ing** : to hit with or destroy by a torpedo

tor·rent *n* **1** : a rushing stream of liquid **2** : a large amount of something especially that is released suddenly

tor·rid *adj* : very hot and usually dry

tor·so *n* : the human body except for the head, arms, and legs

tor·ti·lla *n* : a round flat bread made of corn or wheat flour and usually eaten hot with a filling

tor·toise *n* **1** : a usually large turtle that lives on land **2** : TURTLE

tor·toise·shell *n* **1** : a hard brown and yellow material that covers the shell of a sea tortoise used especially in the past for ornamental objects **2** : a brightly colored butterfly

tor·tu·ous *adj* : having many twists and turns

¹**tor·ture** *n* **1** : the act of causing great pain especially to punish or to obtain a confession **2** : distress of body or mind

²**torture** *vb* **tor·tured; tor·tur·ing** **1** : to punish or force someone to do or say something by causing great pain **2** : to cause great suffering to — **tor·tur·er** *n*

¹**toss** *vb* **tossed; toss·ing** **1** : to throw with a quick light motion **2** : to lift with a sudden

motion **3** : to throw or swing back and forth or up and down **4** : to be thrown about rapidly **5** : to move about restlessly **6** : to stir or mix lightly

²**toss** *n* **1** : an act or instance of throwing something **2** : the act of lifting with a sudden motion

tot *n* : a young child

¹**to·tal** *adj* **1** : being such to the fullest degree **2** : making up the whole **3** : of or relating to the whole of something **4** : making use of every means to do something — **to·tal·ly** *adv*

²**total** *n* : the entire number or amount counted : SUM

³**total** *vb* **to·taled** *or* **to·talled; to·tal·ing** *or* **to·tal·ling** **1** : to add up **2** : to amount to : NUMBER

tote *vb* **tot·ed; tot·ing** : CARRY 1, HAUL

to·tem *n* **1** : an object (as an animal or plant) serving as the emblem of a family or clan **2** : a carving or picture representing such an object

totem pole *n* : a usually wooden pole or pillar carved and painted with totems and set up by American Indian tribes of the northwest coast of North America

tot·ter *vb* **tot·tered; tot·ter·ing** **1** : to sway or rock as if about to fall **2** : to move unsteadily : STAGGER

tou·can *n* : a brightly colored tropical bird that has a very large beak and feeds mostly on fruit

¹**touch** *vb* **touched; touch·ing** **1** : to feel or handle (as with the fingers) especially so as to be aware of **2** : to be or cause to be in contact with something **3** : to hit lightly **4** : ²HARM **5** : to make use of **6** : to refer to in passing **7** : to affect the interest of **8** : to have an influence on **9** : to move emotionally

²**touch** *n* **1** : a light stroke or tap **2** : the act or fact of touching or being touched **3** : the special sense by which one is aware of light pressure **4** : an impression gotten through the sense of touch **5** : a state of contact or communication **6** : a small amount : TRACE **7** : a small detail

touch·down *n* : a score made in football by carrying or catching the ball over the opponent's goal line

touch·ing *adj* : causing a feeling of tenderness or pity

touch pad *n* : a flat surface on an electronic device (as a microwave oven) divided into several differently marked areas that are touched to make choices in controlling the device

touch screen *n* : a display screen (as for a computer) on which the user selects options by touching the screen

touch–tone *adj* : relating to or being a telephone with push buttons that produce tones corresponding to the numbers

touchy *adj* **touch·i·er; touch·i·est** **1** : easily hurt or insulted **2** : calling for tact or careful handling

tough *adj* **tough·er; tough·est** **1** : strong or firm but flexible and not brittle **2** : not easily chewed **3** : physically or emotionally strong enough to put up with strain or hardship **4** : very strict, firm, or determined **5** : very difficult to do or deal with **6** : LAWLESS 2 — **tough·ness** *n*

tough·en *vb* **tough·ened; tough·en·ing** : to make or become tough

¹**tour** *n* **1** : a trip usually involving a series of stops and ending at the point where it started **2** : a fixed period of duty

²**tour** *vb* **toured; tour·ing** : to make a tour of : travel as a tourist

tour·ist *n* : a person who travels for pleasure

tour·na·ment *n* **1** : a series of contests played for a championship **2** : a contest between knights wearing armor and fighting with blunted lances or swords

tour·ni·quet *n* : a device (as a bandage twisted tight) for stopping bleeding or blood flow

tou·sle *vb* **tou·sled; tou·sling** : to put into disorder by rough handling

¹**tow** *vb* **towed; tow·ing** : to draw or pull along behind

²**tow** *n* : an act or instance of drawing or pulling along behind : the fact or state of being drawn or pulled along behind

³**tow** *n* : short broken fiber of flax, hemp, or jute used for yarn, twine, or stuffing

to·ward *or* **to·wards** *prep* **1** : in the direction of **2** : along a course leading to **3** : in regard to **4** : so as to face **5** : ²NEAR **6** : as part of the payment for

tow·el *n* : a cloth or piece of absorbent paper for wiping or drying

¹**tow·er** *n* : a building or structure that is higher than its length or width, is higher than most of what surrounds it, and may stand by itself or be attached to a larger structure

²**tower** *vb* **tow·ered; tow·er·ing** : to reach or rise to a great height

tow·er·ing *adj* **1** : rising high : TALL **2** : very powerful or intense **3** : going beyond proper bounds

tow·head *n* : a person having soft whitish hair

town *n* **1** : a thickly settled area that is usually larger than a village but smaller than a city **2** : the people of a town

town hall *n* : a public building used for offices and meetings of town government

town·ship *n* **1** : a unit of local government in some northeastern and north central states **2** : a division of territory in surveys of United States public lands containing 36 square miles (about 93 square kilometers)

tox·ic *adj* : containing, being, or caused by poisonous or dangerous material

tox·in *n* : a poison produced by a living thing (as an animal or bacterium)

¹toy *n* **1** : something for a child to play with **2** : something of little or no value **3** : something small of its kind

²toy *vb* **toyed; toy·ing 1** : to fidget or play with without thinking **2** : to think about something briefly and not very seriously **3** : to flirt with

¹trace *n* **1** : a mark left by something that has passed or is past **2** : a very small amount

²trace *vb* **traced; trac·ing 1** : ²SKETCH 1 **2** : to form (as letters) carefully **3** : to copy (as a drawing) by following the lines as seen through a transparent sheet placed over the thing copied **4** : to follow the footprints, track, or trail of **5** : to study or follow the development of in detail **6** : to follow something back to its cause or beginning

³trace *n* : either of the two straps, chains, or ropes of a harness that fasten a horse to a vehicle

tra·chea *n, pl* **tra·che·ae 1** : a stiff-walled tube of the respiratory system that connects the pharynx with the lungs **2** : a breathing tube of an insect that connects with the outside of the body and carries oxygen directly to the cells

trac·ing *n* : a copy of something traced from an original

¹track *n* **1** : a mark left by something that has gone by **2** : PATH 1, TRAIL **3** : the rails of a railroad **4** : a course laid out for racing **5** : awareness of things or of the order in which things happen or ideas come **6** : either of two endless metal belts on which a vehicle (as a tank) travels **7** : track-and-field sports

²track *vb* **tracked; track·ing 1** : to follow the marks or traces of **: to search for someone or something **2** : to bring indoors on the bottom of the shoes, feet, or paws

track–and–field *adj* : relating to or being sports events (as racing, throwing, and jumping contests) held on a running track and on the enclosed field

¹tract *n* **1** : an indefinite stretch of land **2** : a defined area of land **3** : a system of body parts or organs that serve some special purpose

²tract *n* : a pamphlet of political or religious ideas and beliefs

trac·tion *n* : the force that causes a moving thing to slow down or to stick against the surface it is moving along

trac·tor *n* **1** : a vehicle that has large rear wheels or moves on endless belts and is used especially for pulling farm implements **2** : a short truck for hauling a trailer

¹trade *n* **1** : the business or work in which a person takes part regularly : OCCUPATION **2** : the business of buying and selling items : COMMERCE **3** : an occupation requiring manual or mechanical skill : CRAFT **4** : an act of trading : TRANSACTION **5** : the persons working in a business or industry **6** : a firm's customers

²trade *vb* **trad·ed; trad·ing 1** : to give in exchange for something else **2** : to take part in the exchange, purchase, or sale of goods **3** : to deal regularly as a customer

trade·mark *n* : a device (as a word) that points clearly to the origin or ownership of merchandise to which it is applied and that is legally reserved for use only by the owner

trad·er *n* **1** : a person who trades **2** : a ship engaged in commerce

trades·man *n, pl* **trades·men 1** : a person who runs a retail store **2** : CRAFTSMAN 1

trades·peo·ple *n pl* : people engaged in occupations requiring manual or mechanical skill

trade wind *n* : a wind blowing steadily toward the equator from an easterly direction

trading post *n* : a store set up in a thinly settled region

tra·di·tion *n* **1** : the handing down of information, beliefs, or customs from one generation to another **2** : a belief or custom handed down from one generation to another

tra·di·tion·al *adj* **1** : handed down from age to age **2** : based on custom : CONVENTIONAL — **tra·di·tion·al·ly** *adv*

¹traf·fic *n* **1** : the movement (as of vehicles or pedestrians) along a route **2** : the people or goods carried by train, boat, or airplane or passing along a road, river, or air route **3** : the business of carrying passengers or goods **4** : the business of buying and selling : COMMERCE **5** : exchange of information

²traffic *vb* **traf·ficked; traf·fick·ing** : ²TRADE 2

traffic light *n* : a visual signal (as a set of colored lights) for controlling the flow of vehicles

trag·e·dy *n, pl* **trag·e·dies 1** : a disastrous event **2** : a serious play that has a sad or disastrous ending

trag·ic *adj* **1** : very unfortunate **2** : of or relating to tragedy

¹trail *vb* **trailed; trail·ing 1** : to drag or draw along behind **2** : to become weak, soft, or less **3** : to follow in the tracks of : PURSUE **4** : to hang down, rest on, or creep over the ground **5** : to lag behind

²trail *n* **1** : a trace or mark left by something that has passed or been drawn along **2** : a beaten path **3** : a path marked through a forest or mountainous region

trail·er *n* **1** : a platform or frame with wheels that is pulled behind a vehicle and used to transport things (as a boat) **2** : a vehicle designed to serve wherever parked as a dwelling or a place of business **3** : PREVIEW

¹train *n* **1** : a connected series of railway cars usually hauled by a locomotive **2** : a part of a gown that trails behind the wearer **3** : a connected series **4** : a moving line of persons, vehicles, or animals **5** : the followers of an important person

²train *vb* **trained; train·ing 1** : to give or receive instruction, discipline, or drill **2** : to teach in an art, profession, or trade **3** : to make ready (as by exercise) for a test of skill **4** : to teach (an animal) to obey **5** : to make (a plant) grow in a particular way usually by bending, trimming, or tying **6** : to aim something at a target — **train·er** *n*

train·ing *n* **1** : the course followed by a person or animal who trains or is being trained **2** : the skill, knowledge, or experience acquired by a person or animal who has trained

training wheels *n pl* : a pair of small wheels connected to the rear axle of a bicycle to help a beginning rider keep balance

traipse *vb* **traipsed; traips·ing** : to walk or wander about

trait *n* : a quality that makes one person, animal, or thing different from another : CHARACTERISTIC

trai·tor *n* **1** : a person who is not loyal or true to a friend, duty, cause, or belief or is false to a personal duty **2** : a person who betrays his or her country : a person who commits treason

trai·tor·ous *adj* **1** : guilty or capable of treason **2** : amounting to treason

¹tramp *vb* **tramped; tramp·ing 1** : to travel or wander through on foot **2** : to walk heavily

²tramp *n* **1** : a person who wanders from place to place, has no home or job, and often lives by begging or stealing **2** : the sounds made by the beat of marching feet **3** : ²HIKE

tram·ple *vb* **tram·pled; tram·pling 1** : to tramp or tread heavily so as to bruise, crush, or injure something **2** : to crush under the feet **3** : to treat as if worthless or unimportant

tram·po·line *n* : a canvas sheet or web supported by springs in a metal frame used for springing and landing in acrobatic tumbling

trance *n* **1** : a condition like sleep (as deep hypnosis) **2** : a state of being so deeply absorbed in thought about something as to be aware of anything else **3** : STUPOR

tran·quil *adj* : very calm and quiet : PEACEFUL

tran·quil·iz·er *n* : a drug used to make someone calm and relaxed

tran·quil·li·ty *or* **tran·quil·i·ty** *n* : the state of being calm : QUIET

trans. *abbr* transitive

trans- *prefix* **1** : on or to the other side of : across : beyond **2** : so as to change or transfer

trans·act *vb* **trans·act·ed; trans·act·ing** : to carry on : MANAGE, CONDUCT

trans·ac·tion *n* **1** : a business deal **2 transactions** *pl* : the record of the meeting of a club or organization

trans·at·lan·tic *adj* : crossing or being beyond the Atlantic Ocean

tran·scend *vb* **tran·scend·ed; tran·scend·ing 1** : to rise above the limits of **2** : to do better or more than

trans·con·ti·nen·tal *adj* : crossing, extending across, or being on the farther side of a continent

tran·scribe *vb* **tran·scribed; tran·scrib·ing** : to make a copy of

tran·script *n* **1** : ¹COPY 1 **2** : an official copy of a student's school record

¹trans·fer *vb* **trans·ferred; trans·fer·ring 1** : to move from one person or place to another **2** : to pass or cause to pass from one person, place, or condition to another **3** : to move to a different place, region, or job **4** : to give over the possession or ownership of **5** : to copy (as by printing) from one surface to another by contact **6** : to change from one vehicle or transportation line to another

²trans·fer *n* **1** : the act of giving over right, title, or interest in property to another person or other persons **2** : an act or process of moving someone or something from one place to another **3** : someone who has changed schools **4** : a ticket allowing a passenger on a bus or train to continue the journey on another route without paying more fare

trans·fix *vb* **trans·fixed; trans·fix·ing** : to hold motionless by or as if by piercing through with a pointed weapon

trans·form *vb* **trans·formed; trans·form·ing** : to change completely

trans·for·ma·tion *n* : the act or process of changing completely : a complete change

trans·form·er *n* : a device for changing the voltage of an electric current

trans·fu·sion *n* **1** : the process of passing a fluid (as blood) into a vein of a person or animal **2** : the act of giving something a fresh supply

trans·gres·sion *n* : a violation of a command or law

¹tran·sient *adj* : not lasting or staying long

²transient *n* : a person traveling about usually in search of work

tran·sis·tor *n* : a small solid electronic device used for controlling the flow of electricity

tran·sit *n* **1** : the act of passing through or across **2** : the act or method of carrying things from one place to another **3** : local transportation of people in public vehicles **4** : a surveyor's instrument for measuring angles

tran·si·tion *n* : an act or the process of passing from one state, stage, place, or subject to another : CHANGE

tran·si·tive *adj* : having or containing a direct object

trans·late *vb* **trans·lat·ed; trans·lat·ing 1** : to turn from one language into another **2** : to change from one form to another

trans·la·tion *n* : the act, process, or result of changing from one form or language into another

trans·lu·cent *adj* : not transparent but clear enough to allow rays of light to pass through

trans·mis·sion *n* **1** : an act or process of transmitting, spreading, or passing along **2** : the gears that pass power from the engine to the axle that gives motion to a motor vehicle

trans·mit *vb* **trans·mit·ted; trans·mit·ting 1** : to transfer, pass, or spread from one person or place to another **2** : to pass on by or as if by inheritance **3** : to pass or cause to pass through space or through a material **4** : to send out (a signal) by means of radio waves

trans·mit·ter *n* **1** : someone or something that transmits something **2** : the part of a telephone that includes the mouthpiece and a device that picks up sound waves and sends them over the wire **3** : a device that sends out radio or television signals

tran·som *n* **1** : a piece that lies crosswise in a structure (as in the frame of a window or of a door that has a window above it) **2** : a window above a door or another window

trans·par·en·cy *n, pl* **trans·par·en·cies** : the quality or state of being transparent **2** : a picture or design on glass or film that can be viewed by shining a light through it

trans·par·ent *adj* **1** : clear enough or thin enough to be seen through **2** : easily detected — **trans·par·ent·ly** *adv*

trans·pi·ra·tion *n* : the process by which plants give off water vapor through openings in their leaves

trans·pire *vb* **trans·pired; trans·pir·ing 1** : to come to pass : HAPPEN **2** : to become known or apparent **3** : to give off water vapor through openings in the leaves

¹trans·plant *vb* **trans·plant·ed; trans·plant·ing 1** : to dig up and plant again in another soil or location **2** : to remove from one place and settle or introduce elsewhere **3** : to transfer (a body organ or tissue) from one part or individual to another

²trans·plant *n* **1** : something or someone planted or moved elsewhere **2** : the process or act of planting or moving elsewhere

¹trans·port *vb* **trans·port·ed; trans·port·ing 1** : to carry from one place to another **2** : to fill with delight

²trans·port *n* **1** : the act of carrying from one place to another : TRANSPORTATION **2** : a ship for carrying soldiers or military equipment **3** : a vehicle used to carry people or goods from one place to another **4** : a state of great joy or pleasure

trans·por·ta·tion *n* **1** : an act, instance, or means of carrying people or goods from one place to another or of being carried from one place to another **2** : public carrying of passengers or goods especially as a business

trans·pose *vb* **trans·posed; trans·pos·ing 1** : to change the position or order of **2** : to write or perform in a different musical key

trans·verse *adj* : lying or being across : placed crosswise — **trans·verse·ly** *adv*

¹trap *n* **1** : a device for catching animals **2** : something by which one is caught or stopped by surprise **3** : a light one-horse carriage with springs **4** : a device that allows something to pass through but keeps other things out

²trap *vb* **trapped; trap·ping 1** : to catch or be caught in a trap **2** : to put or get in a place or position from which escape is not possible — **trap·per** *n*

trap·door *n* : a lifting or sliding door covering an opening in a floor or roof

tra·peze *n* : a short horizontal bar hung from two parallel ropes and used by acrobats

trap·e·zoid *n* : a flat geometric figure with four sides but with only two sides parallel

trap·pings *n pl* **1** : ornamental covering especially for a horse **2** : outward decoration or dress

trash *n* **1** : something of little or no value

that is thrown away **2** : people who deserve little respect

¹trav·el *vb* **trav·eled** *or* **trav·elled; trav·el·ing** *or* **trav·el·ling 1** : to journey from place to place or to a distant place **2** : to get around : pass from one place to another **3** : to journey through or over — **trav·el·er** *or* **trav·el·ler** *n*

²travel *n* **1** : the act or a means of journeying from one place to another **2** : ¹JOURNEY, TRIP — often used in pl. **3** : the number journeying

tra·verse *vb* **tra·versed; tra·vers·ing** : to pass through, across, or over

¹trawl *vb* **trawled; trawl·ing** : to fish or catch with a large net dragged along the sea bottom

²trawl *n* : a large net in the shape of a cone dragged along the sea bottom in fishing

trawl·er *n* : a boat used for fishing with a large net dragged along the sea bottom

tray *n* : an open container with a flat bottom and low rim for holding, carrying, or showing articles

treach·er·ous *adj* **1** : not safe because of hidden dangers **2** : not trustworthy : guilty of betrayal or likely to betray — **treach·er·ous·ly** *adv*

treach·ery *n, pl* **treach·er·ies 1** : the behavior of a person who betrays trust or faith **2** : an act or instance of betraying trust or faith

¹tread *vb* **trod; trod·den** *or* **trod; tread·ing 1** : to step or walk on or over **2** : to beat or press with the feet **3** : to move on foot : WALK — **tread water** : to keep the body upright in water and the head above water by moving the legs and arms

²tread *n* **1** : the action, manner, or sound of stepping or walking **2** : a mark made by a tire rolling over the ground **3** : the part of something (as a shoe or tire) that touches a surface **4** : the part of a step that is stepped on

trea·dle *n* : a device worked by the foot to drive a machine

tread·mill *n* **1** : a device having an endless belt on which an individual walks or runs in place for exercise **2** : a tiresome routine

trea·son *n* : the crime of trying or helping to overthrow the government of the criminal's own country or cause its defeat in war

¹trea·sure *n* **1** : wealth (as money or jewels) stored up or held in reserve **2** : something of great value

²treasure *vb* **trea·sured; trea·sur·ing** : to treat as precious : CHERISH

trea·sur·er *n* : a person (as an officer of a club or business) who has charge of the money

trea·sury *n, pl* **trea·sur·ies 1** : a place in which money and valuable objects are kept

2 : a place where money collected is kept and paid out **3** *cap* : a government department in charge of finances

¹treat *vb* **treat·ed; treat·ing 1** : to handle, deal with, use, or act toward in a usually stated way **2** : to pay for the food or entertainment of **3** : to give medical or surgical care to : use medical care on **4** : to expose to some action (as of a chemical)

²treat *n* **1** : an often unexpected or unusual source of pleasure or amusement **2** : a food that tastes very good and is not eaten very often **3** : an instance of paying for someone's food or entertainment

treat·ment *n* **1** : the act or manner of treating someone or something **2** : medical or surgical care **3** : a substance or method used in treating

trea·ty *n, pl* **trea·ties** : an agreement between two or more states or sovereigns

¹tre·ble *n* **1** : the highest part in harmony having four parts : SOPRANO **2** : an instrument having the highest range or part **3** : a voice or sound that has a high pitch **4** : the upper half of the musical pitch range

²treble *adj* **1** : being three times the number or amount **2** : relating to or having the range of a musical treble

³treble *vb* **tre·bled; tre·bling** : to make or become three times as much

¹tree *n* **1** : a long-lived woody plant that has a single usually tall main stem with few or no branches on its lower part **2** : a plant of treelike form **3** : something shaped like a tree — **tree·less** *adj* — **tree·like** *adj*

²tree *vb* **treed; tree·ing** : to force to go up a tree

tree fern *n* : a tropical fern with a tall woody stalk and a crown of often feathery leaves

tree house *n* : a structure (as a playhouse) built among the branches of a tree

tree·top *n* : the highest part of a tree

tre·foil *n* **1** : a clover or related plant having leaves with three leaflets **2** : a fancy design with three leaflike parts

¹trek *vb* **trekked; trek·king** : to walk a long way with difficulty

²trek *n* : a slow or difficult journey

trel·lis *n* : a frame of lattice used especially as a screen or a support for climbing plants

¹trem·ble *vb* **trem·bled; trem·bling 1** : to shake without control (as from fear or cold) : SHIVER **2** : to move, sound, or happen as if shaken **3** : to have strong fear or doubt

²tremble *n* : the act or a period of shaking

tre·men·dous *adj* **1** : astonishingly large, strong, or great **2** : very good or excellent — **tre·men·dous·ly** *adv*

trem·or *n* **1** : a trembling or shaking especially from weakness or disease **2** : a shaking motion of the earth during an earthquake

trem·u·lous *adj* **1** : marked by trembling or shaking **2** : FEARFUL 2, TIMID

trench *n* : a long narrow ditch

trend *n* : general direction taken in movement or change

trendy *adj* **trend·i·er; trend·i·est** : currently fashionable or popular

trep·i·da·tion *n* : a state of alarm or nervousness

¹tres·pass *n* **1** : unlawful entry upon someone's land **2** : ¹SIN, OFFENSE

²trespass *vb* **tres·passed; tres·pass·ing 1** : to enter upon someone's land unlawfully **2** : to do wrong : SIN — **tres·pass·er** *n*

tress *n* : a long lock of hair

tres·tle *n* **1** : a braced frame consisting usually of a horizontal piece with spreading legs at each end that supports something (as the top of a table) **2** : a structure of timbers or steel for supporting a road or railroad over a low place

T. rex *n* : TYRANNOSAUR

tri- *prefix* : three

tri·ad *n* : a chord made up usually of the first, third, and fifth notes of a scale

tri·al *n* **1** : the hearing and judgment of something in court **2** : a test of someone's ability to do or endure something **3** : an experiment to test quality, value, or usefulness **4** : the action or process of trying or testing

tri·an·gle *n* **1** : a flat geometric figure that has three sides and three angles **2** : something that has three sides and three angles **3** : a musical instrument made of a steel rod bent in the shape of a triangle with one open angle

tri·an·gu·lar *adj* **1** : having three angles, sides, or corners **2** : of, relating to, or involving three parts or persons

trib·al *adj* : relating to a tribe

tribe *n* **1** : a group of people including many families, clans, or generations **2** : a group of people who are of the same kind or have the same occupation or interest

tribes·man *n, pl* **tribes·men** : a member of a tribe

trib·u·la·tion *n* **1** : an experience that is hard to bear **2** : distress or suffering resulting from cruel and unjust treatment or misfortune

tri·bu·nal *n* : a court of justice

trib·u·tary *n, pl* **trib·u·tar·ies** : a stream flowing into a larger stream or a lake

trib·ute *n* **1** : something done, said, or given to show respect, gratitude, or affection **2** : a payment made by one ruler or state to another especially to gain peace

tri·cer·a·tops *n, pl* **triceratops** : a large plant-eating dinosaur with three horns, a large bony crest around the neck, and hoofed toes

¹trick *n* **1** : an action intended to deceive or cheat **2** : a mischievous act : PRANK **3** : an action designed to puzzle or amuse **4** : a quick or clever way of doing something **5** : the cards played in one round of a game

²trick *vb* **tricked; trick·ing** : to deceive with tricks

³trick *adj* : relating to or involving actions intended to deceive or puzzle

trick·ery *n* : the use of actions intended to deceive or cheat

¹trick·le *vb* **trick·led; trick·ling 1** : to run or fall in drops **2** : to flow in a thin slow stream **3** : to move slowly or in small numbers

²trickle *n* : a thin slow stream

trick or treat *n* : a children's Halloween practice of going around usually in costume asking for treats

trick·ster *n* : a person who uses tricks

tricky *adj* **trick·i·er; trick·i·est 1** : requiring special care and skill **2** : likely to use tricks

tri·cy·cle *n* : a vehicle with three wheels that is usually moved by pedals

tri·dent *n* : a spear with three prongs

tried *past and past participle of* TRY

tried–and–true *adj* : found good or trustworthy through experience or testing

¹tri·fle *n* : something of little value or importance

²trifle *vb* **tri·fled; tri·fling** : to treat (someone or something) as unimportant

tri·fling *adj* **1** : not serious : FRIVOLOUS **2** : of little value

trig·ger *n* : the part of the lock of a gun that is pressed to release the hammer so that it will fire

¹trill *n* **1** : ¹WARBLE 1 **2** : the rapid vibration of one speech organ against another (as the tongue against the teeth) **3** : a quick movement back and forth between two musical tones one step apart

²trill *vb* **trilled; trill·ing** : to utter as or with a trill

tril·lion *n* : a thousand billions

tril·li·um *n* : a plant related to the lilies that has three leaves and a single flower with three petals and that blooms in the spring

¹trim *vb* **trimmed; trim·ming 1** : to put decorations on : ADORN **2** : to make neat especially by cutting or clipping **3** : to free of unnecessary matter **4** : to adjust (as a sail) to a desired position — **trim·mer** *n*

²trim *adj* **trim·mer; trim·mest** : neat and compact in line or structure — **trim·ly** *adv*

³trim *n* **1** : material used for ornament or trimming **2** : the woodwork in the finish of a building especially around doors and windows **3** : an act or instance of cutting or clipping

trim·ming *n* : something that ornaments, seasons, or completes

trin·ket *n* : a small object of little value

trio *n, pl* **tri·os** **1** : a group or set of three **2** : a group of three musicians who perform together

¹trip *vb* **tripped; trip·ping** **1** : to catch the foot against something so as to stumble : cause to stumble **2** : to make or cause to make a mistake **3** : to move (as in dancing) with light quick steps **4** : to release (as a spring) by moving a catch

²trip *n* **1** : an instance of traveling from one place to another **2** : a brief errand having a certain aim or being more or less regular **3** : the action of releasing something mechanically **4** : a device for releasing something by tripping a mechanism

tripe *n* : a part of the stomach of a cow used for food

¹tri·ple *vb* **tri·pled; tri·pling** : to make or become three times as great or as many

²triple *n* **1** : a sum, amount, or number that is three times as great **2** : a combination, group, or series of three **3** : a hit in baseball that lets the batter reach third base

³triple *adj* **1** : having three units or parts **2** : being three times as great or as many **3** : repeated three times

trip·let *n* **1** : a combination, set, or group of three **2** : one of three offspring born at one birth

tri·pod *n* **1** : something (as a container or stool) resting on three legs **2** : a stand (as for a camera) having three legs

trite *adj* **trit·er; trit·est** : so common that the newness and cleverness have worn off : STALE

¹tri·umph *n* **1** : the joy of victory or success **2** : an outstanding victory

²triumph *vb* **tri·umphed; tri·umph·ing** **1** : to celebrate victory or success in high spirits **2** : to gain victory : WIN

tri·um·phal *adj* : following or in celebration of victory

tri·um·phant *adj* **1** : VICTORIOUS, SUCCESSFUL **2** : rejoicing for or celebrating victory — **tri·um·phant·ly** *adv*

triv·ia *n* : interesting facts that are not well-known

triv·i·al *adj* : of little worth or importance

trod *past and past participle of* TREAD

trodden *past participle of* TREAD

Tro·jan War *n* : a 10-year war resulting in the destruction of the anciety city of Troy by the Greeks

¹troll *n* : a dwarf or giant of folklore living in caves or hills

²troll *vb* **trolled; troll·ing** **1** : to sing the parts of (a song) in succession **2** : to fish with a hook and line pulled along through the water

³troll *n* : a lure or a line with its lure and hook drawn through the water in fishing

trol·ley *n, pl* **trolleys** **1** : a passenger car that runs on tracks and gets its power through electricity **2** : a wheeled cart

trom·bone *n* : a brass musical instrument made of a long bent tube that has a wide opening at one end and one section that slides in and out to make different tones

¹troop *n* **1** : a group of soldiers **2 troops** *pl* : armed forces : MILITARY **3** : a group of beings or things **4** : a unit of boy or girl scouts under a leader

²troop *vb* **trooped; troop·ing** : to move or gather in groups

troop·er *n* **1** : a soldier in a cavalry unit **2** : a state police officer

tro·phy *n, pl* **trophies** **1** : something given to celebrate a victory or as an award for achievement **2** : something taken in battle or conquest especially as a memorial

trop·ic *n* **1** : either of two parallels of the earth's latitude of which one is about 23½ degrees north of the equator and the other about 23½ degrees south of the equator **2 tropics** *pl, often cap* : the region lying between the Tropic of Cancer and the Tropic of Capricorn

trop·i·cal *adj* : of, or occurring in the tropics

tropical fish *n* : a small often brightly colored fish kept in aquariums

tropical storm *n* : a storm that begins in the tropics with winds that are not as strong as those of a hurricane

¹trot *n* **1** : a gait of an animal with four feet that is faster than walking but slower than galloping and in which a front foot and the opposite hind foot move as a pair **2** : a human jogging pace slower than a run

²trot *vb* **trot·ted; trot·ting** **1** : to ride, drive, go, or cause to go at a trot **2** : to go along quickly : HURRY

¹trou·ble *n* **1** : something that causes worry or distress : MISFORTUNE **2** : an instance of distress or disturbance **3** : extra work or effort **4** : ill health : AILMENT **5** : failure to work normally

²trouble *vb* **trou·bled; trou·bling** **1** : to become or make worried or upset **2** : to produce physical disorder in : AFFLICT **3** : to put to inconvenience **4** : to make an effort

trou·ble·some *adj* **1** : giving distress or anxiety **2** : difficult to deal with

trough *n* **1** : a long shallow open container especially for water or feed for livestock **2** : GUTTER **3** : a long channel or hollow

trounce *vb* **trounced; trounc·ing** **1** : to beat severely : FLOG **2** : to defeat thoroughly

troupe *n* : a group especially of performers who act or work together

trou·sers *n pl* : PANTS

trout *n, pl* **trout** : a freshwater fish related to the salmon that is often caught for food or sport

trow·el *n* **1** : a small hand tool with a flat blade used for spreading and smoothing mortar or plaster **2** : a small hand tool with a curved blade used by gardeners

tru·an·cy *n, pl* **tru·an·cies** : an act or an instance of staying out of school without permission

tru·ant *n* **1** : a student who stays out of school without permission **2** : a person who neglects his or her duty

truce *n* : an agreement between enemies or opponents to stop fighting for a certain period of time

¹truck *n* : a vehicle (as a strong heavy wagon or motor vehicle) for carrying heavy articles or hauling a trailer

²truck *n* : close association

³truck *vb* **trucked; truck·ing** : to transport on or in a truck

trudge *vb* **trudged; trudg·ing** : to walk or march steadily and usually with much effort

¹true *adj* **tru·er; tru·est** **1** : agreeing with the facts : ACCURATE **2** : completely loyal : FAITHFUL **3** : consistent or in accordance with **4** : properly so called : GENUINE **5** : placed or formed accurately : EXACT **6** : being or holding by right : LEGITIMATE **7** : fully realized or fulfilled

²true *adv* **1** : in agreement with fact : TRUTHFULLY **2** : in an accurate manner : ACCURATELY

³true *n* : the quality or state of being accurate (as in alignment)

⁴true *vb* **trued; true·ing** *also* **tru·ing** : to bring to exactly correct condition as to place, position, or shape

true–blue *adj* : very faithful

tru·ly *adv* : in a manner that is actual, genuine, honest, or without question

¹trum·pet *n* **1** : a brass musical instrument that consists of a tube formed into a long loop with a wide opening at one end and that has valves by which different tones are produced **2** : something that is shaped like a trumpet

²trumpet *vb* **trum·pet·ed; trum·pet·ing** **1** : to blow a trumpet **2** : to make a sound like that of a trumpet **3** : to praise (something) loudly and publicly — **trum·pet·er** *n*

trun·dle *vb* **trun·dled; trun·dling** : to roll along : WHEEL

trundle bed *n* : a low bed on small wheels that can be rolled under a taller bed

trunk *n* **1** : the thick main stem of a tree not including the branches and roots **2** : a box or chest for holding clothes or other articles especially for traveling **3** : the enclosed space in the rear of an automobile for carrying articles **4** : the long round muscular nose of an elephant **5 trunks** *pl* : a swimsuit for a man or boy **6** : the body of a person or animal not including the head, arms, and legs

¹truss *vb* **trussed; truss·ing** **1** : to bind or tie firmly **2** : to support, strengthen, or stiffen by a framework of beams

²truss *n* : a framework of beams or bars used in building and engineering

¹trust *vb* **trust·ed; trust·ing** **1** : to rely on or on the truth of : BELIEVE **2** : to place confidence in someone or something **3** : to be confident : HOPE

²trust *n* **1** : firm belief in the character, strength, or truth of someone or something **2** : a person or thing in which confidence is placed **3** : confident hope **4** : a property interest held by one person or organization (as a bank) for the benefit of another **5** : a combination of firms or corporations formed by a legal agreement and often held to reduce competition **6** : an organization in which money is held or managed by someone for the benefit of another or others **7** : responsibility for safety and well-being

trust·ee *n* : a person who has been given legal responsibility for someone else's property

trust·ful *adj* : full of trust — **trust·ful·ness** *n*

trust·ing *adj* : having or showing faith, confidence, or belief in someone or something

trust·wor·thy *adj* : deserving faith and confidence — **trust·wor·thi·ness** *n*

trusty *adj* **trust·i·er; trust·i·est** : worthy of being depended on

truth *n, pl* **truths** **1** : the body of real events or facts **2** : the quality or state of being true **3** : a true or accepted statement or idea — **in truth** : in actual fact : REALLY

truth·ful *adj* : telling or being in the habit of telling facts or making statements that are true — **truth·ful·ly** *adv* — **truth·ful·ness** *n*

¹try *vb* **tried ; try·ing** **1** : to make an effort or attempt at **2** : to put to a test **3** : to examine or investigate in a court of law **4** : to conduct the trial of **5** : to test to the limit — **try on** : to put on (a garment) to test the fit — **try out** : to compete to fill a part (as on an athletic team or in a play)

²try *n, pl* **tries** : an effort to do something : ATTEMPT

try·ing *adj* : hard to bear or put up with

try·out *n* : a test of the ability (as of an athlete or an actor) to fill a part or meet standards

T–shirt *also* **tee shirt** *n* : a shirt with short sleeves and no collar and usually made of cotton

tsp. *abbr* teaspoon

tsu·na·mi *n* : a large sea wave produced especially by an earthquake or volcanic eruption under the sea : TIDAL WAVE

Tu. *abbr* Tuesday

tub *n* **1** : a wide low container **2** : BATHTUB **3** : an old or slow boat **4** : the amount that a tub will hold

tu·ba *n* : a brass musical instrument of lowest pitch with an oval shape and valves for producing different tones

tub·by *adj* **tub·bi·er; tub·bi·est** : short and somewhat fat

tube *n* **1** : a long hollow cylinder used especially to carry fluids **2** : a long soft container whose contents (as toothpaste or glue) can be removed by squeezing **3** : a slender channel within a plant or animal body : DUCT **4** : a hollow cylinder of rubber inside a tire to hold air **5** : ELECTRON TUBE **6** : TELEVISION 2 — **tube·like** *adj*

tu·ber *n* : a short thick fleshy usually underground stem (as of a potato plant) having buds that can produce new plants

tu·ber·cu·lo·sis *n* : a serious disease that mostly affects the lungs and in which there is fever, cough, and difficulty in breathing

tu·bu·lar *adj* **1** : having the form of or made up of a tube **2** : made with tubes

¹tuck *vb* **tucked; tuck·ing 1** : to put or fit into a snug or safe place **2** : to push in the edges of **3** : to pull up into or as if into a fold **4** : to cover by pushing in the edges of bedclothes **5** : to eat or drink with obvious pleasure **6** : to make stitched folds in

²tuck *n* : a fold stitched into cloth usually to alter it

tuck·er *vb* **tuck·ered; tuck·er·ing** : to cause to tire

Tue., Tues. *abbr* Tuesday

Tues·day *n* : the third day of the week

tuft *n* **1** : a small bunch of long flexible things (as hairs or blades of grass) growing close together **2** : ¹CLUMP 1 — **tuft·ed** *adj*

¹tug *vb* **tugged; tug·ging 1** : to pull hard **2** : to move by pulling hard : DRAG **3** : to tow with a tugboat

²tug *n* **1** : an act of pulling hard : a hard pull **2** : TUGBOAT **3** : a strong pulling force **4** : a struggle between two people or forces

tug·boat *n* : a small powerful boat used for towing ships

tug–of–war *n, pl* **tugs–of–war 1** : a contest in which two teams pull against each other at opposite ends of a rope **2** : a struggle to win

tu·ition *n* : money paid for instruction (as at a college)

tu·lip *n* : a plant related to the lily that grows from a bulb and has a large cup-shaped flower in early spring

¹tum·ble *vb* **tum·bled; tum·bling 1** : to fall suddenly and helplessly **2** : to fall while rolling or bouncing **3** : to move or go in a hurried or confused way **4** : to toss together into a confused mass **5** : to perform gymnastic feats of rolling and turning **6** : to suffer a sudden downward turn or defeat

²tumble *n* **1** : an act or instance of falling often while rolling or bouncing **2** : a messy state or collection

tum·ble·down *adj* : DILAPIDATED

tum·bler *n* **1** : a person (as an acrobat) who tumbles **2** : a drinking glass **3** : a movable part of a lock that must be adjusted (as by a key) before the lock will open

tum·ble·weed *n* : a plant that breaks away from its roots in autumn and tumbles about in the wind

tum·my *n, pl* **tummies 1** : ¹STOMACH 1 **2** : ¹STOMACH 2

tu·mor *n* : an abnormal growth of body tissue

tu·mult *n* **1** : UPROAR **2** : great confusion of mind

tu·mul·tu·ous *adj* : characterized by uproar

tu·na *n, pl* **tuna** *or* **tunas** : a large sea fish caught for food and sport

tun·dra *n* : a treeless plain of arctic regions having a permanently frozen layer below the surface of the soil

¹tune *n* **1** : a series of pleasing musical tones : MELODY **2** : correct musical pitch or key **3** : AGREEMENT 1, HARMONY **4** : general attitude — **tune·ful** *adj*

²tune *vb* **tuned; tun·ing 1** : to adjust a radio or television so that it receives clearly **2** : to adjust in musical pitch **3** : to come or bring into harmony **4** : to put (as an engine) in good working order — often used with *up* — **tun·er** *n* — **tune out** : to ignore what is happening or being said

tung·sten *n* : a grayish-white hard metallic chemical element used especially for electrical parts (as for the fine wire in an electric light bulb) and to make alloys (as steel) harder

tu·nic *n* **1** : a usually knee-length belted garment worn by ancient Greeks and Romans **2** : a shirt or jacket reaching to or just below the hips

tuning fork *n* : a metal instrument that gives a fixed tone when struck and is useful for tuning musical instruments

¹tun·nel *n* : a passage under the ground

²**tunnel** *vb* **tun·neled** *or* **tun·nelled; tun·nel·ing** *or* **tun·nel·ling :** to make a passage under the ground

tun·ny *n, pl* **tun·nies :** TUNA

tur·ban *n* **1 :** a head covering worn especially by Muslims and made of a long cloth wrapped around the head or around a cap **2 :** a woman's small soft hat with no brim

tur·bid *adj* **:** dark or discolored with sediment

tur·bine *n* **:** an engine whose central driving shaft is fitted with a series of winglike parts that are spun by the pressure of water, steam, or gas

tur·bu·lence *n* **:** irregular movements of air currents

tur·bu·lent *adj* **:** causing or being in a state of unrest, violence, or disturbance

tu·reen *n* **:** a deep bowl from which food (as soup) is served

turf *n* **1 :** the upper layer of soil bound into a thick mat by roots of grass and other plants **2 :** land covered with grass **3 :** an area that is or is felt to be under an individual's control

Turk *n* **:** a person born or living in Turkey

tur·key *n, pl* **turkeys :** a large North American bird related to the chicken and widely raised for food

¹**Turk·ish** *adj* **:** of or relating to Turkey, the Turks, or Turkish

²**Turkish** *n* **:** the language of the Turks

tur·moil *n* **:** a very confused or disturbed state or condition

¹**turn** *vb* **turned; turn·ing 1 :** to change in position usually by moving through an arc of a circle **2 :** to change course or direction **3 :** to move or direct toward or away from something **4 :** to become or cause to become a certain way **5 :** ¹CHANGE 1, TRANSFORM **6 :** to move or cause to move around a center **7 :** to twist so as to bring about a desired end **8 :** to go around **9 :** to reach or pass beyond **10 :** to become or make very unfriendly **11 :** to pass from one state to another **:** BECOME **12 :** EXECUTE 1, PERFORM **13 :** to set in another and especially an opposite direction **14 :** ¹WRENCH 2 **15 :** to think over **:** PONDER **16 :** ¹UPSET 2 **17 :** to make an appeal **18 :** to make or become spoiled **19 :** TRANSLATE 1 **20 :** to give a rounded form to (as on a lathe) — **turn down 1 :** to lower by using a control **2 :** ¹REFUSE 1, REJECT **3 :** to fold back or under — **turn off 1 :** to stop by using a control **2 :** to change direction — **turn on :** to make work by using a control — **turn out 1 :** to prove to be **2 :** to turn off — **turn over :** to give control or responsibility of to someone — **turn tail :** to turn so as to run away — **turn up 1 :** to be found or happen unexpect-

edly **2 :** to raise by or as if by using a control **3 :** ARRIVE 1

²**turn** *n* **1 :** the act of moving about a center **2 :** a change or changing of direction, course, or position **3 :** a place at which something changes direction **4 :** a period of action or activity **:** SPELL **5 :** proper place in a waiting line or time in a schedule **6 :** a change or changing of the general state or condition **7 :** an act affecting another **8 :** a short walk or ride **9 :** a special purpose or need **10 :** special quality **11 :** the beginning of a new period of time **12 :** a single circle or loop (as of rope passed around an object) **13 :** natural or special skill — **at every turn :** all the time **:** CONSTANTLY, CONTINUOUSLY — **by turns :** one after another — **in turn :** one after the other in order — **to a turn :** precisely right

turn·about *n* **:** a change from one direction or one way of thinking or acting to the opposite

tur·nip *n* **:** the thick white or yellow root of a plant related to the cabbage that is cooked and eaten as a vegetable

turn·out *n* **:** a gathering of people for a special reason

turn·over *n* **:** a filled pastry with one half of the crust turned over the other

turn·pike *n* **:** a road that people must pay a toll to use

turn·stile *n* **:** a post having arms that turn around which is set at an entrance or exit so that people can pass through only on foot one by one

tur·pen·tine *n* **:** an oil made from resin and used as a solvent and as a paint thinner

tur·quoise *n* **:** a blue to greenish gray mineral used in jewelry

tur·ret *n* **1 :** a little tower often at a corner of a building **2 :** a low usually rotating structure (as in a tank, warship, or airplane) in which guns are mounted

tur·tle *n* **:** a reptile that lives on land, in water, or both and has a toothless horny beak and a shell of bony plates which covers the body and into which the head, legs, and tail can usually be drawn

tur·tle·dove *n* **:** a small wild pigeon that has a low soft cry

tur·tle·neck *n* **1 :** a high turned-over collar **2 :** a garment having a high turned-over collar

tusk *n* **:** a very long large tooth (as of an elephant or walrus) that sticks out when the mouth is closed and is used especially in digging and fighting

¹**tus·sle** *n* **1 :** a short fight or struggle **2 :** a rough argument or a struggle against difficult odds

²**tussle** *vb* **tus·sled; tus·sling 1 :** to struggle

roughly : SCUFFLE **2** : to argue or compete with

¹tu·tor *n* : a teacher who works with an individual student

²tutor *vb* **tu·tored; tu·tor·ing** : to teach usually individually

tu·tu *n, pl* **tu·tus** : a short skirt that extends out and is worn by a ballerina

tux·e·do *n, pl* **tux·e·dos** *or* **tux·e·does** : a formal suit for a man

TV *n* : TELEVISION

twain *n* : ²TWO 1

¹twang *n* **1** : a harsh quick ringing sound **2** : speech that seems to be produced by the nose as well as the mouth

²twang *vb* **twanged; twang·ing** : to sound or cause to sound with a harsh quick ringing noise

'twas : it was

¹tweak *vb* **tweaked; tweak·ing** : to pinch and pull with a sudden jerk and twist

²tweak *n* : an act of pinching and pulling with a sudden jerk and twist

tweed *n* **1** : a rough woolen cloth **2 tweeds** *pl* : clothing (as a suit) made of rough woolen cloth

¹tweet *n* : a chirping sound

²tweet *vb* **tweet·ed; tweet·ing** : ²CHIRP

tweez·ers *n pl* : a small instrument that is used like pincers in grasping or pulling something

¹twelfth *adj* : coming right after eleventh

²twelfth *n* : number twelve in a series

¹twelve *adj* : being one more than eleven

²twelve *n* : one more than eleven : three times four : 12

twelve-month *n* : YEAR

¹twen·ti·eth *adj* : coming right after 19th

²twentieth *n* : number 20 in a series

¹twen·ty *adj* : being one more than 19

²twenty *n* : one more than 19 : four times five : 20

twice *adv* : two times

twid·dle *vb* **twid·dled; twid·dling** : ¹TWIRL

twig *n* : a small shoot or branch

twi·light *n* **1** : the period or the light from the sky between full night and sunrise or between sunset and full night **2** : a period of decline

twill *n* : a way of weaving cloth that produces a pattern of diagonal lines

¹twin *n* **1** : either of two offspring produced at one birth **2** : one of two persons or things closely related to or very like each other

²twin *adj* **1** : born with one other or as a pair at one birth **2** : made up of two similar, related, or connected members or parts **3** : being one of a pair

¹twine *n* : a strong string of two or more strands twisted together

²twine *vb* **twined; twin·ing 1** : to twist together **2** : to coil around a support

¹twinge *n* : a sudden sharp stab (as of pain or emotion)

²twinge *vb* **twinged; twing·ing** *or* **twinge·ing** : to affect with or feel a sudden sharp pain or emotion

¹twin·kle *vb* **twin·kled; twin·kling 1** : to shine or cause to shine with a flickering or sparkling light **2** : to appear bright with amusement **3** : to move or flutter rapidly

²twinkle *n* **1** : ²SPARKLE 1, FLICKER **2** : a very short time

twin·kling *n* : ²TWINKLE 2

¹twirl *vb* **twirled; twirl·ing** : to turn or cause to turn rapidly — **twirl·er** *n*

²twirl *n* : an act of turning or causing to turn rapidly

¹twist *vb* **twist·ed; twist·ing 1** : to turn a part of the body around **2** : to follow a winding course **3** : to form into an unnatural shape : CONTORT **4** : to unite by winding one thread, strand, or wire around another **5** : ²TWINE 2 **6** : to turn so as to sprain or hurt **7** : to pull off, rotate, or break by a turning force **8** : to turn (something) in a circular motion with the hand **9** : to change the meaning of

²twist *n* **1** : something that has been turned upon itself, coiled, or rotated **2** : an act of turning with force, coiling, or rotating : the state of being turned with force, coiled, or rotated **3** : a spiral turn or curve **4** : a turn or development that is both surprising and strange **5** : an act of changing the meaning

twist·er *n* **1** : TORNADO **2** : WATERSPOUT 2

¹twitch *vb* **twitched; twitch·ing 1** : to move or cause to move with a slight trembling or jerky motion : QUIVER **2** : to move or pull with a sudden motion : JERK

²twitch *n* **1** : a slight tremble or jerk of a muscle or body part **2** : a short sudden pull or jerk

¹twit·ter *vb* **twit·tered; twit·ter·ing 1** : to make a series of chirping noises **2** : to talk in a chattering fashion

²twitter *n* **1** : the chirping of birds **2** : a light chattering or laughing **3** : a nervous upset state

¹two *adj* : being one more than one

²two *n* **1** : one more than one : 2 **2** : the second in a set or series

two–dimensional *adj* : having the two dimensions of length and width

two-fold *adj* : being twice as great or as many

two–way *adj* **1** : moving or acting or allowing movement or action in either direction **2** : involving two persons or groups **3** : made to send and receive messages

TX *abbr* Texas

ty·coon *n* : a very powerful and wealthy business person

tying *present participle of* TIE

¹type *n* **1** : a particular kind or group of things or people : VARIETY **2** : a set of letters or figures that are used for printing or the letters or figures printed by them **3** : the special qualities or characteristics by which members of a group are set apart from other groups

²type *vb* **typed; typ·ing 1** : to write with a keyboard (as on computer or typewriter) **2** : to identify as belonging to a certain group

type·writ·er *n* : a machine that prints letters or figures when a person pushes its keys down

type·writ·ing *n* **1** : the use of a typewriter **2** : writing done with a typewriter

ty·phoid *n* : TYPHOID FEVER

typhoid fever *n* : a disease that spreads through contaminated food and water and in which there is fever, diarrhea, and great weakness

ty·phoon *n* : a tropical cyclone in the region of the Philippines or the China Sea

ty·phus *n* : a disease spread especially by body lice and in which there is high fever, delirium, severe headache, and a dark red rash

typ·i·cal *adj* : combining or showing the special characteristics of a group or kind — **typ·i·cal·ly** *adv*

typ·i·fy *vb* **typ·i·fied; typ·i·fy·ing 1** : REPRESENT **2** : to have the usual characteristics of : be a typical part of

typ·ist *n* : a person who uses a typewriter

ty·ran·ni·cal *adj* : relating to or like that of tyranny or a tyrant

ty·ran·no·saur *n* : a very large North American meat-eating dinosaur that had small forelegs and walked on its hind legs

ty·ran·no·sau·rus *n* : TYRANNOSAUR

tyr·an·ny *n, pl* **tyr·an·nies 1** : an act or the pattern of harsh, cruel, and unfair control over other people **2** : a government in which all power is in the hands of a single ruler

ty·rant *n* **1** : a ruler who has no legal limits on his or her power **2** : a ruler who exercises total power harshly and cruelly **3** : a person who uses authority or power harshly

U

u *n, pl* **u's** *or* **us** *often cap* **1** : the 21st letter of the English alphabet **2** : a grade rating a student's work as unsatisfactory

ud·der *n* : a large bag-shaped organ (as of a cow) enclosing two or more milk-producing glands each draining into a separate nipple on the lower surface

ugh *interj* — used to express disgust or horror

ug·ly *adj* **ug·li·er; ug·li·est 1** : unpleasant to look at : not attractive **2** : ¹OFFENSIVE 3 **3** : likely to cause bother or discomfort : TROUBLESOME **4** : showing a mean or quarrelsome disposition — **ug·li·ness** *n*

UK *abbr* United Kingdom

uku·le·le *n* : a musical instrument like a small guitar with four strings

ul·cer *n* : a slow-healing open painful sore (as of the lining of the stomach) in which tissue breaks down

ul·na *n, pl* **ul·nas** *or* **ul·nae** : the bone on the little-finger side of the arm between the wrist and elbow

ul·te·ri·or *adj* : kept hidden usually on purpose

ul·ti·mate *adj* **1** : last in a series : FINAL **2** : most extreme **3** : relating to or being the chief or most important — **ul·ti·mate·ly** *adv*

ul·ti·ma·tum *n, pl* **ul·ti·ma·tums** *or* **ul·ti·ma·ta** : a final condition or demand that if rejected

could end future negotiations and lead to forceful or undesirable action

ul·tra *adj* : ¹EXTREME 1

ultra- *prefix* **1** : beyond in space : on the other side **2** : beyond the limits of : SUPER- **3** : beyond what is ordinary or proper

ul·tra·vi·o·let *adj* : relating to, producing, or being energy that is like light but has a slightly shorter wavelength and lies beyond the violet end of the spectrum

um·bil·i·cal cord *n* : a cord that contains blood vessels and connects a developing fetus with the placenta of the mother

um·brel·la *n* : a fabric covering stretched over a circular folding frame of rods attached to a pole and used as a protection against rain or sun

um·pire *n* : an official in a sport (as baseball) who enforces the rules

UN *abbr* United Nations

¹un- *prefix* **1** : not : IN-, NON- **2** : opposite of : contrary to

²un- *prefix* **1** : do the opposite of : DE-, DIS- **2** : remove a specified thing from or free or release from **3** : completely

un·able *adj* : not able

un·ac·cept·able *adj* : not pleasing or welcome : not acceptable

un·ac·count·able *adj* : not to be explained : STRANGE — **un·ac·count·ably** *adv*

un·ac·cus·tomed *adj* : not used to something

un·af·fect·ed *adj* **1** : not influenced or changed **2** : free from false behavior intended to impress others : GENUINE

un·afraid *adj* : not afraid

un·aid·ed *adj* : without help : not aided

un·al·loyed *adj* : PURE 1

unan·i·mous *adj* **1** : having the same opinion : agreeing completely **2** : agreed to by all

un·armed *adj* : having no weapons or armor

un·as·sum·ing *adj* : MODEST 1

un·at·trac·tive *adj* : not attractive : PLAIN

un·avoid·able *adj* : not preventable : INEVITABLE — **un·avoid·ably** *adv*

¹**un·aware** *adv* : UNAWARES

²**unaware** *adj* : not having knowledge : not aware

un·awares *adv* **1** : without warning : by surprise **2** : without knowing : UNINTENTIONALLY

un·bear·able *adj* : seeming too great or too bad to put up with — **un·bear·ably** *adv*

un·be·com·ing *adj* : not suitable or proper : not becoming

un·be·knownst *also* **un·be·known** *adj* : happening without someone's knowledge : UNKNOWN

un·be·liev·able *adj* **1** : too unlikely to be believed **2** : very impressive or amazing — **un·be·liev·ably** *adv*

un·bi·ased *adj* : free from bias

un·bind *vb* **un·bound** ; **un·bind·ing 1** : to remove a band from : UNTIE **2** : to set free

un·born *adj* : not yet born

un·bound·ed *adj* : having no limits

un·break·able *adj* : not easily broken

un·bri·dled *adj* : not controlled or restrained

un·bro·ken *adj* **1** : not damaged : WHOLE **2** : not interrupted : CONTINUOUS **3** : not tamed for use

un·buck·le *vb* **un·buck·led; un·buck·ling** : to unfasten the buckle of (as a belt)

un·bur·den *vb* **un·bur·dened; un·bur·den·ing** : to free from a burden and especially from something causing worry or unhappiness

un·but·ton *vb* **un·but·toned; un·but·ton·ing** : to unfasten the buttons of

un·called–for *adj* : not needed or wanted : not proper

un·can·ny *adj* **1** : strange or unusual in a way that is surprising or mysterious **2** : suggesting powers or abilities greater than normal — **un·can·ni·ly** *adv*

un·cer·tain *adj* **1** : not exactly known or decided on **2** : not sure **3** : not known for sure **4** : likely to change : not dependable — **un·cer·tain·ly** *adv*

un·cer·tain·ty *n, pl* **un·cer·tain·ties 1** : lack of certainty : DOUBT **2** : something that is doubtful or unknown

un·change·able *adj* : not changing or capable of being changed

un·changed *adj* : not changed

un·chang·ing *adj* : not changing or able to change

un·char·ac·ter·is·tic *adj* : not typical or characteristic — **un·char·ac·ter·is·ti·cal·ly** *adv*

un·civ·il *adj* : IMPOLITE

un·civ·i·lized *adj* **1** : having, relating to, or being like a culture that is not advanced **2** : not having or showing good manners : RUDE

un·cle *n* **1** : the brother of a person's father or mother **2** : the husband of a person's aunt

un·clean *adj* **1** : DIRTY 1, FILTHY **2** : not pure and innocent **3** : not allowed for use by religious law

un·clear *adj* : difficult to understand or make sense of

un·cleared *adj* : not cleared especially of trees or brush

un·clothed *adj* : not wearing or covered with clothes

un·com·fort·able *adj* **1** : causing discomfort or uneasiness **2** : feeling discomfort or uneasiness — **un·com·fort·ably** *adv*

un·com·mon *adj* **1** : not often found or seen : UNUSUAL **2** : not ordinary : REMARKABLE — **un·com·mon·ly** *adv*

un·com·pro·mis·ing *adj* : not willing to give in even a little — **un·com·pro·mis·ing·ly** *adv*

un·con·cern *n* : lack of care or interest

un·con·cerned *adj* **1** : free of worry **2** : not involved or interested

un·con·di·tion·al *adj* : without any special exceptions — **un·con·di·tion·al·ly** *adv*

un·con·quer·able *adj* : not capable of being beaten or overcome

un·con·scious *adj* **1** : not aware **2** : having lost consciousness **3** : not intentional or planned — **un·con·scious·ly** *adv* — **un·con·scious·ness** *n*

un·con·sti·tu·tion·al *adj* : not according to or agreeing with the constitution of a country or government

un·con·trol·la·ble *adj* : hard or impossible to control — **un·con·trol·la·bly** *adv*

un·con·trolled *adj* : not being controlled

un·co·op·er·a·tive *adj* : not showing a desire to act or work with others in a helpful way

un·couth *adj* : impolite in conduct or speech : CRUDE

un·cov·er *vb* **un·cov·ered; un·cov·er·ing 1** : to make known usually by investigation **2** : to make visible by removing some covering **3** : to remove the cover from

un·curl *vb* **un·curled; un·curl·ing** : to make

or become straightened out from a curled position

un·cut *adj* **1** : not cut down or cut into **2** : not shaped by cutting

un·daunt·ed *adj* : not discouraged or afraid to continue

un·de·cid·ed *adj* **1** : not yet settled or decided **2** : not having decided : uncertain what to do

un·de·clared *adj* : not made known : not declared

un·de·feat·ed *adj* : having no losses

un·de·ni·able *adj* : clearly true : impossible to deny — **un·de·ni·ably** *adv*

¹un·der *adv* **1** : in or into a position below or beneath something **2** : below some quantity or level

²under *prep* **1** : lower than and topped or sheltered by **2** : below the surface of **3** : in or into such a position as to be covered or hidden by **4** : commanded or guided by **5** : controlled or managed by **6** : affected or influenced by the action or effect of **7** : within the division or grouping of **8** : less or lower than (as in size, amount, or rank)

³under *adj* **1** : lying or placed below or beneath **2** : lower in position or authority — often used in combination

un·der·arm *n* : ARMPIT

un·der·brush *n* : shrubs and small trees growing among large trees

un·der·clothes *n pl* : UNDERWEAR

un·der·cooked *adj* : not cooked enough

un·der·cur·rent *n* **1** : a flow of water that moves below the surface **2** : a hidden feeling or tendency often different from the one openly shown

un·der·dog *n* : a person or team thought to have little chance of winning (as an election or a game)

un·der·foot *adv* **1** : under the feet **2** : close about a person's feet : in the way

un·der·gar·ment *n* : a garment to be worn under another

un·der·go *vb* **un·der·went; un·der·gone; un·der·go·ing** : to experience or endure (something)

¹un·der·ground *adv* **1** : below the surface of the earth **2** : in or into hiding or secret operation

²un·der·ground *n* **1** : SUBWAY **2** : a secret political movement or group

³un·der·ground *adj* **1** : located under the surface of the ground **2** : done or happening secretly

un·der·growth *n* : low growth on the floor of a forest that includes shrubs, herbs, and saplings

¹un·der·hand *adv* : with an upward movement of the hand or arm

²underhand *adj* **1** : done in secret or so as to deceive **2** : made with an upward movement of the hand or arm

un·der·hand·ed *adj* : ²UNDERHAND 1

un·der·lie *vb* **un·der·lay; un·der·lain; un·der·ly·ing** **1** : to lie or be located under **2** : to form the foundation of : SUPPORT

un·der·line *vb* **un·der·lined; un·der·lin·ing** **1** : to draw a line under **2** : EMPHASIZE

un·der·mine *vb* **un·der·mined; un·der·min·ing** **1** : to dig out or wear away the supporting earth beneath **2** : to weaken secretly or little by little

¹un·der·neath *prep* : directly under

²underneath *adv* **1** : below a surface or object : BENEATH **2** : on the lower side

un·der·nour·ished *adj* : given too little food for proper health and growth

un·der·pants *n pl* : underwear worn on the lower part of the body

un·der·part *n* : a part lying on the lower side (as of a bird or mammal)

un·der·pass *n* : a road or passage that runs under something (as another road)

un·der·priv·i·leged *adj* : having fewer advantages than others especially because of being poor

un·der·rate *vb* **un·der·rat·ed; un·der·rat·ing** : to rate too low : UNDERVALUE

un·der·score *vb* **un·der·scored; un·der·scor·ing** **1** : UNDERLINE l **2** : EMPHASIZE

un·der·sea *adj* **1** : being or done under the sea or under the surface of the sea **2** : used under the surface of the sea

un·der·shirt *n* : a collarless garment with or without sleeves that is worn as an undergarment

un·der·side *n* : the side or surface lying underneath

un·der·stand *vb* **un·der·stood; un·der·stand·ing** **1** : to get the meaning of **2** : to know thoroughly **3** : to have reason to believe **4** : to take as meaning something not clearly made known **5** : to have a sympathetic attitude **6** : to accept as settled

un·der·stand·able *adj* **1** : possible or easy to get or realize the meaning of : capable of being understood **2** : normal and reasonable for a particular situation — **un·der·stand·ably** *adv*

¹un·der·stand·ing *n* **1** : ability to get the meaning of and judge **2** : an agreement of opinion or feeling **3** : a willingness to show kind or favorable feelings toward others **4** : the particular way in which someone understands something

²understanding *adj* : having or showing

kind or favorable feelings toward others : SYMPATHETIC

un·der·state·ment *n* : a statement that makes something seem smaller or less important or serious than it really is

un·der·study *n, pl* **un·der·stud·ies** : an actor who is prepared to take over another actor's part if necessary

un·der·take *vb* **un·der·took; un·der·tak·en; un·der·tak·ing 1** : to plan or try to accomplish **2** : to take on as a responsibility : AGREE

un·der·tak·er *n* : a person whose business is to prepare the dead for burial and to take charge of funerals

un·der·tak·ing *n* : an important or difficult task or project

un·der·tone *n* **1** : a low or quiet voice **2** : a partly hidden feeling or meaning

un·der·tow *n* : a current beneath the surface of the water that moves away from or along the shore while the surface water above it moves toward the shore

un·der·val·ue *vb* **un·der·val·ued; un·der·valu·ing** : to value below the real worth

¹un·der·wa·ter *adj* : lying, growing, worn, performed, or operating below the surface of the water

²un·der·wa·ter *adv* : under the surface of the water

un·der·wear *n* : clothing worn next to the skin and under other clothing

un·der·weight *adj* : weighing less than what is normal, average, or necessary

underwent *past of* UNDERGO

un·der·world *n* : the world of crime

un·de·sir·able *adj* : having qualities that are not pleasing or wanted

un·de·vel·oped *adj* **1** : not used for farming or building on **2** : having few large industries and a simple economic system **3** : not fully grown or matured

un·dig·ni·fied *adj* : lacking proper seriousness or self-control in behavior or appearance : not showing dignity

un·dis·cov·ered *adj* : not discovered

un·dis·put·ed *adj* : not disputed : UNQUESTIONABLE

un·dis·turbed *adj* **1** : not moved, interrupted, or interfered with **2** : not upset

un·di·vid·ed *adj* : complete or total

un·do *vb* **un·did; un·done; un·do·ing; un·does 1** : UNTIE 2, UNFASTEN **2** : to cancel the effect of : REVERSE **3** : to cause the ruin or failure of

un·do·ing *n* : a cause of ruin or failure

un·done *adj* : not done or finished

un·doubt·ed *adj* : definitely true or existing : not doubted

un·doubt·ed·ly *adv* : without doubt : SURELY

un·dress *vb* **un·dressed; un·dress·ing** : to remove the clothes or covering of

un·du·late *vb* **un·du·lat·ed; un·du·lat·ing** : to move in or as if in a wavy or flowing way

un·dy·ing *adj* : lasting forever : IMMORTAL

un·earth *vb* **un·earthed; un·earth·ing 1** : to bring up from underground : dig up **2** : to bring to light : UNCOVER

un·easy *adj* **un·eas·i·er; un·eas·i·est 1** : not comfortable in manner : AWKWARD **2** : showing or filled with worry : APPREHENSIVE — **un·eas·i·ly** *adv* — **un·eas·i·ness** *n*

un·ed·u·cat·ed *adj* **1** : lacking in education and especially schooling **2** : based on little or no knowledge or fact

un·em·ployed *adj* : having no job : not employed

un·em·ploy·ment *n* **1** : the state of being out of work **2** : the number of people who do not have jobs

un·end·ing *adj* : having no ending : ENDLESS

un·equal *adj* **1** : not alike (as in size or value) **2** : badly balanced or matched **3** : not having the needed abilities — **un·equal·ly** *adv*

un·equaled *adj* : having no equal or match

un·even *adj* **1** : ODD 2 **2** : not level, straight, or smooth **3** : IRREGULAR 4 **4** : varying in quality **5** : UNEQUAL 2 — **un·even·ly** *adv* — **un·even·ness** *n*

un·event·ful *adj* : having nothing exciting, interesting, or important happening : not eventful — **un·event·ful·ly** *adv*

un·ex·pect·ed *adj* : not expected : UNFORESEEN — **un·ex·pect·ed·ly** *adv*

un·fail·ing *adj* : not failing or likely to fail : CONSTANT — **un·fail·ing·ly** *adv*

un·fair *adj* : not fair, honest, or just — **un·fair·ly** *adv* — **un·fair·ness** *n*

un·faith·ful *adj* : not faithful : DISLOYAL

un·fa·mil·iar *adj* **1** : not well known : STRANGE **2** : lacking good knowledge of something

un·fas·ten *vb* **un·fas·tened; un·fas·ten·ing** : to make or become loose

un·fa·vor·able *adj* **1** : expressing or showing disapproval **2** : likely to make difficult or unpleasant — **un·fa·vor·ably** *adv*

un·feel·ing *adj* : having no kindness or sympathy : CRUEL

un·fin·ished *adj* : not finished

un·fit *adj* **1** : not suitable **2** : not qualified **3** : physically unhealthy

un·fold *vb* **un·fold·ed; un·fold·ing 1** : to open the folds of : open up **2** : to lay open to view or understanding : REVEAL **3** : to develop gradually

un·fore·seen *adj* : not known beforehand : UNEXPECTED

un·for·get·ta·ble *adj* : not likely to be forgotten : lasting in memory — **un·for·get·ta·bly** *adv*

un·for·giv·able *adj* : not to be forgiven or pardoned — **un·for·giv·ably** *adv*

un·for·tu·nate *adj* **1** : not fortunate : UNLUCKY **2** : accompanied by or resulting in bad luck **3** : not proper or suitable — **un·for·tu·nate·ly** *adv*

un·found·ed *adj* : not based on facts or proof : GROUNDLESS

un·friend·ly *adj* **un·friend·li·er; un·friend·li·est 1** : not friendly or kind **2** : not agreeable : UNFAVORABLE

un·furl *vb* **un·furled; un·furl·ing** : to open out from a rolled or folded state

un·gain·ly *adj* **un·gain·li·er; un·gain·li·est** : CLUMSY 1, AWKWARD

un·god·ly *adj* **un·god·li·er; un·god·li·est 1** : SINFUL, WICKED **2** : not normal or bearable

un·gra·cious *adj* : not kind or polite

un·grate·ful *adj* : not feeling or showing thanks

un·gu·late *n* : a usually plant-eating animal (as a cow, horse, or sheep) with hooves

un·hap·py *adj* **un·hap·pi·er; un·hap·pi·est 1** : not cheerful : SAD **2** : not pleased or satisfied **3** : full of or showing feelings of sadness or misery **4** : not fortunate : UNLUCKY **5** : not suitable : INAPPROPRIATE — **un·hap·pi·ly** *adv* — **un·hap·pi·ness** *n*

un·healthy *adj* **un·health·i·er; un·health·i·est 1** : not good for someone's health : promoting a state of poor health **2** : not in good health : SICKLY **3** : HARMFUL, BAD — **un·health·i·ly** *adv*

un·heard *adj* : not heard

un·heard–of *adj* : not known before

un·hin·dered *adj* : not kept back : proceeding freely

un·hitch *vb* **un·hitched; un·hitch·ing** : to free from being hitched

un·ho·ly *adj* **un·ho·li·er; un·ho·li·est 1** : not holy : WICKED **2** : UNGODLY 2

un·hook *vb* **un·hooked; un·hook·ing 1** : to remove from a hook **2** : to unfasten the hooks of

un·horse *vb* **un·horsed; un·hors·ing** : to cause to fall from or as if from a horse

un·hur·ried *adj* : not in a rush

uni- *prefix* : one : single

uni·corn *n* : an imaginary animal that looks like a horse with one horn in the middle of the forehead

un·iden·ti·fi·able *adj* : impossible to identify : not recognizable

un·iden·ti·fied *adj* : having an identity that is not known or determined

uni·fi·ca·tion *n* : the act, process, or result of bringing or coming together into or as if into a single unit or group

¹uni·form *adj* : always the same in form, manner, appearance, or degree throughout or over time — **uni·form·ly** *adv*

²uniform *n* : special clothing worn by members of a particular group (as an army)

uni·formed *adj* : dressed in uniform

uni·for·mi·ty *n, pl* **uni·for·mi·ties** : the quality or state of being the same in form, manner, appearance, or degree

uniform resource lo·ca·tor *n* : URL

uni·fy *vb* **uni·fied; uni·fy·ing** : to bring or come together into or as if into a single unit or group : UNITE

un·imag·in·able *adj* : not possible to imagine or understand

un·im·por·tant *adj* : not important

un·in·hab·it·ed *adj* : not lived in or on

un·in·tel·li·gi·ble *adj* : impossible to understand

un·in·ten·tion·al *adj* : not done on purpose : not intentional — **un·in·ten·tion·al·ly** *adv*

un·in·ter·est·ed *adj* : not interested

un·in·ter·est·ing *adj* : not attracting or keeping interest or attention

un·in·ter·rupt·ed *adj* : not interrupted : CONTINUOUS

un·in·vit·ed *adj* : not having been invited

union *n* **1** : an act or instance of uniting or joining two or more things into one **2** : something (as a nation) formed by a combining of parts or members **3** *cap* : the United States **4** *cap* : the group of states that supported the United States government in the American Civil War **5** : a device for connecting parts (as pipes) **6** : LABOR UNION

Union *adj* : relating to the group of states that supported the United States government in the American Civil War

union suit *n* : an undergarment with shirt and pants in one piece

unique *adj* **1** : being the only one of its kind **2** : very unusual : NOTABLE — **unique·ly** *adv* — **unique·ness** *n*

uni·son *n* : the state of being tuned or sounded at the same pitch or at an octave — **in unison 1** : in exact agreement **2** : at the same time

unit *n* **1** : a single thing, person, or group forming part of a whole **2** : the least whole number : ONE **3** : a fixed quantity (as of length, time, or value) used as a standard of measurement **4** : a part of a school course with a central theme

unite *vb* **unit·ed; unit·ing 1** : to put or come

together to form a single unit **2** : to bind by legal or moral ties **3** : to join in action

unit·ed *adj* **1** : made one **2** : having the same goals, ideas, and principles

uni·ty *n, pl* **uni·ties 1** : the quality or state of being one **2** : the state of those who are in full agreement — HARMONY

uni·ver·sal *adj* **1** : including, covering, or taking in all or everything **2** : present or happening everywhere — **uni·ver·sal·ly** *adv*

universal resource lo·ca·tor *n* : URL

uni·verse *n* : all created things including the earth and heavenly bodies viewed as making up one system

uni·ver·si·ty *n, pl* **uni·ver·si·ties** : an institution of higher learning that gives degrees in special fields and where research is performed

un·just *adj* : not just : UNFAIR — **un·just·ly** *adv*

un·kempt *adj* **1** : not combed **2** : not neat and orderly : UNTIDY

un·kind *adj* **un·kind·er; un·kind·est** : not kind or sympathetic — **un·kind·ly** *adv* — **un·kind·ness** *n*

¹**un·known** *adj* : not known

²**unknown** *n* : one (as a quantity) that is unknown

un·lace *vb* **un·laced; un·lac·ing** : to undo the laces of

un·latch *vb* **unlatched; unlatch·ing** : to open by lifting a latch

un·law·ful *adj* : not lawful : ILLEGAL — **un·law·ful·ly** *adv*

un·learned *adj* **1** : not educated **2** : not based on experience : INSTINCTIVE

un·leash *vb* **un·leashed; un·leash·ing** : to free from or as if from a leash

un·less *conj* : except on the condition that

un·lik·able *adj* : difficult to like

¹**un·like** *prep* **1** : different from **2** : unusual for **3** : differently from

²**unlike** *adj* : DIFFERENT, UNEQUAL

un·like·ly *adj* **un·like·li·er; un·like·li·est 1** : not likely **2** : not promising

un·lim·it·ed *adj* **1** : having no restrictions or controls **2** : BOUNDLESS, INFINITE

un·load *vb* **un·load·ed; un·load·ing 1** : to take away or off : REMOVE **2** : to take a load from **3** : to get rid of or be freed from a load or burden

un·lock *vb* **un·locked; un·lock·ing 1** : to unfasten the lock of **2** : to make known

un·looked–for *adj* : not expected

un·loose *vb* **un·loosed; un·loos·ing 1** : to make looser : RELAX **2** : to set free

un·lucky *adj* **un·luck·i·er; un·luck·i·est 1** : not fortunate : having bad luck **2** : marked by bad luck or failure **3** : likely to bring

misfortune **4** : causing distress or regret — **un·luck·i·ly** *adv*

un·man·age·able *adj* : hard or impossible to handle or control

un·man·ner·ly *adj* : not having or showing good manners

un·mar·ried *adj* : not married : SINGLE

un·mis·tak·able *adj* : impossible to mistake for anything else — **un·mis·tak·ably** *adv*

un·moved *adj* **1** : not being stirred by deep feelings or excitement **2** : staying in the same place or position

un·nat·u·ral *adj* **1** : different from what is found in nature or happens naturally **2** : different from what is usually considered normal behavior **3** : not genuine — **un·nat·u·ral·ly** *adv*

un·nec·es·sary *adj* : not needed — **un·nec·es·sar·i·ly** *adv*

un·nerve *vb* **un·nerved; un·nerv·ing** : to cause to lose confidence, courage, or self-control

un·no·tice·able *adj* : not easily noticed

un·num·bered *adj* **1** : not numbered **2** : INNUMERABLE

un·ob·served *adj* : not noticed

un·oc·cu·pied *adj* **1** : not being used, filled up, or lived in : EMPTY **2** : not busy

un·of·fi·cial *adj* : not official — **un·of·fi·cial·ly** *adv*

un·pack *vb* **un·packed; un·pack·ing 1** : to separate and remove things that are packed **2** : to open and remove the contents of

un·paid *adj* : not paid

un·par·al·leled *adj* : having no counterpart or equal

un·pleas·ant *adj* : not pleasing or agreeable — **un·pleas·ant·ly** *adv* — **un·pleas·ant·ness** *n*

un·prec·e·dent·ed *adj* : not done or experienced before

un·pop·u·lar *adj* : not widely favored or approved

un·prof·it·able *adj* : not producing a profit

un·pre·dict·able *adj* : impossible to predict

un·prej·u·diced *adj* : not resulting from or having a bias for or against

un·pre·pared *adj* : not being or made ready

un·prin·ci·pled *adj* : not having or showing high moral principles

un·ques·tion·able *adj* : being beyond doubt — **un·ques·tion·ably** *adv*

un·ques·tion·ing *adj* : accepting without thinking or doubting

un·rav·el *vb* **un·rav·eled** *or* **un·rav·elled; un·rav·el·ing** *or* **un·rav·el·ling 1** : to separate the threads of : UNTANGLE **2** : SOLVE

un·re·al *adj* : not actual or genuine

un·rea·son·able *adj* : not fair, sensible, ap-

propriate, or moderate — **un·rea·son·ably**
adv

un·re·lent·ing *adj* **1 :** not giving in or soften-
ing in determination : STERN **2 :** not letting
up or weakening in energy or pace — **un·re·**
lent·ing·ly *adv*

un·re·li·able *adj* : not worthy of trust

un·rest *n* **:** a disturbed or uneasy state

un·ripe *adj* : not ripe or mature

un·ri·valed *or* **un·ri·valled** *adj* : having no
rival

un·roll *vb* **un·rolled; un·roll·ing 1 :** to un-
wind a roll of **2 :** to become unrolled

un·ruf·fled *adj* **1 :** not upset or disturbed **2**
: ¹SMOOTH 4

un·ruly *adj* **un·rul·i·er; un·rul·i·est :** difficult
to control — **un·rul·i·ness** *n*

un·safe *adj* **:** exposed or exposing to danger

un·san·i·tary *adj* **:** likely to cause sickness or
disease : dirty or full of germs

un·sat·is·fac·to·ry *adj* **:** not what is needed or
expected — **un·sat·is·fac·to·ri·ly** *adv*

un·sat·is·fied *adj* **1 :** not fulfilled **2 :** not
pleased

un·scathed *adj* **:** completely without harm or
injury

un·schooled *adj* : not trained or taught

un·sci·en·tif·ic *adj* **:** not using or applying the
methods or principles of science : not scientific

un·scram·ble *vb* **un·scram·bled; un·scram·**
bling : to make orderly or clear again

un·screw *vb* **un·screwed; un·screw·ing 1**
: to loosen or withdraw by turning **2 :** to remove the screws from

un·scru·pu·lous *adj* **:** not having or showing
regard for what is right and proper — **un·**
scru·pu·lous·ly *adv*

un·seal *vb* **un·sealed; un·seal·ing :** to break
or remove the seal of : OPEN

un·sea·son·able *adj* **:** happening or coming
at the wrong time — **un·sea·son·ably** *adv*

un·sea·soned *adj* **:** not made ready or fit for
use (as by the passage of time)

un·seat *vb* **un·seat·ed; un·seat·ing 1 :** to remove from a position of authority **2 :** to
cause to fall from a seat or saddle

un·seem·ly *adj* **un·seem·li·er; un·seem·li·est**
: not polite or proper

un·seen *adj* **:** not seen : INVISIBLE

un·self·ish *adj* **:** not selfish — **un·self·ish·ly**
adv — **un·self·ish·ness** *n*

un·set·tle *vb* **un·set·tled; un·set·tling :** to
disturb the quiet or order of : UPSET

un·set·tled *adj* **1 :** not staying the same **2**
: feeling nervous, upset, or worried **3 :** not
finished or determined **4 :** not paid **5 :** not
lived in by settlers

un·sheathe *vb* **un·sheathed; un·sheath·ing**
: to draw from or as if from a sheath

un·sight·ly *adj* **:** not pleasant to look at
: UGLY

un·skilled *adj* **1 :** not having skill **2 :** not
needing skill

un·skill·ful *adj* **:** not skillful : not having skill
— **un·skill·ful·ly** *adv*

un·sound *adj* **1 :** not based on good reasoning or truth **2 :** not firmly made or placed **3**
: not healthy or in good condition **4 :** being
or having a mind that is not normal

un·speak·able *adj* **1 :** impossible to express
in words **2 :** extremely bad — **un·speak·**
ably *adv*

un·spec·i·fied *adj* **:** not mentioned or named

un·spoiled *adj* **:** not damaged or ruined

un·sta·ble *adj* **:** not stable

un·steady *adj* **un·stead·i·er; un·stead·i·**
est : not steady : UNSTABLE — **un·stead·i·**
ly *adv*

un·strap *vb* **un·strapped; un·strap·ping :** to
remove or loosen a strap from

un·stressed *adj* **:** not accented

un·suc·cess·ful *adj* **:** not ending in or having
gained success — **un·suc·cess·ful·ly** *adv*

un·suit·able *adj* **:** not fitting : INAPPROPRIATE

un·sup·port·ed *adj* **1 :** not proved **2 :** not
held up

un·sur·passed *adj* **:** not exceeded (as in excellence)

un·sus·pect·ing *adj* **:** without suspicion

un·tan·gle *vb* **un·tan·gled; un·tan·gling 1**
: to remove a tangle from **2 :** to straighten
out

un·think·able *adj* **:** not to be thought of or
considered as possible or reasonable

un·think·ing *adj* **:** not thinking about actions
or words and how they will affect others

un·ti·dy *adj* **un·ti·di·er; un·ti·di·est :** not neat
— **un·ti·di·ly** *adv* — **un·ti·di·ness** *n*

un·tie *vb* **un·tied; un·ty·ing** *or* **un·tie·ing 1**
: to undo the knots in **2 :** to free from something that fastens or holds back

¹un·til *prep* **:** up to the time of

²until *conj* **:** up to the time that

un·time·ly *adj* **1 :** happening or done before
the expected, natural, or proper time **2**
: coming at the wrong time

un·tir·ing *adj* **:** not becoming tired

un·to *prep* **:** ¹TO

un·told *adj* **1 :** not told or made public **2**
: too great or too numerous to be counted
: VAST

un·touched *adj* **1 :** not tasted **2 :** not affected

un·to·ward *adj* **:** unexpected and unpleasant
or improper

un·trou·bled *adj* **:** not troubled : free from
worry

un·true *adj* **1 :** not correct : FALSE **2 :** not
faithful : DISLOYAL

un·truth *n* **1** : the state of being false **2** : ³LIE

un·truth·ful *adj* : not containing or telling the truth : FALSE — **un·truth·ful·ly** *adv*

un·used *adj* **1** : not accustomed **2** : not having been used before **3** : not being used

un·usu·al *adj* : not done, found, used, experienced, or existing most of the time — **un·usu·al·ly** *adv*

un·veil *vb* **un·veiled; un·veil·ing** : to show or make known to the public for the first time

un·voiced *adj* : VOICELESS 2

un·want·ed *adj* : not desired or needed

un·wary *adj* **un·war·i·er; un·war·i·est** : easily fooled or surprised

un·washed *adj* : not having been washed : DIRTY

un·well *adj* : being in poor health

un·whole·some *adj* : not good for bodily, mental, or moral health

un·wieldy *adj* : hard to handle or control because of size or weight — **un·wield·i·ness** *n*

un·will·ing *adj* : not willing : RELUCTANT — **un·will·ing·ly** *adv* — **un·will·ing·ness** *n*

un·wind *vb* **un·wound ; un·wind·ing 1** : to uncoil a strand of **2** : RELAX **3**

un·wise *adj* : FOOLISH — **un·wise·ly** *adv*

un·wor·thy *adj* **un·wor·thi·er; un·wor·thi·est 1** : not deserving someone or something **2** : not appropriate for a particular kind of person or thing — **un·wor·thi·ness** *n*

un·wrap *vb* **un·wrapped; un·wrap·ping** : to remove the wrapping from

un·writ·ten *adj* : not in writing : followed by custom

un·yield·ing *adj* **1** : not soft or flexible : HARD **2** : showing or having firmness or determination

¹up *adv* **1** : in or to a high or higher place or position **2** : in or into a vertical position **3** : from beneath a surface (as ground or water) **4** : with greater force or to a greater level **5** : so as to make more active **6** : so as to appear or be present **7** : COMPLETELY **8** : so as to approach or be near **9** : from below the horizon **10** : out of bed **11** : in or into a better or more advanced state **12** : for consideration or discussion **13** : into the control of another **14** — used to show completeness **15** : so as to be closed **16** : in or into pieces **17** : to a stop **18** : into a working or usable state

²up *adj* **1** : risen above the horizon or ground **2** : being out of bed **3** : unusually high **4** : having been raised or built **5** : moving or going upward **6** : being busy and moving about **7** : well prepared **8** : happy or excited **9** : going on **10** : at an end **11** : well informed **12** : functioning correctly

³up *prep* **1** : to, toward, or at a higher point of **2** : to or toward the beginning of **3** : ¹ALONG 1 — **up to 1** : as far as **2** : in accordance with **3** : to the limit of

⁴up *n* : a period or state of doing well

⁵up *vb* **upped; up·ping 1** : to act suddenly or surprisingly **2** : to make or become higher

up–and–down *adj* **1** : switching between upward and downward movement or action **2** : PERPENDICULAR

¹up·beat *n* : a beat in music that is not accented and especially one just before a downbeat

²upbeat *adj* : cheerful and positive

up·braid *vb* **up·braid·ed; up·braid·ing** : to criticize or scold severely

up·bring·ing *n* : the process of raising and training

up·com·ing *adj* : coming soon

¹up·date *vb* **up·dat·ed; up·dat·ing 1** : to give or include the latest information **2** : to make more modern

²up·date *n* : something that gives or includes the latest information

up·draft *n* : an upward movement of air

up·end *vb* **up·end·ed; up·end·ing** : to set, stand, or rise on end

up·grade *vb* **up·grad·ed; up·grad·ing 1** : to raise to a higher grade or position **2** : to improve or replace old software or an old device

up·heav·al *n* : a period of great change or violent disorder

¹up·hill *adv* : in an upward direction

²up·hill *adj* **1** : going up **2** : DIFFICULT 1

up·hold *vb* **up·held ; up·hold·ing 1** : to give support to **2** : to lift up

up·hol·ster *vb* **up·hol·stered; up·hol·ster·ing** : to provide with or as if with upholstery — **up·hol·ster·er** *n*

up·hol·stery *n, pl* **up·hol·ster·ies** : materials used to make a soft covering for a seat

up·keep *n* : the act or cost of keeping something in good condition

up·land *n* : high land usually far from a coast or sea

¹up·lift *vb* **up·lift·ed; up·lift·ing 1** : to lift up **2** : to make feel happy or hopeful

²up·lift *n* : an increase in happiness or hopefulness

up·on *prep* : ¹ON

¹up·per *adj* **1** : higher in position or rank **2** : farther inland

²upper *n* : something (as the parts of a shoe above the sole) that is upper

up·per·case *adj* : having the form A, B, C rather than a, b, c — **uppercase** *n*

upper hand *n* : ADVANTAGE 2

up·per·most *adj* 1 : farthest up 2 : being in the most important position

up·raise *vb* **up·raised; up·rais·ing** : to raise or lift up

¹up·right *adj* 1 : ¹VERTICAL 2 : straight in posture 3 : having or showing high moral standards — **up·right·ly** *adv*

²upright *adv* : in or into a vertical position

up·rise *vb* **up·rose ; up·ris·en ; up·ris·ing** 1 : to rise to a higher position 2 : to get up from sleeping or sitting

up·ris·ing *n* : REBELLION

up·roar *n* : a state of commotion, excitement, or violent disturbance

up·root *vb* **up·root·ed; up·root·ing** 1 : to take out by or as if by pulling up by the roots 2 : to take, send, or force away from a country or a traditional home

¹up·set *vb* **up·set; up·set·ting** 1 : to worry or make unhappy 2 : to make somewhat ill 3 : to force or be forced out of the usual position : OVERTURN 4 : to cause confusion in 5 : to defeat unexpectedly

²up·set *n* 1 : an unexpected defeat 2 : a feeling of illness in the stomach 3 : a period of worry or unhappiness

³up·set *adj* : emotionally disturbed or unhappy

up·shot *n* : the final result

up·side–down *adj* 1 : having the upper part underneath and the lower part on top 2 : showing great confusion

up·side down *adv* 1 : in such a way that the upper part is underneath and the lower part is on top 2 : in or into great confusion

¹up·stairs *adv* : up the stairs : on or to an upper floor

²up·stairs *adj* : being on or relating to an upper floor

³up·stairs *n* : the part of a building above the ground floor

up·stand·ing *adj* : HONEST 2

up·start *n* : a person who gains quick or unexpected success and shows off that success

up·stream *adv* : at or toward the beginning of a stream

up·swing *n* : a great increase or rise

up·tight *adj* : being tense, nervous, or uneasy

up–to–date *adj* 1 : including the latest information 2 : knowing, being, or making use of what is new or recent

up·town *adv* : to, toward, or in what is thought of as the upper part of a town or city

¹up·turn *vb* **up·turned; up·turn·ing** : to turn upward or up or over

²up·turn *n* : an upward turning (as toward better conditions)

¹up·ward *or* **up·wards** *adv* 1 : in a direction from lower to higher 2 : toward a higher or

better state 3 : toward a greater amount or a higher number or rate 4 : toward the head

²upward *adj* : turned toward or being in a higher place or level — **up·ward·ly** *adv*

up·wind *adv or adj* : in the direction from which the wind is blowing

ura·ni·um *n* : a radioactive metallic chemical element used as a source of atomic energy

Ura·nus *n* : the planet that is seventh in order of distance from the sun and has a diameter of about 32,000 miles (51,000 kilometers)

ur·ban *adj* : of, relating to, or being a city

ur·chin *n* 1 : a mischievous or disrespectful youngster 2 : SEA URCHIN

-ure *suffix* 1 : act : process 2 : office : duty 3 : body performing an office or duty

urea *n* : a compound of nitrogen that is the chief solid substance dissolved in the urine of a mammal and is formed by the breaking down of protein

¹urge *vb* **urged; urg·ing** 1 : to try to get (something) accepted : argue in favor of 2 : to try to convince 3 : ²FORCE 1, DRIVE

²urge *n* : a strong desire

ur·gen·cy *n* : the quality or state of requiring immediate action or attention

ur·gent *adj* 1 : calling for immediate action 2 : having or showing a sense of requiring immediate action — **ur·gent·ly** *adv*

uri·nary *adj* : of or relating to urine or the parts of the body through which it passes

uri·nate *vb* **uri·nat·ed; uri·nat·ing** : to pass urine out of the body

uri·na·tion *n* : the act of urinating

urine *n* : the yellowish liquid produced by the kidneys and given off from the body as waste

URL *n* : the address of a computer or a document on the Internet

urn *n* 1 : a container usually in the form of a vase resting on a stand 2 : a closed container with a faucet used for serving a hot beverage

us *pron, objective case of* WE

US *abbr* United States

USA *abbr* United States of America

us·able *adj* : suitable or fit for use

us·age *n* 1 : usual way of doing things 2 : the way in which words and phrases are actually used 3 : the action of using : USE

¹use *vb* **used; us·ing** 1 : to put into action or service : make use of 2 — used with *to* to show a former custom, fact, or state 3 : to take into the body 4 : to do something by means of 5 : to behave toward : TREAT — **us·er** *n* — **use up** : to make complete use of : EXHAUST

²use *n* 1 : the act of putting something into action or service 2 : the fact or state of being put into action or service **3** : way of putting into action or service **4** : the ability or power to put something into action or service **5** : the quality or state of being useful **6** : a reason or need to put into action or service **7** : LIKING

used *adj* **1** : SECONDHAND 1 **2** : having the habit of doing or putting up with something

use·ful *adj* **1** : capable of being put to use : USABLE **2** : helpful in doing or achieving something — **use·ful·ly** *adv* — **use·ful·ness** *n*

use·less *adj* : being of or having no use — **use·less·ly** *adv* — **use·less·ness** *n*

us·er–friend·ly *adj* : easy to learn, use, understand, or deal with — **user–friendliness** *n*

¹ush·er *n* : a person who shows people to seats (as in a theater, at a game, or at a wedding)

²usher *vb* **ush·ered; ush·er·ing 1** : to show or be shown to a place **2** : to come before as if to lead in or announce

usu. *abbr* **1** usual **2** usually

usu·al *adj* : done, found, used or existing most of the time — **usu·al·ly** *adv*

usurp *vb* **usurped; usurp·ing** : to take and hold unfairly or by force — **usurp·er** *n*

USVI *abbr* United States Virgin Islands

UT *abbr* Utah

uten·sil *n* **1** : a tool or container used in a home and especially a kitchen **2** : a useful tool

uter·us *n, pl* **uterus** *or* **uteri** : the organ of a female mammal in which the young develop before birth

util·i·ty *n, pl* **util·i·ties 1** : the quality or state of being useful **2** : a business that supplies a public service (as electricity or gas) under special regulation by the government

uti·li·za·tion *n* : the action of making use of : the state of being used

uti·lize *vb* **uti·lized; uti·liz·ing** : to make use of especially for a certain job

¹ut·most *adj* : of the greatest or highest degree or amount

²utmost *n* : the greatest or highest degree or amount

¹ut·ter *adj* : in every way : TOTAL — **ut·ter·ly** *adv*

²utter *vb* **ut·tered; ut·ter·ing 1** : to send forth as a sound **2** : to express in usually spoken words

ut·ter·ance *n* **1** : something said **2** : the act of saying something

V

v *n, pl* **v's** *or* **vs** *often cap* **1** : the 22nd letter of the English alphabet **2** : five in Roman numerals

v. *abbr* verb

Va., VA *abbr* Virginia

va·can·cy *n, pl* **va·can·cies 1** : something (as an office or hotel room) that is vacant **2** : empty space **3** : the state of being vacant

va·cant *adj* **1** : not filled, used, or lived in **2** : showing a lack of thought or expression **3** : free from duties or care — **va·cant·ly** *adv*

va·cate *vb* **va·cat·ed; va·cat·ing** : to leave empty or not used

¹va·ca·tion *n* **1** : a period during which activity (as of a school) is stopped for a time **2** : a period spent away from home or business in travel or amusement

²vacation *vb* **va·ca·tioned; va·ca·tion·ing** : to take or spend a period away from home or business in travel or amusement — **va·ca·tion·er** *n*

vac·ci·nate *vb* **vac·ci·nat·ed; vac·ci·nat·ing** : to give a vaccine to usually by injection

vac·ci·na·tion *n* : the act of vaccinating

vac·cine *n* : a preparation containing usually killed or weakened microorganisms (as bacteria or viruses) that is given usually by in-

jection to increase protection against a particular disease

vac·il·late *vb* **vac·il·lat·ed; vac·il·lat·ing** : to hesitate between courses or opinions : be unable to choose

¹vac·u·um *n, pl* **vac·u·ums** *or* **vac·ua 1** : a space completely empty of matter **2** : a space from which most of the air has been removed (as by a pump) **3** : VACUUM CLEANER

²vacuum *vb* **vac·u·umed; vac·u·um·ing** : to use a vacuum cleaner on

vacuum cleaner *n* : an electrical appliance for cleaning (as floors or rugs) by suction

¹vag·a·bond *adj* : moving from place to place without a fixed home

²vagabond *n* : a person who moves from place to place without a fixed home

va·gi·na *n* : a canal that leads from the uterus to the outside of the body

¹va·grant *n* : a person who has no steady job and wanders from place to place

²vagrant *adj* **1** : wandering about from place to place **2** : having no fixed course

vague *adj* **vagu·er; vagu·est 1** : not clearly expressed **2** : not clearly understood or

sensed **3** : not clearly outlined — **vague·ly**
adv — **vague·ness** *n*

vain *adj* **vain·er; vain·est 1** : having no success **2** : having or showing the attitude of a
person who thinks too highly of his or her
looks or abilities — **vain·ly** *adv* — **in vain 1**
: without success **2** : in an unholy way

vale *n* : VALLEY

val·e·dic·to·ri·an *n* : a student usually of the
highest standing in a class who gives the
farewell speech at the graduation ceremonies

val·en·tine *n* **1** : a greeting card or gift sent or
given on Valentine's Day **2** : a sweetheart
given something as a sign of affection on
Valentine's Day

Valentine's Day *n* : February 14 observed in
honor of Saint Valentine and as a time for
exchanging valentines

va·let *n* **1** : a person who parks cars for
guests (as at a restaurant) **2** : a male servant
or hotel employee who takes care of a man's
clothes and does personal services

val·iant *adj* **1** : boldly brave **2** : done with
courage : HEROIC — **val·iant·ly** *adv*

val·id *adj* **1** : having legal force or effect **2**
: based on truth or fact — **val·id·ly** *adv*

val·i·date *vb* **val·i·dat·ed; val·i·dat·ing 1** : to
have legal force or effect **2** : to prove to be
true, worthy, or justified

va·lid·i·ty *n* : the quality or state of being true
or legally in force or effect

va·lise *n* : SUITCASE

val·ley *n, pl* **valleys** : an area of lowland between ranges of hills or mountains

val·or *n* : COURAGE

val·or·ous *adj* : having or showing courage
: BRAVE — **val·or·ous·ly** *adv*

¹valu·able *adj* **1** : worth a large amount of
money **2** : of great use or service

²valuable *n* : a personal possession of great
value

¹val·ue *n* **1** : a fair return in goods, services,
or money for something exchanged **2**
: worth in money **3** : worth, usefulness, or
importance in comparison with something
else **4** : a principle or quality that is valuable
or desirable

²value *vb* **val·ued; val·u·ing 1** : to estimate
the worth of **2** : to think highly of

valve *n* **1** : a structure in the body that temporarily closes to prevent passage of material or allow movement of a fluid in one direction only **2** : a mechanical device by
which the flow of liquid, gas, or loose material may be controlled by a movable part **3**
: a device on a brass musical instrument that
changes the pitch of the tone **4** : one of the
separate pieces that make up the shell of

some animals (as clams) and are often
hinged

vam·pire *n* : the body of a dead person believed to come from the grave at night and
suck the blood of sleeping people

vampire bat *n* : a bat of tropical America that
feeds on the blood of birds and mammals

van *n* : a usually closed wagon or truck for
moving goods or animals

va·na·di·um *n* : a metallic chemical element
used in making a strong alloy of steel

van·dal *n* : a person who destroys or damages
property on purpose

van·dal·ism *n* : intentional destruction of or
damage to property

van·dal·ize *vb* **van·dal·ized; van·dal·iz·ing**
: to destroy or damage property on purpose

vane *n* **1** : WEATHER VANE **2** : a flat or
curved surface that turns around a center
when moved by wind or water

van·guard *n* **1** : the troops moving at the
front of an army **2** : FOREFRONT

va·nil·la *n* : a substance extracted from vanilla
beans and used as a flavoring especially for
sweet foods and beverages

vanilla bean *n* : the long pod of a tropical
American orchid from which vanilla is extracted

van·ish *vb* **van·ished; van·ish·ing** : to pass
from sight or existence : DISAPPEAR

van·i·ty *n, pl* **van·i·ties 1** : the quality or fact
of being vain **2** : something that is vain **3** : a
small box for cosmetics

van·quish *vb* **van·quished; van·quish·ing**
: OVERCOME 1

va·por *n* **1** : fine bits (as of fog or smoke)
floating in the air and clouding it **2** : a substance in the form of a gas

va·por·ize *vb* **va·por·ized; va·por·iz·ing** : to
turn from a liquid or solid into vapor — **va-
por·iz·er** *n*

var. *abbr* variant

¹var·i·able *adj* **1** : able to change : likely to
be changed : CHANGEABLE **2** : having differences **3** : different from what is normal
or usual — **var·i·ably** *adv*

²variable *n* **1** : something that changes or
can be changed **2** : PLACEHOLDER

¹var·i·ant *adj* : differing from others of its
kind or class

²variant *n* **1** : one of two or more things that
show slight differences **2** : one of two or
more different spellings or pronunciations
of a word

var·i·a·tion *n* **1** : a change in form, position,
or condition **2** : amount of change or difference **3** : departure from what is usual to a
group

var·ied *adj* : having many forms or types

var·ie·gat·ed *adj* **1** : having patches, stripes,

or marks of different colors **2** : full of variety

va·ri·ety *n, pl* **va·ri·et·ies 1** : a collection of different things **2** : the quality or state of having different forms or types **3** : something (as a plant or animal) that differs from others of the same general kind or of the group to which it belongs **4** : entertainment made up of performances (as dances and songs) that follow one another and are not related

var·i·ous *adj* **1** : of different kinds **2** : different one from another : UNLIKE **3** : made up of an indefinite number greater than one

¹var·nish *n* : a liquid that is spread on a surface and dries into a hard coating

²varnish *vb* **var·nished; var·nish·ing** : to cover with or as if with a liquid that dries into a hard coating

var·si·ty *n, pl* **var·si·ties** : the main team that represents a school or club in contests

vary *vb* **var·ied; vary·ing 1** : to make a partial change in **2** : to make or be of different kinds **3** : to show or undergo change **4** : to differ from the usual members of a group

vas·cu·lar *adj* : of, relating to, containing, or being bodily vessels that carry fluid (as blood in an animal or sap in a plant)

vase *n* : an often round container of greater depth than width used chiefly for ornament or for flowers

vas·sal *n* : a person in the Middle Ages who received protection and land from a lord in return for loyalty and service

vast *adj* : very great in size or amount — **vast·ly** *adv* — **vast·ness** *n*

vat *n* : a large container (as a tub) especially for holding liquids in manufacturing processes

vaude·ville *n* : theatrical entertainment made up of songs, dances, and comic acts

¹vault *n* **1** : a room or compartment for storage or safekeeping **2** : something like a vast ceiling **3** : an arched structure of stone or concrete forming a ceiling or roof **4** : a burial chamber

²vault *vb* **vault·ed; vault·ing** : to leap with the aid of the hands or a pole

³vault *n* : ²LEAP

vb. *abbr* verb

VCR *n* : a device for recording (as television programs) on videocassettes and playing them back

veal *n* : the meat of a young calf used for food

vec·tor *n* : a living thing (as a mosquito, fly, or tick) that carries and passes on a disease-causing microorganism

vee·jay *n* : an announcer of a program (as on television) that features music videos

veer *vb* **veered; veer·ing** : to change direction

¹veg·e·ta·ble *adj* : containing or made from plants or parts of plants

²vegetable *n* **1** : a plant or plant part (as lettuce, broccoli, or peas) grown for use as food and eaten raw or cooked usually as part of a meal **2** : ²PLANT 1

veg·e·tar·i·an *n* : a person who does not eat meat

veg·e·ta·tion *n* : plant life or cover (as of an area)

veg·e·ta·tive *adj* : of, relating to, or functioning in nutrition and growth rather than reproduction

ve·he·mence *n* : the quality or state of being vehement

ve·he·ment *adj* **1** : showing great force or energy **2** : highly emotional **3** : expressed with force — **ve·he·ment·ly** *adv*

ve·hi·cle *n* **1** : something used to transport people or goods **2** : a means by which something is expressed, achieved, or shown

¹veil *n* **1** : a piece of cloth or net worn usually by women over the head and shoulders and sometimes over the face **2** : something that covers or hides like a veil

²veil *vb* **veiled; veil·ing** : to cover with or as if with a piece of cloth or net for the head and shoulders or face

vein *n* **1** : one of the blood vessels that carry the blood back to the heart **2** : a long narrow opening in rock filled with a specific mineral **3** : a streak of different color or texture (as in marble) **4** : a style of expression **5** : one of the bundles of fine tubes that make up the framework of a leaf and carry food, water, and nutrients in the plant **6** : one of the slender parts that stiffen and support the wing of an insect — **veined** *adj*

ve·loc·i·ty *n, pl* **ve·loc·i·ties** : quickness of motion : SPEED

¹vel·vet *n* : a fabric with short soft raised fibers

²velvet *adj* **1** : made of or covered with velvet **2** : VELVETY

vel·vety *adj* : soft and smooth

vend *vb* **vend·ed; vend·ing** : to sell or offer for sale — **ven·dor** *also* **vend·er** *n*

vending machine *n* : a machine for selling merchandise operated by putting money into a slot

ve·neer *n* : a layer of material that provides a finer surface or a stronger structure

ven·er·a·ble *adj* **1** : deserving to be venerated — often used as a religious title **2** : deserving honor or respect

ven·er·ate *vb* **ven·er·at·ed; ven·er·at·ing 1** : to consider holy **2** : to show deep respect for

ven·er·a·tion *n* **1** : the act of showing respect for : the state of being shown respect **2** : a feeling of deep respect

ve·ne·tian blind *n* : a blind having thin horizontal slats that can be adjusted to keep out light or to let light come in between them

ven·geance *n* : harm done to someone usually as punishment in return for an injury or offense — **with a vengeance 1** : with great force or effect **2** : to an extreme or excessive degree

venge·ful *adj* : wanting revenge

ven·i·son *n* : the meat of a deer used for food

Venn diagram *n* : a diagram that shows the relationship between two groups of things by means of overlapping circles

ven·om *n* : poison produced by an animal (as a snake or scorpion) and passed to a victim usually by biting or stinging

ven·om·ous *adj* : having or producing venom : POISONOUS

¹vent *vb* **vent·ed; vent·ing 1** : to provide with an outlet **2** : to serve as an outlet for **3** : ³EXPRESS 1

²vent *n* **1** : an opening for the escape of a gas or liquid or for the relief of pressure **2** : an opportunity or means of release

ven·ti·late *vb* **ven·ti·lat·ed; ven·ti·lat·ing 1** : to let in air and especially a current of fresh air **2** : to provide with fresh air **3** : to discuss freely and openly

ven·ti·la·tion *n* **1** : the act or process of ventilating **2** : a system or means of providing fresh air

ven·ti·la·tor *n* : a device for letting in fresh air or driving out bad or stale air

ven·tral *adj* : of, relating to, or being on or near the surface of the body that in human beings is the front but in most animals is the lower surface

ven·tri·cle *n* : the part of the heart from which blood passes into the arteries

ven·tril·o·quist *n* : a person skilled in speaking in such a way that the voice seems to come from a source other than the speaker

¹ven·ture *vb* **ven·tured; ven·tur·ing 1** : to offer at the risk of being criticized **2** : to go ahead in spite of danger **3** : to face the risks and dangers of **4** : to expose to risk

²venture *n* **1** : a task or an act involving chance, risk, or danger **2** : a risky business deal

ven·ture·some *adj* **1** : tending to take risks **2** : involving risk

ven·tur·ous *adj* : VENTURESOME

Ve·nus *n* : the planet that is second in order of distance from the sun and has a diameter of about 7,500 miles (12,100 kilometers)

ve·ran·da *or* **ve·ran·dah** *n* : a long porch extending along one or more sides of a building

verb *n* : a word that expresses an act, occurrence, or state of being

ver·bal *adj* **1** : of, relating to, or consisting of words **2** : spoken rather than written **3** : of, relating to, or formed from a verb — **ver·bal·ly** *adv*

ver·dant *adj* : green with growing plants

ver·dict *n* **1** : the decision reached by a jury **2** : JUDGMENT 2, OPINION

ver·dure *n* : green vegetation

¹verge *n* **1** : THRESHOLD 2, BRINK **2** : something that borders, limits, or bounds : EDGE

²verge *vb* **verged; verg·ing** : to come near to being

ver·i·fi·ca·tion *n* : the act or process of confirming or checking the accuracy of : the state of being confirmed or having the accuracy of checked

ver·i·fy *vb* **ver·i·fied; ver·i·fy·ing 1** : to prove to be true or correct : CONFIRM **2** : to check or test the accuracy of

ver·i·ta·ble *adj* : ACTUAL, TRUE — often used to emphasize similarity to something else

ver·min *n, pl* **vermin** : small common harmful or objectionable animals (as fleas or mice) that are difficult to get rid of

ver·nal *adj* : marking the beginning of spring

ver·sa·tile *adj* **1** : able to do many different kinds of things **2** : having many uses

ver·sa·til·i·ty *n* : the quality or state of having many uses or being able to do many different kinds of things

verse *n* **1** : a portion of a poem or song : STANZA **2** : writing in which words are arranged in a rhythmic pattern **3** : one of the short parts of a chapter in the Bible

versed *adj* : having knowledge or skill as a result of experience, study, or practice

ver·sion *n* **1** : an account or description from a certain point of view **2** : a translation especially of the Bible **3** : a form of a type or original

ver·sus *prep* : AGAINST 1

ver·te·bra *n, pl* **ver·te·brae** : one of the bony sections making up the backbone

¹ver·te·brate *adj* : having vertebrae or a backbone

²vertebrate *n* : an animal (as a fish, amphibian, reptile, bird, or mammal) that has a backbone extending down the back of the body

ver·tex *n, pl* **ver·ti·ces** *also* **ver·tex·es 1** : the point opposite to and farthest from the base of a geometric figure **2** : the common endpoint of the sides of an angle

¹ver·ti·cal *adj* : rising straight up and down from a level surface — **ver·ti·cal·ly** *adv*

²vertical *n* : something (as a line or plane) that rises straight up and down

ver·ti·go *n, pl* **ver·ti·goes** *or* **ver·ti·gos** : a feeling of dizziness

¹very *adv* **1** : to a great degree : EXTREMELY **2** : in actual fact : TRULY

²very *adj* **1** : ²EXACT, PRECISE **2** : exactly suitable or necessary **3** : MERE, BARE **4** : exactly the same

ves·pers *n pl, often cap* : a late afternoon or evening church service

ves·sel *n* **1** : a craft larger than a rowboat for navigation of the water **2** : a hollow utensil (as a cup or bowl) for holding something **3** : a tube (as an artery) in which a body fluid is contained and carried or circulated

¹vest *n* : a sleeveless garment usually worn under a suit coat

²vest *vb* **vest·ed; vest·ing 1** : to place or give into the possession or control of some person or authority **2** : to clothe in vestments

ves·ti·bule *n* : a hall or room between the outer door and the inside part of a building

ves·tige *n* : a tiny amount or visible sign of something lost or vanished : TRACE

ves·ti·gial *adj* : of, relating to, or being the last remaining amount or visible sign of something lost or vanished

vest·ment *n* : an outer garment especially for wear during ceremonies or by an official

¹vet *n* : VETERINARIAN

²vet *n* : ¹VETERAN

¹vet·er·an *n* **1** : a person who has had long experience **2** : a former member of the armed forces especially in war

²veteran *adj* : having gained skill through experience

vet·er·i·nar·i·an *n* : a doctor who gives medical treatment to animals

¹vet·er·i·nary *adj* : of, relating to, specializing in, or being the medical care of animals

²veterinary *n, pl* **vet·er·i·nar·ies** : VETERINARIAN

¹ve·to *n, pl* **vetoes 1** : the act of forbidding something by a person in authority **2** : the power of a president, governor, or mayor to prevent something from becoming law

²veto *vb* **ve·toed; ve·to·ing 1** : FORBID, PROHIBIT **2** : to prevent from becoming law by use of the power to do so

vex *vb* **vexed; vex·ing 1** : to bring trouble, distress, or worry to **2** : to annoy by small irritations

vex·a·tion *n* **1** : the quality or state of being annoyed by small irritations **2** : the act of bringing trouble, distress, or worry to **3** : a cause of trouble or worry

VG *abbr* very good

v.i. *abbr* verb intransitive

VI *abbr* Virgin Islands

via *prep* : by way of

vi·a·ble *adj* **1** : capable of living or growing **2** : possible to use or apply

via·duct *n* : a bridge for carrying a road or railroad over something (as a gorge or highway)

vi·al *n* : a small container (as for medicines) that is usually made of glass or plastic

vi·brant *adj* : having or giving the sense of life, vigor, or action — **vi·brant·ly** *adv*

vi·brate *vb* **vi·brat·ed; vi·brat·ing** : to move or cause to move back and forth or from side to side very quickly

vi·bra·tion *n* **1** : a rapid motion (as of a stretched cord) back and forth **2** : the action of moving or causing to move back and forth or from side to side very quickly : the state of being swung back and forth **3** : a trembling motion

vic·ar *n* : a minister in charge of a church who serves under the authority of another minister

vi·car·i·ous *adj* : sharing in someone else's experiences through the use of imagination or sympathetic feelings — **vi·car·i·ous·ly** *adv* — **vi·car·i·ous·ness** *n*

vice *n* **1** : evil conduct or habits **2** : a moral fault or weakness

vice- *prefix* : one that takes the place of

vice pres·i·dent *n* : an official (as of a government) whose rank is next below that of the president and who takes the place of the president when necessary

vice ver·sa *adv* : with the order turned around

vi·cin·i·ty *n, pl* **vi·cin·i·ties 1** : a surrounding area : NEIGHBORHOOD **2** : the state of being close

vi·cious *adj* **1** : very dangerous **2** : filled with or showing unkind feelings **3** : violent and cruel **4** : very severe — **vi·cious·ly** *adv* — **vi·cious·ness** *n*

vic·tim *n* **1** : a person who is cheated, fooled, or hurt by another **2** : an individual injured or killed (as by disease, violence, or disaster) **3** : a living being offered as a religious sacrifice

vic·tim·ize *vb* **vic·tim·ized; vic·tim·iz·ing** : to make a victim of

vic·tor *n* : WINNER, CONQUEROR

vic·to·ri·ous *adj* : having won a victory — **vic·to·ri·ous·ly** *adv*

vic·to·ry *n, pl* **vic·to·ries 1** : the act of defeating an enemy or opponent **2** : success in a struggle against difficulties

vict·uals *n pl* : food and drink

vi·cu·ña *or* **vi·cu·na** *n* : an animal of the Andes that is related to the llama and has long soft woolly hair

¹**vid·eo** n 1 : TELEVISION 1 2 : the visual part of television 3 : ¹VIDEOTAPE 1 4 : a recorded performance of a song

²**video** adj 1 : relating to or used in the sending or receiving of television images 2 : being, relating to, or involving images on a television screen or computer display

video camera n : a camera (as a camcorder) that records video and usually also audio

vid·eo·cas·sette n 1 : a case containing videotape for use with a VCR 2 : a recording (as of a movie) on a videocassette

videocassette recorder n : VCR

video game n : a game played with images on a video screen

¹**vid·eo·tape** n 1 : a recording of visual images and sound (as of a television production) made on magnetic tape 2 : the magnetic tape used for such a recording

²**videotape** vb **vid·eo·taped; vid·eo·tap·ing** : to make a videotape of

videotape recorder n : a device for recording on videotape

vie vb **vied; vy·ing** : COMPETE

¹**Viet·nam·ese** n 1 : a person born or living in Vietnam 2 : the language of the Vietnamese

²**Vietnamese** adj : of or relating to Vietnam, the Vietnamese people, or their language

¹**view** n 1 : OPINION 1 2 : all that can be seen from a certain place 3 : range of vision 4 : ¹PURPOSE 5 : a picture that represents something that can be seen

²**view** vb **viewed; view·ing** 1 : to look at carefully 2 : ¹SEE 1 3 : ²REGARD 5 — **view·er** n

view·find·er n : a device on a camera that shows the view to be included in the picture

view·point n : POINT OF VIEW, STANDPOINT

vig·il n : an act of keeping watch especially when sleep is usual

vig·i·lance n : the quality or state of staying alert especially to possible danger

vig·i·lant adj : alert especially to avoid danger

vig·i·lan·te n : a member of a group of volunteers who are not police but who decide on their own to stop crime and punish criminals

vig·or n 1 : strength or energy of body or mind 2 : active strength or force

vig·or·ous adj 1 : very healthy and strong 2 : done with force and energy — **vig·or·ous·ly** adv

Vi·king n : one of the Scandinavians who raided or invaded the coasts of Europe in the eighth to tenth centuries

vile adj **vil·er; vil·est** 1 : WICKED 1 2 : very bad or unpleasant

vil·i·fy vb **vil·i·fied; vil·i·fy·ing** : to speak of harshly and often unfairly

vil·la n : a large house or estate usually in the country

vil·lage n 1 : a place where people live that is usually smaller than a town 2 : the people living in a village

vil·lag·er n : a person who lives in a village

vil·lain n 1 : a wicked person 2 : a character in a story or play who opposes the hero or heroine

vil·lain·ous adj : WICKED 1

vil·lainy n, pl **vil·lain·ies** : bad or evil behavior or actions

vil·lus n, pl **vil·li** : one of the tiny extensions shaped like fingers that line the small intestine and are active in absorbing nutrients

vim n : great energy and enthusiasm

vin·di·cate vb **vin·di·cat·ed; vin·di·cat·ing** 1 : to free from blame or guilt 2 : to show to be true or correct

vin·dic·tive adj 1 : likely to seek revenge 2 : meant to be harmful

vine n : a plant whose stem requires support and which climbs by tendrils or twining or creeps along the ground — **vine·like** adj

vin·e·gar n : a sour liquid made from cider, wine, or malt and used to flavor or preserve foods

vine·yard n : a field of grapevines

¹**vin·tage** n 1 : the grapes grown or wine made during one season 2 : the time when something started or was made

²**vintage** adj 1 : produced in a particular year 2 : of old and continuing interest, importance, or quality

vi·nyl n : a substance or product (as a fiber) made from an artificial plastic

¹**vi·o·la** n : a garden plant that looks like but is smaller than a pansy

²**vi·o·la** n : a stringed musical instrument like a violin but slightly larger and lower in pitch

vi·o·late vb **vi·o·lat·ed; vi·o·lat·ing** 1 : to fail to keep : BREAK 2 : to treat in a very disrespectful way 3 : DISTURB 1 — **vi·o·la·tor** n

vi·o·la·tion n : an act or instance of violating something and especially a failure to do what is required or expected by a law, rule, or agreement

vi·o·lence n 1 : the use of force to harm a person or damage property 2 : great force or strength especially of a kind that involves destruction

vi·o·lent adj 1 : showing very strong force 2 : ¹EXTREME 1, INTENSE 3 : using or likely to use harmful force 4 : caused by force — **vi·o·lent·ly** adv

vi·o·let n 1 : a wild or garden plant related to the pansies that has small often fragrant white, blue, purple, or yellow flowers 2 : a bluish purple

vi·o·lin n : a stringed musical instrument with

four strings that is usually held against the shoulder under the chin and played with a bow

vi·o·lin·ist *n* : a person who plays the violin

vi·per *n* : a poisonous heavy-bodied snake with long hollow fangs

vir·eo *n, pl* **vir·e·os** : a small songbird that eats insects and is olive-green or grayish in color

¹vir·gin *n* : a person who has not had sexual intercourse

²virgin *adj* : not yet disturbed or changed by human activity

Vir·go *n* **1** : a constellation between Leo and Libra imagined as a young woman **2** : the sixth sign of the zodiac or a person born under this sign

vir·ile *adj* : having qualities generally associated with men

vir·tu·al *adj* : being in effect but not in fact or name : close to but not quite something — **vir·tu·al·ly** *adv*

virtual reality *n* : an artificial environment which is experienced through sights and sounds provided by a computer and in which a person's actions partly decide what happens in the environment

vir·tue *n* **1** : morally good behavior or character **2** : a good moral or desirable quality **3** : the good result that comes from something — **by virtue of** : because of : through the force of

vir·tu·o·so *n, pl* **vir·tu·o·sos** *or* **vir·tu·o·si** : a person who is an outstanding performer especially in music

vir·tu·ous *adj* : morally good : having or showing virtue — **vir·tu·ous·ly** *adv*

vir·u·lent *adj* : spreading quickly and causing serious harm

vi·rus *n* **1** : a disease-causing agent that is too tiny to be seen by the ordinary microscope, that may be a living organism or may be a very special kind of protein molecule, and that can only multiply when inside the cell of an organism **2** : a disease caused by a virus **3** : a usually hidden computer program that causes harm by making copies of itself and inserting them into other programs

vis·count *n* : a British nobleman ranking below an earl and above a baron

vis·count·ess *n* **1** : the wife or widow of a viscount **2** : a woman who holds the rank of a viscount in her own right

vise *n* : a device with two jaws that can be opened and closed by a screw or lever for holding or clamping work

vis·i·bil·i·ty *n* : the ability to see or be seen

vis·i·ble *adj* **1** : capable of being seen **2** : easily seen or understood : OBVIOUS — **vis·i·bly** *adv*

vi·sion *n* **1** : the special sense by which the qualities of an object (as color) that make up its appearance are perceived through a process in which light rays entering the eye are transformed into signals that pass to the brain **2** : the act or power of seeing : SIGHT **3** : something dreamt or imagined **4** : exceptional ability to know or believe what should happen or be done in the future

vi·sion·ary *n, pl* **vi·sion·ar·ies** : a person who has an exceptional ability to plan or have ideas for the future

¹vis·it *vb* **vis·it·ed; vis·it·ing 1** : to go to see for a particular purpose **2** : to stay with for a time as a guest **3** : to come to or upon

²visit *n* **1** : an act of going to see a person, place, or thing for a particular purpose **2** : a stay as a guest — **vis·i·tor** *n*

vi·sor *n* **1** : the movable front upper piece of a helmet that is brought down to protect the face **2** : a part (as on a cap) that sticks out to protect or shade the eyes

vis·ta *n* : a large and scenic view in the distance

vi·su·al *adj* **1** : obtained by the use of sight **2** : of, relating to, or used in seeing **3** : appealing to the sense of sight — **vi·su·al·ly** *adv*

vi·su·al·ize *vb* **vi·su·al·ized; vi·su·al·iz·ing** : to see or form a mental image : IMAGINE

vi·tal *adj* **1** : concerned with or necessary to the continuation of life **2** : full of life and energy **3** : very important — **vi·tal·ly** *adv*

vi·tal·i·ty *n, pl* **vi·tal·i·ties 1** : capacity to live and develop **2** : ENERGY 1, VIGOR

vi·tals *n pl* : the bodily organs (as the heart, lungs, and liver) that are needed to stay alive

vi·ta·min *n* : any of a group of substances that are found naturally in many foods, are necessary in small quantities for good health and normal development and functioning, and are designated by a capital letter and sometimes a number

vi·va·cious *adj* : full of energy and good spirits

vi·vac·i·ty *n* : the quality or state of being full of energy and good spirits

viv·id *adj* **1** : producing strong mental images **2** : very strong or bright **3** : acting clearly and powerfully **4** : seeming full of life and freshness — **viv·id·ly** *adv* — **viv·id·ness** *n*

vix·en *n* : a female fox

vo·cab·u·lary *n, pl* **vo·cab·u·lar·ies 1** : a list or collection of words and their meanings **2** : the words used in a language, by a group or individual, or in relation to a subject

vo·cal *adj* **1** : uttered by the voice : ORAL **2** : composed or arranged for or sung by the human voice **3** : speaking freely or loudly

: OUTSPOKEN **4** : relating to or involved in producing the voice — **vo·cal·ly** *adv*

vocal cords *n pl* : a pair of folds of tissue that extend across the inside of the larynx and that produce the voice when air exhaled from the lungs causes them to tighten and vibrate

vo·cal·ist *n* : a person who sings : SINGER

vo·ca·tion *n* **1** : a strong desire for a certain career or course of action **2** : the work in which a person is regularly employed : OCCUPATION

vo·ca·tion·al *adj* **1** : of, relating to, or concerned with an occupation **2** : relating to or providing training in a skill or trade to be pursued as a career

vod·ka *n* : a colorless alcoholic liquor

vogue *n* **1** : the quality or state of being popular at a certain time **2** : something that is in fashion at a certain time

¹voice *n* **1** : sound that passes out of the mouth and throat of vertebrates and especially human beings and is produced mainly by the vibration of the vocal cords within the larynx (as in speaking or shouting) **2** : musical sounds produced by singing **3** : the power to use the voice **4** : a sound similar to vocal sound **5** : the right to express a wish, choice, or opinion **6** : a means of expression

²voice *vb* **voiced; voic·ing** : to express in words

voice box *n* : LARYNX

voiced *adj* **1** : having a voice of a specified kind **2** : spoken with vibration of the vocal cords : not silent

voice·less *adj* **1** : having no voice **2** : spoken without vibration of the vocal cords

voice mail *n* : an electronic communication system in which spoken messages are recorded to be played back later

¹void *adj* **1** : containing nothing : EMPTY **2** : being without : DEVOID **3** : having no legal effect

²void *n* : empty space

vol. *abbr* **1** volume **2** volunteer

vol·a·tile *adj* **1** : easily becoming a gas at a fairly low temperature **2** : likely to change suddenly

vol·ca·nic *adj* : of, relating to, or produced by a volcano

vol·ca·no *n, pl* **vol·ca·noes** *or* **vol·ca·nos** **1** : an opening in the earth's crust from which hot or melted rock and steam erupt **2** : a hill or mountain composed of material thrown out in a volcanic eruption

vole *n* : a small animal that is a rodent which looks like a fat mouse or rat and is sometimes harmful to crops

vo·li·tion *n* : the act or power of making choices or decisions without being influenced by other people : WILL

¹vol·ley *n, pl* **volleys** **1** : a group of missiles (as arrows or bullets) passing through the air **2** : the firing of many weapons (as rifles) at the same time **3** : a bursting forth of many things at once **4** : a hit or kick of the ball while it is in the air before it touches the ground

²volley *vb* **vol·leyed; vol·ley·ing** : to hit an object (as a ball) while it is in the air before it touches the ground

vol·ley·ball *n* **1** : a game played by two teams that hit a ball filled with air over a net without letting the ball touch the ground **2** : the ball used in volleyball

volt *n* : a unit for measuring the force that moves an electric current

volt·age *n* : electric force measured in volts

vol·ume *n* **1** : ¹BOOK 1 **2** : one of a series of books that together form a complete work or collection **3** : an amount of space that can be measured in cubic units **4** : ²AMOUNT **5** : a large amount **6** : the degree of loudness of a sound

vo·lu·mi·nous *adj* **1** : of great size or amount : LARGE **2** : ¹FULL 4

vol·un·tary *adj* **1** : done, given, or acting of free choice **2** : done or acting with no expectation of payment **3** : relating to or controlled by the will — **vol·un·tar·i·ly** *adv*

¹vol·un·teer *n* : a person who does something by free choice usually with no payment expected or given

²volunteer *adj* : relating to or done by volunteers

³volunteer *vb* **vol·un·teered; vol·un·teer·ing** : to offer or give without being asked or forced and usually with no expectation of payment

¹vom·it *n* : material from the stomach brought up suddenly through the mouth

²vomit *vb* **vom·it·ed; vom·it·ing** : to bring up the contents of the stomach through the mouth

vo·ra·cious *adj* **1** : very hungry : having a huge appetite **2** : very eager — **vo·ra·cious·ly** *adv*

¹vote *n* **1** : a formal expression of opinion or choice (as by ballot in an election) **2** : the decision reached by voting **3** : the right to vote **4** : the act or process of voting **5** : a group of voters with some common interest or quality

²vote *vb* **vot·ed; vot·ing** **1** : to express a wish or choice by a vote **2** : to elect, decide, pass, defeat, grant, or make legal by a vote **3** : to declare by general agreement **4** : to offer as a suggestion

vot·er *n* : a person who votes or who has the legal right to vote

vouch *vb* **vouched; vouch·ing** : to give a guarantee

vouch·safe *vb* **vouch·safed; vouch·saf·ing** : to give or grant as a special favor

¹vow *n* : a solemn promise or statement

²vow *vb* **vowed; vow·ing** : to make a solemn promise : SWEAR

vow·el *n* **1** : a speech sound (as \ə\, \ā\, or \ó\) produced without obstruction in the mouth **2** : a letter (as *a, e, i, o, u*) representing a vowel

¹voy·age *n* : a journey especially by water to a distant or unknown place

²voyage *vb* **voy·aged; voy·ag·ing** : to take a long trip usually by boat — **voy·ag·er** *n*

VP *abbr* vice president

vs. *abbr* versus

v.t. *abbr* verb transitive

Vt., VT *abbr* Vermont

vul·ca·nize *vb* **vul·ca·nized; vul·ca·niz·ing** : to treat rubber with chemicals in order to give it more strength or flexibility

vul·gar *adj* **1** : having or showing poor taste or manners : COARSE **2** : offensive in language or subject matter

vul·gar·i·ty *n, pl* **vul·gar·i·ties 1** : the quality or having or showing poor taste or manners **2** : rude or offensive language or behavior

vul·ner·a·ble *adj* **1** : capable of being easily hurt or injured **2** : open to attack or damage

vul·ture *n* : a large bird related to the hawks and eagles that has a head bare of feathers and feeds mostly on dead animals

vying *present participle of* VIE

W

w *n, pl* **w's** *or* **ws** *often cap* : the 23rd letter of the English alphabet

W *abbr* **1** west **2** western

WA *abbr* Washington

wacky *also* **whacky** *adj* **wack·i·er** *also* **whack·i·er; wack·i·est** *also* **whack·i·est** : CRAZY 2, INSANE

¹wad *n* **1** : a small mass or lump of soft material **2** : a thick pile of folded money

²wad *vb* **wad·ded; wad·ding** : to crush or press into a small tight mass

¹wad·dle *vb* **wad·dled; wad·dling** : to walk with short steps swaying like a duck

²waddle *n* : a way of walking by taking short steps and swaying from side to side

wade *vb* **wad·ed; wad·ing 1** : to walk through something (as water, snow, or a crowd) that makes it hard to move **2** : to pass or cross by stepping through water **3** : to proceed with difficulty

wading bird *n* : a bird (as a heron) with long legs that wades in water in search of food

wa·fer *n* : a thin crisp cake or cracker

waf·fle *n* : a crisp cake of batter baked in a waffle iron and often indented with a pattern of small squares

waffle iron *n* : a cooking utensil with two hinged metal parts that come together for making waffles

¹waft *vb* **waft·ed; waft·ing** : to move or be moved lightly by or as if by the action of waves or wind

²waft *n* : a slight breeze or puff of air

¹wag *vb* **wagged; wag·ging** : to swing to and fro or from side to side

²wag *n* : a movement back and forth or from side to side

³wag *n* : a person full of jokes and humor

¹wage *n* : payment for work done especially when figured by the hour or day

²wage *vb* **waged; wag·ing** : to engage in : carry on

¹wa·ger *n* **1** : ¹BET **2 2** : the act of betting

²wager *vb* **wa·gered; wa·ger·ing** : to bet on the result of a contest or question

wag·gish *adj* : showing or done in a spirit of harmless mischief

wag·gle *vb* **wag·gled; wag·gling** : to move backward and forward, from side to side, or up and down

wag·on *n* : a vehicle having four wheels and used for carrying goods

waif *n* : a homeless child

¹wail *vb* **wailed; wail·ing 1** : to make a long, loud cry of pain or grief **2** : to complain with a loud voice

²wail *n* : a long cry of grief or pain

wain·scot *n* : the bottom part of an inside wall especially when made of material different from the rest

wain·scot·ing *or* **wain·scot·ting** *n* : WAIN-SCOT

waist *n* **1** : the part of the body between the chest and the hips **2** : the part of a garment that fits around a person's waist

¹wait *vb* **wait·ed; wait·ing 1** : to stay in a place looking forward to something that is expected to happen **2** : to stop moving or doing something **3** : to remain not done or dealt with **4** : to serve food as a waiter or waitress

²**wait** *n* **1** : an act or period of waiting **2** : a hidden place from which a surprise attack can be made — usually used in the expression *lie in wait*

wait·er *n* : a person who serves food to people at tables

waiting room *n* : a room (as in a station or an office) for the use of people waiting

wait·ress *n* : a girl or woman who serves food to people at tables

waive *vb* **waived; waiv·ing** : to give up claim to

¹**wake** *vb* **woke** *also* **waked; wo·ken** *or* **waked** *also* **woke; wak·ing** **1** : to arouse from sleep : AWAKE — often used with *up* **2** : to become alert or aware

²**wake** *n* : a watch held over the body of a dead person before burial

³**wake** *n* : a track or mark left by something moving especially in the water

wake·ful *adj* : not sleeping or able to sleep — **wake·ful·ness** *n*

wak·en *vb* **wak·ened; wak·en·ing** : ¹WAKE 1

¹**walk** *vb* **walked; walk·ing** **1** : to move or cause to move along on foot at a natural slow pace **2** : to cover or pass over on foot **3** : to go with (a person or animal) by walking **4** : to go or cause to go to first base after four balls in baseball — **walk·er** *n* — **walk out 1** : to leave suddenly and unexpectedly **2** : to go on strike

²**walk** *n* **1** : the act of moving along on foot at a natural slow pace **2** : a place or path for walking **3** : distance to be walked often measured in time required by a walker to cover **4** : way of walking **5** : an advance to first base after four balls in baseball **6** : position in life or the community **7** : a slow way of moving by a horse

walk·ie–talk·ie *n* : a small portable radio set for receiving and sending messages

walking stick *n* **1** : a stick used to maintain balance when walking **2** : STICK INSECT

walk·out *n* **1** : a labor strike **2** : the act of leaving a meeting or organization to show disapproval

¹**wall** *n* **1** : one of the sides of a room or building **2** : a solid structure (as of stone) built to enclose or shut off a space **3** : something that separates one thing from another **4** : a layer of material enclosing space — **walled** *adj*

²**wall** *vb* **walled; wall·ing** : to build or have a wall in or around

wall·board *n* : a building material (as of wood pulp) made in large stiff sheets and used especially inside walls and ceilings

wal·let *n* : a small flat case for carrying paper money and personal papers

wall·eye *n* : a large North American freshwa-

ter fish that has large glassy eyes and is caught for food and sport

¹**wal·lop** *vb* **wal·loped; wal·lop·ing** : to hit hard

²**wallop** *n* : a hard blow

¹**wal·low** *vb* **wal·lowed; wal·low·ing** **1** : to roll about in or as if in deep mud **2** : to seem to want to be unhappy

²**wallow** *n* : a muddy or dust-filled area where animals roll about

wall·pa·per *n* : decorative paper for covering the walls of a room

wal·nut *n* : a wrinkled edible nut that comes from a tall tree with hard strong wood

wal·rus *n* : a large animal of northern seas that is related to the seal and has long ivory tusks, a tough wrinkled hide, and flippers used in swimming, diving, and moving about on land

¹**waltz** *n, pl* **waltz·es** : a dance in which couples glide to music having three beats to a measure

²**waltz** *vb* **waltzed; waltz·ing** : to dance a waltz

Wam·pa·noag *n, pl* **Wampanoag** *or* **Wam·pa·noags** : a member of an American Indian people of eastern Rhode Island and neighboring parts of Massachusetts

wam·pum *n* : beads made of shells and once used for money or ornament by North American Indians

wan *adj* **wan·ner; wan·nest** **1** : having a pale or sickly color **2** : showing little effort or energy — **wan·ly** *adv*

wand *n* : a slender rod

wan·der *vb* **wan·dered; wan·der·ing** **1** : to move about without a goal or purpose : RAMBLE **2** : to get off the right path or leave the right area : STRAY **3** : to lose concentration **4** : to follow a winding course — **wan·der·er** *n*

wane *vb* **waned; wan·ing** **1** : to grow smaller or less **2** : to grow shorter

¹**want** *vb* **want·ed; want·ing** **1** : to desire, wish, or long for something **2** : to feel or suffer the need of something **3** : to be without : LACK

²**want** *n* **1** : ²LACK 2, SHORTAGE **2** : the state of being very poor **3** : a wish for something : DESIRE

want·ing *adj* : falling below a standard, hope, or need

wan·ton *adj* **1** : not modest or proper : INDECENT **2** : showing no thought or care for the rights, feelings, or safety of others — **wan·ton·ly** *adv* — **wan·ton·ness** *n*

¹**war** *n* **1** : a state or period of fighting between states or nations **2** : a struggle between opposing forces or for a particular end

²**war** *vb* **warred; war·ring** : to engage in a series of battles

¹**war·ble** *n* **1** : low pleasing sounds that form a melody (as of a bird) **2** : the action of making low pleasing sounds that form a melody

²**warble** *vb* **war·bled; war·bling** : to sing a melody of low pleasing sounds

war·bler *n* **1** : an Old World bird related to the thrush and noted for its musical song **2** : a brightly colored American bird having a song that is usually weak and not musical

¹**ward** *n* **1** : a large room in a hospital where a number of patients often needing similar treatment are cared for **2** : one of the parts into which a town or city is divided for management **3** : a person under the protection of a guardian

²**ward** *vb* **ward·ed; ward·ing** : to avoid being hit or affected by

¹**-ward** *also* **-wards** *adj suffix* **1** : that moves, faces, or is pointed toward **2** : that is found in the direction of

²**-ward** *or* **-wards** *adv suffix* **1** : in a specified direction **2** : toward a specified place

war·den *n* **1** : a person who sees that certain laws are followed **2** : the chief official of a prison

ward·robe *n* **1** : a room or closet where clothes are kept **2** : the clothes a person owns

ware *n* **1** : manufactured articles or products of art or craft — often used in combination **2** : items (as dishes) of baked clay : POTTERY **3** : an article of merchandise

ware·house *n, pl* **ware·hous·es** : a building for storing goods and merchandise

war·fare *n* **1** : military fighting between enemies **2** : conflict between opposing forces or for a particular end

war·like *adj* **1** : fond of war **2** : fit for or characteristic of war

war·lock *n* : a man who practices witchcraft

¹**warm** *adj* **warm·er; warm·est** **1** : somewhat hot **2** : giving off a little heat **3** : making a person feel heat or experience no loss of body heat **4** : having a feeling of warmth **5** : showing strong feeling **6** : newly made : FRESH **7** : near the object sought **8** : of a color in the range yellow through orange to red — **warm·ly** *adv*

²**warm** *vb* **warmed; warm·ing** **1** : to make or become warm **2** : to give a feeling of warmth **3** : to become more interested than at first — **warm up** **1** : to exercise or practice lightly in preparation for more strenuous activity or a performance **2** : to run (as a motor) at slow speed before using

warm–blood·ed *adj* : able to keep up a relatively high constant body temperature that is independent of that of the surroundings

warmth *n* **1** : gentle heat **2** : strong feeling

warm–up *n* : the act or an instance of preparing for a performance or a more strenuous activity

warn *vb* **warned; warn·ing** **1** : to put on guard : CAUTION **2** : to notify especially in advance

warn·ing *n* : something that cautions of possible danger or trouble

¹**warp** *n* **1** : the threads that go lengthwise in a loom and are crossed by the woof **2** : a twist or curve that has developed in something once flat or straight

²**warp** *vb* **warped; warp·ing** **1** : to curve or twist out of shape **2** : to cause to judge, choose, or act wrongly

¹**war·rant** *n* **1** : a reason or cause for an opinion or action **2** : a document giving legal power

²**warrant** *vb* **war·rant·ed; war·rant·ing** **1** : to be sure of or that **2** : ²GUARANTEE 2 **3** : to call for : JUSTIFY

warrant officer *n* : an officer in the armed forces in one of the grades between commissioned officers and noncommissioned officers

war·ren *n* : a place where rabbits live or are kept

war·rior *n* : a person who is or has been in warfare

war·ship *n* : a ship armed for combat

wart *n* : a small hard lump of thickened skin caused by a virus

wart·hog *n* : a wild African hog with pointed tusks and in the male thick growths of skin on the face which resemble warts

wary *adj* **war·i·er; war·i·est** : very cautious — **war·i·ly** *adv* — **war·i·ness** *n*

was *past first person & third person sing of* BE

¹**wash** *vb* **washed; wash·ing** **1** : to cleanse with water and usually a cleaning agent (as soap) **2** : to wet completely with liquid **3** : to flow along or overflow against **4** : to remove or carry away by the action of water **5** : to stand being cleansed without injury

²**wash** *n* **1** : articles in the laundry **2** : an act or instance of cleansing or of being cleansed **3** : the flow, sound, or action of water **4** : a backward flow of water (as made by the motion of a boat) **5** : material carried or set down by water

Wash. *abbr* Washington

wash·able *adj* : capable of being cleansed without damage

wash·bowl *n* : a large bowl for water to wash the hands and face

wash·cloth *n* : a small towel for washing the face and body

wash·er *n* **1** : WASHING MACHINE **2** : a ring (as of metal) used to make something fit tightly or to prevent rubbing

washing machine *n* : a machine used for washing clothes and household linen

wash·out *n* **1** : a place where earth has been washed away **2** : a complete failure

wash·tub *n* : a tub for washing clothes or for soaking them before washing

wasn't : was not

wasp *n* : a winged insect related to the bee and ant that has a slender body with the abdomen attached by a narrow stalk and that in females and workers is capable of giving a very painful sting

wasp·ish *adj* : ³CROSS 3, IRRITABLE — **wasp·ish·ly** *adv*

¹waste *n* **1** : the action of spending or using carelessly or uselessly : the state of being spent or used carelessly or uselessly **2** : material left over or thrown away **3** : material (as carbon dioxide in the lungs or urine in the kidneys) produced in and of no further use to the living body **4** : a large area of barren land : WASTELAND

²waste *vb* **wast·ed; wast·ing 1** : to spend or use carelessly or uselessly **2** : to lose or cause to lose weight, strength, or energy **3** : to bring to ruin

³waste *adj* **1** : being wild and without people or crops : BARREN **2** : of no further use

waste·bas·ket *n* : an open container for odds and ends to be thrown away

waste·ful *adj* : spending or using in a careless or foolish way — **waste·ful·ly** *adv* — **waste·ful·ness** *n*

waste·land *n* : land that is barren or not fit for crops

¹watch *vb* **watched; watch·ing 1** : to keep in view **2** : to be on the lookout **3** : to take care of : TEND **4** : to be careful of **5** : to keep guard **6** : to stay awake — **watch·er** *n* — **watch out** : to be aware of and ready for

²watch *n* **1** : a small timepiece worn on the wrist or carried **2** : close observation **3** : ¹GUARD 2 **4** : the time during which someone is on duty to guard or be on the lookout **5** : an act of keeping awake to guard or protect

watch·dog *n* : a dog kept to guard property

watch·ful *adj* : ATTENTIVE 1, VIGILANT — **watch·ful·ly** *adv* — **watch·ful·ness** *n*

watch·man *n, pl* **watch·men** : a person whose job is to guard property at night or when the owners are away

watch·tow·er *n* : a tower for a guard or watchman

watch·word *n* : PASSWORD

¹wa·ter *n* **1** : the liquid that comes from the clouds as rain and forms streams, lakes, and seas **2** : a body of water or a part of a body of water

²water *vb* **wa·tered; wa·ter·ing 1** : to wet or supply with water **2** : to fill with liquid (as tears or saliva) **3** : to add water to

wa·ter·bird *n* : a swimming or wading bird

water buffalo *n* : a buffalo of Asia with large curving horns that is often used as a work animal

wa·ter·col·or *n* **1** : a paint whose liquid part is water **2** : a picture painted with watercolor **3** : the art of painting with watercolor

wa·ter·course *n* **1** : a channel in which water flows **2** : a stream of water (as a river or brook)

wa·ter·cress *n* : a plant that grows in or near water and has sharp-tasting leaves used especially in salads

wa·ter·fall *n* : a fall of water from a height

water flea *n* : a tiny often brightly colored freshwater animal related to the crab and lobster

wa·ter·fowl *n* **1** : a bird that is typically found in or near water **2** : a swimming bird (as a duck or goose) often hunted as game

wa·ter·front *n* : land that borders on a body of water

water hyacinth *n* : a floating water plant that often clogs streams in the southern United States

water lily *n* : a water plant with rounded floating leaves and showy often fragrant flowers

wa·ter·line *n* : any of several lines marked on the outside of a ship that match the surface of the water when the ship floats evenly

wa·ter·logged *adj* : so filled or soaked with water as to be heavy or hard to manage

wa·ter·mark *n* **1** : a mark that shows a level to which water has risen **2** : a mark made in paper during manufacture that is visible when the paper is held up to the light

wa·ter·mel·on *n* : a large edible fruit with a hard rind and a sweet red juicy pulp

water moccasin *n* : a poisonous snake of the southern United States that lives in or near water

water park *n* : an amusement park with pools and wetted slides

wa·ter·pow·er *n* : the power of moving water used to run machinery

¹wa·ter·proof *adj* : not letting water through

²waterproof *vb* **wa·ter·proofed; wa·ter·proof·ing** : to make something resistant to letting water through

wa·ter·shed *n* **1** : a dividing ridge (as a mountain range) separating one drainage area from others **2** : the whole area that drains into a lake or river

wa·ter–ski *vb* **wa·ter–skied; wa·ter–ski·ing** : to ski on water while being pulled by a speedboat

water ski *n, pl* **water skis** : a ski used in water-skiing

wa·ter·spout *n* **1** : a pipe for carrying off water from a roof **2** : a slender cloud that is shaped like a funnel and extends down to a cloud of spray torn up from the surface of a body of water by a whirlwind

water strid·er *n* : a bug with long legs that skims over the surface of water

wa·ter·tight *adj* : so tight as to be waterproof

wa·ter·way *n* : a channel or a body of water by which ships can travel

wa·ter·wheel *n* : a wheel turned by a flow of water against it

wa·ter·works *n pl* : a system of dams, reservoirs, pumps, and pipes for supplying water (as to a city)

wa·tery *adj* **1** : full of or giving out liquid **2** : containing or giving out water or a thin liquid **3** : like water especially in being thin, soggy, pale, or without flavor **4** : lacking in strength or determination

watt *n* : a unit for measuring electric power

wat·tle *n* : a fleshy flap of skin that hangs usually from the neck (as of a bird)

¹wave *vb* **waved; wav·ing** **1** : to move (as the hand) to and fro as a signal or in greeting **2** : to move (something) back and forth **3** : to curve slightly **4** : to flutter with a rolling movement

²wave *n* **1** : a moving ridge on the surface of water **2** : a waving motion **3** : something that swells and dies away **4** : a rolling movement passing along a surface or through the air **5** : a curving shape or series of curving shapes **6** : a sudden increase in something **7** : a motion that is somewhat like a wave in water and transfers energy from point to point

wave·length *n* : the distance in the line of advance of a wave from any one point to the next similar point

wa·ver *vb* **wa·vered; wa·ver·ing** **1** : to be uncertain in opinion **2** : to move unsteadily or to and fro **3** : to give an unsteady sound

wavy *adj* **wav·i·er; wav·i·est** : like, having, or moving in waves — **wav·i·ness** *n*

¹wax *n* **1** : a yellowish sticky substance made by bees and used in building the honeycomb : BEESWAX **2** : a material (as paraffin) that resembles the wax made by bees (as by being soft and easily molded when warm)

²wax *vb* **waxed; wax·ing** : to treat or polish with wax

³wax *vb* **waxed; waxing** **1** : to grow larger or stronger **2** : BECOME 1, GROW

wax bean *n* : a string bean with yellow waxy pods

wax·en *adj* : lacking vitality or animation : PALE

wax myrtle *n* : a shrub or small tree that has bluish gray waxy berries and is related to the bayberry

wax·wing *n* : a crested mostly brown bird having yellow on the tip of the tail and often a waxy substance on the tip of some wing feathers

waxy *adj* **wax·i·er; wax·i·est** **1** : being like wax **2** : made of or covered with wax **3** : marked by smooth or shiny whiteness

¹way *n* **1** : the manner in which something is done or happens **2** : the course traveled from one place to another : ROUTE **3** : a noticeable point **4** : ¹STATE 1 **5** : distance in time or space **6** : a special or personal manner of behaving **7** : a talent for handling something **8** : room to advance or pass **9** : DIRECTION 3 **10** : a track for travel : PATH, STREET **11** : a course of action **12** : personal choice as to situation or behavior : WISH **13** : progress along a course **14** : a particular place **15** : CATEGORY, KIND — **by the way** : apart from that — **by way of 1** : for the purpose of **2** : by the route through — **in someone's way** *also* **in the way** : in a position to hinder or obstruct — **out of the way 1** : in or to a place away from public view **2** : done fully

²way *adv* **1** : ¹FAR 1 **2** : ¹FAR 2

way·far·er *n* : a traveler especially on foot

way·lay *vb* **way·laid ; way·lay·ing** : to attack from hiding

-ways *adv suffix* : in such a way, direction, or manner

way·side *n* : the edge of a road — **by the wayside** : into a condition of neglect or disuse

way·ward *adj* **1** : DISOBEDIENT **2** : not following a rule or regular course of action

we *pron* : I and at least one other

We. *abbr* Wednesday

weak *adj* **1** : lacking strength of body, mind, or spirit **2** : not able to stand much strain or force **3** : easily overcome **4** : not able to function well **5** : not rich in some usual or important element **6** : lacking experience or skill **7** : not loud or forceful **8** : relating to or being the lightest of three levels of stress in pronunciation — **weakly** *adv*

weak·en *vb* **weak·ened; weak·en·ing** : to make or become weak or weaker

weak·ling *n* : a person or animal that lacks strength

weak·ness *n* **1** : lack of strength **2** : a weak

point : FLAW **3** : a special fondness or the object of a special fondness

wealth *n* **1** : a large amount of money or possessions **2** : a great amount or number

wealthy *adj* **wealth·i·er; wealth·i·est** : having a lot of money or possessions : RICH

wean *vb* **weaned; wean·ing 1** : to get a child or young animal used to food other than its mother's milk **2** : to make someone stop desiring a thing he or she has been fond of

weap·on *n* : something (as a gun, knife, or club) to fight with

weap·on·ry *n* : a particular grouping of weapons

¹**wear** *vb* **wore ; worn ; wear·ing 1** : to use as an article of clothing or decoration **2** : to carry or use on the body **3** : ¹SHOW 1 **4** : to damage, waste, or produce by use or by scraping or rubbing **5** : to make tired **6** : to last through long use **7** : to diminish or fail with the passing of time — **wear·er** *n* — **wear out 1** : to make useless by long or hard use **2** : ¹TIRE 1

²**wear** *n* **1** : the act of wearing : the state of being worn **2** : clothing for a particular group or for a particular occasion **3** : the result of wearing or use

wea·ri·some *adj* : TEDIOUS, DULL

¹**wea·ry** *adj* **wea·ri·er; wea·ri·est 1** : having lost strength, energy, or freshness : TIRED **2** : having lost patience, pleasure, or interest **3** : causing a loss of strength or interest — **wea·ri·ly** *adv* — **wea·ri·ness** *n*

²**weary** *vb* **wea·ried; wea·ry·ing** : to make or become weary

wea·sel *n* : a small slender active animal related to the mink that feeds on small birds and animals (as mice)

¹**weath·er** *n* : the state of the air and atmosphere in regard to how warm or cold, wet or dry, or clear or stormy it is

²**weather** *vb* **weath·ered; weath·er·ing 1** : to expose to the weather **2** : to change (as in color or structure) by the action of the weather **3** : to be able to last or come safely through

weath·er·man *n, pl* **weath·er·men** : a person who reports and forecasts the weather

weath·er·per·son *n* : WEATHERMAN

weather vane *n* : a movable device usually attached to a roof to show which way the wind is blowing

¹**weave** *vb* **wove; wo·ven; weav·ing 1** : to move back and forth, up and down, or in and out **2** : to form (as cloth) by lacing together strands of material **3** : ¹SPIN 4 **4** : to make by or as if by lacing parts together — **weav·er** *n*

²**weave** *n* : a method or pattern of lacing together strands of material

¹**web** *n* **1** : SPIDERWEB, COBWEB **2** : a network of threads spun especially by the larvae of certain insects (as tent caterpillars) and usually serving as a nest or shelter **3** : something that catches and holds like a spider's web **4** : a complex pattern like something woven **5** : a layer of skin or tissue that joins the toes of an animal (as a duck) **6** *cap* : WORLD WIDE WEB

²**web** *vb* **webbed; web·bing** : to join or surround with strands woven together

webbed *adj* : having or being toes joined by a layer of skin or tissue

web–foot·ed *adj* : having toes joined by a layer of skin or tissue

Web site *n* : a group of World Wide Web pages usually containing links to each other and made available online by an individual, company, or organization

wed *vb* **wed·ded** *also* **wed; wed·ding 1** : MARRY **2** : to connect closely

Wed. *abbr* Wednesday

we'd : we had : we should : we would

wed·ding *n* : a marriage ceremony

¹**wedge** *n* **1** : a piece of wood or metal that tapers to a thin edge and is used for splitting logs or for tightening by being forced into a space **2** : something with a triangular shape

²**wedge** *vb* **wedged; wedg·ing 1** : to crowd or squeeze in **2** : to fasten, tighten, or separate with a triangular piece of wood or metal

wed·lock *n* : MARRIAGE 1

Wednes·day *n* : the fourth day of the week

wee *adj* : very small : TINY

¹**weed** *n* : a plant that tends to grow where not wanted and to crowd out more desirable plants

²**weed** *vb* **weed·ed; weed·ing 1** : to remove weeds from **2** : to get rid of what is not wanted

weedy *adj* **weed·i·er; weed·i·est 1** : full of or consisting of weeds **2** : like a weed especially in having strong rapid growth **3** : very skinny

week *n* **1** : seven days in a row especially beginning with Sunday and ending with Saturday **2** : the working or school days that come between Sunday and Saturday

week·day *n* : a day of the week except Sunday or sometimes except Saturday and Sunday

week·end *n* : the period between the close of one work or school week and the beginning of the next

¹**week·ly** *adj* **1** : happening, done, or produced every week **2** : figured by the week

²**weekly** *n, pl* **weeklies** : a newspaper or magazine published every week

weep *vb* **wept; weep·ing** : to shed tears : CRY

weep·ing *adj* : having slender drooping branches

weeping willow *n* : a willow originally from Asia that has slender drooping branches

wee·vil *n* : a small beetle that has a long snout and often feeds on and is harmful to plants or plant products (as nuts, fruit, and grain)

weigh *vb* **weighed; weigh·ing** 1 : to have weight or a specified weight 2 : to find the weight of 3 : to think about as if weighing 4 : to lift an anchor before sailing — **weigh down** : to cause to bend down

¹**weight** *n* 1 : the amount that something weighs 2 : the force with which a body is pulled toward the earth 3 : a unit (as a pound) for measuring weight 4 : an object (as a piece of metal) of known weight for balancing a scale in weighing other objects 5 : a heavy object used to hold or press down something 6 : a heavy object lifted during exercise 7 : ¹BURDEN 2 8 : strong influence

²**weight** *vb* **weight·ed; weight·ing** 1 : to load or make heavy with a weight 2 : to trouble with a burden

weight·less *adj* 1 : having little or no weight 2 : not affected by gravity

weighty *adj* **weight·i·er; weight·i·est** 1 : having much weight : HEAVY 2 : very important

weird *adj* **weird·er; weird·est** : very unusual : STRANGE

weirdo *n, pl* **weird·os** : a very strange person

¹**wel·come** *vb* **wel·comed; wel·com·ing** 1 : to greet with friendship or courtesy 2 : to receive or accept with pleasure

²**welcome** *adj* 1 : greeted or received gladly 2 : giving pleasure : PLEASING 3 : willingly permitted to do, have, or enjoy something 4 — used in the phrase "You're welcome" as a reply to an expression of thanks

³**welcome** *n* : a friendly greeting

¹**weld** *vb* **weld·ed; weld·ing** 1 : to join two pieces of metal or plastic by heating and allowing the edges to flow together 2 : to be capable of being joined by heating and allowing the edges to flow together 3 : to join closely — **weld·er** *n*

²**weld** *n* : a joint made by heating and allowing the edges to flow together

wel·fare *n* 1 : the state of being or doing well especially in relation to happiness, well-being, or success 2 : aid in the form of money or necessities for people in need

¹**well** *adv* **bet·ter; best** 1 : in a skillful or expert manner 2 : by as much as possible : COMPLETELY 3 : in such a way as to be pleasing : as wanted 4 : without trouble 5 : in a thorough manner 6 : in a familiar manner 7 : by quite a lot 8 : so as to be right : in a satisfactory way 9 : in a complimentary or generous way 10 : with reason or courtesy — **as well** 1 : in addition : ALSO 2 : with the same result

²**well** *interj* 1 — used to express surprise or doubt 2 — used to begin a conversation or remark or to continue one that was interrupted

³**well** *n* 1 : a hole made in the earth to reach a natural deposit (as of water, oil, or gas) 2 : a source of supply 3 : something like a deep hole

⁴**well** *adj* 1 : being in a satisfactory or good state 2 : free or recovered from ill health : HEALTHY 3 : FORTUNATE 1

⁵**well** *vb* **welled; well·ing** : to rise to the surface and flow out

we'll : we shall : we will

well–be·ing *n* : WELFARE 1

well–bred *adj* : having or showing good manners : POLITE

well–done *adj* 1 : done right 2 : cooked thoroughly

well–known *adj* : known by many people

well–nigh *adv* : ALMOST

well–off *adj* 1 : being in good condition or in a good situation 2 : WELL-TO-DO

well–to–do *adj* : having plenty of money and possessions

¹**Welsh** *adj* : of or relating to Wales or the people of Wales

²**Welsh** *n* : the people of Wales

welt *n* : a ridge raised on the skin (as by a blow)

wel·ter *n* : a confused jumble

wend *vb* **wend·ed; wend·ing** : to go from one place to another

went *past of* GO

wept *past and past participle of* WEEP

were *past second person sing, past pl, or past subjunctive of* BE

we're : we are

weren't : were not

were·wolf *n, pl* **were·wolves** : a person in folklore who is changed or is able to change into a wolf

¹**west** *adv* : to or toward the direction of sunset

²**west** *adj* : placed toward, facing, or coming from the direction of sunset

³**west** *n* 1 : the direction of sunset : the compass point opposite to east 2 *cap* : regions or countries west of a point that is mentioned or understood

west·bound *adj* : going west

west·er·ly *adj or adv* 1 : toward the west 2 : from the west

¹**west·ern** *adj* 1 *often cap* : of, relating to, or

like that of the West **2** : lying toward or coming from the west

²**western** *n, often cap* : a story, film, or radio or television show about life in the western United States especially in the last part of the 19th century

west·ward *adv or adj* : toward the west

¹**wet** *adj* **wet·ter; wet·test** **1** : containing, covered with, or soaked with liquid (as water) **2** : RAINY **3** : not yet dry — **wet·ness** *n*

²**wet** *vb* **wet** *or* **wet·ted; wet·ting** : to make wet

³**wet** *n* : rainy weather : RAIN

we've : we have

¹**whack** *vb* **whacked; whack·ing** : to hit with a hard noisy blow

²**whack** *n* **1** : a hard noisy blow **2** : the sound of a hard noisy blow — **out of whack** : not in good working order or shape

whacky *variant of* WACKY

¹**whale** *n* : a very large sea mammal that has flippers and a flattened tail and breathes through an opening on the top of the head

²**whale** *vb* **whaled; whal·ing** : to hunt whales

whale·bone *n* : BALEEN

whal·er *n* : a person or ship that hunts whales

wharf *n, pl* **wharves** *also* **wharfs** : a structure built on the shore for loading and unloading ships

¹**what** *pron* **1** : which thing or things **2** : which sort of thing or person **3** : that which **4** — used to ask someone to repeat something **5** : ¹WHATEVER 1 — **what for** : ¹WHY — **what if** **1** : what would happen if **2** : what does it matter if

²**what** *adv* **1** : in what way : HOW **2** — used before one or more phrases that tell a cause

³**what** *adj* **1** — used to ask about the identity of a person, object, or matter **2** : how remarkable or surprising **3** : ²WHATEVER 1

¹**what·ev·er** *pron* **1** : anything or everything that **2** : no matter what **3** : what in the world

²**whatever** *adj* **1** : any and all : any. . .that **2** : of any kind at all

what·so·ev·er *pron or adj* : WHATEVER

wheat *n* : a cereal grain that grows in tight clusters on the tall stalks of a widely cultivated grass, that is typically made into fine white flour used mostly in breads, baked goods (as cakes and crackers), and pasta, and that is also used in animal feeds

wheat·en *adj* : containing or made from wheat

whee·dle *vb* **whee·dled; whee·dling** **1** : to get (someone) to think or act a certain way by flattering : COAX **2** : to gain or get by coaxing or flattering

¹**wheel** *n* **1** : a disk or circular frame that can

turn on a central point **2** : something that is round **3** : STEERING WHEEL **4** : something having a wheel as its main part **5 wheels** *pl* : moving power : necessary parts — **wheeled** *adj*

²**wheel** *vb* **wheeled; wheel·ing** **1** : to carry or move on wheels or in a vehicle with wheels **2** : ROTATE 1 **3** : to change direction as if turning on a central point

wheel·bar·row *n* : a cart with two handles and usually one wheel for carrying small loads

wheel·chair *n* : a chair with wheels used especially by sick, injured, or disabled people to get about

¹**wheeze** *vb* **wheezed; wheez·ing** **1** : to breathe with difficulty and usually with a whistling sound **2** : to make a whistling sound like someone having difficulty breathing

²**wheeze** *n* : a whistling sound like that made by someone having difficulty breathing

whelk *n* : a large sea snail that has a spiral shell and is sometimes used for food in Europe

whelp *n* : one of the young of an animal that eats flesh and especially of a dog

¹**when** *adv* **1** : at what time **2** : the time at which **3** : at, in, or during which

²**when** *conj* **1** : at, during, or just after the time that **2** : in the event that : IF **3** : ALTHOUGH 1 **4** : the time at which

³**when** *pron* : what or which time

whence *adv* **1** : from what place, source, or cause **2** : from or out of which

when·ev·er *conj or adv* : at whatever time

¹**where** *adv* **1** : at, in, or to what place **2** : at or in what way or direction

²**where** *conj* **1** : at, in, or to the place indicated **2** : every place that

³**where** *n* : what place, source, or cause

¹**where·abouts** *adv* : near what place

²**whereabouts** *n pl* : the place where someone or something is — used as singular or plural

where·as *conj* **1** : since it is true that **2** : while just the opposite

where·by *adv* : by or through which

where·fore *adv* : ¹WHY

where·in *adv* **1** : in what way **2** : in which

where·of *conj* : of what : that of which

where·up·on *conj* : and then : at which time

¹**wher·ev·er** *adv* **1** : where in the world **2** : any place at all

²**wherever** *conj* **1** : at, in, or to whatever place **2** : in any situation in which : at any time that

whet *vb* **whet·ted; whet·ting** **1** : to sharpen the edge of by rubbing on or with a stone **2** : to make (as the appetite) stronger

wheth·er *conj* **1** : if it is or was true that **2**

: if it is or was better **3** — used to introduce two or more situations of which only one can occur

whet·stone *n* : a stone on which blades are sharpened

whew *n* : a sound almost like a whistle made as an exclamation chiefly to show amazement, discomfort, or relief

whey *n* : the watery part of milk that separates from the curd after the milk sours and thickens

¹which *adj* : what certain one or ones

²which *pron* **1** : which one or ones **2** — used in place of the name of something other than people at the beginning of a clause

¹which·ev·er *adj* : being whatever one or ones : no matter which

²whichever *pron* : whatever one or ones

¹whiff *n* **1** : a small gust **2** : a small amount (as of a scent or a gas) that is breathed in **3** : HINT 2 **4** : STRIKEOUT

²whiff *vb* **whiffed; whiff·ing 1** : to blow out or away in small amounts **2** : to breathe in an odor

¹while *conj* **1** : during the time that **2** : ALTHOUGH 1

²while *n* **1** : a period of time **2** : time and effort used in doing something

³while *vb* **whiled; whil·ing** : to cause to pass especially in a pleasant way

whim *n* : a sudden wish or desire : a sudden change of mind

¹whim·per *vb* **whim·pered; whim·per·ing** : to cry in low broken sounds : WHINE

²whimper *n* : a whining cry

whim·si·cal *adj* **1** : full of whims **2** : unusual in a playful or amusing way

¹whine *vb* **whined; whin·ing 1** : to make a high-pitched troubled cry or a similar sound **2** : to complain by or as if by whining

²whine *n* : a high-pitched troubled or complaining cry or sound

¹whin·ny *vb* **whin·nied; whin·ny·ing** : to neigh usually in a low gentle way

²whinny *n, pl* **whinnies** : a low gentle neigh

¹whip *vb* **whipped; whip·ping 1** : to move, snatch, or jerk quickly or with force **2** : to hit with something long, thin, and flexible : LASH **3** : to defeat thoroughly **4** : to beat into foam **5** : to cause a strong emotion (as excitement) in **6** : to move back and forth in a lively way **7** : to make in a hurry

²whip *n* **1** : a long thin strip of material (as leather) used in punishing or urging on **2** : a dessert made by whipping some part of the mixture

whip·poor·will *n* : a bird of eastern North America that is active at night and has a loud call that sounds like its name

¹whir *vb* **whirred; whir·ring** : to fly, operate, or turn rapidly with a buzzing sound

²whir *n* : a buzzing sound made by something spinning or operating quickly

¹whirl *vb* **whirled; whirl·ing 1** : to turn or move in circles rapidly **2** : to feel dizzy **3** : to move or carry around rapidly

²whirl *n* **1** : a rapid movement in circles **2** : something that is or seems to be moving in circles **3** : a state of busy movement : BUSTLE **4** : a brief or experimental try

whirl·pool *n* : a rapid swirl of water with a low place in the center into which floating objects are drawn

whirl·wind *n* : a small windstorm in which the air turns rapidly in circles

¹whisk *vb* **whisked; whisk·ing 1** : to move suddenly and quickly **2** : to brush with or as if with a whisk broom **3** : to stir or beat with a whisk or fork

²whisk *n* **1** : a quick sweeping or brushing motion **2** : a kitchen utensil of wire used for whipping (as eggs or cream)

whisk broom *n* : a small broom with a short handle used for cleaning small areas or as a clothes brush

whis·ker *n* **1 whiskers** *pl* : the part of the beard that grows on the sides of the face and on the chin **2** : one hair of the beard **3** : a long bristle or hair growing near the mouth of an animal (as a cat)

whis·key *or* **whis·ky** *n, pl* **whis·keys** *or* **whis·kies** : a strong alcoholic drink usually made from grain (as of rye or barley)

¹whis·per *vb* **whis·pered; whis·per·ing 1** : to speak softly and quietly **2** : to tell by speaking softly and quietly **3** : to make a low rustling sound

²whisper *n* **1** : a soft quiet way of speaking that can be heard only by people who are near **2** : the act of speaking softly and quietly **3** : something said softly and quietly **4** : ¹HINT 1

¹whis·tle *n* **1** : a device by which a loud high-pitched sound is produced **2** : a high pitched sound (as that made by forcing the breath through puckered lips)

²whistle *vb* **whis·tled; whis·tling 1** : to make a high-pitched sound by forcing the breath through the teeth or lips **2** : to move, pass, or go with a high-pitched sound **3** : to produce a high-pitched sound by forcing air or steam through a device **4** : to express by forcing breath through the teeth or lips

whit *n* : a very small amount

¹white *adj* **whit·er; whit·est 1** : of the color of fresh snow : colored white **2** : light or pale in color **3** : pale gray : SILVERY **4** : belonging to a race of people having light-colored skin **5** : ¹BLANK 1 **6** : not intended to cause harm **7** : SNOWY 1 — **white·ness** *n*

²**white** *n* **1** : the color of fresh snow : the opposite of black **2** : the white part of something (as an egg) **3** : white clothing **4** : a person belonging to a race of people having light-colored skin

white blood cell *n* : one of the tiny colorless cells of the blood that help fight infection

white·cap *n* : the top of a wave breaking into foam

white cell *n* : WHITE BLOOD CELL

white·fish *n* : a freshwater fish related to the trout that is greenish above and silvery below and is sometimes used for food

white flag *n* : a flag of plain white raised in asking for a truce or as a sign of surrender

whit·en *vb* **whit·ened; whit·en·ing** : to make or become white or whiter

white–tailed deer *n* : a common North American deer with the underside of the tail white

¹**white·wash** *vb* **white·washed; white·washing** **1** : to cover with a mixture that whitens **2** : to try to hide the wrongdoing of

²**whitewash** *n* : a mixture (as of lime and water) for making a surface (as a wall) white

whith·er *adv* : to what place or situation

whit·ish *adj* : somewhat white

whit·tle *vb* **whit·tled; whit·tling** **1** : to cut or shave off chips from wood : shape by cutting or shaving off chips from wood **2** : to reduce little by little

¹**whiz** *or* **whizz** *vb* **whizzed; whiz·zing** : to move, pass, or fly rapidly with a buzzing sound

²**whiz** *or* **whizz** *n, pl* **whizz·es** : a buzzing sound

³**whiz** *n, pl* **whizzes** : WIZARD 2

who *pron* **1** : what or which person or people **2** — used to stand for a person or people at the beginning of a clause

whoa *vb* — used as a command to an animal carrying a rider or pulling a load to stop

who·ev·er *pron* : whatever person

¹**whole** *adj* **1** : made up of all its parts : TOTAL, ENTIRE **2** : all the **3** : not cut up or ground **4** : not scattered or divided **5** : having all its proper parts : COMPLETE **6** : completely healthy or sound in condition — **whole·ness** *n*

²**whole** *n* **1** : something that is full or complete **2** : a sum of all the parts and elements — **on the whole 1** : all things considered **2** : in most cases

whole-heart·ed *adj* : not holding back — **whole-heart·ed·ly** *adv*

whole number *n* : a number that is zero or any of the natural numbers

¹**whole·sale** *n* : the sale of goods in large quantities to dealers

²**wholesale** *adj* **1** : of, relating to, or working at selling to dealers **2** : done or happening on a large scale

³**wholesale** *vb* **whole·saled; whole·sal·ing** : to sell to dealers usually in large quantities — **whole·sal·er** *n*

whole·some *adj* **1** : helping to improve or keep the body in good condition **2** : healthy for the mind or morals — **whole·someness** *n*

whole wheat *adj* : made from or containing wheat kernels that were ground in their entirety

whol·ly *adv* : to the limit : COMPLETELY

whom *pron, objective case of* WHO

whom·ev·er *pron, objective case of* WHO-EVER

¹**whoop** *vb* **whooped; whoop·ing** **1** : to shout or cheer loudly and strongly **2** : to make the high-pitched gasping sound that follows a coughing attack in whooping cough

²**whoop** *n* : a loud strong shout or cheer

whooping cough *n* : a bacterial disease especially of children in which severe attacks of coughing are often followed by a high-pitched gasping intake of breath

whooping crane *n* : a large white nearly extinct North American crane that has a loud trumpeting call

¹**whoosh** *vb* **whooshed; whoosh·ing** : to pass or move along with a sound like that of something moving quickly

²**whoosh** *n, pl* **whoosh·es** : the sound created by something moving quickly

whop·per 1 : something huge of its kind **2** : a big lie

whorl *n* **1** : a row of parts (as leaves or petals) encircling a stem **2** : something that whirls or winds

¹**whose** *adj* : of or relating to whom or which

²**whose** *pron* : that or those belonging to whom

¹**why** *adv* : for what cause or reason

²**why** *conj* **1** : the cause or reason for which **2** : for which

³**why** *interj* — used to express surprise, uncertainty, approval, disapproval, or impatience

WI *abbr* Wisconsin

wick *n* : a cord, strip, or ring of loosely woven material through which a liquid (as oil) is drawn to the top in a candle, lamp, or oil stove for burning

wick·ed *adj* **1** : bad in behavior, moral state, or effect : EVIL **2** : DANGEROUS 2 **3** : of exceptional quality or degree — **wick·ed·ly** *adv* — **wick·ed·ness** *n*

¹**wick·er** *n* **1** : a flexible twig (as of willow)

used especially in making baskets or furniture **2** : WICKERWORK

²wicker *adj* : made of wicker

wick·er·work *n* : something (as a basket or chair) made of wicker

wick·et *n* **1** : an arch (as of wire) through which the ball is hit in the game of croquet **2** : a small gate or door in or near a larger gate or door **3** : a small window (as in a bank) through which business is conducted **4** : either of the two sets of three rods topped by two crosspieces at which the ball is bowled in cricket

¹wide *adj* **wid·er; wid·est 1** : having a large measure across : BROAD **2** : opened as far as possible **3** : covering a very large area **4** : measured across or at right angles to length **5** : not limited : having a large extent **6** : to the side of : away from — **wide·ly** *adv* — **wide·ness** *n*

²wide *adv* **wid·er; wid·est 1** : over a wide area **2** : to the limit : COMPLETELY

wide–awake *adj* **1** : fully awake **2** : very alert

wid·en *vb* **wid·ened; wid·en·ing** : to make or become wide or wider

wide·spread *adj* **1** : widely stretched out **2** : widely scattered

¹wid·ow *n* : a woman whose husband is dead

²widow *vb* **wid·owed; wid·ow·ing** : to make a widow or widower of

wid·ow·er *n* : a man whose wife is dead

width *n* **1** : the measurement of the shortest or shorter side of an object : BREADTH **2** : a measured piece of something

wield *vb* **wield·ed; wield·ing 1** : to use (as a tool) in an effective way **2** : ²EXERCISE 1

wie·ner *n* : FRANKFURTER

wife *n, pl* **wives** : a married woman — **wife·ly** *adj*

wig *n* : a manufactured covering of natural or artificial hair for the head

¹wig·gle *vb* **wig·gled; wig·gling 1** : to move up and down or from side to side with quick short motions **2** : to proceed with twisting and turning movements

²wiggle *n* : a twisting turning motion

wig·gly *adj* **wig·gli·er; wig·gli·est 1** : constantly moving with twisting turning motions **2** : WAVY

wig·wam *n* : a cone-shaped tent formerly used as a house or shelter by some American Indians

¹wild *adj* **wild·er; wild·est 1** : living in a state of nature and not under human control and care : not tame **2** : growing or produced in nature : not cultivated by people **3** : not civilized : SAVAGE **4** : not kept under control : not restrained **5** : made without knowledge **6** : done without accuracy **7** : going beyond

what is usual **8** : ENTHUSIASTIC — **wild·ly** *adv* — **wild·ness** *n*

²wild *n* : WILDERNESS

wild boar *n* : a wild pig of Europe and Asia that is the ancestor of the domestic pig

wild·cat *n* : a wild animal (as an ocelot or lynx) of the cat family that is of small or medium size

wil·de·beest *n* : a large African antelope with a head like that of an ox, curving horns, a short mane, and long tail

wil·der·ness *n* : an area in its natural state in which few or no people live

wild·fire *n* : an uncontrollable fire that destroys a wide area

wild·flow·er *n* : the flower of a wild plant or the plant bearing it

wild·life *n* : wild animals living in their natural environment

¹wile *n* : a trick meant to trap or deceive

²wile *vb* **wiled; wil·ing** : ²LURE

¹will *helping verb, past* **would** ; *present sing & pl* **will 1** : wish to **2** : am, is, or are willing to **3** : am, is, or are determined to **4** : am, is, or are going to **5** : is or are commanded to **6** : is or are able to **7** : is or are likely or bound to

²will *n* **1** : a firm desire or determination **2** : the power to decide or control emotions or actions **3** : a particular person's decision or choice **4** : a legal paper in which a person states to whom his or her property is to be given after death

³will *vb* **willed; will·ing 1** : to intend or order **2** : to bring to a certain condition by the power of the will **3** : to decide on by choice **4** : to leave by will

will·ful *or* **wil·ful** *adj* **1** : STUBBORN 1 **2** : INTENTIONAL — **will·ful·ly** *adv* — **will·ful·ness** *n*

wil·lies *n pl* : a fit of nervousness

will·ing *adj* **1** : feeling no objection **2** : not slow or lazy **3** : made, done, or given by choice : VOLUNTARY — **will·ing·ly** *adv* — **will·ing·ness** *n*

wil·low *n* : a tree or bush with narrow leaves, catkins for flowers, and tough flexible stems sometimes used in making baskets

will·pow·er *n* : strong determination

¹wilt *vb* **wilt·ed; wilt·ing 1** : to lose freshness and become limp **2** : to lose strength

²wilt *n* : a plant disease (as of tomatoes) in which wilting and browning of leaves leads to death of the plant

wily *adj* **wil·i·er; wil·i·est** : full of tricks : CRAFTY

¹win *vb* **won** ; **win·ning 1** : to achieve the victory in a contest **2** : to obtain by victory **3** : to be the victor in **4** : to get by effort or

skill : GAIN 5 : to ask and get the favor of —
win·ner n

²win n : an act or instance of winning

wince vb **winced; winc·ing :** to draw back
(as from pain)

winch n : a machine that has a roller on
which rope is wound for pulling or lifting

¹wind n **1 :** a natural movement of the air **2**
: power to breathe **3 :** limited knowledge especially about something secret **4 winds** pl
: wind instruments of a band or orchestra

²wind vb **wind·ed; wind·ing :** to cause to be
out of breath

³wind vb **wound ; wind·ing 1 :** to move in or
be made up of a series of twists and turns **2**
: to twist around **3 :** to cover with something
twisted around : WRAP **4 :** to make the
spring of tight — **wind up 1 :** to bring to an
end : CONCLUDE **2 :** to reach a place or situation that was not expected **3 :** to swing the
arm before pitching a baseball

wind·break n : something (as a growth of
trees and shrubs) that reduces the force of
the wind

wind·fall n **1 :** something (as fruit from a
tree) blown down by the wind **2 :** an unexpected gift or gain

wind·ing adj **1 :** having a course made up of
a series of twists and turns **2 :** having a
curved or spiral form

wind instrument n : a musical instrument (as
a clarinet, harmonica, or trumpet) sounded
by the vibration of a stream of air and especially by the player's breath

wind·mill n : a mill or a machine (as for
pumping water) worked by the wind turning
sails or vanes at the top of a tower

win·dow n **1 :** an opening in a wall to let in
light and air **2 :** the glass and frame that fill
a window opening **3 :** any of the areas into
which a computer display may be divided
and on which different types of information
may be shown — **win·dow·less** adj

win·dow·pane n : a pane in a window

win·dow·sill n : SILL 1

wind·pipe n : TRACHEA 1

wind·proof adj : protecting from the wind

wind·shield n : a clear screen (as of glass) attached to the body of a vehicle (as a car) in
front of the riders to protect them from the
wind

wind·storm n : a storm with strong wind and
little or no rain

wind·up n **1 :** the last part of something
: FINISH **2 :** a swing of a baseball pitcher's
arm before the pitch is thrown

¹wind·ward adj : moving or placed toward
the direction from which the wind is blowing

²windward n : the side or direction from
which the wind is blowing

windy adj **wind·i·er; wind·i·est :** having much
or strong wind

wine n **1 :** an alcoholic beverage made from
the fermented juice of grapes **2 :** an alcoholic beverage made from the usually fermented juice of fruits (as peaches) other
than grapes

win·ery n, pl **win·er·ies :** a place where wine
is made

¹wing n **1 :** one of the paired limbs or limb-
like parts with which a bird, bat, or insect
flies **2 :** something like a wing in appearance, use, or motion **3 :** a part (as of a building) that sticks out from the main part **4 :** a
division of an organization **5 wings** pl : an
area just off the stage of a theater — **wingless** adj — **wing·like** adj — **on the wing**
: in flight

²wing vb **winged; wing·ing 1 :** to move by
means of wings : FLY **2 :** THROW 1

winged adj : having wings or winglike parts

wing·span n : the distance from the tip of one
wing to the tip of the other wing

¹wink vb **winked; wink·ing 1 :** to close and
open one eye quickly as a signal or hint **2**
: to close and open the eyelids quickly
: BLINK

²wink n **1 :** a hint or sign given by closing
and opening one eye quickly **2 :** a brief period of sleep **3 :** an act of closing and opening usually one eye quickly **4 :** a very short
time

¹win·ning n **1 :** the act of a person or people
who win **2 :** something won especially in
gambling — often used in pl.

²winning adj **1 :** being someone or something that wins, has won, or wins often **2**
: tending to please or delight

win·now vb **win·nowed; win·now·ing 1 :** to
remove (as waste from grain) by a current of
air **2 :** to sort or separate from a larger group

win·some adj : ²WINNING 2

¹win·ter n **1 :** the season between autumn
and spring (as from December to March in
the northern half of the earth) **2 :** one of the
years of a person's life

²winter vb **win·tered; win·ter·ing 1 :** to pass
the winter **2 :** to keep, feed, or manage during the winter

win·ter·green n : a low evergreen plant with
shiny leaves which produce an oil used in
medicine and flavoring

win·ter·time n : the winter season

win·try adj **win·tri·er; win·tri·est 1 :** marked
by or characteristic of winter **2 :** not
friendly : COLD

¹wipe vb **wiped; wip·ing 1 :** to clean or dry
by rubbing **2 :** to remove by or as if by rub-

...dly–wise *adj* : aware of and having ...ledge about the things and ways of this

...wide *adj* : extending over or involving ...tire world

...wide *adv* : throughout the world

...Wide Web *n* : a part of the Internet de-...d to allow easier navigation of the net-...through the use of text and graphics ...nk to other documents

...n 1 : a usually long creeping or ...ing animal (as a tapeworm) that has a ...ody 2 : EARTHWORM 3 : a person ...or pitied 4 **worms** *pl* : infection ...d by parasitic worms living in the body ...orm·like *adj*

...vb **wormed; worm·ing** 1 : to move ...y by creeping or wriggling 2 : to get ...f or escape from by trickery 3 : to rid ...rasitic worms

...y *adj* **worm·i·er; worm·i·est** : contain-...orms

...*past participle of* WEAR

...out *adj* 1 : useless from long or hard ...2 : very weary

...some *adj* 1 : worrying a lot 2 : caus-...orry

...vb **wor·ried; wor·ry·ing** 1 : to feel or ...s great concern 2 : to make anxious ...et 3 : to shake and tear with the teeth ...r·ri·er *n*

...n, *pl* **worries** 1 : concern about ...hing that might happen : ANXIETY 2 ...se of great concern

...*adj, comparative of* BAD *or of* ILL 1 ...bad or evil 2 : being in poorer health ...re unfavorable, difficult, or unpleas-...: of poorer quality, value, or condition ...ss skillful 6 : less happy 7 : more ...or unsuitable

...n : something worse

...*adv, comparative of* BADLY *or of* ILL ...s well : in a worse way

...vb **wors·ened; wors·en·ing** : to get

...ip *n* 1 : deep respect toward God, a ...r a sacred object 2 : too much respect ...iration

...ip *vb* **wor·shipped** *also* **wor·shiped; ...ip·ping** *also* **wor·ship·ing** 1 : to ...or respect as a divine being 2 : to re-...ith respect, honor, or devotion 3 : to ...rt in worship or an act of worship —...ip·per *or* wor·ship·er *n*

...*adj, superlative of* BAD *or of* ILL 1 ...bad, ill, or evil 2 : most unfavorable, ...t, or unpleasant 3 : least appropriate ...ptable 4 : least skillful 5 : most trou-

²**worst** *adv, superlative of* ILL *or of* BADLY : in the worst way possible

³**worst** *n* : a person or thing that is worst

⁴**worst** *vb* **worst·ed; worst·ing** : to get the better of : DEFEAT

wor·sted *n* 1 : a smooth yarn spun from long fibers of wool 2 : a fabric woven from a worsted yarn

¹**worth** *prep* 1 : equal in value to 2 : having possessions or income equal to 3 : deserving of 4 : capable of

²**worth** *n* 1 : the value or usefulness of something or someone 2 : value as expressed in money or in amount of time something will last 3 : EXCELLENCE 1

worth·less *adj* 1 : lacking worth 2 : USELESS

worth·while *adj* : being worth the time spent or effort used

wor·thy *adj* **wor·thi·er; wor·thi·est** 1 : having worth or excellence 2 : having enough value or excellence — **wor·thi·ness** *n*

would *vb, past of* ¹WILL 1 — used as a helping verb to show that something might be likely or meant to happen under certain conditions 2 — used to describe what someone said, expected, or thought 3 — used as a polite form of *will* 4 : prefers or prefer to 5 : was or were going to 6 : is or are able to : COULD 7 : strongly desire : WISH

wouldn't : would not

¹**wound** *n* 1 : an injury that involves cutting or breaking of bodily tissue 2 : an injury or hurt to a person's feelings or reputation

²**wound** *vb* **wound·ed; wound·ing** 1 : to hurt by cutting or breaking bodily tissue 2 : to hurt the feelings or pride of

³**wound** *past and past participle of* WIND

wove *past of* WEAVE

woven *past participle of* WEAVE

¹**wran·gle** *vb* **wran·gled; wran·gling** 1 : to argue angrily 2 : to care for and herd livestock and especially horses

²**wrangle** *n* : ¹QUARREL 2

wran·gler *n* 1 : a person who quarrels 2 : a worker on a ranch who tends horses or cattle

¹**wrap** *vb* **wrapped; wrap·ping** 1 : to cover by winding or folding 2 : to enclose in a package 3 : to wind or fold around 4 : to involve the attention of completely — **wrap up** 1 : to bring to an end 2 : to put on warm clothing

²**wrap** *n* : a warm loose outer garment (as a shawl, cape, or coat)

wrap·per *n* 1 : a protective covering 2 : a person who wraps merchandise 3 : a garment that is worn wrapped about the body

wrap·ping *n* : something used to wrap something else : WRAPPER

wrath *n* : violent anger : RAGE

bing — **wip·er** *n* — **wipe out** : to destroy completely

²**wipe** *n* : an act of wiping : RUB

¹**wire** *n* 1 : metal in the form of a thread or slender rod 2 : a number of strands grouped together and used to send or receive electrical signals 3 : TELEGRAM

²**wire** *vb* **wired; wir·ing** 1 : to provide or equip with wire 2 : to bind with wire 3 : to send or send word to by telegraph

¹**wire·less** *adj* : relating to communication by electromagnetic waves but without connecting wires : RADIO

²**wireless** *n* : a computer, telephone, or network that uses radio waves to send and receive electronic signals

wiry *adj* **wir·i·er; wir·i·est** 1 : being slender yet strong and muscular 2 : coarse and stiff

Wis., Wisc. *abbr* Wisconsin

wis·dom *n* 1 : knowledge or learning gained over time 2 : good sense 3 : a wise attitude, belief, or course of action

wisdom tooth *n* : the last tooth of the full set of teeth on each side of the upper and lower jaws

¹**wise** *adj* **wis·er; wis·est** 1 : having or showing good sense or good judgment : SENSIBLE 2 : having knowledge or information 3 : rude or insulting in speech — **wise·ly** *adv*

²**wise** *n* : MANNER 2, WAY — used in phrases such as *in any wise, in no wise,* or *in this wise*

-**wise** *adv suffix* 1 : in the manner of 2 : in the position or direction of 3 : with regard to

wise·crack *n* : a clever and often insulting statement usually made in joking

¹**wish** *vb* **wished; wish·ing** 1 : to have a desire for : WANT 2 : to form or express a desire concerning 3 : to request by expressing a desire

²**wish** *n* 1 : an act or instance of having or expressing a desire usually in the mind 2 : something wanted 3 : a desire for happiness or luck

wish·bone *n* : a bone in front of a bird's breastbone that is shaped like a V

wish·ful *adj* : having, showing, or based on a wish

wishy–washy *adj* : lacking spirit, courage, or determination : WEAK

wisp *n* 1 : a thin piece or strand 2 : a thin streak 3 : a small amount of something

wispy *adj* **wisp·i·er; wisp·i·est** : being thin and light

wis·te·ria *also* **wis·tar·ia** *n* : a woody vine that is grown for its long clusters of violet, white, or pink flowers

wist·ful *adj* : feeling or showing a quiet long-

ing especially for something in the past — **wist·ful·ly** *adv* — **wist·ful·ness** *n*

wit *n* 1 : normal mental state — usually used in pl. 2 : power to think, reason, or decide 3 : clever and amusing comments, expressions, or talk 4 : a talent for making clever and usually amusing comments 5 : a person with a talent for making clever and amusing comments

witch *n* 1 : a person and especially a woman believed to have magic powers 2 : an ugly or mean old woman

witch·craft *n* : the use of sorcery or magic

witch doctor *n* : a person who uses magic to cure illness and fight off evil spirits

witch·ery *n, pl* **witch·er·ies** 1 : WITCHCRAFT 2 : power to charm or fascinate

witch ha·zel *n* 1 : a shrub with small yellow flowers in late fall or early spring 2 : a soothing alcoholic lotion made from the bark of the witch hazel

with *prep* 1 : in the company of 2 : by the use of 3 : having in or as part of it 4 : in regard to 5 : in possession of 6 : AGAINST 1 7 : in shared relation to 8 : compared to 9 : in the opinion or judgment of 10 : so as to show 11 : as well as 12 : FROM 2 13 : because of 14 : DESPITE 15 : if given 16 : at the time of or shortly after 17 : in support of 18 : in the direction of

with·draw *vb* **with·drew; with·drawn; with·draw·ing** 1 : to draw back : take away 2 : to take back (as something said or suggested) 3 : to go away especially for privacy or safety

with·draw·al *n* : an act or instance of withdrawing

with·er *vb* **with·ered; with·er·ing** : to shrivel or cause to shrivel from or as if from loss of moisture : WILT

with·ers *n pl* : the ridge between the shoulder bones of a horse

with·hold *vb* **with·held ; with·hold·ing** : to refuse to give, grant, or allow

¹**with·in** *adv* : ²INSIDE

²**within** *prep* 1 : ⁴INSIDE 1 2 : not beyond the limits of 3 : before the end of

¹**with·out** *prep* 1 : not accompanied by or showing 2 : completely lacking 3 : ⁴OUTSIDE 4 : not using something

²**without** *adv* 1 : ³OUTSIDE 2 : not having something

with·stand *vb* **with·stood; with·stand·ing** 1 : to hold out against 2 : to oppose (as an attack) successfully

wit·less *adj* : lacking in wit or intelligence

¹**wit·ness** *n* 1 : a person who sees or otherwise has personal knowledge of something 2 : a person who gives testimony in court 3 : a person who is present at an action (as the

signing of a will) so as to be able to say who did it **4** : TESTIMONY

²witness *vb* **wit·nessed; wit·ness·ing 1** : to see or gain personal knowledge of something **2** : to act as a witness to **3** : to be or give proof of

wit·ted *adj* : having wit or understanding — used in combination

wit·ty *adj* **wit·ti·er; wit·ti·est** : having or showing cleverness

wives *pl of* WIFE

wiz·ard *n* **1** : SORCERER, MAGICIAN **2** : a very clever or skillful person

wiz·ard·ry *n* : the art or practice of a sorcerer

wk. *abbr* week

¹wob·ble *vb* **wob·bled; wob·bling** : to move from side to side in a shaky manner — **wob·bly** *adj*

²wobble *n* : a rocking motion from side to side

woe *n* **1** : great sorrow, grief, or misfortune : TROUBLE **2** : something that causes a problem

woe·ful *adj* **1** : full of grief or misery **2** : bringing woe or misery **3** : very bad — **woe·ful·ly** *adv*

woke *past of* WAKE

woken *past participle of* WAKE

¹wolf *n, pl* **wolves 1** : a large bushy-tailed wild animal that resembles the related domestic dog, eats meat, and often lives and hunts in packs **2** : a crafty or fierce person — **wolf·ish** *adj*

²wolf *vb* **wolfed; wolf·ing** : to eat fast or greedily

wolf dog *n* **1** : WOLFHOUND **2** : the offspring of a wolf and a domestic dog

wolf·hound *n* : a large dog used especially in the past for hunting large animals

wol·fram *n* : TUNGSTEN

wol·ver·ine *n* : a mostly dark brown wild animal with shaggy fur that resembles a small bear but is related to the weasel, eats meat, and is found chiefly in the northern forests of North America

wolves *pl of* WOLF

wom·an *n, pl* **wom·en 1** : an adult female person **2** : women considered as a group

wom·an·hood *n* **1** : the state of being a woman **2** : womanly characteristics **3** : WOMAN 2

wom·an·kind *n* : WOMAN 2

wom·an·ly *adj* : having the characteristics typical of a woman

womb *n* : UTERUS

wom·en·folk *or* **wom·en·folks** *n pl* : women especially of one family or group

won *past and past participle of* WIN

¹won·der *vb* **won·dered; won·der·ing 1** : to

be curious or have doubt **2** : to feel surprise or amazement

²wonder *n* **1** : something extraordinary : MARVEL **2** : a feeling (as of astonishment) caused by something extraordinary

won·der·ful *adj* **1** : causing marvel : MARVELOUS **2** : very good or fine — **won·der·ful·ly** *adv*

won·der·ing·ly *adv* : in or as if in astonishment

won·der·land *n* : a place of wonders or surprises

won·der·ment *n* : AMAZEMENT

won·drous *adj* : WONDERFUL 1

¹wont *adj* : being in the habit of doing

²wont *n* : HABIT 3

won't : will not

woo *vb* **wooed; woo·ing 1** : to try to gain the love of **2** : to try to gain

¹wood *n* **1** : a thick growth of trees : a small forest — often used in pl. **2** : a hard fibrous material that makes up most of the substance of a tree or shrub beneath the bark and is often used as a building material or fuel

²wood *adj* **1** : WOODEN 1 **2** : used for or on wood **3** *or* **woods** : living or growing in woodland

wood·chuck *n* : a reddish brown burrowing animal that is a plant-eating rodent that hibernates during the winter : GROUNDHOG

wood·cock *n* : a brownish bird that has a long bill and feeds chiefly on earthworms

wood·cut·ter *n* : a person who cuts wood especially as an occupation

wood·ed *adj* : covered with trees

wood·en *adj* **1** : made of wood **2** : lacking spirit, ease, or charm

wood·land *n* : land covered with trees and shrubs : FOREST

wood·lot *n* : a small area of trees that is set aside to be used for firewood or to provide wood for building things

wood louse *n* : a tiny flat gray animal that is a crustacean usually found living under stones or bark

wood·peck·er *n* : a bird that climbs trees and drills holes in them with its bill in search of insects

wood·pile *n* : a pile of wood and especially firewood

wood·shed *n* : a shed for storing firewood

woods·man *n, pl* **woods·men** : a person who works in the forest and who is knowledgeable about trees and wood

woodsy *adj* **woods·i·er; woods·i·est** : being, located in, or suggesting woodland

wood·wind *n* : one of the group of wind instruments consisting of the flutes, oboes, clarinets, bassoons, and sometimes saxophones

wood·work *n* : work (as the edge around doorways) made of wood

wood·work·ing *n* : the art or process of shaping or working with wood

woody *adj* **wood·i·er; wood·i·est 1** : having or covered with trees **2** : of or containing wood or wood fibers **3** : very much like wood

¹woof *n* : a deep harsh sound made by a dog

²woof *vb* **woofed; woof·ing** : to make the deep harsh sound of a dog

³woof *n* **1** : the threads that cross the warp in weaving a fabric **2** : a woven fabric or its texture

wool *n* **1** : soft wavy or curly usually thick hair especially of the sheep **2** : a substance that looks like a mass of wavy hair **3** : a material (as yarn) made from wool

wool·en *or* **wool·len** *adj* **1** : made of wool **2** : producing cloth made of wool

wool·ly *adj* **wool·li·er; wool·li·est** : made of or resembling wool

woolly mammoth *n* : an extinct mammal that was a heavy-coated mammoth of cold northern regions

woo·zy *adj* **woo·zi·er; woo·zi·est** : slightly dizzy, nauseous, or weak

¹word *n* **1** : a sound or combination of sounds that has meaning and is spoken by a human being **2** : a written or printed letter or letters standing for a spoken word **3** : a brief remark or conversation **4** : ²COMMAND 2, ORDER **5** : NEWS **6** : ¹PROMISE 1 **7 words** *pl* : remarks said in anger or in a quarrel

²word *vb* **word·ed; word·ing** : to express in words : PHRASE

word·ing *n* : the way something is put into words

word processing *n* : the production of printed documents (as business letters) with automated and usually computerized equipment

word processor *n* **1** : a computer used for creating, storing, and printing text **2** : software designed to perform word processing

wordy *adj* **word·i·er; word·i·est** : using or containing many words or more words than are needed — **word·i·ness** *n*

wore *past of* WEAR

¹work *n* **1** : the use of a person's physical or mental strength or ability in order to get something done or get some desired result **2** : OCCUPATION 1, EMPLOYMENT **3** : the place where someone works **4** : something that needs to be done or dealt with : TASK, JOB **5** : DEED 1, ACHIEVEMENT **6** : something produced by effort or hard work **7 works** *pl* : a place where industrial labor is done : PLANT, FACTORY **8 works** *pl*

: the working or mo
ical device **9** : t
forms labor : wor
pl : everything poss
longing

²work *vb* **worked** *or*
: to do something th
mental effort especi
cause of a need i
: labor or cause to la
: to perform or act
planned : OPERATE
crea
thing that involves
soft
fort **5** : to move or
hate
or with effort **6**
caus
: ¹MAKE 2, SHAPE **8** :
cially for a long per
²wor
VOKE **10** : to carry
slow
through, or along —
hold
or solve by effort **2**
of pa
cise routine
wor

work·able *adj* : capab
ing v
done

work·bench *n* : a be
worn
done (as by mechani
worn

work·book *n* : a book
wear
problems or practice
wor·i
to use as part of a co
ing v

worked up *adj* : emo
¹wor·
pecially angry or ups
expr
or u

work·er *n* **1** : a perso
— w
the members of a
²wor
wasps, or termites th
some
of the colony
: a ca

work·ing *adj* **1** : doi
¹wors
living **2** : relating t
: mor
to allow work or fur
3 :

work·ing·man *n, pl*
ant 4
who works for wa
5 : l
labor
faulty

work·man *n, pl* **work**
²wors
2 : a skilled worker
³wors

work·man·ship *n* 1
: not a
workman **2** : the q
wors·

work·out *n* : an exer
worse
improve ability or

work·shop *n* : a sho
¹wor·s
cially skilled work
god,
or ad

work·sta·tion *n* 1
²wors
for the performanc
wor·s
ally by one person
honor
connected to a larg
gard v

world *n* **1** : EARTH
take p
: HUMANITY **3** :
wor·s
great number or an
¹worst
of the earth **6** : an
: mos

world·ly *adj* **world**
diffic
relating to the affai
or acc
spiritual affairs
bled

world·li·ness *n*

wrath·ful *adj* **1** : full of wrath **2** : showing wrath

wreak *vb* **wreaked; wreak·ing** : to bring down as or as if punishment

wreath *n, pl* **wreaths** : something twisted or woven into a circular shape

wreathe *vb* **wreathed; wreath·ing 1** : to form into wreaths **2** : to crown, decorate, or cover with or as if with a wreath

¹wreck *n* **1** : the remains (as of a ship or vehicle) after heavy damage usually by storm, collision, or fire **2** : a person who is very tired, ill, worried, or unhappy **3** : the action of damaging or destroying something **4** : something in a state of ruin

²wreck *vb* **wrecked; wreck·ing 1** : to damage or destroy by or as if by force or violence **2** : to bring to ruin or an end **3** : ²SHIP-WRECK 2

wreck·age *n* **1** : the remains of a wreck **2** : the act of wrecking : the state of being wrecked

wreck·er *n* **1** : a truck for removing wrecked or broken-down vehicles **2** : a person who wrecks something

wren *n* : a small brown songbird with a short tail that points upward

¹wrench *vb* **wrenched; wrench·ing 1** : to pull or twist with sudden sharp force **2** : to injure by a sudden sharp twisting or straining

²wrench *n* **1** : a tool used in turning nuts or bolts **2** : a violent twist to one side or out of shape **3** : an injury caused by twisting or straining : SPRAIN

wrest *vb* **wrest·ed; wrest·ing 1** : to pull away by twisting or wringing **2** : to obtain only by great and steady effort

¹wres·tle *vb* **wres·tled; wres·tling 1** : to fight by grasping and attempting to turn, trip, or throw down an opponent or to prevent the opponent from being able to move **2** : to struggle to deal with — **wres·tler** *n*

²wrestle *n* : ²STRUGGLE 1

wres·tling *n* : a sport in which two opponents wrestle each other

wretch *n* **1** : a miserable unhappy person **2** : a very bad person

wretch·ed *adj* **1** : very unhappy or unfortunate : suffering greatly **2** : causing misery or distress **3** : of very poor quality : INFE-RIOR — **wretch·ed·ly** *adv* — **wretch·ed·ness** *n*

wrig·gle *vb* **wrig·gled; wrig·gling 1** : to twist or move like a worm : SQUIRM, WIGGLE **2** : to advance by twisting and turning

wrig·gler *n* **1** : someone or something that squirms **2** : a mosquito larva

wring *vb* **wrung ; wring·ing 1** : to twist or

press so as to squeeze out moisture **2** : to get by or as if by twisting or pressing **3** : to twist with a forceful or violent motion **4** : to affect as if by wringing **5** : to twist (hands) together as a sign of anguish

wring·er *n* : a machine or device for squeezing liquid out of something (as laundry)

¹wrin·kle *n* **1** : a crease or small fold (as in the skin or in cloth) **2** : a clever notion or trick **3** : a surprise in a story or series of events

²wrinkle *vb* **wrin·kled; wrin·kling** : to develop or cause to develop creases or small folds

wrist *n* : the joint or the region of the joint between the hand and arm

wrist·band *n* **1** : the part of a sleeve that goes around the wrist **2** : a band that goes around the wrist (as for support or to absorb sweat)

wrist·watch *n* : a watch attached to a bracelet or strap and worn on the wrist

writ *n* : an order in writing signed by an officer of a court ordering someone to do or not to do something

write *vb* **wrote; writ·ten; writ·ing 1** : to form letters or words with pen or pencil **2** : to form the letters or the words of (as on paper) **3** : to put down on paper **4** : to make up and set down for others to read **5** : to compose music **6** : to communicate with someone by sending a letter

writ·er *n* : a person who writes especially as a business or occupation

writhe *vb* **writhed; writh·ing** : to twist and turn from side to side

writ·ing *n* **1** : the act of a person who writes **2** : HANDWRITING **3** : something (as a letter or book) that is written

¹wrong *adj* **1** : not the one wanted or intended **2** : not correct or true : FALSE **3** : not right : SINFUL, EVIL **4** : not satisfactory : causing unhappiness **5** : not suitable **6** : made so as to be placed down or under and not to be seen **7** : not proper **8** : not working correctly — **wrong·ly** *adv*

²wrong *n* : something (as an idea, rule, or action) that is not right

³wrong *adv* : in the wrong direction, manner, or way

⁴wrong *vb* **wronged; wrong·ing** : to treat badly or unfairly

wrong·do·er *n* : a person who does wrong and especially a moral wrong

wrong·do·ing *n* : bad behavior or action

wrong·ful *adj* **1** : ¹WRONG 3, UNJUST **2** : UN-LAWFUL

wrote *past of* WRITE

¹wrought *past and past participle of* WORK

²wrought *adj* **1** : beaten into shape by tools **2** : much too excited

wrung *past and past participle of* WRING

wry *adj* **wry·er; wry·est 1** : funny in a clever or ironic way **2** : expressing irony

wt. *abbr* weight

WV, W.Va. *abbr* West Virginia

www *abbr* World Wide Web

WY, Wyo. *abbr* Wyoming

X

x *n, pl* **x's** *or* **xs** *often cap* **1** : the 24th letter of the English alphabet **2** : ten in Roman numerals **3** : an unknown quantity

X–ax·is *n* : the horizontal line on a coordinate graph

XL *abbr* extra large

Xmas *n* : CHRISTMAS

x–ray *vb* **x–rayed; x–ray·ing** *often cap* X : to examine, treat, or photograph with X–rays

X–ray *n* **1** : a powerful invisible ray made up of very short waves that is somewhat similar to light and that is able to pass through some solids and acts on photographic film like light **2** : a photograph taken by the use of X–rays

xy·lo·phone *n* : a musical instrument consisting of a series of wooden bars of different lengths that are struck by special mallets to produce musical notes

Y

y *n, pl* **y's** *or* **ys** *often cap* : the 25th letter of the English alphabet

¹-y *also* **-ey** *adj suffix* **-i·er; -i·est 1** : showing, full of, or made of **2** : like **3** : devoted to : enthusiastic about **4** : tending to **5** : somewhat : rather

²-y *n suffix, pl* **-ies 1** : state : condition : quality **2** : activity, place of business, or goods dealt with **3** : whole body or group

³-y *n suffix, pl* **-ies** : occasion or example of a specified action

⁴-y — see -IE

yacht *n* : a small ship used for pleasure cruising or racing

yacht·ing *n* : the activity or recreation of racing or cruising in a yacht

yak *n* : a wild or domestic ox of the uplands of central Asia that has very long hair

yam *n* **1** : the starchy thick underground tuber of a climbing plant that is an important food in many tropical regions **2** : a sweet potato with a moist and usually orange flesh

¹yank *n* : a strong sudden pull : JERK

²yank *vb* **yanked; yank·ing** : to pull suddenly or forcefully

Yan·kee *n* **1** : a person born or living in New England **2** : a person born or living in the northern United States **3** : a person born or living in the United States

¹yap *vb* **yapped; yap·ping 1** : to bark often continuously with quick high-pitched sounds **2** : to talk continuously and often loudly : CHATTER

²yap *n* : a quick high-pitched bark

¹yard *n* **1** : an outdoor area next to a building that is often bordered (as by shrubs or fences) **2** : the grounds of a building **3** : a fenced area for livestock **4** : an area set aside for a business or activity **5** : a system of railroad tracks especially for keeping and repairing cars

²yard *n* **1** : a measure of length equal to three feet or 36 inches (about 0.91 meter) **2** : a long pole pointed toward the ends that holds up and spreads the top of a sail

yard·age *n* **1** : a total number of yards **2** : the length or size of something measured in yards

yard·arm *n* : either end of the yard of a square-rigged ship

yard·stick *n* **1** : a measuring stick a yard long **2** : a rule or standard by which something is measured or judged

yarn *n* **1** : a natural or manufactured fiber (as of cotton, wool, or rayon) formed as a continuous thread for use in knitting or weaving **2** : an interesting or exciting story

yaw *vb* **yawed; yaw·ing** : to turn suddenly from a straight course

yawl *n* : a sailboat having two masts with the shorter one behind the point where the stern enters the water

¹yawn *vb* **yawned; yawn·ing 1** : to open the mouth wide and take a deep breath usually as an involuntary reaction to being tired or bored **2** : to open wide

²yawn *n* : an opening of the mouth while taking a deep breath usually as an involuntary reaction to being tired or bored

y–ax·is *n* : the vertical line on a coordinate graph

yd. *abbr* yard

ye *pron* : YOU 1

¹yea *adv* : ¹YES 1 — used when a person is voting aloud for something

²yea *n* **1** : a vote in favor of something **2** : a person casting a yea vote

year *n* **1** : the period of about 365¼ days required for the earth to make one complete trip around the sun **2** : a period of 365 days or in leap year 366 days beginning January 1 **3** : a fixed period of time **4** : the age of a person **5** : a long time

year·book *n* **1** : a book published once a year especially as a report or summary of a certain topic (as new discoveries in science) **2** : a publication that shows a school's current students and staff and the activities that took place during the school year

year·ling *n* : an animal that is between one and two years old

year·ly *adj* : occurring, made, or done every year : ANNUAL

yearn *vb* yearned; yearn·ing : to desire very much

yearn·ing *n* : an eager desire

year–round *adj* : active, present, or done throughout the entire year

yeast *n* **1** : a single-celled fungus that ferments sugar to produce alcohol and carbon dioxide **2** : a commercial product containing living yeast cells that is used in baking to make dough rise and in the making of alcoholic beverages (as wine)

¹yell *vb* yelled; yell·ing : to speak, call, or cry out loudly (as in anger or to get someone's attention)

²yell *n* : a loud call or cry : SHOUT

¹yel·low *adj* **1** : of the color of a lemon : colored yellow **2** : COWARDLY

²yellow *n* **1** : the color of a lemon **2** : something (as the yolk of an egg) yellow in color

³yellow *vb* yel·lowed; yel·low·ing : to turn yellow

yellow fever *n* : a disease carried by mosquitoes in parts of Africa and South America

yel·low·ish *adj* : somewhat yellow

yellow jacket *n* : a small wasp with yellow markings that usually nests in colonies in the ground and can sting repeatedly and painfully

¹yelp *n* : a quick high-pitched bark or cry

²yelp *vb* yelped; yelp·ing : to make a quick high-pitched bark or cry

yen *n* : a strong desire : LONGING

yeo·man *n*, *pl* yeo·men **1** : a petty officer in the navy who works as a clerk **2** : a person who owns and cultivates a small farm

-yer — see ²-ER

¹yes *adv* **1** — used to express agreement in answer to a question, request, or offer or with an earlier statement **2** — used to introduce a phrase with greater emphasis or clearness **3** — used to show uncertainty or polite interest **4** — used to indicate excitement

²yes *n* : a positive reply

¹yes·ter·day *adv* : on the day before today

²yesterday *n* **1** : the day before today **2** : the past in general

yes·ter·year *n* : a time in the past

¹yet *adv* **1** : in addition **2** : ²EVEN **4 3** : up to now : so far **4** : at this time **5** : up to the present : STILL **6** : at some later time **7** : NEVERTHELESS

²yet *conj* : in spite of the fact that

yew *n* : a tree or shrub with stiff needlelike evergreen leaves and seeds having a red juicy covering

Yid·dish *n* : a language related to German that was originally spoken by Jews of central and eastern Europe

¹yield *vb* yield·ed; yield·ing **1** : to give (something) over to the power or control of another : SURRENDER **2** : to give in **3** : to produce as a natural product **4** : to produce or give back as interest or profit **5** : to be productive : bring good results **6** : to stop opposing or objecting to something **7** : to give way under physical force so as to bend, stretch, or break **8** : to allow another person or vehicle to go first

²yield *n* **1** : the amount produced or returned **2** : RETURN 5

¹yip *vb* yipped; yip·ping : ¹YAP 1

²yip *n* : ²YAP

YK *abbr* Yukon Territory

¹yo·del *vb* yo·deled *or* yo·delled; yo·del·ing *or* yo·del·ling : to sing or call with frequent sudden changes from the natural voice range to a higher range and back — **yo·del·er** *n*

²yodel *n* : a song or call made by yodeling

yo·gurt *n* : a thick soft food that is made of milk soured by the addition of bacteria and that is often flavored and sweetened

¹yoke *n* **1** : a wooden bar or frame by which two work animals (as oxen) are harnessed at the heads or necks for drawing a plow or load **2** : a frame fitted to a person's shoulders to carry a load in two equal parts **3** : a clamp that holds or connects two parts **4** *pl usually* **yoke** : two animals yoked together **5** : something that brings about pain, suffering, or a loss of freedom **6** : SLAVERY 1 **7** : a fitted or shaped piece at the shoulder of a garment or at the top of a skirt

²yoke *vb* yoked; yok·ing **1** : to put a yoke on **2** : to attach a work animal to

yo·kel *n* : a person from a small town or the

country who has little education or experience

yolk *n* : the yellow inner part of the egg of a bird or reptile containing stored food material for the developing young

Yom Kip·pur *n* : a Jewish holiday observed in September or October with fasting and prayer

¹**yon** *adj* : ²YONDER

²**yon** *adv* **1** : ¹YONDER **2** : THITHER

¹**yon·der** *adv* : at or in that place

²**yonder** *adj* **1** : more distant **2** : being at a distance within view

yore *n* : time long past

you *pron* **1** : the person, thing, or group these words are spoken or written to **2** : anyone at all

you'd : you had : you would

you'll : you shall : you will

¹**young** *adj* **youn·ger; youn·gest 1** : being in the first or an early stage of life, growth, or development **2** : lacking in experience **3** : recently formed, produced, or come into being : NEW **4** : YOUTHFUL 1

²**young** *n pl* **1** : young people **2** : immature or recently born offspring

youn·gest *n, pl* **youngest** : the least old member especially of a family

young·ster *n* **1** : a young person : YOUTH **2** : CHILD 3

your *adj* **1** : relating to or belonging to you **2** : by or from you **3** : relating to people in general **4** — used before a title of honor in addressing a person

you're : you are

yours *pron* : that which belongs to you

your·self *pron, pl* **your·selves 1** : your own self **2** : your normal or healthy self

youth *n, pl* **youths 1** : the time of life between being a child and an adult **2** : a young man **3** : young people **4** : the quality or state of being young

youth·ful *adj* **1** : belonging to, relating to, or characteristic of youth **2** : not old or mature **3** : having the appearance, spirit, or energy of youth — **youth·ful·ness** *n*

you've : you have

¹**yowl** *vb* **yowled; yowl·ing** : to utter a loud long cry (as of pain or suffering)

²**yowl** *n* : a loud long cry (as of pain or suffering)

yo–yo *n, pl* **yo–yos** *also* **yo–yoes** : a small round toy that has two flattened disks with a string attached to the center and that is made to fall and rise to the hand by unwinding and rewinding on the string

yr. *abbr* year

YT *abbr* Yukon Territory

yuc·ca *n* : a plant that grows in warm dry regions and has stiff pointed leaves at the base and a tall stiff stalk of usually whitish flowers

yucky *adj* **yuck·i·er; yuck·i·est** : causing discomfort, disgust, or a strong feeling of dislike

yule *n, often cap* : CHRISTMAS

yule log *n, often cap Y* : a large log once put in the fireplace on Christmas Eve as the foundation of the fire

yule·tide *n, often cap* : the Christmas season

yum·my *adj* **yum·mi·er; yum·mi·est** : very pleasing especially to the taste

Z

z *n, pl* **z's** *or* **zs** *often cap* : the 26th letter of the English alphabet

za·ny *adj* **za·ni·er; za·ni·est** : very strange and silly

zap *vb* **zapped; zap·ping** : to hit with or as if with a jolt of electricity

zeal *n* : eager desire to get something done or see something succeed

zeal·ous *adj* **1** : filled with or showing a strong and energetic desire to get something done or see something succeed **2** : marked by passionate support for a person, cause, or ideal — **zeal·ous·ly** *adv*

ze·bra *n* : an African animal that is related to the horse and has a hide striped in black and white or black and buff

ze·bu *n* : an Asian domestic ox that has a large hump over the shoulders and loose skin with hanging folds

ze·nith *n* **1** : the point in the sky directly overhead **2** : the highest point or stage

zeph·yr *n* : a gentle breeze

zep·pe·lin *n* : an airship resembling a huge long balloon that has a metal frame and is driven through the air by engines carried on its underside

ze·ro *n, pl* **zeros** *or* **zeroes 1** : the numerical symbol 0 meaning the absence of all size or quantity **2** : the point on a scale (as on a thermometer) from which measurements are made **3** : the temperature shown by the zero mark on a thermometer **4** : a total lack of anything : NOTHING

zest *n* **1** : a piece of the peel of a citrus fruit (as an orange or lemon) used to flavor foods **2** : an enjoyable or exciting quality **3** : keen enjoyment

¹**zig·zag** *n* **1** : one of a series of short sharp

turns or angles in a line or course **2** : a line, path, or pattern with a series of short sharp angles

²zigzag *adv* : in or by a line or course that has short sharp turns or angles

³zigzag *adj* : having short sharp turns or angles

⁴zigzag *vb* **zig·zagged; zig·zag·ging** : to form into or move along a line or course that has short sharp turns or angles

zil·lion *n* : an extremely large number

zinc *n* : a bluish white metal that tarnishes only slightly in moist air and is used mostly to make alloys and to give iron and steel a protective coating

¹zing *n* **1** : a high-pitched humming sound **2** : a lively or energetic quality **3** : a sharp or spicy flavor

²zing *vb* **zinged; zing·ing** : to move very quick with a high-pitched humming sound

zin·nia *n* : a garden plant grown for its long-lasting colorful flowers

¹zip *vb* **zipped; zip·ping** : to move or act quickly and often with energy and enthusiasm

²zip *n* : energy and enthusiasm

³zip *vb* **zipped; zip·ping** : to close or open with a zipper

zip code *n* : a number that identifies each postal delivery area in the United States

zip·per *n* : a fastener (as for a jacket) consisting of two rows of metal or plastic teeth and a sliding piece that closes an opening by bringing the teeth together — **zip·pered** *adj*

zip·py *adj* **zip·pi·er; zip·pi·est 1** : SPEEDY **2** : full of energy : LIVELY

zith·er *n* : a musical instrument with usually 30 to 40 strings that are plucked with the fingers or with a pick

zo·di·ac *n* : an imaginary belt in the sky that includes the paths of the planets and is divided into twelve constellations or signs each with a special name and symbol

zom·bie *also* **zom·bi** *n* : a person who is believed to have died and been brought back to life without speech or free will

¹zone *n* **1** : a region or area set off or characterized as different from surrounding or neighboring parts **2** : one of the sections of an area created for or serving a particular use or purpose

²zone *vb* **zoned; zon·ing** : to divide into sections for different uses or purposes

zoo *n, pl* **zoos** : a place where living usually wild animals are kept for showing to the public

zoo·keep·er *n* : a person who cares for animals in a zoo

zoo·log·i·cal *adj* : of or relating to zoology

zoological garden *n* : ZOO

zoological park *n* : ZOO

zo·ol·o·gist *n* : a person who specializes in zoology

zo·ol·o·gy *n* **1** : a branch of biology concerned with the study of animals and animal life **2** : animal life (as of a region)

¹zoom *vb* **zoomed; zoom·ing 1** : to move quickly often with a loud low hum or buzz **2** : to move upward quickly

²zoom *n* **1** : an act or process of moving quickly along or upwards **2** : a loud low humming or buzzing sound

zuc·chi·ni *n* : a smooth cylinder-shaped green-skinned vegetable that is a type of squash

zwie·back *n* : a usually sweetened bread made with eggs that is baked and then sliced and toasted until dry and crisp

zy·gote *n* : the new cell formed when a sperm cell joins with an egg cell

Ten General Spelling Rules

1) In general, 'i' comes before 'e' except after 'c' or in words like 'neighbor' and 'weigh'.

2) Words that end in a /seed/ sound: 'supersede' is the only word ending in 'sede'; 'exceed', 'proceed' and 'succeed' are the only three words ending in 'ceed'; all others end in 'cede'.

3) Words ending in a hard 'c' sound usually change to 'ck' before adding 'e', 'i', or 'y': picnic → picnicked, picnicking but picnics.

4) Words ending in a stressed single vowel + single consonant usually double the consonant before a suffix: abet → abetted, abetting; begin → beginner.

5) Words ending in silent 'e' usually drop the 'e' before a suffix that begins with a vowel but not before a suffix beginning with a consonant: bone → boned, boning but boneless.

6) Words ending in stressed 'ie' usually change to 'y' before a suffixal 'i': die → dying.

7) Words ending in a double vowel usually remain unchanged before a suffix: agree → agreeable; blue → blueness; coo → cooing.

8) Words ending in a consonant plus 'y' usually change the 'y' to 'i' before a suffix: beauty → beautiful; happy → happiness.

9) Words ending in a vowel plus 'y' usually do not change before a suffix: boy → boys; enjoy → enjoying.

10) Words ending in 'll' usually drop one 'l' when adding another word to form a compound: all + ready → already; full + fill → fulfill; hate + full → hateful.

Ten Rules for Forming Plurals

1) Most nouns form the plural by adding 's': bag → bags.
2) Words that end in silent 'e' usually just add 's': college → colleges.
3) Nouns ending in 'x', 'z', 'ch', 'sh', and 'ss' usually add 'es': fox → foxes; buzz → buzzes; church → churches; bush → bushes; boss → bosses.
4) Words ending in a consonant + 'y' usually change the 'y' to 'i' and add 'es': army → armies; sky → skies.
5) Words ending in a vowel + 'y' usually add 's' with no change: day → days; boy → boys; key → keys.
6) Words ending in a vowel + 'o' usually add 's' with no change: duo → duos; studio → studios.
7) Words ending in a consonant + 'o': some add 's' and some add 'es': ego → egos; piano → pianos; echo → echoes; tomato → tomatoes.
8) Words ending in 'f' usually change the 'f' to 'v' and add 'es': leaf → leaves; self → selves; thief → thieves; but chief → chiefs.
9) Words ending in 'fe' usually change the 'fe' to 'v' and add 'es': knife → knives; life → lives.
10) Words that are the names of fishes, birds, and mammals usually have an unchanging form for the plural or have the unchanging form and an 's' plural, depending on meaning.